Sir Philip Sidney

The Manchester Spenser

The Manchester Spenser is a monograph and text series devoted to historical and textual approaches to Edmund Spenser – to his life, times, places, works and contemporaries.

A growing body of work in Spenser and Renaissance studies, fresh with confidence and curiosity and based on solid historical research, is being written in response to a general sense that our ability to interpret texts is becoming limited without the excavation of further knowledge. So the importance of research in nearby disciplines is quickly being recognised, and interest renewed: history, archaeology, religious or theological history, book history, translation, lexicography, commentary and glossary – these require treatment for and by students of Spenser.

The Manchester Spenser, to feed, foster and build on these refreshed attitudes, aims to publish reference tools, critical, historical, biographical and archaeological monographs on or related to Spenser, from several disciplines, and to publish editions of primary sources and classroom texts of a more wide-ranging scope.

The Manchester Spenser consists of work with stamina, high standards of scholarship and research, adroit handling of evidence, rigour of argument, exposition and documentation.

The series will encourage and assist research into, and develop the readership of, one of the richest and most complex writers of the early modern period.

General Editors Joshua Reid, Kathryn Walls and Tamsin Badcoe
Editorial Board Sukanta Chaudhuri, Helen Cooper, Thomas Herron, J. B. Lethbridge, James Nohrnberg and Brian Vickers

To buy or to find out more about the books currently available in this series, please go to: https://manchesteruniversitypress.co.uk/series/the-manchester-spenser/

Sir Philip Sidney
The Countess of Pembroke's Arcadia

The New Arcadia, Second Revised Edition

Edited by

Victor Skretkowicz, Elisabeth Chaghafi and
J.B. Lethbridge

MANCHESTER UNIVERSITY PRESS

Copyright ©Manchester University Press 2024

While copyright in the volume as a whole is vested in Manchester University Press, copyright in individual chapters belongs to their respective authors, and no chapter may be reproduced wholly or in part without the express permission in writing of both author and publisher.

Published by Manchester University Press
Oxford Road, Manchester, M13 9PL

www.manchesteruniversitypress.co.uk

British Library Cataloguing-in-Publication Data
A catalogue record for this book is available from the British Library

ISBN 978 1 5261 7497 0   hardback
ISBN 978 1 5261 9546 3   paperback

First published 2024
Paperback published 2026

The publisher has no responsibility for the persistence or accuracy of URLs for any external or third-party internet websites referred to in this book, and does not guarantee that any content on such websites is, or will remain, accurate or appropriate.

EU authorised representative for GPSR:
Easy Access System Europe – Mustamäe tee 50,
10621 Tallinn, Estonia
gpsr.requests@easproject.com

Typeset in MinionPro
by Elisabeth Chaghafi

GENERAL PREFACE

EVEN several decades after its publication, Victor Skretkowicz's 1987 edition of the *New Arcadia* remains the authoritative edition of the text. The present edition therefore pursues a twofold aim: to make Skretkowicz's edition widely available again, and to supplement and expand it.

In 2008, after the copyright of his authoritative 1987 edition of the *New Arcadia* had reverted to him, Victor Skretkowicz approached J. B. Lethbridge, then general editor of the Manchester Spenser series, about the possibility of a corrected edition, which TMS gladly accepted. Unfortunately, Skretkowicz's health forced him to prioritize the revising and preparing for the press of his TMS monograph *European Erotic Romance*, and he asked Lethbridge to take over the project, making use of what few corrections Skretkowicz had already made up to this point. The text had to be reset from scratch, which was an opportunity but also a considerable labour that was only just short of that of preparing a wholly new edition, since it also had to be corrected. J. B. Lethbridge enlisted the help of Stefanie Lethbridge of Freiburg University to incorporate corrections into the text and carry out several rounds of proofing of the main text and its footnotes. Eleonora Sereni (also of Freiburg University) compiled the first incarnation of the index of rhetorical figures. The revision and expansion of the commentary, glossary and appendices were done by Elisabeth Chaghafi, along with the final proofreading and the typesetting. A number of people provided various forms of assistance and moral support along the way, most notably Roger Kuin, Anne Prescott and Robert Stillman, while Mariëlla Beukers and Steve Schmidt gave knowledgeable advice on food- and wine-related questions.

While the contents of the original commentary and glossary have been preserved, more than 500 commentaries and glossary entries have been added, and the introductory section has been expanded by notes on the history of *Arcadia* in print and Sidney's use of rhetorical figures, topics that were previously covered only relatively briefly in the Textual Introduction. Additions to the commentary and glossary for the most part do not aim to qualify entries from the 1987 edition but aim to offer further explanations of Sidney's imagery or word choice and additional cross-references to other early printed books. All additions to the 1987 commentary and glossary are clearly indicated by square brackets. The only exception to this rule are Skretkowicz's references to the *OED*. In order to illustrate the innovativeness of Sidney's style, his 1987 edition frequently referred to the *OED* to explain typical (or atypical) sixteenth-century usages and to point out when Sidney's use of a word antedated the earliest example in an *OED* entry. Since then, the *OED* has seen two new editions, however: the second edition, published just two years after the 1987 *New Arcadia*, and the third, online, edition, which is still continuing and aims to revise all remaining entries from the first edition. As a result, a large number of *OED* entries have been reorganized or merged since 1987, definitions have been rephrased, examples have been replaced and words have been antedated (sometimes substantially so). For this reason, all of the *OED* references in the introductions, commentary and glossary of 1987 have been reviewed and updated wherever necessary, so they now reflect the present state of the dictionary. Since these updates merely reflect the changes that the *OED* has undergone since the 1980s and are intended to increase the usefulness of the present edition, they have not been explicitly flagged up. Additionally, the character index has been supplemented by brief summaries, to help readers to locate specific episodes in the text more easily.

Overall, then, this edition does not aim to undo the work of its predecessor, but to enhance and update it for a new century. In this aim, it consequently resembles the third *Arcadia* edition of 1598 more than the second edition of 1593. Throughout, the support and, sad necessity, the patience of Victor Skretkowicz's wife have been crucial. This is Carole Skretkowicz's *New Arcadia*.

EC
JBL

Tübingen, September 2023

PREFACE TO THE 1987 EDITION

SIR PHILIP SIDNEY's *New Arcadia* has not before been published in a full critical edition. In setting out to provide one I have been guided by the analyses of the texts done by Professor William A. Ringler, Jr., in *The Poems of Sir Philip Sidney* (Oxford, 1962) and by Dr Jean Robertson in *The Countess of Pembroke's Arcadia (The Old Arcadia)* (Oxford, 1973). These editors showed how variants in the manuscripts of the *Old Arcadia* were related to those in the texts of the *New Arcadia*, and were the first to include the Cambridge University Library manuscript of the *New Arcadia* in their discussions of the texts. Although the Cambridge manuscript is the earliest copy of the *New Arcadia*, the only one made during Sidney's lifetime to have survived, it contains a corrupt representation of the unfinished text. The first readable version, the quarto of 1590, has therefore been used as the copy-text for this edition. The editors of the quarto admitted to dividing the narrative into chapters for which they provided summaries, and to making up from the author's papers the eclogues he never completed himself. These have been relegated to the textual apparatus and Appendix I. Many small changes were made and a lengthy appendix added to the quarto text in the second edition, the folio of 1593. Where these two earliest editions disagree, the manuscripts of the *Old Arcadia*, the Cambridge manuscript, and the editions of 1598 and 1613 have been used to establish the text. The problems encountered, and the procedures involved in reconstructing the text, are described in the Textual Introduction.

With few exceptions the spelling throughout this edition follows modern practice. The texts themselves, being inconsistent in spelling, have been normalized to the modern form. But where there is agreement in reading an old form which significantly affects pronunciation, that form has been normalized and appropriately glossed or commented upon. Where there has been no danger of distorting quotations from Sidney's other works and from other authors, the text has been modernized. Punctuation and paragraph divisions have been introduced in accordance with present conventions.

In the General Introduction the *New Arcadia* is related to events in Sidney's life and to his principal literary and cultural sources. An assessment of his artistry in form, style, and diction is followed by a summary of the early reception and influence of the work.

The Commentary provides further notes on textual matters and interprets specific details and difficult passages not satisfactorily explained by reference to the Glossary. John Hoskyns's observations on the *New Arcadia* in his *Directions for Speech and Style* have been cited, and proverbs have been identified by reference either to Tilley, to the third edition of *The Oxford Dictionary of English Proverbs*, or to other standard collections. Owing to the limited nature of the Commentary, many distinguished books and articles have not been referred to. I hope this may not in any way be misconstrued.

Support for this edition has been considerable. I am grateful to the Canada Council for a Doctoral Fellowship lasting four years; to the University of Reading for a University Fellowship over three years; to the Society for the Humanities at Cornell University for a Junior Fellowship over one year; and to the University of Dundee for a term's leave of absence from my regular teaching duties.

The librarians and staff of many institutions have contributed generously of their time and expertise. I would like especially to thank those of the Bodleian Library, Oxford; of the British Library; of the Fellow's Library, Winchester College; of the Olin Library, Cornell University; and of the libraries of St John's College, Oxford; the University of Dundee, the University of Ottawa, the University of Reading, the University of Southampton, the University College of Swansea, and St Andrews University. I am indebted to the Cambridge University Library for allowing me to use the manuscript of the *New Arcadia*, to the National Library of Wales for providing a copy of the Ottley Manuscript, and to the British Library, the Huntington Library, and the library of the University College of Swansea for their permission to use their copies of various editions of *The Countess of Pembroke's Arcadia*.

Among the many individuals who contributed their specialist knowledge or helped in other ways are Dr Peter Beal, Professor Harold F. Brooks, Mr John Buxton, Professor E. G. Fogel, and Professor Judith M. Kennedy. Dr B. E. Juel-Jensen kindly allowed me to use his collection and to collate his copy of the 1590 edition. Professor John Norton-Smith has sustained for over a decade a learned running commentary on all aspects of the work.

Constant support has been given by the other editors in this series: Professor R. J. P. Kuin and Professor C. S. Levy; Miss K. Duncan-Jones and the late Professor J. van Dorsten; Professor W. A. Ringler, Jr., who made himself available in Chicago and Oxford for discussion of editorial procedures; and especially Dr Jean Robertson, who oversaw the early stages of this edition. Dr Robertson put at my disposal her text of the *Old Arcadia* while it was still in press, and has remained a steady and stimulating correspondent throughout. Her scepticism and prudence have prevented many an error, and what is good in this edition is largely due to her sound scholarship and advice.

To my wife I owe my greatest thanks.

V.S.

The University, Dundee, December 1985

CONTENTS

General Preface	v
Preface to the 1987 Edition	vii
References and Abbreviations	x
General Introduction	xiii
Textual Introduction	xli
The History of *Arcadia* in Print	lxiv
Arcadia Editions Before 1700	lxxi
Rhetorical Figures in the *New Arcadia*	lxxiii
The *New Arcadia*	
The First Book	1
The Second Book	102
The Third Book	266
Appendices	
I. Eclogues from the 1590 edition	404
II. Dedication from the *Old Arcadia*	435
III. Evidence against *T*	436
IV. *New Arcadia* – Rhetorical Figures	441
Commentary	
The First Book	457
The Second Book	487
The Third Book	529
The Eclogues	561
Glossary	565
Index of Characters	584
Index of Other Names	590
Index of Places	592
Index of First Lines of Poems	593
Genealogical Tables	594
General Index to Introduction and Commentary	597

REFERENCES AND ABBREVIATIONS

EDITIONS OF SIDNEY'S WORKS

Misc. Prose *Miscellaneous Prose of Sir Philip Sidney*, ed. K. Duncan-Jones and J. van Dorsten (Oxford, 1973).

Ringler *The Poems of Sir Philip Sidney*, ed. W. A. Ringler, Jr. (Oxford, 1962).

Robertson *The Countess of Pembroke's Arcadia (The Old Arcadia)*, ed. J. Robertson (Oxford, 1973).

Works *The Prose Works of Sir Philip Sidney*, ed. A. Feuillerat, 4 vols. (Cambridge, 1967–9).

TITLES OF SIDNEY'S WORKS

AS *Astrophil and Stella.*
AT 'Wrongly Attributed Poems'.
CS *Certain Sonnets.*
OA *Old Arcadia.*
OP 'Other Poems'.
PP 'Poems Possibly by Sidney'.
PS Sidney's metrical translation of the Psalms.

Reference to one of these works is by the siglum, followed by the poem number assigned by Ringler, by a full stop, and by the line reference.

MANUSCRIPTS OF THE ARCADIA

Abbreviations for the extant manuscripts are given in the List of Sigla, p. lxii–lxiii. Conjectural manuscripts are abbreviated as follows:

A Sidney's draft of the *Old Arcadia* which, after being subjected to minor revision on four occasions designated as A^1, A^2, A^3, and A^4, became the foul copy of the *New Arcadia* as A^5.

T Hypothesized by Ringler (followed by Robertson) and described as a scribal transcript of the *Old Arcadia* foul papers, made for Sidney, used as his working copy, and the source of the extant manuscripts. In Appendix I the evidence for its scribal nature is refuted, and it becomes identified with *A*.

P The manuscript of the *Old Arcadia* referred to by Sidney in his dedication to the Countess of Pembroke; see below, Appendix II.

X The manuscript of the *Old Arcadia* in A^1 from which *Je* and *Hm* were copied.

Y The manuscript of the *Old Arcadia* in A^2 from which *Ph* was copied.

G The manuscript of the *New Arcadia* referred to by Fulke Greville in his letter to Sir Francis Walsingham (see below, p. xlv), identified in this edition with A^5.

OTHER REFERENCES

Abbott	E. A. Abbott, *A Shakespearian Grammar* (London, 1929).
Heliodorus	Heliodore, *Les Ethiopiques*, ed. R. M. Rattenbury and T. W. Lumb, 2nd edn. (Paris, 1960).
Henkel and Schöne	A. Henkel and A. Schöne, eds., *Emblemata* (Stuttgart, 1967).
Hoskyns	John Hoskins [i.e., Hoskyns], *Directions for Speech and Style*, ed. H. H. Hudson (Princeton, 1935).
Juel-Jensen	B. Juel-Jensen, 'Some Uncollected Authors xxxiv, Sir Philip Sidney', *The Book Collector*, xi (1962), 468–79.
Montemayor	J. de Montemayor, *Los Siete Libros de la Diana*, ed. F. Lopez Estrada (Madrid, 1967).
O'Connor	J. J. O'Connor, *Amadis de Gaule and its Influence on Elizabethan Literature* (New Brunswick, NJ, 1970).
Spenser, *Works*	Edmund Spenser, *The Works of Edmund Spenser*, ed. E. Greenlaw and others, 11 vols. (Baltimore, 1932–57).
Tilley	M. P. Tilley, *A Dictionary of the Proverbs in England in the Sixteenth and Seventeenth Centuries* (Ann Arbor, 1966).
Underdowne	Heliodorus, *An Aethiopian History*, trans. T. Underdowne, ed. C. Whibley (London, 1895).
Yong	J. de Montemayor, *A Critical Edition of Yong's Translation of George of Montemayor's Diana and Gil Polo's Enamoured Diana*, ed. J. M. Kennedy (Oxford, 1968).
CELM	*Catalogue of English Literary Manuscripts 1450–1700* (digital resource).
EEBO / TCP	*Early English Books Online / Text Creation Partnership.*
EETS	*Early English Text Society.*
ELH	*Journal of English Literary History.*
ELN	*English Language Notes.*
ELR	*English Literary Renaissance.*
ESTC	*English Short Title Catalogue* (digital resource).
HLQ	*Huntington Library Quarterly.*
JEGP	*Journal of English and Germanic Philology.*
JWCI	*Journal of the Warburg and Courtauld Institutes.*
MLN	*Modern Language Notes.*
MLQ	*Modern Language Quarterly.*
MLR	*Modern Language Review.*
MP	*Modern Philology.*
N & Q	*Notes and Queries.*
ODEP	*The Oxford Dictionary of English Proverbs*, ed. F. P. Wilson, 3rd edn. (Oxford, 1970).
OED	*Oxford English Dictionary.*

Ph. Q	*Philological Quarterly.*
PMLA	*Publications of the Modern Language Association of America.*
RES	*Review of English Studies.*
SP	*Studies in Philology.*
STC	A. W. Pollard and G. R. Redgrave, *A Short-Title Catalogue of Books Printed in England, Scotland, & Ireland* ... 1475–1640, 2nd edn., rev. W. A. Jackson, F. S. Ferguson, and K. F. Pantzer, 2 vols. (London, 1976–86).
TLS	*Times Literary Supplement* .

GENERAL INTRODUCTION

DATE

For some 400 years Sir Philip Sidney's *New Arcadia* has maintained its reputation as one of the most important English books. The text, left unfinished by the author, was published in the quarto of 1590, and in 1593 formed the first and major section of the Countess of Pembroke's folio compilation of Sidney's Arcadian works. Despite the clear acknowledgement there that the appendix printed after the 1590 text constitutes 'the conclusion, not the perfection of *Arcadia*', the *New Arcadia* inevitably lost its distinctive identity and was thenceforth read as the initial heroic part of a work interrupted by the author's 'untimely death'. Few would have recognized that the general outline of the plot as well as the added romantic ending correspond closely to Sidney's earlier *Old Arcadia*, for that circulated only in manuscript. Even fewer would have known to what degree that work had been subjected to editorial alteration or had been revised by the author while he was composing the *New Arcadia*.

In the *New Arcadia* Sidney developed the romantic adventures of the *Old Arcadia* into an epic poem. The essence of the plot remains the same: the two Grecian princes, Pyrocles and Musidorus, fall in love with the Arcadian princesses Philoclea and Pamela. To gain access to the princesses, who are closely watched in a country retreat, Pyrocles disguises himself as an Amazon warrior, Musidorus as a shepherd. Having moved their court to this isolated pastoral location out of fear for an oracle, both King Basilius and Queen Gynecia become affected by loneliness and idleness. Both immediately and passionately fall in love with Pyrocles, impeding his courtship of Philoclea, while Pamela expresses disdain for her shepherd lover. The resolution of this story occupies the whole of the *Old Arcadia*. In the *New Arcadia* it is enmeshed within a succession of martial exploits, and complicated in Book II by a second plot concerning the ruthless ambitions of the bastard Plexirtus. Through conversation, by which the task of narration is shifted from character to character, the past moral, political, and ethical dilemmas, as well as the heroic deeds of the princes, become intertwined with the current political situation in Arcadia. This is brought to a head when Basilius' sister-in-law Cecropia kidnaps Philoclea, Pamela, and the disguised Pyrocles in an attempt to secure the throne for her son Amphialus. Basilius' siege of Cecropia's castle provides the setting for a series of single combats which are interspersed with discussions about and by each of the captives. These battles include those in which the exemplary lovers Argalus and Parthenia are killed, and in which Amphialus is almost mortally wounded. They provide a foil to the final sequence where Pyrocles, still in disguise, single-handedly takes on Zoilus, Lycurgus, and finally Anaxius. The *New Arcadia* comes to an abrupt halt at this juncture, as Musidorus brings a rescue party before the walls, and Pyrocles inside seems to have his remaining captor well in hand.

Sidney never finished this work of revision. Robertson concludes her discussion of the date with the observation that the first draft of the *Old Arcadia* was completed by the spring of 1581, and that Sidney 'continued to tinker' during 1581–2. David Hume of Godscroft indicates an awareness of this progressive revision in reporting that when Sidney visited the Earl of Angus, between June 1581 and August 1582, he 'was then in travail, or had brought forth rather (though not polished and refined it as now it is) ... his *Arcadia*'.[1] The qualification 'not ... as now it is' implies that Hume did not then see the *New Arcadia*. When in 1586 Fulke Greville wrote to Sir Francis Walsingham about the attempted piracy of the *Old Arcadia*, he mentioned 'a correction of that old one don 4 or 5 years since'.[2] He did not make clear whether the 'correction' or the 'old one' was written in 1581 or 1582, but he probably refers to the *Old Arcadia*, as the only concrete evidence about the date, the inscription on the Cambridge University Library manuscript of the *New Arcadia*, reads '1584'.

By 1584 those revisions which constitute the *New Arcadia* were substantially completed. They include the description of a tournament held to celebrate Andromana's wedding anniversary,[3] in which Philisides jousts against an older knight named Lelius before a lady known as the 'star'. As Philisides is in part Sidney himself, these characters have been identified with Sir Henry Lee and with Penelope Devereux, Sidney's 'Stella'.

It may well be that Sidney knew Lee as 'Laelius', but contemporary evidence is scanty. Not until fifteen years after the *New Arcadia* was published did Joshua Sylvester in the Fourth Day of the First Week of his *Divine Weeks* (1605) refer to Lee as 'Hardy Laelius', with the marginal gloss that he was 'now very aged'.[4] Lee was then seventy-five, and he lived until 1610. Much later again, in 1616, three of Lee's houses were named in the Masters' Reports: 'Lelius in Weedon, Lee's Rest and Spilsbury'.[5] In the way that Sidney's work enabled Abraham Fraunce to write of the legal case of 'Mynshew, the very living image of Sir Philip Sidney's Dametas',[6] Lee's nickname may initially have become attached to him by readers of the *New Arcadia*. On the other hand, in his dedication to Sidney of *De Legationibus Libri Tres* (1585) Alberico Gentile described Edward Dyer as 'tuus sophus Laelius', indicating great friendship in the manner of Cicero's *De Amicitia*.[7] Sidney did tilt against Lee in the Accession Day festivities of 17 November 1584, but there is no indication of Lelius' 'willing missing' Philisides. On this occasion they each broke all six lances upon one another.[8] It is the dated tilt list for 17 November 1581 that has caused speculation that the description of Andromana's tournament was written shortly after these celebrations, for among the tilters Sidney is matched against Lee. The undated copy of the same list, however, has 'not' written beside five names in the first three pairs of combatants: Arundel, Lord Windsor, Grey, Lee, and Sidney. Further, as the scored

---

[1] David Hume of Godscroft, *The History of the Houses of Douglas and Angus* (Edinburgh, 1644), 362, cited in Robertson, p. xvii. [2] See below, p. xlv. [3] See below, p. 218–23. [4] Saluste du Bartas, G. de, *Bartas's Divine Weeks and Works*, trans. J. Sylvester (1633), F6ᵛ. [5] J. H. Hanford and S. R. Watson, 'Personal Allegory in the *Arcadia*: Philisides and Lelius', *MP* xxxii (1934), 1–10, citing Public Record Office, Masters' Reports, 1616, F–N, vol. xxv, Hilary term. [6] *The Countess of Pembroke's Ivychurch* (1591), H1. [7] p. *4. [8] R. Strong, *The Cult of Elizabeth* (London, 1977), 206, citing College of Arms MS 4 and 14, and MS Box 37. The score cheque is reproduced in R. Strong, 'Elizabethan Jousting Cheques in the Possession of the College of Arms: II', *The Coat of Arms*, v (1958–9), 64.

jousting cheque which begins with the fourth pair on the tilt list does not include Sidney or Lee, it would appear that they did not even participate.[1]

The other alleged link between the *New Arcadia* and the year 1581 lies in the possibility that Philisides' 'star' is Penelope Devereux. She came to Sidney's attention in that year, and served as the inspiration for *Astrophil and Stella*.[2] In *AS* 41 and 53 Astrophil's performance in the jousts before Stella represents an experience kindred to Philisides' in the *New Arcadia*. But Sidney often adapts his earlier work, using, for example, the same imagery for his description of Mira in *OA* 62, 'What tongue can her perfections tell', and for the praise of Stella's beauty in *AS* song v.[3] In *AS* song viii. 31–2 Sidney does write of '*Stella* star of heavenly fire, / *Stella* lodestar of desire', and in *AS* 73. 5 he addresses her as 'my star'. But amid the abundance of apostrophes to *Stella* such references are scarce, and as Pyrocles addresses Philoclea in the *Old Arcadia* as 'my only star',[4] the image may have no specific connotation. If, unlikely though it may be, Pyrocles and Mira of the *Old Arcadia* became Astrophil and Stella, and they, however indirectly, became Philisides and this 'star', Sidney may have introduced a veiled allusion to Penelope Devereux into Andromana's tournament. Even so, the evidence is too vague to be used for dating. Pyrocles' aside that 'I only remember six verses' of Philisides' eclogue implies a distance in time from any actual event.[5]

Similarly untenable are the relationships which have been posited to lie between the *New Arcadia* and books published in 1584. Analogues have been found in the complexity of the genealogies included in *Leicester's Commonwealth* (1584) and in Sidney's *Defence of the Earl of Leicester*, but such intertwining of family trees is ordinary among the Elizabethan gentry, and there are no specific connections with the *New Arcadia*.[6] The description of 'the decollation of John Baptist' in Reginald Scot's *Discovery of Witchcraft* (1584) no doubt bears an affinity to Cecropia's fake beheading of Philoclea, but the trick was common in fairgrounds, and Scot was not necessarily Sidney's source.[7] Lastly, evidence that Sidney used the 1584 editions of the maps of either Mercator or of Ortelius is equally tenuous, for these were first published in 1578 and 1579 respectively. Nor can they be said definitely to lie behind the Arcadian geographical details: neither contains Rhipa nor Enispe, visited by Musidorus in his search for Pyrocles.[8]

Comparison of the Cambridge University Library manuscript with the other texts reveals that little work, if any, was done on the *New Arcadia* after this copy was made in 1584. Only the complexity of the revision to sections drawn from the *Old Arcadia*, and the great overall length, suggest that Sidney might have begun composition as early as 1582 and continued into 1584.

---

[1] This conclusion is supported by R. C. Yorke, Archivist, The College of Arms, from College of Arms MS M. 4; see R. Strong, *The Cult of Elizabeth*, 206, and S. Anglo, 'Archives of the English Tournament: Score Cheques and Lists', *Journal of the Society of Archivists*, ii (1961), 161.   [2] Ringler, 440, 492.   [3] Ringler, 484, argues that 'this song was composed earlier than the *Astrophil and Stella* sonnets, and that the "Stella" of line 31 was originally "Mira"'.   [4] Robertson, 293, 22.   [5] See below, p. 221, 3.   [6] D. E. Baughan, 'Sidney's *Defence of the Earl of Leicester* and the Revised *Arcadia*', *JEGP* li (1952), 35–41.   [7] See below, p. 373, 25–6 and p. 378, 14 ff.; and S. R. Watson, 'Sidney at Bartholomew Fair', *PMLA* liii (1938), 125–8.   [8] See below, p. 48, 5; and cf. Ringler, 365, 376; D. Connell, *Sir Philip Sidney: The Maker's Mind* (Oxford, 1977), 131–2 and maps; and Robertson, p. lxi and maps.

SOURCES

Strictly speaking, Sidney's principal source is his *Old Arcadia*, of which Greville regarded this second version as 'a correction'. Many of the events and characters are developed from Books I and II, and from the complicated narrative portions of the First and Second Eclogues. Because the remainder of the *Old Arcadia* contains none of this heroic background material, despite its five-act structure the work divides thematically into two.[1] Only the first of these portions is completely rewritten and integrated into the *New Arcadia*, but the Fourth Eclogues are destroyed by the inclusion in the new Book III of the three long poems, *OA* 73, 'Now was our heav'nly vault', *OA* 74, 'Unto a caitiff wretch', and *OA* 75, 'Since that to death'.[2] One poem, 'The fire, to see my woes', is adapted from Sidney's *Certain Sonnets*,[3] while similarities with the prose of Henry Goldwell's *Brief Declaration* (1581) indicate that Sidney may also draw on the assault upon The Fortress of Perfect Beauty, a royal entertainment in which he participated, and which he had a hand in writing.[4]

John Hoskyns notes that 'for the web ... of his story, he followed three: Heliodorus in Greek, Sannazarius' *Arcadia* in Italian, and *Diana* [by] de Montemayor in Spanish'.[5] In the preface to *The English Arcadia, Alluding his Beginning from Sir Philip Sidney's Ending* (1607), Gervase Markham sweeps aside accusations of his own lack of originality by claiming that 'were our age but blessed with his living breath', his model, Sidney, 'would himself confess the honey he drew both from Heliodorus and *Diana*'.[6] And when Sir Thomas Wilson between 1614 and 1620 presents the first book of his 1596 translation of Montemayor's *Diana* to Fulke Greville, he feels assured of a good reception because 'Sir Philip Sidney did very much affect and imitate the excellent author thereof.'[7]

Andromana's desire for both Musidorus and Pyrocles comes from a passage in the *Old Arcadia* based upon Arsace's lust for Thyamis and Theagenes in Heliodorus' *Aethiopian History*.[8] In her attempts to force Theagenes to her will by imprisonment and torture, Arsace becomes a model for Cecropia, capturing and scourging the princesses. Chariclea's efforts to forestall the wrath of Arsace by encouraging Theagenes to promise to fulfil her desires reappear in Pyrocles' plan that Philoclea should feign acquiescence to Amphialus. Like Theagenes, singled out in the *Defence of Poetry* as the model of a true lover,[9] Philoclea prefers physical anguish to perjury.[10] The tale in Heliodorus of the wicked Demaenete who unsuccessfully tries to seduce her stepson Cnemon provides the Second Eclogues of the *Old Arcadia* with the episode of Amasis and his stepmother. Demaenete's tricking of Cnemon into making an armed attack upon his father is transformed in the *New Arcadia* into the

---

[1] Robertson, pp. xx–xxi and xxvii; and R. W. Parker, 'Terentian Structure and Sidney's Original *Arcadia*', *ELR* ii (1972), 61–78. [2] See below, pp. 300, 269, 386 and notes. [3] *CS* 3. See below, p. 340, 1 and note. [4] In J. Nichols, *Progresses of Queen Elizabeth* (1823), ii. 310–29. E. G. Fogel, 'A Possible Addition to the Sidney Canon', *MLN* lxxv (1960), 389–94, presents evidence of Sidney's authorship of the verse, pp. 4 and 5; cf. Ringler, 518–19. See the entries for The Fortress of Perfect Beauty in the Index, which may indicate that Sidney contributed to the prose of that work. [5] Hoskyns, 41. [6] A2ᵛ. [7] British Library MS Add. 18638, ff. 4ᵛ–5, cited in Yong, pp. xxxii, xxxiv. [8] See below, p. 215, 28–9; Robertson, 155; Heliodorus, VII. iv. 2; Underdowne, 178. [9] *Misc. Prose*, 79. [10] See below, p. 372, 17–23; Heliodorus, VII. xxi. 4–5; Underdowne, 197.

rejected Andromana's vengeful plot to have Plangus caught while apparently trying to murder his father.¹ But Andromana's affair with Plangus prior to becoming his stepmother parallels the long and close adaptation of this scene from Heliodorus in Gil Polo's *Enamoured Diana*, a continuation of Montemayor's *Diana*. There the ageing and rejected shepherdess Felisarda, 'because she thought by these means to enjoy the dishonest love of Montanus', marries 'old Filenus' his father.² Following Heliodorus, Montanus is trapped by Felisarda's ruse and is publicly denounced as a parricide. Rather than being sentenced like Cnemon to perpetual exile, Montanus, as does Plangus, flees his persecutors.³

All that remains in the *New Arcadia* of Sannazaro's influence upon the *Old Arcadia* is the plan to separate the books by eclogues, which was never accomplished, the imagery from Sannazaro's eleventh Eclogue in *OA* 75, and the title itself.⁴ Links forged with Montemayor's *Diana* were much stronger. Through them Sidney continues to signal to his readers the sources and the traditional nature of his work. He begins the *New Arcadia* with a close imitation of the easily recognizable opening of the *Diana*, the passage from which he translated *CS* 28 and 29. Strephon's lament for *remembrance* echoes Sireno's for *memoria*; the mutual love of Strephon and Claius for Urania resembles Sireno and Sylvano's for Diana; the association of places with memories of Urania parallels Sireno's memories of where he saw Diana, and her recollections of where she and Sireno were last together; and Claius' imagery in 'what needs this score to reckon up only our losses' follows Sireno's in 'mi cuenta' and 'la summa'.⁵ From the description of Felicia's palace in Book IV of *Diana* Sidney may have gleaned the word *mosaical* and the outline of Kalander's fountain. The tale of Zelmane, the disguised daughter of Plexirtus, could have come either directly from Montemayor, where Felicia disguises herself as a page in order to follow her beloved Felix, or through any of several adaptations of the Siennese drama *Gl'Ingannati*, including Bandello's.⁶ But the comic passions of a series of sighing and frustrated lovers in idyllic country surroundings proved a great influence upon the *New Arcadia*, for they are reflected in Sidney's own tragic love sequence of Philoxenus, Helen, Amphialus, and Philoclea.⁷

For other details Sidney returned to the *Amadis de Gaule*.⁸ Through the medium of the *Old Arcadia*, from Book XI of the *Amadis* came the amorous adventures of two young men. Arlanges falls in love with Cléophile and pretends to be the maid Garaye, an episode which, in Sidney's version, is combined with another from Book IX in which Florisel dresses himself as a shepherd to woo Silvie. Agesilan, attracted to Diane through seeing her picture, disguises himself as the Amazon Daraïde, becomes separated from Arlanges, is shipwrecked, and reaches Galdap. There King Galanides, fooled by his appearance, and Queen Salderne, undeceived, become enamoured of him. From Book VIII Sidney drew on the story of the Soudan

---

¹ See below, p. 191, 9–37; Robertson, 156–8; Heliodorus, I. ix. I–I. xiv. I; Underdowne, 17–22.   ² Yong, 308.   ³ Ibid. 313.   ⁴ See below, p. 386, 25 and note; Ringler, 419–21.   ⁵ See below, p. 2, 15–16; Montemayor, 11–25; Yong, 12–22 and pp. xxxv–xxxix, where the relationship with the *Arcadia* is explored.   ⁶ Montemayor, 105 ff.; Yong, 87 ff.; Bandello, ii. 36; see Yong, 1, J. Robertson, 'Sidney and Bandello', *The Library*, 5th Ser. xxi (1966), 326, and G. Bullough, *Narrative and Dramatic Sources of Shakespeare*, (1957–75), ii. 269 ff., on the sources of *Twelfth Night*.   ⁷ See below, pp. 11, 1–11; 76, 19–23.   ⁸ O'Connor, 183–201; Robertson, pp. xxi–xxii.

Bazilique who keeps his daughter Niquée in a forest lodge, warned by an astrologer that any man seeing her will be brought to madness through love, or to certain death. Amadis de Grèce, moved to love by a picture of Niquée, poses as the Amazon Néreïde in order to see her, but Bazilique falls in love with him and makes lecherous advances. Into the *New Arcadia* Sidney introduced from the *Amadis* the episodes of Queen Helen and her coachmen, of Phalantus and Artesia, of Pyrocles' reactions at the princess's bath, of the scourging of Pamphilus, and of the comic battle between Dametas and Clinias. While Dametas prepares for that encounter, Sidney has him quote from Sir Thomas More's epigram 'In Malum Pictorem' in order to reveal his ignorance about the function of mottos in imprese.[1]

Analogues with classical literature have long been noted. The annotations by W. Blount in his copy of the 1593 edition, and by Issac Vossius in his copy of the 1613 edition, represent such numerous recollections from their classical knowledge as the *Arcadia* elicited.[2] Though Blount read the *Arcadia* with a current mythography at hand, Abraham Fraunce's *Third Part of the Countess of Pembroke's Ivychurch* (1592),[3] neither he nor Vossius caught the deliberate echo of Alcyone's parting from Ceyx in Ovid's *Metamorphoses* xi, woven prominently into Strephon's lament on remembrance, though diffuse and suppressed in Montemayor.[4] They did not identify the closing lines of Virgil's *Aeneid* in the description of the death of Lycurgus,[5] or note the resemblance with Lucian's *Alexander* in the attempt to assassinate the princes on shipboard and the divulgence of the plot.[6] Neither recognized in the blind king of Paphlagonia being led by Leonatus reminiscences of Macrobius' legend of the first Scipio, or of Antigone's leading of the blind Oedipus in Seneca's *Phoenissae*.[7]

Other sources for the *New Arcadia* were Sidney's own interests and experiences. Benoît de Sainte-Maure in the *Roman de Troie* (c. 1160) introduced into the tradition of the story of Troy medieval knights who tilted and tourneyed a thousand years before these sports were known in Greece – Cantacuzenus records that they were imported from Italy in 1326.[8] Sidney therefore had good precedents for including in his own fictional history of a Greek province those activities at which he was most adept. Evidence survives of his participation in major tilts of 1577, 1579, 22 January 1581, 15–16 May 1581, 6 December 1584, and 17 November 1584.[9] The traditional figures and pageantry of these festive occasions were incorporated into the *New*

---

[1] See below, p. 330, 25. [2] Blount's copy is in the Folger Shakespeare Library, Vossius's in the Leiden University Library. [3] Blount's gloss on Apollo, cited in Ringler, 398, is word for word from Fraunce, I4ᵛ. All on Fraunce after 1592 in the *DNB* is in error; see V. Skretkowicz, 'Abraham Fraunce and Abraham Darcie', *The Library*, 5th Ser. xxxi (1976), 239–42. [4] See below, p. 1, 30 ff. and note. [5] See below, p. 369, 17–37 and note. [6] Lucian, *Alexander*, trans. A. M. Harmon, in *Works* (London, 1913–67), iv. 247–9. [7] Macrobius, *Saturnalia*, I. vi. 26; Seneca, *Phoenissae*, I. [8] *Historiarum Libri IV* (1603), Book I, chap. 42, p. 146, cited by Milton in his 'Commonplace Book', trans. R. Mohl, in *The Complete Prose Works of John Milton*, ed. D. M. Wolfe et al (New Haven, 1953–82), i. 489; see M. R. Scherer, *The Legends of Troy* (New York, 1963), p. xiii. [9] Ringler, 474; R. Strong, *The Cult of Elizabeth*, 206. S. Anglo, 'Archives of the English Tournament: Score Cheques and Lists', *Journal of the Society of Archivists*, ii (1961), 161, notes Sidney's name on a list for tourney and tilt dated 1574 (College of Arms MS M. 4, item iv of those mounted between the first blank leaves); but on seeing the copy supplied by Mr R. C. Yorke, Archivist, The College of Arms, it is evident from the opening match between Sir Christopher Hatton and Mʳ Sidney that the erroneous date has been added: Hatton was not knighted till 1 Dec. 1578. See above, p. xiv.

Arcadia in such characters as the 'wild man... full of withered leaves',[1] in Phalantus' Tree of Chivalry, and in Artesia's entry in an allegorical chariot;[2] but the imprese, devices, and costumes worn by the knights were invented according to the requirements of the allegory and symbolism of the plot.

Sidney's fascination with imprese extended at least from 19 December 1573, when in a letter to Hubert Languet he remarked upon the elegance of Ruscelli, *Le Imprese Illustri*.[3] At Nuremberg, between 1 and 4 April 1577, while travelling with Fulke Greville and Languet he visited Joachim Camerarius, the younger, whose *Symbolorum et Emblematum* [1593] includes several emblems similar to those used for imprese in the *New Arcadia*.[4] Other acquaintances showed an appreciation of Sidney's knowledge. Probably in 1582 Abraham Fraunce presented him with a manuscript of original verse to accompany forty emblems, thirty-eight from Giovio and two from Symeoni, copied out of one of the many editions of Giovio's *Dialogo dell'Imprese* in which Symeoni's *Imprese* was published.[5] No doubt Fraunce knew that Sidney's interest went beyond the academic to the practical, and that like so many of his contemporaries he designed his own imprese.[6] Indeed, so important was his contribution to this aspect of chivalric entertainments that soon after he died his prowess in the 'expressing of a perfect device' was noted by Sir Henry Sidney's secretary, Edmund Molyneux.[7] Even in later years Sidney is named among the foremost English practitioners of the art by Camden in the Remains (1605),[8] and by Peacham in *Minerva Britanna* (1612) and in *The Complete Gentleman* (1622).[9]

Unique to English literature of the renaissance period is the detailed description in the *New Arcadia* of horsemanship, both in battle and exhibition. Elizabethan gentlemen were adept not only at jousting, but also at the tourney, the mounted fight with the sword. Sidney recommended to his brother Robert that he practise the blow as well as the thrust with the sword daily, as it would 'make you a strong man at the Tourney and Barriers'[10] – the two events at the Iberian jousts.[11] These, along with running at the ring, formed part of the training recommended by Sir Humphrey Gilbert to Lord Burleigh in his proposals for an officers' academy, written about 1570.[12]

---

[1] S. Anglo, *Spectacle Pageantry, and Early Tudor Policy* (Oxford, 1969), 111, 113, 119, 151; R. Bernheimer, *Wild Men in the Middle Ages* (Cambridge, Mass., 1952), *passim*. In 1575 Sidney was at Leicester's entertainment at Kenilworth where Gascoigne appeared as a wild man; see C. T. Prouty, *George Gascoigne* (New York, 1942), 177 ff., and Robert Langham, *A Letter*, ed. R. J. P. Kuin (Leiden, 1983), 45. See below, p. 221, 31-3.   [2] G. Kipling, *The Triumph of Honour* (Leiden, 1977), 116-36.   [3] *Works*, iii. 81.   [4] Analogues are noted in the Commentary. See V. Skretkowicz, 'Devices and Their Narrative Function in Sidney's *Arcadia*', *Emblematica* i (1986), 267-292; A. P. McMahon, 'Sir Philip Sidney's Letter to the Camerarii', *PMLA* lxii (1947), 83-95; C. S. Levy, 'The Sidney-Hanau Correspondence', *ELR* ii (1972), 19-28; J. A. van Dorsten, *Poets, Patrons, and Professors* (Leiden, 1962), 51 n. 2.   [5] Bodleian Library MS Rawl. D. 345. See J. Buxton, *Sir Philip Sidney and the English Renaissance*, 2nd edn. (London, 1964), 148-50, and K. Duncan-Jones, 'Two Elizabethan Versions of Giovio's Treatise on Imprese', *English Studies*, lii (1971), 118-23.   [6] See K. Duncan-Jones, 'Sidney's Personal Imprese', *JWCI* xxxii (1970), 321-4, and P. Beal, 'Poems by Sir Philip Sidney: The Ottley Manuscript', *The Library*, 5th Ser. xxxiii (1978), 284-95.   [7] See Molyneux's note in Stow's continuation of Holinshed, *Chronicles* (1587, uncensored version), iii. 1555.   [8] Camden, 165, 174.   [9] Peacham, *Minerva Britanna*, 27; *Complete Gentleman*, 199.   [10] *Works*, iii. 133.   [11] See below, pp. 220, 20-222, 11.   [12] Sir Humphrey Gilbert, *Queen Elizabeth's Academy*, ed. F. J. Fumivall, *EETS*, ES viii (1869), pp. ii n., and 4-5. See E. M. Parkinson, 'Sidney's Portrayal of Mounted Combat with Lances', *Spenser Studies*, v (1985), 231-51 and 301-5 (plates 26-30). See below, p. 132, 7-10 and note.

When in 1585 Christopher Clifford dedicated to Sidney his *School of Horsemanship*, a practical manual 'in training horse for service and travail', he both acknowledged Sidney's 'great knowledge and experience in horsemanship' and, in his address 'To the Reader', warned against teaching a war horse to curvet, for fear that it should be overthrown as was Phalantus'.[1] These imaginative leaps and paces of the school horse were evidently a part of the art of riding that Sidney enjoyed, and when he wrote about Musidorus' performance before Pamela he drew not on a literary source but on first-hand information.[2] In *A Defence of Poetry* he recalled his studies under John Pietro Pugliano in the Spanish Riding School in Vienna, founded in 1572, only two years before.[3] By 1580 he was well enough versed in the text-books on horsemanship to urge his brother Robert, in conjunction with his riding exercises, to read Federico Grisone, Claudio Corte, and Pasqual Carracciolo.[4]

It would have been difficult for Sidney not to have known these writers. The riding school tradition established in Naples by Grisone in 1532 had been imported into England by Henry VIII and continued under Elizabeth. It was fostered by Sidney's uncle Robert Dudley, Earl of Leicester, who was named Master of the Horse on 11 January 1558–9.[5]

About 1560 Thomas Blundeville dedicated to him an adaptation of Grisone's treatise on *The Art of Riding*, and in 1565 a translation of Grisone's *Four Chiefest Offices ... Horsemanship*. In the dedication to the *Four Chiefest Offices* he comments on Grisone's continuous influence in the English court through Henry's Riding Master, Robert Alexander, now known as 'old Alexander', the first Master of the Esquires and Riders of the Queen's stable, and 'sometime Grisone's scholar'.[6] And to bring the work up to date, he intends in future to add a supplement to include the recent writings by 'your Honour's most excellent Rider, called Master Claudio Corte'.[7] By bringing into England the top Italian teachers and by sponsoring writers on the art of riding, Leicester spread an appreciation of fine horsemanship widely among the English gentry. Perhaps urged by his patron, Corte in turn publicized the renown of Leicester and of English horses and horsemen on the continent through the dedications to the Italian nobility of his book *Il Cavallerizzo* (Venice, 1572), a compliment which returned to England in Thomas Bedingfield's translation, *The Art of Riding ... Reduced* (1584). Such universal interest in riding ensured that the *New Arcadia* strongly appealed to all who knew Sidney, and with whom, like Edward Denny, he shared his knowledge. When he prepared a reading-list for Denny, he wrote, 'I do in this with you as we do one to another in horsemanship, teach before we have well learned'.[8] Readers would also have appreciated the variations of colour and marking of the Arcadian horses, and recognized where they followed and where they deviated from the descriptions, with associated characteristics, given in Blundeville's *Four Chiefest Offices*.[9]

In all respects, behind Sidney's literary sources lies a kaleidoscope of personal

---

[1] Clifford, 'To the Reader', inserted leaf; see below, p. 319, 31–5 and note. [2] See below, p. 131. [3] *Misc. Prose*, 73. [4] *Works*, iii. 133. [5] *DNB*. [6] See H. Handler, *The Spanish Riding School*, trans. R. Stockman (New York, 1972), 58; C. C. Trench, *A History of Horsemanship* (New York, 1970), 104; and E. Rosenberg, *Leicester Patron of Letters* (New York, 1955), 46–50. [7] Blundeville, A2ᵛ. [8] J. Buxton, 'An Elizabethan Reading-List', *TLS* (24 Mar. 1972), 344. [9] See for example p. 317, 34–6 and note.

experience – in horsemanship, in falconry, in swordsmanship, and in the chase. From his travels to Prague he learned about and possibly even saw Ferdinand of Tirol's star-shaped lodge.[1] Such materials as this and the fair-ground trick used for the false execution of Philoclea, not any the less important for its association with Christian martyrdom, he imbued with symbolic overtones, while, significantly, these elements of the real world lent an atmosphere of credibility to a mythical Arcadia where the accepted currency was Elizabethan crowns.[2]

FORM

In absorbing into the *New Arcadia* recognizable passages from other authors, Sidney loosely used the patchwork technique of the cento. He extended this obvious borrowing to include the various types of literary form which gave the work its shape. Thus Hoskyns could directly point to those three authors who he thought had provided Sidney with his 'web', Heliodorus, Sannazaro, and Montemayor. Along with Xenophon's *Cyropaedia*, Sidney regarded the *Aethiopian History* of Heliodorus as 'an absolute heroical poem'.[3] Its epic structure was praised by Amyot in the proem to his 1547 translation as unique among Greek prose romances, creating suspense by having the story begin in the middle, return to the same point by the conclusion of the first half, then continue in chronological sequence to the end.[4] Like Virgil in the *Aeneid*, Heliodorus followed the form used by Homer in the *Odyssey*.[5]

Sidney imitated this epic form when rearranging his presentation of the narrative from the first two Books and Eclogues of the *Old Arcadia*. After the brief introductory dialogue between Strephon and Claius, the *New Arcadia* begins *in medias res* with the body of Musidorus floating ashore. Sidney complicated this structure by creating within it a second cycle of events, beginning in Book II with the discovery of Leonatus and the blind king of Paphlagonia being attacked by the bastard Plexirtus. Both plots together are brought full circle at the end of Book II, where for the first time their actions and characters intermingle: Pyrocles hears from Basilius that Plangus, believing that the princes have been assassinated through Plexirtus' plotting, has gone to enlist the aid of Euarchus to rescue Erona. Book III goes on from this theoretical mid-point in chronological progression towards an indeterminate ending, which within the requirements of the form must have been intended to be equal to the burden of completing both beginnings.

This doubling of the structure provided the opportunity to exploit another convention. In the manner of Guillaume de Machaut in the 'Dit dou Roy de Behaingne' and 'Dit dou Roy de Navarre', Sidney set his contrasting themes in opposing seasons of the year. The comic and the tragic were represented in separate epic cycles. After the formulaic 'It was in the ...', the opening comic plot begins with an extravagant

---

[1] See V. Skretkowicz, 'Symbolic Architecture in Sidney's *New Arcadia*', *RES* NS xxxiii (1982), 175–80.
[2] See below, p. 373, 25–6 and p. 148, 10. [3] *Misc. Prose*, 81. [4] See V. Skretkowicz, 'Sidney and Amyot: Heliodorus in the Structure and Ethos of the *New Arcadia*', *RES*, NS xxvii (1976), 170–4. [5] C. W. Keyes, 'The Structure of Heliodorus' *Aethiopica*', *SP* xix (1922), 42–51.

periphrasis for spring announcing the theme of love, followed by the pastoral love-laments of Strephon and Claius. This mitigates the results of the tragic second plot, in the fire and fight on shipboard which occur prior to the beginning of the narrative. The tragic theme is announced in Book II by shipwreck and the princes' heroic practice of ethical and political theory, also beginning 'It was in the ...', with the realistic description of winter's bitterness and Plexirtus' armed attack.[1] These two predominant themes, love in the first book and war in the second, are intermingled in the third.

In completion of a general pattern of repetition inherent in epic poetry,[2] the main action of all three books is preceded by complaints of lovers, an abrupt catastrophe, and then by movement of the distressed characters towards those with whom they will interact. In Book I, the lamentations of Strephon and Claius are followed by the discovery of the shipwrecked heroes and by the passage of Musidorus and Pyrocles into Arcadia; in Book II, the anxious pleas of Gynecia, Pyrocles, Basilius (whose distinctness as a trio becomes stressed by the repeated action of Basilius pleading upon his knees),[3] and of Musidorus, Philoclea, and Pamela precede the shipwreck and succeeding travels of Musidorus and Pyrocles through Pontus and Phrygia to Galatia; in Book III, Musidorus' letter to Pamela leads into the kidnapping and the shift of scene to Amphialus' castle. In each book a crisis is followed by a comic interlude provided by Dametas; but whereas the triumphant lyrics in Books I and II seem to dictate that even more outrageous claims of bravery be sung by Dametas after his defeat of Clinias in Book III, Sidney instead delays the anticipated good-humoured lyrical summary of events, substituting for it the sombre recapitulation in the epitaph for Argalus and Parthenia.

These larger forms embrace smaller sections, following Sannazaro's model in the plan to provide predominantly verse eclogues as pastoral interludes between the books, or Montemayor's design in integrating both long and short poems into the narrative, as had Belleforest in his renderings of Bandello. Montemayor also interwove several interrupted tales which progressed in tandem towards their conclusion. Scaliger had praised these in Heliodorus because they imitated nature and created suspense[4] and Sir John Harington defended abrupt divisions in Ariosto because they were in 'the printed' *Arcadia*, where one could read the 'tale of Phalanto and his company women', and commented, 'this doubtless is a point of great art, to draw a man with a continual thirst to read out the whole work, and toward the end of the book to close up the diverse matters briefly and cleanly. If S[ir] Philip Sidney had counted this a fault, he would not have done so himself in his *Arcadia*.'[5] Sidney was at pains to relate these suspended units to the action, as if they took the form of scenes naturally interrupting one another as the series of events unfolded in dramatic sequence.[6]

The simple device of verbal repetition successfully counteracts the fragmenting effect of these shorter scenes, at times creating an illusory sense of unity, as in the

---

[1] See below, p. 154, 6. [2] See the note to p. 57, 28. [3] See below, pp. 107, 3–4; 195, 24. [4] J. C. Scaliger, *Poetices Libri Septem (1561)* (Stuttgart, 1964) III. xcvi. 144. [5] Harington, in the Moral to Books xi and xx, and in the Preface to his translation, *Luduvico Ariosto's Orlando Furioso*, ed. R. McNulty (Oxford, 1972), 13. [6] See E. Jones, *Scenic Form in Shakespeare* (Oxford, 1971), 49–50.

deliberate echoes of Musidorus' chastising of Pyrocles in Pyrocles' own speeches to Basilius and to Philoclea,[1] or in Anaxius' 'blaspheming heaven' for its powers over him.[2] After the deaths of Philoxenus and Timotheus, when, as Ismenus tells Queen Helen, Amphialus abandons society, taking only his sword, 'waited on by his dog ... seeking out the most solitary places', he appears to flee directly to the banks of the Ladon, where, armed only with his sword, he claims that 'he had only been to seek solitary places ... guided to that place by his spaniel'.[3] His explanation of how at midday 'a dream waked him, and made him see that whereof he had dreamed' is thrown into juxtaposition with his dream of Mira, the embodiment of Diana and Venus which he wrongly takes to be Philoclea, 'the night before he fell in love with her'. But through this dream, which adapted Tottel's version of Petrarch's description of the day he fell in love with Laura, Sidney makes it clear that Amphialus' Mira is Queen Helen, who bears Laura's emblem of chastity, the ermine, and who is described as 'a Diana apparelled in the garments of Venus'. It was fitting, therefore, to draw this circle of events to a close with Amphialus once more appearing with only his sword, this time to confront his mother, to attempt suicide symbolically with the knives he carries as love tokens from Philoclea, and to be taken off to be cured by his true Mira, Helen, in whose arms he seems destined to awake.[4]

Dramatic form descends naturally from the five-act structure of the *Old Arcadia*, and Sidney reinforces the expectation of dramatic action by imitating Heliodorus and those authors such as Bandello who constantly refer to drama in their metaphors.[5] In the convention of morality plays, Erona's dilemma becomes a monologue spoken by love;[6] but there is an even closer relationship with drama in the unity and form of the *New Arcadia*, for the interrupted scenes designed to create epic suspense both blend naturally and cohere through dramatic irony and its attendant foreknowledge.

Although Sidney erred in his revision by having Pyrocles refer, as in the *Old Arcadia*, to 'uncertainty of his [Basilius'] estate' being a cause of the rebellion, a topic not introduced until Clinias' later speech,[7] there are nevertheless several examples of carefully planned disclosure, either of themes, as inconstancy among men and constancy in God,[8] or of episodes which will be developed. Pyrocles' narration of Plexirtus' quest for Artaxia, qualified by her condition that she would only marry a 'prince who would give sure proof that by his means we were destroyed', precedes Plexirtus' attempt on their lives.[9] In 'telling Zelmane he was afraid she had stolen away his daughters', Basilius anticipates the abduction of the princesses.[10] Cecropia informs Philoclea 'that if her son would follow her counsel, he should take another course with her', which presages her urging of him towards rape.[11] The suggestion that on the island 'could no secret treachery be wrought; and for manifest violence,

---

[1] See below, pp. 59, 25–60, 3; 63, 37–64, 2; 195, 8–9; 200, 1–2.   [2] See below, pp. 342, 1–2; 401, 21.   [3] See below, pp. 56, 39–57, 1; 170, 28–30.   [4] See below, pp. 170, 32–3; 299, 36 ff.; 86, 35; 219, 30; 381, 21 ff.   [5] See A. Heiserman, *The Novel Before the Novel* (Chicago, 1977), 96, and E. R. Curtius, *European Literature and the Latin Middle Ages*, trans. W. R. Trask (London, 1979), 138–44.   [6] See below, p. 179, 30–180, 16.   [7] See below, pp. 248, 12–13; 252, 12–13.   [8] See below, pp. 207, 19 ff.; 311, 23–5; 312, 22–4.   [9] See below, pp. 233, 20–1; 236, 14–16.   [10] See below, p. 192, 35–6.   [11] See below, pp. 321, 10–11; 348, 22 ff.

either side might have time enough to succour their party', prepares the reader for the sending of rescuers to retrieve Amphialus and Musidorus.[1] Cecropia's taking of both Philoclea and Pamela to watch the battles sets the stage for both Amphialus and Musidorus to seek inspiration from the windows, and causes them to believe themselves rivals;[2] and her telling Philoclea, 'since they were not to be gotten, there was no way for her son's quiet but to know that they were past getting', suggests that her idle threat might become her next course of action, for she plans 'secretly to empoison them – thinking, since they were not to be won, her son's love would no otherwise be mitigated'.[3] That Amphialus 'had good cause to repent' breaking his good sword after he kills Parthenia anticipates his serious predicament when he breaks a weaker blade over Musidorus and is left unarmed.[4] And information about the string of participants in Phalantus' tourney, especially as it concludes with Zelmane, who resembles Philoclea,[5] prepares the reader for the action of the second plot.

These straightforward connections between scenes are interwoven with a wealth of complex symbolic patterns. The dominance of the theme of love is established from the outset by the laments of Claius and Strephon over the departure of Urania for Cythera, home of a cult to Venus. Traditional associations of Urania with celestial love make it no surprise that the mutual love experienced by these shepherd philosophers cannot be fulfilled in earthly terms, and Sidney exploits this in an allegory by which they deliver Musidorus and, by implication, Pyrocles into the care of Kalander – a devotee not of Urania but of the cult of that Venus who was mother of the mortal Aeneas, and patroness of heroic love. The fountain in Kalander's garden is not merely decorative, but a quasi-religious idol appropriate to a temple.[6] It serves as a notice to the reader that Musidorus and Pyrocles will become subject to heroic love, and elaborates upon the earlier allusion to Pyrocles as 'some god begotten between Neptune and Venus'.[7] On the surface this provides the rationale for the fishermen sailing past and the separation of the heroes. But in the underlying pattern Pyrocles appropriately becomes the son of the patrons of chivalry and love, and by his surrogate mother is metaphorically identifiable as the brother of Aeneas and Cupid. Pyrocles' wiliness in love is emblematized by his association with Jupiter, when he possessed Danae in a golden shower.[8]

To accentuate this theme of the divine nature of love, Sidney built in a series of contrasts. Erona's desecration of the icons of the cult of Cupid brings retribution against her. Venus is seen as the worn-out sister of Diana in Amphialus' dream vision, and as the patroness of sluts such as Mopsa or of courtesans like Artesia, wooed by Phalantus in a style compared to that of Mercury, god of deceivers.[9] And even Aeneas, according to Dido's scathing description of Pamphilus, is the exemplar of false love.[10]

---

[1] See below, pp. 318, 13–15; 357, 17 ff. [2] See below, pp. 317, 28; 320, 35–321, 2; 351, 19–20. [3] See below, pp. 368, 17–18; 381, 19–21. [4] See below, pp. 346, 31; 356, 13–26. [5] See below, pp. 57, 28; 66, 31; 83, 31–6 (where Pyrocles hints at her death); 232, 16. [6] See below, pp. 11, 6–11; 302, 33–6. [7] See below, p. 5, 21–2 and note. [8] See below, p. 195, 25–6 and note; cf. p. 71, 31–2 and note. [9] See below, pp. 177, 20 ff; 301, 33–36; 14, 13; 79, 16–17. [10] See below, p. 207, 37.

The course love was to take is depicted in the symbolic pictures in Kalander's garden house, in itself not unlike Lydgate's *Temple of Glas*. The painting of 'Diana, when Actaeon saw her bathing' implies that chastity will impede the fulfilment of love by transforming the lover into an unfortunate wretch. In this picture, Diana's nymph 'weeping and withal louring' at Actaeon is reflected in Pamela's 'louring beauty' as she rejects Musidorus' advances. But the myth is overtly parodied in Philoclea's reaction to Amphialus. Wearing her 'nymphlike apparel', she departs 'not without so mighty a lour as that face could yield' after he watches her bathing, while Pyrocles, who has already undergone a metamorphosis, escapes her wrath by virtue of his disguise.[1] The second in this pair of pictures depicts Atalanta, cruelly chaste but won by Hippomenes through a ruse supported by Venus, and as such symbolic of the triumph of love over chastity. The triad of 'Helena, Omphale, Iole' is used to hint at complications which love will bring about. The kidnapping of the princesses is foreshadowed in Helen of Troy; in Omphale the analogy is drawn between the enforced humiliation of Hercules in woman's apparel 'by Omphale's commandment' and the new roles taken on by Pyrocles and Musidorus as dictated by their situations; and the picture of Iole, out of love for whom Hercules was said to have died, is indicative of Amphialus' fatal love for Philoclea. While the captive Pyrocles wears his device of Hercules in Omphale's power, Cecropia's lying taunts to Amphialus that he rape the princesses again unite Helen and Iole to point towards the success of the siege and Amphialus' death – or, at least, the death of his passion for Philoclea.[2]

Merely by his connection with Amphialus and Hercules, Argalus seems to share their doom. Among all Arcadians, Amphialus is 'only accounted likely to match' Argalus, whose Herculean labours have helped him win Parthenia. In contrast to Amphialus, the emblem of manliness conquered by love, Argalus goes out to fight Amphialus 'like a man in whom honour could not be rocked on sleep by affection', breaking away from reading the stories of Hercules to Parthenia.[3] To such forebodings are added dreams and prophecies, such as Amphialus' dream of Philoclea which 'not obscurely signified that he felt the smart of his own doings'; those experienced by the victims of war; and Parthenia's dream that brings her to Argalus' side.[4] These support the atmosphere established in the early prognostications of Basilius' death. Strephon and Claius' echo of Alcyone's lament for Ceyx, drowned on his way to consult an oracle, and the comet-shaped lodge, are omens of death reiterated in Gynecia's dream of a decaying body which seems to be her husband's, and in the oracle where Basilius has been 'made dead' and lies upon a bier.[5] Such foreknowledge is directed at the reader to set the overall tone: Musidorus' floating ashore in the manner of Ceyx, but then being found to be alive, betokens the note of optimism that pervades the work.

---

[1] See below, pp. 11, 14 ff; 267, 2; 71, 28; 170, 35–6; 'lour' is also used at p. 345, 34.   [2] See below, pp. 58, 26; 348, 27–32; and V. Skretkowicz, 'Hercules in Sidney and Spenser', *N & Q* xxvii (1980), 306–10.   [3] See below, pp. 22, 6; 23, 38; 322, 5–26.   [4] See below, pp. 170, 33–4; 244, 2–4; 295, 8 ff.; 326, 15.   [5] See below, pp. 1, 28–2, 24; 3, 15–18; 73, 18; 239, 37–240, 9; 255, 35–6. In the *Old Arcadia* Gynecia recalls her dream while looking upon Basilius' body (Robertson, 117, 280, 287).

Sidney wrote for a knowledgeable audience with a wide appreciation of the symbolic and the emblematic. According to Grisone, Amphialus' horse which has a white left forefoot ('left foot before') possesses a serious flaw; but it stands auspiciously with its right or 'further foot' forward and triumphs in battle by pushing over Phalantus' curvetting mount.[1] Other symbolism serves a double purpose, partly foreboding, partly ironic. Phalantus in his horse's mane and tail, and Artesia in her chariot, bear the colour of desire, carnation, enhancing the scathing description of them as Mercury wooing Venus, dishonesty courting prostitution.[2] Befitting one who dies in her ambition to marry Prince Amphialus, Artesia is depicted as the aspiring mortal, Phaeton, on his fatal ride in his father Phoebus' chariot, despite being warned that what he desired was fit only for a god.[3] Phalantus, who easily lies about being twice unhorsed,[4] is primarily desirous of the pleasure denoted by his Bacchic furniture, reins and bit. His armour at the triumph may apply either to his or to Artesia's egotism, both being 'a heaven' surrounded by a bevy of captured beauties. His impresa is 'full of stars, with a speech signifying that it was the beauty which gave it the praise': 'so hath his lance brought ... a forced false testimony to Artesia's excellency'.[5] His own vanity is equally demonstrated when he meets Amphialus in armour 'blue like the heaven, which a sun did ... gild', exhibiting a self confidence lacking in more heroic knights whose unfulfilled aspirations are indicated by their mottoes: 'From whose I am, banished', 'the poor beast wanted the moon's light', and 'The best place [among the stars] yet reserved'.[6] Phalantus' inconstancy is expressed by the waving water of his furniture. The nets in which caught fish strive for freedom refer to his own condition as Artesia's victim, a theme reiterated in Pamela's accusation to her that 'now the time is come that thy wicked wiles have caught thyself in thine own net' – compare Andromana's attempt to bring Musidorus and Pyrocles '(as willingly-caught fishes) to bite at her bait'.[7] But this was also a traditional emblem for the plight of married men, a depth to which Phalantus did not dare plunge.[8] He wears his device as lightly as his commitment either to Artesia or to battle, for 'it was rather choice than nature that led him to matters of arms, so, as soon as the spur of honour ceased, he willingly rested in peaceable delights'.[9] And when he sportingly challenges Amphialus under the motto 'The glory, not the prey' to demonstrate to Artesia 'whom she had so lightly forsaken', Sidney takes care to have the symbolism ironically redound upon him, reversing the roles of victor and vanquished. As the greyhound frees the hare, so Amphialus spares Phalantus.[10]

Other imprese and symbols, though less systematically related, are more directly applied. Amphialus' deadly torpedo fish signals his defeat of Phalantus, Argalus, and Parthenia; but when he appears 'not in his wonted furniture' but under the aegis of a mere shadow to face Musidorus' basilisk-eyed catoblepta, he is clearly foredoomed.[11] Before he challenges Amphialus, Argalus' fate is intimated in his

---

[1] See below, pp. 317, 34–6, 318, 39–40; 319, 33–4.   [2] See below, pp. 318, 18–19; 80, 33–4; 79, 16–17.   [3] See below, p. 80, 34–6; Ovid, *Met.* ii. 53–6.   [4] See below, pp. 88, 36–9; 320, 4–5.   [5] See below, pp. 80, 30–2; 80, 9–15.   [6] See below, pp. 318, 26–8; 350, 20; 350, 32–3; 357, 7.   [7] See below, pp. 84, 14–18; 337, 15–16; 215, 37.   [8] See J. Camerarius, *Symbolorum et Emblematum*, IV. xxi.   [9] See below, p. 78, 2–4.   [10] See below, pp. 318, 30; 316, 10–11.   [11] See below, pp. 318, 6; 350, 10–20; 350, 30.

desire that Parthenia's tears should not be 'a presage unto me of that which you would not should happen', in his claim that he was not given so great a blessing as Parthenia 'so soon to be deprived of it', and in her death-like swoon because of which he fails 'to print his heart in her sweet lips'. The gilt knots of woman's hair over his armour are both love tokens and symbols of mourning. The bleeding hearts in his sleeve, made by Parthenia for him to wear in jousts during their frustrated courtship, hold a premonition of renewed sorrow. Most overtly symbolic is the destruction of his shield with its two palm trees, the emblem of perfect union in love. Amphialus' onslaught is so severe that Argalus' 'shield had almost fallen piecemeal to the earth'. But when the weakened Argalus gathers his strength into a devastating twohanded blow, requiring him first to cast 'away the lillie remnant of his shield',[1] the reader knows even before Argalus does that his life with Parthenia is over.

While device and symbol alert the reader to the outcome of events, their absence introduces the element of surprise. There is no indication that Pyrocles is captain of the helots or that Philoclea is the 'poor gentlewoman' who visits Pyrocles in his cell.[2] Much as identification of the cured Parthenia is delayed until after Argalus' love has been tested,[3] Sidney increases suspense by preserving the anonymity of the Knight of the Tomb. In other circumstances devices become clues in a mystery. The ominous sepulchre, cypress, and the black worms in which she is costumed, along with her impresa of a child with two heads, 'whereon, the one showed that it was already dead; the other alive, but ... looking for death', clearly symbolize Parthenia's vow to follow Argalus, who with her made 'one life double because they made a double life one', and who regarded her as his 'better half'.[4] But in addition, Sidney uses Parthenia's death in a scheme to epitomize the tragic effects of love on Arcadia. Events become related not in the usual sequence of expectation and fulfilment, but rather through loose repetitions which connect them in retrospect. The descriptive catalogue of Parthenia's hair, eyes, lips, and cheeks as she lies preparing for her marriage in death to Argalus, witnessed by Amphialus, both follows the description of her eyes, lips, cheeks, and hair at her wedding, and parodies Pyrocles' encomium upon the naked Philoclea, again watched by Amphialus. As Philoclea's breasts 'of marble clear, / Where azured veins well mixed appear' in that instance relate her to the blue veined statue of Venus, so Philoclea's blood running through 'sapphire-coloured brooks' which 'Sweet islands make' establishes a further relationship with Parthenia, both through her heroic love and through her wound, for 'here was a river of purest red, there, an island of perfittest white'.[5] Such an idyllic geographical description couched in a parallel structure hearkens back to the innocence of Musidorus' first vision of Arcadia with its ideal of pastoral love: 'here, a shepherd's boy piping, as though he should never be old; there, a young shepherdess knitting and withal singing'.[6] Through these echoes of one scene in another, the misery of the state is contrasted against the happiness it once appeared to promise.

The classical device of formulaic repetition also draws together contrasting scenes, as in the statement of Anaxius' intention 'with his own hands to kill the

---

[1] See below, pp. 323, 15–23; 324, 14–25; 325, 20–1; 326, 6–7.   [2] See below, pp. 31, 28–30; 376, 1.   [3] See below, p. 37, 20.   [4] See below, pp. 342, 33 ff.; 327, 24–5; 322, 11; 327, 31.   [5] See below, pp. 344, 14–22; 40, 10–16; 165, 23–4; 11, 8; 167, 26–8; 344, 23–4.   [6] See below, p. 7, 40–8, 1.

two sisters' and its restatement twice within a few hundred words,[1] or in the simple repetition of *live* by Philoclea in despair over Pamela, and by Pyrocles in despair over Philoclea, and of *lived* by Amphialus in despair over himself.[2] Repeating words based upon *conquer* focuses attention on the variety of ethical motivations behind Parthenia's mother's hatred of Argalus, Phalantus' superficiality in capturing pictures of women, the princes' willingness to sacrifice themselves for one another in Phrygia, Pyrocles' jealous challenge of Amphialus, Pyrocles' and Musidorus' heroic stand against the rebels, Cecropia's fruitless rhetoric directed at Pamela and her reply, both Argalus' and Musidorus' honourable fights against the dishonourable Amphialus, and Amphialus' attempted suicide.[3] When Amphialus in artificially rusty armour rides up to Musidorus prior to their final encounter, he greets him with the words, 'because we are men and should know reason why we do things, tell me the cause that makes you thus eager to fight with me'. Through this easily recognizable parody of Musidorus' earlier caution to Pyrocles, 'if we will be men, the reasonable part of our soul is to have absolute commandment', Sidney forces the reader to consider the relative merits of their sense of honour. The association is reinforced because Musidorus and Pyrocles themselves have twice met in combat where rusty armour is worn, Musidorus in the stratagem to deceive the helots, and Pyrocles as the ill-apparelled Knight.[4] Sidney brings Amphialus into direct comparison with Pyrocles when Amphialus accidentally kills Musidorus' horse. He dismounts before continuing the fight 'because he would not have fortune come to claim any part of the victory', echoing Pyrocles' account of his actions after killing Anaxius' horse, 'because I would not be beholding to fortune for any part of the victory, I descended'.[5] Shortly prior to Artesia's treachery, Phalantus' claim when pushed over by Amphialus that 'never yet did any man bring me to the like fortune' brings into contrast his being driven from his horse by Pyrocles when 'that disgrace befell him which he had never before known', much to Artesia's sorrow.[6] Finally, using as his basis for comparison Queen Helen's exclamation, 'what sorrow, what amazement, what shame was in Amphialus when he saw his dear foster-father find him the killer of his only son', Sidney creates a double contrast; for when Musidorus is banished from Pamela, 'It was not an amazement, it was not a sorrow, but it was even a death which then laid hold of Dorus', and when Pyrocles looks upon the severed head of Philoclea, 'It was not a pity; it was not an amazement; it was not a sorrow which then laid hold on Pyrocles, but a wild fury of desperate agony'.[7]

It is no accident that these repetitions, embracing as they do the whole of Amphialus' career, bring his character into disrepute. As the anti-hero, Amphialus is relentlessly pilloried by being the only character to bear the formulaic epithet of classical heroes. Pamela is repeatedly associated with 'majesty' and Philoclea with 'humility' and 'sweetness', but Amphialus by design has the attribute he most lacks attached to his name, *courteous*. Sidney uses 'the courteous Amphialus', an ironic

---

[1] See below, pp. 384, 2–3; 390, 30–1; 392, 6–7; and the note to p. 57, 28.   [2] See below, pp. 372, 25 ff.; 374, 3–4; 375, 4 ff.; 382, 1 ff.   [3] See below, pp. 24, 4–5; 82, 14; 147, 27–8; 149, 7; 170, 3–4; 243, 9; 308, 36–7; 309, 12–14; 326, 38–9; 354, 9; 383, 13–4.   [4] See below, pp. 351, 4–6; 60, 4–5; 29, 1; 87, 15.   [5] See below, pp. 353, 20–1; 209, 15–16; see the note to p. 294, 23.   [6] See below, pp. 336, 19 ff.; 320, 4–5; 88, 38–9.   [7] See below, pp. 54, 35–7; 267, 9–10; 373, 35–6.

imitation of Virgil's incantatory *pius Aeneas*, to establish a cynical brotherhood between him and 'The courteous Vulcan, when he wrought... Aeneas an armour'.¹ In this way Amphialus appears to be an old-fashioned, classical hero whose actions and free will are controlled by superior forces. Even worse, he is wholly governed by his mother within the scenario she creates in order to exploit his passion to her own ends. In contrast, Sidney's modern princes, Musidorus and Pyrocles, actively pursue their chosen humanitarian course as individuals within the renaissance mould. Philoclea remarks that they are 'following the course which virtue and fortune led them'.² But Musidorus more precisely describes how they decided to 'employ those gifts esteemed rare in them to the good of mankind' by going 'privately to seek exercises of their virtue, thinking it not so worthy to be brought to heroical effects by fortune or necessity (like Ulysses and Aeneas) as by one's own choice and working'.³

Nor does Sidney omit to unite the various symbols and episodes concerning the lives of Musidorus and Pyrocles into a coherent whole. In having Phalantus 'considering the Arcadian manner in marching, encamping, and fighting' as they entrench themselves to besiege Amphialus, the improved Arcadian force is compared with its undisciplined state in Book I. Musidorus there observed that 'neither cunning use of their weapons, nor art showed in their marching or encamping' as they prepared to engage the helots. This earlier minor episode, where Clitophon and Argalus are rescued, is exploited as a device to foreshadow the outcome of the major crisis in Book III. Even as an armed force advances against Amphialus' castle, and Pyrocles hopes 'that Musidorus would find some means to deliver them', the reader senses that Musidorus will again unexpectedly find his objective in Pyrocles' control.⁴ Likewise, Musidorus' skirmish with Amphialus between their warring armies, 'worthy to have had more large lists, and more quiet beholders', is contrasted verbally against Pyrocles' more heroic but entirely private combat with Anaxius, 'such a combat as might have demanded as a right, of fortune, whole armies of beholders', and in the lists of their attributes while fighting.⁵

Using a similar technique, Sidney creates a series of parallel situations to substantiate Musidorus' admission that neither he 'nor any man living' could perform any feat more strongly, nimbly, gracefully, or virtuously than Pyrocles – a reputation befitting the lover of Philoclea, to whose 'memory principally all this long matter', the *New Arcadia*, 'is intended'.⁶ Pyrocles' martial superiority is established early when as captain of the helots he defeats Musidorus.⁷ When Musidorus triumphs over Amphialus at their third meeting, he does so with so slight an edge that both were 'filling the veins with rage instead of blood'.⁸ Evidently Amphialus' victory over Argalus is easier, for of the two Argalus alone resorts to 'filling his veins with spite instead of blood'.⁹ Amphialus' true match is Anaxius, whom he has been unable to beat on four occasions, and to whom he is even indebted for saving his life, until he reciprocates by rescuing Anaxius from the Black Knight, Musidorus.¹⁰ With

---

¹ See below, p. 351, 29–30.   ² See below, p. 178, 18–19.   ³ See below, p. 153, 32–7.   ⁴ See below, pp. 316, 3–4; 28, 4–5; 397, 36; 398, 23.   ⁵ See below, pp. 298, 32–3; 402, 3–4.   ⁶ See below, pp. 141, 4–7; 123, 4.   ⁷ See below, p. 31, 17–21.   ⁸ See below, p. 355, 12–13.   ⁹ See below, p. 326, 4.   ¹⁰ See below, pp. 338, 10–11; 342, 3–5.

Anaxius' ability equalled on four occasions by Amphialus, Amphialus defeated by Musidorus at the third attempt, and Musidorus himself clearly bettered by Pyrocles, Pyrocles' success over Anaxius in their meeting, which has been so long delayed and with which the *New Arcadia* ends, is completely ensured.

The conclusions drawn from such simple equations are supported by a complex set of allusions to the shields and armour used in battles between Aeneas and Turnus in the *Aeneid* and between Aeneas and Achilles in the *Iliad*. These round out the relationship of Pyrocles and Musidorus to the statue of Venus with her babe Aeneas which stands symbolically in Kalander's garden.[1] When Musidorus triumphantly encounters Amphialus, 'The courteous Vulcan, when he wrought at his now courteous wives request Aeneas an armour, made not his hammer beget a greater sound than the swords of those noble knights did'. In the *Aeneid*, Venus has armour made to protect Aeneas, arguing that such a request had previously been granted to Nereus' daughter, Thetis, mother of Achilles.[2] It is by the later description of Pyrocles killing Lycurgus, in which Sidney so overtly imitates the closing lines of the *Aeneid* where Aeneas defeats and slays Turnus, his rival for Lavinia, that the application of the first allusion is brought into focus.[3] It signifies Musidorus' victory over his mistaken *rival* (the word is repeated) Amphialus. This event finds its parallel in the fight between Anaxius and Pyrocles, where they are depicted as Achilles and Aeneas. Completing the comparison of Musidorus and Amphialus to 'the lion that beats himself with his own tail to make himself the more angry', which follows Homer's account of Achilles as he begins his fight with Aeneas, and the description of Philoclea being scourged 'like a fair, gorgeous armour hammered upon by an ill-favoured smith', in this final battle the boastful Anaxius 'had a huge shield – such, perchance, as Achilles showed to the pale walls of Troy'.[4] But in Pyrocles Sidney conflates the Homeric with the Virgilian Aeneas. For though Aeneas has to be rescued by Poseidon when he fights Achilles in the dispute over Helen,[5] he decisively defeats Turnus. Thus, in the *New Arcadia* there is no doubt of the outcome. Sidney's artistry has already made it clear that Pyrocles is destined to conquer Anaxius, his newest rival for the hand of the abducted Philoclea. What remains unresolved is whether, having adapted the end of the *Aeneid*, Sidney, like Vegio in his Thirteenth Book, felt that a romantic sequel ought to follow after the heroic section of the epic had come to its natural conclusion.[6]

STYLE

The high degree of artificiality in the form of the *New Arcadia* is equalled by the controlled manipulation of prose, verse, and characterization.[7] Imitation of highly figured Graeco-Roman style creates an elevated atmosphere reminiscent of classical epic and romance. Appropriate to this tone are the amorous and martial activities

---

[1] See below, p. 11, 6–10.　[2] See below, p. 351, 29–31.　[3] See below, p. 400, 30–401, 11; *Aeneid*, xii. 930 ff.　[4] See below, pp. 355, 4–5; 364, 35–6; 402, 22–3.　[5] *Iliad*, xx. 321 ff.　[6] In addition to continental editions, there were three published in England appended to the *Aeneid*, in 1553, 1580, and 1584; see the *STC* under *Vegius*.　[7] For the development of Sidney's style, see Robertson, pp. xxix–xxxiv.

of the central characters. In a plot designed to exhibit personal virtue through a variety of testing circumstances, each episode is couched in a style suited to its context. Whereas Parthenia's wound is beautified, set as it is within a series of idyllic metaphors, the five drunken rebels are placed in an anti-heroic parody of the battle between the Centaurs and Lapiths, from which 'the painter returned well-skilled in wounds, but with never a hand to perform his skill'.[1] In such verbal repetition, seldom does the same meaning attach twice to any word, a device which enhances the blending of rhetorical figures into one another with a rhythmic fluency that seems to have baffled pedantic readers. More than one deliberately unbalanced sentence was subjected to balancing, and imaginative flights of verbal relationships grounded into logicality by the editor of the second edition, which is probably why Hoskyns selected his examples of speech and style out of the 1590 quarto.[2]

The formal structure of longer speeches is seldom developed from exordium to peroration;[3] more usually, it is interrupted by some twist in the plot or fragmented to reflect emotional turmoil.[4] The impression of formality is sustained, however, by metaphors comparing broken speeches with the structures they were intended to fulfil,[5] and in references to delivery through 'gesture' which derives strength from the eyes – as in the blind king of Paphlagonia who 'needed not take to himself the gestures of pity, since his face could not put off the marks thereof'.[6] Such allusions to rhetoric lend an appearance of consistency, and are perhaps what led Jonson to criticize Sidney for 'making every one speak as well as himself'. Such an accusation, levelled also at Lucan and Guarini,[7] just as strongly reflects the opinion of a dramatist with experience of Marlowe and Shakespeare as it indicates defective dialogue in the *New Arcadia*, for what Sidney's characters say, and how they speak, tends to indicate how their given personalities become shaded by psychological states. Idealistic *naïveté* is reflected in Strephon's exaggerated 'sweetest fairness and fairest sweetness'; hesitation in the parentheses which fragment Pyrocles' disclosure of his identity to Philoclea; despair in Amphialus' self-depreciatory anaphora, 'Thou hast lived ... thou hast lived', and mental derangement in his apostrophe to his 'filthy hand'.[8] What Jonson completely overlooked was the gentle understanding of a countryman which contributes to the style of Sidney's rustics, in Dametas' swearing, Lalus' challenge to Phalantus, and the miller's rural usage in 'two milch-kine'.[9] With rustic disorganization Mopsa 'tumbled into her matter' when she recounts the enigma of the princess who runs away for love,[10] and Miso's corrupt 'anothergaines' is as earthy as her tale of her salacious past.[11]

Such contrived lowering of the tone is distinct from Sidney's own usage. Although he 'shunned usual phrases' in his inventive use of diction,[12] ordinary

---

[1] See below, pp. 344, 18–26; 243, 17–244, 12.   [2] Hoskyns, 1; see the Index, under *Hoskyns*.   [3] See L. Challis, 'The Use of Oratory in Sidney's *Arcadia*', *SP* lxii (1965), 561–76, and P. A. Duhamel, 'Sidney's *Arcadia* and Elizabethan Rhetoric', *SP* xlv (1948), 134–50.   [4] See, for example, p. 129, 36–130, 8.   [5] See below, pp. 59, 22–4; 311, 14–17; 335, 38–336, 2; 371, 40–372, 6.   [6] See below, p. 157, 19–20; and also pp. 224, 5–6; 362, 16.   [7] In 'Conversations with Drummond of Hawthornden', in Jonson, *Works*, ed. C. H. Herford and P. Simpson (Oxford, 1925–52), i. 132, 134, 149.   [8] See below, pp. 2, 13; 199, 15–200, 17; 382, 1–11, 16–19.   [9] See below, pp. 68, 27–8; 85, 13–23; 243, 35.   [10] See below, p. 185, 6.   [11] See below, p. 182, 4. [This is the only citation in *OED* (using the spelling 'another-gaines', introduced in the 1622/3 edition).]   [12] Hoskyns, 47.

Elizabethan sentence structure and idiom underlie much of his artifice. His lengthy periods, praised by Harvey as being preferable to 'the tricksiest page in *Euphues* or *Paphatchet*',[1] are so loosely constructed and unwieldy that they were often printed as several short sentences.[2] Following contemporary practice, royal titles are preceded by the definite article, which can be altered to the demonstrative pronoun,[3] and there may be found a general usage of grammatical irregularities such as ellipsis,[4] the gerundial use of the infinitive,[5] transposing or omitting the pronoun,[6] the redundant pronoun,[7] substituting a verb for a noun,[8] using a noun as an adjective,[9] or the adjective as an adverb,[10] the emphatic double negative,[11] and the uninflected genitive.[12]

The technical aspects of dramatic style are inherited from the *Old Arcadia*, as in the stichomythic debate between Musidorus and Pyrocles;[13] but in the new sections, and most noticeably in Book III, Sidney explores the varying relationships between direct and indirect speech. In addition to normal dialogue, direct speech occurs in challenges and letters, whose counterparts in indirect speech come in Cecropia's proclamation to Basilius that 'she would cause the heads of the three ladies, prisoners, to be cut off', and Amphialus' propaganda statement published to support his rebellion.[14] Related to this is the inclusion as part of the narrative of Kalander's idiomatic complaint, 'never having heard him his beloved guests since they parted', misunderstood by the editor of the second edition who substituted *from* for *him*; and of Dametas' colloquialism when 'he bad the page carry back his letter, like a naughty boy as he was, for he was in no humour, he told him, of reading letters'.[15] More obliquely, the indirect speech of Anaxius to his brothers, disguised as part of the narrative, conveys word for word his message to the princesses that he will kill them and send their heads 'for tokens to their father';[16] while the most complex construction incorporates the words of Queen Helen's indirect speech to Lycurgus into Lycurgus' indirect speech conveying her message to Anaxius.[17]

More subtle is the problem of thought regarded as speech. Both Helen's report of talking to herself and thinking to herself are treated as direct speech in ' "Why sure," said I to myself, "Helen, be not afraid" ' and in ' "How well," thought I, "doth love between those lips!" '[18] But when Pamela is contemplating whether to read Musidorus' letter, a transition is made from direct speech into a thought expressed as indirect speech: ' "The paper came from him, and therefore not worthy to be received – and yet the paper", she thought, was not guilty."[19] Thinking is also construed as indirect speech. This occurs when Argalus hypothetically exchanges circumstances with Amphialus in order to conclude that, in the same predicament, Amphialus would be as defiant as he, and in describing how Philoclea's attention

---

[1] Gabriel Harvey, *Pierce's Supererogation*, S2, in *Works*, ed. A. B. Grosart (1884), ii. 218. [2] See below, pp. 281, 1–282, 7. [3] See below, pp. 17, 29–30 and *passim*; 78, 18. [4] See below, pp. 3, 38–4, 1; 4, 17–18; 71, 14–15; 201, 31–5; 220, 36; 383, 18. [5] See below, pp. 205, 31; 315, 5. [6] See below, pp. 229, 28–9; 180, 22–3. [7] See below, p. 231, 5–6. [8] See below, p. 219, 21. [9] See below, pp. 10, 9; 174, 35; 219, 5. [10] See below, p. 350, 12. [11] See below, p. 322, 12. [12] See below, pp. 3, 19; 18, 9; 39, 18; 51, 22; 94, 35; 167, 17 (*phoenix wings*); 220, 12; 250, 35; 311, 28; 364, 1; and see Ringler, 480. [13] See below, pp. 63, 24–64, 8 and Robertson, 23. [14] See below, pp. 359, 20–1; 281, 6–282, 7. [15] See below, pp. 360, 17–18; 331, 9–10. [16] See below, pp. 390, 31; 392, 6–7. [17] See below, pp. 384, 10–25. [18] See below, p. 52, 37–40; and cf. p. 117, 26–28. [19] See below, p. 268, 26–8.

drifts towards Pyrocles, 'for whom, how well, she thought, many of those sayings might have been used' which Cecropia is busy applying to Amphialus.[1]

Through this technique of shifts in perspective, Sidney creates a style calculated to produce the illusion of participating in a continuously unfolding drama. It is because of this that Sidney's central characters do not remain static. Although they are preceded in the action by summaries of their attributes, and parallel both Heliodoran moral examplars and Theophrastan types as Hoskyns notes, and as Sidney plainly demonstrates in having Dametas imitate More's 'In Malum Pictorem'[2] – such traditional methods of characterization are enhanced and complicated in two ways. In the first, groups of characters become associated with one another through shared comparisons, as Pyrocles, Musidorus, and Phalantus with Aeneas; or Pyrocles, Argalus, and Amphialus with Hercules. In the second, individuals are portrayed by the method of accretion of attributes. Philoclea especially is idealized to an extent which would strain the device of the descriptive catalogue even beyond those ridiculous limits reached in the mock-encomium upon Mopsa, *OA* 3. Through Amphialus' dream, she becomes both the reincarnation of Petrarch's saintly Laura and the embodiment of the perfections of Venus and Diana. She is associated with Diana and her nymphs in louring at Amphialus after he spies upon her while bathing; with Venus bewailing the death of Adonis; with Venus' bird, the dove, attacked by kites, and her body a 'Diana's temple' to be destroyed during her scourging while Cupid and Venus weep with her; and with Venus again in that her hand 'was wont to be one of the chief fire brands of Cupid'.[3] When chased by Pyrocles with his lion's head, she is compared to Arethusa – and implicitly, because the Ovidian description has been transferred, to Daphne; through Pyrocles' device she is Omphale; through Basilius' going to his knees before Zelmane, she becomes Danae with a Jupiter figure as her lover, and as Basilius' envoy, Proserpina; through Cecropia's list of happily raped women, she is related to Antiope, Iole, and Helen of Troy; and through comparisons of Pyrocles with Aeneas, she is identified with Lavinia.[4] The extent of these relationships suggests that Sidney is striving to evoke a variety of responses to his characters, and to maintain a style equal to that established in the more readily noticeable embroidery of rhetorical figures and poetic forms.

EARLY RECEPTION AND INFLUENCE

If he is not simply distinguishing between Sidney's *Arcadia* and the universally known work of Sannazaro, William Temple's comment, 'Arcadiae docuit fabrica texta novae',[5] is the only pronouncement of the several upon the *Arcadia* by Sidney's elegists which might betray knowledge of the incompletely revised manuscript that

---

[1] See below, pp. 327, 2–5; 288, 27–8.   [2] See below, p. 330, 25; Hoskyns, 41; cf. V. Skretkowicz, 'Sidney and Amyot: Heliodorus in the Structure and Ethos of the *New Arcadia*', *RES*, NS xxvii (1976), 170–4, and J. Buxton, 'Sidney and Theophrastus', *ELR* ii (1972), 79–82.   [3] See below, pp. 300, 1–304, 35; 170, 35–6; 287, 1–2; 364, 3–13; 280, 2.   [4] See below, pp. 96, 22; 58, 26; 195, 25; 197, 20; 348, 22–37.   [5] In A. Neville, *Academiae Cantabrigiensis Lachrymae* (1587), 85.

Sidney left with Fulke Greville, and which Greville thought 'fitter to be printed than that first' version 'which is so common'.[1] Despite his vigorous praise of the edition of 1590 in *Pierce's Supererogation* (1593), Gabriel Harvey noted in *Four Letters* (1592) that to readers of shifting taste or 'queasy stomachs' Sidney's *Arcadia* was out of fashion.[2] When in 1593 the remains of the manuscript were published as an appendix to the *New Arcadia*, the overtly romantic nature of the *Old Arcadia* appeared to predominate, giving rise to puritan condemnation. In his *Lectures Upon Jonas, Delivered at York in ... 1594* (1597), the Bishop of London, John King, denounced the '*Arcadia*, and *The Faerie Queene*, and *Orlando Furioso*, with such like frivolous stories', for it seemed to be 'the sin of this land and age of ours (perhaps the mother of our atheism) to commit idolatry with such books'.[3] M. P. Anderson in his dedication in James Caldwell's book of meditations, *The Countess of Mar's Arcadia, or Sanctuary* (1625), hinted at a morally pernicious influence, stating that '*The Countess of Pembroke's Arcadia* is for the body; but the *Countess of Mar's Arcadia* is for the soul'.[4] Wye Saltonstall in *Picturae Loquentes* (1631) pointed directly towards the problem in his character of a maid, who 'reads now love's histories, as *Amadis de Gaule* and the *Arcadia*, and in them courts the shadow of love, till she know the substance' – an affliction for which Thomas Powell in *Tom of all Trades* (1631) suggested the antidote: 'instead of reading Sir Philip Sidney's *Arcadia*, let them read the ground of good huswifery. I like not a female poetess at any hand.'[5] But in defence, Anthony Stafford's reply to these railers in *The Guide of Honour* (1634) was equally blunt: 'Some of them lately have not spared even Apollo's first-born, incomparable and inimitable Sir Philip Sidney, whose *Arcadia* they confine only to the reading of chambermaids – a censure that can proceed from none but the sons of kitchenmaids.'[6]

A broader acceptance of the work was cultivated through the efforts of European literati. Although Jean Loiseau de Tourval, translator to James I, began but never completed his version in French,[7] both Jean Baudoin and Geneviève Chappelain (who depended on Baudoin's work) published translations in France in 1624-5.[8] Chappelain's became the text from which the *Arcadia* was rendered into German by Valentinus Theocritus von Hirschberg (1629), into Dutch by Sambix de Jonghe (1639), and into Italian by Livio Alessandri (1659); and it was the inspiration for André Mareschal's *La Cour Bergère ou l'Arcadie de Messire Phillippe Sidney* (1640).[9] Martin Opitz reworked Valentinus Theocritus' German, particularly in the poems, for the editions of 1638 onwards, though it is not clear which was used by Heinrich Schalvius for his four-act play based on 'Philippsen von Sidney Arcadia' (1650) or for the musical masque *Arkadische Schäfer-Lust*, performed in 1679.[10] Flamineo

---

[1] See the Textual Introduction, p. xlv. [2] Cited in G. G. Smith, *Elizabethan Critical Essays* (Oxford, 1904), ii. 263-5 and ii. 231. [3] Z2; cited in *OED* story, n. 3b. [4] *4. [5] Cited in L. B. Wright, 'The Reading of Renaissance English Women', *SP* xxviii (1931), 680-1. [6] Cited in Ben Jonson, *Works*, ed. C. H. Herford and P. Simpson (Oxford, 1925-52), iv. 139. [7] Bodleian Library MS Rawl. D. 920, ff. 365-382, printed in A. W. Osborn, *Sir Philip Sidney en France* (Paris, 1932), Appendix. [8] Osborn, 116 and 85-6. [9] Ed. L. Desvignes (Saint-Étienne, 1981); see id. 'De l'*Arcadie* de Sidney à *La Cour Bergère*, ou du roman pastoral à la tragi-comédie', in C. Longeon, ed., *Le Genre Pastoral en Europe du XVe au XVIIe Siècle* (Saint-Étienne, 1980), 311-18. [10] Osborn, 90-1; and J. Leighton, 'On the Reception of Sir Philip Sidney's *Arcadia* in Germany from Opitz to Anton Ulrich', in D. H. Green, ed., *From Wolfram and Petrarch to Goethe and Grass* (Baden-Baden, 1982), 483-5.

Parisetti's libretto for the opera *Il Re Pastore uvere il Basilio in Arcadia*, performed in Brunswick in 1691, imported Alessandri's translation as an influence, for Friedrich Christian Bressand turned Parisetti into *Der königliche Schäfer/ oder Basilius in Arcadien* which was played in Brunswick, 1691, and in Hamburg, 1694, and was published in 1696.[1] But the German translation directly influenced Grimmelshausen's description of his battle of Wittstock in *Simplicissimus* (1666–7),[2] and was among the sources for examples of good style published by Justus Georg Schottelius in *Teutsche Sprachkunst* (1641).[3]

In England the *Arcadia* was also seen as a manual of style, without doubt prompted by the publication of Fraunce's *Arcadian Rhetoric* (1588), which drew its examples from the *Old Arcadia*.[4] In adapting Petrus Ramus' Latin grammar, Paul Greaves introduced a few brief lines of verse and phrases of prose, without identifying them, into *Grammatica Anglicana* (1594), as did Alexander Gill in *Logonomia Anglica* (1619); but John Hoskyns made serious and extensive use of the edition of 1590 in preparing his *Directions for Speech and Style* for a student of the Temple, in about 1599. Thomas Blount printed much of these *Directions* without acknowledgement in his *Academy of Eloquence* (1654), and many of the examples from the *Arcadia* were in turn gleaned from Blount by John Smith for his *Mystery of Rhetoric Unveil'd* (1657).[5] Inevitably the advice given in these manuals was abused and the bogus rhetoricians lampooned, as in Jonson's *Every Man Out of His Humour* (1600), 'she does observe as pure a phrase, and use as choice figures in her ordinary conference, as any be i'the *Arcadia*',[6] and in John Stephens, *Satirical Essays* (1615), 'he woos with bawdry in text, and with jests or speeches stolen from plays, or from the common-helping *Arcadia*'.[7] Lawyers' clerks such as this one did not need to read Sidney to seek wisdom, for many *sententiae* with similes had been published in twelve editions of Nicholas Ling's *Politeuphuia: Wit's Commonwealth* (1597) by 1640, a tradition reiterated in Jane Porter's *Aphorisms of Sir Philip Sidney* (1807), and instinctive to keepers of commonplace-books.[8]

Although Everard Guilpin in *Skialetheia* (1598) recorded that Sidney was 'not exempt from prophanation, / But censur'd for affectation',[9] the *Arcadia* inspired sequels, imitations, expansions, and borrowings, in prose fiction, in verse, and in drama. The impetus to fill the narrative gap between the end of the *New Arcadia* and the additional material first published from Sidney's working papers in 1593 lay in the notice printed there. In 1593 it read simply:

> How this combat ended, how the ladies by the coming of the discovered forces were delivered and restored to Basilius, and how Dorus again returned to his old master, Dametas, is altogether unknown. What afterwards chanced, out of the author's own writings and conceits hath been supplied as followeth.

---

[1] Osborn, 90–1, and Leighton, 485. [2] H. Guelen, '"Arkadische" Simpliciana. Zu einer Quelle Grimmelshausens und ihrer strukturellen Bedeutung für seinen Roman', *Euphorion*, lxiii (1969), 426–37. [3] Leighton, 481. [4] Ringler, 562; Robertson, pp. xlv–xlvi and Commentary. [5] Hoskyns, pp. xxx–xxxviii. [6] II. iii. 224–6. [7] Cited in Jonson, *Works*, ed. C. H. Herford and P. Simpson (Oxford, 1925–52), ix. 439. [8] See P. Beal, *Index of English Literary Manuscripts* (London, 1980), ii. 466, and Ringler, 366 and 552–61, non-substantive copies. [9] E1^v, in Shakespeare Assoc. Facs., 2 (London, 1931).

But in 1613 it was expanded, partly with reference to Sidney's letter of dedication:

> Thus far the worthy author had revised or enlarged that first written *Arcadia* of his, which only passed from hand to hand and was never printed, having a purpose likewise to have new ordered, augmented, and concluded the rest had he not been prevented by untimely death; so that all which followeth here of this work remained as it was done and sent away in several loose sheets, being never after reviewed, nor so much as seen all together by himself, without any certain disposition or perfect order; yet for that it was his, howsoever deprived of the just grace it should have had, was held too good to be lost. And therefore with much more labour were the best coherencies that could be gathered out of those scattered papers made and afterwards printed, as now it is, only by her noble care to whose dear hand they were first committed, and for whose delight and entertainment only undertaken. What conclusion it should have had, or how far the work have been extended had it had his last hand thereunto, was only known to his own spirit, where only those admirable images were – and nowhere else – to be cast.
>
> And here we are likewise utterly deprived of the relation how this combat ended, and how the ladies by discovery of the approaching forces were delivered and restored to Basilius, how Dorus returned to his old master, Dametas, all which unfortunate maim we must be content to suffer with the rest.[1]

This 'unfortunate maim' attracted uninventive repairers. Sir William Alexander's 'Supplement of the said defect' was entered in the Stationers' Register on 31 August 1616 and bound into copies of the still current 1613 edition; James Johnstoun's 'Supplement to the Third Book of *Arcadia*' was added to the 1638 edition. They continued to be published with the *Arcadia* until 1674. As a tribute to their inspiration, both accounts end with the death of Philisides.[2]

Sequels to the entire printed version took their cues from the variant closing of the *Old Arcadia* printed in 1593, where they found suggestions for additional episodes which 'may awake some other spirit to exercise his pen in that wherewith mine is already dulled'.[3] Gervase Markham in *The English Arcadia, Alluding his Beginning from Sir Philip Sidney's Ending* (1607), advertised on the head-title as 'The Moral English Arcadia', and *The Second and Last Part of the First Book of the English Arcadia* (1613), wrote the tale of Pyrophilus and Melidora, the offspring of Pyrocles and Musidorus, and left Queen Helen awaiting a champion to defend her against accusations of infidelity during the absence of her husband Amphialus. This sustained literary effort drew freely upon episodes from Ariosto, Tasso, and Montemayor, besides Sidney. No further Books were published. Sir Richard Belling in *A Sixth Book to the Countess of Pembroke's Arcadia* (Dublin, 1624), first included in the Sidney volume in 1627, married Amphialus and Helen, involved Plexirtus, Artaxia, Plangus, and Erona, and concluded with Coridon's challenge to Menalcas

---

[1] Ee3. [2] See Juel-Jensen, 473–4, 477; A. Mitchell and K. Foster, 'Sir William Alexander's *Supplement* to Book III of Sidney's *Arcadia*', *The Library*, 5th Ser. xxiv (1969), 234–41; A. G. D. Wiles, 'Sir William Alexander's Continuation of the Revised Version of Sir Philip Sidney's *Arcadia*', *Studies in Scottish Literature*, iii (1965), 22–9; id., 'James Johnstoun and the Arcadian Style', *Renaissance Papers* (1957), 72–81.
[3] Robertson, 417 (var.).

for the hand of Kalodoulus' daughter in an appended Eclogue of prose and verse.[1] And Anne Weamys in *A Continuation of Sir Philip Sidney's Arcadia* (1651) united Plangus to Erona, Amphialus to Helen, Urania to Strephon, as well as Musidorus to Pamela and Pyrocles to Philoclea, with the final expiration of Philisides from unrequited love upon Klaius' tomb.

Variations on minor episodes or on the story of Basilius' family, as these appear in the 1593 edition, inspired both drama and verse. The most original was John Day's *Isle of Gulls* (1606), a vulgar burlesque imbrued with cryptic political satire.[2] The author of *Love's Changelings' Change* in a derivative manner attempted to cover all the material in the volume except the tale of Argalus and Parthenia.[3] He included the preparations for Clitophon's marriage, cut from the 1613 *Arcadia*, and details drawn from Alexander's *Supplement* printed with that edition. James Shirley in *A Pastoral Called the Arcadia* (1640) omitted the action of Book III of the New Arcadia but otherwise followed the central plot, as did the author of the later 'Arcadian Lovers or Metamorphosis of Princes',[4] though minor alterations were introduced in McNamara Morgan's tragedy *Philoclea* (Dublin, 1754). The royalist poem, 'A Draught of Sir Phillip Sidney's Arcadia', developed both Sidney's diction and examples of statecraft into an argument suggesting that those events which resulted in the Civil War could have been foreseen by an astute reader of the *Arcadia*.[5]

In his *Amorous Songs, Sonnets, and Elegies* (1606) Alexander Craig proved his arguments by alluding to individual episodes: Lalus' promises to Kala, Demagoras poisoning Parthenia and Argalus' steadfastness, Musidorus finding Pyrocles in his arbour, Philoxenus' death and Amphialus' dog, Euarchus' condemnation of Pyrocles; and in *The Poetical Recreations* (1609) he wrote of the unrepentant Plexirtus.[6] The episode of Plangus, Erona, Andromana, and Zelmane provided the basis of Beaumont and Fletcher's *Cupid's Revenge* (1615) and through that play influenced *Philaster* (1620), and the play by the unidentified J. S., *Andromana, or the Merchant's Wife* (1660).[7] The tragedy of Argalus and Parthenia gave Francis Quarles the narrative of his celebrated poem *Argalus and Parthenia* (1629)[8] and Henry Glapthorne his dramatic version with the same title, perhaps produced in 1632 but published in 1639.[9] Francis Quarles's poem not only led to a sequel in verse by John Quarles, *The History of the Most Vile Dimagoras* (1658), but also to two prose adaptations with varying titles, but generally known as *The Most Pleasant and Delightful History of Argalus and Parthenia* (1672 onwards) and *The Unfortunate Lovers; the History of Argalus and Parthenia* (c. 1700 onwards).[10]

---

[1] See Juel-Jensen, 476; his birth in 1613 as in H. J. Rose, *Biographical Dictionary* (1857) is rejected in *DNB*.
[2] M. C. Andrews, 'The Isle of Gulls as Travesty', *The Yearbook of English Studies*, iii (1973), 78–84. [3] Ed. F. Rota, in *L' Arcadia di Sidney e il teatro* (Bari, 1966), and J. P. Cutts (Fennimore, 1974). [4] Bodleian Library MS Rawl. Poet. 3, ff. 1–41; see Rota, 103–22. [5] Ed. J. Buxton, in *Historical Essays 1600–1750 Presented to David Ogg*, ed. H. E. Bell and R. L. Ollard (London, 1963), 60–77. [6] *Amorous Songs*, C5^v, C8, D2^v, E1, E2; *Poetical Recreations*, C2, in *The Poetical Works of Alexander Craig of Rose-Craig*, ed. D. Laing, Hunterian Club, ii (Glasgow, 1873). [7] J. E. Savage, 'Beaumont and Fletcher's *Philaster* and Sidney's *Arcadia*', *ELH* xiv (1947), 194–206; M. C. Andrews, 'The Sources of Andromana', *RES* xix (1968), 295–300. [8] See J. Horden, *A Bibliography of Francis Quarles* (Oxford, 1953), 22–30. [9] G. E. Bentley, *The Jacobean and Caroline Stage* (Oxford, 1941–68), iv. 480. [10] B. S. Field, Jr., 'Sidney's Influence: The Evidence of the Publication of the History of Argalus and Parthenia', *ELN* xvii (1979), 98–102.

Shakespeare recognized the dramatic possibilities offered by Sidney's development of the relationship between psychological turmoil and tragic potential. Hardly any major character in the Histories or Tragedies remains unaffected by the spectrum of mental anguish portrayed in the *Arcadia*, and in *King Lear* (1608) the tensions between Gloucester, Edgar, and Edmund originate in the tale of the blinded Paphlagonian king and his sons.[1] The anonymous author of *The Trial of Chivalry* (1605) used Sidney's phrasing and episodes – Helen, Philoxenus, and Amphialus lie behind Katharine, Ferdinand, and Pembroke, and the story of Argalus, Parthenia, and Demagoras is adapted into that of Bellamira, Philip, and Bourbon.[2] In Sir William Alexander's *Tragedy of Croesus* (1604), Parthenia's protests at Argalus' departure are paralleled by Caelia's to Atis, and the lamentations of Parthenia and Amphialus over Argalus by those of Caelia and Adrastus over Atis.[3] In *Love's Sacrifice* (1633), John Ford drew upon the confrontation of Pamphilus and his concubines, incidentally taking over phrases from Sidney. Similarly, non-dramatic writings leaned heavily upon the *Arcadia*: Emmanuel Ford in *Parismus* (1590) adapted Cecropia's scourging of Philoclea and fall to death for Adamasia,[4] Robert Anton in *Moriomachia* (1613) compared the comic duel between the Knights of the Sun and the Moon with the battle between Clinias and Dametas,[5] and Robert Baron in *The Cyprian Academy* (1647) lifted chunks of Sidney's prose and verse.[6]

Although Baron's *Mirza* (1655) contained acknowledged references to the *Arcadia*, in the *Apology for Paris* (1649) and *Pocula Castalia* (1650) he used Sidney's work for verbal assistance within original contexts. Overt borrowings such as these may have been meant to be recognized, as in Shakespeare's *Sonnets* (3–6, 8, 9, 12–14).[7] Others, working from notes or commonplace-books, surreptitiously blended Sidney's material into their own, as did John Weever in *Faunus and Melliflora* (1600);[8] William Browne in *Britannia's Pastorals* ([1613]–16); Phineas Fletcher in *Britain's Ida* (1628), otherwise known as *Venus and Anchises*,[9] and in *Siceledes* (1631), *Purple Island* (1633), and *Piscatory Eclogues* (1633). John Webster followed the same practice in *The White Devil* (1612), *A Monumental Column* (1613), the additions to Overbury's *Characters* (1615), *The Duchess of Malfi* (1623), and *The Devil's Law-Case* (1623).[10] In a letter of 1640, Henry Oxinden expressed himself in a combination of phrases from the *Arcadia*.[11] One image alone was used by George Wilkins in translating *The History of Justine* (1606) and in *The Painful Adventures of Pericles* (1608), apparently through the medium of the anonymous *Two Most Unnatural*

---

[1] K. Muir, ed., *King Lear* (London, 1969), pp. xxxvii–xlii. [2] C. R. Baskerville, 'Sidney's *Arcadia* and *The Trial of Chivalry*', *MP* x (1912), 197–201. [3] Following the textual variants in L. E. Kastner and H. B. Charlton, eds., *The Poetical Works of Sir William Alexander*, Scottish Text Society, NS xi (Edinburgh, 1921), the diminishing influence of the *Arcadia* may be noted between the editions of 1604–7 and 1616–37. [4] Chs. xxii–xxiii, noted in O'Connor, 265. [5] O'Connor, 216. [6] See H. J. Todd, ed., *Poetical Works of John Milton* (1801), vi. 401–6; G. C. Moore Smith, 'Robert Baron, author of *Mirza, a Tragedy* ', *N & Q*, 11th Ser. ix (1914), 1–3, 22–4, 43–4, 61–3, 206; and C. R. Forker, 'Robert Baron's Use of Webster, Shakespeare, and Other Elizabethans', *Anglia*, lxxxiii (1965), 176–98. [7] T. W. Baldwin, *On the Literary Genetics of Shakespeare's Poems and Sonnets* (Urbana, 1950), 194–209. [8] See the notes by A. Davenport, ed. (Liverpool, 1948). [9] Ed. E. Seaton (London, 1926). [10] R. W. Dent, *John Webster's Borrowing* (Berkeley, 1960). [11] E. E. Duncan-Jones, 'Henry Oxinden and Sidney's *Arcadia*', *N & Q* cxcviii (1953), 322–3.

and Bloody Murthers (1605);[1] and a few clusters of words appear in the fictional verse epistles between Sidney and Lady Penelope Rich.[2]

Further examples are rather more oblique, as in Charles Cotton's 'Surprise', or in the play *Mucedorus* (1598), where the closest resemblances to Musidorus' killing of the bear and the flight of the lovers are in the 1610 edition. Small echoes can be found in Drummond of Hawthornden's 'Song I',[3] many of Shakespeare's plays,[4] John Marston's *Malcontent* (1604),[5] Henry Constable's 'Of His Mistress, upon occasion of her walking in a garden',[6] Marvell's 'Definition of Love' and 'Last Instructions to a Painter',[7] and Milton's *Lycidas, Paradise Lost*, and *Samson Agonistes*.[8] Fulke Greville in 'A Treatise of Monarchy' referred to *OA* 66, the beast fable;[9] in *The New Metamorphosis* one tale was set in Arcadia where Musidorus and Pyrocles were listed as friends;[10] and the anonymous prose romance, *The Heroical Adventures of the Knight of the Sea ... Prince Oceander* (1600), portrayed in a burlesque of the tradition a hermit named Kalander and a ruthless, lecherous King Basileon.[11] Other prose romances with vague indebtedness were Lady Mary Wroth's *Countess of Montgomery's Urania* (1621), Roger Boyle, Earl of Orrery's *Parthenissa* (1660), Sir George Mackenzie's *Aretina, or the Serious Romance* (1660), and John Crowne's *Pandion and Amphigenia, or the History of the Coy Lady of Thessalia* (1665) which followed the new tastes developed by continental literature, though characters' names were dependent upon those in the *Arcadia*. Even the religious allegory in Nathaniel Ingelo's *Bentivolio and Urania* (1660-4) was couched in Sidney's language. Others were content to take only their titles from it, as Anthony Scoloker in *Daiphantus, or the Passions of Love* (1604), the anonymous *Zelmane, or the Corinthian Queen*,[12] Samuel Richardson in *Pamela* (1742), where Pamela refers to Sidney's work,[13] and Richard Brathwaite in *The Two Lancashire Lovers: or the Excellent History of Philocles and Doriclea* (1640).

By far the most debased use made of the *Arcadia* was to discredit the dead king. In later editions of Gauden's *Eikon Basilike* (1649) Pamela's prayer was introduced at the head of the list of those used by Charles I the night before his execution. This led to Milton's vitriolic response in *Eikonoklastes* (1649):

> a prayer stol'n word for word from the mouth of a heathen fiction praying to a heathen God, & that in no serious book, but the vain amatorious poem of Sr Philip Sidney's *Arcadia*; a book in that kind full of worth and wit, but among

---

[1] See below, p. 232, 16–17, 'perfection ... dying', noted in E. A. J. Honigmann, *The Stability of Shakespeare's Text* (London, 1965), 193–4. [2] J. A. Roberts, 'The Imaginary Epistles of Sir Philip Sidney and Lady Penelope Rich', *ELR* xv (1985), 59–77. [3] See L. E. Kastner, ed., *Poetical Works* (Edinburgh, 1913), i. 170–6. [4] See the notes in J. C. Maxwell, ed., *Pericles* (Cambridge, 1965); A. D[avenport]., 'Possible Echoes from Sidney's *Arcadia* in Shakespeare, Milton and Others', *N & Q* cxciv (1949), 554–5; J. Rees, 'Juliet's Nurse: Some Branches of a Family Tree', *RES*, NS xxxiv (1983), 43–7. [5] See A. J. Axelrad, *Un Malcontent Elizabéthan: John Marston (1576-1634)* (Paris, 1955), 281–2; and J. F. Finkelpearl, *John Marston of the Middle Temple* (Cambridge, Mass., 1969), 240–1. [6] See J. Grundy, ed., *The Poems of Henry Constable* (Liverpool, 1966), 228. [7] See H. M. Margoliouth, ed., *The Poems and Letters of Andrew Marvell*, rev. P. Legouis and E. E. Duncan-Jones, 3rd edn. (Oxford, 1971), i. 259, 368. [8] See A. D[avenport]., 'Possible Echoes', *N & Q* cxciv (1949), 554–5; and E. G. Fogel, 'Milton and Sir Philip Sidney's *Arcadia*', *N & Q* cxcvi (1951), 115–17. [9] In *The Remains*, ed. G. A. Wilkes (Oxford, 1919), II. ii and p. 62. [10] J. H. H. Lyon, *A Study of the New Metamorphosis* (New York, 1919), II. ii and p. 62. [11] O'Connor, 217–20. [12] Rota, 175–6. [13] iii. 141; iv. 116, 165; see W. M. Sale, Jr., *Samuel Richardson: Master Printer* (Ithaca, 1950), 204.

religious thoughts and duties not worthy to be nam'd; nor to be read at any time without good caution, much less in time of trouble and affliction to be a Christian's prayer-book.[1]

Though this catalogue could be expanded still further,[2] the impact of the *Arcadia* upon the visual arts was limited to the title-page of the 1593 edition, illustrations in Chappelain's French translation which were republished in the German derivative,[3] twenty-six panels in the Single Cube room of Wilton House by Emanuel de Critz, finished 1654,[4] and Edmund Marmion's illustrations in Quarles's *Argalus and Parthenia* (1656).[5] Through its portrayal of Elizabeth I in the guise of Queen Helen of Corinth the *Arcadia* may even by 1585 have influenced the symbolism of the 'Ermine' portrait of the queen,[6] but a less direct visual contribution to society was made in its enhancement and support of such spectacular tournaments as were later described by Thomas Nashe in *The Unfortunate Traveller* (1594).[7] It was in the *Arcadia* that these events received sanction as legitimate inclusions within the literature of the day. Indirectly, therefore, Sidney's work provided directions for the special effects required by the producers of *King Lear*, in Edgar's battle with Edmund,[8] and of *Pericles*, in the tournament of the six knights.[9]

---

[1] *The Complete Prose Works of John Milton*, ed. D. M. Wolfe et al (New Haven, 1953-82), iii. 362-3; see F. F. Madan, *A New Bibliography of the Eikon Basilike* (Oxford, 1950), no. 22 and pp. 119-21; and M. Y. Hughes, 'New Evidence on the Charge that Milton Forged the Pamela Prayer in the *Eikon Basilike*' *RES*, NS iii (1952), 130-40. [2] I have not included in this account the many suggestions for which the evidence is not clear. See also P. Salzman, *English Prose Fiction 1558-1700* (Oxford, 1985). [3] Osborn, 85, 90. [4] See Sidney, 16th Earl of Pembroke, *A Catalogue of the Paintings & Drawings in the Collection at Wilton House, Salisbury, Wiltshire* (London, 1968), 91 (five are published in Mona Wilson, *Sir Philip Sidney* (London, 1931), plates viii-xi). The fashion for room decoration from the romances is studied in W. Stechow, 'Heliodorus' *Aethiopica* in Art', *JWCI* xvi (1953), 144-52. [5] J. Horden, 'Edmund Marmion's Illustrations for Francis Quarles' *Argalus and Parthenia*', *Trans. of the Cambridge Bibliographical Society*, ii (1954), 55-62. [6] See below, p. 86, 36 and note. [7] K. Duncan-Jones, 'Nashe and Sidney: The Tournament in *The Unfortunate Traveller*', *MLR* lxiii (1968), 3-6. [8] V. iii. 100 ff. [9] II. ii. 16 ff.

TEXTUAL INTRODUCTION

THE TEXTS

Old Arcadia manuscripts[1]

Group 1

[*Je*] Jesus College, Oxford, MS 150.
[*Hm*] British Library MS Additional 61821 (Helmingham Hall MS), formerly in the collection of Arthur A. Houghton, Jr.
[*Qu*] Queen's College, Oxford, MS R 38/301.

Group 2

[*Da*] British Library MS Additional 41204 (Davies MS).
[*Ph*] British Library MS Additional 38892 (Phillipps MS).

The manuscript was made for, and is partly in the hand of, Sir John Harington, who seems to have been responsible for the numerous spurious passages.[2] These have been printed in the Commentary in Robertson (cf. Robertson, p. liii). The manuscript was in the catalogue *Bibliotheca Heberiana*, pt. xi, lot 1433, in the sale beginning 10 February 1836, before passing through Thorpe into the Phillipps collection.[3] The British Library, North Library, copy of the Heber catalogue notes that it fetched 4*s*.

Group 3

[*Cl*] Folger Shakespeare Library MS H.b.1 (Clifford MS).
[*Le*] British Library MS Additional 41498 (Lee MS).
[*As*] Huntington Library MS HM 162 (Ashburnham MS).
[*O*]   National Library of Wales, Ottley (Ottley MS).

---

[1] Apart from the Ottley MS which has subsequently been reported, these texts have been fully described by Ringler, pp. x and 525–38, and by Robertson, pp. xlii–lii. To their accounts I have added notes on the Phillipps and the Ottley MSS. The groups of manuscripts reflect the four different states of composition established by Ringler, 369–70. The Houghton Library, Harvard University, and the Library of Congress confirm that the entry in the *National Union Catalog: Pre-1956 Imprints*, 0532163, 'The Countess of Pembroke's Arcadia. A manuscript in the Houghton Library, Harvard University', is a ghost. [A fragmentary manuscript (Cambridgeshire Record Office, Huddleston Papers 488/M) is discussed, with a facsimile, in H.R. Woudhuysen, 'A New Manuscript Fragment of Sidney's Old Arcadia: The Huddleston Manuscript', *EMS* 11 (2002), 52–69. *Bo*, *Cl*, *Fl*, *Ha*, *Hm*, and *Ph* have been fully digitised and can be freely accessed through the respective libraries' digital repositories.]   [2] P. J. Croft, 'Sir John Harington's Manuscript of Sir Philip Sidney's *Arcadia*', in S. Parks and P. J. Croft, *Literary Autographs* (Los Angeles, 1983), 39 ff., reviewed by J. Robertson, *RES*, NS xxxvi, (1985), 258–62.   [3] Ringler, 526; cf. W. W. Greg, ed., Jonson, *Masque of Gipsies* (London, 1952), 6–7, for the Heber-Thorpe-Phillipps connection of the Heber-Huntington manuscript.

6 ff. in a single secretary hand with italic for Latin and some proper nouns, containing 48 poems: CS 1, 2, 13–25, 31, 32 (and Edward Dyer's CS 16a); AT 19, 21; three poems of unknown authorship and one poem attributed to Queen Elizabeth I; OA 2, 3, 11, 12 (ll. 1–24), 13 (ll. 116–21, 123, 125, 129, 131–2, 136–7, 141), 14–22, 27, 28 (ll. 37–48), 31, 33–5, 38, 60, 62 (ll. 1–24, 27–8, 37–146), 77, and the prose Nota on rules of verse in Robertson, 80–1. The manuscript was owned by Adam Ottley (1685–1752), Registrar of the diocese of St David's, 1713–52. It was first described by P. Beal, 'Poems by Sir Philip Sidney: The Ottley Manuscript', *The Library*, 5th Ser. xxxiii (1978), 284–95, and was placed in the stemma of the *Old Arcadia* by Jean Robertson, 'A Note on "Poems by Sir Philip Sidney: The Ottley Manuscript"', *The Library*, 6th Ser. ii (1980), 202–5, where the influence upon the text is assessed.

Group 4

[St]   St John's College, Cambridge, MS I. 7.
[Bo]   Bodleian Library MS e Museo 37.

Extracts from the *Old Arcadia*

[Dd]   Cambridge University Library MS Dd.5. 75 (2)
       OA 2, 3, 62; CS 3.
[Eg]   British Library MS Egerton 2421.
       OA 62. 143–6.
[Fl]   Folger Shakespeare Library MS V.a.339.
       OA 17.
[Ha]   British Library MS Harleian 6910.
       OA 3, 15. 1–8 and 13–14.
[Hn]   Arundel Castle, His Grace the Duke of Norfolk, 'Harrington MS. Temp. Eliz.'; ed. Ruth Hughey, *The Arundel Harington Manuscript of Tudor Poetry*, 2 vols. (Columbus, Ohio, 1960).
       OA 74; CS 3.
[Hy]   British Library MS Harleian 7392 (2).
       OA 3; CS 3.
[Ma]   Marsh's Library, Dublin MS Z. 3. 5. 21.
       OA 17.
[Ra]   Bodleian Library MS Rawlinson Poetical 85.
       OA 21, 22; CS 3.
[Fr]   Fraunce, Abraham, *The Arcadian Rhetoric* (1588).
       CS 3.
[Bn]   B[reton]., N[icholas]., *The Arbour of Amorous Devices* (1597).
       CS 3.

Texts of the *New Arcadia*[1]

[Cm] Cambridge University Library MS Kk. 1 5 (2).

Folio, 210 ff., numbered as follows: [4 leaves unnumbered], 5–103, 105–144, [1 leaf unnumbered], 145–187, 185–200, 202–208. 20 cm × 27.5 cm (trimmed for binding). Watermark 1.7 cm × 3.8 cm, a large-brimmed pot topped by a single fleur-de-lis, not in C. M. Briquet, *Les Filigranes*, ed. A. H. Stevenson (Amsterdam, 1968). Untitled. The manuscript is dated 1584 on the upper left corner of f. 1, and written in the same italic hand as the Norwich MS of *A Defence of Poetry*.[2] It was in the catalogue of the library of Richard Holdsworth (1590–1645), Cambridge University Library MS Ff. 4. 27, f. 250, item 50 (2), and in the copy, Cambridge University Library MS Dd. 8. 45.[3] It was listed on the table pasted into the front of the binding of the composite manuscript MS Kk. 1. 5 and in the *Catalogue of the Manuscripts* (1856–67), iii. 559, and was mentioned in editions of other sections of the manuscript: J. Stevenson, ed., *Lancelot Du Lak* (Edinburgh, 1839), p. xiv (not followed by W. W. Skeat, EETS, os vi (1865), but by M. M. Gray, Scottish Text Society (1912), p. viii); and J. R. Lumby, ed., *Ratis Raving*, EETS, os xliii (1870), p. v.

Cm begins at the beginning of the *New Arcadia* but ends mid-page in mid-sentence (below, p. 391, 38) with deliberate, final, treble punctuation: 'comaundement and./.' There is little punctuation or paragraph division. On f. 65 the prose of Book I runs into Book II, 'pastimes. In', and after the end of Book II, ff. 148^v, 149, and 149^v have been left blank before Book III begins. There is no indication of chapter division or of eclogues. The poems are as follows: *OA* 3, 2, 4, 5, 14, 15, 16, 17, 18 (blank), 19 (blank), 62 (ll. 1–8), 30 (ll. 5–37), 8 (incipit), 20, 21; *OP* 1; *OA* 22, 25, 1 (blank), 26 (ll. 1–4), 74 (ll. 1–16), 73 (blank); *OP* 2; *CS* 3 (incipit); *OP* 3 (blank); and *OA* 75 (blank).[4] There are four lacunae in Cm which are common to all texts of the *New Arcadia*: on f. 33, a description of Amphialus' device (below, p. 48, 25); on f. 99, a tree catalogue (p. 162, 11); on f. 127^v Lelius' impresa (p. 220, 25); and on f. 168^v, following *OA* 73, where the scribe of Cm also omitted the preceding clause (p. 299, 36). On f. 164 for 'bound all over' (p. 294, 32) Cm has these numbers, with spaces between: 7 9 10 3. In general, names are written in spaces left for them with a broader and less cursive script, as are some epistles, challenges, and mottoes. Some spaces contain several names, but many are left blank, especially towards the end of the manuscript.

---

[1] I list only the substantive texts here. Non-substantive texts of the poems are mentioned in the Commentary; those with prose extracts are described in Ringler, 366 and 553–61, and in P. Beal, *Index of English Literary Manuscripts* (London, 1980), ii. 466. A full list of editions is in the *STC* and in Juel-Jensen [as well as the digital *ESTC*. A more recent account of the different *Arcadia* versions can be found in chapter 8 (262–82) of Gavin Alexander's *Writing After Sidney* (Oxford, 2006). For a comprehensive list of manuscripts known to contain extracts from Sidney's works (including a number of seventeenth-century miscellanies copied from printed books, demonstrating *Arcadia*'s enduring popularity) see the author page for Sidney on *CELM*]. [2] The manuscript, in the Norfolk County Record Office, is described in *Misc. Prose*, 65. [3] On Holdsworth, see J. A. Trentman, 'The Authorship of *Directions for a Student in the Universitie*', *Trans. of the Cambridge Bibliographical Society*, vii (1978), 170–83. [4] Ringler, 530–1; the line reference to *OA* 74 is emended here.

[90] *The Countess of Pembroke's Arcadia*, written by Sir Philip Sidney. Printed for William Ponsonby, 1590.

Quarto in eights. STC 22539a; Juel-Jensen, 1a [variant imprint] *Printed by John Windet for William Ponsonby*, 1590. STC 22539; Juel-Jensen, 1b.
Entered in the Stationers' Register on 23 August 1588.
   Some copies have the following note on A4^v:

> The division and summing of the chapters was not of Sir Philip Sidney's doing, but adventured by the overseer of the print for the more ease of the readers. He therefore submits himself to their judgement, and if his labour answer not the worthiness of the book, desireth pardon for it. As also if any defect be found in the Eclogues, which although they were of Sir Philip Sidney's writing, yet were they not perused by him, but left till the work had been finished, that then choice should have been made which should have been taken and in what manner brought in. At this time they have been chosen and disposed as the overseer thought best.

The woodcut of the Sidney coat of arms on the title-page belonged to John Wolfe who had previously printed it in two books he published himself, Richard Robinson's translation of John Leland's *A Learned and True Assertion of... the most Noble, Valiant, and Renowned Prince Arthur* (1582), and Scipione Gentile's *Nereus sive de natali Elizabethae Illustriss. Philippi Sidnaei Filiae* (1585) which was dedicated to Sidney. Wolfe held a stock of pictorial blocks and was at the time printing Spenser's *Faerie Queene* (1590) for Ponsonby, with the same St George he used in G. D., *A Brief Discovery of Doctor Allen's Seditious Drifts* (1588), printed for Francis Coldock, Ponsonby's father-in-law. Inevitably the close community of publishers and printers encouraged the sharing of such blocks among them.[1]

Three compositors in Windet's house worked on the printing, as in the early edition of Hooker's *Laws of Ecclesiastical Polity* (1597) of which the manuscript printer's copy survives.[2] The work of one, which seems to be a literatim transcript of printer's copy, is similar in spelling and punctuation to *Cm*. This is preserved in the cancelled B3–B6^v of the Huntington Library 69441 copy (Juel-Jensen, 1a. 4). The work of the two other compositors can be distinguished by their use of O and ô (for O and oh), most noticeable on Q6^v–Q7^v (below, pp. 127, 8–128, 29), and by inconsistencies between catchword and text when composition was begun on a new forme, as in *Which* E6 and *which* E6^v, *applied* H4 and *applie* H4^v, *one of* Rr6^v and *of* Rr7, *veying* Rr7 and *ing* Rr7^v, *to her* Ss6^v and *her* Ss7.

Proof correction, though extensive, was mainly restricted to case and punctuation, and was made without reference to copy.[3] Blanks were left, as in *Cm*, for the description of Amphialus' device (G2), the tree catalogue (V5), Lelius' impresa (Cc4), and to designate the hiatus after *OA* 73 (Nn3^v), where three asterisks were printed between *feet*, and *But*. An ornamental border was printed around the blank

---

[1] A. C. Judson, *The Life of Edmund Spenser*, in *Works*, xi. 140–1; P. Gaskell, *A New Introduction to Bibliography* (Oxford, 1972), 176.   [2] Bodleian Library MS Add. C. 165; see P. Simpson, *Proof-Reading in the Sixteenth Seventeenth and Eighteenth Centuries* (Oxford, 1935), 78.   [3] Examples are in the textual apparatus, and below, p. lvi.

left for the epitaph (Rr7ᵛ; below, p. 346, 14–22) and the text ended partly down the page in mid-sentence, as had *Cm*, but some three thousand words beyond the point where it broke off in *Cm* (Zz8ᵛ).

In his letter of November 1586 to Sidney's father-in-law Sir Francis Walsingham, Fulke Greville asked that the translation of de Mornay's 'book on Atheism' be stayed and that the pirated publication of the *Old Arcadia* be prevented,

> for I haue sent my lady yor daughter at her request, a correction of that old one don 4 or 5 years since which he left in trus⟨t⟩ with me wherof ther is no more copies, & fitter to be printed then that first which is so common, notwithstanding euen that to be amended by a direction sett doun vndre his own hand how & why, so as in many respects espetially the care of printing it i[s] to be don with more deliberation, – besyds … many other works … which requyre the care of his frends, not to amend for I think it fales within the reache of no man liuing, but only to see to the paper and other common errors of mercenary printing.¹

In his later *Dedication to Sir Philip Sidney*, Greville wrote of 'the Arcadian antiques', 'I liked them too well – even in that unperfected shape they were – to condescend that such delicate, though inferior, pictures of himself should be suppressed', although he recalled that Sidney 'bequeathed no other legacy but the fire to this unpolished embryo'.² That Greville prepared the edition of 1590 for the press was recorded in a book of epigrams published in 1589, *De Caede et Interitu Gallorum Regis, Henrici Tertii*, where the anonymous dedication to Greville begins, 'Dum tu Sidnaei regale poema recudis'.³ This is confirmed by Thomas Wilson who, in dedicating his translation of the first Book of Montemayor's *Diana* to Greville, refers to the *Arcadia*, 'which by your noble virtue the world so happily enjoys'.⁴

Matthew Gwinne's involvement in producing the volume is signalled in an inscription on the flyleaf of the Huntington Library 69441 copy of *90*: 'May. 29. 1590. pr[etium]: vˢ. published by D. Guin, Doctor in physick, fellow of S. Iohns in Oxon.' This attribution of editorship must have been written after 17 July 1593 when the MB and MD were conferred upon Gwinne, but it is none the less not improbable.⁵ In the Oxford volume *Exequiae* (1587), D2ᵛ–D3ᵛ, Gwinne mentioned Sidney's translations of du Bartas and de Mornay as well as the *Arcadia*; he spent the winter of 1587-8 on the continent with Greville on business for Walsingham;⁶ and in John Florio's translation of the Second Book of Montaigne's *Essays* (1603) he addressed sonnets to Sidney's daughter Elizabeth, Countess of Rutland, and to Lady Penelope Rich. In dedicating this volume to them, Florio praised 'that perfect-unperfect *Arcadia*' and lamented that Sidney

---

¹ Public Record Office, SP 12/195/33, transcribed in Ringler, 530, and in W. W. Greg, *A Companion to Arber* (Oxford, 1967), 145. A facsimile is in V. Skretkowicz, 'Building Sidney's Reputation: Texts and Editors of the *Arcadia*', in J. van Dorsten, D. Baker-Smith, and A. F. Kinney, eds., *Sir Philip Sidney: 1586 and The Creation of a Legend* (Leiden, 1986), 111–24.   ² *The Prose Works of Fulke Greville, Lord Brooke*, ed. J. Gouws (Oxford, 1986), 134, 11.   ³ H. H. Hudson, 'An Oxford Epigram-Book of 1589', *HLQ* ii [1939] 216, translates this as, 'While you are printing the royal poem of Sidney'.   ⁴ British Library MS Additional 18638, ff. 4ᵛ–5, cited in Yong, p. xxxiv.   ⁵ A. Clark, *Register of the University of Oxford* (Oxford, 1887), II. i. 127, 150, 190.   ⁶ V. Skretkowicz, 'Greville and Sidney: Biographical Addenda', *N & Q*, NS xxi (1974), 408–10, and Sir George Clark, *A History of the Royal College of Physicians* (Oxford, 1964), i. 170 ff.

lived not to mend or end-it: since this end we see of it, though at first above all, now is not answerable to the precedents: and though it were much easier to mend out of an original and well corrected copy than to make-up so much out of a most corrupt, yet see we more marring that was well, than mending what was amiss.[1]

Such knowledge of the state of the author's papers and of the editorial process suggests that Florio, who had been associated with Greville and Gwinne from before 1583,[2] was also involved in preparing the first edition for publication. Certainly he retaliated in the Preface to his *World of Words* (1598) to an attack on him by H. S. (Hugh Sanford). In his address to the reader in the 1593 edition of the *Arcadia* (see below), Sanford commented scathingly about the editing of 90. He made hostile puns on the words 'flowers' and 'roses' – Florio's wife was called Rose, which was 'the proper name of a whore' in Italian proverbs[3] – and he began the address with 'The disfigured face', possibly a slur on Florio's appearance.[4]

Sidney's dedication 'To My Dear Lady and Sister, The Countess of Pembroke' (A3–A4) referred to 'this idle work of mine ... done in loose sheets of paper, most of it in your presence, the rest by sheets sent unto you as fast as they were done'. Although in the following discussion of the relationships of the texts it becomes clear that the *New Arcadia* grew out of the foul papers of the *Old Arcadia*, this dedication properly belongs to the earlier text. It is printed below in Appendix II.

[93] *The Countess of Pembroke's Arcadia. Written by Sir Philip Sidney Knight. Now since the first edition augmented and ended. Printed for William Ponsonby*, 1593.

Folio in sixes. STC 22540; Juel-Jensen, 2.

It was suggested by G. W. Williams, 'The Printer of the First Folio of Sidney's *Arcadia*', *The Library*, 5th Ser. xii (1957), 274–5, that the printer was John Windet. This can be confirmed by the factotum on B1 in 90 and on both ¶3 and X1 in 93, which seems to be the only one of the headpieces, factotums, and initials in 90 and 93 to be found exclusively in Windet's books. In it the crowned Tudor rose is supported (sinister) by Justice holding her sword, and (dexter) by Prudence bearing a serpent and mirror, both suppressing underfoot snaky-haired Envy who struggles to arise.

The engraved title-page border (McKerrow and Ferguson, 212), and a summary of scholarship on it are in Robertson, frontispiece and p. xlix, and in M. Corbett and R. Lightbown, *The Comely Frontispiece* (London, 1979), 58–65. The pig and marjoram device represented a tradition in English publishing,[5] and Musidorus' posture and shepherd's stave with a spud are in the convention of the illustration to Spenser's

---

[1] Cited in F. A. Yates, *John Florio* (Cambridge, 1934), 200.   [2] Yates, *Florio*, 48, 55, 92. Florio was in Cork on 26 May 1587 when his godson Alexander (?) Teregli wrote to him from London; see *State Papers Supplementary*, Pt. 1, List & Index Society, ix (1966), SP 46/125, ff. 163, 163d   [3] G. Torriano, *The Second Alphabet Consisting of Proverbial Phrases* (1662), Zz1ᵛ.   [4] The tendency to comment on Florio's face is noted in Yates, *Florio*, 55, 167–8, and in her *Study of Love's Labours Lost* (Cambridge, 1936), 44.
[5] See R. Tottel, 'The Printer to the Reader', in *Tottel's Miscellany (1557–1587)*, ed. H. E. Rollins, rev. edn. (Cambridge, Mass., 1965), i. 3: 'I exhort the unlearned by reading to learn to be more skilful, and to purge that swinelike grossness that maketh the sweet marjoram not to smell to their delight.'

'January', though in the text Musidorus' stave is double ended, with a crook and a spud.¹ John Aubrey in *The Natural History and Antiquities of the County of Surrey* (1719) compared the staves of Surrey with that on the title-page of the *Arcadia*.²

The volume opened by reprinting from 90 Sidney's dedication to the Countess of Pembroke. Following this, Hugh Sanford, the Earl of Pembroke's secretary, published his criticism of the first edition and laid down his own editorial policy:

> *To the Reader.*
>
> The disfigured face, gentle reader, wherewith this work not long since appeared to the common view, moved that noble lady, to whose honour consecrated, to whose protection it was committed, to take in hand the wiping away those spots wherewith the beauties thereof were unworthily blemished. But, as often in repairing a ruinous house the mending of some old part occasioneth the making of some new, so here her honourable labour, begun in correcting the faults, ended in supplying the defects; by the view of what was ill done guided to the consideration of what was not done.³ Which part with what advice entered into, with what success it hath been passed through, most by her doing, all by her directing, if they may be entreated not to define, which are unfurnished of means to discern, the rest (it is hoped) will favourably censure. But this they shall, for their better satisfaction, understand, that though they find not here what might be expected, they may find nevertheless as much as was intended, the conclusion, not the perfection *of Arcadia;* and that no further than the author's own writings or known determinations could direct. Whereof who sees not the reason must consider there may be reason which he sees not. Albeit I dare affirm he either sees, or from wiser judgements than his own may hear, that Sir Philip Sidney's writings can no more be perfected without Sir Philip Sidney than Apelles' pictures without Apelles. There are that think the contrary; and no wonder. Never was Arcadia free from the cumber of such cattle. To us, say they, the pastures are not pleasant; and as for the flowers, such as we light on we take no delight in, but the greater part grow not within our reach. Poor souls! What talk they of flowers? They are roses,⁴ not flowers, must do men good, which if they find not here, they shall do well to go feed elsewhere. Any place will better like them; for without Arcadia nothing grows in more plenty than lettuce suitable to their lips.⁵ If it be true that likeness is a great cause of liking,⁶ and that contraries infer contrary consequences, men is it true that the worthless reader can never worthily esteem of so worthy a writing; and as true that the noble, the wise, the virtuous, the courteous, as many as have had any acquaintance with true learning and knowledge, will with all love and dearness entertain it, as well for affinity with themselves, as being child to such a father. Whom albeit it do not exactly and in every lineament represent, yet considering the father's untimely death prevented the

---

¹ See below, p. 108, 13–14. ² ii. 306–7; see L. F. Salzman, 'Some Notes on Shepherd's Staves', *The Agricultural History Review*, v, (1957), 91–4. ³ Sanford here imitates one of the passages that Sidney added to Book III of the *OA* and which was printed in 93: 'remembering what might have been done to considering what was now to be done' (Robertson, 237, 22–3). ⁴ Camerarius, *Symbolorum et Emblematum*, I. xciii, 'Non Tibi Spiro', the emblem adapted by Sanford for the title-page, compares the variant proverb, 'Sus per rosas'; see Corbett and Lightbown, 63, and Reusner, *Emblemata* (1581), ii. 21, cited in Henkel and Schöne, 548, where ignorant swine flee marjoram and tread roses underfoot.
⁵ Tilley, L326. ⁶ Tilley, L294. [Cf. also p. 22, 38–9.]

timely birth of the child, it may happily seem a thank-worthy labour, that the defects being so few, so small, and in no principal part, yet the greatest unlikeness is rather in defect than in deformity. But howsoever it is, it is now by more than one interest *The Countess of Pembroke's Arcadia*; done, as it was, for her; as it is, by her. Neither shall these pains be the last (if no unexpected accident cut off her determination) which the everlasting love of her excellent brother will make her consecrate to his memory.

H. S.

The emended text was printed from a copy of *90*, and a long appendix added from manuscript. This appendix consisted substantially of Books III–V of the *Old Arcadia*, but with those minor additions and alterations noted in Robertson's textual apparatus. Proof correction was slight, but many errors were introduced by the compositors.[1]

[98]   *The Countess of Pembroke's Arcadia. Written by Sir Philip Sidney Knight. Now the third time published, with sundry new additions of the same author. Imprinted for William Ponsonby*, 1598.

Folio in sixes. STC 22541; Juel-Jensen, 3.

The printer has been identified as Richard Field, and the price 9s per copy (H. R. Plomer, 'The Edinburgh Edition of Sidney's "Arcadia"', *The Library*, NS i (1900), 196). This was the first collected edition of Sidney's works. The text of *93* was reproduced with few editorial emendations.

Variants from the editions of 1599, the Edinburgh piracy, and 1605, a reprint of *98*, have not been cited. Following Ringler, 536, the next and last edition of importance was that of 1613.

[13]   *The Countess of Pembroke's Arcadia. Written by Sir Philip Sidney Knight. Now the fourth time published, with some new additions. Imprinted by H[umphrey]. L[ownes]. for Simon Waterson*, 1613.

Folio in sixes. STC 22544; Juel-Jensen, 6a
[variant imprint] *Imprinted by H[umphrey]. L[ownes]. for Matthew Lownes*, 1613. STC 22544a; Juel-Jensen, 6 b.

Variants demonstrate that *13* was printed from *98*. Conjectural emendations were made by the editor, including the removal of the three references to Clitophon's marriage (below, pp. 15, 21–2; 20, 35–6; 118, 7). Sir William Alexander's *Supplement* was added in later issues; see STC 22544a. 3 and following; Ringler, 536; Juel-Jensen, 473; and A. Mitchell and K. Foster, 'Sir William Alexander's *Supplement* to Book III of Sidney's *Arcadia*' *The Library*, 5th Ser. xxiv (1969), 234–41.

---

[1] H. E. Rollins, ed., *Tottel's Miscellany (1557–1587)*, rev. edn., ii. 34, observes that when Windet printed the 1585 edition from a copy of the 1574 edition he added errors 'in almost incredible profusion', and gives examples.

THE RELATIONSHIPS OF THE TEXTS

The relationships of the texts of *The Countess of Pembroke's Arcadia* have been closely studied by William A. Ringler, Jr., in *The Poems of Sir Philip Sidney* (Oxford, 1962), and by Dr Jean Robertson in her edition of the *Old Arcadia* (Oxford, 1973). These editors agree that a single lost scribal transcript (*T*) of the foul papers of the *Old Arcadia* was the source of all the extant copies of that text. A small number of those readings which Ringler, 367, supposed to be errors, and on which he based his hypothesis of the scribal nature of *T*, were accepted by Robertson into her text;[1] but she also added to Ringler's list of apparent errors within the manuscript tradition. This established a strong precedent for absolving Sidney of responsibility for extremely difficult and unusual readings, and for introducing hypothetical emendation at these points.

Ringler, 371–2, and Robertson, p. lvii, convincingly argue that the poems (excepting CS 3 and OP 3) and the eclogues in 90 were printed from *T*, and that Sidney continued to use *T* 'when he altered and expanded the prose of the *Old Arcadia*'. They suggest that the copy of the foul papers of the *New Arcadia* (*G*), described by Greville in his letter to Walsingham as having been left with him by Sidney,[2] became the basis of the prose of the 1590 edition, and had previously been copied in *Cm*. The scribal nature of *G* was ascertained by Ringler, 371, and Robertson, p. lvi, who pointed out errors common to *Cm* and 90. To further complicate matters, Robertson, p. lix, noted that 'some of the corrections to 90 in 93 restore the *Old Arcadia* readings. These may simply be the correct *New Arcadia* readings taken from *G*, but they could have come from the Countess of Pembroke's own *Old Arcadia* manuscript (*P*).'[3]

To the editor of the *New Arcadia* this set of textual relationships is fraught with problems. Where the *Old Arcadia* forms the basis of the *New Arcadia*, but the text of the *New Arcadia* departs from it, the source of the disparity may equally be author or scribe. In cases of divided agreement between *Cm* or 90 or 93 with some or other of the manuscripts of the *Old Arcadia*, all or any of the scribes or compositors may be at fault. Where 93 'restores' a reading which corresponds with one in the *Old Arcadia*, the emendation cannot be determined to belong to the *New Arcadia*. In new passages where *Cm*, 90, and 93 contain an awkward reading, or where they differ from one another, scribal error in *G* may be the cause, and the solution lie in hypothetical emendation.

With this in mind, the evidence for the scribal nature of *T* and *G* has been subjected to extensive examination. In Appendix III below is set out the evidence for *T*. In each case reasons are presented which either support the reading of the manuscript tradition, or at the very least suggest some alternative to scribal incompetence causing the crux in question. This vitiates two of Ringler's premises: that all the difficult readings in the *Old Arcadia* are not Sidney's, and that the foul copy of the *Old Arcadia* could not independently, directly or indirectly, lie behind each

---

[1] Those in the text of this volume are *Iris* (p. 14, 14); *watered eyes* (p. 198, 13); *keep* (p. 406, 28); and *rayed* (p. 426, 16), and notes.   [2] See above, p. xlv.   [3] See Appendix II.

of those manuscripts that he designated as descending from *T*. Without the force of these arguments to support its existence, the hypothetical manuscript *T* must be replaced in the stemma of the *Old Arcadia* by that which it was purported to be a copy of, that is, Sidney's own foul papers. These may be designated by the letter '*A*'.[1] Accepting that the manuscripts of the *Old Arcadia* reflect in their variant readings the four states of composition established by Ringler, *Je*, *Hm* (*Qu*) become A^1; *Da*, *Ph* become A^2; *Cl*, *Le*, *As* with the addition of *O* become A^3; and *St*, *Bo* (cited in that order by Robertson) become A^4.

The evidence for *G* in the apparently inexplicable readings in the *New Arcadia* is similar to that mustered for *T*. In much the same way these readings can be demonstrated to be difficult but not inscrutable, many being fairly regular Elizabethan usages. I have incorporated a number of these into the following discussion, and mention the others in the Commentary. As now no problems remain throughout the textual tradition of the *New Arcadia* that can with certainty be said to arise in scribal corruption, it is not possible to maintain that *G* is any other than Sidney's foul papers of the *New Arcadia*. Indeed, comparison of all the texts of the two versions indicates that the single manuscript behind *Cm*, *90*, and the majority of the alterations and additions in *93*, was *A*, though in a form consistent with its continuous use by Sidney as his working copy. In addition, as *A* and *G* are synonymous, the stemma can be relieved of *G*. The remainder of this discussion is occupied with setting out other evidence for *A* being the sole source of the texts, with ascertaining what the characteristics of *A* were when Sidney gave it to Greville, and with understanding how *A* was used in *Cm*, *90*, and *93*.

One of the indications that the texts of both versions of the *Arcadia* descend from the single ancestor *A* is in the haphazard agreement in variants between groups of texts, as may be seen on p. 42, 8 *say of OA* (ex. *Ph*), *Cm*; *say to Ph*, *90*, *93*; on p. 60, 16 *imperfections OA* (ex. *Je*), *Cm*, *93*; *affections Je*, *90*; on p. 91, 16 *secret Cl*, *As*, *Ph*, *Cm*, *93*; *sacred St*, *Bo*, *Da*, *Hm*, *90*; and on p. 200, 29 where *growing* [*proving Cm*] is the revised version of *grow* [*prove Qu*]. Use of *A* would also encourage transmission into the *New Arcadia* of readings which reflect the development of the *Old Arcadia* text, as *lockes* [sic] *made of Cm*, an erroneous variant of the A^{1-3} reading, *laces made of*, p. 164, 3 (var.), where *St*, *Bo*, *90*, *93* read *threads of finest*. On p. 114, 12 in a passage only lightly revised *Cm*, *90*, *93* read *rage* with *Cl*, *Le*, *As* against *heat* in the other manuscripts of the *Old Arcadia*. Robertson writes that in this case 'Sidney himself may have hesitated between the two words',[2] which would both have been in *A*. On p. 201, 11 another variant lies within a passage heavily revised and then transcribed by the author. Here the agreement between *Cm*, *90*, *93* and *Cl*, *As* in reading *labour* rather than *seek* in the other manuscripts shows that the author chose one of his alternatives when rewriting,[3] as at p. 254, 35 where he evidently preferred *be assured Cm*, *90*, *93*, *Cl*, *As* over *assure her St*, *Da*, *Ph*, *Je*, *Hm* (*measure Bo*).

In addition to these relationships with manuscripts from A^3, the working copy for the *New Arcadia* also contained readings related only to A^4. On p. 96, 14–18, Pyrocles fighting with the lion 'strake him such a blow' and came away 'with a little

---

[1] The diagram of the stemma is below on p. lx.   [2] Robertson, p. lxv.   [3] Ibid., pp. xxx–xxxi n. and 121, 23.

scratch'. In *St, Bo* where Pyrocles 'strake him so great a blow', the lion only 'did hurt a little' in retaliation. This contrasts with the version in A^{1-3} where Pyrocles 'thrust the lion through', receiving in return 'a sore [shrewd *Da*] wound' (Robertson, 47, 23).

These are variants in which earlier and later states of the composition of the *Old Arcadia* are represented in the text of the *New Arcadia*. They support the theory that the working papers for the *New Arcadia* consisted of the whole of *A* with some sections slightly revised, some sections heavily revised and then written out by the author, and with newly written passages of prose and verse added. Even the text of *CS* 3 as it was in *A* preserves authorial alternatives in p. 340, 24, *makes of Bo, Dd, Hn, Hy, Ra, 93, 98* (*CS*), *Bn* and *sets by St, Cl, 90*. But the first line of the poem at p. 340, 1 seems to have been altered to suit the context in which it was set in the *New Arcadia*, reading *woes Cm, 90, Hn* instead of *wrongs* (*ex.* wrong *Dd*). Again adapting Ringler's terminology, this amalgam of the foul copy of the *Old Arcadia* which, with additions, became the foul copy of the *New Arcadia*, is hereafter referred to as A^5.

General characteristics of A^5 may be seen in the texts of the *New Arcadia*. That there were no chapter divisions was stated by the 'overseer of the print' of *90*, who admitted to supplying them. This was attested to by their absence from *Cm* and their removal from *93*, where only some of the surrounding prose, adjusted in *90* to accommodate the chapter summaries, was restored to the form preserved in *Cm*. In all three texts are the four lacunae mentioned above in the description of *Cm*. Agreements between *Cm* and *90* or *93*, or with both, are also useful in determining information about A^5, for though the scribe of *Cm* at times became inattentive, on p. 337, 20 writing 'he and the Nurse' for 'heard the noise', they demonstrate a strong relationship with a common source, as in the omission in *Cm, 90* of the epitaph, OP 3 (p. 346, 14–22).

In *93* the *New Arcadia* was printed from a copy of *90*, seen on K5^v where the distinguishing typography in O and ô of the two compositors of *90* was reproduced from Q6^v–Q7^v. The text reprinted the errors from such uncorrected sheets as were bound in that copy of *90*, and as at p. 57, 32 (*var.*) compounded them. The editor of *93* corrected this copy of *90* from A^5, as at p. 254, 18 where the change from bold *St, Bo, Cl, Da, Ph, 90* to bobbed *As, Je, Hm, Cm, 93* (as in *St*) required careful consideration of the manuscript. He allowed several errors to remain, and those were carried over into *93*. Many are indicated by agreements between *OA* and *Cm* as in p. 43, 8 *here OA, Cm; thereof 90, 93*; or in p. 240, 27 *other OA, Cm; otherwise 90, 93*. Most of the changes to *90* are unsupported by any text. Some may be errors by the compositor, but many represent editorial interference.[1] Even so, characteristics of A^5 are revealed through readings which did receive sanction in *93*. On p. 102, 15, in a passage considerably revised, the editor agreed that *Cm, 90* rightly omitted the same material which had been accidentally left out of *As* by skipping from *was* to *was*. Variant readings introduced to agree with the *Old Arcadia*, as on p. 93, 35 *learn Cm, 90* and *discern OA, 93* or p. 250, 31 *coldly Cm, 90* and *wildly OA, 93*; and readings introduced to agree with *Cm* as at p. 98, 4 *bloody Cm, 93* for *fearful OA, 90*

---

[1] These are discussed on pp. lvi–lvii.

or p. 106, 4 *homage Cm*, 93 for *honour OA*, 90, indicate that Sanford was often faced with having to decide which of the author's jottings in *A* he preferred.

The uncorrected sheets of *90* divulge a great deal about *A⁵*. Errors in common with *Cm* reveal unwanted punctuation in *A⁵*, as in the full stop after *years* at p. 10, 24; difficulty in distinguishing between *u* and *n*, reading *Enarchus* at p. 136, 8 (here *Euarelius Cm* is a departure from the usual *Enarchus*) and at p. 137, 29; between *e* and *c* in *Elegiae* instead of *Elegiac* at p. 267, 38; between *ct* and *il* in *fact* instead of *fail* at p. 363, 35; and in deciphering minims, as in *iminate* for *innate* at p. 359, 34 – an error also made in *Cm* alone at p. 247, 22 (see *var.*) and p. 258, 33. But the proof correction in *90* in addition preserves evidence of tampering with the text by standardizing the spelling of *A⁵*, not only in the cancelled B3–B6ᵛ, but also on p. 362, 8 where *dispaire Cm, 90* (uncorr.) became *despaire*; on p. 363, 38 where *whott Cm* and *whot 90* (uncorr.) became *hot*; on p. 366, 11 where *seperated Cm, 90* (uncorr.) became *separated*; on p. 236, 14 where *endewed Cm, 90* (uncorr.) became *endowed* – an example of the proof corrector unnecessarily changing the diction. Other instances of this are at p. 14, 6 where *These* became *The*; p. 138, 18 where *employed to* became *employed but to*; p. 306, 31 where *her* became *their* (by consulting *A* the corrector would have seen that the compositor erred at the second *her* rather than the first); and p. 307, 37 *destres Cm, distresse 90* (uncorr.) which became *dress* through association with *dressing* a few lines above at p. 307, 31. Conversely, the corrector made no attempt to standardize either the manuscript spelling at p. 191, 19 *flower Cm, 90, 93* for *floor*, or the possessive ending in *-es* after *Mopsa*, *Pamela*, and *Erona*; indeed, at times he seemed to prefer *Pamelaes* and *Eronaes* where *Cm* read simply *Pamelas, Eronas*. At p. 94, 34 he left unconnected *shewed Cm, 90* for *sued 93*, the single instance where the compositor misread Sidney's long *s* (written second in the ligature *ss*) as *h*, an error frequent in *Cm* in such words as *eternishe, ishewe, purshewed*, where the related misreading as *s* of the second letter of the ligature *ph* abounds in *Strepson, Ompsale, Clitopson, Delpsos*, and *Psilanax*.

Other readings in *Cm* directly represent the unfinished state of *A⁵*. In newly written passages as well as those adapted from the *Old Arcadia Cm* reads *duke* or *duke's* for *king* or *king's*,[1] and once at p. 106, 29 reads *duchess* for *queen*. *Cleophila* or *Cleofila*, especially in sections adapted from the *Old Arcadia*, is more frequent than *Zelmane* or the more usual *Zelmana* or *Selmana*, and in many places *Zelmane* is written over *Cleophila*, which infrequently is stroked through. Evidently Sidney had originally avoided the awkwardness at p. 83, 34 where *Zelmane* (*Cleophila* in *Cm*) comments upon *Zelmane*, a duplication originating in *90* through the not unreasonable desire of the editors for consistency. Although the scribe of *Cm* at times without reference to copy entered the wrong names into the spaces he had left, as at p. 51, 3 where *Kalander* is written above *Clitophon* and *Thimothus* (for *Timotheus*, the correct name), other names coupled in *Cm* reflect drafting in *A⁵*. Through much of Book I *Palladius* is written above *Musidorus*, which has on few occasions been stroked out. At p. 249, 17, 24 *Amphiales* is written above *Hipponax*, evidence that *Hipponax* in *Cm* at p. 181, 30 was the reading in *A⁵* before alteration

---

[1] See pp. 106, 24, 30; 107, 12, 20, 21; 116, 29, 34; 120, 35.

in 90 to *Amphialus*. Similarly, on pp. 250, 39 and 251, 3 *Clinias* is above *Callias*, though *Callias* alone is in *Cm* at p. 253, 36. At p. 93, 19 *Clinias* in *Cm* seems to be an error for *Calodoulus* 90, 93 made without reference to copy and perhaps at a later time, for Clinias is not named in the text until p. 249, 6. In *Cm Claius* begins with *K* as in the *Old Arcadia* only at p. 9, 29 and p. 118, 12; in 90 it is *Claius* except in the unrevised Eclogues where *Klaius* prevails, the only *Claius* there being at p. 432, 37. *Pirocles,Pirocleas*, and *Perocleas* are the spellings in *Cm* of *Pyrocles*, although *Philantus* and *Phalantus* are used interchangeably. In *Cm*, *Musidory* at p. 147, 15, 17; *Plexirty* at p. 158, 4, 7; *Menelay* at p. 348, 35, and *Amphialy* at p. 349, 21 indicate both that the abbreviation for final *us* was at times used in A^5, and that the scribe of *Cm* did not recognize it.

Place names in A^5 were similarly left in an inconsistent state, as at p. 179, 13 where Plangus' home was called *Colchis* (*Colehos Cm*) which lies west of *Iberia* 90, 93. Throughout 90 and on seven occasions in *Cm*, 93 Erona's kingdom is *Lycia*; however, at p. 177, 17, 20 in a passage from the *Old Arcadia*, and at p. 177, 26 in a newly written clause, *Lydia* is the reading in *Cm*, 93, reflecting the disparity in A^5. As the Lydian attack upon Thessalia at p. 139, 19 is not mentioned in connection with Erona, *Lydia* seems accidentally to have persisted in *A*, and by proximity suggested itself to the author for his new clause. In only three of the ten occurrences does *Cm* read *Phrygia* with 90. Once a blank space was left, but on six occasions the reading copied into *Cm* from *A* was *Pergamum*, a city of Mysia north of Phrygia, though at times part of it. Such lack of final revision may have been behind the three readings in *Cm* of *Lacedaemon* for *Laconia* 90, 93 and of *Lacedaemonian discipline* at p. 34, 18 for *Spartan discipline* 90, 93, though these may have been added later by the scribe of *Cm* without reference to copy. At p. 68, 7 *Ithonia Cm*, 90, 93 seems to be an outright error in *A* for *Ithome*, caused by homoeoteleuton with *Messenia, Laconia, Arcadia*.

Agreements among the variants in the independent witnesses to *A* show some of the difficulties in reproducing its text. At p. 199, 35-6 the agreement between *OA* and *Cm* in reading *I say* twice reveals the omission in 90 which was carried into 93. At p. 244, 18 *succour OA, Cm*, 93 indicates substitution in *help* 90, while p. 244, 28-9 *the court gate OA*, 93 suggests omission in *the gate Cm*, 90. At p. 306, 29 *relieved* 90 may have come about through hasty reading of *rescued Cm*, 93, as perhaps did p. 310, 11 *hid* 90 where the correction in 93 to *hidden* is supported by *hid he Cm*, indicating that such a form as *hidne* may have been in *A*. At p. 157, 2 *so well Cm* receives support both from *soul* 90 (cf. *souel* 90 (uncorr.) at p. 92, 9) and from *well* 93, where the correction was partial, as at p. 1, 20 *grace Cm* where *gaze* 90 became hybridized in *graze* 93.

In several instances there was complete disagreement between *Cm* and 90 and 93. Evidently in these cases the difficult reading preserved in *Cm* was in *A* but became simplified in 90. On comparison with *A* the editor of 93 rejected the simplification and substituted his own version. At p. 144, 28 *they had, they had left* the contraction to *they had left* 90 was corrected and expanded in 93 to *they lately had, they had left*. At p. 146, 11-12 *of those desperate ambition Cm*, *those* as the demonstrative adjective meaning *such* (see note) was misread as the pronoun antecedent of the following relative *who* and changed into *those desperate ambitious* 90, and partially corrected in 93 to *those of desperate ambition* where the words were juggled to suit the interpretation. At p. 217, 17–18 the negative in 'not knowing any other, but that', which reduced to 'only knowing' before *all her pleasures* to *Cm*, was interpreted as the beginning of a new clause for which different verbs were supplied in *all her pleasures bent to* 90 and *all her pleasures were directed to* 93. At p. 220, 36 the ellipsis in *among there Cm* was expanded to *among them there* 90 and *among whom there* 93. At p. 255, 13 Pyrocles' recollection of *cruel Dido Cm* became reversed in 90 to refer to Pamphilus' *cruelty to Dido* and in 93 to his *cruel handling Dido*. At p. 274, 29 *younger than Cm* (evidently spelled *then* in *A*) was altered to *then younger* in 90 and to *younger* in 93. At p. 291, 15 lack of punctuation to separate argument from proof in *A*, where *Cm* read *fortune she would* for *fortune – she would*, led to the conjectural *fortune, if she would* 90 and *fortune, which should* 93. At p. 306, 27 by ignoring the terminology of confinement in *unvisited* (cf. p. 390, 28 which is the earliest citation in *OED* (b))¹ the editors of both editions read the preceding *departed* as intransitive and altered *not unvisited Cm* to *not having visited* 90 and *not visiting* 93. At p. 313, 31 where *this* was used in place of *these* (*OED* II, 5f) in *this beastly absurdities* the editor of 90 read *these beastly absurdities* while the editor of 93 regularized the agreement towards the singular in *this beastly absurdity*. At p. 314, 30 the synoeciosis in *ugly shamefastness Cm* was destroyed in *ugly shamelessness* 90 and retrieved in *ugly shamefulness* 93 where the medial *f* was reinstated, though in a simpler contrast. At p. 324, 3 the ellipsis in *quickly received Cm* was expanded to *quickly he received* 90 and altered to *he quickly received* 93. At p. 336, 36 the uncommon *admonished Cm* was rejected in favour of *acknowledge* 90 and again some of the letters at least were restored in *a promised* 93. At p. 337, 34 the difficult adjective in *occasionable by Cm* was construed as *occasioned by* 90 and changed to a noun in *occasion of* 93, 98, though almost given its correct meaning in *by occasion of* 13. At p. 351, 29 reference to Vulcan's *now courteous* wife – Venus seduced him to make him courteously grant her request for Aeneas' armour – was interpreted as a mere comparative in *now more courteous* 90, reduced to *more courteous* 93. At p. 351, 34 *yᵗ* [sic] *was Cm* was expanded to *it was* 90, and then both words were read as contractions and both expanded in 93 to *that way as*. At p. 354, 15 *storm of cunning*, 'heavy downfall of blows guided by cunning', was altered to avoid the forthcoming repetition in *storm of fury*, 'violence of fury', by editors who missed the difference in meaning and were prepared to create their own in reading *stream of cunning* 90 and *stern of cunning* 93. At p. 366, 21 the figurative use of *set* as in 'set gems' in *set – in the eyes of her*, which without punctuation was the reading in *Cm*, was misinterpreted as 'placed' with the necessity of *her* as a possessive requiring completion in *set in the eyes of her creatures* 90 and *set in the eyes of men* 93. At p. 368, 28–9 *look out to another Cm* was made personal in *look out to one another* 90, then reduced to *look one to another* 93. At p. 390, 16 *all such numbers men's mourning*, the unusual usage of *number* in the plural without *of* (cf. *OED* 9c for the singular) is supported by the determination by the scribe of *Cm* to correct his own error in writing *of mens* ['mens'

---

¹ [Thomas North's translation of Plutarch's *Lives* (1579) also contains an example, however.]

deleted] all such numbers mens mourning. Here the printed editions simplified to *all such numbers' mourning* 90 and *whose mourning* 93.

Other difficulties in working from *A* are indicated by p. 83, 19 *the coupled Cm, their coupled* 90, *that coupled* 93; p. 99, 5 *delight Cm, discern* 90, *decipher* 93; p. 143, 34 *waves Cm, vows* 90, *voices* 93; or by p. 251, 39 *not Cm, knows* 90, *wot* 93 where the manuscript seems to have been virtually illegible. At p. 97, 6 *her Cm,* 90 for *his OA,* 93 and at p. 122, 2 *her Cm,* 90, 93 arise from the author loosely referring to the male lion and the male heron by the rustic feminine (cf. *OED* under *she* 1a (b)). p. 104, 22 (*var.*) *and the more ... hoping* and p. 119, 28 (*var.*) *high* are readings imported into 90 through lack of clear deletion in *A*, but rejected in *Cm*, 93. Some errors were mechanical. At p. 58, 26–7 the scribe of *Cm* skipped from *with a* to *with a* and the compositor of 90 transposed *set with* and *a distaff.* At p. 395, 5–6 the compositor of 90 skipped from *own* to *own*, losing the concept that abuse by one's parents and family may be worse than abuse by strangers.

Many apparent textual cruces arose not from copy but from misinterpretation and simplification of unusual syntax and style. At p. 3, 37–8 the cryptic combination of zeugma and syllepsis in *cast destruction and himself* became diffused in 93 by shifting *destruction* to the end of the preceding question and omitting *and.* At p. 77, 4–6 by syllepsis the relative *who* applies to both clauses in *who ... thinking* and *who ... made.* This distorts the syntax indicated by *caused*, which requires completion by *to make*, as in 'caused all the kites ... to make the poor kite find'– a difficulty avoided by changing *caused* to *called* in 90. At p. 120, 22 the apparent tautology in *spare or stop his horses* is caused by syllepsis of the preceding negatives. These ought to have been understood to have applied equally to the second element in the construction, as 'neither for our praises nor curses will [neither] spare [n]or stop his horses', but the editor of 93 changed his text to *spur or stop his horses.* At p. 123, 13–15 in *Philoclea ... which tender youth* where the antecedent is repeated indirectly in 'tender youth',[1] the construction was missed by the editor of 90 who expanded to *which from the tender youth*, and by the editor of 93 who contracted to the simplified *whose tender youth*, coincidentally agreeing with the reading in the *Old Arcadia.* At p. 138, 3 the early use of *actions* as 'conduct' seems to have prompted the editor of 93 to read *axioms*, altering the parallel structure and adding the figure anadiplosis by repeating *laws.* Certainly this sort of misinterpretation lay behind the destruction of the pun or paronomasia at p. 97, 22–3 where the contrast to *virtuous courage* in *courage Cm*, 90, 'haughtiness' or 'pride' was lost in the explanatory substitution of *cowards* 93.

Colloquial usage in both direct and indirect speech was made formal. At p. 134, 31 *time a day Cm*, 93 became *time of the day* in 90; at p. 216, 20 *a request* was correctly expanded in 93 to *on request*, though the spelling *one* could be ambiguous; at p. 183, 4 Miso's dialectal *ballets Cm*, 90, 93 was altered in 98, 13 to the more proper *ballads*; and at p. 318, 32–3 Amphialus' challenge to Phalantus that he was *ready to know whether he had anything to him* became the debased and mild message in 93 that he was *ready to know whether he had anything to say to him.* At p. 98, 24–5 Pamela's

---

[1] Cf. Abbott, 184.

pejorative reference to Musidorus as a mere 'this' in *But this – no other weapon but that knife* (*Cm* reads *But this noe other weapon, but that knyfe*) was interpreted as an ellipsis requiring clarification, becoming *But this shepherd, having no other weapon but that knife* in 90, embellished in 93 into *But this young shepherd with a wonderful courage, having no other weapon but that knife*.

A small number of readings omitted from *Cm* were printed in 90 but rejected from 93. At p. 65, 12–13 *as if his tears had been outflowing blood, his arms an overpressing burthen* was an addition to a passage taken almost word for word from the *Old Arcadia*; at p. 147, 29–30 *that wished none well, to them worse than others, and to him worst of all* was an unnecessary comment in the triplet style of p. 156, 23–4; at p. 312, 2–3 *as now, being; then, not being* is a gloss on the preceding 'of chanceable, not eternal', altered to *if chanceable* in 93, revealing that the editor misunderstood this comment upon the nature of the 'chanceable'. At p. 312, 22–4 *or fortune the efficient of these ... and eternity the fruit of her inconstancy* a further concept is introduced into the argument; at p. 20, 27 *and attend* seems tautological after *wait*; and at p. 60, 26, in a passage from the *Old Arcadia* containing both slight alterations and variants which suggest lack of clarity in *A*, 'right' in *right reason* might have seemed optional. In all of these instances of omission by *Cm* and 93 some markings of an unspecific nature, whether for inclusion or omission, seem to have guided those reading *A* towards opposite conclusions. I have accepted these readings from 90, but have printed them in square brackets.

In 93 outright departures from *Cm* and 90 arose partly from errors by the compositor (as at p. 159, 8 where *men* was omitted at the end of a line), partly through incomplete understanding by the editor. At p. 77, 31–2 where Phalantus, 'The Fair Man-of-Arms', was known chiefly because *of his own good*, his fairness or goodness, the editor of 93 transformed him into one known only for *his good justing*. At p. 87, 33 the antagonists in the imitation matachin where every one had *adversaries* were specifically given *two adversaries*. At p. 187, 32–4 the addition of *garments* after *mourning* created an unwarranted parallel with the following *mourning garments*. At p. 190, 10 *tedious*, 'disagreeable', describing Andromana's interpretation of all Plangus' actions, was changed to *hideous* to relate strictly to the comparison with Proteus. At p. 276, 33 the intimacy of Cecropia's teasing her son in *I have brought* was lost in the factually correct but unemotional *my policy hath brought*. At p. 318, 39 Phalantus' overall glittering appearance, 'as when the *sun shines* upon a waving water', was narrowed to reflect the image of his blue armour 'which a sun did ... gild': 93 reads, 'as when the *sun in a clear day shines* upon a waving water'. At p. 319, 19 misinterpretation *of disdained*, 'disdainful', led to the more accustomed *disdaining*; and at p. 359, 18 Cecropia's devotion to and control over Amphialus became minimized in changing *he should* to *she would*, which simply reasserted her dominance.

Unlike these examples, the alteration in 93 of p. 141, 21–2 *now, finding him able Cm*, 90 to *now, being both sent for by Euarchus, and finding Pyrocles able* is less likely to be expansion by the editor than an attempt at fidelity to copy. This added information is previously given at p. 115, 32–4 where 'the king of Macedon ... did at this time send both for the prince, his son ... and for Musidorus', the subject of the following paragraph. In *Cm* this sentence ends after *the king of Macedon*, followed by the exclamation in all texts, 'But alas ...!', omitting the reference to the princes being sent for. It would seem that here is an instance of alternative readings in *A* some pages apart, where the scribe of *Cm* felt directed to leave out both, the editors of *90* and *93* to include the fuller version on p. 115, and the editor of *93* alone to add the second on p. 141.

The most significant departure from *Cm* and *90* in *93* is the massive appendix which the editor of *93* termed 'the conclusion, not the perfection of *Arcadia*'. Before it, he inserted this note:

> How this combat ended, how the ladies by the coming of the discovered forces were delivered and restored to Basilius, and how Dorus again returned to his old master, Dametas, is altogether unknown. What afterward chanced, out of the author's own writings and conceits hath been supplied, as followeth.

The appendix closely resembles Books III–V of the *Old Arcadia*, but contains small additions, substitutions, and omissions. Such changes are slight and in no way begin to approach the complexity or fullness of even the simplest of the alterations to Books I and II.

The addition to *A* of the bulky manuscript of Book III left the remaining section in need of radical revision in plot, character, and style. To fulfil the predictions of the oracles within this new framework would necessitate a serious reconsideration of the romantic plot. The purpose and content of the severely depleted Eclogues would have to be reassessed. Except in Philisides' eclogue which may have been written earlier, the epitaph, and Dametas' one-line motto, Sidney showed no willingness to compose new poems for the *New Arcadia*. For the prose, he could return to the old Books III–V, or could invent a new ending. He did neither.

The differences between the appendix and Books III–V of the *Old Arcadia* clearly demonstrate that the remains of *A* served as printer's copy for *93*, and that *A* had been altered by Sidney mainly during the revision of Books I and II. Passages about Philanax and Menalcas, which lie behind the descriptions of those characters in the *New Arcadia*, are omitted.[1] From a sequence of four images in a passage deleted in *A*, 'his heart ... one ... to discover ... upon what slippery grounds', the last is used early in the new Book III at p. 266, 22–3, *the ground he stood upon ... slippery*. The preceding three are reworked, along with topics from another sentence, into the revised beginning of the appendix.[2] One line from the deletion at the opening of the old Book III, 'counterfeit a love to Mopsa, and tell her whatsoever he would have Pamela understand', becomes p. 130, 21–2 in the *New Arcadia*, 'counterfeiting love to Mopsa, and saying to Mopsa whatsoever he would have her know'.[3] Another, 'the heart stuffed up with woefulness ... air of comfort', is moved to the long passage which in *93* replaces the end of Book III of the *Old Arcadia*.[4] In this new passage the aphorism is preceded by lines transferred from the description of Pyrocles' thoughts as he approaches Philoclea's chamber, 'long as Gynecia ... missed favour', and followed by an adaptation of lines formerly describing Musidorus and Pamela

---

[1] Cf. pp. 253, 32–4; 255, 7–16 and Robertson, 285, 26–286, 13; and cf. pp. 93, 13–14; 93, 18–22 and Robertson, 409, 1–4.   [2] Robertson, 174, 5–9; 172, 25–9 (*var.*)   [3] Ibid., 172, 19–20.   [4] Ibid., 172, 8–9; 237, 30–1.

asleep in the old Book IV, 'thoughts even ... together'. These in turn are replaced by a new sentence retaining the original phrase from the *Old Arcadia*, *delicately wound up one in another's arms*, omitting *up*.¹ The opening sentence of Book IV is rewritten incorporating 'the instrument of revealing'.² The opening words, 'The everlasting justice ... chastisement', are moved well into the book as a substitution for the simpler 'the everlasting justice to be chastisers'.³

These variants illustrate that the mechanics of revision, in splitting and reallocating passages, are similar to those used by Sidney in Books I and II. The influence of this method is felt in the *New Arcadia* only as far as the beginning of Book III at p. 266, 23. The change in method at this point, from adaptation of old material to fresh composition, corresponds to the enormous gap in thematic unity between the rest of Book III and this appendix. Up to that point a certain amount of continuity has been achieved. Removal from the earlier part of *A* of Musidorus kissing Pamela 'a hundred times' while she lies in a swoon after he kills the bear accords with the excision from the appendix of his designs upon her virtue.⁴ Passages about Pyrocles' 'due bliss' and 'mutual satisfaction' with Philoclea⁵ are replaced by references to an earlier addition describing his plan to elope with Philoclea to 'some town of the helots ... newly again up in arms against the nobility', having first 'put on a slight undersuit of man's apparel'.⁶ Their taking refuge with the helots is anticipated in the *New Arcadia* at p. 34, 39–35, 1 in Pyrocles' promise to return should the treaty with the Lacedaemonians be broken. In the new passage added to *A* near the beginning of Book V, the new information that this treaty has not held falls within Plangus' report of events which occur at the end of Book II in the *New Arcadia*.⁷ Plangus' report itself is in part a substitution in *A* for the description of Euarchus, redeveloped in the *New Arcadia* at p. 136, 13 ff. Of a similar nature is the added reference in *A* to the 'late mutiny' (cf. below, p. 306, 2) in the revised narrative about Philanax. Excerpts from the *Old Arcadia* version of this are integrated into the *New Arcadia*, particularly at p. 253, 32–4 where 'principal Arcadian lords' becomes *principal noblemen*, 'placed garrisons in all the towns and villages anything near the lodges' becomes *place such garrisons in all the towns and villages near unto him*, and 'five hundred horse' becomes reduced at p. 255, 8 to *a hundred horse*.⁸

These revisions in the latter part of *A* were made as material was withdrawn from the *Old Arcadia* for use in the *New Arcadia*. One of the latest seems to be the addition of three references, by Philoclea, the narrator, and Philanax himself to his being 'preserved by Philoclea what time, taken by Amphialus, he was like to suffer a cruel death',⁹ drawing on p. 305, 15 ff. The other is Musidorus' ironic repudiation of 'our services done to Basilius in the late war with Amphialus, importing no less than his daughters' lives and his state's preservation', alluding to the triumphant outcome of the siege prescribed by the second oracle at p. 396, 33, but nowhere described.¹⁰

Another characteristic of the appendix is the mingling of authorial variants which cut across the states of *A*. Such a mixture attests to the presence in the copy of

---

¹ Ibid., 228, 15–20; 314, 10–21 and *var.* ² Ibid., 265, 7 and *var.* ³ Ibid., 265, 2–4; 307, 10 and *var.*
⁴ Ibid., 306, 14–19; 52, 11–13. ⁵ Ibid., 243, 5; 273, 6. ⁶ Ibid., 236, 28–9; 273, 19 (*var.*); 217, 2–3 (*var.*).
⁷ Ibid., 357 (*var.*) ⁸ Ibid., 285, 26–286, 13 (*var.*) ⁹ Ibid., 303, 24 (*var.*); 304, 10 (*var.*), 22 (*var.*), and 27 (*var.*) ¹⁰ Ibid., 400, 37 (*var.*).

both early and late readings which are not clearly distinguished from one another. Individual readings in 93 agree at times with A^{1-2}, or with A^{1-3}, or with A^{3-4}. Most noticeably, 93 agrees with A^{1-3} in omitting the comment on Agelastus at Robertson, 284, 5-7; with A^{1-2} and *Cl* alone from A^3 in reading *and then ... offered unto it* in the penultimate prose, and *remembering Cleophila's [Zelmane's 93] hurt* in the final prose of its First Eclogues.[1] Seven readings which agree with A^{1-2} are closely inter-spersed with five agreeing with A^{3-4} in a passage corresponding to Robertson, 389-96 (see the textual apparatus).

Like the scribe of *Cm*, the editor of 93 failed to alter completely *Cleophila* (*Cleofila* in 93) to *Zelmane*,[2] *Kerxenus* to *Kalander*[3] *duchess* to *princess*,[4] *duke* to *king*,[5] *dukedom* to *kingdom*,[6] and one reference to Musidorus as a *duke*.[7] In other respects the editor remained faithful to his copy where he could understand it, not altering the text to bring Pyrocles' execution into line with his new sentence,[8] and not altering the discrepancy in the ages of Musidorus and Pyrocles from one year in the *Old Arcadia* to accord with the 'three or four years' of the *New Arcadia*, as on p. 140, 33-4.[9] Given the editor's determination to print the Fourth Eclogues, his removal of the elegy, *OA* 75, from Book III of the *New Arcadia* (p. 386, 25 ff.) became a necessity – and provides evidence that Sidney had not supplied a replacement for the poem in the Fourth Eclogues. In retaining in the appendix some eleven of twenty-one authorial intrusions in the prose, the editor seems to have been guided by selective revision in his copy, for authorial comments are included both in revised and in new passages,[10] and in the *New Arcadia* itself at p. 123, 3-6.

In *OA* 8 (below, p. 183, 13 ff.) and *OA* 30 (below, p. 172, 1 ff.) the editor of 93 rejected readings unique to 90 in favour of agreement with the readings of the *Old Arcadia*. This policy continued in the new Eclogues in *OA* 7 and *OA* 31.[11] However, in *OA* 31, *OA* 13, and *OA* 63 he also introduced several words which differ from those in any earlier texts,[12] continuing to demonstrate a preference for certain variants in *A*, as he had at p. 98, 4, *bloody Cm*, 93 against *fearful OA*, 90 and at p. 106, 4, *homage Cm*, 93 against *honour OA*, 90. Apparently alternative readings could be found throughout the prose and verse of *A*, both in the Books and in the Eclogues. The Eclogues themselves, disarranged in *A*, led the editor of 93 to vary those first published in 90, and to add his own version of the Third and Fourth in the appendix. In addition to the missing epitaph for Argalus and Parthenia, below, p. 346, 14 ff., he included *OP* 4 and *OP* 5, apparently preserving whatever remained in Sidney's working papers that could be associated with the *Arcadia*.

It had been a work in progress, reaching one plateau in the *Old Arcadia* and another in the *New Arcadia*. The unfinished remains of the foul copy are preserved in the appendix to 93. Above all, their incomplete nature indicates how great was the chasm between the level actually achieved and Sidney's ultimate goal.

The diagram of the stemma which follows is simpler than those produced by Ringler, 380, and Robertson, p. lxiv. The scribal intermediaries hypothesized by

---

[1] Ibid., 88, 19-21, 24. [2] Ibid., 416, 16. [3] Ibid., 412, 11; 415, 9. [4] Ibid., 193, 19. [5] Ibid., 193, 12; 222, 8; 415, 4, 12. [6] Ibid., 417, 5. [7] Ibid., 410, 19. [8] Ibid., 408, 2-3; 405, 26 (var.) [9] Ibid., 377, 26. [10] Ibid., 237, 38; 314, 9-23 (var.); 356, 29-30. [11] Ibid., 58, 34; 62, 30-2; 63, 4-22; 64, 1; 160, 6 ff. [12] Ibid., 82, 25 ff.; 245, 29 ff.

these editors, T, P, and G, have been removed. The theory put forth in this edition favours the descent of the extant texts from a single set of foul papers, A, used for both versions of *The Countess of Pembroke's Arcadia*. Their variants reflect five stages of composition.

```
    A¹           A²              A³              A⁴           A⁵
    |           /  \           / | \           /   \        / | \
    X          Da   Y         Cl Le As  O     Bo   St      Cm 90 93
   / \              |                                          |
  Je  Hm            Ph                                         98
      |                                                        |
      Qu                                                       13
```

Summary

When Sidney began to revise and expand the foul papers of the *Old Arcadia* (A¹⁻⁴) they became the foul papers of the *New Arcadia* (A⁵). In 1584 the prose and a small amount of verse were badly copied from A⁵ into *Cm*. After *Cm* was copied, only one small passage of prose was added. In a heavily edited form A⁵ served as printer's copy for the whole of *90*. It was used again to emend the text of *90* and for the Eclogues and appendix in *93*. Minor emendations were made in *98* and *13*.

THIS EDITION

The object of this edition is to reconstruct Sidney's *New Arcadia* from the three witnesses to his foul papers (A⁵): *Cm*, *90*, and *93*. *Cm* is incomplete and greatly inaccurate. As A⁵ was well reproduced in *90*, I have used *90* as my copy-text and collated several examples. Apart from the silent emendation of minor printer's errors, departures from *90* are in the textual apparatus. The text of *90* was corrected in *93* from A⁵. Agreement between two of the texts has generally been taken to represent the reading in the archetype. Exceptions are discussed above, under the Relationships of the Texts.

Although the textual traditions of the *Old Arcadia* and the *New Arcadia* originated in the same body of foul papers, they became divorced when the author began his revision. Discrepancies between the traditions are not recorded. Variants among the manuscripts of the *Old Arcadia* are given only when they are related to at least one of the texts of the *New Arcadia*, and assist in reconstructing the archetype. This occurs, for example, in agreements between *OA* and *Cm* against *90*, *93* which demonstrate that *93* may be reprinting an error in *90*. *Old Arcadia* variants which cast no light upon the nature of the archetype are not given. These occur where a minority of manuscripts haphazardly departs from the readings of A¹⁻⁴. They are printed in Robertson.

Where *Cm* reads against *90* and *93* without support from *OA*, *98*, or *13* its variant is not recorded. This frees the textual apparatus of hundreds of errors unique to *Cm*. All the variants in *93* which were reprinted in *98* or *13* are included, but variants first introduced in *98* or *13* have not been admitted where no textual crux exists.

The chapter headings in *90*, not having the support of *Cm* or *93*, have been treated as textual variants and placed in the textual apparatus. *Cm* and *93* indicate that the prose was adjusted to accommodate the chapter headings. These alterations were not all restored in *93* to the reading in *Cm*. On such occasions the reading in *Cm* has been considered carefully, and at times adopted. The First and Second Eclogues from *90* have also been excluded from the text. These ought to have been represented in the textual apparatus, but because of their length have been printed separately in Appendix I. Within themselves, these Eclogues possess two distinct textual traditions. The author had revised the verse in A^5, which contained such unfinished draft lines and alterations as in *OA* 7. But as the prose was stitched together and considerably altered by the editor, it must be regarded as the composition of that editor, with its genesis in A^5 but with no textual tradition behind it. The equally unauthorized version of the Eclogues in *93* has no claim to be further associated with the *New Arcadia*. Like the appendix in *93* they are relics of textual history. The verse which they contain is in Ringler and Robertson, except for OP 4 and OP 5 which are in Ringler alone.

In the Introduction and Commentary, quotations from Sidney's other works and from the writings of other authors have in general been put into modern spelling, with modern punctuation. Whereas the punctuation in this edition has been modernized, the spelling has been normalized so that forms may be retained which differ in sound from modern usage but which appear from the texts to have been authorial, as *alablaster*, pp. 166, 13–4 and 344, 22; *furder*, *farder* and *fardest*, pp. 180, 25; 366, 35 and 378, 1; or *thorough* where it is used for *through*. In verbs the spelling has generally been determined by the textual tradition, as *dost*, *doest*, *doost*, but has been normalized where there is lack of unanimity: *dooth* becomes *doth* and, except where required by the rhyme, *hard* becomes *heard*. In other cases the spelling considered to be normal in the *OED* has been preferred, as *sound* for *sowne* or *sownde*, meaning 'swoon'. Where the spelling of the textual tradition and the mo-dern spelling are virtual homophones, the words have been normalized to the mo-dern, as *blue* for *blew*, *cheer* for *chere*, *eager* for *eger*, *feign* for *fain*, *float* for *flote*, *hearken* for *herken*, *known* for *knowen*, *show* for *shew*, and *virtue* for *vertue*, as well as in the ending of the past participle in *-ed* for *-t*, or in *-t* for *-ed in past* for *passed*. The textual tradition has determined in each case the usage of suffixes such as *-ward* or *-wards* and *-time* or *-times*, but not the prefixes *en-* and *in-* which regularly read contrary to present practice, with which they have been brought into line to avoid confusion. The initial silent *h* in *hable*, which the *OED* notes was a peculiarity of spelling adopted by classicists such as Sidney during the sixteenth and seventeenth centuries, has been dropped. As *you* and *ye* are used throughout inconsistently and read against one another in *Cm*, *90*, *93*, *you* has been preferred in the text. Possessives formed by addition of *-s* as in *Omphales*, or of *-es* as in

Cupides and *Pamelaes*, or of the possessive pronoun as in *Argalus his* (abbreviated in *Philanaxis*) have been changed to agree with modern practice, but the uninflected genitive before *sake*, as in *pity sake*, or following a sibilant, as in *Philanax letter*, has been retained.[1] In spelling the name *Euarchus* I have been guided by the textual tradition and by the arguments assembled by Jean Robertson.[2]

In the textual apparatus, when the lemma is the reading of *90* it is followed by a square bracket and then by its variants. Texts in agreement are not listed. The textual authority of each variant is given by the sigla, separated by commas; variants are separated from one another by semicolons. When the lemma is a departure from *90* it is followed by the sigla of its authorities, and by a colon; variants and their sigla follow this colon. In such cases every text not lacking the lemma is represented. The punctuation of the lemma follows the punctuation of this edition; that of the variants is as it would be had the variants been accepted into the text. Spelling in the textual apparatus has been normalized, unless old spelling is necessary to understand textual transmission. The siglum *OA* represents a reading of all the manuscripts of the *Old Arcadia* which are not defective at that point, and the siglum *93* represents a reading common to *93, 98, 13*.

The abbreviation *corr. to* indicates alterations in manuscripts, while *corr.* and *uncorr.* indicate corrected and uncorrected sheets in the printed editions. '*OA (ex. As)*' means that all the manuscripts of the *Old Arcadia* except *As* are in agreement – in such cases the reading of *As* is listed as a variant. '*93 (only)*' indicates a reading found only in *93*.

Following Robertson, I use Ringler's sigla for the texts, adding *Hm* and *O*, and cite them, when not lacking, in this order: *OA (St, Bo, Cl, Le, As, O, Da, Ph, Je, Hm (Qu)), Dd, Eg, Fl, Ha, Hn, Hy, Ma, Ra, Bn, Fr, Cm, 90, 93 (98, 13)*. The poems are referred to by Ringler's terminology, *A, AT, CS, LM, OA, OP, PP, PS*, and by his line numbering.

LIST OF SIGLA

Manuscripts of the *Old Arcadia*

As	Huntington Library MS HM 162 (Ashburnham MS)
Bo	Bodleian Library MS e Museo 37
Cl	Folger Shakespeare Library MS H.b.1 (Clifford MS)
Da	British Library MS Additional 41204 (Davies MS)
Hm	British Library MS Additional 61821 (Helmingham Hall MS)
Je	Jesus College, Oxford, MS 150
Le	British Library MS Additional 41498 (Lee MS)
O	National Library of Wales (Ottley MS)
Ph	British Library MS Additional 38892 (Phillipps MS)

---

[1] See above, p. xxxii, and Abbott, 32, 144. [2] J. Robertson, 'Euarchus/Evarchus in Sidney's *Arcadia*', *Renaissance Quarterly*, xxviii (1975), 298–9.

TEXTUAL INTRODUCTION   lxiii

Qu Queen's College, Oxford, MS R 38/301
St St John's College, Cambridge, MS I. 7
OA All the manuscripts of the *Old Arcadia* except (*ex.*) any indicated by its siglum

Manuscripts containing poems from the *New Arcadia*

Dd Cambridge University Library MS Dd.5.75 (2)
Eg British Library MS Egerton 2421
Fl Folger Shakespeare Library MS V.a.339
Ha British Library MS Harleian 6910
Hn Duke of Norfolk, 'Arundel Harington' MS
Hy British Library MS Harleian 7392 (2)
Ma Marsh's Library, Dublin, MS Z. 3. 5. 21
Ra Bodleian Library MS Rawlinson Poetical 85

Printed books containing poems from the *New Arcadia*

Bn N[icholas]. B[reton]., *The Arbour of Amorous Devices* (1597)
Fr Abraham Fraunce, *The Arcadian Rhetoric* (1588)

Texts of the *New Arcadia*

Cm Cambridge University Library MS Kk. 1. 5 (2)
90   *The Countess of Pembroke's Arcadia* (1590)
93   *The Countess of Pembroke's Arcadia* (1593)
98   *The Countess of Pembroke's Arcadia* (1598)
13   *The Countess of Pembroke's Arcadia* (1613)
93   If there are no variants among 93, 98, 13 this siglum represents the editions of 1593, 1598, and 1613 together

THE HISTORY OF *ARCADIA* IN PRINT

THE 1590 quarto edition of *Arcadia* is characterized not only by its incompleteness but by the fact that the book's editors appear to make no attempt to acknowledge or account for it, although by placing Sidney's dedication (see Appendix II) at the beginning of the book, they are implicitly making the author apologize for the lack of closure as one of the text's 'deformities'. This is surprising, because the 1590 version of *Arcadia* ends not only in mid-chapter but in mid-sentence, so the editors could hardly have hoped that the lack of an ending would pass unnoticed. The preface by the 'ouer-seer of the print' included in some copies of the quarto refers to the incompleteness of the text only indirectly, in the statement that the eclogues had been left unrevised by Sidney 'till the worke had bene finished, that then choice should haue bene made, which should haue bene taken, and in what manner brought in', leaving readers to draw the logical conclusion that since the choice was not made, the work could not have been finished.[1] Instead of expressing regret at *Arcadia*'s unfinished state or the unrevised eclogues, however, the preface concludes by simply stating that 'at this time [the eclogues] haue bene chosen and disposed as the ouer-seer thought best'. This statement is peculiar for two reasons: the 'ouer-seer' openly admits that he did not know what Sidney's intentions were and followed his own intuition instead, exposing his edition to criticism, but also the openness of the phrase 'at this time', which implies that closure may be forthcoming at a later time – but does not fully promise that it will. In a sense, then, the 1590 preface is as conspicuously lacking in closure as the version of *Arcadia* that it introduces.

The cautious tone of the 1590 preface, which suggests that the 'ouer-seer of the print' is scrupulous not to be regarded as passing off editorial choices as authorial intention and reluctant to impose his reading of Sidney's text (and of Sidney himself) on other readers, makes the vehemence of its 1593 counterpart all the more surprising. Rather than merely noting that the 1593 version of the text is, as its title page suggests, 'now since the first edition augmented and ended', and concluding that this makes his edition the definitive one with the Pembroke seal of approval, Hugh Sanford's preface, which contains deliberate echoes of Sidney's dedication, attacks his predecessors' efforts. For the purpose of highlighting the 1593 edition's superiority to the first and establishing it as the only authoritative version that the author himself might have approved of, it might have sufficed to portray the editors of the 1590 edition as well-meaning but misguided. Instead, Sanford compares the editorial choices in the 1590 edition to spots and blemishes that are so numerous and so prominent as to 'disfigure' the work and thus implicitly groups the editors themselves among the 'worthless' readers, who 'can neuer worthely esteeme of so worthye a writing'. In his claim that the textual inadequacies that had to be repaired through the Countess of Pembroke's 'honourable labour' reflect on the 1590 editors' moral shortcomings, Sanford thus places his predecessors in opposition to the book's author and dedicatee, adding injury to insult.

---

[1] For the full text see the Textual Introduction.

The second conspicuous absence in the 1590 text, the missing epitaph for Argalus and Parthenia, represented in the text by an empty frame of printer's flowers, is even more puzzling than the ending in mid-sentence, because its omission from the text could easily have been concealed by changing the wording in the final sentence of Chapter 16 from 'this Epitaphe' to 'an Epitaphe'. Following the publication of the 1593 edition, which did include the epitaph, some early readers of the 1590 edition, including the owners of two copies at the Huntington Library (call numbers 69441 and 69442), interpreted the blank space as an invitation to interact with the printed page and supply the epitaph themselves.[1]

In addition to the textual differences discussed in the textual preface, the first two *Arcadia* editions differ noticeably in their presentation of the text. Those differences are partly caused by the difference in format, which affects the overall page layout. The contrast between the two editions is particularly striking on the first few pages, because the printer used decorated initials from the same set, which are the same size but appear disproportionately larger in the 1590 layout than they do in 1593. In the main body of the text, one of the defining features of the 1590 quarto is its consistent use of decorated initials at the beginnings of chapters – in addition to the two initials used in the prefatory materials and three larger initials at the beginning of each book, the quarto contains 76 initials indicating chapter beginnings. The 1593 folio, by contrast, uses decorated initials only to indicate the beginnings of books.[2] Generous use of decorated initials is relatively uncommon among early printed texts of this length, because inserting the wooden blocks containing the initials slowed down the typesetting process and reduced the compositor's flexibility in arranging the type on the page. In the 1590 *Arcadia*, the function of the decorated initials is not purely aesthetic, however; they also draw attention to the structure of the book by emphasizing another defining feature of the edition: the chapter divisions and summaries 'aduentured by the ouer-seer of the print, for the more ease of the Readers' (A4^v).[3] While they were not authorial and Sanford was consequently justified in removing them, the chapter summaries, which direct readers to numbered glosses in order to locate specific passages in the text, did have the intended effect of making the 1590 quarto the most reader-friendly version of *Arcadia*.

A somewhat puzzling feature of the 1590 edition are the inverted commas that sporadically appear on the margin to indicate sententiae. The inverted commas are virtually absent from Book I (apart from one set of inverted commas to highlight the phrase 'The noblest kinde reiects no others woes' in a poem from the first Eclogues) and 35 out of 40 appear in the second half of the book, between gatherings Aa and Zz, with noticeable clusters in gatherings Kk (four sententiae), Rr (also four sententiae), Tt (six sententiae) and Zz (five sententiae), while gatherings Nn–Qq contain no inverted commas at all. This clustering suggests they were not a feature

---

[1] Although in both of the Huntington copies the writers attempted to write in a neat, scribal-looking hand, slanting lines, uneven letter sizes and misjudged line lengths make it unlikely that either of them was a professional scribe. [2] The only exception to this is Pyrocles' song ('Transformd in shew, but more transformd in minde'), which is given a small decorated T. [3] For a counterexample cf. another quarto published by William Ponsonby in 1590, the first instalment of Edmund Spenser's *Faerie Queene*, which uses decorated initials to highlight the beginnings of books but not of cantos.

of the manuscript that formed the basis of the edition but were probably introduced by a compositor who was presumably trying to be helpful and enhance the reading experience by alerting readers to phrases that struck him as particularly suitable for commonplacing.[1]

Without the help of the chapter divisions, readers of later editions were forced to find alternative ways of navigating a text that was more densely printed than the quarto version – up to 48 lines per page, compared to the quarto's 32 – and offered no subdivisions below the level of books. Some early readers went to considerable lengths to make the text easier to navigate. William Blount, the owner of the most heavily annotated copy of the 1593 folio at the Folger Library, compiled his own alphabetical index of characters and key events, consisting of six pages and over 300 main entries, densely written on the endpapers of the book, followed by an index of the first lines of poems arranged in the order in which they occur in the text.[2] The alphabetical arrangement and the fact that there are no gaps or added entries suggest the index was prepared separately and Blount later copied it into the book. In a copy of the 1613 folio in the Houghton Library's collection, a late seventeenth-century owner even went to the trouble of reinstating the chapter summaries and numbered glosses of the 'former edition'.

Just as the 1590 quarto is visually shaped by its aim of reader-friendliness, the 1593 folio is shaped by its aim to undo the first edition. The title page not only announces that Sidney's work is 'now since the first edition augmented and ended', but the edition's intention to discredit and replace the previous one is also signalled by the title frame, whose most prominent feature is the pig in marjoram, used as an emblem of previous editors' pig-ignorance and inability to appreciate the sweetness of Sidney's writing.[3] At the same time, the posture and orientation of the pig contrast with the Sidney porcupine displayed at the top of the frame, echoing the preface's claim that the 1590 edition had 'vnworthely' blemished the beauty of Sidney's work by misrepresenting it to its readers, implying it had turned a warrior-like porcupine into a cowering hog.

While the 1593 edition removes chapter divisions and numbered sections, it introduces line numbering as an alternative, though perhaps less practical, way of assisting readers with navigating a long text. As a side effect, the numbered lines signal textual stability to readers by implying they will be able to cite from the text more specifically than merely by page numbers. While this may not have been a deliberate choice on Sanford's part, it nevertheless chimes with the aim of the 1593

---

[1] The compositors working on subsequent editions appear to have struggled to make sense of those inverted commas, however. The 1593 edition preserved them next to just thirteen passages, but it misplaced or partially misplaced them for four of those passages (additionally, the inverted commas on 99^v were mistakenly carried over to 100^v). Of those thirteen passages, the 1598 folio preserved the inverted commas for only four (including two on p. 305 in which the inverted commas had been misplaced). The 1605 edition preserved two – in the poems 'What tongue can her perfections tell' and 'Alas how long this pilgrimage doth last' – and dropped the misplaced inverted commas for the remaining two passages, while the 1613 edition did the exact opposite and reinstated the misplaced inverted commas on p. 305 but dropped the inverted commas the 1605 edition had preserved. Editions printed after 1613 omitted the inverted commas altogether. [2] STC 22540 copy 1 at the Folger Shakespeare Library. For Blount's annotations, which focus predominantly on noting references to classical texts, see the General Introduction. [3] See xlii, n. 5.

edition to present a stable and definitive version of Sidney as well as his work. On a similar note, the 1593 edition adds a full stop to the unfinished half-sentence that had concluded the book in 1590, providing not so much closure as finality.[1] The note that follows the break in the text, which declares the end of the combat and subsequent events to be 'altogether vnknowne', follows the same strategy. It is printed in italics and indented, to distinguish it from Sidney's text, and the continuation supplied 'out of the Authors owne writings and conceits', which adjoins it without a significant gap, is given an (undecorated) initial. As a result, the transition is visible but subtle.[2]

The title page of the 1598 folio reuses the decorative frame of the 1593 edition and is structured very similarly, although the line 'now since the first edition augmented and ended' has been changed to 'now the third time published with sundry new additions of the same author'. None of those additions, which collectively account for 104 pages, are named (perhaps because most of them are not strictly 'new'); although their inclusion effectively turns the edition into Sidney's collected works, Ponsonby appears to have decided that a new edition of *Arcadia* plus extras would appeal more to readers. The layout of the text closely resembles that of the 1593 folio, although in 1598, the text of Arcadia takes up fifteen fewer pages than in the previous edition. While this may seem like an insignificant number in the context of a book of several hundred pages, it is in fact a considerable achievement on the part of the 1598 compositors: those pages in the 1593 edition contain over 11,000 words and the saved space corresponds to more than half of the *Defence of Poesie* in the same volume. More importantly from Ponsonby's point of view, they correspond to three and a half sheets of saved paper per book.

While the compositors working on the 1593 edition had been able to save space by dropping chapter summaries and initials and taking advantage of the folio format, which allowed them to put more words in each line and more lines on each page, the 1598 compositors were faced with the challenge of trying to save space on a text already printed in the same format. For this reason, they are likely to have welcomed the line numbers, which facilitated their task by enabling them to judge more quickly how much more text might be fitted on a page, or to save time by setting lines as they had been set in the earlier edition. Thus the first of the 1598 compositors begins by saving five lines through using a smaller initial at the beginning of Book I, resulting in different line breaks, but after reaching the end

---

[1] The 1590 edition has no full stop and concludes with three asterisks as a substitute for FINIS. [2] In the editions of 1598, 1605 and 1613, the note appears at the top of p. 333, giving it the appearance of a section heading. Having the break in the text coincide with a page break also allowed for the insertion of Sir William Alexander's *Supplement* (which, as the pagination indicates, had been printed separately) in some copies of the 1613 edition, followed by the second textual note, 'Thus far the worthy Author had reuised …'. After the 1613 edition, the break appears on p. 326, with the second textual note taking up the rest of the page and the supplement continuing on p. 327, introduced either through a heading or through a marginal gloss that reads 'Here this Story, left vnperfect by the Authour, is continued by Sr. W. A.'. After the *Supplement*, the later editions continue with the 1593 text on p. 347, introduced with a heading derived from the 1593 note: 'From hence the History is againe continued out of the Authors owne writings and conceits, as followeth'. What is conspicuously absent is the 1593 edition's statement that it is 'altogether vnknowne' how Sidney intended to continue. Perhaps by coincidence, the editions published after 1613 also remove the 1593 edition's ungrammatical full stop at the end of the half-sentence.

of the first section ('a wast of fire in the midst of the water', see 5, 4–5), the edition mostly follows the line breaks of 1593 and saves space by adding another line at the bottom of most pages.[1] By the time they have reached the second song, which the 1593 edition had printed on the recto of leaf 23 (the equivalent of page 45), the 1598 compositors have already gained one and a half pages on their predecessors, bringing the song forward to page 43. This pattern continues until the end of the volume, enabling the compositors to average three saved pages per book, although their space-saving efforts are hampered by the fact that they need to consider aesthetics as well as space, so after the end of each book they are forced to start over on a new page, meaning some of the space gained over the course of the book is lost again at the end of Book I and Book II.

Nevertheless, the 1598 compositors succeed in having Book III and Book IV end at the bottom of a page, so that only about a page's worth of space is 'wasted' in this manner (compared to nearly two in the 1593 edition). Towards the end of Book III, on pages 385 and 389, the running title wrongly reads 'Lib. 4' instead of 'Lib. 3' – a mistake that may have happened in the excitement of being able to fit the end of a book neatly onto a page for the first time. The 1605 edition, printed for Simon Waterson and Matthew Lownes, who had taken over the publishing rights following Ponsonby's death, replicates the mistake, but the 1613 edition printed by Humphrey Lownes (which exists in two versions, whose title pages identify it as having been printed for Waterson or Matthew Lownes) corrects it.[2] Although there are minor differences between them, such as the fact that the 1605 edition omits the line numbers, both the 1605 edition and the 1613 edition mirror the layout and page breaks of the 1598 folio so closely that pages missing from a copy of one edition might be replaced with pages from a copy of one of the others. The only exception to this occurs at the point at which the 1590 edition had ended. Some copies of the 1613 edition at this point insert Sir William Alexander's *Supplement* and temporarily deviate from the pagination of 1598 and 1605 (first skipping from page 332 to 335, then numbering the two subsequent leaves '334' and '335' before ceasing altogether for the remaining eight leaves), although the original pagination resumes on page 333.

The 1613 folio of Sidney's works contains visual echoes of the folio edition of Spenser's works, printed between 1611 and 1613. Both books not only reuse the frame that had already featured on the title page of the 1593 folio, they also share decorative elements and contain initials from the same sets. The Spenser folio makes more generous use of space and decorative elements, however, owing to the fact that unlike the Sidney folio, it was produced in individual components to be sold separately, and the layout of the Spenser folio's poetry, which often included stanza divisions, was harder for the compositor to manipulate than the prose of *Arcadia*.[3] While the visual similarities are perhaps unsurprising, since both books were pro-

---

[1] In the 1593 folio, most pages contain 47 lines, which increases to 48 in the 1598 edition. [2] The 1605 edition exists in two variants whose only difference is the publisher's name on the title page, an indication that Lownes and Waterson shared the production costs to reduce their financial risk. Humphrey Lownes, who printed the 1613 edition, was also one of the printers of the 1605 edition (along with George Eld). [3] S. K. Galbraith, 'Spenser's First Folio: The Build-It-Yourself Edition', *Spenser Studies* xi (2006), 21–49.

duced by the same printer for the same publisher around the same time, they are likely to have contributed to early readers' association of the two poets.

Like the 1605 and 1613 editions, the two editions printed outside England – Robert Waldegrave's 1599 edition published in Edinburgh and the 1621 Dublin edition whose impressum simply reads 'printed by the Societie of Stationers' – were based on the 1598 folio. Unlike the later English editions, however, the Edinburgh edition, which was intended for the Scottish market and thus not technically pirated, is characterized by its consistency in trying to save space at all costs. While the compositors of the 1598 folio had aimed for, and largely achieved, an optimized but balanced layout, their Scottish counterparts were clearly instructed to prioritize economy over aesthetics. The Edinburgh edition consequently uses slightly smaller type and begins by compressing both Sidney's dedication and Sanford's preface to the reader so that each fits on a single page. This is an uncommon practice: dedications in early printed books typically use larger type and a more generous layout (often featuring large initials and decorative elements) as a form of visual tribute to patrons, even if the rest of the book uses a plain, practical layout. Sidney's dedicatory epistle to the Countess of Pembroke spanned three pages in the 1590 quarto and two in every subsequent folio edition except Waldegrave's. In the main body of *Arcadia*, the Scottish compositors attempt to save space not only through the smaller type but through dropping most of the blank lines used to set off the songs, resulting in a compressed-looking layout in which prose and verse appear to have been glued together. This strategy continues until the end of the volume and enables the compositors to save a substantial amount of space overall, but the highly condensed layout of the text sacrifices readability as well as aesthetics in order to maximize the amount of print on each page.[1]

The Dublin edition, by contrast, whose title page declares it to be 'now the fift time published', is identical to the folio sold as the sixth edition by Waterson and Lownes in 1622–1623. The dates and title pages differ between copies, but the books use identical line and page breaks and the decorative devices and initials match exactly.[2] This suggests the books were printed at the same time in 1621 and sold over the course of several years with different title pages (perhaps an indication that thirty-five years after Sidney's death, the market for editions of his works had become saturated). The edition follows the line breaks of the previous folio editions relatively closely, although it often uses 49 lines of text per page, which enables the compositors to save a modest amount of space. In some versions the text is nevertheless longer than in the 1598 folio, because it includes Sir William Alexander's *Supplement*. While they do not go so far as to use decorated initials, the compositors of the fifth / sixth edition frequently use very large initials at the beginnings of songs, which creates an interesting contrast on the page. Since the line breaks in verse are predefined, initials have no impact on the number of lines required to set

---

[1] For *Astrophil and Stella*, the Edinburgh compositors even adopt the dubious strategy of setting some of the songs (4, 6, and 8–11, which have relatively short lines) in two columns and reverting to a single-column layout for the sonnets.   [2] This includes an uncommon style of decorated W at the beginning of *The Defence of Poesie*, which depicts two heavily overlapping V's that suggest a V rather than a W, before a floral background.

it, so the edition's large initials are an aesthetic choice rather than a practical one and highlight the songs' significance in the text.

The subsequent edition, sold with varying title pages identifying it as the sixth or seventh between 1628 and 1629, is a faithful reprint of the preceding one. It includes the supplement to Book III, as well as Richard Bellings' *Sixth Booke to the Countesse of Pembrokes Arcadia*, which is given a separate title page, although the pagination continues from *Arcadia*. One version of the title page contains the line 'sold by R[ichard] Moore in S. Dunstons Churchyard', which suggests that even following Matthew Lownes' death in 1625, Waterson preferred not to be the sole publisher of Sidney's works. The eighth and ninth editions of 1633 and 1638 respectively are likewise reprints that preserve the pagination of the previous edition and introduce no layout changes to the text. Both include Sir William Alexander's *Supplement* in Book III and add the *Sixth Booke*. The title page of the ninth edition highlights that it also contains an alternative supplement by 'Mr Ia. Iohnstoun Scoto-Brit. dedicated to K. Iames, and now annexed to this work, for the Readers benefit'. The addition of an alternative, evidently dated, supplement (in 1638, James had been dead for thirteen years) seems rather a small and arbitrarily chosen 'benefit' to entice readers to a book that at this point had been in print for nearly fifty years, and suggests the publishers may have struggled to shift copies of Sidney's works, since most potential readers already owned copies of the older folio editions, which they had inherited from their fathers or grandfathers.

The pattern of adding further extras in the hope of rekindling interest in *Arcadia* continues in the remaining three editions published in the seventeenth century: the title pages of the tenth, eleventh and twelfth editions (published in 1655, 1662 and 1674) all feature the line 'with his Life and Death; a brief Table of the principal Heads, and some other new Additions' (although the 'new Additions' are the same in all three versions). Perhaps in an attempt to direct readers' attention to the new features, all three editions insert the biography of Sidney, an extract from Camden, thirteen pages of elegies for Sidney and a short passage from Peter Heylyn's *Cosmographie* in a counter-intuitive place: between Sanford's preface and the beginning of *Arcadia*. The rest of the text, including Sir William Alexander's *Supplement*, Richard Bellings' *Sixth Booke*, and Sidney's other works, is again reprinted from the previous editions with identical pagination and unchanged (as a side effect of this, the subtitle of *Certain Sonnets* first introduced in 1598 – 'never before imprinted' – still appears in the 1674 edition). This is followed by Johnstoun's supplement, the poem 'A Remedie for Love' (attributed to Sidney) and a brief index to *Arcadia* of fewer than a hundred main entries.

No further editions of *Arcadia* were published until 1725, when it was included in a three-volume edition of Sidney's works printed for Edmund Curll and a group of other booksellers. However, the extent to which interest in *Arcadia* had diminished by the early eighteenth century can be seen from two other titles. *The Famous History of Heroick Acts: or The Honour of Chivalry, Being an Abstract of Pembroke's Arcadia* (1701) is a small, cheaply produced book subdivided into chapters and accompanied by crude woodcuts – effectively a chapbook *Arcadia* in 154 pages. Sir

Philip Sidney's Arcadia Moderniz'd by Mrs. Stanley (1725), while longer and aimed at a more genteel audience – a list of subscribers, which features a 'Mrs Sidney', is included towards the beginning of the book – bears just as little resemblance to Sidney's Arcadia as The Honour of Chivalry. In her dedication to the Princess of Wales, Mrs Stanley praises Sidney as 'the politest Author of his Age' and her preface mentions only in passing that the author has decided to omit all of Sidney's poetry in accordance with the subscribers' wishes, 'and as it is to them alone I think my self accountable, I shall esteem their Approbation a sufficient Reason'. Arguably, the two eighteenth-century Arcadia adaptations are also aiming for reader-friendliness. The fact that they do so by focusing on the plot, omitting the songs and simplifying Sidney's language, however, illustrates how dramatically the perception of Arcadia had shifted, from the chief work of an author valued both for his poetry and for his complex prose style, to a classic that needed to be made more accessible through abbreviation or 'modernization' before it could be read. – EC

ARCADIA EDITIONS BEFORE 1700

1. *The Countesse of Pembrokes Arcadia, written by Sir Philippe Sidnei.* Printed by Iohn Windet for william Ponsonbie (London, 1590).
2. *The Countesse of Pembrokes Arcadia. Written by Sir Philip Sidney Knight. Now Since the first edition augmented and ended.* Printed [by John Windet] for William Ponsonbie (London, 1593).
3. *The Countesse of Pembrokes Arcadia. Written by Sir Philip Sidney Knight. Now the third time published, with sundry new additions of the same Author.* Imprinted [by Richard Field] for William Ponsonbie (London, 1598).
3a. *The Countesse of Pembrokes Arcadia. Written by Sir Philip Sidney Knight. Now the third time published, with sundry new additions of the same Author.* Printed by Robert walde-graue, Printer to the Kings Majestie (Edinburgh, 1599).
4. *The Countesse of Pembrokes Arcadia. Written by Sir Philip Sidney Knight. Now the fourth time published, with sundry new additions of the same author.* Imprinted [by George Eld and Humphrey Lownes] for Matthew Lownes / Simon Waterson (London, 1605)
5. *The Countesse of Pembrokes Arcadia. Written by Sir Philip Sidney Knight. Now the fourth [sic] time published, with some new additions.* Imprinted by H[umphrey]. L[ownes]. for Matthew Lownes / Simon Waterson (London, 1613)
6. *The Countesse of Pembrokes Arcadia. Written by Sir Philip Sidney Knight. Now the sixt time published.* Imprinted by H[umphrey]. L[ownes]. for Matthew Lownes / Simon Waterson (London 1622/3)
6a. *The Countesse of Pembrokes Arcadia. Written by Sir Philip Sidney Knight. Now the fift [sic] time published, with some new Additions. Also a supplement of a defect in the third part of this History. By Sir W. Alexander.* Printed by the Societie of Stationers (Dublin, 1621)

7a. *The Countesse of Pembrokes Arcadia. Written by Sir Philip Sidney Knight. Now the sixt [sic] time published, with some new Additions. Also a supplement of a defect in the third part of this Historie, By Sir W. Alexander.* Printed by W[illiam] S[tansby, Humphrey Lownes, and Robert Young] for Simon Waterson (London, 1627 [i.e. 1628])

7. *The Countesse of Pembrokes Arcadia. Written by Sir Philip Sidney Knight. Now the seuenth time published, with some new Additions. With the supplement of a Defect in the third part of this History, by Sir W.A. Knight. Whereunto is now added a sixth Booke, By R.B. of Lincolnes Inne, Esq.* Printed by [William Stansby,] H[umphrey]. L[ownes]. and R[obert]. Y[oung]. and are sold by S[imon]. Waterson in S. Pauls Churchyard / R[ichard]. Moore in S. Dunstons Churchyard (London, 1629)

8. *The Countesse of Pembrokes Arcadia. Written by Sir Philip Sidney Knight. Now the eighth time published, with some new Additions. With the supplement of a Defect in the third part of this History, by Sir W. A. Knight. Whereunto is now added a sixth Booke, By R.B. of Lincolnes Inne, Esq.* Printed [by Robert Young] for Simon Waterson and R[obert]. Young [and Thomas Downes] (London, 1633)

9. *The Countesse of Pembrokes Arcadia, Written by Sir Philip Sidney Knight. Now the ninth time published, with a twofold supplement of a defect in the third Book: the one by Sr W.A. Knight; the other, by Mr Ja. Johnstoun Scoto-Brit. dedicated to K. James, and now annexed to this work, for the Readers benefit. Whereunto is also added a sixth Booke, By R.B. of Lincolnes Inne, Esq.* Printed [by Robert Young and Thomas Harper] for J[ohn] Waterson and R[obert]. Young [and Thomas Downes] (London, 1638)

10. *The Countess of Pembroke's Arcadia written by Sr Philip Sidney Knight. The tenth Edition. With his Life and Death; a brief Table of the principal heads, and som other new Additions.* Printed by William Du-Gard: and are to bee sold by George Calvert, at the half Moon in the new buildings in Paul's Church-yard; and Thomas Pierrepont, at the Sun in Paul's Church-yard (London, 1655)

11. *The Countess of Pembroke's Arcadia written by Sir Philip Sidney Knight. The eleventh Edition. With his Life and Death; a brief Table of the principal Heads, and som other new Additions.* Printed by Henry Lloyd, for William Du-Gard: and are to bee sold by George Calvert, at the half Moon in the new buildings; and Thomas Pierrepont, at the Sun in St. Paul's Church-yard (1662)

12. *The Countess of Pembroke's Arcadia written by Sir Philip Sidney Knight. The Thirteenth [sic] Edition. With his Life and Death; a brief Table of the principal Heads, and some other new Additions.* Printed for George Calvert, at the Golden-Ball in Little-Britain (London, 1674)

RHETORICAL FIGURES IN THE *NEW ARCADIA*

STUDIES on Sidney's prose rhetoric tend to stress that his use of rhetorical figures is not, or not merely, ornamental.[1] One disadvantage of the underlying argument that unites most twentieth-century studies is that it makes scholars sound almost apologetic about the aesthetic and ornate (though not purely ornamental) qualities of Sidney's 'artificial' style.[2] Yet to adopt an apologetic attitude towards Sidney's style is to neglect the fact that it is precisely those 'artificial' qualities that account for *Arcadia*'s appeal as one of the most beautifully crafted pieces of Renaissance prose written in English.[3]

Ironically, Sidney himself would probably have been pleased to see his style described as 'artificial', because in the sixteenth century, the word was predominantly used in the positive senses of 'artful', 'skilfully crafted' or 'cleverly constructed' – all of which were of course desirable qualities in a piece of literary prose. The *OED* entry contains just four sixteenth-century examples that use the word 'artificial' in a negative sense (meanings 3 'affected, pretentious', 4a 'contrived or fabricated' and 8 'artful, cunning'). Of the remaining sixteen examples from this period, eight use the adjective in a neutral sense (meanings 1a 'made or constructed by human skill', 2a 'brought about by human skill or invention', 2b 'produced or resulting from human skill or design' 6 'according to an art or science' and 7 'of or designating the practical arts or crafts') and eight in a positive sense (9a 'skilfully made or contrived', 9b 'technically or artistically adept', 10 'expert, ingenious', 11 'relying on sound rational principles'). Sidney himself repeatedly uses it in a positive sense in *Arcadia*, for example in Pyrocles' description of Basilius' artistically made star-shaped lodge and its surroundings (p. 73, 6-34).

The artificiality of Sidney's style is mainly created by his extensive use of rhetorical figures. The range of figures he uses is broad and varied, and they feature in

---

[1] Examples include P. Albert Duhamel's 1948 article on 'Sidney's *Arcadia* and Elizabethan Rhetoric' (*SP* 45 (1948), 134-50), which compares speeches from the *New Arcadia* to a 'euphuistic' speech from John Lyly's *Euphues*; Lorna Challis' article on 'The Use of Oratory in Sidney's *Arcadia*' published nearly two decades later in the same journal (*SP* 62 (1965), 561-76); John Carey's essay on 'Structure and Rhetoric in Sidney's *Arcadia*' (first published in *Poetica* in 1982 and subsequently reprinted in Dennis Kay (ed.), *Sir Philip Sidney: An Anthology of Modern Criticism* (Oxford, 1987), 254-64), which begins with the disclaimer that 'Sidney's *Arcadia*, to a modern reader, can seem an ornate and frivolous work', before moving on to argue for the functionality of Sidney's rhetoric for establishing what Carey views as the overarching themes of *Arcadia* as a whole; and Ann Dobyns' article on 'Style and Character in the "New Arcadia"' (1986), which focuses on Sidney's use of dialogue to establish characters through their manner of speaking and uses a similar opening move, by stating that 'few, if any, critics of Sir Philip Sidney's prose would deny his skill as a craftsman', adding that consequently the real question has always been 'whether Sidney's superbly crafted style represents merely his concern for ornament or functions, rather, as an important determiner of the meaning of the text' (*Style* xx (1986), 90-102; 90). [2] See Victor Skretkowicz's section on style in the General Introduction, which begins by referring to the 'high degree of artificiality in the form of the *New Arcadia*' (xxvi). [3] Gavin Alexander's more recent article 'Sidney, Scott, and the Proportion of Poetics' (*Sidney Journal* xxx (2015)), which focuses on William Scott's reading of Sidney's use of proportion in *The Model of Poesy*, but also considers the aesthetic and rhetorical aspects of Sidney's prose as well as his poetry more widely, is a notable exception to this pattern, as is Alexander's preface to his edition of *The Model of Poesy* (Cambridge, 2013).

nearly every sentence; it is not uncommon for Sidney's sentences to contain combinations of two or more different figures, which collectively can have what Sidney might have called a 'cloying' effect on modern readers. Even his description of the plain-speaking Arcadian who persuades the helots to open their gates in Book I is far from plain, since he is introduced as

> ... a cunning fellow (so much the cunninger as that he could mask it under rudeness) who with such a kind of rhetoric as weeded out all flowers of rhetoric delivered unto the helots assembled together that they were country people of Arcadia, no less oppressed by their lords, and no less desirous of liberty than they, and therefore had put themselves in the field, and had already, besides a great number slain, taken nine or ten score gentlemen prisoners, whom they had there well and fast chained. (p. 29, 9–16)

Although Sidney's style is not ornamental in the sense that his rhetorical 'flowers' are purely decorative, they do of course have an aesthetic function as well, which is most apparent when they are examined on a smaller scale, at figure- or sentence-level. At this level, it is possible to appreciate the ways in which Sidney's use of figures highlights the specific purpose of individual sentences – such as the switch from an elaborate combination of polyptoton, parenthesis, periphrasis and metaphor to a straightforward anaphora that introduces relatively plain syntax in the sentence above, which re-enacts the muted rhetoric it describes.[1] At the same time, considering how Sidney's 'flowers' – a selection of which can be found in the list in Appendix IV – work at sentence-level also makes it easier to recognize their aesthetic, 'artificial' pleasantness as a strength rather than as a weakness of a text that Sidney's contemporaries rightly admired as a pattern of English prose. Ironically, two of the greatest and best-known admirers among those contemporaries may have been indirectly responsible for leading later readers to think of Sidney's figures as ornamental: Hoskyns and Fraunce often cite figures from *Arcadia* without providing the context that might have explained why a particular scene in the text lends itself to a particular figure. However, they were only able to decontextualize Sidney's figures to such an extent because they could expect their readers both to have read *Arcadia* in detail[2] and to have had sufficient instruction in rhetoric to be aware that 'flowers' were not simply there to be admired but were inseperable from their practical function.

Twentieth-century criticism on Sidney's rhetoric in particular has had a tendency to focus either on his purpose (as in Carey and Dobyns) or on the theoretical framework that underpins his work (as in Duhamel and Challis), but both approaches regard the rhetorical figures themselves as decorative stylistic obstacles that readers need to overcome in order to grasp Sidney's meaning and that can be glossed over by pointing to the stylistic preferences among Sidney's contemporaries

---

[1] All rhetorical terms are briefly defined in Appendix IV. Anaphora is a figure which Sidney particularly associates with persuasive rhetoric (see below for further examples). [2] Although Abraham Fraunce's *Arcadian Rhetorike* was published in 1588, before the first printed edition of *Arcadia*, the fact that the book contains no preface to readers (the first sections are preceded only by a multilingual dedicatory poem to the Countess of Pembroke) and that the term 'Arcadian' is never explained suggests it was meant for the use of readers who already understood the reference because they had read the *Old Arcadia*.

and stressing how different they are from our own. This attitude towards Sidney's style effectively tolerates its ornateness, but it does not treat it as one of his strengths. Sidney and his contemporaries did not wish to draw such distinctions between form and function; rhetoric was effectively taught as a practical, 'applied' art that had clearly defined aims. So, for example, the first book of Thomas Wilson's *Arte of Rhetorique* (1553) contains sections whose titles indicate a focus on application, such as 'The ende of Rhetorique', 'By what meanes Eloquence is attained' and 'To what purpose this arte [i.e. rhetoric] is set furthe'. Later, in the third book, Wilson notes that 'By ... Figures, euerye Oration maye be muche beautified, and without the same, not one can attaine to be counted an Oratoure, thoughe his learninge otherwise be neuer so greate' (fol. 81o^v (*sic*) [i.e. 90^v]), which implies that figures are an integral part of rhetoric, without which it cannot serve its 'end' (to teach, delight and persuade). Consequently, the ornateness of Sidney's style is evidence of his purposeful sophistication as a writer. A perhaps more constructive (and historically sound) attitude towards the ornateness of Sidney's rhetoric and the proliferation of figures in his sentences, then, is to embrace the aesthetic artificiality of his sentences as an integral feature of his style and to direct our attention to the subtle, creative and humorous ways in which Sidney uses figures to construct rather than obscure meaning and purpose in each individual sentence.

The function of stylistic features to highlight and enhance the meaning of the sentences in which they appear is something that holds generally true for Sidney's use of rhetorical figures in *Arcadia*. For this purpose, Sidney also frequently combines several figures, which can in turn make the resulting phrases hard to assign unambiguously to a particular figure, so examples of antithesis or epanalepsis in *Arcadia* often also include elements of parison, as in the phrase 'neither that did hurt her, nor any contrary mean help her' (p. 197, 29–30), or 'their strength failed them sooner than their skill, and yet their breath failed them sooner than their strength' (p. 402, 32–3).[1] If a particular phrase is considered within its full syntactic context, matters become yet more complex. For example, Hoskyns identifies the phrase 'absented presence' (p. 57, 17) as synoeciosis, but on closer inspection, the 'absented presence' turns out to be part of a longer phrase: 'the universal lamenting his absented presence assured him of his present absence'. In matching 'absented presence' with its mirror image 'present absence' (p. 57, 16–18), Sidney does not simply combine two oxymorons, but effectively crafts a chiastic antithesis out of two oxymorons in order to create one larger oxymoron. That antithetical phrase is itself part of a sentence that occurs towards the beginning of 'Chapter 12' and charts part of Musidorus' unsuccessful search for Pyrocles, before he returns to Arcadia – and promptly encounters his friend disguised as Zelmane. In full, the sentence runs:

> There indeed he found his fame flourishing, his monuments engraved in marble, and yet more durable in men's memories – but the universal lamenting

---

[1] See Appendix IV. The two phrases are quoted by Hoskyns as examples of contentio and epanalepsis respectively. Similarly, some of the phrases he quotes as examples of parison contain contrasting elements that could be regarded as antithesis, such as 'rather seek to obtain that constantly by courtesy which you can never, assuredly, enjoy by violence' (p. 306, 18–20).

his absented presence assured him of his present absence; thence into the Elean province, to see whether at the Olympian games there celebrated he might in such concourse bless his eyes with so desired an encounter – but that huge and sportful assembly grew to him a tedious loneliness, esteeming nobody found, since Daiphantus was lost. (p. 57, 15–21)

In its syntactic context, then, the oxymoronic phrase 'absented presence' serves to express the paradox that Pyrocles is absent from Laconia but present both in the minds of the Laconians and in the shape of physical traces (the monuments that preserve his fame). At the same time, it contributes to a larger contrast between Musidorus' search for Pyrocles by retracing their steps and returning to Laconia, and by looking for him in Olympia, a place they have not previously visited but that Pyrocles (as a man most frequently described through superlatives) might conceivably want to visit. Olympia turns out to generate further paradoxes, however, because the crowds there only increase Musidorus' sense of isolation in the absence of his friend. Collectively, then, the sentence expresses the central idea of Musidorus' growing loneliness, made worse by the fact that although Pyrocles' fame is everywhere, Pyrocles himself is nowhere to be found. The pithy oxymoron 'absented presence' is thus used by Sidney not for its own sake as a pleasant-sounding turn of phrase (although it is that), but as one of several constituent parts from which he builds this larger idea.

Pyrocles' 'absented presence' is not an isolated example. While *Arcadia* is a text that lends itself to figure-spotting and was frequently used for this purpose by early readers, who extracted *sententiae*, similes or other interesting turns of phrase from it, the precise function of Sidney's rhetorical figures is often best understood through the context of the sentences in which they appear and of the other figures that accompany them.[1] As the list in Appendix IV illustrates, the range of figures Sidney uses is broad, although this does not imply they are all equally prominent. The figure that is perhaps most evident in Sidney's prose is parenthesis, the insertion of words or phrases that interrupt the main clause. While modern punctuation tends to disguise Sidney's parentheses on the page, early modern punctuation often serves to highlight this aspect of the text, so that on the pages of the 1590 edition, the interruption becomes visual as well as grammatical. Sidney's use of parenthesis is one of the main reasons why some of the sentences in the *New Arcadia* can appear unwieldy at first sight and, in addition to their most obvious function of incorporating asides by characters or the narrator into the text, they can also serve

---

[1] One example of such an early reader is John Ward, a future vicar of Stratford, whose reading notes (which he wrote as a nineteen-year-old student) reveal an interest in extracting examples of unusual imagery from the text, as well as mining it for aphorisms – some of which he created himself through selective quotation. See Elisabeth Chaghafi, 'Visible Fruits and "Selected Sentences": How John Ward Misread his (Father's) Sidney', *Sidney Journal* 38 (2020), 51–76. Ward's *Arcadia* notes are uncommonly extensive. For accounts of the commonplacing habits of some of Ward's contemporaries cf. Heidi Brayman Hackel, 'Noting readers of the *Arcadia* in marginalia and commonplace books', in *Reading Material in Early Modern England: Print, Gender, Literacy* (Cambridge, 2005), 137–95, and Fred Schurink, 'Lives and Letters: Three Early Seventeenth-Century Manuscripts with Extracts from Sidney's *Arcadia*', *English Manuscript Studies* 16 (2011), 170–96.

more subtle purposes.[1] When the shipwrecked Musidorus opens his eyes again after having been revived by the two shepherds, for example (see p. 3, 30–7), the narrative repeatedly darts back and forth between description and simultaneous commentary (separated from the main clause through brackets), culminating in a clause that in *90* has a single word framed by two sets of brackets: 'They therefore continued on their charitable office, vntil (his spirits being well returned,) hee (without so much as thanking them for their paines) gate vp …' (3ᵛ).

At first sight, these two parentheses, which were a visual irritant to readers of the 1590 edition and even in modern punctuation are likely to make readers stumble briefly, appear to be a needless complication of an otherwise simple sentence. They serve an important purpose here, however, because they draw attention to the peculiar narrative situation at the beginning of the *New Arcadia* and indicate an impending shift in perspective. Book I opens with a scene between the shepherds Claius and Strephon, and the first few pages, including their discovery of the seemingly drowned Musidorus, are essentially told from their perspective. As soon as Musidorus fetches breath, however, the focus begins to shift towards him through the parentheses that respectively comment on his state of health and his strange lack of gratitude towards the shepherds who have just saved his life. The latter is subsequently explained through his exclamation 'and shall Musidorus live after Pyrocles?' (which the reader notes but the shepherds apparently fail to overhear), followed by his unsuccessful attempt to drown himself. The parentheses in this scene, then, act as an early clue to readers that the Laconian shepherds are only minor characters and the suicidal stranger is the hero of the story – or at least one of the heroes.

At other points, Sidney's parentheses suggest motivations for a character's actions, as for example in the evil king of Pontus' execution of the two faithful servants Leucippus and Nelsus, as told to Pamela by the disguised Musidorus towards the beginning of Book II:

> … but he (swelling in their humbleness like a bubble swollen up with a small breath, broken with a great) forgetting, or never knowing humanity, caused their heads to be stricken off (by the advice of his envious counsellor, who now hated them so much the more as he foresaw the happiness in having such, and so fortunate, masters), and sent them with unroyal reproaches to Musidorus and Pyrocles. (pp. 151, 36–152, 2)

Here the parentheses offer speculative explanations of the king's irrational behaviour – that he was emboldened by Musidorus' and Pyrocles' decision to petition for the release of the prisoners before attacking, and that he was egged on by his counsellor, who had taken a dislike to them. At the same time, however, it is central to Musidorus' account of his life before the shipwreck in Book I that he is telling it in the character of his alias, 'Dorus the shepherd', who has not yet revealed his true identity to Pamela. Musidorus' speculative asides, which even include a hint of doubt whether the servants' lives might have been preserved had their masters

---

[1] The second cause of Sidney's long sentences (which can fill whole pages in *90*) is what Carey identifies as an underlying peripatetic tendency of Sidney's writing: 'The phrasing loops round elegantly on itself, returning in a circle or figure-of-eight to its starting-point' (Carey, 246).

chosen a less 'humble' approach, consequently signal his emotional involvement in the story he is telling, which, along with his knowledge of details, leads Pamela to the conclusion that 'Dorus' is telling his own story.

As Duhamel observed, Sidney's prose contains far fewer examples of alliteration than Lyly's. Figures based on the repetition of words or phrases, on the other hand, are fairly common in *Arcadia*. Two of those, epizeuxis and anadiplosis, in which the second instance of a word directly follows the first, typically occur only in passages containing direct speech. More specifically, they tend to occur in passages in which the text draws attention to a character's deliberate use of the figure in order to appeal to another character. Musidorus' love-letter to Pamela via Mopsa in Book II is a particularly interesting and complex example of such a situation, because it is framed as a rhetorical performance both of Musidorus himself – who pretends to be addressing Mopsa but is really addressing Pamela – and of Pamela, who, after having previously read it to Mopsa, reads it again to Philoclea. Its conclusion runs:

> For since you will not that he live – alas! alas! what followeth? What followeth of the most ruined Dorus but his end? End then, evil-destinied Dorus, end! And end, thou woeful letter, end! for it sufficeth her wisdom to know that her heavenly will shall be accomplished. (p. 133, 32–6)

The defining purpose of this letter is Musidorus' rhetorical balancing act of seeking to amuse Pamela through the conceit that the object of his affections is Mopsa, while also seeking to persuade Pamela that his affection for herself is genuine. In the letter's conclusion, this double purpose is echoed in its use of repetitions to achieve a finely balanced mixture of pathos and comedy. While the repetition of 'alas' and 'what followeth' could by themselves pass for a serious emotional appeal to the recipient of the letter, the repetition of 'end' is so excessive that the letter briefly crosses over into self-parody, before concluding on a more serious note. Musidorus' use of repetitions at the end of his letter, then, reminds both Pamela and the reader of the fact that the letter-writer is self-consciously performing to a double audience: Pamela herself, who is likely to prefer the elegant appeal to her wisdom and her heavenly will at the end of the letter, and the unsubtle Mopsa, who can be expected to favour the excessive repetition that precedes it.

A similarly ambiguous moment occurs slightly earlier, during Gynecia's 'love-complaints' at the beginning of Book II. While Gynecia's anguish that her passion for her daughter's suitor has created a conflict of interest may be as real as Philoclea's anguish at the realization she has fallen in love with her friend, Gynecia's inner conflict nevertheless serves as a source of humour at this point. This is particularly apparent halfway through Gynecia's lament, when she complains about her fate in these terms:

> … if there were but one hope for all my pains, or but one excuse for all my faultiness! But wretch that I am, my torment is beyond all succour, and my evil-deserving doth exceed my evil-fortune. For nothing else did my husband take this strange resolution to live so solitarily, for nothing else have the winds delivered this strange guest to my country, for nothing else have the destinies reserved my life to this time, but that only I, most wretched I, should become a plague to myself, and a shame to womankind. (p. 103, 2–9)

Here Gynecia's repeated use of the phrase 'for nothing else' reinforces the self-blame expressed in the preceding sentences ('my evil-deserving doth exceed my evil-fortune'). At the same time, however, the repetition draws attention to the note of self-pity in Gynecia's self-centred assumption that the sole purpose of Basilius' decision to leave his court (and of Pyrocles' shipwreck) was to punish her by placing her in this dilemma. The humour stems both from the fact that this is clearly not how the narrative has presented the significance of those events to the reader and from Gynecia's misguided assumption that this is all about her, which clashes with the reader's knowledge that (like Mopsa) she is merely a supporting character.

An example of anaphora in the narrative rather than in the voice of a character occurs later in Book II, in a sentence that describes how the scheming Plexirtus takes advantage of his good brother Leonatus:

> But Plexirtus finding that, if nothing else, famine would at last bring him to destruction, thought better by humbleness to creep where by pride he could not march; for certainly, so had nature formed him (and the exercise of craft conformed him) to all turningness of sleights, that though no man had less goodness in his soul than he, no man could better find the places whence arguments might grow of goodness to another; though no man felt less pity, no man could tell better how to stir pity; no man more impudent to deny, where proofs were not manifest; no man more ready to confess, with a repenting manner of aggravating his own evil, where denial would but make the fault fouler. (p. 159, 9–18)

What makes this sentence so long is, once again, the device that Sidney has used to structure and define it: the second half of the sentence consists almost entirely of clauses beginning with the words '(though) no man'. The purpose of the somewhat excessive anaphora becomes clearer, however, when the content of the sentence is considered: it characterises Plexirtus not just as a dissembling manipulator but as a manipulator through rhetoric, who is able to exploit another person's goodness by tailoring his arguments to it, to move his audience to feel pity he does not feel himself and to lie without reservations if there is insufficient proof against him. All of these are of course the hallmarks of an orator who abuses the power of rhetoric. In repeating the phrase 'no man' slightly too often, then, the sentence effectively mimics Plexirtus' manipulation through rhetoric, while at the same time making it too obvious for the reader to miss (although in the story, Plexirtus does succeed in deceiving his brother, culminating in a 'reconciliation' that cannot last).

In addition to the figures based on the repetition of words, figures connected to the repetition of sounds frequently appear in *Arcadia*. Unlike Lyly, however, Sidney favours more complex figures that hinge not only on the straightforward repetition of sounds but on variations of sound and meaning, such as polyptoton (which repeats the root of a word, but with varying endings), paronomasia (which creates a connection between different though similar-sounding words) and antanaclasis (a subform of paronomasia that is essentially a pun on homophones or words that have multiple meanings).[1] None of these are figures that are likely to appeal to modern

---

[1] Although polyptoton is typically classed as a figure of repetition, it is the cadence of sound that creates its characteristic effect, so it is arguably also a figure of sound.

readers, who may perceive them as tedious wordplay, but a closer examination of the way Sidney uses them reveals that those seemingly unsubtle figures are in fact concerned with subtleties of meaning and of the connections between words and what they express. When in Book I Kalander's steward tells Musidorus the story of Argalus and Parthenia, for example, he uses the following sentence to express the idea that the two were destined to fall in love with each other:

> I think you think that these perfections meeting could not choose but find one another and delight in that they found, for likeness of manners is likely, in reason, to draw liking with affection. (p. 22, 36–9)

Here the polyptoton ('likeness ... likely ... liking') is used to reinforce the central idea of the sentence – that Argalus and Parthenia could not help falling for each other because they were so well matched in their perfections – by echoing their 'likeness of manners' in the likeness of words and sounds. Sidney's choice to use a figure associated with drawing attention to affinities between words is particularly apt here, since he uses it to express the two lovers' affinity that forms the basis for their relationship. An example of polyptoton put to a very different use occurs in Book III. Basilius has sent his regent Philanax to Delphi in order to consult the oracle on the question whether he should allow Anaxius and his brothers to marry his daughters. The oracle's uncharacteristically straightforward advice is followed by a direct reprimand to Philanax for his excessive faith in human (as opposed to divine) wisdom, which had prompted his attempt to dissuade Basilius from following the advice of the first oracle. Philanax's reaction to the unexpected divine rebuke is described in a sentence whose first half is dominated by polyptoton:

> Philanax, then finding that reason cannot show itself more reasonable than to leave reasoning in things above reason, returns to his lord; and like one that preferred truth before the maintaining of an opinion, hid nothing from him, nor from thenceforth durst any more dissuade him from that which he found by the celestial providence directed. (pp. 396, 38–397, 3)

Rather than questioning (or even abandoning) his faith in human reason, Philanax's response is to make subtle adjustments to his definition of rational behaviour and to persuade himself that this is a situation in which it is reasonable to refrain from reasoning. This is of course not quite what the oracle had asked of him, but it is in character for him to reframe even seemingly irrational behaviour as the product of reason, and the subtle change of the endings in the polyptoton (which loops back to uninflected 'reason') both reflects Philanax's sophistry and shows up the circularity in his argument.[1] Although the oracle prompts a change in his behaviour, Philanax ultimately remains unconvinced, which is also expressed in the pointed use of 'like' in the second half of the sentence (suggesting that secretly, Philanax continues to prefer the maintaining of an opinion, provided it is supported by reason).

The rhetorical figure that is perhaps most likely to be misunderstood – and underappreciated – by modern audiences is paronomasia, specifically its subform antanaclasis, because punning is now associated almost exclusively with humour,

---

[1] The second 'reason' at the end of the phrase introduces an element of epanalepsis, although it is still primarily an example of polyptoton.

whereas in the sixteenth century it was primarily thought of as a witty, pithy way of making visible an otherwise invisible truth about the relationship between words or ideas. The flexibility offered by early modern spelling conventions can also be employed to accentuate this further, as for example in a couplet from the song 'What tongue can her perfections tell' that in 90 reads 'Waste it is calde, for it doth waste / Mens liues, vntill it be imbraste' (p. 165, 33–4). There is nothing unusual about the spellings 'waist' and 'waste' being used interchangeably in a late sixteenth-century text, but the spelling 'imbraste' / 'embraste' that is used here is very uncommon (even more so than 'imbrast' / 'embrast' without the final -e) and does not appear elsewhere in 90, where the word appears eight more times and is spelt either 'embraced' or 'imbraced'.[1] Clearly, then, the purpose of the spelling 'imbraste' is to support the antanaclasis of 'waste' used as a noun followed by its use as a verb, but also the contrast between wasting and embracing that is central to the image – and in this context it is perhaps worth remembering that 'waste' in sixteenth-century usage is strongly connoted with destruction and death (as in the violent 'wasting' of cities and their inhabitants or 'waste' as another word for consumption). So the antanaclasis contained in the couplet is in fact more complex and more serious than the feeble pun as which we might perceive it at first sight. Additionally, it links back to a sentence that introduces the song as a spontaneous composition by Zelmane:

> And so together went the utterance and the invention that one might judge it was Philoclea's beauty which did speedily write it in her eyes, or the sense thereof which did word by word indite it in her mind, whereto she, but as an organ, did only lend utterance. (p. 163, 35–9)

This notion of utterance and invention going together and the sense 'inditing' the words in Zelmane's mind is, in essence, the central idea of antanaclasis and paronomasia more generally. An example of antanaclasis that is even more unambiguously non-humorous occurs in Book III, after Philoclea has withstood Cecropia's attempts to bully her into submission, which have just culminated in a vicious beating. Before giving Philoclea's own reaction (which is to ask her aunt to kill her rather than continue tormenting her), the focus of the text briefly moves away from the two central characters of the scene and instead describes the 'reaction' of Philoclea's surroundings:

> The sun drew clouds up to hide his face from so pitiful a sight, and the very stone walls did yield drops of sweat for agony of such a mischief. Each senseless thing had sense of pity – only they, that had sense, were senseless. (p. 364, 8–10)

Here the central idea is, of course, that the sun and the walls respond to the beating of Philoclea with empathy and pity, the qualities that Cecropia evidently lacks. That idea is not so much encapsulated in the image of the perspiring walls and sun's hidden face, however, as in the highly condensed double antanaclasis of the subsequent sentence, which reflects on this contrast by juxtaposing different meanings of

---

[1] The EEBO / TCP corpus lists 26 examples for the spelling 'imbraste', 32 for 'embraste', 37 for 'imbrast', and 43 for 'embrast', compared to 2,755 examples for 'imbraced' and 6,291 for 'embraced'. The unconventional spelling 'imbraste' was preserved until the seventh edition of 1628/9. The 1633 edition changed it to 'imbrac't' (still an uncommon spelling at 110 examples, but far less so than 'imbraste'), which was preserved until the 1674 edition.

'senseless' (inanimate / unfeeling) and 'sense' (sensation / a mind capable of perception and reason). The conclusion to be drawn is that 'sense' is not always a safeguard against cruel, 'senseless' behaviour – which becomes particularly significant considering the pronoun used in the final phrase is not 'she' but 'they', implying that the reproach includes Amphialus (who unlike his mother is not a fully-fledged villain, but who is suppressing his own sense of pity). The function of the seemingly unsubtle device of repeating the words 'senseless ... sense ... sense ... senseless', then, is to bring out subtle nuances of meaning and to create a moment of reflection in the middle of a scene of violence.

This is not to say that Sidney's use of paronomasia cannot also be humorous. One of the less memorable participants at Phalantus' challenge in Book I is Polycetes, an Arcadian whose main claim to fame is that he is known to worship Gynecia – honourably, as the text reminds us several times. His failure, which has a comical function because Gynecia is not upset to see her champion fail, only embarrassed to see him fail before Zelmane, is commented on through two different instances of paronomasia: 'neither her fair picture nor his fair running could warrant him from overthrow' and, in the subsequent sentence, 'her champion went away as much discomforted as discomfited' (p. 84, 29–33). The latter in particular is an evident verbal joke, on 'discomforted' (discouraged or distressed) and 'discomfited' (defeated in battle), two words that are in fact closely etymologically related, so the observation that to be discomfited is to be discomforted is arguably paronomasia turned truism.

Figures relating to imagery are of course also central to Sidney's style in the *New Arcadia*. The images Sidney chooses are often colourful and a little peculiar, which might explain why John Ward, his young seventeenth-century reader (see p. lxxvi, n. 1 above), included so many similes and metaphors among his notes. Yet even the more fanciful images are carefully selected to suit the sentences in which they appear and their context, which is particularly apparent in Sidney's similes. So, for example, when Musidorus encounters the disguised Pyrocles in Book I and berates him at great length for having lost his way, the analogy he draws is 'as if you should drown your ship in the long-desired haven, or like an ill player, should mar the last act of his tragedy' (p. 60, 2–3). Musidorus offers the two images as alternative illustrations of the ways in which he believes his friend has jeopardized his reputation as a prince and a hero by becoming transformed in show and (more worryingly) transformed in mind, and they are highly appropriate for a survivor of two shipwrecks who is dressed up in Amazon gear. A slightly more surprising imagery is applied to the elderly Basilius, who in Book II has just heard from Philoclea that Zelmane (who rebuked him in their last encounter) has agreed to meet him after all. His eagerness to see Zelmane again, because he believes she might be willing to give him a second chance, is compared to the eagerness of a young heir who, after having been raised by a controlling guardian, has finally come of age: 'and straight, like a hard-kept ward new come to his lands, would fain have used the benefit of that grant in laying his sickness before his only physician' (p. 257, 26–7). The incongruity of the comparison – Basilius is eighty years old and consequently about as far from being a ward as possible – highlights both the silliness and the imprudence of his pursuit of an eighteen-year-old (a hard-kept ward new come to his lands is particularly prone to overenthusiastic spending and rash decisions), but it also casts Philoclea and Zelmane in the role of the responsible grown-ups.

A figure associated with imagery that Sidney uses comparatively often is catachresis, a type of metaphor that hinges on the unconventional use of one or more words. Finding that the introduction to Arcadia and its eccentric ruler that he meant to give his visitor has turned into a list of complaints about Dametas and his family, Kalander, towards the beginning of Book I, checks himself and apologizes to Musidorus for giving so much attention to such an undeserving subject: 'But in sooth I am afraid I have given your ears too great a surfeit with the gross discourses of that heavy piece of flesh' (p. 15, 13–15). Kalander's image of overfeeding Musidorus' ears with food that will lead to indigestion at once serves as an apology for having talked at length about an uninteresting subject, an apology for being a bad host (who ought to take greater care in selecting the type and the quantity of food he serves to his guests) – and a final barb against that big oaf Dametas in comparing him to an indigestible lump of meat. Another assault on the ears by that same heavy piece of flesh takes place in Book II, when Dametas escorts Zelmane back to Basilius' lodge and entertains her with a long, incoherent discourse on the art of husbandry (with a particular focus on the correct way of dunging fields). Zelmane's pointed silence is described: 'poor Zelmane yielded her ears to those tedious strokes, not warding them so much as with any one answer' (p. 121, 9–10). The odd image – 'warding' the strokes of tedious conversation with answers is of course likely to prolong rather than end it (which does not fit with the idea of parrying blows) – heightens the comedy of the situation, by acting as a reminder that even the greatest warrior is helpless when assaulted by boring conversation.

Sententiae – proverb-like aphorisms that readers were able to copy into their commonplace books and that were consequently likely to receive particular attention – also feature in *Arcadia*. However, the pithy phrases tend to be clothed in much longer sentences that either qualify them or invoke them in a specific context, introduced by the statement 'I / he / she found that', so that in many cases it could be argued that strictly speaking, Sidney is citing a sententia rather than writing one himself. Thus one of Hoskyns' examples, 'Who stands only upon defence stands upon no defence', occurs in Book II, when Zelmane attacks Amphialus, who infuriatingly refuses to engage in a serious fight and only parries or avoids her blows – a scene that the text compares to 'the image of innocency against violence' (p. 169, 33–4).[1] This is followed by the sentence containing the sententia cited by Hoskyns:

> But at length he found that, both in public and private respects, who stands only upon defence stands upon no defence, for Zelmane seeming to strike at his head, and he going to ward it withal stepped back as he was accustomed, she stopped her blow in the air, and suddenly turning the point ran full at his breast, so as he was driven with the pommel of his sword (having no other

---

[1] Note, however, that this comparison is introduced by the words 'at that time seeming', alerting readers that Amphialus is not in fact as innocent and Zelmane not as violent as they momentarily appear in this emblem-like scene.

weapon of defence) to beat it down; but the thrust was so strong that he could not so wholly beat it away but that it met with his thigh, thorough which it ran; but Zelmane retiring her sword, and seeing his blood, victorious anger was conquered by the before-conquered pity. (p. 169, 34–170, 4)

While the context does not change the sententious character of the phrase, it does to some extent modify it, because in this scene, the reader is hardly supposed to condemn Amphialus for not killing or seriously injuring one of the heroes of the story, who has rashly picked a fight with him. Amphialus' real mistake here is not his refusal to fight a lady, but his failure to take his hot-headed opponent seriously. At other times, Sidney tucks away *sententiae* in parentheses, which on the one hand makes them more visible through the brackets used for parentheses in *90* and other early editions, but on the other hand removes the wording that makes them sententious in the first place, as in 'the child of peace, good husbandry' (p. 8, 20) or 'the prince of weapons, the sword' (p. 294, 13). Although early readers could and did extract *sententiae* from *Arcadia*, either by using the same strategy as Hoskyns and selecting their 'sentences' from a much longer and more complex sentence, or by rephrasing, it is rare for Sidney to present his readers with sentences containing straightforward commonplaces that are not modified in some way. The notable exception to this is Cecropia, whose use of the figure is clearly problematic. While trying to coerce Philoclea into marrying Amphialus, she repeatedly tries to harness the persuasive power of *sententiae* such as 'men's experience is woman's best eyesight' (p. 288, 1–2) or 'beauty goes away, devoured by time – but where remains it ever flourishing, but in the heart of a lover' (p. 309, 27–9). She adopts a similar strategy when trying to persuade Amphialus to stop being upset about the fact that Philoclea does not love him and take more decisive action, by telling him things like ' "no" is no negative in a woman's mouth' (p. 348, 15) or 'each virtue has his time' (p. 348, 19). In both cases, however, it is clear that Cecropia has neither Philoclea's nor Amphialus' interests at heart but is acting on her own ambition to be queen mother (if she cannot be queen herself). Cecropia's extensive use of *sententiae* – which Hoskyns stresses should be used only sparingly – as well as the fact that she presents them as general truths that do not require the qualification or contextualization that *Arcadia* otherwise provides them with, characterize her as a manipulative speaker (much like Plexirtus in his overuse of anaphora). – EC

THE FIRST BOOK

It was[1] in the time that the earth begins to put on her new apparel against the approach of her lover, and that the sun, running a most even course, becomes an indifferent arbiter between the night and the day, when the hopeless shepherd Strephon was come to the sands which lie against the island of Cythera, where, viewing the place with a heavy kind of delight, and sometimes casting his eyes to the isleward, he called his friendly rival, the pastor Claius, unto him; and setting first down in his darkened countenance a doleful copy of what he would speak, 'O my Claius,' said he, 'hither we are now come to pay the rent for which we are so called unto by over-busy remembrance – remembrance, restless remembrance, which claims not only this duty of us but, for it, will have us forget ourselves. I pray you, when we were amid our flock, and that of other shepherds some were running after their sheep strayed beyond their bounds, some delighting their eyes with seeing them nibble upon the short and sweet grass, some medicining their sick ewes, some setting a bell for an ensign of a sheepish squadron, some with more leisure inventing new games of exercising their bodies and sporting their wits, did remembrance grant us any holiday either for pastime or devotion, nay, either for necessary food or natural rest, but that still it forced our thoughts to work upon this place where we last (alas, that the word *last* should so long last!) did grace[2] our eyes upon her ever-flourishing beauty? Did it not still cry within us, "Ah, you base-minded wretches, are your thoughts so deeply bemired in the trade of ordinary worldlings as, for respect of gain some paltry wool may yield you, to let so much time pass without knowing perfectly her estate, especially in so troublesome a season; to leave that shore unsaluted from whence you may see to the island where she dwelleth; to leave those steps unkissed wherein Urania printed the farewell of all beauty?"

'Well then, remembrance commanded, we obeyed; and here we find that, as our remembrance came ever clothed unto us in the form of this place, so this place gives new heat to the fever of our languishing remembrance. Yonder, my Claius, Urania lighted. The very horse, methought, bewailed to be so disburdened; and as for thee, poor Claius, when thou wentst to help her down, I saw reverence and desire so divide thee that thou didst at one instant both blush and quake, and instead of bearing her, wert ready to fall down thyself. There, she sate vouchsafing my cloak (then most gorgeous) under

---

[1] The First Book. It was 93: It was *Cm*; The First Book. Chap. 1. The shepherdish complaints of the absented lovers Strephon and Claius; the second shipwreck of Pyrocles and Musidorus; their strange saving, interview, and parting. It was 90   [2] grace *Cm*: gaze 90; graze 93

her. At yonder rising of the ground, she turned herself, looking back toward her wonted abode and, because of her parting, bearing much sorrow in her eyes, the lightsomeness whereof had yet so natural a cheerfulness as it made even sorrow seem to smile. At that turning, she spake unto[1] us all, opening the cherry of her lips – and Lord! how greedily mine ears did feed upon the sweet words she uttered! And here, she laid her hand over thine eyes when she saw the tears springing in them, as if she would conceal them from other, and yet herself feel some of thy sorrow. But (woe is me) yonder, yonder did she put her foot into the boat, at that instant, as it were, dividing her heavenly beauty between the earth and the sea. But when she was embarked did you not mark how the winds whistled and the seas danced for joy, how the sails did swell with pride, and all because they had Urania? O Urania, blessed be thou, Urania, the sweetest fairness and fairest sweetness – .'

With that word his voice brake so with sobbing that he could say no further; and Claius thus answered: 'Alas, my Strephon,' said he, 'what needs this score to reckon up only our losses? What doubt is there but that the light of this place doth call our thoughts to appear at the court of affection, held by that racking steward, remembrance? As well may sheep forget to fear when they spy wolves as we can miss such fancies when we see any place made happy by her treading. Who can choose, that saw her, but think where she stayed, where she walked, where she turned, where she spoke? But what is all this? Truly no more, but as this place served us to think of those things, so those things serve as places to call to memory more excellent matters.

'No, no: let us think with consideration, and consider with acknowledging, and acknowledge with admiration, and admire with love, and love with joy in the midst of all woes; let us in such sort think, I say, that our poor eyes were so enriched as to behold, and our low hearts so exalted as to love a maid who is such that, as the greatest thing the world can show is her beauty, so the least thing that may be praised in her is her beauty. Certainly as her eyelids are more pleasant to behold than two white kids climbing up a fair tree and browsing on his tenderest branches, and yet are nothing compared to the day-shining stars contained in them; and as her breath is more sweet than a gentle south-west wind which comes creeping over flowery fields and shadowed waters in the extreme heat of summer, and yet is nothing compared to the honey-flowing speech that breath doth carry, no more all that our eyes can see of her (though when they have seen her, what else they shall ever see is but dry stubble after clover's grass) is to be matched with the flock of unspeakable virtues laid up delightfully in that best-builded fold. But, indeed, as we can better consider the sun's beauty by

---

[1] unto] to 93

marking how he gilds these waters and mountains than[1] by looking upon his own face, too glorious for our weak eyes, so it may be our conceits, not able to bear her sun-staining excellency, will better weigh it by her works upon some meaner subject employed. And, alas, who can better witness that than we whose experience is grounded upon feeling? Hath not the only love of her made us, being silly ignorant shepherds, raise up our thoughts above the ordinary level of the world so as great clerks do not disdain our conference? Hath not the desire to seem worthy in her eyes made us, when others were sleeping, to sit viewing the course of heavens; when others were running at base, to run over learned writings; when other mark their sheep, we to mark our selves? Hath not she thrown reason upon our desires and, as it were, given eyes unto Cupid? Hath in any, but in her, love-fellowship maintained friendship between rivals, and beauty taught the beholders chastity?'

He was going on with his praises, but Strephon bad him stay and look; and so they both perceived a thing which floated drawing nearer and nearer to the bank, but rather by the favourable working of the sea than by any self-industry. They doubted awhile what it should be, till it was cast up even hard before them, at which time they fully saw that it was a man; whereupon running for pity sake unto him, they found his hands (as it should appear, constanter friends to his life than his memory) fast griping upon the edge of a square small coffer which lay all under his breast; else in himself no show of life, so as the board seemed to be but a bier to carry him aland to his sepulchre. So drew they up a young man of so goodly shape and well pleasing favour that one would think death had, in him, a lovely countenance, and that though he were naked, nakedness was to him an apparel. That sight increased their compassion, and their compassion called up their care; so that lifting his feet above his head, making a great deal of salt water to come[2] out of his mouth, they laid him upon some of their garments and fell to rub and chafe him till they brought him to recover both breath the servant, and warmth the companion, of living. At length opening his eyes, he gave a great groan – a doleful note but a pleasant ditty, for by that they found not only life, but strength of life in him. They therefore continued on their charitable office until, his spirits being well returned, he, without so much as thanking them for their pains, gate up; and looking round about to the uttermost limits of his sight, and crying upon the name of *Pyrocles*, nor seeing nor hearing cause of comfort, 'What,' said he, 'and shall Musidorus live after Pyrocles?' Therewithal he offered wilfully to cast destruction and himself again[3] into the sea – a strange sight to the shepherds, to whom it seemed that before, being in appearance dead had yet saved his life, and

---

[1] than] them *90 (uncorr.)*   [2] water to come] water come *93*   [3] Pyrocles? ... again] Pyrocles' destruction? Therewithal he offered wilfully to cast himself again *93*

now, coming to his life should be a cause to procure his death! But they ran unto him, and pulling him back (then too feeble for them) by force stickled that unnatural fray.

'I pray you,' said he, 'honest men, what such right have you in me as not to suffer me to do with myself what I list? And what policy have you to bestow a benefit where it is counted an injury?'

They hearing him speak in Greek, which was their natural language, became the more tender-hearted towards him; and considering by his calling and looking that the loss of some dear friend was great cause of his sorrow, told him they were poor men that were bound by course of humanity to prevent so great a mischief, and that they wished him, if opinion of somebody's perishing bred such desperate anguish in him, that he should be comforted by his own proof, who had lately escaped as apparent danger as any might be.

'No, no,' said he, 'it is not for me to attend so high a blissfulness. But since you take care of me, I pray you find means that some bark may be provided that will go out of the haven, that if it be possible we may find the body, far, far too precious a food for fishes; and for the hire,' said he, 'I have within this casket of value sufficient to content them.'

Claius presently went to a fisherman, and having agreed with him and provided some apparel for the naked stranger, he embarked, and the shepherds with him; and were no sooner gone beyond the mouth of the haven, but that some way into the sea they might discern, as it were, a stain of the water's colour, and by times some sparks and smoke mounting thereout. But the young man no sooner saw it but that, beating his breast, he cried that there was the beginning of his ruin, entreating them to bend their course as near unto it as they could, telling how that smoke was but a small relic of a great fire which had driven both him and his friend rather to commit themselves to the cold mercy of the sea than to abide the hot cruelty of the fire; and that therefore, though they both had abandoned the ship, that he was (if anywhere) in that course to be met withal. They steered, therefore, as near thitherward as they could; but when they came so near as their eyes were full masters of the object, they saw a sight full of piteous strangeness: a ship, or rather the carcass of the ship, or rather some few bones of the carcass, hulling there, part broken, part burned, part drowned – death having used more than one dart to that destruction. About it floated great store of very rich things, and many chests which might promise no less. And amidst the precious things were a number of dead bodies which likewise did not only testify both elements' violence, but that the chief violence was grown of human inhumanity, for their bodies were full of grisly wounds, and their blood had, as it were, filled the wrinkles of the sea's visage, which, it seemed, the sea would not wash away, that it might witness it is not always his fault when we condemn his cruelty: in sum, a defeat where the conquered kept both field and spoil, a shipwreck without storm or ill-footing, and a waste of fire in the midst of water.[1]

But a little way off they saw the mast whose proud height now lay along, like a widow having lost her make, of whom she held her honour; but upon the mast they saw a young man (at least, if he were a man) bearing show of about eighteen years of age, who sate as on horseback, having nothing upon him but his shirt which, being wrought with blue silk and gold, had a kind of resemblance to the sea on which the sun then near his western home did shoot some of his beams. His hair, which the young men of Greece used to wear very long, was stirred up and down with the wind, which seemed to have a sport to play with it, as the sea had to kiss his feet; himself full of admirable beauty set forth by the strangeness both of his seat and gesture, for, holding his head up full of unmoved majesty, he held a sword aloft with his fair arm which often he waved about his crown as though he would threaten the world in that extremity. But the fishermen, when they came so near him that it was time to throw out a rope by which hold they might draw him, their simplicity bred such amazement, and their amazement such a superstition,[2] that (assuredly thinking it was some god begotten between Neptune and Venus that had made all this terrible slaughter) as they went under sail by him, held up their hands and made their prayers – which when Musidorus saw, though he were almost as much ravished with joy as they with astonishment, he leapt to the mariner and took the rope[3] out of his hand; and saying, 'Doest thou live, and art well?' (who answered, 'Thou canst tell best, since most of my well-being stands in thee') threw it out. But already the ship was passed beyond Pyrocles, and therefore Musidorus could do no more but persuade the mariners to cast about again, assuring them that he was but a man (although of most divine excellencies) and promising great rewards for their pain.

And now they were already come upon the stays, when one of the sailors descried a galley which came with sails and oars directly in the chase of them, and straight perceived it was a well-known pirate who hunted not only for goods but for bodies of men, which he employed either to be his galley-slaves or to sell at the best market; which when the master understood, he commanded forthwith to set on all the canvas they could and fly homeward, leaving in that sort poor Pyrocles, so near to be rescued. But what did not Musidorus say? What did he not offer to persuade them to venture the fight?

---

[1] of water] of the water 93   [2] such a superstition] such superstition 93   [3] rope] cord 93

But fear standing at the gates of their ears put back all persuasions, so that he had nothing wherewith to[1] accompany Pyrocles but his eyes, nor to succour him but his wishes. Therefore praying for him, and casting a long look that way, he saw the galley leave the pursuit of them and turn to take up the spoils of the other wrack; and lastly, he might well see them lift up the young man.

'And alas,' said he to himself, 'dear Pyrocles, shall that body of thine be enchained? Shall those victorious hands of thine be commanded to base offices? Shall virtue become a slave to those that be slaves to viciousness? Alas, better had it been thou hadst ended nobly thy noble days. What death is so evil as unworthy servitude?'

But that opinion soon ceased when he saw the galley setting upon another ship which held long and strong fight with her, for then he began afresh to fear the life of his friend and to wish well to the pirates whom before he hated, lest in their ruin he might perish. But the fishermen made such speed into the haven that they absented his eyes from beholding the issue, where being entered, he could procure neither them nor any other as then to put themselves into the sea. So that being as full of sorrow for being unable to do anything as void of counsel how to do anything, besides that sickness grew something upon him, the honest shepherds Strephon and Claius (who being themselves true friends did the more perfectly judge the justness of his sorrow) advise him that he should mitigate somewhat of his woe since he had gotten an amendment in fortune, being come from assured persuasion of his death to have no cause to despair of his life – as one that had lamented the death of his sheep, should after know they were but strayed, would receive pleasure, though readily he knew not where to find them.

'Now[2] sir,' said they, 'thus for ourselves it is. We are in profession but shepherds, and in this country of Laconia little better than strangers, and therefore neither in skill nor ability of power greatly to stead you. But what we can present unto you is this: Arcadia, of which country we are, is but a little way hence. And even upon the next confines there[3] dwelleth a gentleman, by name Kalander, who vouchsafeth much favour unto us – a man who for his hospitality is so much haunted that no news stir but comes to his ears; for his upright dealing so beloved of his neighbours that he hath many ever ready to do him their uttermost service; and by the great goodwill our prince bears him, may soon obtain the use of his name and credit, which hath a principal sway not only in his own Arcadia but in all these countries

---

[1] nothing wherewith to *Cm*, 93: nothing to 90   [2] them. 'Now *Cm*, 93: them. Chap. 2. The pastors' comforts to the wracked Musidorus; his passage into Arcadia; the descriptions of Laconia, Arcadia, Kalander's person, house, and entertainment to Musidorus, now called Palladius; his sickness, recovery, and perfections. 'Now 90   [3] confines there *Cm*, 93: confines. There 90

of Peloponnesus; and (which is worth all) all these things give him not so much power as his nature gives him will to benefit, so that it seems no music is so sweet to his ear as deserved thanks. To him we will bring you. And there you may recover again your health, without which you cannot be able to make any diligent search for your friend; and therefore, but in that respect,[1] you must labour for it. Besides, we are sure the comfort of courtesy and ease of wise counsel shall not be wanting.'

Musidorus, who besides he was merely unacquainted in the country had his wits astonished with sorrow, gave easy consent to that from which he saw no reason to disagree. And therefore, defraying the mariners with a ring bestowed upon them, they took their journey together through Laconia, Claius and Strephon by course carrying his chest for him, Musidorus only bearing in his countenance evident marks of a sorrowful mind supported with a weak body, which they perceiving, and knowing that the violence of sorrow is not at the first to be striven withal (being like a mighty beast, sooner tamed with following than overthrown by withstanding), they gave way unto it for that day and the next, never troubling him either with asking questions or finding fault with his melancholy, but rather fitting to his dolour dolorous discourses of their own and other folks' misfortunes – which speeches, though they had not a lively entrance to his senses shut up in sorrow, yet like one half asleep he took hold of much of the matters spoken unto him, so (as a man may say) ere sorrow was aware they made his thoughts bear away something else beside his own sorrow; which wrought so in him that at length he grew content to mark their speeches, then to marvel at such wit in shepherds, after, to like their company, and lastly, to vouchsafe conference.

So that the third day after, in the time that the morning did strow roses and violets in the heavenly floor against the coming of the sun, the nightingales, striving one with the other which could in most dainty variety recount their wrong-caused sorrow, made them put off their sleep; and rising from under a tree which that night had been their pavilion, they went on their journey, which by and by welcomed Musidorus' eyes (wearied with the wasted soil of Laconia) with delightful prospects. There were hills, which garnished their proud heights with stately trees; humble valleys, whose base estate seemed comforted with refreshing of silver rivers; meadows enamelled with all sorts of eye-pleasing flowers; thickets, which being lined with most pleasant shade, were witnessed so to by the cheerful deposition of many well-tuned birds; each pasture stored with sheep feeding with sober security, while the pretty lambs with bleating oratory craved the dams' comfort; here, a shepherd's boy piping, as though he should never be old; there, a

---

[1] but in that respect] om. 93

young shepherdess knitting and withal singing, and it seemed that her voice comforted her hands to work, and her hands kept time to her voice's music. As for the houses of the country (for many houses came under their eye), they were all scattered, no two being one by th'other, and yet not so far off as that it barred mutual succour – a show as it were of an accompanable solitariness, and of a civil wildness.

'I pray you,' said Musidorus, then first unsealing his long-silent lips, 'what countries be these we pass through which are so diverse in show, the one wanting no store, th'other having no store but of want?'

'The country,' answered Claius, 'where you were cast ashore and now are passed through is Laconia, not so poor by the barrenness of the soil (though in itself not passing fertile) as by a civil war which, being these two years within the bowels of that estate between the gentlemen and the peasants (by them named helots), hath in this sort as it were disfigured the face of nature and made it so unhospital as now you have found it, the towns neither of the one side nor the other willingly opening their gates to strangers, nor strangers willingly entering for fear of being mistaken. But this country where now you set your foot is Arcadia (and even hard by is the house of Kalander whither we lead you), this country being thus decked with peace and, the child of peace, good husbandry. These houses you see so scattered are of men as we two are that live upon the commodity of their sheep, and therefore in the division of the Arcadian estate are termed shepherds – a happy people, wanting little because they desire not much.'

'What cause then,' said Musidorus, 'made you venter to leave this sweet life and put yourself in yonder unpleasant and dangerous realm?'

'Guarded with poverty,' answered Strephon, 'and guided with love.'

'But now,' said Claius, 'since it hath pleased you to ask anything of us whose baseness is such as the very knowledge is darkness, give us leave to know something of you and of the young man you so much lament, that at least we may be the better instructed to inform Kalander, and he the better know how to proportion his entertainment.'

Musidorus, according to the agreement between Pyrocles and him to alter their names, answered that he called himself Palladius and his friend Daiphantus. 'But till I have him again,' said he, 'I am indeed nothing, and therefore my story is of nothing. His entertainment, since so good a man he is, cannot be so low as I account my estate; and in sum, the sum of all his courtesy may be to help me by some means to seek my friend.'

They perceived he was not willing to open himself further; and therefore without further questioning brought him to the house about which they might see (with fit consideration both of the air, the prospect, and the nature of the ground) all such necessary additions to a great house as might well show Kalander knew that provision is the foundation of hospitality, and thrift the fuel of magnificence. The house itself was built of fair and strong stone, not affecting so much any extraordinary kind of fineness as an honourable representing of a firm stateliness; the lights, doors, and stairs rather directed to the use of the guest than to the eye of the artificer, and yet, as the one chiefly heeded, so the other not neglected; each place handsome without curiosity and homely without loathsomeness, not so dainty as not to be trode on, nor yet slubbered up with good fellowship – all more lasting than beautiful (but that the consideration of the exceeding lastingness made the eye believe it was exceeding beautiful); the servants not so many in number as cleanly in apparel and serviceable in behaviour, testifying even in their countenances that their master took as well care to be served as of them that did serve. One of them was forthwith ready to welcome the shepherds as men who, though they were poor, their master greatly favoured. And understanding by them that the young man with them was to be much accounted of – for that they had seen tokens of more than common greatness, howsoever now eclipsed with fortune – he ran to his master, who came presently forth; and pleasantly welcoming the shepherds, but especially applying him to Musidorus, Strephon privately told him all what he knew of him – and particularly that he found this stranger was loath to be known.

'No,' said Kalander, speaking aloud, 'I am no herald to inquire of men's pedigrees. It sufficeth me if I know their virtues, which, if this young man's face be not a false witness, do better apparel his mind than you have done his body.'

While he was speaking[1] there came a boy (in show like a merchant's prentice) who taking Strephon by the sleeve delivered him a letter written jointly both to him and Claius from Urania, which they no sooner had read but that with short leave-taking of Kalander, who quickly guessed and smiled at the matter, and once again (though hastily) recommending the young man unto him, they went away, leaving Musidorus even loath to part with them for the good conversation he had of them, and obligation he accounted himself tied in unto them; and therefore, they delivering his chest unto him, he opened it and would have presented them with two very rich jewels, but they absolutely refused them, telling him they[2] were more than enough rewarded in the knowing of him; and without hearkening unto a reply, like men whose hearts disdained all desires but one, gate speedily away, as if the letter had brought wings to make them fly. But by that sight

---

[1] was speaking] was thus speaking 93   [2] him they] him that they 93

Kalander soon judged that his guest was of no mean calling, and therefore the more respectfully entertaining him.

Musidorus found his sickness which the fight, the sea, and late travel had laid upon him grow greatly, so that fearing some sudden accident, he delivered the chest to Kalander – which was full of most precious stones gorgeously and cunningly set in divers manners – desiring him he would keep those trifles and, if he died, he would bestow so much of it as was needful to find out and redeem a young man naming himself Daiphantus, as then in the hands of Laconia pirates. But Kalander, seeing him faint more and more, with careful speed conveyed him to the most commodious lodging in his house where, being possessed with an extreme burning fever, he continued some while with no great hope of life. But youth at length got the victory of sickness, so that in six weeks the excellency of his returned beauty was a credible embassador of his health, to the great joy of Kalander, who, as in this time he had by certain friends of his that dwelt near the sea in Messenia set forth a ship and a galley to seek and succour Daiphantus, so at home did he omit nothing which he thought might either profit or gratify Palladius. For having found in him, besides his bodily gifts beyond the degree of admiration, by daily discourses which he delighted himself to have with him, a mind of most excellent composition, a piercing wit quite void of ostentation, high-erected thoughts seated in a heart of courtesy, an eloquence as sweet in the uttering as slow to come to the uttering, a behaviour so noble as gave a majesty to adversity – and all in a man whose age could not be above one and twenty years – the good old man was even enamoured with a fatherly love towards him, or rather, became his servant by the bonds such virtue laid upon him, once he acknowledged himself so to be by the badge of diligent attendance.

But[1] Palladius having gotten his health and only staying there to be in place where he might hear answer of the ships set forth, Kalander one afternoon led him abroad to a well-arrayed ground he had behind his house, which he thought to show him before his going as the place himself, more than in any other, delighted. The backside of the house was neither field, garden, nor orchard – or rather it was both field, garden, and orchard – for as soon as the descending of the stairs had delivered them down, they came into a place cunningly set with trees of the most taste-pleasing fruits; but scarcely they had taken that into their consideration but that they were suddenly stepped into a delicate green, of each side of the green a thicket bend, behind[2] the thickets again new beds of flowers, which being under the

---

[1] attendance. But *Cm, 93*: attendance. Chap. 3. The pictures of Kalander's dainty garden-house; his narration of the Arcadian estate, the king, the queen, their two daughters, and their guardians with their qualities, which is the ground of all this story. But *90*   [2] thicket bend, behind] thicket, and behind *93*

trees, the trees were to them a pavilion, and they to the trees, a mosaical floor, so that it seemed that art therein would needs be delightful by counterfeiting his enemy, error, and making order in confusion. In the middest of all the place was a fair pond whose shaking crystal was a perfect mirror to all the other beauties, so that it bare show of two gardens, one indeed, the other in shadows; and in one of the thickets was a fine fountain made thus: a naked Venus of white marble wherein the graver had used such cunning that the natural blue veins of the marble were framed in fit places to set forth the beautiful veins of her body. At her breast she had her babe Aeneas who seemed, having begun to suck, to leave that to look upon her fair eyes which smiled at the babe's folly, the mean while[1] the breast running.

Hard by was a house of pleasure built for a summer retiring-place, whither Kalander leading him, he found a square room full of delightful pictures made by the most excellent workman of Greece. There was Diana, when Actaeon saw her bathing, in whose cheeks the painter had set such a colour as was mixed between shame and disdain, and one of her foolish nymphs, who weeping and withal louring, one might see the workman meant to set forth tears of anger. In another table was Atalanta, the posture of whose limbs was so lively expressed that (if the eyes were the only judges as they be the only seers) one would have sworn the very picture had run; besides many mo, as of Helena, Omphale, Iole. But in none of them all beauty seemed to speak so much as in a large table which contained a comely old man with a lady of middle age – but of excellent beauty – and more excellent would have been deemed but that there stood between them a young maid whose wonderfulness took away all beauty from her, but that which it might seem she gave her back again by her very shadow. And such difference (being known that it did indeed counterfeit a person living) was there between her and all the other, though goddesses, that it seemed the skill of the painter bestowed on the other new beauty, but that the beauty of her bestowed new skill of the painter.

Though he thought inquisitiveness an uncomely guest, he could not choose but ask who she was that, bearing show of one being indeed, could with natural gifts go beyond the reach of invention. Kalander answered that it was made by Philoclea, the younger daughter of his prince, who, also with his wife, were contained in that table, the painter meaning to represent the present condition of the young lady who stood watched by an over-curious eye of her parents, and that he would also have drawn her eldest sister (esteemed her match for beauty) in her shepherdish attire, but that the rude clown her guardian would not suffer it; neither durst he ask leave

---

[1] folly, the mean while] folly, mean while 93

of the prince for fear of suspicion. Palladius perceived that the matter was wrapped up in some secrecy, and therefore would for modesty demand no further; but yet his countenance could not but with dumb eloquence desire it – which Kalander perceiving, 'Well,' said he, 'my dear guest, I know your mind and I will satisfy it. Neither will I do it like a niggardly answerer, going no further than the bounds of the question, but I will discover unto you as well that wherein my knowledge is common with others, as that which by extraordinary means is delivered unto me, knowing so much in you, though not long acquainted, that I shall find your ears faithful treasurers.' So then, sitting down in two chairs, and sometimes casting his eye to the picture, he thus spake:

'This country, Arcadia, among all the provinces of Greece hath ever been had in singular reputation, partly for the sweetness of the air and other natural benefits, but principally for the well-tempered minds of the people who, finding that the shining title of glory so much affected by other nations doth indeed help little to the happiness of life, are the only people which, as by their justice and providence give neither cause nor hope to their neighbours to annoy them, so are they not stirred with false praise to trouble others' quiet, thinking it a small reward for the wasting of their own lives in ravening that their posterity should long after say they had done so. Even the muses seem to approve their good determination by choosing this country for their chief repairing place, and by bestowing their perfections so largely here that the very shepherds have their fancies lifted to so high conceits as the learned of other nations are content both to borrow their names and imitate their cunning.

'Here dwelleth and reigneth this prince, whose picture you see, by name Basilius – a prince of sufficient skill to govern so quiet a country where the good minds of the former princes had set down good laws, and the well bringing-up of the people doth[1] serve as a most sure bond to hold them. But to be plain with you, he excels in nothing so much as in the zealous love of his people, wherein he doth not only pass all his own foregoers, but (as I think) all the princes living; whereof the cause is that, though he exceed not in the virtues which get admiration – as depth of wisdom, height of courage, and largeness of magnificence, yet is he notable in those which stir affection – as truth of word, meekness, courtesy, mercifulness, and liberality. He being already well stricken in years, married a young princess named Gynecia, daughter to the king of Cyprus, of notable beauty (as by her picture you see), a woman of great wit, and in truth of more princely virtues than her husband, of most unspotted chastity, but of so working a mind and so vehement spirits as a man may say it was happy she took a good course, for otherwise it would have been terrible.

---

[1] doth] did *OA, 93 (uncorr.)*

'Of these two are brought to the world two daughters, so beyond measure excellent in all the gifts allotted to reasonable creatures that we may think they were born to show that nature is no stepmother to that sex, how much soever some men (sharp-witted only in evil speaking) have sought to disgrace them. The elder is named Pamela, by many men not deemed inferior to her sister. For my part, when I marked them both, methought there was (if at least such perfections may receive the word of *more*) more sweetness in Philoclea, but more majesty in Pamela; methought love played in Philoclea's eyes and threatened in Pamela's; methought Philoclea's beauty only persuaded – but so persuaded as all hearts must yield, Pamela's beauty used violence – and such violence as no heart could resist. And it seems that such proportion is between their minds: Philoclea, so bashful as though her excellencies had stolen into her before she was aware, so humble that she will put all pride out of countenance – in sum, such proceeding as will stir hope but teach hope good manners; Pamela, of high thoughts, who avoids not pride with not knowing her excellencies, but by making that one of her excellencies to be void of pride, her mother's wisdom, greatness, nobility – but, if I can guess aright, knit with a more constant temper.

'Now then, our Basilius (being so publicly happy as to be a prince, and so happy in that happiness as to be a beloved prince, and so in his private blessed as to have so excellent a wife and so over-excellent children) hath of late taken a course which yet makes him more spoken of than all these blessings; for having made a journey to Delphos and safely returned, within short space he brake up his court and retired himself, his wife, and children into a certain forest hereby which he calleth his desert, wherein, besides a house appointed for stables and lodgings for certain persons of mean calling who do all household services, he hath builded two fine lodges. In the one of them himself remains with his younger daughter, Philoclea – which was the cause they three were matched together in this picture – without having any other creature living in that lodge with him; which though it be strange, yet not so strange as the course he hath taken with the Princess Pamela whom he hath placed in the other lodge – but how think you accompanied? Truly with none other but one Dametas, the most arrant, doltish clown that I think ever was, without the privilege of a bauble, with his wife Miso and daughter Mopsa[1] – in whom no wit can devise anything wherein they may pleasure her, but to exercise her patience, and to serve for a foil of her perfections. This loutish clown is such that you never saw so ill-favoured a visor, his behaviour such that he is beyond the degree of ridiculous, and for his apparel, even as I would wish him. Miso, his wife (so handsome a beldam that only her face and her splay-foot have made her accused for a

---

[1] daughter Mopsa] daughter of Mopsa *Hm*, 93; daughter to Mopsa *corr. to* daughter Mopsa *St*

witch), only one good point she hath – that she observes decorum, having a froward mind in a wretched body. Between[1] these two personages (who never agreed in any humour but in disagreeing) is issued forth Mistress Mopsa, a fit woman to participate of both their perfections; but because a pleasant fellow of my acquaintance set forth her praises in verse, I will only repeat them and spare mine[2] own tongue, since she goes for a woman. These verses are these,[3] which I have so often caused to be sung that I have them without book:

> What length of verse can serve brave Mopsa's good to show,
> Whose virtues strange, and beauties such, as no man them may know?
> Thus shrewdly burdened then, how can my muse escape?
> The gods must help, and precious things must serve to show her shape:
> Like great god Saturn, fair, and like fair Venus, chaste;
> As smooth as Pan; as Juno, mild; like goddess Iris, fast;
> With Cupid she foresees, and goes god Vulcan's pace,
> And for a taste of all these gifts, she steals god Momus' grace;
> Her forehead, jacinth-like; her cheeks of opal hue;
> Her twinkling eyes, bedecked with pearl; her lips, as sapphire, blue;
> Her hair like crapal stone; her mouth, O, heav'nly wide;
> Her skin like burnished gold; her hands like silver ore untried.
>   As for her parts unknown, which hidden sure are best,
>   Happy be[4] they which well[5] believe, and never seek the rest.

'Now, truly having made these descriptions unto you, methinks you should imagine that I rather feign some pleasant device than recount a truth – that a prince not banished from his own wits could possibly make so unworthy a choice. But truly, dear guest, so it is, that princes whose doings have been often soothed with good success think nothing so absurd which they cannot make honourable.

'The beginning of his credit was by the prince's straying out of the[6] way one time he hunted, where, meeting this fellow and asking him the way, and so falling into other questions, he found some of his answers (as a dog, sure if he could speak, had wit enough to describe his kennel) not unsensible, and all uttered with such rudeness[7] (which he interpreted plainness – though there be great difference between[8] them) that Basilius, conceiving a sudden delight, took him to his court with apparent show of his good opinion – where the flattering courtier had no sooner taken the prince's mind but that there were straight reasons to confirm the prince's doing, and shadows

---

[1] Between] Betwixt *OA* (*ex. Da*)   [2] mine] my *Bo, As, Da, Cm*   [3] These] The *90* (*corr.*), *93*   [4] be] are *Le, O, Ph, Dd*   [5] well] will *St, Bo, As, O, Dd*   [6] of the] of his *OA* (*ex. Hm*)   [7] rudeness] a rudeness *OA* (*ex. Ph, Hm*)   [8] between] betwixt *OA* (*ex. Da, Ph*)

of virtues found for Dametas. His silence grew wit, his bluntness integrity, his beastly ignorance virtuous simplicity; and the prince (according to the nature of great persons in love with that he had done himself) fancied that his weakness, with his presence, would much be mended. And so, like a creature of his own making, he liked him more and more, and thus having first given him the office of principal herdman, lastly (since he took this strange determination) he hath in a manner put the life of himself and his children into his hands – which authority (like too great a sail for so small a boat) doth so oversway poor Dametas that, if before he were a good fool in a chamber, he might be allowed it now in a comedy. So as I doubt me (I fear me, indeed) my master will in the end, with his cost, find that his office is not to make men, but to use men as men are – no more than a horse will be taught to hunt or an ass to manage. But in sooth I am afraid I have given your ears too great a surfeit with the gross discourses of that heavy piece of flesh; but the zealous grief I conceive to see so great an error in my lord hath made me bestow more words than, I confess, so base a subject deserveth.

'Thus[1] much now that I have told you is nothing more than in effect any Arcadian knows; but what moved him to this strange solitariness hath been imparted, as I think, but to one person living. Myself can conjecture – and indeed more than conjecture – by this accident that I will tell you.

'I have an only son, by name Clitophon, who is now absent preparing for his own marriage which I mean shortly shall be here celebrated. This son of mine, while the prince kept his court, was of his bedchamber; now, since the breaking up thereof, returned home and showed me (among other things he had gathered) the copy which he had taken of a letter, which, when the prince had read, he had laid in a window, presuming nobody durst look in his writings. But my son not only took a time to read it but to copy it. In truth, I blamed Clitophon for the curiosity which made him break his duty in such a kind whereby kings' secrets are subject to be revealed, but since it was done, I was content to take so much profit as to know it.

'Now here is the letter that I ever since for my good liking have carried about me – which before I read unto you, I must tell you from whom it came. It is a nobleman of this country, named Philanax, appointed by the prince regent in this time of his retiring, and most worthy so to be; for there lives no man whose excellent wit more simply embraceth integrity, besides his unfeigned love to his master wherein never yet any could make question, saving whether he loved Basilius or the prince better – a rare temper, while[2] most men either servilely yield to all appetites, or with an obstinate austerity

---

[1] deserveth. 'Thus *Cm*, *93*: deserveth.' Chap. 4. The cause of Basilius' discourting; Philanax's dissuasive letter; Basilius' privileged company; four causes why old men are discoursers; the state, the skill, and exercise of the Arcadian shepherds. 'Thus *90*   [2] while] whilst *OA* (*ex. Da, Ph*)

looking to that they fancy good, in effect neglect the prince's person. This then being the man whom of all other (and most worthy) the prince chiefly loves, it should seem (for more than the letter I have not to guess by) that the prince upon his return from Delphos (Philanax then lying sick) had written unto him his determination, rising, as evidently appears, upon some oracle he had there received; whereunto he wrote this answer:

'"Most[1] redoubted and beloved prince, if as well it had pleased you at your going to Delphos, as now, to have used my humble service, both I should in better season and to better purpose have spoken, and you, if my speech had prevailed, should have been at this time,[2] as no way more in danger, so much more in quietness. I would then have said that wisdom and virtue be the only destinies appointed to man to follow, whence we ought to seek all our knowledge, since they be such guides as cannot fail, which, besides their inward comfort, do lead so direct a way of proceeding as either prosperity must ensue, or, if the wickedness of the world should oppress it, it can never be said that evil happeneth to him who falls accompanied with virtue. I would then have said the heavenly powers to be reverenced, and not searched into, and their mercies rather by prayers to be sought than their hidden counsels by curiosity; these kind of soothsayers[3] – since they have left us in ourselves sufficient guides to be nothing but fancy, wherein there must either be vanity or infallibleness, and so either not to be respected, or not to be prevented.

'"But since it is weakness too much to remember what should have been done, and that your commandment stretcheth to know what is to be done, I do, most dear lord, with humble boldness say that the manner of your determination doth in no sort better please me than the cause of your going. These thirty years you have so governed this region that neither your subjects have wanted justice in you, nor you obedience in them; and your neighbours have found you so hurtlessly strong that they thought it better to rest in your friendship than make new trial of your enmity. If this, then, have proceeded out of the good constitution of your state, and out of a wise providence generally to prevent all those things which might encumber your happiness, why should you now seek new courses, since your own ensample comforts you to continue, and that it is to me most certain (though it please you not to tell me the very words of the oracle) that yet no destiny nor influence whatsoever can bring man's wit to a higher point than wisdom and goodness? Why should you deprive yourself of government for fear of losing your government, like one that should kill himself for fear of death?

---

[1] answer: '"Most *Cm*: answer. *Philanax's letter to Basilius.* '"Most 90, 93   [2] should ... time] at this time should have been *OA (ex. Da)*   [3] kind of soothsayers] kinds of soothsayings 93

Nay rather, if this oracle be to be accounted of, arm up your courage the more against it; for who will stick to him that abandons himself? Let your subjects have you in their eyes, let them see the benefits of your justice daily more and more; and so must they needs rather like of present sureties than uncertain changes. Lastly, whether your time call you to live or die, do both like a prince.

' "Now for your second resolution, which is to suffer no worthy prince to be a suitor to either of your daughters, but while you live to keep them both unmarried, and as it were to kill the joy of posterity which in your time you may enjoy – moved perchance by a misunderstood oracle. What shall I say if the affection of a father to his own children cannot plead sufficiently against such fancies? Once, certain it is: the god which is god of nature doth never teach unnaturalness. And even the same mind hold I touching your banishing them from company, lest I know not what strange loves should follow. Certainly, sir, in my ladies, your daughters, nature promiseth nothing but goodness, and their education by your fatherly care hath been hitherto such as hath been most fit to restrain all evil, giving their minds virtuous delights, and not grieving them for want of well-ruled liberty. Now to fall to a sudden straitening them, what can it do but argue suspicion, a thing no more unpleasant than unsure for the preserving of virtue? Leave women's minds, the most untamed that way of any. See whether any cage can please a bird, or whether a dog grow not fiercer with tying. What doth jealousy but stir up the mind to think what it is from which they are restrained? For they are treasures, or things of great delight, which men use to hide for the aptness they have to catch[1] men's[2] fancies; and the thoughts once awaked to that, harder sure it is to keep those thoughts from accomplishment than it had[3] been before to have kept the mind (which being the chief part, by this means is defiled) from thinking.

' "Lastly, for the recommending so principal a charge of the Princess Pamela (whose mind goes beyond the governing of many thousands such) to such a person as Dametas is – besides that the thing in itself is strange, it comes of a very evil ground that ignorance should be the mother of faithfulness. Oh no, he cannot be good that knows not why he is good, but stands so far good as his fortune may keep him unassayed. But coming once to that, his rude simplicity is either easily changed or easily deceived; and so grows that to be the last excuse of his fault which seemed to have been the first foundation of his faith.

' "Thus far hath your commandment and my zeal drawn me, which I, like a man in a valley that may discern hills, or like a poor passenger that may spy

---

[1] catch] each 93 (*uncorr.*), 98, 13   [2] men's] man's *Ph*,93   [3] than it had] than had 93 (*uncorr.*), 98, 13

a rock, so humbly submit to your gracious consideration, beseeching you again to stand wholly upon your own virtue as the surest way to maintain you in that you are, and to avoid any evil which may be imagined."

'By the contents of this letter you may perceive that the cause of all hath been the vanity which possesseth many, who (making a perpetual mansion of this poor baiting-place of man's life) are desirous to know the certainty of things to come, wherein there is nothing so certain as our continual uncertainty. But what in particular points the oracle was, in faith I know not; neither, as you may see by one place of Philanax letter, he himself distinctly knew. But this experience shows us that Basilius' judgement, corrupted with a prince's fortune, hath rather heard than followed the wise (as I take it) counsel of Philanax. For having left[1] the stern of his government with much amazement to the people, among whom many strange bruits are received for current; and with some apparence of danger in respect of the valiant Amphialus, his nephew; and much envy in the ambitious number of the nobility against Philanax to see Philanax so advanced (though to speak simply he deserve more than as many of us as there be in Arcadia), the prince himself hath hidden his head in such sort as I told you, not sticking plainly to confess that he means not while he breathes that his daughters shall have any husband, but keep them thus solitary with him, where he gives no other body leave to visit him at any time but a certain priest, who being excellent in poetry, he makes him write out such things as he best likes, he being no less delightful in conversation than needful for devotion, and about twenty specified shepherds in whom, some for exercises and some for eclogues, he taketh greater recreation.

'And now you know as much as myself, wherein if I have held you over long, lay hardly the fault upon my old age, which in the very disposition of it is talkative – whether it be,' said he smiling, 'that nature loves to exercise that part most which is least decayed – and that is our tongue; or that knowledge being the only thing whereof we poor old men can brag, we cannot make it known but by utterance; or that mankind, by all means seeking to eternize himself so much the more as he is near his end, doth it not only by the children that come of him, but by speeches and writings recommended to the memory of hearers and readers. And yet thus much I will say for myself: that I have not laid these matters either so openly or largely to any as yourself, so much (if I much fail not) do I see in you which makes me both love and trust you.'

'Never may he be old,' answered Palladius, 'that doth not reverence that age whose heaviness, if it weigh down the frail and fleshly balance, it as much lifts up the noble and spiritual part; and well might you have alleged

---

[1] left *Cm, 93*: lost *90*

another reason – that their wisdom makes them willing to profit others, and that have I received of you, never to be forgotten but with ungratefulness. But among many strange conceits you told me which have showed effects in your prince, truly even the last – that he should conceive such pleasure in shepherds' discourses – would not seem the least unto me, saving that you told me at the first that this country is notable in those wits and that, indeed, myself having been brought not only to this place but to my life by Strephon and Claius, in their conference found wits as might better become such shepherds as Homer speaks of, that be governors of peoples, than such senators who hold their council in a sheepcote.'

'For them two,' said Kalander, 'especially Claius, they are beyond the rest by so much as learning commonly doth add to nature; for having neglected their wealth in respect of their knowledge, they have not so much impaired the meaner as they bettered the better – which all (notwithstanding it is a sport to hear how) they impute to love, which hath endued their thoughts, say they, with such a strength.

'But certainly, all the people of this country from high to low is given to those sports of the wit, so as you would wonder to hear how soon even children will begin to versify. Once, ordinary it is among the meanest sort to make songs and dialogues in metre, either love whetting their brain or, long peace having begun it, example and emulation amending it – not so much but the clown Dametas will stumble sometimes upon some songs that might become a better brain. But no sort of people so excellent in that kind as the pastors, for their living standing but upon the looking to their beasts, they have ease, the nurse of poetry. Neither are our shepherds such as I hear they be in other countries, but they are the very owners of the sheep to which either themselves look, or their children give daily attendance. And then truly it would delight you, under some tree or by some river's side, when two or three of them meet together, to hear their rural muse; how prettily it will deliver out sometimes joys, sometimes lamentations, sometimes challengings one of the other, sometimes under hidden forms uttering such matters as otherwise they durst not deal with. Then have they[1] most commonly one who judgeth the price to the best doer – of which they are no less glad than great princes are of triumphs – and his part is to set down in writing all that is said, save that it may be his pen with more leisure doth polish the rudeness of an unthought-on song.

'Now the choice of all (as you may well think) either for goodness of voice or pleasantness of wit the prince hath, among whom also there are two or three strangers, whom inward melancholies having made weary of the world's eyes have come to spend their lives among the country people of

---

[1] have they *Cm, 93*: they have *90*

Arcadia, and their conversation being well approved, the prince vouchsafeth them his presence; and not only by looking on, but by great courtesy and liberality, animates the shepherds the more exquisitely to labour for his good liking; so that there is no cause to blame the prince for sometimes hearing them. The blameworthiness is that to hear them he rather goes to solitariness than makes them come to company. Neither do I accuse my master for advancing a countryman, as Dametas is – since, God forbid, but where worthiness is, as truly it is among divers of that fellowship, any outward lowness should hinder the highest raising – but that he would needs make election of one, the baseness of whose mind is such that it sinks a thousand degrees lower than the basest body could carry the most base fortune, which, although it might be answered for the prince that it is rather a trust he hath in his simple plainness than any great advancement, being but chief herdman, yet all honest hearts feel that the trust of their lord goes beyond all advancement.

'But I am ever too long upon him when he crosseth the way of my speech, and by the shadow of yonder tower I see it is a fitter time with our supper to pay the duties we owe to our stomachs, than to break the air with my idle discourses. And more wit I might have learned of Homer, whom even now you mentioned, who never entertained either guests or hosts with long speeches, till the mouth of hunger be throughly stopped.'

So withal he rose, leading Palladius through the garden again to the parlour where they used to sup, Palladius assuring him that he had already been more fed to his liking than he could be by the skilfullest trencher-men of Media. But[1] being come to the supping place, one of Kalander's servants rounded in his ear, at which, his colour changing, he retired himself into his chamber, commanding his men diligently to wait [and attend][2] upon Palladius, and to excuse his absence with some necessary business he had presently to dispatch – which they accordingly did, for some few days forcing themselves to let no change appear. But though they framed their countenances never so cunningly, Palladius perceived there was some ill-pleasing accident fallen out. Whereupon being again set alone at supper, he called to the steward and desired him to tell him the matter of his sudden alteration; who, after some trifling excuses, in the end confessed unto him that his master had received news that his son, before the day of his near marriage, chanced to be at a battle which was to be fought between the

---

[1] Media. But *Cm, 93*. Media. Chap. 5. The sorrow of Kalander for his son Clitophon; the story of Argalus and Parthenia: their perfections, their love, their troubles, her empoisoning, his rare constancy, her strange refusal, their pathologies, her flight, his revenge on his rival the mischief-worker Demagoras, then captain of the rebel helots who take him, and Clitophon that sought to help him – but both are kept alive by their new captain. But *90*   [2] and attend] *om. Cm, 93*

gentlemen of Lacedaemon and the helots – who winning the victory, he was there made prisoner, going to deliver a friend of his taken prisoner by the helots; that the poor young gentleman had offered great ransom for his life, but that the hate those peasants conceived against all gentlemen was such that every hour he was to look for nothing but some cruel death, which hitherunto had only been delayed by the captain's vehement dealing for him, who seemed to have a heart of more manly pity than the rest; which loss had stricken the old gentleman with such sorrow as, if abundance of tears did not seem sufficiently to witness it, he was alone retired tearing his beard and hair and cursing his old age that had not made his grave to stop his ears from such advertisements; but that his faithful servants had written in his name to all his friends, followers, and tenants (Philanax the governor refusing to deal in it – as a private cause – but yet giving leave to seek their best redress so as they wronged not the state of Lacedaemon) of whom there were now gathered upon the frontiers good forces that, he was sure, would spend their lives by any way to redeem or revenge Clitophon.

'Now, sir,' said he, 'this is my master's nature: though his grief be such as to live is a grief unto him, and that even his reason is darkened with sorrow, yet the laws of hospitality long and holily observed by him give still such a sway to his proceeding that he will no way suffer the stranger lodged under his roof to receive as it were any infection of his anguish – especially you, toward whom I know not whether his love or admiration be greater.'

But Palladius could scarce hear out his tale with patience, so was his heart torn in pieces with compassion of the case, liking of Kalander's noble behaviour, kindness for his respect to himward, and desire to find some remedy – besides the image of his dearest friend Daiphantus, whom he judged to suffer either a like or a worse fortune. Therefore, rising from the board, he desired the steward to tell him particularly the ground and event of this accident, because by knowledge of many circumstances there might perhaps some way of help be opened; whereunto the steward easily, in this sort, condescended:

'My lord,' said he, 'when our good King Basilius, with better success than expectation, took to wife even in his more than decaying years the fair young Princess Gynecia, there came with her a young lord, cousin-german to herself, named Argalus – led hither partly with the love and honour of his noble kinswoman, partly with the humour of youth which ever thinks that good whose goodness he sees not. And in this court he received so good increase of knowledge that, after some years spent, he so manifested a most virtuous mind in all his actions that Arcadia gloried such a plant was transported unto them – being a gentleman indeed most rarely accomplished, excellently learned, but without all vainglory; friendly without factiousness; valiant so as, for my part, I think the earth hath no man that hath done more heroical acts than he, howsoever now of late the fame flies of the two princes of Thessalia and Macedon, and hath long done of our noble Prince Amphialus, who indeed in our parts is only accounted likely to match him – but I say, for my part, I think no man for valour of mind and ability of body to be preferred, if equalled, to Argalus, and yet so valiant as he never durst do anybody injury; in behaviour, some will say ever sad – surely sober and somewhat given to musing, but never uncourteous; his word ever led by his thought and followed by his deed; rather liberal than magnificent, though the one wanted not and the other had ever good choice of the receiver: in sum, for I perceive I shall easily take a great draught of his praises, whom both I and all this country love so well, such a man was, and I hope is, Argalus as hardly the nicest eye can find a spot in – if the over-vehement constancy of yet spotless affection may not in hardwrested constructions be counted a spot, which in this manner began that work in him which hath made both him (and itself in him) over all this country famous. My master's son, Clitophon, whose loss gives the cause to this discourse, and yet gives me cause to begin with Argalus since his loss proceeds from Argalus, being a young gentleman (as of great birth being our king's sister's son, so truly of good nature, and one that can see good and love it) haunted more the company of this worthy Argalus than of any other; so as, if there were not a friendship – which is so rare as it is to be doubted whether it be a thing indeed or but a word – at least there was such a liking and friendliness as hath brought forth the effects which you shall hear.

'About two years since it so fell out that he brought him to a great lady's house, sister to my master, who had with her her only daughter, the fair Parthenia – fair indeed (fame, I think, itself daring not to call any fairer, if it be not Helena, queen of Corinth, and the two incomparable sisters of Arcadia), and that which made her fairness much the fairer was that it was but a fair embassador of a most fair mind full of wit, and a wit which delighted more to judge itself than to show itself; her speech being as rare as precious, her silence without sullenness, her modesty without affectation, her shamefastness without ignorance: in sum, one, that to praise well, one must first set down with himself what it is to be excellent – for so she is. I think you think that these perfections meeting could not choose but find one another and delight in that they found, for likeness of manners is likely, in reason, to draw liking with affection. Men's actions do not always cross with reason; to be short, it did so indeed. They loved – although for awhile

BOOK ONE

the fire thereof (hope's wings being cut off) were blown by the bellows of despair, upon this occasion.

'There had been a good while before, and so continued, a suitor to this same lady, a great nobleman (though of Laconia, yet near neighbour to Parthenia's mother) named Demagoras – a man mighty in riches and power, and proud thereof; stubbornly stout, loving nobody but himself, and for his own delight's sake, Parthenia. And pursuing vehemently his desire, his riches had so gilded over all his other imperfections that the old lady (though contrary to my lord her brother's mind) had given her consent; and using a mother's authority upon her fair daughter had made her yield thereunto, not because she liked her choice, but because her obedient mind had not yet taken upon it to make choice. And the day of their assurance drew near when my young Lord Clitophon brought this noble Argalus, perchance principally to see so rare a sight as Parthenia by all well-judging eyes was judged. But though few days were before the time of assurance appointed, yet love that saw he had a great journey to make in short time hasted so himself that, before her word could tie her to Demagoras, her heart hath vowed her to Argalus – with so grateful a receipt in mutual affection that, if she desired above all things to have Argalus, Argalus feared nothing but to miss Parthenia. And now Parthenia had learned both liking and misliking, loving and loathing, and out of passion began to take the authority of judgement – insomuch that when the time came that Demagoras (full of proud joy) thought to receive the gift of herself, she with words of resolute refusal (though with tears showing she was sorry she must refuse) assured her mother she would first be bedded in her grave than wedded to Demagoras.

'The change was no more strange than unpleasant to the mother, who being determinately – lest I should say of a great lady, *wilfully* – bent to marry her to Demagoras, tried all ways which a witty and hard-hearted mother could use upon so humble a daughter, in whom the only resisting power was love. But the more she assaulted, the more she taught Parthenia to defend; and the more Parthenia defended, the more she made her mother obstinate in the assault; who at length finding that Argalus standing between them was it that most eclipsed her affection from shining upon Demagoras, she sought all means how to remove him, so much the more as he manifested himself an unremovable suitor to her daughter, first by employing him in as many dangerous enterprises as ever the evil stepmother Juno recommended to the famous Hercules. But the more his virtue was tried, the more pure it grew, while all the things she did to overthrow him did set him up upon the height of honour – enough to have moved her heart, especially to a man every way so worthy as Argalus; but she struggling against all reason because she would have her will, and show her authority in matching her with Demagoras, the more virtuous Argalus was, the more she hated him, thinking herself conquered in his conquests, and therefore still employing him in more and more dangerous attempts. Meanwhile[1] she used all extremities possible upon her fair daughter to make her give over herself to her direction – but it was hard to judge whether he in doing or she in suffering showed greater constancy of affection; for, as to Argalus the world sooner wanted occasions than he valour to go through them, so to Parthenia malice sooner ceased than her unchanged patience. Lastly, by treasons Demagoras and she would have made away Argalus; but he with providence and courage so passed over all, that the mother took such a spiteful grief at it that her heart brake withal, and she died.

'But then Demagoras – assuring himself that now Parthenia was her own she would never be his, and receiving as much by her own determinate answer, not more desiring his own happiness than envying Argalus, whom he saw with narrow eyes even ready to enjoy the perfection of his desires – strengthening his conceit with all the mischievous counsels which disdained love and envious pride could give unto him, the wicked wretch taking a time that Argalus was gone to his country to fetch some of his principal friends to honour the marriage which Parthenia had most joyfully consented unto, the wicked Demagoras, I say, desiring to speak with her, with unmerciful force (her weak arms in vain resisting) rubbed all over her face a most horrible poison, the effect whereof was such that never leper looked more ugly than she did; which done, having his men and horses ready, departed away in spite of her servants, as ready to revenge as they could be in such an unexpected mischief. But the abominableness of this fact being come to my Lord Kalander, he made such means both by our king's intercession and his own that by the king and senate of Lacedaemon Demagoras was upon pain of death banished the country; who hating the punishment where he should have hated the fault, joined himself with all the powers he could make unto the helots, lately in rebellion against that state – and they, glad to have a man of such authority among them, made him their general, and under him have committed divers the most outrageous villainies that a base multitude full of desperate revenge can imagine.

'But within awhile after this pitiful fact committed upon Parthenia, Argalus returned, poor gentleman, having her fair image in his heart, and already promising his eyes the uttermost of his felicity, when they (nobody else daring to tell it him) were the first messengers to themselves of their

---

[1] attempts. Meanwhile] attempts. In the meanwhile 93

own misfortune. I mean not to move passions with telling you the grief of both when he knew her – for at first he did not, nor at first knowledge could possibly have virtue's aid so ready as not even weakly to lament the loss of such a jewel, so much the more as that skilful men in that art assured it was unrecoverable. But within a while, truth of love which still held the first face in his memory, a virtuous constancy and even a delight to be constant, faith given, and inward worthiness shining through the foulest mists, took so full hold of the noble Argalus that, not only in such comfort which witty arguments may bestow upon adversity, but even with the most abundant kindness that an eye-ravished lover can express, he laboured both to drive the extremity of sorrow from her and to hasten the celebration of their marriage – whereunto he unfeignedly showed himself no less cheerfully earnest than if she had never been disinherited of that goodly portion which nature had so liberally bequeathed unto her; and for that cause deferred his intended revenge upon Demagoras, because he might continually be in her presence, showing more humble serviceableness and joy to content her than ever before.

'But as he gave this rare ensample, not to be hoped for of any other but of another Argalus, so of the other side she took as strange a course in affection; for where she desired to enjoy him more than to live, yet did she overthrow both her own desire and his, and in no sort would yield to marry him – with a strange encounter of love's affects and effects, that he by an affection sprung from excessive beauty should delight in horrible foulness, and she, of a vehement desire to have him, should kindly build a resolution never to have him – for truth is that so in heart she loved him as she could not find in her heart he should be tied to what was unworthy of his presence.

'Truly, sir, a very good orator might have a fair field to use eloquence in if he did but only repeat the lamentable and truly affectionated speeches, while he conjured her by remembrance of her affection, and true oaths of his own affection, not to make him so unhappy as to think he had not only lost her face, but her heart; that her face, when it was fairest, had been but as a marshal to lodge the love of her in his mind, which now was so well placed as it needed no further help of any outward harbinger; beseeching her even with tears to know that his love was not so superficial as to go no further than the skin, which yet now to him was most fair, since it was hers; how could he be so ungrateful as to love her the less for that which she had only received for his sake; that he never beheld it but therein he saw the loveliness of her love toward him, protesting unto her that he would never take joy of his life if he might not enjoy her, for whom principally he was glad he had life. But (as I heard by one that overheard them) she, wringing him by the hand, made no other answer but this:

'"My lord," said she, "God knows, I love you. If I were princess of the whole world, and had withal all the blessings that ever the world brought forth, I should not make delay to lay myself and them under your feet; or if I had continued but as I was, though I must confess far unworthy of you, yet would I (with too great a joy for my heart now to[1] think of) have accepted your vouchsafing me to be yours, and with faith and obedience would have supplied all other defects – but first let me be much more miserable than I am, ere I match Argalus to such a Parthenia. Live happy, dear Argalus. I give you full liberty, and I beseech you take it; and I assure you I shall rejoice, whatsoever become of me, to see you so coupled as may be fit both for your honour and satisfaction."

'With that she burst out in crying and weeping, not able longer to contain herself from blaming her fortune, and wishing her own death. But Argalus with a most heavy heart still pursuing his desire, she fixed of mind to avoid further entreaty and to fly all company, which even of him grew unpleasant unto her, one night she stole away – but whither as yet is unknown, or indeed, what is become of her. Argalus sought her long and in many places. At length, despairing to find her (and the more he despaired, the more enraged), weary of his life, but first determining to be revenged of Demagoras, he went alone disguised into the chief town held by the helots; where coming into his presence guarded about by many of his soldiers, he could delay his fury no longer for a fitter time, but setting upon him in despite of a great many that helped him, gave him divers mortal wounds; and himself no question had been there presently murthered, but that Demagoras himself desired he might be kept alive, perchance with intention to feed his own eyes with some cruel execution to be laid upon him. But death came sooner than he looked for, yet having had leisure to appoint his successor, a young man not long before delivered out of the prison of the king of Lacedaemon, where he should have suffered death for having slain the king's nephew; but him he named, who at that time was absent making roads upon the Lacedaemonians, but being returned, the rest of the helots, for the great liking they conceived of that young man, especially because they had none among themselves to whom the others would yield, were content to follow Demagoras' appointment. And well hath it succeeded with them, he having since done things beyond the hope of the youngest heads, of whom I speak the rather because he hath hitherto preserved Argalus alive, under pretence

---

[1] heart now to *Cm*, *98*, *13*: heart to *90*, *93*

to have him publicly and with exquisite torments executed after the end of these wars, of which they hope for a soon and prosperous issue.

'And he hath likewise hitherto kept my young Lord Clitophon alive, who to redeem his friend went with certain other noblemen of Laconia, and forces gathered by them, to besiege this young and new successor. But he issuing out, to the wonder of all men defeated the Laconians, slew many of the noblemen, and took Clitophon prisoner – whom with much ado he keepeth alive, the helots being villainously cruel. But he tempereth them so, sometimes by following their humour, sometimes by striving with it, that hitherto he hath saved both their lives – but in different estates, Argalus being kept in a close and hard prison, Clitophon at some liberty. And now, sir, though to say the truth we can promise ourselves little of their safeties while they are in the helots' hands, I have delivered all I understand touching the loss of my lord's son and the cause thereof, which though it was not necessary to Clitophon's case to be so particularly told, yet the strangeness of it made me think it would not be unpleasant unto you.'

Palladius[1] thanked him greatly for it, being even passionately delighted with hearing so strange an accident of a knight so famous over the world as Argalus, with whom he had himself a long desire to meet, so had fame poured a noble emulation in him towards him. But then well bethinking himself, he called for armour, desiring them to provide him of horse and guide; and armed all saving the head he went up to Kalander, whom he found lying upon the ground, having ever since banished both sleep and food as enemies to the mourning which passion persuaded him was reasonable. But Palladius raised him up, saying unto him:

'No more, no more of this, my Lord Kalander; let us labour to find before we lament the loss. You know myself miss one who, though he be not my son, I would disdain the favour of life after him. But while there is hope left, let not the weakness of sorrow make the strength of it languish; take comfort, and good success will follow.'

And with those words, comfort seemed to lighten in his eyes, and that in his face and gesture was painted victory. Once, Kalander's spirits were so revived withal, that receiving some sustenance and taking a little rest, he armed himself and those few of his servants he had left unsent, and so, himself guided Palladius to the place upon the frontiers where already there were assembled between three and four thousand men, all well disposed for Kalander's sake to abide any peril – but like men disused with a long

---

[1] you.' Palladius *Cm*, 93: you.' Chap. 6. Kalander's expedition against the helots; their estate; Palladius' stratagem against them, which prevaileth; the helots' resistance, discomfiture, and reinforce by the return of their new captain; the combat and interknowledge of Daiphantus and Palladius, and by their means a peace, with the release of Kalander and Clitophon. Palladius *90*

peace, more determinate to do than skilful how to do, lusty bodies and brave armours, with such courage as rather grew of despising their enemies whom they knew not, than of any confidence for anything which in themselves they knew, but neither cunning use of their weapons, nor art showed in their marching or encamping;[1] which Palladius soon perceiving, he desired to understand, as much as could be delivered unto him, the estate of the helots.

And he was answered by a man well acquainted with the affairs of Laconia that they were a kind of people, who having been of old freemen and possessioners, the Lacedaemonians had conquered them, and laid not only tribute but bondage upon them, which they had long borne till of late (the Lacedaemonians through greediness growing more heavy than they could bear, and through contempt less careful how to make them bear) they had with a general consent, rather springing by the generalness of the cause than of any artificial practice, set themselves in arms. And whetting their courage with revenge, and grounding their resolution upon despair, they had proceeded with unlooked-for success, having already taken divers towns and castles with the slaughter of many of the gentry, for whom no sex nor age could be accepted for an excuse. And that although at the first they had fought rather with beastly fury than any soldierly discipline, practice had now made them[2] comparable to the best of the Lacedaemonians; and more of late than ever, by reason first of Demagoras, a great lord who had made himself of their party, and since his death of another captain they had gotten, who had brought up their ignorance and brought down their fury to such a mean of good government, and withal led them so valorously, that besides the time wherein Clitophon was taken, they had the better in some other great conflicts – in such wise that the estate of Lacedaemon had sent unto them, offering peace with most reasonable and honourable conditions.

Palladius having gotten this general knowledge of the party against whom (as he had already of the party for whom) he was to fight, he went to Kalander and told him plainly that by plain force there was small apparence of helping Clitophon, but some device was to be taken in hand wherein no less discretion than valour was to be used, whereupon the council of the chief men was called. And at last, this way Palladius (who by some experience, but especially by reading histories, was acquainted with stratagems) invented, and was by all the rest approved, that all the men there should dress themselves like the poorest sort of the people in Arcadia, having no banners but bloody shirts hanged upon long staves, with some bad bagpipes instead of drum and fife; their armour they should, as well as might

---

[1] encamping] in camping 93   [2] them *Cm, 93*: then *90*

be, cover, or at least make them look so rustily and ill-favouredly as might well become such wearers. And this the whole number should do, saving two hundred of the best-chosen gentlemen for courage and strength, whereof Palladius himself would be one, who should have their arms chained and be put in carts like prisoners.

This being performed according to the agreement, they marched on towards the town of Cardamyla, where Clitophon was captive. And being come two hours before sunset within view of the walls, the helots already descrying their number and beginning to sound the alarum, they sent a cunning fellow (so much the cunninger as that he could mask it under rudeness) who with such a kind of rhetoric as weeded out all flowers of rhetoric delivered unto the helots assembled together that they were country people of Arcadia, no less oppressed by their lords and no less desirous of liberty than they, and therefore had put themselves in the field, and had already, besides a great number slain, taken nine or ten score gentlemen prisoners, whom they had there well and fast chained. Now because they had no strong retiring-place in Arcadia and were not yet of number enough to keep the field against their prince's forces, they were come to them for succour, knowing that daily more and more of their quality would flock unto them, but that in the meantime, lest their prince should pursue them, or the Lacedaemonian king and nobility for the likeness of the cause fall upon them, they desired that, if there were not room enough for them in the town, that yet they might encamp under the walls, and for surety have their prisoners (who were such men as were ever able to make their peace) kept within the town.

The helots made but a short consultation, being glad that their contagion had spread itself into Arcadia, and making account that if the peace did not fall out between them and their king that it was the best way to set fire in all the parts of Greece (besides their greediness to have so many gentlemen in their hands in whose ransoms they already meant to have a share), to which haste of concluding two things well helped: the one, that their captain with the wisest of them was at that time absent about confirming or breaking the peace with the state of Lacedaemon; the second, that over-many good fortunes began to breed a proud recklessness in them. Therefore sending to view the camp, and finding that by their speech they were Arcadians with whom they had had no war (never suspecting a private man's credit could have gathered such a force) and that all other tokens witnessed them to be of the lowest calling – besides, the chains upon the gentlemen, they granted not only leave for the prisoners, but for some others of the company; and to all, that they might harbour under the walls. So opened they the gates and received in the carts; which being done, and Palladius seeing fit time, he gave the sign; and shaking off their chains (which were made with such art that, though they seemed most strong and fast, he that ware them might easily loose them) drew their swords hidden in the carts, and so, setting upon the ward, made them to fly either from the place or from their bodies, and so give entry to all the force of the Arcadians before the helots could make any head to resist them.

But the helots being men hardened against dangers gathered as well as they could together in the market-place, and thence would have given a shrewd welcome to the Arcadians, but that Palladius (blaming those that were slow, heartening them that were forward, but especially with his own ensample leading them) made such an impression into the squadron of the helots that, at first the great body of them beginning to shake and stagger, at length every particular body recommended the protection of his life to his feet. Then Kalander cried to go to the prison where he thought his son was, but Palladius wished him (first scouring the streets) to house all the helots, and make themselves masters of the gates. But ere that could be accomplished the helots had gotten new heart, and with divers sorts of shot from corners of streets and house windows galled them; which courage was come unto them by the return of their captain, who, though he brought not many with him, having dispersed most of his companies to other of his holds, yet meeting a great number running out of the gate (not yet possessed by the Arcadians), he made them turn face, and with banners displayed, his trumpet gave[1] the loudest testimony he could of his return; which once heard, the rest of the helots which were otherwise scattered bent thitherward with a new life of resolution – as if their captain had been a root out of which, as into branches, their courage had sprung.

Then began the fight to grow most sharp, and the encounters of more cruel obstinacy, the Arcadians fighting to keep that they had won, the helots to recover what they had lost; the Arcadians (as in an unknown place) having no succour but in their hands, the helots (as in their own place) fighting for their livings, wives, and children. There was victory and courage against revenge and despair, safety of both sides being no otherwise to be gotten but by destruction. At length, the left wing of the Arcadians began to lose ground; which Palladius seeing, he straight thrust himself with his choice band against the throng that oppressed them, with such an overflowing of valour that the captain of the helots (whose eyes soon judged of that wherewith themselves were governed) saw that he alone was worth all the rest of the Arcadians; which he so wondered at that it was hard to say whether he more liked his doings, or misliked the effects of his doings; but determining that upon that cast the game lay, and disdaining to fight with any other,

---

[1] gave *Cm*, 93: give 90, 98, 13

sought only to join with him – which mind was no less in Palladius, having easily marked that he was as the first mover of all the other hands.

And so, their thoughts meeting in one point, they consented (though not agreed) to try each other's fortune. And so, drawing themselves to be the uttermost of the one side, they began a combat which was so much inferior to the battle in noise and number as it was surpassing it in bravery of fighting and, as it were, delightful terribleness. Their courage was guided with skill and their skill was armed with courage. Neither did their hardiness darken their wit, nor their wit cool their hardiness; both valiant, as men despising death, both confident, as unwonted to be overcome – yet doubtful by their present feeling, and respectful by what they had already seen; their feet steady, their hands diligent, their eyes watchful, and their hearts resolute. The parts either not armed or weakly armed were well known, and according to the knowledge should have been sharply visited, but that the answer was as quick as the objection; yet some lighting,[1] the smart bred rage and the rage bred smart again; till both sides beginning to wax faint, and rather desirous to die accompanied than hopeful to live victorious, the captain of the helots, with a blow whose violence grew of fury not of strength, or of strength proceeding of fury, strake Palladius upon the side of the head, that he reeled astonied, and withal the helmet fell off, he remaining bareheaded. But other of the Arcadians were ready to shield him from any harm might rise of that nakedness; but little needed it, for his chief enemy, instead of pursuing that advantage, kneeled down, offering to deliver the pommel of his sword in token of yielding, withal speaking aloud unto him that he thought it more liberty to be his prisoner than any others' general.

Palladius standing upon himself and misdoubting some craft, and the helots that were next their captain wavering between looking for some stratagem or fearing treason, 'What!' said the captain, 'hath Palladius forgotten the voice of Daiphantus?'

By that watchword Palladius knew that it was his only friend Pyrocles whom he had lost upon the sea. And therefore both (most full of wonder so to be met, if they had not been fuller of joy than wonder) caused the retrait to be sounded – Daiphantus by authority and Palladius by persuasion, to which helped well the little advantage that was of either side, and that of the helots' party their captain's behaviour had made as many amazed as saw or heard of it, and of the Arcadian side the good old Kalander, striving more than his old age could achieve, was newly taken prisoner. But indeed the chief parter of the fray was the night, which with her black arms pulled their malicious sights one from the other.

---

[1] lighting] lightning *Cm*, 93 (*uncorr.*), 98

But he that took Kalander meant nothing less than to save him – but only so long as the captain might learn the enemy's secrets, towards whom he led the old gentleman when he caused the retreat to be sounded, looking for no other delivery from that captivity but by the painful taking away of all pain; when whom should he see next to the captain, with good tokens how valiantly he had fought that day against the Arcadians, but his son Clitophon! But now the captain had caused all the principal helots to be assembled, as well to deliberate what they had to do, as to receive a message from the Arcadians – among whom Palladius' virtue, besides the love Kalander bare him, having gotten principal authority, he had persuaded them to seek rather by parley to recover the father and the son than by the sword, since the goodness of the captain assured him that way to speed, and his value, wherewith he was of old acquainted, made him think any other way dangerous. This therefore was done in orderly manner, giving them to understand that, as they came but to deliver Clitophon, so, offering to leave the footing they already had in the town, to go away without any further hurt, so as they might have the father and the son without ransom delivered. Which conditions being heard and conceived by the helots, Daiphantus persuaded them without delay to accept them.

'For first,' said he, 'since the strife is within our own home, if you lose, you lose all that in this life can be dear unto you; if you win, it will be a bloody victory with no profit but the flattering in ourselves that same bad humour of revenge; besides, it is like to stir Arcadia upon us, which now, by using these persons well, may be brought to some amity; lastly, but especially, lest the king and nobility of Laconia (with whom now we have made a perfect peace) should hope by occasion of this quarrel to join the Arcadians with them, and so break off the profitable agreement already concluded. In sum, as in all deliberations weighing the profit of the good success with the harm of the evil success, you shall find this way most safe and honourable.'

The helots, as much moved by his authority as persuaded by his reasons, were content therewith – whereupon Palladius took order that the Arcadians should presently march out of the town taking with them their prisoners, while the night with mutual diffidence might keep them quiet, and ere day came they might be well on of their way, and so avoid those accidents which in late enemies a look, a word, or a particular man's quarrel might engender. This being on both sides concluded on, Kalander and Clitophon (who now with infinite joy did know each other) came to kiss the hands and feet of Daiphantus, Clitophon telling his father how Daiphantus, not without danger to himself, had preserved him from the furious malice of the helots,

BOOK ONE 33

and even that day going to conclude the peace, lest in his absence he might receive some hurt, he had taken him in his company and given him armour upon promise he should take the part of the helots; which he had in this[1] fight performed, little knowing that it was against his father.

'But,' said Clitophon, 'here is he who as a father hath new-begotten me, and as a god hath saved me from many deaths which already laid hold on me'; which Kalander with tears of joy acknowledged, besides his own deliverance, only his benefit.

But Daiphantus, who loved doing well for itself and not for thanks, brake off those ceremonies, desiring to know how Palladius (for so he called Musidorus) was come into that company, and what his present estate was; whereof receiving a brief declaration of Kalander, he sent him word by Clitophon that he should not as now come unto him because he held himself not so sure a master of the helots' minds that he would adventure him in their power, who was so well-known with an unfriendly acquaintance, but that he desired him to return with Kalander, whither also he within few days, having dispatched himself of the helots, would repair. Kalander would needs kiss his hand again for that promise, protesting he would esteem his house more blessed than a temple of the gods if it had once received him; and then desiring pardon for Argalus, Daiphantus assured them that he would die but he would bring him – though till then kept in close prison, indeed for his safety, the helots being so animated against him as else he could not have lived. And so, taking their leave of him, Kalander, Clitophon, Palladius, and the rest of the Arcadians swearing that they would no further in any sort molest the helots, they straightway marched out of the town carrying both their dead and wounded bodies with them, and by morning were already within the limits of Arcadia.

The[2] helots of the other side shutting their gates, gave themselves to bury their dead, to cure their wounds, and rest their wearied bodies, till the next day bestowing the cheerful use of the light upon them, Daiphantus, making a general convocation, spake unto them in this manner:

'We are first,' said he, 'to thank the gods that, further than we had either cause to hope or reason to imagine, have delivered us out of this gulf of danger wherein we were already swallowed; for all being lost, had they not[3] directed my return so just as they did, it had been too late to recover that which, being had, we could not keep. And had I not happened to know one of the principal men among them, by which means the truce began between

---

[1] his *Cm, 93*: this *90, 98, 13* [2] Arcadia. The *Cm, 93*: Arcadia. Chap. 7. The articles of peace between the Lacedaemonians and helots: Daiphantus' departure from the helots with Argalus to Kalander's house; the offer of a strange lady to Argalus, his refusal, and who she was. The *90* [3] had they not *Cm, 93*: had they had not *90*

us, you may easily conceive what little reason we have to think but that, either by some supply out of Arcadia, or from the nobility of this country who would have made fruits of wisdom grow out of this occasion, we should have had our power turned to ruin, our pride to repentance and sorrow. But now the storm, as it fell,[1] so it ceased; and the error committed in retaining Clitophon more hardly than his age or quarrel deserved becomes a sharply learned experience to use in other times more moderation.

'Now have I to deliver unto you the conclusion between the kings, with the nobility of Lacedaemon, and you, which is in all points as yourselves desired, as well for that you would have granted, as for the assurance of what is granted. The towns and forts you presently have are still left unto you, to be kept either with or without garrison, so as you alter not the laws of the country and pay such duties as the rest of the Laconians do; yourselves are made by public decree freemen, and so capable both to give and receive voice in election of magistrates; the distinction of names between *helots* and *Lacedaemonians* to be quite taken away, and all indifferently to enjoy both names and privileges of Laconians; your children to be brought up with theirs in Spartan[2] discipline; and so you, framing yourselves to be good members of that estate, to be hereafter fellows and no longer servants – which conditions, you see, carry in themselves no more contentation than assurance, for this is not a peace which is made with them, but this is a peace by which you are made of them; lastly, a forgetfulness decreed of of all[3] what is past, they showing themselves glad to have so valiant men as you are joined with them – so that you are to take minds of peace since the cause of war is finished, and as you hated them before like oppressors, so now to love them as brothers, to take care of their estate because it is yours, and to labour by virtuous doing that the posterity may not repent your joining.

'But now, one article only they stood upon which in the end I with your commissioners have agreed unto, that I should no more tarry here, mistaking perchance my humour and thinking me as seditious as I am young; or else it is the King Amiclas' procuring, in respect that it was my ill hap to kill his nephew Eurileon. But howsoever it be, I have condescended.'

'But so will not we!' cried almost the whole assembly, counselling one another rather to try the uttermost event than to lose him by whom they had been victorious. But he, as well with general orations as particular dealing with the men of most credit, made them throughly see how necessary it was to prefer such an opportunity before a vain affection, but yet could not prevail till openly he sware that he would, if at any time the Lacedaemonians

---

[1] fell *Cm, 93*: fell out *90* [2] in Spartan] in Lacedaemonian *Cm*; in the Spartan *93* [3] decreed of of all] om. *Cm*; decreed of all *93*

brake this treaty, come back again and be their captain. So then, after a few days' settling¹ them in perfect order, he took his leave of them, whose eyes bad him farewell with tears, and mouths with kissing the places where he stepped, and (after) making temples unto him as to a demigod, thinking it beyond the degree of humanity to have a wit so far overgoing his age, and such dreadful terror proceed from so excellent beauty. But he, for his sake, obtained free pardon for Argalus, whom also, upon oath never to bear arms against the helots, he delivered. And taking only with him certain principal jewels of his own, he would have parted alone with Argalus (whose countenance well showed, while Parthenia was lost he counted not himself delivered) but that the whole multitude would needs guard him into Arcadia, where, again leaving them all to lament his departure, he by inquiry got to the well-known house of Kalander.

There was he received with loving joy of Kalander, with joyful love of Palladius, with humble (though doleful) demeanour of Argalus (whom specially² both he and Palladius regarded), with grateful serviceableness of Clitophon, and honourable admiration of all – for being now well-viewed to have no hair of his face to witness him a man, who had done acts beyond the degree of a man, and to look with a certain almost bashful kind of modesty, as if he feared the eyes of men, who was unmoved with sight of the most horrible countenances of death, and as if nature had mistaken her work to have a Mars' heart in a Cupid's body, all that beheld him (and all that might behold him did behold him) made their eyes quick messengers to their minds that there they had seen the uttermost that in mankind might be seen. The like wonder Palladius had before stirred, but that Daiphantus, as younger and newer come, had gotten now the advantage in the moist and fickle impression of eyesight.

But while all men, saving poor Argalus, made the joy of their eyes speak for their hearts towards Daiphantus, fortune (that belike was bid to that banquet and meant then to play the good-fellow) brought a pleasant adventure among them. It was that, as they had newly dined, there came in to Kalander a messenger that brought him word, a young noble lady, near kinswoman to the fair Helen, queen of Corinth, was come thither and desired to be lodged in his house. Kalander, most glad of such an occasion, went out, and all his other worthy guests with him – saving only Argalus, who remained in his chamber, desirous that this company were once broken up that he might go in his solitary quest after Parthenia. But when they met this lady, Kalander straight thought he saw his niece Parthenia, and was about in such familiar sort to have spoken unto her; but she in grave and

---

¹ settling] setting 93   ² specially] especially *Cm*, 13

honourable manner giving him to understand that he was mistaken, he (half ashamed) excused himself with the exceeding likeness was between them, though indeed it seemed that this[1] lady was of the more pure and dainty complexion.

She said, 'It might very well be, having been many times taken one for another.'

But as soon as she was brought into the house, before she would rest her she desired to speak with Argalus publicly, who she heard was in the house. Argalus came in hastily,[2] and as hastily thought as Kalander had done, with sudden changes of joy into sorrow. But she, when she had stayed their thoughts with telling them her name and quality, in this sort spake unto him:

'My Lord Argalus,' said she, 'being of late left in the court of Queen Helen of Corinth as chief in her absence, she being upon some occasion gone thence, there came unto me the Lady Parthenia, so disfigured[3] as I think Greece hath nothing so ugly to behold. For my part, it was many days before with vehement oaths and some good proofs she could make me think that she was Parthenia. Yet at last finding certainly it was she, and greatly pitying her misfortune (so much the more as that all men had ever told me, as now you do, of the great likeness between us), I took the best care I could of her, and of her understood the whole tragical history of her undeserved adventure, and therewithal of that most noble constancy in you, my Lord Argalus, which whosoever loves not shows himself to be a hater of virtue, and unworthy to live in the society of mankind. But no outward cherishing could salve the inward sore of her mind, but a few days since she died, before her death earnestly desiring and persuading me to think of no husband but of you, as of the only man in the world worthy to be loved. Withal she gave me this ring to deliver you, desiring you, and by the authority of love commanding you, that the affection you bare her you should turn to me, assuring you that nothing can please her soul more than to see you and me matched together. Now my lord, though this office be not perchance suitable to my estate nor sex (who should rather look to be desired), yet an extraordinary desert requires an extraordinary proceeding, and therefore I am come with faithful love built upon your worthiness to offer myself, and to beseech you to accept the offer; and if these noble gentlemen present will say it is great folly, let them withal say it is great love.'

And then she stayed, earnestly attending Argalus' answer, who, first making most hearty sighs do such obsequies as he could to Parthenia, thus answered her:

---

[1] this *Cm, 93*: his *90*   [2] came in hastily] came hastily *93*   [3] disfigured *Cm, 93*: disguised *90*

'Madam,' said he, 'infinitely bound am I[1] unto you for this no more rare than noble courtesy, but most bound for the goodness I perceive you showed to the Lady Parthenia.'

With that, the tears ran down his eyes, but he followed on:

'And as much as so unfortunate a man, fit to be the spectacle of misery, can do you service, determine you have made a purchase of a slave, while I live, never to fail you. But this great matter you propose unto me, wherein I am not so blind as not to see what happiness it should be unto me, excellent lady, know that, if my heart were mine to give, you before all other should have it – but Parthenia's it is, though dead. There I began, there I end all matter of affection. I hope I shall not long tarry after her, with whose beauty if I had only been in love, I should be so with you who have the same beauty. But it was Parthenia's self I loved, and love, which no likeness can make one, no commandment dissolve, no foulness defile, nor no death finish.'

'And shall I receive,' said she, 'such disgrace as to be refused?'

'Noble lady,' said he, 'let not that hard word be used, who know your exceeding worthiness far beyond my desert; but it is only happiness I refuse, since, of the only happiness I could and can desire, I am refused.'

He had scarce spoken those words when she ran to him; and embracing him, 'Why then, Argalus,' said she, 'take thy Parthenia!'

And Parthenia it was indeed. But because sorrow forbad him too soon to believe, she told him the truth with all circumstances – how being parted alone, meaning to die in some solitary place, as she happened to make her complaint, the Queen Helen of Corinth, who likewise felt her part of miseries being then walking also alone in that lonely[2] place, heard her, and never left till she had known the whole discourse; which the noble queen greatly pitying, she sent her to a physician of hers, the most excellent man in the world, in hope he could help her; which in such sort (as they saw) performed.[3] And she, taking with her of the queen's servants, thought yet to make this trial whether he would quickly forget his true Parthenia, or no. Her speech was confirmed by the Corinthian gentleman who before had kept her counsel, and Argalus easily persuaded to what more than ten thousand years of life he desired.

And Kalander would needs have the marriage celebrated in his house – principally the longer to hold his dear guests towards whom he was now, besides his own habit of hospitality, carried with love and duty, and therefore omitted no service that his wit could invent and his power minister; but[4] no way he saw he could so much pleasure them as by leaving

---

[1] bound am I] am I bound 93   [2] lonely 93: lovely Cm, 90   [3] saw) performed] saw) he had performed 93   [4] minister; but Cm, 93: minister. Chap. 8. The adventures first of Musidorus, then of Pyrocles, since their shipwrack to their meeting; the marriage of Argalus and Parthenia. But 90

the two friends alone, who being shrunk aside to the banqueting house where the pictures were, there Palladius recounted unto him that, after they had both abandoned the burning ship and either of them taken something under him the better to support him to the shore, he knew not how, but either with over-labouring in the fight and sudden cold, or the too much receiving of salt water, he was past himself; but yet holding fast (as the nature of dying men is to do) the chest that was under him, he was cast on the sands where he was taken up by a couple of shepherds, and by them brought to life again, and kept from drowning himself when he despaired of his safety; how after having failed to take him into the fisher-boat he had (by the shepherds' persuasion) come to this gentleman's house, where, being dangerously sick, he had yielded to seek the recovery of health only for that he might the sooner go seek the delivery of Pyrocles, to which purpose Kalander by some friends of his in Messena[1] had already set a ship or two abroad, when this accident of Clitophon's taking had so blessedly procured their meeting. Then did he set forth unto him the noble entertainment and careful cherishing of Kalander towards him; and so, upon occasion of the pictures present, delivered with the frankness of a friend's tongue, as near as he could, word by word what Kalander had told him touching the strange story, with all the particularities belonging, of Arcadia; which did in many sorts so delight Pyrocles to hear that he would needs have much of it again repeated, and was not contented till Kalander himself had answered him divers questions. But first, at Musidorus' request (though in brief manner, his mind much running upon the strange story of Arcadia) he did declare by what course of adventures he was come to make up their mutual happiness in meeting.

'When, cousin,' said he, 'we had stripped ourselves and were both leapt into the sea and swum a little toward the shore, I found by reason of some wounds I had that I should not be able to get the land, and therefore turned back again to the mast of the ship where you found me, assuring myself that if you came alive to the shore[2] you would seek me; if you were lost, as I thought it as good to perish as to live, so that place as good to perish in as another. There I found my sword among some of the shrouds, wishing (I must confess) if I died to be found with that in my hand, and withal waving it about my head, that sailors by it might[3] have the better glimpse of me. There, you missing me, I was taken up by pirates, who putting me underboard prisoner, presently set upon another ship, and maintaining a long fight in the end put them all to the sword – amongst whom I might hear them greatly praise one young man who fought most valiantly, whom (as

---

[1] Messena *Cm, 93*: Messenia *90* [2] to the shore] to shore *93, 13* [3] by it might] by might *93*

love is careful, and misfortune subject to doubtfulness) I thought certainly to be you.

'And so, holding you as dead from that time till the time I saw you, in truth I sought nothing more than a noble end, which perchance made me more hardy than otherwise I would have been – trial whereof came within two days after. For the kings of Lacedaemon having set out some galleys under the charge of one of their nephews to scour the sea of the pirates, they met with us, where our captain, wanting men, was driven to arm some of his prisoners, with promise of liberty for well-fighting – among whom I was one. And being boarded by the admiral, it was my fortune to kill Eurileon, the kings' nephew. But in the end they prevailed, and we were all taken prisoners, I not caring much what became of me, only keeping the name of *Daiphantus* according to the resolution you know is between us.

'But being laid in the jail of Taenaria with special hate to me for the death of Eurileon, the popular sort of that town conspired with the helots, and so by night opened them the gates, where entering and killing all of the gentle and rich faction, for honesty sake brake open all prisons, and so delivered me. And I, moved with gratefulness and encouraged with carelessness of life, so behaved myself in some conflicts they had within[1] few days, that they barbarously thinking unsensible wonders of me, and withal so much the better trusting me as they heard I was hated of the king of Lacedaemon, their chief captain being slain as you know by the noble Argalus (who helped thereunto by his persuasion, having borne a great affection unto me), and to avoid the dangerous emulation which grew among the chief, who should have the place, and also so[2] affected as rather to have a stranger than a competitor, they elected me (God wot, little proud of that dignity!), restoring unto me such things of mine as, being taken first by the pirates and then by the Lacedaemonians, they had gotten in the sack of the town. Now being in it, so good was my success with many victories that I made a peace for them to their own liking the very day that you delivered Clitophon, whom I with much ado had preserved. And in my peace the King Amiclas of Lacedaemon would needs have me banished and deprived of the dignity whereunto I was exalted, which (and you may see how much you are bound to me!) for your sake I was content to suffer, a new hope rising in me that you were not dead, and so meaning to travel over the world to seek you. And now here, my dear Musidorus, you have me.'

And with that, embracing and kissing each other, they called Kalander, of whom Daiphantus desired to hear the full story which before he had

---

[1] within *Cm*, 93: in *90*   [2] also so *Cm*: all so *90*; also *93*

recounted to Palladius, and to see the letter of Philanax, which he read and well marked.

But within some days after, the marriage between Argalus and the fair Parthenia being to be celebrated, Daiphantus and Palladius, selling some of their jewels, furnished themselves of very fair apparel, meaning to do honour to their loving host, who as much for their sakes as for the marriage set forth each thing in most gorgeous manner. But all the cost bestowed did not so much enrich, nor all the fine deckings so much beautify, nor all the dainty devices so much delight, as the fairness of Parthenia, the pearl of all the maids of Mantinea; who as she went to the temple to be married, her eyes themselves seemed a temple wherein love and beauty were married; her lips, although[1] they were kept close with modest silence, yet with a pretty kind of natural swelling they seemed to invite the guests that looked on them; her cheeks blushing, and withal when she was spoken unto a little smiling, were like roses when their leaves are with a little breath stirred; her hair being laid at the full length down her back bare show as, if the vaward failed, yet that would conquer.

Daiphantus marking her, 'O Jupiter!' said he, speaking to Palladius. 'How happens it that beauty is only confined to Arcadia?'– but Palladius not greatly attending his speech. Some days were continued in the solemnizing the marriage, with all conceits that might deliver delight to men's fancies, but[2] such a change was grown in Daiphantus that (as if cheerfulness had been tediousness, and good entertainment were turned to discourtesy) he would ever get himself alone – though almost when he was in company he was alone, so little attention he gave to any that spake unto him. Even the colour and figure of his face began to receive some alteration, which he showed little to heed. But every morning early going abroad, either to the garden or to some woods towards the desert, it seemed his only comfort was to be without a comforter; but long it could not be hid from Palladius, whom true love made ready to mark, and long knowledge able to mark. And therefore being now grown weary of his abode in Arcadia, having informed himself fully of the strength and riches of the country, of the nature of the people and manner of their laws, and seeing the court could not be visited, prohibited to all men but to certain shepherdish people, he greatly desired a speedy return to his own country after the many mazes of fortune he had trodden. But perceiving this great alteration in his friend, he thought first to break with him thereof, and then to hasten his return – whereto he found him but smally inclined; whereupon one day, taking him alone with certain

---

[1] although] though 93   [2] fancies, but *Cm*, 93: fancies. Chap. 9. Pyrocles' inclination to love; his and Musidorus' disputation thereabouts broken off by Kalander. But *90*

graces and countenances as if he were disputing with the trees, began in this manner to say unto him:

'A mind well trained and long exercised in virtue, my sweet and worthy cousin, doth not easily change any course it once undertakes but upon well-grounded and well-weighed causes, for being witness to itself of his own inward good, it finds nothing without it of so high a price for which it should be altered. Even the very countenance and behaviour of such a man doth show forth images of the same constancy by maintaining a right harmony betwixt it and the inward good in yielding itself suitable to the virtuous resolutions[1] of the mind. This speech I direct to you, noble friend Pyrocles, the excellency of whose mind and well-chosen course in virtue if I do not sufficiently know (having seen such rare demonstrations of it) it is my weakness and not your unworthiness. But as indeed I know[2] it, and knowing it most dearly love both it and him that hath it, so must I needs say that since our late coming into this country I have marked in you, I will not say an alteration, but a relenting, truly, and a slacking of the main career you had so notably begun and almost performed – and that in such sort as I cannot find sufficient reasons[3] in my great love toward you how to allow it. For to leave off other secreter arguments which my acquaintance with you makes me easily find, this in effect to any man may be manifest: that whereas you were wont in all places you came to give yourself vehemently to the knowledge of those things which might better your mind, to seek the familiarity of excellent men in learning and soldiery, and lastly, to put all these things in practice both by continual wise proceeding[4] and worthy enterprises, as occasions[5] fell for them, you now leave all these things undone; you let your mind fall asleep; besides,[6] your countenance troubled – which surely comes not of virtue, for virtue, like the clear heaven, is without clouds; and lastly, you subject yourself to solitariness, the sly enemy that doth most separate a man from well-doing.'

Pyrocles' mind was all this while so fixed upon another devotion that he no more attentively marked his friend's discourse than the child that hath leave to play marks the last part of his lesson, or the diligent pilot in a dangerous tempest doth attend the[7] unskilful words of a[8] passenger. Yet the very sound having imprinted the general points[9] of his speech in his heart, pierced with any mislike of so dearly an esteemed friend, and desirous by degrees to bring him to a gentler consideration of him, with a shamefast look

---

[1] resolutions *OA* (*ex. Ph*), *Cm*: resolution *Ph*, *90*, *93* [2] I know] I do know *OA* (*ex. Cl*) [3] reasons *OA* (*ex. Ph*), *Cm*: reason *Ph*, *90*, *93* [4] proceeding] proceedings *Cl*, *Da*, *Ph*, *Hm*, *Cm* [5] occasions *St*, *Cl*, *As*, *Je*, *Hm*, *Cm*: occasion *Bo*, *Da*, *90*, *93*; actions *Ph* [6] besides *OA*, *Cm*: beside *90*, *93* [7] attend the] attend to the *OA* (*ex. As*) [8] words of a] words of the *OA* (*ex. Cl*, *Je*); om. *Cl* [9] points *OA*, *Cm*, *98*, *13*: point *90*, *93*

witnessing he rather could not help than did not know his fault, answered him to this purpose:

'Excellent Musidorus, in the praises[1] you gave me in the beginning of your speech I easily acknowledge the force of your goodwill unto me; for neither could you have thought so well of me if extremity of love had not made your judgement partial, nor you could have loved me so entirely if you had not been apt to make so great (though undeserved) judgements[2] of me. And even so must I say of[3] those imperfections, to which though I have ever through weakness been subject, yet you by the daily mending of your mind have of late been able to look into them, which before you could not discern; so that the change you speak[4] of falls not out by my impairing[5] but by your bettering. And yet, under the leave of your better judgement, I must needs say thus much, my dear cousin, that I find not myself wholly to be condemned because I do not with a continual[6] vehemency follow those knowledges which you call the bettering of my mind; for both the mind itself must like other things sometimes be unbent, or else it will be either weakened or broken; and these[7] knowledges, as they are of good use, so are they not all the mind may stretch itself unto. Who knows whether I feed not my mind with higher thoughts? Truly, as I know not all the particularities, so yet I see the bounds of all these knowledges; but the workings of the mind I find much more infinite than can be led unto by the eye, or imagined by any that distract their thoughts without themselves. And in such contemplation, or (as I think) more excellent, I enjoy my solitariness, and my solitariness perchance is the nurse of these contemplations. Eagles, we see, fly alone; and they are but sheep which always herd together. Condemn not, therefore, my mind sometime to enjoy itself, nor blame not the taking of such times as serve most fit for it. And alas, dear Musidorus, if I be sad, who knows better than you the just causes I have of sadness?'

And here Pyrocles suddenly stopped, like a man unsatisfied in himself – though his wit might well have served to have satisfied another. And so, looking with a countenance as though he desired he should know his mind without hearing him speak, and yet desirous to speak to breathe out some part of his inward evil, sending again new blood to his face, he continued his speech in this manner:

'And Lord! dear cousin,' said he, 'doth not the pleasantness of this place carry in itself sufficient reward for any time lost in it? Do you not see how all things conspire together to make this country a heavenly dwelling? Do you not see the grass, how in colour they excel the emeralds, everyone striving to

---

[1] praises *OA, Cm*: praise *90, 93* [2] judgements] judgement *OA (ex. Cl, As)* [3] say of *OA (ex. Ph), Cm*: say to *Ph, 90, 93* [4] speak] spake *St, Cl* [5] by my impairing] by impairing *Da, Cm* [6] with a continual *OA, Cm*: with continual *90, 93* [7] these] those *St, Bo, As, Da, Je, Hm*

pass his fellow – and yet they are all kept of an equal height? And see you not the rest of these beautiful flowers, each of which would require a man's wit to know, and his life to express? Do not these stately trees seem to maintain their flourishing old age with the only happiness of their seat, being clothed with a continual spring because no beauty here should ever fade? Doth not the air breathe health, which the birds, delightful both to ear and eye, do daily solemnize with the sweet concent of their voices? Is not every echo here[1] a perfect music? And these fresh and delightful brooks, how slowly they slide away, as loath to leave the company of so many things united in perfection! And with how sweet a murmur they lament their forced departure! Certainly, certainly, cousin, it must needs be that some goddess inhabiteth this region, who is the soul of this soil; for neither is any less than a goddess worthy to be shrined in such a heap of pleasures, nor any less than a goddess could have made it so perfect a plot of the celestial dwellings' – and so ended with a deep sigh, ruefully casting his eye upon Musidorus, as more desirous of pity, than pleading.

But Musidorus had all this while held his look fixed upon Pyrocles' countenance, and with no less loving attention marked how his words proceeded from him. But in both these he perceived such strange diversities that they rather increased new doubts than gave him ground to settle any judgement; for besides his eyes sometimes even great with tears, the oft changing of his colour, with a kind of shaking unstaidness over all his body, he might see in his countenance some great determination mixed with fear, and might perceive in him store of thoughts rather stirred than digested, his words interrupted continually with sighs which served as a burthen to each sentence, and the tenor of his speech (though of his wonted phrase) not knit together to one constant end but rather dissolved in itself as the vehemency of the inward passion prevailed: which made Musidorus frame his answer nearest to that humour which should soonest put out the secret. For having in the beginning of Pyrocles' speech which defended his solitariness framed in his mind a reply against it in the praise of honourable action (in showing that such a kind[2] of contemplation is but a glorious title to idleness; that in action a man did not only better himself but benefit others; that the gods would not have delivered a soul into the body which hath arms and legs, only instruments of doing, but that it were intended the mind should employ them; and that the mind should best know his own good or evil by practice – which knowledge was the only way to increase the one and correct the other; besides many other better arguments[3] which the plentifulness of the matter yielded to the sharpness of his wit), when he found Pyrocles leave

---

[1] here *OA, Cm*: thereof *90, 93*   [2] such a kind] such kind *OA (ex. Bo)*   [3] other better arguments *OA, Cm*: other arguments *90, 93*

that and fall into such an affected praising of the place, he left it likewise, and joined with him therein because he found him in that humour utter more[1] store of passion. And even thus, kindly embracing him, he said:

'Your words are such, noble cousin, so sweetly and strongly handled in the praise of solitariness, as they would make me likewise yield myself up into it, but that the same words make me know it is more pleasant to enjoy the company of him that can speak such words than by such words to be persuaded to follow solitariness. And even so do I give you leave, sweet Pyrocles, ever to defend solitariness, so long as, to defend it, you ever keep company. But I marvel at the excessive praises you give to this country. In truth, it is not unpleasant; but yet, if you would return into Macedon, you should see either[2] many heavens, or find this no more than earthly. And even Tempe in my Thessalia, where you and I to my great happiness were brought up together, is nothing inferior unto it. But I think you will make me see that the vigour of your wit can show itself in any subject; or else you feed sometimes your solitariness with the conceits of the poets, whose liberal pens can as easily travel over mountains as molehills, and so (like well-disposed men) set up everything to the highest note – especially when they put such words in the mouths of one of these fantastical mind-infected people that children and musicians call lovers!'

This word *lover*[3] did no less pierce poor Pyrocles than the right tune of music toucheth him that is sick of the tarantula. There was not one part of his body that did not feel a sudden motion, while his heart with panting seemed to dance to the sound of that word. Yet after some pause lifting up his eyes a little from the ground, and yet not daring to place them in the eyes of Musidorus, armed with the very countenance of the poor prisoner at the bar whose answer is nothing but 'guilty,' with much ado he brought forth this question:

'And alas,' said he, 'dear cousin, what if I be not so much the poet, the freedom of whose pen can exercise itself in anything, as even that very[4] miserable subject of his cunning whereof you speak?'[5]

'Now the eternal Gods forbid,' mainly cried out Musidorus, 'that ever my ear should be poisoned with so evil news of you! Oh, let me never know that any base affection should get any lordship in your thoughts.'

But as he was speaking more, Kalander came and brake off their discourse with inviting them to the hunting of a goodly stag, which being harboured in a wood thereby, he hoped would make them good sport and drive away some part of Daiphantus' melancholy. They condescended; and so,

---

[1] more] most *OA (ex. Cl, Ph)* [2] see either] either see 93 [3] word *lover*] word of *lover OA (ex. Cl, As)*
[4] very *OA (ex. Cl, Ph), Cm*: om. *Cl, Ph, 90, 93* [5] speak] spake *Cl*; speak of *St, Da, Je, Hm*; spake of *Cm*

going to their lodgings, furnished themselves as liked them, Daiphantus writing a few words which he left in a sealed[1] letter against their return.[2] Then went they together abroad, the good Kalander entertaining them with pleasant discoursing how well he loved the sport of hunting when he was a young man; how much, in the comparison thereof, he disdained all chamber delights; that the sun, how great a journey soever he had to make, could never prevent him with earliness, nor the moon with her sober countenance dissuade him from watching till midnight for the deer's feeding.

'Oh,' said he, 'you will never live to my age without you keep yourselves in breath with exercise, and in heart with joyfulness. Too much thinking doth consume the spirits, and oft it falls out that while one thinks too much of his doing, he leaves to do the effect of his thinking.'

Then spared he not to remember how much Arcadia was changed since his youth, activity and good fellowship being nothing in the price it was then held in, but according to the nature of the old-growing world, still worse and worse. Then would he tell them stories of such gallants as he had known, and so with pleasant company beguiled the time's haste and shortened the way's length, till they came to the side of the wood where the hounds were in couples staying their coming, but with a whining accent craving liberty – many of them in colour and marks so resembling that it showed they were of one kind; the huntsmen handsomely attired in their green liveries as though they were children of summer, with staves in their hands to beat the guiltless earth when the hounds were at a fault, and with horns about their necks to sound an alarum upon a silly fugitive.

The hounds were straight uncoupled, and ere long the stag thought it better to trust to the[3] nimbleness of his feet than to the slender fortification of his lodging. But even his feet betrayed him, for howsoever they went, they themselves uttered themselves to the scent of their enemies, who one taking it of another, and sometimes believing the wind's advertisements, sometimes the view of their faithful counsellors, the huntsmen, with open mouths then denounced war when the war was already begun – their cry being composed of so well-sorted mouths that any man would perceive therein some kind of proportion, but the skilful woodmen did find a music. Then delight and variety of opinion drew the horsemen sundry ways; yet cheering their hounds with voice and horn, kept still as it were together. The wood seemed to conspire with them against his own citizens, dispersing their noise through all his quarters, and even the nymph Echo left to bewail

---

[1] in a sealed] sealed in a 93 [2] return. Then *Cm*, 93: return. Chap. 10. Kalander's hunting; Daiphantus' close departure and letter; Palladius' care and quest after him, accompanied with Clitophon; his finding and taking on Amphialus' armour; their encounter with Queen Helen's attendants; her mistaking Palladius. Then 90 [3] trust to the *Cm*, 93: trust the 90

the loss of Narcissus, and became a hunter. But the stag was in the end so hotly pursued that, leaving his flight, he was driven to make courage of despair; and so, turning his head, made the hounds with change of speech to testify that he was at a bay[1] – as if from hot pursuit of their enemy they were suddenly come to a parley. But Kalander by his skill of coasting the country was among the first that came in to the besieged deer, whom, when some of the younger sort would have killed with their swords, he would not suffer, but with a crossbow sent a death to the poor beast, who with tears showed the unkindness he took of man's cruelty.

But by the time that the whole company was assembled, and that the stag had bestowed himself liberally among them that had killed him, Daiphantus was missed – for whom Palladius carefully inquiring, no news could be given him but by one that said he thought he was returned home, for that he marked him in the chief of the hunting take a by-way which might lead to Kalander's house. That answer for the time satisfying, and they having performed all duties, as well for the stag's funeral as the hounds' triumph, they returned, some talking of the fatness of the deer's body, some of the fairness of his head, some of the hounds' cunning, some of their speed, and some of their cry; till coming home about the time that the candle begins[2] to inherit the sun's office, they found Daiphantus was not to be found; whereat Palladius greatly marvelling, and a day or two passing while neither search nor inquiry could help him to knowledge, at last he lighted upon the letter which Pyrocles had written before he went a-hunting, and left in his study among other of his writings. The letter was directed to Palladius himself, and contained these words:

'My only friend, violence of love leads me into such a course whereof your knowledge may much more vex you than help me. Therefore pardon my concealing it from you, since if I wrong you, it is in respect[3] I bear you. Return into Thessalia, I pray you, as full of good fortune as I am of desire; and if I live, I will in short time follow you – if I die, love my memory.' This was all, and this Palladius read twice or thrice over.

'Ah,' said he, 'Pyrocles, what means this alteration? What have I deserved of thee to be thus banished of thy counsels? Heretofore I have accused the sea, condemned the pirates, and hated my evil fortune that deprived me of thee; but now thyself is the sea which drowns my comfort; thyself is the pirate that robs thyself of me; thy own will becomes my evil fortune.'

Then turned he his thoughts to all forms of guesses that might light upon the purpose and course of Pyrocles – for he was not so sure, by his words,

---

[1] at a bay *Cm, 93*: at bay *90* (*Cm* could read at abay)   [2] candle begins] candle begin *Cm*; candles begin *93*   [3] in respect] in the respect *93*

that it was love, as he was doubtful where the love was. One time he thought some beauty in Laconia had laid hold of his eyes. Another time he feared that it might be Parthenia's excellency which had broken the bands of all former resolution. But the more he thought, the more he knew not what to think, armies of objections rising against any accepted opinion.

Then as careful he was what to do himself, at length, determined never to leave seeking him till his search should be either by meeting accomplished or by death ended. Therefore, for all the unkindness bearing tender respect that his friend's secret determination should be kept from any suspicion in others, he went to Kalander and told him that he had received a message from his friend, by which he understood he was gone back again into Laconia about some matters greatly importing the poor men whose protection he had undertaken, and that it was, in any sort, fit for him to follow him, but in such private wise as not to be known; and that therefore he would as then bid him farewell – arming himself in a black armour as either a badge or prognostication of his mind, and taking only with him good store of money and a few choice jewels, leaving the greatest number of them and most of his apparel with Kalander; which he did partly to give the more cause to Kalander to expect their return, and so to be the less curiously inquisitive after them, and partly to leave those honourable thanks unto him for his charge and kindness, which he knew he would no other way receive.

The good old man, having neither reason to dissuade, nor hope to persuade, received the things with mind of a keeper, not of an owner; but before he went, desired he might have the happiness fully to know what they were, which, he said, he had ever till then delayed, fearing to be any way importune; but now he could not be so much an enemy to his desires as any longer to imprison them in silence. Palladius told him that the matter was not so secret, but that so worthy a friend deserved the knowledge and should have it as soon as he might speak with his friend, without whose consent (because their promise bound him otherwise) he could not reveal it; but bad him hold for most assured that, if they lived but a while, he should find that they which bare the names of Daiphantus and Palladius would give him, and his, cause to think his noble courtesy well employed. Kalander would press him no further; but desiring that he might have leave to go, or at least to send his son and servants with him, Palladius brake off all ceremonies by telling him his case stood so, that his greatest favour should be in making least ado of his parting; wherewith Kalander, knowing it to be more cumber than courtesy to strive, abstained from further urging him – but not from hearty mourning the loss of so sweet a conversation. Only Clitophon by vehement importunity obtained to go with him, to come again to Daiphantus, whom he named (and accounted) his lord.

And in such private guise departed Palladius; though having a companion to talk withal, yet talking much more with unkindness. And first they went to Mantinea, whereof because Parthenia was, he suspected there might be some cause of his abode. But finding there no news of him, he went to Tegea, Rhipa, Enispe, Stymphalus, and Pheneus (famous for the poisonous Stygian water), and through all the rest of Arcadia, making their eyes, their ears, and their tongue serve almost for nothing but that inquiry – but they could know nothing, but that in none of those places he was known. And so went they, making one place succeed to another, in like uncertainty to their search, many times encountering strange adventures worthy to be registered in the rolls of fame.

But this may not be omitted: as they passed in a pleasant valley, of either side of which high hills lifted up their beetle brows as if they would overlook the pleasantness of their under-prospect, they were, by the daintiness of the place and the weariness of themselves, invited to light from their horses; and pulling off their bits that they might something refresh their mouths upon the grass which plentifully grew, brought up under the care of those well shading trees, they themselves laid them down hard by the murmuring music of certain waters which spouted out of the side of the hills, and in the bottom of the valley made, of many springs, a pretty brook, like a commonwealth of many families. But when they had awhile hearkened to the persuasion of sleep, they rose and walked onward in that shady place, till Clitophon espied a piece of armour; and not far off another piece; and so, the sight of one piece teaching him to look for more, he at length found all, with headpiece and shield, by the device whereof, which was ..., he straight knew it to be the armour of his cousin, the noble Amphialus; whereupon fearing some inconvenience happened unto him, he told both his doubt and his cause of doubt[1] to Palladius, who considering thereof thought best to make no longer stay but to follow on, lest perchance some violence were offered to so worthy a knight, whom the fame of the world seemed to set in balance with any knight living. Yet with a sudden conceit, having long borne great honour to the name of Amphialus, Palladius thought best to take that armour, thinking thereby to learn (by them that should know that armour) some news of Amphialus, and yet not hinder him in the search of Daiphantus too; so he by the help of Clitophon quickly put on that armour, whereof there was no one piece wanting, though hacked in some places, bewraying some fight not long since passed. It was something too great, but yet served well enough.

---

[1] and his cause of doubt] and cause of doubt *93, 98*; and cause of his doubt *13*

And so, getting on their horses, they travelled but a little way when, in opening of the mouth of the valley into a fair field, they met with a coach drawn with four milk-white horses furnished all in black, with a blackamoor boy upon every horse – they all apparelled in white, the coach itself very richly furnished in black and white. But before they could come so near as to discern what was within, there came running upon them above a dozen horsemen who cried to them to yield themselves prisoners, or else they should die. But Palladius, not accustomed to grant over the possession of himself upon so unjust titles, with sword drawn gave them so rude an answer that divers of them never had breath to reply again; for being well-backed by Clitophon, and having an excellent horse under him, when he was overpressed by some he avoided them; and ere th'other thought of it, punished in him his fellow's faults; and so, either with cunning or with force, or rather with a cunning force, left none of them either living, or able to make his life serve to other's hurt; which being done, he approached the coach, assuring the black boys they should have no hurt (who were else ready to have run away), and looking into the coach, he found in the one end a lady of great beauty, and such a beauty as showed forth the beams both of wisdom and good nature, but all as much darkened as might be with sorrow; in the other, two ladies who by their demeanour showed well they were but her servants, holding before them a picture in which was a goodly gentleman – whom he knew not – painted, having in their faces a certain waiting sorrow, their eyes being infected with their mistress's weeping; but the chief lady having not so much as once heard the noise of this conflict, so had sorrow closed up all the entries of her mind, and love tied her senses to that beloved picture.

Now the shadow of him falling upon the picture made her cast up her eye. And seeing the armour which too well she knew, thinking him to be Amphialus, the lord of her desires; blood coming more freely into her cheeks as though it would be bold, and yet, there, growing new again pale for fear; with a pitiful look, like one unjustly condemned, 'My Lord Amphialus,' said she, 'you have enough punished me. It is time for cruelty to leave you, and evil fortune me. If not, I pray you (and to grant my prayer, fitter time nor place you can have), accomplish the one even now – and finish the other.'

With that, sorrow (impatient to be slowly uttered in her often staying speeches) poured itself so fast in tears that Palladius could not hold her longer in error; but pulling off his helmet, 'Madam,' said he, 'I perceive you mistake me. I am a stranger in these parts, set upon without any cause given by me by some of your servants; whom, because I have in my just defence evil entreated, I came to make my excuse to you; whom seeing such as I do, I find greater cause why I should crave pardon of you.'

When she saw his face and heard his speech, she looked out of the coach; and seeing her men, some slain, some lying under their dead horses and striving to get from under them, without making more account of the matter, 'Truly,' said she, 'they are well served that durst lift up their arms against that armour. But, Sir Knight,' said she, 'I pray you tell me, how come you by this armour, for if it be by the death of him that owed it, then have I more to say unto you.'

Palladius assured her it was not so, telling her the true manner how he found it.

'It is like enough,' said she, 'for that agrees with the manner he hath lately used. But I beseech you, sir,' said she, 'since your prowess hath bereft me of my company, let it yet so far heal the wounds itself hath given as to guard me to the next town.'

'How great soever my business be, fair lady,' said he, 'it shall willingly yield to so noble a cause. But first, even by the favour you bear to the lord of this noble armour, I conjure you to tell me the story of your fortune herein, lest hereafter, when the image of so excellent a lady in so strange a plight come before mine eyes, I condemn myself of want of consideration in not having demanded thus much. Neither ask I it without protestation that, wherein my sword and faith may avail you, they shall bind themselves to your service.'

'Your conjuration, fair knight,' said she, 'is too strong for my poor spirit to disobey, and that shall make me without any other hope, my ruin being but by one unrelievable, to grant your will herein; and to say the truth, a strange niceness were it in me to refrain that from the ears of a person representing so much worthiness, which I am glad even to rocks and woods to utter.

'Know[1] you then that my name is Helen, queen by birth, and hitherto, possession, of the fair city and territory of Corinth. I can say, no more of myself, but beloved of my people – and may justly say "beloved", since they are content to bear with my absence and folly. But I being left by my father's death, and accepted by my people in the highest degree that country could receive, as soon, or rather, before that my age was ripe for it, my court quickly swarmed full of suitors – some perchance loving my state, others my person; but once I know (all of them!), howsoever my possessions were in their hearts, my beauty, such as it is, was in their mouths – many strangers of princely and noble blood, and all of mine own country to whom either birth

---

[1] utter. 'Know *Cm*, 93: utter.' Chap. 11. The story of Queen Helen; Philoxenus, her suitor; Amphialus, an intercessor for his friend; his praises, birth, and education; her love won to himself; his refusal and departure; Philoxenus' wrong-rage against him; their fight; the death of son and father; Amphialus' sorrow and detestation of the queen; a new onset on Palladius for Amphialus' armour; whose grief is amplified by meeting his dead friend's dog; Palladius' parting with Helen and Clitophon. 'Know 90

or virtue gave courage to avow so high a desire.

'Among the rest, or rather before the rest, was the Lord Philoxenus, son and heir to the virtuous nobleman, Timotheus; which Timotheus was a man both in power, riches, parentage, and (which passed all these) goodness, and (which followed all these) love of the people, beyond any of the great men of my country. Now this son of his (I must say, truly not unworthy of such a father), bending himself by all means of serviceableness to me, and setting forth of himself to win my favour, wan thus far of me that in truth I less misliked him than any of the rest; which in some proportion my countenance delivered unto him, though I must protest it was a very false embassador if it delivered at all any affection, whereof my heart was utterly void – I as then esteeming myself born to rule, and thinking foul scorn willingly to submit myself to be ruled. But whiles Philoxenus in good sort pursued my favour, and perchance nourished himself with overmuch hope because he found I did in some sort acknowledge his value, one time among the rest he brought with him a dear friend of his.'

With that, she looked upon the picture before her, and straight sighed, and straight tears followed, as if the idol, of duty, ought to be honoured with such oblations; and then her speech stayed, the tale having brought her to that look, but that look having quite put her out of her tale. But Palladius, greatly pitying so sweet a sorrow in a lady whom by fame he had already known and honoured, besought her, for her promise sake, to put silence so long unto her moaning till she had recounted the rest of this story.

'Why,' said she, 'this is the picture of Amphialus! What need I say more to you? What ear is so barbarous but hath heard of Amphialus? Who follows deeds of arms, but everywhere finds monuments[1] of Amphialus? Who is courteous, noble, liberal, but he that hath the example before his eyes of Amphialus? Where are all heroical parts, but in Amphialus? O Amphialus, I would thou were not so excellent; or I would I thought thee not so excellent; and yet would I not, that I would so.'

With that, she wept again; till he again soliciting the conclusion of her story, 'Then must you,' said she, 'know the story of Amphialus; for his will is my life, his life my history. And indeed, in what can I better employ my lips than in speaking of Amphialus?

'This knight, then, whose figure you see, but whose mind can be painted by nothing but by the true shape of virtue, is brother's son to Basilius, king of Arcadia, and in his childhood esteemed his heir; till Basilius, in his old years marrying a young and a fair lady, had of her those two daughters (so famous for their perfection in beauty), which put by their young cousin from

---

[1] monuments *Cm, 93*: monument *90*

that expectation; whereupon his mother (a woman of a haughty heart, being daughter to the king of Argos), either disdaining or fearing that her son should live under the power of Basilius, sent him to that Lord Timotheus (between whom and her dead husband there had passed strait bands of mutual hospitality) to be brought up in company with his son, Philoxenus – a happy resolution for Amphialus, whose excellent nature was by this means trained on with as good education as any prince's son in the world could have (which otherwise, it is thought, his mother, far unworthy of such a son, would not have given him), the good Timotheus no less loving him than his own son.

'Well they grew in years, and shortly occasions fell aptly to try Amphialus – and all occasions were but steps for him to climb fame by. Nothing was so hard but his valour overcame; which yet still he so guided with true virtue, that although no man was in our parts spoken of but he for his manhood, yet as though therein he excelled himself, he was commonly called "the courteous Amphialus". An endless thing it were for me to tell how many adventures, terrible to be spoken of, he achieved – what monsters, what giants, what conquests[1] of countries; sometimes using policy, sometimes force, but always virtue, well-followed (and but followed) by Philoxenus; between whom and him so fast a friendship by education was knit that at last Philoxenus having no greater matter to employ his friendship in than to win me, therein desired, and had his uttermost furtherance.

'To that purpose brought he him to my court, where (truly I may justly witness) with him, that what his wit could conceive (and his wit can conceive as far as the limits of reason stretch) was all directed to the setting forward the suit of his friend, Philoxenus. My ears could hear nothing from him but touching the worthiness of Philoxenus, and of the great happiness it would be unto me to have such a husband, with many arguments which, God knows, I cannot well remember because I did not much believe. For why should I use many circumstances to come to that where already I am, and ever while I live must continue? In few words, while he pleaded for another, he wan me for himself; if, at least,' with that she sighed, 'he would account it a winning, for his fame had so framed the way to my mind that his presence (so full of beauty, sweetness, and noble conversation) had entered there before he vouchsafed to call for the keys.

'Oh Lord! How did my soul hang at his lips while he spake! Oh! When he in feeling manner would describe the love of his friend, "How well", thought I, "doth love between those lips!" When he would with daintiest eloquence stir pity in me toward Philoxenus, "Why sure," said I to myself, "Helen, be not afraid. This heart cannot want pity." And when he would extol the deeds

---

[1] conquests *Cm, 93*: conquest *90*

of Philoxenus who, indeed, had but waited of him therein, "Alas," thought I, "good Philoxenus, how evil doth it become thy name to be subscribed to his letter!"

'What should I say? Nay, what should I not say, noble knight, who am not ashamed, nay, am delighted thus to express mine own passions?

'Days passed. His eagerness for his friend never decreased; my affection to him ever increased. At length, in way of ordinary courtesy I obtained of him (who suspected no such matter) this his picture, the only Amphialus, I fear, that I shall ever enjoy. And grown bolder, or madder, or bold with madness, I discovered my affection unto him. But Lord! I shall never forget how anger and courtesy at one instant appeared in his eyes when he heard that motion; how with his blush he taught me shame. In sum, he left nothing unassayed which might disgrace himself to grace his friend, in sweet terms making me receive a most resolute refusal of himself. But when he found that his presence did far more persuade for himself than his speech could do for his friend, he left my court, hoping that forgetfulness which commonly waits upon absence would make room for his friend – to whom he would not utter thus much, I think for a kind fear not to grieve him, or perchance (though he cares little for me) of a certain honourable gratefulness not[1] yet to discover[2] so much of my secrets; but as it should seem meant to travel into far countries until his friend's affection either ceased or prevailed. But within a while Philoxenus came to see how onward the fruits were of his friend's labour, when, as in truth I cared not much how he took it, he found me sitting beholding this picture, I know not with how affectionate countenance, but I am sure with a most affectionate mind. I straight found jealousy and disdain took hold of him; and yet the froward pain of mine own heart made me so delight to punish him, whom I esteemed the chiefest let in my way, that when he with humble gesture and vehement speeches sued for my favour, I told him that I would hear him more willingly if he would speak for Amphialus as well as Amphialus had done for him.

'He never answered me; but pale and quaking went straight away – and straight my heart misgave me some evil success. And yet, though I had authority enough to have stayed him, as in these fatal things it falls out that the high-working powers make second causes unwittingly accessary to their determinations, I did no further, but sent a footman of mine whose faithfulness to me I well knew, from place to place to follow him and bring me word of his proceedings; which, alas, have brought forth that which I fear I must ever rue – for he had travelled scarce a day's journey out of my country, but that not far from this place he overtook Amphialus (who by succouring a distressed lady had been here stayed), and by and by called

---

[1] not *Cm, 98, 13*: nor *90, 93*   [2] discover *Cm, 93*: discourse *90*

him to fight with him, protesting that one of them two should die. You may easily judge how strange it was to Amphialus whose heart could accuse itself of no fault but too much affection toward him, which he, refusing to fight with him, would fain have made Philoxenus understand. But (as my servant since told me) the more Amphialus went back, the more he followed, calling him "traitor", and "coward", yet never telling the cause of this strange alteration.

'"Ah Philoxenus," said Amphialus, "I know I am no traitor, and thou well knowest I am no coward. But I pray thee, content thyself with this much; and let this satisfy thee that I love thee, since I bear thus much of thee."

'But he, leaving words, drew his sword and gave Amphialus a great blow or two, which but for the goodness of his armour would have slain him; and yet, so far did Amphialus contain himself, stepping aside, and saying to him:

'"Well Philoxenus, and thus much villainy am I content to put up, not any longer for thy sake (whom I have no cause to love, since thou dost injure[1] me and wilt not tell me the cause), but for thy virtuous father's sake, to whom I am so much bound. I pray thee, go away and conquer thy own passions, and thou shalt make me soon yield to be thy servant."

'But he would not attend his words, but still strake so fiercely at Amphialus that in the end, nature prevailing above determination, he was fain to defend himself and withal so to[2] offend him that by an unlucky blow the poor Philoxenus fell dead at his feet, having had time only to speak some words whereby Amphialus knew it was for my sake; which when Amphialus saw, he forthwith gave such tokens of true-felt sorrow that, as my servant said, no imagination could conceive greater woe – but that by and by an unhappy occasion made Amphialus pass himself in sorrow: for Philoxenus was but newly dead when there comes to the same place the aged and virtuous Timotheus, who having heard of his son's sudden and passionate manner of parting from my court, had followed him as speedily as he could, but (alas) not so speedily but that he found him dead before he could overtake him.

'Though my heart be nothing but a stage for tragedies, yet I must confess it is even unable to bear the miserable representation thereof, knowing Amphialus and Timotheus as I have done. Alas, what sorrow, what amazement, what shame was in Amphialus when he saw his dear foster-father find him the killer of his only son! In my heart I know, he wished mountains had lain upon him to keep him from that meeting. As for Timotheus, sorrow of his son, and I think principally unkindness of Amphialus, so devoured his vital

---

[1] injure] injury 93   [2] withal so to *Cm*, 98, 13: withal, to 90, 93

spirits that, able to say no more but, "Amphialus! Amphialus! Have I – ", he sank to the earth and presently died.

'But not my tongue, though daily used to complaints; no, nor if my heart which is nothing but sorrow were turned to tongues, durst it undertake to show the unspeakableness of his grief, but because this serves to make you know my fortune. He threw away his armour – even this which you have now upon you, which at the first sight I vainly hoped he had put on again; and then as ashamed of the light he ran into the thickest[1] of the woods, lamenting, and even crying out so pitifully that my servant (though of a fortune not used to much tenderness) could not refrain weeping when he told it me. He once overtook him; but Amphialus drawing his sword, which was the only part of his arms (God knows to what purpose!) he carried about him, threatened to kill him if he followed him, and withal, bad him deliver this bitter message: that he well enough found I was the cause of all this mischief, and that if I were a man he would go over the world to kill me – but bad me assure myself that, of all creatures in the world, he most hated me.

'Ah, Sir Knight (whose ears I think by this time are tired with the rugged ways of these misfortunes), now weigh my case – if, at least, you know what love is. For this cause have I left my country, putting in hazard how my people will in time deal by me, adventuring what perils or dishonours might ensue, only to follow him who proclaimeth hate against me and to bring my neck unto him, if that may redeem my trespass and assuage his fury. And now, sir,' said she, 'you have your request, I pray you take pains to guide me to the next town, that there I may gather such of my company again as your valour hath left me.'

Palladius willingly condescended. But ere they began to go, there came Clitophon, who having been something hurt by one of them, had pursued him a good way; at length overtaking him and ready to kill him, understood they were servants to the fair Queen Helen, and that the cause of this enterprise was for nothing but to make Amphialus prisoner, whom they knew their mistress sought – for she concealed her sorrow, nor cause of her sorrow, from nobody. But Clitophon, very sorry for this accident, came back to comfort the queen, helping such as were hurt in the best sort that he could, and framing friendly constructions of this rashly undertaken enmity – when in comes another (till that time unseen) all armed, with his beaver down; who first looking round about upon the company, as soon as he spied Palladius he drew his sword, and making no other prologue let fly at him. But Palladius (sorry for so much harm as had already happened) sought rather

---

[1] into the thickest] into thickest 93

to retire and ward, thinking he might be someone that belonged to the fair queen, whose case in his heart he pitied; which Clitophon seeing, stepped between them, asking the new-come knight the cause of his quarrel; who answered him that he would kill that thief who had stolen away his master's armour if he did not restore it. With that, Palladius looked upon him and saw that he, of the other side, had Palladius' own armour upon him.

'Truly,' said Palladius, 'if I have stolen this armour, you did not buy that. But you shall not fight with me upon such a quarrel. You shall have this armour willingly, which I did only put on to do honour to the owner.'

But Clitophon straight knew by his words and voice that it was Ismenus, the faithful and diligent page of Amphialus. And therefore telling him that he was Clitophon, and willing him to acknowledge his error to the other who deserved all honour, the young gentleman pulled off his head-piece, and lighting, went to kiss Palladius' hands, desiring him to pardon his folly, caused by extreme grief which easily might bring forth anger.

'Sweet gentleman,' said Palladius, 'you shall only make me this amends: that you shall carry this, your lord's armour, from me to him; and tell him, from an unknown knight who admires his worthiness, that he cannot cast a greater mist over his glory than by being unkind to so excellent a princess as this queen is.'

Ismenus promised he would, as soon as he durst find his master; and with that went to do his duty to the queen whom, in all these encounters, astonishment made hardy. But as soon as she saw Ismenus, looking to her picture, 'Ismenus,' said she, 'here is my lord; where is yours? Or come you to bring me some sentence of death from him? If it be so, welcome be it. I pray you, speak – and speak quickly.'

'Alas, madam,' said Ismenus, 'I have lost my lord;' with that, tears came unto his eyes; 'for as soon as the unhappy combat was concluded with the death both of father and son, my master casting off his armour went his way, forbidding me upon pain of death to follow him. Yet divers days I followed his steps, till lastly I found him, having newly met with an excellent spaniel belonging to his dead companion, Philoxenus. The dog straight fawned on my master for old knowledge; but never was there thing more pitiful than to hear my master blame the dog for loving his master's murtherer, renewing afresh his complaints with the dumb counsellor, as if they might comfort one another in their miseries. But my lord having spied me rase up in such rage that in truth I feared he would kill me; yet as then he said only, if I would not displease him, I should not come near him till he sent for me – too hard a commandment for me to disobey. I yielded, leaving him only waited on by his dog, and (as I think) seeking out the most solitary places that this or any other country can grant him. And I, returning where I had left his armour, found another instead thereof; and disdaining (I must confess) that any should bear the armour of the best knight living, armed myself therein to play the fool, as even now I did.'

'Fair Ismenus,' said the queen, 'a fitter messenger could hardly be to unfold my tragedy. I see the end. I see my end!'

With that, sobbing, she desired to be conducted to the next town, where Palladius left her to be waited on by Clitophon – at Palladius' earnest entreaty, who desired alone to take that melancholy course of seeking his friend. And therefore changing armours again with Ismenus, who went withal to a castle belonging to his master, he continued his quest for his friend Daiphantus.

And so[1] directed he his course to Laconia, as well among the helots as Spartans. There indeed he found his fame flourishing, his monuments[2] engraved in marble, and yet more durable[3] in men's memories – but the universal lamenting his absented presence assured him of his present absence; thence into the Elean province, to see whether at the Olympian games there celebrated he might in such concourse bless his eyes with so desired an encounter – but that huge and sportful assembly grew to him a tedious loneliness,[4] esteeming nobody found, since Daiphantus was lost. Afterward, he passed through Achaia and Sicyonia to the Corinthians, proud of their two seas, to learn whether by the strait of that isthmus it were[5] possible to know of his passage. But finding every place more dumb than other to his demands, and remembering that it was late-taken love which had wrought this new course, he returned again after two months' travel in vain to make a fresh[6] search in Arcadia – so much the more as then first he bethought himself of the picture of Philoclea, in[7] resembling her he had once loved, might perhaps awake again that sleeping passion. And having already passed over the greatest part of Arcadia, one day coming under the side of the pleasant mountain, Maenalus, his horse, nothing guilty of his inquisitiveness, with flat tiring[8] taught him that discreet stays make speedy journeys. And therefore lighting down and unbridling his horse, he himself went to repose himself in a little wood he saw thereby, where lying under the pro-

---

[1] Daiphantus. And so *Cm*: Daiphantus. Chap. 12. Palladius, after long search of Daiphantus, lighteth on an Amazon lady; her habit, song, and who she was; objections of the one against women, and love of them; the answers of the other for them both; their passionate conclusion in relenting kindness. So *90*; Daiphantus. So *93* [2] monuments *Cm, 93*: monument *90* [3] durable] durably *93* [4] loneliness] loveliness *Cm, 93* (*only*) [5] were *Cm, 93*: was *90* [6] make a fresh *Cm, 93*: make fresh *90* [7] in] which *93* [8] flat tiring] flattering *90* (*uncorr.*); flat-tryng *93* (*uncorr.*)

tection of a shady tree with intention to make forgetting sleep comfort a sorrowful memory, he saw a sight which persuaded, and obtained of his eyes, that they would abide yet awhile open.

It was the appearing of a lady, who, because she walked with her side toward him, he could not perfectly see her face – but so much he might see of her, that was a surety for the rest that all was excellent. Well might he perceive the hanging of her hair in fairest quantity, in locks, some curled and some as it were forgotten, with such a careless care and an art so hiding art that she seemed she would lay them for a pattern,[1] whether nature simply, or nature helped by cunning be the more[2] excellent; the rest whereof was drawn into a coronet of gold, richly set with pearl,[3] and so joined all over with gold wires and covered with feathers of divers colours that it was not unlike to an helmet,[4] such a glittering show it bare, and so bravely it was held up from the head. Upon her body she ware a doublet of sky-colour satin covered with plates of gold, and as it were, nailed with precious stones, that in it she might seem armed. The nether part[5] of her garment was so full of stuff and cut after such a fashion that, though the length of it reached to the ankles, yet in her going one might sometimes discern the small of the leg,[6] which with the foot was dressed in a short pair of crimson velvet buskins, in some places open (as the ancient manner was) to show the fairness of the skin. Over all this she ware a certain mantle, made in such manner that, coming under her right[7] arm, and covering most of that side, it had no fastening of the left side, but only upon the top of the shoulder where the two ends met and were closed together with a very rich jewel, the device whereof (as he after saw) was this: a Hercules made in little form, but set with a distaff in his hand (as he once was by Omphale's commandment), with a word[8] in Greek, but thus to be interpreted: 'Never more valiant.' On the same side, on her thigh she ware a sword, which as it witnessed her to be an Amazon or one following that profession, so it seemed but a needless weapon, since her other forces were without withstanding.

But this lady walked outright till he might see her enter into a fine, close arbour. It was of trees whose branches so lovingly interlaced one the other that it could resist the strongest violence of eyesight. But she went into it by a door she opened – which moved him as warely as he could to follow her; and by and by he might hear her sing this song, with a voice no less beautiful to her ears than her goodliness was full of harmony to his eyes:

---

[1] pattern] trial *St, Bo*; paragon *Cl, Da, Ph, Je, Hm* (pattern *corr. to* paragon *Cl*) [2] be the more *OA, 93*: be more *Cm, 90* [3] pearl] pearls *St, Bo, Da*; om. *Cl* [4] an helmet] a helmet *St, Cl, Da, Je, Hm* [5] part *OA, 93*: parts *Cm, 90* [6] the leg *St, Bo, Da, Cm*: his leg *Cl, As, Je, Hm*; his legs *Ph*; her leg *90, 93* [7] her right *Cm, 93*: his right *OA*; the right *90* [8] but set with a distaff in his ... with a word *93*: but set with a word *Cm*; but a distaff set within his ... with a word *90*

Transformed in show, but more transformed in mind,
I cease to strive, with double conquest foiled;
For (woe is me) my powers all I find
With outward force and inward treason spoiled.
For from without came to mine eyes the blow,
Whereto mine inward thoughts did faintly yield;
Both these conspired poor reason's overthrow;
False in myself, thus have I lost the field.
Thus are my eyes still captive to one sight;
Thus all my thoughts are slaves to one thought still;
Thus reason to his servants yields his right;
Thus is my power transformed to your will.
    What marvel, then, I take a woman's hue,
    Since what I see, think, know, is all but you?

The ditty gave him some suspicion, but the voice gave him almost assurance who the singer was. And therefore boldly thrusting open the door and entering into the arbour, he perceived indeed that it was Pyrocles thus disguised; wherewith, not receiving so much joy to have found him as grief so to have found him, amazedly looking upon him (as Apollo is painted when he saw Daphne suddenly turned to[1] a laurel), he was not able to bring forth a word; so that Pyrocles (who had as much shame as Musidorus had sorrow) rising to him would have formed a substantial excuse – but his insinuation being of blushing, and his division of sighs, his whole oration stood upon a short narration – 'What was the causer of this metamorphosis?' But by that time Musidorus had gathered his spirits together; and yet casting a ghastful countenance upon him, as if he would conjure some strange spirits, he thus spake unto him:

'And is it possible that this is Pyrocles, the only young prince in the world formed by nature and framed by education to the true exercise of virtue? Or is it indeed some Amazon that hath counterfeited the face of my friend, in this sort to vex me – for likelier sure I would have thought it that any outward face might have been disguised, than that the face of so excellent a mind could have been thus blemished. O sweet Pyrocles, separate yourself a little, if it be possible, from yourself, and let your own mind look upon your own proceedings. So shall my words be needless, and you best instructed. See with yourself how fit it will be for you, in this your tender youth, born so great a prince and of so rare not only expectation but proof, desired of your old father and wanted of your native country, now so near your home, to divert your thoughts from the way of goodness; to lose, nay, to abuse your

---

[1] turned to *St, Bo, Je, Hm, Cm*: turned into *Cl, As, Da, Ph, 90, 93*

time; lastly, to overthrow all the excellent things you have done which have filled the world with your fame – as if you should drown your ship in the long-desired haven, or like an ill player, should mar the last act of his tragedy.

'Remember, for I know you know it, that if we will be men, the reasonable part of our soul is to have absolute commandment, against which if any sensual weakness arise, we are to yield all our sound forces to the overthrowing of so unnatural a rebellion; wherein, how can we want courage, since we are to deal against so weak an adversary that in itself is nothing but weakness? Nay, we are to resolve that if reason direct it, we must do it; and if we must do it, we will do it – for to say "I cannot" is childish; and "I will not", womanish.

'And see how extremely every way you endanger your mind – for to take this womanish[1] habit, without you frame your behaviour accordingly, is wholly vain. Your behaviour can never come kindly from you but as the mind is proportioned unto it; so that you must resolve, if you will play your part to any purpose, whatsoever peevish imperfections[2] are in that sex,[3] to soften your heart to receive them – the very first down step to all wickedness. For do not deceive yourself, my dear cousin, there is no man suddenly either excellently good[4] or extremely evil, but grows either as he holds himself up in virtue or lets himself slide to viciousness.

'And let us see what power is the author of all these troubles: forsooth, love – love, a passion, and the basest and fruitlessest of all passions. Fear breedeth wit; anger is the cradle of courage; joy openeth and enableth the heart; sorrow, as it closeth, so it draweth[5] it inward to look to the correcting of itself. And so all of them generally[6] have power towards some good by the direction of [right][7] reason. But this bastard love (for indeed the name of *love* is unworthily[8] applied[9] to so hateful a humour[10] as it is, engendered betwixt lust and idleness), as the matter it works upon is nothing but a certain base weakness which some gentle fools call a gentle heart; as his adjoined companions be unquietness, longings, fond comforts, faint discomforts, hopes, jealousies, ungrounded rages, causeless yieldings; so is the highest end it aspires unto a little pleasure, with much pain before and great repentance after. But that end, how endless[11] it runs to infinite evils, were fit enough for the matter we speak of – but not for your ears, in whom indeed there is so much true disposition to virtue. Yet thus[12] much of his worthy

---

[1] womanish] woman's *St, Bo*; womanly *Cl, Da, Je, Hm*; om. *Ph* [2] imperfections *OA* (ex. *Je*), *Cm, 93*: affections *Je, 90* [3] sex, to soften *OA, 93*; sex, soften *Cm, 90* [4] suddenly either excellently good *OA* (ex. *As, Je*), *93*: suddenly good *Je*; suddenly either excellent good *As*; suddenly excellently good *Cm, 90* [5] it draweth] yet draweth *OA* (ex. *As, Da*) [6] all of them generally *OA, 93*: all generally *Cm, 90* [7] right] om. *OA, Cm, 93* [8] unworthily *OA, Cm*: most unworthily *90, 93* [9] applied *OA, Cm, 90* (catchword), *93*: applie *90* [10] a humour] an humour *OA* (ex. *Da*) [11] endless] endlessly *St, Bo, Da, Ph* [12] thus] this *Je, Hm, 13*

effects in yourself is to be seen: that besides your breaking laws of hospitality with Kalander and of friendship with me, it utterly subverts the course of nature in making reason give place to sense, and man to woman.

'And truly, I think hereupon it first gate the name of love, for indeed, the true love hath that excellent nature in it that it doth transform the very essence of the lover into the thing loved, uniting and as it were incorporating it with a secret and inward working. And herein do these kind of loves[1] imitate the excellent, for as the love of heaven makes one heavenly, the love of virtue virtuous, so doth the love of the world make one become worldly – and this effeminate love of a woman doth so womanize[2] a man that, if you[3] yield to it, it will not only make you[4] an Amazon, but a launder, a distaff-spinner, or whatsoever other vile occupation their idle heads can imagine and their weak hands perform. Therefore, to trouble you no longer with my tedious but loving words, if either you remember what you are, what you have been, or what you must be; if you consider what it is that moved you, or for[5] what kind of creature you are moved, you shall find the cause so small, the effect[6] so dangerous, yourself so unworthy to run into the one or to be driven by the other, that I doubt not I shall quickly have occasion rather to praise you for having conquered it than to give you further[7] counsel how to do it.'

But in Pyrocles this speech wrought no more but that he, who before he was espied was afraid, after being perceived was ashamed, now being hardly rubbed upon left both fear and shame, and was moved to anger; but the exceeding goodwill he bare to Musidorus striving with it, he thus (partly to satisfy him, but principally to loose the reins to his own motions) made him answer:

'Cousin, whatsoever good disposition nature hath bestowed upon me,[8] or howsoever that disposition hath been by bringing up confirmed, this must I confess: that I am not yet come to that degree of wisdom to think light[9] of the sex of whom I have my life; since if I be anything (which your friendship rather finds, than I acknowledge), I was to come to it born of a woman, and nursed of a woman. And certainly (for this point of your speech doth nearest touch me) it is strange to see the unmanlike cruelty of mankind, who not content with their tyrannous ambition to have brought the others' virtuous patience under them, like childish[10] masters think their masterhood nothing without doing injury to them, who (if we will argue by

---

[1] kind of loves *St, Bo, As, Je, Hm, 93*: kinds of love *Cl, Ph, Cm, 90*; kind of love *Da* [2] womanize *Bo, Je, Hm, Cm, 93*: womanish *St, Cl, As, Da, Ph, 90* [3] if you *OA, Cm (Cm reads if ye)*: if he *90, 93* [4] make you *OA, Cm (Cm reads you corr. to ye)*: make him *90, 93* [5] or for *OA (ex. Cl), Cm*: or with *Cl*; or by *90, 93* [6] effect] effects *St, Bo, As, Cl, Da* [7] you further] you any further *St, Bo, As, Da, Ph*; you any *Je* [8] upon me] on me *St, Bo, Cl, Da, Je, Hm* [9] light] lightly *St, Bo, Da, Je, Hm*; little *Ph* [10] like childish *OA, 93*: like to childish *Cm, 90*

reason) are framed of nature with the same parts of the mind for the exercise of virtue as we are. And for example, even this estate of Amazons, which I now for my greatest honour do seek to counterfeit, doth well witness that, if generally the sweetness of their disposition[1] did not make them see the vainness of these things which we account glorious, they neither want valour of mind, nor yet doth their fairness take away their force. And truly, we men and praisers of men should remember, that if we have such excellencies, it is reason to think them excellent creatures of whom we are, since a kite never brought forth a good flying hawk. But to tell you true, as I think it superfluous to use any words of such a subject which is so praised in itself as it needs no praises, so withal I fear lest my conceit, not able to reach unto them, bring forth words which for their unworthiness may be a disgrace to them[2] I so inwardly honour. Let this suffice: that they are capable of virtue, and virtue, you yourselves say, is to be loved; and I, too, truly. But this I willingly confess: that it likes me much better when I find virtue in a fair lodging than when I am bound to seek it in an ill-favoured creature, like a pearl in a dunghill.

'As for my fault of being an uncivil guest to Kalander, if you could feel what an inward guest myself am host unto, you would think it very excusable, in that I rather perform the duties of an host than the ceremonies of a guest. And for my breaking the laws of friendship with you, which I would rather die than effectually do, truly I could find in my heart to ask you pardon for it, but that your handling[3] of me gives me reason to my former dealing.'

And here Pyrocles stayed, as to breathe himself, having been transported with a little vehemency because it seemed him Musidorus had over bitterly glanced against the reputation of womankind. But then quieting his countenance, as well as out of an unquiet mind it might be, he thus proceeded on:

'And poor love,' said he, 'dear cousin, is little beholding unto you, since you are not contented to spoil it of the honour of the highest power of the mind, which notable men have attributed unto it, but you deject it below all other passions – in truth, somewhat[4] strangely, since if love receive any disgrace, it is by the company of these passions you prefer before it. For those kinds[5] of bitter objections (as that lust, idleness, and a weak heart should be, as it were, the matter and form of love) rather touch me, dear Musidorus, than love. But I am good witness of mine own imperfections, and therefore will not defend myself. But herein I must say you deal contrary to yourself; for if I be so weak, then can you not with reason stir me up, as you did,

---

[1] disposition *OA, 93*: dispositions *Cm, 90*   [2] to them *St, As, Da, Ph, Hm, 93*: unto them *Bo, Cl, Je, Cm, 90*   [3] your handling] your now handling *93*   [4] somewhat] something *OA (ex. Ph, Je)*; sometimes *Je*   [5] kinds] kind *OA (ex. Da)*

by the remembrance[1] of my[2] own virtue. Or if indeed I be virtuous, then must you confess that love hath his working in a virtuous heart – and so no doubt hath it, whatsoever I be, for if we love virtue, in whom shall we love it but in a virtuous creature – without your meaning be I should love this word *virtue*[3] where I see it written in a book? Those troublesome effects you say it breeds be[4] not the faults[5] of love, but of him that loves, as an unable vessel to bear such a liquor – like evil eyes not able to look on the sun, or like an ill[6] brain soonest overthrown with best[7] wine. Even that heavenly love you speak of is accompanied in some hearts with hopes, griefs, longings, and despairs. And in that heavenly love, since there are two parts (the one, the love itself; th'other, the excellency of the thing loved), I (not able at the first leap to frame both in me) do now, like a diligent workman, make ready the chief instrument and first part of that great work, which is love itself; which, when I have a while practised in this sort, then you shall see me turn it to greater matters. And thus gently you may, if it please you, think of me. Neither doubt you because I wear a woman's apparel I will be the more womanish, since, I assure you, for all my apparel there is nothing I desire more than fully to prove myself a man in this enterprise. Much might be said in my defence, much more for love, and most of all for that divine creature which hath joined me and love together – but these disputations are fitter for quiet schools than my troubled brains, which are bent rather in deeds to perform, than in words to defend, the noble desire that[8] possesseth me.'

'O Lord!' said Musidorus, 'how sharp-witted you are to hurt yourself!'

'No,' answered he, 'but it is the hurt you speak of which makes me so sharp-witted.'

'Even so,' said Musidorus, 'as every base occupation makes one sharp in that practice, and foolish in all the rest.'

'Nay rather,' answered Pyrocles, 'as each excellent thing, once well learned, serves for a measure of all other knowledges.'

'And is that become,' said Musidorus, 'a measure for other things, which never received measure in itself?'

'It is counted without measure,' answered Pyrocles, 'because the workings of it are without measure; but otherwise, in nature it hath measure, since it hath an end allotted unto it.'

'The beginning being so excellent, I would gladly know the end.'[9]

'Enjoying,' answered Pyrocles, with a deep[10] sigh.

---

[1] by the remembrance *OA, Cm*: by remembrance *90, 93* [2] my] mine *St, Cl, Ph, Hm, 98, 13* [3] word virtue] word of *virtue OA (ex. As)*; world virtue *Cm* [4] be] is *OA (ex. Cl)* [5] faults] fault *OA (ex. Cl)* [6] an ill] a weak *OA, 93* [7] with best] with the best *OA, 93* [8] that *OA, 93*: which *Cm, 90* [9] the end] his end *St, Da, Ph, Je, Hm* [10] deep *OA, Cm, 93*: great *90*

'Oh,' said Musidorus, 'now set you forth the baseness of it, since if it end in enjoying, it shows all the rest was nothing.'

'You mistake me,' answered Pyrocles. 'I spake of the end to which it is directed; which end ends not, no sooner than the life.'

'Alas! Let your own brain disenchant you,' said Musidorus.

'My heart is too far possessed,' said Pyrocles.

'But the head gives you direction.'

'And the heart gives me life,' answered Pyrocles.

But Musidorus was so grieved to see his well-beloved friend obstinate, as he thought to his own destruction, that it forced him with more than accustomed vehemency to speak these words:

'Well, well,' said he, 'you list to abuse yourself. It was a very white and red virtue which you could pick out of a painterly gloss of a visage. Confess the truth, and you shall find the utmost was but beauty; a thing which, though it be in as great excellency in yourself as may be in any, yet I am sure you make no further reckoning of it than of an outward fading benefit nature bestowed upon you. And yet, such is your want of a true grounded virtue (which must be like itself in all points) that what you wisely account a trifle in yourself, you fondly become a slave unto in another. For my part, I now protest I have left nothing unsaid which my wit could make me know, or my most entire friendship to you requires of me. I do now beseech you, even for the love betwixt us (if this other love have left any in you towards me), and for the remembrance of your old careful father (if you can remember him, that forget yourself), lastly, for Pyrocles' own sake (who is now upon the point of falling or rising), to purge your self of this vile infection. Otherwise, give me leave to leave off this name of friendship as an idle title of a thing which cannot be, where virtue is abolished.'

The length of these speeches before had not so much cloyed Pyrocles (though he were very impatient[1] of long deliberations) as this[2] last farewell of him he loved as his own life did wound his soul, for thinking[3] himself afflicted, he was the apter to conceive unkindness deeply; insomuch that, shaking his head, and delivering some show of tears, he thus uttered his griefs:

'Alas,' said he, 'Prince Musidorus, how cruelly you deal with me! If you seek the victory, take it; and if you list, triumph.[4] Have you all the reason of the world, and with me remain all the imperfections – yet such as I can no more lay from me than the crow can be persuaded by the swan to cast off all his black feathers. But truly, you deal with me like a physician that, seeing his

---

[1] impatient *OA* (*ex. Ph*), *Cm*, 93: unpatient *Ph*, 90   [2] this *OA*, *Cm*, 93: the 90   [3] soul, for thinking *Cm*, 93: soul, thinking 90   [4] list, triumph] list the triumph 90 (*uncorr.*), 93, 98

patient in a pestilent fever, should chide him instead of ministering help, and bid him be sick no more; or rather, like such a friend that, visiting his friend condemned to perpetual prison and loaden with grievous fetters, should will him to shake off his fetters, or he would leave him. I am sick, and sick to the death. I am prisoner;[1] neither is there[2] any redress but by her to whom I am slave.[3] Now, if you list, leave[4] him that loves you in the highest degree; but remember ever to carry this with you, that you abandon your friend in his greatest extremity.'

And herewith, the deep wound of his love being rubbed afresh with this new unkindness began as it were to bleed again, in such sort that he was not able[5] to bear it any longer; but gushing out abundance of tears, and crossing his arms over his woeful heart, [as if his tears had been out-flowing blood, his arms an over-pressing burthen,] he sank[6] down to the ground – which sudden trance went so to the heart of Musidorus that, falling down by him, and kissing the weeping eyes of his friend, he besought him not to make account of his speech, which if it had been over vehement, yet was it to be borne withal, because it came out of a love much more vehement; that he had not thought fancy could have received so deep a wound, but now finding in him the force of it, he would no further contrary it, but employ all his service to medicine it in such sort as the nature of it required. But even this kindness made Pyrocles the more melt in the former unkindness, which his manlike tears well showed, with a silent look upon Musidorus, as who should say, 'And is it possible that Musidorus should threaten to leave me?' And this strook Musidorus' mind and senses so dumb too that, for grief being not able to say anything, they rested with their eyes placed one upon another, in such sort as might well paint out the true passion of unkindness to be never aright but betwixt them that most dearly love.

And thus remained they a time, till at length, Musidorus embracing him, said, 'And will you thus shake off your friend?'

'It is you that shake me off,' said Pyrocles, 'being for my unperfectness unworthy of your friendship.'

'But this,' said Musidorus, 'shows you more[7] unperfect, to be cruel to him that submits himself unto you. But since you are unperfect,' said he, smiling, 'it is reason you be governed by us wise and perfect men. And that authority will I begin to take upon me with three absolute commandments: the first, that you increase not your evil with further griefs; the second, that you love her with all the powers of your mind; and the last commandment shall be,

---

[1] am prisoner *OA (ex. Cl, As), 93*: am a prisoner *Cl, As, Cm, 90* [2] is there *OA, 93*: is *Cm, 90* [3] am slave] am a slave *Cl, As, Da, 98, 13* [4] list, leave *OA, 93*: list to, leave *Cm, 90* [5] not able] not unable *corr. to* not able *Cm*; unable *OA, 93* [6] heart... sank] heart, he sank *OA, Cm*; heart, he sunk *93* [7] you more] you much more *OA (ex. Je)*

you command me to do what service I can towards the attaining of your desires.'

Pyrocles' heart was not so oppressed with the two mighty[1] passions of love and unkindness but that it yielded to some mirth at this commandment of Musidorus that he should love, so that something clearing his face from his former shows of grief, 'Well,' said he, 'dear cousin, I see by the well choosing of your commandments that you are far fitter[2] to be a prince than a councillor, and therefore I am resolved to employ all my endeavour to obey you, with this condition: that the commandments you command me to lay upon you shall only be that you continue to love me, and look upon my imperfections with more affection than judgement.'

'Love you!' said he. 'Alas, how can my heart be separated from the true embracing of it, without it burst by being too full of it? But,' said he, 'let us leave off these flowers of new-begun friendship. And now I pray you again, tell me (but tell it me fully, omitting no circumstance) the story of your affection's both beginning and proceeding, assuring yourself that there is nothing so great which I will fear to do for you, nor nothing so small which I will disdain to do for you. Let me therefore receive a clear understanding, which many times we miss while those things we account small, as a speech or a look, are omitted – like as a whole sentence may fail of his congruity by wanting one particle. Therefore between friends all must be laid open, nothing being superfluous nor tedious.'

'You shall be obeyed,' said Pyrocles. 'And here are we in as fit a place for it as may be, for this arbour nobody offers to come into but myself, I using it as my melancholy retiring-place, and therefore that respect is borne unto it; yet if by chance any should come, say that you are a servant sent from the queen of the Amazons to seek me, and then let me alone for the rest.' So sate they down, and Pyrocles thus said:

'Cousin,[3] then[4] began the fatal overthrow of all my liberty when, walking among the pictures in Kalander's house, you yourself delivered unto me what you had understood of Philoclea, who much resembling, though I must say much surpassing the Lady Zelmane whom too[5] well I loved, there were mine eyes infected, and at your mouth did I drink my poison. Yet alas, so sweet was it unto me that I could not be contented till Kalander had made it more and more strong with his declaration; which the more I questioned, the more pity I conceived of her unworthy fortune; and when with pity

---

[1] the two mighty *OA, 93*: the mighty *Cm, 90*   [2] are far fitter *OA (ex. As), 93*: are fitter *As, Cm, 90*   [3] said: 'Cousin *Cm, 93*: said: Chap. 13. How Pyrocles fell in love with Philoclea; his counsel and course therein; his disguising into Zelmane; her meeting with Dametas, Basilius, the queen, and her daughters; and their speeches; her abode there over-entreated; and the place thereof described. 'Cousin *90*   [4] 'Cousin, then *Cm*: 'Cousin, and then *corr. to* 'Cousin, then *Cm*; 'Cousin,' said he, ' then *90, 93*   [5] too] so *93*

once my heart was made tender, according to the aptness of the humour, it received quickly a cruel impression of that wonderful passion which to be defined is impossible, because no words reach to the strange nature of it. They only know it which inwardly feel it; it is called love.

'Yet did I not, poor wretch, at first know my disease, thinking it only such a wonted kind of desire to see rare sights, and my pity to be no other but the fruits of a gentle nature. But even this arguing with myself came of further thoughts, and the more I argued, the more my thoughts increased. Desirous I was to see the place where she remained – as though the architecture of the lodges would have been much for my learning; but more desirous to see herself – to be judge, forsooth! of the painter's cunning! for thus at the first did I flatter myself, as though my wound had been no deeper. But when within short time I came to the degree of uncertain wishes, and that those[1] wishes grew to unquiet longings; when I could fix my thoughts upon nothing but that, within little varying, they should end with Philoclea; when each thing I saw seemed to figure out some part[2] of my passions; when even Parthenia's fair face became a lecture to me of Philoclea's imagined beauty; when I heard no word spoken but that methought it carried the sound[3] of Philoclea's name; then indeed, then I did yield to the burthen, finding myself prisoner before I had leisure to arm myself, and that I might well, like the spaniel, gnaw upon the chain that ties him, but I should sooner mar my teeth than procure liberty.

'Yet I take to witness the eternal spring of virtue that I had never read, heard, nor seen anything; I had never any taste of philosophy, nor inward feeling in myself which, for a while, I did not call for[4] my succour. But alas, what resistance was there when ere long my very reason was – you will say corrupted – I must needs confess,[5] conquered; and that methought even reason did assure me that all eyes did degenerate from their creation which did not honour such beauty? Nothing in truth could hold any plea with it but the reverent friendship I bare unto you, for as it went against my heart to break any way from you, so did I fear, more than any assault, to break it to you, finding (as it is indeed) that to a heart fully resolute counsel is tedious, but reprehension is loathsome; and that there is nothing more terrible to a guilty heart than the eye of a respected friend. This made me determine with myself (thinking it a less fault in friendship to do a thing without your knowledge than against your will) to take this secret course; which conceit was most built up in me the last day of my parting and speaking with you, when upon your speech with me, and my but naming *love*, when else perchance I would have gone further, I saw your voice and countenance so

---

[1] those *OA, 93*: the *Cm, 90* [2] part *OA, Cm, 93*: parts *90* [3] sound *OA, 93*: sonn *Cm*; sum *90* [4] call for] call to *93* [5] must needs confess] must confess *93*

change as it assured me my revealing it should but purchase your grief, with my cumber; and therefore, dear Musidorus, even ran away from thy well-known chiding. For having written a letter (which I know not whether you found or no) and taken[1] my chief jewels with me, while you were in the middest of your sport I got a time, as I think unmarked, to[2] steal away – I cared not whither, so I might scape you.

'And so came I to Ithonia in the province of Messenia, where lying secret, I put this in practice which before I had devised. For remembering by Philanax's letter and Kalander's speech how obstinately Basilius was determined not to marry his daughters, and therefore fearing lest any public dealing should rather increase her captivity than further my love, love, the refiner of invention, had put in my head thus to disguise myself, that under that mask I might, if it were possible, get access; and what access could bring forth, commit to fortune and industry, determining to bear the countenance of an Amazon. Therefore in the closest manner I could, naming myself Zelmane for that dear lady's sake to whose memory I am so much bound, I caused this apparel to be made; and bringing it near the lodges which are hard at hand, by night thus dressed myself, resting till occasion might make me to be found[3] by them whom I sought; which the next morning happened as well as my own plot could have laid it.

'For after I had run over the whole pedigree of my thoughts, I gave myself to sing a little; which, as you know I ever delighted in, so now especially, whether it be the nature of this clime to stir up poetical fancies, or rather as I think, of love, whose scope being pleasure, will not so much as utter his griefs but in some form of pleasure. But I had sung very little, when as I think displeased with my bad music, comes Master Dametas with a hedging-bill in his hand, chafing, and swearing by the pantable[4] of Pallas and such other oaths as his rustical bravery could imagine. And when he saw me, I assure you my beauty was no more beholding to him than my harmony; for leaning his hands upon his bill and his chin upon his hands, with the voice of one that playeth Hercules in a play[5] but never had his fancy in his head, the first word he spake to me was: "Am not I Dametas? Why, am not I Dametas?"

'He needed not name himself, for Kalander's description had set such a note upon him as made him very notable unto me; and therefore the height of my thoughts would not descend so much as to make him any answer, but continued on my inward discourses; which he (perchance witness of his own unworthiness, and therefore the apter to think himself contemned)

---

[1] taken *Cm, 93*: taking *90*   [2] unmarked, to] unmarked by any, to *93*   [3] me to be found *Cm, 93*: me sound *90*   [4] pantable] pantople *St*; pantaple *Cl*; pantables *As*; pantofle *Ph, 13*; pantople *Je*   [5] in a play] in the play *Ph*; in play *St, As, Hm*

took in so heinous manner that standing upon his tiptoes, and staring as if¹ he would have had a² mote pulled out of his eye, "Why," said he, "thou woman, or boy, or both! Whatsoever thou be, I tell thee here is no place for thee. Get thee gone. I tell thee it is the prince's pleasure; I tell thee it is Dametas' pleasure."

'I could not choose but smile at him, seeing him look so like an ape that had newly taken a purgation; yet taking myself with the manner, spake these words to myself: "O spirit", said I, "of mine, how canst thou receive any mirth in the midst of thine agonies? And thou, mirth, how darest thou enter into a mind so grown of late thy professed enemy?"

'"Thy spirit?" said Dametas. "Dost thou think me a spirit? I tell thee I am Basilius' officer, and have charge of him and his daughters."

'"O only pearl!" said I, sobbing, "that so vile an oyster should keep thee!"

'"By the combcase of Diana!" sware Dametas, "this woman is mad! Oysters and pearls! Dost thou think I will buy oysters? I tell thee once again, get thee packing", and with that, lifted up his bill to hit me with the blunt end of it.

'But indeed, that put me quite out of my lesson, so that I forgat all Zelmaneship; and drawing out my sword, the baseness of the villain yet made me stay my hand. And he, who as Kalander told me, from his childhood ever feared the blade of a sword, ran back³ backward with his hands above his head at least twenty paces, gaping and staring with the very grace, I think, of the clowns that by Latona's prayers were turned into frogs. At length staying, finding himself without the compass of blows, he fell to a fresh scolding in such mannerly manner as might well show he had passed through the discipline of a tavern. But seeing me walk up and down without marking what he said, he went his way, as I perceived after, to Basilius; for within a while he came unto me, bearing indeed shows in his countenance of an honest and well-minded gentleman. And with as much courtesy, as Dametas with rudeness, saluting me, "Fair lady," said he, "it is nothing strange that such a solitary place as this should receive solitary persons; but much do I marvel how such a beauty as yours is should be suffered to be thus alone."

'I that now knew it was my part to play, looking with a grave majesty upon him as if I found in myself cause to be reverenced, "They are never alone", said I, "that are accompanied with noble thoughts."

'"But those thoughts", replied Basilius, "cannot in this your loneliness neither warrant you from suspicion in others, nor defend you from melancholy in yourself."

---

¹ as if *OA (ex. As)*, *93*: as though *As*, *Cm*, *90*   ² have had a *OA*, *93*: have a *Cm*, *90*   ³ back] *om. Bo, Cl, As, Ph, 13*

'I then showing a mislike that he pressed me so far, "I seek no better warrant", said I, "than my[1] own conscience, nor no greater pleasure[2] than mine own[3] contentation."

'"Yet virtue seeks to satisfy others", said Basilius.

'"Those that be good," said I; "and they will be satisfied as long as they see no evil."

'"Yet will the best in this country", said Basilius, "suspect so excellent a beauty,[4] being so weakly guarded."

'"Then are the best but stark nought," answered I; "for open suspecting others comes of secret condemning themselves. But in my country, whose manners I am in all places to maintain and reverence, the general goodness which is nourished in our hearts makes every one think the[5] strength of virtue in another, whereof they find the assured foundation in themselves."

'"Excellent lady," said he, "you praise so greatly and yet so wisely your country that I must needs desire to know what the nest is out of which such birds do fly."

'"You must first deserve it", said I, "before you may obtain it."

'"And by what means", said Basilius, "shall I deserve to know your estate?"

'"By letting me first know yours", answered I.

'"To obey you", said he, "I will do it, although it were so much more reason yours should be known first, as you do deserve in all points to be preferred. Know you, fair lady, that my name is Basilius, unworthily[6] lord of this country; the rest either fame hath already brought[7] to your ears, or if it please you to make this place happy by your presence, at more leisure you shall understand of me."

'I that from the beginning assured myself it was he, but would not seem I did so, to keep my gravity the better, making a piece of reverence unto him, "Mighty prince," said I, "let my not knowing you serve for the excuse of my boldness, and the little reverence I do you, impute it to the manner of my country, which is the invincible land of the Amazons; myself, niece to Senicia, queen thereof, lineally descended of the famous Penthesilea, slain by the bloody hand of Pyrrhus. I having in this my youth determined to make the world see the Amazons' excellencies as well in private as in public virtue, have passed some dangerous adventures in divers countries, till the unmerciful sea deprived me of my company; so that shipwrack casting me not far hence, uncertain wandering brought me to this place."

---

[1] my] mine *St, Cl, Ph, Hm*   [2] pleasure *OA, Cm, 93*: pleasures *90*   [3] mine own] my *Bo, Da*   [4] excellent a beauty] excellent beauty *93*   [5] think the] think that *OA (ex. As)*   [6] unworthily] unworthy *OA (ex. Bo, Cl)*   [7] hath already brought *OA, 93*: hath brought *Cm, 90*

'But Basilius (who now began to taste that[1] which since he hath swallowed up, as I will tell you) fell to more cunning entreating my abode than any greedy host would use to well-paying passengers. I thought nothing could shoot righter at the mark of my desires; yet had I learned already so much, that it was against my womanhood to be forward in my own wishes. And therefore he, to prove whether intercessions in fitter mouths might better prevail, commanded Dametas to bring forthwith[2] his wife and daughters thither – three ladies, although of diverse, yet all of[3] excellent beauty: his wife in grave matronlike attire, with countenance and gesture suitable, and of such fairness (being in the strength of her age) as, if her daughters had not been by, might with just price have purchased admiration; but they being there, it was enough that the most dainty eye would think her a worthy mother of such children. The fair Pamela, whose noble heart I find doth greatly disdain that the trust of her virtue is reposed in such a lout's hands as Dametas, had yet, to show an obedience, taken on a shepherdish[4] apparel which was but of russet cloth cut after their fashion, with a straight body, open breasted, the nether part full of pleats, with long and wide sleeves. But believe me, she did apparel her apparel, and with the preciousness of her body made it most sumptuous: her hair at the full length, wound about with gold lace – only by the comparison to show[5] how far her hair doth excel in colour; betwixt her breasts, which sweetly rase up like two fair mountainets[6] in the pleasant vale[7] of Tempe, there hung a very rich diamond set but in a black horn – the word, I have since read, is this: "Yet still myself." And thus particularly have I described them, because you may know that mine eyes are not so partial but that marked *them* too!

'But when the ornament of the earth, the model of heaven, the triumph of nature, the light[8] of beauty, the queen[9] of love, young Philoclea, appeared in her nymphlike apparel, so near nakedness as one might well discern part of her perfections, and yet so apparelled as did show she kept best store of her beauty to herself – her hair (alas, too poor a word; why should I not rather call them her beams?) drawn up into a net able to have caught[10] Jupiter when he was in the form of an eagle; her body (oh, sweet body!) covered with a light taffeta garment, so cut as the wrought smock came through it in many places – enough to have made *your* restrained imagination have thought what was under it; with the cast of her black eyes (black indeed, whether nature so made them that we might be the more able to behold and bear their

---

[1] taste that] taste of that 93   [2] forthwith] forth OA, 13   [3] yet all of] yet of Hm, 98, 13   [4] on a shepherdish] on shepherdish Cm, 90 (uncorr.), 93   [5] show OA, 93: see Cm, 90   [6] mountainets] mountains St, Bo, Da, Ph, Hm, Cm; mountaints 90 (uncorr.)   [7] vale OA, 93: valley Cm, 90   [8] light] like Cm; life 93   [9] beauty, the queen Cm, 93: beauty, queen 90   [10] have caught OA, Cm, 93: take 90

wonderful shining, or that she, goddess like, would work this miracle in herself,[1] in giving blackness the price above all beauty) – then, I say, indeed, methought the lilies grew pale for envy; the roses, methought, blushed to see sweeter roses in her cheeks; and the apples, methought, fell down from the trees to do homage to the apples of her breast. Then the clouds gave place that the heavens might more freshly[2] smile upon her; at the least,[3] the clouds of my thoughts quite vanished, and my sight, then more clear and forcible than ever, was so fixed there that I imagine I stood like a well wrought image, with some life in show, but none in practice. And so had I been like enough to have stayed long time, but that Gynecia stepping between[4] my sight and the only Philoclea, the change of object made me recover my senses, so that I could with reasonable good manner receive the salutation of her and of the Princess Pamela, doing them yet no further reverence than one prince[5] useth to another. But when I came to the never-enough praised Philoclea, I could not but fall down on my knees; and taking by force her hand and kissing it, I must confess with more than womanly ardency, "Divine lady," said I, "let not the world nor these great princes[6] marvel to see me, contrary to my manner, do this especial honour unto you, since all, both men and women, do owe this to the perfection of your beauty."

'But she, blushing like a fair morning in May at this my singularity, and causing me to rise, "Noble lady," said she, "it is no marvel to see your judgement much mistaken[7] in my beauty, since you begin with so great an error as to do more honour unto me than to them, to whom[8] I myself owe all service."

' "Rather," answered I with a bowed-down countenance, "that shows the power of your beauty, which forced me to do such an error, if it were an error."

' "You are so well acquainted", said she, sweetly, most sweetly smiling, "with your own beauty that it makes you easily fall into the discourse of beauty."

' "Beauty in me!" said I, truly sighing. "Alas, if there be any it is in my[9] eyes, which your blessed presence hath imparted unto them."

'But then, as I think, Basilius willing her so to do,[10]

"Well", said she, "I must needs confess I have heard that it is a great happiness to be praised of them that are most praiseworthy. And well I find that you are an invincible Amazon, since you will overcome, though in a

---

[1] in herself] with herself 93   [2] freshly] freely 93   [3] at the least] at least *OA* (ex. *Da*)   [4] between] betwixt *OA* (ex. *Bo*, *Hm*)   [5] prince] princess *OA*, 93   [6] princes] princess *St*, *Cl*; princesses *Bo*, 93   [7] judgement much mistaken *OA*, *Cm*, 93: judgement mistaken 90   [8] them, to whom *OA*, 93: them whom *Cm*, 90   [9] my] mine *St*, *Da*, *Ph*, *Hm*; your *Bo*   [10] so to do *Cm*, 93: so do 90

wrong matter. But if my beauty be anything, then let it obtain thus much of you: that you will remain some while in this company, to ease your own travail and our solitariness."

'"First let me die", said I, "before any word spoken by such a mouth should come in vain."

'And thus with some other words of entertaining was my staying concluded, and I led among them to the lodge, truly a place for pleasantness, not unfit to flatter solitariness; for it being set upon such an unsensible rising of the ground as you are come to a pretty height before almost you perceive that you ascend, it gives the eye lordship over a good large circuit; which according to the nature of the country being diversified between hills and dales, woods and plains, one place more clear and the other[1] more darksome, it seems a pleasant picture of nature, with lovely lightsomeness and artificial shadows. The lodge is of a yellow stone, built in the form of a star, having, round about, a garden framed into like points; and beyond the garden, ridings cut out, each answering the angles of the lodge. At the end of one of them is the other, smaller, lodge, but of like fashion, where the gracious Pamela liveth; so that the lodge seemeth not unlike a fair comet whose tail stretcheth itself to a star of less greatness.

'So[2] Gynecia herself bringing me to my lodging, anon after I was invited and brought down to sup with them in the garden, a place not fairer in natural ornaments than artificial inventions, where in a[3] banqueting house among certain pleasant trees, whose heads seemed curled with the wrappings-about of vine branches, the table was set near to an excellent waterwork, for by the casting of the water in most cunning manner it makes with the shining of the sun upon it a perfect rainbow, not more pleasant to the eye than to the mind, so sensibly to see the proof of the heavenly Iris. There were birds also, made so finely that they did not only deceive the sight with their figure, but the hearing with their songs which the watery instruments did make their gorge deliver. The table at which we sate was round; which being fast to the floor whereon we sate, and that divided from the rest of the buildings, with turning a vice (which Basilius at first did to make me sport) the table, and we about the table, did all turn round by means of water which ran under, and carried it about as a mill.

'But alas, what pleasure did it to me to make divers times the full circle round about, since Philoclea, being also set, was carried still in equal distance from me, and that only my eyes did overtake her; which when the table was stayed and we began to feed, drank much more eagerly of her beauty

---

[1] and the other] another 93   [2] greatness. 'So *Cm, 93*: greatness.' Chap. 14. The devices of the first banquet to Zelmane; her crosses in love by the love of Basilius and Gynecia; the conclusion between Musidorus and Zelmane. 'So *90*   [3] where in a *Cm, 93*: wherein is a *90*

than my mouth did of any other liquor? And so was my common sense deceived, being chiefly bent to her, that as I drank the wine and withal stale a look on her, meseemed I tasted her deliciousness. But alas, the one thirst was much more inflamed than the other quenched. Sometimes my eyes would lay themselves open to receive all the darts she did throw, sometimes close up with admiration, as if, with a contrary fancy, they would preserve the riches of that sight they had gotten, or cast my lids[1] as curtains over the image of beauty her presence had painted in them. True it is that my reason, now grown a servant to passion, did yet often tell his master that he should more moderately use his delight, but he, that of a rebel was become a prince, disdained almost to allow him the place of a councillor; so that my senses' delights being too strong for any other resolution, I did even loose the reins unto them, hoping that, going for a woman, my looks would pass either unmarked or unsuspected.

'Now thus I had, as methought, well played my first act, assuring myself that under that disguisement I should find opportunity to reveal myself to the owner of my heart. But who would think it possible, though I feel it true, that in almost eight weeks' space I have lived here, having no more company but her parents, and I being familiar, as being a woman, and watchful, as being a lover, yet could never find opportunity to have one minute's leisure of private[2] conference; the cause whereof is as strange as the effects are to me miserable. And alas, this it is.

'At the first sight that Basilius had of me (I think Cupid having headed his arrows with my misfortune) he was stricken, taking me to be such as I profess, with great affection towards me, which since is grown to such a doting love, that (till I was fain to get this place, sometimes to retire unto freely) I was even choked with his tediousness. You never saw fourscore years dance up and down more lively in a young lover, now as fine in his apparel as if he would make me in love with a cloak, and verse for verse with the sharpest-witted lover in Arcadia. Do you not think that this is a salad of wormwood, while mine eyes feed upon the ambrosia of Philoclea's beauty?

'But this is not all. No, this is not the worst! For he, good man, were easy enough to be dealt with; but as I think, love and mischief having made a wager, which should have most power in me, have set Gynecia also on such a fire towards me as will never, I fear, be quenched but with my destruction; for she being a woman of excellent wit and of strong-working thoughts, whether she suspected me by my over-vehement shows of affection to Philoclea, which love forced me unwisely to utter while hope of my mask foolishly encouraged me, or that she hath taken some other mark of me that I am not

---

[1] lids *Cm, 93*: lid *90*   [2] private *Cm, 93*: privie *90*

a woman, or what devil it is hath revealed it unto her, I know not; but so it is, that all her countenances, words, and gestures are miserable[1] portraitures of a desperate affection, whereby a man may learn that these avoidings of company do but make the passions more violent when they meet with fit subjects.

'Truly it were a notable dumb show of Cupid's kingdom to see my eyes, languishing with over-vehement longing, direct themselves to Philoclea; and Basilius as busy about me as a bee, and indeed as cumbersome, making such suits[2] to me who neither could if I would, nor would if I could, help him, while the terrible wit of Gynecia, carried with the beer of violent love, runs thorough us all. And so jealous is she of my love to her daughter that I could never yet begin to open my mouth to the unevitable Philoclea, but that her unwished presence gave my tale a conclusion before it had a beginning. And surely, if I be not deceived, I see such shows of liking (and if I be acquainted with passions, of almost a passionate liking) in the heavenly Philoclea towards me that I may hope her ears would not abhor my discourse. And for good Basilius, he thought it best to have lodged us together, but that the eternal hatefulness of my destiny made Gynecia's jealousy stop that and all other my blessings – yet must I confess that one way her love doth me pleasure, for since it was my foolish fortune or unfortunate folly to be known by her, that keeps her from bewraying me to Basilius. And thus, my Musidorus, you have my tragedy played unto you by myself, which, I pray the gods, may not indeed prove a tragedy' – and there he[3] ended, making a full point of a hearty sigh.

Musidorus recommended to his best discourse all which Pyrocles had told him, but therein he found such intricateness that he could see no way to lead him out of the maze. Yet perceiving his affection so grounded that striving against it did rather anger than heal the wound, and rather call his friendship in question than give place to any friendly counsel, 'Well,' said he, 'dear cousin, since it hath pleased the gods to mingle your other excellencies with this humour of love, yet happy it is that your love is employed upon so rare a woman, for certainly a noble cause doth ease much a grievous case. But as it stands now, nothing vexeth me as that I cannot see wherein I can be serviceable unto you.'

'I desire no greater service of you,' answered Pyrocles, 'than that you remain secretly in this country and sometimes come to this place, either late in the night or early in the morning, where you shall have my key to enter; because as my fortune either amends or impairs, I may declare it unto you and have your counsel and furtherance. And hereby I will of purpose

---

[1] are miserable] are even miserable 93   [2] such suits] such vehement suits 93   [3] there he] therewith he 93

lead her, that is the praise and yet the stain of all womankind, that you may have so good a view as to allow my judgement; and as I can get the most convenient time, I will come unto you. For though by reason of yonder wood you cannot see the lodge, it is hard at hand. But now,' said she, 'it is time for me to leave you. And towards evening we will walk out of purpose hitherward; therefore keep yourself close in that time.'

But Musidorus, bethinking himself that his horse might happen to bewray them, thought it best to return for that day to a village not far off, and dispatching his horse in some sort, the next day early to come afoot thither, and so to keep that course afterward; which Pyrocles very well liked of.

'Now farewell, dear cousin,' said he, 'from me – no more Pyrocles, nor Daiphantus now, but Zelmane. Zelmane is my name; Zelmane is my title; Zelmane is the only hope of my advancement.' And with that word, going out and seeing that the coast was clear, Zelmane dismissed Musidorus, who departed as full of care to help his friend as before he was to dissuade him;[1] and Zelmane returned to the lodge, where inflamed by Philoclea, watched by Gynecia, and tired by Basilius, she was like a horse desirous to run and miserably spurred, but so short-reined as he cannot stir forward.

Zelmane sought occasion to speak with Philoclea, Basilius with Zelmane, and Gynecia hindered them all. If Philoclea happened to sigh (and sigh she did often), as if that sigh were to be waited on, Zelmane sighed also – whereto Basilius and Gynecia soon made up four parts of sorrow. Their affection increased their conversation, and their conversation increased their affection; the respect borne bred due ceremonies, but the affection shined so through them that the ceremonies seemed not ceremonious; Zelmane's eyes were like children afore[2] sweetmeat, eager, but fearful of their ill-pleasing governors; time in one instant seeming both short and long unto them – short in the pleasingness of such presence, long in the stay of their desires.

But Zelmane failed not to entice them all many times abroad, because she was desirous her friend Musidorus, near whom of purpose she led them, might have full sight of them, sometimes angling, to a little river near hand, which for the moisture it bestowed upon roots of some flourishing trees, was rewarded with their shadow. There would they sit down, and pretty wagers be made between Pamela and Philoclea, which could soonest beguile silly fishes; while Zelmane protested that the fit prey for them was hearts of princes. She also had an angle in her hand, but the taker was so taken that she

---

[1] him; and Zelmane: him; And Zelmane/Cleophila *Cm* him; Chap. 15. The labyrinth of Zelmane's love; the ladies' exercises; the challenge of Phalantus in paragon of Artesia's beauty; the description of their persons and affections, and occasion of this challenge; the success thereof abroad. Zelmane 90; him. Zelmane 93   [2] afore] before 93

had forgotten taking. Basilius in the meantime would be the cook himself of what was so caught, and Gynecia sit still, but with no still pensiveness. Now she brought them to see a seeled dove, who the blinder she was, the higher she strave; another time, a kite, which having a gut cunningly pulled out of her, and so let fly, caused[1] all the kites in that quarter, who as oftentimes the world is deceived, thinking her prosperous when indeed she was wounded, made the poor kite find that opinion of riches may well be dangerous.

But these recreations were interrupted by a delight of more gallant show; for one evening as Basilius returned from having forced his thoughts to please themselves in such small conquests, there came a shepherd who brought him word that a gentleman desired leave to do a message from his lord unto him. Basilius granted, whereupon the gentleman came, and after the dutiful ceremonies observed, in his master's name told him that he was sent from Phalantus of Corinth to crave license that, as he had done in many other courts, so he might in his presence defy all Arcadian knights in the behalf of his mistress's beauty, who would, besides, herself in person be present to give evident proof what his lance should affirm. The conditions of his challenge were that the defendant should bring his mistress's picture, which being set by the image of Artesia (so was the mistress of Phalantus named), who in six courses should have better of the other in the judgement of Basilius, with him both the honours and the pictures should remain. Basilius, though he had retired himself into that solitary dwelling with intention to avoid rather than to accept any matters of drawing company, yet because he would entertain Zelmane, that she might not think the time, so gainful to him, loss to her, granted him to pitch his tent for three days not far from the lodge, and to proclaim his challenge; that what Arcadian knight (for none else, but upon his peril, was licensed to come) would defend what he honoured against Phalantus should have the like freedom of access and return.

This obtained and published, Zelmane being desirous to learn what this Phalantus was (having never known him further than by report of his own good,[2] insomuch as he was commonly called 'The Fair Man-of-Arms'), Basilius told her that he had had occasion, by one very inward with him, to know in part the discourse of his life, which was that he was bastard brother to the fair Helen, queen of Corinth, and dearly esteemed of her for his exceeding good parts, being honourably courteous and wronglessly valiant, considerately pleasant in conversation, and an excellent courtier without unfaithfulness; who finding his sister's unpersuadable melancholy thorough the love of Amphialus, had for a time left her court and gone into Laconia,

---

[1] caused *Cm, 93*: called *90*   [2] his own good] his good justing *93*

where in the war against the helots he had gotten the reputation of one that both durst and knew. But as it was rather choice than nature that led him to matters of arms, so, as soon as the spur of honour ceased, he willingly rested in peaceable delights, being beloved in all companies for his lovely qualities and, as a man may term it, winning[1] cheerfulness, whereby to the prince and court of Laconia none was more agreeable than Phalantus; and he, not given greatly to struggle with his own disposition, followed the gentle current of it, having a fortune sufficient to content, and he content with a sufficient fortune. But in that court he saw and was acquainted with this Artesia whose beauty he now defends; became her servant; said himself, and perchance thought himself, her lover.

'But certainly,' said Basilius, 'many times it falls out that these young companions make themselves believe they love at the first liking of a likely beauty, loving because they will love for want of other business, not because they feel indeed that divine power which makes the heart find a reason in passion, and so, God knows, as inconstantly lean,[2] upon the next chance that beauty casts before them. So therefore, taking love upon him like a fashion, he courted this Lady Artesia, who was as fit to pay him in his own money as might be; for she, thinking she did wrong to her beauty if she were not proud of it, called her disdain of him chastity, and placed her honour in little setting by his honouring her, determining never to marry but him whom she thought worthy of her – and that was one in whom all worthiness were harboured. And to this conceit not only nature had bent her, but the bringing up she received at my sister-in-law Cecropia had confirmed her, who having in her widowhood taken this young Artesia into her charge because her father had been a dear friend of her dead husband's, and taught[3] her to think that there is no wisdom but in including heaven[4] and earth in one's self, and that love, courtesy, gratefulness, friendship, and all other virtues, are rather to be taken on than taken in one's self. And so good a disciple[5] she found of her, that liking the fruits of her own planting, she was content, if so her son could have liked of it, to have wished her in marriage to my nephew Amphialus – but I think that desire hath lost some of his heat since she hath known that such a queen as Helen is doth offer so great a price as a kingdom to buy his favour, for if I be not deceived in my good sister Cecropia, she thinks no face so beautiful as that which looks under a crown. But Artesia indeed liked well of my nephew Amphialus (for I can never deem that *love* which in haughty hearts proceeds of a desire only to please, and as it were, peacock themselves); but yet she hath showed vehemency

---

[1] winning *Cm, 93*: cunning *90* [2] lean] leave *93* [3] and taught] had taught *93* [4] including heaven] including both heaven *93* [5] good a disciple *Cm, 93*: good discipline *90*

of desire that way, I think because all her desires be vehement, insomuch that she hath both placed her only brother, a fine youth called Ismenus, to be his squire, and herself is content to wait upon my sister till she may see the uttermost what she may work in Amphialus; who being of a melancholy, though I must needs say courteous[1] and noble mind, seems to love nothing less than love.

'And of late, having through some adventure or inward miscontentment withdrawn himself from anybody's knowledge, where he is, Artesia the easier condescended to go to the court of Laconia, whither she was sent for by the king's wife, to whom she is somewhat allied. And there after the war of the helots, this knight Phalantus, at least for tongue-delight, made himself her servant; and she, so little caring as not to show mislike thereof, was content only to be noted to have a notable servant. For truly, one in my court nearly acquainted with him within these few days made me a pleasant description of their love: while he with cheerful looks would speak sorrowful words, using the phrase of his affection in so high a style that Mercury would not have wooed Venus with more magnificient eloquence, but else neither in behaviour nor action accusing in himself any great trouble in mind whether he sped or no; and she of the other side well finding how little it was, and not caring for more, yet taught him that often it falleth out but a foolish wittiness to speak more than one thinks. For she made earnest benefit of his jest, forcing him in respect of his profession[2] to do her such service as were both cumbersome and costly unto him, while he still thought he went beyond her, because his heart did not commit the idolatry. So that lastly, she I think having in mind to make the fame of her beauty an orator for her to Amphialus, persuading herself perhaps that it might fall out in him as it doth in some that have delightful meat before them, and have no stomach to it before other folks praise it, she took the advantage one day upon Phalantus' unconscionable praisings of her, and certain castaway vows how much he would do for her sake, to arrest his word as soon as it was out of his mouth, and by the virtue thereof to charge him to go with her thorough all the courts of Greece, and with the challenge now made, to give her beauty the principality over all other.

'Phalantus was entrapped, and saw round about him but could not get out. Exceedingly perplexed he was, as he confessed to him that told me the tale, not for doubt he had of himself, for indeed he had little cause, being accounted with his lance especially – whereupon the challenge is to be tried – as perfect as any that Greece knoweth, but because he feared to offend his sister Helen; and withal (as he said) he could not so much believe his

---

[1] must needs say courteous] must say truly courteous 93   [2] profession *Cm, 93*: promise *90*

love but that he might[1] think in his heart (whatsoever his mouth affirmed) that both she, my daughters, and the fair Parthenia, wife to a most noble gentleman, my wives near kinsman, might far better put in their claim for that prerogative; but his promise had bound him prentice, and therefore it was now better with willingness to purchase thanks than with a discontented doing to have the pain and not the reward, and therefore went on as his faith, rather than love, did lead him. And now hath he already passed the courts of Laconia, Elis, Argos, and Corinth, and, as many times it happens that a good pleader makes a bad cause to prevail, so hath his lance brought captives to the triumph of Artesia's beauty – such as, though Artesia be among the fairest, yet in that company were to have the pre-eminence; for in those courts many knights that had been in other far countries defended such as they had seen and liked in their travel, but their defence had been such as they had forfeited the picture[2] of their ladies to give a forced false testimony to Artesia's excellency. And now, lastly, is he come hither, where he hath leave to try his fortune.

'But I assure you, if I thought it not in due and true consideration an injurious service and churlish courtesy to put the danger of so noble a title in the deciding of such a dangerless combat, I would make young Master Phalantus know that your eyes can sharpen a blunt lance, and that age (which my grey hairs, only gotten by the loving care of others, make seem more than it is) hath not diminished in me the power to protect an undeniable verity.' With that, he bustled up himself as though his heart would fain have walked abroad. Zelmane with an inward smiling gave him outward thanks, desiring him to reserve his force for worthier causes.

And so,[3] passing their time according to their wont, they waited for the coming of Phalantus, who the next morning, having already caused his tents to be pitched near to a fair tree hard by the lodge, had upon the tree made a shield to be hanged up, which the defendant should strike that would call him to the maintaining his challenge. The impresa in the shield was a heaven full of stars, with a speech signifying that it was the beauty which gave it the praise.

Himself came in next after a triumphant chariot, made of carnation velvet enriched with purl and pearl, wherein Artesia sat, drawn by four winged horses with artificial flaming mouths and fiery wings, as if she had newly borrowed them of Phoebus. Before her marched, two after two, certain footmen pleasantly attired, who between them held one picture after another of them that by Phalantus' well running had lost the prize in the race of beauty;

---

[1] might] must 93   [2] picture] pictures 93   [3] causes. And so *Cm*: causes. Chap. 16. Phalantus and Artesia's pompous entrance; the painted muster of an eleven conquered beauties. So *90*; causes. So *93*

and at every pace they stayed, turning the pictures to each side so leisurely that with perfect judgement they might be discerned.

The first that came in (following the order of the time wherein they had been won) was the picture of Andromana, queen of Iberia, whom a Laconian knight having sometime and with special favour served, though some years since returned home, with more gratefulness than good fortune defended. But therein fortune had borrowed wit, for indeed she was not comparable to Artesia, not because she was a good deal elder, for time had not yet been able to impoverish her store thereof, but an exceeding red hair with small eyes did, like ill companions, disgrace the other assembly of most commendable beauties.

Next after her was borne the counterfeit of the princess of Elis, a lady that taught the beholders no other point of beauty but this: that as liking is not always the child of beauty, so whatsoever liketh is beautiful – for in that visage there was neither majesty, grace, favour, nor fairness; yet she wanted not a servant that would have made her fairer than the fair Artesia – but he wrote her praises with his helmet in the dust, and left her picture to be as true a witness of his overthrow as his running was of her beauty.

After her was the goodly Artaxia, great queen of Armenia, a lady upon whom nature bestowed and well placed her delightful[1] colours, and withal had proportioned her without any fault quickly to be discovered by the senses, yet altogether seemed not to make up that harmony that Cupid delights in; the reason whereof might seem a mannish countenance which overthrew that lovely sweetness, the noblest power of womankind, far fitter to prevail by parley than by battle.

Of a far contrary consideration was the representation of her that next followed, which was Erona, queen of Lycia; who though of so brown a hair as no man should have injured it to have called it black, and that in the mixture of her cheeks the white did so much overcome the red (though what was, was very pure) that it came near to paleness, and that her face was a thought longer than the exact symmetrians perhaps would allow, yet love played his part so well in every part that it caught hold of the judgement before it could judge, making it first love, and after acknowledge it fair; for there was a certain delicacy which in yielding conquered, and with a pitiful look made one find cause to crave help himself.

After her came two ladies of noble but not of royal birth. The former was named Baccha, who though very fair and of a fatness rather to allure than to mislike, yet her breasts over-familiarly laid open, with a mad[2] countenance about her mouth between simpering and smiling, her head bowed some-

---

[1] her delightful] her most delightful 93 [2] mad] made 93

what down, seemed to languish with overmuch idleness; with[1] an inviting look cast upward, dissuaded[2] with too much persuading, while hope might seem to overcome[3] desire. The other, whose name was written 'Leucippe,' was of a fine daintiness of beauty, her face carrying in it a sober simplicity, like one that could do much good and meant no hurt; her eyes having in them such a cheerfulness as nature seemed to smile in them, though her mouth and cheeks obeyed that[4] pretty demureness, which the more one marked,[5] the more one would judge the poor soul apt to believe, and therefore the more pity to deceive her.

Next came the queen of Laconia, one that seemed born in the confines of beauty's kingdom, for all her lineaments were neither perfect possessions[6] thereof nor absolute[7] strangers thereto – but she was a queen, and therefore beautiful.

But she that followed conquered indeed with being conquered, and might well have made all the beholders wait upon her triumph while herself were led captive. It was the excellently fair Queen Helen, whose jacinth hair, curled by nature and intercurled[8] by art, like a fine brook through golden sands, had a rope of fair pearls[9] which, now hiding, now hidden by the hair, did as it were play at fast and loose[10] each with other, mutually giving and receiving riches;[11] in her face so much beauty and favour expressed as, if Helen had not been known, some would rather have judged it the painter's exercise to show what he could do than counterfeiting[12] of any living pattern; for no fault the most fault-finding wit could have found, if it were not that to the rest of the body the face was somewhat too little – but that little was such a spark of beauty as was able to inflame a world of love; for everything was full of a choice fineness, that if it wanted anything in majesty, it supplied it with increase of pleasure,[13] and if at the first it strake not admiration, it ravished with delight. And no indifferent soul there was, which if it could resist from subjecting itself to make it his princess, that would not long to have such a playfellow. As for her attire, it was costly and curious, though the look (fixed with more sadness than it seemed nature had bestowed to any that knew her fortune) bewrayed that, as she used those ornaments not for herself but to prevail with another, so she feared that all would not serve.

Of a far differing, though esteemed equal, beauty was the fair Parthenia who next waited on Artesia's triumph, though far better she might have sit in

---

[1] idleness; with] idleness, and with 93   [2] dissuaded Cm, 93: dissuading 90   [3] overcome] overrun 93   [4] obeyed that] obeyed to that 93   [5] marked Cm, 93: marks 90   [6] possessions] possessioners 93   [7] absolute Cm, 93: absent 90   [8] and intercurled] but intercurled 93   [9] pearls] pearl 93   [10] and loose Cm, 93: or loose 90   [11] riches] richness 93   [12] than counterfeiting] the counterfeiting Cm; than the counterfeiting 93   [13] of pleasure] in pleasure 93

the throne, for in her everything was goodly and stately, yet so that it might seem that great-mindedness was but the ancient-bearer to humbleness;[1] for her great grey eye (which might seem full of her own beauties),[2] a large and exceedingly fair forehead, with all the rest of her face and body cast in the mould of nobleness, was yet so attired as might show the mistress thought it either not to deserve or not to need any exquisite decking, having no adorning but cleanliness, and so far from all art that it was full of carelessness – unless that carelessness itself, in spite of itself, grew artificial. But Basilius could not abstain from praising Parthenia as the perfect picture of a womanly virtue and wively faithfulness, telling withal Zelmane how he had understood that, when in the court of Laconia her picture, maintained by a certain Sicyonian knight, was lost thorough want rather of valour than justice, her husband, the famous Argalus, would in a chafe have gone and redeemed it with a new trial; but she, more sporting than sorrowing for her undeserved champion, told her husband she desired to be beautiful in nobody's eye but his, and that she would rather mar her face as evil as ever it was than that it should be a cause to make Argalus put on armour. Then would Basilius have told Zelmane that which she already knew of the rare trial of their coupled[3] affection, but the next picture made the mouth[4] give place to their eyes.

It was of a young maid which sate pulling out a thorn out of a lamb's foot, with her look so attentive upon it, as if that little foot could have been the circle of her thoughts; her apparel so poor as it had nothing but the inside to adorn it, a sheephook lying by her, with a bottle upon it. But with all that poverty, beauty played the prince, and commanded as many hearts as the greatest queen there did. Her beauty and her estate made her quickly to be known to be the fair shepherdess Urania, whom a rich knight called Lacemon, far in love with her, had unluckily defended.

The last of all in place, because last in the time of her being captive, was Zelmane, daughter to the King Plexirtus, who at the first sight seemed to have some resembling of Philoclea; but with more marking, comparing it to the present Philoclea, who indeed had no paragon but her sister, they might see it was but such a likeness as an unperfect glass doth give, answerable enough in some features and colours, but erring in others. But Zelmane sighing, turning to Basilius, 'Alas, sir,' said she, 'here be some pictures which might better become the tombs of their mistresses than the triumph of Artesia.'

'It is true, sweetest lady,' said Basilius. 'Some of them be dead, and some other captive; but that hath happened so late as it may be the knights that

---

[1] to humbleness] to the humbleness 93   [2] beauties] beauty 93   [3] their coupled] the coupled *Cm*; that coupled 93   [4] the mouth] their mouths 93

defended their beauty knew not so much, without we will say (as in some hearts I know it would fall out) that death itself could not blot out the image which love hath engraven in them. But divers besides these,' said Basilius, 'hath Phalantus won, but he leaves the rest, carrying only such who either for greatness of estate or of beauty may justly glorify the glory of Artesia's triumph.'

Thus[1] talked Basilius with Zelmane, glad to make any matter subject to speak of with his mistress, while Phalantus in this pompous manner brought Artesia with her gentlewomen into one tent, by which he had another, where they both waited who would first strike upon the shield, while Basilius, the judge, appointed sticklers and trumpets to whom the other should obey. But none that day appeared; nor the next, till already it had consumed half his allowance of light. But then there came in a knight, protesting himself as contrary to him in mind as he was in apparel – for Phalantus was all in white, having in his bases and caparison embroidered a waving water, at each side whereof he had nettings cast over in which were divers fishes naturally made, and so prettily, that as the horse stirred the fishes seemed to strive and leap in the net. But the other knight, by name Nestor, by birth an Arcadian, and in affection vowed to the fair shepherdess, was all in black, with fire burning both upon his armour and horse. His impresa in his shield was a fire made of juniper, with this word: 'More easy, and more sweet.' But this hot knight was cooled with a fall which at the third course he received of Phalantus, leaving his picture to keep company with the other of the same stamp; he going away, remedilessly chafing at his rebuke.

The next was Polycetes, greatly esteemed in Arcadia for deeds he had done in arms, and much spoken of for the honourable love he had long borne to Gynecia, which Basilius himself was content not only to suffer, but to be delighted with, he carried it in so honourable and open plainness, setting to his love no other mark than to do her faithful service. But neither her fair picture nor his fair running could warrant him from overthrow, and her from becoming as then the last of Artesia's victories, a thing Gynecia's virtues would little have recked at another time, nor then, if Zelmane had not seen it. But her champion went away as much discomforted as discomfited. Then Telamon for Polixena,[2] and Eurileon[3] for Elpine, and Leon for Zoana (all brave knights, all fair ladies), with their going down lifted up the balance of his praise for activity, and hers for fairness.

---

[1] triumph.' Thus *Cm, 93*: triumph.' Chap. 17. The overthrow of five Arcadian knights; the young shepherd's pretty challenge; what passions the sixth knight's foil bred in Zelmane; Clitophon hardly overmatched by Phalantus; the Ill-arrayed and the Black Knights' contention for priority against Phalantus; the Halting Knight's complaint against the Black Knight; Phalantus' fall by the Ill-furnished Knight; the cross-parting of Phalantus with Artesia; and who the victor was. Thus *90*   [2] Polixena] Polexena *93*   [3] Eurileon *Cm, 93*: Eurimelon *90*

Upon whose loss, as the beholders were talking, there comes into the place where they ran a shepherd stripling (for his height made him more than a boy, and his face would not allow him a man), brown of complexion (whether by nature or by the sun's familiarity), but very lovely withal; for the rest, so perfectly proportioned that nature showed she doth not, like men, who slubber up matters of mean account. And well might his proportion be judged, for he had nothing upon him but a pair of slops, and upon his body a goatskin which he cast over his shoulder (doing all things with so pretty grace[1] that it seemed ignorance could not make him do amiss, because he had a heart to do well), holding in his right hand a long staff. And so, coming with a look full of amiable fierceness (as in whom choler could not take away the sweetness), he came towards the king; and making a reverence which in him was comely because it was kindly, 'My liege lord,' said he, 'I pray you hear a few words, for my heart will break if I say not my mind to you. I see here the picture of Urania, which (I cannot tell how nor why) these men, when they fall down, they say is not so fair as yonder gay woman. But pray God I may never see my old mother alive, if I think she be any more match to Urania than a goat is to a fine lamb, or than the dog that keeps our flock at home is like your white greyhound that pulled down the stag last day. And therefore I pray you, let me be dressed as they be, and my heart gives me I shall tumble him on the earth, for indeed he might as well say that a cowslip is as white as a lily; or else, I care not, let him come with his great staff and I with this in my hand, and you shall see what I can do to him.'

Basilius saw it was the fine shepherd Lalus, whom once he had afore him in pastoral sports, and had greatly delighted in his wit full of pretty simplicity; and therefore laughing at his earnestness, he bad him be content, since he saw the pictures of so great queens were fain to follow their champions' fortune. But Lalus, even weeping-ripe, went among the rest, longing to see somebody that would revenge Urania's wrong, and praying heartily for everybody that ran against Phalantus; then began[2] to feel poverty, that he could not set himself to that trial.

But by and by, even when the sun (like a noble heart) began to show his greatest countenance in his lowest estate, there came in a knight called Phebilus, a gentleman of that country, for whom hateful fortune had borrowed the dart of love to make him miserable by the sight of Philoclea, for he had even from her infancy loved her, and was stricken by her before she was able to know what quiver of arrows her eyes carried. But he loved and despaired, and the more he despaired, the more he loved; he saw his own unworthiness, and thereby made her excellency have more terrible aspect

---

[1] pretty grace] pretty a grace 93   [2] began] beginning 93

upon him. He was so secret therein (as not daring to be open) that to no creature he ever spake of it; but his heart made such silent complaints within itself that, while all his senses were attentive thereto, cunning judges might perceive his mind, so that he was known to love though he denied; or rather, was the better known because he denied it. His armour and his attire was of a sea colour; his impresa, the fish called sepia, which being in the net casts a black ink about itself, that in the darkness thereof it may escape. His word was 'Not so.'

Philoclea's picture, with almost an idolatrous magnificence, was borne in by him. But straight jealousy was a harbinger for disdain in Zelmane's heart, when she saw any but herself should be avowed a champion for Philoclea, insomuch that she wished his shame, till she saw him shamed; for at the second course he was stricken quite from out of the saddle, so full of grief and rage withal that he would fain with the sword have revenged it. But that being contrary to the order set down, Basilius would not suffer, so that wishing himself in the bottom of the earth, he went his way, leaving Zelmane no less angry with his loss than she would have been with his victory – for if she thought before a rival's praise would have angered her, her lady's disgrace did make her much more forget what she then thought while that passion reigned, so much the more as she saw a pretty blush in Philoclea's cheeks bewray a modest discontentment. But the night commanded truce for those sports, and Phalantus, though entreated, would not leave Artesia, who in no case would come into the house, having as it were sucked of Cecropia's breath a mortal mislike against Basilius.

But the night, measured by the short ell of sleep, was soon passed over, and the next morning had given the watchful stars leave to take their rest, when a trumpet summoned Basilius to play his judge's part; which he did, taking his wife and daughters with him – Zelmane having locked her door so as they would not trouble her for that time, for already there was a knight in the field ready to prove Helen of Corinth had received great injury, both by the erring judgement of the challenger, and the unlucky weakness of her former defender. The new knight was quickly known to be Clitophon (Kalander's son, of Basilius' sister) by his armour, which all gilt, was so well handled that it showed like a glittering sand and gravel, interlaced with silver rivers. His device he had put in the picture of Helen which he defended. It was the ermion, with a speech that signified, 'Rather dead than spotted.' But in that armour, since he had parted from Helen (who would no longer his company, finding him to enter into terms of affection) he had performed so honourable actions (still seeking for his two friends by the names of Palladius and Daiphantus) that though his face were covered, his being was discovered; which yet Basilius, which had brought him up in his court, would not seem to do. But glad to see trial of him of whom he had heard very well, he commanded the trumpets to sound; to which the two brave knights obeying, they performed their courses, breaking their six staves with so good both skill in the hitting and grace in the manner that it bred some difficulty in the judgement. But Basilius in the end gave sentence against Clitophon because Phalantus had broken more staves upon the head, and that once Clitophon had received such a blow that he had lost the reins of his horse, with his head well nigh touching the crupper of the horse.

But Clitophon was so angry with the judgement, wherein he thought he had received wrong, that he omitted his duty to his prince and uncle, and suddenly went his way, still in the quest of them whom as then he had left by seeking, and so yielded the field to the next comer; who coming in about two hours after, was no less marked than all the rest before, because he had nothing worth the marking; for he had neither picture nor device; his armour of as old a fashion (besides the rusty poorness) that it might better seem a monument of his grandfather's courage; about his middle he had, instead of bases, a long cloak of silk, which as unhandsomely (as it needs must) became the wearer; so that all that looked on measured his length on the earth already, since he had to meet one who had been victorious of so many gallants. But he went on towards the shield, and with a sober grace strake it. But as he let his sword fall upon it, another knight, all in black, came rustling in, who strake the shield almost as soon as he, and so strongly that he brake the shield in two.

The Ill-appointed Knight (for so the beholders called him) angry with that (as he accounted) insolent injury to himself, hit him such a sound blow that they that looked on said it well became a rude arm. The other answered him again in the same case, so that lances were put to silence, the swords were so busy. But Phalantus, angry of this defacing his shield, came upon the Black Knight, and with the pommel of his sword set fire to his eyes; which presently was revenged not only by the Black, but the Ill-apparelled Knight, who disdained another should enter into his quarrel; so as, whoever saw a matachin dance to imitate fighting, this was a fight that did imitate the matachin, for they being but three that fought, every one had adversaries[1] striking him who struck the third, and revenging perhaps that of him which he had received of the other. But Basilius rising, himself came to[2] part them, the sticklers' authority scarcely able to persuade choleric hearers; and part them he did.

But before he could determine, comes in a fourth, halting on foot, who complained to Basilius, demanding justice on the Black Knight for having by force taken away the picture of Pamela from him, which in little form

---

[1] had adversaries] had two adversaries 93   [2] himself came to *Cm*, 93: himself to 90

he ware in a tablet, and covered with silk had fastened it to his helmet, purposing for want of a bigger to paragon the little one with Artesia's length, not doubting but in[1] that little quantity the excellency of that would shine thorough the weakness of the other, as the smallest star doth thorough the whole element of fire. And by the way he had met with this Black Knight who had, as he said, robbed him of it. The injury seemed grievous, but when it came fully to be examined, it was found that the Halting Knight meeting the other, asking the cause of his going thitherward, and finding it was to defend Pamela's divine beauty against Artesia's, with a proud jollity commanded him to leave that quarrel only for him, who was only worthy to enter into it. But the Black Knight obeying no such commandments, they fell to such a bickering that he gat a halting and lost his picture. This understood by Basilius, he told him he was now fitter to look to his own body than another's picture; and so uncomforted therein, sent him away to learn of Aesculapius that he was not fit for Venus.

But then the question arising who should be the former against Phalantus, of the Black, or the Ill-apparelled Knight (who now had gotten the reputation of some sturdy lout, he had so well defended himself), of the one side was alleged the having a picture which the other wanted, of the other side the first striking the shield; but the conclusion was that the Ill-apparelled Knight should have the precedence if he delivered the figure of his mistress to Phalantus, who asking him for it, 'Certainly,' said he, 'her liveliest picture, if you could see it, is in my heart, and the best comparison I could make of her is of the sun and of all other the[2] heavenly beauties. But because perhaps all eyes cannot taste the divinity of her beauty, and would rather be dazzled than taught by the light if it be not clouded by some meaner thing, know you then that I defend that same lady whose image Phebilus so feebly lost yesternight; and instead of another, if you overcome me, you shall have me your slave to carry that image in your mistress's triumph.'

Phalantus easily agreed to the bargain, which already he made his own. But when it came to the trial, the Ill-apparelled Knight choosing out the greatest staves in all the store, at the first course gave his head such a remembrance that he lost almost his remembrance, he himself receiving the encounter of Phalantus without any extraordinary motion; and at the second, gave him such a counterbuff that, because Phalantus was so perfect a horseman as not to be driven from the saddle, the saddle with broken girths was driven from the horse, Phalantus remaining angry and amazed, because now being come almost to the last of his promised enterprise, that disgrace befell him which he had never before known. But the victory being by the

---

[1] but in] but even in 93 [2] all other the] all the other 93

judges given, and the trumpets witnessed, to the Ill-apparelled Knight, Phalantus' disgrace was engrieved, in lieu of comfort, by[1] Artesia, who telling him she never looked for other, bad him seek some other mistress. He excusing himself and turning over the fault to fortune, 'Then let that be your ill fortune too,' said she, 'that you have lost me!'

'Nay truly, madam,' said Phalantus, 'it shall not be so, for I think the loss of such a mistress will prove a great gain!' and so concluded – to the sport of Basilius, to see young folks' love, that came in masked with so great pomp, go out with so little constancy. But Phalantus, first professing great service to Basilius for his courteous intermitting his solitary course for his sake, would yet conduct Artesia to the castle of Cecropia, whither she desired to go, vowing in himself that neither heart nor mouth-love should ever any more entangle him.

And with that resolution, he left the company; whence all being dismissed (among whom the Black Knight went away repining at his luck that had kept him from winning the honour, as he knew he should have done, to the picture of Pamela), the Ill-apparelled Knight, who was only desired to stay because Basilius meant to show him to Zelmane, pulled off his helmet, and then was known himself to be Zelmane – who that morning, as she told, while the others were busy, had stolen out to the prince's stable which was a mile off from the lodge, had gotten a horse (they knowing it was Basilius' pleasure she should be obeyed), and borrowing that homely armour for want of a better, had come upon the spur to redeem Philoclea's picture which, she said, she could not bear (being one of that little wilderness-company) should be in captivity, if the cunning she had learned in her country of the noble Amazons could withstand it – and under that pretext, fain she would have given a secret passport to her affection. But this act painted, at one instant, redness in Philoclea's face and paleness in Gynecia's, but brought forth no other countenances but of admiration, no speeches but of commendations – all these few, besides love, thinking they honoured themselves in honouring so accomplished a person as Zelmane, whom daily they sought with some or other sports to delight; for which purpose Basilius had, in a house not far off, servants, who though they came not uncalled, yet at call were ready. And[2] so, many days were spent, and many ways used, while Zelmane was like one that stood in a tree waiting a good occasion to shoot, and Gynecia, a blancher which kept the dearest deer from her.

But the day being come, which[3] according to an appointed course, the shepards were to assemble and make their pastoral sports afore Basilius,

---

[1] by] of 93   [2] ready. And *Cm*, 93: ready. Chap. 18. Musidorus disguised; his song; his love; the cause thereof; his course therein. And 90   [3] come, which] come, on which 93

Zelmane fearing lest many eyes, and coming divers ways, might hap to spy Musidorus, went out to warn him thereof. But before she could come to the arbour, she saw walking from herward a man in shepherdish apparel, who being in the sight of the lodge, it might seem he was allowed there. A long cloak he had on, but that cast under his right arm, wherein he held a sheephook so finely wrought that it gave a bravery to poverty; and his raiments, though they were mean, yet received they handsomeness by the grace of the wearer, though he himself went but a kind of languishing pace, with his eyes sometimes[1] cast up to heaven as though his fancies strave to mount higher, sometimes thrown down to the ground as if the earth could not bear the burthen[2] of his sorrows. At length, with a lamentable tune, he sung these few verses.

> Come, shepherd's weeds, become your master's mind:
> Yield outward show, what inward change[3] he tries;
> Nor be abashed, since such a guest you find,
> Whose strongest hope in your weak comfort lies.
>
> Come, shepherd's weeds, attend my woeful cries:
> Disuse yourselves from sweet Menalcas' voice,
> For other be those tunes which sorrow ties
> From those clear notes which freely may rejoice.
>   Then pour out plaint, and in one word say this:
>   Helpless his plaint who spoils himself of bliss.

And having ended, he strake himself on the breast, saying 'O miserable wretch, whither do thy destinies guide thee?'

The voice made Zelmane hasten her pace to overtake him; which having done, she plainly perceived that it was her dear friend Musidorus. Whereat marvelling not a little, she demanded of him whether the goddess of those woods had such a power to transform everybody, or whether, as in all enterprises else he had done, he meant thus to match her in this new alteration.

'Alas,' said Musidorus, 'what shall I say, who am loath to say, and yet fain would have said? I find indeed that all is but lip-wisdom which wants experience. I now (woe is me!) do try what love can do. O Zelmane, who will resist it must either have no wit, or put out his eyes. Can any man resist his creation? Certainly, by love we are made, and to love we are made. Beasts only cannot discern beauty; and let them be in the roll of beasts that do not honour it.'

The perfect friendship Zelmane bare him, and the great pity she, by good trial, had of such cases, could not keep her from smiling at him, remem-

---

[1] sometimes *OA, 93*: somewhat *Cm, 90*   [2] burthen *OA, 93*: burdens *Cm*; burthens *90*   [3] change *OA (ex. Hm), Cm, 93*: chance *Hm, 90*

bering how vehemently he had cried out against the folly of lovers. And therefore a little to punish him, 'Why, how now, dear cousin!' said she. 'You that were last day so high in the pulpit[1] against lovers, are you now become so mean an auditor? Remember that love is a passion, and that a worthy man's reason must ever have the masterhood.'

'I recant, I recant!' cried Musidorus; and withal falling down prostrate, 'O thou celestial or infernal spirit of love, or what other heavenly or hellish title thou list to have – for effects of both I find in myself, have compassion of me, and let thy glory be as great in pardoning them that be submitted to thee, as in conquering those that were rebellious!'

'No, no,' said Zelmane, 'I see you well enough; you make but an interlude of my mishaps, and do but counterfeit thus to make me see the deformity of my passions. But take heed that this jest do not one day turn to[2] earnest.'

'Now I beseech thee,' said Musidorus, taking her fast by the hand, 'even for[3] the truth of our[4] friendship, of which, if I be not altogether an unhappy man, thou hast some remembrance, and by those secret[5] flames which I know have likewise nearly touched thee, make no jest of that which hath so earnestly pierced me thorough; nor let that be light to thee which is to me so burdenous that I am not able to bear it.'

Musidorus both in words and behaviour did so lively deliver out his inward grief that Zelmane found indeed he was thoroughly wounded. But there rose a new jealousy in her mind, lest it might be with Philoclea, by whom, as Zelmane thought, in right, all hearts and eyes should be inherited. And therefore desirous to be cleared of that doubt, Musidorus shortly, as in haste, and full of passionate perplexedness, thus recounted his case unto her.

'The day,' said he, 'I parted from you, I being in mind to return to a town from whence I came hither, my horse (being before tired) would scarce bear me a mile hence; where being benighted, the light of a candle I saw a good way off guided me to a young shepherd's house, by name Menalcas, who seeing me to be a straying stranger, with the right honest hospitality which seems to be harboured in the Arcadian breasts, and though not with curious costliness, yet with cleanly sufficiency, entertained me. And having by talk with him found the manner of the country something more in particular than I had by Kalander's report, I agreed to sojourn with him in secret, which he faithfully promised to observe; and so, hither to your arbour divers times repaired, and here by your means had the sight (oh that it had never been so! nay, oh that it might ever be so!) of a goddess[6] who in a definite

---

[1] in the pulpit *OA, 93*: in pulpit *Cm, 90* [2] to] into *OA (ex. Cl)* [3] for] by *OA (ex. Cl, As)* [4] our] your *Ph, Cm* [5] secret *Cl, As, Ph, Cm, 93*: sacred *St, Bo, Da, Hm, 90* [6] a goddess] the goddess *93*

compass can set forth infinite beauty.' All this while Zelmane was racked with jealousy. But he went on:

'For,' said he, 'I lying close, and in truth thinking of you, and saying thus to myself, "O sweet Pyrocles, how art thou bewitched! Where is thy virtue? Where is the use of thy reason? How much[1] am I inferior to thee in the state of the mind! And yet know I that all the heavens cannot bring me to such thraldom" – scarcely, think I, had I spoken these words[2] when the ladies came forth; at which sight, I think the very words returned back again to strike my soul – at least, an unmeasurable sting I felt in myself that I had spoken such words.'

'At which sight?' said Zelmane, not able to bear him any longer.

'Oh!' said Musidorus, 'I know your suspicion. No, no – banish all such fear. It was, it is, and must be, Pamela!'

'Then all is safe,' said Zelmane. 'Proceed, dear Musidorus.'

'I will not,' said he, 'impute it to my late solitary life (which yet is prone to affections), nor to the much thinking of you (though that called the consideration of love into my mind, which before I ever neglected), nor to the exaltation of Venus, nor revenge of Cupid; but even to her, who is the planet, nay, the goddess against which the only shield must be my sepulchre. When I first saw her, I was presently stricken, and I (like a foolish child, that when anything hits him will strike himself again upon it) would needs look again, as though I would persuade mine eyes that they were deceived. But alas, well have I found that love to a yielding heart is a king, but to a resisting is a tyrant. The more with arguments I shaked the stake which he had planted in the ground of my heart, the deeper still it sank into it. But what mean I to speak of the causes of my love, which is as impossible to describe as to measure the backside of heaven? Let this word suffice: I love. And that you may know I do so, it was I that came in black armour to defend her picture, where I was both prevented and beaten by you. And so, I that waited here to do you service, have now myself most need of succour.'

'But whereupon got you yourself this apparel?' said Zelmane.

'I had forgotten to tell you,' said Musidorus, 'though that were one principal matter of my speech – so much am I now master of my own mind! But thus it happened: being returned to Menalcas' house full of tormenting desire, after awhile fainting under the weight, my courage stirred up my wit to seek for some relief before I yielded to perish. At last this came into my head, that very evening that I had to no purpose last used my horse and armour. I told Menalcas that I was a Thessalian gentleman, who by

---

[1] How much] Much *OA (ex. Cl, As)*   [2] these words *Cl, As, Hm, Cm*: those words *St, Bo, Da, Ph*; this word *90, 93*

mischance having killed a great favourite of the prince of that country, was pursued so cruelly that in no place, but either by favour or corruption, they would obtain my destruction; and that therefore I was determined, till the fury of my persecutions[1] might be assuaged, to disguise myself among the shepherds of Arcadia, and if it were possible, to be one of them that were allowed the prince's presence, because if the worst should fall, that I were discovered, yet having gotten the acquaintance of the prince, it might happen to move his heart to protect me.

'Menalcas, being of an honest disposition, pitied my case, which my face through my inward torment made credible; and so, I giving him largely for it, let me have this raiment, instructing me in all the particularities touching himself, or myself, which I desired to know. Yet not trusting so much to his constancy as that I would lay my life, and life of my life, upon it, I hired him to go into Thessalia to a friend of mine, and to deliver him a letter from me, conjuring him to bring me as speedy an answer as he could because it imported me greatly to know whether certain of my friends did yet possess any favour, whose intercessions I might use for my restitution. He willingly took my letter, which being well sealed, indeed contained other matter. For I wrote to my trusty servant Calodoulus, whom you know, that as soon as he had delivered the letter, he should keep him prisoner in his house, not suffering him to have conference with anybody till he knew my further pleasure; in all other respects, that he should use him as my brother. And thus is Menalcas gone, and I here, a poor shepherd, more proud of this estate than of any kingdom, so manifest it is that the highest point outward things can bring one unto is the contentment of the mind, with which no estate, without which all estates, be miserable. Now have I chosen this day because, as Menalcas told me, the other shepherds are called to make their sports, and hope that you will, with your credit, find means to get me allowed among them.'

'You need not doubt,' answered Zelmane, 'but that I will be your good mistress. Marry, the best way of dealing must be by Dametas, who since his blunt brains[2] hath perceived some favour the prince doth bear unto me (as without doubt, the most servile flattery is lodged most easily in the grossest capacity – for their ordinary conceit draweth a yielding to their greaters, and then have they not wit to learn the right[3] degrees of duty) is much more serviceable unto me than I can find any cause to wish him. And therefore despair not to win him, for every present occasion will catch his senses, and

---

[1] persecutions] persecutors 93   [2] brains *OA, Cm*: brain *90, 93*   [3] learn the right] discern right *St, Da*; discern the right *Bo, Cl, As, Ph, Hm, 93*

his senses are masters of his silly mind. Only reverence him and reward him, and with that bridle and saddle you shall well ride him.'

'O heaven and earth!' said Musidorus. 'To what a pass are our minds brought, that from the right line of virtue are wried to these crooked shifts! But O love, it is thou that doost it. Thou changest name upon name; thou disguisest our bodies and disfigurest our minds; but indeed thou hast reason, for though the ways be foul, the journey's end is most fair and honourable.'

'No[1] more, sweet Musidorus,' said Zelmane, 'of these philosophies, for here comes the very person of Dametas.'

And so he did indeed, with a sword by his side, a forest-bill on his neck, and a chopping-knife under his girdle – in which provided[2] sort he had ever gone since the fear Zelmane had put him in. But he no sooner saw her, but with head and arms he laid his reverence afore her, enough to have made any[3] man forswear all courtesy, and then in Basilius' name he did invite her to walk down to the place where that day they were to have the pastorals.

But when he spied Musidorus to be none of the shepherds allowed in that place, he would fain have persuaded himself to utter some anger, but that he durst not; yet muttering, and champing as though his cud troubled him, he gave occasion to Musidorus to come near him, and feign this tale of his own life: that he was a younger brother of the shepherd Menalcas, by name Dorus, sent by his father in his tender age to Athens, there to learn some cunning more than ordinary, that he might be the better liked of the prince; and that after his father's death, his brother Menalcas, lately gone thither to fetch him home, was also deceased; where, upon his death, he had charged him to seek the service of Dametas, and to be wholly and ever guided by him, as one in whose judgement and integrity the prince had singular confidence – for token whereof, he gave to Dametas a good sum of gold in ready coin, which Menalcas had bequeathed unto him, upon condition he should receive this poor Dorus into his service, that his mind and manners[4] might grow the better by his daily example. Dametas, that of all manners of style could best conceive of golden eloquence, being withal tickled by Musidorus' praises, had his brain so turned that he became slave to that which he that sued to be his servant offered to give him; yet for countenance sake he seemed very squeamish, in respect of the charge he

---

[1] honourable.' 'No *Cm, 93*: honourable.' Chap. 19. The means of Musidorus' apprenticeage unto Dametas; the preparation and place of the pastorals; the lion's assault on Philoclea, and death by Zelmane; the she-bear's on Pamela, and death by Dorus; the Io Paean of Dametas, and his scape from the bear; the victors' praises; whence those beasts were sent. 'No *90*   [2] which provided] which well-provided *93*   [3] any] a *OA (ex. Bo, Cl)*; a *corr. to* any *Bo*   [4] manners *OA (ex. Je)*, *93*: manner *Je, Cm, 90*

had of the Princess Pamela. But such was the secret operation of the gold, helped with the persuasion[1] of the Amazon Zelmane, who said it was pity so handsome a young man should be anywhere else than with so good a master, that in the end he agreed, if that day he behaved himself so to the liking of Basilius as he might be contented, that then he would receive him into his service.

And thus went they to the lodge, where they found Gynecia and her daughters ready to go to the field to delight themselves there awhile until the shepherds' coming; whither also taking Zelmane with them, as they went Dametas told them of Dorus, and desired he might be accepted there that day instead of his brother Menalcas. As for Basilius, he stayed behind to bring the shepherds (with whom he meant to confer, to breed the better Zelmane's liking, which he only regarded), while the other beautiful band came to the fair field appointed for the shepherdish pastimes. It was indeed a place of delight, for thorough the middest of it there ran a sweet brook which did both hold the eye open with her azure streams, and yet seek to close the eye with the purling noise it made upon the pibble-stones it ran over; the field itself being set in some places with roses, and in all the rest constantly preserving a flourishing green. The roses added such a ruddy show unto it, as though the field were bashful at his own beauty. About it, as if it had been to enclose a theatre, grew such a sort[2] of trees as either excellency of fruit, stateliness of growth, continual greenness, or poetical fancies have made at any time famous; in most part of which there had been framed by art such pleasant arbours that, one answering[3] another, they became a gallery aloft, from tree to tree, almost[4] round about, which below gave a perfect shadow, a pleasant refuge then from the choleric look of Phoebus.

In this place, while Gynecia walked hard by them carrying many unquiet contentions about her, the ladies sate them down, inquiring many[5] questions of the shepherd Dorus, who keeping his eye still upon Pamela, answered with such a trembling voice and abashed countenance, and often-times so far from the matter, that it was some sport to[6] the young ladies, thinking it want of education which made him so discountenanced with unwonted presence. But Zelmane, that saw in him the glass of her own misery, taking the hand of Philoclea, and with burning kisses setting it close to her lips (as if it should stand there, like a hand in the margin of a book, to note some saying worthy to be marked) began to speak these words: 'O love, since thou art so changeable in men's estates, how art thou so constant in their torments' – when suddenly there came out of a wood a monstrous

---

[1] persuasion] persuasions *St, Bo, Da, Ph* [2] such a sort] such sort *93, 98*; such sorts *13* [3] one answering *Cm, 93*: one tree to tree answering *90* [4] from tree to tree, almost *Cm, 93*: from almost *90* [5] many] divers *93* [6] to] for *Je, 13*

lion, with a she-bear not far from him of little less fierceness; which as they guessed, having been hunted in forests far off were by chance come thither, where before such beasts had never been seen.

Then care, not fear – or fear not for themselves, altered something the countenances of the two lovers, but so as any man might perceive was rather an assembling of powers than dismayedness of courage. Philoclea no sooner espied the lion but that, obeying the commandment of fear, she leapt up and ran to the lodge-ward as fast as her delicate legs could[1] carry her, while Dorus drew Pamela behind a tree, where she stood quaking like the partridge on which the hawk is even ready to seize. But the lion seeing Philoclea run away, bent his race to her-ward, and was ready to seize himself on the prey, when Zelmane, to whom danger then was a cause of dreadlessness, all the compositions[2] of her elements being nothing but fiery, with swiftness of desire crossed him, and with force of affection strake him such a blow upon his chine that she opened all his body; wherewith the valiant beast turning upon her with open jaws, she gave him such a thrust thorough his breast that all the lion could do was, with his paw, to tear off the mantle and sleeve of Zelmane, with a little scratch rather than a wound, his death-blow having taken away the effect of his force. But therewithal he fell down, and gave Zelmane leisure to take off his head to carry it for a present to her Lady Philoclea; who all this while, not knowing what was done behind her, kept on her course like Arethusa when she ran from Alpheus, her light apparel being carried up with the wind, that much of those beauties she would at another time have willingly hidden were[3] present[4] to the sight of the twice-wounded Zelmane; which made Zelmane not follow her over-hastily lest she should too soon deprive herself of that pleasure, but carrying the lion's head in her hand, did not fully overtake her till they came to[5] the presence of Basilius.

Neither were they long there but that Gynecia came thither also, who had been in such a trance of musing that Zelmane was fighting with the lion before she knew of any lion's coming. But then affection resisting, and the soon ending of the fight preventing all extremity of fear, she marked Zelmane's fighting. And when the lion's head was off, as Zelmane ran after Philoclea, so she could not find in her heart but run after Zelmane, so that it was a new sight fortune had prepared to those woods, to see these great personages thus run one after the other, each carried forward with an inward violence (Philoclea with such fear that she thought she was still in the lion's mouth; Zelmane with an eager and impatient delight; Gynecia with wings of love) flying they[6] neither knew nor cared to know whither.

---

[1] could] would *OA* (*ex. Je, Hm*)   [2] compositions] composition *93*   [3] were *OA, Cm*: was *90, 93*
[4] present] presently *corr. to* present *Cm*; presented *OA, 93*   [5] to] in *St, Da*; into *Bo, Cl, As, Je, Hm*
[6] they] she *93*

But now being all come before Basilius, amazed with this sight, and fear having such possession in the fair Philoclea that her blood durst not yet to come to her face to take away the name of paleness from her most pure whiteness, Zelmane kneeled down; and presenting[1] the lion's head unto her, 'Only lady,' said she, 'here see you the punishment of that unnatural beast, which contrary to her[2] own kind would have wronged prince's blood, guided with such traitorous eyes as durst rebel against your beauty.'

'Happy am I and my beauty both,' answered the sweet Philoclea, then blushing, for fear had bequeathed his room to his kinsman bashfulness, 'that you, excellent Amazon, were there to teach him good manners.'

'And even thanks to that[3] beauty,' answered Zelmane, 'which can give an edge to the bluntest swords.'

There Philoclea told her father how it had happened. But as she had turned her eyes in her tale to Zelmane, she perceived some blood upon Zelmane's shoulder; so that starting with the lovely grace of pity, she showed it to her father and mother, who as the nurse sometimes with overmuch kissing may forget to give the child[4] suck, so had they with too much delighting in beholding and praising Zelmane left off to mark whether she needed succour. But then they ran both unto her, like a father and mother to an only child, and though Zelmane assured them it was nothing, would needs see it, Gynecia having skill in surgery – an art in those days much esteemed because it served to virtuous courage, which even ladies would, ever[5] with the contempt of courage,[6] seem to cherish. But looking upon it (which gave more inward bleeding wounds to Zelmane, for she might sometimes feel Philoclea's touch whiles she helped her mother), she found it was indeed of no importance;[7] yet applied she a precious balm unto it, of power to heal a greater grief.

But even then, and not before, they remembered Pamela; and therefore Zelmane, thinking of her friend Dorus, was running back to be satisfied when they might all see Pamela coming between Dorus and Dametas, having in her hand the paw of a bear which the shepherd Dorus had newly presented unto her, desiring her to accept it, as of such a beast, which though she deserved death for her presumption, yet was her wit[8] to be esteemed since she could make so sweet a choice. Dametas for his part came piping and dancing, the merriest man in a parish. But when he came so near as he might be heard of Basilius, he would needs break thorough his ears with this joyful song of their good success:

---

[1] presenting *Cm, 93, 98*: presented *90, 13* [2] her] his *OA, 93* [3] thanks to that] thank that *OA*; thank to that *Cm* [4] child *OA, Cm*: babe *90, 93* [5] ever *Cm, 93*: even *90* [6] courage] cowards *93* [7] of no importance *93*: of importance *Cm*; of no great importance *90* [8] wit *OA, 93* will *Cm, 90*

> Now thanked be the great god Pan
> Which thus preserves my loved life;
> Thanked be I that keep a man
> Who ended hath this bloody[1] strife;
>   For if my man must praises have,
>   What then must I that keep the knave?
>
> For as the moon the eye[2] doth please
> With gentle beams not hurting sight,
> Yet hath Sir Sun the greatest praise,
> Because from him doth come her light:
>   So if my man must praises have,
>   What then must I that keep the knave?

Being all now come together, and all desirous to know each other's adventures, Pamela's noble heart would needs gratefully make known the valiant mean of her safety, which, directing her speech to her mother, she did in this manner.

'As soon,' said she, 'as you were all run away and that I hoped to be in safety, there came out of the same woods a foul horrible bear, which fearing belike to deal while the lion was present, as soon as he was gone came furiously towards the place where I was, and this young shepherd left alone by me – I truly (not guilty of any wisdom, which since they lay to my charge because they say it is the best refuge against that beast, but even pure fear bringing forth that effect of wisdom) fell down flat of my face, needing not counterfeit being dead, for indeed I was little better. But this – no[3] other weapon but that knife you see, standing before the place where I lay so behaved himself that the first sight I had (when I thought myself nearer[4] Charon's ferry) was the shepherd showing me his bloody knife in token of victory.'

'I pray you,' said Zelmane, speaking to Dorus, whose valour she was careful to have manifested, 'in what sort, so ill-weaponed, could you achieve this enterprise?'

'Noble lady,' said Dorus, 'the manner of these beasts' fighting with any man is to stand up upon their hinder feet; and so this did; and being ready to give me a shrewd embracement, I think the god Pan, ever careful of the chief blessings of Arcadia, guided my hand so just to the heart of the beast that neither she could once touch me, nor (which is the only matter in this worthy remembrance) breed any danger to the princess. For my part, I am rather with all subjected humbleness to thank her excellencies (since the

---

[1] bloody *Cm, 93*: fearful *OA, 90*   [2] eye *OA, 93*: eye *corr. to* eyes *Cm*; eyes *90*   [3] this – no *Cm*: this shepherd, having no *90*; this young shepherd with a wonderful courage, having no *93*   [4] myself nearer] myself already near *93*

duty thereunto gave me heart to save myself) than to receive thanks for a deed which was her only inspiring.'

And this Dorus spake, keeping affection, as much as he could, back from coming into his eyes and gestures. But Zelmane, that had the same character in her heart, could easily discern[1] it; and therefore to keep him the longer in speech, desired to understand the conclusion of the matter, and how the honest Dametas was escaped.

'Nay!' said Pamela, 'none shall take that office from myself, being so much bound to him as I am for my education!' And with that word, scorn borrowing the countenance of mirth, somewhat she smiled, and thus spake on. 'When,' said she, 'Dorus made me assuredly perceive that all cause of fear was passed, the truth is, I was ashamed to find myself alone with this shepherd; and therefore looking about me if I could see anybody, at length we both perceived the gentle Dametas lying with his head and breast[2] as far as he could thrust himself into a bush, drawing up his legs as close unto him as he could, for like a man of a very kind nature, soon to take pity of himself, he was full resolved not to see his own death. And when this shepherd pushed him, bidding him be[3] of good cheer, it was a great[4] while ere we could persuade him that Dorus was not the bear; so that he was fain to pull him out by the heels and show him the beast as dead as he could wish it – which, you may believe me, was a very joyful sight unto him. But then he forgate all courtesy, for he fell upon the beast, giving it many a manful wound, swearing by much it was not well such beasts should be suffered in a commonwealth. And then my governor, as full of joy as before of fear, came dancing and singing before, as[5] even now you saw him.'

'Well, well,' said Basilius, 'I have not chosen Dametas for his fighting, nor for his discoursing, but for his plainness and honesty; and therein I know he will not deceive me.'

But then he told Pamela, not so much because she should know it as because he would tell it, the wonderful act Zelmane had performed, which Gynecia likewise spake of – both in such extremity of praising, as was easy to be seen, the construction[6] of their speech might best be made by the grammar rules of affection. Basilius told with what a gallant grace she ran with the lion's head in her hand, like another Pallas with the spoils of Gorgon; Gynecia sware she saw the very face[7] of the young Hercules killing the Nemean lion; and all with a grateful assent confirmed the same praises. Only poor Dorus, though of equal desert, yet not proceeding of equal estate, should have been left forgotten, had not Zelmane again with great admira-

---

[1] discern] delight *Cm*; decipher *93* [2] head and breast *OA, 93*: breast and head *Cm, 90* [3] him be *OA, Cm*: him to be *90, 93* [4] great *OA, 93*: good *Cm, 90* [5] before, as *Cm, 93, 98*: before us as *90, 13* [6] construction *Cm, 93*: constructions *90* [7] the very face *OA, Cm, 93*: the face *90*

tion begun to speak of him asking whether it were the fashion or no, in Arcadia, that shepherds should perform such valorous enterprises. This Basilius (having the quick sense of a lover) took as though his mistress had given him a[1] secret reprehension that he had not showed more gratefulness to Dorus, and therefore as nimbly as he could inquired of his estate, adding promise of great rewards – among the rest, offering to him, if he would exercise his courage in soldiery, he would commit some charge unto him under his lieutenant Philanax.

But Dorus, whose ambition climbed by another stair, having first answered, touching his estate, that he was brother to the shepherd Menalcas, who among other was wont to resort to the prince's presence, and excused his going to soldiery by the unaptness he found in himself that way, he told Basilius that his brother in his last testament had willed him to serve Dametas; and therefore, for due obedience thereunto,[2] he would think his service greatly rewarded if he might obtain by that mean to live in the sight of his prince, and yet practise his own chosen vocation.

Basilius, liking well his goodly shape and handsome manner, charged Dametas to receive him like a son into his[3] house, saying that his valour and Dametas' truth would be good bulwarks against such mischiefs as, he sticked not to say, were threatened to his daughter Pamela. Dametas, no whit out of countenance with all that had been said, because he had no worse to fall into than his own, accepted Dorus; and withal telling Basilius that some of the shepherds were come, demanded in what place he would see their sports; who first curious to know whether it were not more requisite for Zelmane's hurt to rest than sit up at those pastimes, and she that felt no wound but one earnestly desiring to have pastorals,[4] Basilius commanded it should be at the gate of the lodge; where the throne of the prince being according to the ancient manner, he made Zelmane sit between him and his wife therein (who thought herself between drowning and burning), and the two young ladies of either side the throne; and so prepared their eyes and ears to be delighted by the shepherds.

But before all of them were assembled to begin their sports, there came a fellow, who being out of breath (or seeming so to be) for haste, with humble hastiness told Basilius that his mistress, the Lady Cecropia, had sent him to excuse the mischance of her beasts ranging in that dangerous sort, being happened by the folly of the keeper, who thinking himself able to rule them, had carried them abroad and so was deceived; whom yet, if Basilius would punish for it, she was ready to deliver. Basilius made no other answer but that his mistress, if she had any more such beasts, should cause them to be

---

[1] given him a OA, 93: given a Cm, 90   [2] thereunto] thereto OA (ex. Hm)   [3] into his] in his St, Bo, Cl, Da, Ph   [4] have pastorals] have the pastorals 93

killed. And then he told his wife and Zelmane of it, because they should not fear those woods as though they harboured such beasts, where the like had never been seen.

But Gynecia took a further conceit of it, mistrusting greatly Cecropia[1] because she had heard much of the devilish wickedness of her heart, and that, particularly, she did her best to bring up her son Amphialus, being brother's son to Basilius, to aspire to the crown as next heir male after Basilius; and therefore saw no reason but that she might conjecture it proceeded rather of some mischievous practice than of misfortune. Yet did she only utter her doubt to her daughters, thinking, since the worst was past, she would attend a further occasion, lest overmuch haste might seem to proceed of the ordinary mislike between sisters-in-law; only they marvelled that Basilius looked no further into it, who, good man, thought so much of his late-conceived commonwealth that all other matters were but digressions unto him.

But the shepherds were ready, and with well handling themselves called their senses to attend their pastimes.

---

[1] mistrusting greatly Cecropia *Cm*, *93*: mistrusting Cecropia *90*

THE SECOND BOOK

In these[1] pastoral[2] pastimes a great number of days were sent[3] to follow their flying predecessors, while the cup of poison, which was deeply tasted of this noble company, had left no sinew of theirs without mortally[4] searching into it; yet never manifesting his venomous work, till once that the night, parting away angerly[5] that she could distil no more sleep into the eyes of lovers, had no sooner given place to the breaking out of the morning[6] light, and the sun bestowed his beams upon the tops of the mountains, but that the woeful Gynecia to whom rest was no ease had left her loathed lodging and gotten herself into the solitary places those deserts[7] were[8] full of, going up and down with such unquiet motions as the[9] grieved and hopeless[10] mind is wont to bring forth. There appeared unto the eyes of her judgement the evils she was like to run into, with ugly infamy waiting upon them; she felt the terrors[11] of her own conscience; she was guilty of a long-exercised virtue, which made this vice the fuller of deformity. The uttermost of the good she could aspire unto was a mortal[12] wound to her vexed spirits, and lastly, no small part of her evils was that she was wise to see her evils, insomuch that having a great while thrown her countenance ghastly about her as if she had called all the powers of the world to be witness[13] of her wretched estate, at length casting up her watery eyes to heaven, 'O sun,' said she, 'whose unspotted light directs the steps of mortal mankind, art thou not ashamed to impart the clearness of thy presence to such a dust-creeping worm as I am? O you heavens, which continually keep the course allotted unto you, can none of your influences prevail so much upon the miserable Gynecia as to make her preserve a course so long embraced by her? O deserts, deserts, how fit a guest am I[14] for you, since my heart can people you with wild ravenous beasts which in you are wanting! O virtue, where doost thou hide thyself? Or what[15] hideous thing is this which doth eclipse thee? Or is it true that thou wert[16] never but a vain name, and no essential thing, which hast thus left thy professed servant when she had most need of thy lovely

---

[1] pastimes. The Second Book In these: pastimes. In these *Cm*; pastimes. The First Eclogues [*See Appendix I*]. The end of the first Book. The Second Book of *The Countess of Pembroke's Arcadia*. Chap. 1. The love-complaints of Gynecia, Zelmane, and Basilius; her, and his, wooing of Zelmane; and her shifting of both to bemoan herself. In these 90; pastimes, [pastimes. 98, 13] The First Eclogues.... The end of the First Book. The Second Book of *The Countess of Pembroke's Arcadia*. In these 93 [2] pastoral] pastorals *Da, Hm*; pastorical *Je* [3] sent] spent *Cl, Da, Ph* [4] mortally] mortality *Je, Cm* [5] angerly] angry 93 [6] morning] morning's *OA (ex. As, Je)* [7] deserts] desert *St, Bo* [8] were] was *St, Bo, As*; blank left *Cl* [9] as the *OA, Cm*: as a 90, 93 [10] hopeless] helpless *corr. to* hopeless *Cm*; hapless *Da, Je, Hm* [11] terrors *OA, Cm, 93*: terrous 90 [12] was a mortal] was but a fountain of danger; and the least of her dangers was a mortal *OA (ex. As)* [13] to be witness *OA Cm, 93*: to witness 90 [14] am I] I am *St, Bo, Ph* [15] thyself? Or what] thyself? What 93 [16] wert] art *Ph*; wast *Je*

presence? O imperfect proportion of reason, which can too much[1] foresee, and too little prevent! Alas, alas,' said she, 'if there were but one hope for[2] all my pains, or but one excuse for all my faultiness! But wretch that I am, my torment is beyond all succour, and my evil-deserving doth exceed my evil-fortune. For nothing else did my husband take this strange resolution to live so solitarily,[3] for nothing else have[4] the winds delivered this strange guest to my country, for nothing else have the destinies reserved my life to this time, but that only I, most wretched I, should become a plague to myself, and a shame to womankind. Yet if my desire, how unjust so ever it be, might take effect, though a thousand deaths followed it, and every death were followed with a thousand shames, yet should not my sepulchre receive me without some contentment. But alas, though sure I am that Zelmane is such as can answer my love, yet as sure I am that this disguising must needs come for some foretaken conceit. And then, wretched Gynecia, where canst thou find any small groundplot for hope to dwell upon? No, no, it is Philoclea his heart is set upon; it is my daughter I have borne to supplant me. But if it be so, the life I have given thee, ungrateful Philoclea, I will sooner with these hands bereave thee of[5] than my birth shall glory she hath bereaved me of my desires. In shame there is no comfort but to be beyond all bounds[6] of shame.'

Having spoken this[7], she began to make a piteous war with her fair hair when she might hear not far from her an extremely doleful[8] voice, but so suppressed[9] with a kind of whispering note that she could not conceive the words distinctly. But as a lamentable tune is the sweetest music to a woeful mind, she drew thither near away in hope to find some companion[10] of her misery. And as she paced[11] on, she was stopped with a number of trees so thickly placed together that she was afraid she should, with rushing thorough, stop the speech of the lamentable party, which she was so desirous to understand. And therefore setting her down as softly as she could (for she was now in distance to hear), she might first perceive a lute, excellently well played upon, and then the same doleful voice accompanying it with these verses:

> In vain, mine eyes, you labour to amend
>   With flowing tears your fault[12] of hasty sight;
> Since to my heart her shape you so did[13] send
>   That her I see, though you did lose your light.

---

[1] can too much] can much *Da*; can so much *Je*   [2] hope for] hope of *corr. to* hope for *St*; hope of *Ph, Je*   [3] solitarily] solitary *OA* (*ex. Cl*)   [4] have] did *Cl*; hath *Ph*   [5] bereave thee of] bereave thereof *Ph, Cm* (*St could be read thus*); bereaveth of *Hm*   [6] bounds] bonds *Cl, Da, Hm*   [7] this *OA, Cm*: thus *90, 93*   [8] an extremely doleful] an extreme doleful *Bo*; a piteous a doleful *Cl*; an extremity a doleful *As*; a doleful *Da, Ph, Je, Hm*   [9] suppressed] suspected *Ph*; oppressed *Je*   [10] companion] company *Da, Je*   [11] paced *OA* (*ex. Cl, Je, Hm*), *93*: passed *Cl, Je, Hm, Cm, 90*   [12] fault] faint *Cl*; fate *Je, Hm*   [13] so did] did so *O, 98*

>   In vain, my heart, now you with sight are burned,
>   With sighs you seek to cool your hot desire;
>   Since sighs (into mine[1] inward furnace turned)
>   For bellows serve to kindle more the fire.
>   Reason, in vain (now you have lost my heart)
>   My head you seek, as to your strongest fort;
>   Since there mine eyes have played so false a part
>   That to your strength your foes have sure resort.
>   Then since in vain I find were all my strife,
>   To this strange death I vainly yield my life.

The ending of the song served but for a beginning of new plaints; as if the mind, oppressed with too heavy a[2] burthen of cares, was fain to discharge itself of all sides, and as it were paint out the hideousness[3] of the pain in all sorts of colours. For the woeful person, as if the lute had evil joined with[4] the voice, threw it to[5] the ground with such like words: 'Alas, poor lute, how much art thou[6] deceived to think that in my miseries thou couldst[7] ease my woes, as in my careless times[8] thou wert[9] wont to please my fancies! The time is changed, my lute, the time is changed; and no more did my joyful mind then receive everything to a joyful consideration than my careful mind now makes each thing taste like the bitter juice of care. The evil is inward, my lute, the evil is inward; which all thou doost doth serve but to make me think more freely of; and alas,[10] what is then thy harmony but the sweetmeats of sorrow? The discord of my thoughts, my lute, doth ill agree to the concord of thy strings; therefore, be not ashamed to leave thy master, since he is not afraid to forsake himself.'

And thus much spoken,[11] instead of a conclusion, was closed up with so hearty a groaning that Gynecia could not refrain to show herself, thinking such griefs could serve fitly for nothing but her[12] own fortune. But as she came into the little arbour of this sorrowful music, her eyes met with the eyes of Zelmane (which was the party that thus had indicted herself of misery), so that either of them remained confused with a sudden astonishment, Zelmane fearing lest she had heard some part of those[13] complaints, which she had risen up that morning early of purpose[14] to breathe out in secret to herself. But Gynecia a great while stood still, with a kind of dull amazement,

---

[1] mine] my *Bo, Da, Je*   [2] heavy a] heavy *Cl, s*   [3] hideousness] sharpness *OA (ex. St, Bo)*   [4] joined with] joined to *OA (ex. Cl, As)*   [5] it to] it down to *OA (ex. As)*   [6] art thou] thou art *OA (ex. As)*   [7] couldst] could *St, Bo, Ph*; om. *As*   [8] times] tunes *Cl*; time *Ph*; mind *Hm*   [9] wert *OA (ex. Hm, Ph), Cm*: were *Ph*; wast *Hm*; was *90, 93*   [10] of; and alas *Cm, 93*: of; and the more I think, the more cause I find of thinking, but less of hoping; and alas *90*   [11] spoken] spoke *93*   [12] her] *Hm missing from here ff. 33–45*   [13] those] these *Ph, Qu*   [14] that morning early of purpose *OA (ex. Cl, Ph, Qu), Cm, 93*: early that morning of purpose *Cl, Qu*; that morning of purpose early *Ph*; that morning of purpose *90*

looking steadfastly upon her. At length returning to some use of herself, she began to ask Zelmane what cause carried her so early abroad. But as if the opening of her mouth to Zelmane had opened some great flood-gap[1] of sorrow, whereof her heart could not abide the violent issue, she sank to the ground with her hands over her face, crying vehemently: 'Zelmane, help me! O Zelmane, have pity on[2] me!'

Zelmane ran to her, marvelling what sudden sickness had thus possessed her; and beginning to ask her the cause of her pain, and offering her service to be employed by her, Gynecia opening her eyes wildly upon her, pricked with the flames of love and the torments of her own conscience: 'O Zelmane, Zelmane,' said she, 'doost though offer me physic which art my only poison, or wilt thou do me service which hast already brought me into eternal slavery?'

Zelmane then knowing well at what mark she shot, yet loath to enter into it, 'Most excellent lady,' said she, 'you were best retire[3] yourself into your lodging that you the better may[4] pass this[5] sudden fit.'

'Retire myself!' said Gynecia, 'if I had retired myself into myself when thou (to me[6] unfortunate guest) came[7] to draw me from myself, blessed had I been, and no need had I had of this counsel. But now, alas, I am forced to fly to thee for succour, whom I accuse of all my hurt; and make thee judge of my cause, who art the only author of my mischief.'

Zelmane, the more astonished, the more she understood her, 'Madam,' said she, 'whereof do you accuse me that I will not clear myself? Or wherein may I stead you that you may not command me?'

'Alas,' answered Gynecia, 'what shall I say more? Take pity of me, O Zelmane – but not as Zelmane. And disguise not with me in words, as I know thou doost in apparel.'

Zelmane was much troubled with that word, finding herself brought to this strait. But as she was thinking what to answer her, they might see old Basilius pass hard by[8] them, without ever seeing them, complaining likewise of love very freshly, and ending his complaint with this song, love having renewed both his invention and voice:

Let not old age disgrace my high desire,
   O heav'nly soul in human shape contained.
Old wood inflamed doth yield the bravest fire,
   When younger doth in smoke his virtue spend.

---

[1] flood-gap *OA* (*ex. Bo, Je*), *Cm*: flood-gape *Bo*; flood-gates *Je*; flood-gate *90, 93* [2] on] of *OA* (*ex. Cl, Ph, Qu*) [3] best retire] best to retire *OA* (*ex. Cl, As*) [4] the better may] may the better *As, Da* [5] pass this] pass over this *OA* (*ex. Cl, As*) [6] to me] *om. Da, Je* [7] came *OA, Cm*: camest *90, 93* [8] hard by] by *Cl, Je*

>   Ne let white hairs (which on my face do[1] grow)
>   Seem to your eyes of a disgraceful hue;
>   Since whiteness doth present the sweetest[2] show,
>   Which makes all eyes do homage[3] unto you.
>   Old age is wise and full of constant truth;
>   Old age well stayed from ranging humour[4] lives;
>   Old age hath known whatever was in youth;
>   Old age orecome, the greater honour gives.
>   And to old age since you yourself aspire,
>   Let not old age disgrace my high desire.

Which being done, he looked very curiously upon himself, sometimes fetching a little skip, as if he had said his strength had not yet forsaken him. But Zelmane having in this time gotten some leisure[5] to think for an answer, looking upon Gynecia as if she thought she did her some wrong, 'Madam,' said she, 'I am not acquainted with those[6] words of disguising; neither is it the profession of an Amazon, neither are you a party with whom it is to be used. If my service may please you, employ it, so long as you do me no wrong in misjudging of me.'

'Alas, Zelmane,' said Gynecia, 'I perceive you know full little how piercing the eyes are of a true lover. There is no one beam of those[7] thoughts you have planted in me but is able to discern[8] a greater cloud than you do go in. Seek not to conceal yourself further from me, nor force not the passion of love into violent extremities!'

Now was Zelmane brought to an exigent, when the king, turning his eyes[9] that way thorough the trees, perceived his wife and mistress together; so that framing the most lovely countenance he could, he came straightway towards them, and at the first word thanking his wife for having entertained Zelmane, desired her she would now return into the lodge because he had certain matters of estate to impart to the Lady Zelmane. The queen, being nothing troubled with jealousy in that point, obeyed the king's commandment, full of raging agonies and determinately bent that, as she would seek all loving means to win Zelmane, so she would stir up terrible tragedies rather than fail of her intent. And so went she from them to the lodgeward with such a battle in her thoughts, and so deadly an overthrow given to her best resolutions, that even her body, where the field was fought, was oppressed withal, making a languishing sickness wait upon the triumph of passion; which the more it prevailed in her, the more it made her jealousy

---

[1] do] doth *Cl*, *Le*, *Qu*   [2] sweetest] bravest *Je*; clearest *Ha*   [3] homage *Cm, 93*: honour *OA, 90*   [4] humour] honour *Cl, Le*; humours *Ph*   [5] gotten some leisure *OA, 93*: gotten leisure *Cm, 90*   [6] those] these *OA (ex. Ph)*   [7] those] the *As*; these *Qu*   [8] able to discern *OA, Cm, 93*: able discern *90*   [9] eyes] eye *OA (ex. Je)*

watchful both over her daughter and Zelmane, having ever one of them entrusted to her own eyes.

But as soon as Basilius was rid of his wives presence, falling down on[1] his knees, 'O lady,' said he, 'which have[2] only had the power to stir up again those[3] flames which had so long lain dead in me, see in me the power of your beauty, which can make old age come to ask counsel of youth, and a prince unconquered to become a slave to a stranger. And when you see that power of yours, love that at least in me, since it is yours, although of me[4] you see nothing to be loved.'

'Worthy prince,' answered Zelmane, taking him up from his kneeling, 'both your manner and your speech are so strange unto me as I know not how to answer it better than with silence.' 'If silence please you,' said the king, 'it shall never displease me, since my heart is wholly pledged to obey you. Otherwise, if you would vouchsafe mine ears such happiness as to hear you, they shall convey your words to such a mind which is with the humblest degree of reverence to receive them.'

'I disdain not to speak to you, mighty prince,' said Zelmane, 'but I disdain to speak to any matter which may bring my[5] honour into[6] question.'

And therewith, with a brave counterfeited[7] scorn, she departed from the king, leaving him not so sorry for his[8] short answer, as proud in himself that he had broken the matter. And thus did the king, feeding his mind with these[9] thoughts, pass great time in writing of verses,[10] and making more of himself than he was wont to do; that with a little help he would have grown into a pretty kind of dotage.

But Zelmane, being rid of this loving, but little loved company, 'Alas,' said she, 'poor Pyrocles! Was there ever one but I that had received wrong and could blame nobody, that having more than I desire, am still in want of that I would? Truly, love, I must needs say thus much on thy behalf, thou hast employed my love there where all love is deserved; and for recompense hast[11] sent me more love than ever I desired. But what wilt thou do, Pyrocles? Which way canst thou find to rid thee of thy intricate troubles? To her whom I would be known to, I live in darkness; and to her am revealed[12] from whom I would be most secret. What shift shall I find against the diligent love of Basilius; what shield against the violent passion[13] of Gynecia? And if that be done, yet how am I the nearer to quench the fire that consumes me? Well, well, sweet Philoclea, my whole confidence must be built in thy

---

[1] on] of *St, Bo, As, Ph, Qu*   [2] have *OA, Cm*: hast *90, 93*   [3] those] the *As*; these *Je*   [4] of me] in me *Cl, Da, Je, Qu*   [5] my] mine *OA (ex. Bo, Da, Qu)*   [6] into] in *As, Qu*   [7] counterfeited] counterfeit *As, Da*   [8] for his] for this *St, Bo, Ph*   [9] with these *OA (ex. Qu), Cm*: with his *Qu*; with those *90, 93*   [10] of verses *OA (ex. Bo), Cm*; verses *Bo, 90, 93*   [11] hast] hath *St, Bo, Cl, Da*; om. *Ph, Qu*   [12] am revealed] am I revealed *Da, Je, Qu*   [13] passion *OA, Cm*: passions *90, 93*

divine spirit, which cannot be ignorant of the cruel wound I have received by you.'

But[1] as sick folks when they are alone think company would relieve them, and yet having company do find it noisome, changing willingly outward objects when indeed the evil is inward, so poor Zelmane was no more weary of Basilius than she was of herself when Basilius was gone, and ever the more, the more she turned her eyes to become her own judges. Tired wherewith, she longed to meet her friend Dorus, that upon the shoulders of friendship she might lay the burthen of sorrow, and therefore went toward the other lodge, where among certain beeches she found Dorus, apparelled in flannen, with a goat's skin cast upon him and a garland of laurel mixed with cypress leaves on his head, waiting on his master Dametas, who at that time was teaching him how with his sheephook to catch a wanton lamb, and with[2] the same to cast a little clod at any one that strayed out of company. And while Dorus was practising, one might see Dametas hold[3] his hand under his girdle behind him, nodding from the waist upwards, and swearing he never knew man go more awkwardly to work, and that they might talk of book-learning what they would, but for his part he never saw more unfeatly[4] fellows than great clerks were; but Zelmane's coming saved Dorus from further chiding. And so, she beginning to speak with him of the number of his master's sheep, and which province of Arcadia bare the finest wool, drew him on to follow her in such country discourses till, being out of Dametas' hearing, with such vehemency of passion, as though her heart would climb into her mouth to take her tongue's office, she declared unto him upon what briars the roses of her affections grew; how time still seemed to forget her, bestowing no one hour of comfort upon her, she remaining still in one plight of ill-fortune, saving so much worse as continuance of evil doth in itself increase evil.

'Alas, my Dorus,' said she, 'thou seest how long and languishingly the weeks are passed over us since our last talking; and yet am I the same miserable I that I was, only stronger in longing and weaker in hoping.'

Then fell she to so pitiful a declaration of the insupportableness of her desires that Dorus' ears, not able to show what wounds that discourse gave unto them, procured his eyes with tears to give testimony how much they suffered for her suffering; till passion, a most cumbersome guest to itself, made Zelmane, the sooner to shake it off, earnestly entreat Dorus that he also with like freedom of discourse would bestow a map of his little world upon her, that she might see whether it were troubled with such unhabitable

---

[1] you.' But *Cm, 93*: you.' Chap. 2. Dametas' instructing of Dorus; Zelmane's discourse to Dorus of her difficulties, and his to her of his success in love; his love-suits made to Mopsa, meant to Pamela, with their answers. But *90*   [2] and with] and how with *93*   [3] hold] holding *93*   [4] unfeatly] unfeatie *93*

climes of cold despairs and hot rages as hers was. And so, walking under a few palm trees, which being loving in their own nature seemed to give their shadow the willinglier because they held discourse of love, Dorus thus entered to the description of his fortune:

'Alas,' said he, 'dear cousin, that it hath pleased the high powers to throw us to such an estate as the only intercourse of our true friendship must be a bartering of miseries! For my part, I must confess indeed that from a huge darkness of sorrows I am crept, I cannot say to a lightsomeness, but to a certain dawning, or rather, peeping out of some possibility of comfort; but woe is me, so far from the mark of my desires that I rather think it such a light as comes through a small hole to a dungeon, that the miserable caitiff may the better remember the light of which he is deprived, or like a scholar who is only come to that degree of knowledge to find himself utterly ignorant.

'But thus stands it with me. After that by your means I was exalted to serve in yonder blessed lodge, for awhile I had in the furnace of my agonies this refreshing, that because of the service I had done in killing of the bear it pleased the princess, in whom indeed stateliness shines through courtesy, to let fall some gracious look upon me, sometimes to see my exercises, sometimes to hear my songs. For my part, my heart would not suffer me to omit any occasion whereby I might make the incomparable Pamela see how much extraordinary devotion I bare to her service, and withal strave to appear more worthy in her sight, that small desert joined to so great affection might prevail something in the wisest lady. But too well, alas, I found that a shepherd's service was but considered of as from a shepherd, and the acceptation limited to no further proportion than of a good servant. And when my countenance had once given notice that there lay affection under it, I saw straight majesty sitting in the throne of beauty draw forth such a sword of just disdain that I remained as a man thunder-stricken, not daring, no, not able to behold that power. Now to make my estate known seemed again impossible by reason of the suspiciousness of Dametas, Miso, and my young mistress, Mopsa. For Dametas, according to the constitution of a dull head, thinks no better way to show himself wise than by suspecting everything in his way, which suspicion Miso, for the hoggish shrewdness of her brain, and Mopsa, for a very unlikely envy she hath stumbled upon against the princess's unspeakable beauty, were very glad to execute; so that I, finding my service by this means lightly regarded, my affection despised, and myself unknown, remained no fuller of desire than void of comfort[1] how to come to my desire, which, alas, if these trees could speak, they might well witness. For many times have I stood here bewailing myself unto them, many times

---

[1] comfort] counsel 93

have I, leaning to yonder palm, admired the blessedness of it that it could[1] bear love without sense of pain, many times, when my master's cattle came hither to chew their cud in this fresh place, I might see the young bull testify his love – but how? – with proud looks, and joyfulness.

'"O wretched mankind," said I then to myself, "in whom wit which should be the governor of his welfare becomes the traitor to his blessedness! These beasts, like children to nature, inherit her blessings quietly; we, like bastards, are laid abroad even as foundlings to be trained up by grief and sorrow. Their minds grudge not their[2] bodies' comfort, nor their senses are letted from enjoying their objects; we have the impediments of honour, and the torments of conscience."

'Truly, in such cogitations have I sometimes so long stood that methought my feet began to grow into the ground, with such a darkness and heaviness of mind that I might easily have been persuaded to have resigned over my very essence. But love, which one time layeth burthens, another time giveth wings, when I was at the lowest of my downward thoughts, pulled up my heart to remember that nothing is achieved before it be throughly attempted, and that lying still doth never go forward; and that therefore it was time, now or never, to sharpen my invention, to pierce thorough the hardness of this enterprise, never ceasing to assemble all my conceits, one after the other, how to manifest both my mind and estate; till at last I lighted and resolved on this way, which yet perchance you will think was a way rather to hide it.

'I began to counterfeit the extremest love towards Mopsa that might be; and as for the love, so lively it was indeed within me (although to another subject) that little I needed to counterfeit any notable demonstrations of it. And so, making a contrariety the place of my memory, in her foulness I beheld Pamela's fairness, still looking on Mopsa, but thinking on Pamela, as if I saw my sun shine in a puddled water. I cried out of nothing but Mopsa; to Mopsa my attendance was directed; to Mopsa the best fruits I could gather were brought; to Mopsa it seemed still that mine eye conveyed my tongue, so that Mopsa was my saying, Mopsa was my singing; Mopsa, that is only suitable in laying a foul complexion upon a filthy favour, setting forth both in sluttishness – she was the lodestar of my life, she the blessing of mine eyes, she the overthrow of my desires and yet the recompense of my overthrow, she the sweetness of my heart, even sweetening the death which her sweetness drew upon me. In sum, whatsoever I thought of Pamela, that I said of Mopsa, whereby, as I gate my master's goodwill (who before spited me, fearing lest I should win the princess's favour from him), so did the same

---

[1] that it could *Cm, 93*: that could *90* [2] not their] not at their *93*

make the princess be¹ better content to allow me her presence – whether indeed it were that a certain spark of noble indignation did rise in her not to suffer such a baggage to win away anything of hers, how meanly soever she reputed of it; or rather, as I think, my words being so passionate, and shooting so quite contrary from the marks of Mopsa's worthiness, she perceived well enough whither they were directed, and therefore, being so masked, she was contented as a sport of wit to attend them. Whereupon one day determining to find some means to tell, as of a third person, the tale of mine own love and estate, finding Mopsa, like a cuckoo by a nightingale, alone with Pamela, I came in unto them, and with a face, I am sure, full of cloudy fancies, took a harp and sung this song:

Since so mine eyes are subject to your sight,
That in your sight they fixed have my brain;
Since so my heart is filled with that light,
That only light doth all my life maintain;
Since in sweet you all goods so richly reign,
That where you are no wished good can want;
Since so your living image lives in me,
That in myself yourself true love doth plant;
   How can you him unworthy then decree,
   In whose chief part² your worths³ implanted be?

'The song being ended, which I had often broken off in the middest with grievous sighs which overtook every verse I sang, I let fall my harp from me, and casting my eye⁴ sometime upon Mopsa, but settling⁵ my sight principally upon Pamela, "And is it the only⁶ fortune, most beautiful Mopsa," said I, "of wretched Dorus, that fortune must be the measure⁷ of his mind? Am I only he that, because I am in misery, more misery must be laid upon me? Must that which should be cause of compassion become an argument of cruelty against me? Alas, excellent Mopsa, consider that a virtuous prince requires the life of his meanest subject, and the heavenly sun disdains not to give light to the smallest worm. O Mopsa, Mopsa! If my heart could be as manifest to you⁸ as it is uncomfortable to me, I doubt not the height of my thoughts should well countervail the lowness⁹ of my quality. Who hath not heard of the greatness of your estate? Who seeth not that your estate is much excelled¹⁰ with that sweet uniting of all beauties¹¹ which

---

¹ be] the 93   ² part] plant Bo; parts As, Le, Ph, Qu   ³ worths] worthies Le, Da, Je   ⁴ eye] eyes Je, Qu (eyes corr. to eye St)   ⁵ settling OA (ex. Ph, Je), 93: setting Ph, Je, Cm, 90   ⁶ the only] only the OA (ex. Ph, Qu); only Ph   ⁷ must be the measure OA (ex. Qu), 93: should be measure Qu, 90; should be the measure Cm   ⁸ to you] unto you Je; unto thee Cm   ⁹ lowness] lowliness Cl, Da   ¹⁰ excelled] extolled Da; excellent Je (excellent corr. to excelled St, Qu)   ¹¹ all beauties] your beauties Ph; beauties Qu, Cm

remaineth and dwelleth with you? Who knows not that all these are but ornaments of that divine spark within[1] you which, being descended from heaven, could not elsewhere pick out so sweet a mansion? But if you will know what is the band[2] that ought to knit all these excellencies together, it is a kind mercifulness[3] to such a one as is in his soul[4] devoted to those perfections."

'Mopsa (who already had had[5] a certain smackering[6] towards me) stood all this while with her hand sometimes before her face, but most commonly with a certain special grace of her own, wagging her lips and grinning, instead of smiling. But all the words I could get of her was (wrying[7] her waist, and thrusting out her chin), "In faith, you jest with me! you are a merry man indeed!"

'But the ever-pleasing Pamela, that well found the comedy would be marred if she did not help Mopsa to her part, was content to urge a little further of me. "Master Dorus," said the fair Pamela, "methinks you blame your fortune very wrongfully, since the fault is not in fortune but in you that cannot frame yourself to your fortune; and as wrongfully do require[8] Mopsa to so great a disparagement as to her father's servant, since she is not worthy to be loved[9] that hath not some feeling of her own worthiness."

'I stayed a good while after her words in hope she would have continued her speech, so great a delight I received in hearing her.[10] But[11] seeing her say no further, with a quaking all over my body, I thus answered her: "Lady, most worthy of all duty, how falls it out that you, in whom all virtue shines, will take the patronage[12] of fortune, the only rebellious handmaid against virtue? Especially since before your eyes you have a pitiful spectacle of her wickedness, a forlorn creature which must remain not such as I am but such as she makes me, since she must be the balance of worthiness or disparagement. Yet alas, if the condemned man even at his death have leave to speak, let my mortal wound purchase thus[13] much consideration: since the perfections are such in the party I love as the feeling of them cannot come into any unnoble[14] heart, shall that heart, which doth not only feel them, but hath all the working[15] of his life placed in them, shall that heart, I say, lifted up to such a height, be counted base? Oh, let not an excellent spirit do itself

---

[1] within] which is in *As, Je* [2] band] bond *OA (ex. Je)* [3] kind mercifulness *St, Bo, As, Da, Ph, Qu,* 93: kind of mercifulness *Cl, Le, Je, Cm,* 90 [4] in his soul] in soul *OA (ex. Le*; in his soul *corr. to* in soul *St)* [5] already had had] had had already *Bo, Ph*; already had *Je* [6] smackering] smacking *Le*; smickering *Je*; smytering *Qu* [7] wrying *OA (ex. Ph, Je, Qu),* 93: om. *Ph*; wringing *Je, Qu, Cm,* 90 (wringe *corr. to* wringeing *Cm*) [8] do require] you do require *St, Bo, Cl, Da, Ph*; do you require *As, Je, Qu* [9] loved] beloved *Ph, Qu* [10] hearing her] hearing of her *Cl, Da* [11] But] And *Le, As, Cm* [12] patronage] patrony *St, Cl*; patriconie *Bo*; pattern *Le*; patrocinie *As, Je*; patrimony *Da*; patronicy *Qu* [13] thus] this *Je, Cm* [14] unnoble] unmovable *Da*; humble *Ph*; immovable *Je*; unable *Qu* [15] working] workings *OA (ex. Je)*

such wrong, as where[1] it is placed, embraced, and loved, there can be any unworthiness![2] since the weakest mist is not easilier driven away by the sun, than that is chased away with so high thoughts."

'"I will not deny", answered the gracious Pamela, "but that the love you bear to Mopsa hath brought you to the consideration of her virtues, and the[3] consideration may have made you the more[4] virtuous, and so the more worthy. But even that, then, you must confess you have received of her, and so are rather gratefully to thank her than to press any further till you bring something of your own whereby[5] to claim it. And truly, Dorus, I must in Mopsa's behalf say thus much to you, that if her beauties have so overtaken you, it becomes[6] a true love to have your heart more set upon her good than your own, and to bear a tenderer[7] respect to her honour than your[8] satisfaction."

'"Now, by my hallidame, madam!" said Mopsa, throwing a great number of sheep's eyes upon me, "you have even touched mine[9] own mind to the quick, forsooth!"

'I, finding that the policy I[10] had used had at leastwise procured thus much happiness unto me as that I might even in my lady's presence discover the sore which had deeply festered within me, and that she could[11] better conceive my reasons applied to Mopsa than she would have vouchsafed them whilst herself was a party, thought good to pursue on my good beginning using this fit occasion of Pamela's wit and Mopsa's ignorance. Therefore with an humble, piercing[12] eye looking upon Pamela, as if I had rather been[13] condemned by her mouth than highly exalted by the other, turning myself to Mopsa, but keeping mine eye where it was, "Fair Mopsa," said I, "well do I find by the wise knitting together of your answer that any disputation I can use is as much too weak as I unworthy. I find my love shall be proved no[14] love, without I leave to love, being too unfit a vessel in whom so high thoughts should be engraved. Yet since the love I bear you hath so joined itself to the best part of my life, as the one cannot depart but that th'other will follow, before I seek to obey you in making my last passage, let me know which is my[15] unworthiness, either of mind, estate, or both."

'Mopsa was about to say, "In neither", for her heart, I think, tumbled with overmuch kindness, when Pamela with a more favourable countenance than before, finding how apt I was to fall into despair, told me I might therein have

---

[1] as where *St, Bo, Le, As, Ph, Je, Cm*: as to think where *Cl, 90, 93*; as once to imagine where *Da*; as when *Qu* [2] unworthiness] worthiness *Qu, Cm* [3] and the *OA, Cm*: and that *90, 93* [4] you the more] you more *Bo, Le, Ph, Qu* [5] whereby] by which *OA (ex. Le, As)* [6] becomes] becometh *OA (ex. Cl, Le, As)* [7] tenderer] tender *Le, Cm*; more tender *Da* [8] than your] than to your *Cl, Da* [9] mine] my *Bo, As, Da* [10] policy I *OA, Cm*: policy that I *90, 93* [11] could] would *Cl, Le* [12] humble, piercing] humble but piercing *OA (ex. Cl, Le, As)* [13] been] be *OA (ex. Cl, Ph, Je)* [14] no] in *Cl, As, Ph* [15] is my] is mine *Bo, Ph, Qu*

answered myself, for besides that it was granted me that the inward feeling of Mopsa's perfections had greatly beautified my mind, there was none could deny but that my mind and body deserved[1] great allowance. "But Dorus," said she, "you must be so far master of your love as to consider that, since the judgement of the world stands upon matter of fortune, and that the sex of womankind of all other is most bound to have regardful[2] eye to men's judgements, it is not for us to play the philosophers[3] in seeking out your[4] hidden virtues, since that which in[5] a wise prince would be counted wisdom, in us will be taken for a light-grounded affection; so is not one thing one, done by divers persons."

'There is no man in a burning fever feels so great contentment in cold water greedily received (which as soon as the drink ceaseth, the rage[6] reneweth) as poor I found my soul refreshed with her sweetly pronounced words, and newly and more violently again inflamed as soon as she had closed up her delightful speech with no less well-graced silence. But remembering in myself that as well the soldier dieth which standeth still as he that gives the bravest onset, and seeing that to the making up of my fortune there wanted nothing so much as the making known of mine estate, with a face well witnessing how deeply my soul was possessed, and with the most submissive behaviour that a thralled heart could express, even as if[7] my words had been too thick[8] for my mouth, at length spake to this purpose: "Alas, most worthy princess," said I, "and do not then your own sweet words sufficiently testify that there was never man could have a juster action against filthy fortune than I, since all other things being granted me, her blindness is my only let? O heavenly God![9] I would either she had such eyes as were able to discern my deserts, or I were blind not to see the daily cause[10] of my misfortune! But yet," said I, "most honoured lady, if my miserable speeches have not already cloyed you, and that the very presence of such a wretch become not hateful in your eyes, let me reply thus much further against my mortal sentence by telling you a story which happened in this same country[11] long since (for woes make the shortest time seem long), whereby you shall see that my[12] estate is not so contemptible but that a prince hath been content to take the like upon him, and by that only hath aspired to enjoy a mighty princess."

---

[1] body deserved] body of themselves deserved *OA* (ex. *Le, Qu*); om. *Qu* [2] have regardful] have a regardful *As, Da, Je* [3] philosophers] philosopher *Le, Je* [4] your] the *As, Qu, Cm* [5] which in] within *St, Da, Ph*; which is in *As*; in *Je, Qu* [6] rage] heat *OA* (ex. *Cl, Le, As*) [7] as if *OA, Cm*: as 90, 93 [8] thick] think *Da, Ph*; big *Je* [9] God] gods *OA* (ex. *Cl, Le*) [10] daily cause of my] cause of my daily *Da*; cause of my *Je* [11] this same country] this country *Da, Je* [12] my] mine *Cl, Le*

'Pamela graciously hearkened, and I told my tale in this sort: "In[1] the country of Thessalia (alas, why name I that accursed country which brings forth nothing but matters for[2] tragedies – but name it I must), in Thessalia, I say, there was – well may I say[3] there was – a prince. No! no[4] prince, whom bondage wholly possessed, but yet accounted a prince, and named Musidorus. O Musidorus! Musidorus! But to what serve[5] exclamations where there are no ears to receive the sound? This Musidorus, being yet in the tenderest age, his worthy father paid to nature with a violent death her[6] last duties, leaving his child to the faith of his friends and the proof of time. Death gave him not such pangs as the foresightful care he had of his silly successor – and yet, if in his foresight he could have seen so much, happy was that good prince in his timely departure which barred him from the knowledge of his son's miseries, which his knowledge could neither[7] have prevented nor relieved.[8] The young Musidorus being thus (as for the first pledge of the destinies' goodwill) deprived of his principal stay, was yet for some years after (as if the stars would breathe[9] themselves for a greater mischief) lulled up in as much good luck as the heedful love of his doleful mother and the flourishing estate of his country could breed unto[10] him. But when the time now came that misery seemed to be ripe for him, because he had age to know misery, I think there was a conspiracy in all heavenly and earthly things to frame fit occasions[11] to lead him unto it. His people (to whom all foreign matters in foretime were odious) began to[12] wish in their beloved prince experience by travel. His dear mother (whose eyes were held open only with the joy of looking upon him) did now dispense with the comfort of her widowhead[13] life, desiring the same her subjects did, for the increase of her son's worthiness. And hereto did Musidorus' own virtue (see how virtue can be a minister to mischief!) sufficiently provoke him. For indeed, thus much I must[14] say for him (although the likeness of our mishaps makes me presume to pattern myself unto him) that well doing was at that time his scope, from which no faint pleasures[15] could withhold him. But the present occasion (which did knit all these[16] together) was his uncle, the king of Macedon, who having lately before gotten such victories as were beyond expectation, did at this time send both for the prince, his son (brought up together, to avoid the wars, with Musidorus) and for Musidorus

---

[1] sort: " In *OA, Cm, 93*: sort.' Chap. 3. Dorus' tale of his own education, travel, enamouring, metamorphosing, saving from sea, and being Musidorus; his octave; Pamela's and Mopsa's answer to his suit; his present to them, and perplexity in himself." In *90* [2] for] of *Cl, Ph, Je, Qu* (of *corr. to* for *St*) [3] well may I say] well I may say *St, Bo, As, Da, Ph*; well I say *Qu* [4] No! no] now no *As*; no *Da* [5] serve] serves *St, As, Da, Ph*; service *Qu* [6] her] his *Ph, Cm* [7] neither] never *Ph, Qu* [8] relieved] revealed *Da, Je* [9] breathe *OA, Cm*: breath *90, 93* [10] unto] into *As*; in *Qu* [11] occasions *OA (ex. Je, Qu), 93*: occasion *Je, Qu, Cm, 90* [12] began to] began now to *OA (ex. Qu)* [13] widowhead] widowed *St, Bo, Da, Je*; widowhood *Cl, Ph, Qu* [14] I must] must I *Cl, Le, Je*; om. *Ph* [15] pleasures *OA, Cm*: pleasure *90, 93* [16] these *OA (ex. Ph), Cm*: those *Ph*; this *90, 93*

himself, that his joy might be the more full having such partakers of it. But alas, to what a sea of miseries my plaintful tongue doth lead me!"

'And thus out of breath, rather with that I thought than that[1] I said, I stayed my speech, till Pamela showing by countenance that such was her pleasure, I thus continued it: "These two young princes, to satisfy the king, took their way by sea towards Thrace, whither they would needs go with a navy to succour him, he being at that time before Byzantium (with a mighty army besieging it) where at that time his court was. But when the conspired heavens had gotten this subject of their wrath upon so fit a place as the sea was, they straight began to breathe out in boisterous winds some part of their malice against him, so that with the loss of all his navy,[2] he only with the prince, his cousin, were cast aland, far off from the place whither their desires would have guided them. O cruel winds in your unconsiderate[3] rages! Why either began you this fury, or why did you not end it in his end? But your cruelty was such as you would spare his life for many deathful torments. To tell you what pitiful mishaps fell to the young prince of Macedon, his cousin, I should too much fill your ears with strange horrors; neither will I stay[4] upon those laboursome adventures, nor loathsome misadventures, to which and through which his fortune and courage conducted him – my speech hasteneth itself to come to the full point[5] of Musidorus' infortunes. For as we find the most pestilent diseases do gather into themselves all the infirmities[6] with which the body before was annoyed, so did his last misery embrace in the extremity of itself all his former mischiefs.[7] Arcadia, Arcadia was the place prepared to be the stage of his endless overthrow. Arcadia was (alas, well might I say *it is*) the charmed circle where all his spirits for ever should be enchanted. For here, and nowhere else, did his infected eyes make his mind know what power heavenly beauty hath to throw it down to hellish agonies. Here, here did he see the Arcadian king's eldest daughter, in whom he forthwith placed so all his hopes of joy and joyful parts of his heart, that he left in himself nothing but a maze of longing[8] and a dungeon of sorrow. But alas, what can saying make them believe, whom seeing cannot persuade? Those pains must be felt before they can be understood; no outward utterance can command a conceit. Such was as then the state of the king as it was no time by direct means to seek her; and such was the state of his captived will as he could delay no time of seeking her. In this entangled case,[9] he clothed himself in a shepherd's

---

[1] than that] than with that *OA* (*ex. Je*)   [2] navy] navies *OA* (*ex. Cl, As, Du*); name *Da*   [3] unconsiderate] inconsiderate *Bo, As, Qu*; unconstant *Ph*; considerate *Je*   [4] stay] stand *Ph*; seem *Qu*   [5] the full point] the point *St*; the full points *Cm*   [6] infirmities *OA, Cm, 93*: infirmity *90*   [7] mischiefs] mischief *Cl, Le, Je*   [8] longing] lodging *Cl* (lodging corr. to longing *Cm*); language *Ph*; lingering *Qu*   [9] case] care *Ph*; sort *Qu*; cause *98*

weed, that under the baseness of that form he might at least have free access to feed his eyes with that which should at length eat up his heart. In which doing, thus much without doubt he hath manifested: that this estate is not always to be rejected, since under that veil[1] there may be hidden things to be esteemed. And if[2] he might, with taking on a shepherd's look, cast up his eyes to the fairest princess nature in that time created, the like, nay, the same desire of mine need no more to be disdained or held for disgraceful. But now, alas, mine eyes wax dim, my tongue begins to falter, and my heart to want force to help either, with the feeling remembrance I have in what heap of miseries the caitiff prince lay at this time buried. Pardon therefore, most excellent princess, if I cut off the course of my dolorous tale, since (if I be understood) I have said enough for the defence of my baseness. And for that which after might befall to that[3] pattern of ill fortune, the matters are too monstrous[4] for my capacity. His hateful destinies must best declare their own workmanship."

'Thus having delivered my tale in this perplexed manner, to the end the princess might judge that he meant himself who spake so feelingly, her answer was both strange and in some respect comfortable, for (would you think it?) she hath heard heretofore of us both by means of the valiant Prince Plangus, and particularly of our casting away; which she, following my own style, thus delicately brought forth: "You have told," said she, "Dorus, a pretty tale. But you are much deceived in the latter end of it, for the Prince Musidorus with his cousin Pyrocles did both perish upon the coast of Laconia, as a noble gentleman called Plangus, who was well acquainted with the history, did assure my father."

'Oh how that speech of hers did pour joys in my heart! "O blessed name", thought I, "of mine, since thou hast been in that tongue and passed through those lips – though I can never hope to approach them."

'"As for Pyrocles," said I, "I will not deny it but that he is perished" – which I said lest sooner suspicion might arise of your being here than[5] yourself would have it, and yet affirmed no lie unto her, since I only said I would not deny it. "But for Musidorus," said I, "I perceive indeed you have either[6] heard or read the story of that unhappy prince, for this was the very objection which that peerless princess did make unto him when he sought to appear such as he was before her wisdom. And thus, as I have read it fair written in the certainty of my knowledge, he might answer her that

---

[1] under that veil] under the veil St, As, Ph [2] And if] And that if OA (ex. Le, As) [3] to that] to the As, Ph, Qu [4] too monstrous OA, Cm, 93: monstrous 90 [5] being here than Cm, 93: being than 90
[6] either Cm, 93: neither 90

indeed the ship wherein he came by a treason was perished, and therefore that Plangus might easily be deceived; but that he himself was cast upon the coast of Laconia where he was taken up by a couple of shepherds who lived in those days famous (for that both loving one fair maid, they yet remained constant friends – one of whose songs not long since was sung before you by the shepherd Lamon) and brought by them to a nobleman's house near Mantinea, whose son had a little before his marriage[1] been taken prisoner, and by the help of this Prince Musidorus (though naming himself by another name) was delivered."

'Now these circumlocutions I did use because of the one side I knew the princess would know well the parties I meant, and of the other, if I should have named Strephon, Claius, Kalander, and Clitophon, perhaps it would have rubbed some conjecture into the heavy head of Mistress Mopsa.

'"And therefore," said I, "most divine lady, he justly was to[2] argue against such suspicions; that the prince[3] might easily by those parties be satisfied that upon that wrack such a one was taken up, and therefore that Plangus might well err, who knew not of any's taking up again; that he that was so preserved brought good tokens to be one of the two chief of that wracked company, which two, since Plangus knew to be Musidorus and Pyrocles, he must needs be one of them, although, as I said, upon a foretaken vow he was otherwise at that time called. Besides, the princess must needs judge that no less than a prince durst undertake such an enterprise, which, though he might get the favour of the princess, he could never defend with less than a prince's power against the force of Arcadia. Lastly, said he for a certain demonstration, he presumed to show unto the princess a mark he had on his face, as I might", said I, "show this of my neck to the rare Mopsa", and withal showed my neck to them both, where, as you know, there is a red spot bearing figure, as they tell me, of a lion's paw, "that she may ascertain herself that I am Menalcas' brother. And so did he, beseeching her to send someone she might trust into Thessalia, secretly to be advertised whether the age, the complexion, and particularly that notable sign, did not fully agree with their[4] Prince Musidorus."

'"Do you not know further", said she, with a settled countenance not accusing any kind of inward motion, "of that story?"

'"Alas, no," said I, "for even here the historiographer stopped, saying the rest belonged to astrology." And therewith, thinking her silent imaginations began to work upon somewhat, to mollify them (as the nature of music is to do), and withal to show what kind of shepherd I was, I took up my harp and sang these few verses:

---

[1] before his marriage been] before marriage been *Cm*; before been *13*   [2] was to] was thus to *93*
[3] prince] princess *Cm, 13*   [4] their *Cm, 93*: this *90*

My sheep are thoughts, which I both guide and serve:
Their pasture is fair hills of fruitless love:
On¹ barren sweets they feed, and feeding starve:
I wail their lot, but will not other prove.
My sheephook is wanhope which all upholds:
My weeds, desire, cut out in endless folds.
   What wool my sheep shall bear, whiles thus they² live,
   In you it is, you must the judgement give.

And then, partly to bring Mopsa again to the matter, lest she should too much take heed to our discourses, but principally, if it were possible, to gather some comfort out of her answers, I kneeled down to the princess, and humbly besought her to move Mopsa in my behalf, that she would unarm her heart³ of that steely resistance against the sweet blows of love; that since all her parts were decked with some particular ornament – her face with beauty, her head with wisdom, her eyes with majesty, her countenance with gracefulness, her lips with loveliness, her tongue with victory – that she would make her heart the throne of pity, being the most excellent raiment of the most excellent part.

'Pamela, without show either of favour or disdain, either of heeding or neglecting what I had said, turned her speech to Mopsa, and with such a voice and action as might show she spake of a matter which little did concern her, "Take heed⁴ to yourself," said she, "Mopsa, for your shepherd can speak well. But truly, if he do fully prove himself such as he saith (I mean the honest shepherd Menalcas' brother and heir), I know no reason why you should think scorn of him."

'Mopsa, though in my conscience she were even then far spent towards me, yet she answered her, that for all my quaint speeches she would keep her honesty close enough, and that as for the way⁵ of matrimony, she would step never a foot further till my master, her father, had spoken the whole word himself, no she would not. But ever and anon turning her muzzle towards me, she threw such a prospect upon me as might well have given a surfeit to any weak lover's stomach. But Lord, what a fool am I to mingle that drivel's speeches among my noble thoughts – but because she was an actor in this tragedy, to give you a full knowledge, and to leave nothing that I can remember unrepeated.

'Now the princess being about to withdraw herself from us, I took a jewel made in the figure of a crabfish, which because it looks one way and goes another, I thought it did fitly pattern out my looking to Mopsa but bending to Pamela – the word about it was "By force, not choice" – and still kneeling,

---

¹ On] In *OA (ex. Bo, Da)*, *Fl*, *Ma*; O *Da*   ² they] I *Fl*, *Ma*   ³ her heart] her noble heart *93*   ⁴ Take heed] take good heed *OA (ex. Ph)*   ⁵ the way *Cm*, *93*: the high way *OA*, *90*

besought the princess that she would vouchsafe to give it Mopsa, and with the blessedness of her hand to make acceptable unto her that toy which I had found, following of late an acquaintance of mine at the plough. "For," said I, "as the earth was turned up, the ploughshare lighted upon a great stone. We pulled that up, and so found both that and some other pretty things" – which we had divided betwixt us.

'Mopsa was benumbed with joy when the princess gave it her – but in the princess I could find no apprehension of what I either said or did, but with a calm carelessness letting each thing slide (justly as we do by their speeches who neither in matter nor person do any way belong unto us); which kind of cold temper, mixed with that lightning of her natural majesty, is of all others most terrible unto me. For yet if I found she contemned me, I would desperately labour both in fortune and virtue to overcome it; if she only misdoubted me, I were in heaven, for quickly I would bring sufficient assurance; lastly, if she hated me, yet I should know what passion to deal with, and either with infiniteness of desert I would take away the fuel from that fire, or if nothing would serve, then I would give her my heart-blood to quench it. But this cruel quietness, neither retiring to mislike nor proceeding to favour; gracious, but gracious still after one manner (all her courtesies having this engraven in them, that "what is done is for virtue's sake, not for the party's"); ever keeping her course, like the sun, who neither for our praises nor curses will spare[1] or stop his horses; this, I say, heavenliness of hers (for howsoever my misery is, I cannot but so entitle it) is so impossible to reach unto that I almost begin to submit myself to the tyranny of despair, not knowing any way of persuasion where wisdom seems to be unsensible. I have appeared to her eyes like myself, by a device I used with my master, persuading him that we two might put on certain[2] rich apparel I had provided, and so practise something on horseback before Pamela, telling him it was apparel I had gotten for playing well the part of a king in a tragedy at Athens. My horse indeed was it I had left at Menalcas' house, and Dametas got one by friendship out of the prince's stable. But howsoever I show I am no base body, all I do is but to beat a rock and get foam.'

But[3] as Dorus was about to tell further, Dametas, who came whistling, and counting upon his fingers how many load of hay his seventeen fat oxen eat up in a year, desired Zelmane from the king that she would come into the lodge where they stayed for her.

'Alas,' said Dorus, taking his leave, 'the sum is this: that you may well find you have beaten your sorrow against such a wall, which with the force of rebound may well make your sorrow stronger.'

---

[1] spare] spur 93   [2] on certain *Cm*, 93: on a certain 90   [3] foam.' But *Cm*, 93: foam.' Chap. 4. Basilius' hawking; Gynecia's hurt by Dametas overturning her coach; her jealousy over Zelmane; Philoclea's love-passions, vow of chastity, revocation, lamentation. But 90

But Zelmane turning her speech to Dametas, 'I shall grow,' said she, 'skilful in country matters if I have often conference with your servant.'

'In sooth,' answered Dametas with a graceless scorn, 'the lad may prove well enough if he over-soon think not too well of himself, and will bear away that he heareth of his elders.'

And therewith, as they walked to the other lodge, to make Zelmane find she might have spent her time better with him, he began with a wild method to run over all the art of husbandry, especially employing his tongue about well-dunging of a field; while poor Zelmane yielded her ears to those tedious strokes, not warding them so much as with any one answer, till they came to Basilius and Gynecia who attended for her in a coach, to carry her abroad to see some sports prepared for her. Basilius and Gynecia sitting in the one end, placed her at the other with her left side to Philoclea. Zelmane was moved in her mind to have kissed their feet for the favour of so blessed a seat, for the narrowness of the coach made them join from the foot to the shoulders very close together, the truer touch whereof, though it were barred by their envious apparel, yet as a perfect magnes, though put[1] in an ivory box, will thorough the box send forth his embraced[2] virtue to a beloved needle, so this imparadised neighbourhood made Zelmane's soul cleave unto her, both thorough the ivory case of her body, and the apparel which did overcloud it; all the blood of Zelmane's body stirring in her, as wine will do when sugar is hastily put into it, seeking to suck the sweetness of the beloved guest; her heart, like a lion new imprisoned seeing him that restrains his liberty before the grate, not panting, but striving violently, if it had been possible, to have leapt into the lap of Philoclea.

But Dametas, even then proceeding from being Master of a Cart to be Doctor of a Coach, not a little proud in himself that his whip at that time guided the rule of Arcadia, drave the coach (the cover whereof was made with such joints that, as they might to avoid the weather pull it up close when they listed, so when they would they might put each end down, and remain as discovered and opensighted as on horseback); till upon the side of the forest, they had both greyhounds, spaniels, and hounds – whereof the first might seem the lords; the second, the gentlemen; and the last, the yeomen of dogs. A cast of merlins there was besides, which flying of a gallant height over certain bushes, would beat the birds that rose down unto the bushes, as falcons will do wild-fowl over a river. But the sport which for that day Basilius would principally show to Zelmane was the mounty at a hern, which getting up on his waggling wings with pain till he was come to some height, as though the air next to the earth were not fit for his great body to fly thorough, was now growen to diminish the sight of himself, and to give

---

[1] put] but 93   [2] embraced] embracing 93

example to great persons that, the higher they be, the less they should show; when a gerfalcon was cast off after her; who straight spying where the prey was, fixing her eye with desire and guiding her wing by her eye, used no more strength than industry, for as a good builder, to a high tower, will not make his stair upright, but winding almost the full compass about, that the steepness be the more unsensible, so she, seeing the towering of her pursued chase, went circling and compassing about, rising so with the less sense of rising, and yet finding that way scantly serve the greediness of her haste. As an ambitious body will go far out of the direct way to win to a point of height which he desires, so would she, as it were, turn tail to the heron and fly quite out another way; but all was to return in a higher pitch, which once gotten, she would either beat with cruel assaults the heron, who now was driven to the best defence of force since flight would not serve, or else clasping with him, come down together to be parted by the over-partial beholders.

Divers of which flights Basilius showing to Zelmane, thus was the richesse of the time spent, and the day deceased before it was thought of, till night, like a degenerating successor, made his departure the better remembered. And therefore, so constrained, they willed Dametas to drive homeward; who half sleeping, half musing about the mending of a vine-press,[1] guided the horses so ill, that the wheel coming over a great stub of a tree, it overturned the coach, which though it fell violently upon the side where Zelmane and Gynecia sat, yet for Zelmane's part, she would have been glad of the fall which made her bear the sweet burthen of Philoclea, but that she feared she might receive some hurt. But indeed, neither she did, nor any of the rest, by reason they kept their arms and legs within the coach, saving Gynecia, who with the only bruise of the fall had her shoulder put out of joint – which, though by one of the falconers' cunning it was set well again, yet with much pain was she brought to the lodge; and pain fetching his ordinary companion, a fever, with him, drave her to entertain them both in her bed.

But neither was the fever of such impatient heat as the inward plague-sore of her affection, nor the pain half so noisome as the jealousy she conceived of her daughter Philoclea, lest this time of her sickness might give apt occasion to Zelmane, whom she misdoubted. Therefore she called Philoclea to her, and though it were late in the night, commanded her in her ear to go to the other lodge and send Miso to her, with whom she would speak, and she lie with her sister Pamela; the meanwhile Gynecia kept Zelmane with her, because she would be sure she should be out of the lodge before she licensed Zelmane. Philoclea, not skilled in anything better than obedience, went quietly down; and the moon then full, not thinking scorn to be a torch-

---

[1] vine-press] wine-press 93

bearer to such beauty, guided her steps – whose motions bare a mind which bare in itself far more stirring motions.

And alas, sweet Philoclea, how hath my pen till now forgot thy passions, since to thy memory principally all this long[1] matter is intended? Pardon the slackness to come to those woes, which having caused in others,[2] thou didst feel in thyself. The sweet-minded Philoclea was in their degree[3] of well doing to whom the not knowing of evil serveth for a ground of virtue, and hold their inward powers in better form with an unspotted simplicity than many, who rather cunningly seek to know what goodness is than willingly take[4] into themselves the following of it. But as that sweet and simple breath of heavenly goodness is the easier to be altered because it hath not passed through the worldly wickedness, nor feelingly[5] found the evil that evil carries with it, so now the Lady Philoclea, whose eyes and senses had received nothing but according as the natural course of each thing required (which tender[6] youth had obediently lived under her parents' behests without framing out of her own will the forechoosing of anything), when now she came to appoint (wherein her judgement was to be practised in knowing faultiness by his first tokens), she was like a young fawn, who coming in the wind of the hunters, doth not know whether it be a thing or no to be eschewed – whereof at this time she began to get a costly experience.

For after that Zelmane had a while lived in the lodge with her, and that her only being a noble stranger had bred a kind of heedful attention, her coming to that lonely[7] place (where she had nobody but her parents) a willingness of conversation, her wit and behaviour a liking and silent admiration, at length, the excellency of her natural gifts joined with the extreme shows she made of most devout honouring Philoclea (carrying thus in one person the only two bands of goodwill, loveliness and lovingness) brought forth in her heart a yielding to a most friendly affection; which when it had gotten so full possession of the keys of her mind that it would receive no message from her senses without that affection were the interpreter, then straight grew an exceeding delight still to be with her, with an unmeasurable liking of all that Zelmane did – matters being so turned in her that, where at first, liking her manners did breed goodwill, now goodwill became the chief cause of liking her manners, so that within a while Zelmane was not prized for her demeanour, but the demeanour was prized because it was Zelmane's.

Then followed that most natural effect of conforming oneself to that which she did like, and not only wishing to be herself such another in all

---

[1] long] om. Ph, Qu [2] others] other St, Bo, Da [3] their degree] the way As; the very degree Da; the degree Ph [4] take] to take Cl, Qu [5] nor feelingly] nor yet feelingly Cl, As [6] which tender Cm: which from the tender 90; whose tender OA, 93 [7] lonely] lovely Cm, 13

things, but to ground an imitation upon so much an esteemed authority; so that the next degree was to mark all Zelmane's doings, speeches, and fashions, and to take them into herself as a pattern of worthy proceeding, which when once it was enacted, not only by the commonalty of passions, but agreed unto by her most noble thoughts, and that by reason[1] itself (not yet experienced in the issues of such matters) had granted his royal assent, then friendship, a diligent officer, took care to see the statute thoroughly observed. Then grew on that not only she did imitate the soberness of her countenance, the gracefulness of her speech, but even their particular gestures; so that, as Zelmane did often eye her, she would often eye Zelmane, and as Zelmane's eyes would deliver a submissive but vehement desire in their look, she, though as yet she had not the desire in her, yet should her eyes answer in like-piercing kindness of a look. Zelmane, as much as Gynecia's jealousy would suffer, desired to be near Philoclea; Philoclea, as much as Gynecia's jealousy would suffer, desired to be near Zelmane. If Zelmane took her hand and softly strained it, she also, thinking the knots of friendship ought to be mutual, would with a sweet fastness show she was loath to part from it. And if Zelmane sighed, she would sigh also. When Zelmane was sad, she deemed it wisdom, and therefore she would be sad too. Zelmane's languishing countenance, with crossed arms, and sometimes cast-up eyes, she thought to have an excellent grace, and therefore she also willingly put on the same countenance; till at the last, poor soul, ere she were aware, she accepted not only the band,[2] but the service; not only the sign, but the passion signified. For whether it were that her wit in continuance did find that Zelmane's friendship was full of impatient desire, having more than ordinary limits, and therefore she was content to second Zelmane, though herself knew not the limits, or that in truth true love, well considered, have an infective power, at last she fell in acquaintance with love's harbinger, wishing.

First she would wish that they two might live all their lives together like two of Diana's nymphs – but that wish she thought not sufficient, because she knew there would be more nymphs besides them who also would have their part in Zelmane. Then would she wish that she were her sister, that such a natural band might make her more special to her – but against that, she considered that though being her sister, if she happened to be married, she should be robbed of her. Then, grown bolder, she would wish either herself or Zelmane a man, that there might succeed a blessed marriage betwixt them – but when that wish had once displayed his ensign in her mind, then

---

[1] that by reason] that her reason *Cm*; that reason *13*   [2] band] badge *93*

followed whole squadrons of longings that so it might be, with a main battle of mislikings and repinings against their creation that so it was not. Then dreams by night began to bring more unto her than she durst wish by day, whereout waking,[1] did make her know herself the better by the image of those fancies. But as some diseases, when they are easy to be cured they are hard to be known, but when they grow easy to be known they are almost impossible to be cured, so the sweet Philoclea, while she might prevent it she did not feel it, now she felt it when it was past preventing – like a river, no rampires being built against it till already it have overflowed, for now indeed love pulled off his mask, and showed his face unto her, and told her plainly that she was his prisoner.

Then needed she no more paint her face with passions, for passions shone thorough her face. Then her rosy colour was often increased with extraordinary blushing, and so, another time, perfect whiteness ascended[2] to a degree of paleness – now hot, then cold, desiring she knew not what, nor how, if she knew what. Then her mind, though too late, by the smart was brought to think of the disease, and her own proof taught her to know her mother's mind, which, as no error gives so strong assault as that which comes armed in the authority of a parent, so greatly fortified her desires, to see that her mother had the like desires. And the more jealous her mother was, the more she thought the jewel precious which was with so many looks guarded. But that prevailing so far as to keep the two lovers from private conference, then began she to feel the sweetness of a lover's solitariness, when freely with words and gestures, as if Zelmane were present, she might give passage to her thoughts, and so as it were utter out some smoke of those flames, wherewith else she was not only burned but smothered.

As this night, that going from the one lodge to the other (by her mother's commandment) with doleful gestures and uncertain paces, she did willingly accept the time's offer to be a while alone, so that going a little aside into the wood where many times before she had delighted to walk, her eyes were saluted with a tuft of trees so close set together as, with the shade the moon gave thorough it, it might breed a fearful kind of devotion to look upon it. But true thoughts of love banish[3] all vain fancy of superstition. Full well she did both remember and like the place, for there had she often with their shade beguiled Phoebus of looking upon her; there had she enjoyed herself often, while[4] she was mistress of herself, and had no other thoughts but such as might arise out of quiet senses. But the principal cause that invited

---

[1] waking *Cm, 13*: making *90, 93* [2] ascended] descended *93* [3] banish] banished *93* [4] while] whilst *Ph*; when *Qu*

her remembrance was a goodly white marble stone that should seem had been dedicated in ancient time to the sylvan gods; which she finding there a few days before Zelmane's coming, had written these words upon it as a testimony of her mind against the suspicion her captivity made her think she lived in. The writing was this:

> You living pow'rs enclosed in stately shrine
> Of growing trees, you[1] rural gods that wield
> Your sceptres here, if to your ears divine
> A voice may come which troubled soul doth yield,
>   This vow[2] receive, this vow O gods maintain:
>   My virgin life no spotted thought shall stain.
>
> Thou purest stone, whose pureness doth present
> My purest mind; whose temper hard[3] doth show
> My tempered heart; by thee my promise sent
> Unto myself let after-livers know.
>   No fancy mine, nor others' wrong suspect
>   Make me, O virtuous shame, thy laws neglect.
>
> O chastity, the chief of heav'nly lights,
> Which makst[4] us most immortal shape to wear,
> Hold thou my heart, establish thou my sprites;
> To only thee my constant course I bear.
>   Till spotless soul unto thy bosom fly,
>   Such life to lead, such death I vow to die.

But now that her memory served as an accuser of her change, and that her own hand-writing was there to bear testimony against her fall, she went in among those few trees, so closed in the tops[5] together as they might seem a little chapel; and there might she by the help of the moonlight perceive the goodly stone which served as an altar in that woody devotion. But neither the light was enough to read the words, and the ink was already foreworn and in many places blotted; which, as she perceived, 'Alas,' said she, 'fair marble, which never receivedst[6] spot but by my writing, well do these blots become a blotted writer; but pardon her which did not dissemble then, although she have[7] changed since. Enjoy, enjoy the glory of thy nature which can so constantly bear the marks of my inconstancy!'

And herewith hiding her eyes with her soft hand, there came into her head certain verses which, if she had had present commodity, she would have adjoined as a retractation[8] to the other. They were to this effect:

---

[1] you] ye *St, Bo, Cl, Le, As*; the *Ph, Qu* [2] This vow] This voice *As, Ph* [3] hard] heart *St*; hear *Da* [4] makst] makes *OA (ex. Le)* [5] tops] top *OA (ex. Je)* [6] receivedst] received *St, Bo, Cl, As, Ph*; receivest *Qu* [7] have] hath *Ph*; had *Je* [8] retractation] retraction *Cl, Ph, Je, Qu, Cm*

My words, in hope to blaze my[1] steadfast mind,
This marble chose, as of like temper known:
But lo, my words defaced, my fancies blind,
Blots to the stone, shame[2] to myself I find;
    And witness am, how ill agree in one,
    A woman's hand with constant marble stone.

My words full weak, the marble full of might;
My words in store, the marble all alone;
My words black ink, the marble kindly white;
My words unseen, the marble still in sight,
    May witness bear, how ill agree in one,
    A woman's hand with constant marble stone.

But seeing she could not see means to join as then this recantation to the former vow, laying all her fair length under one of the trees, for a while she did nothing but turn up and down, as if she had hoped to turn away the fancy that mastered her, and hid her face, as if she could have hidden herself from her own fancies. At length, with a whispering note to herself, 'O me, unfortunate wretch,' said she, 'what poisonous heats be these which thus torment me? How hath the sight of this strange guest invaded my soul? Alas, what entrance found this desire, or what strength had it thus to conquer me?'

Then, a cloud passing between her sight and the moon, 'O Diana,' said she, 'I would either the cloud that now hides the light of my virtue would as easily pass away as you will quickly overcome this let; or else that you were for ever thus darkened, to serve for an excuse of my outrageous folly.'

Then looking to the stars, which had perfitly as then beautified the clear sky, 'My parents,' said she, 'have told me that in these fair heavenly bodies there are great hidden deities which have their working in the ebbing and flowing of our estates. If it be so, then, O you stars, judge rightly of me, and if I have with wicked intent made myself a prey to fancy, or if by any idle lusts I framed my heart fit for such an impression, then let this plague daily increase in me till my name be made odious to womankind. But if extreme and unresistable violence have oppressed me, who will ever do any of you sacrifice, O you stars, if you do not succour me? No, no, you will not help me. No, no, you cannot help me! Sin must be the mother, and shame the daughter of my affection. And yet are these but childish objections, simple Philoclea. It is the impossibility that doth torment me; for unlawful desires are punished after the effect of enjoying, but unpossible desires are punished in the desire itself. Oh, then, oh ten times unhappy that I am, since where in all other hope kindleth love, in me despair should be the bellows of my

---

[1] blaze my] blaze in *Qu*; blaze a *98, 13*   [2] shame] shames *St, Le, As, O, Je, 93*: shame is *Qu*

affection! and of all despairs, the most miserable, which is drawn from impossibility. The most covetous man longs not to get riches out of a ground which never can bear anything. Why? Because it is impossible. The most ambitious wight vexeth not his wits to climb into heaven. Why? Because it is impossible. Alas, then, O love, why doost thou in thy beautiful sampler set such a work for my desire to take out, which is as much impossible? And yet, alas, why do I thus condemn my fortune before I hear what she can say for herself? What do I, silly wench, know what love hath prepared for me? Do I not see my mother as well, at least as furiously as myself, love Zelmane? And should I be wiser than my mother? Either she sees a possibility in that which I think impossible, or else impossible loves need not misbecome me. And do I not see Zelmane, who doth not think a thought which is not first weighed by wisdom and virtue – doth not she vouchsafe to love me with like ardour? I see it. Her eyes depose it to be true. What then? And if she can love poor me, shall I think scorn to love such a woman as Zelmane? Away, then, all vain examinations of why and how. Thou lovest me, excellent Zelmane, and I love thee!' And with that, embracing the very ground whereon she lay, she said to herself (for even to herself she was ashamed to speak it out in words), 'O my Zelmane! Govern and direct me, for I am wholly given over unto thee.'

In[1] this depth of muses and divers sort[2] of discourses would she ravingly have[3] remained, but that Dametas and Miso who were round about to seek her, understanding she was to come to their lodge that night, came hard by her, Dametas saying that he would not deal in other body's matters, but for his part he did not like that maids should once stir out of their fathers' houses, but if it were to milk a cow or save a chicken from a kite's foot, or some such other matter of importance; and Miso swearing that, if it were her daughter Mopsa, she would give her a lesson for walking so late that should make her keep within doors for one fortnight. But their jangling made Philoclea rise; and pretending as though she had done it but to sport with them, went with them (after she had willed Miso to wait upon her mother) to the lodge, where being now accustomed by her parents' discipline, as well as her sister, to serve herself, she went alone up to Pamela's chamber; where meaning to delight her eyes and joy her thoughts with the sweet conversation of her beloved sister, she found her (though it were in the time that the wings of night doth blow sleep most willingly into mortal creatures) sitting in a chair, lying backward, with her head almost over the

---

[1] thee.' In *Cm*, *93*: thee.' Chap. 5. The bedfellow communication of Philoclea and Pamela; Pamela's narration of her shepherd's making love, of Dorus and Dametas' horsemanship, of his hot pursuit, and her cold acceptance; his letter; her relenting; and Philoclea's sole complaint. In *90*   [2] sort *OA (ex. Qu)*, *Cm*: sorts *Qu, 90, 93*   [3] ravingly have *OA (ex. Ph), 93*: have ravingly *Ph*; have re: ravingly have (re: deleted) *Cm*; have ravingly *90*

back of it, and looking upon a wax candle which burnt before her, in one hand holding a letter, in the other her handkerchief which had lately drunk up the tears of her eyes, leaving instead of them crimson circles, like red flakes in the element when the weather is hottest; which Philoclea finding, for her eyes had learned to know the badges of sorrows,[1] she earnestly entreated to know the cause thereof, that either she might comfort or accompany her doleful humour.

But Pamela, rather seeming sorry that she had perceived so much than willing to open any further, 'O my Pamela,' said Philoclea, 'who are to me a sister in nature, a mother in counsel, a princess by the law of our country, and, which name methink of all other is the dearest, a friend by my choice and your favour, what means this banishing me from your counsels? Do you love your sorrow so well as to grudge me part of it? Or do you think I shall not love a sad Pamela so well as a joyful? Or be my ears unworthy, or my tongue suspected? What is it, my sister, that you should conceal from your sister, yea, and servant Philoclea?'

These words wan no further of Pamela; but that telling her they might talk better as they lay together, they impoverished their clothes to enrich their bed, which for that night might well scorn the shrine of Venus. And there, cherishing one another with dear though chaste embracements, with sweet though cold kisses, it might seem that love was come to play him there without dart, or that weary of his own fires, he was there to refresh himself between their sweet-breathing lips. But Philoclea earnestly again entreated Pamela to open her grief, who drawing the curtain that the candle might not complain of her blushing, was ready to speak; but the breath, almost formed into words, was again stopped by her and turned into sighs; but at last, 'I pray you,' said she, 'sweet Philoclea, let us talk of some other thing. And tell me whether you did ever see anything so amended as our pastoral sports be, since that Dorus came hither.'

O love, how far thou seest with blind eyes! Philoclea had straight found her; and therefore, to draw out more, 'Indeed,' said she, 'I have often wondered to myself how such excellencies could be in so mean a person, but belike fortune was afraid to lay her treasures where they should be stained with so many perfections. Only I marvel how he can frame himself to hide so rare gifts under such a block as Dametas!'

'Ah!' said Pamela, 'if you knew the cause – but no more do I, neither – and to say the truth – but Lord! How are we fallen to talk of this fellow? And yet, indeed, if you were sometimes with me to mark him, while Dametas reads his rustic lecture unto him (how to feed his beasts before noon, where to shade them in the extreme heat, how to make the manger handsome for

---

[1] sorrows] *om. Cm*; sorrow 93

his oxen, when to use the goad and when the voice), giving him rules of a herdman though he pretend[1] to make him a shepherd, to see all the while with what a grace (which seems to set a crown upon his base estate) he can descend to those poor matters, certainly you would – but to what serves this? No doubt we were better sleep than talk of these idle matters.'

'Ah, my Pamela!' said Philoclea, 'I have caught you! The constantness[2] of your wit was not wont to bring forth such disjointed speeches. You love! Dissemble no further!'

'It is true,' said Pamela. 'Now you have it – and with less ado should, if my heart could have thought those words suitable for my mouth. But indeed, my Philoclea, take heed, for I think virtue itself is no armour of proof against affection. Therefore, learn by my example.'

'Alas,' thought Philoclea to herself, 'your shears come too late to clip the bird's wings that already is flown away.'

But then Pamela, being once set in the stream of her love, went away amain withal, telling her how his noble qualities had drawn her liking towards him – but yet ever weighing his meanness, and so held continually in due limits; till seeking many means to speak with her, and ever kept from it, as well because she shunned it (seeing and disdaining his mind), as because of her jealous jailers, he had at length used the finest policy that might be, in counterfeiting love to Mopsa, and saying to Mopsa whatsoever he would have her know; and in how passionate manner he had told his own tale in a third person, making poor Mopsa believe that it was a matter fallen out many ages before.

'And in the end, because you shall know my tears come not neither of repentance nor misery, who think you is my Dorus fallen out to be? Even the Prince Musidorus, famous over all Asia for his heroical enterprises (of whom, you remember, how much good the stranger Plangus told my father), he not being drowned as Plangus thought, though his cousin Pyrocles indeed perished. Ah, my sister, if you had heard his words or seen his gestures when he made me know what and to whom his love was, you would have, matched in yourself, those two rarely matched together, pity and delight. Tell me, dear sister (for the gods are my witnesses, I desire to do virtuously), can I without the detestable stain of ungratefulness abstain from loving him, who far exceeding the beautifulness of his shape with the beautifulness of his mind, and the greatness of his estate with the greatness of his acts, is content so to abase himself as to become Dametas' servant for my sake? You will say, but how know I him to be Musidorus? Since the handmaid of wisdom is slow belief,[3] that consideration did not want in me; for the nature of desire itself

---

[1] pretend *Cm, 93*: pretended *90*   [2] constantness] constancy *93*   [3] is slow belief] is belief *Cm*; is slow of belief *98, 13*

is no easier to receive belief than it is hard to ground belief, for, as desire is glad to embrace the first show of comfort, so is desire desirous of perfect assurance – and that have I had of him, not only by necessary arguments to any of common sense, but by sufficient demonstrations. Lastly, he would have me send to Thessalia; but truly, I am not as now in mind to do my honourable love so much wrong as so far to suspect him. Yet, poor soul, knows he no other but that I do both suspect, neglect – yea, and detest him; for every day he finds one way or other to set forth himself unto me, but all are rewarded with like coldness of acceptation.

'A few days since, he and Dametas had furnished themselves very richly to run at the ring before me. Oh, how mad a sight it was to see Dametas like rich tissue! furred with lambskins! But oh, how well it did with Dorus! to see with what a grace he presented himself before me on horseback, making majesty wait upon humbleness: how at the first, standing still, with his eyes bent upon me, as though his motions were chained to my look, he so stayed till I caused Mopsa bid him do something upon his horse; which no sooner said, but with a kind rather of quick gesture than show of violence, you might see him come towards me, beating the ground in so due time as no dancer[1] can observe better measure. If you remember the ship we saw once when the sea went high upon the coast of Argos, so went the beast; but he, as if centaur-like he had been one piece with the horse, was no more moved than one is with the going of his own legs, and in effect, so did he command him as his own limbs. For though he had both spurs and wand, they seemed rather marks of sovereignty than instruments of punishment; his hand and leg with most pleasing grace commanding without threatening, and rather remembering than chastising (at least, if sometimes he did, it was so stolen as neither our eyes could discern it, nor the horse with any change[2] did complain of it), he ever going so just with the horse, either forthright or turning, that it seemed, as he borrowed the horse's body, so he lent the horse his mind (in the turning, one might perceive the bridle-hand something gently stir, but indeed so gently as it did rather distil virtue than use violence); himself (which methinks is strange!) showing at one instant both steadiness and nimbleness – sometimes making him turn close to the ground like a cat when scratchingly she wheels about after a mouse, sometimes with a little more rising before, now like a raven, leaping from ridge to ridge, then like one of Dametas' kids bound over the hillocks – and all so done, as neither the lusty kind showed any roughness, nor the easier any idleness, but still like a well-obeyed master, whose beck is enough for a discipline; ever concluding each thing he did with his face to me-wards, as

---

[1] dancer *Cm, 93*: dance *90*   [2] change *Cm, 93*: chance *90*

if thence came not only the beginning, but ending, of his motions.

'The sport was to see Dametas. How he was tossed! from the saddle, to the mane of the horse, and thence to the ground, giving his gay apparel almost as foul an outside as it had an inside (but, as before he had ever said he wanted but horse and apparel to be as brave a courtier as the best, so now, bruised with proof, he proclaimed it a folly for a man of wisdom to put himself under the tuition of a beast), so as Dorus was fain alone to take the ring – wherein truly, at least my womanish eyes could not discern, but that taking his staff from his thigh, the descending it a little down, the getting of it up into the rest, the letting of the point fall, and taking the ring, was but all one motion; at least, if they were divers motions, they did so stealingly slip one into another as the latter part was ever in hand before the eye could discern the former was ended. Indeed, Dametas found fault that he showed no more strength in shaking of his staff, but to my conceit the fine clearness[1] of bearing it was exceeding delightful.

'But how delightful soever it was, my delight might well be in my soul, but it never went to look out of the window to do him any comfort; but how much more I found reason to like him, the more I set all the strength of mind to suppress it – or at least to conceal it. Indeed, I must confess, as[2] some physicians have told me, that when one is cold outwardly he is not inwardly, so truly, the cold ashes laid upon my fire did not take the nature of fire from it. Full often hath my breast swollen with keeping my sighs imprisoned. Full often have the tears I drave back from mine eyes turned back to drown my heart. But alas, what did that help poor Dorus, whose eyes, being his diligent intelligencers, could carry unto him no other news but discomfortable? I think no day passed but by some one invention he would appear unto me to testify his love. One time, he danced the matachin dance in armour (Oh, with what a graceful dexterity!), I think to make me see that he had been brought up in such exercises. Another time, he persuaded his master, to make my time seem shorter, in manner of a dialogue to play Priamus while he played Paris. Think, sweet Philoclea, what a Priamus we had! But truly, my Paris was a Paris – and more than a Paris! who, while in a savage apparel, with naked neck, arms, and legs he made love to Oenone, you might well see by his changed countenance – and true tears – that he felt the part he played. Tell me, sweet Philoclea, did you ever see such a shepherd? Tell me, did you ever hear of such a prince? And then, tell me if a small or unworthy assault have conquered me. Truly, I would hate my life if I thought vanity led me – but since my parents deal so cruelly with me, it is time for me to trust something to my own judgement. Yet hitherto have my looks

---

[1] clearness] cleanness 93   [2] confess, as] confess, that as 93

been as I told you, which, continuing after many of these, his fruitless trials, have wrought such change in him as, I tell you true' – with that word, she laid her hand upon her quaking side – 'I do not a little fear him. See what a letter this is' – then drew she the curtain, and took the letter from under the pillow – 'which today with an afflicted humbleness he delivered me, pretending before Mopsa that I should read it unto her, to mollify – forsooth! – her iron stomach!' With that, she read the letter, containing thus much:

' "Most blessed paper, which shalt[1] kiss that hand whereto all blessedness is in nature a servant, do not yet disdain to carry with thee the woeful words of a miser now despairing; neither be afraid to appear before her, bearing the base title of the sender; for no sooner shall that divine hand touch thee, but that thy baseness shall be turned to most high preferment. Therefore mourn boldly, my ink, for while she looks upon you, your blackness will shine. Cry out boldly, my lamentation, for while she reads you, your cries will be music. Say then, O happy messenger of a most unhappy message, that the too soon born, too[2] late dying, creature (which dares not speak; no, not look; no, not scarcely think, as from his miserable self unto her heavenly highness) only presumes to desire thee, in the time that her eyes and voice do exalt thee, to say (and in this manner to say, not from him – oh, no, that were not fit – but of him) thus much unto her sacred judgement: 'O you, the only, the only honour[3] to women – to men, the only admiration; you that, being armed by love, defy him that armed you; in this high estate wherein you have placed me, yet let me remember him to whom I am bound for bringing me to your presence – and let me remember him, who since he is yours, how mean soever it be,[4] it is reason you have an account of him. The wretch, yet your wretch, though with languishing steps, runs fast to his grave. And will you suffer a temple, how poorly built soever, but yet a temple of your deity, to be rased? But he dieth. It is most true. He dieth. And he, in whom you live, to obey you, dieth; whereof, though he plain, he doth not complain – for it is a harm, but no wrong, which he hath received. He dies because in woeful language all his senses tell him that such is your pleasure. For since you will not that he live – alas! alas! what followeth? What followeth of the most ruined Dorus but his end?' End then, evil-destinied Dorus, end! And end, thou woeful letter, end! for it sufficeth her wisdom to know that her heavenly will shall be accomplished."

'O my Philoclea, is he a person to write these words? And are these words lightly to be regarded? But if you had seen, when with trembling hand he had delivered it, how he went away, as if he had been but the coffin that

---

[1] shalt] shall *Cm, 13*   [2] born, too] born, and too *93*   [3] the only, the only honour] the only honour *93*
[4] soever it be] soever he be *93*

carried himself to his sepulchre! Two times, I must confess, I was about to take courtesy into mine eyes, but both times the former resolution stopped the entry of it, so that he departed without obtaining any further kindness. But he was no sooner out of the door but that I looked to the door kindly. And truly, the fear of him ever since hath put me into such perplexity as now you found me.'

'Ah my Pamela,' said Philoclea, 'leave sorrow. The river of your tears will soon lose his fountain. It is in your hand, as well to stitch up his life again, as it was before to rent it.'

And so, though with self-grieved mind, she comforted her sister till sleep came to bathe himself in Pamela's fair weeping eyes; which when Philoclea found, wringing her hands, 'O me,' said she, 'indeed the only subject of the destinies' displeasure, whose greatest fortunateness is more unfortunate than my sister's greatest unfortunateness, alas, she weeps because she would be no sooner happy; I weep because I can never be happy. Her tears flow from pity; mine, from being too far lower than the reach of pity. Yet do I not envy thee, dear Pamela. I do not envy thee – only I could wish that, being thy sister in nature, I were not so far off a kin in fortune.'

But[1] the darkness of sorrow overshadowing her mind, as the night did her eyes, they were both content to hide themselves under the wings of sleep, till the next morning had almost lost his name before the two sweet-sleeping sisters awaked from dreams, which flattered them with more comfort than their waking could, or would, consent unto; for then they were called up by Miso, who having been with Gynecia, had received commandment to be continually with her daughters, and particularly not to let Zelmane and Philoclea have any private conference – but that she should be present to hear what passed. But Miso,[2] having now her authority increased, came[3] with scowling eyes to deliver a slavering good morrow to the two ladies, telling them it was a shame for them to mar their complexions, yea, and conditions too, with long lying abed, and that when she was of their age, she trowed, she would have made a handkerchief by that time a day.[4] The two sweet princes[5] with a smiling silence answered her entertainment; and obeying her direction, covered their dainty beauties with the glad clothes.

But as soon as Pamela was ready (and sooner she was than her sister), the agony of Dorus giving a fit to herself (which the words of his letter, lively imprinted in her mind, still remembered her of), she called to Mopsa and

---

[1] fortune.' But *Cm, 93*: fortune.' Chap. 6. The ladies' uprising and interrogatories to Dorus concerning Pyrocles and Euarchus; his historiology of Euarchus' kingly excellencies, his entry on a most corrupt estate, and reformation thereof by royal arts and actions; his and Dorilaus' cross-marriage to each other's sister, having by each a son; their mutual defence, with Dorilaus' death. But *90* [2] passed. But Miso] passed. Miso *93* [3] increased, came] increased, but came *93, 98* [4] time a day *Cm, 93*: time of the day *90* [5] princes] princesses *Cm, 13*

willed her to fetch Dorus to speak with her, because, she said, she would take further judgement of him before she would move Dametas to grant her in marriage unto him. Mopsa, as glad as of sweetmeat to go of such an arrant, quickly returned with Dorus to Pamela, who intended both by speaking with him to give some comfort to his passionate heart, and withal to hear some part of his life past, which although fame had already delivered unto her, yet she desired in more particular certainties to have it from so beloved an historian. Yet the sweetness of virtue's disposition, jealous even over itself, suffered her not to enter abruptly into questions of Musidorus (whom she was half ashamed she did love so well, and more than half sorry she could love no better), but thought best first to make her talk arise of Pyrocles and his virtuous father, which thus she did:

'Dorus,' said she, 'you told me the last day that Plangus was deceived, in that he affirmed the Prince Musidorus was drowned. But withal you confessed his cousin Pyrocles perished, of whom certainly in that age there was a great loss, since, as I have heard, he was a young prince of whom all men expected as much as man's power could bring forth, and yet, virtue promised for him, their expectation should not be deceived.'

'Most excellent lady,' said Dorus, 'no expectation in others, nor hope in himself, could aspire to a higher mark than to be thought worthy to be praised by your judgement, and made worthy to be praised by your mouth. But most sure it is that, as his fame could by no means get so sweet and noble an air to fly in as in your breath, so could not you (leaving yourself aside) find in the world a fitter subject of commendation – as noble as a long succession of royal ancestors, famous, and famous of[1] victories, could make him; of shape most lovely, and yet of mind more lovely; valiant, courteous, wise – what should I say more? Sweet Pyrocles – excellent Pyrocles – what can my words, but wrong thy perfections, which I would to God in some small measure thou hadst bequeathed to him that ever must have thy virtues in admiration, that masked at least in them, I might have found some more gracious acceptation.' With that, he imprisoned his look for a while upon Mopsa, who thereupon fell into a very wide smiling.

'Truly,' said Pamela, 'Dorus, I like well your mind that can raise itself out of so base a fortune as yours is to think of the imitating so excellent a prince as Pyrocles was. Who shoots at the midday sun, though he be sure he shall never hit the mark, yet as sure he is he shall shoot higher than who aims but at a bush. But I pray you, Dorus,' said she, 'tell me, since I perceive you are well acquainted with that story, what prince was that Euarchus, father to Pyrocles, of whom so much fame goes for his rightly royal virtues, or by

---

[1] famous of] famous of *corr. to* famous if *Cm*; famous for *93*

what ways he got that opinion. And then so descend to the causes of his sending, first away from him, and then to him, for that excellent son of his, with the discourse of his life and loss. And therein you may, if you list, say something of that same Musidorus, his cousin, because they going together, the story of Pyrocles (which I only desire) may be the better understood.'

'Incomparable lady,' said he, 'your commandment doth not only give me the will, but the power to obey you – such influence hath your excellency. And first for that famous King Euarchus: he was, at this time you speak of, king of Macedon, a kingdom which in elder time had such a sovereignty over all the provinces of Greece that even the particular kings therein did acknowledge, with more or less degrees of homage, some kind of fealty thereunto – as among the rest, even this now most noble (and by you ennobled) kingdom of Arcadia. But he, when he came to his crown, finding by his latter[1] ancestors' either negligence or misfortune that in some ages many of those duties had been intermitted, would never stir up old titles how apparent soever, whereby the public peace with the loss of many not guilty souls should be broken; but contenting himself to guide that ship wherein the heavens had placed him, showed no less magnanimity in dangerless despising, than others in dangerous affecting, the multiplying of kingdoms (for the earth hath since borne enow bleeding witnesses that it was no want of true courage); who as he was most wise to see what was best, and most just in the performing what he saw, and temperate in abstaining from anything anyway contrary, so, think I, no thought can imagine a greater heart to see and contemn danger, where danger would offer to make any wrongful threatening upon him; a prince that indeed especially measured his greatness by his goodness – and if for anything he loved greatness, it was because therein he might exercise his goodness; a prince of a goodly aspect, and the more goodly by a grave majesty, wherewith his mind did deck his outward graces; strong of body, and so much the stronger as he by a well-disciplined exercise taught it both to do and suffer; of age so, as he was about fifty years when his nephew Musidorus took on such shepherdish apparel – for the love of the world's paragon – as I now wear.

'This king left orphan both of father and mother, whose father and grandfather likewise had died young, he found his estate, when he came to age[2] which allowed his authority, so disjointed even in the noblest and strongest limbs of government that the name of a king was grown even odious to the people, his authority having been abused by those great lords and little kings, who in those between times of reigning, by unjust favouring those that were partially theirs and oppressing them that would defend their

---

[1] latter *Cm, 93*: later *90*   [2] to age] to the age *93*

liberty against them, had brought in, by a more felt than seen manner of proceeding, the worst kind of oligarchy (that is, when men are governed indeed by a few, and yet are not taught to know what those few be to whom they should obey); for they, having the power of kings but not the nature of kings, used the authority as men do their farms, of which they see within a year they shall go out, making the king's sword strike whom they hated, the king's purse reward whom they loved, and, which is worst of all, making the royal countenance serve to undermine the royal sovereignty. For the subjects could taste no sweeter fruits of having a king than grievous taxations to serve vain purposes; laws made rather to find faults than to prevent faults; the court of a prince rather deemed as a privileged place of unbridled licentiousness than as a biding[1] of him who, as a father, should give a fatherly example unto his people. Hence grew a very dissolution of all estates, while the great men (by the nature of ambition, never satisfied) grew factious among themselves, and the underlings, glad indeed to be underlings to them they hated least, to preserve them from such they hated most; men of virtue suppressed, lest their shining should discover the others' filthiness, and at length virtue itself almost forgotten, when it had no hopeful end whereunto to be directed; old men long nuzzled in corruption scorning them that would seek reformation, young men very fault-finding but very faulty – and so to newfangleness both of manners, apparel, and each thing else by the custom of self-guilty evil glad to change, though oft for a worse; merchandise abused, and so towns decayed, for want of just and natural liberty; offices, even of judging souls, sold; public defences neglected; and in sum, lest too long I trouble you, all awry; and, which wried it to the most wry course of all, wit abused, rather to feign reason why it should be amiss than how it should be amended.

'In this, and a much worse plight than it is fit to trouble your excellent ears withal, did the King Euarchus find his estate when he took upon him the regiment; which, by reason of the long stream of abuse, he was forced to establish by some even extreme severity, not so much for the very faults themselves, which he rather sought to prevent than to punish, as for the faulty ones, who strong even in their faults, scorned his youth, and could not learn to disgest that the man which they so long had used to mask their own appetites should now be the reducer of them into order. But so soon as some few but indeed notable examples had thundered a duty into the subjects' hearts, he soon showed, no baseness of suspicion nor the basest baseness of envy could any whit rule such a ruler; but then shined forth, indeed all love, among them, when an awful fear engendered by justice did make that love

---

[1] as a biding] as abiding *Cm*; as the abiding *93*

most lovely; his first and principal care being to appear unto his people such as he would have them be, and to be such as he appeared – making his life the example of his laws, as it were his actions[1] arising out of his deeds; so that within small time he wan a singular love in his people, and engraffed singular confidence (for how could they choose but love him, whom they found so truly to love them); he, even in reason, disdaining that they that have charge of beasts should love their charge and care for them, and that he that was to govern the most excellent creature should not love so noble a charge. And therefore where most princes, seduced by flattery to build upon false grounds of government, make themselves as it were another thing from the people, and so count it gain what they get[2] from them, and as if it[3] were two counterbalances, that their estate goes highest when the people goes lowest, by a fallacy of argument thinking themselves most kings when the subject is most basely subjected; he contrariwise, virtuously and wisely acknowledging that he with his people made all but one politic body whereof himself was the head, even so cared for them as he would for his own limbs, never restraining their liberty without it stretched to licentiousness, nor pulling from them their goods (which they found were not employed to[4] the purchase of a greater good), but in all his actions showing a delight in[5] their welfare, brought that to pass, that while by force he took nothing, by their love he had all. In sum, peerless princess, I might as easily set down the whole art of government as to lay before your eyes the picture of his proceedings. But in such sort he flourished in the sweet comfort of doing much good, when by an action[6] of leaving his country he was forced to bring forth his virtue of magnanimity as before he had done of justice.

'He had only one sister, a lady, lest I should too easily fall to partial praises of her, of whom it may be justly said that she was no unfit branch to the noble stock whereof she came.[7] Her he had given in marriage to Dorilaus, prince of Thessalia, not so much to make a friendship as to confirm the friendship betwixt[8] their posterity, which between them, by the likeness of virtue, had been long before made – for certainly Dorilaus could need no amplifier's mouth for the highest point of praise.'

'Who hath not heard,' said Pamela, 'of the valiant, wise, and just Dorilaus, whose unripe death doth yet, so many years since, draw tears from virtuous eyes? And indeed, my father is wont to speak of nothing with greater admiration than of the notable friendship (a rare thing in princes – more rare between princes), that so holily was observed to the last, of those two excellent men. But,' said she, 'go on, I pray you.'

---

[1] laws, as it were his actions] laws, and his laws as it were his axioms 93 (*Cm* reads ax^tionnes)   [2] they get *Cm*, 93: they can get 90   [3] as if it] as it *Cm*, 13   [4] employed to] employed but to 90 (*corr.*)   [5] delight in *Cm*, 93: delight to 90   [6] action] occasion 93   [7] came] was come 93   [8] betwixt] between 93

'Dorilaus,' said he, 'having married his sister, had his marriage in short time blessed (for so are folk wont to say, how unhappy soever the children after grow) with a son whom they named Musidorus – of whom I must needs first speak before I come to Pyrocles, because as he was born first, so upon his occasion grew, as I may say, accidentally, the other's birth. For scarcely was Musidorus made partaker of this oft-blinding light when there were found numbers of soothsayers who affirmed strange and incredible things should be performed by that child. Whether the heavens at that time listed to play with ignorant mankind, or that flattery be so presumptuous as even at times to borrow the face of divinity, but certainly so did the boldness of their affirmation accompany the greatness of what they did affirm (even, descending to particularities, what kingdoms he should overcome) that the king of Phrygia, who over-superstitiously thought himself touched in the matter, sought by force to destroy the infant to prevent his after-expectations, because a skilful man, having compared his nativity with the child, so told him: foolish man, either vainly fearing what was not to be feared, or not considering that, if it were a work of the superior powers, the heavens at length are never children. But so he did, and by the aid of the kings of Lydia and Crete, joining together their armies, invaded Thessalia and brought Dorilaus to some behindhand of fortune, when his faithful friend and brother, Euarchus, came so mightily to his succour that with some interchanging changes of fortune they begat, of a just war, the best child – peace; in which time Euarchus made a cross-marriage also with Dorilaus' sister, and shortly left her with child of the famous Pyrocles, driven to return to the defence of his own country, which in his absence, helped with some of the ill-contented nobility, the mighty king of Thrace and his brother, king of Pannonia, had invaded.

'The success of those wars was too notable to be unknown to your ears to which, it seems, all worthy fame hath glory to come unto. But there was Dorilaus, valiantly requiting his friend's help, in a great battle deprived of life,[1] his obsequies being no more solemnized by the tears of his partakers than the blood of his enemies, with so piercing a sorrow to the constant heart of Euarchus that the news of his son's birth could lighten his countenance with no show of comfort – although all the comfort that might be in a child, truth itself in him forthwith delivered; for what fortune only soothsayers foretold of Musidorus, that, all men might see prognosticated in Pyrocles – both heavens and earth giving tokens of the coming forth of an heroical virtue. The senate house of the planets was at no time so[2] set for the decreeing of perfection in a man as at that time, all folks skilful therein did

---

[1] of life *Cm, 93*: of his life *90* [2] so *Cm, 93*: to *90*

acknowledge. Only love was threatened and promised to him, and so to his cousin, as both the tempest and haven of their best years. But as death may have prevented Pyrocles, so unworthiness must be the death of[1] Musidorus.

'But[2] the mother of Pyrocles shortly after her childbirth dying was cause that Euarchus recommended the care of his only son to his sister, doing it the rather because the war continued in cruel heat betwixt him and those evil neighbours of his; in which meantime, those young princes, the only comforters of that virtuous widow, grew on so that Pyrocles taught admiration to the hardest conceits; Musidorus, perchance because among his subjects, exceedingly beloved; and by the good order of Euarchus, well performed by his sister, they were so brought up that all the sparks of virtue which nature had kindled in them were so blown to give forth their uttermost heat that, justly it may be affirmed, they inflamed the affections of all that knew them; for almost before they could perfectly speak they began to receive conceits not unworthy of the best speakers; excellent devices being used to make even their sports profitable, images of battles and fortifications being then delivered to their memory, which, after, their stronger judgements might dispense; the delight of tales being converted to the knowledge of all the stories of worthy princes, both to move them to do nobly, and teach them how to do nobly, the beauty of virtue still being set before their eyes, and that taught them with far more diligent care than grammatical rules; their bodies exercised in all abilities both of doing and suffering, and their minds acquainted by degrees with dangers; and in sum, all bent to the making up of princely minds, no servile fear used towards them, nor any other violent restraint, but still as to princes, so that a habit of commanding was naturalized in them, and therefore the farther from tyranny, nature having done so much for them in nothing as that it made them lords of truth, whereon all the other goods were builded – among which, I nothing[3] so much delight to recount as the memorable friendship that grew betwixt the two princes (such as made them more like than the likeness of all other virtues, and made them more near one to the other than the nearness of their blood could aspire unto), which I think grew the faster, and the faster was tied between them, by reason that Musidorus being elder by three or four years, it was neither so great a difference in age as did take away the delight in society, and yet, by the difference, there was taken away the occasion of childish contentions, till they had both passed over the humour of such contentions, for Pyrocles bare reverence full of love to Musidorus, and Musidorus had a delight full of love in Pyrocles; Musidorus, what he had learned

---

[1] death of *Cm, 93*: death to *90*   [2] Musidorus. 'But *Cm, 93*: Musidorus.' Chap. 7. The education of Pyrocles and Musidorus; their friendship, navigation, and first shipwrack; the strange gratitude of two brothers to them upon their liberality to those two brothers. 'But *90*   [3] I nothing] nothing I *93*

either for body or mind, would teach it to Pyrocles, and Pyrocles was so glad to learn of none as of Musidorus; till Pyrocles, being come to sixteen years of age, he seemed so to overrun his age in growth, strength, and all things following it that not Musidorus, no, nor any man living, I think could perform any action either on horse or foot more strongly, or deliver that strength more nimbly, or become the delivery more gracefully, or employ all more virtuously – which may well seem wonderful, but wonders are no wonders in a wonderful subject.

'At which time understanding that the King Euarchus, after so many years' war and the conquest of all Pannonia and almost Thrace, had now brought the conclusion of all to the siege of Byzantium, to the raising of which siege great forces were made, they would needs fall to the practice of those virtues which they before learned. And therefore, the mother of Musidorus nobly yielding over her own affects to her children's good (for a mother she was in effect to them both) the rather that they might help her beloved brother, they brake off all delays – which Musidorus for his part thought already had devoured too much of his good time, but that he had once granted a boon (before he knew what it was) to his dear friend Pyrocles that he would never seek the adventures of arms until he might go with him, which having fast bound his heart, a true slave to faith, he had bid a tedious delay of following his own humour for his friend's sake, till now, finding him able[1] every way to go thorough with that kind of life, he was as desirous for his sake as for his own to enter into it. So therefore preparing a navy that they might go like themselves, and not only bring the comfort of their presence, but of their power, to their dear parent Euarchus, they recommended themselves to the sea (leaving the shore of Thessalia, full of tears and vows), and were received thereon with so smooth and smiling a face as if Neptune had as then learned falsely to fawn on princes.

'The wind was like a servant, waiting behind them so just that they might fill the sails as they listed, and the best sailers, showing themselves less covetous of his liberality, so tempered it that they all kept together (like a beautiful flock which so well could obey their master's pipe), without, sometimes, to delight the princes' eyes some two or three of them would strive who could, either by the cunning of well-spending the wind's breath, or by the advantageous building of their moving houses, leave their fellows behind them in the honour of speed, while the two princes had leisure to see the practice of that which before they had learned by books: to consider the art of catching the wind prisoner, to no other end but to run away with it; to see how beauty and use can so well agree together that, of all the trinkets

---

[1] now, finding him able] now, being both sent for by Euarchus, and finding Pyrocles able 93

wherewith they are attired, there is not one but serves to some necessary purpose; and – O Lord! – to see the admirable power and noble effects of love, whereby the seeming insensible loadstone, with a secret beauty holding the spirit of iron in it, can draw that hard-hearted thing unto it, and like a virtuous mistress, not only make it bow itself, but with it make it aspire to so high a love as of the heavenly poles, and thereby to bring forth the noblest deeds that the children of the earth can boast of. And so, the princes delighting their conceits with confirming their knowledge, seeing wherein the sea-discipline differed from land-service, they had for a day and almost a whole night as pleasing entertainment as the falsest heart could give to him he means worst to.

'But, by that the next morning began a little to make a gilden show of a good meaning, there arose even with the sun a veil of dark clouds before his face, which shortly, like ink poured into water, had blacked over all the face of heaven, preparing as it were a mournful stage for a tragedy to be played on; for forthwith the winds began to speak louder and, as in a tumultuous kingdom, to think themselves fittest instruments of commandment, and blowing whole storms of hail and rain upon them, they were sooner in danger than they could almost bethink themselves of change; for then the traitorous sea began to swell in pride against the afflicted navy (under which, while the heaven favoured them, it had lain so calmly), making mountains of itself, over which the tossed and tottering ship should climb, to be straight carried down again to a pit of hellish darkness, with such cruel blows against the sides of the ship (that, which way soever it went, was still in his malice) that there was left neither power to stay, nor way to escape; and shortly had it so dissevered the loving company which the day before had tarried together, that most of them never met again, but were swallowed up in his never satisfied mouth.

'Some indeed, as since was known, after long wandering returned into Thessalia; other recovered Byzantium, and served Euarchus in his war. But in the ship wherein the princes were, now left as much alone as proud lords be when fortune fails them, though they employed all industry to save themselves, yet what they did was rather for duty to nature than hope to escape. So ugly a darkness, as if it would prevent the night's coming, usurped the day's right, which, accompanied sometimes with thunders, always with horrible noises of the chafing winds, made the masters and pilots so astonished that they knew not how to direct – and if they knew, they could scarcely, when they directed, hear their own whistle; for the sea strave with the winds which should be louder, and the shrouds of the ship (with a ghastful noise to them that were in it) witnessed that their ruin was the wager of the others' contention; and the heaven, roaring out thunders, the more amazed them, as having those powers for enemies. Certainly there is no danger carries with it more horror than that which grows in those flowing[1] kingdoms, for that dwelling-place is unnatural to mankind; and then the terribleness of the continual motion, the dissolution[2] of the far-being from comfort, the eye and the ear having ugly images ever before it, doth still vex the mind even when it is best armed against it.

'But thus the day passed (if that might be called a day), while the cunningest mariners were so conquered by the storm as they thought it best with stricken[3] sails to yield to be governed by it, the valiantest feeling inward dismayedness, and yet the fearfullest ashamed fully to show it, seeing that the princes (who were to part from the greatest fortunes) did in their countenances accuse no point of fear, but encouraging them to do what might be done, putting their hands to every most painful office, taught them at one instant to promise themselves the best, and yet to[4] despise the worst. But so were they carried by the tyranny of the wind and the treason of the sea all that night (which, the elder it was, the more wayward it showed itself towards them), till the next morning (known to be a morning better by the hour-glass than by the day-clearness), having run fortune as blindly as itself ever was painted, lest the conclusion should not answer to the rest of the play, they were driven upon a rock, which, hidden with those outrageous waves, did as it were closely dissemble his cruel mind, till with an unbelieved violence (but to them that have tried it) the ship ran upon it; and seeming willinger to perish than to have her course stayed, redoubled her blows till she had broken herself in pieces, and as it were tearing out her own bowels to feed the sea's greediness, left nothing within it but despair of safety and expectation of a loathsome end.

'There was to be seen the divers manner of minds in distress. Some sate upon the top of the poop, weeping and wailing till the sea swallowed them. Someone, more able to abide death than fear of death, cut his own throat to prevent drowning. Some prayed, and there wanted not of them which cursed – as if the heavens could not be more angry than they were; but a monstrous cry begotten of many roaring vows[5] was able to infect with fear a mind that had not prevented it with the power of reason. But the princes, using the passions of fearing evil and desiring to escape (only to serve the rule of virtue not to abandon oneself), leapt to a rib of the ship, which broken from his

---

[1] flowing] floating 93   [2] dissolution] desolation 93   [3] stricken *Cm, 93*: striking *90*   [4] yet to *Cm, 93*: yet not to *90*   [5] vows] waves *Cm*; voices *93*

fellows, floated with more likelihood to do service than any other limb of that ruinous body, upon which there had gotten already two brethren, well-known servants of theirs; and straight they four were carried out of sight, in that huge rising of the sea, from the rest of the ship.

'But the piece they were on, sinking by little and little under them, not able to support the weight of so many, the brethren, the elder whereof was Leucippus, the younger, Nelsus, showed themselves right faithful – and grateful – servants unto them. "Grateful", I say, for this cause. Those two gentlemen had been taken prisoners in the great war the king of Phrygia made upon Thessalia in the time of Musidorus' infancy, and having been sold into another country, though peace fell after between these realms, could not be delivered (because of their valour known) but for a far greater sum than either all their friends were able, or the dowager willing to make, in respect of the great expenses her self and people had been put to in those wars. And so had they remained in prison about thirteen years, when the two young princes, hearing speeches of their good deserts, found means (both by selling all the jewels they had of great price, and by giving under their hands great estates when they should come to be kings – which promises, their virtue promised for them, should be kept) to get so much treasure as redeemed them from captivity. This remembered, and kindly remembered, by these two brothers (perchance helped by a natural duty to their princes' blood), they willingly left hold of the board, committing themselves to the sea's rage, and even when they went[1] to die, themselves praying for the princes' lives. It is true that neither the pain nor danger so moved the princes' hearts as the tenderness of that loving part, far from glory – having so few lookers on, far from hope of reward – since themselves were sure to perish.

'But[2] now, of all the royal navy they had, they had left[3] but one piece[4] of one ship whereon they kept themselves, in all truth having interchanged their cares, while either cared for other, each comforting and counselling how to labour for the better, and to abide the worse. But so fell it out that, as they were carried by the tide which there, seconded by the storm, ran exceedingly[5] swiftly, Musidorus seeing, as he thought, Pyrocles not well upon the board, as he would with his right hand have helped him on better, he had no sooner unfastened his hold but that a wave forcibly spoiled his

---

[1] went] meant 93   [2] perish. 'But *Cm*, 93: perish.' Chap. 8. Pyrocles cast on the shore of Phrygia, led prisoner to the king; that suspicious tyrant naturalized, his intent to kill Pyrocles; Musidorus' escape from sea, and offer to die for his friend; their contention for death; preparation for Musidorus' execution, his strange delivery by Pyrocles, and a sudden mutiny; their killing the bad king, and creating a better. 'But 90   [3] they had, they had left *Cm*: they had left 90; they lately had, they had left 93   [4] piece] little piece 93   [5] exceedingly] exceeding 93

weaker hand of hold. And so, for a time, parted those friends, each crying to the other; but the noise of the sea drowned their farewell.

'But Pyrocles, then careless of death, if it had come by any means but his own, was shortly brought out of the sea's fury to the land's comfort, when (in my conscience I know) that comfort was but bitter unto him. And bitter indeed it fell out, even in itself, to be unto him, for being cast on land, much bruised and beaten both with the sea's hard farewell and the shore's rude welcome, and even almost deadly tired with the length of his uncomfortable labour, as he was walking up to discover somebody to whom he might go for relief, there came straight running unto him certain (who, as it was after known, by appointment watched with many others in divers places along the coast) who laid hands of him; and without either questioning with him or showing will to hear him – like men fearful to appear curious – or, which was worse, having no regard to the hard plight he was in, being so wet and weak, they carried him some miles thence to a house of a principal officer of that country, who with no more civility, though with much more business than those under-fellows had showed, began in captious manner to put interrogatories unto him, to which he, unused to such entertainment, did shortly and plainly answer what he was and how he came thither. But that no sooner known, with numbers of armed men to guard him – for mischief, not from mischief – he was sent to the king's court (which as then was not above a day's journey off) with letters from that officer containing his own serviceable diligence in discovering so great a personage, adding withal more than was true of his conjectures, because he would endear his own service.

'This country whereon he fell was Phrygia, and it was to the king thereof to whom he was sent – a prince of a melancholy constitution, both of body and mind: wickedly sad (ever musing of horrible matters), suspecting (or rather, condemning) all men of evil because his mind had no eye to espy goodness – and therefore, accusing sycophants, of all men, did best sort to his nature – but therefore not seeming sycophants, because of no evil they said, they could bring any new or doubtful thing unto him but such as already he had been apt to determine, so as they came but as proofs of his wisdom; fearful, and never secure while the fear he had figured in his mind had any possibility of event; a toad-like retiredness and closeness of mind, nature teaching the odiousness of poison, and the danger of odiousness – yet while youth lasted in him, the exercises of that age, and his humour not yet fully discovered, made him something the more frequentable and less dangerous. But after that years began to come on, with some, though more seldom, shows of a bloody nature, and that the prophecy of Musidorus' destiny came to his ears (delivered unto him, and received of him, with the hardest interpretation, as though his subjects did delight in the hearing thereof), then gave he himself indeed to the full current of his disposition, especially after the war of Thessalia wherein, though in truth wrongly, he deemed his unsuccessings[1] proceeded of their unwillingness to have him prosper; and then thinking himself contemned, knowing no countermine against contempt but terror, began to let nothing pass which might bear the colour of a fault without sharp punishment; and when he wanted faults, excellency grew a fault; and it was sufficient to make one guilty that he had power to be guilty. And as there is no honour[2] to which impudent poverty cannot make itself serviceable, so were there enow of those desperate ambition,[3] who would build their houses upon others' ruins, which after should fall by like practices, so as servitude came mainly upon that poor people (whose deeds were not only punished, but words corrected, and even thoughts by some mean or other pulled out of them), while suspicion bred the mind of cruelty, and the effects of cruelty stirred a new cause of suspicion.

'And in this plight, full of watchful fearfulness, did the storm deliver sweet Pyrocles to the stormy mind of that tyrant, all men that did such wrong to so rare a stranger, whose countenance deserved both pity and admiration, condemning themselves as much in their hearts as they did brag in their forces. But when this bloody king knew what he was, and in what order he and his cousin Musidorus (so much of him feared) were come out of Thessalia, assuredly thinking (because ever thinking the worst) that those forces were provided against him, glad of the perishing (as he thought) of Musidorus, determined in public sort to put Pyrocles to death, for having quite lost the way of nobleness, he strave to climb to the height of terribleness; and thinking to make all men adread to make such one an enemy who would not spare, nor fear, to kill so great a prince; and lastly, having nothing in him why to make him his friend, thought[4] he would make him away for being[5] his enemy. The day was appointed, and all things appointed for that cruel blow in so solemn an order as if they would set forth tyranny in most gorgeous decking, the princely youth, of invincible valour, yet so unjustly subjected to such outrageous wrong, carrying himself in all his demeanour so constantly, abiding extremity, that one might see it was the cutting away of the greatest hope of the world, and destroying virtue in his sweetest growth.

---

[1] unsuccessings] unsuccess 93 [2] honour] humour 93 [3] those desperate ambition *Cm*: those desperate ambitious *90*; those of desperate ambition *93* [4] friend, thought] friend, he thought *93* [5] make him away for being] take him away from being *93*

'But so it fell out that his death was prevented by a rare example of friendship in Musidorus, who being almost drowned, had been taken up by a fisherman belonging to the kingdom of Pontus; and being there and understanding the full discourse (as fame was very prodigal of so notable an accident) in what case Pyrocles was (learning withal that his hate was far more to him than to Pyrocles), he found means to acquaint himself with a nobleman of that country; to whom largely discovering what he was, he found him a most fit instrument to effectuate his desire, for this nobleman had been one who in many wars had served Euarchus, and had been so mind-stricken by the beauty of virtue in that noble king that, though not born his subject, he even[1] professed himself his servant. His desire therefore, to him, was to keep Musidorus in a strong castle of his, and then to make the king of Phrygia understand that, if he would deliver Pyrocles, Musidorus would willingly put himself into his hands – knowing well that, how thirsty soever he was of Pyrocles' blood, he would rather drink that of Musidorus.

'The nobleman was loath to preserve one by the loss of another. But time urging resolution, the importunity of Musidorus who showed a mind not to overlive Pyrocles, with the affection he bare to Euarchus, so prevailed that he carried this strange offer of Musidorus, which by that tyrant was greedily accepted. And so, upon security of both sides, they were interchanged – where I may not omit that[2] work of friendship in Pyrocles, who both in speech and countenance, to Musidorus well showed that he thought himself injured and not relieved by him, asking him what he had ever seen in him why he could not bear the extremities of mortal accidents as well as any man, and why he should envy him the glory of suffering death for his friend's cause, and as it were rob him of his own possession. But in this notable contention, where the conquest must be the conqueror's destruction, and safety the punishment of the conquered, Musidorus prevailed because he was a more welcome prey[3] to the unjust king [that wished none well, to them worse than others, and to him worst of all]; and as[4] cheerfully going towards (as Pyrocles went frowardly fromward) his death, he was delivered to the king, who could not be enough sure of him without he fed his own eyes upon one whom he had begun to fear as soon as the other began to be.

'Yet because he would in one act both make ostentation of his own felicity, into whose hands his most feared enemy was fallen, and withal cut off such hopes from his suspected subjects when they should know certainly he was dead, with much more skilful cruelty and horrible solemnity he caused each thing to be prepared for his triumph of tyranny. And so, the

---

[1] even] ever 93   [2] that] the 93   [3] prey *Cm, 93*: prize *90*   [4] king ... and as] king; and as *Cm, 93*

day being come, he was led forth by many armed men, who often had been the fortifiers of wickedness, to the place of execution; where coming with a mind comforted in that he had done such service to Pyrocles, this strange encounter he had.

'The excelling Pyrocles was no sooner delivered by the king's servants to a place of liberty than he bent his wit and courage – and what would not they bring to pass? – how either to deliver Musidorus, or to perish with him. And finding he could get in that country no forces sufficient by force to rescue him, to bring himself to die with him (little hoping of better event), he put himself in poor raiment; and by the help of some few crowns he took of that nobleman, who full of sorrow, though not knowing the secret of his intent, suffered him to go in such order from him, he, even he, born to the greatest expectation, and of the greatest blood that any prince might be, submitted himself to be servant to the executioner that should put to death Musidorus: a far notabler proof of his friendship, considering the height of his mind, than any death could be. That bad officer not suspecting him (being arrayed fit for such an estate, and having his beauty hidden by many foul spots he artificially put upon his face), gave him leave not only to wear a sword himself, but to bear his sword, prepared for the justified murther. And so Pyrocles, taking his time when Musidorus was upon the scaffold, separated somewhat from the rest, as allowed to say something, he stepped unto him; and putting the sword into his hand – not bound – a point of civility the officers used towards him because they doubted no such enterprise, "Musidorus!" said he, "Die nobly!"

'In truth, never man between joy (before knowledge what to be glad of) and fear (after considering his case) had such a confusion of thoughts as I had when I saw Pyrocles so near me – ' but with that, Dorus blushed; and Pamela smiled. And Dorus the more blushed at her smiling; and she the more smiled at his blushing, because he had, with the remembrance of that plight he was in, forgotten in speaking of himself to use the third person. But Musidorus turned again her thoughts from his cheeks to his tongue, in this sort.

'But,' said he, 'when they were with swords in hands, not turning backs one to the other, for there they knew was no place of defence, but making it[1] a preservation in not hoping to be preserved; and now acknowledging themselves subject to death, meaning only to do honour to their princely birth, they flew amongst them all (for all were enemies) and had quickly either with flight or death left none upon the scaffold to annoy them; wherein Pyrocles – the excellent Pyrocles! – did such wonders beyond belief as was able to lead Musidorus to courage – though he had been born a coward!

---

[1] it *Cm, 93*: that *90*

But indeed, just rage and desperate virtue did such effects that the popular sort of the beholders began to be almost superstitiously amazed, as at effects beyond mortal power. But the king with angry threatenings from out a window, where he was not ashamed the world should behold him a beholder, commanded his guard and the rest of his soldiers to hasten their death; but many of them lost their bodies to loose their souls – when the princes grew almost so weary as they were ready to be conquered with conquering.

'But as they were still fighting (with weak arms and strong hearts), it happened that one of the soldiers, commanded to go up after his fellows against the princes, having received a light hurt, more wounded in his heart, went back with as much diligence as he came up with modesty; which another of his fellows seeing, to pick a thank of the king strake him upon the face, reviling him that so accompanied he would run away from so few. But he, as many times it falls out, only valiant when he was angry, in revenge thrust him through – which with his death was straight revenged by a brother of his, and that again requited by a fellow of the other's. There began to be a great tumult amongst the soldiers, which seen and not understood by the people, used to fears but not used to be bold in them, some began to cry, "Treason!" And that voice straight multiplying itself, the king (oh the cowardice of a guilty conscience!), before any man set upon him, fled away; wherewith a bruit, either by art of some well-meaning men, or by such chance as such things often fall out by, ran from one to the other that the king was slain; wherewith certain young men of the bravest minds cried with loud voice, "Liberty!"; and encouraging the other citizens to follow them, set upon the guard and soldiers as chief instruments of tyranny; and quickly (aided by the princes) they had left none of them alive – nor any other in the city who they thought had in any sort set his hand to the work of their servitude; and, God knows, by the blindness of rage killing many guiltless persons, either for affinity to the tyrant, or enmity to the tyrant-killers. But some of the wisest,[1] seeing that a popular licence is indeed the many-headed tyranny, prevailed with the rest to make Musidorus their chief (choosing one of them – because princes – to defend them, and him because elder and most hated of the tyrant), and by him to be ruled; whom forthwith they lifted up – fortune I think smiling at her work therein, that a scaffold of execution should grow a scaffold of coronation. But by and by there came news, of more certain truth, that the king was not dead but fled to a strong castle of his near hand, where he was gathering forces in all speed possible to suppress this mutiny.

'But now they had run themselves too far out of breath to go back again the same career, and too well they knew the sharpness of his memory to

---

[1] wisest] wiser 93

forget such an injury. Therefore, learning virtue of necessity, they continued resolute to obey Musidorus; who seeing what forces were in the city, with them issued against the tyrant while they were in this heat (before practices might be used to dissever them) and with them met the king; who likewise (hoping little to prevail by time, knowing and finding his people's hate) met him with little delay in the field – where himself was slain by Musidorus, after he had seen his only son, a prince of great courage and beauty, but fostered in blood by his naughty father, slain by the hand of Pyrocles.

'This victory obtained with great (and truly not undeserved) honour to the two princes, the whole estates of the country with one consent gave the crown and all other marks of sovereignty to Musidorus, desiring nothing more than to live under such a government as they promised themselves of him. But he, thinking it a greater greatness to give a kingdom than get a kingdom, understanding that there was left of the blood royal, and next to the succession, an aged gentleman of approved goodness (who had gotten nothing by his cousin's power but danger from him, and odiousness for him, having passed his time in modest secrecy, and as much from intermeddling in matters of government as the greatness of his blood would suffer him), did, after having received the full power to his own hands, resign all to the nobleman, but with such conditions, and cautions of the conditions, as might assure the people with as much assurance as worldly matters bear, that not only that governor, of whom indeed they looked for all good, but the nature of the government, should be no way apt to decline to tyranny.

'This[1] doing set forth no less his magnificence than the other act did his magnanimity. So that greatly praised of all, and justly beloved of the new king (who in all, both words and behaviour, protested himself their tenant and[2] liege man), they were drawn thence to revenge those two servants of theirs, of whose memorable faith I told you, most excellent princess, in willingly giving themselves to be drowned for their sakes. But drowned indeed they were not, but gat with painful swimming upon a rock, from whence, after being come as near famishing as before drowning, the weather breaking up, they were brought to the mainland of Pontus, the same country upon which Musidorus also was fallen, but not in so lucky a place; for they were brought to the king of that country – a tyrant also, not thorough suspicion, greediness, or unrevengefulness,[3] as he of Phrygia, but as I may term it, of a wanton cruelty; inconstant of[4] his choice of friends (or rather, never

---

[1] tyranny. 'This *Cm, 93*: tyranny.' Chap. 9. The two brothers escape to the shore of Pontus; inconstancy and envy portrayed in the king and his counsellor; the advancement and overthrow by them of those two brothers; the revenge thereof by the two princes; the cruelties of two revengeful giants, and their death by the princes; their honours, and their honourable minds. 'This *90*   [2] tenant and *Cm, 93*: tenant or *90*   [3] unrevengefulness] revengefulness *93*   [4] inconstant of] inconstant in *93*

having a friend but a playfellow) of whom, when he was weary, he could not otherwise rid himself than by killing them; giving sometimes prodigally, not because he loved them to whom he gave, but because he lusted to give; punishing, not so much for hate or anger, as because he felt not the smart of punishment; delighted to be flattered, at first for those virtues which were not in him, at length making his vices virtues worthy the flattering; with like judgement glorying when he had happened to do a thing well, as when he had performed some notable mischief.

'He chanced at that time (for indeed long time none lasted with him) to have next in use about him a man of the most envious disposition that I think ever infected the air with his breath; whose eyes could not look right upon any happy man, nor ears bear the burthen of anybody's praise; contrary to the natures of all other plagues, plagued with others' well-being; making happiness the ground of his unhappiness, and good news the argument of his sorrow: in sum, a man whose favour no man could win, but by being miserable.

'And so, because these two faithful servants of theirs came in miserable sort to that court, he was apt enough at first to favour them. And the king (understanding of their adventure, wherein they had showed so constant a faith unto their lords) suddenly falls to take a pride in making much of them, extolling them with infinite praises, and praising himself in his heart, in that he praised them; and by and by were they made great courtiers, and in the way of minions – when advancement, the most mortal offence to envy, stirred up their former friend to overthrow his own work in them. Taking occasion upon the knowledge newly come to the court of the late king[1] of Phrygia, destroyed by their two lords, who having been a near kinsman to this prince of Pontus, by this envious counsellor (partly with suspicion of practice, partly with glory of in part revenging his cousin's death) the king was suddenly turned (and every turn with him was a downfall) to lock them up in prison as servants to his enemies – whom before he had never known, nor, till that time one of his own subjects had entertained and dealt for them, did ever take heed of. But now, earnest in every present humour, and making himself brave in his liking, he was content to give them just cause of offence, when they had power to make just revenge. Yet did the princes send unto him, before they entered into war, desiring their servants' liberty; but he (swelling in their humbleness like a bubble swollen[2] up with a small breath, broken with a great) forgetting, or never knowing humanity, caused their heads to be stricken off (by the advice of his envious counsellor, who now hated them so much the more as he foresaw the happiness[3] in having

---

[1] late king] late death of the king 93   [2] swollen] blown 93   [3] the happiness] their happiness 93

such, and so fortunate, masters), and sent them with unroyal reproaches to Musidorus and Pyrocles, as if they had done traitorously, and not heroically, in killing his tyrannical cousin.

'But that injury went beyond all degree of reconcilement. So that they making forces in Phrygia (a kingdom wholly at their commandment by the love of the people and gratefulness of the king), they entered his country; and wholly conquering it with such deeds as, at least, fame said were excellent, took the king. And by Musidorus' commandment (Pyrocles' heart more inclining[1] to pity) he was slain upon the tomb of their two true servants, which they caused to be made for them, with royal expenses and notable workmanship, to preserve their dead lives. For his wicked servant, he should have felt the like, or worse, but that his heart brake even to death with the beholding the honour done to the dead[2] carcasses. There might Pyrocles quietly have enjoyed that crown, by all the desire of that people, most of whom had revolted unto him; but he finding a sister of the late king's (a fair and well esteemed lady, looking for nothing more than to be oppressed with her brother's ruins), gave her in marriage to the nobleman, his father's old friend, and endowed them with the crown of that kingdom.

'And not content with those public actions of princely and, as it were, governing virtue, they did in that kingdom (and some other near about) divers acts of particular trials, more famous because more perilous; for in that time those regions were full both of cruel monsters and monstrous men, all which in short time, by private combats, they delivered the countries of – among the rest, two brothers of huge both greatness and force (therefore[3] commonly called giants) who kept themselves in a castle seated upon the top of a high rock,[4] impregnable because there was no coming unto it but by one narrow path, where one man's force was able to keep down an army. These brothers had awhile served the king of Pontus, and in all his affairs (especially of war, whereunto they were only apt) they had showed, as unconquered courage, so a rude faithfulness, being men indeed by nature apter to the faults of rage than of deceit; not greatly ambitious more than to be well and uprightly dealt with; rather impatient of injury than delighted with more than ordinary courtesies; and in injuries more sensible of smart or loss than of reproach or disgrace. These men being of this nature (and certainly jewels to a wise man, considering what, indeed, wonders they were able to perform) yet were discarded by that unworthy prince after many notable deserts, as not worthy the holding – which was the more evident to them because it suddenly fell from an excess of favour, which, many examples having taught them, never stopped his race till it

---

[1] inclining *Cm, 93*: inclined *90*   [2] the dead] their dead *93*   [3] force (therefore] force (and therefore *OA, Cm*   [4] a high rock *OA, Cm*: a rock *90, 93*

came to an headlong overthrow. They, full of rage, retired themselves unto this castle, where thinking nothing juster than revenge, nor more noble than the effects of anger (that according to the nature, full of inward bravery and fierceness, scarcely in the glass of reason thinking itself fair but when it is terrible), they immediately gave themselves to make all the country about them, subject to that king, to smart for their lord's folly, not caring how innocent they were, but rather thinking the more innocent they were, the more it testified their spite, which they desired to manifest. And with use of evil growing more and more evil, they took delight in slaughter, and pleasing[1] themselves in making others' wrack the effect of their power. So that where, in the time that they obeyed a master, their anger was a serviceable power of the mind to do public good, so now, unbridled, and blind judge of itself, it made wickedness violent, and praised itself in excellency of mischief – almost to the ruin of the country, not greatly regarded by their careless and loveless king; till now, these princes finding them so fleshed in cruelty as not to be reclaimed, secretly undertook the matter alone, for accompanied they would not have suffered them to have mounted. And so, those great fellows scornfully receiving them as foolish birds fallen into their net, it pleased the eternal justice to make them suffer death by their hands; and so,[2] they were manifoldly acknowledged the savers of that country.

'It were the part of a very idle orator to set forth the numbers of well-devised honours done unto them. But as high honour is not only gotten and born by pain and danger, but must be nursed by the like or else vanisheth as soon as it appears to the world, so the natural hunger thereof which was in Pyrocles suffered him not to account a resting seat of that (which ever either riseth or falleth), but still to make one action[3] beget another, whereby his doings might send his praise to others' mouths, to rebound again true contentment to his spirit.

'And therefore, having well established those kingdoms under good governors, and rid them by their valure of such giants and monsters as beforetime armies were not able to subdue, they determined in unknown order to see more of the world, and to employ those gifts esteemed rare in them to the good of mankind; and therefore would themselves (understanding that the King Euarchus was passed all the cumber of his wars) go privately to seek exercises of their virtue, thinking it not so worthy to be brought to heroical effects by fortune or necessity (like Ulysses and Aeneas) as by one's own choice and working. And so went they away from very unwilling people to leave them, making time haste itself to be a circumstance of their honour, and one place witness to another of the truth of their doings: for

---

[1] pleasing] pleased 93   [2] hands; and so *Cm, 93*: hands; so as *90*   [3] action] occasion *93*

scarcely were they out of the confines of Pontus but that, as they rid alone armed (for alone they went, one serving the other), they met an adventure, which though not so notable for any great effect they performed, yet worthy to be remembered for the unused examples therein, as well of true natural goodness, as of wretched ungratefulness.

'It[1] was in the kingdom of Galatia, the season being (as in the depth of winter) very cold and (as then) suddenly grown to so extreme and foul a storm that never any winter, I think, brought forth a fouler child; so that the princes were even compelled by the hail that the pride of the wind blew into their faces to seek some shrouding place, which,[2] a certain hollow rock offering it unto[3] them, they made it their shield against the tempest's fury. And so, staying there till the violence thereof was passed, they heard the speech of a couple, who not perceiving them (being hid within that rude canopy), held a strange and pitiful disputation – which made them step out, yet in such sort as they might see unseen. There they perceived an aged man, and a young (scarcely come to the age of a man), both poorly arrayed, extremely weather-beaten; the old man blind, the young man leading him. And yet, through all those miseries, in both there[4] seemed to appear a kind of nobleness not suitable to that affliction. But the first words they heard were these of the old man.

'"Well, Leonatus," said he, "since I cannot persuade thee to lead me to that which should end my grief and thy trouble, let me now entreat thee to leave me. Fear not. My misery cannot be greater than it is, and nothing doth become me but misery. Fear not the danger of my blind steps; I cannot fall worse than I am. And do not, I pray thee, do not obstinately continue to infect thee with my wretchedness, but fly, fly from this region only worthy of me."

'"Dear father," answered he, "do not take away from me the only remnant of my happiness. While I have power to do you service, I am not wholly miserable."

'"Ah, my son!" said he – and with that he groaned, as if sorrow strave to break his heart, "How evil fits it me to have such a son; and how much doth thy kindness upbraid my wickedness!"

'These doleful speeches, and some others to like purpose well showing they had not been born to the fortune they were in, moved the princes to go out unto them and ask the younger what they were. "Sirs," answered he

---

[1] ungratefulness. 'It 93: ungratefulness, 'I Cm; ungratefulness.' Chap. 10. The pitiful state and story of the Paphalgonian [sic] unkind king, and his kind son, first related by the son, then by the blind father; the three princes assaulted by Plexirtus and his train, assisted by their king of Pontus and his troops; Plexirtus succoured and saved by two brothers that virtuously loved a most vicious man; besieged by the new king, he submitteth and is pardoned; the two princes depart to aid the queen of Lycia. 'It 90
[2] which Cm, 93: within 90   [3] offering it unto] offering unto 93   [4] there Cm, 93: these 90

with a good grace – and made the more agreeable by a certain noble kind of piteousness, "I see well you are strangers that know not our misery, so well here known that no man dare know, but that we must be miserable. Indeed, our state is such, as though nothing is so needful unto us as pity, yet nothing is more dangerous unto us than to make ourselves so known as may stir pity. But your presence promiseth that cruelty shall not overrun hate. And if it did, in truth, our state is sunk below the degree of fear.

'"This old man whom I lead was lately rightful prince of this country of Paphlagonia; by the hard-hearted ungratefulness of a son of his deprived not only of his kingdom, whereof no foreign forces were ever able to spoil him, but of his sight, the riches which nature grants to the poorest creatures; whereby (and by other his unnatural dealings) he hath been driven to such grief as even now he would have had me to have led him to the top of this rock, thence to cast himself headlong to death; and so would have made me, who received my life of him, to be the worker of his destruction. But, noble gentlemen," said he, "if either of you have a father and feel what dutiful affection is engraffed in a son's heart, let me entreat you to convey this afflicted prince to some place of rest and security. Amongst your worthy acts, it shall be none of the least that a king of such might and fame, and so unjustly oppressed, is in any sort by you relieved."

'But before they could make him answer, his father began to speak. "Ah, my son," said he, "how evil an historian are you, that leave out the chief knot of all the discourse – my wickedness! My wickedness! And if thou doest it to spare my ears, the only sense now left me proper for knowledge, assure thyself thou dost mistake me. And I take witness of that sun which you see," with that, he cast up his blind eyes as if he would hunt for light, "and wish myself in worse case than I do wish myself – which is as evil as may be – if I speak untruly, that nothing is so welcome to my thoughts as the publishing of my shame. Therefore know you, gentlemen, to whom from my heart I wish that it may not prove ominous[1] foretoken of misfortune to have met with such a miser as I am, that whatsoever my son (O God! That truth binds me to reproach him with the name of *my son*!) hath said is true. But besides those truths, this also is true: that having had in lawful marriage, of a mother fit to bear royal children, this son (such one[2] as partly you see, and better shall know by my short declaration), and so enjoyed the expectations in the world of him till he was grown to justify their expectations (so as I needed envy no father for the chief comfort of mortality, to leave another oneself after me), I was carried by a bastard son of mine, if, at least, I be bound to believe the words of that base woman, my concubine – his mother, first to

---

[1] prove ominous] prove some ominous 93   [2] such one] such a one 93

mislike, then to hate, lastly to destroy – to[1] do my best to destroy – this son, I think you think undeserving destruction. What ways he[2] used to bring me to it, if I should tell you, I should tediously trouble you with as much poisonous hypocrisy, desperate fraud, smooth malice, hidden ambition, and smiling envy as in any living person could be harboured. But I list it not. No remembrance, no, of naughtiness[3] delights me, but mine own; and methinks the accusing his traps[4] might in some manner excuse my fault, which certainly I loath to do. But the conclusion is that I gave order to some servants of mine, whom I thought as apt for such charities as myself, to lead him out into a forest, and there to kill him.

'"But those thieves (better natured, to my son, than myself) spared his life, letting him go to learn to live poorly, which he did, giving himself to be a private soldier in a country hereby. But as he was ready to be greatly advanced for some noble pieces of service which he did, he heard news of me – who drunk in my affection to that unlawful and unnatural son of mine, suffered myself so to be governed by him that all favours and punishments passed by him, all offices and places of importance distributed to his favourites, so that, ere I was aware, I had left myself nothing but the name of a king; which he shortly weary of too, with many indignities (if anything may be called an indignity which was laid upon me) threw me out of my seat, and put out my eyes; and then, proud in his tyranny, let me go, neither imprisoning nor killing me, but rather delighting to make me feel my misery – misery indeed, if ever there were any – full of wretchedness, fuller of disgrace, and fullest of guiltiness. And as he came to the crown by so unjust means, as unjustly he kept it by force of stranger soldiers in citadels, the nests of tyranny and murderers of liberty; disarming all his own countrymen, that no man durst show himself a well-willer of mine – to say the truth, I think few of them being so, considering my cruel folly to my good son, and foolish kindness to my unkind bastard. But if there were any who fell to[5] pity of so great a fall, and had yet any sparks of unslain[6] duty left in them towards me, yet durst they not show it, scarcely with giving me alms at their doors – which yet was the only sustenance of my distressed life, nobody daring to show so much charity as to lend me a hand to guide my dark steps; till this son of mine (God knows, worthy of a more virtuous and more fortunate father), forgetting my abominable wrongs, not recking danger, and neglecting the present good way he was in, doing[7] himself good, came hither to do this kind office you see him perform towards me – to my unspeakable grief, not only because his kindness is a glass even to my blind eyes of my

---

[1] destroy – to] destroy, or to 93   [2] he] be 93, 98; she 13   [3] remembrance, no, of naughtiness] remembrance of naughtiness 93   [4] traps Cm, 93: trains 90   [5] fell to] felt a 93   [6] unslain Cm, 93: unstained 90   [7] was in, doing] was in of doing 93

naughtiness, but that, above all griefs, it grieves me he should desperately adventure the loss of his so well-deserving[1] life for mine, that yet owe more to fortune for my deserts, as if he would carry mud in a chest of crystal. For well I know, he that now reigneth, how much soever and with good reason he despiseth me, of all men despised, yet he will not let slip any advantage to make away him whose just title, ennobled by courage and goodness, may one day shake the seat of a never secure tyranny.

'"And for this cause I craved of him to lead me to the top of this rock, indeed, I must confess with meaning to free him from so serpentine a companion as I am; but he finding what I purposed, only therein since he was born showed himself disobedient unto me. And now, gentlemen, you have the true story which I pray you publish to the world, that my mischievous proceedings may be the glory of his filial piety, the only reward now left for so great a merit. And if it may be, let me obtain that of you which my son denies me, for never was there more pity in saving any than in ending me, both because therein my agonies shall end, and so shall you preserve this excellent young man who else wilfully follows his own ruin."

'The matter in itself lamentable, lamentably expressed by the old prince which needed not take to himself the gestures of pity, since his face could not put off the marks thereof, greatly moved the two princes to compassion, which could not stay in such hearts as theirs without seeking remedy. But by and by the occasion was presented: for Plexirtus (so was the bastard called) came thither with forty horse only of purpose to murder his brother, of whose coming he had soon advertisement, and thought no eyes of sufficient credit in such a matter but his own, and therefore came himself to be actor and spectator; and as soon as he came, not regarding the weak (as he thought) guard of but two men, commanded some of his followers to set their hands to his in the killing of Leonatus. But the young prince, though not otherwise armed but with a sword, how falsely soever he was dealt with by others, would not betray himself; but bravely drawing it out, made the death of the first that assaulted[2] him warn his fellows to come more warily after him.

'But then Pyrocles and Musidorus were quickly become parties (so just a defence deserving as much as old friendship) and so did behave them (among that company more injurious than valiant) that many of them lost their lives for their wicked master. Yet perhaps had the number of them at last prevailed, if the king of Pontus (lately by them made so) had not come unlooked for to their succour; who having had a dream (which had fixed his imagination vehemently upon some great danger) presently to follow those

---

[1] so well-deserving *Cm*: soul-deserving *90*; well-deserving *93*   [2] assaulted] assailed *93*

two princes whom he most dearly loved, was come in all haste, following as well as he could their track with a hundreth horses, in that country which he thought, considering who then reigned, a fit place enough to make the stage of any tragedy. But then the match had been so ill made for Plexirtus that his ill-led life and worse-gotten honour should have tumbled together to destruction, had there not come in Tydeus and Telenor with forty or fifty in their suit to the defence of Plexirtus.

'These two were brothers, of the noblest house of that country, brought up from their infancy with Plexirtus; men of such prowess as not to know fear in themselves, and yet to teach it others that should deal with them, for they had often made their lives triumph over most terrible dangers, never dismayed, and ever fortunate; and truly, no more settled in their valure[1] than disposed to goodness and justice – if either they had lighted on a better friend, or could have learned to make friendship a child, and not the father, of virtue. But bringing up (rather than choice) having first knit their minds unto him (indeed, crafty enough either to hide his faults or never to show them, but when they might pay home), they willingly held out the course rather to satisfy him than all the world, and rather to be good friends than good men; so as, though they did not like the evil he did, yet they liked him that did the evil; and though not counsellors of the offence, yet protectors of the offender.

'Now they having heard of this sudden going out with so small a company, in a country full of evil-wishing minds toward him (though they knew not the cause), followed him; till they found him in such case as they were to venture their lives, or else he to lose his – which they did with such force of mind and body that, truly I may justly say, Pyrocles and Musidorus had never till then found any that could make them so well repeat their hardest lesson in the feats of arms. And briefly, so they did, that if they overcame not, yet were they not overcome, but carried away that ungrateful master of theirs to a place of security, howsoever the princes laboured to the contrary. But this matter being thus far begun, it became not the constancy of the princes so to leave it. But in all haste making forces both in Pontus and Phrygia, they had in few days left him but only that one strong place where he was (for fear having been the only knot that had fastened his people unto him, that once untied by a greater force, they all scattered from him like so many birds whose cage had been broken); in which season the blind king, having in the chief city of his realm set the crown upon his son Leonatus' head, with many tears both of joy and sorrow setting forth to the whole people his own fault and his son's virtue, after he had kissed him and forced his son to accept honour of him, as of his new-become subject, even in a moment died – as it

---

[1] in their valure] in valure 93

should seem, his heart, broken with unkindness and affliction, stretched so far beyond his limits with this excess of comfort, as it was able no longer to keep safe his royal[1] spirits.

'But the new king (having no less lovingly performed all duties to him dead than alive) pursued on the siege of his unnatural brother, as much for the revenge of his father as for the establishing of his own quiet – in which siege, truly, I cannot but acknowledge the prowess of those two brothers, than whom the princes never found in all their travel two men of[2] greater ability to perform, nor of abler skill for conduct. But Plexirtus finding that, if nothing else, famine would at last bring him to destruction, thought better by humbleness to creep where by pride he could not march; for certainly, so had nature formed him (and the exercise of craft conformed him) to all turningness[3] of sleights, that though no man had less goodness in his soul than he, no man could better find the places whence arguments might grow of goodness to another; though no man felt less pity, no man could tell better how to stir pity; no man more impudent to deny, where proofs were not manifest; no man more ready to confess, with a repenting manner of aggravating his own evil, where denial would but make the fault fouler. Now he took this way: that having gotten a passport for one (that pretended he would put Plexirtus alive into his hands) to speak with the king his brother, he himself (though much against the minds of the valiant brothers, who rather wished to die in brave defence) with a rope about his neck, barefooted, came to offer himself to the discretion of Leonatus – where what submission he used; how cunningly, in making greater the fault, he made the faultiness the less; how artificially he could set out the torments of his own conscience, with the burdensome cumber he had found of his ambitious desires; how finely, seeming to desire nothing but death, as ashamed to live, he begged life in the refusing it, I am not cunning enough to be able to express – but so fell out of it, that though at first sight Leonatus saw him with no other eye than as the murderer of his father, and anger already began to paint revenge in many colours, ere long he had not only gotten pity, but pardon, and if not an excuse of the fault past, yet an opinion of a future amendment; while the poor villains, chief ministers of his wickedness, now betrayed by the author thereof, were delivered to many cruel sorts of death – he so handling it that it rather seemed he had more[4] come into the defence of an unremediable mischief already committed, than that they had done it, at first, by his consent.

'In such sort the princes left these reconciled brothers, Plexirtus in all his behaviour carrying him in far lower degree of service than the ever-noble

---

[1] royal] vital 93 [2] two men of] two of 93 [3] turningness *Cm, 93*: turnings 90 [4] more *Cm, 93*: rather 90

nature of Leonatus would suffer him. And taking likewise their leaves of their good friend the king of Pontus (who returned to enjoy their benefit, both of his wife and kingdom), they privately went thence, having only with them the two valiant brothers who would needs accompany them through divers places – they four doing acts more dangerous, though less famous, because they were but private chivalries; till hearing of the fair and virtuous Queen Erona of Lycia, besieged by the puissant king of Armenia, they bent themselves to her succour, both because the weaker (and weaker, as being a lady), and partly because they heard the king of Armenia had in his company three of the most famous men living (for matters of arms) that were known to be in the world; whereof one was the Prince Plangus, whose name was sweetened by your breath, peerless lady, when the last day it pleased you to mention him unto me; the other two were two great princes, though holding of him, Barzanes and Euardes,[1] men of giant-like both hugeness and force, in which two especially the trust the king had of victory was reposed. And of them, those two brothers,[2] Tydeus and Telenor (sufficient judges in warlike matters), spake so high commendations that the two young princes[3] had even a youthful longing to have some trial of their virtue.

'And therefore, as soon as they were entered into Lycia, they joined themselves with them that faithfully served the poor queen at that time besieged, and ere long animated in such sort their almost overthrown hearts that they went by force to relieve the town – though they were deprived of a great part of their strength by the parting of the two brothers, who were sent for in all haste to return to their old friend and master, Plexirtus; who willingly hoodwinking themselves from seeing his faults, and binding themselves to believe what he said, often abused the virtue of courage to defend his foul vice of injustice. But now they were sent for to advance a conquest he was about, while Pyrocles and Musidorus pursued the delivery of the Queen Erona.'

'I[4] have heard,' said Pamela, 'that part of the story, of Plangus, when he passed through this country. Therefore you may, if you list, pass over that war of Erona's quarrel, lest if you speak too much of war matters, you should wake Mopsa, which might happily breed a great broil.'

He looked, and saw that Mopsa indeed sat swallowing of sleep with open mouth, making such a noise withal, as nobody could lay the stealing of a nap to her charge. Whereupon willing to use that occasion, he kneeled

---

[1] Euardes] Euandes *Cm*, Euardus *13* [2] those two brothers] those brothers *93* [3] two young princes] two princes *93* [4] Erona.' 'I *Cm, 93*: Erona.' Chap. 11. Dorus' suit to Pamela interrupted by Mopsa's waking; the sisters' going with Zelmane to wash themselves; the pleasantness of the river; the pleasure Zelmane had in seeing them, uttered in speech and song; she led by a spaniel to know and hurt her noble rival; the parting of that fray. 'I *90*

down; and with humble-heartedness and hardy[1] earnestness printed in his graces, 'Alas,' said he, 'divine lady, who have wrought such miracles in me as to make a prince, none of the basest, to think all principalities base in respect of the sheephook which may hold him up in your sight, vouchsafe now at last to hear in direct words my humble suit, while this dragon sleeps, that keeps the golden fruit. If in my desire I wish, or in my hopes aspire, or in my imagination feign to myself anything which may be the least spot to that heavenly virtue which shines in all your doings, I pray the eternal powers that the words I speak may be deadly poisons while they are in my mouth, and that all my hopes, all my desires, all my imaginations, may only work their own confusion. But if love, love of you, love of your virtues, seek only that favour of you which becometh that gratefulness, which cannot misbecome your excellency, oh, do not – '

He would have said further, but Pamela calling aloud, 'Mopsa!', she suddenly start up, staggering; and rubbing her eyes, ran first out of the door, and then back to them, before she knew how she went out, or why she came in again; till at length, being fully come to her little self, she asked Pamela why she had called her.

'For nothing,' said Pamela, 'but that you might hear some tales of your servant's telling; and therefore, now,' said she, 'Dorus, go on.' But as he, who found no so good sacrifice as obedience, was returning to the story of himself, Philoclea came in, and by and by after her, Miso; so as for that time they were fain to let Dorus depart.

But Pamela (delighted even to preserve in her memory the words of so well a beloved speaker) repeated the whole substance to her sister; till their sober dinner being come and gone, to recreate themselves something, even tired with the noisomeness of Miso's conversation, they determined to go while the heat of the day lasted to bathe themselves (such being the manner of the Arcadian nymphs often to do) in the river of Ladon, and take with them a lute, meaning to delight them under some shadow. But they could not stir, but that Miso with her daughter Mopsa was after them. And as it lay in their way to pass by the other lodge, Zelmane out of her window espied them, and so stale down after them – which she might the better do because that Gynecia was sick, and Basilius, that day being his birthday, according to his manner was busy about his devotions; and therefore she went after, hoping to find some time to speak with Philoclea. But not a word could she begin, but that Miso would be one of the audience; so that she was driven to recommend thinking, speaking, and all, to her eyes, who diligently performed her trust; till they came to the river's side, which of all the rivers

---

[1] hardy *Cm*, 93, 98: hearty 90, 13

of Greece had the price for excellent pureness and sweetness, insomuch as the very bathing in it was accounted exceeding healthful.

It ran upon so fine and delicate a ground as one could not easily judge whether the river did more wash the gravel, or the gravel did purify the river; the river not running forthright, but almost continually winding, as if the lower streams would return to their spring, or that the river had a delight to play with itself; the banks of either side seeming arms of the loving earth that fain would embrace it, and the river a wanton nymph which still would slip[1] from it, either side of the bank being fringed with most beautiful trees, which resisted the sun's darts from overmuch piercing the natural coldness of the river. There was the …; but among the rest, a goodly cypress, who bowing her fair head over the water, it seemed she looked into it, and dressed her green locks by that running river.

There the princesses determining to bathe themselves, though it was so privileged a place, upon pain of death, as nobody durst presume to come thither, yet for the more surety they looked round about and could see nothing but a water-spaniel who came down the river, showing that he hunted for a duck, and with a snuffling grace disdaining that his smelling force could not as well prevail thorough the water as thorough the air, and therefore waiting with his eye to see whether he could espy the duck's getting up again. But then a little below them failing of his purpose, he got out of the river; and shaking off the water as great men do their friends, now he had no further cause to use it, inweeded himself so, as the ladies lost the further marking his sportfulness.

And inviting Zelmane also to wash herself with them, and she excusing herself with having taken a late cold, they began by piecemeal to take away the eclipsing of their apparel. Zelmane would have put to her helping hand, but she was taken with such a quivering that she thought it more wisdom to lean herself to a tree and look on, while Miso and Mopsa, like a couple of forswat melters, were getting the pure silver of their bodies out of the ore of their garments. But as the raiments went off to receive kisses of the ground, Zelmane envied the happiness of all – but of the smock was even jealous. And when that was taken away too, and that Philoclea remained (for her Zelmane only marked) like a diamond taken from out the rock, or rather, like the sun getting from under a cloud and showing his naked beams to the full view, then was the beauty too much for a patient sight, the delight too strong for a stayed conceit; so that Zelmane could not choose but run to touch, embrace, and kiss her. But conscience made her come to herself and leave Philoclea, who blushing and withal smiling (making shamefastness pleasant, and pleasure shamefast) tenderly moved her feet, unwonted to feel

---

[1] slip *Cm*, *93*: stir *90*

the naked ground, till the touch of the cold water made a pretty kind of shrugging come over her body – like the twinkling of the fairest among the fixed stars. But the river itself gave way unto her, so that she was straight breast high, which was the deepest that thereabout she could be. And when cold Ladon had once fully embraced them, himself was no more so cold to those ladies; but as if his cold complexion had been heated with love, so seemed he to play about every part he could touch.

'Ah sweet, now sweetest, Ladon,' said Zelmane, 'why dost thou not stay thy course to have more full taste of thy happiness? But the reason is manifest: the upper streams make such haste to have their part of embracing that the nether (though loathly) must needs give place unto them. O happy Ladon! within whom she is, upon whom her beauty falls, thorough whom her eye pierceth. O happy Ladon! which art now an unperfect mirror of all perfection, canst thou ever forget the blessedness of this impression? If thou do, then let thy bed be turned from fine gravel to weeds and mud; if thou do, let some unjust niggards make weirs to spoil thy beauty; if thou do, let some greater river fall into thee to take away the name of Ladon. O Ladon! happy Ladon! rather slide than run by her, lest thou shouldest make her legs slip from her – and then, O happy Ladon, who would then call thee but the most cursed Ladon?'

But as the ladies played them in the water, sometimes striking it with their hands, the water making lines in his face seemed to smile at such beating, and with twenty bubbles – not to be content to have the picture of their face in large upon him, but he would in each of those bubbles set forth the miniature of them. But Zelmane, whose sight was gainsaid by nothing but the transparent veil of Ladon, like a chamber where a great fire is kept, though the fire be at one stay, yet with the continuance continually hath his heat increased, had the coals of her affection so kindled with wonder and blown with delight that now all her parts grudged that her eyes should do more homage than they to the princess of them; insomuch that taking up the lute, her wit began to be with a divine fury inspired, her voice would in so beloved an occasion second her wit, her hands accorded the lute's music to the voice, her panting heart danced to the music – while, I think, her feet did beat the time – while her body was the room where it should be celebrated, her soul the queen which should be delighted. And so together went the utterance and the invention that one might judge it was Philoclea's beauty which did speedily write it in her eyes, or the sense thereof which did word by word indite it in her mind, whereto she, but as an organ, did only lend utterance. The song was to this purpose:

What tongue can her perfections¹ tell
In whose each part all pens may dwell?
Her hair fine threads of finest² gold
In curled knots man's thought³ to hold;
But that her forehead says,⁴ 'In me
A whiter beauty you may see.'
Whiter indeed; more white than snow
Which on cold winter's face doth grow.
    That doth present those⁵ even⁶ brows,
Whose equal line⁷ their angles bows,
Like to the moon when after change
Her horned head abroad⁸ doth range;
And arches be to heav'nly⁹ lids,
Whose wink each bold attempt forbids.
    For the black¹⁰ stars those spheres contain,
The matchless pair, ev'n praise doth stain.
No lamp whose light by art is got,
No sun which shines, and seeth not,
Can liken them without all peer,
Save one as much as other clear;
Which only thus unhappy be
Because themselves they cannot see.
    Her cheeks with kindly claret¹¹ spread,
Aurora-like new out of bed,¹²
Or like the fresh queen-apple's side,
Blushing at sight of Phoebus' pride.¹³
Her nose, her chin, pure¹⁴ ivory wears,
No purer than the pretty ears.¹⁵
So¹⁶ that therein appears some blood,
Like wine and milk that mingled stood,
In¹⁷ whose incirclets if you gaze
Your eyes may tread a lover's maze,

---

¹ perfections] perfection *As, Hm, 13* ² threads of finest] laces made of *Cl, Le, As, O, Da, Ph, Je, Hm*; locks made of *Cm* ³ thought] thoughts *Bo, Le, Da, Je, Hm, Dd* ⁴ says] says *corr. to* said *Bo*; sures *Je*; said *Cm* ⁵ those] these *Bo, Je, Hm* ⁶ even] eben *corr. to* even *St*; eboene *Bo*; pretty *Cl, Le, As, O, Da, Ph, Je, Hm* ⁷ line] lines *OA (ex. Hm), Dd* ⁸ head abroad] face in heav'n *Cl, Le, As, O, Da, Ph, Je, Hm* ⁹ heav'nly] those fair *Cl, Le, As, O, Da, Ph*; these fair *Je, Hm* ¹⁰ For the black] As for the *Cl, Le, As, O, Da, Ph, Je, Hm* ¹¹ claret] scarlet *O*; scarlet *corr. to* claret *Ph* ¹² *om. Bo*; Like crystal underlaid with red *Cl, Le, As, O, Da, Ph* (revised line added in margin), *Je, Hm* ¹³ *om. Cl, Le, As, O, Da, Je, Hm*; added in margin *Ph* ¹⁴ her chin, pure] and chin such *Cl, Le, As, O, Da, Ph, Je, Hm* ¹⁵ No … ears] No elephant so perfect bears *Cl, Le, As, O, Da, Ph, Je, Hm* ¹⁶ So] but *corr. to* Save *Bo*; in *Ph* ¹⁷ In] On *St, Bo, Da*

But with such turns the voice to stray,[1]
No talk untaught can find the way.[2]
The tip no jewel needs[3] to wear;
The tip is jewel of the ear.[4]
   But who those ruddy lips can miss,   5
Which blessed still themselves do kiss?
Rubies, cherries, and roses new,
In worth, in taste, in perfit hue,
Which never part but that they show
Of precious pearl the double row,   10
The second sweetly-fenced ward
Her heav'nly-dewed tongue to guard,
Whence never word in vain did flow.
   Fair under these[5] doth stately grow
The handle of this precious work,   15
The neck, in which strange graces lurk.
Such be, I think, the sumptuous towers
Which skill[6] doth make in princes'[7] bowers.
   So good a say[8] invites the eye
A little downward to espy   20
The lively clusters of her breasts,
Of Venus' babe[9] the wanton nests,
Like pommels round of marble clear,
Where azured veins well mixed appear,
With dearest tops[10] of porphyry.   25
   Betwixt these two a way doth lie,
A way more worthy beauty's fame
Than that which bears the milky name.
This[11] leads into[12] the joyous field
Which only still doth lilies yield;   30
But lilies such whose native[13] smell
The Indian odours doth[14] excel.
Waist it is called, for it doth waste
Men's lives until it be embraced.
   There may one see, and yet not see,   35

---

[1] stray] stay *Da, Ph in margin* [2] *om. Dd* [3] needs] need *Bo, Dd* [4] *om. Cl, Le, As, O, Je, Hm; added in margin Ph* [5] these] this *Le, Dd* [6] skill] still *Le, Hm, Dd* [7] princes'] princely *Cl, Le* [8] So good a say] So true a taste *Cl, Le, As, O, Da, Ph, Je, Hm* (true *corr. to* good *Ph*) [9] babe] babb *Cl*; babes *Da*; baits *Je*; bait *Hm* [10] dearest tops] lickerous (lycoras *Cl*; lickerish *As*) stalks *Cl, Le, As, O, Da, Ph* (*corr. to* dearest tops), *Je, Hm* [11] This] These *Cl, Le* [12] into] unto *OA (ex. Hm)* [13] native] nature *Le*; natures *As* [14] doth] do *Cl, Le, Ph*

Her ribs in white[1] all armed be,
More white than Neptune's foamy face[2]
When struggling rocks he would embrace,[3]
   In those delights the wand'ring thought
5 Might of each side astray be brought,
But that her navel doth unite
In curious circle busy sight,
A dainty seal of virgin-wax
Where nothing but impression lacks.
10   Her[4] belly there[5] glad sight doth fill,
Justly entitled Cupid's hill;
A hill most fit for such a master,
A spotless mine of alablaster,
Like alablaster fair and sleek,
15 But soft and supple, satin-like,
In that sweet seat the boy doth sport.
Loath, I must leave his chief resort;[6]
For such a[7] use the world hath gotten,
The best things still must be forgotten.[8]
20   Yet never shall my song omit[9]
Her thighs[10] (for Ovid's song more fit)
Which, flanked with two sugared flanks,
Lift up their stately swelling banks
That Albion clives in whiteness pass,
25 With haunches smooth as looking glass.[11]
   But bow all knees, now of her knees
My tongue doth tell what fancy sees:[12]
The knots of joy, the gems[13] of love,
Whose motion makes all graces move;
30 Whose bought incaved[14] doth yield such sight,[15]
Like cunning painter[16] shadowing white.
The gart'ring place with childlike sign
Shows easy print in metal fine.
   But then again the flesh doth rise

---

[1] ribs in white] tender ribs *Cl, Le, As, O, Da, Ph, Je*; tender tender ribs *Hm* [2] More... face] Like whitest stone [snow *Cl*) in silver brook *Cl, Le, As O, Da, Ph, Hm* (*revised line added in margin, prefixed by* alius *Da*; *catchword* Like *before missing leaf Je*) [3] When ... embrace] Fair through fair strikes heedful [of heedful *Cl, Hm*] look *Cl, Le, As, O, Da, Ph, Hm* (*revised line added in margin Da*) [4] Her] The *Bo, Cl, Je* [5] there *OA, Dd, 98, 13*: then *90, 93* [6] *om. Cl* [7] a] an *OA (ex. O), Dd* [8] *om. As; added in margin Je* [9] *Je is missing from here* [10] Her thighs *93*: Those thighs *OA* (Her thighs *added in margin Ph*), *Dd*; Thighs *90* [11] *om. Hm* [12] *om. (ex. some initial word in margin) Ph* [13] gems] Gynnes *Cl*; iemes *Le, Dd*; Jinnes *Ph*; Ieames *Hm* [14] incaved] enchained *Cl*; engraved *As* [15] sight] lights *As, Hm* [16] painter] painters *Cl, Hm*

In her brave calves like crystal[1] skies,
Whose Atlas is a[2] smallest small,
More white than whitest bone of all.[3][4]
   Thereout steals out that round clean foot,
This noble cedar's precious root;   5
In show and scent pale violets,
Whose step on earth all beauty sets.
   But back unto her back, my muse,
Where Leda's[5] swan his feathers mews,[6]
Along whose ridge such bones are met,   10
Like comfits round in marchpane set.
   Her shoulders be like two white doves,
Perching within[7] square royal rooves,
Which leaded are, with silver skin,[8]
Passing the hate-spot[9] ermelin[10].   15
   And thence those arms derived are;
The phoenix wings are[11] not so rare
For faultless length and stainless hue.
   Ah, woe is me, my woes renew!
Now course doth lead me to her hand,   20
Of my first love the fatal band,
Where whiteness doth for ever sit;
Nature herself[12] enamelled it.
For there with strange compact doth[13] lie
Warm snow, moist pearl, soft ivory.   25
There fall those sapphire-coloured brooks,
Which conduit-like, with[14] curious crooks,
Sweet islands make[15] in that sweet land.
As for the fingers of the hand,[16]
The bloody shafts of Cupid's war,   30
With amatists they headed are.
   Thus hath each part his beauty's part;
But how the Graces do impart
To all her limbs a special[17] grace,

---

[1] crystal] morning *Cl, Le, As, O, Da, Ph* (corr. to crystal), *Hm*   [2] Whose Atlas is a] That limits have in *Cl, Le, As, Da, Hm*; That limits have on *O, Ph*   [3] More … all] Whose even descent makes equal fall *Cl, Le, As, O, Da, Ph, Hm* (revised line added in margin *Ph*)   [4] all] whale *St, Bo, Dd*   [5] Leda's] lo as *Da*; blank left *Ph*   [6] mews] muse *Bo, Le, As, Da*; om. *Cl*   [7] within] upon *Cl, Le, As, O, Da, Ph, Hm* (upon corr. to within *Ph*)   [8] Which … skin] Whose gentle rays such lustre find *Cl, Le, As, O, Da, Ph, Hm*   [9] hate-spot *Bo, Dd, 93*: hate-sport *St, 90*   [10] Passing … ermelin] Like thinnest lawn [lawns *Le*] with tinsel [twysell *As*] lined *Cl, Le, As, O, Da, Ph, Hm*   [11] are] be *OA (ex. As, Da), Dd*   [12] herself] itself *Ph, Hm*   [13] doth] do *Le, Ph, Hm*   [14] with] om. *Bo, Dd*   [15] make] makes *Cl, Le, As*   [16] the hand] that hand *As, Dd*   [17] a special] especial *Cl, Ph*

    Becoming every time and place,
    Which doth ev'n beauty beautify,
    And most bewitch the wretched eye!
    How all this is but a fair inn
    Of fairer guests[1] which dwell[2] within![3]
    Of whose high praise, and praiseful bliss,
    Goodness the pen, heav'n paper is –
    The ink immortal fame doth lend.
    As I began, so must I end:
        No tongue can her perfections[4] tell,
        In whose each part all tongues may dwell.

But as Zelmane was coming to the latter end of her song, she might see the same water-spaniel which before had hunted come and fetch away one of Philoclea's gloves, whose fine proportion showed well what a dainty guest was wont there to be lodged. It was a delight to Zelmane to see that the dog was therewith delighted, and so let him go a little way withal, who quickly carried it out of sight among certain trees and bushes which were very close together. But by and by he came again, and amongst the raiments (Miso and Mopsa being preparing sheets against their coming out) the dog lighted upon a little book of four or five leaves of paper and was bearing that away too; but then Zelmane, not knowing what importance it might be of, ran after the dog, who going straight to those bushes, she might see the dog deliver it to a gentleman who secretly lay there. But she hastily coming in, the gentleman rose up, and with a courteous though sad countenance presented himself unto her. Zelmane's eyes straight willed her mind to mark him, for, she thought, in her life she had never seen a man of a more goodly presence, in whom strong making took not away delicacy, nor beauty fierceness – being indeed such a right manlike man as nature, often erring, yet shows she would fain make. But when she had a while (not without admiration) viewed him, she desired him to deliver back the glove and paper because they were the Lady Philoclea's, telling him withal that she would not willingly let them know of his close lying in that prohibited place while they were bathing themselves, because she knew they would be mortally offended withal.

    'Fair lady,' answered he, 'the worst of the complaint is already past, since I feel, of my fault, in myself the punishment; but for these things, I assure you it was my dog's wanton boldness, not my presumption.' With that he gave her back the paper. 'But for the glove,' said he, 'since it is my Lady Philoclea's, give me leave to keep it, since my heart cannot persuade itself to part from

---

[1] guests] guest *OA (ex. Bo, Hm), Dd*   [2] dwell] dwells *OA (ex. Bo)*   [3] within] therein *Cl, 13*
[4] perfections] perfection *As, Eg*

it; and I pray you, tell the lady (lady indeed of all my desires) that owes it that I will direct my life to honour this glove with serving her.'

'O villain!' cried out Zelmane, madded with finding an unlooked-for rival, and that he would make her a messenger. 'Dispatch,' said she, 'and deliver it, or by the life of her that owes it I will make thy soul, though too base a price, pay for it'; and with that drew out her sword which, Amazon-like, she ever ware about her.

The gentleman retired himself into an open place from among the bushes, and then drawing out his too, he offered to deliver it unto her, saying withal, 'God forbid I should use my sword against you, since, if I be not deceived, you are the same famous Amazon that both defended my lady's just title of beauty against the valiant Phalantus, and saved her life in killing the lion; therefore I am rather to kiss your hands, with acknowledging myself bound to obey you.'

But this courtesy was worse than a bastinado to Zelmane, so that again (with rageful eyes) she bad him defend himself, for no less than his life should answer it.

'A hard case,' said he, 'to teach my sword that lesson, which hath ever used to turn itself to a shield in a lady's presence.'

But Zelmane, hearkening to no more words, began with such witty fury to pursue him with blows and thrusts that nature and virtue commanded the gentleman to look to his safety; yet still courtesy, that seemed incorporate in his heart, would not be persuaded by danger to offer any offence, but only to stand upon the best defensive guard he could – sometimes going back, being content in that respect to take on the figure of cowardice, sometime with strong and well-met wards, sometime cunning avoidings of his body, and sometimes feigning some blows, which himself pulled back before they needed to be withstood. And so, with play did he a good while fight against the fight of Zelmane, who, more spited with that courtesy that one that did nothing should be able to resist her, burned away with choler any motions which might grow out of her own sweet disposition, determining to kill him if he fought no better; and so, redoubling her blows, drave the stranger to no other shift than to ward and go back, at that time seeming the image of innocency against violence. But at length he found that, both in public and private respects, who stands only upon defence stands upon no defence, for Zelmane seeming to strike at his head, and he going to ward it withal stepped back as he was accustomed, she stopped her blow in the air, and suddenly turning the point ran full at his breast, so as he was driven with the pommel of his sword (having no other weapon of defence) to beat it down; but the thrust was so strong that he could not so wholly beat it away but that it met with his thigh, thorough which it ran; but Zelmane retiring her sword, and seeing his blood, victorious anger was conquered by the before-conquered pity.

And heartily sorry, and even ashamed with herself she was (considering how little he had done, who well she found could have done more), insomuch that she said, 'Truly, I am sorry for your hurt, but yourself gave the cause, both in refusing to deliver the glove, and yet not fighting as I know you could have done. But,' said she, 'because I perceive you disdain to fight with a woman, it may be before a year come about you shall meet with a near kinsman of mine, Pyrocles, prince of Macedon; and I give you my word, he for me shall maintain this quarrel against you.'

'I would,' answered Amphialus, 'I had many more such hurts to meet and know that worthy prince whose virtue I love and admire, though my good destiny hath not been to see his person.'

But as they were so speaking, the young ladies came, to whom Mopsa (curious in anything but her own good behaviour) having followed and seen Zelmane fighting, had cried what she had seen – while they were drying themselves, and the water with some drops seemed to weep that it should part from such bodies. But they careful of Zelmane, assuring themselves that any Arcadian would bear reverence to them, Pamela with a noble mind and Philoclea with a loving, hastily hiding the beauties whereof nature was proud and they ashamed, they made quick work to come to save Zelmane, but already they found them in talk, and Zelmane careful of his wound. But when they saw him they knew it was their cousin-german, the famous Amphialus, whom yet with a sweet-graced bitterness they blamed for breaking their father's commandment, especially while themselves were in such sort retired. But he craved pardon, protesting unto them that he had only been to seek solitary places, by an extreme melancholy that had a good while possessed him, and guided to that place by his spaniel, where, while the dog hunted in the river, he had withdrawn himself to pacify with sleep his overwatched eyes, till a dream waked him, and made him see that whereof he had dreamed, and withal not obscurely signified that he felt the smart of his own doings. But Philoclea, that was even jealous of herself for Zelmane, would needs have her glove, and not without so mighty a lour as that face could yield.

As for Zelmane, when she knew it was Amphialus, 'Lord Amphialus,' said she, 'I have long desired to know you, heretofore I must confess with more good will, but still with honouring your virtue, though I love not your person; and at this time, I pray you, let us take care of your wound, upon condition you shall hereafter promise that a more knightly combat shall be performed between us.'

Amphialus answered in honourable sort, but with such excusing himself that more and more accused his love to Philoclea, and provoked more hate in Zelmane. But Mopsa had already called certain shepherds not far off (who knew and well observed their limits) to come and help to carry away Amphialus, whose wound suffered him not without danger to strain it; and so, he leaving himself with them, departed from them, faster bleeding in his heart than at his wound, which bound up by the sheets wherewith Philoclea had been wrapped, made him thank the wound and bless the sword for that favour. But he[1] being gone, the ladies (with merry anger talking in what naked simplicity their cousin had seen them) returned to the lodge-ward; yet thinking it too early (as long as they had any day) to break off so pleasing a company with going to perform a cumbersome obedience, Zelmane invited them to the little arbour only reserved for her, which they willingly did. And there sitting, Pamela having a while made the lute in his language show how glad it was to be touched by her fingers, Zelmane delivered up the paper which Amphialus had at first yielded unto her, and seeing written upon the backside of it *The Complaint of Plangus*, remembering what Dorus had told her, and desiring to know how much Philoclea knew of her estate, she took occasion in the presenting of it to ask whether it were any secret or no.

'No, truly,' answered Philoclea, 'it is but even an exercise of my father's writing, upon this occasion: he was one day (somewhile before your coming hither) walking abroad, having us two with him, almost a mile hence; and crossing a highway which comes from the city of Megalopolis, he saw this gentleman whose name is there written, one of the properest and best-graced men that ever I saw, being of middle age, and of a mean stature. He lay as then under a tree while his servants were getting fresh post-horses for him. It might seem he was tired with the extreme travel he had taken, and yet not so tired that he forced to take any rest, so hasty he was upon his journey; and withal so sorrowful that the very face thereof was painted in his face, which with pitiful motions, even groans, tears, and passionate talking to himself, moved my father to fall in talk with him; who at first not knowing him, answered him in such a desperate phrase of grief that my father afterward took a delight to set it down in such form as you see, which if you read, what you doubt of my sister and I are able to declare unto you.'

Zelmane willingly opened the leaves and read it, being written dialogue-wise in this manner:

---

[1] favour. But he *Cm*: favour. Chap. 12. How Basilius found Plangus; his lamentation; Philoclea entreated by Zelmane to relate the story of Erona. He *90*; favour. He *93*

                Plangus   *Basilius*

Plangus. Alas, how long this pilgrimage doth last!
    What greater ills have now the heav'ns in store
    To couple coming harms with sorrows past?
Long since my voice is hoarse, and throat is sore,
    With cries to skies, and curses to the ground;
    But more I plain, I feel my woes the more.
Ah, where was first that cruel cunning found
    To frame of earth a vessel of[1] the mind,
    Where it should be to[2] self-destruction bound?
What needed[3] so high sprites such mansions[4] blind?
    Or wrapped in flesh, what do they here obtain,
    But glorious name of wretched human-kind?
Balls to the stars, and thralls to fortune's reign;
    Turned from themselves, infected with their cage[5]
    Where death is feared, and life is held with pain:
Like players placed to fill a filthy stage,
    Where change of thoughts one fool to other shows,
    And all but jests, save only sorrow's rage.
The child feels that; the man that feeling knows,
    With cries first born, the presage of his life,
    Where wit but serves to have true taste of woes.
A shop of shame, a book where blots be[6] rife
    This body is; this body so composed
    As in itself to nourish mortal strife.
So divers be the elements disposed
    In this weak work that it can never be
    Made uniform to any state reposed.
Grief only makes his wretched state to see
    (Ev'n like a top which nought but whipping moves)
    This man, this talking beast, this walking tree.
Grief is the stone which finest judgement proves;
    For who grieves not hath but a blockish brain,
    Since cause of grief no cause from[7] life removes.
Basilius. How long wilt thou with moanful music stain
    The cheerful notes these pleasant places yield,
    Where all[8] good haps a perfect state maintain?

---

[1] vessel of] vessel for *Le*; vessel to *As*   [2] to] *the corr. to* to *Cl*; the *Le*   [3] needed] need *Ph, Hm*   [4] mansions] mansion *Bo, Je*   [5] cage] age *St, Bo, Ph*; rage *As*   [6] be] are *Cl*; are *corr. to* be *Cm*   [7] from] of *Bo, Ph*   [8] all] as *Cl, Le*

Plangus. Cursed be good haps, and cursed be they that build
    Their hopes on haps, and do not make despair
    For all these[1] certain blows the surest shield.
Shall I that saw Erona's shining hair
    Torn with her hands, and those same hands of snow
    With loss of purest blood themselves to tear;
Shall I that saw those breasts where beauties flow,
    Swelling with sighs, made pale with mind's disease,
    And saw those eyes (those suns) such show'rs[2] to show;
Shall I, whose ears her mournful words did[3] seize
    (Her words in syrup laid of sweetest breath),
    Relent those thoughts which then did so displease?
No, no; despair my daily lesson saith,
    And saith, although I seek my life to fly,
    Plangus must live to see Erona's death;
Plangus must live some help for her to try
    Though in despair, for love so forceth[4] me.
    Plangus doth live, and shall[5] Erona die?
Erona die? O heav'n (if heav'n there be)
    Hath all thy[6] whirling course so small effect?
    Serve all thy starry eyes this shame to see?
Let dolts in haste some altars fair erect
    To those high pow'rs which idly sit above,
    And virtue do in greatest need neglect.
Basilius. O man, take heed how thou the gods do move
    To causeful[7] wrath which thou canst not resist.
    Blasphemous words the speaker vain do[8] prove.
Alas, while we are wrapped in foggy mist
    Of our self-love (so passions do deceive)
    We think they hurt when most they do assist.
To harm us worms should that high[9] justice leave
    His nature? nay, himself? for so it is.
    What glory from our loss can he receive?
But still our dazzled eyes their way do miss,
    While that we do at his sweet scourge repine,
    The kindly way to beat us on to[10] bliss.

---

[1] these] those *As*; the *Je, Hm*   [2] show'rs] shows *Le, Da*; shewers *As, Je*; shrowd *Ph*   [3] did] do *Cl, Le*   [4] for love so forceth *OA, 93*: so love enforceth *90*   [5] shall *OA, 93*: must *90*   [6] thy] the *Cl, Le*   [7] causeful *Cl, Le, As, Da, Ph, Je, 93*: careful *St*; causeless *Bo, Hm*; ireful *90*   [8] do] doth *Cl, Le*   [9] high] by *Cl, Le*   [10] on to *OA, 93*: to our *90*

                If she must die, then hath she passed the line
                    Of loathsome days, whose loss how canst thou moan,
                    That doost¹ so well their miseries define?
                But such we are, with inward tempest blown
 5   Of winds² quite³ contrary in waves of will:
                    We moan that lost,⁴ which had we did bemoan.
    Plangus. And shall she die, shall cruel fire spill
                    Those beams that set so many hearts on fire?
                    Hath she not force ev'n death with love to kill?
10   Nay, ev'n cold death inflamed with hot desire
                    Her to enjoy (where joy itself is thrall)
                    Will spoil the earth of his most rich attire.
                Thus death becomes a rival to us all,
                    And hopes with foul embracements her to get,
15   In whose decay virtue's fair shrine must fall.
                O virtue weak, shall death his triumph set
                    Upon thy spoils, which never should lie waste?
                    Let death first die; be thou his worthy let.
                By what eclipse shall that sun be defaced?
20   What mine hath erst thrown down so fair a tower?
                    What sacrilege hath such a saint disgraced?
                The world the garden is; she is the flower
                    That sweetens all the place; she is the guest
                    Of rarest price, both heav'n and earth her bower.
25   And shall (O me!) all this in ashes rest?
                    Alas, if you a phoenix new⁵ will have⁶
                    Burnt by the sun, she first must build her nest –
                But well you know the gentle sun would save
                    Such beams so like his own, which might have might
30   In him the thoughts of Phaeton's dam to grave;
                Therefore, alas, you use vile Vulcan's spite,
                    Which nothing spares, to melt that virgin-wax⁷
                    Which while it is, it is all Asia's light.
                O Mars, for what doth serve thy armed axe?
35   To let that wittold⁸ beast consume in flames⁹
                    Thy¹⁰ Venus' child,¹¹ whose beauty Venus lacks?
                O Venus (if her praise no envy frames

---

¹ doost] durst *Ph*; doth *Je, Hm*   ² winds *OA, 93*: minds *Le, 90*   ³ quite] clean *Cl, Le*   ⁴ lost] loss *Cl, Ph*   ⁵ new] now *Cl, Le, Da*   ⁶ have] save *Je, Hm* (save *corr.* to have *St*)   ⁷ virgin-wax] virgin's wax *St, Da, Ph, Je, Hm*   ⁸ wittold] withold *Bo*; wit hold *Hm*   ⁹ flames] flame *90 (uncorr.)*   ¹⁰ Thy] The *Ph, Hm*   ¹¹ child] shield *Ph, Je, Hm*

    In thy high mind) get her thy husband's grace.
    Sweet speaking oft a currish heart reclaims.
O eyes of mine, where once she saw her face
    (Her face which was more lively in my heart),
    O brain, where thought of her hath only place,   5
O hand, which touched her hand when we[1] did part,
    O lips, that kissed that hand[2] with my tears sprent,
    O tongue, then dumb, not daring tell my smart,
O soul, whose love in her is only spent,
    Whate'er you see, think, touch, kiss, speak, or love,   10
    Let all for her, and unto her, be bent.

Basilius. Thy wailing words do much my spirits move;
    They uttered are in such a feeling fashion
    That sorrow's work against my will I prove.
Methinks I am partaker of thy passion,   15
    And in thy case do glass mine[3] own debility –
    Self-guilty folk most prone[4] to feel compassion.
Yet reason saith, 'Reason should have ability
    To hold these worldly[5] things in such proportion
    As let them come or go with ev'n facility.'   20
But our desire's tyrannical extortion
    Doth force us there to set our chief delightfulness
    Where but a baiting-place is all our portion.
But still, although we fail of perfect rightfulness,
    Seek we to tame these[6] childish superfluities;   25
    Let us not wink, though void of purest sightfulness.
For what can breed[7] more peevish incongruities
    Than man to yield to female lamentations?
    Let us some grammar learn of more[8] congruities.

Plangus. If through mine[9] ears pierce any consolations[10]   30
    By wise discourse, sweet tunes, or poet's fiction;
    If aught I cease these hideous[11] exclamations,
While that my soul, she, she lives[12] in affliction;
    Then let my life long time on earth[13] maintained be,
    To wretched me the last worst malediction.   35

---

[1] we *OA, 93*: she *90*   [2] that hand *OA (ex. Je), 93*: her hand *Je, 90*   [3] mine] my *St, Bo, As*   [4] most prone] must prove *Bo, Cl, Le, As, Ph, Je* (most prove *corr. to* most prone *St*)   [5] worldly] wordly *St, Ph, 93, 98*   [6] these *OA (ex. Je), 93*: those *Je*; the *90*   [7] can breed] can yield *Da, Je, Hm*; yields *Ph*   [8] more] our *Cl, Le*   [9] mine] my *Le, Da*   [10] consolations *Cl, Le, As, Da*; consolation *St, Bo, Ph, Je, Hm, 90, 93*   [11] hideous] odious *Cl, Da*   [12] she lives] liveth *Da, Ph, Je*   [13] long time on earth] on earth long time *Cl, Le, Ph, Je*

Can I, that know¹ her sacred² parts, restrained be
    From³ any joy; know fortune's vile displacing her,
In moral⁴ rules let raging woes contained be?
Can I forget, when they in prison placing her,
    With swelling heart in spite and due disdainfulness,
She lay for dead, till I helped with unlacing her?
Can I forget from how much mourning⁵ plainfulness⁶
    With diamond in window-glass she graved,
'Erona, die, and end this⁷ ugly painfulness?'
Can I forget in how strange phrase she craved
    That quickly they would her burn, drown,⁸ or smother,
As if by death she only might be saved?
Then let me eke forget one hand from other;
    Let me forget that Plangus I am called;
    Let me forget I am son to my mother;
But if my memory must thus be thralled
    To that strange stroke which conquered all my senses,
Can thoughts⁹ still thinking so rest unappalled?¹⁰

Basilius. Who still doth seek against himself offences,
    What pardon can avail? Or who employs him
To hurt himself, what shields¹¹ can be defences?
Woe to poor man: each outward thing annoys him
    In divers kinds; yet, as he were not filled,
He heaps in inward¹² grief that¹³ most destroys him.
Thus¹⁴ is our thought with pain for thistles tilled;
    Thus be our noblest parts dried up with sorrow;
Thus is our mind with too much minding spilled.
One day lays up stuff of grief for the morrow,
    And whose good haps do leave him unprovided,
Condoling cause of friendship he will borrow.
Betwixt the good and shade of good divided,
    We pity deem that which but weakness is –
So are we from our high creation slided.
But Plangus, lest I may your sickness miss,
    Or rubbing, hurt the sore, I here do end.
The ass did hurt when he did think to kiss.

---

¹ know] knew *Cl, Le, 98,13* ² sacred] secret *Ph, Je, Hm* ³ From *OA (ex. Da), 93,* for *Da, 90* ⁴ moral] mortal *Da, Ph, Je* ⁵ mourning] mournful *Bo, Je* ⁶ plainfulness] painfulness *Le, Ph, Je, 98,13* ⁷ this *OA, 93:* thy *90* ⁸ drown] down *Cl, Hm* ⁹ thoughts] thought *Cl, Le* ¹⁰ om. *Je* ¹¹ shields] shield *As, Ph* ¹² inward] outward *Da, 93* ¹³ that *OA, 93:* which *90* ¹⁴ Thus] This *Bo, Le, Je*

When Zelmane had read it over, marvelling very much of the speech of Erona's death and therefore desirous to know further of it (but more desirous to hear Philoclea speak), 'Most excellent lady,' said she, 'one may be little the wiser for reading this[1] dialogue, since it neither sets forth what this Plangus is, nor what Erona is, nor what the cause should be which threatens her with death and him with sorrow; therefore I would humbly crave to understand the particular discourse thereof, because, I must confess, something in my travel I have heard of this strange matter, which I would be glad to find by so sweet an authority confirmed.'

'The truth is,' answered Philoclea, 'that after he knew my father to be prince of this country, while he hoped to prevail something with him in a great request he made unto him, he was content to open fully unto him[2] the estate both of himself and of that lady, which with my sister's help,' said she, 'who remembers it better than I, I will declare unto you; and first, of Erona, being the chief subject of this discourse, this story, with more tears and exclamations than I list to spend about it, he recounted.

'Of[3] late there reigned a king in Lycia,[4] who had for the blessing of his marriage this only daughter of his, Erona, a princess worthy, for her beauty, as much praise as beauty may be praiseworthy. This Princess Erona, being nineteen years of age, seeing the country of Lycia[5] so much devoted to Cupid as that in every place his naked pictures and images were superstitiously adored, either moved thereunto by the esteeming that could be no godhead which could breed wickedness, or the shamefast consideration of such nakedness, procured so much of her father as utterly to pull down and deface all those statues and pictures; which how terribly he punished (for to that the Lycians[6] impute it) quickly after appeared; for she had not lived a year longer when she was stricken with most obstinate love to a young man but of mean parentage in her father's court, named Antiphilus – so mean as that he was but the son of her nurse, and by that means (without other desert) became known of her. Now so evil could she conceal her fire, and so wilfully persevered she in it, that her father offering her the marriage of the great Tiridates, king of Armenia, who desired her more than the joys of heaven, she for Antiphilus' sake refused it. Many ways her father sought to withdraw her from it, sometimes persuasions, sometimes threatenings, once hiding Antiphilus and giving her to understand that he was fled the country; lastly, making a solemn execution to be done of another, under the name of

---

[1] this *Cm, 93*: the *90* [2] unto him] *om. 93* [3] recounted. 'Of *Cm, 93*: recounted.' Chap. 13. Erona, irreligious gainst love, must love the base Antiphilus; is loved, pursued, and beleaguered by the great Tiridates; the two Greek princes aid her; they combat with two kings, Antiphilus with Plangus; they conquerors, he prisoner; Erona's hard-choice to redeem him; Tiridates slain, Antiphilus delivered; Artaxia chased by the two princes, and her hate to them. 'Of *90* [4] Lycia] Lydia *OA, Cm, 93* [5] Lycia] Lydia *OA, Cm, 93* [6] Lycians] Lydians *Cm, 93*

Antiphilus, whom he kept in prison. But neither she liked persuasions, nor feared threatenings, nor changed for absence; and when she thought him dead, she sought all means, as well by poison as knife,[1] to send her soul, at least, to be married in the eternal church with him. This so brake the tender father's heart that, leaving things as he found them, he shortly after died. Then forthwith Erona, being seized of the crown, and arming her will with authority, sought to advance her affection to the holy title of matrimony.

'But before she could accomplish all the solemnities, she was overtaken with a war the King Tiridates made upon her, only for her person, towards whom, for her ruin, love had kindled his cruel heart – indeed cruel, and tyrannous; for being far too strong in the field, he spared not man, woman, and child, but (as though there could be found no foil to set forth the extremity of his love but extremity of hatred) wrote as it were the sonnets of his love in the blood, and tuned them in the[2] cries, of her subjects (although his fair sister Artaxia, who would accompany him in the army, sought all means to appease his fury); till lastly he besieged Erona in her best city, vowing to win her or lose his life. And now had he brought her to the point either of a woeful consent or a ruinous denial, when there came thither (following the course which virtue and fortune led them) two excellent young princes, Pyrocles and Musidorus, the one prince of Macedon, the other of Thessalia – two princes, as Plangus said (and he witnessed his saying with sighs and tears), the most accomplished[3] both in body and mind that the sun ever looked upon.'

While Philoclea spake those words, 'Oh, sweet words!' thought Zelmane to herself, 'which are not only a praise to me, but a praise to praise itself, which out of that mouth issueth!'

'These two princes,' said Philoclea, 'as well to help the weaker (especially being a lady) as to save a Greek people from being ruined by such whom we call and count barbarous, gathering together such of the honestest Lycians as would venture their lives to succour their princess, giving order by a secret message they sent into the city that they should issue with all force at an appointed time, they set upon Tiridates' camp with so well-guided a fierceness that being of both sides assaulted he was like to be overthrown, but that this Plangus, being general of Tiridates' horsemen (especially aided by the two mighty men, Euardes and Barzanes), rescued the footmen, even almost defeated, but yet could not bar the princes with their succours both of men and victual to enter the city; which when Tiridates found would make the war long (which length seemed to him worse than a languishing consumption), he made a challenge of three princes in his retinue against

---

[1] as knife *OA, Cm, 93*: as by knife *90*   [2] the *Cm, 93*: the *90*   [3] accomplished *Cm, 93*: accnoplished *90*

those two princes and Antiphilus, and that thereupon the quarrel should be decided – with compact that neither side should help his fellow, but of whose side the more overcame, with him the victory should remain.

'Antiphilus, though Erona chose rather to bide the brunt of war than venture him, yet could not for shame refuse the offer, especially since the two strangers that had no interest in it did willingly accept it; besides that, he saw it like enough that the people, weary of the miseries of war, would rather give him up if they saw him shrink than for his sake venture their ruin, considering that the challengers were far of greater worthiness than himself. So it was agreed upon, and against Pyrocles was Euardes, king of Bithynia; Barzanes of Hyrcania against Musidorus (two men that thought the world scarce able to resist them); and against Antiphilus he placed this same Plangus, being his own cousin-german and son to the king of Iberia. Now so it fell out that Musidorus slew Barzanes, and Pyrocles Euardes (which victory those princes esteemed above all that ever they had); but of the other side, Plangus took Antiphilus prisoner, under which colour, as if the matter had been equal (though indeed it was not, the greater part being overcome of his side), Tiridates continued his war; and to bring Erona to a compelled yielding sent her word that he would, the third morrow after, before the walls of the town, strike off Antiphilus' head, without his suit in that space were granted; adding withal (because he had heard of her desperate affection) that, if in the meantime she did herself any hurt, what tortures could be devised should be laid upon Antiphilus.

'Then, lo, if Cupid be a god, or that the tyranny of our own thoughts seem as a god unto us – but whatsoever it was, then it did set forth the miserableness of his effects, she being drawn to two contraries by one cause (for the love of him commanded her to yield to no other; the love of him commanded her[1] to preserve his life), which knot might well be cut, but untied it could not be; so that love, in her passions like a right makebate, whispered to both sides arguments of quarrel: "What!" said he of the one side, "doost thou love Antiphilus, O Erona? And shall Tiridates enjoy thy body? With what eyes wilt thou look upon Antiphilus when he shall know that another possesseth thee? But if thou wilt do it, canst thou do it? Canst thou force thy heart? Think with thyself: if this man have thee, thou shalt never have more part of Antiphilus than if he were dead – but thus much more, that the affection shall be still gnawing,[2] and the remorse still present. Death perhaps will cool the rage of thy affection; where thus, thou shalt ever love, and ever lack. Think this beside: if thou marry Tiridates, Antiphilus is so excellent a man that long he cannot be from being in some high place

---

[1] her *Cm, 93*: him *90* [2] be still gnawing *Cm, 93*: be gnawing *90*

married. Canst thou suffer that too? If another kill him, he doth him the wrong; if thou abuse thy body, thou doost him the wrong. His death is a work of nature, and either now or at another time he shall die; but it shall be thy work, thy shameful work which is in thy power to shun, to make him live to see thy faith falsified and his bed defiled."

'But when love had well kindled that part[1] of her thoughts, then went he to the other side: "What!" said he, "O Erona! And is thy love of Antiphilus come to that point, as thou doost now make it a question whether he shall die or no? Oh, excellent affection! which for too much love will see his head off! Mark well the reasons of the other side, and thou shalt see it is but love of thyself which so disputeth: 'Thou canst not abide Tiridates'– this is but love of thyself; 'Thou shalt be ashamed to look upon him afterward'– this is but fear of shame and love of thyself; 'Thou shalt want him as much then'– this is but love of thyself; 'He shall be married'– if he be, well, why should that grieve thee but for love of thyself? No, no. Pronounce these words, if thou canst: 'Let Antiphilus die.'"

'Then the images of each side stood before her understanding: one time she thought she saw Antiphilus dying, another time she thought Antiphilus saw her by Tiridates enjoyed; twenty times calling for a servant to carry message of yielding, but before he came the mind was altered; she blushed when she considered the effect of granting, she was pale when she remembered the fruits of denial. As for[2] weeping, sighing, wringing her hands, and tearing her hair, were indifferent of both sides. Easily she would have agreed to have broken all disputations with her own death, but that the fear of Antiphilus' furder torments stayed her. At length, even the evening before the day appointed of his death, the determination of yielding prevailed, especially growing upon a message of Antiphilus, who with all the conjuring terms he could devise besought her to save his life – upon any condition.[3] But she had no sooner sent her messenger to Tiridates but her mind changed, and she went to the two young princes, Pyrocles and Musidorus; and falling down at their feet desired them to try some way for her deliverance, showing herself resolved not to overlive Antiphilus, nor yet to yield to Tiridates.

'They, that knew not what she had done in private, prepared that night accordingly, and as sometimes it falls out that what is inconstancy seems cunning, so did this change indeed stand in as good stead as a witty dissimulation, for it made the king as reckless as them diligent; so that in the dead time of the night the princes issued out of the town, with whom she would needs go, either to die herself or rescue Antiphilus, having no armour nor weapon but affection. And I cannot tell you how – by what device, though

---

[1] part] party 93   [2] denial. As for] denying. For 93   [3] condition] conditions 93

Plangus at large described it – the conclusion was, the wonderful valour of the two princes so prevailed that Antiphilus was succoured and the king slain. Plangus was then the chief man left in the camp; and therefore, seeing no other remedy, conveyed in safety into her country Artaxia, now queen of Armenia, who with true lamentations made known to the world that her new greatness did no way comfort her in respect of her brother's loss, whom she studied all means possible to revenge upon every one of the occasioners, having (as she thought) overthrown her brother by a most abominable treason; insomuch that, being at home, she proclaimed great rewards to any private man, and herself in marriage to any prince, that would destroy Pyrocles and Musidorus. But thus was Antiphilus redeemed, and (though against the consent of all her nobility) married to Erona, in which case the two Greek princes, being called away by another adventure, left them.

'But[1] now methinks, as I have read some poets, who when they intend to tell some horrible matter they bid men shun the hearing of it, so, if I do not desire you to stop your ears from me, yet may I well desire a breathing-time before I am to tell the execrable treason of Antiphilus that brought her to this misery; and withal wish you all, that from all mankind indeed you stop your ears. Oh most happy were we, if we did set our loves one upon another!' – and as she spake that word, her cheeks in red letters writ more than her tongue did speak. 'And therefore, since I have named Plangus, I pray you, sister,' said she, 'help me with the rest, for I have held the stage long enough; and if it please you to make his fortune known, as I have done Erona's, I will after take heart again to go on with his falsehood, and so between us both my Lady Zelmane shall understand both the cause and parties of this lamentation.'

'Nay, I beshrow me then!' said Miso. 'I will none of that; I promise you, as long as I have the government, I will first have my tale – and then my Lady Pamela, my Lady Zelmane, and my daughter Mopsa,' for Mopsa was then returned from Amphialus, 'may draw cuts, and the shortest cut speak first. For I tell you, and this may be suffered, when you are married you will have first and last word of your husbands.'

The ladies laughed to see with what an eager earnestness she looked, having threatening not only in her ferret-eyes, but, while she spake, her nose seeming to threaten her chin, and her shaking limbs one to threaten another. But there was no remedy; they must obey. And Miso, sitting on the ground with her knees up, and her hands upon her knees, tuning her voice with many a quavering cough, thus discoursed unto them.

---

[1] them. 'But *Cm*, 93: them.' Chap. 14. Philoclea's narration broken off by Miso; her old-wives tale and ballad against Cupid; their drawing cuts for tales; Mopsa's tale of the old cut cut off by the ladies to return to their stories. 'But 90

'I tell you true,' said she, 'whatsoever you think of me, you will one day be as I am; and I, simple though I sit here, thought once my penny as good silver as some of you do; and if my father had not played the hasty fool (it is no lie I tell you) I might have had another-gaines husband than Dametas. But let that pass, God amend him; and yet I speak it not without good cause. You are full of[1] your tittle-tattling[2] of Cupid: here is Cupid, and there is Cupid. I will tell you now what a good old woman told me, what an old wise man told her, what a great learned clerk told him, and gave it him in writing; and here I have it in my prayer-book.'

'I pray you,' said Philoclea, 'let us see it and read it.'

'No haste but good,' said Miso, 'you shall first know how I came by it. I was a young girl of a seven-and-twenty year old, and I could not go thorough the street of our village but I might hear the young men talk: "Oh the pretty little eyes of Miso!", "Oh the fine thin lips of Miso!", "Oh the goodly fat hands of Miso!" – besides how well a certain wrying I had of my neck became me; then the one would wink with one eye, and the other cast daisies at me. I must confess, seeing so many amorous, it made me set up my peacock's tail with the highest; which when this good old woman perceived (Oh the good wold woman! well may the bones rest of the good wold woman!) she called me to her, into her house (I remember full well, it stood in the lane as you go to the barber's shop – all the town knew her! there was a great loss of her!), she called me to her, and taking first a sop of wine to comfort her heart (it was of the same wine that comes out of Candia, which we pay so dear for now-a-days, and in that good world was very good cheap), she called me to her. "Minion," said she – indeed, I was a pretty one in those days, though I say it, "I see a number of lads that love you. Well," said she, "I say no more. Do you know what love is?" With that, she brought me into a corner where there was painted a foul fiend, I trow, for he had a pair of horns like a bull, his feet cloven, as many eyes upon his body as my grey mare hath dapples, and for all the world so placed. This monster sat like a hangman upon a pair of gallows. In his right hand he was painted holding a crown of laurel, in his left hand a purse of money; and out of his mouth hung a lace, of two fair pictures of a man and a woman; and such a countenance he showed, as if he would persuade folks by those allurements to come thither and be hanged. I, like a tender-hearted wench, skriked out, for fear of the devil. "Well," said she, "this same is even love; therefore do what thou list with all those fellows, one after another, and it recks not much what they do to thee, so it be in secret. But, upon my charge, never love none of them." "Why mother," said I, "could such

---

[1] full of] full in 93   [2] tittle-tattling] tittle-tattlings 93

a thing come from the belly of the fair Venus?[1] "– for a few days before, our priest, between him and me, had told me the whole story of Venus. "Tush!" said she, "they are all deceived", and therewith gave me this book, which, she said, a great maker of ballets had given to an old painter, who (for a little pleasure) had bestowed both book and picture of her. "Read there," said she, "and thou shalt see that his mother was a cow, and the false Argus his father." And so, she gave me this book; and there now you may read it.'

With that, the remembrance of the good old woman made her make such a face to weep as, if it were not sorrow, it was the carcass of sorrow that appeared there. But while her tears came out, like rain falling upon dirty furrows, the latter end of her prayer-book was read among these ladies; which contained this:

> Poor painters oft with silly poets join
> To fill the world with strange but vain conceits:
> One brings the stuff, the other stamps the coin,
> Which breeds nought else but glozes of deceits.
>   Thus painters Cupid paint, thus poets do,
>   A naked god, young, blind,[2] with arrows two.
>
> Is he a god, that ever flies the light?
> Or naked he, disguised in all untruth?
> If he be blind, how hitteth he so right?
> How is he young, that tamed old Phoebus' youth?
>   But arrows two, and tipped with gold or lead:
>   Some hurt accuse a third, with horny head.
>
> No, nothing so; an old false knave he is,
> By Argus got on Io, then a cow,
> What time, for her, Juno her Jove did miss,
> And charge of her to Argus did allow.
>   Mercury killed his false sire for this act,
>   His dam, a beast, was pardoned beastly fact.
>
> With father's death, and mother's guilty shame,
> With Jove's disdain at such a rival's seed,
> The wretch, compelled, a runagate became,
> And learned what ill a miser[3] state doth breed;
>   To lie, feign, gloze, to steal, pry, and[4] accuse,
>   Naught in himself, each other to abuse.

---

[1] Venus *Cm, 93*: Fenus *90* [2] young, blind] blind, young *OA, 93* [3] miser] wretched *Bo*; miser's *Le, Da, Je, Hm* [4] feign, gloze, to steal, pry, and] to steal, to pry, and to *OA, 93*

Yet bears he still his parents' stately gifts,
A horned head, cloven foot,[1] and thousand eyes,
Some gazing still, some winking wily shifts,
With long large ears where never rumour dies.
    His horned[2] head doth seem the heaven to spite:
    His cloven foot[3] doth never tread aright.
Thus half a man, with man he daily haunts,
Clothed in the shape which soonest may deceive:
Thus half a beast, each beastly vice he plants
In those weak hearts that his advice receive.
    He prowls each place still in new colours decked,
    Sucking one's ill, another to infect.
To narrow breasts he comes all wrapped in gain;
To swelling hearts he shines in honour's fire;
To open eyes all beauties he doth rain;
Creeping to each with flatt'ring of desire.
    But, for that love's desire most[4] rules the eyes,
    Therein[5] his name, there his chief triumph lies.
Millions of years this old drivel Cupid lives;
While still more wretch, more wicked he doth prove:
Till now at length that Jove him office gives
(At Juno's suit who much did Argus love)
    In this our world a hangman for to be
    Of all those fools that will have all they see.

These[6] ladies made sport at the description and story of Cupid; but Zelmane could scarce suffer those blasphemies (as she took them) to be read, but humbly besought Pamela she would perform her sister's request of the other part of the story.

'Noble lady,' answered she (beautifying her face with a sweet smiling, and the sweetness of her smiling with the beauty of her face), 'since I am born a prince's daughter, let me not give example of disobedience. My governess will have us draw cuts; and therefore I pray you let us do so, and so, perhaps, it will light upon you to entertain this company with some story of your own – and it is reason our ears should be willinger to hear, as your tongue is abler to deliver.'

'I will think,' answered Zelmane, 'excellent princess, my tongue of some value, if it can procure your tongue thus much to favour me.'

---

[1] foot] feet *Cl, Le, Da, Ph,* 93   [2] horned] horny *Bo, Da*   [3] foot] feet *Cl, Le, Ph*   [4] love's desire most] love is worst which *OA* (textitex. *Le, Ph*), 93; love is worse which *Le*; love is most which *Ph*   [5] Therein] Thereon *OA,* 93   [6] These] The 93

But Pamela pleasantly persisting to have fortune their judge, they set hands; and Mopsa (though at the first for squeamishness going up and down with her head, like a boat in a storm) put to her golden golls among them; and blind fortune (that saw not the colour of them) gave her the pre-eminence. And so, being her time to speak, wiping her mouth (as there was good cause), she thus tumbled into her matter.

'In time past,' said she, 'there was a king (the mightiest man in all his country), that had by his wife the fairest daughter that ever did eat pap. Now this king did keep a great house, that everybody might come and take their meat freely. So, one day, as his daughter was sitting in her window playing upon a harp, as sweet as any rose, and combing her head with a comb all of precious stones, there came in a knight into the court upon a goodly horse – one, hair of gold; and the other, of silver. And so, the knight, casting up his eyes to the window, did fall into such love with her that he grew not worth the bread he eat; till many a sorry day going over his head, with daily diligence and grisly groans he wan her affection, so that they agreed to run away together. And so, in May, when all true hearts rejoice, they stale out of the castle, without staying so much as for their breakfast. Now, forsooth, as they went together, often all to-kissing one another, the knight told her he was brought up among the water-nymphs, who had so bewitched him that if he were ever asked his name he must presently vanish away; and therefore charged her upon his blessing that she never ask him what he was, nor whether he would. And so, a great while she kept his commandment; till once, passing through a cruel wilderness, as dark as pitch, her mouth so watered that she could not choose but ask him the question. And then he, making the grievousest complaints (that would have melted a tree to have heard them), vanished quite away; and she lay down, casting forth as pitiful cries as any shritch-owl. But having lain so, wet by the rain and burned by the sun, five days and five nights, she gat up and went over many a high hill and many a deep river, till she came to an aunt's house of hers, and came and cried to her for help. And she, for pity, gave her a nut, and bad her never open her nut till she was come to the extremest misery that ever tongue could speak of. And so, she went, and she went, and never rested the evening where she went in the morning, till she came to a second aunt. And she gave her another nut.'

'Now good Mopsa,' said the sweet Philoclea, 'I pray thee, at my request, keep this tale till my marriage-day, and I promise thee that the best gown I wear that day shall be thine.'

Mopsa was very glad of the bargain, especially that it should grow a festival tale; so that Zelmane, who desired to find the uttermost what these ladies understood touching herself, and having understood the danger of Erona, of which before she had never heard (purposing with herself, as soon as this pursuit she now was in was brought to any effect, to succour her), entreated again that she might know, as well the story of Plangus, as of Erona. Philoclea referred it to her sister's perfecter remembrance, who, with so sweet a voice, and so winning a grace, as in themselves were of most forcible eloquence to procure attention, in this manner to their earnest request soon condescended.

'The[1] father of this Prince Plangus as yet lives, and is king of Iberia – a man, if the judgement of Plangus may be accepted, of no wicked nature, nor willingly doing evil – without himself mistake the evil, seeing it disguised under some form of goodness. This prince, being married at the first to a princess, who both from her ancestors and in herself was worthy of him, by her had this son, Plangus, not long after whose birth the queen, as though she had performed the message for which she was sent into the world, returned again unto her maker. The king, sealing up all thoughts of love under the image of her memory, remained a widower many years after, recompensing the grief of that disjoining from her in conjoining in himself both a fatherly and a motherly care toward her only child, Plangus; who being grown to man's age, as our own eyes may judge, could not but fertilely requite his father's fatherly education.

'This prince, while yet the errors in his nature were excused by the greenness of his youth (which took all the fault upon itself), loved a private man's wife of the principal city of that kingdom – if that may be called love which he rather did take into himself willingly than by which he was taken forcibly. It sufficeth that the young man persuaded himself he loved her, she being a woman beautiful enough, if it be possible that the outside only[2] can justly entitle a beauty. But finding such a chase as only fled to be caught, the young prince brought his affection with her to that point which ought to engrave remorse in her heart, and to paint shame upon her face; and so possessed he his desire without any interruption, he constantly favouring her, and she thinking that the enamelling of a prince's name might hide the spots of a broken wedlock. But as I have seen one that was sick of a sleeping disease could not be made wake but with pinching of him, so out of his sinful sleep, his mind, unworthy so to be lost, was not to be called to itself but by a sharp accident.

---

[1] condescended. 'The *Cm*, 93: condescended. Chap. 15. Plangus' parentage; his trick of youth, espied, and turned over by, and to, his old father; an inveigling-woman's arts; a guilty stepmother's devilish practices against Plangus; her minister's false informations; Plangus' perplexities; his father's jealousies; the queen's complots to feed the one's suspicion and work the other's overthrow; Plangus taken; delivered, flieth; is pursued with old hate and new treason; yet must he serve abroad, while a new heir is made at home; this story broken off by Basilius. 'The 90   [2] outside only] only outside 93

'It fell out that his many-times leaving of the court in undue times began to be noted, and, as princes' ears be manifold, from one to another came unto the king, who, careful of his only son, sought and found by his spies (the necessary evil servants to a king) what it was whereby he was from his better delights so diverted; whereupon the king, to give his fault the greater blow, used such means (by disguising himself) that he found them (her husband being absent) in her house together, which he did to make him the more feelingly ashamed of it; and that way he took, laying threatenings upon her, and upon him reproaches. But the poor young prince, deceived with that young opinion that if it be ever lawful to lie it is for one's lover, employed all his wit to bring his father to a better opinion. And because he might bend him from that, as he counted it, crooked conceit of her, he wrested him as much as he could possibly to the other side, not sticking with prodigal protestations to set forth her chastity – not denying his own attempt,[1] but thereby the more extolling her virtue.

'His sophistry prevailed. His father believed, and so believed that ere long (though he were already stepped into the winter of his age) he found himself warm in those desires, which were in his son far more excusable. To be short, he gave himself over unto it, and, because he would avoid the odious comparison of a young rival, sent away his son with an army to the subduing of a province lately rebelled against him (which he knew could not be a less work than of three or four years), wherein he behaved him so worthily as even to this country the fame thereof came long before his own coming; while yet his father had a speedier success, but in a far unnobler conquest: for while Plangus was away the old man (growing only in age and affection) followed his suit with all means of unhonest servants, large promises, and each thing else that might help to countervail his own unloveliness; and she (whose husband about that time died), forgetting the absent Plangus (or at least not hoping of him to obtain so aspiring a purpose), left no art unused which might keep the line from breaking whereat the fish was already taken, not drawing him violently, but letting him play himself upon the hook which he had greedily[2] swallowed; for accompanying her mourning[3] with a doleful countenance, yet neither forgetting handsomeness in her mourning garments, nor sweetness in her doleful countenance, her words were ever seasoned with sighs; and any favour she showed, bathed in tears, that affection might see cause of pity, and pity might persuade cause of affection.

'And being grown skilful in his humours, she was no less skilful in applying his humours, never suffering his fear to fall to a despair, nor his hope to hasten to an assurance. She was content he should think that she loved

---

[1] attempt *Cm, 93*: attempts *90*   [2] had greedily] had so greedily *93*   [3] mourning with] mourning garments with *93*

him, and a certain stolen look should sometimes (as though it were against her will) bewray it – but if thereupon he grew bold, he straight was encountered with a mask of virtue. And (that which seemeth most impossible unto me, for as near as I can I repeat[1] it as Plangus told it) she could not only sigh when she would (as all can do), and weep when she would (as they say some can do), but being most impudent in her heart, she could, when she would, teach her cheeks blushing, and make shamefastness the cloak of shamelessness. In sum (to leave out many particularities which he recited) she did not only use so the spur that his desire ran on, but so the bit that it ran on even in such a career as she would have it; that within a while the king, seeing with no other eyes but such as she gave him, and thinking no other[2] thoughts but such as she taught him (having at the first liberal measure of favours, then shortened of them when most his desire was inflamed), he saw no other way but marriage to satisfy his longing and her mind, as he thought, loving – but chastely loving; so that by the time Plangus returned from being notably victorious of the rebels, he found his father not only married but already a father of a son and a daughter by this woman, which though Plangus (as he had every way just cause) was grieved at, yet did his grief never bring forth either contemning of her or repining at his father.

'But she who, besides she was grown a mother and a stepmother, did read in his eyes her own fault and made his conscience her guiltiness, thought still that his presence carried her condemnation, so much the more as that she, unchastely attempting his wonted fancies, found, for the reverence of his father's bed, a bitter refusal; which breeding rather spite than shame in her (or if it were a shame, a shame not of the fault but of the repulse), she did not only (as hating him) thirst for a revenge, but (as fearing harm from him) endeavoured to do harm unto him.

'Therefore did she try the uttermost of her wicked wit how to overthrow him in the foundation of his strength, which was in the favour of his father; which because she saw strong both in nature and desert, it required the more cunning how to undermine it. And therefore shunning the ordinary trade of hireling sycophants, she made her praises of him to be accusations, and her advancing him to be his ruin: for first with words nearer admiration than liking she would extol his excellencies (the goodliness of his shape, the power of his wit, the valiantness of his courage, the fortunateness of his successes), so as the father might find in her a singular love towards him – nay, she shunned not to kindle some few sparks of jealousy in him. Thus having gotten an opinion in his father that she was far from meaning mischief to the son, then fell she to praise him with no less vehemency of

---

[1] I can I repeat] I can repeat *Cm, 98, 13*   [2] thinking no other] thinking on other *93*; thinking on no other *98, 13*

affection, but with much more cunning of malice, for then she sets forth the liberty of his mind, the highflying of his thoughts, the fitness in him to bear rule, the singular love the subjects bare him; that it was doubtful whether his wit were greater in winning their favours, or his courage in employing their favours; that he was not born to live a subject-life, each action of his bearing in it majesty ("Such a kingly entertainment! such a kingly magnificence! such a kingly heart for enterprises!"), especially remembering those virtues which in a successor are no more honoured by the subjects than suspected of the princes. Then would she, by putting off objections, bring in objections to her husband's head, already infected with suspicion: "Nay," would she say, "I dare take it upon my death that he is no such son as many, of like might, have been, who loved greatness so well as to build their greatness upon their father's ruin. Indeed, ambition, like love, can abide no lingering, and ever urgeth on his own successes, hating nothing but what may stop them. But the gods forbid we should ever once dream of any such thing in him! who perhaps might be content that you and the world should know what he can do, but the more power he hath to hurt, the more admirable is his praise that he will not hurt"; then ever remembering to strengthen the suspicion of his estate with private jealousy of her love, doing him excessive honour when he was in presence, and repeating his pretty speeches and graces in his absence; besides, causing him to be employed in all such dangerous matters as either he should perish in them, or, if he prevailed, they should increase his glory – which she made a weapon to wound him; until she found that suspicion began already to speak for itself, and that her husband's ears were grown hungry of rumours, and his eyes prying into every accident.

'Then took she help to her of a servant near about her husband, whom she knew to be of a hasty ambition, and such a one who, wanting true sufficiency to raise him, would make a ladder of any mischief. Him she useth to deal more plainly in alleging causes of jealousy, making him know the fittest times, when her husband already was stirred that way. And so, they two with divers ways nourished one humour, like musicians that, singing divers parts, make one music; he sometime with fearful countenance would desire the king to look to himself, for that all the court and city were full of whisperings and expectation of some sudden change, upon what ground himself knew not; another time, he would counsel the king to make much of his son and hold his favour, for that it was too late now to keep him under; now, seeming to fear himself, because, he said, Plangus loved none of them that were great about his father; lastly, breaking with him directly (making a sorrowful countenance and an humble gesture bear false witness for his true meaning) that he found, not only soldiery, but people, weary of his government, and all their affections bent upon Plangus; both he and the queen concurring in strange dreams, and each thing else that in a mind already perplexed might breed astonishment, so that within a while all Plangus' actions began to be translated into the language of suspicion (which, though Plangus found, yet could he not avoid), even contraries being driven to draw one yoke of argument: if he were magnificent, he spent much with an aspiring intent; if he spared, he heaped much with an aspiring intent; if he spake courteously, he angled the people's hearts; if he were silent, he mused upon some dangerous plot – in sum, if he could have turned himself to as many forms as Proteus, every form should have been made tedious.[1]

'But so it fell out that a mere trifle gave them occasion of further proceeding. The king one morning going to a vineyard that lay along the hill where his[2] castle stood, he saw a vine-labourer that, finding a bough broken, took a branch of the same bough for want of another thing, and tied it about the place broken. The king asking the fellow what he did, "Marry," said he, "I make the son bind the father!" This word, finding the king already superstitious through suspicion, amazed him straight, as a presage of his own fortune; so that returning, and breaking with his wife how much he misdoubted his estate, she made such gainsaying answers as, while they strave, strave to be overcome.

'But even while the doubts most boiled, she thus nourished them. She underhand dealt with the principal men of that country that at the great parliament which was then to be held they should, in the name of all the estates, persuade the king, being now stepped deeply into old age, to make Plangus his associate in government with him, assuring them that not only she would join with them, but that the father himself would take it kindly, charging them not to acquaint Plangus withal, for that perhaps it might be harmful unto him if the king should find that he were a party. They, who thought they might do it not only willingly (because they loved him), and truly (because such indeed was the mind of the people), but safely (because she who ruled the king was agreed thereto), accomplished her counsel, she indeed keeping promise of vehement persuading the same, which the more she and they did, the more she knew her husband would fear – and hate the cause of his fear. Plangus found this, and humbly protested against such desire, or will to accept; but the more he protested, the more his father thought he dissembled, accounting his integrity to be but a cunning face of falsehood; and therefore, delaying the desire of his subjects, attended some fit occasion to lay hands upon his son – which his wife thus brought to pass.

'She caused that same minister of hers to go unto Plangus, and enabling

---

[1] tedious] hideous 93   [2] where his] whereupon his 93

his words with great show of faith, and endearing them with desire of secrecy, to tell him that he found his ruin conspired by his stepmother with certain of the noble men of that country, the king himself giving his consent, and that few days should pass before the putting it in practice; withal discovering the very truth indeed, with what cunning his stepmother had proceeded. This, agreeing with Plangus' own opinion, made him give him the better credit, yet not so far as to fly out of his country (according to the naughty fellow's persuasion), but to attend, and to see further; whereupon the fellow, by the direction of his mistress, told him one day that the same night, about one of the clock, the king had appointed to have his wife and those noble men together to deliberate of their manner of proceeding against Plangus, and therefore offered him that, if himself would agree, he would bring him into a place where he should hear all that passed, and so have the more reason (both to himself and to the world) to seek his safety. The poor Plangus, being subject to that only disadvantage of honest hearts, credulity, was persuaded by him; and arming himself because of his late-going, was closely conveyed into the place appointed.

'In the meantime, his stepmother making all her gestures cunningly counterfeit a miserable affliction, she lay almost grovelling on the floor of her chamber, not suffering anybody to comfort her; until, they calling for her husband, and he held off with long inquiry, at length she told him (even almost crying out every word) that she was weary of her life, since she was brought to that plunge either to conceal her husband's murther, or accuse her son, who had ever been more dear than a son unto her. Then, with many interruptions and exclamations, she told him that her son Plangus, soliciting her in the old affection between them, had besought her to put her[1] helping hand to the death of the king, assuring her that, though all the laws in the world were against it, he would marry her when he were king.

'She had not fully said thus much (with many pitiful digressions) when in comes the same fellow that brought Plangus; and running himself out of breath, fell at the king's feet, beseeching him to save himself, for that there was a man with sword[2] drawn in the next room. The king, affrighted, went out and called his guard, who entering the place found indeed Plangus, with his sword in his hand but not naked – but standing suspiciously enough to one already suspicious. The king, thinking he had put up his sword because of the noise, never took leisure to hear his answer, but made him prisoner, meaning the next morning to put him to death in the market-place.

'But the day had no sooner opened the eyes and ears of his friends and followers but that there was a little army of them who came, and by force

---

[1] to put her] to put to her *Cm, 13*   [2] with sword] with a sword *93*

delivered him, although numbers on the other side (abused with the fine framing of their report) took arms for the king. But Plangus, though he might have used the force of his friends to revenge his wrong and get the crown, yet the natural love of his father, and hate to make their suspicion seem just, caused him rather to choose a voluntary exile than to make his father's death the purchase of his life; and therefore went he to Tiridates, whose mother was his father's sister, living in his court eleven or twelve years, ever hoping by his intercession (and his own desert) to recover his father's grace; at the end of which time the war of Erona happened, which my sister, with the cause thereof, discoursed unto you.

'But his father had so deeply engraved the suspicion in his heart that he thought his flight rather to proceed of a fearful guiltiness than of an humble faithfulness, and therefore continued his hate with such vehemency that he did ever[1] hate his nephew Tiridates, and afterwards, his niece Artaxia (because in their court he received countenance), leaving no means unattempted of destroying his son – among other, employing that wicked servant of his, who undertook to empoison him. But his cunning disguised him not so well but that the watchful servants of Plangus did discover him; whereupon the wretch was taken and (before his well-deserved execution) by torture forced to confess the particularities of this, which in general I have told you; which confession autentically set down, though Tiridates with solemn embassage sent it to the king, wrought no effect, for the king, having put the reins of the government into his wives hand, never did so much as read it, but sent it straight by her to be considered, so as they rather heaped more hatred upon Plangus for the death of their servant.

'And now finding that his absence and their reports had much diminished the wavering people's affection towards Plangus (with advancing fit persons for faction, and granting great immunities to the commons), they prevailed so far as to cause the son of the second wife (called Palladius) to be proclaimed successor, and Plangus quite excluded, so that Plangus was driven to continue his serving Tiridates, as he did in the war against Erona, and brought home Artaxia, as my sister told you; when Erona, by the treason of Antiphilus – '.

But at that word she stopped, for Basilius, not able longer to abide their absence, came suddenly among them; and with smiling countenance telling Zelmane he was afraid she had stolen away his daughters, invited them to follow the sun's counsel in going then to their lodging – for indeed, the sun was ready to set. They yielded, Zelmane meaning some other time to understand the story of Antiphilus' treason and Erona's danger, whose case[2]

---

[1] ever] even 93   [2] case] cause 93

she greatly tendered. But Miso had no sooner espied Basilius but that, as spitefully as her rotten voice could utter it, she set forth the sauciness of Amphialus. But Basilius only attended what Zelmane's opinion was, who though she hated Amphialus, yet the nobility of her courage prevailed over it, and she desired he might be pardoned that youthful error (considering the reputation he had, to be one of the best knights in the world), so as hereafter he governed himself as one remembering his fault. Basilius, giving the infinite terms of praises to Zelmane's both valour in conquering and pitifulness in pardoning, commanded no more words to be made of it, since such, he thought, was her pleasure.

And so[1] brought he them up to visit his wife, where between her and him the poor Zelmane received a tedious entertainment, oppressed with being loved almost as much as with loving. Basilius, not so wise in covering his passion, could make his tongue go almost no other pace but to run into those immoderate praises which the foolish lover thinks[2] short of his mistress, though they reach far beyond the heavens; but Gynecia, whom womanly modesty did more outwardly bridle, yet did oftentimes use the advantage of her sex in kissing Zelmane as she sate upon her bedside by her, which was but still more and more sweet incense to cast upon the fire wherein her heart was sacrificed. Once, Zelmane could[3] not stir but that, as if they had been poppets whose motion[4] stood only upon her pleasure, Basilius with serviceable steps, Gynecia with greedy eyes, would follow her. Basilius' mind Gynecia well knew, and could have found in her heart to laugh at, if mirth could have borne any proportion with her fortune; but all Gynecia's actions were interpreted by Basilius as proceeding from jealousy of his amorousness – Zelmane betwixt both, like the poor child whose father, while he beats him, will make him believe it is for love, or like the sick man to whom the physician swears the ill-tasting wallowish medicine he proffers is of a good taste. Their love was hateful, their courtesy troublesome; their presence cause of her absence thence where not only her light, but her life, consisted.

'Alas,' thought she to herself, 'dear Dorus, what odds is there between thy destiny and mine! for thou hast to do in thy pursuit but with shepherdish folks, who trouble thee with a little envious care and affected diligence, but I, besides that I have now Miso, the worst of thy devils, let loose upon me, am waited on by princes, and watched by the two wakeful eyes of love and jealousy. Alas, incomparable Philoclea, thou ever seest me, but dost never

---

[1] pleasure. And so *Cm*: pleasure. Chap. 16. The cumber of Zelmane's love and lovers; Gynecia's love-lamentations; Zelmane's passions and sonnet; Basilius' wooing and Zelmane's answers; Philoclea feed attorney to plead her father's cause. So *90*; pleasure. So *93*   [2] lover thinks] lover ever thinks *OA (ex. Qu)*   [3] could] would *Qu, Cm*   [4] motion] motions *OA (ex. Qu)*

see me as I am; thou hearest willingly all that I dare say, and I dare not say that which were most fit for thee to hear. Alas, who ever but I was imprisoned in liberty, and banished, being still present? To whom but me have lovers been jailers, and honour a captivity?'

But the night coming on with her silent steps upon them, they parted each from other (if, at least, they could be parted, of whom every one did live in another) and went about to flatter sleep with their beds, that disdained to bestow itself liberally upon such eyes which by their will would ever be looking – and in least measure upon Gynecia, who when Basilius after long tossing was gotten asleep, and the cheerful comfort of the lights removed from her, kneeling up in her bed, began with a soft voice and swollen heart to renew the curses of her birth; and then in a manner embracing her bed, 'Ah chastest bed of mine,' said she, 'which never heretofore couldst accuse me of one defiled thought, how canst thou now receive this disastered[1] changeling? Happy, happy be they only which be not; and thy blessedness only in this respect thou mayst feel – that thou hast no feeling!' With that she furiously tare off great[2] part of her fair hair. 'Take here, O forgotten virtue,' said she, 'this miserable sacrifice. While my soul was clothed with modesty, that was a comely ornament; now, why should nature crown that head, which is so wicked as her only despair is she cannot be enough wicked?'

More she would have said, but that Basilius, awaked with the noise, took her in his arms and began to comfort her, the goodman thinking it was all for a jealous love of him – which humour, if she would a little have maintained[3] perchance it might have weakened his new-conceived fancies. But he, finding her answers wandering from the purpose, left her to herself, glad the next morning to take the advantage of a sleep (which a little before day, overwatched with sorrow, her tears had as it were sealed up in her eyes) to have the more conference with Zelmane, who, baited on this fashion by these two lovers, and ever kept from any[4] mean[5] to declare herself, found in herself a daily increase of her violent desires – like a river, the more swelling, the more his current is stopped.

The chief recreation she could find in her[6] anguish was sometimes to visit that place where first she was so happy as to see the cause of her unhap.[7] There would she kiss the ground and thank the trees, bliss the air, and do dutiful reverence to everything that she thought did accompany her at their[8] first meeting; then return again to her inward thoughts, sometimes despair darkening all her imaginations, sometimes the active passion of love chee-

---

[1] disastered] disaltered *Bo*; disordered *Da*; om. *Ph*; distressed *Qu*; dastred *Cm* [2] great] a great *Cl, Ph, Qu* [3] maintained] seconded *Da, Ph, Je, Qu* [4] from any] for many *93 (uncorr.)*; form any *93 (corr.)* [5] mean] means *OA (ex. Je)* [6] in her] in all her *OA (ex. Bo, Ph)* [7] unhap] hap *Da*; unhappiness *Ph*; mishap *Je*; unhappy *Qu* [8] their] the *OA (ex. Cl, Je, Qu)*; her *Je, Qu*

ring and clearing her invention how to unbar that cumbersome hindrance of her two ill-matched lovers. But this morning Basilius himself gave her good occasion to go beyond them, for having combed and tricked himself more curiously than any time forty winters before, coming where Zelmane was he found her given over to her musical muses, to the great pleasure of the good old Basilius, who retired himself behind a tree, while[1] she with a most sweet voice did utter these passionate verses:

> Loved I am, and yet complain of love;
> As loving not, accused, in love I die.
> When pity most I crave, I cruel prove;
> Still seeking love, love found as much I fly.[2]
> Burnt in myself, I muse at others' fire;
> What I call wrong, I do the same, and more;
> Barred of my will, I have beyond desire;
> I wail for want, and yet am choked with store.
> This is thy work, thou god for ever blind;
> Though thousands old, a boy entitled still.
> Thus children do the silly birds they find
> With stroking hurt, and too much cramming kill.
>   Yet thus much love, O love, I crave of thee:
>   Let me be loved, or else not loved be.

Basilius made no great haste from behind the tree till he perceived she had fully ended her music; but then, loath to lose the precious fruit of time, he presented himself unto her, falling down upon both his knees and holding up his hands – as the old governess of Danae is painted when she suddenly saw the golden shower: 'O heavenly woman, or earthly goddess,' said he, 'let not my presence be odious unto you, nor my humble suit seem of small weight in your ears. Vouchsafe your eyes to descend upon this miserable old man whose life hath hitherto been maintained but to serve as[3] an[4] increase of your beautiful triumphs. You only have overthrown me, and in my bondage consists my glory. Suffer not your own work to be despised of you, but look upon him with pity whose life serves for your praise.'

Zelmane, keeping a countenance askances[5] she understood him not, told him it became her evil to suffer such excessive reverence of him, but that it worse became her to correct him to whom she owed duty; that the opinion she had of his wisdom was such as made her esteem greatly of his words, but that the words themselves sounded so as she could not imagine what they might intend.

---

[1] while] whilst *Cl, Qu* [2] fly] die *Cl, Qu* [3] as] for *Cl*; *om. Ph* [4] an] *om. Da*; one *Ph* [5] askances] as though *Ph*; senses *corr. to* seeming *Je*

'Intend!' said Basilius, proud that that was brought in question, 'What may they intend but a refreshing of my soul and a swaging[1] of my heat – and enjoying those your excellencies wherein my life is upheld and my death threatened?'

Zelmane lifting up her face as if she had received a mortal injury of him, 'And is this the devotion your ceremonies have been bent unto?' said she[2] 'Is it the disdain of my estate or the opinion of my lightness that have emboldened such base fancies towards me? "Enjoying", quoth you? Now little joy come to them that yield to such enjoying!'

Poor Basilius was so appalled that his legs bowed under him, his eyes looked as though he would gladly hide himself, and (his old blood going to his heart) a general shaking all over his[3] body possessed him. At length, with a wan mouth, he was about to give a stammering answer, when it came into Zelmane's head by this device to make her profit of his folly; and therefore with a relented[4] countenance thus said unto him: 'Your words, mighty prince, were unfit either for me to hear or you to speak, but yet the large testimony I see of your affection makes me willing to suppress a great number of errors. Only thus much I think good to say: that the[5] same words in my Lady Philoclea's mouth, as from one woman to another – so as there were no other body by – might have had a better grace, and perchance have found a gentler[6] receipt.'

Basilius, whose senses by desire were held open, and conceit was by love quickened, heard scarcely half her answer out but that, as if speedy flight might save his life, he turned away and ran with all the speed his body would suffer him towards his daughter Philoclea, whom he found at that time dutifully watching by her mother, and Miso curiously watching her, having left Mopsa to do the like service to Pamela. Basilius forthwith calling Philoclea aside, with all the conjuring words which desire could indite and authority utter, besought her she would preserve his life in whom her life was begun; she would save his grey hairs from rebuke, and his aged mind from despair; that if she were not cloyed with his company, and that she thought not the earth overburdened with him, she would cool his fiery grief, which was to be done but[7] by[8] her breath; that in fine, whatsoever he was, he was nothing but what it pleased Zelmane – all the powers of his spirit depending of her;[9] that if she continued cruel he could no more sustain his life than the earth remain fruitful in the sun's continual absence. He concluded she should in one payment requite all his deserts, and that she

---

[1] and a swaging] an assuaging *St, Bo, Cl, Da, Ph*; and assuaging *As, Cm*; and an assuaging *Je, Qu* [2] have … she] said she, ' have … unto *OA* (*ex. Bo, Je*); have … unto *Je* [3] all over his] over all his whole *Bo*; over all his *Je* [4] relented] relenting *Ph, Je* [5] the] these *St, Ph, Je, Qu; om. Bo* [6] gentler] gentlier *Da*; gentle *Qu* [7] but] *om. Da, Je* [8] by] with *St, Bo, Je, Qu* [9] of her] in her *Bo, Je, Qu*

needed not disdain[1] any service, though never so mean, which was warranted by the sacred name of a father.

Philoclea, more glad than ever she had known herself that she might by this occasion enjoy the private conference of Zelmane, yet had so sweet a feeling of virtue in[2] her mind that she would not suffer a vile colour to be cast over her fair[3] thoughts, but with humble grace answered her father that there needed neither promise nor persuasion to her to make her do her uttermost for her father's service; that, for Zelmane's favour, she would in all virtuous sort seek it towards him; and that, as she would not pierce further into his meaning than himself should declare, so would she interpret all his doings to be accomplished in goodness; and therefore desired, if otherwise it were, that he would not impart it to her,[4] who then should be forced to begin by true obedience a show of disobedience, rather performing his general commandment (which had ever been to embrace virtue) than any new particular sprung out of passion and contrary to the former.

Basilius, content to take that since he could have no more, thinking it a great point if by her means he could get but a more free access unto Zelmane, allowed her reasons and took her proffer thankfully, desiring only a speedy return of comfort. Philoclea was parting, and Miso straight behind her, like Alecto following Proserpina. But Basilius forced her to stay, though with much ado, she being sharp-set upon the fulfilling of a shrewd office, in overlooking Philoclea, and so said to Basilius that she did as she was commanded, and could not answer it to Gynecia if she were any whit from Philoclea, telling him true that he did evil to take her charge from her. But Basilius, swearing he would put out her eyes if she stirred a foot to trouble his daughter, gave her a stop for that while. And so,[5] away departed Philoclea with a new field of fancies for her travailing mind, for well she saw her father was grown her adverse party, and yet her fortune such as she must favour her rival – and the fortune of that fortune such as neither that did hurt her, nor any contrary mean help her.

But she walked but a little on before she saw Zelmane lying upon a bank, with her face so bent over Ladon that, her tears falling into the water, one might have thought that she began meltingly to be metamorphosed to the under-running river; but by and by with speech she made known as well that she lived as that she sorrowed. 'Fair streams,' said she, 'that do vouchsafe in your clearness to represent unto me my blubbered face, let the tribute-offer of my tears unto you procure your stay a while with me, that I may begin

---

[1] not disdain] not to disdain *Ph, Je, Qu*   [2] in] within *OA (ex. Cl, Je)*   [3] fair] by *St, Bo, As, Je*; high *Cl, Da, Ph*; om. *Qu*   [4] to her] unto her *Cl, As, Da*   [5] while. And so *Cm*: while. Chap. 17. Zelmane's tears and tearful ditty; Philoclea enters conference with her; she shues, and shows herself Prince Pyrocles; Philoclea fears much but loves more; their conclusion, with reentry to their intermitted historiology. So *90*; while. *So93*

yet at last to find something that pities me, and that all things of comfort and pleasure do not fly away from me. But if the violence of your spring command you to haste away to pay your duties to your great prince the sea, yet carry with you these few words, and let the uttermost ends of the world know them. A love more clear than yourselves, dedicated to a love (I fear) more cold than yourselves, with the clearness lays a night of sorrow upon me, and with the coldness inflames a world of fire within me.' With that she took a willow stick and wrote in a sandy bank these few verses:

> Over these brooks, trusting to ease mine eyes
> (Mine eyes ev'n great in labour[1] with their tears),
> I laid my face (my face wherein there lies
> Clusters of clouds which no sun ever clears).
>   In wat'ry[2] glass my watered eyes I see:
>   Sorrows ill eased, where sorrows painted be.
>
> My thoughts, imprisoned in my secret woes,
> With flamy breaths[3] do[4] issue oft in sound:
> The sound to this strange air no sooner goes
> But that it doth with echo's force rebound[5]
>   And make[6] me hear the plaints I would refrain:
>   Thus[7] outward helps my inward griefs[8] maintain.
>
> Now in this sand I would discharge my mind,
> And cast from me part of my burd'nous cares:
> But in the[9] sand[10] my pains[11] foretold I find,
> And see therein how well the writer fares.
>   Since stream, air, sand, mine eyes and ears conspire,
>   What hope to quench where each thing blows the fire?

And as soon as she had written them (a new swarm of thoughts stinging her mind) she was ready with her foot to give the new-born letters both death and burial; but Philoclea, to whom[12] delight of hearing and seeing was before a stay from interrupting her, gave herself to be seen unto[13] her, with such a lightening of beauty upon Zelmane that neither she could look on, nor would look off.

At last, Philoclea (having a little[14] mused how to cut the thread even between her own hopeless affection and her father's unbridled hope) with eyes, cheeks, and lips (whereof each sang their part to make up the harmony

---

[1] great in labour with] in great labour with *Le*; great with labour of *Ph, Cm*; great with *Qu*   [2] wat'ry] watered *Le, Qu, Ra* watered *OA (ex. Bo, Cl), Ra, Cm*: wat'ry *Bo, Cl, 90, 93*   [3] breaths] breath *OA, Ra, 13*   [4] do] doth *Cl, Le*   [5] rebound] resound *O, Ph, Je, Qu, Ra*   [6] make] makes *Cl, Da, Je*   [7] Thus] That *As, Cm*   [8] griefs] grief *St, Bo, Cl, O, 93*   [9] the] these *Je, Qu, Ra*   [10] sand] sands *OA (ex. Le, As), Ra*   [11] pains *OA (ex. Bo), Ra, Cm*: cares *Bo*; tales *90, 93*   [12] to whom] whose *93*   [13] unto] of *Cl, Je, Qu (of corr. to* unto *Bo)*   [14] little] while *OA (ex. As)*

of bashfulness) began to say, 'My father, to whom I owe myself, and therefore – ', when Zelmane (making a womanish habit to be the armour of her boldness), giving up her life to the lips of Philoclea, and taking it again by the sweetness of those kisses, humbly besought her to keep her speech for a while within the paradise of her mind, for well she knew her father's errand, who should soon[1] receive a sufficient answer. But now she demanded leave, not to lose this long-sought-for commodity of time, to ease her heart thus far: that if in her agonies her destiny was to be condemned by Philoclea's mouth, at least Philoclea might know whom she had condemned. Philoclea easily yielded to grant her own desire. And so, making the green bank the situation, and the river the prospect, of the most beautiful buildings of nature, Zelmane doubting how to begin (though her thoughts already had run to the end), with a mind fearing the unworthiness of every word that should be presented to her ears, at length brought it forth in this manner:

'Most beloved lady, the incomparable excellencies of your self, waited on by the greatness of your estate, and the importance of the thing, whereon my life consisteth, doth require both many ceremonies before the beginning, and many circumstances in the uttering, my speech both bold and fearful. But the small opportunity of envious occasion, by the malicious eye hateful love doth cast upon me, and the extreme bent[2] of my affection, which will either break out in words or break my heart, compel me not only to embrace the smallest time, but to pass by the respects[3] due unto you, in respect of your poor caitiff's life, who is now or never to be preserved. I do therefore vow unto you hereafter never more to omit all dutiful form;[4] do you only now vouchsafe to hear the matter of a mind most perplexed. If ever the sound of love have come to your ears, or if ever you have understood what force it hath had to conquer the strongest hearts and change the most settled estates, receive here an example of those[5] strange tragedies – one that in himself containeth the particularities of all those misfortunes, and from henceforth believe that such a thing may be, since you shall see it is. You shall see, I say, a living image and a present story of what love can do when he is bent to ruin.

'But alas, whither goest thou, my tongue; or how doth my heart consent to adventure the revealing his nearest touching secret? But peace, fear! thou comest too late, when already the harm is taken. Therefore I say, again I say,[6] O only princess, attend here a miserable miracle of affection! Behold here before your eyes Pyrocles, prince of Macedon, whom you only have brought to this game of fortune, and unused metamorphosis; whom you

---

[1] soon] om. Cl, Da [2] bent] bents St; beauty Qu [3] by the respects Cm, 93: by respects 90 [4] form] forms OA (ex. As) [5] those] these Ph, Qu [6] I say, again I say Cm: again I say, I say OA (ex. Je, Qu); again I say Je, Qu; I say again 90, 93

only have made neglect his country, forget his father, and lastly, forsake to be Pyrocles – the same Pyrocles who you heard was betrayed by being put in a ship, which being burned, Pyrocles was drowned. Oh, most true presage! for these traitors, my eyes, putting me in¹ a ship of desire which daily burneth, those eyes, I say, which betrayed me, will never leave till they have drowned me. But be not, be not, most excellent lady, you that nature hath made to be the lodestar of comfort, be not the rock of shipwreck; you whom virtue hath made the princess of felicity, be not the minister of ruin; you whom my choice hath made the goddess of my safety, oh let not, let not from you be poured upon me destruction. Your fair face hath many tokens in it of amazement at my words: think then what his amazement is from whence they come, since no words can carry with them the life of the inward feeling. I desire that my desire may be weighed in the balances of honour, and let virtue hold them; for if the highest love in no base person may aspire to grace, then may I hope your beauty will not be without pity. If otherwise you be (alas, but let it never be so) resolved, yet shall not my death be comfortless, receiving it by your sentence.'

The joy which wrought into Pygmalion's mind, while he found his beloved image was softer and warmer in his folded arms till at length it accomplished his gladness with a perfect woman's shape, still beautified with the former perfections, was even such as by each degree of Zelmane's words creepingly entered into Philoclea, till her pleasure was fully made up with the manifesting of his being – which was such as in hope did overcome hope. Yet doubt would fain have played his part in her mind, and called in question how she should be assured that Zelmane was Pyrocles – but love straight stood up, and deposed that a lie could not come from the mouth of Zelmane. Besides, a certain spark of honour² which rose in her well disposed mind made her fear to be alone with him, with whom alone she desired to be – with all the other contradictions growing³ in those minds which neither absolutely climb the rock of virtue nor freely sink into the sea of vanity – but that spark soon gave place, or at least gave no more light in her mind than a candle doth in the sun's presence. But even sick with a surfeit of joy, and fearful of she knew not what (as he that⁴ newly finds huge treasures doubts whether he sleep or no, or like a fearful deer which then looks most about when he comes to the best feed), with a shrugging⁵ kind of tremor through all her principal parts, she gave these affectionate words for answer:

'Alas, how painful a thing it is to a divided mind to make a well-joined answer! How hard it is to bring inward shame to outward confession! And what handsomeness, trow you, can be observed in that speech which is

---

¹ in] into 93   ² honour] humour *As, Ph*   ³ growing] grow *OA* (*ex. Qu*); prove *Qu*; proving *Cm*
⁴ that] which *Cl, Da*   ⁵ shrugging] shaking *Ph*; shrinking *Je*

made, one knows not to whom? Shall I say, "O Zelmane"? Alas, your words be against it! Shall I say, "Prince Pyrocles"? Wretch that I am, your show is manifest against it. But this, this[1] I may well[2] say: if I had continued (as I ought) Philoclea, you had either never been, or ever been, Zelmane; you had either never attempted this change, set on with hope, or never discovered it, stopped with despair. But I fear me my behaviour ill-governed gave you the first comfort. I fear me my affection ill-hid hath given you this last assurance. I fear indeed the weakness of my government before made you think such a mask would be grateful unto me, and my weaker government since makes you to pull off the visor. What shall I do then?[3] Shall I seek far-fetched inventions? Shall I labour[4] to lay marble colours over my ruinous thoughts? Or rather, though the pureness of my virgin[5] mind be stained, let me keep the true simplicity of my word. True it is, alas, too true it is, O Zelmane (for so I love[6] to call thee, since in that name my love first began, and in the shade of that name my love shall best lie[7] hidden), that even while so thou wert[8] – what eye bewitched *me*, I know not – my passions were fitter[9] to desire than to be desired. Shall I say then I am sorry, or that my love must be turned to hate, since thou art turned to Pyrocles? How may that well be, since when thou wert Zelmane the despair thou mightest not be thus did most[10] torment me? Thou hast then the victory; use it with virtue. Thy virtue wan me; with virtue preserve me. Doost thou love me? Keep me then still worthy to be beloved.'

Then held she her tongue, and cast down a self-accusing look, finding that in herself she had as it were shot out of the bow of her affection a more quick opening of her mind than she minded to have done. But Pyrocles, so carried up with joy that he did not envy the gods' felicity, presented her with some jewels of right princely value as some little tokens of his love and quality, and withal showed her letters from his father, King Euarchus, unto him, which even in the sea had amongst his jewels been preserved. But little needed those proofs to one who would have fallen out with herself rather than make any contrary conjectures to Zelmane's speeches, so that with such embracements[11] as it seemed their souls desired to meet and their hearts to kiss as their mouths did, which fain Pyrocles would have sealed with the chief arms of his desire, but Philoclea commanded the contrary – and yet they passed the promise of marriage.

And then at Philoclea's entreaty (who was willing to purloin all occasions of remaining with Zelmane) she told her the story of her life from the time

---

[1] this, this] this *Ph, Je, Qu* [2] may well] well may *OA (ex. Cl, As)* [3] What ... then] What then shall I do *St, Bo, Ph, Je, Qu*; Then what shall I do *Cl, Da* [4] labour] seek *OA (ex. Cl, As)* [5] virgin] virgin's *Ph, Qu* [6] I love] I do love *Cl, Da* [7] lie] be *Cl, Da, Ph* [8] wert] art *As, Qu*; were *Ph* [9] were fitter] were far fitter *OA (ex. Je)* [10] did most] did then most *St, Bo, Ph, Je, Qu*; did most then *Da* [11] embracements] embracings *OA (ex. Qu)*

of their departing from Erona, for the rest she had already understood of her sister: 'For,' said she, 'I have understood how you first in the company of your noble cousin, Musidorus, parted from Thessalia, and of divers adventures which with no more danger than glory you passed through, till your coming to the succour of the Queen Erona; and the end of that war (you might perceive by myself) I had understood of the Prince Plangus. But what since was the course of your doings, until you came after so many victories to make a conquest of poor me, that I know not, the fame thereof having rather showed it by pieces than delivered any full form of it. Therefore, dear Pyrocles (for what can mine ears be so sweetly fed with, as to hear you of you?) be liberal unto me of those things which have made you indeed precious to the world; and now doubt not to tell of your perils, for, since I have you here out of them, even the remembrance of them is pleasant.'

Pyrocles easily perceived she was content with kindness to put off occasion of further kindness – wherein love showed himself a cowardly boy that durst not attempt for fear of offending; but rather, love proved himself valiant, that durst with the sword of reverent duty gainstand the force of so many enraged desires – but so it was that, though he knew this discourse was to entertain him from a more straight parley, yet he durst not but kiss his rod and gladly make much of the[1] entertainment which she allotted unto him; and therefore, with a desirous sigh chastening his breast for too much desiring, 'Sweet princess of my life,' said he, 'what trophies, what triumph, what monuments, what histories may[2] ever make my fame yield so sweet a music to my ears, as that it pleaseth you to lend your mind to the knowledge of anything touching Pyrocles, only therefore of value because he is your Pyrocles? And therefore grow I now so proud as to think it worth the hearing, since you vouchsafe to give it the hearing.[3] Therefore, only height of my hope, vouchsafe to know that after the death of Tiridates and settling Erona in her government, for settled we left her, howsoever since, as I perceived by your speech the last day, the ungrateful treason of her ill-chosen husband overthrew her – a thing in truth never till this time by me either heard or suspected, for who could think, without having such a mind as Antiphilus,' that so great a beauty as Erona's, indeed excellent, could not have held his affection, so great goodness could not have bound gratefulness, and so high advancement could not have satisfied his ambition? But therefore true it is that wickedness may well be compared to a bottomless pit, into which it is far easier to keep oneself from falling than, being fallen, to give oneself any stay from falling infinitely. But for my cousin and me, upon this cause we parted from Erona.

---

[1] the] that 93   [2] may] my *Cm*; might 93   [3] it the hearing *Cm*, 93: it hearing 90

'Euardes, the[1] brave and mighty prince whom it was my fortune to kill in the combat for Erona, had three nephews, sons to a sister of his, all three set among the foremost ranks of fame for great minds to attempt, and great force to perform what they did attempt – especially the eldest, by name Anaxius, to whom all men would willingly have yielded the height of praise, but that his nature was such as to bestow it upon himself before any could give it, for of so unsupportable a pride he was that, where his deed[2] might well stir envy, his demeanour did rather breed disdain; and if it be true that the giants ever made war against heaven, he had been a fit ensign-bearer for that company, for nothing seemed hard to him, though impossible, and nothing unjust while his liking was his justice. Now he in these wars had flatly refused his aid because he could not brook that the worthy Prince Plangus was by his cousin Tiridates preferred before him, for allowing no other weights but the sword and spear in judging of desert, how much he esteemed himself before Plangus in that, so much would he have had his allowance in his service. But now that he understood that his uncle was slain by me, I think rather scorn that any should kill his uncle than any kindness (an unused guest to an arrogant soul) made him seek his revenge – I must confess in manner gallant enough, for he sent a challenge unto[3] me to meet him at a place appointed in the confines of the kingdom of Lycia, where he would prove upon me that I had by some treachery overcome his uncle, whom else many hundreds such as I could not have withstood.

'Youth and success made me willing enough to accept any such bargain, especially because I had heard that your cousin, Amphialus, who for some years hath universally borne the name of the best knight in the world, had divers times fought with him and never been able to master him, but so had left him that every man thought Anaxius in that one virtue of courtesy far short of him, in all other his match – Anaxius still deeming himself for his superior. Therefore to him I would go; and I would needs go alone because so I understood for certain he was, and, I must confess, desirous to do something without the company of the incomparable Prince Musidorus, because in my heart I acknowledge that I owed more to his presence than to anything in myself, whatsoever before I had done; for of him indeed, as of any worldly cause, I must grant as received whatever there is, or may be, good in me. He taught me by word, and best by example, giving me in him so lively an image of virtue as ignorance could not cast such mist over mine eyes as not to see and to love it, and all with such dear friendship and

---

[1] Erona. 'Euardes, the 93: Erona the *Cm*; Erona.' Chap. 18. Anaxius' surquidry, and challenge to Pyrocles accepted; the execution of ladies done on a light of love; Pyrocles' intercession in the cause; the lewd parts of that light lecher; his scoffing excuses; Dido's revenge on him stopped, and his revenge on her stayed by Pyrocles. 'Euardes, the 90   [2] deed] deeds 93   [3] unto *Cm, 93*: to 90

care as, O heaven,[1] how can my life ever requite unto him; which made me indeed find in myself such a kind of depending upon him as without him I found a weakness and a mistrustfulness of myself, as one strayed from his best strength, when at any time I missed him; which humour perceiving to overrule me, I strave against it – not that I was unwilling to depend upon him, in judgement, but by weakness I would not, which, though it held me to him, made me unworthy of him. Therefore I desired his leave and obtained it (such confidence he had in me, preferring my reputation before his own tenderness), and so privately went from him, he determining (as after I knew) in secret manner not to be far from the place where we appointed to meet, to prevent any foul play that might be offered unto me. Full loath was Erona to let us depart from her, as it were forefeeling the harms which after fell to her. But I, rid fully from those cumbers of kindness, and half a day's journey in my way toward Anaxius, met an adventure (though[2] in itself of small importance) I will tell you at large, because by the occasion thereof I was brought to as great cumber and danger as lightly any might escape.

'As I passed through a laund (each side whereof was so bordered both with high timber-trees, and copses of far more humble growth, that it might easily bring a solitary mind to look for no other companions than the wild burgesses of the forest) I heard certain cries, which coming by pauses to mine ears from within the wood, of the right hand, made me well assured by the greatness of the cry it was the voice of a man, though it were a very unmanlike voice so to cry. But making mine ear my guide, I left not many trees behind me before I saw at the bottom of one of them a gentleman, bound with many garters hand and foot, so as well he might tumble and toss, but neither run nor resist he could. Upon him, like so many eagles upon an ox, were nine gentlewomen, truly such as one might well enough say they were handsome. Each of them held bodkins in their hands wherewith they continually pricked him (having been beforehand unarmed of any defence from the waist upward, but only of his shirt), so as the poor man wept and bled, cried and prayed, while they sported themselves in his pain, and delighted in his prayers as the arguments of their victory.

'I was moved to compassion, and so much the more that he straight called to me for succour, desiring me at least to kill him, to deliver him from those tormentors. But before myself could resolve, much less any other tell what I would resolve, there came in choleric haste towards me about seven or eight knights, the foremost of which willed me to get me away and not to trouble the ladies while they were taking their due revenge – but with so

---

[1] heaven *Cm, 93*: heavens *90*   [2] adventure (though] adventure, which (though *93*

overmastering a manner of pride as truly my heart could not brook it; and therefore (answering them that how I would have defended him from the ladies I knew not, but from them I would) I began a combat first with him particularly, and after his death with the others (that had less good manners) jointly. But such was the end of it that I kept the field with the death of some and flight of others – insomuch as the women, afraid what angry victory would bring forth, ran away,[1] saving only one who was so fleshed in malice that neither during nor after the fight she gave any truce to her cruelty, but still used the little instrument of her great spite (to the well-witnessed pain of the impatient patient), and was now about to put out his eyes, which all this while were spared because they should do him the discomfort of seeing who prevailed over him, when I came in, and after much ado brought her to some conference – for some time it was before she would hearken, more before she would speak, and most before she would in her speech leave off that sharp remembrance[2] of her bodkin. But at length, when I pulled off my head-piece and humbly entreated her pardon, or knowledge why she was cruel, out of breath more with choler (which increased in his own exercise) than with the pain she took, much to this purpose she gave her grief unto my knowledge.

' "Gentleman," said she, "much it is against my will to forbear any time the executing of my just revenge upon this naughty creature – a man in nothing but in deceiving women. But because I see you are young and like enough to have the power, if you would have the mind, to do much more mischief than he, I am content upon this bad subject to read a lecture to your virtue.

' "This man called Pamphilus in birth I must confess is noble – but what is that to him, if it shall be a stain to his dead ancestors to have left such an offspring! in shape as you see not uncomely – indeed, the fit mask of his disguised falsehood! in conversation wittily pleasant and pleasantly gamesome, his eyes full of merry simplicity, his words of hearty companableness – and such a one whose head one would not think so staid as to think mischievously! delighted in all such things which, by imparting their[3] delight to others, makes the user thereof welcome, as music, dancing, hunting, feasting, riding, and such like – and to conclude, such a one as who can keep him at arm's end need never wish a better companion!

' "But under these qualities lies such a poisonous adder as I will tell you, for by those gifts of nature and fortune, being in all places acceptable, he creeps – nay, to say truly, he flies so into the favour of poor silly women that I would be too much ashamed to confess, if I had not revenge in my hand as

---

[1] ran away] ran all away 93   [2] that sharp remembrance *Cm*: that remembrance 90; the sharp remembrance 93   [3] their] the 93

well as shame in my cheeks; for his heart being wholly delighted in deceiving us, we could never be warned, but rather one bird caught served for a stale to bring in more; for the more he gat, the more still he showed that he, as it were, gave away to his new mistress when he betrayed his promises to the former. The cunning of his flattery, the readiness of his tears, the infiniteness of his vows were but among the weakest threads of his net. But the stirring our own passions, and by the entrance of them to make himself lord of our forces – there lay his master's part of cunning, making us now jealous; now envious; now, proud of what we had, desirous of more; now giving one the triumph to see him, that was prince of many, subject to her; now with an estranged look making her fear the loss of that mind which, indeed, could never be had; never ceasing humbleness and diligence till he had embarked us in some such disadvantage as we could not return dry-shod; and then suddenly a tyrant – but a crafty tyrant, for so would he use his imperiousness that we had a delightful fear, and an awe which made us loath to lose our hope; and, which is strangest, when sometimes with late repentance I think of it, I must confess even in the greatest tempest of my judgement was I never driven to think him excellent, and yet so could set my mind both to get and keep him, as though therein had lain my felicity – like them I have seen play at the ball grow extremely earnest who should have the ball, and yet everyone knew it was but a ball. But in the end[1] the bitter sauce of the sport was that we had either our hearts broken with sorrow, or our estates spoiled with being at his direction, or our honours forever lost, partly by our own faults, but principally by his faulty using of our faults, for never was there man that could with more scornful eyes behold her at whose feet he had lately lain, nor with a more unmanlike bravery use his tongue to her disgrace, which lately had sung sonnets of her praises (being so naturally inconstant as I marvel his soul finds not some way to kill his body whereto it had been so long united): for so hath he dealt with us (unhappy fools) as we could never tell whether he made greater haste, after he once liked, to enjoy, or after he once enjoyed, to forsake.

'"But making a glory of his own shame, it delighted him to be challenged of unkindness; it was a triumph unto him to have his mercy called for; and he thought the fresh colours of his beauty were painted in nothing so well as in the ruins of his lovers. Yet so far had we engaged ourselves (unfortunate souls) that we listed not complain, since our complaints could not but carry the greatest accusation to ourselves. But every of us, each for herself, laboured all means how to recover him, while he rather daily sent us companions of our deceit than ever returned in any sound and faithful manner – till at length, he concluded all his wrongs with betrothing himself

---

[1] in the end] in end 93

to one, I must confess, worthy to be liked (if any worthiness might excuse so unworthy a changeableness), leaving us nothing but remorse for what was past, and despair of what might follow. Then indeed the common injury made us all join in fellowship,[1] who till that time had employed our endeavours one against the other, for we thought nothing was a more condemning of us than the justifying of his love to her by marriage. Then despair made fear valiant, and revenge gave shame countenance; whereupon we that you saw here devised how to get him among us alone, which he, suspecting no such matter of them whom he had by often abuses (he thought) made tame to be still abused, easily gave us opportunity to do – and a man may see, even in this, how soon rulers grow proud, and in their pride, foolish.

' "He came with such an authority among us, as if the planets had done enough for us that by us once he had been delighted. And when we began in courteous manner one after the other to lay his unkindness unto him, he seeing himself confronted by so many, like a resolute orator went not to denial, but to justify his cruel falsehood, and all with such jests and disdainful passages that, if the injury could not be made greater, yet were our conceits made the apter to apprehend it. Among other of his answers, forsooth, I shall never forget how he would prove it was no inconstancy to change from one love to another, but a great constancy; and contrary, that which we call constancy, to be most changeable: 'For,' said he, 'I ever loved my delight, and delighted always in what was lovely, and wheresoever I found occasion to obtain that, I constantly followed it. But these constant fools you speak of, though their mistress grow by sickness foul or by fortune miserable, yet still will love her, and so commit the absurdest inconstancy that may be, in changing their love from fairness to foulness, and from loveliness to his contrary, like one not content to leave a friend, but will straight give over himself to his mortal enemy – where I, whom you call inconstant, am ever constant: to beauty in others, and delight in myself.'

' "And so, in this jolly scoffing bravery he went over us all, saying he left one because she was over-wayward, another because she was too soon won, a third because she was not merry enough, a fourth because she was over-gamesome, the fifth because she was grown with grief subject to sickness, the sixt because she was so foolish as to be jealous of him, the seventh because she had refused to carry a letter for him to another that he loved, the eight because she was not secret, the ninth because she was not liberal; but to me (who am named Dido – and indeed have met with a false Aeneas!), to me, I say (oh, the ungrateful villain!),[2] he could find no other fault to object but that, pardie, he met with many fairer!

---

[1] fellowship *Cm*, 93: friendship 90   [2] villain] villany 93, 98

' "But when he had thus played the careless prince, we having those servants of ours in readiness (whom you lately so manfully overcame) laid hold of him, beginning at first but that trifling revenge in which you found us busy – but meaning afterwards[1] to have mangled him so, as should have lost his credit for ever abusing more. But as you have made my fellows fly away, so for my part the greatness of his wrong overshadows in my judgement the greatness of any danger; for was it not enough for him to have deceived me, and through the deceit abused me, and after the abuse forsaken me, but that he must now, of all the company, and before all the company, lay want of beauty to my charge? Many fairer! I trow, even in your judgement, sir, if your eyes do not beguile me, not many fairer! And I know, whosoever says the contrary, there are not many fairer. And of whom should I receive this reproach but of him, who hath best cause to know there are not many fairer! And therefore, howsoever my fellows pardon his injuries, for my part I will ever remember, and remember to revenge, this scorn of all scorns!"

'With that, she to him afresh, and surely would have put out his eyes (who lay mute for shame, if he did not sometimes cry for fear) if I had not leapt from my horse and, mingling force with entreaty, stayed her fury. But while I was persuading her to meekness comes a number of his friends, to whom he forthwith cried that they should kill that woman that had thus betrayed and disgraced him. But then I was fain to forsake the ensign under which I had before served, and to spend my uttermost force in the protecting of the lady, which so well prevailed for her that in the end[2] there was a faithful peace promised of all sides.

'And so, I leaving her in a place of security (as she thought) went on my journey towards Anaxius, for whom I was fain to stay two days in the appointed place (he disdaining to wait for me) till he was sure I were there; and so I[3] did patiently abide his angry pleasure, till about that space of time he came, indeed according to promise alone, and that I may not say too little because he is wont to say too much, like a man whose courage was apt to climb over any danger. And as soon as ever he came near me, in fit distance for his purpose he with much fury (but with fury skilfully guided) ran upon me, which I in the best sort I could resisted, having kept myself ready for him because I had understood that he observed few[4] complements in matter[5] of arms, but such as a proud anger did indite unto him. And so, putting our horses into a full career, we hit each other upon the head with our lances.

---

[1] afterwards *Cm*, 93: afterwarwards 90   [2] in the end] in end 93   [3] there, and so I *Cm*: there.' Chap. 19. The monomachy between Anaxius and Pyrocles, adjourned by Pyrocles to re-succour Dido; the course of Dido's danger; the miserableness of her father; his carlish entertainment to Pyrocles, and his treason against him; Pyrocles hard bested, succoured by Musidorus; both saved by the king of Iberia; the execution of the traitors and death of Dido. 'I 90; there. 'I 93   [4] observed few *Cm*, 93: observed but few 90   [5] matter *Cm*, 93: matters 90

I think he felt my blow. For my part, I must confess I never received the like. But I think, though my senses were astonished, my mind forced them to quicken themselves, because I had learned of him how little favour he is wont to show in any matter of advantage – and indeed, he was turned and coming upon me with his sword drawn, both our staves having been broken at that encounter. But I was so ready to answer him that truly I know not who gave the first blow; but whosoever gave the first was[1] quickly seconded by the second. And indeed, excellentest lady, I must say truly, for a time it was well fought between us, he undoubtedly being of singular valour – I would to God it were not abased by his too much loftiness; but, as by the occasion of the combat, winning and losing ground, we changed places, his horse happened to come upon the point of the broken spear which, fallen to the ground, chanced to stand upward; so as, it lighting upon his heart, the horse died. He driven to dismount threatened, if I did not the like, to do as much for my horse as fortune had done for his; but whether for that, or because I would not be beholding to fortune for any part of the victory, I descended.

'So began our foot-fight, in such sort that we were well entered to blood of both sides, when there comes by that unconstant Pamphilus whom I had delivered (easy to be known, for he was barefaced), with a dozen armed men after him. But before him he had Dido (that lady who had most sharply punished him) riding upon a palfrey, he following her, with most unmanlike cruelty beating her with wands he had in his hand, she crying for sense of pain or hope of succour, which was so pitiful a sight unto me that it moved me to require Anaxius to defer our combat till another day, and now to perform the duties of knighthood in helping this distressed lady. But he that disdains to obey anything but his passion (which he calls his mind) bad me leave off that thought, but when he had killed me, he would then (perhaps) go to her succour.

'But I well finding the fight would be long between us, longing in my heart to deliver the poor Dido, giving him so great a blow as somewhat stayed him, to term it aright I flatly ran away from him toward my horse, who trotting after the company, in mine armour I was put to some pain, but that use made me nimble unto it. But as I followed my horse, Anaxius followed me; but his proud heart did so disdain that exercise that I had quickly overrun him and overtaken my horse, being I must confess ashamed to see a number of country folks who happened to pass thereby, who hallowed and hooted after me as at the arrantest coward that ever showed his shoulders to his enemy. But when I had leapt on my horse (with such speedy agility that they all cried, "Oh, see how fear gives him wings!") I turned to

---

[1] first was *Cm, 93*: first it was *90*

Anaxius and aloud promised him to return thither again as soon as I had relieved the injuried lady. But he railing at me with all the base words angry contempt could indite, I said no more but "Anaxius, assure thyself I neither fear thy force nor thy opinion"; and so, using no weapon of a knight as at that time but my spurs, I ran in my knowledge after Pamphilus – but in all their conceits from Anaxius, which, as far as I could hear, I might well hear testified with such laughters and games that I was some few times moved to turn back again.

'But the lady's misery overbalanced my reputation, so that after her I went; and with six hours' hard riding through so wild places as it was rather the cunning of my horse sometimes than of myself so rightly to hit the way, I overgat them a little before night near to an old ill-favoured castle, the place where (I perceived) they meant to perform their unknightly errand, for there they began to strip her of her clothes – when I came in among them. And running through the first with a lance, the justness of the cause so enabled me against the rest (false-hearted in their own wrong-doing) that I had, in as short time almost as I had been fighting with only Anaxius, delivered her from those injurious wretches, most of whom carried news to the other world that amongst men secret wrongs are not always left unpunished. As for Pamphilus, he having once seen and (as it should seem) remembered me, even from the beginning began to be in the rearward, and before they had left fighting he was too far off to give them thanks for their pains.

'But when I had delivered to the lady a full liberty both in effect and in opinion – for some time it was before she could assure herself she was out of their hands, who had laid so vehement apprehension of death upon her – she then told me how, as she was returning toward her father's weakly accompanied (as too soon trusting to the falsehood of reconcilement), Pamphilus had set upon her; and killing those that were with her, carried herself by such force, and with such manner as I had seen, to this place, where he meant in cruel and shameful manner to kill her in the sight of her own father – to whom he had already sent word of it, that out of his castle window (for this castle she said was his) he might have the prospect of his only child's destruction – if my coming (whom she said he feared), as soon as he knew me by the armour, had not warranted her from that near-approaching cruelty. I was glad I had done so good a deed for a gentlewoman not unhandsome, whom before I had in like sort helped. But the night beginning to persuade some retiring-place, the gentlewoman, even out of countenance before she began her speech, much after this manner invited me to lodge that night with her father.

' "Sir," said she, "how much I owe you can be but abased by words, since, the life I have, I hold it now the second time of you, and therefore need not offer service unto you, but only to remember you that I am your servant, and I would my being so might any way yield any small contentment unto you. Now, only I can but desire you to harbour yourself this night in this castle, because the time requires it, and in truth this country is very dangerous for murthering thieves, to trust a sleeping life among them. And yet I must confess that, as the love I bear you makes me thus invite you, so the same love makes me ashamed to bring you to a place where you shall be so – not spoken by ceremony, but by truth – miserably entertained."

'With that, she told me that, though she spake of her father, whom she named Chremes, she would hide no truth from me, which was in sum that, as he was of all that region the man of greatest possessions and riches, so was he either by nature or an evil-received opinion given to sparing in so unmeasurable sort[1] that he did not only bar himself from the delightful, but almost from the necessary, use thereof, scarcely allowing himself fit sustenance of life rather than he would spend of those goods, for whose sake only he seemed to joy in life; which extreme dealing (descending from himself upon her) had driven her to put herself with a great lady of that country, by which occasion she had stumbled upon such mischance[2] as were little for the honour either of her or her family – but so wise had he showed himself therein as, while he found his daughter maintained without his cost, he was content to be deaf to any noise of infamy, which, though it had wronged her much more than she deserved, yet she could not deny, but she was driven thereby to receive more than decent favours. She concluded that there at least I should be free from injuries, and should be assured, to her-wards, to abound as much in the true causes of welcomes, as I should want[3] of the effects thereof.

'I, who had acquainted myself to measure the delicacy of food and rest by hunger and weariness, at that time well-stored of both, did not abide long entreaty, but went with her to the castle, which I found of good strength, having a great moat round about it – the work of a noble gentleman, of whose unthrifty son he had bought it. The bridge drawn up (where we were fain to cry a good while before we could have answer, and to dispute a good while before answer would be brought to acceptance), at length a willingness rather than a joy to receive his daughter (whom he had lately seen so near death), and an opinion rather brought[4] into his head by course because he heard himself called a father, rather than any kindness that he found in his own heart, made him take us in (for my part, by that time grown so weary of such entertainment that no regard of myself, but only the importunity of his daughter, made me enter), where I was met with this Chremes (a drivelling old fellow, lean, shaking both of head and hands – already half earth, and yet

---

[1] unmeasurable sort *Cm, 93*: unmeasurable a sort *90* [2] mischance] mischances *93* [3] should want] should find want *93* [4] opinion rather brought] opinion brought *93*

then most greedy of earth), who scarcely would give me thanks for that[1] I had done, for fear (I suppose) that thankfulness might have an introduction of reward.

'But with a hollow voice giving me a false welcome, I might perceive in his eye to his daughter that it was hard to say whether the displeasure of her company did not overweigh the pleasure of her own coming; but on he brought me, into so bare a house that it was the picture of miserable happiness and rich beggary, served only by a company of rustical villains full of sweat and dust (not one of them other than a labourer in some, as he counted it, profitable drudgery), and all preparations both for food and lodging such as would make one detest niggardness, it is so sluttish a vice – his talk nothing[2] but of his poverty (for fear belike lest I should have proved a young borrower!): in sum, such a man as any enemy could not wish him worse than to be himself. But there that night bid I the burthen of being a tedious guest to a loathsome host, overhearing him sometimes bitterly warn his daughter of bringing such costly mates under his roof; which she grieving at, desired much to know my name (I think partly of kindness to remember who had done something for her, and partly because she assured herself I was such a one as would make even his miser mind contented with what he had done), and accordingly she demanded my name and estate, with such earnestness that I (whom love had not as then so robbed me of myself as to be another than I am) told her directly my name and condition, whereof she was no more glad than her father, as I might well perceive by some ill-favoured cheerfulness which then first began to wrinkle itself in his face.

'But the causes of their joys were far different, for, as the shepherd and the butcher both may look upon one sheep with pleasing conceits, but the shepherd with mind to profit himself by preserving, the butcher with killing him, so she rejoiced to find that mine own benefits had tied me to be her friend, who was a prince of such greatness, and lovingly rejoiced – but his joy grew (as I to my danger after perceived) by the occasion of the Queen Artaxia's setting my head to sale for having slain her brother, Tiridates; which being the sum of an[3] hundreth thousand crowns to whosoever brought me alive into her hands, that old wretch, who had overlived all good nature, though he had lying idly by him much more than that, yet above all things loving money for money's sake, determined to betray me (so well deserving of him) for to have that which he was determined never to use. And so, knowing that the next morning I was resolved to go to the place where I had left Anaxius, he sent in all speed to a captain of a garrison

---

[1] that] what 93   [2] talk nothing] talk of nothing 93   [3] an] a *Cm, 13*

hard¹ by, which though it belonged to the king of Iberia, yet knowing the captain's humour to delight so in riotous spending as he cared not how he came by the means to maintain it, doubted not that, to be half with him in the gain, he would play his quarter's part in the treason: and therefore that night agreeing of the fittest places where they might surprise me.

'In² the morning, the old caitiff was grown so ceremonious as he would needs accompany me some miles in my way – a sufficient token to me, if nature had made me apt to suspect, since a churl's courtesy rathely³ comes but either for gain or falsehood. But I suffered him to stumble into that point of good manner, to which purpose he came out with all his clowns, horsed upon such cart-jades, and so furnished as, in good faith, I thought with myself, if that were thrift, I wished none of my friends or subjects ever to thrive. As for his daughter, the gentle Dido, she would also (but in my conscience, with a far better mind) prolong the time of farewell as long as he. And so,⁴ we went on together (he so old in wickedness that he could look me in the face and freely talk with me, whose life he had already contracted for), till coming into the falling of a way which led us into a place, of each side whereof men might easily keep themselves undiscovered, I was encompassed suddenly by a great troop of enemies, both of horse and foot, who willed me to yield myself to the Queen Artaxia.

'But they could not have used worse eloquence to have persuaded my yielding than that, I knowing the little good will Artaxia bare me. And therefore making necessity and justice my best sword and shield, I used the other weapons I had as well as I could, I am sure to the little ease of a good number, who, trusting to their number more than to their valure, and valuing money higher than equity, felt that guiltlessness is not always with ease oppressed. As for Chremes, he withdrew himself – yet so gilding his wicked conceits with his hope of gain that he was content to be a beholder, how I should be taken, to make his prey. But I was grown so weary that I supported myself more with anger than strength – when the most excellent Musidorus came to my succour, who, having followed my trace as well as he could, after he had found⁵ I had left the fight with Anaxius, came to the niggard's castle, where he found all burned and spoiled by the country-people, who bare mortal hatred to that covetous man and now took the time, when the castle was left almost without guard, to come in and leave monuments of their malice therein; which Musidorus not staying either to further or impeach, came upon the spur after me (because with one voice many told him that, if I were in his company, it was for no good meant unto me) and in this extremity found me.

---

¹ hard] near 93   ² In] *om.* 93   ³ rathely] rarely 93   ⁴ And so *Cm*, 93: So 90   ⁵ he had found] he found 93

'But when I saw that cousin of mine, methought my life was doubled; and where before I thought of a noble death, I now thought of a noble victory, for who can fear that hath Musidorus by him! who, what he did there for me, how many he killed (not stranger for the number than for the strange blows wherewith he sent them to a well-deserved death), might well delight me to speak of, but I should so hold you too long in every particular – but in truth, there if ever (and ever – if ever any man) did Musidorus show himself second to none in able valour.

'Yet what the unmeasureable excess of their number would have done in the end, I know not, but the trial thereof was cut off by the chanceable coming thither of the king of Iberia (that same father of that[1] worthy Plangus, whom it hath pleased you sometimes to mention), who, not yielding over to old age his country delights, especially of hawking, was at that time (following a merlin) brought to see this injury offered unto us; and having great numbers of courtiers waiting upon him, was straight known by the soldiers that assaulted us to be their king, and so most of them withdrew themselves. He by his authority knowing (of the captain's own constrained confession) what was the motive of this mischievous practice, misliking much such violence should be offered in his country to men of our rank, but chiefly disdaining it should be done in respect of his niece (whom, I must confess, wrongfully he hated, because he interpreted that her brother and she had maintained his son Plangus against him), caused the captain's head presently to be stricken off, and the old bad Chremes to be hanged – though truly, for my part, I earnestly laboured for his life, because I had eaten of his bread. But one thing was notable, for a conclusion of his miserable life: that neither the death of his daughter – who, alas, the poor[2] gentlewoman! was by chance slain among his clowns, while she over-boldly for her weak sex sought to hold them from me – nor yet his own shameful end, was so much in his mouth as he was led to execution as the loss of his goods and burning of his house, which often (with more laughter than tears of the hearers) he made pitiful exclamations upon.

'But this[3] justice thus done and we delivered, the king indeed in royal sort invited us to his court not far thence, in all points entertaining us so, as truly I must ever acknowledge a beholdingness unto him, although the stream of it fell out not to be so sweet as the spring; for after some days' being there, curing ourselves of such wounds as we had received (while I, causing diligent search to be made of Anaxius, could learn nothing but

---

[1] of that] of y^t *Cm*; of the 93   [2] the poor] poor 93   [3] upon. 'But this *Cm*: upon.' Chap. 20. The two princes' passage to the Iberian court; Andromana's omniregency; her party-love to them both; her fair and foul means to inveigle them; Palladius' love to Zelmane; Zelmane's love to Pyrocles, and practice with her lover to release her beloved. 'This 90; upon. 'This 93

that he was gone out of the country, boasting in every place how he had made me run away), we were brought to receive the favour of acquaintance with this Queen Andromana, whom the Princess Pamela did in so lively colours describe the last day, as still methinks the figure thereof possesseth mine eyes, confirmed by the knowledge myself had; and therefore I shall need the less to make you know what kind of woman she was, but this only: that first with the rareness[1] of affection, and after with the very use of directing, she had made herself so absolute a master of her husband's mind that a while he would not (and after, he could not) tell how to govern, without being governed by her; but finding an ease in not understanding, let loose his thoughts wholly to pleasure, entrusting to her the entire conduct of all his royal affairs – a thing that may luckily fall out to him that hath the blessing to match with some heroical-minded lady, but in him it was neither guided by wisdom, nor followed by fortune – but thereby was slipped insensibly into such an estate that he lived at her undiscreet discretion (all his subjects having by some years learned so to hope for good, and fear of harm, only from her, that it should have needed a stronger virtue than his to have unwound so deeply an entered vice), so that, either not striving because he was contented, or contented because he would not strive, he scarcely knew what was done in his own chamber, but as it pleased her instruments to frame the relation.

'Now we being brought known unto her the time that we spent in curing some very dangerous wounds, after once we were acquainted – and acquainted we were sooner than ourselves expected – she continually almost haunted us, till, and it was not long a-doing, we discovered a most violent bent of affection (and that so strangely that we might well see, an evil mind in authority doth not only follow the sway of the desires already within it, but frames to itself new desires not before thought of), for with equal ardour she affected us both; and so did her greatness disdain shamefastness that she was content to acknowledge it to both – for having many times torn the veil of modesty, it seemed for a last delight that she delighted in infamy, which often she had used to her husband's shame, filling all men's ears but his with reproach,[2] while he, hoodwinked with kindness, least of all men knew who strake him.

'But her first degree was, by setting forth her beauties (truly, in nature not to be misliked, but as much advanced to the eye as abased to the judgement by art), thereby to bring us (as willingly-caught fishes) to bite at her bait; and thereto had she that scutcheon of her desires supported by certain badly-diligent ministers who often cloyed our ears with her praises, and would

---

[1] rareness] reins 93   [2] with reproach] with his reproach 93

needs teach us a way of felicity by seeking her favour. But when she found that we were as deaf to them as dumb to her, then she listed no longer stay in the suburbs of her foolish desires, but directly entered upon them, making herself an impudent suitor, authorizing herself very much with making us see that all favour and power in that realm so depended upon her that, now being in her hands, we were either to keep or lose our liberty at her discretion – which yet while she[1] so tempered[2] as that we might rather suspect than she threaten. But when our wounds grew so as that they gave us leave to travel, and that she found we were purposed to use all means we could to depart thence, she with more and more importunateness craved which,[3] in all good manners, was either of us to be desired, or not granted.

'Truly, most fair and every way excellent lady, you would have wondered to have seen how, before us, she would confess the contention in her own mind between that lovely – indeed, most lovely – brownness of Musidorus' face, and this colour of mine, which she (in the deceivable style of affection) would entitle beautiful; how her eyes wandered (like a glutton at a feast) from the one to the other; and how her words would begin half of the sentence to Musidorus, and end the other half to Pyrocles; not ashamed (seeing the friendship between us) to desire either of us to be a mediator to the other, as if we should have played, a request,[4] at tennis between us; and often wishing that she might be the angle where the lines of our friendship might meet, and be the knot which might tie our hearts together – which proceeding of hers I do the more largely set before you, most dear lady, that[5] by the foil thereof you may see the nobleness of my desire to you, and the warrantableness of your favour to me.'

At that, Philoclea smiled – with a little nod. 'But,' said Pyrocles, 'when she perceived no hope by suit to prevail, then (persuaded by the rage of affection, and encouraged by daring to do anything) she found means to have us accused to the king (as though we went about some practice to overthrow him in his own estate, which, because of the strange successes we had in[6] the kingdoms of Phrygia, Pontus, and Galatia, seemed not unlikely to him) who, but skimming anything that came before him, was disciplined to leave the through-handling of all to his gentle wife, who forthwith caused us to be put in prison, having while we slept deprived us of our arms[7] – a prison indeed injurious, because a prison, but else well testifying affection, because in all respects as commodious as a prison might be; and indeed so placed as she might at all hours not seen by many (though she cared not much how many had seen her) come unto us. Then fell she to sauce her

---

[1] yet while she *Cm*: yet she *90*; yet a while she *93*   [2] tempered] tempted *93, 98*   [3] craved which *Cm, 93*: craved that which *90*   [4] a request] one request *93*   [5] that] because *93*   [6] had in] had had in *93*   [7] arms *Cm, 93*: armour *90*

desires with threatenings, so that we were in a great perplexity, restrained to so unworthy a bondage, and yet restrained by love (which, I cannot tell how, in noble minds, by a certain duty claims an answering); and how much that love might move us, so much – and more – that faultiness of her mind removed us, her beauty being balanced by her shamelessness.

'But that which did as it were tie us in captivity was that to grant had been wickedly injurious to him that had[1] saved our lives, and to accuse a lady that loved us of her love unto us, we esteemed almost as dishonourable, and but by one of those ways we saw no likelihood of going out of that place, where, the words would be injurious to your ears which should express the manner of her suit, while yet many times earnestness dyed her cheeks with the colour of shamefastness, and wanton languishing borrowed of her eyes the downcast look of modesty. But we in the meantime far from loving her, and often assuring her that we would not so recompense her husband's saving of our lives, to such a ridiculous degree of trusting her she had brought him that she caused him send us word that upon our lives we should do whatsoever she commanded us – good man, not knowing any other, but that all her pleasures to[2] the preservation of his estate. But when that made us rather pity than obey his folly, then fell she to servile entreating us, as though force could have been the school of love, or that an honest courage would not rather strive against than yield to injury – all which yet could not make us accuse her, though it made us almost pine away for spite to lose any of our time in so troublesome an idleness.

'But while we were thus full of weariness of what was past and doubt of what was to follow, love (that I think in the course of my life hath a sport sometimes to poison me with roses, sometimes to heal me with wormwood) brought forth a remedy unto us, which, though it helped me out of that distress, alas, the conclusion was such as I must ever while I live think it worse than a rack so to have been preserved. This king – by this queen – had a son of tender age (but of great expectation) brought up in the hope of themselves (and already acceptation of the inconstant people) as successor of his father's crown, whereof he was as worthy considering his parts, as unworthy in respect of the wrong was thereby done against the most worthy[3] Plangus, whose great deserts now either forgotten or ungratefully remembered, all men set their sails with the favourable wind which blew on the fortune of this young prince – perchance not in their hearts, but surely in[4] their mouths, now giving Plangus (who some years before was their only champion) the poor comfort of calamity, pity.

---

[1] that had saved *Cm*, 93: that saved 90   [2] pleasures to *Cm*: pleasures bent to 90; pleasures were directed to 93   [3] worthy] noble 93   [4] surely in *Cm*, 13: surely not in 90, 93, 98

'This youth therefore accounted prince of that region, by name Palladius, did with vehement affection love a young lady brought up in his father's court, called Zelmane, daughter to that mischievously unhappy Prince Plexirtus (of whom already I have, and sometimes must make – but never honourable – mention) left there by her father because of the intricate changeableness of his estate – he by the motherside being half-brother to this Queen Andromana, and therefore the willinger committing her to her care. But as love, alas, doth not always reflect itself, so fell it out that this Zelmane (though truly, reason there was enough to love Palladius) yet could not ever persuade her heart to yield thereunto, with that pain to Palladius as they feel that feel an unloved love. Yet, loving indeed, and therefore constant, he used still the intercession of diligence and faith, ever hoping, because he would not put himself into that hell to be hopeless – until the time of our being come and captived there brought forth this end, which truly deserves of me a further degree of sorrow than tears.

'Such was therein my ill destiny that this young Lady Zelmane – like some unwisely liberal, that more delight to give presents than pay debts – she chose, alas, for the pity rather to bestow her love (so much undeserved, as not desired) upon me than to recompense him, whose love, besides many other things, might seem even in the court of honour justly to claim it of her. But so it was – alas, that so it was! – whereby it came to pass that, as nothing doth more naturally follow his cause than care to preserve, and benefit doth follow unfeigned affection, she felt with me what I felt of my captivity, and straight laboured to redress my pain (which was her pain), which she could do by no better means than by using the help therein of Palladius, who (true lover) considering what and not why in all her commandments – and indeed, she concealing from him her affection, which she entitled compassion – immediately obeyed to employ his uttermost credit to relieve us, which, though as great as a beloved son with a mother (faulty otherwise, but not hard-hearted toward him), yet it could not prevail to procure us liberty; wherefore he sought to have that by practice which he could not by prayer. And so, being allowed often to visit us (for indeed, our restraints were more or less according as the ague of her passion was either in the fit or intermission), he used the opportunity of a fit time thus to deliver us.

'The[1] time of the marrying that queen was, every year, by the extreme love of her husband and the serviceable love of the courtiers, made notable

---

[1] us. 'The *Cm*, 93: us.' Chap. 21. The cause of the Iberian yearly justs; Queen Helen's praises; the prize borne by her knights, which Palladius and the princes set them to reverse; the inventions and actions of seven tilters; Palladius and the princes' entry into the field, honour in it, and flight from it; Andromana's pursuit of them, to the death of her son and herself. 'The 90

by some public honours which did[1] as it were proclaim[2] to the world how dear she was to that[3] people; among other, none was either more grateful to the beholders, or more noble in itself, than justs both with sword and lance, maintained for a seven-night together; wherein that nation doth so excel both for comeliness and ableness that from neighbour countries they ordinarily come, some to strive, some to learn, and[4] some to behold.

'This day it happened that divers famous knights came thither from the court of Helen, queen of Corinth – a lady whom fame at that time was so desirous to honour that she borrowed all men's mouths to join with the sound of her trumpet: for, as her beauty hath won the prize from all women that stand in degree of comparison (for, as for the two sisters of Arcadia, they are far beyond all conceit of comparison!), so hath her government been such as hath been no less beautiful to men's judgements than her beauty to the eyesight; for being brought by right of birth (a woman – a young woman – a fair woman) to govern a people in nature mutinously proud, and always before so used to hard governors as they knew not how to obey without the sword were drawn, yet could she for some years so carry herself among them that they found cause, in the delicacy of her sex, of admiration, not of contempt; and which was notable, even in the time that many countries were[5] full of wars which, for old grudges to Corinth, were thought still would conclude there, yet so handled she the matter that the threatens ever smarted in the threateners – she using so strange and yet so well-succeeding a temper that she made her people (by peace) warlike, her courtiers (by sports) learned, her ladies (by love) chaste; for, by continual martial exercises without blood, she made them perfect in that bloody art; her sports were such as carried riches of knowledge upon the stream of delight; and such the behaviour both of herself and her ladies as builded their chastity, not upon waywardness, but by[6] choice of worthiness: so as, it seemed that court to have been the marriage place of love and virtue, and that herself was a Diana apparelled in the garments of Venus.

'And this (which fame only delivered unto me, for yet I have never seen her) I am the willinger to speak of to you who, I know, know her better, being your near neighbour, because you may see by her example (in herself wise, and of others beloved) that neither folly is the cause of vehement love, nor reproach the effect; for never, I think, was there any woman that with more unremovable determination gave herself to the counsel of love (after she had once set before her mind the worthiness of your cousin Amphialus),

---

[1] did *Cm, 93*: indeed *90* [2] proclaim *Cm, 93*: proclaimed *90* [3] that *Cm, 93*: the *90* [4] and] *om. 93*
[5] countries were] countries about her were *93* [6] by] *om. 93*

and yet is neither her wisdom doubted of, nor honour blemished; for, O God, what doth better become wisdom than to discern what is worthy the loving? What more agreeable to goodness than to love it, so discerned; and what to greatness of heart than to be constant in it, once loved?

'But, at that time, that love of hers was not so publicly known as the death of Philoxenus and her search of Amphialus hath made it, but then seemed to have such leisure to send thither divers choice knights of her court because they might bring her at least the knowledge, perchance the honour, of that triumph; wherein so they behaved themselves, as for three days they carried the prize; which being come from so far a place to disgrace her servants, Palladius, who himself had never used arms, persuaded the Queen Andromana to be content for the honour sake of her court to suffer us two to have our horse and armour, that he with us might undertake the recovery of their lost honour – which she granted, taking our oath to go no further than her son, and never[1] to abandon him (which she did, not more for saving him than keeping us); and yet, not satisfied with our oath, appointed a band of horsemen to have eye that we should not go beyond appointed limits.

'We were willing to gratify the young prince who, we saw, loved us; and so, the fourth day of that exercise, we came into the field, where, I remember, the manner was that the forenoon they should run at tilt one after the other, the afternoon in a broad field in manner of a battle, till either the strangers, or that country knights, wan the field.

'The first that ran was a brave knight whose device was to come in all chained, with a nymph leading him. His impresa was .... Against him came forth an Iberian, whose manner of entering was with bagpipes instead of trumpets, a shepherd's boy before him for a page, and by him a dozen apparelled like shepherds (for the fashion, though rich in stuff) who carried his lances which, though strong to give a lancely blow indeed, yet so were they coloured, with hooks near the morne, that they prettily represented sheephooks. His own furniture was dressed over with wool, so enriched with jewels artificially placed that one would have thought it a marriage between the lowest and the highest. His impresa was a sheep marked with pitch, with this word: "Spotted to be known". And because I may tell you out his conceit, though that were not done till the running for that time was ended, before the ladies departed from the windows – among there[2] was one, they say, that was the 'star' whereby his course was only directed. The shepherds attending upon Philisides went among them and sang an eclogue, one of

---

[1] and never] nor ever 93   [2] among there *Cm*: among them there *90*; among whom there *93*

them answering another, while the other shepherds, pulling out recorders which possessed the place of pipes, accorded their music to the others' voice. The eclogue had great praise – I only remember six verses – while having questioned one with the other, of their fellow shepherd's sudden growing a man-of-arms, and the cause of his so doing, they thus said:

> Methought some staves he missed – if so, not much amiss,
> For where he most would hit, he ever yet did miss;
> One said he brake across: full well it so might be,
> For never was there man more crossly crossed than he;
> But most cried, "Oh, well broke!" O fool, full gaily blessed,
> Where failing is a shame, and breaking is his best!

'Thus I have digressed, because his manner liked me well; but when he began to run against Lelius, it had near grown, though great love had ever been betwixt them, to a quarrel; for Philisides breaking his staves with great commendation, Lelius, who was known to be second to none in the perfection of that art, ran ever over his head – but so finely, to the skilful eyes, that one might well see he showed more knowledge in missing than others did in hitting, for with so gallant a grace his staff came swimming close over the crest of the helmet, as if he would represent the kiss, and not the stroke, of Mars. But Philisides was much moved with it, while he thought Lelius would show a contempt of his youth; till Lelius (who therefore would satisfy him because he was his friend) made him know: that to such bondage he was, for so many courses, tied by her; whose disgraces to him were graced by her excellency; and whose injuries he could never otherwise return, than honours.

'But so, by Lelius' willing missing, was the odds of the Iberian side, and continued so in the next by the excellent running of a knight, though fostered so by the muses as many times the very rustic people left both their delights and profits to hearken to his songs, yet could he so well perform all armed sports, as if he had never had any other pen than a lance in his hand. He came in like a wild man (but such a wildness as showed his eyesight had tamed him), full of withered leaves which, though they fell not, still threatened falling. His impresa was a mill-horse, still bound to go in one circle, with this word: "Data fata sequutus".

'But after him, the Corinthian knights absolutely prevailed, especially a great nobleman of Corinth, whose device was to come without any device, all in white like a new knight (as indeed he was) but so new as his newness shamed most of the others' long exercise; then another from whose tent, I remember, a bird was made fly with such art to carry a written embassage among the ladies that one might say, "If a live bird, how so taught? If a dead bird, how so made?"; then he, who hidden (man and horse) in a great figure lively representing the phoenix, the fire took so artificially as it consumed the bird, and left him to rise, as it were, out of the ashes thereof; against whom was the fine Frozen Knight (frozen in despair), but his armour so naturally representing ice, and all his furniture so lively answering thereto, as yet did I never see anything that pleased me better.

'But the delight of those pleasing sights have carried me too far in an[1] unnecessary discourse. Let it then suffice, most excellent lady, that you know the Corinthians that morning in the exercise, as they had done the days before, had the better – Palladius neither suffering us, nor himself, to take in hand that party[2] till the afternoon, when we were to fight in troops – not differing otherwise from earnest, but that the sharpness of the weapons was taken away; but in the trial, Palladius – especially led by Musidorus, and somewhat aided by me – himself truly behaving himself nothing like a beginner, brought the honour to rest itself that night of[3] the Iberian side. And the next day, both morning and afternoon being kept by our party, he, that saw the time fit for the delivery[4] he intended, called unto us to follow him, which we (both bound by oath, and willing by good will) obeyed. And so, the guard not daring to interrupt us (he commanding passage), we went after him upon the spur to a little house in a forest near by, which he thought would be the fittest resting-place till we might go further from his mother's fury – whereat he was no less angry and ashamed than desirous to obey Zelmane.

'But his mother, as I learned since, understanding by the guard her son's conveying us away, forgetting her greatness and resigning modesty to more quiet thoughts, flew out from her place and cried to be accompanied, for she herself would follow us. But what she did, being rather with vehemency of passion than conduct of reason, made her stumble while she ran, and by her own confusion hinder her own desires, for so impatiently she commanded as a good while nobody knew what she commanded, so as we had gotten so far the start as to be already past the confines of her kingdom before she overtook us – and overtake us she did, in the kingdom of Bithynia, not regarding shame, or danger, of having entered into another's dominions; but having with her about a threescore horsemen, straight commanded to take us alive and not to regard her son's threatening therein, which they attempted to do first by speech, and then by force. But neither liking their eloquence nor fearing their might, we esteemed few swords in a just defence able to resist many[5] unjust assaulters; and so, Musidorus' incredible valour, beating down all lets, made both me and Palladius so good way that we

---

[1] in an] into an 93 [2] that party] the party 93 [3] of] on 93 [4] the delivery *Cm, 93*: that delivery 90
[5] many *Cm, 93*: any 90

had little to do to overcome weak wrong, and now had the victory in effect without blood – when Palladius, heated with the fight and angry with his mother's fault, so pursued our assailers that one of them (who, as I heard since, had before our coming been a special minion of Andromana's, and hated us for having dispossessed him of her heart) taking him to be one of us, with a traitorous blow slew his young prince; who falling down before our eyes, whom he specially had delivered, judge, sweetest lady, whether anger might not be called justice in such a case. Once, so it wrought in us that many of his subjects' bodies we left there dead, to wait on him more faithfully to the other world.

'All this while, disdain (strengthened by the fury of a furious love) made Andromana stay to the last of the combat; and when she saw us light down to see what help we might do to the helpless Palladius, she came running madly unto us, then no less threatening when she had no more power to hurt. But when she perceived it was her only son that lay hurt, and that his hurt was so deadly as that already his life had lost the use of the reasonable and, almost, sensible part, then only did misfortune lay his own ugliness upon her[1] fault, and make her see what she had done, and to what she was come – especially finding in us rather detestation than pity (considering the loss of that young prince), and resolution presently to depart, which still she laboured to stay. But deprived of all comfort, with eyes full of death she ran to her son's dagger, and (before we were aware of it, who else could[2] have stayed it) strake herself a mortal wound. But then her love (though not her person) awaked pity in us, and I went to her while Musidorus laboured about Palladius; but the wound was past the cure of a better surgeon than myself, so as I could but receive some few of her dying words, which were cursings of her ill-set affection, and wishing unto me many crosses and mischances in my love, whensoever I should love (wherein I fear – and only fear! – that her prayer[3] is from above granted). But the noise of this fight and issue thereof being blazed by the country-people to some noblemen thereabouts, they came thither; and finding the wrong offered us, let us go on our journey, we having recommended those royal bodies unto them to be conveyed to the king of Iberia.'

With that, Philoclea seeing the tears stand in his eyes with remembrance of Palladius, but much more of that which thereupon grew, she would needs drink a kiss from those eyes, and he suck another from her lips – whereat she blushed, and yet kissed him again to hide her blushing – which had almost brought Pyrocles into another discourse, but that she with so sweet a rigour forbad him that he durst not rebel (though he found it a great war to keep

---

[1] upon her *Cm, 93*: upon his *90* [2] could] would *93* [3] prayer] prayers *93, 98*

that peace), but was fain to go on his[1] story, for so she absolutely bad him, and he durst not know how to disobey.

'And so,'[2] said he, 'parting from that place before the sun had much abased himself of his greatest height, we saw sitting upon the dry sands (which yielded at that time a very hot reflection) a fair gentlewoman, whose gesture accused her of much sorrow, and every way showed she cared not what pain she put her body to, since the better part, her mind, was laid under so much agony – and so was she dulled withal that we could come so near as to hear her speeches, and yet she not perceive the hearers of her lamentation. But well we might understand her at times say, "Thou doost kill me with thy unkind falsehood!" and "It grieves me not to die, but it grieves me that thou art the murtherer! Neither doth mine own pain so much vex me as thy error, for, God knows, it would not trouble me to be slain for thee; but much it torments me to be slain by thee!

' "Thou art untrue, Pamphilus! Thou art untrue! And woe is me, therefore! How oft didst thou swear unto me that the sun should lose his light, and the rocks run up and down like little kids, before thou wouldst falsify thy faith to me! Sun, therefore, put out thy shining! And rocks, run mad for sorrow, for Pamphilus is false! But, alas, the sun keeps his light, though thy faith be darkened; the rocks stand still, though thou change like a[3] weathercock!

' "Oh, fool that I am! that thought I could grasp water and bind the wind! I might well have known thee by others – but I would not, and rather wished to learn poison by drinking it myself, while my love helped thy words to deceive me.

' "Well yet, I would thou hadst made a better choice when thou didst foresake thy unfortunate Leucippe – but it is no matter. Baccha, thy new mistress, will revenge my wrongs! But do not, Baccha. Let Pamphilus live happy, though I die!"

'And much more to such-like phrase she spake, but that I, who had occasion to know something of that Pamphilus, stepped to comfort her; and though I could not do that, yet I got thus much knowledge of her: that this being the same Leucippe to whom the unconstant Pamphilus had betrothed himself (which had moved the other ladies to such indignation as I told you), neither her worthiness (which in truth was great) nor his own suffering for her (which is wont to endear affection) could fetter his fickleness, but

---

[1] on his] on in his 93 [2] disobey. 'And so Cm; disobey Chap 22 A new complaint of Pamphilus' new change to a graceless courtesan; Zelmane loves, and as a page serves Pyrocles; the two princes' policy to reconcile two warring brothers; the unbrotherly brave combat of Tydeus and Telenor; Plexirtus' viperine unkindness to the kindest Leonatus; his conquest by the two brothers, and his dogtrick to destroy them by themselves; the regreet of the dying brothers. 'So 90; disobey. 'So 93   [3] like a Cm, 93: like the 90

that, before his marriage-day appointed, he had taken to wife that Baccha of whom she complained, one that in divers places I had heard before blazed as the most impudently unchaste woman of all Asia, and withal, of such an imperiousness therein that she would not stick to employ them whom she made unhappy with her favour to draw more companions of their folly, in the multitude of whom she did no less glory than a captain would do of being followed by brave soldiers – waywardly proud, and therefore bold because extremely faulty, and yet, having no good thing to redeem both these and other unlovely parts but a little beauty disgraced with wandering eyes and unweighed speeches. Yet had Pamphilus for her left Leucippe, and withal left his faith – Leucippe, of whom one look in a clear judgement would have been more acceptable than all her kindnesses so prodigally bestowed. For myself, the remembrance of his cruel Dido,[1] joined to this, stirred me to seek some revenge upon him, but that I thought it should be a gain to him to lose his life, being so matched; and therefore leaving him to be punished by his own election, we conveyed Leucippe to a house thereby, dedicated to Vestal nuns, where she resolved to spend all her years (which her youth promised should be many) in bewailing the wrong, and yet praying for the wrong-doer.

'But the next morning, we, having striven with the sun's earliness, were scarcely beyond the prospect of the high turrets of that building when there overtook us a young gentleman – for so he seemed to us. But indeed, sweet lady, it was the fair Zelmane, Plexirtus' daughter, whom unconsulting affection (unfortunately borne to me-wards) had made borrow so much of her natural modesty as to leave her more decent raiments, and taking occasion of Andromana's tumultuous pursuing us, had apparelled herself like a page, with a pitiful cruelty cutting off her golden hair, leaving nothing but the short curls to cover that noble head – but that she ware upon it a fair headpiece; a shield at her back and a lance in her hand, else disarmed; her apparel of white, wrought upon with broken knots; her horse fair and lusty, which she rid so as might show a fearful boldness (daring to do that which she knew that she knew not how to do) – and the sweetness of her countenance did give such a grace to what she did, that it did make handsome the unhandsomeness, and make the eye force the mind to believe that there was a praise in that unskilfulness.

'But she straight approached me, and with few words (which borrowed the help of her countenance to make themselves understood) she desired me to accept her in[2] my service, telling me she was a nobleman's son of Iberia, her name Daiphantus, who, having seen what I had done in that

---

[1] his cruel Dido *Cm*: his cruelty to Dido *90*; his cruel handling Dido *93*   [2] in] into *93*

court, had stolen from her father to follow me. I inquired the particularities of the manner of Andromana's following me, which by her I understood, she hiding nothing – but her sex – from me. And still methought I had seen that face, but the great alteration of her fortune made her far distant from my memory; but liking very well the young gentleman (such I took her to be), admitted this Daiphantus about me, who well showed there is no service like his that serves because he loves; for though born of princes' blood, brought up with tenderest education, unapt to service because a woman, and full of thoughts because in a strange estate, yet love enjoined such diligence that no apprentice – no, no bondslave – could ever be by fear more ready at all commandments than that young princess was. How often, alas, did her eyes say unto me that they loved! and yet I, not looking for such a matter, had not my conceit open to understand them. How often would she come creeping to me, between gladness to be near me, and fear to offend me! Truly, I remember that then I marvelled[1] to see her receive my commandments with sighs, and yet do them with cheerfulness, sometimes answering me in such riddles as I then thought a childish inexperience[2] – but since, returning to my remembrance, they have come more near[3] unto my knowledge – and pardon me, only dear lady, that I use many words, for her affection to me deserves of me an affectionate speech.

'But in[4] such sort did she serve me, in that kingdom of Bithynia, for two months' space – in which time we brought to good end a cruel war long maintained between the king of Bithynia and his brother; for my excellent cousin and I, dividing ourselves to either side, found means (after some trial we had made, of ourselves) to get such credit with them as we brought them to as great peace between themselves, as love towards us for having made the peace; which done, we intended to return through the kingdom of Galatia toward Thrace, to ease the care of our father and mother, who we were sure, first with the shipwreck and then with the other dangers we daily passed, should have little rest in their thoughts till they saw us.

'But we were not entered into that kingdom, when by the noise of a great fight we were guided to a pleasant valley, which, like one of those circuses which in great cities somewhere doth give a pleasant spectacle of running horses, so of either side, stretching itself in a narrow length, was it hemmed in by woody hills, as if indeed nature had meant therein to make a place for beholders. And there we beheld one of the cruellest fights between two knights that ever hath adorned the martial[5] story, so as, I must confess, a while we stood bewondered,[6] another while delighted, with the rare bravery

---

[1] marvelled *Cm, 93*: marvelling *90* [2] a childish inexperience *Cm, 93*: childish in experience *90*
[3] near] clear *93* [4] But in *Cm, 93*: In *90* [5] the martial] the most martial *93* [6] bewondered *Cm, 93*: wondering *90*

thereof, till seeing such streams of blood as threatened a drowning of life, we galloped toward them to part them. But we were prevented by a dozen armed knights (or rather, villains) who, using this time of their extreme feebleness, all together set upon them. But common danger brake off particular discord, so that, though with a dying weakness, with a lively courage they resisted, and by our help drave away or slew those murdering attempters, among whom we happed to take alive the principal. But going to disarm those two excellent knights, we found (with no less wonder to us than astonishment to themselves) that they were the two valiant and indeed famous brothers, Tydeus and Telenor, whose adventure (as afterward we made that ungracious wretch confess) had thus fallen out.

'After the noble Prince Leonatus had (by his father's death) succeeded in the kingdom of Galatia, he (forgetting all former injuries) had received that naughty Plexirtus into a strait degree of favour – his goodness being as apt to be deceived as the other's craft was to deceive; till by plain proof finding that the ungrateful man went about to poison him, yet would not suffer his kindness to be overcome, not by justice itself; but calling him to him, used words to this purpose.

'"Plexirtus," said he, "this wickedness is found by thee. No good deeds of mine have been able to keep it down in thee. All men counsel me to take away thy life, likely to bring forth nothing but as dangerous, as wicked, effects. But I cannot find it in my heart, remembering what father's son thou art. But since it is the violence of ambition which perchance pulls thee from thine own judgement, I will see whether the satisfying that may quiet the ill-working of thy spirits.

'"Not far hence is the great city of Trebizond, which, with the territory about it, anciently pertained unto this crown – now unjustly possessed, and as unjustly abused, by those who have neither title to hold it, nor virtue to use it.[1] To the conquest of that for thyself, I will lend thee force, and give thee my right. Go therefore, and with less unnaturalness glut thy ambition there; and that done, if it be possible, learn virtue."

'Plexirtus, mingling forsworn excuses with false-meant promises, gladly embraced the offer; and hastily sending back for those two brothers, who at that time were with us succouring the gracious Queen Erona, by their virtue chiefly (if not only) obtained the conquest of that goodly dominion, which indeed done by them, gave them such an authority that, though he reigned, they in effect ruled – most men honouring them because they only deserved honour (and many thinking therein to please Plexirtus, considering how much he was bound unto them), while they likewise, with a certain sincere

---

[1] to use it] *om. Cm*; to rule it 93

boldness of self-warranting friendship, accepted all openly and plainly, thinking nothing should ever by Plexirtus be thought too much in them, since all they were was his. But he, who by the rules of his own mind could construe no other end of men's doings but self-seeking, suddenly feared what they could do; and as suddenly suspected what they would do; and as suddenly hated them, as having both might, and mind, to do. But dreading their power (standing so strongly in their own valour, and others' affection), he durst not take open way against them; and as hard it was to take a secret, they being so continually followed by the best and everyway ablest of that region; and therefore used this devilish sleight which I will tell you, not doubting, most wicked man, to turn their own friendship toward him to their own destruction.

'He, knowing that they well knew there was no friendship between him and the new king of Pontus (never since he succoured Leonatus and us, to his overthrow), gave them to understand that of late there had passed secret defiance between them to meet privately at a place appointed, which though not so fit a thing for men of their greatness, yet was his honour so engaged as he could not go back. Yet feigning to find himself weak by some counterfeit infirmity, the day drawing near, he requested each of them to go in his stead, making either of them swear to keep the matter secret – even[1] each from other; delivering the selfsame particularities to both, but that he told Tydeus the king would meet him in a blue armour, and Telenor that it was a black armour – and with wicked subtilty, as if it had been so appointed, caused Tydeus to take a black armour, and Telenor a blue; appointing them ways how to go, so as he knew they should not meet till they came to the place appointed, where each had promised to keep silence, lest the king should discover it was not Plexirtus. And there in await had he laid these murtherers, that who overlived the other should by them be dispatched – he not daring trust more than those with that enterprise, and yet thinking them too few, till themselves, by themselves, were weakened.

'This we learned chiefly by the chief of those way-beaters after the death of those worthy[2] brothers, whose love was no less than their valour. But well we might find much thereof by their pitiful lamentation, when they knew their mismeeting and saw each other; in despite of the surgery we could do unto them, striving who should run fastest to the goal of death; each bewailing the other, and more dying in the other than in himself; cursing their own hands for doing, and their breasts for not sooner suffering; detesting their unfortunately spent time in having served so ungrateful a tyrant, and accusing their folly in having believed he could faithfully love, who did

---

[1] even *Cm, 93*: ever *90* [2] those worthy] those two worthy *93*

not love faithfulness; wishing us to take heed how we placed our good will upon any other ground than proof of virtue, since length of acquaintance, mutual secrecies, nor height of benefits could bind a savage heart – no man being good to other that is not good in himself; then, while any hope was, beseeching us to leave the care[1] of him that besought, and only look to the other. But when they found by themselves – and us – no possibility, they desired to be joined; and so embracing, and craving that pardon each of other which they denied to themselves, they gave us a most sorrowful spectacle of their death, leaving few in the world behind them their matches in anything – if they had soon enough known the ground and limits of friendship. But with woeful hearts we caused those bodies to be conveyed to the next town of Bithynia, where we learning thus much as I have told you, caused the wicked historian to conclude his history[2] with his own well-deserved death.

'But[3] then, I must tell you, I found such woeful countenances in Daiphantus, that I could not but much marvel (finding them continue beyond the first assault of pity) how the case[4] of strangers (for further I did not conceive) could so deeply pierce. But the truth indeed is that, partly with the shame and sorrow she took of her father's faultiness, partly with the fear that the hate I conceived against him would utterly disgrace her in my opinion whensoever I should know her, so vehemently perplexed her that her fair colour decayed, and daily and hastily grew into the very extreme working of sorrowfulness – which oft I sought to learn and help, but she (as fearful as loving) still concealed it, and so decaying still more and more in the excellency of her fairness – but that whatsoever weakness took away, pity seemed to add. Yet still she forced herself to wait on me, with such care and diligence as might well show had been taught in no other school but love.

'While we returning again to embark ourselves for Greece, understood that the mighty Otanes,[5] brother to Barzanes (slain by Musidorus in the battle of the six princes), had entered upon the kingdom of Pontus, partly upon the pretences he had to the crown, but principally because he would revenge upon him, whom he knew we loved, the loss of his brother, thinking, as indeed he had cause, that wheresoever we were, hearing of his extremity we would come to relieve him – in spite whereof he doubted not to prevail, not only upon the confidence of his own virtue and power, but especially because he had in his company two mighty giants, sons to a couple whom we

---

[1] care *Cm, 93*: cure *90* [2] history] story *93* [3] death. 'But *Cm, 93*: death.' Chap. 23. Zelmane's grief for Plexirtus' fault; Otaves and his giants' war on Pontus; Plexirtus endangered, needs help of the dead brothers; Zelmane thought-sick, unmasks herself; her dying tears and last requests; Musidorus to Pontus, Pyrocles hardly parts to save Plexirtus; the source and course of his death's-doom stayed by Pyrocles; the combat of Pontus well ended; the Asian princes' meeting to honour the two Greeks. 'But *90* [4] case *Cm, 93*: cause *90* [5] Otanes *Cm, 93*: Otaves *90*

slew in the same realm. They having been absent at their father's death, and now returned, willingly entered into his service, hating (more than he) both us and that king of Pontus. We therefore with all[1] speed went thitherward; but by the way this fell out, which, whensoever I remember without sorrow, I must forget withal all humanity.

'Poor Daiphantus fell extreme sick, yet would needs conquer the delicacy of her constitution and force herself to wait on me; till one day, going toward Pontus, we met one who in great haste went seeking for Tydeus and Telenor, whose death as yet was not known unto the messenger – who, being their servant, and knowing how dearly they loved Plexirtus, brought them word how, since their departing, Plexirtus was in present[2] danger of a cruel death if by the valiantness of one of the best knights of the world he were not rescued. We inquired no further of the matter, being glad he should now to his loss find what an unprofitable treason it had been unto him to dismember himself of two such friends, and so let the messenger part, not sticking to make him know his masters' destruction by the falsehood of Plexirtus – but the grief of that (finding a body already brought to the last degree of weakness) so overwhelmed the little remnant of the spirits left in Daiphantus that she fell suddenly into deadly soundings, never coming to herself but that withal she returned to make most pitiful lamentations – most strange unto us, because we were far from guessing the ground thereof. But finding her sickness such as began to print death in her eyes, we made all haste possible to convey her to the next town – but before we could lay her on a bed, both we, and she, might find in herself that the harbingers[3] of over-hasty death had prepared his lodging in that dainty body; which she undoubtedly feeling, with a weak cheerfulness showed comfort therein.

'And then, desiring us both to come near her and that nobody else might be present, with pale and yet even-in-paleness-lovely lips, "Now or never – and never, indeed! But now it is[4] time for me", said she, "to speak. And I thank death, which gave[5] me leave to discover that, the suppressing whereof perchance hath been the sharpest spur that hath hasted my race to this end. Know, then, my lords, and especially you, my lord and master Pyrocles, that your page Daiphantus is the unfortunate Zelmane, who for your sake caused my as unfortunate lover and cousin Palladius to leave his father's court, and consequently both him and my aunt, his mother, to lose their lives. For your sake myself have become, of a princess, a page, and for your sake have put off the apparel of a woman, and – if you judge not more mercifully – the modesty"[6]

'We were amazed at her speech, and then had, as it were, new eyes given us to perceive that which before had been a present stranger to our minds;

---

[1] with all *Cm*, 93: withal 90   [2] present *Cm*, 93: prent 90   [3] harbingers *Cm*, 93: harbinger 90   [4] it is] is it 93   [5] gave] gives 93   [6] the modesty *Cm*, 93: modesty 90

for indeed, we forthwith knew it to be the face of Zelmane, whom before we had known in the court of Iberia. And sorrow and pity laying her pain upon me, I comforted her the best I could by the tenderness of good will, pretending indeed better hope than I had of her recovery.

'But she that had inward ambassadors from the tyrant that should shortly[1] oppress her, "No, my dear master," said she, "I neither hope nor desire to live. I know you would never have loved me;" and with that, she[2] wept, "nor, alas, had it been reason you should, considering many ways my unworthiness. It sufficeth me that the strange course I have taken shall to your remembrance witness my love. And yet this breaking of my heart, before I would discover my pain, will make you, I hope, think I[3] was not altogether unmodest. Think of me so, dear master, and that thought shall be my life." And with that, languishingly looking upon me, "And I pray you," said she, "even by these dying eyes of mine (which are only sorry to die because they shall lose your sight), and by these polled locks of mine (which while they were long were the ornament of my sex; now in their short curls, the testimony of my servitude), and by the service I have done you (which, God knows, hath been full of love), think of me after my death with kindness, though you cannot with love. And whensoever you shall make any other lady happy with your placed[4] affection, if you tell her my folly, I pray you speak of it not with scorn but with pity."

'I assure you, dear princess: of my life – for how could it be otherwise – her words and her manner,[5] with the lively consideration of her love, so pierced me that I, though[6] I had divers griefs before, yet methought I never felt till then how much sorrow enfeebleth all resolution; for I could not choose but yield to the weakness of abundant weeping, in truth with such grief that I could willingly at that time have changed lives with her. But when she saw my tears, "O God!" said she, "How largely am I recompensed for my losses! Why, then", said she, "I may take boldness to make some requests unto you."

'I besought her to do, vowing the performance though my life were the price thereof. She showed great joy. "The first", said she, "is this: that you will pardon my father the displeasure you have justly conceived against him, and for this once succour him out of the danger wherein he is. I hope he will amend; and I pray you, whensoever you remember him to be the faulty Plexirtus, remember withal that he is Zelmane's father. The second is that, when you come into[7] Greece, you will take unto yourself this name (though unlucky) of Daiphantus, and vouchsafe to be called by it, for so shall I be sure you shall have cause to remember me – and let it please your noble cousin

---

[1] should shortly] shortly would 93 [2] that, she] that word, she 93 [3] think I] think that I 93 [4] your placed] your well-placed 93 [5] manner *Cm*, 93: manners 90 [6] that I, though] that, though 93 [7] come into] come once into 93

to be called Palladius, that I do that right to that poor prince, that his name yet may[1] live upon the earth in so excellent a person; and so, between you, I trust sometimes your unlucky page shall be, perhaps with a sigh, mentioned. Lastly, let me be buried here obscurely, not suffering my friends to know my fortune; till, when you are safely returned to your own country, you cause my bones to be conveyed thither, and laid, I beseech you, in some place where yourself vouchsafe sometimes to resort" – alas, small petitions for such a suitor, which yet she so earnestly craved that I was fain to swear the accomplishment.

'And then kissing me, and often desiring me not to condemn her of lightness, in mine arms she delivered her pure soul to the purest place, leaving me as full of agony as kindness, pity, and sorrow could make an honest heart – for I must confess for true, that if my stars had not wholly reserved me for you, there else perhaps I might have loved, and, which had been most strange, begun my love after death; whereof let it be the less marvel, because somewhat she did resemble you, though, as far short of your perfection, as herself dying was of her flourishing.[2] Yet something there was, which, when I saw a picture of yours, brought again her figure into my remembrance, and made my heart as apt to receive the wound, as the power of your beauty with unresistable force to pierce.

'But we in woeful and yet private manner burying her, performed her commandment; and then inquiring of her father's estate, certainly learned that he was presently to be succoured or, by death, to pass the need of succour. Therefore we determined to divide ourselves: I (according to my vow) to help him, and Musidorus toward the king of Pontus who stood in no less need than immediate succour – and even ready to depart one from the other, there came a messenger from him (who after some inquiry found us) giving us to understand that he, trusting upon us two, had appointed the combat between him and us against Otanes[3] and the two giants. Now the day was so accorded as it was impossible for me both to succour Plexirtus and be there, where my honour was not only so far engaged,[4] but, by the strange working of unjust fortune, I was to leave the standing-by Musidorus (whom better than myself I loved) to go save him whom for just causes I hated. But my promise given, and given to Zelmane – and to Zelmane dying – prevailed more with me than my friendship to Musidorus, though certainly, I may affirm, nothing had so great rule in my thoughts as that. But my promise carried me the easier, because Musidorus himself would not suffer me to break it.

'And so with heavy minds, more careful each of other's success than of our own, we parted – I toward the place where I understood Plexirtus was

---

[1] yet may *Cm, 93*: may yet *90* [2] her flourishing] herself flourishing *93* [3] Otanes *Cm, 93*: Otaves *90*
[4] so far engaged *Cm, 93*: gaged so far *90*

prisoner to an ancient lord,[1] absolutely governing a goodly castle with a large territory about it, whereof he acknowledged no other sovereign but himself; whose hate to Plexirtus grew for a kinsman of his whom he maliciously had murdered, because, in the time that he reigned in Galatia, he found him apt to practise for the restoring of his virtuous brother, Leonatus. This old knight, still thirsting for revenge, used as the way to it a policy, which this occasion I will tell you prepared for him.

'Plexirtus in his youth had married Zelmane's mother, who dying of that only child-birth, he (a widower, and not yet a king) haunted the court of Armenia, where, as he was coming[2] to win favour, he obtained great good liking of Artaxia – which he pursued till (being called home by his father) he falsely got his father's kingdom, and then neglected his former love; till (thrown out of that by our means before he was deeply rooted in it, and by and by again placed in Trebizond) understanding that Artaxia by her brother's death was become queen of Armenia, he was hotter than ever in that pursuit; which being understood by this old knight, he forged such a letter as might be written from Artaxia, entreating his present but very private[3] repair thither, giving him faithful promise of present marriage – a thing far from her thought, having faithfully and publicly protested that she would never marry any, but some such prince who would give sure proof that by his means we were destroyed. But he (no more witty to frame, than blind to judge, hopes) bit hastily at the bait, and in private manner posted toward her.

'But by the way he was met by this knight, far better accompanied, who quickly laid hold of him and condemned him to death, cruel enough (if anything may be both cruel and just), for he caused him to be kept in a miserable prison till a day appointed, at which time he would deliver him to be devoured by a monstrous beast of most ugly shape (armed like a rhinoceros, as strong as an elephant, as fierce as a lion, as nimble as a leopard, and as cruel as a tiger), whom he having kept in a strong place from the first youth of it, now thought no fitter match than such a beastly monster with a monstrous tyrant; proclaiming yet withal that if any so well loved him as to venture their lives against his[4] beast for him, if they overcame, he should be saved – not caring how many they were (such confidence he had in that[5] monster's strength), but especially hoping to entrap thereby the great courages of Tydeus and Telenor, whom he no less hated because they had been principal instruments of the other's power.

'I dare say, if Zelmane had known what danger I should have passed, she would rather have let her father perish than me to have bidden that adventure; but my word was passed, and, truly, the hardness of the enterprise

---

[1] lord *Cm, 93*: knight *90* [2] coming] cunning *93* [3] private *Cm, 93*: privy *90* [4] his *Cm, 93*: this *90*
[5] that *Cm, 93*: the *90*

was not so much a bit as a spur unto me, knowing well that the journey of high honour lies not in plain ways. Therefore going thither, and taking sufficient security that Plexirtus should be delivered if I were victorious, I undertook the combat; and (to make short, excellent lady, and not trouble[1] your ears with recounting a terrible matter) so was my weakness blessed from above that without dangerous wounds I slew that monster (which hundreds durst not attempt), to so great admiration of many (who from a safe place might look on) that there was order given to have the fight both by sculpture and picture celebrated in most parts of Asia. And the old nobleman so well liked me that he loved me, only bewailing my virtue had been employed to save a worse monster than I killed, whom yet (according to faith given) he delivered, and accompanied me to the kingdom of Pontus, whither I would needs in all speed go to see whether it were possible for me (if perchance the day had been delayed) to come to the combat – but that, before I came, had been thus finished.

'The virtuous Leonatus, understanding two so good friends of his were to be in that danger, would perforce be one himself; where he did valiantly, and so did the king of Pontus – but the truth is that, both they being sore hurt, the incomparable Musidorus finished the combat by the death of both the giants, and the taking of Otanes[2] prisoner, to whom, as he gave his life, so he got a noble friend – for so he gave his word to be; and he is well known to think himself greater, in being subject to that, than in the greatness of his principality.

'But thither (understanding of our being there) flocked great multitudes of many great persons, and even of princes – especially those whom we had made beholding unto us, as the kings of Phrygia; Bithynia; with those two hurt, of Pontus and Galatia; and Otanes,[3] the prisoner by Musidorus set free; and thither came Plexirtus of Trebizond; and Antiphilus (then king of Lycia), with as many mo great princes, drawn either by our reputation, or by willingness to acknowledge themselves obliged unto us for what we had done for the others, so as, in those parts of the world, I think, in many hundreds of years, there was not seen so royal an assembly, where nothing was let pass to do us the highest honours which such persons, who might command both purses and inventions, could perform – all, from all sides, bringing unto us right royal presents (which we to avoid both unkindness and importunity liberally received); and not content therewith would needs accept, as from us, their crowns, and acknowledge to hold them of us – with many other excessive honours which would not suffer the measure of this short leisure to describe unto you.

---

[1] not trouble] not to trouble 93   [2] Otanes *Cm*, 93 Otaves 90   [3] Otanes *Cm*, 93: Otaves 90

'But[1] we (quickly aweary thereof) hasted to Greece-ward, led thither partly with the desire of our parents, but hastened principally because I understood that Anaxius (with open mouth of defamation) had gone thither to seek me, and was now come to Peloponnesus, where from court to court he made inquiry of me, doing yet himself so noble deeds as might hap to authorize an ill opinion of me. We therefore suffered but short delays, desiring to take this country in our way – so renowmed over the world that no prince could pretend height, nor beggar lowness, to bar him from the sound thereof; renowmed indeed, not so much for the ancient praises attributed thereunto, as for the having in it Argalus and Amphialus, two knights of such rare prowess as we desired especially to know – and yet by far not so much for that, as without suffering of comparison for the beauty of you and your sister, which makes all indifferent judges that speak thereof account this country as a temple of deities.

'But these causes indeed moving us to come by this land, we embarked ourselves in the next port, whither all those princes (saving Antiphilus, who returned – as he pretended – not able to tarry longer[2] from Erona) conveyed us. And there found we a ship most royally furnished by Plexirtus, who made[3] all things so proper, as well for our defence as ease, that all the other princes greatly commended him for it, who, seeming a quite altered man, had nothing but repentance in his eyes, friendship in his gesture, and virtue in his mouth; so that we, who had promised the sweet Zelmane to pardon him, now not only forgave, but began to favour, persuading ourselves with a youthful credulity that perchance things were not so evil as we took them, and, as it were, desiring our own memory that it might be so.

'But so were we licensed from those princes, truly, not without tears, especially of the virtuous Leonatus, who with the king of Pontus would have come with us, but that we (in respect of the one's young wife, and both their new-settled kingdoms) would not suffer it. Then would they have sent whole fleets to guard us, but we, that desired to pass secretly into Greece, made them leave that motion when they found that more ships than one would be displeasing unto us. But so committing ourselves to the uncertain discretion of the wind, we (then determining as soon as we came to Greece to take the names of Daiphantus and Palladius, as well for our own promise to Zelmane, as because we desired to come unknown into Greece) left the Asian shore, full of princely persons, who even upon their knees recommended our safe-

---

[1] you. 'But *Cm, 93*: you.' Chap. 24. The causes and provisions of the princes' embarking for Arcadia; Plexirtus' treason against them disclosed by one, attempted by another of his ministers; sedition and slaughter in the ship about it; their shipwreck by fire; Pyrocles' fight with the captain, and escape from sea; the amorous concluding the old, and beginning a new story; both broken off by Miso. 'But *90*   [2] longer *Cm, 93*: long *90*   [3] who made] who had made *93*

ties to the devotion of their chief desires; among whom, none had been so officious (though I dare affirm, all quite contrary to his unfaithfulness) as Plexirtus.

'And so,[1] having sailed almost two days, looking for nothing but when we might look upon the land, a grave man (whom we had seen of great trust with Plexirtus, and was sent as our principal guide) came unto us; and with a certain kind manner mixed with shame and repentance began to tell us that he had taken such a love unto us, considering our youth and fame, that though he were a servant, and a servant of such trust about Plexirtus as that he had committed unto him even those secrets of his heart (which abhorred all other knowledge), yet he rather chose to reveal at this time a most pernicious counsel, than by concealing it bring to ruin those whom he could not choose but honour. So went he on, and told us that Plexirtus, in hope thereby to have Artaxia (endued[2] with the great kingdom of Armenia) to his wife, had given him order, when we were near Greece, to find some opportunity to murder us, bidding him to take us asleep, because he had seen what we could do waking.

'"Now sirs," said he, "I would rather a thousand times lose my life than have my remembrance while I lived poisoned with such a mischief. And therefore, if it were only I that knew herein the king's order, then should my disobedience be a warrant of your safety – but to one more," said he, "namely, the captain of the ship, Plexirtus hath opened so much touching the effect of murdering you (though, I think, laying the cause rather upon old grudge than his hope of Artaxia), and myself (before the consideration of your excellencies had drawn love and pity into mind) imparted it to such as I thought fittest for such a mischief. Therefore I wish you to stand upon your guard, assuring you that, what I can do for your safety, you shall see, if it come to the push, by me performed."

'We thanked him (as the matter indeed deserved), and from that time would no more disarm ourselves, nor the one sleep, without his friend's eyes waked for him; so that it delayed the going forward of their bad enterprise, while they thought it rather chance than providence which made us so behave ourselves. But when we came within half a day's sailing of the shore, soon[3] they saw it was speedily or not at all to be done. Then, and I remember it was about the first watch in the night, came the captain, and whispered the counsellor in the ear. But he as it should seem dissuading him from it, the captain (who had been a pirate from his youth, and often blooded in it) with a loud voice sware that, if Plexirtus bad him, he would not stick to kill God himself, and therewith called his mates, and in the king's name willed

---

[1] 'And so *Cm, 93*: 'So *90* [2] endued] endowed *90 (corr.), 93* [3] soon] so that *93*

them to take us alive or dead, encouraging them with the spoil of us, which he said (and indeed was true) would yield many exceeding rich jewels. But the counsellor, according to his promise, commanded them they should not commit such a villainy, protesting that he would stand between them and the king's anger therein; wherewith the captain, enraged, "Nay!" said he, "Then we must begin with this traitor himself!" and therewith gave him a sore blow upon the head, who honestly did the best he could to revenge himself.

'But then we knew it time rather to encounter than wait for mischief, and so, against the captain we went – who straight was environed with most part of the soldiers and mariners. And yet the truth is there were some whom either the authority of the counsellor, doubt of the king's mind, or liking of us, made draw their swords of our side, so that quickly it grew a most confused fight; for the narrowness of the place, the darkness of the time, and the uncertainty in such a tumult how to know friends from foes, made the rage of swords rather guide, than be guided by, their masters.

'For my cousin and me, truly, I think we never performed less in any place, doing no other hurt than the defence of ourselves, and succouring them who came for it, drave us to; for not discerning perfectly who were for or against us, we thought it less evil to spare a foe than spoil a friend. But from the highest to the lowest part of the ship there was no place left without cries of murdering and murdered persons. The captain I happed awhile to fight withal, but was driven to part with him by hearing the cry of the counsellor who received a mortal wound, mistaken of one of his own side. Some of the wiser would call to parley, and wish peace, but while the words of peace were in their mouths some of their evil auditors[1] gave them death for their hire, so that no man almost could conceive hope of living, but being left alive[2]; and therefore everyone was willing to make himself room by dispatching almost any other, so that the great number in the ship was reduced to exceeding few, when, of those few, the most part (weary of those troubles) leapt into the boat which was fast to the ship – but while they that were first were cutting of the rope that tied it, others came leaping in so disorderly that they drowned both the boat and themselves.

'But while even in that little remnant, like the children of Cadmus, we continued still to slay one another, a fire which (whether by the desperate malice of some, or intention to separate; or accidentally, while all things were cast up and down) it should seem had taken a good while before, but never heeded of us who only thought to preserve or revenge, now violently burst out in many places, and began to master the principal parts of the ship. Then necessity made us see that a common enemy sets at one a civil war; for

---

[1] their evil auditors *Cm, 93*: their auditors *90*   [2] but being left alive] but by being last alive *93*

that little all we were, as if we had been waged by one man to quench a fire, straight went to resist that furious enemy by all art and labour. But it was too late, for already it did embrace and devour from the stern to the waist of the ship, so as labouring in vain, we were driven to get up to the prow of the ship (by the work of nature seeking to preserve life as long as we could), while, truly, it was a strange and ugly sight to see so huge a fire, as it quickly grew to be, in the sea and in the night, as if it had come to light us to death. And by and by it had burned off the mast which all this while had proudly borne the sail (the wind, as might seem, delighted to carry fire and blood in his mouth), but now it fell overboard. And the fire growing nearer us, it was not only terrible in respect of what we were to attend, but insupportable through the heat of it, so that we were constrained to bide it no longer; but disarming and stripping ourselves, and laying ourselves upon such things as we thought might help our swimming to the land, too far for our own strength to bear us, my cousin and I threw ourselves into the sea.

'But I had swum a very little way when I felt, by reason of a wound I had, that I should not be able to bide the travail; and therefore, seeing the mast (whose tackling had been burnt off) float clear from the ship, I swam unto it; and getting on it, I found mine own sword, which by chance, when I threw it away, caught by a piece of canvas, had hung to the mast. I was glad because I loved it well – but gladder when I saw at the other end the captain of the ship and of all this mischief, who having a long pike, belike had borne himself up with that till he had set himself upon the mast.

'But when I perceived him, "Villain!" said I, "Doost thou think to overlive so many honest men, whom thy falsehood hath brought to destruction?"' With that, bestriding the mast, I gat by little and little towards him (after such a manner as boys are wont, if ever you saw that sport, when they ride the wild mare); and he perceiving my intention, like a fellow that had much more courage than honesty, set himself to resist. But I had in short space gotten within him, and giving him a sound blow, sent him to feed fishes; but there myself remained, until by pirates I was taken up, and among them again taken prisoner, and brought into Laconia.'

'But what,' said Philoclea, 'became of your cousin, Musidorus?'

'Lost!', said Pyrocles.

'Ah, my Pyrocles!' said Philoclea, 'I am glad I have taken you. I perceive you lovers do not always say truly. As though I know[1] not your cousin, Dorus the shepherd!'

'Life of my desires,' said Pyrocles, 'what is mine, even to my soul, is yours; but the secret of my friend is not mine. But if you know so much, then I may truly say he is lost, since he is no more his own – but I perceive your noble sister and you are great friends, and well doth it become you so to be.'

---

[1] know] knew 93

'But go forward, dear Pyrocles. I long to hear out till your meeting me, for there (to me-ward) is the best part of your story.'

'Ah, sweet Philoclea!' said Pyrocles. 'Do you think I can think so precious leisure as this well-spent in talking? Are your eyes a fit book, think you, to read a tale upon? Is my love quiet enough to be an historian? Dear princess, be gracious unto me!' – and then he fain would have remembered to have forgot himself. But she, with a sweetly disobeying grace, desired him that[1] her desire, once for ever, might serve that no spot might disgrace that love, which shortly (she hoped) should be to the world warrantable. Fain he would not have heard – till she threatened anger; and then the poor lover durst not, because he durst not.

'Nay, I pray thee, dear Pyrocles,' said she, 'let me have my story.'

'Sweet princess,' said he, 'give my thoughts a little respite. And if it please you, since this time must so be spoiled, yet it shall suffer the less harm if you vouchsafe to bestow your voice, and let me know how the good Queen Erona was betrayed into such danger, and why Plangus sought me; for indeed, I should pity greatly any mischance fallen to that princess.'

'I will,' said Philoclea, smiling, 'so you give me your word your hands shall be quiet auditors!'

'They shall,' said he, 'because subject.'

Then began she to speak, but with so pretty and delightful a majesty when she set her countenance to tell the matter that Pyrocles could not choose but rebel so far as to kiss her. She would have pulled her head away, and speak – but while she spake, he kissed – and it seemed he fed upon her words. But she gat away.

'How will you have your discourse,' said she, 'without you let my lips alone?'

He yielded, and took her hand. 'On this,' said he, 'will I revenge my wrong!' – and so, began to make much of that hand; when her tale and his delight were interrupted by Miso, who taking her time while Basilius' back was turned, came unto them and told Philoclea she deserved, she knew what, for leaving her mother (being evil at ease) to keep company with strangers. But Philoclea telling her that she was there by her father's commandment, she went away muttering that though her back, and her shoulders, and her neck were broken, yet as long as her tongue would wag, it should do her errand to her mother; and so, went up to Gynecia,[2] who was at that time miserably vexed with this manner of dream.

---

[1] desired him that *Cm, 93*: desired that *90*   [2] mother; and so, went up to Gynecia *Cm, 93*: mother. Chap. 25. Gynecia's divining dream; her passionate jealousy in actions, speech, and song described; her troubling Philoclea and Zelmane; the rebels' troubling her; rebels resisted by Zelmane; Zelmane assisted by Dorus; Dorus and Zelmane's five memorable strokes. So went up Miso to Gynecia *90*

It seemed unto her to be in a[1] place full of thorns, which so molested her as she could neither abide standing still, nor tread safely[2] going forward. In this case she thought Zelmane (being upon a fair hill, delightful to the eye and easy in apparence) called her thither, whither, with much anguish being come, Zelmane was vanished, and she found nothing but a dead body – like unto her husband; which seeming[3] at the first with a strange smell to infect her, as she was ready likewise within a while to die, the dead body (she thought) took her in his arms, and said, 'Gynecia, leave all, for here is thy only rest.' With that she awaked, crying very loud, 'Zelmane! Zelmane!' But remembering herself, and seeing Basilius by (her guilty conscience more suspecting than being suspected), she turned her call, and called for Philoclea.

Miso forthwith, like a valiant shrew, looking at Basilius as though she would speak though she died for it, told Gynecia that her daughter had been a whole hour together in secret talk with Zelmane. 'And,' says she, 'for my part, I could not be heard, your daughters are brought up in such awe – though I told her of your pleasure sufficiently.'

Gynecia, as if she had heard her last doom pronounced against her, with a side-look and changed[4] countenance, 'Oh, my lord,' said she, 'what mean you to suffer these[5] young folks together?'

Basilius, that aimed nothing at the mark of her suspicion, smilingly took her in his arms. 'Sweet wife,' said he, 'I thank you for your care[6] of your child, but they must be youths of other metal than Zelmane that can endanger her.'

'Oh, but – ', cried Gynecia; and therewith she stayed, for then indeed she did suffer a right[7] conflict betwixt the force of love, and rage of jealousy. Many times was she about to satisfy the spite[8] of her mind and tell Basilius how she knew Zelmane to be far other[9] than the outward appearance, but those[10] many times were all put back by the manifold objections of her vehement love. Fain she would have barred her daughter's hap, but loath she was to cut off her own hope. But now, as if her life had been set upon a wager of quick rising, as weak as she was, she gat up – though Basilius (with a kindness flowing only from the fountain of unkindness, being indeed desirous to win his daughter as much time as might be), was loath to suffer it, swearing he saw sickness in her face, and therefore was loath she should adventure the air.

But the great and wretched Lady Gynecia, possessed with those devils of love and jealousy, did rid herself from her tedious husband; and taking

---

[1] be in a] be a *Ph, Je, Qu, Cm*; om. *Da* [2] safely] safely *corr. to* softly *Cl*; softly *As, Da, Je, Qu*; fastly *Ph* [3] seeming] seemed *Bo, Qu*; being *Ph* [4] changed] changing *OA (ex. Cl, As)* [5] these] those *Cl, Ph, Je, Qu* [6] your care] the care *As, Da, Je* [7] right] great *Bo, Cl, Je* [8] spite] spirit *Da, Ph, Je* [9] other *OA, Cm*: otherwise *90, 93* [10] those] these *Cl, Je*

nobody with her, going toward them, 'O jealousy,' said she, 'the frenzy of wise folks, the well-wishing spite and unkind carefulness, the self-punishment for[1] other's fault[2] and self-misery in other's happiness; the cousin of envy, daughter[3] of love, and mother of hate, how couldst thou so quietly get thee a seat in the unquiet heart of Gynecia – Gynecia,' said she, sighing, 'thought wise, and once virtuous? Alas, it is thy breeder's power which plants thee there; it is the inflaming[4] agony of affection that works the chilling access of thy fever, in such sort that nature gives place. The growing of my daughter seems the decay of my self; the blessings of a mother turn to the curses[5] of a competitor, and the fair face of Philoclea appears more horrible in my sight than the image of death.'

Then remembered she this song, which she thought took a right measure of her present mind:

With two strange fires of equal heat possessed,
The one of love, the other jealousy,[6]
Both still do work, in neither find I rest;
For both, alas, their strengths[7] together tie[8];
The one aloft doth hold the other high.
   Love wakes[9] the jealous eye lest thence[10] it moves;
   The jealous eye, the more it looks, it loves.

These fires increase, in these I daily burn:
They feed on me, and with my wings do fly:
My lively[11] joys to doleful ashes turn:
Their flames mount up, my powers prostrate lie:
They live in force, I quite consumed die.
   One wonder yet far passeth my conceit:
   The fuel small, how be the fires[12] so great?

But her unleisured thoughts ran not over the ten first words, but, going with a pace not so much too fast for her body as slow for her mind, she found them together – who after Miso's departure had left their tale and determined what to say to Basilius. But full abashed was poor Philoclea (whose conscience now began to know cause of blushing), for first salutation receiving an eye from her mother full of the same disdainful scorn which Pallas showed to poor[13] Arachne,[14] that durst contend with her for the prize of well-weaving – yet did the force of love so much rule her that, though for

---

[1] for] of *Ph, Je, Qu* [2] fault *OA (ex. Ph, Je)*, 93: faults *Ph, Je, Cm*, 90 [3] daughter] the daughter *Ph, Je* [4] inflaming *OA (ex. Ph, Da), Cm*: flaming *Ph*, 90, 93; inflamed *Da* [5] curses] cursings *Ph, Qu* [6] other jealousy] other of jealousy *Ph, Ra*, 13 (of *deleted St*) [7] strengths] strength *Da, Ra* [8] tie] lie *Cl, Qu*; try *Ra* [9] wakes] marks *Ph, Ra*; makes *Je, Qu* [10] thence] them *As, Cm* [11] lively *OA (ex. O, Da), Cm*: lovely *O*, 90, 93; lives *Da* [12] fires] fire *Le, Ph, Qu* [13] to poor] to the poor *OA (ex. Je)* [14] Arachne] Arkyve *St*; Ariadne *Ph*

Zelmane's sake she did detest her, yet for Zelmane's sake she used no harder words to her[1] than to bid her go home and accompany her solitary father.

Then began she to display to Zelmane the storehouse of her deadly desires – when suddenly the confused rumour of a[2] mutinous multitude gave just occasion to Zelmane to break off any such conference (for well she found[3] they were not friendly voices they heard), and to retire with as much diligence as conveniently they could towards[4] the lodge. Yet before they could win the lodge by twenty paces, they were overtaken by an unruly sort[5] of clowns and other rebels, which like a violent flood were carried, they themselves knew not whither. But as soon as they came within perfect discerning these ladies, like enraged beasts, without[6] respect of their estates or pity of their sex, they began to run against them – as right villains, thinking ability to do hurt to be a great advancement; yet so many as they were, so many almost were their[7] minds, all knit together only in madness. Some cried 'Take!', some 'Kill!', some 'Save!' – but even they that cried 'save' ran for company with them that meant[8] to kill. Every one commanded, none obeyed. He only seemed chief captain that was most rageful.

Zelmane, whose virtuous courage was ever awake, drew out her sword, which upon those ill-armed churls giving as many wounds as blows, and as many deaths (almost) as wounds, lightening courage, and thundering smart upon them, kept them at a bay; while the two ladies got themselves into the lodge, out of the which Basilius (having put on an armour long untried)[9] came to prove his authority among his subjects, or at least to adventure his life with his dear mistress, to whom he brought a shield – while the ladies tremblingly[10] attended the issue of this dangerous adventure. But Zelmane made them perceive the odds between an eagle and a kite, with such a nimble staidness and such an assured nimbleness that, while one was running back for fear, his fellow had her sword in his guts – and by and by was both her heart and help well increased by the coming of Dorus, who (having been making of hurdles for his master's sheep) heard the horrible cries of this mad multitude; and having straight represented before the eyes of his careful love the peril wherein the soul of his soul might be, he went to Pamela's lodge, but found her in a cave hard by with Mopsa and Dametas, who at that time would not have opened the entry to his father; and therefore leaving them there, as in a place safe, both for being strong and unknown, he ran as the noise guided him.

---

[1] to her] om. *Bo*; unto her *Je, Qu*   [2] of a] of *Da*; of the *Qu*   [3] she found] they found *OA (ex. Cl)*   [4] towards] unto *Bo, Je*; to *Qu*   [5] sort] company *As, Je*   [6] without] with *Bo, Da*   [7] their] the *OA (ex. Cl, As)*   [8] meant] went *Da, Ph*; cried *Je*   [9] long untried] long before untried *OA (ex. Je)*   [10] tremblingly] trembling *St, Ph, Je, Qu*

But when he saw his friend in such danger among them, anger and contempt asking no counsel but of courage made him run[1] among them with no other weapon but his sheephook, and with that overthrowing one of the villains, took away a two-hand sword from him, and withal helped him from ever being ashamed of losing it. Then lifting up his brave head, and flashing terror into their faces, he made arms and legs go complain to the earth how evil their masters had kept them. Yet the multitude still growing, and the very killing wearying them, fearing lest in long fight they should be conquered with conquering, they drew back toward the lodge – but drew back in such sort that still their terror went forward, like a valiant mastiff, whom, when his master pulls back by the tail from the bear with whom he hath already interchanged a hateful embracement, though his pace be backward his gesture is forward, his teeth and eyes threatening more in the retiring than they did in the advancing – so guided they themselves homeward, never stepping step backward, but that they proved themselves masters of the ground where they stepped.

Yet among the rebels there was a dapper fellow, a tailor by occupation, who, fetching his courage only from their going back, began to bow his knees and very fencer-like to draw near to Zelmane; but (as he came within her distance) turning his sword very nicely about his crown, Basilius with a side-blow strake off his nose. He being a suitor to a seamster's daughter, and therefore not a little grieved for such a disgrace, stooped down because he had heard that, if it were fresh put to, it would cleave on again – but as his hand was on the ground to bring his nose to his head, Zelmane with a blow sent his head to his nose. That saw a butcher (a butcherly chuff indeed, who that day was sworn brother to him in a cup of wine), and lifted up a great lever, calling Zelmane all the vile names of a butcherly eloquence; but she letting slip the blow of the lever, hit him so surely on[2] the side of his face that she left nothing but the nether jaw, where the tongue still wagged – as willing to say more, if his master's remembrance had served.

'Oh!' said a miller that was half drunk, 'See the luck of a goodfellow!' – and with that word ran with a pitchfork at Dorus. But the nimbleness of the wine carried his head so fast that it made it overrun his feet, so that he fell withal, just between the legs of Dorus; who setting his foot on his neck, though he offered two milch-kine and four fat hogs for his life, thrust his sword quite through from one ear to the other – which took it very unkindly to feel such news before they heard of them, instead of hearing, to be put to such feeling. But Dorus, leaving the miller to vomit his soul

---

[1] run *Cm, 93*: room *90*   [2] on] upon *93*

out in wine and blood, with his two-hand sword strake off another quite by the waist, who the night before had dreamed he was grown a couple, and interpreting it he[1] should be married, had bragged of his dream that morning among his neighbours. But that blow astonished quite a poor painter who stood by with a pike in his hands. This painter was to counterfeit the skirmishing[2] between the Centaurs and Lapiths and had been very desirous to see some notable wounds, to be able the more lively to express them; and this morning, being carried by the stream of this company, the foolish fellow was even delighted to see the effect of blows – but this last happening near him so amazed him that he stood stock still,[3] while Dorus with a turn of his sword strake off both his hands; and so, the painter returned well-skilled in wounds, but with never a hand to perform his skill.

In[4] this manner they recovered the lodge, and gave the rebels a face of wood of[5] the outside. But they then, though no more furious, yet more courageous when they saw no resister, went about with pickax to the wall and fire to the gate to get themselves entrance. Then did the two ladies mix fear with love – especially Philoclea who ever caught hold of Zelmane, so by the folly of love hindering the succour[6] which she desired. But Zelmane seeing no way of defence, nor time to deliberate (the number of those villains still increasing, and their madness still increasing with their number), thought it only the mean[7] to go beyond their expectation with an unused boldness, and with danger to avoid danger, and therefore opened again the gate; and Dorus and Basilius standing ready for her defence, she issued again among them.

The blows she had dealt before, though all in general were hasty, made each of them in particular take breath before they brought them suddenly over-near her, so that she had time to get up to the judgement-seat of the prince, which according to the guise of that country was before the court gate.[8] There she paused awhile, making sign with her hand unto them, and withal speaking aloud that she had something to say unto them that would please them. But she was answered a while with nothing but shouts and cries, and some beginning to throw stones at her, not daring to approach her. But at length a young farmer, who might do most among the country sort, and was caught in a little affection towards Zelmane, hoping by this kindness to have some good of her, desired them, if they were honest men, to hear the woman speak.

---

[1] it he] it that he 93 [2] skirmishing] skirmish 93 [3] stood stock still *Cm*, 93: stood still 90 [4] skill. In *Cm*, 93: skill. Chap. 26. Zelmane's confident attempt to appease the mutiny; a bone of division cast by her, and caught by them; her pacificatory oration; the acceptation and issue of it. In 90 [5] wood of] wood on *Cl, As, Da* [6] succour *OA, Cm*, 93: help 90 [7] mean *St, Bo, Cl, As, Ph, Cm*: way *Da*; means *Je, Hm*, 90, 93 [8] the court gate *OA*, 93: the gate *Cm*, 90

'Fie, fellows, fie!' said he. 'What will all the maids in our town say if so many tall men shall be afraid to hear a fair wench? I swear unto you – by no little ones – I had rather give my team of oxen than we should show ourselves so uncivil wights. Besides – I tell you true – I have heard it of old men counted wisdom to hear much and say little.'

His sententious speech so prevailed that the most part began to listen. Then she (with such efficacy of gracefulness, and such a quiet magnanimity represented in her face in this uttermost peril, as the more the barbarous people looked, the more it fixed their looks upon her) in this sort began unto them.

'It is no small comfort unto me,' said she, 'having to speak something unto you for your own behoofs, to find that I have to deal with such a people who show indeed in themselves the right nature of valour, which, as it leaves no violence unattempted while the choler is nourished with resistance, so, when the subject of their wrath doth of itself unlooked-for offer itself into their hands, it makes them at least[1] take a pause before they determine cruelty. Now then, first, before I come to the principal matter, have I to say unto you that your Prince Basilius himself in person is within this lodge, and was one of the three whom a few of you went about to fight withal' – and this she said, not doubting but they knew it well enough, but because she would have them imagine that the prince might think that they did not know it. 'By him am I sent unto you, as from a prince to his well-approved subjects – nay, as from a father to beloved children – to know what it is that hath bred just quarrel among you, or who they be that have any way wronged you; what it is with which you are displeased, or of which you are desirous. This he requires; and indeed, for he knows your faithfulness, he commands you presently to set down, and to choose among yourselves someone who may relate your griefs or demands unto him.'

This, being more than they hoped for from their prince, assuaged well their fury, and many of them consented – especially the young farmer helping on, who meant to make one of the demands that he might have Zelmane for his wife. But when they began to talk of their grieves, never bees made such a confused humming, the town-dwellers demanding putting down of imposts; the country fellows, laying out of commons; some would have the prince keep his court in one place, some in another; all cried out to have new councillors (but when they should think of any new, they liked them as well as any other that they could remember); especially they would have the treasure so looked unto as that he should never need to take any more subsidies. At length, they fell to direct contrarieties: for the artisans, they would have corn and wine set at a lower price, and bound to be kept so still; the ploughmen, vine-labourers, and farmers would none of that. The

---

[1] least] last *Ph, Hm*

countrymen demanded that every man might be free in the chief towns – that could not the burgesses like of. The peasants would have the[1] gentlemen destroyed; the citizens (especially such as cooks, barbers, and those other that lived most on gentlemen) would but have them reformed. And of each side were like divisions, one neighbourhood beginning to find fault with another.

But no confusion was greater than of particular men's likings and dislikings, one dispraising such a one whom another praised, and demanding such a one to be punished whom the other would have exalted. No less ado was there about choosing him who should be their spokesman, the finer sort of burgesses (as merchants, prentices, and cloth-workers) because of their riches disdaining the baser occupations, and they because of their number as much disdaining them; all they scorning the countrymen's ignorance, and the countrymen suspecting as much their cunning – so that Zelmane, finding that their united rage was now grown not only to a dividing, but to a crossing one of another, and that the mislike grown among themselves did well allay the heat against her, made tokens again unto them (as though she took great care of their well doing and were afraid of their falling out) that she would speak unto them. They now grown jealous one of another – the stay having engendered division, and division having manifested their weakness – were willing enough to hear, the most part striving to show themselves willinger than their fellows; which Zelmane, by the acquaintance she had had with such kind of humours, soon perceiving, with an angerless bravery and an unbashed[2] mildness in this manner spake unto them.

'An unused thing it is, and I think not heretofore seen, O Arcadians, that a woman should give public counsel to men; a stranger to the country people; and that, lastly, in such a presence by a private person the regal throne should be possessed. But the strangeness of your action makes that used for virtue which your violent necessity imposeth. For certainly a woman may well speak to such men who have forgotten all manlike government; a stranger may with reason instruct such subjects that neglect due points of subjection; and is it marvel this place is entered into by another, since your own prince after thirty years' government dare not show his face unto his faithful people? Hear therefore, O Arcadians, and be ashamed!

'Against whom hath this zealous[3] rage been stirred? Whither have been bent these manful weapons of yours? In this quiet harmless[4] lodge there[5] are[6] harboured no Argians, your ancient enemies, nor Laconians, your now feared neighbours. Here be neither hard landlords nor biting usurers. Here

---

[1] have the] have all the 93 [2] unbashed *OA (ex. Ph)*, *Cm*: unbashed *corr. to* unabashed *Ph*; unabashed 90, 93 [3] zealous *OA (ex. As)*, 93: jealous *As*; *om. Cm*, 90 [4] harmless] *om. Bo, Je* [5] there *OA*, 93: *om. Cm*, 90 [6] are] be *As*, 93

lodge none but such as either you have¹ great cause to love or no cause to hate, here being none besides your prince, princess, and their children, but myself. Is it I,² then, O Arcadians, against whom your anger is armed? Am I the mark of your vehement quarrel? If it be so that innocency shall not be a stop for fury; if it be so that the law of hospitality (so long and holily observed among you) may not defend a stranger fled to your arms for succour; if, in fine, it be so that so many valiant men's courages can be inflamed to the mischief of one silly woman, I refuse not to make my life a sacrifice to your wrath. Exercise in me your indignation, so it go no further. I am content to pay the great favours I have received among you with my life, not ill-deserving. I present it³ here unto you, O Arcadians, if that may satisfy⁴ you, rather than you (called over the world 'the wise and quiet Arcadians') should be so vain as to attempt that alone which all the rest of your country will abhor; than you should show yourselves so ungrateful as to forget the fruit of so many years' peaceable government, or so unnatural⁵ as not to have, with the holy name of your natural prince, any fury overmastered – for such a hellish madness I know did never enter into your hearts, as to attempt anything against his person, which no successor, though never so hateful, will ever leave – for his own sake – unrevenged.

'Neither can your wonted valour be turned to such a baseness as, instead of a prince delivered unto you by so many royal ancestors, to take the tyrannous yoke of your fellow subject, in whom the innate⁶ meanness will bring forth ravenous covetousness, and the newness of his estate suspectful cruelty. Imagine, what could⁷ your enemies more wish unto you than to see your own estate with your own hands undermined? Oh, what would your forefathers say if they lived at this time and saw their offspring defacing such an excellent principality, which they with much⁸ labour and blood so wisely have established? Do you think them fools that saw you should not enjoy your vines, your cattle, no, not your wives and children, without government? And that there could be no government without a magistrate, and no magistrate without obedience, and no obedience where every one upon his own private passion may interpret the doings of the rulers?

'Let your wits make your present example to⁹ you. What sweetness, in good faith, find you in your present condition? What choice, of choice, find you if you had lost Basilius? Under whose ensign would you go if your enemies should invade you? If you cannot agree upon one to speak for you, how will you agree upon one to fight for you? But with this fear of I cannot

---

¹ but ... have] but either such as you have *As*; but such as you have *Ph, Je*   ² Is it I] It is I *Ph, Cm* (It is I *corr. to* Is it I *St*); *om. Je*   ³ it] *om. Da, Je*   ⁴ satisfy] suffice *Cl, Je, Hm*   ⁵ unnatural] unmerciful *Cl, As*   ⁶ innate] *blank left Cl, As*; mute *Ph*; imminate *Cm*   ⁷ could] would *St, Bo, Je, Hm*; *om. Da*
⁸ with much *OA (ex. Bo, Ph), 93*: with so much *Bo, Ph, Cm, 90*   ⁹ example to] example a lesson to *93*

tell what, one is troubled; and with that past wrong another is grieved. And I pray you, did the sun ever bring you a fruitful harvest but that it was more hot than pleasant? Have any of you children that be not sometimes cumbersome? Have any of you fathers that be not sometime wearish? What, shall we curse the sun, hate our children, or disobey our fathers?

'But what need I use these words since I see in your countenances, now virtuously settled, nothing else but love and duty to him by whom, for your only[1] sakes, the government is embraced? For all what is done he doth not only pardon you, but thank you, judging the action by the minds, and not the minds by the action. Your grieves and desires, whatsoever and whensoever you list, he will consider of – and to his consideration it is reason you should refer them. So then, to conclude: the uncertainty of his estate made you take arms; now you see him well, with the same love lay them down. If now you end, as I know you will, he will make no other account of this matter but as of a vehement, I must confess over-vehement, affection. The only continuance[2] might prove a wickedness. But it is not so; I see very well you began with zeal, and will end with reverence.'

The action Zelmane used, being beautified by nature and apparelled with skill (her gestures being such that, as her words did paint out her mind, so they served as a shadow to make the picture more lively and sensible; with the sweet clearness of her voice rising and falling kindly, as the nature of the word and efficacy of the matter required), all together in such an admirable[3] person (whose incomparable valour they had well felt, whose beauty did pierce through the thick dullness of their senses) gave such a way unto her speech through the rugged wilderness of their imaginations (who, besides they were stricken in admiration of her, as of more than a human creature, were cooled with taking breath, and had learned doubts out of leisure) that instead of roaring cries there was now heard nothing but a confused muttering, whether her saying were to be followed, betwixt fear to pursue, and loathness to leave. Most of them could have been content it had never been begun, but how to end it (each afraid of his companion) they knew not, finding it far easier to tie than to loose knots.

But Zelmane thinking it no evil way in such mutinies to give the mutinous some occasion of such service as they might think in their own judgement[4] would countervail their trespass, withal to take the more assured possession of their minds which she feared might begin to waver, 'Loyal Arcadians,' said she, 'now do I offer unto you the manifesting of your duties. All those that have taken arms for the prince's safety, let them turn their

---

[1] your only] only your *Cl, As*; your own *Je* [2] continuance] countenance *Cl, As, Hm* [3] such an admirable *Cm, 93*: such admirable *90* [4] judgement] judgements *OA (ex. Bo)*

backs to the gate with their weapons bent against such as would hurt his sacred person.'

'Oh weak trust of the many-headed multitude, whom inconstancy only doth guide to well-doing! Who can set confidence there where company takes away shame, and each may lay the fault on[1] his fellow?' – so said a crafty fellow among them (named Clinias) to himself, when he saw the word no sooner out of Zelmane's mouth, but that there were some shouts of joy, with 'God save Basilius!', and divers of them with much jollity grown to be his guard that but little[2] before meant to be his murderers.[3] This Clinias in his youth had been a scholar (so far as to learn rather words than manners, and of words, rather plenty than order) and oft had used to be an actor in tragedies (where he had learned, besides a slidingness of language, acquaintance with many passions, and to frame his face to bear the figure of them), long used to the eyes and ears of men – and to reckon no fault but shamefastness; in nature a most notable coward – and yet, more strangely than rarely, venturous in privy practices. This fellow was become of near trust to Cecropia, Amphialus' mother, so that he was privy to all the mischievous devices wherewith she went about to ruin Basilius and his children for the advancing of her son; and though his education had made him full of tongue, yet his love to be doing taught him in any evil to be secret, and had by his mistress been used, ever since the strange retiring of Basilius, to whisper rumours into the people's ears; and this time finding great aptness in the multitude, was one of the chief that set them in the uproar – though quite without the consent of Amphialus, who would not for all the kingdoms of the world so have adventured the life of Philoclea.

But now, perceiving the flood of their fury began to ebb, he thought it policy to take the first of the tide, so that no man cried louder than he upon Basilius; and some of the lustiest rebels not yet agreeing to the rest, he caused two or three of his mates that were at his commandment to lift him up; and then, as if he had had a prologue to utter, he began with a nice gravity to demand audience. But few attending what he said, with vehement gesture, as if he would tear the stars from the skies, he fell to crying out so loud that not only Zelmane, but Basilius, might hear him.

'O unhappy men, more mad than the Giants that would have plucked Jupiter out of heaven, how long shall this rage continue? Why do you not all throw down your weapons and submit yourselves to our good prince – our good Basilius, the Pelops of wisdom and Minos of all good government?

---

[1] on *Da, Je, Cm,* 93: in *OA (ex. Da, Je);* of *90*   [2] but little] but then *OA (ex. Ph);* but a little *Ph*
[3] murderers. This *Cm,* 93: murderers. Chap. 27. A verbal crafty coward portrayed in Clinias; his first raising; and with the first, relenting in this mutiny; punished by the farmer; the uproar reinforced and weakened by themselves; Clinias' Sinon-like narration of this drunken rebellion's original; the king's order in it. This *90*

When will you begin to believe me and other honest and faithful subjects, that have done all we could to stop your fury?'

The farmer that loved Zelmane could abide him no longer, for, as at the first he was willing to speak of conditions, hoping to have gotten great sovereignties – and among the rest, Zelmane; so now perceiving that the people, once anything down the hill from their fury, would never stay[1] till they came to the bottom of absolute yielding, and so, that he should be nearer fears of punishment than hopes of such advancement, he was one of them that stood most against the agreement. And to begin withal, disdaining this fellow should play the preacher (who had been one of the chiefest makebates) strake him a great wound upon the face with his sword. The cowardly wretch fell down crying for succour; and scrambling through the legs of them that were about him, gat to the throne, where Zelmane took him and comforted him, bleeding for that was past, and quaking for fear of more.

But as soon as that blow was given, as if Aeolus had broke open the door to let all his winds out, no hand was idle, each one killing him that was next, for fear he should do as much to him; for being divided in minds and not divided in companies, they that would yield to Basilius were intermingled with them that would not yield: these men thinking their ruin stood upon it, those men (to get favour of their prince) converted their ungracious motion into their own bowels, and by a true judgement grew their own punishers. None was sooner killed than those that had been leaders in the disobedience, who by being so had taught them, that they did lead, disobedience to the same leaders. And many times it fell out that they killed them that were of their own faction, anger whetting, and doubt hastening, their fingers.

But then came down Zelmane, and Basilius with Dorus issued; and sometimes seeking to draw together those of their party, sometimes laying indifferently among them, made such havoc (among the rest, Zelmane striking the farmer to the heart with her sword as before she had done with her eyes) that in a while all they of the contrary side were put to flight and fled to certain woods upon the frontiers; where feeding coldly[2] and drinking only water, they were disciplined for their drunken riots – many of them being slain in that[3] chase, about a score only escaping. But when these late rebels, now soldiers, were returned from the chase, Basilius calling them together (partly for policy sake, but principally because Zelmane before had spoken it, which was to him more than a divine ordinance), he pronounced their general pardon, willing them to return to their houses and thereafter be more circumspect in their proceedings – which they did, most of them with share-marks[4] of their folly.[5] But imagining Clinias to be one of the chief

---

[1] stay *Cm, 93*: stop *90* [2] coldly] wildly *OA, 93* [3] that] the *93* [4] share-marks] sharp marks *93*
[5] their folly] their follies *Ph*; their own folly *Je*; their own follies *Hm*

that had bred this good alteration, he gave him particular thanks, and withal willed him to make him know how this frenzy had entered into the people.

Clinias purposing indeed to tell him the truth of all, saving what did touch himself or Cecropia, first dipping his hand in the blood of his wound, 'Now by this blood,' said he, 'which is more dear to me than all the rest that is in my body, since it is spent for your safety, this tongue (perchance unfortunate, but never false) shall not now begin to lie unto my prince, of me most beloved.' Then stretching out his hand, and making vehement countenances the ushers to his speeches, in such manner of terms recounted this accident.

'Yesterday,' said he, 'being your birthday, in the goodly green two mile hence before the city of Enispus, to do honour to the day were a four or five thousand people of all conditions, as I think, gathered together, spending all the day in dancings and other exercises; and when night came, under tents and boughs making great cheer, and meaning to observe a wassailing watch all that night for your sake. Bacchus, the learned say, was begot with thunder; I think that made him ever since so full of stir and debate. Bacchus indeed it was which[1] sounded the first trumpet to this rude[2] alarum, for that barbarous opinion being generally among them, to think with vice to do honour, and with activity in beastliness to show abundance of love, made most of them seek to show the depth of their affection in the depth of their draught. But being once well chafed with wine, having spent all the night and some piece of the morning in such revelling, and emboldened by your absented manner of living, there was no matter their ears had ever heard of that grew not to be a subject of their winy conference.

'I speak it by proof, for I take witness of the gods (who never leave perjuries unpunished) that I often cried out against their impudency, and when that would not serve, stopped mine ears because I would not be partaker of their blasphemies – till with buffets they forced me to have mine ears and eyes defiled. Public affairs were mingled[3] with private grudges, neither was any man thought of wit that did not pretend some cause of mislike. Railing was counted the fruit of freedom, and saying nothing had his uttermost praise in ignorance. At the length, your sacred person – alas, why did I live to hear it? Alas, how do I breathe to utter it? But your commandment doth not only enjoin obedience, but give me force – your sacred person, I say, fell to be their table-talk, a proud word swelling in their stomachs, and disdainful reproaches against so great a greatness having put on the show of greatness in their little[4] minds; till at length, the very unbridled use of words having increased fire in[5] their minds (which, God wot, thought their knowledge

---

[1] which] that *Da, Qu*   [2] rude] om. *Bo, Je*   [3] mingled *OA, Cm, 93*: minlegd *90*   [4] little] base *OA (ex. Cl, As)*   [5] in] to *OA (ex. Qu)* wot *93*: not *Cm*; knows *90*

notable because they had at all no knowledge to condemn their own want of knowledge), they descended (oh, never to be forgotten presumption!) to a direct[1] mislike of your living from among them, whereupon it were tedious to remember their far-fetched constructions, but the sum was, you disdained them; and what were the pomps of your estate if their arms maintained you not; who would call you a prince if you had not a people – when certain of them of wretched estates and worse minds, whose fortunes change could not impair, began to say that your government was to be looked into; how the great treasures you had levied among them had been spent; why none but great men and gentlemen could be admitted into council; that the commons (forsooth!) were too plain-headed to say their opinions, but yet their blood and sweat must maintain all – who could tell whether you were not betrayed in this place where you lived, nay, whether you did live or no; therefore, that it was time to come and see, and if you were here, to know, if Arcadia were grown loathsome in your sight, why you did not rid yourself of the trouble: there would not want those that would[2] take so fair a cumber in good part. Since the country was theirs, and the government an adherent to the country, why should they not consider of the one as well as inhabit the other?'

"Nay, rather", said they, "let us begin that which all Arcadia will follow; let us deliver our prince from danger of practices, and ourselves from want[3] of a prince; let us do that which all the rest think; let it be said that we only are not astonished with vain titles, which have their force but in our force"; lastly, to have said and heard so much was as dangerous as to have attempted – and to attempt, they had the glorious name of[4] liberty with them.

'These words being spoken, like a furious storm presently carried away their well-inclined brains. What I and some other of the honester sort could do was no more than if with a puff of breath one should go about to make a sail go against a mighty wind, or with one hand stay the ruin of a mighty wall, so general grew this madness among them. There needed no drum where each man cried; each spake to other, that spake as fast to him, and the disagreeing sound of so many voices was the chief token of their unmeet agreement. Thus was their banquet turned to a battle, their winy mirths to bloody rages, and the happy prayers for your life to monstrous threatening[5] your estate; the solemnizing[6] your birthday tended to have been the cause of your funerals. But as a drunken rage hath (besides his wickedness) that folly that the more it seeks to hurt, the less it considers how to be able to hurt,

---

[1] direct] great *Ph, Je* [2] those that would] those should *OA (ex. As, Je)*; these that should *As* [3] from want] from the want *OA (ex. Bo)* [4] glorious name of *Cm, 93*: name of glorious *90* [5] threatening *OA (ex. Cl, Hm)*, *Cm*: threatenings *Cl, Hm*; threatening of *90, 93* [6] solemnizing] solemnizing of *Bo, Ph, Je, Hm*

they never weighed how to arm themselves, but took up everything for a weapon that fury offered to their hands. Many swords, pikes, and bills there were; others took pitchforks and rakes, converting husbandry to soldiery; some caught hold of spits (things serviceable for life) to be the instruments of death; and there was some such one who held the same pot wherein he drank[1] to your health, to use it as he could to your mischief.

'Thus armed, thus governed; forcing the unwilling and heartening the willing; adding fury to fury and increasing rage with running, they came headlong toward this lodge, no man I daresay resolved in his own heart[2] what was the uttermost he would do when he came hither. But as mischief is of such nature that it cannot stand but with strengthening one evil by another, and so multiply in itself till it come to the highest, and then fall with his own weight, so to their minds once past the bounds[3] of obedience, more and more wickedness opened itself, so that they who first pretended to preserve you, then to reform you – I speak it in my conscience and with a bleeding heart – now thought no safety for them without murdering you; so as if the gods who preserve you for the preservation of Arcadia had not showed their miraculous power, and that they had not used for instruments both your own valour (not fit to be spoken of by so mean a mouth as mine) and some, I must confess, honest minds – whom, alas, why should I mention, since what we did reached not to the[4] hundreth part of our duty? – our hands (I tremble to think of it!) had destroyed all that for which we have cause to rejoice that we are Arcadians.'

With that, the fellow did wring his hands, and wrang out tears; so as Basilius (that was not the sharpest piercer into masked minds) took a good liking to him – and so much the more as he had tickled him with praise in the hearing of his mistress; and therefore pitying his wound, willed him to get him home and look well unto it, and make the best search he could to know if there were any further depth in this matter, for which he should be well rewarded. But before he went away, certain of the shepherds being come (for that day was appointed for their pastorals), he sent one of them to Philanax, and another to other principal noblemen and cities thereabouts, to make thorough-inquiry of this uproar, and withal to place such garrisons in all the towns and villages near unto him that he might thereafter keep his solitary lodge in more security – upon the making of a fire or ringing of a bell, having them in a readiness for him. This[5] Clinias (having his ear one way when his eye was another) had perceived, and therefore hasted away with mind to tell Cecropia that she was to take some speedy resolution, or

---

[1] drank] had drunk *OA (ex. Bo)*   [2] his own heart] his heart *As, Je*   [3] bounds] bonds *Cl, Da, Ph, Je, Hm*   [4] not to the *Cm, 93*: not the *90*   [5] him. This *Cm, 93*: him. Chap. 28. The praises of Zelmane's act; Dametas' carol for saving himself and his charge; Basilius' conference with Philanax of the oracle (the ground of all this story); his wrong-construction of it; his hymn to Apollo; his courting turned over to tale-telling. This *90*

else it were danger those examinations would both discover and ruin her, and so went his way, leaving that little company with embracements and praising of Zelmane's excellent proceeding, to show that no decking sets forth anything so much as affection; for as, while she stood at the discretion of those[1] undiscreet[2] rebels, every angry countenance any of them made seemed a knife laid upon their own throats,[3] so unspeakable was now their joy that they saw, besides her safety and their own, the same wrought (and safely wrought) by her means, in whom they had placed all their delights. What examples Greece could ever allege of wit and fortitude were set in the rank of trifles, being compared to this action.

But as they were in the midst of those unfeigned ceremonies, a gittern ill played on, accompanied with a hoarse voice (who seemed to sing maugre the muses, and to be merry in spite of fortune), made them look the way of the ill-noised song. The song was this:

> A hateful cure[4] with hate to heal;
> A bloody help with blood to save;
> A foolish thing with fools to deal;
> Let him be bobbed[5] that bobs will have,
>   But who by means of wisdom high
>   Hath saved his charge? It is[6] even I.
>
> Let others[7] deck their pride with scars,
> And of their wounds make brave lame shows;
> First let them die, then pass the stars,
> When rotten fame will tell their blows.
>   But eye from blade, and ear from cry,
>   Who hath saved all? It is even I.

They had soon found it was Dametas, who came with no less lifted up countenance than if he had passed over the bellies of all[8] his enemies – so wise a point he thought he had performed in using the natural strength of the cave.[9] But never was it his doing to come so soon thence, till the coast[10] were more assuredly clear; for it was a rule with him that after a great storm there ever fell[11] a few drops before it be fully finished.

But Pamela, who had now experienced how much care doth solicit a lover's heart, used this occasion of going to her parents and sister; indeed, as well for that cause, as being unquiet till her eye might be assured[12] how her shepherd had gone through the danger. But Basilius with the sight of

---

[1] those] these *As, Je* [2] undiscreet *OA, 93*: indiscreet *Cm, 90* [3] throats] throat *OA (ex. Ph)* [4] cure] cry *Cl*; cur *Ph*; care *Cm* [5] bobbed *As, Je, Hm, Cm, 93*: bold *Bo, Cl, Da, Ph, 90* (bold corr. in another hand to bobbed *St*) [6] It is] It corr. to ' Tis *St*; ' Tis *Ph* [7] others *OA (ex. Cl), Cm, 93*: other *Cl, 90* [8] over ... all] over all the bellies of *Ph, Je, Hm* [9] the cave *Cm, 93*: a cave *90* [10] coast] coasts *St, Cl* [11] fell] fall *Bo, Ph, Hm, 93*; falls *As, Je* [12] be assured] assure her *St, Da, Ph, Je, Hm*; measure *Bo*

Pamela, of whom almost his head (otherwise occupied) had left the wonted remembrance, was suddenly stricken into a devout kind of admiration, remembering the oracle; which according to the fawning humour of false hope he interpreted, now his own, to his own best, and with the willing blindness of affection, because his mind ran wholly upon Zelmane, he thought the gods in their oracles[1] did principally mind her. But as he was deeply thinking of the matter, one of the shepherds told him that Philanax was already come, with a hundred horse in his company; for having by chance rid not far off the little desert, he had heard of this uproar, and so was come upon the spur (gathering a company of gentlemen as fast as he could) to the succour of his master.

Basilius was glad of it; but not willing to have him (nor any other of the noblemen) see his mistress, he himself went out of the lodge. And so, giving order unto him of placing garrisons and examining these matters, and Philanax with humble earnestness beginning to entreat him to leave off his[2] solitary course which already had been so dangerous unto him, 'Well,' said Basilius, 'it may be ere long I will condescend unto your desire. In the mean time, take you the best order you can to keep me safe in my solitariness. But,' said he, 'do you remember how earnestly you wrote unto me that I should not be moved by that oracle's authority which brought me to this resolution?'

'Full well, sir!' answered Philanax, 'for though it pleased you not as then to let me know what the oracle's words were, yet all oracles holding in my conceit one degree of reputation, it sufficed me to know it was but an oracle which led you from your own course.'

'Well,' said Basilius, 'I will now tell you the words (which before I thought not good to do) because, when all the events fall out (as some already have done) I may charge you with your incredulity.' So he repeated them in this sort:

> Thy elder care shall from thy careful face
> By princely mean be stol'n and yet not lost;
> Thy younger shall with nature's bliss embrace
> An[3] uncouth love, which nature hateth most.
> Both they themselves unto such two shall wed,
> Who at thy bier, as at a bar, shall plead
> Why thee (a living man) they had made dead.
> In thy own seat a foreign state shall sit.
> And ere that all these blows thy head do hit,
> Thou with thy wife adult'ry shall commit.

---

[1] oracles] oracle *Ph, Je, Hm*   [2] his] this *93*   [3] An] And *93, 98*

'For you, forsooth,' said he, 'when I told you that some supernatural cause sent me strange visions (which being confirmed with presagious chances, I had gone to Delphos and there received this answer), you replied to me that the only supernatural causes were the humours of my body which bred such melancholy dreams, and that both they framed a mind full of conceits apt to make presages of things which in themselves were merely chanceable,[1] and withal, as I say, you remember what you wrote unto me touching authority of the oracle. But now I have some notable trial of the truth thereof, which hereafter I will more largely communicate unto you. Only now know that the thing I most feared is already performed – I mean, that a foreign state should possess my throne, for that hath been done by Zelmane, but not as I feared to my ruin, but to my preservation.'

But when he had once named Zelmane, that name was as good as a pulley to make the clock of his praises run on, in such sort that Philanax found was more exquisite than the only admiration of virtue breedeth; which his faithful heart inwardly repining at made him shrink away as soon as he could, to go about the other matters of importance which Basilius had enjoined unto him.

Basilius returned into the lodge, thus by himself construing the oracle: that, in that he said his elder care should by princely mean be stolen away from him and yet not lost, it was now performed, since Zelmane had as it were robbed from him the care of his first-begotten child – yet was it not lost, since in his heart the ground of it remained; that his younger should with nature's bliss embrace the love of Zelmane because he had so commanded her for his sake to do – yet should it be with as much hate of nature, for being so hateful an[2] opposite to the jealousy he thought her mother had of him; the sitting in his seat he deemed by her already performed; but that which most comforted him was his interpretation of the adultery, which he thought he should commit with Zelmane whom afterwards he should have to his wife. The point of his daughters' marriage, because it threatened his death withal, he determined to prevent with keeping them, while he lived, unmarried.[3]

But having (as he thought) gotten thus much understanding of the oracle, he determined for three days after to perform certain rites to Apollo, and even then began with his wife and daughters to sing this hymn, by them yearly used:

> Apollo great, whose beams the greater world do light,
> And, in our little world, dost[4] clear our inward sight;

---

[1] chanceable *Cm, 93*: changeable *90* [2] an] and *Ph, Hm* [3] them ... unmarried *Cm, 93*: them unmarried while he lived *90* [4] dost *Cl, As, Da, Je, Hm, Cm*: does *St, Bo*; do *Ph, 90, 93*

Which ever shines[1] (though hid from earth by earthly shade),
Whose lights do ever live (but in our darkness fade);
Thou God, whose youth was decked with spoil[2] of Python's skin
(So humble knowledge can throw down the snakish sin),[3]
Latona's son, whose birth in pain[4] and travail long
Doth teach, to learn the good, what travails do belong;
In travail of our life (a short but tedious space
While brickle hour-glass runs) guide thou our panting race[5]:
Give us foresightful minds; give us minds to obey
What foresight tells; our thoughts upon thy knowledge stay.
Let so our fruits grow up that nature be maintained;
But so our hearts keep down, with vice they be not stained.
Let this assured hold our judgements[6] ever take[7],
That nothing wins the heav'n but what doth earth forsake.

As soon as he had ended his[8] devotion, all the privileged shepherds being now come, knowing well enough he might lay all his care upon Philanax, he was willing to sweeten the taste of this past tumult with some rural pastimes; for which, while the shepherds prepared themselves in their best manner, Basilius took his daughter Philoclea aside, and with such haste as if his ears hunted for words, desired to know how she had found Zelmane. She humbly answered him (according to the agreement betwixt them) that thus much, for her sake, Zelmane was content to descend from her former resolution, as to hear him whensoever he would speak; and further than that, she said, as Zelmane had not granted, so she neither did nor ever would desire.

Basilius kissed her with more than fatherly thanks, and straight, like a hard-kept ward new come to his lands, would fain have used the benefit of that grant in laying his sickness before his only physician. But Zelmane, that had not yet fully determined with herself how to bear herself toward him, made him in a few words understand that the time, in respect of the company, was unfit for such a parley. And therefore, to keep his brains the busier (letting him understand what she had learned of his daughters touching Erona's distress, whom in her travel she had known and been greatly beholding to) she desired him to finish the rest, for so far as Plangus had told him, because, she said – and she said truly, she was full of care for that lady, whose desert (only except an over-base choice) was nothing agreeable to misfortune. Basilius, glad that she would command him anything (but

---

[1] shines *OA*, *Cm*: shine *90*, *93*   [2] spoil *OA* (*ex. Je*), *93*: om. *Je*; spoils *90*   [3] sin *OA* (*ex. Je*), *93*: skin *90*; kin *90*   [4] pain] pains *St*, *Bo*, *Cl*, *As*, *Je*, *Hm*   [5] race *OA* (*ex. Da*): pace *Da*, *90*, *93*   [6] judgements] judgement *Da*, *Je*   [7] ever take *OA* (*ex. Je*): overtake *Je*, *90*, *93*   [8] his] their *Bo*, *As*, *Da*, *Je*

more glad that in excusing the unfitness of that time she argued an intention to grant a fitter), obeyed her in this manner.

'Madam,'[1] said he, 'it is very true that, since years enabled me to judge what is or is not to be pitied, I never saw anything that more moved me to justify a vehement compassion in myself than the estate of that prince, whom, strong against all his own afflictions (which yet were great, as I perceive you have heard), yet true and noble love had so pulled down as to lie under sorrow for another; insomuch as I could not temper my long-idle pen in that subject, which I perceive you have seen.

'But then, to leave that unrepeated which I find my daughters have told you, it may please you to understand (since it pleaseth you to demand) that Antiphilus being crowned, and so left by the famous princes, Musidorus and Pyrocles, led thence by the challenge of Anaxius who is now in these provinces of Greece making a dishonourable inquiry after that excellent Prince Pyrocles, already perished, Antiphilus, I say, being crowned, and delivered from the presence of those two whose virtues, while they were present good schoolmasters, suppressed his vanities, he had not strength of mind enough in him to make long delay of discovering what manner of man he was. But straight, like one carried up to so high a place that he loseth the discerning of the ground over which he is, so was his mind lifted so far beyond the level of his own discourse that, remembering only that himself was in the high seat of a king, he could not perceive that he was a king of reasonable creatures who would quickly scorn follies and repine at injuries. But imagining no so true property of sovereignty as to do what he listed, and to list whatsoever pleased his fancy, he quickly made his kingdom a tennis-court where his subjects should be the balls (not, in truth, cruelly, but licentiously abusing them), presuming so far upon himself that what he did was liked of everybody – nay, that his disgraces were favours, and all because he was a king; for, in nature not able to conceive the bonds of great matters, suddenly borne into an unknown ocean of absolute power he was swayed withal (he knew not how) as every wind of passions puffed him, whereto nothing helped him better than that poisonous sugar of flattery – which some used out of the innate baseness of their heart, straight like dogs fawning upon the greatest; others (secretly hating him and disdaining his great rising so suddenly, so undeservedly), finding his humour, bent their exalting him only to his overthrow, like the bird that carries the shellfish

---

[1] manner. 'Madam *Cm*, 93; manner. Chap. 29. Antiphilus' base-born pride borne high by flattery; his unkind hating the loving Erona, and fond loving of hating Artaxia; Artaxia's trap to take them both; the man's weakness and the woman's strength in bearing captivity; Plangus' love to her employed by her to save Antiphilus, who again betrays himself and them; his execution by women; Plangus' hardy attempts to save Erona; the conditions of her death; her sorrow for Antiphilus, and Plangus' travail for her, with his crosses, and course therein. 'Madam 90

high to break him the easier with his fall. But his mind, being an apt matter to receive what form their amplifying speeches would lay upon it, danced so pretty a music to their false measure that he thought himself the wisest, the worthiest, and best beloved that ever gave honour to a royal title; and being but obscurely born, he had found out unblushing pedigrees that made him not only of the blood royal, but true heir[1] – though unjustly dispossessed by Erona's ancestors; and like the foolish bird that, when it so hides the head that it sees not itself, thinks nobody else sees it, so did he imagine that nobody knew his baseness while he himself turned his eyes from it.

'Then vainness, a meagre friend to gratefulness, brought him so to despise Erona, as of whom he had received no benefit, that within half a year's marriage he began to pretend barrenness; and making first an unlawful law of having mo wives than one, he (still keeping Erona) underhand by messages[2] sought Artaxia, who no less hating him than loving (as unlucky a choice) the naughty King Plexirtus, yet to bring to pass what he[3] purposed, was content to train him into false hopes, till already his imagination had crowned him king of Armenia, and had made that but the foundation of more and more monarchies – as if fortune had only gotten eyes to cherish him. In which time a great assembly of most part of all the princes of Asia being, to do honour to the never sufficiently praised Pyrocles and Musidorus, he would be one – not to acknowledge his obligation (which was as great as any of the others'), but looking to have been young-mastered[4] among those great estates, as he was among his abusing underlings. But so many valorous princes indeed far nearer to disdain him than otherwise, he was quickly (as standing upon no true ground inwardly) out of countenance with himself, till his seldom-comfortless flatterers, persuading him it was envy and fear of his expected greatness, made him haste away from that company; and without further delay appointed the meeting with Artaxia, so incredibly blinded with the over-bright shining of his royalty that he could[5] think such a queen could be content to be joined patent with another to have such an husband.

'Poor Erona to all this obeyed, either vehemency of affection making her stoop to so over-base a servitude; or astonished with an unlooked-for fortune, dull to any behoofeful resolution; or, as many times it falls out even in great hearts when they can accuse none but themselves, desperately bent to maintain it – for so went she on in that way of her love that, poor lady! to be beyond all other examples of ill-set affection, she was brought to write to Artaxia that she was content for the public good to be a second wife, and yield the first place to her – nay, to extol him, and even woo Artaxia for him.

---

[1] heir – though unjustly *Cm, 93*: heir – unjustly *90* [2] messages *Cm, 93*: message *90* [3] he] she *93*
[4] young-mastered *Cm, 93*: young master *90*   [5] could] would *93*

But Artaxia, mortally hating them both for her brother's sake, was content to hide her hate till she had time to show it; and pretending that all her grudge was against the two paragons of virtue, Musidorus and Pyrocles, even met them half-way in excusing her brother's murder (as not being principal actors, and, of the other side, driven to what they did by the ever-pardonable 'necessity'), and so well handled the matter as, though she promised nothing, yet Antiphilus promised himself all that she would have him think.

'And so, a solemn interview was appointed – but, as the poets say, Hymen had not there his saffron-coloured coat; for Artaxia laying men secretly (and easily they might be secret, since Antiphilus thought she overran him in love), when he came even ready to embrace her (showing rather a countenance of accepting than offering), they came forth; and having much advantage both in number, valure, and fore-preparation, put all his company to the sword, but such as could fly away.

'As for Antiphilus, she caused him and Erona both to be put in irons, hasting back toward her brother's tomb upon which she meant to sacrifice them, making the love of her brother stand between her and all other motions of grace, from which by nature she was alienated. But great diversity in them two quickly discovered itself for the bearing of that affliction, for Antiphilus that had no greatness but outward, that taken away, was ready to fall faster than calamity could thrust him, with fruitless begging where[1] reason might well assure him his death was resolved, and weak bemoaning his fortune, to give his enemies a most pleasing music, with many promises and protestations to as little purpose, as from a little mind. But Erona, sad indeed (yet like one rather used than new-fallen to sadness, as who had the joys of her heart already broken) seemed rather to welcome than to shun that end of misery, speaking little – but what she spake was for Antiphilus, remembering his guiltlessness (being at that time prisoner to Tiridates when the valiant princes slew him), to the disgrace of men showing that there are women both more[2] wise to judge what is to be expected, and more constant to bear it when it is happened.

'But her wit endeared by her youth, her affliction by her birth, and her sadness by her beauty, made this noble Prince Plangus (who, never almost from his cousin Artaxia, was now present at Erona's taking) to perceive the shape of loveliness more perfectly in woe than in joyfulness (as in a picture, which receives greater life by the darkness of shadows than by more glittering colours); and seeing, to like; and liking, to love; and loving, straight to feel the most incident effects of love: to serve and preserve. So borne by the hasty tide of short leisure, he did hastily deliver together his affection

---

[1] begging where] begging of life where 93   [2] women both more *Cm, 93*: women more *90*

and affectionate care; but she, as if he had spoken of a small matter (when he mentioned her life) to which she had not leisure to attend, desired him if he loved her to show it in finding some way to save Antiphilus. For her, she found the world but a wearisome stage unto her, where she played a part against her will, and therefore besought him not to cast his love in so unfruitful a place as could not love itself; but for a testimony of constancy, and a suitableness to his word, to do so much comfort to her mind as that, for her sake, Antiphilus were saved.

'He told me how much he argued against her tendering him, who had so ungratefully betrayed her and foolishly cast away himself. But perceiving she did not only bend her very good wits to speak for him against herself, but when such a cause could be allied to no reason, yet love would needs make itself a cause and bar her rather from hearing than yield that she should yield to such arguments, he (likewise in whom the power of love, as they say of spirits, was subject to the love in her) with grief consented and, though backwardly, was diligent to labour the help of Antiphilus, a man whom he not only hated as a traitor[1] to Erona, but envied as a possessor of Erona. Yet love sware, his heart, in spite of his heart, should make him become a servant to his rival – and so did he, seeking all the means of persuading Artaxia which the authority of so near and so virtuous a kinsman would[2] give unto him. But she, to whom the eloquence of hatred had given revenge the face of delight, rejected all such motions; but rather the more closely imprisoning them in her chief city, where she kept them with intention, at the birthday of Tiridates which was very near, to execute Antiphilus, and at the day of his death which was about half a year after, to use the same rigour towards[3] Erona.

'Plangus, much grieved because much loving, attempted the humours of the Lycians to see whether they would come in with forces to succour their princess. But there the next inheritor to the crown (with the true play that is used in the game of kingdoms) had no sooner his mistress in captivity but he had usurped her place; and making her odious to her people because of the unfit election she had made, had so left no hope there, but (which is worse) had sent to Artaxia persuading the justicing her, because that unjustice might give his title the name of justice.

'Wanting that way, Plangus practised with some dear friends of his to save Antiphilus out of prison – whose day because it was much nearer than Erona's, and that he well found she had twisted her life upon the same thread with his, he determined first to get him out of prison. And to that end having prepared all matters as well as in such case he could (where Artaxia had

---

[1] traitor *Cm, 93*: trairor *90*   [2] would] could *93*   [3] towards *93*: toward *Cm*; towars *90*

set many of Tiridates' old servants to have well-marking eyes), he conferred with Antiphilus, as by the authority he had he found means to do, and agreed with him of the time and manner how he should by the death of some of his jailers escape. But all being well ordered, and Plangus willingly putting himself into the greatest danger, Antiphilus (who, like a bladder swelled ready to break while it was full of the wind of prosperity, that being out, was so abjected as apt to be trode on by everybody), when it came to the point that with some hazard he might be in apparent likelihood to avoid the uttermost harm, his heart fainted, and (weak fool!) neither hoping nor fearing as he should, gat a conceit that with bewraying his[1] practice, he might obtain pardon; and therefore, even a little before Plangus should have come unto him, opened the whole practice to him that had the charge, with unpitied tears idly protesting he had rather die by Artaxia's commandment than against her will escape, yet begging life upon any the hardest and wretchedest conditions that she would lay upon him.

'His keeper provided accordingly, so that when Plangus came he was like himself to have been entrapped. But that finding with a lucky insight that it was discovered, he retired, and calling his friends about him, stood upon his guard – as he had good cause, for Artaxia (accounting him most ungrateful, considering that her brother and she had not only preserved him against the malice of his father, but ever used him much liker his birth than his fortune) sent forces to apprehend him. But he among the martial men had gotten so great love that he could not only keep himself from the[2] malice, but work in their minds a compassion of Erona's adversity – but for the succour of Antiphilus he could get nobody to join with him, the contempt of him having not been able to qualify the hatred, so that Artaxia might easily upon him perform her will, which was, at the humble[3] suit of all the women of that city, to deliver him to their censure; who mortally hating him for having made a law of polygamy, after many tortures forced him to throw himself from a high pyramis which was built over Tiridates' tomb, and so to end his false-hearted life which had planted no strong thought in him but that he could be unkind.

'But Plangus well perceiving that Artaxia stayed only for the appointed day that the fair Erona's body, consumed to ashes, should make a notorious testimony how deeply her brother's death was engraven in her breast, he assembled good numbers of friends (whom his virtue, though a stranger, had tied unto him) by force to give her liberty. Contrariwise Artaxia (to whom anger gave more courage than her sex did fear) used her regal authority the most she could to suppress that sedition and have her will, which,

---

[1] his] this 93 [2] the] her 93 [3] at the humble *Cm, 93*: at humble *90*

she thought, is the most princely thing that may be. But Plangus, who indeed as all men witness is one of the best captains both for policy and valour that are trained in the school of Mars, in a conflict overthrew Artaxia's power, though of far greater number, and there took prisoner a base son of her brother's whom she dearly affected, and then sent her word that he should run the same race of fortune, whatsoever it was, that Erona did – and happy was that threatening for her, for else Artaxia had hastened the day of her death, in respect of those tumults.

'But now some principal noblemen of that country interposing themselves, it was agreed that all persons else fully pardoned, and all prisoners except Erona delivered, she should be put into the hands of a principal nobleman who had a castle of great strength, upon oath that if by the day two year from Tiridates' death Pyrocles and Musidorus did not in person combat and overcome two knights whom she appointed to maintain her quarrel, against Erona and them, of having by treason destroyed her brother, that then Erona should be that same day burned to ashes; but if they came and had the victory she should be delivered; but upon no occasion neither freed nor executed till that day – and hereto of both sides all took solemn oath. And so, the peace was concluded, they of Plangus' party forcing him to agree, though he himself the sooner condescended, knowing the courtesy of those two excellent princes not to refuse so noble a quarrel, and their power such, as two more like the other two were not able to resist. But Artaxia was more and upon better ground pleased with this action, for she had even newly received news from Plexirtus that upon the sea he had caused them both to perish – and therefore she held herself sure of the match.

'But poor Plangus knew not so much, and therefore (seeing his party, as most times it falls out in like case, hungry of conditions[1] of peace) accepted them, and then obtained leave of the lord that indifferently kept her to visit Erona, whom he found full of desperate sorrow – not suffering neither his unworthiness, nor his wrongs, nor his death (which is the natural conclusion of all worldly acts) either to cover with forgetfulness or diminish with consideration the affection she had borne him. But even glorying in affliction and shunning all comfort, she seemed to have no delight but in making herself the picture of misery, so that when Plangus came to her she fell in deadly trances, as if in him she had seen the death of Antiphilus because he had not succoured him. And yet, her virtue striving, she did at one time acknowledge herself bound and profess herself injured; instead of allowing the conclusion they had made or writing to the princes (as he wished her to do), craving nothing but some speedy death to follow her (in spite of just

---

[1] of conditions] of any conditions 93

hate) beloved Antiphilus; so that Plangus, having nothing but a ravished kiss from her hand at their parting, went away toward Greece, whitherward he understood the princes were embarked.

'But by the way it was his fortune to intercept letters written by Artaxia to Plexirtus, wherein she signified her accepting him to her husband whom she had ever favoured, so much the rather as he had performed the conditions of her marriage in bringing to their deserved end her greatest enemies, withal thanking the sea in such terms as he might well perceive it was by some treason wrought in Plexirtus' ship; whereupon, to make more diligent search, he took ship himself and came into Laconia, inquiring and, by his inquiry, finding that such a ship was indeed with fight and fire perished, none almost escaping – but for Pyrocles and Musidorus, it was assuredly determined that they were cast away, for the name of such princes, especially in Greece, would quickly else have been a large witness to the contrary.

'Full of grief with that, for the loss of such who left the world poor of perfection, but more sorry for Erona's sake who now by them could not be relieved, a new advertisement from Armenia overtook him which multiplied the force of his anguish. It was a message from the nobleman who had Erona in ward, giving him to understand that, since his departure, Artaxia using the benefit of time had beseiged him in his castle, demanding present delivery of her – whom yet (for his faith given) he would not before the day appointed, if possibly he could resist, which he foresaw long he should not do for want of victual, which he had not so wisely provided because he trusted upon the general oath taken for two years' space; and therefore willed him to make haste to his succour, and come with no small forces, for all they that were of his side in Armenia were consumed, and Artaxia had increased her might by marriage of Plexirtus, who (now crowned king there) sticked not to glory in the murder of Pyrocles and Musidorus, as having just cause thereto in respect of the deaths of his sister, Andromana; her son, his nephew; and his own daughter, Zelmane, all whose loss he unjustly charged them withal, and now openly sticked not to confess what a revenge his wit had brought forth.

'Plangus (much astonished herewith) bethought himself what to do, for to return to Armenia was vain, since his friends there were utterly overthrown. Then thought he of going to his father, but he had already, even since the death of his stepmother and brother, attempted the recovering his favour, and all in vain; for they, that had before joined with Andromana to do him the wrong, thought now no life for them if he returned, and therefore kept him still, with new-forged suspicions, odious to his father – so that Plangus, reserving that for a work of longer time than the saving of Erona could bear, determined to go to the mighty and good King Euarchus, who lately having to his eternal fame fully, not only conquered his enemies, but established good government in their countries, he hoped he might have present succour of him, both for the justness of the cause and revenge of his children's death, by so heinous a treason murthered.

'Therefore with diligence he went to him; and by the way passing through my country, it was my hap to find him, the most overthrown man with grief that ever I hope to see again (for still it seemed he had Erona at a stake before his eyes, such an apprehension he had taken of her danger), which, in despite of all the comfort I could give him, he poured out in such lamentations that I was moved not to let him pass till he had made full declaration – which by pieces my daughters and I have delivered unto you. Fain he would have had succour of myself, but the course of my life being otherwise bent, I only accompanied him with some that might safely guide him to the great Euarchus; for my part, having had some of his speeches so feelingly in my memory that at an idle time, as I told you, I set them down dialogue-wise, in such manner as you have seen.

'And thus, excellent lady, I have obeyed you in this story, wherein, if it well please you to consider what is the strange power of love and what is due to his authority, you shall exercise therein the true nobleness of your judgement, and do the more right to the unfortunate historian.'

Zelmane, sighing for Erona's sake (yet inwardly comforted in that she assured herself Euarchus would not spare to take in hand the just delivering of her, joined with the just revenge of his children's loss), having now what she desired of Basilius, to avoid his further discourses of affection encouraged the shepherds to begin, whom she saw all ready[1] for them.

---

[1] all ready] already ready 93

THE THIRD BOOK

THIS[1] last day's danger, having made Pamela's love discern what a loss it should have suffered if Dorus had been destroyed, bred such tenderness of kindness in her toward him that she could no longer keep love from looking through[2] her eyes and going forth in her words, whom before as a close prisoner she had to her heart only committed. So as finding not only by his speeches and letters, but by the pitiful oration of a languishing behaviour and the easily deciphered character of a sorrowful face that despair began now to threaten him destruction, she grew content both to pity him and let him see she pitied him – as well by making her own beautiful beams thaw[3] away the former iciness of her behaviour, as by entertaining his discourses whensoever he did use them in the third person of Musidorus – to so far a degree that in the end she said, that if she had been the princess whom that disguised prince had virtuously loved, she would have requited his faith with faithful affection, finding in her heart that nothing could so heartily love as virtue (with many mo words to the same sense, of noble favour, and chaste plainness); which, when at the first it made that expected bliss shine upon Dorus, he was like one frozen with extremity of cold over-hastily brought to a great fire – rather oppressed than relieved with such a lightening of felicity. But after the strength of nature had made him able to feel the sweetness of joyfulness, that again being a child of passion, and never acquainted with mediocrity, could not set bounds upon his happiness, nor be content to give desire a kingdom but that it must be an unlimited monarchy; so that the ground he stood upon being over-high in happiness and slippery through affection, he could not hold himself from falling into such an error, which with sighs blew all comfort out of his breast and washed away all cheerfulness of his cheer with tears: for this favour filling him with hope, hope encouraging his desire, and desire considering nothing but opportunity, one time Mopsa being called away by her mother and he left alone with Pamela, the sudden occasion called love – and that never stayed to ask reason's leave, but made the too-much loving Dorus take her in his arms, offering to kiss her, and as it were to establish a trophy of his victory.

But she, as if she had been ready to drink a wine of excellent taste and colour which suddenly she perceived had poison in it, so did she put him away from her, looking first unto[4] heaven, as amazed to find herself so be-

---

[1] them. The Third Book This. them. This *Cm;* them. The Second Eclogues *[See Appendix I].* The end of the second Book. The Third Book of *The Countess of Pembroke's Arcadia.* Chap. 1. Dorus' fair and foul weather in his love; his forlorn agonies; his doubts to write, and Pamela's to read, his elegy. This 90; them. The second Eclogues .... The end of the second Eclogues. The Third Book of *The Countess of Pembroke's Arcadia.* This 93 [2] looking through] looking out through 93 [3] beams thaw] beams to thaw 93 [4] unto] up to 93

guiled in him, then laying the cruel punishment upon him of angry love and louring beauty; showing disdain – and a despising disdain. 'Away!' said she, 'unworthy man, to love, or to be loved! Assure thyself, I hate myself for being so deceived. Judge, then, what I do thee for deceiving me: let me see thee no more, the only fall of my judgement and stain of my conscience!' With that, she called Mopsa, not staying for any answer – which was no other but a flood of tears which she seemed not to mark, much less to pity – and chid her for having so left her alone.

It was not an amazement, it was not a sorrow, but it was even a death which then laid hold of Dorus – which certainly at that instant would have killed him, but that the fear to tarry longer in her presence contrary to her commandment gave him life to carry himself away from her sight, and to run into the woods, where, throwing himself down at the foot of a tree, he did not fall to lamentation (for that proceeded of pitying), or grieving for himself (which he did no way), but to curses of his life, as one that detested himself; for finding himself not only unhappy, but unhappy after being fallen from all happiness, and to be fallen from all happiness not by any misconceiving but by his own fault, and his fault to be done to no other but to Pamela, he did not tender his own estate, but despised it, greedily drawing into his mind all conceits which might more and more torment him. And so remained he two days in the woods, disdaining to give his body food or his mind comfort, loving in himself nothing but the love of her – and indeed, that love only strave with the fury of his anguish, telling it that, if it destroyed Dorus, it should also destroy the image of her that lived in Dorus; and when the thought of that was crept in unto him, it began to win of him some compassion to the shrine of the image,[1] and to bewail, not for himself whom he hated, but that so notable a love should perish. Then began he only so far to wish his own good as that Pamela might pardon him the fault, though not the punishment; and the uttermost height he aspired unto was that, after his death, she might yet pity his error, and know that it proceeded of love, and not of boldness.

That conceit found such friendship in his thoughts that at last he yielded, since he was banished her presence, to seek some means by writing to show his sorrow and testify his repentance; therefore, getting him the necessary instruments of writing, he thought best to counterfeit his hand (fearing that, as already she knew his, she would cast it away as soon as she saw it), and to put it in verse (hoping that would draw her on to read the more), choosing the elegiac[2] as fittest for mourning. But pen did never more[3] quakingly perform his office, never was paper more double moistened with ink and

---

[1] the image] that image 93 [2] elegiac] Elegiae *Cm, 90 (uncorr)* [3] pen did never more] never pen did more 93

tears, never words more slowly married together, and never the muses more tired than now with changes and rechanges of his devices – fearing how to end before he had resolved how to begin, mistrusting each word, condemning each sentence. This word was not significant, that word was too plain: this would not be conceived, the other would be ill-conceived. Here, sorrow was not enough expressed; there, he seemed too much for his own sake to be sorry. This sentence rather showed art than passion; that sentence, rather foolishly passionate than forcibly moving. At last, marring with mending, and putting out better than he left, he made an end of it – and being ended, was[1] divers times ready to tear it; till his reason assuring him, the more he studied, the worse it grew, he folded it up, devoutly invoking good acceptation unto it; and watching his time when they were all gone one day to dinner – saving Mopsa – to the other lodge, stale up into Pamela's chamber, and in her standish (which first he kissed, and craved of it a safe and friendly keeping) left it there to be seen at her next using her ink (himself returning again to be true prisoner to desperate sorrow), leaving her standish upon her bed's head to give her the more occasion to mark it – which also fell out; for she finding it at her afternoon return in another place than she left it, opened it. But when she saw the letter her heart gave her from whence it came; and therefore clapping it to again, she went away from it as if it had been a contagious garment of an infected person, and yet was not long away but that she wished she had read it, though she were loath to read it.

'Shall I', said she, 'second his boldness so far as to read his presumptuous letters? And yet,' said she, 'he sees me not, to[2] grow the bolder thereby. And how can I tell whether they be presumptuous? The paper came from him, and therefore not worthy to be received – and yet the paper,' she thought, 'was not guilty'. At last, she concluded, it were not much amiss to look it over, that she might out of his words pick some further quarrel against him. Then she opened it; and threw it away; and took it up again; till, ere she were aware, her eyes would needs read it, containing this matter.

Unto a[3] caitiff wretch whom long affliction holdeth,
   And now fully believes help to be quite perished,
Grant yet, grant yet a look to the last monument[4] of his anguish,
   O you (alas, so I find) cause of his only ruin.
Dread not a whit, O goodly cruel, that pity may enter
   Into thy heart by the sight of this epistle I send,
And so refuse to behold of these strange wounds the recital,

---

[1] was *Cm, 93*: and *90* [2] not, to] not now to *93* [3] a] the *OA, Hn* (the *corr. in another hand to a St*)
[4] monument] moment *As, Ph, Hm*

BOOK THREE

Lest it might thee[1] allure home to thyself to return
 (Unto thyself I do mean, those graces dwell so within thee,
Gratefulness, sweetness, holy love, hearty regard).
Such thing cannot I seek (despair hath giv'n me my answer,
 Despair, most tragical clause[2] to a deadly request);   5
Such thing cannot he hope that knows thy determinate hardness;
 Hard like a rich marble; hard, but a fair diamond.
Can those[3] eyes, that of eyes drowned in most hearty flowing tears
 (Tears, and tears of a man) had no return to remorse,
Can those eyes now yield to the kind conceit of a sorrow   10
 Which ink only relates, but ne laments, ne replies?
Ah, that, that do I[4] not conceive, though that to my bliss were
 More than Nestor's years, more than a king's diadem.[5]
Ah, that, that do I[6] not conceive[7] – to the heav'n when a mouse climbs,
 Then may I hope t'achieve grace of a heavenly tiger.   15
But, but alas, like a man condemned doth crave to be heard speak –
 Not that he hopes for amends of the disaster he feels,
But finding th'approach of death, with an inly[8] relenting
 Gives an adieu to the world, as to his only delight –
Right so[9] my boiling heart inflamed with fire of a fair eye,   20
 Bubbling out, doth breathe signs of his hugy dolours,
Now that he finds to what end his life and love be reserved,
 And that he thence[10] must part where, to live only, he lived,[11]
O fairest, are such thy[12] triumphs to thy fairness?
 Can death beauty become? Must I be such[13] monument?   25
Must I be only the mark shall prove that virtue is angry,
 Shall prove that[14] fierceness can with a white dove abide,
Shall to the world appear that faith and love be rewarded
 With mortal disdain bent to[15] unendly revenge?
Unto revenge? O sweet, on a wretch wilt thou be revenged?   30
 Shall such high planets tend[16] to the loss of a worm?
And to revenge, who do bend, would in that kind be revenged[17]
 As th'offence was[18] done, and go beyond if he can.
All my'offence was love; with love then must I be[19] chastened,

---

[1] thee *OA (ex. Bo, As)*: the *Bo, As, Cm*; the *corr. to* th' *Hn*; th' *90, 93*   [2] clause] cause *As, Hm*   [3] those] these *Da, Hm*   [4] that do I *OA (ex. Bo, Cl), Hn, 13*: that I do I *Bo, 90, 93, 98*; I do *Cl*   [5] *om. Da*   [6] that do I *OA (ex. Cl, Da), 93, 13*: I do *Cl, Da*; that I do *Hn, 90, 98*   [7] though … conceive] *om. As*   [8] inly *OA, Hn, 93*: ugly *90*   [9] so] to *Bo, Ph*   [10] thence *OA (ex. Cl), Hn, 93*: hence *Cl, 90*   [11] lived *OA, Hn, 93*: lov'd *90*   [12] such thy] such the *OA (ex. Bo, As, Da), Hn, 90 (uncorr.)*; such to the *Bo*; such *As*   [13] I be such *Bo, Cl, Je, Hm, Hn, 93*: I be such a *St, Le, As, Da, Ph*; be such a *90*   [14] that] the *Ph (the corr. to* that *Cl)*   [15] to] the *Da, Je*   [16] tend *OA (ex. Da), Hn, 93*: tread *Da*; end *90*   [17] *om. Cl*   [18] was] is *Cl, Ph*; were *Da*   [19] must I be] must be *Ph, Hm*

And with more, by the laws that to revenge do[1] belong.
If that love be a fault, more fault in you to be lovely:
  Love never had me oppressed, but that I saw to be loved.
You be the cause that I loved – what reason blameth a shadow
  That with a body't goes, since by a body it is?
If that[2] love you did hate, you should your beauty have hidden:
  You should those fair eyes have, with a veil, covered
(But fool, fool that I am! Those eyes would shine from a dark cave.
  What veils then do prevail, but to a more miracle?),
Or those golden locks, those locks which lock[3] me to bondage,
  Torn you should disperse unto the blasts of a wind
(But fool, fool that I am! Though I had but a hair of her head found,
  Ev'n as I am, so I should[4] unto that hair be a thrall);
Or with fair[5] hand's nails (O hand, which nails me to this[6] death!)
  You should have your face, since love is ill, blemished
(Oh, wretch! What do[7] I say? Should that fair face be defaced?
  Should my too much sight cause so true a sun to be lost?
First let Cimmerian darkness be my onl' habitation,
  First be mine[8] eyes pulled out, first be my brain perished
Ere that I should consent to do such[9] excessive a[10] damage
  Unto the earth, by the hurt of this her heavenly jewel.)[11]
Oh, not[12] but such love, you say, you could have afforded,
  As might learn temp'rance, void of a rage's[13] events[14]
(Oh, sweet simplicity! From whence should love be so[15] learned?
  Unto Cupid – that boy! – shall[16] a pedante[17] be found?);
Well, but faulty I was: reason to my passion yielded,
  Passion unto my rage, rage to a hasty revenge –
But what's this for a fault, for which such faith be[18] abolished,
  Such faith, so stainless, inviolate, violent?
Shall I not, oh, may I not thus yet refresh the remembrance
  What sweet joys I had once, and what a place I did hold?
Shall I not, once, object that you, you[19] granted a favour
  Unto the man whom now such miseries you award?
Bend your thoughts to the dear sweet words which then to me giv'n were;
  Think what a world is now, think who hath altered her heart.

---

[1] do] om. Bo; doth Hn [2] that] the OA (ex. Ph) [3] lock] locks Le, Ph; looked Da; locked Je [4] I should] should I Da, Hm [5] with fair] with a fair Bo, Cl, Le, As, Ph, Hm, Hn [6] this] om. Cl, Le, As, Da [7] do] did OA (ex. St), Hn [8] mine] my As, Je [9] such] so 93 [10] a] om.Le, Hm [11] jewel] Ivill Bo; evil Cl [12] not OA, Hn, 93: no 90 [13] a rage's] outrageous Cl; rages Le, Ph, Je [14] events] event Le, As, Ph, Hn [15] be so OA, Hn, 93: so be 90 [16] shall] should Cl, Le, As [17] a pedante] a padante St, a pechante Bo; a pendaunt Cl, Le; a picture Ph; apelante Je; a pendantes Hm; a pedantee Hn [18] faith be OA (ex. Le), Hn, 93: faith is Le; fault is 90 [19] you, you] yon you Bo; you me Ph; you have Je; you now Hm

What, was I then worthy such¹ good, now worthy such¹ evil²;
  Now fled, then cherished; then so nigh, now so remote?
Did not a rosed³ breath, from lips more rosy proceeding,
  Say that I well should⁴ find in what a care I was had,
With⁵ much more? Now what do I find, but care to abhor me,
  Care that I sink in grief, care that I live banished?
And banished do I live, nor now will seek a recov'ry,
  Since so she will, whose will is to me more than a law.
If then a man in most ill case may give you a farewell,
  Farewell, long farewell, all my woe, all my delight.

What⁶ this would have wrought in her, she herself could not tell; for before her reason could moderate the disputation between favour and faultiness, her sister and Miso called her down to entertain Zelmane, who was come to visit the two sisters (about whom, as about two poles, the sky of beauty was turned) – while Gynecia wearied her bed with her melancholy sickness, and made Miso's shrewdness (who like a sprite set to keep a treasure barred Zelmane from any further conference) to be the lieutenant of her jealousy, both she and her husband driving Zelmane to such a strait of resolution, either of impossible granting or dangerous refusing, as the best escape she had was, as much as she could, to avoid their company; so as, this day being the fourth day after the uproar, Basilius being with his sick wife conferring upon such examinations as Philanax and other of his noblemen had made of this late sedition (all touching Cecropia with vehement suspicion of giving either flame or fuel unto it), Zelmane came with her body to find her mind – which was gone long before her and had gotten his seat in Philoclea, who now with a bashful cheerfulness, as though she were ashamed that she could not choose but be glad, joined with her sister in making much of Zelmane.

And so, as they sat devising how to give more feathers to the wings of time, there came to the lodge door six maids, all in one livery of scarlet petticoats which were tucked up almost to their knees, the petticoats themselves being in many places garnished with leaves; their legs naked, saving that above the ankles they had little black silk laces upon which did hang a few silver bells – like which they had a little above their elbows upon their bare arms; upon their hair they ware garlands of roses and gillyflowers – and

---

¹ worthy such] worthy of such *St, Cl, As, Hn* ² such evil] so much evil *OA (ex. Ph, Le)*; too much evil *Ph* ³ a rosed] arosed *Bo*; a rosy *Le, Hn* ⁴ well should *OA (ex. As), Hn, 98, 13*: will should *As*; should well *90, 93* ⁵ With] What *As*; Which *Ph* ⁶ delight. What *93*: [blank] What *Cm*; delight. Chap. 2. The young ladies met; invited to the country wenches' sports; go thither; mere are taken and thence carried to Amphialus' castle; their entertainment there; Cecropia's auricular confession of her proud carriage in prosperity, and ambitious practices in adversity; Amphialus' affection in these actions. What *90*

the hair was so dressed as that came again above the garlands, interchanging a mutual covering, so as it was doubtful whether the hair dressed the garlands or the garlands dressed the hair; their breasts, liberal to the eye; the face of the foremost of them[1] in excellency fair, and of the rest lovely, if not beautiful – and beautiful would[2] have been if they had not suffered greedy Phoebus, over-often and hard, to kiss them; their countenances, full of a graceful gravity, so as (the gesture matched with the apparel) it might seem a wanton modesty, and an enticing soberness. Each of them had an instrument of music in their hands, which, consorting their well-pleasing tunes, did charge each ear with unsensibleness that did not lend itself unto them.

The music entering alone into the lodge, the ladies were all desirous to see from whence so pleasant a guest was come, and therefore went out together, where, before they could take the pains to doubt, much less to ask the question of their quality, the fairest of them, with a gay but yet discreet demeanour, in this sort spake unto them.

'Most excellent ladies, whose excellencies have power to make cities envy these woods, and solitariness to be accounted the sweetest company, vouchsafe our message your gracious hearing, which, as it comes from love, so comes it from lovely persons. The maids of all this coast of Arcadia, understanding the often access that certain shepherds of these quarters are allowed to have in this forbidden place, and that their rural sports are not disdained of you, have been stirred with emulation to them (and affection to you) to bring forth something which might as well breed your contentment; and therefore, hoping that the goodness of their intention and the hurtlessness of their sex shall excuse the breach of the commandment in coming to this place unsent for, they chose out us to invite both your princely parents and yourselves to a place in the woods about half a mile hence, where they have provided some such sports as they trust your gracious acceptations will interpret to be delightful. We have been at the other lodge, but finding them there busied in weightier affairs, our trust is that you yet will not deny the shining of your eyes upon us.'

The ladies stood in some doubt whether they should go or not, lest Basilius might be angry withal; but Miso, that had been at none of the pastorals, and had a great desire to lead her old senses abroad to some pleasure, told them plainly, they should nor will nor choose, but go thither, and make the honest country-people know that they were not so squeamish as folks thought of them. The ladies, glad to be warranted by her authority, with a smiling humbleness obeyed her, Pamela only casting a seeking look whether

---

[1] of them *Cm, 93*: of of them *90* [2] would] might *93*

she could see Dorus, who, poor wretch, wandered half mad for sorrow in the woods, crying for pardon of her who could not hear him – but indeed was grieved for his absence, having given the wound to him through her own heart. But so, the three ladies and Miso went with those six nymphs, conquering the length of the way with the force of music, leaving only Mopsa behind, who disgraced weeping with her countenance because her mother would not suffer her to show her new-scoured face among them – but the place appointed, as they thought, met them half in their way, so well were they pleased with the sweet tunes and pretty conversation of their inviters.

There found they in the midst of the thickest part of the wood a little square place, not burdened with trees, but with a board covered and beautified with the pleasantest fruits that sunburned autumn could deliver unto them. The maids besought the ladies to sit down and taste of the swelling grapes, which seemed great with child of Bacchus, and of the divers-coloured plums, which gave the eye a pleasant taste before they came to the mouth. The ladies would not show to scorn their provision, but eat, and drank a little of their cool wine, which seemed to laugh for joy to come to such lips.

But after the collation was ended, and that they looked for the coming forth of such devices as were prepared for them, there rushed out of the woods twenty armed men who round about environed them; and laying hold of Zelmane before she could draw her sword, and taking it from her, put hoods over the heads of all four; and so muffled, by force set them on horseback and carried them away, the sisters in vain crying for succour, while Zelmane's heart was rent in pieces with rage of the injury and disdain of her fortune. But when they had carried them a four or five mile further, they left Miso with a gag in her mouth and bound hand and foot, so to take her fortune, and brought the three ladies, by that time that the[1] night seemed with her silence to conspire to their treason, to a castle about ten mile off[2] from the lodges – where they were fain to take a boat which waited for them, for the castle stood in the midst of a great lake, upon a high rock, where partly by art, but principally by nature, it was by all men esteemed impregnable. But at the castle gate their faces were discovered, and there were met with a great number of torches, after whom the sisters knew their aunt-in-law Cecropia. But that sight increased the deadly terror of the princesses, looking for nothing but death since they were in the power of the wicked Cecropia, who yet came unto them making courtesy the outside of mischief, and desiring them not to be discomforted, for they were in a place dedicated to their service.

---

[1] time that the] time the *Cm, 98, 13*   [2] off] *om. 93*

Philoclea, with a look where love shined through the mist of fear, besought her to be good unto them, having never deserved evil of her; but Pamela's high heart disdaining humbleness to injury, 'Aunt,' said she, 'what you have determined of us, I pray you, do it speedily. For my part, I look for no service where I find violence.'

But Cecropia, using no more words with them, conveyed them all three to several lodgings (Zelmane's heart so swelling with spite that she could not bring forth a word) and so left them, first taking from them their knives, because they should do themselves no hurt before she had determined of them; and then, giving such order that they wanted nothing but liberty and comfort, she went to her son (who yet kept his bed because of his wound he had received of Zelmane) and told him whom now he had in his power. Amphialus was but even then returned from far countries (where he had won immortal fame both of courage and courtesy) when he met with the princesses and was hurt by Zelmane, so as he was utterly ignorant of all his mother's wicked devices – to which he would never have consented, being, like a rose out of a briar, an excellent son of an evil mother – and now, when he heard of this, was as much amazed as if he had seen the sun fall to the earth, and therefore desired his mother that she would tell him the whole discourse how all these matters had happened.

'Son,' said she, 'I will do it willingly. And since all is done for you, I will hide nothing from you; and howsoever I might be ashamed to tell it strangers, who would think it wickedness, yet what is done for your sake, how evil soever to others, to you is virtue.

'To begin, then, even with the beginning: this doting fool Basilius that now reigns, having lived unmarried till he was nigh threescore years old, and in all his speeches affirming, and in all his doings assuring, that he never would marry, made all the eyes of this[1] country to be bent upon your father, his only brother (but younger than[2] by thirty years) as upon the undoubted successor, being indeed a man worthy to reign, thinking nothing enough for himself – where this goose, you see, puts down his head before there be anything near to touch him; so that he, holding place and estimation as heir of Arcadia, obtained me of my father, the king of Argos (his brother helping to the conclusion with protesting his bachelorly intention – for else, you may be sure, the king of Argos, nor his daughter, would have suffered their royal blood to be stained with the base name of subjection); so that I came into this country as apparent princess thereof, and accordingly was courted, and followed, of all the ladies of this country.

---

[1] this *Cm, 93*: the *90* [2] younger than *Cm*: then younger *90*; younger *93*

'My port and pomp did well become a king of Argos' daughter. In my presence, their tongues were turned into ears, and their ears were captives unto my tongue. Their eyes admired my majesty; and happy was he or she on whom I would suffer the beams thereof to fall. Did I go to church? It seemed the very gods waited for me, their devotions not being solemnized till I was ready. Did I walk abroad to see any delight? Nay, my walking was the delight itself, for to it was the concourse, one thrusting upon another who might show himself most diligent and serviceable towards me. My sleeps were inquired after, and my wakings never unsaluted; the very gate of my house, full of principal persons who were glad if their presents had received a grateful acceptation.

'And in this felicity wert thou born, the very earth submitting itself unto thee to be trodden on, as by his prince (and to that pass had my husband's virtue by my good help within short time brought it, with a plot we laid, as we should not have needed to have waited the tedious work of a natural end of Basilius), when the heavens, I think envying my great felicity, then stopped thy father's breath, when he breathed nothing but power and sovereignty. Yet did not thy orphancy or my widowhood deprive us of the delightful prospect which the hill of honour doth yield, while expectation of thy succession did bind dependencies unto us; but before, my son, thou wert come to the age to feel the sweetness of authority, this beast (whom I can never name with patience) falsely and foolishly married this Gynecia, then a young girl, and brought her to sit above me in all feasts – to turn her shoulder to me-ward in all our solemnities.

'It is certain it is not so great a spite to be surmounted by strangers as by one's own allies. Think then what my mind was, since, withal, there is no question the fall is greater from the first to the second, than from the second to the undermost. The rage did swell in my heart – so much the more as it was fain to be suppressed in silence, and disguised with humbleness. But above all the rest, the grief of grieves was when, with these daughters,[1] now thy prisoners, she cut off all hope of thy succession. It was a tedious thing to me that my eyes should look lower than anybody's; that, myself being by, another's voice than mine should be more respected – but it was insupportable unto me to think that not only I, but thou, shouldst spend all thy time in such misery, and that the sun should see my eldest son less than a prince. And though I had been a saint, I could not choose finding the change this change of fortune bred unto me – for now, from the multitude of followers, silence grew to be at my gate, and absence in my presence; the

---

[1] these daughters] these two daughters 93

guess of my mind could prevail more before than, now, many of my earnest requests; and thou my dear son, by the fickle multitude, no more than an[1] ordinary person born of the mud of the people, regarded.

'But I, remembering that in all miseries weeping becomes fools, and practice wise folks, have tried divers means to pull us out of the mire of subjection; and though many times fortune failed me, yet did I never fail myself. Wild beasts I kept in a cave hard by the lodges, which I caused by night to be fed in the place of their pastorals (I as then living in my house hard by the place); and against the hour they were to meet, having kept the beasts without meat, then let them loose, knowing that they would seek their food there and devour what they found – but blind fortune, hating sharp-sighted inventions, made them unluckily to be killed. After, I used my servant Clinias to stir a notable tumult of country-people – but those louts were too gross instruments for delicate conceits. Now, lastly finding Philanax's examinations grow dangerous, I thought to play double or quit, and with a sleight I used of my fine-witted wench, Artesia, with other maids of mine, would have sent these good[2] inheritrixes of Arcadia to have pleaded their cause before Pluto – but that over-fortunately for them, you made me know the last day how vehemently this childish passion of love doth torment you; therefore I have brought them unto you, yet wishing rather hate than love in you, for hate often begetteth victory – love commonly is the instrument of subjection. It is true that I would also by the same practice have entrapped the parents, but my maids failed of it, not daring to tarry long about it. But this sufficeth, since, these being taken away, you are the undoubted inheritor, and Basilius will not long overlive this loss.'

'O mother!' said Amphialus. 'Speak not of doing them hurt – no more than to mine eyes, or my heart, or (if I have anything more dear than eyes or heart) unto me. Let others find what sweetness they will in ever fearing, because they are ever feared; for my part, I will think myself highly entitled if I may be once by Philoclea accepted for a servant.'

'Well,' said Cecropia, 'I would I had borne you of my mind, as well as of my body – then should you not have sunk under base[3] weaknesses. But since you have tied your thoughts in so wilful a knot, it is happy I have brought[4] matters to such a pass as you may both enjoy affection and, upon that, build your sovereignty.'

'Alas,' said Amphialus, 'my heart would fain yield you thanks for setting me in the way of felicity, but that fear kills them in me before they are fully born: for if Philoclea be displeased, how can I be pleased; if she count it

---

[1] an *Cm, 93*: any *90* [2] good] goodly *93* [3] under base] under these base *93* [4] happy I have brought] happy my policy hath brought *93*

unkindness, shall I give tokens of kindness? Perchance she condemns me of this action – and shall I triumph? Perchance she drowns now the beauties I love with sorrowful tears – and where is then my rejoicing?'

'You have reason,' said Cecropia, with a feigned gravity. 'I will therefore send her away presently, that her contentment may be recovered.'

'No, good mother,' said Amphialus, 'since she is here! I would not for my life constrain presence – but rather would I die than consent to absence!'

'Pretty, intricate follies!' said Cecropia. 'But get you up and see how you can prevail with her, while I go to the other sister; for after we shall have our hands full to defend ourselves, if Basilius hap to besiege us.' But remembering herself, she turned back and asked him what he would have done with Zelmane, since now he might be revenged of his hurt.

'Nothing but honourably,' answered Amphialus, 'having deserved no other of me, especially being, as I hear, greatly cherished of Philoclea; and therefore I could wish they were lodged together.'

'Oh, no!' said Cecropia. 'Company confirms resolutions, and loneliness breeds a weariness of one's thoughts, and so, a sooner consenting to reasonable proffers.'

But[1] Amphialus, taking of his mother Philoclea's knives – which he kept as a relic, since she had worn them – gat up. And calling for his richest apparel, nothing seemed sumptuous enough for his mistress's eyes; and that which was costly, he feared were not dainty; and though the invention were delicate, he misdoubted the making. As careful he was too of the colour, lest, if gay, he might seem to glory in his injury, and her wrong; if mourning, it might strike some evil presage unto her of her fortune. At length, he took a garment more rich than glaring, the ground being black velvet, richly embrodered, with great pearl and precious stones – but they set so, among certain tuffs of cypress, that the cypress was like black clouds through which the stars might yield a dark lustre. About his neck, he ware a broad and gorgeous collar, whereof, the pieces interchangeably answering, the one was of diamonds and pearl set with a white enamel so as, by the cunning of the workman, it seemed like a shining ice; and the other piece, being of rubies and opals, had a fiery glistering – which he thought pictured the two passions of fear and desire, wherein he was enchained.

His hurt not yet fully well made him a little halt, but he strave to give the best grace he could unto his halting, and in that sort he went to Philoclea's chamber – whom he found, because her chamber was over lightsome, sitting of that side of her bed which was from the window (which did cast such a

---

[1] proffers.' But *Cm*, 93: proffers.' Chap. 3. Amphialus' addressing him to Philoclea; her melancholy habit; his humble suit; her pitiful answer, and his compassionate reply; their parting with cold comfort. But *90*

shadow upon her as a good painter would bestow upon Venus, when under the trees she bewailed the murther of Adonis), her hands and fingers as it were indented one within the other, her shoulder leaning to her bed's head, and over her head a scarf which did eclipse almost half her eyes, which under it fixed their beams upon the wall by, with so steady a manner, as if in that place they might well change, but not mend, their object – and so remained they a good while after his coming in, he not daring to trouble her, nor she perceiving him; till that, a little varying her thoughts something quickening her senses, she heard him as he happed to stir his upper garment, and perceiving him rose up with a demeanour where, in the book of beauty, there was nothing to be read but sorrow – for kindness was blotted out, and anger was never there.

But Amphialus, that had entrusted his memory with long and forcible speeches, found it so locked up in amazement that he could pick nothing out of it but the beseeching her to take what was done in good part, and to assure herself there was nothing but honour meant unto her person. But she making no other answer but letting her hands fall one from the other, which before were joined, with eyes something cast aside and a silent sigh, gave him to understand that considering his doings she thought his speech as full of incongruity as her answer would be void of purpose – whereupon he kneeling down and kissing her hand (which she suffered, with a countenance witnessing captivity but not kindness), he besought her to have pity of him whose love went beyond the bounds of conceit – much more, of uttering; that in her hands the balance of his life or death did stand, whereto the least motion of hers would serve to determine, she being indeed the mistress of his life, and he, her eternal slave; and with true vehemency besought her that he might hear her speak – whereupon she suffered her sweet breath to turn itself into these kind of words.

'Alas, cousin,' said she, 'what shall my tongue be able to do, which is informed by the ears one way and by the eyes another? You call for pity – and use cruelty; you say you love me – and yet do the effects of enmity; you affirm your death is in my hands – but you have brought me to so near a degree to death as, when you will, you may lay death upon me, so that while you say I am mistress of your life, I am not mistress of mine own; you entitle yourself my slave – but I am sure I am yours. If then violence, injury, terror, and depriving of that which is more dear than life itself, liberty, be fit orators for affection, you may expect that I will be easily persuaded. But if the nearness of our kinred breed any remorse in you, or there be any such thing in you, which you call love, toward me, then let not my fortune be disgraced with the name of imprisonment; let not my heart waste itself by being vexed with feeling evil – and fearing worse; let not me be a cause of my parents' woeful destruction. But restore me to myself and, so doing, I shall account I have received myself of you – and what I say for myself, I say for my dear sister, and my friend Zelmane, for I desire no well-being without they may be partakers.'

With that, her tears rained down from her heavenly eyes, and seemed to water the sweet and beautiful flowers of her face. But Amphialus was like the poor woman, who loving a tame doe she had above all earthly things, having long played withal and made it feed at her hand and lap, is constrained at length by famine (all her flock being spent, and she fallen into extreme poverty) to kill the deer to sustain her life: many a pitiful look doth she cast upon it, and many a time doth she draw back her hand before she can give the stroke – for even so, Amphialus by a hunger-starved affection was compelled to offer this injury, and yet the same affection made him with a tormenting grief think unkindness in himself that he could find in his heart any way to restrain her freedom. But at length, neither able to grant nor deny, he thus answered her.

'Dear lady,' said he, 'I will not say unto you, how justly soever I may do it, that I am neither author nor accessory unto this your withholding, for since I do not redress it, I am as faulty as if I had begun it. But this I protest unto you – and this protestation of mine, let the heavens hear; and if I lie, let them answer me with a deadly thunderbolt – that in my soul I wish I had never seen the light, or rather, that I had never had a father to beget such a child, than that by my means those eyes should overflow their own beauties, than by my means the sky of your virtue should be overclouded with sorrow. But woe is me! Most excellent lady, I find myself most willing to obey you; neither, truly, do mine ears receive the least word you speak with any less reverence than as absolute and unresistable commandments – but alas! that tyrant, love, which now possesseth the hold of all my life and reason, will no way suffer it. It is love! It is love, not I, which disobey you. What then shall I say, but that I who am ready to lie under your feet; to venture, nay, to lose my life at your least commandment, I am not the stay of your freedom, but love – love, which ties you in your own knots. It is you yourself that imprison yourself! It is your beauty which makes these castle walls embrace you! It is your own eyes which reflect upon themselves this injury! Then is there no other remedy but that you some way vouchsafe to satisfy this love's vehemency, which, since it grew in yourself, without question you shall find it – far more than I – tractable.'

But with these words Philoclea fell to so extreme a quaking, and her lively whiteness did degenerate to so dead a[1] paleness, that Amphialus feared

---

[1] so dead a] such a deadly 93

some dangerous trance; so that taking her hand, and feeling that it (which was wont to be one of the chief firebrands of Cupid) had all the sense of it wrapped up in coldness, he began humbly to beseech her to put away all fear, and to assure herself (upon the vow he made thereof unto God and herself) that the uttermost forces he would ever employ to conquer her affection should be desire and desert. That promise brought Philoclea again to herself, so that slowly lifting up her eyes upon him, with a countenance ever courteous (but then languishing), she told him that he should do well to do so (if indeed he had ever tasted what true love was), for that where now she did bear him goodwill, she should, if he took any other way, hate and abhor the very thought of him, assuring[1] him withal that, though his mother had taken away her knives, yet the house of death had so many doors as she would easily fly into it, if ever she found her honour endangered.

Amphialus, having the cold ashes of care cast upon the coals of desire, leaving some of his mother's gentlewomen to wait upon Philoclea (himself indeed a prisoner to his prisoner, and making all his authority to be but a footstool to humbleness), went from her to his mother, to whom with words which affection indited but amazement uttered, he delivered what had passed between him and Philoclea, beseeching her to try what her persuasions could do with her, while he gave order for all such things as were necessary against such forces as he looked daily Basilius would bring before his castle. His mother bad him quiet himself, for she doubted not to take fit times, but that the best way was first to let her own passion a little tire itself;[2] and so, they calling Clinias and some other of their council, advised upon their present affairs.

First, he dispatched private letters to all those principal lords and gentlemen of the country whom he thought either alliance or friendship to himself might draw, with special motions, from the general consideration of duty; not omitting all such whom either youthful age or youth-like minds did fill with unlimited desires; besides, such whom any discontentment made hungry of change, or an over-spended want made want a civil war – to each (according to the counsel of his mother) conforming himself, after their humours: to his friends, friendliness; to the ambitious, great expectations; to the displeased, revenge; to the greedy, spoil – wrapping their hopes with such cunning, as they rather seemed given over unto them, as partakers, than promises sprong of necessity; then sent he to his mother's brother, the king of Argos, but he was as then so overlaid with war himself, as from thence he could attend small succour.

---

[1] assuring *Cm, 93*: offering *90*   [2] itself; and so *Cm*: itself. Chap. 4. Amphialus' warlike preparations; his justification; his fortifications; his art of men; his love passions and passionate complaints. So *90*; itself; so *93*

But because he knew how violently rumours do blow the sails of popular judgements, and how few there be that can discern between truth and truth-likeness, between shows and substance, he caused a justification of this his action to be written (whereof were sowed abroad many copies) which with some glosses of probability might hide indeed the foulness of his treason, and from true commonplaces fetch down most false applications; for beginning how much the duty which is owed to the country goes beyond all other duties, since in itself it contains them all (and that for the respect thereof not only all tender respects of kinred, or whatsoever other friendships, are to be laid aside, but that even long-held opinions – rather builded upon a secret of government than any ground of truth – are to be forsaken), he fell by degrees to show, that since the end whereto anything is directed is ever to be of more noble reckoning than the thing thereto directed, that, therefore, the weal-public was more to be regarded than any person or magistrate that thereunto was ordained; the feeling consideration whereof had moved him, though as near of kin to Basilius as could be, yet to set principally before his eyes the good estate of so many thousands over whom Basilius reigned rather than so to hoodwink himself with affection as to suffer the realm to run to manifest ruin – the care whereof did kindly appertain to those who (being subaltern magistrates and officers of the crown) were to be employed, as from the prince, so for the people – and of all other, especially himself, who being descended of the royal race and next heir male, nature had no sooner opened his eyes but that the soil whereupon they did look was to look for, at his hands, a continual carefulness; which, as from his childhood he had ever carried, so now, finding that his uncle had not only given over all care of government, but had put it into the hands of Philanax (a man neither in birth comparable to many, nor for his corrupt, proud, and partial dealing, liked of any), but beside, had set his daughters (in whom the whole estate, as next heirs thereunto, had no less interest than himself) in so unfit and ill-guarded a place as it was not only dangerous for their persons but (if they should be conveyed to any foreign country) to the whole commonwealth pernicious – that, therefore, he had brought them into this strong castle of his (which way, if it might seem strange, they were to consider that new necessities require new remedies), but there they should be served and honoured as belonged to their greatness until, by the general assembly of the estates, it should be determined how they should to their best (both private and public) advantage be matched, vowing all faith and duty both to the father and children, never by him to be violated; but if in the meantime (before the estates could be assembled) he were[1] assailed, he would then for his own defence take arms, desiring all that either tendered the dangerous case

---

[1] were] should be 93

of their country, or in their hearts loved justice, to defend him in this just action; and if the prince should command them otherwise, yet to know that therein he was no more to be obeyed than if he should call for poison to hurt himself withal, since all that was done was done for his service, howsoever he might, seduced by Philanax, interpret of it – he protesting that whatsoever he should do for his own defence should be against Philanax, and no way against Basilius.

To this effect, amplified with arguments and examples, and painted with rhetorical colours, did he sow abroad many discourses, which, as they prevailed with some of more quick than sound conceit to run his fortune with him, so in many did it breed a coolness to deal violently against him, and a false-minded neutrality to expect the issue. But besides the ways he used to weaken the adverse party, he omitted nothing for the strengthening of his own, the chief trust whereof, because he wanted men to keep the field, he reposed in the surety of his castle – which at least would win him much time, the mother of many mutations. To that, therefore, he bent both his[1] outward and inward eyes, striving to make art strive with nature, to whether of them two that fortification should be most beholding. The seat nature bestowed, but art gave the building; which, as his rocky hardness would not yield to undermining force, so, to open assaults, he took counsel of skill how to make all approaches, if not impossible, yet difficult, as well at the foot of the castle as round about the lake, to give unquiet lodgings to them whom only enmity would make neighbours. Then omitted he nothing of defence (as well simple defence as that which did defend by offending), fitting instruments of mischief to places whence the mischief might be most liberally bestowed. Neither was his smallest care for victuals, as well for the providing that which should suffice both in store and goodness, as in well-preserving it and wary distributing it, both in quantity and quality, spending that first which would keep least.

But wherein he sharpened his wits to the piercingest point was touching his men, knowing them to be the weapon of weapons, and master-spring, as it were, which makes all the rest to stir, and that, therefore, in the art of man stood the quintessence and ruling skill of all prosperous government, either peaceable or military. He chose in number as many as (without pestering, and so, danger of infection) his victual would seem[2] for two year to maintain, all of able bodies, and some few of able minds to direct – not seeking many commanders, but contenting himself that the multitude should have obeying wills,[3] every one knowing whom he should command and whom he should obey, the place where, and the matter wherein; distributing each office as near as he could to the disposition of the person that should exercise

---

[1] bent both his *Cm, 93*. bent his *90* [2] seem] serve *93* [3] wills] wits *93*

it, knowing no love, danger, nor discipline can suddenly alter an habit in nature: therefore would he not employ the still man to a shifting practice, nor the liberal man to be a dispenser of his victuals, nor the kind-hearted man to be a punisher, but would exercise their virtues in sorts where they might be profitable – employing his chief care to know them all particularly and throughly – regarding also the constitution of their bodies, some being able better to abide watching; some, hunger; some, labour; making his benefit of each ability, and not forcing beyond power. Time to everything, by just proportion, he allotted, and, as well in that as in everything else, no small error winked at lest greater should be animated. Even of vices he made his profit, making the cowardly Clinias to have care of the watch, which, he knew, his own fear would make him very wakefully perform. And before the siege began, he himself caused rumours to be sowed and libels to be spread against himself (fuller of malice than witty persuasion), partly to know those that would be apt to stumble at such motions (that he might cull them from the faithfuller band), but principally because in necessity they should not know (when any such thing were in earnest attempted) whether it were or not of his own invention.

But even then (before the enemy's face came near, to breed any terror) did he exercise his men daily in all their charges, as if danger had presently presented his most hideous presence, himself rather instructing by example than precept, being neither more sparing in travail nor spending in diet than the meanest soldier, his hand and body disdaining no base matters, nor shrinking from the heavy. The only odds was that, when others took breath, he sighed, and when others rested, he crossed his arms; for love, passing thorough the pikes of danger, and tumbling itself in the dust of labour, yet still made him remember his sweet desire, and beautiful image. Often, when he had begun to command one, somewhat before half the sentence were ended his inward guest did so entertain him that he would break it off, and a pretty while after end it when he had, to the marvel of the standers-by, sent himself in to talk with his own thoughts. Sometimes, when his hand was lifted up to do[1] something, as if with the sight of Gorgon's head he had been suddenly turned into a stone, so would he there abide with his eyes planted and hands[2] lifted, till at length coming to the use of himself he would look about whether any had perceived him. Then would he accuse and (in himself) condemn all those wits that durst affirm idleness to be the well-spring of love.

'O', would he say, 'all you that affect the title of wisdom by ungrateful scorning the ornaments of nature, am I now piping in a shadow, or do slothful feathers now enwrap me? Is not hate before me and doubt behind me?

---

[1] to do 93: to d *Cm*; to 90   [2] hands] hand 93

Is not danger of the one side and shame of the other? And do I not stand upon pain and travail, and yet, over all, my affection triumphs? The more I stir about urgent affairs, the more methinks the very stirring breeds a breath to blow the coals of my love; the more I exercise my thoughts, the more they increase the appetite of my desires. O sweet Philoclea!' With that, he would cast up his eyes, wherein some water did appear, as if they would wash themselves against they should see her. 'Thy heavenly face is my astronomy! thy sweet virtue, my sweet philosophy! Let me profit therein – and farewell, all other cogitations. But, alas, my mind misgives me, for your planets bear a contrary aspect unto me. Woe, woe is me! They threaten my destruction. And whom do they threaten this destruction? Even him that loves them. And by what means will they destroy? But by loving them. O dear (though killing) eyes! Shall death head his dart with the gold of Cupid's arrow? Shall death take his aim from the rest of beauty? O beloved (though hating) Philoclea, how, if thou beest merciful, hath cruelty stolen into thee? Or how, if thou beest cruel, doth cruelty look more merciful[1] than ever mercy did? Or, alas, is it my destiny that makes mercy cruel, like an evil vessel which turns sweet liquor to sourness; so, when thy grace falls upon me, my wretched constitution makes it become fierceness?'

Thus would he exercise his eloquence when she could not hear him – and be dumb-stricken when her presence gave him fit occasion of speaking; so that his wit could find out no other refuge but the comfort and counsel of his mother, desiring her (whose thoughts were unperplexed) to use for his sake the most prevailing manners of intercession.

She[2] seeing her son's safety depend thereon, though her pride much disdained the name of a 'desire,'[3] took the charge upon her, not doubting the easy conquest of an unexpert virgin, who had already with subtilty and impudency begun to undermine a monarchy; therefore, weighing Philoclea's resolutions by the counterpease of her own youthful thoughts (which she then called to mind), she doubted not at least to make Philoclea receive the poison distilled in sweet liquor, which she with little disguising had drunk up thirstily. Therefore she went softly to Philoclea's chamber. And peeping through the side of the door, then being a little open, she saw Philoclea sitting low upon a cushion, in such a given-over manner that one would have thought silence, solitariness, and melancholy were come there (under the ensign of mishap) to conquer delight and drive him from his natural seat of beauty. Her tears came dropping down like rain in sunshine, and she

---

[1] merciful] beautiful 93   [2] intercession. She *Cm*, 93: intercession. Chap. 5. Subtle Cecropia visits sad Philoclea; the shameless aunt's shrewd temptations to love and marriage; the modest niece's maidenly resistance. Cecropia 90   [3] desire] desirer 93

not taking heed to wipe the tears, they ran down[1] upon her cheeks and lips as upon cherries, which the dropping tree bedeweth. In the dressing of her hair and apparel, she might see neither a careful art nor an art of carelessness, but even left to a neglected chance, which yet could no more unperfect her perfections than a die any way cast could lose his squareness.

Cecropia, stirred with no other pity but for her son, came in; and haling kindness into her countenance, 'What ails this sweet lady?', said she. 'Will you mar so good eyes with weeping? Shall tears take away the beauty of that complexion which the women of Arcadia wish for, and the men long after? Fie of this peevish sadness! In sooth, it is untimely for your age. Look upon your own body, and see whether it deserve to pine away with sorrow. See whether you will have these hands,' with that, she took one of her hands and, kissing it, looked upon it as if she were enamoured with it, 'fade from their whiteness (which makes one desire to touch them) and their softness (which rebounds again a desire to look on them) and become dry, lean, and yellow, and make everybody wonder at the change, and say, that sure you had used some art before, which now you had left – for, if the beauties had been natural, they would never so soon have been blemished. Take a glass and see whether these tears become your eyes – although, I must confess, those eyes are able to make tears comely.'

'Alas, madam,' answered Philoclea, 'I know not whether my tears become mine eyes, but I am sure mine eyes, thus beteared, become my fortune.'

'Your fortune,' said Cecropia, 'if she could see to attire herself, would put on her best raiments! For I see – and I see it with grief, and, to tell you true, unkindness – you misconster everything that only for your sake is attempted: you think you are offended, and are indeed defended; you esteem yourself a prisoner, and are in truth a mistress; you fear hate, and shall find love. And truly, I had a thing to say to you – but it is no matter. Since I find you are so obstinately melancholy as that you woo his fellowship, I will spare my pains and hold my peace' – and so stayed, indeed thinking Philoclea would have had a female inquisitiveness of the matter.

But she (who rather wished to unknow what she knew than to burden her heart with more hopeless knowledge) only desired her to have pity of her, and, if indeed she did mean her no hurt, then to grant her liberty, for else the very grief and fear would prove her unappointed executioners.

'For that,' said Cecropia, 'believe me, upon the faith of a king's daughter, you shall be free so soon as your freedom may be free of mortal danger, being brought hither for no other cause but to prevent such mischiefs as you know

---

[1] ran down] hung 93

not of. But if you think indeed to win me to have care of you, even as of mine own daughter, then lend your ears unto me, and let not your mind arm itself with a wilfulness to be flexible to nothing – but if I speak reason, let reason have his due reward, persuasion.

'Then, sweet niece,' said she, 'I pray you, presuppose that now, even in the midst of your agonies (which you paint unto yourself most horrible), wishing with sighs and praying with vows for a soon and safe delivery; imagine, niece, I say, that some heavenly spirit should appear unto you and bid you follow him through the door that goes into the garden, assuring you that you should thereby return to your dear mother, and what other delights soever your mind esteems delights – would you, sweet niece, would you refuse to follow him, and say that, if he led you not through the chief gate, you would not enjoy your over-desired liberty? Would you not drink the wine you thirst for, without it were in such a glass as you especially fancied? Tell me, dear niece – but I will answer for you, because I know your reason and will[1] is such as must needs conclude, that such niceness can no more be in you to disgrace such a mind, than disgracefulness can have any place in so faultless a beauty; your wisdom would assuredly determine how the mark were hit, not whether the bow were of yew or no wherein you shot.

'If this be so (and thus, sure, my dear niece, it is), then I pray you imagine that I am that same good angel, who, grieving in your grief, and in truth not able to suffer that bitter sighs should be sent forth with so sweet a breath, am come to lead you not only to your desired and imagined happiness, but to a true and essential happiness; not only to liberty, but to liberty with commandment. The way I will show you, which, if it be not the gate builded hitherto in your private choice, yet shall it be a door to bring you through a garden of pleasures as sweet as this life can bring forth – nay, rather, which makes this life to be a life.

'My son – let it be no blemish to him that I name him my son, who was your father's own nephew, for you know I am no small king's daughter – my son, I say, far passing the nearness[2] of his kinred with the nearness of goodwill, and striving to match your matchless beauty with a matchless affection, doth by me present unto you the full enjoying of your liberty – so as, with this gift, you will accept a greater (which is this castle, with all the rest which you know he hath in honourable quantity), and will confirm his gift, and your receipt of both, with accepting him to be yours. I might say much both for the person and the matter – but who will cry out, "The sun shines!"? It is so manifest a profit unto you as the meanest judgement

---

[1] will] wit 93   [2] with the nearness] with nearness 93

must straight apprehend it; so, far is it from the sharpness of yours thereof to be ignorant. Therefore, sweet niece, let your gratefulness be my intercession, and your gentleness my eloquence, and let me carry comfort to a heart which greatly needs it.'

Philoclea looked upon her, and cast down her eye again. 'Aunt,' said she, 'I would I could be so much a mistress of my own mind as to yield to my cousin's virtuous request – for so I construe of it. But my heart is already set,' and staying a while on that word, she brought forth afterwards, 'to lead a virgin's life to my death, for such a vow I have in myself devoutly made.'

'The heavens prevent such a mischief!' said Cecropia. '"A vow", quoth you? No, no, my dear niece. Nature, when you were first born, vowed you a woman; and as she made you child of a mother, so, to do your best to be mother of a child, she gave you beauty to move love, she gave you wit to know love, she gave you an excellent body to reward love – which kind of liberal rewarding is crowned with unspeakable[1] felicity; for this, as it bindeth the receiver, so it makes happy the bestower: this doth not impoverish, but enrich the giver. Oh, the sweet name of a mother! Oh, the comfort of comforts! to see your children grow up, in whom you are as it were eternized. If you could conceive what a heart-tickling joy it is to see your own little ones with awful love come running to your lap, and like little models of yourself still carry you about them, you would think unkindness in your own thoughts that ever they did rebel against the mean unto it. But perchance I set this blessedness before your eyes as captains do victory before their soldiers, to which they might[2] come through many pains, grieves, and dangers. No, I am content you shrink from this my counsel if the way to come unto it be not, most of all, pleasant.'

'I know not,' answered the sweet Philoclea, fearing lest silence would offend her[3] sullenness, 'what contentment you speak of, but I am sure the best you can make of it, which is marriage, is a burdenous yoke.'

'Ah, dear niece,' said Cecropia, 'how much you are deceived! A yoke indeed we all bear, laid upon us in our creation, which by marriage is not increased, but thus far eased that you have a yoke-fellow to help to draw through the cloddy cumbers of this world. O widow-nights, bear witness with me of the difference! How often, alas, do I embrace the orphan side of my bed, which was wont to be imprinted by the body of my dear husband, and with tears acknowledge that I now enjoy such a liberty as the banished man hath, who may, if he list, wander over the world, but is forever[4] restrained from his most delightful home; that I have now such a liberty as the seeled dove hath, which, being first deprived of eyes, is then by the falconer

---

[1] with unspeakable] with an unspeakable 93   [2] might] must 93   [3] her] for 93   [4] forever *Cm*, 93: ever 90

cast off. For believe me, niece, believe me, man's experience is woman's best eyesight. Have you ever seen a pure rose-water kept in a crystal glass? How fine it looks! How sweet it smells, while that beautiful glass imprisons it! Break the prison, and let the water take his own course: doth it not embrace dust, and lose all his former sweetness and fairness! Truly, so are we, if we have not the stay – rather than the restraint – of crystalline marriage. My heart melts to think of the sweet comforts I in that happy time received when I had never cause to care, but the care was doubled; when I never rejoiced but that I saw my joy shine in another's eyes. What shall I say of the free delight which the heart might embrace – without the accusing of the inward conscience, or fear of outward shame? And is a solitary life as good as this? Then can one string make as good music as a consort; then can one colour set forth a beauty.

'But it may be the general consideration of marriage doth not so much mislike you as the applying of it to him. He is my son. I must confess I see him with a mother's eyes, which if they do not much deceive me, he is no such one over whom contempt may make any just challenge. He is comely; he is noble; he is rich. But that which in itself should carry all comeliness, nobility, and riches – he loves you; and he loves you, who is beloved of others. Drive not away his affection, sweet lady, and make no other lady hereafter proudly brag that she hath robbed you of so faithful and notable a servant.'

Philoclea heard some pieces of her speeches no otherwise than one doth when a tedious prattler cumbers the hearing of a delightful music, for her thoughts had left her ears in that captivity and conveyed themselves to behold, with such eyes as imagination could lend them, the estate of her Zelmane – for whom, how well, she thought, many of those sayings might have been used with a far more grateful acceptation! Therefore, listing not to dispute in a matter whereof herself was resolved,[1] and desired not to inform the other, she only told her that whilst she was so captived she could not conceive of any such persuasions (though never so reasonable) any otherwise than as constraints; and as constraints, must needs even in nature abhor them, which at her liberty, in their own force of reason might more prevail with her; and so, fain would have returned the strength of Cecropia's persuasions, to have procured freedom.[2] But neither her witty words, in an enemy, nor those words (made more than eloquent with passing through such lips) could prevail in Cecropia – no more than her persuasions could win Philoclea to disavow her former vow, or to leave the

---

[1] resolved *Cm, 93*: resolute *90*   [2] freedom. But *Cm, 93*: freedom. Chap. 6. Fresh motives to Philoclea; Cecropia's new fetch to attempt Pamela; Pamela's prayer and saint-like graces in it; her aunt's fruitless arguments. But *90*

prisoner Zelmane for the commanding Amphialus; so that both sides being desirous, and neither granters, they brake off conference, Cecropia sucking up more and more spite out of her denial, which yet, for her son's sake, she disguised with a vizard of kindness, leaving no office unperformed which might either witness, or endear, her son's affection.

Whatsoever could be imagined likely to please her was with liberal diligence performed: musics at her window, and especially such musics as might with doleful embassage call the mind to think of sorrow, and think of it with sweetness – with ditties so sensibly expressing Amphialus' case that every word seemed to be but a diversifying of the name of Amphialus; daily presents (as it were, oblations to pacify an angry deity) sent unto her, wherein, if the workmanship of the form had striven with the sumptuousness of the matter, as much did the invention, in the application, contend to have the chief excellency – for they were as so many stories of his disgraces and her perfections, where the richness did invite the eyes, the fashion did entertain the eyes, and the device did teach the eyes the present misery of the presenter himself – awfully serviceable (which was the more notable, as his authority was manifest); and for the bondage wherein she lived, all means used to make known that, if it were a bondage, it was a bondage only knit in love-knots. But in heart already understanding no language but one, the music wrought indeed a dolefulness – but it was a dolefulness to be in his power; the ditty intended for Amphialus, she translated to Zelmane; the presents seemed so many tedious clogs of a thralled obligation; and his service, the more diligent it was, the more it did exprobrate, as she thought, unto her, her unworthy estate: that even he that did her service had authority of commanding her – only construing her servitude in his own nature, esteeming it a right (and a right bitter) servitude.

So that, all their shots, how well soever levelled, being carried awry from the mark by the storm of her mislike, the Prince Amphialus affectionately languished; and Cecropia, spitefully cunning, disdained at the barrenness of their success – which willingly Cecropia would have revenged, but that she saw her hurt could not be divided from her son's mischief; wherefore she bethought herself to attempt Pamela, whose beauty being equal, she hoped, if she might be won, that her son's thoughts would rather rest on a beautiful gratefulness than still be tormented with a disdaining beauty; wherefore[1] giving new courage to her wicked inventions, and using the more industry because she had missed in this, and taking even precepts of prevailing in Pamela by her failing in Philoclea, she went to her chamber and (according to her own ungracious method of a subtile[2] proceeding) stood listening at

---

[1] wherefore] Therefore 93   [2] of a subtile] of subtile 93

the door, because that out of the circumstance of her present behaviour there might kindly arise a fit beginning of her intended discourse.

And so, she might perceive that Pamela did walk up and down full of deep though patient thoughts, for her look and countenance was settled, her pace soft and almost still of one measure, without any passionate gesture or violent motion; till at length, as it were, awaking and strengthening herself, 'Well,' said she, 'yet this is the best. And of this I am sure, that howsoever they wrong me, they cannot overmaster God. No darkness blinds his eyes; no jail bars him out. To whom, then, else should I fly, but to him for succour?'

And therewith kneeling down even in the same place where[1] she stood, she thus said: 'O all-seeing light and eternal life of all things, to whom nothing is either so great that it may resist or so small that it is contemned, look upon my misery with thine eye of mercy, and let thine infinite power vouchsafe to limit out some proportion of deliverance unto me, as to thee shall seem most convenient. Let not injury, O Lord, triumph over me; and let my faults by thy hands[2] be corrected; and make not mine unjust enemy the minister of thy justice. But yet, my God, if in thy wisdom this be the aptest chastisement for my inexcusable[3] folly, if this low bondage be fittest for my over-high desires, if the pride of my not-enough-humble heart be thus to be broken, O Lord, I yield unto thy will, and joyfully embrace what sorrow thou wilt have me suffer. Only thus much let me crave of thee (let my craving, O Lord, be accepted of thee, since even that proceeds from thee): let me crave, even by the noblest title which in my greatest affliction I may give myself – that I am thy creature – and by thy goodness which is thyself, that thou wilt suffer some beam of thy majesty so to shine into my mind that it may still depend confidently upon thee. Let calamity be the exercise, but not the overthrow of my virtue; let their power prevail, but prevail not to destruction; let my greatness be their prey; let my pain be the sweetness of their revenge; let them, if so it seem good unto thee, vex me with more and more punishment – but, O Lord, let never their wickedness have such a hand but that I may carry a pure mind in a pure body.' And pausing a while, 'And, O most gracious Lord,' said she, 'whatever become of me, preserve the virtuous Musidorus.' The other part Cecropia might well hear, but this latter prayer for Musidorus, her heart held it as so jewel-like a treasure that it would scarce trust her own lips withal.

But this prayer, sent to heaven from so heavenly a creature (with such a fervent grace, as if devotion had borrowed her body to make of itself a most beautiful representation); with her eyes so lifted to the skyward that one would have thought they had begun to fly thitherward to take their place

---

[1] even in the same place where] even where 93   [2] hands] hand 93   [3] inexcusable] unexcusable 93

among their fellow stars; her naked hands raising up their whole length and, as it were, kissing one another (as if the right had been the picture of zeal, and the left of humbleness, which both united themselves to make their suits more acceptable); lastly all her senses being rather tokens than instruments of her inward motions – all together had so strange a working power that even the hard-hearted wickedness of Cecropia, if it found not a love of that goodness, yet it felt an abashment at that goodness; and if she had not a kindly remorse, yet had she an irksome accusation of her own naughtiness; so that she was put from the bias of her fore-intended lesson, for well she found there was no way at that time to take that mind but with some, at least, image of virtue – and what the figure thereof was, her heart knew not.

Yet did she prodigally spend her uttermost eloquence, leaving no argument unproved which might with any force invade her excellent judgement: the justness of the request – being but for marriage; the worthiness of the suitor; then, her own present fortune – she would[1] not only have amendment but felicity (besides, falsely making her believe that her sister would think herself happy if now she might have his love which before she contemned, and obliquely touching what danger it should be for her if her son should accept Philoclea in marriage, and so match the next heir apparent, she being in his power); yet plentifully perjuring how extremely her son loved her, and excusing the little shows he made of it with the dutiful respect he bare unto her, and taking upon herself that she restrained him, since she found she could set no limits to his passions. And, as she did to Philoclea, so did she to her, with the tribute of gifts seek to bring her mind into servitude; and all other means that might either establish a beholdingness, or at the least[2] awake a kindness, doing it so as, by reason of their imprisonment, one sister knew not how the other was wooed, but each might think that only she was sought. But if Philoclea with sweet and humble dealing did avoid their assaults, she with the majesty of virtue did beat them off.

But[3] this day their speech was the sooner broken off, by reason that he who stood as watch upon the top of the keep did not only see a great dust arise which the earth sent up as if it would strive to have clouds as well as the air, but might spy sometimes, especially when the dust wherein the naked wind did apparel itself was carried aside from them, the shining of armour, like flashing of lightning, wherewith the clouds did seem to be with child; which the sun gilding with his beams, it gave a sight delightful to any, but to them that were to abide the terror. But the watch gave a quick alarum

---

[1] fortune – she would *Cm*: fortune, if she would *90*; fortune, which should *93*   [2] at the least] at least *93*
[3] off. But *Cm, 93*: off. Chap. 7. An alarm to the Amphialians; base cowardice in Clinias, brave courage imaged in Amphialus; his onset, with the death of two friends, his foes; the horror of Mars' game; two deaths taken where they were not looked for, the third, delayed where it was expected. But *90*

to the soldiers within, whom practice already having prepared, began each with unabashed hearts, or at least countenances, to look to their charge or obedience which was allotted unto them.

Only Clinias and Amphialus did exceed the bounds of mediocrity – the one in his natural coldness of cowardice, the other in heat of courage; for Clinias, who was bold only in busy whisperings, and even in that whisperingness rather indeed confident in his cunning that it should not be bewrayed than any way bold if ever it should be bewrayed, now that the enemy gave a dreadful aspect unto the castle, his eyes saw no terror, nor ear heard any martial sound, but that they multiplied the hideousness of it to his mated mind. Before their coming he had many times felt a dreadful expectation, but yet his mind, that was willing to ease itself of the burden of fear, did sometimes feign unto itself possibility of let, as the death of Basilius, the discord of the nobility; and when other cause failed him, the nature of chance served as a cause unto him. And sometimes the hearing other men speak valiantly, and the quietness of his unassailed senses, would make himself believe that he durst do something.

But now that present danger did display itself unto his eye, and that a dangerous doing must be the only mean to prevent the danger of suffering, one that had marked him would have judged that his eyes would have run into him and his soul out of him, so unkindly did either take a scent of danger. He thought the lake was too shallow and the walls too thin. He misdoubted each man's treason and conjectured every possibility of misfortune (not only forecasting likely perils, but such as all the planets together could scarce[1] have conspired), and already began to arm himself though it was determined he should tarry within doors, and while he armed himself, imagined in what part of the vault he might[2] hide himself if the enemies won the castle. Desirous he was that everybody should do valiantly but himself, and therefore was afraid to show his fear, but for very fear would have hid his fear lest it should discomfort others; but the more he sought to disguise it, the more the unsuitableness of a weak broken voice to high brave words, and of a pale shaking countenance to a gesture of animating, did discover him – but quite contrarily Amphialus, who before the enemies came was careful, providently diligent, and not sometimes without doubting of the issue; now, the nearer danger approached, like the light of a glow-worm, the less still it seemed.

And now his courage began to boil in choler, and with such impatience to desire to pour out both upon the enemy that he issued presently into certain boats he had of purpose; and carrying with him some choice men, went to

---

[1] scarce] scarcely 93 [2] might] would 93

the fortress he had upon the edge of the lake, which he thought would be the first thing that the enemy would attempt because it was a passage which, commanding all that side of the country,[1] and being lost, would stop victual or other supply that might be brought into the castle. And in that fortress having some force of horsemen, he issued out with two hundred horse and five hundred footmen; embushed his footmen in the falling of a hill which was overshadowed with a wood. He with his horsemen went a quarter of a mile further, aside-hand of which he might perceive the many troops of the enemy, who came but to take view where best to encamp themselves.

But as if the sight of the enemy had been a magnes-stone to his courage, he could not contain himself; but showing his face to the enemy and his back to his soldiers, used that action as his only oration both of denouncing war to the one, and persuading help of the other; who faithfully following an example of such authority, they made the earth to groan under their furious burden, and the enemies to begin to be angry with them, whom in particular they knew not – among whom there was a young man, youngest brother to Philanax, whose face as yet did not bewray his sex with so much as show of hair, of a mind having no limits of hope, not[2] knowing why to fear, full of jollity in conversation, and lately grown a lover. His name was Agenor, of all that army the most beautiful; who having ridden in sportful conversation among the foremost, all armed saving that his beaver was up to have his breath in more freedom, seeing Amphialus come a pretty way before his company, neither staying the commandment of the captain, nor recking whether his face were armed or no, set spurs to his horse; and with youthful bravery casting his staff about his head, put it then in his rest – as careful of comely carrying it as if the mark had been but a ring, and the lookers-on ladies.

But Amphialus' lance was already come to the last of his descending line, and began to make the full point of death against the head of this young gentleman, when Amphialus perceiving his youth and beauty, compassion so rebated the edge of choler that he spared that fair nakedness and let his staff fall to Agenor's vamplate, so as both with brave breaking should hurtlessly have performed that match – but that the pitiless lance of Amphialus, angry with being broken, with an unlucky counterbuff full of unsparing splinters lighted upon that face far fitter for the combats of Venus, giving not only a sudden, but a foul death, leaving scarcely any tokens of his former beauty. But his hands abandoning the reins and his thighs the saddle, he fell sideward from the horse – which sight coming to Leontius, a dear friend of his who in vain had lamentably cried unto him to stay when

---

[1] of the country *Cm, 93*: of of that country *90*   [2] not *Cm, 98, 13*: nor *90, 93*

he saw him begin his career, it was hard to say whether pity of the one or revenge of[1] the other held as then the sovereignty in his passions. But while he directed his eye to his friend and his hand[2] to his enemy, so wrongly consorted a power could not resist the ready-minded force of Amphialus, who perceiving his ill-directed direction against him, so paid him his debt before it was lent that he also fell to the earth, only happy that one place and one time did finish both their loves and lives together.

But by this time there had been a furious meeting of either side, where, after the terrible salutation of warlike noise, the shaking of hands was with sharp weapons. Some lances, according to the metal they met and skill of the guider, did stain themselves in blood. Some flew up in pieces as if they would threaten heaven because they failed on earth – but their office was quickly inherited either by the prince of weapons, the sword, or by some heavy mace or biting axe, which, hunting still the weakest chase, sought ever to light there where smallest resistance might worse prevent mischief. The clashing of armour and crushing of staves, the justling of bodies, the resounding of blows, was the first part of that ill-agreeing music which was beautified with the grisliness of wounds, the rising of dust, the hideous falls – and groans of the dying.

The very horses, angry in their masters' anger, with love and obedience brought forth the effects of hate and resistance, and with minds of servitude did as if they affected glory. Some lay dead under their dead masters, whom unknightly wounds had unjustly punished for a faithful duty; some lay upon their lords by like accidents, and in death had the honour to be borne by them whom in life they had borne; some having lost their commanding burthens ran scattered about the field, abashed with the madness of mankind.

The earth itself, wont to be a burial of men, was now as it were buried with men, so was the face thereof hidden with dead bodies to whom death had come, masked in divers manners. In one place lay disinherited heads, dispossessed of their natural seigniories; in another, whole bodies to see to, but that their hearts, wont to be bound all over so close, were now with deadly violence opened; in others, fouler deaths had uglily displayed their trailing guts. There lay arms whose fingers yet moved, as if they would feel for him that made them feel, and legs which, contrary to common nature,[3] by being discharged of their burden were grown heavier.

But no sword paid so large a tribute of souls to the eternal kingdom as that of Amphialus, who like a tiger from whom a company of wolves did seek to ravish a new-gotten pray, so he, remembering they came to take away

---

[1] revenge of] revenge against 93   [2] hand] hind 93, 98   [3] nature] reason 93

Philoclea, did labour to make valure, strength, hatred, and choler[1] to answer the proportion of his love – which was infinite. There died of his hands the old knight Æschylus, who though by years might well have been allowed to use rather the exercise[2] of wisdom than of courage, yet having a lusty body and a merry heart, he ever took the summons of time in jest (or else it had so creepingly stolen upon him that he had heard scarcely the noise of his feet), and therefore was as fresh in apparel and as forward in enterprises as a far younger man. But nothing made him bolder than a certain prophecy had been told him, that he should die in the arms of his son; and therefore feared the less the arm of an enemy. But now, when Amphialus' sword was passed through his throat, he thought himself abused, but that before he died his son indeed, seeing his father begin to fall, held him up in his arms – till a pitiless soldier of the other side with a mace brained him, making father and son become twins in their[3] never again dying birth.

As for Drialus, Memnon, Nisus, and Policrates, the first had his eyes cut out, so as he could not see to bid the near-following death welcome. The second had met with the same prophet that old Æschylus had; and having found many of his speeches true, believed this too, that he should never be killed but by his own companions; and therefore no man was more valiant than he against an enemy, no man more suspicious of his friends, so as he seemed to sleep in security when he went to a battle, and to enter into a battle when he began to sleep, such guards he would set about his person – yet mistrusting the very guards that[4] they would murther him. But now Amphialus helped to unriddle his doubts, for he overthrowing him from his horse, his own companions coming with a fresh supply pressed him to death. Nisus, grasping with Amphialus, was with a short dagger slain. And for Policrates, while he shunned as much as he could, keeping only his place for fear of punishment, Amphialus with a memorable blow strake off his head, where, with the convulsions of death setting his spurs to his horse, he gave so brave a charge upon the enemy as it grew a proverb that Policrates was only valiant after his head was off.

But no man escaped so well his hands as Phebilus did, for he having long loved Philoclea, though for the meanness of his estate he never durst reveal it, now knowing Amphialus, setting the edge of a rival upon the sword of an enemy, he held strong fight with him. But Amphialus had already in the dangerousest places disarmed him and was lifting up his sword to send him away from him[5] when, he thinking indeed to die, 'O Philoclea!' said he, 'Yet this joys me – that I die for thy sake!' The name of Philoclea first stayed his sword; and when he heard him out, though he abhorred him

---

[1] hatred, and choler] choler, and hatred 93   [2] exercise] exercises 93   [3] their] the 93   [4] the very guards that] those very guards lest 93   [5] him] himself 93

much worse than before, yet could he not vouchsafe him the honour of dying for Philoclea but turned his sword another way, doing him no hurt, for overmuch hatred. But what good did that to poor Phebilus if, escaping a valiant hand, he was slain by a base[1] soldier, who seeing him so disarmed thrust him through?

But thus[2] with the well-followed valour of Amphialus were the other almost overthrown – when Philanax, who was the marshal of the army, came in with new force, renewing the almost decayed courage of his soldiers; for crying to them, and asking them whether their backs or their arms were better fighters, he himself thrust into the press, and making force and fury wait upon discretion and government, he might seem a brave lion who taught his young lionets how, in taking of a prey, to join courage with cunning. Then fortune, as if she had made chases enow of the one side of that bloody tennis-court, went of the other side the line, making as many fall down of Amphialus' followers as before had done of Philanax's, they losing the ground as fast as before they had won it, only leaving them to keep it who had lost themselves in keeping it. Then those that had killed inherited the lot of those that had been killed, and cruel death[3] made them lie quietly together who most in their lives had sought to disquiet each other, and many of those first overthrown had the comfort to see the murtherers overrun them to Charon's ferry.

Codrus, Ctesiphon, and Milo lost their lives upon Philanax's sword. But nobody's case was more pitied than of a young esquire of Amphialus called Ismenus, who never abandoning his master, and making his tender age aspire to acts of the strongest manhood, in this time that his side was put to the worst and that Amphialus' valure was the only stay of them from delivering themselves over to a shameful flight, he saw his master's horse killed under him; whereupon asking no advice, of no thought[4] but of faithfulness and courage, he presently lighted from his own horse and, with the help of some choice and faithful servants, gat his master up. But in the multitude that came of either side, some to succour, some to save Amphialus, he came under the hand of Philanax; and the youth perceiving he was the man that did most hurt to his party, desirous even to change his life for glory, strake at him as he rode by him, and gave him a hurt upon the leg that made Philanax turn towards him. But seeing him so young and of a most

---

[1] by a base] by base 93, 98 [2] through? But thus *Cm, 93.* through? Chap. 8. The Basilians re-embattled first by Philanax, then by the Black Knight; Ismenus slain by Philanax; Philanax captived by Amphialus; the Black Knight's exploits; his encounter with Amphialus, parted by a by-blow; the Amphialians' retrait and departure of the Black Knight. Thus 90   [3] death] deaths 93   [4] asking no advice, of no thought] asking advice of no thought *Cm*; asking advice of no other thought 13

lovely presence, he rather took pity of him, meaning to make him prisoner and then to give him to his brother Agenor to be his companion because they were not much unlike, neither in years nor countenance. But as he looked down upon him with that thought, he spied where his brother lay dead, and his friend Leontius by him, even almost under the squire's feet. Then sorrowing not only his own sorrow, but the past-comfort sorrow which he foreknew his mother would take, who with many tears and misgiving sighs had suffered him to go with his elder brother, Philanax blotted out all figures of pity out of his mind; and putting forth his horse while Ismenus doubled two or three more valiant than well-set blows, saying to himself, 'Let other mothers bewail an[1] untimely death, as well as mine,' he thrust him through. And the boy, fierce though beautiful, and beautiful though dying, not able to keep his failing feet, fell down to the earth which he bit for anger – repining at his fortune and as long as he could resisting death, which might seem unwilling too, so long he was in taking away his young, struggling soul.

Philanax himself could have wished the blow ungiven when he saw him fall – like a fair apple which some uncourteous body, breaking his bough, should throw down before it were ripe; but the case of his brother made him forget both that and himself, so as over-hastily pressing upon the retiring enemies, he was, ere he was aware, further engaged than his own soldiers could relieve him; where being overthrown by Amphialus, Amphialus (glad of him) kept head against his enemies while some of his men carried away Philanax. But Philanax's men, as if with the loss of Philanax they had lost the fountain of their valure, had their courages so dried up in fear that they began to set honour at their backs, and to use the virtue of patience in an untimely time – when into the press comes, as hard as his horse (more afraid of the spur than the sword) could carry him, a knight in armour as dark as blackness could make it, followed by none, and adorned by nothing; so far without authority that he was without knowledge. But virtue quickly made him known, and admiration bred him such authority that, though they of whose side he came knew him not, yet they all knew it was fit to obey him; and while he was followed by the valiantest, he made way for the vilest, for taking part with the besiegers, he made the Amphialians' blood serve for a caparison to his horse, and a decking to his armour.

His arm no oftener gave blows than the blows gave wounds, than the wounds gave deaths, so terrible was his force – and yet was his quickness more forcible than his force, and his judgement more quick than his quick-

---

[1] an] and 93, 98

ness, for though his sword[1] went faster than eyesight could follow it, yet his own judgement went still before it. There died of his hand Sarpedon, Plistonax, Strophilus, and Hippolitus, men of great proof in wars, and who had that day undertaken the guard of Amphialus; but while they sought to save him, they lost the fortresses that nature had placed them in. Then slew he Megalus, who was a little before proud to see himself stained in the blood of his enemies; but when his own blood came to be married to theirs, he then felt that cruelty doth never enjoy a good cheap glory. After him sent he Palemon, who had that day vowed with foolish bravery to be the death of ten; and nine already he had killed, and was careful to perform his almost-performed vow, when the Black Knight helped him to make up the tenth himself.

And now the often-changing fortune began also to change the hue of the battles, for at the first, though it were terrible, yet terror was decked so bravely with rich furniture, gilt swords, shining armours, pleasant pencels, that the eye with delight had scarce leisure to be afraid; but now all universally defiled with dust, blood, broken armours, mangled bodies, took away the mask and set forth horror in his own horrible manner. But neither could danger be dreadful to Amphialus' undismayable courage, nor yet seem ugly to him whose truly-affected mind did still paint it over with the beauty of Philoclea. And therefore he, rather inflamed than troubled with the increase of dangers, and glad to find a worthy subject to exercise his courage, sought out this new knight – whom he might easily find, for he like a wanton rich man that throws down his neighbours' houses to make himself the better prospect, so had his sword made him so spacious a room that Amphialus had more cause to wonder at the finding than labour for the seeking, which, if it stirred hate in him to see how much harm he did to the one side, it provoked as much emulation in him to perceive how much good he did to the other side.

Therefore they approaching one to the other (as in two beautiful folks love naturally stirs a desire of joining, so in their two courages hate stirred a desire of trial), then began there a combat between them worthy to have had more large lists, and more quiet beholders, for with the spur of courage and the bit of respect, each so guided himself that one might well see the desire to overcome made them not forget how to overcome, in such time and proportion they did employ their blows that none of Ceres' servants could more cunningly place his flail; while the left-foot spur set forward his own horse, the right set backward the contrary horse, even sometimes by the advantage of the enemy's leg, while the left hand, like him that held the

---

[1] his sword *Cm, 93*: the sword *90*

stern, guided the horses' obedient courage – all done in such order that it might seem the mind was a right prince indeed, who sent wise and diligent lieutenants into each of those well-governed parts.

But the more they fought, the more they desired to fight; and the more they smarted, the less they felt the smart; and now were like to make a quick proof to whom fortune or valour would seem most friendly – when in comes an old governor of Amphialus (always a good knight, and careful of his charge), who giving a sore wound to the Black Knight's thigh while he thought not of him, with another blow slew his horse under him.

Amphialus cried to him that he dishonoured him. 'You say well,' answered the old knight. 'To stand now like a private soldier, setting your credit upon particular fighting while, you may see, Basilius with all his host is getting between you and your town!'

He looked that way and found that true indeed, that the enemy was beginning to encompass him about and stop his return; and therefore causing the retreat to be sounded, his governor led his men homeward, while he kept himself still hindmost, as if he had stood at the gate of a sluice to let the stream go with such proportion as should seem good unto him, and with so manful discretion performed it that, though with loss of many of his men, he returned in himself safe, and content that his enemies had felt how sharp the sword could bite of Philoclea's lover.

The other party, being sorry for the loss of Philanax, was yet sorrier when the Black Knight could not be found, for he having gotten a[1] horse whom his dying master had bequeathed to the world, finding himself sore hurt, and not desirous to be known, had in the time of the enemy's retiring retired away also, his thigh not bleeding blood so fast as his heart bled revenge. But Basilius, having attempted in vain to bar the safe return of Amphialus, encamped himself as strongly as he could, while he, to his grief, might hear the joy was made in the town by his own subjects, that he had that day sped no better; for Amphialus being well-beloved of that people, when they saw him not vanquished, they esteemed him as victorious, his youth setting a flourishing show upon his worthiness, and his great nobility ennobling his dangers.

But[2] the first thing Amphialus did, being returned, was to visit Philoclea – and first presuming to cause his dream to be sung unto her, which he had seen the night before he fell in love with her, making a fine boy he had accord a pretty dolefulness unto it. The song was this:

---

[1] gotten a *Cm, 93*: gotten on a *90* [2] dangers. But *Cm, 93*: dangers. Chap. 9. The love-divining dream of Amphialus sung to Philoclea; Philanax's captivity and death's-doom, for Philoclea's sake turned to life and liberty; his loyal answer of his lord's intents; Cecropia's arts to persuade the sisters. But *90*

Now was our heav'nly vault deprived of the light
With sun's depart, and now the darkness of the night
Did light those beamy stars which greater light did dark;
Now each thing that[1] enjoyed that fiery quick'ning spark
(Which life is called) were moved their spirits to repose,
And wanting use of eyes, their eyes began to close
(A[2] silence sweet, each where with one concent embraced –
A music sweet, to one in careful musing[3] placed),
And mother earth, now clad in mourning weeds, did breathe
A dull desire to kiss the image of our death –
When I, disgraced wretch (not wretched then) did give
My senses such relief as they which quiet live
(Whose brains broil not in woes, nor breasts with beatings[4] ache)
With nature's praise are wont in safest[5] home to take.
Far from my thoughts was aught, whereto their minds aspire
Who under courtly pomps do hatch a base desire;
Free all my powers were from those captiving snares
Which heav'nly purest gifts defile, in muddy cares;
Ne could my soul itself accuse of such a fault
As tender conscience might with furious pangs assault –
But like the feeble flow'r whose stalk cannot sustain
His weighty top, his top doth downward[6] drooping[7] lean,
Or as the silly bird in well-acquainted nest
Doth hide his head, with cares but only how to rest,
So I, in simple course and unentangled[8] mind,
Did suffer drowsy lids mine[9] eyes (then clear) to blind,
And laying down my head, did nature's rule observe,
Which senses up doth shut the senses to preserve:
They first their use forgot, then fancies lost their force,
Till deadly sleep at length possessed my living corse.
A living corse I lay,[10] but ah, my wakeful mind
(Which made of heav'nly stuff, no mortal change doth blind)[11]
Flew up with freer[12] wings, of fleshly bondage free,
And having placed my thoughts, my thoughts thus placed me:
Methought – nay, sure, I was – I was in fairest wood
Of Samothea land, a land which whilom stood

---

[1] thing that] thing which *OA (ex. Je)* [2] A] And *Cl, As, IIm* [3] musing] music *Cl, Ph, IIm* [4] beatings] heating *Da*; bitings *Ph*; heatings *Je* [5] safest] safety *Cl, Le*; saftest *Je* [6] doth downward] downward *90 (uncorr.)*; downward doth *93* [7] drooping] dropping *Bo, Cl, Da, Ph* [8] unentangled] unitangled *Cl*; uninfangled *As*; in untangled *Da* [9] mine] my *Bo, As, Da* [10] lay] say *As, Ph, Hm* [11] blind] bind *OA (ex. St, Da)* [12] freer] cleer *90 (uncorr.)*

An honour to the world (while honour was their end,
And while their line of years they did in virtue spend);
But there I was, and there my calmy thoughts I fed
On nature's sweet repast, as healthful senses led.
Her gifts my study was, her beauties were my sport;   5
My work, her works to know; her dwelling, my resort:
Those lamps of heav'nly fire to fixed motion bound;
The ever-turning spheres; the never-moving ground;
What essence dest'ny hath; if fortune be, or no;
Whence[1] our immortal souls to mortal earth do flow;   10
What life it is; and how that all these lives do gather[2]
With outward maker's force, or like an inward father.
Such thoughts (methought) I thought, and strained my single mind,
Then void of nearer cares, the depth[3] of things to find,
When[4] lo! with hugest noise (such noise a[5] tower makes   15
When it blown down with wind a fall of ruin takes,
Or[6] such a noise it was as highest thunders send,
Or cannons thunder-like all shot together lend)
The moon asunder rent, whereout with sudden fall
More swift than falcon's stoop to feeding falconer's call   20
There came a chariot fair, by doves and sparrows guided,
Whose storm-like course stayed not, till hard by me it bided.
I, wretch, astonished was, and thought the deathful doom
Of heav'n, of earth, of hell, of time and place was come.
But straight there issued forth two ladies (ladies sure   25
They seemed[7] to me) on whom did wait a virgin pure.
Strange were the ladies' weeds, yet more unfit than strange;
The first with clothes tucked up as nymphs in woods do range,
Tucked up ev'n with[8] the knees; with bow and arrows prest;
Her right arm naked was; discovered was her breast;   30
But heavy was her pace, and such a meagre cheer
As little hunting mind (God knows!) did there[9] appear.
The other had with art (more than our women know)
As stuff meant for the sale set out to glaring show
A wanton woman's face, and with curled knots had twined   35
Her hair, which by the help of painter's cunning shined.
When I such guests did see come out of such a house,
The mountains, great with child, I thought brought forth a mouse.

---

[1] Whence] When *Da, Hm*   [2] do gather] doth gather *St, Bo, Hm*; together *As*   [3] depth] depths *Cl, Da*
[4] When] Who *Cl, Ph, Hm*   [5] a] as *Cl, Le*; no *Da, Ph, Je, Hm*   [6] Or] But *Da, Ph, Je, Hm*   [7] seemed] seem *Da, Je*   [8] ev'n with] ev'n to *Cl, Le*   [9] did there] there did *Da, Hm*

But walking forth, the first thus to the second said:
'Venus, come on!' Said she, 'Diane,[1] you are obeyed.'
Those names abashed me much, when those great names I hard,
Although their fame, meseemed, from truth had greatly jarred!
As I thus musing stood, Diana called to her
The[2] waiting nymph, a nymph that did excel as far
All things that erst I saw (as orient pearls exceed
That which their mother hight, or else their silly seed);
Indeed, a perfect hue; indeed, a sweet concent
Of all those graces' gifts the heav'ns have ever lent;
And so she was attired as one that did not prize
Too[3] much her peerless parts, nor yet could them despise.
But called, she came apace – a pace wherein did move
The band of beauties all, the little world of love.
And bending humbled eyes (O eyes, the sun[4] of sight)[5]
She waited mistress' will, who thus disclosed her sprite:
'Sweet Mira mine,' quoth she, 'the pleasure of my mind,
In whom of all my rules the perfect proof I find,
To only thee, thou seest, we grant this special grace
Us to attend in this most private time and place.
Be silent therefore now, and so be silent still
Of that thou seest; close up in secret knot thy will.'
She answered was with look, and well performed behest;
And Mira I admired – her shape sunk in my breast.
But thus, with ireful eyes and face that shook[6] with spite,
Diana did begin: 'What moved me to invite
Your presence, sister dear, first to my moony[7] sphere
And hither now, vouchsafe to take with willing ear.
I know full well you know what discord long hath reigned
Betwixt us two; how much that discord foul hath stained
Both our estates, while each the other did deprave –
Proof speaks too much to us that feeling trial have:
Our names are quite forgot; our temples are defaced;
Our off'rings[8] spoiled; our priests[9] from priesthood are displaced.
Is this the[10] fruit of[11] strife, those thousand churches high,
Those thousand altars fair, now in the dust to lie?
In mortal minds, our minds but planets' names preserve.

---

[1] Diane] Diana *Cl, Le, Da, Ph, Hm*   [2] The] Her *OA (ex. St)*   [3] Too] So *St, Cl, Le, Da*   [4] sun] sum *St, Bo, Le, As, Je, 13*   [5] sight] light *Cl, Da, Ph*   [6] face that shook] face trembling *Ph, Je*; trembling face *Hm*   [7] moony] moovy *Cl*; moonish *As*; mani *Da*; mony *Ph*   [8] off'rings] offsprings *As, Je* (offsprings *corr. to* offrings *St, Da*)   [9] priests *OA, 93*: priest *90*   [10] the] thy *St, Bo, Cl, Le, As, Hm*   [11] of] O *St, Bo, Le, Da, Ph, Hm*; or *As*

No knees[1] once bowed – forsooth, for them, they say, we serve!
Are we their servants grown? No doubt, a noble stay:
Celestial pow'rs, to worms; Jove's children serve to clay!
But such they say we be – this praise our discord bred,
While we for mutual spite a striving passion fed.   5
But let us wiser be; and what foul discord brake,
So much more strong again let fastest[2] concord make.
Our years do it[3] require; you see we both do feel
The weak'ning work of time's for ever whirling wheel.
Although we be divine, our grandsire Saturn is   10
With age's force decayed – yet once the heav'n was his.
And now, before we seek by wise Apollo's skill
Our young years to renew (for so he saith[4] he will),
Let us a perfect peace between us two resolve,
Which, lest the ruinous want of government dissolve,   15
Let one the princess be, to her the other yield,
For vain equality is but contention's[5] field;
And let her have the gifts that should in both remain:
In her let beauty both and chasteness fully reign;
So as, if I prevail, you give your gifts to me;   20
If you, on you I lay what in my office be.
Now resteth only this: which of us two is she
To whom precedence[6] shall of both accorded be[7].
For that (so that you like) hereby doth lie a youth,'
She beckoned unto me, 'as yet of spotless truth,   25
Who may this doubt discern; for better wit than lot
Becometh us; in us, fortune determines not.
This crown of amber fair' – an amber crown she held –
'To worthiest let him give when both he hath beheld;
And be it as he saith.' Venus was glad to hear   30
Such proffer made, which she well showed with smiling cheer,
As though she were the same as when by Paris' doom
She had chief goddesses in beauty overcome,
And smirkly thus gan say: 'I never sought debate,
Diana dear. My mind to love and not to hate   35
Was ever apt, but you my pastimes did despise.
I never spited you, but thought you over[8] wise.
Now kindness proferred is, none kinder is than I,

---

[1] knees] knee OA (ex. St)   [2] fastest] safest Cl; fattest Da   [3] it] yet Cl, Le, Da, Ph, Hm   [4] he saith] saith he Le, Ph   [5] contention's] a contentious Ph, Hm; contentious 90 (uncorr.)   [6] precedence] precedents St, Cl, Le, Hm; president As   [7] Now resteth ... accorded be om. Je   [8] over] ever Da, Hm

And so most ready am this mean of peace to try.
And let him be our judge; the lad doth please me well.'
Thus both did come to me, and both began to tell
(For both together spake, each loath to be behind)
That they by solemn oath their deities would bind
To stand unto my will; their will they made me know.
I that was first aghast when first I saw their show,
Now bolder waxed, waxed proud that I such sway must bear,
For near acquaintance doth diminish reverent fear;
And having bound them fast, by Styx, they should obey
To all what[1] I decreed, did thus my verdict say:
'How ill both you can rule, well hath your discord taught;
Ne yet, for aught[2] I see, your beauties merit aught.
To yonder nymph, therefore,' to Mira I did point,
'The crown above you both for ever I appoint.'
I would have spoken out, but out they both did cry:
'Fie, fie, what have we done? Ungodly rebel, fie!
But now we needs must yield to that[3] our oaths require.'
'Yet thou shalt not go free!' quoth Venus. 'Such a fire
Her beauty kindle shall within thy foolish mind
That thou full oft shalt[4] wish thy judging eyes were blind.'
'Nay! Then,' Diana said, 'the[5] chasteness I will give,
In ashes of despair, though burnt, shall make thee live.'
'Nay! Thou,' said both, 'shalt see such beams shine in her face
That thou shalt never dare seek help of wretched case.'
And with that cursed curse, away to heav'n[6] they fled,
First having all their gifts upon fair Mira spread.
The rest I cannot tell, for therewithal I waked
And found with deadly fear that all my sinews[7] shaked.
Was it a dream? O dream, how hast thou wrought in me
That I things erst unseen should first in dreaming see?
And thou,[8] O traitor sleep, made for to be our rest,
How hast thou framed the pain wherewith I am oppressed?
O coward Cupid, thus doost thou thy honour keep,
Unarmed, alas, unwarned,[9] to take a man asleep?'[10]

– laying not only the conquests, but the heart of the conqueror, at her feet.

...

---

[1] what] that *Le, Je, Hm, 13* (that *corr. to* what *St*)   [2] for aught] for what *OA (ex. Cl, Le)*; om. *Le*   [3] that] what *OA (ex. St)*   [4] shalt] shall *Bo, Hm*   [5] the] thee *Cl, Le, Ph*   [6] heav'n] heav'ns *Cl, Le, As*   [7] sinews] senses *Le, Hm*   [8] thou] then *Bo, Cl, Da, Ph*   [9] unwarned *St, Bo, Le, 93*: unarmed *Cl, As, Da, Ph, Hm*; unwares *90*   [10] The crown above you ... take a man asleep?' om. *Je*

But she receiving him after her wonted sorrowful (but otherwise unmoved) manner, it made him think his good success was but a[1] pleasant monument of a doleful burial, joy itself seeming bitter unto him since it agreed not to her taste; therefore, still craving his mother's help to persuade her, he himself sent for Philanax unto him, whom he had not only long hated, but now had his hate greatly increased by the death of his squire, Ismenus – besides, he had made him as one of the chief causes that moved him to this rebellion and therefore was inclined (to colour the better his action, and the more to imbrue the hands of his accomplices by making them guilty of such a trespass) in some formal sort to cause him to be executed, being also greatly egged thereunto by his mother, and some other who long had hated Philanax only because he was more worthy to be loved than they.[2]

But while that deliberation was handled, according rather to the humour than the reason of each speaker, Philoclea coming to knowledge of the hard plight wherein Philanax stood, she desired one of the gentlewomen appointed to wait upon her to go in her name and beseech Amphialus that, if the love of her had any power of persuasion in his mind, he would lay no further punishment than imprisonment upon Philanax. This message was delivered even as Philanax was entering to the presence of Amphialus, coming, according to the warning was given him, to receive a judgement of death. But when he with manful resolution attended the fruit of such a tyrannical sentence (thinking it wrong, but no harm, to him that should die in so good a cause), Amphialus turned quite the form of his pretended speech, and yielded him humble thanks that by his means he had come to that happiness as to receive a commandment of his lady; and therefore he willingly gave him liberty to return in safety whither he would, quitting him not only of all former grudge, but assuring him that he would be willing to do him any friendship and service – only desiring thus much of him, that he would let him know the discourse and intent of Basilius' proceeding.

'Truly, my lord,' answered Philanax, 'if there were any such, known to me, secret in my master's counsel as that the revealing thereof might hinder his good success, I should loath the keeping of my blood with the loss of my faith, and would think the just name of a traitor a hard purchase of a few years' living. But since it is so that my master hath indeed no way of privy practice, but means openly and forcibly to deal against you, I will not stick in few words to make your required declaration.'

Then told he him in what a maze[3] of amazement[4] both Basilius and Gynecia were when they missed their children and Zelmane, sometimes apt

---

[1] but a] but as a 93   [2] to be loved than they] than they to be loved 93   [3] a maze *Cm, 93*: amaze *90*
[4] amazement] a mazement *90 (corr.), 93, 98*

to suspect some practice of Zelmane because she was a stranger, sometimes doubting some relics of the late mutiny; which doubt was rather increased than any way satisfied by Miso, who being found almost dead for hunger by certain country-people, brought home word with what cunning they were trained out, and with what violence they were carried away; but that within a few days they came to knowledge where they were, with[1] Amphialus' own letters, sent abroad to procure confederates in his attempts; that Basilius' purpose was never to leave the siege of this town till he had taken it and revenged the injury done unto him; that he meant rather to win it by time and famine than by force of assault, knowing how valiant men he had to deal withal in the town; that he had sent order that supplies of soldiers, pioneers, and all things else necessary should daily be brought unto him; 'so as, my lord,' said Philanax, 'let me now (having received my life by your grace), let me give you your life and honour by my counsel, protesting unto you that I cannot choose but love you, being my master's nephew, and that I wish you well in all causes but this. You know his nature is as apt to forgive as his power is able to conquer. Your fault past is excusable, in that love persuaded, and youth was persuaded. Do not urge the effects of angry victory, but rather seek to obtain that constantly by courtesy which you can never, assuredly, enjoy by violence.'

One might easily have seen in the cheer of Amphialus that disdainful choler would fain have made the answer for him, but the remembrance of Philoclea served for forcible[2] barriers between anger and angry effects, so as he said no more, but that he would not put him to the trouble to give him any further counsel, but that he might return, if he listed, presently.

Philanax, glad to receive an uncorrupted liberty, humbly accepted his favourable convoy out of the town, and so departed, not unvisited,[3] the princesses, thinking it might be offensive to Amphialus and no way fruitful to them, who were no way but by force to be rescued[4] – the poor ladies indeed not suffered either to meet together, or to have conference with any other but such as Cecropia had already framed to sing all her songs to their tune,[5] she herself omitting no day and catching hold of every occasion to move forward her son's desire and remove their own[6] resolutions, using the same arguments to the one sister as to the other, determining that whom she could win first, the other should (without her son's knowledge) by poison be made away. But though the reasons were the same to both, yet the handling was diverse (according as she saw their humours) to prepare[7] a more or less aptness of apprehension, this day having used long speech to Philoclea

---

[1] with] by 93   [2] forcible *Cm, 93*: forcibie *90*   [3] unvisited *Cm*: having visited *90*; visiting *93*   [4] rescued *Cm, 93*: relieved *90*   [5] her songs to their tune *Cm*: her songs to her tune *90 (uncorr.)*; her songs to her tune *90 (corr.), 93*   [6] own *Cm, 93*: known *90*   [7] prepare *Cm, 93*: prefer *90*

amplifying not a little the great dutifulness her son had showed in delivering Philanax – of whom she could get no answer but a silence, sealed up in virtue and so sweetly graced as that in one instant it carried with it both resistance and humbleness.

Cecropia[1] (threatening in herself to run a more ragged[2] race with her) went to her sister Pamela, who that day having wearied herself with reading, and with the height of her heart disdaining to keep company with any of the gentlewomen appointed to attend her, whom she accounted her jailers, was working upon a purse certain roses and lilies, as by the fineness of the work, one might see she had borrowed her wits of the sorrow that then owed[3] them, and lent them wholly to that exercise – for the flowers she had wrought carried such life in them that the cunningest painter might have learned of her needle, which with so pretty a manner made his careers to and fro through the cloth as if the needle itself would have been loath to have gone fromward such a mistress, but that it hoped to return thenceward[4] very quickly again, the cloth looking with many eyes upon her, and lovingly embracing the wounds she gave it. The shears also were at hand to behead the silk that was grown too short, and if at any time she put her mouth to bite it off, it seemed that, where she had been long in making of a rose with her hands,[5] she would in an instant make roses with her lips – as the lilies seemed to have their whiteness rather of the hand that made them than of the matter whereof they were made, and that they grew there by[6] the suns of her eyes, and were refreshed by the most, in discomfort, comfortable air which an unwares sigh might bestow upon them. But the colours for the ground were so well chosen (neither sullenly dark nor glaringly lightsome) and so well-proportioned (as that though much cunning were in it, yet it was but to serve for an ornament of the principal work) that it was not without marvel to see how a mind, which could cast a careless semblant upon the greatest conflicts of fortune, could command itself to take care for so small matters.

Neither had she neglected the dainty dressing of herself, but, as if it[7] had been her marriage time to affliction, she rather seemed to remember her own worthiness than the unworthiness of her husband; for well one might perceive she had not rejected the counsel of a glass, and that her hands had pleased themselves in paying the tribute of undeceiving skill to so high perfections of nature – the sight whereof, so diverse from her sister who rather suffered sorrow to distress[8] itself in her beauty than that she would

---

[1] humbleness. Cecropia 93: humbleness, [*blank space for the name*] *Cm*; humbleness. Chap. 10. Pamela's exercise; Cecropia's talk with her of beauty and the use thereof; the aunt's atheism refuted by the niece's divinity. Cecropia 90   [2] ragged] rugged 93   [3] that then owed 93: that they owed *Cm*; that owed 90   [4] thenceward] thitherward 93   [5] hands *Cm*, 93: hand 90   [6] there by] thereby 93   [7] as if it *Cm*, 93: as it 90   [8] distress] dress 90 (*corr.*), 93

bestow any entertainment of so unwelcome a guest, made Cecropia take a sudden assuredness of hope that she should obtain somewhat of Pamela, thinking, according to the squaring out of her own good nature, that beauty carefully set forth would soon prove a sign of an unrefusing harborough.

Animated wherewith, she sate down by Pamela; and taking the purse, and with affected curiosity looking upon the work, 'Full happy is he,' said she,' – at least if he knew his own happiness – to whom a purse in this manner, and by this hand wrought, is dedicated; in faith, he shall have cause to account it not as a purse for treasure, but as a treasure itself, worthy to be pursed up in the purse of his own heart.'

'And think you so indeed!' said Pamela, half smiling. 'I promise you, I wrought it but to make some tedious hours believe that I thought not of them; for else, I valued it but even as a very purse.'

'It is the right nature,' said Cecropia, 'of beauty to work unwitting effects of wonder.'

'Truly,' said Pamela, 'I never thought till now that this outward glass entitled beauty, which it pleaseth you to lay to my, as I think, unguilty charge, was but a pleasant mixture of natural colours, delightful to the eye as music is to the ear, without any further consequence, since it is a thing which not only beasts have, but even stones and trees – many of them do greatly excel in it.'

'That other things,' answered Cecropia, 'have some portion of it takes not away the excellency of it where indeed it doth excel, since we see that even those beasts, trees, and stones are in the name of beauty only highly praised. But that the beauty of human persons be beyond all other things, there is great likelihood of reason, since to them only is given the judgement to discern beauty – and among reasonable wights (as it seems) that our sex hath the pre-eminence, so that, in that pre-eminence, nature countervails all other liberalities wherein she may be thought to have dealt more favourably toward mankind.

'How do men crown – think you – themselves with glory! for having either by force brought others to yield to their mind, or with long study and premeditated orations persuaded what they would have persuaded. And see, a fair woman shall not only command without authority, but persuade without speaking. She shall not need to procure attention, for their own eyes will chain their ears unto it. Men venture lives to conquer; she conquers lives without venturing. She is served and obeyed (which is the most notable) not because the laws so command it, but because they become laws to themselves[1] to obey her – not for her parents' sake, but for her own sake. She need

---

[1] laws to themselves] laws themselves 93

not dispute whether to govern by fear or by love[1] since, without her thinking thereof, their love will bring forth fear, and their fear will fortify their love; and she need not seek offensive or defensive force, since her lips[2] may stand for ten thousand shields, and ten thousand unevitable shot go from her eyes. Beauty, beauty, dear niece, is the crown of the feminine greatness; which gift on whomsoever the heavens, therein most niggardly, do bestow, without question she is bound to use it to the noble purpose for which it is created, not only winning, but preserving – since that indeed is the right happiness which is not only in itself happy, but can also derive the happiness to another.'

'Certainly, aunt,' said Pamela, 'I fear me you will make me not only think myself fairer than ever I did, but think my fairness a matter of greater value than heretofore I could imagine it, for I ever till now conceived these conquests you spake[3] of rather to proceed from the weakness of the conquered than from the strength of the conquering power. As they say, the cranes overthrow whole battles of Pygmies, not so much of their cranish courage, as because the other are Pygmies; and that we see, young babes think babies of wonderful excellency, and yet the babies are but babies. But since your elder years and abler judgement find beauty to be worthy of so incomparable estimation, certainly, methinks, it ought to be held in dearness according to the excellency; and no more than we would do of things which we account precious, ever to suffer it to be defiled.'

'Defiled!' said Cecropia. 'Marry, God forbid that my speech should tend to any such purpose as should deserve so foul a title! My meaning is to join your beauty to love, your youth to delight; for truly, as colours should be as good as nothing if there were no eyes to behold them, so is beauty nothing without the eye of love behold it, and therefore, so far is it from defiling it, that it is the only honouring of it, the only preserving of it; for beauty goes away, devoured by time – but where remains it ever flourishing, but in the heart of a true lover? And such a one (if ever there were any) is my son, whose love is so subjected unto you that, rather than breed any offence unto you, it will not delight itself in beholding you.'

'There is no effect of his love,' answered Pamela, 'better pleaseth me than that! But as I have often answered you, so resolutely I say unto you that he must get my parent's consent, and then he shall know further of my mind; for without that I know I should offend God.'

'O sweet youth!' said Cecropia. 'How untimely subject it is to devotion! No, no, sweet niece! Let us old folks think of such precise considerations. Do you enjoy the heaven of your age, whereof you are sure; and like good householders which spend those things that will not be kept, so do you

---

[1] fear or by love] fear or love 93   [2] her lips] her only lips 93   [3] spake] speak 93

pleasantly enjoy that – which else will bring an over-late repentance when your glass shall accuse you to your face what a change there is in you. Do you see how the spring-time is full of flowers, decking itself with them, and not aspiring to the fruits of autumn? What lesson is that unto you, but that in the April of your age you should be like April? Let not some of them for whom already the grave gapeth, and perhaps envy the felicity in you which themselves cannot enjoy, persuade you to lose the hold of occasion while it may not only be taken, but offers, nay, sues to be taken; which, if it be not now taken, will never hereafter be overtaken. Yourself know how your father hath refused all offers made by the greatest princes about you – and will you suffer your beauty to be hidden[1] in the wrinkles of his peevish thoughts?'

'If he be peevish,' said Pamela, 'yet is he my father; and how beautiful soever I be, I am his daughter, so as God claims at my hands obedience, and makes me no judge of his imperfections.'

These often replies upon conscience in Pamela made Cecropia think that there was no righter way for her than, as she had in her opinion set her in liking of beauty with persuasion not to suffer it to be void of purpose, so, if she could make her less feeling of those heavenly conceits, that then she might easily wind her to her crooked bias. Therefore, employing the uttermost of her mischievous wit, and speaking the more earnestly because she spake as she thought, she thus dealt with her.

'Dear niece (or rather, dear daughter, if my affection and wish might prevail therein), how much doth it increase – trow you – the earnest desire I have of this blessed match, to see these virtues of yours knit fast with such zeal of devotion! – indeed the best bond which the most politic wits have found, to hold man's wit in well doing; for, as children must first by fear be induced to know that which after, when they do know, they are most glad of, so are these bugbears of opinions brought by great clerks into the world to serve as shewels to keep them from those faults whereto else the vanity of the world and weakness of senses might pull them – but in you, niece, whose excellency is such as it need not to be held up by the staff of vulgar opinions, I would not you should love virtue servilely, for fear of I know not what which you see not, but even for the good effects of virtue which you see.

'Fear – and indeed, foolish fear – and fearful ignorance – was the first inventor of those conceits; for when they heard it thunder, not knowing the natural cause, they thought there was some angry body above that spake so loud; and ever, the less they did perceive, the more they did conceive. Whereof they knew no cause, that grew straight a miracle – foolish folks, not

---

[1] hidden 93: hid he *Cm*; hid 90

marking that the alterations be but upon particular accidents, the universality being always one.

'Yesterday was but as today, and tomorrow will tread the same footsteps of his foregoers; so as it is manifest enough that all things follow but the course of their own nature – saving only man, who, while by the pregnancy of his imagination he strives to things supernatural, meanwhile he loseth his own natural felicity.

'Be wise, and that wisdom shall be a god unto thee; be contented, and that is thy heaven; for else, to think that those powers – if there be any such – above are moved either by the eloquence of our prayers or in a chafe by[1] the folly of our actions carries as much reason as if flies should think that men take great care which of them hums sweetest, and which of them flies nimblest.'

She would have spoken further, to have enlarged and confirmed her discourse, but[2] Pamela, whose cheeks were dyed in the beautifullest grain of virtuous anger, with eyes which glistered forth beams of disdain, thus interrupted her:

'Peace, wicked woman! Peace! Unworthy to breathe, that doest not acknowledge the breath giver; most unworthy to have a tongue, which speakest against him through whom thou speakest – keep your affection to yourself, which, like a bemired dog, would defile with fawning! You say yesterday was as today. O foolish woman – and most miserably foolish, since wit makes you foolish – what doth that argue but that there is a constancy in the everlasting governor? Would you have an inconstant God, since we count a man foolish that is inconstant?

'He is not seen, you say. And would you think him a God who might be seen by so wicked eyes as yours – which yet might see enough, if they were not like such who, for sport sake, willingly hoodwink themselves to receive blows the easier? But though I speak to you without any hope of fruit in so rotten a heart, and there be nobody else here to judge of my speeches, yet be thou my witness, O captivity, that my ears shall not be willingly guilty of my creator's blasphemy.

'You say, because we know not the causes of things, therefore fear was the mother of superstition. Nay, because we know that each effect hath a cause, that hath engendered a true and lively devotion; for this goodly work of which we are, and in which we live, hath not his being by chance (on which opinion it is beyond marvel by what chance any brain could stumble!) – for if it be eternal as you would seem to conceive of it, eternity and chance are things unsufferable together, for that is chanceable which happeneth; and

---

[1] chafe by] chafe at 93   [2] but] *om. Cm*; when 93

if it happen, there was a time before it happened when it might not have[1] happened, or else it did not happen – and so, of[2] chanceable, not eternal: [as now, being; then, not being.][3]

'And as absurd it is to think that, if it had a beginning, his beginning was derived from chance, for chance could never make all things of nothing. And if there were substances before, which by chance should meet to make up this work, thereon follows another bottomless pit of absurdities – for then those substances must needs have been from ever, and so, eternal; and that eternal causes should bring forth chanceable effects is as sensible as that the sun should be the author of darkness.

'Again, if it were chanceable, then was it not necessary – whereby you take away all consequents. But we see in all things, in some respect or other, necessity of consequence; therefore, in reason, we must needs know that the causes were necessary.

'Lastly, chance is variable, or else it is not to be called chance – but we see this work is steady and permanent. If nothing but chance had glued those pieces of this all, the heavy parts would have gone infinitely downward, the light infinitely upward, and so never have met to have made up this[4] goodly body; for before there was a heaven or a earth, there was neither a heaven to stay the height of the rising, nor an earth which, in respect of the round walls of heaven, should become a centre. Lastly, perfect order, perfect beauty, perfect constancy: if these be the children of chance, [or fortune the efficient of these,] let[5] wisdom be counted the root of wickedness [and eternity the fruit of her inconstancy.][6]

'But you will say, "It is so by nature" – as much as if you said, "It is so, because it is so." If you mean, of many natures conspiring together, as in a popular government, to establish this fair estate – as if the elementish and ethereal parts should in their town-house set down the bounds of each one's office! – then consider what follows: that there must needs have been a wisdom which made them concur; for their natures being absolute contrary, in nature rather would have sought each other's ruin than have served as well-consorted parts to such an unexpressable harmony. For that contrary things should meet to make up a perfection, without a force and wisdom above their powers, is absolutely impossible – unless you will fly to that hissed-out opinion of chance again.

'But you may perhaps affirm that one universal nature, which hath been for ever, is the knitting together of these many parts to such an excellent unity. If you mean a nature of wisdom, goodness, and providence, which

---

[1] not have] have not 93   [2] of] if 93   [3] eternal … being] eternal Cm, 93   [4] this] his 93, 98   [5] chance … let] chance, let Cm, 93   [6] wickedness … inconstancy] wickedness Cm, 93

knows what it doth, then say you that which I seek of you, and cannot conclude those blasphemies with which you defiled your mouth and mine ears. But if you mean a nature, as we speak of the fire which goeth upward, it knows not why, and of the nature of the sea which in ebbing and flowing seems to observe so just a dance, and yet understands no music, it is but still the same absurdity superscribed[1] with another tide. For this word "one", being attributed to that which is all, is but "one", mingling of many and many "ones" (as, in a less matter, when we say "one kingdom", which contains many cities, or "one city", which contains many persons), wherein the under-ones, if there be not a superior power and wisdom, cannot by nature regard to any preservation but of themselves (no more we see they do, since the water willingly quenches the fire and drowns the earth), so far are they from a conspired unity – but that a right heavenly nature, indeed as it were unnaturing them, doth so bridle them.

'Again, it is as absurd in nature that from an unity many contraries should proceed, still kept in an unity, as that from the number of contrarieties an unity should arise. I say still, if you banish both a singularity and plurality of judgement from among them, then (if so earthly a mind can lift itself up so high) do but conceive how a thing whereto you give the highest and most excellent kind of being, which is eternity, can be of the base[2] and vilest degree of being, and next to a not-being – which is so to be as not to enjoy his own being.

'I will not here call all your senses to witness, which can hear nor see nothing (which yields not most evident evidence) of the unspeakableness of that wisdom. Each thing being directed to an end, and an end of preservation, so, proper effects of judgement, as speaking and laughing, are of mankind; but what mad fury can ever so inveigle any conceit as to see our mortal and corruptible selves to have a reason, and that this universality, whereof we are but the least pieces, should be utterly devoid thereof – as if one should say that one's foot might be wise, and himself foolish! This heard I once alleged against such a godless mind as yours, who being driven to acknowledge this beastly absurdities,[3] that our bodies should be better than the whole world if it had the knowledge whereof the other were void, he sought (not able to answer directly) to shift it off in this sort: that if that reason were true, then must it follow also that the world must have in it a spirit that could write and read to, and be learned, since that was in us so commendable[4] – wretched fool, not considering that books be but supplies of defects (and so are praised because they help our want) and therefore cannot be incident

---

[1] superscribed *Cm, 93*: subscribed *90* [2] the base] a base *93* [3] this beastly absurdities *Cm*: these beastly absurdities *90*; this beastly absurdity *93* [4] us so commendable] us commendable *corr. to* us a commendable *Cm*; us commendable *93*

to the eternal intelligence, which needs no recording of opinions to confirm his knowledge, no more than the sun wants wax to be the fuel of his glorious lightfulness.

'This world, therefore, cannot otherwise consist but by a mind of wisdom which governs it, which, whether you will allow to be the creator thereof – as undoubtedly he is, or the soul and governor thereof, most certain it is that whether he govern all, or make all, his power is above either his creatures or his government. And if his power be above all things, then consequently it must needs be infinite, since there is nothing above it to limit it; for beyond which there is nothing must needs be boundless and infinite. If his power be infinite, then likewise must his knowledge be infinite, for else there should be an infinite proportion of power which he should not know how to use (the unsensibleness whereof, I think even you can conceive), and if infinite, then must nothing, no, not the estate of flies (which you with so unsavoury scorn did jest at) be unknown unto him; for if it were, then there were his knowledge bounded, and so, not infinite. If knowledge and power be infinite, then must needs his goodness and justice march in the same rank; for infiniteness of power and knowledge, without like measure of goodness, must necessarily bring forth destruction and ruin, and not ornament and preservation.

'Since, then, there is a God, and an all-knowing God so as he sees into the darkest of all natural secrets, which is the heart of man, and sees therein the deepest dissembled thoughts – nay, sees the thoughts before they be thought; since he is just to exercise his might, and mighty to perform his justice, assure thyself, most wicked woman, that hast so plaguily a corrupted mind as thou canst not keep thy sickness to thyself, but must most wickedly infect others, assure thyself, I say – for what I say depends of everlasting and unremovable causes – that the time will come when thou shalt know that power by feeling it, when thou shalt see his wisdom in the manifesting thy ugly shamefastness,[1] and shalt only perceive him to have been a creator in thy destruction!'

Thus[2] she said; thus, she ended, with so fair a majesty of unconquered virtue that captivity might seem to have authority over tyranny, so foully was the filthiness of impiety discovered by the shining of her unstained goodness – so far, as either Cecropia saw indeed, or else the guilty amazement of a[3] self-accusing conscience made her eyes untrue judges of their natural object: that there was a light more than human which gave a lustre

---

[1] shamefastness *Cm*: shamelessness *90*; shamefulness *93* [2] destruction!' Thus *Cm, 93*: destruction!' Chap. 11. Cecropia, malcontent, still practiseth; the besiegers' discipline, and attempts of the besieged; Phalantus challengeth by letter Amphialus, who by letter accepteth it; Amphialus' and Phalantus' militar accoutrements; their foe-like combat, but friendly conclusion. Thus *90* [3] of a *Cm, 93*: of her *90*

to her perfections. But Cecropia, like a bat which, though it have eyes to discern that there is a sun, yet hath so evil eyes that it cannot delight in the sun, found a truth but could not love it; but, as great persons are wont to make the wrong they have done to be a cause to do the more wrong, her knowledge rose to no higher point but to envy a worthier, and her will was no otherwise bent but the more to hate, the more she found her enemy provided against her.

Yet all the while she spake (though with eyes cast like a horse that would strike at the stirrup, and with colour which blushed through yellowness), she sate rather still than quiet, and after her speech rather muttered than replied (for the war of wickedness in her self brought forth disdainful pride to resist cunning dissimulation); so as saying little more unto her but that she should have leisure enough better to bethink herself, she went away, repining but not repenting, condemning greatly (as she thought) her son's over-feeble humbleness, and purposing to egg him forward to a course of violence; for herself, determining to deal with neither of them both any more in manner of a suitor, for what majesty of virtue did in the one, that did silent humbleness in the other.

But finding her son over-apt to lay both condemnation and execution of sorrow upon himself, she sought to mitigate his mind with feigned delays of comfort; who, having this inward overthrow in himself, was the more vexed that he could not utter the rage thereof upon his outward enemies, for Basilius, taught by the last day's trial what dangerous effects chosen courages can bring forth, rather used the spade than the sword (or the sword but to defend the spade), girding about the whole town with trenches; which beginning a good way off from the town, with a number of well-directed pioneers, he still carried before him till they came to a near distance, where he builded forts, one answering the other in such sort as it was a pretty consideration, in the discipline of war to see building used for the instrument of ruin, and the assailer entrenched as if he were besieged. But many sallies did Amphialus make to hinder their working, but they (exercising more melancholy than choler in their resolution) made him find that, if by the advantage of place few are able to defend themselves from many, that many must needs have power, making themselves strong in seat to repel few, referring the revenge rather to the end than a present requital.

Yet oftentimes they dealt some blows in light skirmishes (each side having a strong retiring-place, and rather fighting with many alarums to vex the enemy than for any hope of great success), which every way was a tedious cumber to the impatient courage of Amphialus – till the fame of this war bringing thither divers both strangers and subjects, as well of princely as noble houses, the gallant Phalantus (who restrained[1] his sportful delights as then to serve Basilius, whom he honoured for received honours), when he had spent some time in considering the Arcadian manner in marching, encamping, and fighting, and had learned in what points of government and obedience their discipline differed from others, and too, had[2] satisfied his mind in the knowledges[3] both for the cutting off the enemy's helps, and furnishing oneself, which Basilius' orders could deliver unto him – his young spirits, weary of wanting cause to be weary, desired to keep his valure in knowledge by some private act, since the public policy restrained him, the rather because his old mistress, Artesia, might see whom she had so lightly forsaken. And therefore demanding and obtaining leave of Basilius, he caused a herald to be furnished with apparel of his office and tokens of a peaceable message, and so sent him to the gate of the town to demand audience of Amphialus, who understanding thereof, caused him both safely and courteously to be brought into his presence; who, making lowly reverence unto him, presented his letters, desiring Amphialus that, whatsoever they contained, he would consider that he was only the bearer, but[4] not the inditer.

Amphialus with noble gentleness assured him both by honourable speeches, and a demeanour which answered for him, that his revenge, whensoever, should sort unto itself a higher subject. But opening the letters, he found them to speak in this manner.

'Phalantus of Corinth to Amphialus of Arcadia sendeth the greeting of a hateless enemy. The liking of martial matters, without any mislike of your person, hath brought me rather to the company than to the mind of your besiegers, where languishing in idleness, I desire to refresh my mind with some exercise of arms which might make known the doers, with delight of the beholders. Therefore, if there be any gentleman in your town that either for the love of honour or honour of his love, well[5] armed on horseback, with lance and sword, win[6] another or lose himself to be a prisoner at discretion of the conqueror, I will tomorrow morning by sunrising, with a trumpet and a squire only, attend him in like order furnished. The place I think fittest, the island within the lake – because it stands so well in the view of your castle as that the ladies may have the pleasure of seeing the combat; which though it be within the commandment of your castle, I desire no better security than the promise I make to myself of your virtue. I attend your answer, and wish you such success as may be to your honour, rather in yielding to that which is just, than in maintaining wrong by much[7] violence.'

---

[1] restrained] refrained 93　[2] and too, had *Cm*: and had 90; and so, had 93　[3] knowledges *Cm*, 93: knowledge 90　[4] but] and 93　[5] well] will 93　[6] win *Cm*, 93: will win 90　[7] much] mith [*underscored*] *Cm*; om. 93

Amphialus read it with cheerful countenance; and thinking but a little with himself, called for ink and paper, and wrote this answer:

'Amphialus of Arcadia to Phalantus of Corinth wisheth all his own wishes, saving those which may be hurtful to another. The matter of your letters so fit for a worthy mind, and the manner so suitable to the nobleness of the matter, give me cause to think how happy I might account myself if I could get such a friend, who esteem it no small happiness to have met with so noble an enemy. Your challenge shall be answered and both time, place, and weapon accepted. For your security from[1] any treachery, having no hostage worthy to countervail you, take my word, which I esteem above all respects. Prepare therefore your arms to fight, but not your heart to malice, since true valure needs no other whetstone than desire of honour.'

Having writ and sealed his letter, he delivered it to the herald, and withal took a fair chain from off his own neck and gave it him; and so, with safe convoy, sent him away from out his city. And he being gone, Amphialus showed unto his mother and some other of his chief councillors what he had received, and how he had answered, telling them withal that he was determined to answer the challenge in his own person.

His mother with prayers authorized by motherly commandment, his old governor with persuasions mingled with reprehensions that he would rather affect the glory of a private fighter than of a wise general, Clinias with falling down at his feet and beseeching him to remember that all their lives depended upon his safety, sought all to dissuade him. But Amphialus, whose heart was inflamed with courage, and courage inflamed with affection, made an imperious resolution cut off the tediousness of replies, giving them in charge what they should do upon all occasions (and particularly to deliver the ladies) if otherwise than well happened unto him, only desiring his mother that she would bring Philoclea to a window where[2] she might with ease perfectly discern the combat.

And so, as soon as the morning began to draw dew from the fairest greenness to wash her face withal against the approach of the burning sun, he went to his stable where himself chose out a horse whom, though he was near twenty year old, he preferred for a piece of sure service before a great number of younger. His colour was of a brown bay, dappled thick with black spots; his forehead marked with a white star, to which in all his body there was no part suitable but the left foot before; his mane and tail black and thick; of goodly and well-proportioned greatness. He caused him to be trimmed with a sumptuous saddle of tawny and gold enamel, enriched with precious stones. His furniture was made into the fashion of the branches of a tree from

---

[1] from *Cm, 93*: for *90*   [2] where] whence *93*

which the leaves were falling – and so artificially were the leaves made that, as the horse moved, it seemed indeed that the leaves wagged, as when the wind plays with them; and being made of a pale cloth of gold, they did bear the straw-coloured livery of ruin. His armour was also of tawny and gold, but formed into the figure of flames, darkened as when they newly break the prison of a smoky furnace. In his shield he had painted the torpedo fish.

And so appointed, he caused himself with his trumpet and squire (whom he had taken since the death of Ismenus) to be ferried over into the island – a place well chosen for such a purpose, for it was so plain as there was scarcely any bush or hillock, either to unlevel or shadow it; of length and breadth enough to try the uttermost both of lance and sword; and the one end of it facing of the[1] castle, the other extending itself toward the camp, and no access to it but by water. There could no secret treachery be wrought; and for manifest violence, either side might have time enough to succour their party.

But there he found Phalantus already waiting for him upon a horse, milk-white, but that upon his shoulder and withers he was fretened[2] with red stains, as when a few strawberries are scattered into a dish of cream. He had caused his mane and tail to be dyed in carnation. His reins were vine branches, which engendering one with the other, at the end when it came to the bit, there for the boss brought forth a cluster of grapes, by the workman made so lively that it seemed, as the horse champed on his bit, he chopped for them, and that it did make his mouth water to see the grapes so near him. His furniture behind was of vines so artificially made as it seemed the horse stood in the shadow of the vine, so prettily were clusters of ruby grapes dispersed among the trappers which embraced his sides. His armour was blue like the heaven, which a sun did, with his rays proportionately delivered, gild in most places. His shield was beautified with this device: a greyhound, which overrunning his fellow and taking the hare, yet hurts it not when it takes it. The word was 'The glory, not the prey.'

But as soon as Amphialus landed, he sent his squire to Phalantus to tell him that there was the knight ready to know whether he had anything to him.[3] Phalantus answered that his answer now must be in the language of lances; and so each attended the warning of the trumpets which were to sound at the appointment of four judges – who, with consideration of the same, had divided the ground.

Phalantus' horse, young, and feeling the youth of his master, stood corvetting; which being well-governed by Phalantus gave such a glittering grace as when the sun shines[4] upon a waving water. Amphialus' horse stood panting upon the ground, with his further foot before, as if he would for his

---

[1] facing of the] facing the 93   [2] fretened] freetned *Cm*; freckned 93   [3] to him] to say to him 93
[4] sun shines] sun in a clear day shines 93

master's cause begin to make himself angry; till the trumpet sounding[1] together, together they set spurs to their horses, together took their lances from their thighs; conveyed them up into their rests together; together let them sink downward – so as it was a delectable sight in a dangerous effect, and a pleasant consideration that there was so perfect agreement in so mortal disagreement, like a music made of cunning discords. But their horses (keeping an even line their masters had skilfully allotted unto them) passed one by another without encountering, although either might feel the angry breath of other; but the staves (being come to a just descent, but even), when the mark was ready to meet them, Amphialus was run through the vamplate and under the arm, so as, the staff appearing behind him, it seemed to the beholders he had been in danger – but he strake Phalantus just upon the gorget, so as he battered the lames thereof, and made his head almost touch the back of his horse.

But either side having stayed the spur and used the bit to stop their horses' fury, casting away the truncheons of their staves and drawing their swords, they attended the second summons of the death-threatening trumpet, which quickly followed; and they as soon, making their horses answer their hands, with a gentle gallop set the one[2] toward the other; till being come in the nearness of little more than a stave's length, Amphialus, trusting more to the strength than to the nimbleness of his horse, put him forth with speedy violence, and making his head join to the other's flank (guiding his blow with discretion, and strengthening it with the course of his horse), strake Phalantus upon the head in such sort that his feeling sense did both dazzle his sight and astonish his hearing. But Phalantus, not accustomed to be ungrateful to such benefits, strake him upon the side of his face, with such force[3] that he thought his jaw had been cut asunder, though the faithfulness of his armour indeed guarded him from further damage.

And so remained they awhile, rather angry with fighting than fighting for anger, till Amphialus' horse leaning hard upon the other and winning ground, the other horse, feeling himself pressed, began to rise a little before, as he was wont to do in his corvet; which advantage Amphialus taking, set forward his own horse with the further spur, so as Phalantus' horse came over, with his master under him; which Amphialus seeing, lighted with intention to help Phalantus. But his horse, that had faulted rather with untimely art than want of force gat up from burdening his burden, so as Phalantus, in the fall having gotten his feet free of the[4] stirrup, could, though something bruised, arise; and seeing[5] Amphialus near him, he asked him whether he had given him any help in removing his horse.

---

[1] sounding *Cm, 93*: sounded *90*   [2] set the one] set one *93*   [3] such force *Cm, 93*: such a force *90*   [4] of the *Cm, 93*: of and the *90*   [5] and seeing *Cm, 93*: seeing *90*

Amphialus said, 'No.'

'Truly,' said Phalantus, 'I asked it because I would not willingly have fought with him that had had my life in his mercy. But now,' said Phalantus, 'before we proceed further, let me know who you are – because never yet did any man bring me to the like fortune.'

Amphialus, listing to keep himself unknown, told him he was a gentleman, to whom Amphialus that day had given armour and horse to try his valour, having never before been in any combat worthy remembrance.

'Ah!' said Phalantus in a rage. 'And must I be the exercise of your prenticeage?' And with that, choler took away either the bruise, or the feeling of the bruise, so as he entered afresh into the combat; and boiling into[1] his arms the disdain of his heart, strake so thick upon Amphialus as if every blow would fain have been foremost. But Amphialus, that many like trials had taught great spending to leave small remnants, let pass the storm with strong wards and nimble avoidings; till seeing his time fit both for distance and nakedness, he strake him so cruel a blow on the knee that the poor gentleman fell down withal in a sound. But Amphialus, pitying approved valour made precious by natural courtesy, went to him; and taking off his head-piece to give him air, the young knight, disdained[2] to buy life with yielding, bad him use his fortune, for he was resolved never to yield.

'No more you shall,' said Amphialus, 'if it be not to my request that you will account yourself to have great interest in me.'

Phalantus (more overcome by his kindness, than by his fortune) desired yet once again to know his name, who in his first beginning had showed such fury in his force, and yet such stay in his fury. Amphialus then named himself, telling him withal, he would think his name much bettered if it might be honoured by the title of his friend. But no balm could be more comfortable to his wound than the knowledge thereof was to his mind, when he knew his mishap should be excused by the renowned valour of the other; and so, promising each to other assuredness of goodwill, Phalantus (of whom Amphialus would have no other ransom but his word of friendship) was conveyed into the camp, where he would but little remain among the enemies of Amphialus, but went to seek his adventures otherwhere.[3] As for Amphialus, he was received with triumph into the castle, although one might see, by his eyes humbly lifted up to the window where Philoclea stood, that he was rather suppliant than victorious – which occasion Cecropia ta-

---

[1] boiling into *Cm*, 93: boiling in 90   [2] disdained] disdaining 93   [3] otherwhere. As *Cm*, 93: otherwhere.

Chap. 12. Philoclea's ill-taking Amphialus' well-meaning; his challenge and conquests continued for love, and his love; Argalus sent for to this challenge; the conjugal happiness of him and his wife; the passions stirred by this message; their sorrow-sounding farewell; Argalus' defy; Amphialus' answer; Argalus' furniture; their combat, bloody to both, deadly to Argalus; Parthenia comes to the end of it, and him; her and his lamentations; the funerals. As 90

king (who as then stood by Philoclea, and had lately left Pamela in another room whence also she might see the combat), 'Sweet lady,' said she, 'now you may see whether you have cause to love my son, who then lies under your feet when he stands upon the neck of his bravest enemies.'

'Alas,' said Philoclea, 'a simple service to me, methinks it is, to have those who come to succour me destroyed! If it be my duty to call it love, be it so; but the effects it brings forth, I confess I account hateful.'

Cecropia grew so angry with this unkind answer that she could not abstain from telling her that she was like them that could not sleep when they were softly laid; but that if her son would follow her counsel, he should take another course with her – and so, flang away from her; yet knowing the desperate melancholy of Amphialus in like cases, framed to him a very thankful message, powdering it with some hope-giving phrases, which were of such joy to Amphialus that he, though against public respect and importunity of dissuaders, presently caused it to be made known to the camp that, whatsoever knight would try the like fortune as Phalantus did, he should in like sort be answered; so as divers of the valiantest, partly of themselves, partly at the instigation of Basilius, attempted the combat with him.

And according to every one's humour, so were the causes of the challenge grounded, one laying treason to his charge; another preferring himself in the worthiness to serve Philoclea; a third exalting some lady's beauty beyond either of the sisters'; a fourth laying disgraces to love itself, naming it the bewitcher of the wit, the rebel to reason, the betrayer of resolution, the defiler of thoughts, the underminer of magnanimity, the flatterer of vice, the slave to weakness, the infection of youth, the madness of age, the curse of life, and reproach of death; a fifth, disdaining to cast at less than at all, would make the cause of his quarrel the causers of love, and proclaim his blasphemies against womankind, that namely that sex was the oversight of nature, the disgrace of reasonableness; the obstinate cowards, the slave-born tyrants, the shops of vanities, the gilded weathercocks – in whom conscience is but peevishness, chastity waywardness, and gratefulness a miracle.

But all these challenges, how well soever indited, were so well answered that some by death taught others (though past learning themselves), and some by yielding gave themselves the lie for having blasphemed – to the great grief of Basilius, so to see his rebel prevail, and in his own sight to crown himself with deserved honour; whereupon thirsting for revenge, and else not hoping to prevail, the best of his camp being already overthrown, he sent a messenger to Argalus (in whose approved courage and force he had – and had cause – to have great confidence) with a letter requiring him to take this quarrel in hand, from which he had hitherto spared him in respect of his late marriage. But now his honour, and (as he esteemed it) felicity standing upon it, he could no longer forbear to challenge of him his faithful service.

The messenger made speed and found Argalus at a castle of his own, sitting in a parlour with the fair Parthenia; he reading in a book the stories of Hercules, she by him, as to hear him read – but while his eyes looked on the book, she looked on his eyes, and sometimes staying him with some pretty question, not so much to be resolved of the doubt as to give him occasion to look upon her – a happy couple, he joying in her, she joying in herself (but in herself because she enjoyed him); both increasing their riches by giving to each other; each making one life double because they made a double life one, where desire never[1] wanted satisfaction, nor satisfaction never bred satiety; he ruling because she would obey – or rather, because she would obey, she therein ruling.

But when the messenger came in with letters in his hand and haste in his countenance, though she knew not what to fear, yet she feared because she knew not; but she rose and went aside while he delivered his letters and message. Yet, afar off, she looked now at the messenger, and then at her husband – the same fear which made her loath to have cause of fear, yet making her seek cause to nourish her fear; and well she found there was some serious matter, for her husband's countenance figured some resolution between loathness and necessity. And once his eye cast upon her; and finding hers upon him, he blushed – and she blushed because he blushed, and yet straight grew paler,[2] because she knew not why he had blushed.

But when he had read and heard, and dispatched away the messenger (like a man in whom honour could not be rocked on sleep[3] by affection) with promise quickly to follow, he came to Parthenia; and as sorry as might be for parting (and yet more sorry for her sorrow), he gave her the letter to read. She with fearful slowness took it, and with fearful quickness read it; and having read it, 'Ah, my Argalus!' said she. 'And have you made such haste to answer? And are you so soon resolved to leave me?'

But he discoursing unto her how much it imported[4] his honour (which since it was dear to him he knew it would be dear unto her), her reason, overclouded with sorrow, suffered her not presently to reply, but left the charge thereof to tears and sighs; which he not able to bear, left her alone and went to give order for his present departure. But by[5] that time he was armed and ready to go, she had recovered a little strength of spirit again; and coming out, and seeing him armed and wanting nothing for his departure but her farewell, she ran to him; took him by the arm; and kneeling down,

---

[1] never] ever 93   [2] paler] pale 93   [3] on sleep] a sleep 93, 98; asleep 13   [4] imported Cm, 93: imparted 90   [5] But by Cm, 93: By 90

without regard who either heard her speech or saw her demeanour, 'My Argalus! My Argalus!' said she. 'Do not thus forsake me! Remember, alas! remember that I have interest in you, which I will never yield shall be thus adventured. Your valour is already sufficiently known. Sufficiently have you already done for your country. Enow, enow there are besides you to lose less worthy lives. Woe is me! What shall become of me if you thus abandon me? Then was it time for you to follow these adventures when you adventured nobody but yourself and were nobody's but your own – but now (pardon me, that now or never I claim mine own!) mine you are, and without me you can undertake no danger. And will you endanger Parthenia? Parthenia shall be in the battle of your fight! Parthenia shall smart in your pain; and your blood must be bled by Parthenia!'

'Dear Parthenia,' said he, 'this is the first time that ever you resisted my will. I thank you for it – but persevere not in it, and let not the tears of those most beloved eyes be a presage unto me of that which you would not should happen. I shall live, doubt not; for so great a blessing as you are was not given unto me so soon to be deprived of it. Look for me, therefore, shortly – and victorious, and prepare a joyful welcome, and I will wish for no other triumph.'

She answered not, but stood as it were thunder-stricken with amazement, for true love made obedience stand up against all other passions. But when he took her in his arms and sought to print his heart in her sweet lips, she fell in a sound, so as he was fain to leave her to her gentlewomen; and carried away by the tyranny of honour (though with many a back-cast look and hearty groan) went to the camp, where[1] understanding the notable victories of Amphialus, he thought to give him some days' respite of rest, because he would not have his victory disgraced by the other's weariness – in which days he sought by all means, having leave to parley with him, to dissuade him from his enterprise; and then (imparting his mind to Basilius, because he found Amphialus was inflexible) wrote his defy unto him, in this manner.

'Right famous Amphialus, if my persuasion in reason or prayer in goodwill might prevail with you, you should by better means be like to obtain your desire: you should make many brave enemies become your faithful servants, and make your honour fly up to the heaven,[2] being carried up by both the wings of valure and justice, whereof now it wants the latter. But since my suit nor counsel can get no place in you, disdain not to receive a mortal challenge from a man so far inferior unto you in virtue, as that[3] I do not so much mislike of the deed as I have the doer in admiration. Prepare

---

[1] where *Cm*, *93*: when *90* [2] to the heaven] to heaven *93* [3] virtue, as that] virtue, as I that *Cm*; virtue, that *13*

therefore yourself according to the noble manner you have used, and think not lightly of never so weak an arm, which strikes with the sword of justice.'

To this, quickly received[1] this answer: 'Much more famous Argalus, I, whom never threatenings could make afraid, am now terrified by your noble courtesy, for well I know from what height of virtue it doth proceed, and what cause I have to doubt such virtue bent to my ruin. But love, which justifieth the unjustice you lay unto me, doth also animate me against all dangers, since I come full of him, by whom yourself have been (if I be not deceived) sometimes conquered. I will therefore attend your appearance in the isle carrying this advantage with me, that, as it shall be a singular honour if I get the victory, so there can be no dishonour in being overcome by Argalus.'

The challenge thus denounced and accepted, Argalus was armed in a white armour which was gilded[2] over with knots of woman's hair, which came down from the crest of his head-piece and spread itself in rich quantity over all his armour. His furniture was cut out into the fashion of an eagle – whereof the beak, made into a rich jewel, was fastened to the saddle; the tail covered the crupper of the horse, and the wings served for trappers, which falling of each side, as the horse stirred, the bird seemed to fly. His peitrel and reins were embrodered with features, suitable unto it. Upon his right arm he ware a sleeve which his dear Parthenia had made for him to be worn in a justs, in the time that success was ungrateful to their well-deserved love; it was full of bleeding hearts, though never intended to any bloody enterprise. In this[3] shield, as his own device, he had two palm trees near one another, with a word signifying, 'In that sort flourishing.' His horse was of a fiery sorrel, with black feet and black list on his back, who with open nostrils breathed war before he could see an enemy, and now up with one leg, and then with another, seemed to complain of nature that she had made him any whit earthy.

But he had scarcely viewed the ground of the island and considered the advantages, if any were thereof, before the castle boat had delivered Amphialus, in all points provided to give a hard entertainment. And then sending each to other their squires in honourable manner to know whether they should attend any further ceremony, the trumpets sounding, the horses with smooth running, their staves[4] with unshaked motion, obediently performed their choleric commandments. But when they drew near, Argalus' horse, being hot, pressed in with his head; which Amphialus perceiving, knowing if he gave him his side it should be to his disadvantage, pressed in also with him, so as both the horses and men met shoulder to shoulder, so as the

---

[1] quickly received *Cm*: quickly he received *90*; he quickly received *93* [2] was gilded] was all gilded *93* [3] this] his *93* [4] their staves] the staves *93*

horses, hurt as much with the striking as being stricken, tumbled down to the earth, dangerously to their master,[1] but that they, by strength nimble, and by use skilful, in the falling shunned the harm of the fall; and without more respite drew out their swords with a gallant bravery, each striving to show himself the less endamaged, and to make known that they were glad they had now nothing else to trust to but their own virtue.

True it is that Amphialus was the sooner up, but Argalus had his sword out the sooner. And then fell they to the cruellest combat that any present eye had seen, their swords, first, like cannons, battering down the walls of their armour, making breaches almost in every place for troops of wounds to enter. Among the rest, Argalus gave a great wound to Amphialus' disarmed face, though part of the force of it Amphialus warded upon his shield; and withal (first casting his eye up to Philoclea's window, as if he had fetched his courage thence) feigning to intend the same sort of blows,[2] turned his sword, and with a mighty reverse gave a cruel wound to the right arm of Argalus, the unfaithful armour yielding to the sword's strong-guided sharpness. But though the blood accused the hurt of Argalus, yet would he in no action of his confess it; but keeping himself in a lower ward, stood watching with timely thrusts to repair his loss – which quickly he did, for Amphialus, following his fawning fortune, laid on so thick upon Argalus that his shield had almost fallen piecemeal to the earth, when Argalus, coming in with his right foot, and something stooping to come under his armour, thrust him into the belly dangerously; and mortally it would have been but that with the blow before Amphialus had overthrown[3] himself, so as he fell sideward down, and with falling saved himself from ruin, the sword by that means slipping aside, and not piercing more deeply.

Argalus seeing him fall, threatening with voice and sword, bad him yield. But he striving without answer to rise, Argalus strake with all his might upon his head. But his hurt arm, not able to master so sound a force, let the sword fall so, as Amphialus, though astonished with the blow, could arise; which Argalus considering, ran in to grasp with him; and so, closed together, falling so to the ground, now one getting above and then the other, at length, both weary of so unlovely embracements with a dissenting[4] consent gate up and went to their swords – but happened each of his enemy's; where Argalus finding his foe's sword garnished in his blood, his heart rase with the same sword to revenge it, and on that blade to ally their bloods together. But his mind was evil waited on by his lamed force, so as he received still more and more wounds, which made all his armour seem to blush that it had defended his master no better.

---

[1] master] masters 93   [2] blows] blow 93   [3] overthrown] overstricken 93   [4] dissenting] dissending 93; descending 98

But Amphialus perceiving it, and weighing the small hatefulness of their quarrel with the worthiness of the knight, desired him to take pity of himself. But Argalus (the more repining, the more he found himself in disadvantage) filling his veins with spite instead of blood, and making courage arise against faintness, like a candle which a little before it goes out gives then the greatest blaze, so did he unite all his force that casting away the little remnant of his shield, and taking his sword in both hands, he stroke such a notable blow that he cleft his shield, armour, and arm almost to the bone. But then Amphialus forgat all ceremonies, and with cruel blows made more of his blood[1] succeed the rest; till his hand being stayed by his ear, his ear filled with a pitiful cry, the cry guided his sight to an excellent fair lady who came running as fast as she could, and yet, because she could not as fast as she would, she sent her lamentable voice before her; and being come, and being known to them both to be the beautiful Parthenia (who had that night dreamed she saw her husband in such estate as she then found him, which made her make such haste thither), they both marvelled.

But Parthenia ran between them (fear of love making her forget the fear of nature) and then fell down at their feet, determining so to part them till she could get breath to sigh out her doleful speeches. And when her breath, which running had spent and dismayedness made slow to return, had by sobs gotten into her sorrow-closed breast, for a while she could say nothing but, 'Oh, wretched eyes of mine! Oh, wailful sight! Oh, day of darkness!' At length turning her eyes, wherein sorrow swam, to Amphialus, 'My lord,' said she, 'it is said you love. In the power of that love, I beseech you to leave off this combat. As even[2] your heart may find comfort in his affection, even for her sake I crave it. Or if you be mortally determined, be so pitiful unto me as first to kill me, that I may not see the death of Argalus.'

Amphialus was about to have answered, when Argalus, vexed with his fortune, but most vexed that she should see him in that fortune, 'Ah Parthenia,' said he, 'never till now unwelcome unto me, do you come to get my life by request? And cannot Argalus live but by request? Is that a[3] life?' With that he went aside for fear of hurting her, and would have begun the combat afresh.

But Amphialus, not only conjured by that which held the monarchy of his mind, but even in his noble heart melting with compassion at so passionate a sight, desired him to withhold his hands, for that he should strike one who sought his favour and would not make resistance – a notable example[4] of the wonderful effects of virtue, where the conqueror sought for friendship of the conquered, and the conquered would not pardon the conqueror, both

---

[1] his blood] his best blood 93   [2] even] ever 93   [3] that a 93: yt a *Cm*; it a 90   [4] example *Cm*, 93: examble 90

indeed being of that mind to love each other for accepting but not for giving mercy, and neither affected to overlive a dishonour; so that Argalus not so much striving with Amphialus (for if he had had him in the like sort, in like sort he would have dealt with him, as labouring against his own power which he chiefly despised) set himself forward, stretching his strength to the uttermost. But the fire of that strife, blown with his inward rage, boiled out his blood in such abundance that he was driven to rest him upon the pommel of his sword; and then, each thing beginning to turn round in the dance of death before his eyes, his sight both dazzled and dimmed; till, thinking to sit down, he fell in a sound.

Parthenia and Amphialus both hastily went unto him. Amphialus took off his helmet, and Parthenia laid his head in her lap, tearing off her linen sleeves and partlet to serve about his wounds, to bind which she took off her hair-lace, and would have cut off her fair hair herself, but that the squires and judges came in with fitter things for the purpose, while she bewailed herself with so lamentable sweetness as was enough to have taught sorrow to the gladdest thoughts, and have engraved it in the minds of hardest metal.

'O Parthenia – no more Parthenia!' said she. 'What art thou? What seest thou? How is thy bliss in a moment fallen! How art thou – even now before all ladies the example of perfect happiness, and now the gazing-stock of endless misery? O God, what hath been my desert to be thus punished; or, if such have been my desert, why was I not in myself punished? O wandering life, to what wilderness wouldst thou lead me?[1] But, sorrow, I hope thou art sharp enough to save my labour from other remedies. Argalus! Argalus, I will follow thee! I will follow thee!'

But with that Argalus came out of his sound; and lifting up his languishing eyes which a painful rest and iron sleep did seek to lock up, seeing her in whom even dying he lived and himself seated in so beloved a place, it seemed a little cheerful blood came up to his cheeks, like a burning coal almost dead, if some breath a little revive it; and forcing up the best he could his feeble voice, 'My dear – my dear – my[2] better half – ' said he, 'I find I must now leave thee; and by that sweet hand and fair eyes of thine, I swear that death brings nothing with it to grieve me but that I must leave thee, and cannot remain to answer part of thy infinite deserts with being some comfort unto thee. But since so it pleaseth him whose wisdom and goodness guideth all, put thy confidence in him, and one day we shall blessedly meet again, never to depart. Meanwhile, live happily, dear Parthenia; and I persuade myself it will increase the blessedness of my soul so to see thee. Love well the remembrance of thy loving – and truly loving – Argalus. And let

---

[1] me *Cm, 93*: one *90*   [2] dear – my dear – my] dear – my *93*

not – ' with that word he sighed, 'this disgrace of mine make thee one day think thou hadst an unworthy husband.'

They could scarcely understand the last words, for death began to seize himself of his heart. Neither could Parthenia make answer, so full was her breast of anguish. But while the other sought to stanch his remediless wounds, she with her kisses made him happy, for his last breath was delivered into her mouth.

But when indeed she found his ghost was gone, then sorrow lost the wit of utterance and grew rageful and mad, so that she tare her beautiful face and rent her hair, as though they could serve for nothing since Argalus was gone; till Amphialus (so moved with pity of that sight as that he honoured his adversary's death with tears) caused her, with the help of her women that came with her, partly by force to be conveyed into the boat[1] with the dead body of Argalus, from which she could[2] not depart. And being come of the other side, there she was received by Basilius himself, with all the funeral pomp of military discipline – trailing all their ensigns upon the ground, making the warlike[3] instruments sound doleful notes; and Basilius, with comfort in his mouth and woe in his face, sought to persuade some ease into Parthenia's mind. But all was as easeful to her as the handling of sore wounds – all the honour done being to her but the triumph of her ruin, she finding no comfort but in desperate yielding to sorrow, and rather determined to hate herself if ever she should find ease thereof. And well might she hear as she passed through the camp the great praises spoken of her husband, which all were records of her loss.

But the more excellent he was, being indeed accounted second to none in all Greece, the more did the breath of those praises bear up the wings of Amphialus' fame, to whom, yet such was his case that trophy upon trophy still did but build up the monument of his thraldom, he ever finding himself in such favour of Philoclea that she was most absent when he was present with her, and ever sorriest when he had best success – which would have made him renounce all comfort, but that his mother with diversity of devices kept up his heart. But while he allayed thus his outward glory with inward discomfort, he was like to have been overtaken with a notable treason, the beginning whereof, though merely ridiculous, had like to have brought forth unto him a weeping effect.

Among[4] other that attended Basilius in this expedition, Dametas was one – whether to be present with him, or absent from Miso; once, certain it

---

[1] into the boat *Cm, 93*: into boat *90* [2] could] would *93* [3] the warlike *Cm*: his warlike *90*; these warlike *93, 98*; their warlike *13* [4] effect. Among *Cm, 93*: effect. Chap. 13. Dametas put in heart to defy Clinias; Clinias out of heart to see the vie; Dametas' bravery, adubments, and imprese; Clinias drawn to answer him; their passions in coming to the field; their actions in it not so doughty as their fortune doubtful; Clinias' yielding to triumphant Dametas. Among *90*

was without any mind to make his sword cursed by any widow! Now, being in the camp, while each talk seemed injurious which did not acknowledge some duty to the fame of Amphialus, it fell out sometimes in communication that, as the speech of heaven doth often beget the mention of hell, so the admirable prowess of Amphialus, by a contrary, brought forth the remembrance of the cowardice of Clinias (insomuch as it grew almost to a proverb, 'As very a coward as Clinias'), describing him in such sort that in the end Dametas began to think with himself that, if he made a challenge unto him, he would never answer it, and that then he should greatly increase the favourable conceit of Basilius.

This fancy of his he uttered to a young gentleman that waited upon Philanax, in whose friendship he had especial confidence because he haunted his company, laughing often merrily at his speeches, and not a little extolling the goodly dotes of Mopsa. The young gentleman, as glad as if he had found a hare sitting, egged him on, breaking the matter with Philanax. And then, for fear the humour should quail in him, wrote a challenge himself for Dametas, and brought it to him.

But when Dametas read it (putting his head on his shoulder and somewhat smiling) he said it was pretty indeed, but that it had not a lofty style enough; and so would needs indite it in this sort: 'O Clinias! Thou, Clinias, the wickedest worm that ever went upon two legs! the very fritter of fraud and seething pot of iniquity! I, Dametas, Chief Governor of All the Royal Cattle (and also of Pamela, whom thy master most perniciously hath suggested out of my dominion), do defy thee in a mortal affray, from the bodkin, to the pike, upward; which if thou doost presume to take in hand, I will out of that superfluous body of thine make thy soul to be evacuated.'

The young gentleman seemed dumb-stricken with admiration, and presently took upon him to be the bearer thereof while the heat of the fit lasted; and having gotten leave of Basilius (every one[1] helping on to ease his mind, overcharged with melancholy), he went into the town according to the manner beforetime used, and in the presence of Amphialus delivered this letter to Clinias, desiring to have an answer which might be fit for his reputation. Clinias opened it and read[2] it, and in the reading, his blood, not daring to be in so dangerous a place, went out of his face and hid itself more inwardly, and his very words, as if they were afraid of blows, came very slowly out of his mouth; but as well as his panting[3] breath would utter it, he bad him tell the lout that sent him that he disdained to have anything to do with him. But Amphialus, perceiving the matter, took him aside and very earnestly dealt with him not to shame himself – Amphialus only[4] desirous to bring it to pass to make some sport to Philoclea; but not being able to persuade with

---

[1] every one] everybody 93   [2] it and read] it, read 93   [3] panting *Cm*, 93: painting 90   [4] Amphialus only *Cm*, 93: Amphialus not only 90

him, Amphialus licensed the gentleman, telling him by the[1] next morning he should have answer.

The young gentleman, sorry he had sped no better, returned to Dametas, who had fetched many a sour-breathed sigh for fear Clinias would accept the challenge. But when he perceived by his trusty messenger that this delay was in effect a denial, there being no disposition in him to accept it, then lo! Dametas began to speak his loud voice, to look big, to march up and down (and in his march to lift his legs higher than he was wont), swearing by no mean devotions that the walls should not keep the coward from him, but he would fetch him out of his cony-berry; and then was hotter than ever to provide himself of horse and armour, saying he would go to the island bravely adubbed and show himself to his charge, Pamela.

To this purpose many willing hands were about him, letting him have reins, peitrel, with the rest of the furniture, and very brave bases – but all coming from divers houses, neither in colour nor[2] fashion showing any kinred one with another. But that liked Dametas the better; for that, he thought, would argue that he was master of many brave furnitures. Then gave he order to a painter for his device, which was a plough (with the oxen loosed from it), a sword (with a great many of arms[3] and legs cut off), and lastly, a great army of pen and inkhorns, and books. Neither did he stick to tell the secret of his intent, which was that he had left off the plough to do such bloody deeds with his sword as many inkhorns and books should be employed about the historifying of them. And being asked why he set no word unto it, he said that was indeed like the painter that sayeth in his picture, 'Here is the dog, and there[4] is the hare' – and with that, he laughed so perfectly as was great consolation to the beholders. Yet remembering that Miso would not take it well at his return if he forgat his duty to her, he caused about, in a border,[5] to be written,

Miso, mine own pigsney, thou shalt hear news of[6] Dametas.

Thus, all things being condignly ordered, with an ill-favoured impatiency[7] he waited until the next morning, that he might make a muster of himself in the island, often asking them that very diligently waited upon him whether it were not pity that such a coward as Clinias should set his runaway feet upon the face of the earth. But as he was by divers principal young gentlemen (to his no small glory) lifted up on horseback, comes me a page of Amphialus, who with humble smiling reverence delivered a letter unto him from Clinias – whom Amphialus had brought to this, first, with persuasions

---

[1] him by the] him that by 93 [2] nor *Cm, 93*: or *90* [3] many of arms *Cm*: many arms *90*; number of arms *93* [4] there *Cm, 93*: here *90* [5] about, in a border] in a border about *93* [6] of *Cm, 93*: o' *90* [7] impatiency] impatience *Cm, 13*

that for certain, if he did accept the combat, Dametas would never dare to appear, and that then the honour should be his; but principally, threatening him that if he refused it he would turn him out of the town to be put to death for a traitor by Basilius; so as the present fear (ever to a coward most terrible) of being turned out of the town made him though full unwillingly undertake the other fear, wherein he had some show of hope that Dametas might hap either to be sick, or not to have the courage to perform the matter.

But when Dametas heard the name of Clinias, very aptly suspecting what the matter might be, he bad the page carry back his letter, like a naughty boy as he was, for he was in no humour, he told him, of reading letters. But Dametas' friend, first persuading him that for certain it was some submission, took upon him so much boldness as to open his letter, and to read it aloud, in this sort:

'Filthy drivel (unworthy to have thy name set in any letter by a soldier's hand written), could thy wretched heart think it was timorousness that made Clinias suspend a while his answer? No, caitiff, no! It was but as a ram, which goes back to return with the greater force. Know therefore that thou shalt no sooner appear (appear now, if thou darest!) – I say, thou shalt no sooner appear in the island (O happy thou, if thou do not appear!) but that I will come upon thee with all my force, and cut thee in pieces – mark what I say – joint after joint, to the eternal terror of all presumptuous villains. Therefore look what thou doost, for I tell thee, horrible smart and pain shall be thy lot if thou wilt needs be so foolish, I having given thee no such cause, as to meet with me.'

These terrible words Clinias used, hoping they would give a cooling to the heat of Dametas' courage – and so indeed they did that he did groan to hear the thundering of those threatenings; and when the gentleman had ended the reading of them, Dametas told them that, in his opinion, he thought his[1] answer came too late, and that, therefore, he might very well go and disarm himself, especially considering the other had in courteous manner warned him not to come. But they, having him now on horseback, led him unto[2] the ferry, and so into the island, the clashing of his own armour striking miserable fear into him, and in his mind thinking great unkindness in his friend that he had brought him to a matter so contrary to his complexion.

There stayed he but a little (the gentlemen that came with him teaching him how to use his sword and lance, while he cast his eye about to see which way he might run away), cursing all islands in[3] being evil situated, when Clinias with a brave sound of trumpets landed at the other end – who came

---

[1] thought his] thought this 93   [2] unto] on to *Cm*; into 13   [3] in] for 93

all the way debating with himself what he had deserved of Amphialus to drive him to those inconveniences. Sometimes his wit made him bethink himself what was best to be done, but fear did so corrupt his wit that, whatsoever he thought was best, he still found danger therein (fearfulness, contrary to all other vices, making him think the better of another, the worse he found himself), rather imagining in himself what words he would use if he were overcome to get his life of Dametas, than how to overcome, whereof he could think with no patience. But oftentimes (looking to the earth, pitifully complaining that a man of such sufficiency as he thought himself should in his best years be swallowed up by so base an element) fain he would have prayed – but he had not heart enough to have confidence in prayer, the glittering of the armour and sounding of the trumpets giving such an assault to the weak-breach of his false senses that he grew, from the degree of fear, to an amazement not, almost, to know what he did; till two judges chosen for the purpose making the trumpets cease, and taking the oath of those champions that they came without guile or witchcraft, set them at wonted distance one from the other.

Then the trumpets sounding, Dametas' horse, used to such causes – when he thought least of the matter – started out so lustily that Dametas was jogged back with head and body, and pulling withal his bridle-hand. The horse that was tender of mouth made half a stop and fell to bounding, so that Dametas threw away his lance and with both his hands held by the pommel, the horse half running, half leaping – till he met with Clinias, who fearing he should miss his rest, had put his staff therein before he began his career – neither would he then have begun but that at the trumpets' warning one that stood behind strake on his horse – who running swiftly, the wind took such hold of his staff that it crossed quite over his breast, and in that sort gave a flat bastinado to Dametas, who half out of his saddle, went near to his old occupation of digging the earth – but with the crest of his helmet.

Clinias, when he was past him, not knowing what he had done but fearing lest Dametas were at his back, turned with a wide turn; and seeing him on the ground, he thought then was his time, or never, to tread him under his horse's feet, and withal if he could, hurt him with his lance – which had not broken, the encounter was so easy. But putting forth his horse, what with the falling of the staff too low before the legs of the horse, and the coming upon Dametas who was then scrambling up, the horse fell over and over and lay upon Clinias – which Dametas (who was gotten up) perceiving, drew out his sword, prying which way he might best come to kill Clinias behind. But the horse that lay upon him kept such a pawing with his feet that Dametas durst not approach but very leisurely; so as the horse being lusty gat up, and withal fell to strike and leap, that Dametas started up[1] a good way and gave Clinias time to rise – but so bruised in body and broken in heart that he meant to yield himself to mercy; and with that intent drew out his sword, intending when he came nearer to present the pommel of it to Dametas.

But Dametas, when he saw him come with his sword drawn (nothing conceiving of any such intent), went back as fast as his back and heels would[2] lead him. But as Clinias found that, he began to think a possibility in the victory, and therefore followed, with the cruel haste of a prevailing coward laying upon Dametas – who did nothing but cry out to him, to hold his hand; sometimes, that he was dead; sometimes, that he would complain to Basilius; but still bare the blows ungratefully, going back – till at length, he came into the water with one of his feet. But then a new fear, of drowning, took him; so that not daring to go back, nor to deliberate – the blows still so lighted on him, nor to yield – because of the cruel threatenings of Clinias, fear (being come to the extremity) fell to a madness of despair; so that winking, as hard as ever he could he began to deal some blows, and, his arm being used to a flail in his youth, laid them on so thick that Clinias now began with lamentable eyes to see his own blood come out in many places – and before he had lost half an ounce, finding in himself that he fainted, cried out aloud to Dametas that he yielded.

'Throw away thy sword then!' said Dametas, 'and I will save thee!' – but still laying on as fast as he could.

Clinias straight obeyed, and humbly craved mercy, telling him his sword was gone. Then Dametas first opened his eyes; and seeing him indeed unweaponed, made him stand a good way off from it; and then willed him to lie down upon the earth as flat as he could. Clinias obeyed. And Dametas, who never could think himself safe till Clinias were dead, began to think with himself that if he strake at him with his sword, if he did not kill him at the first blow, that then Clinias might hap to arise and revenge himself. Therefore he thought best to kneel down upon him, and with a great whittle he had, having disarmed his head, to cut his throat – which he had used so with calves as he had no small dexterity in it. But while he sought for his knife which under his armour he could not well find out, and that Clinias lay with so sheepish[3] a countenance[4] as if he would have been glad to have his throat cut for fear of more pain, the judges came in and took Dametas from off him, telling him he did against the law of arms, having promised life if he threw away his sword. Dametas was loath to consent – till they sware they would not suffer him to fight any more when he was up. And then, more

---

[1] up] back 93   [2] would] could 93   [3] sheepish] sleepish *Cm*, 98   [4] countenance] quietness 93

forced than persuaded, he let him rise, crowing over him, and warning him to take heed how he dealt any more with any that came of his father's kinred.

But thus this combat of cowards being finished, Dametas was with much mirth and melody received into the camp as victorious, never a page there failing to wait upon this triumph. But[1] Clinias, though he wanted heart to prevent shame, yet he wanted not wit to feel shame – not so much repining at it for the abhorring of shame as for the discommodities that, to them that are shamed, ensue, for well he deemed it would be a great bar to practice[2] and a pulling on of injuries when men needed not care how they used him; insomuch that Clinias, finding himself the scorning-stock of every company, fell with repining to hate the cause thereof – and hate in a coward's heart could set itself no other limits but death; which purpose was well egged on by representing unto himself what danger he lately was in, which still kept no less ugly figure in his mind than when it was present. And quickly, even in his dissembling countenance, might be discerned a concealed grudge: for though he forced in himself a far more diligent officiousness toward Amphialus than ever before, yet a leering eye upon the one side at him, a countenance still framed to smiling before him – how little cause soever there was of smiling, and grumbling behind him at any of his commandments, with an uncertain manner of behaviour (his words coming out, though full of flattery, yet slowly and hoarsely pronounced), might well have blazed what arms his false heart bare.

But despised because of his cowardliness, and not marked because despised, he had the freer scope of practice, which he did the more desperately enter into because the daily dangers Amphialus did submit himself into made Clinias assuredly look for his overthrow – and for his own, consequently, if he did not redeem his former treason to Basilius with a more treasonable falsehood toward Amphialus. His chief care therefore was to find out, among all sorts of Amphialus,[3] whom either like fear, tediousness of the siege, or discontentment of some unsatisfied ambition, would make apt to dig in the same mine that he did; and some already of wealthy, weary folks, and unconstant youths who had not found such sudden success as they had promised themselves, he had made stoop to the[4] lure.

But of none he made so good account as of Artesia (sister to the late-slain Ismenus, and the chief of six[5] maids who had trained out the princesses to their banquet of misery), so much did the sharpness of her wit countervail, as he thought, any other defects of her sex; for she had undertaken that

---

[1] triumph. But *Cm, 93*: triumph. Chap. 14. Clinias, a sly traitor; Artesia, his malcontent accomplice; Zelmane's passions; her practice with Artesia; the complot revealed to the disliking sisters, bewrayed by Pamela. But *90*   [2] to practice] to his practice *93*   [3] sorts of Amphialus] sorts of [*blank space left for name*] *Cm*; sorts of the Amphialians *93*   [4] the] his *93*   [5] of six] of the six *93*

dangerous practice by the persuasion of Cecropia, who assured her that the two princesses should be made away, and then Amphialus would marry her – which she was the apter to believe by some false persuasion her glass had given her of her own incomparable excellencies, and by the great favour she knew he bare to her brother Ismenus, which, like a self-flattering woman, she conceived was done for her sake. But when she had achieved her attempt, and that she found the princesses were so far from their intended death as that the one of them was like to be her sovereign, and that neither her service had won of Amphialus much more than ordinary favour, nor her over-large offering herself (to a mind otherwise owed) had obtained a looked-for acceptation, disdain to be disdained, spite of a frustrate hope, and perchance[1] unquenched lust-grown rage, made her unquiet thoughts find no other rest but malice, which was increased by the death of her brother, whom she judged neither succoured against Philanax, nor revenged upon Philanax.

But all these coals were well blown by the company she especially kept with Zelmane, all this time of her imprisonment. For finding her presence uncheerful to the mourning Philoclea and contemned of the high-hearted Pamela, she spent her time most with Zelmane – who though at the first hardly brooking the instrument of their misery, learning cunning in the school of adversity, in time framed herself to yield her acceptable entertainment. For Zelmane, when she had by that unexpected mischief her body imprisoned, her valure overmastered, her wit beguiled, her desires barred, her love eclipsed; assured of evil, fearing worse; able to know Philoclea's misfortune and not able to succour her, she was a great while before the greatness of her heart could descend to sorrow, but rather rose, boiling up in spite and disdain, reason hardly making courage believe that it was distressed – but as if the walls would be afraid of her, so would her looks shoot out threatening upon them. But the fetters of servitude (growing heavier with wearing) made her feel her case, and the little prevailing of repining. And then grief gat seat[2] in her softened mind, making sweetness of past comforts by due title claim tears of present discomfort,[3] and, since her fortune made her able to help as little as anybody, yet to be able to wail as much as anybody, solitary sorrow, with a continual circle in herself, going out at her own mouth, to come in again at her own ears. Then was the name of Philoclea graved in the glass windows, and, by the foolish idolatry of affection, no sooner written than adored; and no sooner adored than pitied, all the wonted praises she was wont to give unto her being now but figures of rhetoric to amplify the injuries of misfortune, against which, being alone,

---

[1] perchance *Cm*, 93: perchauce 90 [2] gat seat] gat a seat 93 [3] discomfort] discomforts 93

she would often make invective declamations methodized only by raging sorrow.

But when Artesia did insinuate herself into her acquaintance, she gave the government of her courage to wit, and was content to familiarize herself with her, so much the rather as that she perceived in her certain flaws of ill-concealed discontentment – insomuch that when Zelmane would sweeten her mouth with the praises of the sisters (especially setting forth their noble gratefulness in never forgetting well-intended services, and invoking the justice of the gods not to suffer such treasures to be wrongfully hidden), and sometimes with a kind unkindness charging Artesia that she had been abused to abuse so worthy persons, Artesia, though falsely, would protest that she had been beguiled in it, never meaning other matter than recreation. And yet withal, by alleging how ungratefully she was dealt with, it was easy to be seen it was the unrewarding, and not the evil-employing her service, which grieved her.

But Zelmane, using her own bias to bowl near the mistress of her own thoughts, was content to lend her belief and withal to magnify her desert, if willingly she would deliver whom unwillingly she had imprisoned, leaving no argument which might tickle ambition or flatter revenge; so that Artesia, pushed forward by Clinias and drawn onward by Zelmane, bound herself to that practice, wherein Zelmane for her part desired no more but to have armour and weapons brought into her chamber, not doubting therewith to perform anything, how impossible soever, which longing love can persuade and invincible valour dare promise. But Clinias, whose faith could never comprehend the mysteries of courage, persuaded Artesia, while he by corruption had drawn the guard of one gate to open it (when he would appoint the time) to the enemy, that she should empoison Amphialus, which she might the easier do because she herself had used to make the broths when Amphialus, either wearied or wounded, did use such diet.

And all things already were ready to be put in execution, when they thought best to break the matter with the two excellent sisters, not doubting of their consent in a thing so behoofeful to themselves – their reasons being that the princesses, knowing their service, might be sure to preserve them from the fury of the entering soldiers (whereof Clinias, even so, could scarcely be sufficiently certain) and withal making them privy to their action to bind them afterwards to admonished[1] gratefulness towards them. They went therefore, at one time when they knew them to be alone, Clinias to Philoclea and Artesia to Pamela. And Clinias with no few words did set forth what an exploit was intended for her service; but Philoclea (in whose clear

---

[1] admonished *Cm*: acknowledge *90*; a promised *93*

mind treason could find no hiding-place) told him that she would be glad if he could persuade her cousin to deliver her, and that she would never forget his service therein, but that she desired him to lay down any such way of mischief, for that, for her part, she would rather yield to perpetual imprisonment than consent to the destroying her cousin, who, she knew, loved her, though wronged her.

This unlooked-for answer amazed Clinias, so that he had no other remedy in his mind but to kneel down to Philoclea and beseech her to keep it secret, considering that the intention was for her service, and vowing, since she misliked it, to proceed no further therein. She comforted him with promise of silence, which she performed. But that little availed; for Artesia having in like sort opened this device to Pamela, she (in whose mind virtue governed with the sceptre of knowledge) hating so horrible a wickedness, and straight judging what was fit to do, 'Wicked woman!' said she, 'whose unrepenting heart can find no way to amend treason but by treason, now the time is come that thy wicked[1] wiles have caught thyself in thine own net! As for me, let the gods dispose of me as shall please them – but sure, it shall be no such way, nor way-leader, by which I will come to liberty!'

This she spake something with a louder voice than she was wont to use, so as Cecropia heard the noise (who was, sooner than Artesia imagined she would, come up to bring Pamela to a window where she might see a notable skirmish happened in the camp, as she thought, among themselves); and being a cunning fisher in troubled waters, straight found by their voices and gestures there was some matter of consequence, which she desired Pamela to tell her.

'Ask of her!' said Pamela. 'And learn to know that who do falsehood to their superiors, teach falsehood to their inferiors.'

More she would not say. But Cecropia taking away the each-way-guilty Artesia, with fear of torture gat of her the whole practice, so as Zelmane was the more closely imprisoned, and Clinias with the rest of his corrupted mates (according to their merits) executed; for as for Artesia, she was but locked up in her chamber, Amphialus not consenting, for the love he bare Ismenus,[2] that further punishment should be laid upon her.

But[3] the noise they heard in the camp was occasionable by[4] the famous Prince Anaxius, nephew to the giant Euardes whom Pyrocles slew: a prince of body exceedingly strong, in arms so skilful and fortunate as no man was thought to excel him, of courage that knew not how to fear – parts worthy

---

[1] wicked] wretched 93   [2] bare Ismenus] bare to Ismenus 93   [3] her. But *Cm*, 93: her. Chap. 15. Proud Anaxius breaketh through the besiegers; his welcome by Amphialus; the music and lovesong made to Philoclea; the sally of Anaxius, and his, on the Basilians, backed by Amphialus, beaten back by three unknown knights; the retrait of both sides. But 90   [4] occasionable by *Cm*: occasioned by 90; occasion of 93, 98; by occasion of 13

praise, if they had not been guided by pride and followed by unjustice; for by a strange composition of mind, there was no man more tenderly sensible in anything offered to himself which, in the farthest-fet construction, might be wrested to the name of wrong; no man that in his own actions could worse distinguish between valour and violence; so proud as he could not abstain from a Thraso-like boasting, and yet (so unlucky a lodging his virtues had gotten) he would never boast more than he would accomplish; falsely accounting an unflexible anger a courageous constancy; esteeming fear and astonishment righter causes of admiration than love and honour.

This man had four sundry times fought with Amphialus, but Mars had been so unpartial an arbiter that neither side gate advantage of the other. But in the end it happened that Anaxius found Amphialus, unknown, in a great danger, and saved his life; whereupon loving his own benefit, began to favour him, so much the more as, thinking so well of himself, he could not choose but like him whom he found a match for himself – which at last grew to as much friendship towards him as could by a proud heart be conceived; so as in this travel (seeking Pyrocles, to be revenged of his uncle's death), hearing of this siege (never taking pains to examine the quarrel, like a man whose will was his god and his hand his law), taking with him his two brothers (men accounted little inferior to himself in martial matters) and two hundred chosen horsemen (with whom he thought himself able to conquer the world, yet commanding the rest of his forces to follow), he himself upon such an unexpected suddenness entered in upon the back of Basilius that many with great unkindness took their death, not knowing why nor how they were so murdered. There if ever did he make known the wonderfulness of his force. But the valiant and faithful Philanax with well-governed speed made such head against him as would have showed how soon courage falls in the ditch which hath not the eye of wisdom – but that Amphialus at the same time issued out; and winning with an abundance of courage one of the sconces which Basilius had builded, made way for his friend Anaxius, with great loss of both sides, but especially of the Basilians, such notable monuments had those two swords especially left of their masters' redoubted worthiness.

There, with the respect fit to his estate, the honour due to his worthiness, and the kindness which accompanies friendship made fast by interchanged benefits, did Amphialus enforce himself (as much as in a besieged town he could) to make Anaxius know that his succour was not so needful as his presence grateful; for causing the streets and houses of the town to witness his welcome (making both soldiers and magistrates in their countenances to show their gladness of him), he led him to his mother, whom he besought to entertain him with no less love and kindness than as one who once had saved her son's life, and now came to save both life and honour.

'Tush!' said Anaxius speaking aloud, looking upon his brothers, 'I am only sorry there are not half a dozen kings more about you, that what Anaxius can do might be the better manifested.'

His brothers smiled, as though he had over-modestly spoken, far underneath the pitch of his power. Then was he disarmed, at the earnest request of Amphialus (for Anaxius boiled with desire to issue out upon the enemies, persuading himself that the sun should not be set before he had overthrown them); and having reposed himself, Amphialus asked him whether he would visit the young princesses.

But Anaxius whispered him in the ear, 'In truth,' said he, 'dear friend Amphialus, though I am none of those that love to speak of themselves, I never came yet in company of ladies but that they fell in love with me; and I, that in my heart scorn them as a peevish, paltry sex, not worthy to communicate with my virtues, would not do you the wrong, since, as I hear, you do debase yourself so much as to affect them.'

The courteous Amphialus could have been angry with him for those words, but knowing his humour, suffered him to dance to his own music, and gave himself to entertain both him and his brothers with as cheerful a manner as could issue from a mind whom unlucky love had filled with melancholy, for to Anaxius he yielded the direction of all: he gave the watchword; and if any grace were granted, the means were to be made to Anaxius; and that night, when supper was ended (wherein Amphialus would needs himself wait upon him), he caused in boats upon the lake an excellent music to be ordered – which, though Anaxius might conceive was for his honour, yet indeed he was but the brickwall to convey it to the ears of the beloved Philoclea.

The music was of cornets, whereof one answering the other (with a sweet emulation striving for the glory of music) and striking upon the smooth face of the quiet lake, was then delivered up to the castle-walls, which with a proud reverberation spreading it into the air, it seemed before the harmony came to the ear that it had enriched itself in travel, the nature of those places adding melody to that melodious instrument. And when a while that instrument had made a brave proclamation, to all unpossessed minds, of attention, an excellent consort straight followed of five viols and as many voices, which all (being but orators of their master's passions) bestowed this song upon her that thought upon another matter:

The fire, to see my woes,[1] for anger burneth;
The air, in rain, for my[2] affliction weepeth;
The sea, to ebb, for grief his flowing turneth;
The earth, with pity dull, his[3] centre keepeth[4];
    Fame is with wonder blazed;
    Time runs away for sorrow;
    Place standeth still, amazed
To see my night[5] of evils,[6] which[7] hath[8] no morrow.
      Alas, alonely[9] she no pity taketh
      To know[10] my miseries;[11] but chaste and cruel,
      My fall her glory maketh –
      Yet still her eyes give to my flames their[12] fuel.

Fire, burn me quite[13] till sense of burning leave me[14];
Air, let me draw thy breath no more[15] in anguish;
Sea, drowned[16] in thee, of tedious life bereave me;
Earth, take this earth wherein my[17] spirits languish;
    Fame, say I was not born;
    Time, haste my dying[18] hour;
    Place, see my grave uptorn;
Fire, air, sea, earth, fame, time, place, show your power.
      Alas, from all their[19] helps[20] I am exiled,
      For hers am I,[21] and death fears her displeasure.
      Fie,[22] death! Thou art beguiled:
      Though I be hers, she makes of me[23] no treasure.

But Anaxius, seeming aweary before it was ended, told Amphialus that for his part he liked no music but the neighing of horses, the sound of trumpets, and the cries of yielding persons; and therefore desired that the next morning they should issue upon the same place where they had entered that day, not doubting to make them quickly aweary of being the besiegers of Anaxius. Amphialus, who had no whit less courage, though nothing blown up with pride, willingly condescended.

---

[1] woes] wrongs *St, Bo, Cl, Hy, Ra, Bn, Fr, 93, 98* (CS); wrong *Dd*   [2] my] mine *Ra, Bn*   [3] his] the *Dd, Hn, Hy, Ra, Bn, Fr, 98* (CS)   [4] keepeth] *St, Bo, Cl, Hn, Hy, Ra, Bn, Fr, 93, 98* (CS): turneth *90*; keeps *Dd*   [5] night] nights *Ra, Bn*   [6] evils *St, Bo, Cl, Dd, 93, 98* (CS): woes *Hn*; evil *Hy, Bn*; grief *Ra*; ill *Fr*; ills *90*   [7] which] that *Hn, Ra, Fr*   [8] hath] have *Bo, Hy, Bn*   [9] alonely] onely *Hy, Bn*; a lovely *98* (CS)   [10] know] see *Hn, Ra, Bn*   [11] miseries] mysteries *Hn*; misery *Hy, Ra*   [12] their] the *Cl, Fr*; onely *Hn*   [13] quite] quick *Hy, Bn*   [14] leave me] leave *Ra, Bn*   [15] thy breath no more] no more thy breath *St, Bo, Dd, 98* (CS), *Fr*; no more my breath *Cl, Hy*; no more this breath *Hn*; my breath no more *Ra, Bn*   [16] drowned] drowned me *Hy*; drown me *Ra, Bn*   [17] my] these *Hy, Ra, Bn*   [18] haste my dying] draw my dismal *Hy, Bn*   [19] their] your *Cl, Ra*   [20] helps *Bo, Dd, Hn, Hy, Ra, 93, 98, Bn, Fr*: help *St, Cl, 90, 98* (CS)   [21] hers am I] I am hers *Hn*; hers I am *Hy, Ra*   [22] Fie] O *Hy, Ra, Bn*   [23] she makes of me *Bo, Dd, Hn, Hy, Ra, 93, 98* (CS), *Bn*: she sets by me *St, Cl, 90*; of me she makes *Fr*

And so, the next morning giving false alarum to the other side of the camp, Amphialus at Anaxius' earnest request staying within the town to see it guarded, Anaxius and his brethren, Lycurgus and Zoilus, sallied out with the best chosen men. But Basilius having been the last day somewhat unprovided, now had better fortified the overthrown sconce, and so well had prepared everything for defence that it was impossible for any valour from within to prevail. Yet things were performed by Anaxius beyond the credit of the credulous, for thrice, valiantly followed by his brothers, did he set up his banner upon the rampire of the enemy, though thrice again by the multitude and advantage of the place, but especially by the coming of three valiant knights, he were driven down again.

Numbers there were that day whose deaths and overthrows were executed[1] by the well-known sword of Anaxius, but the rest, by the length of time and injury of historians have been wrapped up in dark forgetfulness: only Tressennius is spoken of, because when all abandoned the place, he only made head to Anaxius; till having lost one of his legs, yet not lost the heart of fighting, Lycurgus, second brother to Anaxius, cruelly murthered him – Anaxius himself disdaining any further to deal with him. But so far had Anaxius at the third time prevailed that now the Basilians began to let their courage descend to their feet, Basilius and Philanax in vain striving, with reverence of authority, to bridle the flight of astonishment, and to teach fear discretion; so that Amphialus, seeing victory show such a flattering countenance to him, came out with all his force, hoping that day to end the siege.

But that fancy altered quickly by the sudden coming to the other side of three knights, whereof the one was in white armour, the other in green, and the third, by his black armour and device, straight known to be the notable knight who the first day had given fortune so short a stop with his notable deeds and fighting hand to hand with the[2] deemed-invincible Amphialus; for the very cowards no sooner saw him but, as borrowing some of his spirit, they went like young eagles to the prey under the wing of their dam; for the three adventurers, not content to keep them from their rampire, leapt down among them and entered into a brave combat with the three valiant brothers.

But to whether side fortune would have been partial could not be determined, for the Basilians, lightened with the beams of these strangers' valure, followed so thick that the Amphialians were glad with some haste to retire to the walls-ward; though Anaxius, neither reason, fear, nor example could make him assuage the fury of his fight, until one of the Basilians, unworthy to have his name registered since he did it cowardly, sideward, when he least

---

[1] executed] excused 93   [2] hand with the] hand the 93

looked that way almost cut off one of his legs, so as he fell down, blaspheming heaven that all the influences thereof had power to overthrow him – and there death would have seized of his proud heart, but that Amphialus took in hand the Black Knight while some of his soldiers conveyed away Anaxius, so requiting life for life unto him. And for the love and example of Amphialus, the fight began to enter into a new fit of heat, when Basilius, that thought enough to be done for that day, caused retrait to be sounded, fearing lest his men following over-earnestly[1] might be the loss of those excellent knights, whom he desired to know.

The knights, as soon as they heard the retrait, though they were eagerly set, knowing that courage without discipline is nearer beastliness than manhood, drew back their swords, though hungry of more blood – especially the Black Knight, who knowing Amphialus, could not refrain to tell him that this was the second time he escaped out of his hands, but that he would shortly bring him a bill of all the former accounts. Amphialus seeing it fit to retire also, most of his people being hurt both in bodies and hearts, withdrew himself – with so well-seated a resolution (that it was as far from anger as from dismayedness) answering no other to the Black Knight's threats, but that when he brought him his account he should find a good paymaster.

But the[2] fight being ceased and each side withdrawn within their strengths, Basilius sent Philanax to entertain the strange knights, and to bring them unto him that he might acknowledge what honour was due to their virtue; but they excused themselves, desiring to be known first by their deeds before their names should accuse their unworthiness. And though the other replied according as they deserved, yet finding that unwelcome courtesy is a degree of injury, he suffered them to retire themselves to a tent of their own without the camp, where they kept themselves secret, Philanax himself being called away to another strange knight – strange not only by the unlookedforness of his coming, but by the strange manner of his coming; for he had before him four damosels, and so many behind him, all upon palfreys, and all apparelled in mourning weeds; each of them, servant[3] of each side, with like liveries of sorrow; himself in an armour all painted over with such a cunning of shadow that it represented a gaping sepulchre. The furniture of his horse was all of cypress branches, wherewith in old time they were wont to dress graves. His bases, which he ware so long as they came almost to his ankle, were embrodered only with black worms, which seemed to crawl up and down, as ready already to devour him. In his shield for

---

[1] over-earnestly *Cm, 93*: over-hastily *90*   [2] paymaster. But the *Cm*: paymaster. Chap. 16. The unknown knights will not be known; the Knight of the Tomb's show, and challenge accepted by Amphialus; their fight, with the death of the Tomb-Knight; who that knight was; the dying speeches, and the lamentable funerals. The *90*; paymaster. The *93*   [3] servant *Cm*: servants *90*; a servant *93*

impresa he had a beautiful child, but having two heads – whereon,[1] the one showed that it was already dead; the other alive, but in that case necessarily looking for death. The word was 'No way to be rid from death, but by death.'

This Knight of the Tomb (for so the soldiers termed him) sent to Basilius to demand leave to send in a damosel into the town to call out Amphialus, according as beforetime some others had done; which being granted, as glad any would undertake the charge which nobody else in that camp was known willing to do, the damosel went in. And having with tears sobbed out a brave challenge to Amphialus from the Knight of the Tomb, Amphialus (honourably entertaining the gentlewoman and desiring to know the knight's name, which the doleful gentlewoman would not discover) accepted the challenge, only desiring the gentlewoman to say thus much to the strange knight from him, that, if his mind were like to his title, there were more cause of affinity than enmity between them.

And therefore presently, according as he was wont, as soon as he perceived the Knight of the Tomb (with his damosels and judge) was come into the island, he also went over in accustomed manner; and yet, for the courtesy of his nature, desired to speak with him. But the Knight of the Tomb (with silence, and drawing his horse back) showed no will to hear nor speak, but with lance on thigh made him know it was fit for him to go to the other end of the career; whence (waiting the start of the unkown knight) he likewise made his spurs claim haste of his horse. But when his staff was in his rest, coming down to meet with the knight, now very near him, he perceived the knight had missed his rest; wherefore the courteous Amphialus would not let his lance descend, but with a gallant grace ran over the head of his therein-friended enemy. And having stopped his horse (and with the turning of him, blessed his sight with the window where he thought Philoclea might stand), he perceived the knight had lighted from his horse and thrown away his staff, angry with his misfortune, as having[2] missed his rest, and drawn his sword to make that supply his fellow's fault. He also lighted and drew his sword, esteeming victory by advantage rather robbed than purchased. And so, the other coming eagerly toward him, he with his shield out and sword aloft with more bravery than anger drew unto him – and straight made their swords speak for them a pretty while with equal fierceness.

But Amphialus, to whom the earth brought forth few matches, having both much more skill to choose the places, and more force to work upon the chosen, had already made many windows in his armour for death to come in at when (in the[3] nobleness of his nature abhorring to make the punishment

---

[1] whereon] whereof 90 (*uncorr.*)   [2] as having] as of having 93   [3] in the *Cm*, 93: in 90

overgo the offence) he stepped a little back, and withal, 'Sir Knight,' said he, 'you may easily see that it pleaseth God to favour my cause. Employ your valour against them that wish you hurt. For my part, I have not deserved hate of you.'

'Thou liest, false traitor!' said the other, with an angry but weak voice.

But Amphialus, in whom abused kindness became spiteful rage, 'Ah, barbarous wretch!' said he, 'only courageous in discourtesy! Thou shalt soon see whether thy tongue hath betrayed thy heart or no!' – and with that, redoubling his blows, gave him a great wound upon his neck; and closing with him, overthrew him, and with the[1] fall thrust him mortally into the body; and with that, went to pull off his helmet with intention to make him give himself the lie for having so said, or to cut off his head.

But the head-piece was no sooner off but that there fell about the shoulders of the overcome knight the treasure of fair golden hair, which, with the face soon known by the badge of excellency, witnessed that it was Parthenia, the unfortunately virtuous wife of Argalus – her beauty then, even in despite of the past sorrow, or coming death, assuring all beholders that it was nothing short of perfection: for her exceeding fair eyes having with continual weeping gotten a little redness about them; her roundy, sweetly swelling lips a little trembling, as though they kissed their neighbour, death; in her cheeks, the whiteness striving by little and little to get upon the rosiness of them; her neck (a neck indeed of alablaster) displaying the wound which with most dainty blood laboured to drown his own beauties, so as here was a river of purest red, there, an island of perfittest white, each giving lustre to the other – with the sweet countenance, God knows, full of an unaffected languishing. Though these things to a grossly-conceiving sense might seem disgraces, yet indeed were they but apparelling beauty in a new fashion, which, all looked upon thorough the spectacles of pity, did even increase the lines of her natural fairness, so as Amphialus was astonished with grief, compassion, and shame, detesting his fortune that made him unfortunate in victory. Therefore putting off his head-piece and gauntlet, kneeling down unto her, and with tears testifying his sorrow, he offered his by-himself-accursed hands to help her, protesting his life and power to be ready to do her honour.

But Parthenia, who had inward messengers of the desired death's approach; looking upon him – and straight turning away her feeble sight, as from a delightless object; drawing out her words which her breath, loath to depart[2] from so sweet a body, did faintly deliver, 'Sir,' said she, 'I pray you – if prayers have place in enemies – to let my maids take my body, untouched by

---

[1] with the] in the 93   [2] depart *Cm*, 93: part 90

you. The only honour I now desire, by your means, is that I have no honour of you. Argalus made no such bargain with you that the hands which killed him should help me. I have of them – and I do not only pardon you, but thank you for it – the service which I desired. There rests nothing now but that I go live with him, since whose death I have done nothing but die.'

Then pausing; and a little fainting; and again coming to herself, 'O sweet life! Welcome!' said she. 'Now feel I the bands untied of the cruel death which so long hath held me. And, O life! O death! answer for me that my thoughts have not so much as in a dream tasted any comfort, since they were deprived of Argalus. I come, my Argalus! I come! And, O God, hide my faults in thy mercies; and grant, as I feel thou doost grant, that, in thy eternal love, we may love each other eternally. And this, O Lord – '. But there Atropos cut off her sentence; for with that, casting up both eyes and hands to the skies, the noble soul departed – one might well assure himself to heaven, which left the body in so heavenly a demeanour.

But Amphialus, with a heart oppressed with grief because of her request, withdrew himself. But the judges, as full of pity, had been all this while disarming her, and her gentlewomen with lamentable cries labouring to stanch the remediless wounds; and a while she was dead before they perceived it, death being able to divide the soul, but not the beauty, from that body. But when the infallible tokens of death assured them of their loss, one of[1] the women would have killed herself, but that the squire of Amphialus perceiving it, by force held her; others that had as strong passions[2] though weaker resolution fell to cast dust upon their heads, to tear their garments – all falling upon and[3] crying upon their sweet mistress, as if their cries could persuade the soul to leave the celestial happiness, to come again into the elements of sorrow: one time, calling to remembrance her virtue, chasteness, sweetness, goodness to them; another time, accursing themselves[4] that they had obeyed her, they having been deceived by her words, who assured them that it was revealed unto her that she should have her heart's desire in the battle against Amphialus, which they wrongly understood; then kissing her cold hands and feet, weary of the world, since she was gone, who was their world.

The very heavens seemed with a cloudy countenance to lour at the loss, and fame itself, though by nature glad to tell of rare[5] accidents, yet could not choose but deliver it in lamentable accents. And in such sort went it quickly all over the camp, and as if the air had been infected with sorrow, no heart was so hard but was subject to that contagion, the rareness of the accident

---

[1] one of *Cm, 90 (catchword), 93*: of *90*   [2] passions] passion *93*   [3] upon and] upon the earth and *93*
[4] themselves *Cm, 93*: themselves *90*   [5] of rare *Cm*: rare *90*; such rare *93*

matching together the rarely matched together – pity with admiration. Basilius himself came forth, and brought forth the¹ fair Gynecia with him – who was gone² into the camp under colour of visiting her husband and hearing of her daughters, but indeed, Zelmane was the saint to which her pilgrimage was intended, cursing, envying, blessing, and in her heart kissing the walls which imprisoned her. But both they, with Philanax and the rest of the principal nobility, went out to make honour triumph over death, conveying³ that excellent body (whereto Basilius himself would needs lend⁴ his shoulder) to a church a mile from the camp, where the valiant Argalus lay entombed, recommending to that sepulchre the blessed relics of faithful and virtuous love, giving order for the making of marble images to represent them, and each way enriching the tomb, upon which Basilius himself caused this epitaph to be written:

> His⁵ being was in her alone,
> And he not being, she was none.
>   They joyed one joy; one grief they grieved;
>   One love they loved; one life they lived.
>   The hand was one; one was the sword
>   That did his death, her death, afford.
> As all the rest, so now the stone
> That tombs the two is justly one.
>   Argalus and Parthenia.⁶

And then,⁷ with eyes full of tears and mouths full of her praises, returned they to the camp with more and more hate against Amphialus, who (poor gentleman) had therefore greater portion of woe than any of them – for that courteous heart, which would have grieved but to have heard the like adventure, was rent with remembering himself to be the author, so that his wisdom could not so far temper his passion, but that he took his sword (counted the best in the world, which with much blood he had once conquered of a mighty giant) and brake it into many pieces – which afterwards he had good cause to repent – saying that neither it was worthy to serve the noble exercise of chivalry, nor any other worthy to feel that sword which had stroken so excellent a lady; and withal banishing all cheerfulness of his countenance, he returned home where he gate him to his bed, not so much to rest his restless mind as to avoid all company, the sight whereof was tedious unto him.

---

¹ forth the] the *93*   ² gone] come *93*   ³ conveying *Cm, 90 (catchword), 93*: con-/ing *90*   ⁴ lend *Cm, 93*: bend *90*   ⁵ written: His: written *Cm, 90*; written: The Epitaph. His *93*   ⁶ His … Parthenia *93*: *blank space left Cm*; *printed border enclosing blank space 90*   ⁷ And then *Cm*: Chap. 17. The remorse of Amphialus for his last deed, and lasting destiny; his reverent respect in love; his mother's ghosty counsel to a rape. Then *90*; Then *93*

And then melancholy, only rich in unfortunate remembrances, brought before him all the mishaps with which his life had wrestled, taking this not only as a confirming of the former, but a presage of following misery; and to his heart already overcome by sorrowfulness, even trifling misfortunes came to fill up the roll of a grieved memory, labouring only his wits to pierce farther and farther into his own wretchedness. So all[1] that night, in despite of darkness he held his eyes open, and the[2] morning when the light began to restore to each body his colour, then with curtains barred he himself from the enjoying of it, neither willing to feel the comfort of the day nor the ease of the night, until his mother, who never knew what love meant, but only to himward, came to his bedside. And beginning with loving earnestness to lay a kind chiding upon him because he would suffer the weakness of sorrow to conquer the strength of his virtues, he did with a broken, piecemeal speech, as if the tempest of passion unorderly blew out his words, remember the mishaps of his youth; the evils he had been cause of; his rebelling with shame, and that shame increased with shameful accidents; the deaths of Philoxenus and Parthenia – wherein he found himself hated of the ever-ruling powers; but especially, and so especially[3] as the rest seemed nothing when he came to that, his fatal love to Philoclea, to whom he had so governed himself as one that could neither conquer nor yield, being of the one side a slave, and of the other a jailer – and withal almost upbraiding unto his mother the little success of her large-hoping promises, he in effect finding Philoclea nothing mollified, and now himself so cast down as he thought him unworthy of better.

But his mother, as she had plentiful cause, making him see that of his other griefs there was little or no fault in himself, and therefore there ought to be little or no grief in him, when she came to the head of the sore (indeed seeing that she could not[4] patch up her former promises, he taking a desperate deafness to all delaying hopes) she confessed plainly that she could prevail nothing – but the fault was his own, who had marred the young girl by seeking to have that by prayer which he should have taken by authority; that, as it were an absurd cunning to make high ladders to go in a plain way, so was it an untimely and foolish flattery there to beseech where one might command, puffing them up by being besought with such a self-pride of superiority that it was not, forsooth, to be held out, but by a denial.

'O God!' said Amphialus. 'How well I thought my fortune would bring forth this end of your labours! Assure yourself, mother, I will sooner pull out these eyes than they shall look upon the heavenly Philoclea but as upon a heaven whence they have their light, and to which they are subject. If

---

[1] So all] So as all 93   [2] and the] and in the 13 (and in the *corr. to* and the *Cm*)   [3] so especially] so espeically 90 (*uncorr.*)   [4] not] no longer 93

they will pour down any influences of comfort, oh happy I! But if, by the sacrifice of a faithful heart, they will not be called unto me, let me languish, and wither with languishing, and grieve with withering, but never so much as repine with never so much grieving. Mother, O mother! Lust may well be a tyrant, but true love, where it is indeed, it is a servant. Accursed more than I am may I be, if ever I did approach her, but that I freezed as much in a fearful reverence as I burned in a vehement desire. Did ever man's eye look thorough love upon the majesty of virtue shining through beauty, but that he became – as it well became him – a captive? And is it the style of a captive to write, "Our will and pleasure"?'

'Tush, tush, son!' said Cecropia. If you say you love, but withal you fear, you fear lest you should offend. Offend! And how know you that you should offend? Because she doth deny. Deny! Now, by my truth! If your sadness would let me laugh, I could laugh heartily to see that yet you are ignorant that "no" is no negative in a woman's mouth. My son, believe me – a woman, speaking of women: a lover's modesty among us is much more praised than liked – or if we like it, so well we like it that, for marring of his modesty, he shall never proceed further!

'Each virtue hath his time. If you command your soldier to march foremost, and he for courtesy put others before him, would you praise his modesty? Love is your general. He bids you dare. And will Amphialus be a dastard? Let examples serve. Do you think Theseus should ever have gotten Antiope with sighing and crossing his arms? He ravished her – and ravished her that was an Amazon and therefore had gotten a habit of stoutness above the nature of a woman. But having ravished her, he got a child of her – and I say no more, but that, they say, is not gotten without consent of both sides! Iole had her own father killed by Hercules, and herself ravished – by force ravished. And yet, ere long this ravished and unfathered lady could sportfully put on the lion's skin upon her own fair shoulders, and play with the club with her own delicate hands; so easily had she pardoned the ravisher that she could not but delight in those weapons of ravishing. But above all, mark Helen, daughter to Jupiter, who could never brook her mannerly-wooing Menelaus, but disdained his humbleness and loathed his softness. But so well she could like the force of enforcing Paris that for him she could abide what might be abidden. But what? Menelaus takes heart. He recovers her by force; by force carries her home; by force enjoys her – and she, who could never like him for serviceableness, ever after loved him for violence; for what can be more agreeable than upon force to lay the fault of desire, and in one instant to join a dear delight with a just excuse? Or rather, the true cause is (pardon me, O womankind, for revealing to mine own son the truth of this mystery) we think there wants fire where we find no sparkles (at least) of fury.

'Truly, I have known a great lady, long sought by most great, most wise, most beautiful, most valiant persons – never won because they did over-superstitiously¹ solicit her; the same lady, brought under by another inferior to all them, in all those qualities, only because he could use that imperious masterfulness which nature gives to men above women. For indeed, son, I confess unto you, in our very creation we are servants – and who praiseth² his servants shall never be well obeyed; but, as a ready horse straight yields when he finds one that will have him yield, the same falls to bounds when he feels a fearful horseman. Awake thy spirits, good Amphialus, and assure thyself that though she refuseth, she refuseth but to endear the obtaining. If she weep and chide and protest before it be gotten, she can but weep and chide and protest when it is gotten. Think: she would not strive but that she means to try thy force. And, my Amphialus, know thyself a man; and show thyself a man – and believe me, upon my word, a woman is a woman.'

Amphialus³ was about to answer her, when a gentleman of his made him understand that there was a messenger come who had brought a letter unto him from out of the camp, whom he presently calling for, took, opened, and read the letter, importing this:

'To thee, Amphialus of Arcadia, the Forsaken Knight wisheth health and courage, that by my hand thou mayest receive punishment for thy treason according to thine own offer, which wickedly occasioned, thou hast proudly begun and accursedly maintained. I will presently, if thy mind faint thee not for his own guiltiness, meet thee in thy island in such order as hath by the former been used; or if thou likest not the time, place, or weapon, I am ready to take thine own reasonable choice in any of them, so as thou do perform the substance. Make me such answer as may show that thou hast some taste of honour. And so I leave thee, to live till I meet thee.'

Amphialus read it, and with a deep sigh (according to the humour of inward affection)⁴ seemed even to condemn himself, as though indeed his reproaches were true. But howsoever the dullness of melancholy would have languishingly yielded thereunto, his courage (unused to such injuries) desired help of anger to make him this answer:

'Forsaken Knight, though your nameless challenge might carry in itself excuse for a man of my birth and estate, yet herein set your heart at rest: you

---

¹ over-superstitiously *Cm, 93*: over-suspiciously 90   ² praiseth] praise *Cm*; prayeth 13   ³ woman.' Amphialus *Cm, 93*: woman.' Chap. 18. The Forsaken Knight's defy; Amphialus' answer; the one and other's armour and imprese; the issue of their quarrel; their heroical monomachy on horse and foot; their breathings and re-encounters; Amphialus rescued by Anaxius' brethren, the Black Knight by the Green and White; the supply of both sides to carry away the breathless knights; the Black Knight's grieves. Amphialus 90   ⁴ affection] affliction 93

shall not be forsaken. I will without stay answer you in the wonted manner, and come both armed in your foolish threatenings, and yet the more fearless, expecting weak blows where I find so strong words. You shall not, therefore, long attend me in the island before proof teach you that, of my life, you have made yourself too large a promise. In the meantime, farewell.'

This being written and delivered, the messenger told him that his lord would, if he liked the same, bring two knights with him to be his patrons, which Amphialus accepted. And withal shaking off with resolution his mother's importunate dissuasions, he furnished himself for the fight – but not in his wonted furniture, for now, as if he would turn his inside outward, he would needs appear all in black, his decking both for himself and horse being cut out into the fashion of very rags – yet all so dainty joined[1] together with precious stones as it was a brave raggedness and a rich poverty; and so cunningly had a workman followed his humour in his armour that he had given it a rusty show, and yet so, as any man might perceive was by art and not negligence, carrying at one instant a disgraced handsomeness and a new oldness. In his shield he bare for his device a night, by an excellent painter excellently painted[2] with a sun with a shadow, and upon the shadow, with a speech signifying that it only was barred from enjoying that whereof it had his life, or, 'From whose I am, banished.' In his crest he carried Philoclea's knives – the only token of her forward[3] favour.

So passed he over into the island, taking with him the two brothers of Anaxius – where he found the Forsaken Knight attired in his own livery, as black as sorrow itself could see itself in the blackest glass; his ornaments of the same hue, but formed into[4] the figure of ravens which seemed to gape for carrion – only his reins were snakes, which finely wrapping themselves one within the other, their heads came together to the cheeks and bosses of the bit where they might seem to bite at the horse, and the horse, as he champed the bit, to bite at them; and that the white foam was engendered by the poisonous fury of the combat. His impresa was a catoblepta, which so long lies dead as the moon, whereto it hath so natural a sympathy, wants her light. The word signified that the moon wanted not the light, but the poor beast wanted the moon's light. He had in his head-piece a whip to witness a self-punishing repentance. Their very horses were coal-black too, not having so much as one star to give light to their night of blackness – so as one would have thought they had been the two sons of sorrow, and were come thither to fight for their birthright in that sorry inheritance; which alliance of passions so moved Amphialus (already tender-minded by the afflictions

---

[1] dainty joined *Cm*: dainty, joined *90*; daintily joined *93*   [2] excellent painter excellently painted *Cm, 93*: excellently painter *90*   [3] forward] forced *93*   [4] into *Cm, 93*: in *90*

of love) that without staff, or sword drawn, he trotted fairly to the Forsaken Knight, willing to have put off his combat,[1] to which his melancholy heart did, more than ever in like occasion, misgive him.

And therefore saluting him, 'Good knight,' said he, 'because we are men and should know reason why we do things, tell me the cause that makes you thus eager to fight with me.'

'Because I affirm,' answered the Forsaken Knight,' that thou dost most rebellious injury to those ladies, to whom all men owe service.'

'You shall not fight with me,' said Amphialus, 'upon that quarrel, for I confess the same too – but it proceeds from their own beauty to enforce love to offer this force.'

'I maintain, then,' said the Forsaken Knight, 'that thou art not worthy so to love.'

'And that confess I too,' said Amphialus, 'since the world is not so richly blessed as to bring forth anything worthy thereof – but no more unworthy than any other, since in none can be a more worthy love.'

'Yes! more unworthy than myself!' said the Forsaken Knight. 'For though I deserve contempt, thou deservest both contempt and hatred!'

But Amphialus by that thinking (though wrongly – each indeed mistaking other) that he was his rival, forgat all mind of reconciliation. And having all his thoughts bound up in choler, never staying either judge, trumpet, or his own lance, drew out his sword; and saying, 'Thou liest, false villain!' unto him, his words and blows came so quick together as the one seemed a lightning of the other's thunder. But he found no barren ground of such seed, for it yielded him his own with such increase that, though reason and amazement go rarely together, yet the most reasonable eyes that saw it found reason to be amazed at the fury of their combat – never game of death better played; never fury set itself forth in greater bravery.

The courteous Vulcan, when he wrought at his now[2] courteous wives request Aeneas an armour, made not his hammer beget a greater sound than the swords of those noble knights did. They needed no fire to their forge, for they made the fire to shine at the meeting of their swords and armours. Each side fetching still new[3] spirit from the castle window, and careful of keeping their sight, that was[4] a matter of greater consideration in their combat than either the advantage of sun or wind; which sun and wind, if the astonished eyes of the beholders were not by the astonishment deceived, did both stand still to be beholders of this rare match, for neither could their amazed eyes discern motion in the sun, and no breath of wind stirred – as if, either for

---

[1] his combat] this combat *93*   [2] his now *Cm*: his now more *90*; his more *93*   [3] fetching still new *Cm, 93*: fetching new *90*   [4] sight, that was *Cm*: sight, it was *90*; sight that way as *93*

fear it would not come among such blows, or with delight had his eyes so busy, as it had forgot to open his mouth.

This fight, being the more cruel since both love and hatred conspired to sharpen their humours, that hard it was to say whether love with one trumpet, or hatred with another, gave the louder alarum to their courages. Spite, rage, disdain, shame, revenge came waiting upon hatred. Of the other side came, with love-longing desire, both invincible hope and fearless despair, with rival-like jealousy – which although brought up within doors in the school of Cupid, would show themselves no less forward than the other dusty band of Mars to make themselves notable in the notableness of this combat; of either side, confidence unacquainted with loss – but assured trust to overcome, and good experience how to overcome: now seconding their terrible blows with cunning labouring the horses to win ground of the enemy; now unlooked-for parting one from the other, to win advantage by an advantageous return. But force against force, skill against skill, so interchangeably encountered that it was not easy to determine whether enterprising or preventing came former, both sometimes at one instant doing and suffering wrong, and choler no less rising of the doing than of the suffering.

But as the fire, the more fuel is put to it, the more hungry still it is to devour more, so the more they strake, the more unsatisfied they were with striking. Their very armour by piecemeal fell away from them, and yet their flesh abode the wounds constantly, as though it were less sensible of smart than the senseless armour; their blood in most places staining the black colour,[1] as if it would give a more lively colour of mourning than black can do. And so, a long space they fought while neither virtue nor fortune seemed partial of either side, which so tormented the unquiet heart of Amphialus that he resolved to see a quick end. And therefore, with the violence of courage adding strength to his blow, he strake in such wise upon the side of the other's head that his remembrance left that battered lodging, so as he was quite from himself, casting his arms abroad and ready to fall down. His sword likewise went out of his hand, but that being fast by a chain to his arm, he could not lose. And Amphialus used the favour of occasion, redoubling his blows.

But the horse, weary to be beaten (as well as the master), carried his master away till he came unto himself. But then who could have seen him might well have discerned shame in his cheeks and revenge in his eyes, so as, setting his teeth together with rage, he came running upon Amphialus, reaching out his arm which had gathered up the sword, meaning with that

---

[1] the black colour *Cm*: the black *90*; their black colour *93*

blow to have cleaved Amphialus in two. But Amphialus, seeing the blow coming, shunned it with nimble turning his horse aside, wherewith the Forsaken Knight overstrake himself so, as almost he came down with his own strength. But the more hungry of[1] his purpose, the more he was barred the food of it.

Disdaining the resistance both of force and fortune, he returned upon the spur again, and ran with such violence upon Amphialus that his horse with the force of the shock rose up before, almost overturned; which Amphialus perceiving, with rein and spur put forth his horse, and withal gave a mighty blow in the descent of his horse upon the shoulder of the Forsaken Knight, from whence sliding, it fell upon the neck of his horse, so as horse and man fell to the ground – but he was scarce down before he was up on his feet again, with brave gesture showing rising of courage in the falling of fortune. But the courteous Amphialus excused himself for having, against his will, killed his horse.

'Excuse thyself for viler faults!' answered the Forsaken Knight, 'and use this poor advantage the best thou canst, for thou shalt quickly find thou hast need of more.'

'Thy folly,' said Amphialus, 'shall not make me forget myself, and therewith trotting a little aside, alighted from his horse, because he would not have fortune come to claim any part of the victory – which courteous act would have mollified the noble heart of the Forsaken Knight, if any other had done it besides the jailer of his mistress.

But that was a sufficient defeasance for the firmest bond of good nature; and therefore he was no sooner alighted but that he ran unto him, re-entering into as cruel a fight as eye did ever see or thought could reasonably imagine, far beyond the reach of weak words to be able to express it – for what they had done on horseback was but as a morsel to keep their stomachs in appetite, in comparison of that which now, being themselves, they did; nor ever glutton by the change of dainty diet could be brought to fetch[2] feeding (when he might have been satisfied before) with more earnestness, than those, by the change of their manner of fight, fell clean to a new fight, though any else would have thought they had had their fill already.

Amphialus being the taller man for the most part stood with his right leg before, his shield at the uttermost length of his arm, his sword high but with the point toward his enemy; but when he strake, which came so thick as if every blow would strive to be foremost, his arm seemed still a postilion of death. The Forsaken Knight showed with like skill unlike gesture, keeping himself in continual motion, proportioning the distance between them to

---

[1] hungry of *Cm*, 93: hungry he was of 90 [2] fetch] fresh 93

anything that Amphialus attempted. His eye guided his foot and his foot conveyed his hand; and since nature had made him something the lower of the two, he made art follow and not strive with nature, shunning rather than warding his blows (like a cunning mastiff who knows the sharpness of the horn and strength of the bull fights low to get his proper advantage), answering mightiness with nimbleness, and yet at times employing his wonderful force wherein he was second to none. In sum, the blows were strong, the thrusts thick, and the avoidings cunning. But the Forsaken Knight, that thought it a degree of being conquered to be long in conquering, strake so[1] mighty a blow that he made Amphialus put knee to the ground – without any humbleness. But when he felt himself stricken down, and saw himself stricken down by his rival, then shame seemed one arm and disdain another, fury in his eyes and revenge in his heart. Skill and force gave place, and they took the place of skill and force, with so unweariable a manner that the Forsaken Knight was also[2] driven to leave the storm[3] of cunning, and give himself wholly to be guided by the storm of fury – there being in both, because hate would not suffer admiration, extreme disdain to find themselves so matched.

'What!' said Amphialus to himself. 'Am I Amphialus, before whom so many monsters and giants have fallen dead when I only sought causeless adventures? And can one knight now withstand me, in the presence of Philoclea and fighting for Philoclea? Or since I lost my liberty, have I lost my courage? Have I gotten the heart of a slave as well as the fortune? If an army were against me, in the sight of Philoclea could it resist me? O beast! One man resists thee! Thy rival resists thee! Or am I indeed Amphialus? Have not passions killed him, and wretched I – I know not how – succeeded into his place?'

Of the other side, the Forsaken Knight with no less spite fell out with himself. 'Hast thou broken,' said he to himself, 'the commandment of thy only princess, to come now into[4] her presence – and in her presence to prove thyself a coward? Doth Asia and Egypt set up trophies unto thee, to be matched here by a traitor? O noble Barzanes, how shamed will thy soul be that he that slew thee should be resisted by this one man! O incomparable Pyrocles, more grieved wilt thou be with thy friend's shame than with thine own imprisonment, when thou shalt know how little I have been able to do for the delivery of thee and those heavenly princesses. Am I worthy to be friend to the most valorous prince that ever was entitled valorous, and show myself so weak a wretch? No! Shamed Musidorus! worthy for nothing but

---

[1] strake so] strake him so 93   [2] was also] also was 93   [3] storm *Cm*: stream 90; stern 93   [4] into *Cm*, 90 (*catchword*), 93: in- 90

to keep sheep! Get thee a sheephook again, since thou canst use a sword no better!'

Thus at times did they, now with one thought, then with another, sharpen their over-sharp humours (like the lion that beats himself with his own tail to make himself the more angry), these thoughts indeed not staying, but whetting their angry swords, which now had put on the apparel of cruelty – they bleeding so abundantly that everybody that saw them fainted for them. And yet, they fainted not in themselves, their smart being more sensible to others' eyes than to their own feeling, wrath and courage barring the common sense from bringing any message of their case to the mind; pain, weariness, and weakness not daring to make known their case, though already in the limits of death, in the presence of so violent fury; which filling the veins with rage instead of blood, and making the mind minister spirits to the body, a great while held out their fight – like an arrow, shot upward by the force of the bow, though by his own nature he would go downward.

The Forsaken Knight had the more wounds, but Amphialus had the sorer, which the other, watching time and place, had cunningly given unto him. Whoever saw a well-manned galley fight with a tall ship might make unto himself some kind of comparison of the difference of these two knights, a better couple than which the world could not brag of. Amphialus seemed to excel in strength, the Forsaken Knight in nimbleness; and yet did the one's strength excel in nimbleness, and the other's nimbleness excel in strength – but now strength and nimbleness were both gone, and excess of courage only maintained the fight.

Three times had Amphialus with his mighty blows driven the Forsaken Knight to go staggering backward, but every one of those times he requited pain with smart and shame with repulse. And now, whether he had cause, or that over-much confidence (an over-forward scholar of unconquered courage) made him think he had cause, he began to persuade himself he had the advantage of the combat – though the advantage he took himself to have was only that he should be the later to die; which hopes,[1] hate, as unsecret as love, could not conceal, but (drawing himself a little back from him) brake out in these manner of words:

'Ah, Amphialus,' said the Forsaken Knight, 'this third time thou shalt not escape me, but thy death shall satisfy thy injury and my malice, and pay for the cruelty thou showedst in killing the noble Argalus and the fair Parthenia.'

'In troth,' said Amphialus, 'thou art the best knight that ever I fought withal, which would make me willing to grant thee thy life, if thy wit were

---

[1] hopes] hope 93

as good as thy courage, that, besides other follies, layest that to my charge which most against my will was committed. But whether my death be in thy power or no, let this tell thee!' – and upon the word waited a blow which parted his shield into two pieces, and despising the weak resistance of his already broken armour, made a great breach into his heart-side, as if he would make a passage for his love to get out at.

But pain rather seemed to increase life than to weaken life in those champions, for the Forsaken Knight coming in with his right leg, and making it guide the force of the blow, strake Amphialus upon the belly so horrible a wound that his guts came out withal; which Amphialus perceiving, fearing death only because it should come with overthrow, he seemed to conjure all his strength for one moment's service, and so, lifting up his sword with both hands, hit the Forsaken Knight upon the head a blow wherewith his sword brake. But as if it would do a notable service before it died, it prevailed so, even in the instant of breaking, that the Forsaken Knight fell to the ground, quite for that instant forgetting both love and hatred. And Amphialus, finding himself also in such weakness as he looked for speedy death, glad of the victory though little hoping to enjoy it, pulled up his visor, meaning with his dagger to give him death. But instead of death he gave him life, for the air so revived his spirits that coming to himself, and seeing his present danger, with a life conquering death he took Amphialus by the thigh, and together rose himself and overturned him; but Amphialus scrambled up again – both now so weak indeed as their motions rather seemed the afterdrops to a storm than any matter of great fury.

But Amphialus might repent himself of his wilful breaking his good sword, for the Forsaken Knight (having with the extremity of justly-conceived hate, and the unpitifulness of his own near-threatening death, blotted out all complements of courtesy) let fly at him so cruelly that, though the blows were weak, yet weakness upon a weakened subject proved such strength that Amphialus, having attempted in vain once or twice to close with him, receiving wound upon wound, sent his whole burden to strike the earth with falling, since he could strike his foe no better in standing, giving no other tokens of himself than as of a man even ready to take his oath to be death's true servant; which, when the hardy brothers of Anaxius perceived, not recking law of arms nor use of chivalry, they flew in to defend their friend, or revenge their loss of him.

But they were forthwith encountered with the two brave companions of the Forsaken Knight, whereof the one being all in green, both armour and furniture, it seemed a pleasant garden wherein grew orange-trees, which with their golden fruits cunningly beaten in and embroidered greatly enriched the eye-pleasing colour of green. In his shield was a sheep feeding in a pleasant field, with this word, 'Without fear or envy', and therefore was called the Knight of the Sheep. The other knight was all in milk-white, his attiring else all cut in stars, which made of cloth of silver and silver spangles, each way seemed to cast many aspects. His device was the very pole itself, about which many stars stirring, but the place itself left void. The word was 'The best place yet reserved.'

But these four knights inheriting the hate of their friends began a fierce[1] combat, the Forsaken Knight himself not able to help his side, but was driven to sit him down with the extreme faintness of his more and more fainting body. But those valiant couples seeking honour by dishonouring, and to build safety upon ruin, gave new appetites to the almost glutted eyes of the beholders. And now blood began to put sweat from the full possession of their outsides, no advantage being yet to be seen, only the Knight of the Sheep seeming most deliver, and affecting most all that viewed him – when a company of soldiers sent by Cecropia came out in boats to the island, and all came running to the destruction of the three knights, whereof the one was utterly unable to defend himself.

But then did the other two knights show their wonderful courage and fidelity, for turning back to back, and both bestriding the black Forsaken Knight (who had fainted so long till he had lost the feeling of faintness), they held play against the rest, though the two brothers unknightly helped them – till Philanax, who watchfully attended such traitorous practices, sent likewise over both by boat and swimming so choice a number as did put most of the other to the sword, only the two brothers (with some of the bravest of them) carrying away the body of Amphialus, which they would rather have died than have left behind them.

So was the Forsaken Knight, laid upon cloaks, carried home to the camp; but his two friends (knowing his earnest desire not to be known) covering him from anybody's eyes, conveyed him to their own tent, Basilius himself conquering his earnest desire to see him with fear to displease him, who had fought so notably in his quarrel. But fame set the honour upon his back which he would not suffer to shine in his face, no man's mouth being barren of praises to the noble knight that had bettered the most esteemed knight in the world, everybody praying for his life – and thinking that therein they prayed for themselves.

But he himself, when by the diligent care of friends and well-applied cunning of surgeons he came to renew again the league between his mind and body, then fell he to a fresh war with his own thoughts, wrongfully

---

[1] a fierce] a most fierce 93

condemning his manhood, laying cowardice to himself, whom the impudentest backbiter would not so have wronged; for his courage, used to use victory as an inheritance, could brook no resistance at any time. But now that he had promised himself not only the conquest of him, but the scaling of the walls and delivery of Pamela, though he had done beyond all others' expectation, yet so short was he of his own that he hated to look upon the sun that had seen him do so weakly, and so much abhorred all visitation or honour (whereof he thought himself unworthy) that he besought his two noble friends to carry him away to a castle not far off, where he might cure his wounds and never be known till he made success excuse this, as he thought, want in him. They lovingly obeyed him, leaving Basilius and all the camp very sorry for the parting of these three unknown knights in whose prowess they had reposed greatest trust of victory.

But[1] they being gone, Basilius and Philanax gave good order to the strengthening of the siege, fortifying themselves so as they feared no more any such sudden onset as that of Anaxius; and they within, by reason of Anaxius' hurt, but especially of Amphialus,' gave themselves only to diligent watch and ward, making no sallies out, but committing the principal trust to Zoilus and Lycurgus, for Anaxius was yet forced to keep his chamber. And as for Amphialus, his body had such wounds (and he gave[2] such wounds to his mind) as easily it could not be determined whether death or he made the greater haste one to the other; for when the diligent care of cunning surgeons had brought life to the possession of his own right, sorrow and shame, like two corrupted servants, came waiting of it, persuading nothing but the giving over of itself to destruction. They laid before his eyes his present case, painting every piece of it in most ugly colours. They showed him his love wrapped in despair, his fame blotted by overthrow; so that if before he languished because he could not obtain his desiring, he now lamented because he durst not desire the obtaining.

'Recreant Amphialus!' would he say to himself. 'How darest thou entitle thyself the lover of Philoclea, that hast neither showed thyself a faithful coward nor a valiant rebel, but both rebellious and cowardly, which no law can quite nor grace have pity of? Alas, life, what little pleasure thou doost me! to give me nothing but sense of reproach and exercise of ruin. I would, sweet Philoclea, I had died before thy eyes had seen my weakness, and then perchance with some sigh thou wouldest have confessed thou hadst lost a worthy servant – but now, caitiff that I am, whatever I have done serves but to build up my rival's glory.'

---

[1] victory. But *Cm*, 93: victory. Chap. 19. The state of the leaguer and beleaguered; the agonies of Amphialus; the wit-craft of Cecropia to threaten Basilius with the three ladies' death; Kalander's compassion; Philanax's counter-counsel; the breaking up the siege. But 90   [2] he gave *Cm*, 93: gave 90

To these speeches he would couple such gestures of vexation, and would fortify the gestures with such effects of fury (as sometimes offering to tear up his wounds, sometimes to refuse the sustenance of meat and counsel of physicians) that his perplexed mother was driven to make him by force to be tended, with extreme corsie to herself and annoyance to him; till in the end he was contented to promise her he would attempt no violence upon himself, upon condition he might be troubled by nobody, but only his physicians – his melancholy detesting all company, so as not the very surgeons, nor servants, durst speak unto him in doing him service. Only he had prayed his mother, as she tendered his life, she would procure him grace, and that without that she would never come at him more.

His mother, who had confined all her love only unto him, set only such about him as were absolutely at her commandment, whom she forbad to let him know anything that passed in the castle till his wounds were cured, but as she from time to time should instruct them, she for herself being resolved (now she had the government of all things in her own hands) to satisfy her son's love by their yielding, or satisfy her own revenge in their punishment. Yet first, because he should[1] be the freer from outward force, she sent a messenger to the camp to denounce unto Basilius that, if he did not presently raise his siege, she would cause the heads of the three ladies, prisoners, to be cut off before his eyes – and to make him the more fear a present performance, she caused his two daughters and Zelmane to be led unto the walls (where she had made a scaffold easy to be seen by Basilius) and there caused them to be kept, as ready for the slaughter, till answer came from Basilius.

A sight full of pity it was to see those three (all excelling in all those excellencies wherewith nature can beautify any body – Pamela giving sweetness to majesty, Philoclea enriching nobleness with humbleness, Zelmane setting in womanly beauty manlike valour) to be thus subjected to the basest injury of unjust fortune. One might see in Pamela a willingness to die rather than to have life at other's discretion, though sometimes a princely disdain would sparkle out of her princely eyes that it should be in other's power to force her to die. In Philoclea, a pretty fear came up to endamask her rosy cheeks, but it was such a fear as rather seemed a kindly child to her innate[2] humbleness than any other dismayedness, or if she were dismayed, it was more for Zelmane than for herself, or if more for herself, it was because Zelmane should lose her. As for Zelmane, as she went with her hands bound, for they durst not adventure on her well-known valour, especially among people[3] which perchance might be moved by such a spectacle to some revolt,

---

[1] he should] she would 93   [2] innate] iminate *Cm, 90 (uncorr.)*   [3] among people] among a people 93

she was the true image of overmastered courage and of spite that sees no remedy – for her breast swelled withal; the blood burst out at her nose; and she looked paler than accustomed, with her eyes cast on the ground with such a grace as if she were fallen out with the heavens for suffering such an injury.

The lookers on were so moved withal as they misliked what themselves did, and yet still did what themselves misliked: for some, glad to rid themselves of the dangerous annoyance of this siege; some, willing to shorten the way to Amphialus' succession whereon they were dependents; some – and the greatest some – doing because others did (and suffering because none durst begin to hinder), did in this sort set their hands to this, in their own conscience, wicked enterprise.

But when this message was brought to Basilius, and that this pitiful preparation was a sufficient letter of credit for him to believe it, he called unto him his chief councillors, among which those he chiefly trusted were Philanax and Kalander – lately come to the camp at Basilius' commandment; and in himself weary of his solitary life, wanting his son's presence; and never having heard him[1] his beloved guests since they parted from him. Now in this doubt what he should do, he willed Kalander to give him his advice, who spake much to this purpose:

'You command me, sir,' said he, 'to speak rather because you will keep your wonted grave and noble manner to do nothing of importance without counsel, than that in this cause which indeed hath but one way your mind needs to have any counsel, so as my speech shall rather be to confirm what you have already determined than to argue against any possibility of other determination. For what sophistical scholar can find any question in this: whether you will have your incomparable daughters live or die; whether, since you be here to cause their deliverance, you will make your being here the cause of their destruction – for nothing can be more unsensible than to think what one doth, and to forget[2] the end why it is done. Do therefore as I am sure you mean to do. Remove the siege, and after seek by practice or other gentle means to recover that which by force you cannot; and thereof is indeed, when it please you, more counsel to be taken. Once, in extremities the winning of time is the purchase of life – and worse by no means, than their deaths, can befall unto you. A man might use more words if it were to any purpose to gild gold, or that I had any cause to doubt of your mind; but you are wise, and are a father.'

He said no more, for he durst not attempt to persuade the marrying of his daughter to Amphialus, but left that to bring in at another consultation. But

---

[1] heard him] heard from 93   [2] forget] froget 90 (uncorr.)

Basilius made sign to Philanax, who standing a while in a maze, as inwardly perplexed, at last thus delivered his opinion.

'If ever I could wish my faith untried and my counsel untrusted, it should be at this time, when in truth I must confess I would be content to purchase silence with discredit. But since you command, I obey – only let me say thus much, that I obey not to these excellent ladies' father, but to my prince; and a prince it is to whom I give counsel. Therefore, as to a prince, I say that the grave and I well know true-minded counsel of my Lord Kalander had come in good time when you first took arms, before all your subjects gate notice of your intention, before so much blood was spent – and before they were driven to seek this shift for their last remedy. But if now this force you away, why did you take arms, since you might be sure whenever they were in extremity they would have recourse to this threatening? And for a wise man to take in hand that which his enemy may with a word overthrow hath, in my conceit, great incongruity; and as great not to forethink what his enemy in reason will do.

'But they threaten they will kill your daughters. What if they promised you, if you removed your siege, they would honourably send home your daughters? Would you be angled by their promises? Truly, no more ought you be terrified by their threatenings, for yet, of the two, promise binds faith more than threatening. But indeed, a prince of judgement ought not to consider what his enemies promise or threaten, but what the promisers and threateners in reason will do; and the nearest conjecture thereunto is what is best, for their own behoof, to do.

'They threaten, if you remove not, they will kill your daughters. And if you do remove, what surety have you but that they will kill them, since if the purpose be to cut off all impediments of Amphialus' ambition, the same cause will continue when you are away – and so much the more encouraged as the revenging power is absent, and they have the more opportunity to draw their factious friends about them. But if it be for their security only, the same cause will bring forth the same effect, and for their security they will preserve them.

'But, it may be said, no man knows what desperate folks will do. It is true, and as true that no reason nor policy can prevent what desperate folks will do; and therefore they are among those dangers which, wisdom is, not to recken. Only let it suffice to take away their despair, which may be by granting pardon for what is past, so as the ladies may be freely delivered. And let them (that are your subjects) trust you, that are their prince. Do not you subject yourself to trust them, who are so untrusty as to be manifest traitors; for if they find you so base-minded as by their threatening to remove your force, what indignity is it that they would not bring you unto still, by the same threatening?

'Since, then, if love stir them, love will keep them from murthering what they love; and if ambition provoke them, ambitious they will be when you are away as well as while you are here. Take not away your force, which bars not the one, and bridles the other; for as for their shows and words, they are but fear-babes,[1] not worthy once to move a worthy man's conceit – which must still consider what in reason they are like to do. Their despair, I grant, you shall do well to prevent, which, as it is the last of all resolutions, so no man falls into it while so good a way as you may offer is open unto them. In sum, you are a prince – and a father – of people,[2] who ought with the eye of wisdom, the hand of fortitude, and the heart of justice to set down all private conceits in comparison of what, for the public, is profitable.'

He would have proceeded on, when Gynecia came running in, amazed for her daughter Pamela – but mad for Zelmane; and falling at Basilius' feet besought him to make no delay, using such gestures of compassion, instead of stopped words, that Basilius (otherwise enough tender-minded) easily granted to raise the siege which he saw dangerous to his daughters – but indeed, more careful for Zelmane, by whose besieged person the poor old man was straitly besieged; so as, to rid him of the famine of his mind, he went in speed away, discharging his soldiers, only leaving the authority, as before, in Philanax's hands. He himself went with Gynecia to a strong castle of his, where he took counsel how first to deliver Zelmane (whom he called 'the poor stranger,' as though only law of hospitality moved him), and for that purpose sent divers messengers to traffic with Cecropia.

But she[3] by this means rid of the present danger of the siege, desiring Zoilus and Lycurgus to take the care till their brother recovered of revictualling and furnishing the city both with men and what else wanted, against any new occasion should urge them, she herself, disdaining to hearken to Basilius without he would grant his daughter in marriage to her son, which by no means he would be brought unto, bent all the sharpness of her malicious wit how to bring a comfortable grant to her son, whereupon she well found no less than his life depended. Therefore, for a while she attempted all means of eloquent praying and flattering persuasion, mingling sometimes gifts, sometimes threatenings, as she had cause to hope that either open force or undermining would best win the castle of their resolution. And ever as much as she did to Philoclea, so much did she to Pamela, though in manner

---

[1] but fear-babes *Cm, 93*: but to fear babes *90*   [2] of people] of a people *93*   [3] Cecropia. But she *93*: [*blank space*]. But she *Cm*; Cecropia. Chap. 20. The sweet resistance of the true sisters to the sour assaults of their false aunt; the whipping of Philoclea and Pamela; the patience of both, and passions for their lovers. Cecropia *90*

sometimes differing as she found fit to level at the one's noble height and the other's sweet lowliness; for though she knew her son's heart had wholly given itself to Philoclea, yet seeing the equal gifts in Pamela, she hoped a fair grant would recover the sorrow of a fair refusal, cruelly intending the present empoisoning the one as soon as the other's affection were purchased.

But in vain was all her vain oratory employed. Pamela's determination was built upon so brave a rock that no shot of hers could reach unto it; and Philoclea, though humbly seated, was so environed with sweet rivers of clear virtue as could neither be battered nor undermined. Her witty persuasions had wise answers; her eloquence, recompensed with sweetness; her threatenings, repelled with disdain in the one and patience in the other; her gifts, either not accepted, or accepted to obey but not to bind – so as Cecropia (in nature violent; cruel because ambitious; hateful for old-rooted grudge to their mother, and now spiteful because she could not prevail with girls, as she counted them; lastly, drawn on by her love to her son and held up by a tyrannical authority) forthwith followed the bias of her own crooked disposition, and doubling and redoubling her threatenings, fell to confirm some of her threatened effects: first, withdrawing all comfort both of servants and service from them – but that those excellent ladies had been used unto, even at home, and then found in themselves how much good the hardness of education doth to the resistance of misery; then, dishonourably using them both in diet and lodging, by a contempt to pull down their thoughts to yielding – but as before the consideration of a prison had disgraced all ornaments, so now the same consideration made them attend all diseasefulness; then still, as she found those not prevail, would she go forward with giving them terrors – sometimes with noises[1] of horror, sometimes with sudden frightings in the night, when the solitary darkness thereof might easier astonish the disarmed senses – but to all, virtue and love resisted, strengthened one by the other when each found itself over-vehemently assaulted; Cecropia still sweetening her fierceness with fair promises if they would promise fair; that feeling evil, and seeing a way[2] far better, their minds might the sooner be mollified – but they, that could not taste her behaviour when it was pleasing, indeed, could worse now when they had lost all taste by her injuries.

She, resolving all extremities rather than fail[3] of conquest, pursued on her rugged way, letting no day pass without new and new perplexing the poor ladies' minds and troubling their bodies. And still swelling the more she was stopped, and growing hot with her own doings, at length abominable rage carried her to absolute tyrannies, so that taking with her certain

---

[1] noises] voices *Cm*; noise *13* [2] feeling evil, and seeing a way] seeing feeling evil, and a way *90 (uncorr.)*
[3] fail] fact *Cm, 90 (uncorr.)*

old women of wicked dispositions (and apt for envy sake to be cruel to youth and beauty), with a countenance empoisoned with malice flew to the sweet Philoclea, as if so many kites should come about a white dove; and matching violent gestures with mischievous threatenings, she having a rod in her hand, like a Fury that should carry wood to the burning of Diana's temple fell to scourge that most beautiful body, love in vain holding the shield of beauty against her blind cruelty.

The sun drew clouds up to hide his face from so pitiful a sight, and the very stone walls did yield drops of sweat for agony of such a mischief. Each senseless thing had sense of pity – only they, that had sense, were senseless. Virtue rarely found her worldly weakness more, than by the oppression of that day; and weeping Cupid told his weeping mother that he was sorry he was not deaf as well as blind, that he might never know so lamentable a work. Philoclea with tearful eyes and sobbing breast, as soon as her weariness rather than compassion gave her respite, kneeled down[1] to Cecropia; and making pity – in her face – honourable and torment delightful, besought her, since she hated her – for what cause, she took God to witness, she knew not – that she would at once take away her life, and not please herself with the tormenting of a poor gentlewoman.

'If', said she, 'the common course of humanity[2] cannot move you, nor the having me in your own walls cannot claim pity – nor womanly mercy, nor near alliance, nor remembrance (how miserable soever now) that I am a prince's daughter – yet let the love you have often told me your son bears me so much procure, that for his sake one death may be thought enough for me. I have not lived so many years but that one death may be able to conclude them, neither have my faults, I hope, been so many but that one death may satisfy them. It is no great suit to an enemy when but death is desired; I crave but that. And as for the granting your request, know for certain, you lose your labours, being every day further-off-minded from becoming his wife, who useth me like a slave.'

But that, instead of getting grace, renewed again Cecropia's fury, so that, excellent creature, she was newly again tormented by those hellish monsters, Cecropia using no other words but that she was a proud and ungrateful wench, and that she would teach her to know her own good, since of herself she would not conceive it; so that with[3] silence and patience, like a fair, gorgeous armour hammered upon by an ill-favoured smith, she abode their pitiless dealing with her, till rather reserving her for more than meaning to end, they left her to an uncomfortable leisure to consider with herself her fortune, both helpless herself, being a prisoner, and hopeless, since Zelmane

---

[1] down *Cm*, 93: dowe 90   [2] humanity] hunanitie 90 (*uncorr.*)   [3] so that with *Cm*, 93: So with 90

was a prisoner – who therein only was short of the bottom of misery, that she knew not how unworthily her angel by these devils was abused, but wanted, Got wot, no stings of grief when those words did but strike upon her heart that Philoclea was a captive, and she not able to succour her; for well she knew the confidence Philoclea had in her, and well she knew Philoclea had cause to have confidence, and all trodden under foot by the wheel of senseless fortune.

Yet if there be that imperious power in the soul as it can deliver knowledge to another without bodily organs, so vehement were the workings of their spirits as one met with other, though themselves perceived it not, but only thought it to be the doubling of their own loving fancies; and that was the only worldly thing whereon Philoclea rested her mind – that she knew she should die beloved of Zelmane, and should die rather than be false to Zelmane. And so, this most dainty nymph easing the pain of her mind with thinking of another's pain, and almost forgetting the pain of her body through the pain of her mind, she wasted, even longing for the conclusion of her tedious tragedy. But for a while she was unvisited, Cecropia employing her time in using the like cruelty upon Pamela, her heart growing not only to desire the fruit of punishing them, but even to delight in the punishing them.

But if ever the beams of perfection shined through the clouds of affliction, if ever virtue took a body to show his else-unconceivable beauty, it was in Pamela; for when reason taught her there was no resistance, for to just resistance first her heart was inclined, then with so heavenly a quietness and so graceful a calmness did she suffer the divers kinds of torments they used to her that, while they vexed her fair body, it seemed that she rather directed than obeyed the vexation. And when Cecropia ended, and asked whether her heart would yield, she a little smiled – but such a smiling as showed no love, and yet could not but be lovely.

And then, 'Beastly woman!' said she. 'Follow on! Do what thou wilt and canst upon me, for I know thy power is not unlimited. Thou mayest well rack this silly body, but me thou canst never overthrow. For my part, I will not do thee the pleasure to desire death of thee. But assure thyself, both my life and death shall triumph with honour, laying shame upon thy detestable tyranny.'

And so, in effect conquering their doing with her suffering (while Cecropia tried as many sorts of pains as might rather vex them than spoil them – for that she would not do while she were in any hope to win either of them for her son), Pamela remained almost as much content with trial in herself what virtue could do, as grieved with the misery wherein she found herself plunged. Only sometimes her thoughts softened in her, when with open wings they flew to Musidorus; for then she would think with herself how grievously Musidorus would take this her misery, and she, that wept not for herself, wept yet Musidorus' tears which he would weep for her, for gentle love did easilier yield to lamentation than the constancy of virtue would else admit. Then would she remember the case wherein she had left her poor shepherd; and she that wished death for herself, feared death for him; and she that condemned in herself the feebleness of sorrow, yet thought it great reason to be sorry for his sorrow; and she that long had prayed for the virtuous joining themselves together, now thinking to die herself, heartily prayed that long time their fortunes might be separated.

'Live long, my Musidorus!' would she say. 'And let my name live in thy mouth; in thy heart, my memory. Live long, that thou mayest love long the chaste love of thy dead Pamela.'

Then would she wish to herself that no other woman might ever possess his heart – and yet scarcely the wish was made a wish when herself would find fault with it, as being too unjust that so excellent a man should be banished from the comfort of life. Then would she fortify her resolution with bethinking the worst, taking the counsel of virtue, and comfort of love.

And so,[1] these diamonds of the world (whom nature had made to be preciously set – in the eyes of her,[2] to be the chief works of her workmanship, the chief ornaments of the world, and princesses of felicity) by rebellious injury were brought to the uttermost distress that an enemy's heart could wish, or a woman's spite invent, Cecropia daily in one or other sort punishing them still with her evil torments, giving them fear of worse, making the fear itself the sorriest[3] torment of all; that in the end, weary of their bodies, they should be content to bestow them at her appointment. But as in labour, the more one doth exercise it, the more by the doing one is enabled to do (strength growing upon the work so as what at first would have seemed impossible after grows easy), so these princesses, second to none (and far from any second, only to be matched by themselves), with the use of suffering their minds gat the habit of suffering, so as all fears and terrors were to them but summons to a battle whereof they knew beforehand they would be victorious, and which in the suffering was painful, being suffered, was a trophy to itself – whereby Cecropia found herself still farder[4] off; for where at first she might perchance have persuaded them to have visited her son and have given him some comfort (in his sickness drawing near to the confines

---

[1] love. And so *Cm*: love. Chap. 21. Cecropia's indurate tyrannies; her device, with the death of one to threaten another; Philoclea threatened, persisteth; the execution done in sight of Philoclea and Zelmane; Philoclea's sorrow for her sister. So 90; love. So 93   [2] of her *Cm*: of her creatures 90; of men 93
[3] sorriest] sorest 93   [4] farder] fardest *Cm*; further 98, 13

of death's kingdom), now they protested that they would never otherwise speak to him than as to the enemy of most unjust cruelty towards them, that any time or place could ever make them know.

This made the poison swell in her cankered breast, perceiving that, as in water, the more she grasped, the less she held. But yet, now having run so long the way of rigour, it was too late in reason, and too contrary to her passion, to return to a course of meekness. And therefore taking counsel of one of her old associates, who so far excelled in wickedness as that she had not only lost all feeling of conscience, but had gotten a very glory in evil, in the end they determined that beating and other such sharp dealing did not so much pull down a woman's heart as it bred anger, and that nothing was more enemy to yielding than anger, making their tender hearts take on the armour of obstinacy (for thus did their wicked minds, blind to the light of virtue, and owly-eyed in the night of wickedness, interpret of it), and that therefore that was no more to be tried. And for fear of death, which, no question, would do most with them, they had been so often threatened as they began to be familiarly acquainted with it, and learned to esteem threatening words to be but words. Therefore the last but best way now was that the one, seeing indeed the other's death, should perceive there was no dallying meant – and then there was no doubt that a woman's soul would do much, rather than leave so beautiful a body.

This being concluded, Cecropia went to Philoclea, and told her that now she was to come to the last part of the play. For her part, though she found her hard-hearted obstinacy such that neither the sweetness of loving means, nor the force of hard means, could prevail with her, yet before she would pass to a further degree of extremity, she had sought to win her sister, in hope that her son might be with time satisfied with the love of so fair a lady. But finding her also rather more, than less, wilful, she was now minded that one of their deaths should serve for an example to the other that despising worthy folks was more hurtful to the despiser than the despised; that yet, because her son especially affected her, and that in her own self she was more inclinable to pity her than she had deserved, she would begin with her sister, who that afternoon should have her head cut off before her face, if in the mean time one of them did not pull out their ill-wrought stitches of unkindness. She bad her look for no other, nor longer time, than she told her.

There was no assault given to the sweet Philoclea's mind that entered so far as this; for where to all pains and dangers of herself, foresight with his lieutenant resolution had made ready defence, now with the love she bare her sister she was driven to a stay before she determined. But long she stayed not before this reason did shine unto her; that since in herself she preferred death before such a base servitude, love did teach her to wish the same to her sister.

Therefore crossing her arms and looking sideward upon the ground, 'Do what you will,' said she, 'with us. For my part, heaven shall melt before I be removed. But if you will follow my counsel, for your own sake – for as for prayers for my sake, I have felt how little they prevail – let my death first serve for example to win her, who perchance is not so resolved against Amphialus; and so shall you not only justly punish me, who indeed do hate both you and your son, but, if that may move you, you shall do more virtuously in preserving one most worthy of life, and killing another most desirous of death. Lastly, in winning her instead of a peevish, unhappy creature that I am, you shall bless your son with the most excellent woman in all praiseworthy things that the world holdeth.'

But Cecropia, who had already set down to herself what she would do, with bitter both terms and countenance told her that she should not need to woo death over-eagerly, for if her sister going before her did not teach her wit, herself should quickly follow; for since they were not to be gotten, there was no way for her son's quiet but to know that they were past getting.

And so, since no entreating nor threatening might prevail, she bad her prepare her eyes for a new play which she should see within few hours in the hall of that castle – a place indeed over-fit for so unfit a matter; for being so stately made that, the bottom of it being even with the ground, the roof reached as high as any part of the castle. At either end it had convenient lodgings. In the one end was, one story from the ground, Philoclea's abode; in the other, of even height, Pamela's; and Zelmane's in a chamber above her – but all so vaulted of strong and thickly built stone as one could no way hear the other. Each of these chambers had a little window to look into the hall, but because the sisters should not have so much comfort as to look out to another,[1] there was of the outsides curtains drawn, which they could not reach with their hands, so barring the reach of their sight.

But when the hour came that the tragedy should begin, the curtains were withdrawn from before the windows of Zelmane and of Philoclea – a sufficient challenge to call their eyes to defend themselves in such an encounter. And by and by came in at one end of the hall, with about a dozen armed soldiers, a lady led by a couple, with her hands bound before her (from above her eyes to her lips muffled with a fair kerchief, but from her mouth to the shoulders all bare), and so was led on to a scaffold raised a good deal from the floor and all covered with crimson velvet. But neither Zelmane nor Philoclea needed to be told who she was, for the apparel she ware made

---

[1] out to another *Cm*: out to one another *90*; one to another *93*

them too well assured that it was the admirable Pamela, whereunto the rare whiteness of her naked neck gave sufficient testimony to their astonished senses. But the fair lady being come to the scaffold, and then made to kneel down, and so left by her unkind supporters, as it seemed that she was about to speak somewhat (whereunto Philoclea, poor soul, earnestly listened – according to her speech, even minded[1] to frame her mind, her heart never till then, almost, wavering to save her sister's life) before the unfortunate lady could pronounce three words, the executioner cut off the one's speech and the other's attention with making his sword do his cruel office upon that beautiful neck.

Yet the pitiless sword had such pity of so precious an object that at first it did but hit flatlong – but little availed that, since the lady falling down astonished withal, the cruel villain forced the sword with another blow to divorce the fair marriage of the head and body. And this was done so in an instant that the very act did overrun Philoclea's sorrow – sorrow not being able so quickly to thunderbolt her heart thorough her senses, but first only oppressed her with a storm of amazement. But when her eyes saw that they did see, as condemning themselves to have seen it they became weary of their own power of seeing. And her soul then drinking up woe with great draughts, she fell down to deadly trances; but her waiting jailors with cruel pity brought loathed life unto her, which yet many times took his leave as though he would indeed depart. But when he was stayed by force, he kept with him deadly sorrow, which thus exercised her mourning speech:

'Pamela! My sister! My sister Pamela! Woe is me for thee! I would I had died for thee! Pamela, never more shall I see thee; never more shall I enjoy thy sweet company and wise counsel. Alas, thou art gone to beautify heaven.[2] And hast thou left[3] me here, who have nothing good in me but that I did ever love thee, and ever will lament thee? Let this day be noted of all virtuous folks for most unfortunate. Let it never be mentioned but among curses. And cursed be they that did this mischief – and most accursed be mine eyes that beheld it.

'Sweet Pamela! That head is stricken off where only wisdom might be spoken withal. That body is destroyed which was the living book of virtue. Dear Pamela, how hast thou left me to all wretchedness and misery? Yet while thou livedst, in thee I breathed – of thee I hoped. O Pamela, how much did I for thy excellency honour thee more than my mother, and love thee more than myself! Never more shall I lie with thee. Never more shall we bathe in the pleasant river together. Never more shall I see thee in thy shepherd apparel. But thou art gone – and where am I? Pamela is dead! and

---

[1] minded] minding 93   [2] beautify] be beautified Cm; a beautified 13   [3] hast thou left] hast left 93

live I? My God[1] – '. And with that, she fell again in a sound, so as it was a great while before they could bring her to herself again.

But being come to herself, 'Alas!' said she. 'Unkind women! Since you have given me so many deaths, torment me not now with life. For God's sake, let me go, and excuse your hands of more blood. Let me follow my Pamela, whom ever I sought to follow.

'Alas, Pamela! They will not let me come to thee. But if they keep promise, I shall tread thine own steps after thee – for to what am I born, miserable soul, but to be most unhappy in myself, and yet more unhappy in others? But, oh! that a thousand more miseries had happened[2] unto me, so thou hadst not died! Pamela! My sister Pamela!'

And so, like lamentable Philomela, complained she the horrible wrong done to her sister; which if it stirred not in the wickedly closed minds of her tormenters a pity of her sorrow, yet bred it a weariness of her sorrow, so as, only leaving one to prevent any harm she should do herself, the rest went away, consulting again with Cecropia how to make profit of this, their late bloody act. In[3] the end, that woman that used most to keep company with Zelmane told Cecropia that she found by many most sensible proofs in Zelmane that there was never woman so loved another as she loved Philoclea, which was the cause that she, further than the commandment of Cecropia, had caused Zelmane's curtains to be also drawn – because having the same spectacle that Philoclea had, she might stand in the greater fear for her whom she loved so well; and that indeed she had hit the needle in that device, for never saw she creature so astonished as Zelmane – exceedingly sorry for Pamela, but exceedingly exceeding that exceedingness in fear for Philoclea. Therefore, her advice was, she should cause Zelmane to come and speak with Philoclea, for there being such vehemency of friendship between them, it was both likely[4] to move Zelmane to persuade, and Philoclea to be persuaded.

Cecropia liked well of the counsel, and gave order to the same woman to go deal therein with Zelmane, and to assure her with oath that Cecropia was determined Philoclea should pass the same way that Pamela had done, without she did yield to satisfy the extremity of her son's affection; which the woman did, adding thereunto many, as she thought, good reasons to make Zelmane think Amphialus a fit match for Philoclea. But Zelmane, who had from time to time understood the cruel dealing they had used to the sisters, and now had her own eyes wounded with the sight of one's death,

---

[1] My God] O my God 93   [2] happened] chanced 93   [3] act. In *Cm*, 93: act. Chap. 22. Cecropia's policy to use Zelmane's intercession; Zelmane's self-conflict; her motion to Philoclea rather to dissemble than die; Philoclea's resolution rather to die than dissemble; at sight of Philoclea's head, Zelmane's ecstasies, desperate designs, and comfortless complaints. In *90*   [4] both likely] most likely both 93

was so confused withal (her courage still rebelling against her wit, desiring still with force to do impossible matters) that, as her desire was stopped with power, so her conceit was darkened with a mist of desire – for blind love and invincible valure still would cry out that it could not be Philoclea should be in so miserable estate, and she not relieve her; and so, while she haled her wit to her courage, she drew it from his own limits. But now Philoclea's death (a word able to marshal all his thoughts in order) being come to so short a point, either with small delay to be suffered, or by the giving herself to another to be prevented, she was driven to think, and to desire some leisure of thinking; which the woman granted for that night unto her – a night that was not half so black as her mind, not half so silent as was fit for her musing thoughts.

At last he, that would fain have desperately lost a thousand lives for her sake, could not find in his heart that she should lose any life for her own sake; and he, that despised his own death in respect of honour, yet could well nigh dispense with honour itself in respect of Philoclea's death – for, once, the thought could not enter into his heart nor the breath issue out of his mouth which could consent to Philoclea's death, for any bargain. Then how to prevent the next degree to death (which was her being possessed by another) was the point of his mind's labour, and in that he found no other way but that Philoclea should pretend a yielding unto Cecropia's request, and so, by speaking with Amphialus, and making fair but delaying promises, procure liberty for Zelmane – who only wished but to come by a sword, not doubting then to destroy them all and deliver Philoclea, so little did both the men and their forces seem in her eyes, looking down upon them from the high top of affection's tower.

With that mind therefore, but first well-bound, she was brought to Philoclea, having already plotted out in her conceit how she would deal with her. And so came she (with heart and eyes which did each sacrifice either to love, upon the altar of sorrow), and there had she the pleasing-displeasing sight of Philoclea – Philoclea, whom already the extreme sense of sorrow had brought to a dullness therein, her face not without tokens that beauty had been by many miseries cruelly battered; and yet showed it most the perfection of the beauty[1] which could remain unoverthrown, by such enemies. But when Zelmane was set down by her, and the women gone away (because she might be the better persuaded when nobody was by) that had heard her say she would not be persuaded, then began first the eyes to speak and the hearts to cry out. Sorrow a while would needs speak his own language, without using their tongues to be his interpreters. At last, Zelmane brake silence, but spake with the only eloquence of

---

[1] the beauty] that beauty 93

amazement, for all her long methodized oration was inherited only by such kind of speeches:

'Dear lady, in extreme necessities we must not – '; 'But alas! unfortunate wretch that I am, that I live to see this day!'; 'And I take heaven and earth to witness that nothing – '; and with that, her breast swelled so with spite and grief that her breath had not leisure to turn herself[1] into words.

But the sweet Philoclea (that had already died in Pamela, and of the other side had the heaviness of her heart something quickened in the most beloved sight of Zelmane) guessed somewhat at Zelmane's mind, and therefore spake unto her in this sort:

'My Pyrocles,' said she, 'I know this exceeding comfort of your presence is not brought unto me for any goodwill that is owed unto me, but, as I suppose, to make you persuade me to save my life with the ransom of mine honour – although nobody should be so unfit a pleader in that cause as yourself! Yet perchance you would have me live – '.

'Your honour! God forbid,' said Zelmane, 'that ever, for any cause, I should yield to any touch of it! But a while to pretend some affection till time or my liberty might work something for your service – this, if my astonished senses would give me leave, I would fain have persuaded you.'

'To what purpose, my Pyrocles?' said Philoclea. 'Of a miserable time, what gain is there? Hath Pamela's example wrought no more in me? Is a captive life so much worth? Can ever it go out of these lips that I love any other but Pyrocles? Shall my tongue be so false a traitor to my heart as to say I love any other but Pyrocles? And why should I do all this? To live? O Pamela! Sister Pamela, why should I live? Only for thy sake, Pyrocles, I would live – but to thee I know too well I shall not live; and if not to thee, hath thy love so base allay, my Pyrocles, as to wish me to live? For dissimulation – my Pyrocles, my simplicity is such that I have hardly been able to keep a straight way; what shall I do in a crooked? But in this case there is no mean of dissimulation, not for the cunningest. Present answer is required, and present performance upon the answer. Art thou so terrible, O death? No, my Pyrocles. And for that I do thank thee – and in my soul thank thee, for I confess the love of thee is herein my chiefest virtue. Trouble me not therefore, dear Pyrocles, nor double not my death by tormenting my resolution. Since I cannot live with thee, I will die for thee. Only remember me, dear Pyrocles, and love the remembrance of me; and if I may crave so much of thee, let me be thy last love, for though I be not worthy of thee who indeed art the worthiest creature living, yet remember that my love was a worthy love.'

But Pyrocles was so overcome with sorrow (which wisdom and virtue made just in so excellent a lady's case, full of so excellent kindness) that

---

[1] herself] itself 93

words were ashamed to come forth, knowing how weak they were to express his mind and her merit, and therefore so stayed in a deadly silence, forsaken of hope and forsaking comfort – till the appointed guardians came in to see the fruits of Zelmane's labour. And then Zelmane, warned by their presence, fell again to persuade, though scarcely herself could tell what – but in sum, desirous of delays; but Philoclea sweetly continuing constant, and in the end punishing her importunity with silence, Zelmane was fain to end.

Yet craving another time's conference, she obtained it, and divers others, till at the last Cecropia found it was to no purpose, and therefore determined to follow her own way – Zelmane yet still desirous to win by any means respite (even wasted with sorrow, and uncertain whether in worse case in her presence or absence), being able to do nothing for Philoclea's succour but by submitting the greatest courage of the earth to fall at the feet of Cecropia, and crave stay of their sentence till the uttermost was seen what her persuasions might do. Cecropia seemed much to be moved by her importunity, so as divers days were won of painful life to the excellent Philoclea, while Zelmane suffered some hope to cherish her mind, especially trusting upon the help of Musidorus, who, she knew, would not be idle in this matter; till one morning a noise awaked Zelmane from whose over-watchful mind the tired body had stolen a little sleep. And straight with the first opening of her eyes, care taking the wonted[1] place, she ran to the window which looked into the hall, for that way the noise guided her. And there might she see, the curtain being left open ever since the last execution, seven or eight persons in a cluster upon the scaffold, who by and by retiring themselves, nothing was to be seen thereupon but a basin of gold, pitifully enamelled with blood; and in the midst of it, the head of the most beautiful Philoclea.

The horribleness of the mischief was such, as Pyrocles could not at first believe his own senses, but bent his woeful eyes to discern it better; where too well he might see it was Philoclea's self, having no veil but beauty over the face, which still appeared to be alive, so did those eyes shine even as they were wont – and they were wont more than any other. And sometimes, as they moved, it might well make the beholder think that death therein had borrowed her[2] beauty, and not they any way disgraced by death, so sweet and piercing a grace they carried with them.

It was not a pity; it was not an amazement; it was not a sorrow which then laid hold on Pyrocles, but a wild fury of desperate agony – so that he cried out, 'O tyrant heaven! Traitor earth! Blind providence! No justice? How is this done? How is this suffered? Hath this world a government? If it have, let it pour out all his mischiefs upon me, and see whether it have power to make me more wretched than I am. Did she excel for this? Have I prayed

---

[1] the wonted] his wonted 93   [2] her Cm, 93: their 90

for this? Abominable hand that did it! Detestable devil that commanded it! Cursed light that beheld it! And if the light be cursed, what are then mine eyes that have seen it? And have I seen Philoclea dead? And do I live? And have I lived not to help her, but to talk of her? And stand I, still talking?'

And with that, carried with the madness of anguish, not having a readier way to kill himself, he ran as hard as ever he could with his head against the wall, with intention to brain himself. But the haste to do it made the doing the slower, for as he came to give the blow, his foot tripped, so as it came not with the full force – yet forcible enough to strike him down, and withal to deprive him of his sense, so that he lay a while, comforted by the hurt in that he felt not his discomfort. And when he came again to himself, he heard (or he thought he heard) a voice which cried, 'Revenge! Revenge!'[1] Whether indeed it were his good angel which used that voice to stay him from unnatural murdering of himself, or that his wandering spirits lighted upon that conceit, and by their weakness, subject to apprehensions, supposed they heard it – but that indeed, helped with virtue and her valiant servant, anger, stopped him from present destroying himself, yielding in reason and manhood first to destroy man, woman, and child that were any way of kin to them that were accessary to this cruelty, then to raze the castle and to build a sumptuous monument for her sister, and a most sumptuous for herself, and then himself to die upon her tomb.

This determining in himself to do, and to seek all means how (for that purpose) to get out of prison, he was content a while to bear the thirst of death; and yet went he again to the window to kiss the beloved head with his eyes. But there saw he nothing but the scaffold all covered over with scarlet, and nothing but solitary silence to mourn this mischief. But then, sorrow having dispersed itself from his heart into[2] all his noble parts, it proclaimed his authority in cries and tears, and with a more gentle dolefulness could pour out his inward evil.

'Alas!' said he. 'And is that head taken away too, so soon, from mine eyes? What, mine eyes! Perhaps they envy the excellency of your sorrow. Indeed there is nothing now left to become the eyes of all mankind, but tears; and woe be to me if any exceed me in woefulness. I do conjure you, all my senses, to accept no object but of sorrow! Be ashamed – nay, abhor to think of comfort! Unhappy eyes! you have seen too much that ever the light should be welcome to you. Unhappy ears! you shall never hear the music, of music in her voice. Unhappy heart, that hast lived to feel these pangs!

'Thou hast done thy worst, world. And cursed be thou – and cursed art thou, since to thine own self thou has done the worst thou couldest

---

[1] Revenge!'] Revenge!', unto him 93   [2] into *Cm*, 93: in 90

do. Exiled beauty, let only now thy beauty be blubbered faces! Widowed music, let now thy tunes be roarings and lamentations! Orphan virtue, get thee wings and fly after her into heaven – here is no dwelling-place for thee.

'Why lived I, alas? Alas, why loved I? To die wretched! and to be the example of the heavens' hate! And hate, and spare not! for your worst blow is stricken. Sweet Philoclea, thou art gone and hast carried with thee my love, and hast thy[1] love in me, and I, wretched man, do live. I live to die continually, till thy revenge do give me leave to die. And then die I will. My Philoclea, my heart willingly makes this promise to itself.

'Surely he did not look upon thee that gave the cruel blow! for no eye could have abidden to see such beauty overthrown by such mischief. Alas! why should they divide such a head from such a body? No other body is worthy of that head; no other head is worthy of that body. Oh, yet if I had taken my last leave! If I might have taken a holy kiss from that dying mouth!

'Where art thou, hope, which promisest never to leave a man while he liveth? Tell me, what canst thou hope for? Nay, tell me, what is there which[2] I would willingly hope after? Wishing-power, which is accounted infinite, what now is left to wish for? She is gone! and gone with her, all my hope, all my wishing.

'Love, be ashamed to be called love! Cruel hate, unspeakable hate is victorious over thee. Who is there now left that can justify thy tyranny, and give reason to thy passion? O cruel divorce of the sweetest marriage that ever was in nature! Philoclea is dead – and dead is with her all goodness, all sweetness, all excellency! Philoclea is dead – and yet life is not ashamed to continue upon the earth. Philoclea is dead! O deadly word, which containeth in itself the uttermost of all misfortunes – but happy word, when thou shalt be said of me! And long it shall not be before it be said.'

Then[3] stopping his words with sighs, drowning his sighs in tears, and drying again his tears in rage, he would sit a while in a wandering muse which represented nothing but vexations unto him; then throwing himself sometimes[4] upon the floor, and sometimes upon the bed, then up again – till walking was wearisome, and rest loathsome. And so, neither suffering food nor sleep to help his afflicted nature, all that day and night he did nothing but weep, 'Philoclea!'; sigh, 'Philoclea!'; and cry out, 'Philoclea!' – till (as it happened, at that time upon his bed) toward the dawning of the day, he heard one stir in his chamber by the motion of garments, and he[5] with an angry voice asked who was there.

---

[1] hast thy] hast left thy 93   [2] which] *om. Cm*; that 13   [3] said.' Then *Cm*, 93: said.' Chap. 17. A lady's kind comforts to Pyrocles' comfortless unkindness; his hardly knowing her; her unmasking of Cecropia's fruitless sophistry; their medley of solace and sorrow. Then 90   [4] sometimes] sometime 93   [5] and he] and 93

'A poor gentlewoman,' answered the party, 'that wish long life unto you.'

'And I, soon death to you!' said he, 'for the horrible curse you have given me.'

'Certainly,' said she, 'an unkind answer, and far unworthy the excellency of your mind – but not suitable to the rest of your behaviour! For most part of this night I have heard you, being let into your chamber – you never perceiving it, so was your mind estranged from your senses – and have heard nothing of Zelmane in Zelmane; nothing but weak wailings, fitter for some nurse of a village than so famous a creature as you are.'

'O God!' cried out Pyrocles. 'That thou wert a man that usest these words unto me! I tell thee, I am sorry. I tell thee, I will be sorry – in despite of thee and all them that would have me joyful.'

'And yet,' replied she, 'perchance Philoclea is not dead, whom you so much bemoan.'

'I would we were both dead, of that condition,' said Pyrocles.

'See the folly of your passion!' said she. 'As though you should be nearer to her, you being dead and she alive, than she being dead and you alive! And if she be dead, was she not born to die? What then do you cry out for? Not for her, who must have died one time or other, but for some few years – so as, it is time and this world that seem so lovely things, and not Philoclea, unto you.'

'O noble sisters!' cried Pyrocles. 'Now you be gone, who were the only exalters of all womankind, what is left in that sex but babbling and business?'

'And truly,' said she, 'I will yet a little longer trouble you – '.

'Nay, I pray you, do!' said Pyrocles. 'For I wish for nothing in my short life but mischiefs and cumbers – and I am content you shall be one of them!'

'In truth!' said she. 'You would think yourself a greatly privileged person! if, since the strongest buildings[1] and lastingest monarchies are subject to end, only your Philoclea, because she is yours, should be exempted! But indeed, you bemoan yourself, who have lost a friend – you cannot her, who hath in one act both preserved her honour and left the miseries of this world.'

'Oh, woman's philosophy! Childish folly!' said Pyrocles. 'As though, if I do bemoan myself, I have not reason to do so, having lost more than any monarchy – nay, than my life can be worth unto me.'

'Alas!' said she. 'Comfort yourself nature did not forget her skill when she had made them. You shall find many their superiors, and perchance such as, when your eyes shall look abroad, yourself will like better.'

But that speech put all good manners out of the conceit of Pyrocles, insomuch that, leaping out of his bed, he ran to have stricken her. But coming near her, the morning then winning the field of darkness, he saw (or

---

[1] buildings] building 93

he thought he saw) indeed the very face of Philoclea – the same sweetness, the same grace, the same beauty – with which, carried into a divine astonishment, he fell down at her feet.

'Most blessed angel!' said he. 'Well hast thou done to take that shape, since thou wouldest submit thyself to mortal sense; for a more[1] angelical form could not have been created for thee. Alas, even by that excellent beauty so beloved of me, let it be lawful for me to ask of thee what is the cause that she, that heavenly creature whose form you have taken, should by the heavens be destined to so unripe an end? Why should unjustice so prevail? Why was she seen to the world, so soon to be ravished from us? Why was she not suffered to live, to teach the world perfection?'

'Do not deceive thyself,' answered she; 'I am no angel, I am Philoclea! the same Philoclea, so truly loving you, so truly beloved of you.'

'If it be so,' said he, 'that you are indeed the soul of Philoclea, you have done well to keep your own figure, for no heaven could have given you a better. Then, alas, why have you taken the pains to leave your blissful seat to come to this place, most wretched to me, who am wretchedness itself, and not rather obtain for me that I might come where you are, there eternally to behold, and eternally to love, your beauties? You know – I know – that I desire nothing but death, which I only stay to be justly revenged of your unjust murtherers.'

'Dear Pyrocles,' said she, 'I am thy Philoclea! and as yet living, not murdered as you supposed; and therefore be[2] comforted' – and with that, gave him her hand.

But the sweet touch of that hand seemed to his estrayed powers so heavenly a thing that it rather for a while confirmed him in his former belief, till she with vehement protestations (and desire that it might be so, helping to persuade that it was so) brought him to yield – yet doubtfully to yield – to this height of all comfort, that Philoclea lived; which witnessing with tears[3] of joy, 'Alas,' said he, 'how shall I believe mine eyes any more? Or do you yet but appear thus unto me to stay me from some desperate end; for, alas! I saw the excellent Pamela beheaded, I saw your head – the head indeed, and chief part of all nature's works – standing in a dish of gold, too mean a shrine, God wot, for such a relic. How can this be, my only dear, and you live? Or if this be not so, how can I believe mine[4] own senses? And if I cannot believe them, why should I now believe these blessed tidings they bring me?'

'The truth is,' said she, 'my Pyrocles, that neither I, as you find, nor yet my dear sister, is dead – although the mischievously subtle Cecropia used sleights to make either of us think so of other; for having in vain attempted

---

[1] for a more *Cm, 93*: for a a more *90* [2] therefore be *Cm, 93*: therefore to be *90* [3] with tears *Cm, 93*: with the tears *90* [4] believe mine *Cm, 93*: beleeeve mine *90*

the fardest of her wicked eloquence to make either of us yield to her son, and seeing that neither it (accompanied with great flatteries and rich presents) could get any ground of us, nor yet the violent way she fell into of cruelty (tormenting[1] our bodies) could prevail with us, at last she made either of us think the other dead, and so hoped to have wrested our minds to the forgetting of virtue. And first, she gave to mine eyes the miserable spectacle of my sister's (as I thought) death – but indeed, not my sister. It[2] was only Artesia, she who so cunningly brought us to this misery. Truly I am sorry for the poor gentlewoman, though justly she be punished for her double falsehood. But Artesia, muffled so as you could not easily discern her, and in my sister's apparel, which they had taken from her under colour of giving her other, did they execute. And when I, for thy sake especially, dear Pyrocles, could by no force nor fear be won, they assayed the like with my sister – by bringing me down under the scaffold, and making me thrust my head up through a hole they had made therein. They did put about my poor neck a dish of gold whereout they had beaten the bottom, so as, having set blood in it, you saw how I played the part of death – God knows, even willing to have done it in earnest; and so had they set me that I reached but on tiptoes to the ground, so as scarcely I could breathe, much less speak. And truly, if they had kept me there any whit longer, they had strangled me instead of beheading me; but then they took me away.

'And seeking to see their issue of this practice, they found my noble sister (for the dear love she vouchsafeth to bear me) so grieved withal that she willed them to do their uttermost cruelty unto her, for she vowed never to receive sustenance of them that had been the causers of my murther. And finding both of us even given over, not like to live many hours longer, and my sister Pamela rather worse than myself (the strength of her heart worse bearing those indignities), the good woman, Cecropia, with the same pity as folks keep fowl when they are not fat enough for their eating, made us know her deceit, and let us come one to another – with what joy you can well imagine, who I know feel the like; saving that we only thought ourselves reserved to miseries, and therefore fitter for condoling than congratulating. For my part, I am fully persuaded, it is but with a little respite to have a more feeling sense of the torments she prepares for us.

'True it is that one of my guardians would have me to believe that this proceeds of my gentle cousin Amphialus, who having heard some inkling that we were evil entreated, had called his mother to his bedside (from whence he never rose since his last combat), and besought and charged her upon all the love she bare him to use us with all kindness, vowing with all

---

[1] cruelty (tormenting)] cruelly tormenting 93   [2] indeed, not my sister. It] indeed it Cm; indeed, it was not my sister, it 93

the imprecations he could imagine, that if ever he understood, for his sake, that I received further hurt than the want of my liberty, he would not live an hour longer. And the good woman sware to me that he would kill his mother if he knew how I had been dealt with, but that Cecropia keeps him from understanding things, how they pass; only having heard a whispering, and myself named, he had – of abundance, forsooth, of honourable love! given this charge for us, whereupon this enlargement of mine was grown. For my part, I know too well their cunning, who leave no money unoffered that may buy mine honour, to believe any word they say, but, my dear Pyrocles, even look for the worst, and prepare myself for the same.

'Yet I must confess I was content to rob from death, and borrow of my misery the sweet comfort of seeing my sweet sister and, most sweet comfort, of thee, my Pyrocles. And so, having leave, I came stealing into your chamber, where, O Lord! what a joy it was unto me to hear you solemnize the funerals of the poor Philoclea; that I myself might live to hear my death bewailed – and by whom? – by my dear Pyrocles; that I saw death was not strong enough to divide thy love from me. O my Pyrocles, I am too well paid for my pains I have suffered. Joyful is my woe for so noble a cause! And welcome be all miseries! since to thee I am so welcome.

'Alas, how I pitied to hear thy pity of me! And yet a great while I could not find in my heart to interrupt thee, but often had even pleasure to weep with thee; and so kindly came forth thy lamentations that they enforced me to lament too, as if indeed I had been a looker-on to see poor Philoclea die; till at last I spake with you, to try whether I could remove thee from sorrow – till I had almost procured myself a beating!' And with that, she prettily smiled; which, mingled with her tears, one could not tell whether it were a mourning pleasure or a delightful sorrow – but like when a few April drops are scattered by a gentle Zephyrus among fine-coloured flowers.

But Pyrocles who had felt (with so small distance of time) in himself the overthrow both of hope and despair, knew not to what key he should tune his mind, either of joy or sorrow; but finding perfit reason in neither, suffered himself to be carried by the tide of his imagination, and his imaginations to be raised even by the sway which hearing or seeing might give unto them. He saw her alive; he was glad to see her alive. He saw her weep; he was sorry to see her weep. He heard her comfortable speeches nothing more gladsome; he heard her prognosticating her own destruction nothing more doleful. But when he had a little taken breath from the panting motion of such contrariety in passions, he fell to consider with her of her present estate, both comforting her that certainly the worst of this storm was past (since already they had done the worst which man's wit could imagine), and that if they had determined to have killed her, now they would have[1] done it; and also earnestly counselling her (and enabling his counsels with vehement prayers) that she would so far second the hopes of Amphialus as that she might but procure him liberty, promising then as much to her as the liberality of loving courage durst promise to himself.

But[2] who would lively describe the manner of these speeches should paint out the lightsome colours of affection shaded with the deepest shadows of sorrow, finding then[3] (between hope and fear) a kind of sweetness in tears; till Philoclea (content to receive a kiss – and but a kiss – of Pyrocles) sealed up his[4] moving[5] lips, and closed them up in comfort. And herself, for the passage was left between them open, went to her sister, with whom she had stayed but a while, fortifying one another, while Philoclea tempered Pamela's just disdain and Pamela ennobled Philoclea's sweet humbleness, when Amphialus came unto them; who never since he had heard Philoclea named could be quiet in himself, although none of them about him, fearing more his mother's violence than his power, would discover what had passed. And many messages he sent to know her estate, which brought answers[6] back according as it pleased Cecropia to indite them; till his heart (full of unfortunate affection)[7] more and more misgiving him, having impatiently borne the delay of the night's unfitness, this morning he gat up. And though full of wounds which not without danger could suffer such exercise, he apparelled himself; and with a countenance that showed strength in nothing but in grief, he came where the sisters were. And weakly kneeling down, he besought them to pardon him if they had not been used in that castle according to their worthiness and his duty, beginning to excuse small matters – poor gentleman! not knowing in what sort they had been handled.

But Pamela's high heart, having conceived mortal hate for the injury offered to her and her sister, could scarcely abide his sight, much less hear out his excuses, but interrupted him with these words:

'Traitor,' said she, 'to thine own blood! and false to the profession of so much love as thou hast vowed! Do not defile our ears with thy excuses, but pursue on thy cruelty that thou and thy goodly mother have used towards us. For my part, assure thyself – and so do I answer for my sister whose mind I know – I do not more desire mine own safety than thy destruction.'

Amazed with this speech, he turned his eye (full of humble sorrowfulness) to Philoclea. 'And is this, most excellent lady, your doom of me also?'

---

[1] now they would have *Cm, 93*: they would have now *90*   [2] himself. But *Cm, 93*: himself. Chap. 24. Amphialus excuseth; the princesses accuse; Cecropia, seeking their death, findeth her own; Amphialus' death-pangs and self-killing; the woeful knowledge of it. But *90*   [3] then *Cm, 93*: them *90*   [4] his *Cm, 93*: with *90*   [5] moving] moaning *Cm* [*spelled* moninge], *98, 13* [*spelled* moning in *98, 13*]   [6] answers *Cm, 93*: answer *90*   [7] affection *Cm, 93*: affliction *90*

She, sweet lady, sate weeping, for as her most noble kinsman, she had ever favoured him, and loved his love, though she could not be in love with his person. And now, partly unkindness of his wrong, partly pity of his case, made her sweet mind yield some tears before she could answer. And her answer was no other but that she had the same cause as her sister had.

He replied no further, but delivering from his heart two or three untaught sighs, rose, and with most low reverence went out of their chamber; and straight (by threatening torture) learned of one of the women in what terrible manner those princesses had been used. But when he heard it (crying out 'O God – ', and then not able to say any more, for his speech went back to rebound woe upon his heart), he needed no judge to go upon him, for no man could ever think any other worthy of greater punishment than he thought himself. Full therefore of the horriblest despair which a most guilty conscience could breed, with wild looks promising some terrible issue, understanding his mother was on[1] the top of the leads, he caught one of his servant's swords from him.

And none of them daring to stay him, he went up (carried by fury instead of strength) where she was, at that time musing how to go thorough with this matter, and resolving to make much of her nieces in show, and secretly to empoison them – thinking, since they were not to be won, her son's love would no otherwise be mitigated. But when she saw him come in, with a sword drawn, and a look more terrible than the sword, she straight was stricken with the guiltiness of her own conscience. Yet the well-known humbleness of her son somewhat animated her; till he coming nearer her and crying to her, 'Thou damnable creature! only fit to bring forth such a monster of unhappiness as I am!' – she, fearing he would have stricken her (though indeed he meant it not, but only intended to kill himself in her presence), went back so far till ere she were aware she overthrew herself from over the leads to receive her death's kiss at the ground. And yet was she not so happy as presently to die, but that she had time with hellish agony to see her son's mischief (whom she loved so well) before her end, when she confessed with most desperate but not repenting mind the purpose she had to empoison the princesses – and would then have had them murthered, but everybody seeing (and glad to see) her end, had left obedience to her tyranny; and – if it could be – her ruin increased woe in the noble heart of Amphialus, who when he saw her fall, had his own rage stayed a little with the suddenness of her destruction.

'And was I not enough miserable before,' said he, 'but that before my end I must be the death of my mother – who, how wicked soever, yet I would she had received her punishment by some other. O Amphialus! Wretched

---

[1] on] upon 93

Amphialus! Thou hast lived to be the death of thy most dear companion and friend, Philoxenus, and of his father, thy most careful foster-father. Thou hast lived to kill a lady with thine own hands – and so excellent and virtuous a lady as the fair Parthenia was. Thou hast lived to see thy faithful Ismenus slain in succouring thee – and thou not able to defend him. Thou hast lived to show thyself such a coward as that one unknown knight could overcome thee – in thy lady's presence. Thou hast lived to bear arms against thy rightful prince – thine own uncle. Thou hast lived to be accounted – and justly accounted – a traitor, by the most excellent persons that this world holdeth. Thou hast lived to be the death of her that gave thee life. But ah! wretched Amphialus! Thou hast lived, for thy sake and by thy authority, to have Philoclea tormented. O heavens! In Amphialus' castle! Where Amphialus commanded! Tormented! Tormented! Torment of my soul! Philoclea tormented! And thou hast had such comfort in thy life as to live all this while!

'Perchance this hand, used only to mischievous acts, thinks it were too good a deed to kill me. Or else, filthy hand! only worthy to kill women! thou art afraid to strike a man. Fear not, cowardly hand, for thou shalt kill but a cowardly traitor. And do it gladly – for thou shalt kill him whom Philoclea hateth!'

With that, furiously he tare open his doublet; and setting the pommel of the sword to the ground and the point to his breast, he fell upon it. But the sword more merciful than he to himself, with the slipping of the pommel the point swerved, and razed him but upon the side. Yet with the fall his other wounds opened, so as he bled in such extremity that Charon's boat might very well be carried in that flood – which yet he sought to hasten, by this means.

As he opened his doublet and fell, there fell out Philoclea's knives (which Cecropia at the first had taken from her and delivered to her son, and he had ever worn them next his heart as the only relic he had of his saint); now seeing them by him (his sword being so, as weakness could not well draw it out from his doublet), he took the knives; and pulling one of them out and many times kissing it, and then first (with the passions of kindness and unkindness) melting in tears, 'O dear knives! You are come in a good time to revenge the wrong I have done you all this while, in keeping you from her blessed side, and wearing you without your mistress's leave. Alas, be witness with me yet before I die – and well you may, for you have lain next my heart – that, by my consent, your excellent mistress should have had as much honour as this poor place could have brought forth for so high an excellency. And now I am condemned to die by her mouth. Alas, other, far other hope would my desire often have given me – but other event it hath pleased her to lay upon me. Ah Philoclea!' – with that, his tears gushed out as though they would strive to overflow his blood, 'I would yet thou knewest how I love thee. Unworthy I am! Unhappy I am! False I am! But to thee, alas, I am not false. But what a traitor am I, any way to excuse him whom she condemneth! Since there is nothing left me wherein I may do her service, but in punishing him who hath so offended her, dear knife, then do your noble mistress's commandment!'

With that, he stabbed himself into divers places of his breast and throat, until those wounds – with the old freshly bleeding – brought him to the senseless gate of death; by which time, his servants having with fear of his fury abstained a while from coming unto him, one of them (preferring dutiful affection before fearful duty) came in, and there found him swimming in his own blood – there giving[1] a pitiful spectacle, where the conquest was the conqueror's overthrow, and self-ruin the only triumph of a battle fought between him and himself.

The time full of danger, the person full of worthiness, the manner full of horror did greatly astonish all the beholders, so as by and by all the town was full of it; and then, of all ages came running up to see the beloved body, everybody thinking their safety bled in his wounds, and their honour died in his destruction. But[2] when it came – and quickly it came – to the ears of his proud friend Anaxius, who by that time was grown well of his wound but never had come abroad, disdaining to abase himself to the company of any other but of Amphialus, he was exceedingly vexed (either with kindness, or if a proud heart be not capable thereof, with disdain) that he who had the honour to be called the friend of Anaxius should come to such an unexpected ruin.

Therefore, then coming abroad with a face red in anger and engrained in pride, with lids raised and[3] eyes levelling from top to the toe[4] of them that met him, treading as though he thought to make the earth shake under him, with his hand upon his sword, short speeches and disdainful answers, giving straight order to his two brothers to go take the oath of obedience in his name of all the soldiers and citizens in the town, and withal to swear them to revenge the death of Amphialus upon Basilius, he himself went to see him – calling for all the surgeons and physicians there, spending some time in viewing the body, and threatening them all to be hanged if they did not heal him. But they taking view of his wounds and falling down at Anaxius' feet assured him that they were mortal, and no possible means

---

[1] there giving] giving 93 [2] destruction. But *Cm, 93*: destruction. Chap. 25. Anaxius' rages for the death, Queen Helen's coming for the cure, of Amphialus; her complaints over him; her passport and safe-conduct to carry him to her chirurgeon; the people's sorrow set down in a song. But *90* [3] raised and *Cm, 93*: raised up and *90* [4] top to the toe] *om. Cm*; top to toe *93*

to keep him above two days alive. And he stood partly in doubt to kill or save them, between his own fury and their humbleness, but vowing with his own hands to kill the two sisters as causers of his friend's death – when his brothers came to him and told him they had done his commandment in having received the oath of allegiance with no great difficulty, the most part terrified by their valure and force of their servants, and many that had been forward actors in the rebellion willing to do anything rather than come under the subjection of Basilius again; and such few as durst gainsay, being cut off by present slaughter.

But withal, as the chief matter of their coming to him, they told Anaxius that the fair Queen Helen was come with an honourable retinue to the town, humbly desiring leave to see Amphialus, whom she had sought in many places of the world; and lastly being returned into her own country, she heard together of the late siege, and of his combat with the strange knight who had dangerously hurt him; whereupon, full of loving care which she was content even to publish to the world, how ungratefully soever he dealt with her, she had gotten leave of Basilius to come by his frontiers to carry away Amphialus with her to the excellentest surgeon then known, whom she had in her country, but so old as not able to travel – but had given her sovereign anointments to preserve his body withal, till he might be brought unto him; and that Basilius had granted leave, either natural kindness prevailing over all the offences done, or, rather, glad to make any passage which might lead him out of his country, and from his daughters.

This discourse Lycurgus understanding of Helen, delivered to his brother, with her vehement desire to see the body and take her last farewell of him. Anaxius, though he were fallen-out with all womankind in respect of the hate he bare the sisters, whom he accounted murtherers of Amphialus, yet at his brother's request granted her leave; and she, poor lady, with grievous expectation and languishing desire, carried her faint legs to the place where he lay, either not breathing, or in all appearance breathing nothing but[1] death; in which piteous plight, when she saw him, though sorrow had set before her mind the pitifullest conceit thereof that it could paint, yet the present sight went beyond all former apprehensions, so that beginning to kneel by the body, her sight ran from her service rather than abide such a sight, and she fell in a sound upon him as if she could not choose but die of his wounds. But when her breath, aweary to be closed up in woe, broke the prison of her fair lips, and brought memory with his servant, senses, to his natural office, she yet made the breath convey these doleful words with it:

'Alas,' said she, 'Amphialus! What strange diseases[2] be these! that having sought thee so long, I should be now sorry to find thee; that these eyes

---

[1] breathing nothing but *Cm*, *93*: breathing but *90*   [2] diseases] *om. Cm*; disasters *93*

should look upon Amphialus and be grieved withal; that I should have thee in my power without glory, and embrace thee without comfort! How often have I blessed the means that might bring me near thee! Now, woe worth the cause that brings me so near thee!

'Often, alas! often hast thou disdained my tears – but now, my dear Amphialus, receive them. These eyes can serve for nothing else but weep[1] for thee. Since thou wouldest never vouchsafe them thy comfort, yet disdain not them thy sorrow. I would they had been more dear unto thee, for then hadst thou lived.

'Woe is me! that thy noble heart could love who hated thee, and hate who loved thee. Alas, why should not my faith to thee cover my other defects, who only sought to make my crown thy footstool, myself thy servant? That was all my ambition; and alas, thou disdainedst it to serve them by whom thy incomparable self wert[2] disdained!

'Yet, O Philoclea (wheresoever you are, pardon me if I speak in the bitterness of my soul), excellent may you be in all other things – and excellent sure you are, since he loved you – your want of pity where the fault only was infiniteness of desert cannot be excused. I would, O God I would! that you had granted his deserved suit of marrying you – and that I had been your serving-maid to have made my estate the foil of your felicity, so he had lived.

'How many weary steps have I trodden after thee, while my only complaint was that thou wert unkind! Alas, I would now thou wert, to be unkind! Alas, why wouldest thou not command my service in persuading Philoclea to love thee? Who could, or, if every one could, who would have recounted thy perfections so well as I? Who with such kindly passions could have stirred pity for thee as I? Who should have delivered not only the words but the tears I had of thee? And so shouldest thou have exercised thy disdain in me, and yet used my service for thee.'

With that, the body moving somewhat and giving a groan full of death's music, she fell upon his face and kissed him, and withal cried out, 'O miserable I! that have only favour by misery!' And then would she have returned to a fresh career of complaints, when an aged and wise gentleman came to her and besought her to remember what was fit for her greatness, wisdom, and honour, and withal that it was fitter to show her love in carrying the body to her excellent surgeon, first applying such excellent medicines as she had received of him for that purpose, rather than only show herself a woman-lover in fruitless lamentations.

She was straight warned, with the obedience of an overthrown mind; and therefore (leaving some surgeons of her own to dress the body) went herself to Anaxius, and humbling herself to him as low as his own pride could wish,

---

[1] but weep] but to weep 93   [2] wert *Cm, 98, 13*: were *90, 93*

besought him, that since the surgeons there had utterly given him over, that he would let her carry him away in her litter with her, since the worst he could have should be to die – and to die in her arms that loved him above all things, and where he should have such monuments erected over him as were fit for her love, and his worthiness; beseeching him withal, since she was in a country of enemies where she trusted more to Anaxius' valour than Basilius' promise, that he would convey them safely out of those territories.

Her reasons something moved him, but nothing thoroughly persuaded him but the last request, of his help – which he straight promised, warranting all security as long as that sword had his master alive. She (as happy therein as unhappiness could be), having received as small comfort of her own surgeons as of the others, caused yet the body to be easily conveyed into the litter, all the people then beginning to roar and cry, as though never till then they had lost their lord. And if the terror of Anaxius had not kept them under, they would have mutinied rather than suffered his body to be carried away. But Anaxius himself riding before the litter with the choice men of that place, they were afraid even to cry, though they were ready to cry for fear; but because that they might do, everybody forced (even with harming themselves) to do honour to him – some throwing themselves upon the ground, some tearing their clothes and casting dust upon their heads, and some even wounding themselves and sprinkling their own blood in the air. Among the rest, one accounted good in that kind, and made the better by the true feeling of sorrow, roared out a song of lamentation, which, as well as might be, was gathered up in this form:

> Since that to death is gone the shepherd high
> Who[1] most the silly shepherd's pipe did prize,
> Your doleful tunes, sweet muses, now apply.
> And you, O trees (if any life there lies
> In trees), now through your porous barks receive
> The strange resound of these my causeful cries,
> And let my breath upon your branches cleave[2]
> (My breath, distinguished into words of woe),
> That so I may signs of my sorrow[3] leave.
> But if among yourselves some one tree grow
> That aptest is to figure misery,
> Let it embassage[4] bear, your grieves to show;
> The weeping myrrh, I think, will not deny
> Her help to this, this justest cause of plaint.
> Your doleful tunes, sweet muses, now apply.

---

[1] Who *OA, 93*: Whom *90*   [2] cleave *OA, 93*: leave *90*   [3] sorrow] sorrows *OA (ex. Le)*   [4] embassage] ambassade *Bo, As*; embasshade *St*; (embraced) *Cl*; imbassage *Le*; ambassage *Da, Je*; imbusshed *Ph*; embashed *Hm*

And thou, poor earth (whom fortune doth attaint
   In nature's name to suffer such a harm
   As for to lose thy gem, and such a saint),
Upon thy face let coaly ravens swarm;
   Let all the sea thy tears accounted be;
   Thy bowels with all killing metals arm;
Let gold now rust, let diamonds waste in thee;
   Let pearls be wan, with woe their dam doth bear;
   Thyself henceforth the light do never see.
And you, O flow'rs, which sometimes princes were
   Till these strange alt'rings you did hap to try,
   Of prince's loss, yourselves for tokens rear.
Lily, in mourning[1] black thy whiteness dye[2];
   O hyacinth, let 'ai' be on thee still.
   Your doleful tunes, sweet muses, now apply.
O echo, all these woods with roaring[3] fill,
   And do not only mark the accents last,
   But all, for all reach out my wailful will;
One echo to another, echo, cast[4]
   Sound of my griefs, and let it never end
   Till that it hath all woods and waters passed;
Nay, to the heav'ns your just complaining[5] send,
   And stay the stars' inconstant constant[6] race
   Till that they do unto our[7] dolours bend,
And ask the reason of that special grace
   That they, which have no lives, should live so long,
   And virtuous souls so soon should lose their place;
Ask if, in great men, good men do so[8] throng
   That he for want of elbow-room must die,
   Or, if that they be scant, if this be wrong.
Did wisdom this our wretched time espy,
   In one true chest, to rob all virtue's treasure?
   Your doleful tunes, sweet muses, now apply –
And if that any counsel you to measure
   Your doleful tunes, to them still plaining[9] say,
   'To well-felt grief, plaint is the only pleasure.'

---

[1] in mourning] in morning *Cl, Le*; O mourn in *Da, Hm*; O morn in *Ph, Je* [2] thy whiteness dye] and whiteness fly *Da, Ph, Je, Hm* [3] roaring] roarings *St, Bo, Je*; scritching *Ph* [4] And do not only mark the accents last, But all, for all reach out my wailful will; One echo to another, echo, cast om. *As* [5] complaining] complainings *St, Bo, Cl, Le, As, Je* [6] inconstant] unconstant *Cl, Le*; inconst *As*; in constant *Da, Ph* [7] our] your *As, Ph* [8] do so] so do OA (ex. *Da, Ph*) [9] plaining] playing *Bo, Cl, Da*

O light of sun, which is entitled day,
   Oh, well thou doost that thou no longer bidest,
   For mourning light[1] her black weeds may display;
O Phoebus, with good cause thy face thou hidest,
   Rather than have thy all-beholding eye
   Fouled[2] with this sight, while thou thy[3] chariot guidest;
And well, methinks, becomes this vaulty sky
   A stately tomb to cover him deceased.
   Your doleful tunes, sweet muses, now apply.
O Philomela (with thy breast oppressed
   By shame and grief), help, help me to lament
   Such cursed harms as cannot be redressed;
Or if thy mourning notes be fully spent,
   Then give a quiet ear unto my plaining,
   For I, to teach the world complaint, am bent.
You dimmy clouds, which well employ your staining
   This cheerful air with your obscured cheer,
   Witness your woeful tears with daily raining.
And if, O sun,[4] thou ever didst appear
   In shape which by man's eye might be perceived –
   Virtue is dead, now set thy triumph here,
Now set thy triumph in this world, bereaved
   Of what was good, where now no good doth lie,
   And by thy[5] pomp our loss will be conceived.
O notes of mine, yourselves together tie;
   With too much grief methinks you are dissolved.
   Your doleful tunes, sweet muses, now apply.
Time, ever old and young, is still revolved
   Within itself, and never tasteth end;
   But mankind is for ay to nought resolved.[6]
The filthy snake her aged coat can mend,
   And getting youth again, in youth[7] doth flourish;
   But unto man, age ever death doth send.
The very trees with grafting we can cherish,
   So that we can long time produce their time;
   But man, which helpeth them, helpless must perish.
Thus, thus, the minds which over all do climb,
   When they by years' experience get best graces,

---

[1] light] night *OA, 13* [2] Fouled] Iould *St, Bo, Da, Je;* Would *Ph* [3] thy] the *Cl, Ph* [4] sun] sin *93, 13* [5] thy] the *Cl, Da, Ph, 93 (only)* [6] resolved] dissolved *Le, As, Da, Ph, Je, Hm* [7] again, in youth] in youth again *Cl, Le*

Must finish then by death's detested crime:
We last short while, and build long-lasting places.
   Ah, let us all against foul nature cry,
   We nature's works do help, she us defaces;
For how can nature unto this reply[1]:
   That she her child, I say, her best child, killeth?
   Your doleful tunes, sweet muses, now apply.

Alas, methinks my weakened voice but spilleth
   The vehement course of this just lamentation;
   Methinks my sound no place with sorrow filleth.
I know not I; but once, in detestation
   I have myself and all what life containeth,
   Since death on virtue's fort hath made invasion.
One word of woe another after traineth;
   Ne do I care how rude be my invention,
   So it be seen what sorrow in me reigneth.
O elements, by whose, men say, contention
   Our bodies be in living pow'r[2] maintained,
   Was this man's death the fruit of your dissension?
O physic's power, which some say hath restrained[3]
   Approach of death, alas, thou helpest meagrely
   When once one is for Atropos distrained.
Great be physicians' brags, but aid is beggarly;
   When rooted moisture fails or groweth dry,
   They leave off all, and say, 'Death comes,' too eagerly.
They are but words, therefore, that men do buy
   Of any, since god[4] Aesculapius ceased.
   Your doleful tunes, sweet muses, now apply.

Justice, justice is now, alas, oppressed;
   Bountifulness hath made his last conclusion;
   Goodness, for best attire, in dust is dressed.
Shepherds, bewail your uttermost confusion,
   And see, by[5] this picture to you presented,
   Death is our home, life is but a delusion;
For see, alas, who is from you absented.
   Absented? Nay, I say for ever banished
   From such as were to die for him contented.
Out of our sight (in turn of hand) is vanished

---

[1] reply] apply *Cl, Le*   [2] power] powers *Le, Hm*   [3] restrained] refrained *OA (ex. Cl)*   [4] god] good *Bo, Ph, Je, Hm; om. Cl*   [5] by] with *Da, Je*

> Shepherd of shepherds, whose well-settled order,
> Private with wealth, public with quiet, garnished.
> While he did live, far, far was all disorder;
> Example more prevailing than direction,
> Far was home-strife, and far was foe from border;
> His life a law, his look a full correction;
> As in his health we healthful were preserved,
> So in his sickness grew our sure infection;
> His death, our death. But ah, my muse hath swarved
> From such deep plaint[1] as should such woes descry,
> Which he of us for ever hath deserved.
> The style of heavy heart can never fly
> So high as should make such a pain notorious.
> Cease, muse, therefore; thy dart, O death, apply;
> And farewell, prince, whom goodness hath made glorious.

The[2] general consort of all such numbers men's[3] mourning performed so the natural times[4] of sorrow that even to them (if any such were) that felt not the loss, yet others' grief taught them grief, having before their compassionate sense so passionate a spectacle, of a young man of great beauty, beautified with great honour, honoured by great valure – made of inestimable valure by[5] the noble using of it, to lie there languishing under the arrest of death, and a death where the manner could be no comfort to the discomfortableness of the matter. But when the body was carried thorough the gate, and the people (saving such as were appointed) not suffered to go further, then was such an universal cry as if they had all had but one life, and all received but one blow; which so moved Anaxius to consider the loss of his friend that (his mind apter to revenge than tenderness), he presently giving order to his brother to keep the prisoners safe and unvisited till his return from conveying Helen, he sent a messenger to the sisters to tell them this courteous message: that at his return, with his own hands, he would cut off their heads and send them for tokens to their father.

This message was brought unto the sisters as they sate at that time together with Zelmane, conferring how to carry themselves, having heard of the death of Amphialus; and as no expectation of death is so painful as where the resolution is hindered by the intermixing of hopes, so did this new alarum, though not remove, yet move somewhat the constancy

---

[1] plaint] plaints *Le, Hm*   [2] glorious. The *93*: [blank] The *Cm*; glorious. Chap. 26. The public grief amplified; Anaxius' death-threatening to the princesses; their resoluteness in it; his return and stop; Zelmane's brave challenge unto him scorned by him; his love to Pamela scorned by her; his brothers' brave loves have as mean success. The *90*   [3] all such numbers men's *Cm*: all such numbers' *90*; whose *93*   [4] times] tunes *93*   [5] valure by] value by *93*

of their minds, which were so unconstantly dealt with. But within a while, the excellent Pamela had brought her mind again to his old acquaintance; and then, as careful for her sister whom most dearly she loved, 'Sister,' said she, 'you see how many acts our tragedy hath. Fortune is not yet aweary of vexing us. But what? A ship is not counted strong for biding one storm. It is but the same trumpet of death, which now perhaps gives the last sound; and let us make that profit of our former miseries, that in them we learned to die willingly.'

'Truly,' said Philoclea, 'dear sister, I was so beaten with the evils of life that, though I had not virtue enough to despise the sweetness of it, yet my weakness bred that strength to be weary of the pains of it. Only I must confess that little hope, which by these late accidents was awaked in me, was at the first angry withal. But even in the darkness of that horror, I see a light of comfort appear – and how can I tread amiss, that see Pamela's steps? I would only – oh, that my wish might take place! – that my schoolmistress might live to see me say my lesson truly.'

'Were that a life, my Philoclea?' said Pamela. 'No, no,' said she; 'let it come – and put on his worst face, for at the worst it is but a bugbear. Joy is it to me to see you so well resolved; and since the world will not have us, let it lose us. Only – ', with that, she stayed a little, and sight, only, my Philoclea – ', then she bowed down, and whispered in her ear, 'only Musidorus, my shepherd, comes between me and death, and makes me think I should not die – because I know he would not I should die.'

With that, Philoclea sighed also – saying no more, but looking upon Zelmane, who was walking up and down the chamber, having heard this message from Anaxius; and having in times past heard of his nature, thought him like enough to perform it, which winded her again into the former maze of perplexity. Yet, debating with herself of the manner how to prevent it, she continued her musing humour, little saying, or indeed little finding in her heart to say, in a case of such extremity where peremptorily death was threatened. And so stayed they, having yet that comfort that they might tarry together, Pamela nobly, Philoclea sweetly, and Zelmane sadly and desperately, none of them entertaining sleep, which they thought should shortly begin, never to awake.

But Anaxius came home, having safely conducted Helen – and safely he might well do it, for though many of Basilius' knights would have attempted something upon Anaxius, by that means to deliver the ladies, yet Philanax having received his master's commandment, and knowing[1] his word was given, would not consent unto it; and the Black Knight, who by then[2] was

---

[1] and knowing] *Cm ends after and* [2] then] them *93, 98*

able to carry abroad his wounds, did not know thereof, but was bringing forces,[1] by force to deliver his lady; so as Anaxius (interpreting it rather fear than faith, and making even chance an argument of his virtue) returned. And as soon as he was returned, with a felon heart calling his brothers up with him, he went into the chamber where they were all three together, with full intention to kill the sisters with his own hands, and send their heads for tokens to their father; though his brothers, who were otherwise inclined, dissuaded him; but his reverence stayed their persuasions.

But when he was come into the chamber, with the very words of choleric threatening climbing up his throat, his eyes first lighted upon Pamela; who, hearing he was coming, and looking for death, thought she would keep her own majesty in welcoming it. But the beams thereof so strake his eyes with such a counterbuff unto his pride that, if his anger could not so quickly love, nor his pride so easily honour, yet both were forced to find a worthiness; which while it bred a pause in him, Zelmane (who had ready in her mind both what and how to say) stepped out unto him, and with a resolute staidness void either of anger, kindness, disdain, or humbleness, spake in this sort:

'Anaxius,' said she, 'if fame have not been over-partial to thee, thou art a man of exceeding valour; therefore I do call thee, even before that virtue, and will make it the judge between us. And now I do affirm that, to the eternal blot of all the fair acts that thou hast done, thou doest weakly in seeking without danger to revenge his death, whose life with[2] danger thou mightst perhaps have preserved. Thou doost cowardly in going about, by the death of these excellent ladies, to prevent the just punishment that hereafter they, by the powers which they (better than their father or any other) could make, might lay upon thee; and doost most basely in once presenting thyself as an executioner, a vile office upon men and in a just cause, beyond the degree of any vile word in so unjust a cause – and upon ladies, and such ladies; and therefore, as a hangman, I say thou art unworthy to be counted a knight or to be admitted into the company of knights. Neither for what I say will I allege other reasons of wisdom or justice to prove my speech, because I know thou doost disdain to be tied to their rules, but even in thine own virtue, whereof thou so much gloriest, I will make my trial, and therefore defy thee, by the death of one of us two, to prove or disprove these reproaches. Choose thee what arms thou likest. I only demand that these ladies whom I defend may in liberty see the combat.'

When Zelmane began her speech, the excellency of her beauty and grace made him a little content to hear – besides that, a new lesson he had read

---

[1] forces] force 93   [2] with 93: wfth 90

in Pamela had already taught him some regard. But when she entered into bravery of speech, he thought at first a mad and railing humour possessed her, till finding the speeches hold well together, and at length come to flat challenge of combat, he stood leaning back with his body and head, sometimes (with bent brows) looking upon the one side of her, sometimes of the other, beyond marvel marvelling that he who had never heard such speeches from any knight should be thus rebuffed by a woman. And that marvel made him hear out her speech; which ended, he turned his head to his brother Zoilus, and said nothing, but only (lifting up his eyes) smiled.

But Zelmane finding his mind, 'Anaxius,' said she, 'perchance thou disdainest to answer me because, as a woman, thou thinkest me not fit to be fought withal. But I tell thee that I have been trained up in martial matters, with so good success that I have many times overcome better[1] knights than thyself, and am well known to be equal in feats of arms to the famous Pyrocles who slew thy valiant uncle, the giant Euardes.'

The remembrance of his uncle's death something nettled him, so as he answered thus: 'Indeed,' said he, 'any woman may be as valiant as that coward and traitorly boy who slew my uncle traitorously, and after, ran from me in the plain field. Five thousand such could not have overcome Euardes but by falsehood. But I sought him all over Asia, following him still from one of his cony-holes to another, till coming into this country, I heard of my friend's being besieged, and so came to blow away the wretches that troubled him. But wheresoever the miserable boy fly, heaven nor hell shall keep his heart from being torn by these hands.'

'Thou liest in thy throat,' said Zelmane. 'That boy, wherever he went, did so noble acts as thy heart, as proud as it is, dares not think of, much less perform. But to please thee the better with my presence, I tell thee no creature can be nearer of kin to him than myself; and so well we love that he would not be sorrier for his own death than for mine, I being begotten by his father of an Amazon lady. And therefore thou canst not devise to revenge thyself more upon him than by killing me, which, if thou darest do manfully, do it. Otherwise, if thou harm these incomparable ladies or myself without daring to fight with me, I protest before these knights – and before heaven and earth that will reveal thy shame – that thou art the beggarliest dastardly villain that dishonoureth! the earth with his steps. And if thou lettest me overlive them, so will I blaze thee.'

But all this could not move Anaxius, but that he only said, 'Evil should it become the terror of the world to fight, much less[2] to scold with thee. But,' said he, 'for the death of these same,' pointing to the princesses, 'of my grace

---

[1] better] braver 93   [2] less] worse 93

I give them life.' And withal, going to Pamela and offering to take her by the chin, 'And as for you, minion,' said he, 'yield but gently to my will, and you shall not only live, but live so happily – '.

He would have said further, when Pamela (displeased both with words, matter, and manner), putting him away with her fair hand, 'Proud beast,' said she; 'yet thou playest worse thy comedy than thy tragedy. For my part, assure thyself, since my destiny is such that at each moment my life and death stand in equal balance, I had rather have thee – and think thee far fitter – to be my hangman than my husband!'

Pride and anger would fain have cruelly revenged so bitter an answer, but already Cupid had begun to make it his sport to pull his plumes, so that, unused to a way of courtesy, and put out of his bias of pride, he hastily went away, grumbling to himself (between threatening and wishing), leaving his brothers with them, the elder of whom, Lycurgus, liked Philoclea, and Zoilus would needs love Zelmane – or at least entertain themselves with making them believe so.

Lycurgus, more braggard and near his brother's humour, began with setting forth their blood, their deeds, how many they had despised of most excellent women, how much they were bound to them that would seek that of them – in sum, in all his speeches more like the bestower than the desirer of felicity; whom, it was an excellent pastime (to those that would delight in the play of virtue) to see with what a witty ignorance she would not understand, and how, acknowledging his perfections, she would make that one of his perfections not to be injurious[1] to ladies. But when he knew not how to reply, then would he fall to touching and toying, still viewing his graces in no glass but self-liking – to which Philoclea's shamefastness and humbleness were as strong resisters as choler and disdain; for though she yielded not, he thought she was to be overcome, and that thought a while stayed him from further violence. But Zelmane had eye to his behaviour, and set in her memory upon the score of revenge, while she herself was no less attempted by Zoilus, who, less full of brags, was forwardest in offering indeed dishonourable violence.

But[2] when after their fruitless labours they had gone away, called by their brother who began to be perplexed between new-conceived desires and disdain to be disdained, Zelmane, who with most assured quietness of judgement looked into their present estate, earnestly persuaded the two sisters that, to avoid the mischiefs of proud outrage, they would only so

---

[1] injurious 93: injurions 90   [2] violence. But 93: violence. Chap. 27. Zelmane's persuasions to temporize, and refer them to Basilius; Anaxius' embassage to treat the marriage; Basilius' recourse to a new oracle, and his negative thereon; the flattering relation of his Mercury; the brothers' course to resist force without, and use force within. But 90

far suit their behaviour to their estates as they might win time, which, as it could not bring them to worse case than they were, so it might bring forth inexpected relief.

'And why,' said Pamela, 'shall we any longer flatter adversity? Why should we delight to make ourselves any longer balls to injurious fortune? Since our own parents are content to be tyrants over us, since our own kin[1] are content traitorously to abuse us, certainly, in mishap it may be some comfort to us that we are lighted in these fellows' hands, who yet will keep us from having cause of being miserable by our friends' means. Nothing grieves me more than that you, noble Lady Zelmane, to whom the world might have made us able to do honour, should receive only hurt by the contagion of our misery. As for me and my sister, undoubtedly it becomes our birth to think of dying nobly, while we have done or suffered nothing which might make our soul ashamed at the parture from these bodies. Hope is the fawning traitor of the mind. While under colour of friendship, it robs it of his chief force of resolution.'

'Virtuous and fair lady,' said Zelmane, 'what you say is true, and that truth may well make up a part in the harmony of your noble thoughts – but yet the time, which ought always to be one, is not tuned for it. While that may bring forth any good, do not bar yourself thereof, for then would[2] be the time to die nobly when you cannot live nobly.'

Then so earnestly she persuaded with them both to refer themselves to their father's consent (in obtaining whereof they knew some while would be spent, and by that means to temper the minds of their proud wooers), that in the end Pamela yielded to her because she spake reason, and Philoclea yielded to her reason because she spake it. And so, when they were again solicited in that little-pleasing petition, Pamela forced herself to make answer to Anaxius that, if her father gave his consent, she would make herself believe that[3] such was the heavenly determination, since she had no means to avoid it.

Anaxius, who was the most frank promiser to himself of success, nothing doubted of Basilius' consent, but rather assured himself he would be his orator in that matter. And therefore he chose out an officious servant (whom he esteemed very wise because he never found him but just of his opinion), and willed him to be his embassador to Basilius, and to make him know that, if he meant to have his daughter both safe and happy, and desired himself to have such a son-in-law as would not only protect him in his quiet course but, if he listed to accept it, would give him the monarchy of the world, that then he should receive Anaxius, who never before knew what it was to pray

---

[1] own parents ... own kin 93: own kin 90   [2] would] will 93   [3] that 93: rhat 90

anything; that if he did not, he would make him know that the power of Anaxius was in everything beyond his will, and yet his will not to be resisted by any other power.

His servant, with smiling and cast-up look, desired God to make his memory able to contain the treasure of that wise speech, and therefore besought him to repeat it again, that by the oftener hearing it his mind might be the better acquainted with the divineness thereof. And that being graciously granted, he then doubted not, by carrying with him in his conceit the grace wherewith Anaxius spake it, to persuade rocky minds to their own harm, so little doubted he to win Basilius to that which, he thought, would make him think the heavens opened when he heard but the proffer thereof.

Anaxius gravely allowed the probability of his conjecture, and therefore sent him away, promising him he should have the bringing-up of his second son by Pamela. The messenger with speed performed his lord's commandment to Basilius, who, by nature quiet and by superstition made doubtful, was loath to take any matter of arms in hand wherein already he had found so slow success, though Philanax vehemently urged him thereunto, making him see that his retiring back did encourage injuries. But Basilius (betwixt the fear of Anaxius' might, the passion of his love, and jealousy of his estate) was so perplexed that, not able to determine, he took the common course of men, to fly only then to devotion when they want resolution.

So,[1] detaining the messenger with delays, he deferred the directing of his course to the counsel of Apollo; which, because himself at that time could not well go to require, he entrusted the matter to his best-trusted Philanax, who, as one in whom obedience was a sufficient reason unto him, went with diligence to Delphos; where being entered into the secret place of the temple, and having performed the sacrifices usual, the spirit that possessed the prophesying[2] woman with a sacred fury attended not his demand, but, as if it would argue him of incredulity, told him not in dark, wonted speeches, but plainly to be understood, what he came for, and that he should return to Basilius and will him to deny his daughters to Anaxius and his brothers, for that they were reserved for such as were better beloved of the gods; that he should not doubt, for they should return unto him safely and speedily; and that he should keep on his solitary course till both Philanax and Basilius fully agreed in the understanding of the former prophecy; withal, commanding Philanax from thence forward to give tribute, but not oblation, to human wisdom.

Philanax, then finding that reason cannot show itself more reasonable than to leave reasoning in things above reason, returns to his lord; and like

---

[1] So] Therefore 93   [2] prophesying 98, 13: prohesying 90, 93

one that preferred truth before the maintaining of an opinion, hid nothing from him, nor from thenceforth durst any more dissuade him from that which he found by the celestial providence directed. But he himself looking to repair the government as much as in so broken an estate by civil dissension he might, and fortifying with notable art both the lodges so as they were almost made unapproachable, he left Basilius to bemoan the absence of his daughters – and to bewail the imprisonment of Zelmane. Yet wholly given holily to obey the oracle, he gave a resolute negative unto the messenger of Anaxius, who all this while had waited for it – yet, in good terms, desiring him to show himself in respect of his birth and profession so princely a knight as, without forcing him to seek the way of force, to deliver in noble sort those ladies unto him; and so should the injury have been in Amphialus, and the benefit in him.

The messenger went back with this answer. Yet having ever used to sugar anything which his master was to receive, he told him that, when Basilius first understood his desires, he did overreach so far all his most hopeful expectations that he thought it were too great a boldness to hearken to such a man, in whom the heavens had such interest, without asking the gods' counsel, and therefore had sent his principal councillor to Delphos; who, although he kept the matter never so secret, yet his diligence (inspired by Anaxius' privilege over all worldly things) had found out the secret; which was that he should not presume[1] to marry his daughters to one who already was enrolled among the demigods, and yet much less he should dare the attempting to take them out of his hands.

Anaxius, who till then had made fortune his creator and force his god, now began to find another wisdom to be above, that judged so rightly of him. And where in this time of his servant's waiting for Basilius' resolution he and his brothers had courted their ladies (as whom they vouchsafed to have for their wives), he resolved now to dally no longer in delays, but to make violence his orator, since he had found persuasions had gotten nothing but answers; which intention he opened to his brothers, who having all this while wanted nothing to take that way but his authority, gave spurs to his running. And, unworthy men, neither feeling virtue in themselves nor tendering it in others, they were headlong to make that evil consort of love and force, when Anaxius had word that from the tower there were descried some companies of armed men marching towards the town; wherefore he gave present order to his servants and soldiers to go to the gates and walls, leaving none within but himself and his brothers – his thoughts then so full of their intended prey that Mars' loudest trumpet could scarcely have

---

[1] presume 93: presnme 90

awaked him. But[1] while he was directing what he would have done, his youngest brother, Zoilus, glad that he had the commission, went in the name of Anaxius to tell the sisters, that since he had answer from their father that he and his brother Lycurgus should have them in what sort it pleased them, that they would now grant them no longer time, but presently to determine whether they thought it more honourable comfort to be compelled, or persuaded.

Pamela made him answer that in a matter whereon the whole state of her life depended, and wherein she had ever answered she would not lead, but follow her parents' pleasure, she thought it reason she should, either by letter or particular messenger, understand something from themselves and not have her belief[2] bound to the report of their partial servants.[3] And therefore, as to their words she and her sister had ever a simple and true resolution, so against their unjust force, God, they hoped, would either arm their lives, or take away their lives.

'Well, ladies,' said he, 'I will leave my brothers, who by and by will come unto you to be their own embassadors. For my part, I[4] must now do myself service.' And with that, turning up his mustachos, and marching as if he would begin a paven, he went toward Zelmane.

But Zelmane having had[5] all this while of the messenger's being with Basilius much to do to keep those excellent ladies from seeking by the passport of death to escape those base dangers whereunto they found themselves subject; still hoping that Musidorus would find some means to deliver them (and therefore had often, both by her own example and comfortable reasons, persuaded them to overpass many insolent indignities of their proud suitors, who thought it was a sufficient favour not to do the uttermost injury), now come again to the strait she most feared for them, either of death or dishonour – if heroical courage would have let her, she had been beyond herself amazed. But that yet held up her wit, to attend the uttermost occasion – which even then brought his hairy forehead unto her.

For Zoilus smacking his lips as for the prologue of a kiss, and something advancing himself, 'Darling!' said he. 'Let thy heart be full of joy! And let thy fair eyes be of counsel with it, for this day thou shalt have Zoilus, whom many have longed for – but none shall have him, but Zelmane. And oh! how much glory I have to think what a race will be between us! The world, by the heavens! the world will be too little for them!' And with that, he would have put his arm about her neck.

---

[1] him. But 93: him. Chap. 28. Zoilus, the messenger and first offerer of force, is forced to fly and die; Lycurgus, pointed to kill, is fought withal, foiled, and killed; Anaxius-the-Revenger with Pyrocles-the-Punisher, brave, and bravely combatted. But 90   [2] belief] be led 90 (uncorr.)   [3] servants] servant 93   [4] I] you 90 (uncorr.)   [5] had] heard 90 (uncorr.)

But she withdrawing herself from him, 'My lord,' said she, 'much good may your thoughts do you. But that I may not dissemble with you, my nativity being cast by one that never failed in any of his prognostications, I have been assured that I should never be apt to bear children. But since you will honour me with so high favour, I must only desire that I may perform a vow which I made among my countrywomen, the famous Amazons, that I would never marry none, but such one as was able to withstand me in arms. Therefore, before I make mine own desire serviceable to yours, you must vouchsafe to lend me armour and weapons, that at least with a blow or two of the sword I may not find myself perjured to myself.'

But Zoilus but laughing with a hearty loudness went by force to embrace her, making no other answer but, since she had a mind to try his knighthood, she should quickly know what a man-of-arms he was; and so, without reverence to the ladies, began to struggle with her.

But in Zelmane, then disdain became wisdom, and anger gave occasion. For abiding no longer abode in the matter, she (that had not put off, though she had disguised Pyrocles) being far fuller of strong nimbleness, tripped up his feet so that he fell down at hers; and withal meaning to pursue what she had begun, pulled out his sword which he ware about him. But before she could strike him withal, he gat up and ran to a fair chamber – where he had left his two brethren preparing themselves to come down to their mistresses; but she followed at his heels, and even as he came to throw himself into their arms for succour, she hit him with his own sword such a blow upon the waist that she almost cut him asunder. Once, she sundered his soul from his body, sending it to Proserpina, an angry goddess against ravishers.

But Anaxius seeing before his eyes the miserable end of his brother, fuller of despite than wrath, and yet fuller of wrath than sorrow, looking with a woeful eye upon his brother Lycurgus, 'Brother,' said he, 'chastise this vile creature, while I go down and take order lest further mischief arise'; and so, went down to the ladies, whom he visited, doubting there had been some further practice than yet he conceived. But finding them only strong in patience, he went and locked a great iron gate, by which only anybody might mount to that part of the castle (rather to conceal the shame of his brother, slain by a woman, than for doubt of any other annoyance), and then went up to receive some comfort of the execution he was sure his brother had done of Zelmane.

But Zelmane no sooner saw those brothers, of whom (reason assured her) she was to expect revenge, but that she leapt to a target, as one that well knew the first mark of valure to be defence. And then accepting the opportunity of Anaxius' going away, she waited not the pleasure of Lycurgus, but without any words, which she ever thought vain when resolution took the place of persuasion, gave her own heart the contentment to be the assailer.

Lycurgus, who was in the disposition of his nature hazardous, and by the lucky passing through many dangers grown confident in himself, went toward her rather as to spoil[1] than to fight – so far from fear that his assuredness disdained to hope. But when her sword made demonstrations above all flattery of arguments, and that he found she pressed so upon him as showed that her courage sprang not from blind despair but was guarded both with cunning and strength, self-love then first in him divided itself from vainglory, and made him find that the world of worthiness had not his whole globe comprised in his breast, but that it was necessary to have strong resistance against so strong assailing. And so between them – for a few blows – Mars himself might have been delighted to look on.

But Zelmane, who knew that in her case slowness of victory was little better than ruin, with the bellows of hate blew the fire of courage. And he striking a main blow at her head, she warded it with the shield (but so warded that the shield was cut in two pieces while it protected her), and withal she ran in to him; and thrusting at his breast, which he put by with his target, as he was lifting up his sword to strike again, she let fall the piece of her shield, and with her left hand catching his sword of the inside of the pommel, with nimble and strong sleight she had gotten his sword out of his hand before his sense could convey to his imagination what was to be doubted. And having now two swords against one shield, meaning not foolishly to be ungrateful to good fortune, while he was no more amazed with his being unweaponed than with the suddenness thereof, she gave him such a wound upon his head in despite of the shield's over-weak resistance, that withal he fell to the ground astonished with the pain, and aghast with fear.

But seeing Zelmane ready to conclude her victory in his death, bowing up his head to her with a countenance that had forgotten all pride, 'Enough! excellent lady,' said he. 'The honour is yours – whereof you shall want the best witness if you kill me. As you have taken from men the glory of manhood, return so now again to your own sex for mercy. I will redeem my life of you with no small services, for I will undertake to make my brother obey all your commandments. Grant life, I beseech you – for your own honour, and for the person's sake that you love best.'

Zelmane repressed a while her great heart – either disdaining to be cruel, or pitiful, and therefore not cruel. And now the image of human condition began to be an orator unto her of compassion, when she saw, as he lifted

---

[1] to spoil] to a spoil 93

up his arms with a suppliant's grace, about one of them unhappily tied a garter with a jewel, which, given to Pyrocles by his aunt of Thessalia and greatly esteemed by him, he had presented to Philoclea, and with inward rage promising extreme hatred had seen Lycurgus (with a proud force and not without some hurt unto her) pull away from Philoclea, because at entreaty she would not give it him. But the sight of that was like a cipher signifying all the injuries which Philoclea had of him suffered; and that remembrance, feeding upon wrath, trod down all conceits of mercy. And therefore saying no more but, 'No villain, die! It is Philoclea that sends thee this token for thy love,' with that, she made her sword drink the blood of his heart – though he wresting his body, and with a countenance prepared to excuse, would fain have delayed the receiving of death's embassadors.

But neither that stayed Zelmane's hand, nor yet Anaxius' cry unto her, who having made fast the iron gate, even then came to the top of the stairs, when, contrary to all his imaginations, he saw his brother lie at Zelmane's mercy. Therefore crying, promising, and threatening to her to hold her hand, the last groan of his brother was the only answer he could get to his unrespected eloquence.

But then pity would fain have drawn tears, which fury in their spring dried; and anger would fain have spoken, but that disdain sealed up his lips – but in his heart he blasphemed heaven that it could have such a power over him, no less ashamed of the victory he should have of her than of his brothers' overthrow, and no more spited that it was yet unrevenged than that the revenge should be no greater than a woman's destruction. Therefore, with no speech but such a groaning cry as often is the language of sorrowful anger, he came running at Zelmane, use of fighting then serving, instead of patient consideration what to do; guided wherewith, though he did not with knowledge, yet did he according to knowledge, pressing upon Zelmane in such a well-defended manner that in all the combats that ever she had fought she had never more need of quick senses and ready virtue; for being one of the greatest men of stature then living, as he did fully answer that stature in greatness of might, so did he exceed both in greatness of courage, which, with a countenance formed by the nature both of his mind and body to an almost horrible fierceness, was able to have carried fear to any mind that was not privy to itself of a true and constant worthiness.

But Pyrocles, whose soul might well be separated from his body, but never alienated from the remembering what was comely, if at the first he did a little apprehend the dangerousness of his adversary (whom once before he had something tried, and now perfectly saw as the very picture of forcible fury), yet was that apprehension quickly stayed in him, rather strengthening than weakening his virtue by that wrestling (like wine, growing the stronger by being moved); so that they both, prepared in hearts and able in hands, did honour solitariness there with such a combat as might have demanded as a right, of fortune, whole armies of beholders.

But no beholders needed there, where manhood blew the trumpet and satisfaction did whet as much as glory. There was strength against nimbleness, rage against resolution, fury against virtue, confidence against courage, pride against nobleness – love in both breeding mutual hatred; and desire of revenging the injury of his brothers' slaughter, to Anaxius, being like Philoclea's captivity, to Pyrocles. Who had seen the one would have thought nothing could have resisted; who had marked the other would have marvelled that the other had so long resisted. But like two contrary tides, either of which are able to carry worlds of ships and men upon them with such swiftness as nothing seems able to withstand them, yet, meeting one another with mingling their watery forces and struggling together, it is long to say whether stream gets the victory, so between these, if Pallas had been there she could scarcely have told whether she had nursed better in the feats of arms. The Irish greyhound against the English mastiff, the swordfish against the whale, the rhinoceros against the elephant might be models, and but models, of this combat.

Anaxius was better armed defensively, for, beside a strong cask bravely covered wherewith he covered his head, he had a huge shield – such, perchance, as Achilles showed to the pale walls of Troy – wherewithal that body[1] was covered. But Pyrocles, utterly unarmed for defence, to offend had the advantage, for in either hand he had a sword, and with both hands nimbly performed that office. And according as they were diversely furnished, so did they differ in the manner of fighting, for Anaxius, most by warding, and Pyrocles, oftenest by avoiding, resisted the adversary's assault; both hasty to end, yet both often staying for advantage. Time, distance, and motion – custom made them so perfect in that, as if they had been fellow councillors and not enemies, each knew the other's mind, and knew how to prevent it; so as their strength failed them sooner than their skill, and yet their breath failed them sooner than their strength – and breathless indeed they grew before either could complain of any loss of blood.

So,[2] [3] consenting by the mediation of necessity to a breathing-time of truce, being withdrawn a little one from the other, Anaxius stood leaning upon his sword with his grim eye so settled upon Zelmane as is wont to be the look of an earnest thought; which Zelmane marking and, according to the Pyroclean nature, fuller of gay bravery in the midst than in the beginning

---

[1] that body] that great body 93 [2] blood. So 93: blood. Chap. 29. The combatants' first breathing, re-encounter, and – . So 90 [3] So] So that 93

of danger, 'What is it,' said she, 'Anaxius, that thou so deeply musest on? Doth thy brothers' example make thee think of thy fault past, or of thy coming punishment?'

'I think,' said he, 'what spiteful god it should be, who envying my glory hath brought me to such a wayward case that neither thy death can be a revenge, nor thy overthrow a victory.'

'Thou doost well indeed,' said Zelmane, 'to impute thy case to the heavenly providence – which will have thy pride find itself, even in that whereof thou art most proud, punished by the weak sex, which thou most contemnest.'

But then, having sufficiently rested themselves, they renewed again their combat, far more terribly than before – like nimble vaulters, who at the first and second leap do but stir and as it were awake the fiery and aery parts, which after, in the other leaps, they do with more excellency exer-cise – for in this pausing each had brought to his thoughts the manner of the other's fighting, and the advantages which, by that and by the quality of their weapons, they might work themselves; and so again repeated the lesson they had said before, more perfectly by the using of it.

Anaxius oftener used blows, his huge force as it were more delighting therein, and the large protection of his shield animating him unto it. Pyrocles, of a more fine and deliver strength, watching his time when to give fit thrusts, as with the quick obeying of his body to his eyes' quick commandment he shunned any harm Anaxius could do to him, so would he soon have made an end of Anaxius if he had not found him a man of wonderful and almost matchless excellency in matters of arms. Pyrocles used divers feignings to bring Anaxius on into some inconvenience, but Anaxius keeping a sound manner of fighting never offered, but seeing fair cause, and then followed it with well-governed violence.

Thus spent they a great time striving to do, and with striving to do wearying themselves more than with the very doing. Anaxius, finding Zelmane so near unto him that with little motion he might reach her, knitting all his strength together, at that time mainly foined at her face. But Zelmane, strongly putting it by with her right-hand sword, coming in with her left foot and hand would have given him a[1] sharp visitation to his right side, but that he was fain to leap away – whereat ashamed, as having never done so much before in his life –[2]

---

[1] given him a] given a 93   [2] life –] *The* New Arcadia *ends here*

APPENDICES

APPENDIX I

The First Eclogues [1590]

BASILIUS, because Zelmane so would have it, used the artificial day of torches to lighten the sports their inventions could minister. And yet, because many more shepherds were newly come than at the first, he did in a gentle manner chastise the cowardice of the fugitive shepherds with making them for that night the torch bearers; and the others later come, he willed with all freedom of speech and behaviour to keep their accustomed method, which while they prepared to do, Dametas, who much disdained (since his late authority) all his old companions, brought his servant Dorus in good acquaintance and allowance of them, and himself stood like a director over them, with nodding, gaping, winking, or stamping showing how he did like or mislike those things he did not understand. The first sports the shepherds showed were full of such leaps and gambols as (being accorded to the pipe which they bare in their mouths even as they danced) made a right picture of their chief god Pan and his companions, the satyrs. Then would they cast away their pipes and, holding hand in hand, dance as it were in a brawl by the only cadence of their voices, which they would use in singing some short couplets, whereto the one half beginning, the other half should answer; as, the one half saying:

> We love, and have our loves rewarded.

The others would answer:

> We love, and are no whit regarded.

The first again:

> We find most sweet affection's snare.

With like tune it should be as in choir sent back again:

> That sweet, but sour despairful care.

A third time likewise thus:

> Who can despair whom hope doth bear?

The answer:

> And who can hope that feels despair?

Then all joining their voices, and dancing a faster measure, they would conclude[1] with some such words:

> As without breath no pipe doth move,
> No music kindly without love.

---

[1] conclude: couclude *90*

APPENDIX I

Having thus varied both their songs and dances into divers sorts of inventions, their last sport was one of them to provoke another to a more large expressing of his passions: which Lalus, accounted one of the best singers amongst them, having marked in Dorus' dancing no less good grace and handsome behaviour than extreme tokens of a travailed mind, began first with his pipe and then with his voice thus to challenge Dorus, and was by him answered in the underwritten sort:

Lalus and Dorus

Lalus. Come, Dorus, come, let songs thy sorrows signify;
    And if, for want of use, thy mind ashamed is,
    That very shame with love's high title dignify.
       No style is held for base where love well named is:
    Each ear sucks up the words a true love scattereth,
    And plain speech oft than quaint phrase better framed is.

Dorus. Nightingales seldom sing, the pie still chattereth;
    The wood cries most before it throughly kindled be;
    Deadly wounds inward bleed, each slight sore mattereth;
       Hardly they herd which by good hunters singled be;
    Shallow brooks murmur most, deep silent slide away,
    Nor true love loves those loves with others mingled be.

Lalus. If thou wilt not be seen, thy face go hide away,
    Be none of us, or else maintain our fashion:
    Who frowns at others' feasts doth better bide away.
       But if thou hast a love, in that love's passion,
    I challenge thee, by show of her perfection,
    Which of us two deserveth most compassion.

Dorus. Thy challenge great, but greater my protection:
    Sing, then, and see (for now thou hast inflamed me)
    Thy health too mean a match for my infection.
       No, though the heav'ns for high attempts have blamed me,
    Yet high is my attempt. O muse, historify
    Her praise, whose praise to learn your skill hath framed me.

Lalus. Muse, hold your peace! But thou, my god Pan, glorify
    My Kala's gifts, who with all good gifts filled is.
    Thy pipe, O Pan, shall help, though I sing sorrily.
       A heap of sweets she is, where nothing spilled is,
    Who, though she be no bee, yet full of honey is:
    A lily field, with plough of rose, which tilled is.
       Mild as a lamb, more dainty than a cony is:
    Her eyes my eyesight is, her conversation

More glad to me than to a miser money is.
   What coy account she makes of estimation!
How nice to touch! How all her speeches peised be!
A nymph thus turned, but mended in translation.

Dorus. Such Kala is; but ah, my fancies raised be
In one whose name to name were high presumption,
Since virtues all, to make her title, pleased be.
   O happy gods, which by inward assumption
Enjoy her soul, in body's fair possession,
And keep it joined, fearing your seat's consumption.
   How oft with rain of tears skies make confession
Their dwellers rapt with sight of her perfection,
From heav'nly throne to her heav'n use digression!
   Of best things, then, what world can yield confection
To liken her? Deck yours with your comparison:
She is herself of best things the collection.

Lalus. How oft my doleful sire cried to me, 'Tarry, son,'
When first he spied my love! How oft he said to me,
'Thou art no soldier fit for Cupid's garrison.
   My son, keep this that my long toil hath laid to me:
Love well thine own. Methinks, wool's whiteness passeth all:
I never found long love such wealth hath paid to me.'
   This wind he spent; but when my Kala glasseth all
My sight in her fair limbs, I then assure myself,
Not rotten sheep, but high crowns she surpasseth all.
   Can I be poor, that her gold hair procure myself?
Want I white wool, whose eyes her white skin garnished?
Till I get her, shall I to keep inure myself?

Dorus. How oft, when reason saw love of her harnished[1]
With armour of my heart, he cried, 'O vanity,
To set a pearl in steel so meanly varnished!
   Look to thyself; reach not beyond humanity;
Her mind, beams, state, far from thy weak wings banished;
And love which lover hurts is inhumanity.'
   Thus reason said: but she came, reason vanished;
Her eyes so mast'ring me that such objection
Seemed but to spoil the food of thoughts long famished.
   Her peerless height my mind to high erection
Draws up; and if hope-failing end live's pleasure,
Of fairer death how can I make election?

---

[1] harnished: harnised *90*

Lalus. Once my well-waiting eyes espied my treasure,
    With sleeves turned up, loose hair, and breast enlarged,
    Her father's corn (moving her fair limbs) measure.
        'Oh,' cried I, 'of so mean work be discharged:
    Measure my case, how by thy beauty's filling 5
    With seed of woes my heart brim-full is charged.
        Thy father bids thee save, and chides for spilling.
    Save then my soul, spill not my thoughts well heaped:
    No lovely praise was ever got by killing.'
        These bold words she did hear, this fruit I reaped, 10
    That she, whose look alone might make me blessed,
    Did smile on me; and then away she leaped.

Dorus. Once – oh, sweet once! – I saw, with dread oppressed,
    Her whom I dread; so that with prostrate lying,
    Her length the earth in love's chief clothing dressed. 15
        I saw that richess fall, and fell a-crying:
    'Let not dead earth enjoy so dear a cover,
    But deck therewith my soul, for your sake dying.
        Lay all your fear upon your fearful lover;
    Shine, eyes, on me, that both our lives be guarded: 20
    So I your sight, you shall yourselves recover.'
        I cried, and was with open rays rewarded;
    But straight they fled, summoned by cruel honour,
    Honour, the cause desert is not regarded.

Lalus. This maid, thus made for joys, O Pan, bemoan her, 25
    That without love she spends her years of love:
    So fair a field would well become an owner.
        And if enchantment can a hard heart move,
    Teach me what circle may acquaint her sprite
    Affection's charms in my behalf to prove. 30
        The circle is my round-about-her sight:
    The power I will invoke dwells in her eyes:
    My charm should be she haunt me day and night.

Dorus. Far other care, O muse, my sorrow tries,
    Bent to such one, in whom, myself must say, 35
    Nothing can mend that point that in her lies.
        What circle, then, in so rare force bears sway,
    Whose sprite all sprites can spoil, raise, damn, or save?
    No charm holds her, but well possess she may;
        Possess she doth, and makes my soul her slave: 40

My eyes the bands, my thoughts the fatal knot;
No thralls like them, that inward bondage have.

Lalus. Kala, at length, conclude my ling'ring lot:
    Disdain me not, although I be not fair.
5   Who is an heir of many hundred sheep
    Doth beauties keep, which never sun can burn,
    Nor storms do turn: fairness serves oft to wealth.
    Yet all my health I place in your goodwill,
    Which, if you will (oh, do) bestow on me,
10 Such as you see, such still you shall me find:
    Constant and kind. My sheep your food shall breed,
    Their wool your weed; I will you music yield
    In flow'ry field; and as the day begins,
    With twenty gins we will the small birds take,
15 And pastimes make, as nature things hath made.
    But when in shade we meet of myrtle boughs,
    Then love allows, our pleasures to enrich,
    The thought of which doth pass all worldly pelf.

Dorus. Lady, yourself, whom neither name I dare,
20 And titles are but spots to such a worth,
    Hear plaints come forth from dungeon of my mind:
    The noblest kind rejects not others' woes.
    I have no shows of wealth: my wealth is you,
    My beauty's hue your beams, my health your deeds;
25 My mind for weeds your virtue's liv'ry wears.
    My food is tears; my tunes waymenting yield;
    Despair my field; the flowers spirit's wars;
    My day new cares; my gins my daily sight,
    In which do light small birds of thoughts o'erthrown.
30 My pastimes none; time passeth on my fall.
    Nature made all, but me of dolours made.
    I find no shade, but where my sun doth burn;
    No place to turn; without, within, it fries;
    Nor help by life or death who living dies.

35 *Lalus.* But if my Kala this my suit denies,
    Which so much reason bears,
    Let crows pick out mine eyes which saw too much.
    If still her mind be such,
    My earthy mould will melt in wat'ry tears.

Dorus. My earthy mould doth melt in wat'ry tears,
   And they again resolve
   To air of sighs, sighs to the heart's fire turn,
   Which doth to ashes burn:
   So doth my life within itself dissolve.   5

Lalus. So doth my life within itself dissolve
   That I am like a flower
   New plucked from the place where it did breed,
   Life showing, dead indeed;
   Such force hath love above poor nature's power.   10

Dorus. Such force hath love above poor nature's power
   That I grow like a shade,
   Which being nought seems somewhat to the eyen,
   While that one body shine;
   Oh, he is marred that is for other made!   15

Lalus. Oh, he is marred that is for others made,
   Which thought doth mar my piping declaration,
   Thinking how it hath marred my shepherd's trade.
     Now my hoarse voice doth fail this occupation,
   And others long to tell their loves' condition: 20
   Of singing take to thee the reputation.

Dorus. Of singing take to thee the reputation,
   New friend of mine; I yield to thy ability:
   My soul doth seek another estimation.
     But ah, my muse, I would thou hadst agility   25
   To work my goddess so by thy invention
   On me to cast those eyes, where shine nobility:
     Seen and unknown; heard, but without attention.

    This eclogue betwixt Lalus and Dorus of every one of the beholders received great commendations – when Basilius called to a young shepherd who neither had danced nor sung with them, but lain all this while upon the ground at the foot of a cypress tree, in so deep a melancholy as though his mind were banished from the place he loved, to be in prison in his body; and desired him he would begin some eclogue with some other of the shepherds according to the accustomed guise, or else declare the discourse of his own fortune, unknown to him, as being a stranger in that country. But he prayed the king to pardon him, the time being far too joyful to suffer the rehearsal of his miseries; yet, to satisfy Basilius some way, he sang this song he had learned before he had subjected his thoughts to acknowledge no master but a mistress:

> As I my little flock on Ister bank
> (A little flock, but well my pipe they couth)
> Did piping lead, the sun already sank
> Beyond our world, and ere I got my booth
> Each thing with mantle black the night doth scothe;
>   Saving the glow-worm, which would courteous be
>   Of that small light oft watching shepherds see.
>
> The welkin had full niggardly enclosed
> In coffer of dim clouds his silver groats,
> Ycleped stars; each thing to rest disposed:
> The caves were full, the mountains void of goats;
> The birds' eyes clos'd, closed their chirping notes.
>   As for the nightingale, wood-music's king,
>   It August was; he deigned not then to sing.
>
> Amid my sheep, though I saw nought to fear,
> Yet (for I nothing saw) I feared sore;
> Then fond I which thing is a charge to bear,
> As, for my sheep, I dradded mickle more
> Than ever for myself since I was bore.
>   I sate me down, for see to go ne could,
>   And sang unto my sheep lest stray they should.
>
> The song I sang old Languet[1] had me taught,
> Languet,[2] the shepherd best swift Ister knew,
> For clerkly rede, and hating what is naught,
> For faithful heart, clean hands, and mouth as true.
> With his sweet skill my skilless youth he drew
>   To have a feeling taste of him that sits
>   Beyond the heav'n, far more beyond your wits.
>
> He said the music best thilk powers pleased
> Was jump concord between our wit and will,
> Where highest notes to godliness are raised,
> And lowest sink not down to jot of ill.
> With old true tales he wont mine ears to fill:
>   How shepherds did of yore, how now they thrive,
>   Spoiling their flock, or while twixt them they strive.

---

[1] Languet: Lanquet *90*   [2] Languet: Lanquet *90*

He liked me, but pitied lustful youth.
His good strong staff my slipp'ry years upbore.
He still hoped well, because he loved truth;
Till forced to part, with heart and eyes ev'n sore,
To worthy Coriden he gave me o'er.   5
   But thus in oak's true shade recounted he
   Which now in night's deep shade sheep heard of me.
Such manner time there was (what time I not)
When all this earth, this dam or mould of ours,
Was only won'd with such as beasts begot;   10
Unknown as then were they that builded towers.
The cattle, wild or tame, in nature's bowers
   Might freely roam or rest, as seemed them;
   Man was not man their dwellings in to hem.
The beasts had sure some beastly policy,   15
For nothing can endure where order nis.
For once the lion by the lamb did lie;
The fearful hind the leopard did kiss;
Hurtless was tiger's paw and serpent's hiss.
   This think I well: the beasts with courage clad   20
   Like senators a harmless empire had.
At which, whether the others did repine
(For envy harb'reth most in feeblest hearts)
Or that they all to changing did incline
(As ev'n in beasts their dams leave changing parts),   25
The multitude to Jove a suit imparts,
   With neighing, blaying, braying, and barking,
   Roaring, and howling, for to have a king.
A king in language theirs they said they would
(For then their language was a perfect speech);   30
The birds likewise with chirps and puing could,
Cackling, and chatt'ring, that of Jove beseech.
Only the owl still warned them not to seech
   So hastily that which they would repent;
   But saw they would, and he to deserts went.   35
Jove wisely said (for wisdom wisely says):
'O beasts, take heed what you of me desire.
Rulers will think all things made them to please,
And soon forget the swink due to their hire.
But since you will, part of my heav'nly fire   40

  I will you lend; the rest yourselves must give,
  That it both seen and felt may with you live.'

Full glad they were, and took the naked sprite,
Which straight the earth yclothed in his clay.
The lion, heart; the ounce gave active might;
The horse, good shape; the sparrow, lust to play;
Nightingale, voice, enticing songs to say.
  Elephant gave a perfect memory;
  And parrot, ready tongue, that to apply.

The fox gave craft; the dog gave flattery;
Ass, patience; the mole, a working thought;
Eagle, high look; wolf, secret cruelty;
Monkey, sweet breath; the cow, her fair eyes brought;
The ermion, whitest skin, spotted with nought;
  The sheep, mild-seeming face; climbing, the bear;
  The stag did give the harm-eschewing fear.

The hare, her sleights; the cat, his melancholy;
Ant, industry; and cony, skill to build;
Cranes, order; storks, to be appearing holy;
Chameleon, ease to change; duck, ease to yield;
Crocodile, tears, which might be falsely spilled;
  Ape great thing gave, though he did mowing stand,
  The instrument of instruments, the hand.

Each other beast likewise his present brings;
And (but they drad their prince they ought should want)
They all consented were to give him wings.
And ay more awe towards him for to plant,
To their own work this privilege they grant:
  That from thenceforth to all eternity
  No beast should freely speak, but only he.

Thus man was made; thus man their lord became;
Who at the first, wanting or hiding pride,
He did to beasts' best use his cunning frame,
With water drink, herbs' meat, and naked hide,
And fellow-like let his dominion slide;
  Not in his sayings saying 'I', but 'we;'
  As if he meant his lordship common be.

But when his seat so rooted he had found
That they now skill'd not how from him to wend,

Then gan in guiltless earth full many a wound,
Iron to seek, which gainst itself should bend,
To tear the bowels, that good corn should send.
    But yet the common dam none did bemoan,
    Because (though hurt) they never heard her groan.   5
Then gan the factions in the beasts to breed;
Where helping weaker sort, the nobler beasts
(As tigers, leopards, bears, and lions' seed)
Disdained with this, in deserts sought their rests;
Where famine ravin taught their hungry chests,   10
    That craftily he forced them to do ill,
    Which being done, he afterwards would kill
For murthers done, which never erst was seen,
By those great beasts. As for the weakers' good,
He chose themselves his guarders for to been   15
Gainst those of might, of whom in fear they stood,
As horse and dog; not great, but gentle blood.
    Blithe were the commons, cattle of the field,
    Tho when they saw their foen of greatness killed.
But they, or spent or made of slender might,   20
Then quickly did the meaner cattle find,
The great beams gone, the house on shoulders light;
For by and by the horse fair bits did bind;
The dog was in a collar taught his kind.
    As for the gentle birds, like case might rue   25
    When falcon they, and goshawk, saw in mew.
Worst fell to smallest birds, and meanest herd,
Whom now his own, full like his own he used.
Yet first but wool, or feathers, off he teared;
And when they were well used to be abused   30
For hungry teeth their flesh with teeth he bruised;
    At length for glutton taste he did them kill;
    At last for sport their silly lives did spill.
But yet, O man, rage not beyond thy need;
Deem it no gloire to swell in tyranny.   35
Thou art of blood; joy not to see things bleed.
Thou fearest death; think they are loath to die.
A plaint of guiltless hurt doth pierce the sky.
    And you, poor beasts, in patience bide your hell,
    Or know your strengths, and then you shall do well.   40

> Thus did I sing and pipe eight sullen hours
> To sheep whom love, not knowledge, made to hear,
> Now fancy's fits, now fortune's baleful stours.
> But then I homewards called my lambkins dear;
> 5 For to my dimmed eyes began t'appear
>   The night grown old, her black head waxen grey,
>   Sure shepherd's sign that morn should soon fetch day.

According to the nature of diverse ears, diverse judgements straight followed, some praising his voice, others his words fit to frame a pastoral style, others the strangeness of the tale, and scanning what he should mean by it. But old Geron (who had borne him a grudge ever since in one of their eclogues he had taken him up over-bitterly) took hold of this occasion to make his revenge, and said he never saw thing worse proportioned than to bring in a tale of he knew not what beasts at such a sport-meeting when rather some song of love, or matter for joyful melody, was to be brought forth. 'But,' said he, 'this is the right conceit of young men, who think then they speak wiseliest when they cannot understand themselves.' But little did the melancholic shepherd regard either his dispraises or the others' praises, who had set the foundation of his honour there where he was most despised. And therefore, he returning again to the train of his desolate pensiveness, Geron invited Histor to answer him in eclogue-wise; who, indeed, having been long in love with the fair Kala, and now by Lalus overgone, was grown into a detestation of marriage. But thus it was:

         Geron   Histor

> 25 *Geron.* In faith, good Histor, long is your delay
>   From holy marriage, sweet and surest mean
> Our foolish lust in honest rules to stay.
>   I pray thee do to Lalus' sample lean.
> Thou seest how frisk and jolly now he is
> 30 That last day seemed he could not chew a bean.
>   Believe me, man, there is no greater bliss
> Than is the quiet joy of loving wife,
> Which whoso wants, half of himself doth miss.
>   Friend without change, playfellow without strife,
> 35 Food without fullness, counsel without pride,
> Is this sweet doubling of our single life.
>
> *Histor.* No doubt to whom so good chance did betide
>   As for to find a pasture strawed with gold,
> He were a fool if there he did not bide.

Who would not have a phoenix if he could?
The humming wasp, if it had not a sting,
Before all flies the wasp accept I would.
   But this bad world few golden fields doth bring;
Phoenix but one, of crows we millions have;   5
The wasp seems gay, but is a cumbrous thing.
   If many Kalas our Arcadia gave,
Lalus' example I would soon ensue;
And think I did myself from sorrow save.
   But of such wives we find a slender crew;   10
Shrewdness so stirs, pride so puffs up the heart,
They seldom ponder what to them is due;
   With meagre looks, as if they still did smart,
Puiling and whimp'ring, or else scolding flat,
Make home more pain than following of the cart;   15
   Either dull silence, or eternal chat;
Still contrary to what her husband says;
If he do praise the dog, she likes the cat.
   Austere she is, when he would honest plays;
And gamesome then, when he thinks on his sheep;   20
She bids him go, and yet from journey stays.
   She war doth ever with his kinsfolk keep,
And makes them fremb'd who friends by nature are,
Envying shallow toys with malice deep.
   And if, forsooth, there come some new-found ware,   25
The little coin his sweating brows have got
Must go for that, if for her lours he care;
   Or else: 'Nay, faith, mine is the lucklest lot
That ever fell to honest woman yet;
No wife but I hath such a man, God wot!'   30
   Such is their speech who be of sober wit;
But who do let their tongues show well their rage,
Lord, what bywords they speak! what spite they spit!
   The house is made a very loathsome cage,
Wherein the bird doth never sing, but cry   35
With such a will as nothing can assuage.
   Dearly the servants do their wages buy,
Reviled for each small fault, sometimes for none;
They better live that in a jail do lie.
   Let other fouler spots away be blown,   40

>　　　For I seek not their shame; but still, methinks,
>　　　A better life it is to lie alone.
>
> *Geron.* Who for each fickle fear from virtue shrinks
>　　　　Shall in his life embrace no worthy thing;
> 5　　　No mortal man the cup of surety drinks.
>　　　　　The heav'ns do not good haps in handfuls bring,
>　　　But let us pick our good from out much bad,
>　　　That still our little world may know his king.
>　　　　But certainly so long we may be glad
> 10　　While that we do what nature doth require,
>　　　And for th'event we never ought be sad.
>　　　　　Man oft is plagued with air; is burnt with fire;
>　　　In water drowned; in earth his burial is –
>　　　And shall we not therefore their use desire?
> 15　　　　Nature above all things requireth this:
>　　　That we our kind do labour to maintain;
>　　　Which drawn-out line doth hold all human bliss.
>　　　　　Thy father justly may of thee complain
>　　　If thou do not repay his deeds for thee,
> 20　　In granting unto him a grandsire's gain.
>　　　　　Thy commonwealth may rightly grieved be,
>　　　Which must by this immortal be preserved,
>　　　If thus thou murther thy posterity.
>　　　　　His very being he hath not deserved
> 25　　Who for a self-conceit will that forbear
>　　　Whereby that being ay must be conserved.
>　　　　　And God forbid women such cattle were
>　　　As you paint them; but well in you I find,
>　　　No man doth speak aright who speaks in fear.
> 30　　　Who only sees the ill is worse than blind.
>　　　These fifty winters married have I been,
>　　　And yet find no such faults in womankind.
>　　　　　I have a wife worthy to be a queen,
>　　　So well she can command, and yet obey;
> 35　　In ruling of a house so well she's seen.
>　　　　　And yet in all this time, betwixt us tway,
>　　　We bear our double yoke with such consent
>　　　That never passed foul word, I dare well say.
>　　　　　But these be your love-toys which still are spent
> 40　　In lawless games, and love not as you should,

But with much study learn late to repent.
    How well last day before our prince you could
Blind Cupid's works with wonder testify!
Yet now the root of him abase you would.
    Go to, go to, and Cupid now apply   5
To that where thou thy Cupid mayst avow,
And thou shalt find in women virtues lie:
    Sweet supple minds which soon to wisdom bow,
Where they by wisdom's rule directed are,
And are not forced fond thraldom to allow.   10
    As we to get are framed, so they to spare;
We made for pain, our pains they made to cherish;
We care abroad, and they of home have care.
    O Histor, seek within thyself to flourish;
Thy house by thee must live, or else be gone –   15
And then who shall the name of Histor nourish?
    Riches of children pass a prince's throne,
Which touch the father's heart with secret joy
When without shame he saith: 'These be mine own.'
    Marry therefore, for marriage will destroy   20
Those passions which to youthful head do climb,
Mothers and nurses of all vain annoy.

All the assembly laughed at the lustiness of the old fellow, and easily perceived in Histor, he liked Lalus' fortune better than he loved his person. But Basilius, to intermix with these light notes of liberty some sadder tune   25
set to the key of his own passion, not seeing there Strephon or Klaius (who, called thence by Urania's letter, were both gone to continue their suit, like two true runners, both employing their best speed but not one hindering the other), he called to one Lamon, of their acquaintance, and willed him to sing some one of their songs, which he readily performed in this double sestine: 30

Strephon   Klaius

Strephon. You goat-herd gods, that love the grassy mountains,
    You nymphs, that haunt the springs in pleasant valleys,
    You satyrs, joyed with free and quiet forests,
    Vouchsafe your silent ears to plaining music   35
    Which to my woes gives still an early morning,
    And draws the dolour on till weary evening.

Klaius. O Mercury, foregoer to the evening,
    O heav'nly huntress of the savage mountains,

O lovely star, entitled of the morning,
While that my voice doth fill these woeful valleys,
Vouchsafe your silent ears to plaining music,
Which oft hath Echo tired in secret forests.

5 *Strephon.* I that was once free burgess of the forests,
Where shade from sun, and sports I sought at evening,
I that was once esteemed for pleasant music,
Am banished now among the monstrous mountains
Of huge despair, and foul affliction's valleys,
10 Am grown a shritch-owl to myself each morning.

Klaius. I that was once delighted every morning,
Hunting the wild inhabiters of forests,
I that was once the music of these valleys,
So darkened am that all my day is evening,
15 Heart-broken so, that molehills seem high mountains,
And fill the vales with cries instead of music.

Strephon. Long since, alas, my deadly swannish music
Hath made itself a crier of the morning,
And hath with wailing strength climbed highest mountains.
20 Long since my thoughts more desert be than forests.
Long since I see my joys come to their evening,
And state thrown down to over-trodden valleys.

Klaius. Long since the happy dwellers of these valleys
Have prayed me leave my strange exclaiming music,
25 Which troubles their day's work, and joys of evening.
Long since I hate the night, more hate the morning.
Long since my thoughts chase me like beasts in forests,
And make me wish myself laid under mountains.

Strephon. Meseems I see the high and stately mountains
30 Transform themselves to low dejected valleys.
Meseems I hear in these ill-changed forests
The nightingales do learn of owls their music.
Meseems I feel the comfort of the morning
Turned to the mortal serene of an evening.

35 *Klaius.* Meseems I see a filthy cloudy evening
As soon as sun begins to climb the mountains.
Meseems I feel a noisome scent the morning
When I do smell the flowers of these valleys.
Meseems I hear (when I do hear sweet music)
40 The dreadful cries of murdered men in forests.

Strephon. I wish to fire the trees of all these forests;
   I give the sun a last farewell each evening;
   I curse the fiddling finders-out of music;
   With envy I do hate the lofty mountains,
   And with despite despise the humble valleys;   5
   I do detest night, evening, day, and morning.
Klaius. Curse to myself my prayer is, the morning;
   My fire is more than can be made with forests;
   My state more base than are the basest valleys.
   I wish no evenings more to see, each evening;   10
   Shamed I have myself in sight of mountains,
   And stop mine ears, lest I grow mad with music.
Strephon. For she, whose parts maintained a perfect music,
   Whose beauty shined more than the blushing morning,
   Who much did pass in state the stately mountains,   15
   In straightness passed the cedars of the forests,
   Hath cast me, wretch, into eternal evening,
   By taking her two suns from these dark valleys.
Klaius. For she, to whom compared the Alps are valleys,
   She, whose least word brings from the spheres their music,   20
   At whose approach the sun rose in the evening,
   Who, where she went, bare in her forehead morning,
   Is gone, is gone from these our spoiled forests,
   Turning to deserts our best pastured mountains.
Stephon. These mountains witness shall, so shall these valleys,   25
Klaius. These forests eke, made wretched by our music,
   Our morning hymn is this, and song at evening.

    Zelmane seeing nobody offer to fill the stage, as if her long-restrained conceits had new burst out of prison, she thus desiring her voice should be accorded to nothing but Philoclea's ears, laying fast hold on her face with   30
her eyes, she sang these sapphics, speaking as it were to her own hope:

   If mine eyes can speak to do hearty errand,
   Or mine eyes' language she do hap to judge of,
   So that eyes' message be of her received,
       Hope, we do live yet.   35

   But if eyes fail then, when I most do need them,
   Or if eyes' language be not unto her known,
   So that eyes' message do return rejected,
       Hope, we do both die.

> Yet dying, and dead, do we sing her honour;
> So become our tombs monuments of her praise;
> So becomes our loss the triumph of her gain;
>   Hers be the glory.
>
> If the spheres senseless do yet hold a music,
> If the swan's sweet voice be not heard but at death,
> If the mute timber when it hath the life lost
>   Yieldeth a lute's tune,
>
> Are then human minds privileged so meanly
> As that hateful death can abridge them of power,
> With the vow of truth to record to all worlds
>   That we be her spoils?
>
> Thus not ending, ends the due praise of her praise;
> Fleshly veil consumes, but a soul hath his life,
> Which is held in love; love it is that hath joined
>   Life to this our soul.
>
> But if eyes can speak to do hearty errand,
> Or mine eyes' language she do hap to judge of,
> So that eyes' message be of her received,
>   Hope, we do live yet.

What exclaiming praises Basilius gave to Zelmane's song, any man may guess that knows love is better than a pair of spectacles to make everything seem greater which is seen through it; and then is it never tongue-tied where fit commendation (whereof womankind is so lickerous) is offered unto it. Yea, he fell prostrate on the ground, and thanked the gods they had preserved his life so long as to hear the very music they themselves used, in an earthly body. But the wasting of the torches served as a watch unto them to make them see the time waste; and therefore the king, though unwilling, rose from the seat (which he thought excellently settled on the one side), and considering Zelmane's late hurt, persuaded her to take that far spent night's rest. And so, of all sides they went to recommend themselves to the elder brother of death.

The end of the first Book.

The Second Eclogues [1590]

THE rude tumult of the Enispians gave occasion to the honest shepherds to begin their pastorals this day with a dance which they called the skirmish betwixt Reason and Passion. For seven shepherds, which were named the reasonable shepherds, joined themselves, four of them making a square and the other two going a little wide of either side, like wings for the main battle, and the seventh man foremost, like the forlorn hope, to begin the skirmish. In like order came out the seven appassionated shepherds, all keeping the pace of their foot by their voice and sundry consorted instruments they held in their arms. And first the foremost of reasonable side began to sing:

| R. | Thou rebel vile, come, to thy master yield. |

And the other that met with him answered:

P.	No tyrant, no; mine, mine shall be the field.
Reason.	Can Reason then a tyrant counted be?
Passion.	If Reason will that Passions be not free.
R.	But Reason will that Reason govern most.
P.	And Passion will that Passion rule the roast.
R.	Your will is will; but Reason reason is.
P.	Will hath his will when Reason's will doth miss,
R.	Whom Passion leads unto his death is bent.
P.	And let him die, so that he die content.
R.	By nature you to Reason faith have sworn.
P.	No so, but fellowlike together born.
R.	Who Passion doth ensue lives in annoy.
P.	Who Passion doth forsake lives void of joy.
R.	Passion is blind, and treads an unknown trace.
P.	Reason hath eyes to see his own ill case.

Then, as they approached nearer, the two of Reason's sides, as if they shot at the other, thus sang:

R.	Dare Passions then abide in Reason's light?
P.	And is not Reason dimmed with Passion's might?
R.	O foolish thing, which glory doth destroy!
P.	O glorious title of a foolish toy!
R.	Weakness you are; dare you with our strength fight?
P.	Because our weakness weak'neth all your might.
R.	O sacred Reason, help our virtuous toils!
P.	O Passion, pass on feeble Reason's spoils!
R.	We with ourselves abide a daily strife.

P.		We gladly use the sweetness of our life.
R.		But yet our strife sure peace in end doth breed.
P.		We now have peace; your peace we do not need.

Then did the two square battles meet and, instead of fighting, embrace one another, singing thus:

R.		We are too strong; but Reason seeks no blood.
P.		Who be too weak do feign they be too good.
R.		Though we cannot o'ercome, our cause is just.
P.		Let us o'ercome, and let us be unjust.
R.		Yet Passion, yield at length to Reason's stroke.
P.		What shall we win by taking Reason's yoke?
R.		The joys you have shall be made permanent.
P.		But so we shall with grief learn to repent.
R.		Repent indeed, but that shall be your bliss.
P.		How know we that, since present joys we miss?
R.		You know it not; of Reason therefore know it.
P.		No Reason yet had ever skill to show it.
R.P.		Then let us both to heav'nly rules give place,
		Which Passions skill, and Reason do, deface.

Then embraced they one another, and came to the king, who framed his praises of them according to Zelmane's liking – whose unrestrained parts (the mind and eye) had their free course to the delicate Philoclea, whose look was not short in well requiting it, although she knew it was a hateful sight to her jealous mother. But Dicus, that had in this time taken a great liking of Dorus for the good parts he found above his age in him, had a delight to taste the fruits of his wit, though in a subject which he himself most of all other despised; and so entered to speech with him in the manner of this following eclogue:

Dicus   Dorus

Dicus. Dorus, tell me, where is thy wonted motion
   To make these woods resound thy lamentation?
Thy saint is dead, or dead is thy devotion.
   For who doth hold his love in estimation,
To witness that he thinks his thoughts delicious,
   Thinks to make each thing badge of his sweet passion.

Dorus. But what doth make thee, Dicus, so suspicious
   Of my due faith, which needs must be immutable?
Who others' virtue doubt, themselves are vicious.
   Not so; although my metal were most mutable,

Her beams have wrought therein most fair impression:
　　To such a force some change were nothing suitable.
Dicus. The heart well set doth never shun confession:
　　If noble be thy bands, make them notorious:
　　Silence doth seem the mask of base oppression.
　　　Who glories in his love doth make love glorious:
　　But who doth fear, or bideth muet wilfully,
　　Shows guilty heart doth deem his state opprobrious.
　　　Thou, then, that fram'st both words and voice most skilfully,
　　Yield to our ears a sweet and sound relation,
　　If love took thee by force, or caught thee guilefully.
Dorus. If sunny beams shame heav'nly habitation;
　　If three-leaved grass seem to the sheep unsavoury,
　　Then base and sour is love's most high vocation.
　　　Or if sheep's cries can help the sun's own bravery,
　　Then may I hope my pipe may have ability
　　To help her praise, who decks me in her slavery.
　　　No, no; no words ennoble self-nobility.
　　As for your doubts, her voice was it deceived me,
　　Her eye the force beyond all possibility.
Dicus. Thy words well voiced, well graced, had almost heaved me
　　Quite from myself to love love's contemplation;
　　Till of these thoughts thy sudden end bereaved me.
　　　Go on, therefore, and tell us by what fashion
　　In thy own proof he gets so strange possession;
　　And how possessed, he strengthens his invasion.
Dorus. Sight is his root; in thought is his progression;
　　His childhood, wonder; prenticeship, attention;
　　His youth, delight; his age, the soul's oppression.
　　　Doubt is his sleep; he waketh in invention;
　　Fancy his food; his clothing is of carefulness;
　　Beauty his boot; his play, lover's dissension;
　　　His eyes are curious search, but veiled with warefulness;
　　His wings, desire, oft clipped with desperation;
　　Largess, his hands, could never skill of sparefulness.
　　　But how he doth by might or by persuasion
　　To conquer, and his conquest[1] how to ratify,
　　Experience doubts, and schools hold disputation.

---

[1] conquest: conqnest *90*

Dicus. But so thy sheep may thy good wishes satisfy
    With large increase, and wool of fine perfection,
  So she thy love, her eyes thy eyes may gratify,
    As thou wilt give our souls a dear refection
5   By telling how she was, how now she framed is,
  To help or hurt in thee her own infection.

Dorus. Blessed be the name wherewith my mistress named is;
    Whose wounds are salves, whose yokes please more than pleasure doth:
  Her stains are beams; virtue the fault she blamed is.
10   The heart, eye, ear here only find his treasure doth;
  All numbering arts her endless graces number not;
    Time, place, life, wit scarcely her rare gifts measure doth.
  Is she in rage? So is the sun in summer hot,
    Yet harvest brings. Doth she, alas, absent herself?
15 The sun is hid; his kindly shadows cumber not.
    But when to give some grace she doth content herself,
  Oh, then it shines, then are the heav'ns distributed,
    And Venus seems, to make up her, she spent herself.
  Thus then (I say) my mischiefs have contributed
20   A greater good by her divine reflection;
  My harms to me, my bliss to her attributed.
    Thus she is framed: her eyes are my direction;
  Her love, my life; her anger, my destruction;
    Lastly, what so she is, that's my protection.

25 *Dicus.* Thy safety sure is wrapped in destruction,
    For that construction thine own words do bear.
  A man to fear a woman's moody eye
    Makes reason lie a slave to servile sense;
  A weak defence where weakness is thy force;
30   So is remorse in folly dearly bought.

Dorus. If I had thought to hear blasphemous words,
    My breast to swords, my soul to hell have sold
  I rather would than thus mine ears defile
    With words so vile, which viler breath doth breed.
35 O herds, take heed! for I a wolf have found
    Who, hunting round the strongest for to kill,
  His breast doth fill with earth of others' joys,
    And loaden so, pulls down; pulled down, destroys.
  O shepherds' boys, eschew these tongues of venom
40   Which do envenom both the soul and senses!

Our best defences are to fly these adders.
O tongues, like ladders made to climb dishonour,
Who judge that honour which hath scope to slander!

Dicus. Dorus, you wander far in great reproaches,
   So love encroaches on your charmed reason; 5
   But it is season for to end our singing,
   Such anger bringing. As for me, my fancy
     In sickman's frenzy rather takes compassion
   Than rage for rage; rather my wish I send to thee,
   Thou soon may have some help or change of passion. 10
     She oft her looks, the stars her favour, bend to thee:
   Fortune store, nature health, love grant persuasion.
     A quiet mind none but thyself can lend to thee –
   Thus I commend to thee all our former love.

Dorus. Well do I prove error lies oft in zeal; 15
   Yet it is seal (though error) of true heart.
   Nought could impart such heats to friendly mind
   But for to find thy words did her disgrace,
   Whose only face the little heaven is,
     Which, who doth miss, his eyes are but delusions 20
   Barred from their chiefest object of delightfulness,
   Thrown on this earth, the chaos of confusions.
     As for thy wish to my enraged spitefulness –
   The lovely, blown with rare reward – my prayer is
   Thou mayest love her, that I may see thy sightfulness. 25
     The quiet mind (whereof myself impairer is,
   As thou doest think) should most of all disquiet me
   Without her love, than any mind who fairer is.
     Her only cure from surfeit-woes can diet me:
   She holds the balance of my contentation: 30
   Her cleared eyes (nought else) in storms can quiet me.
     Nay, rather than my ease discontentation
   Should breed to her, let me for aye dejected be
   From any joy which might her grief occasion.
     With so sweet plagues my happy harms infected be: 35
   Pain wills me die, yet will of death I mortify;
   For though life irks, in life my loves protected be.
     Thus, for each change, my changeless heart I fortify.

When they had ended to the good pleasing of the assistants, especially of
Zelmane who never forgat to give due commendations to her friend Dorus, 40

the more to advance him in his pursuit (although therein he had brought his matters to a more wished conclusion than yet she knew of), out start a jolly younker – his name was Nico – whose tongue had borne a very itching silence all this while; and having spied one Pas, a mate of his, as mad as himself – both indeed lads to climb any tree in the world – he bestowed this manner of salutation upon him, and was with like reverence requited:

          Nico   *Pas*[1]

Nico. And are you there, old Pas? In troth, I ever thought,
    Among us all, we should find out some thing of nought.
Pas. And I am here the same, so mote I thrive and thee;
    Despaired in all this flock to find a knave, but thee.
Nico. Ah, now I see why thou art in thyself so blind:
    Thy grey hood hides the thing that thou despair'st to find.
Pas. My grey hood is mine own, all be it be but grey,
    Not like the scrip thou stol'st while Dorcas sleeping lay.
Nico. Mine was the scrip; but thou, that seeming rayed with love,
    Didst snatch from Cosma's hand her greeny wroughten glove.
Pas. Ah fool, so courtiers do. But who did lively skip
    When, for a treen dish stol'n, thy father did thee whip?
Nico. Indeed, the witch, thy dam, her crouch from shoulder spread,
    For pilf'ring Lalus' lamb, with crouch to bless thy head.
Pas. My voice the lamb did win; Menalcas was our judge
    Of singing match was made, whence he with shame did trudge.
Nico. Couldst thou make Lalus fly? So nightingales avoid
    When with the cawing crows their music is annoyed.
Pas. Nay, like to nightingales the other birds give ear,
    My pipe and song made him both pipe and song forswear.
Nico. I think it well: such voice would make one music hate –
    But if I had been there, th'adst met another mate.
Pas. Another sure, as is a gander from a goose;
    But still when thou dost sing, methinks a colt is loose.
Nico. Well aimed, by my hat; for as thou sangst last day,
    The neighbours all did cry, 'Alas, what ass doth bray?'
Pas. But here is Dicus old; let him then speak the word
    To whether, with best cause, the nymphs fair flowers afford.
Nico. Content; but I will lay a wager hereunto,
    That profit may ensue to him that best can do.

---

[1] Pas: Dorus *90*

I have (and long shall have) a white great nimble cat,
A king upon a mouse, a strong foe to the rat;
Fine ears, long tail he hath, with lion's curbed claw
Which oft he lifteth up, and stays his lifted paw,
Deep musing to himself, which after-mewing shows,   5
Till with licked beard, his eye of fire espy his foes.
If thou (alas, poor if!) do win, then win thou this;
And if I better sing, let me thy Cosma kiss.

Pas. Kiss her? Now mayst thou kiss – I have a better match –
  A pretty cur it is; his name, iwis, is Catch.   10
No ear nor tail he hath, lest they should him disgrace,
A ruddy hair his coat, with fine long speckled[1] face.
He never musing stands, but with himself will play,
Leaping at every fly, and angry with a flea;
He eft would kill a mouse, but he disdains to fight,   15
And makes our home good sport with dancing bolt upright.
This is my pawn; the price let Dicus' judgement show:
Such odds I willing lay; for him and you I know.

Dicus. Sing then, my lads, but sing with better vein than yet,
  Or else who singeth worst, my skill will hardly hit!   20

Nico. Who doubts but Pas' fine pipe again will bring
  The ancient praise to Arcad shepherds' skill?
Pan is not dead, since Pas begins to sing.

Pas. Who evermore will love Apollo's quill,
  Since Nico doth, to sing, so widely gape?   25
Nico his place far better furnish will.

Nico. Was not this he who did for Syrinx scape,
  Raging in woes, teach pastors first to plain?
Do you not hear his voice, and see his shape?

Pas. This is not he that failed her to gain,   30
  Which made a bay, made bay a holy tree;
But this is one that doth his music stain.

Nico. O fauns, O fairies all, and do you see
  And suffer such a wrong? A wrong, I trow,
That Nico must with Pas compared be?   35

Pas. O nymphs, I tell you news, for Pas you know:
  While I was warbling out your wonted praise,
Nico would needs with Pas his bagpipe blow.

---

[1] speckled: spectled *90*

Nico. If never I did fail your holy-days,
    With dances, carols, or with barley-break,
    Let Pas now know how Nico makes the lays.
Pas. If each day hath been holy for your sake
5   Unto my pipe, O nymphs – help now my pipe,
    For Pas well knows what lays can Nico make.
Nico. Alas, how oft I look on cherries ripe,
    Methinks I see the lips my Leuca hath,
    And wanting her, my weeping eyes I wipe.
10 *Pas.* Alas, when I in spring meet roses rathe,
    And think from Cosma's sweet red lips I live,
    I leave mine eyes unwiped my cheeks to bathe.
Nico. As I of late near bushes used my sieve,
    I spied a thrush where she did make her nest;
15   That will I take, and to my Leuca give.
Pas. But long have I a sparrow gaily dressed,
    As white as milk, and coming to the call,
    To put it with my hand in Cosma's breast.
Nico. I oft do sue, and Leuca saith I shall,
20   But when I did come near with heat and hope,
    She ran away and threw at me a ball.
Pas. Cosma once said she left the wicket ope
    For me to come, and so she did; I came,
    But in the place found nothing but a rope.
25 *Nico.* When Leuca doth appear, the sun for shame
    Doth hide himself, for to himself he says,
    'If Leuca live, she darken will my fame.'
Pas. When Cosma doth come forth, the sun displays
    His utmost light; for well his wit doth know,
30   Cosma's fair beams emblemish much his rays.
Nico. Leuca to me did yester-morning show
    In perfect light, which could not me deceive,
    Her naked leg, more white than whitest snow.
Pas. But yesternight by light I did receive
35   From Cosma's eyes, which full in darkness shine,
    I saw her arm, where purest lilies cleave.
Nico. She once stark nak'd did bathe a little tine,
    But still (methought) with beauties from her fell,
    She did the waters wash, and make more fine.

Pas. She once, to cool herself, stood in a well,
 But ever since that well is well besought,
 And for rose-water sold of rarest smell.

Nico. To river's bank, being on-walking brought,
 She bad me spy her baby in the brook:
 'Alas,' said I, 'this babe doth nurse my thought!'

Pas. As in a glass I held she once did look,
 I said my hands well paid her for mine eyes,
 Since in my hands' self goodly sight she took.

Nico. Oh, if I had a ladder for the skies,
 I would climb up, and bring a pretty star
 To wear upon her neck that open lies.

Pas. Oh, if I had Apollo's golden car,
 I would come down and yield to her my place,
 That (shining now) she then might shine more far.

Nico. Nothing, O Leuca, shall thy fame deface,
 While shepherds' tunes be heard, or rhymes be read,
 Or while that shepherds love a lovely face.

Pas. Thy name, O Cosma, shall with praise be spread
 As far as any shepherds piping be,
 As far as love possesseth any head.

Nico. Thy monument is laid in many a tree,
 With name engraved; so though thy body die,
 The after-folks shall wonder still at thee.

Pas. So oft these woods have heard me 'Cosma' cry,
 That after death to heav'n, in woods' resound,
 With Echo's help, shall 'Cosma, Cosma' fly.

Nico. Peace, peace, good Pas! Thou weariest ev'n the ground
 With sluttish song. I pray thee learn to blea,
 For good thou mayst yet prove in sheepish sound.

Pas. My father hath at home a pretty jay.
 Go win of him (for chattering) praise or shame,
 For so yet of a conquest speak thou may.

Nico. Tell me (and be my Pan) the monster's name
 That hath four legs, and with two only goes,
 That hath four eyes, and only two can frame.

Pas. Tell me (and Phoebus be) what monster grows
 With so strong lives that body cannot rest
 In ease, until that body life forgoes?

Dicus. Enough! Enough! So ill hath done the best
    That, since the having them to neither's due,
    Let cat and dog fight which shall have both you.

  Some speech there straight grew among the hearers what they should mean by the riddles of the two monsters. But Zelmane, whose heart better delighted in wailful ditties as more according to her fortune, she desired Lamon he would again repeat some other lamentation of the still absent Strephon and Klaius. Basilius, as soon as he understood Zelmane's pleasure, commanded Lamon upon pain of his life (as though everything were a matter of life and death that pertained to his mistress's service) immediately to sing it; who, with great cunning varying his voice according to the diversity of the persons, began this dizain, answered in that kind of verse which is called the crown:

           Strephon   Klaius

Strephon. I joy in grief, and do detest all joys;
    Despise delight, and tired with thought of ease
    I turn my mind to all forms of annoys,
    And with the change of them my fancy please.
    I study that which may me most displease,
    And in despite of that displeasure's might
    Embrace that most that most my soul destroys.
    Blinded with beams, fell darkness is my sight;
    Dole on my ruin feeds, with sucking smart;
    I think, from me – not from my woes, to part.

Klaius. I think, from me – not from my woes, to part,
    And loath this time called life; nay, think that life
    Nature to me for torment did impart;
    Think my hard haps have blunted death's sharp knife,
    Not sparing me in whom his works be rife;
    And thinking this: think nature, life, and death
    Place sorrow's triumph on my conquered breast,
    Whereto I yield, and seek none other breath
    But from the scent of some infectious grave,
    Nor of my fortune aught but mischief crave.

Strephon. Nor of my fortune aught but mischief crave,
    And seek to nourish that which now contains
    All what I am. If I myself will save,
    Then must I save what in me chiefly reigns,
    Which is the hateful web of sorrow's pains.

APPENDIX I

> Sorrow, then cherish me, for I am sorrow –
> No being now but sorrow I can have –
> Then deck me as thine own; thy help I borrow,
> Since thou my riches art, and that thou haste
> Enough to make a fertile mind lie waste.   5

Klaius. Enough to make a fertile mind lie waste
> Is that huge storm which pours itself on me:
> Hailstones of tears, of sighs a monstrous blast,
> Thunders of cries, lightnings my wild looks be;
> The darkened heav'n, my soul which nought can see;   10
> The flying sprites which trees by roots uptear
> Be those despairs which have my hopes quite waste.
> The difference is: all folks those storms forbear,
> But I cannot, who then myself should fly,
> So close unto myself my wracks do lie.   15

Strephon. So close unto myself my wracks do lie,
> Both cause, effect, beginning, and the end
> Are all in me. What help then can I try?
> My ship, myself, whose course to love doth bend,
> Sore beaten doth her mast of comfort spend;   20
> Her cable, reason, breaks from anchor, hope;
> Fancy, her tackling, torn away doth fly;
> Ruin, the wind, hath blown her from her scope,
> Bruised with waves of cares – but broken is
> On rock, despair, the burial of my bliss.   25

Klaius. On rock, despair, the burial of my bliss,
> I long do plough with plough of deep desire.
> The seed, fast-meaning is, no truth to miss;
> I harrow it with thoughts, which all conspire
> Favour to make my chief and only hire.   30
> But, woe is me, the year is gone about,
> And now I fain would reap, I reap but this:
> Hate fully grown, absence new sprongen out,
> So that I see, although my sight impair,
> Vain is their pain who labour in despair.   35

Strephon. Vain is their pain who labour in despair,
> For so did I when with my angle, will,
> I sought to catch the fish torpedo fair.
> Ev'n then despair did hope already kill –
> Yet fancy would perforce employ his skill,   40

And this hath got: the catcher now is caught,
Lamed with the angle which itself did bear,
And unto death, quite drowned in dolours, brought
To death, as then disguised in her fair face.
Thus, thus I had, alas, my loss in chase.

Klaius. Thus, thus I had, alas, my loss in chase
When first that crowned basilisk I knew,
Whose footsteps I with kisses oft did trace,
Till by such hap as I must ever rue
Mine eyes did light upon her shining hue,
And hers on me, astonished with that sight.
Since then, my heart did lose his wonted place,
Infected so with her sweet poison's might
That, leaving me for dead, to her it went:
But ah! her flight hath my dead relics spent.

Strephon. But ah! her flight hath my dead relics spent –
Her flight from me – from me! though dead to me,
Yet living still in her, while her beams lent
Such vital spark that her mine eyes might see.
But now those living lights absented be,
Full dead before, I now to dust should fall,
But that eternal pains my soul should hent,
And keep it still within this body thrall,
That thus I must, while in this death I dwell,
In earthly fetters feel a lasting hell.

Klaius. In earthly fetters feel a lasting hell,
Alas, I do; from which to find release,
I would the earth, I would the heavens fell.
But vain it is to think these pains should cease
Where life is death, and death cannot breed peace.
O fair, O only fair, from thee, alas,
These foul, most foul distresses, to me fell,
Since thou from me (O me!), O sun, didst pass.
Therefore, esteeming all good blessings toys,
I joy in grief, and do detest all joys.

Strephon. I joy in grief, and do detest all joys.
And now an end, O Claius, now an end,
For ev'n the herbs our mournful music stroys,
And from our burning breath the trees do bend.

So well did Lamon's voice express the passions of those shepherds that all the princely beholders were stricken in a silent consideration of them; indeed, every one making that he heard of another the balance of his own troubles. And Basilius, perceiving such melancholic music best consorted to the humour of his mistress, entreated again the young melancholy shepherd that he would impart some part of the sorrow his countenance so well witnessed unto them; which he, in part to satisfy, began an eclogue betwixt himself and the echo, framing his voice in those desert places as, what words he would have the echo reply, unto those he would sing higher than the rest, and so kindly framed a disputation betwixt himself and it, which, with these hexameters in the following order, he uttered:

	Echo
Fair rocks, goodly rivers, sweet woods, when shall I see peace?	Peace.
Peace? Who debars me my tongue? Who is it that comes me so nigh?	I.
Oh! I do know what guest I do meet; it is echo!	'Tis[1] echo.
Well met, echo; approach, and tell me thy will too.	I will too.
Echo, what do I get yielding my sprite to my grieves?	Grieves.
What medicine may I find for a pain that draws me to death?	Death.
Oh, pois'nous medicine! What worse to me can be than it?	It.
In what state was I then, when I took this deadly disease?	Ease.
And what manner a mind, which had to that humour a vein?	Vain.
Hath not reason enough vehemence the desire to reprove?	Prove.
Oft prove I; but what salve, when reason seeks to be gone?	One.
Oh, what is it? What is it that may be a salve to my love?	Love.
What do lovers seek for, long seeking for t'enjoy?	Joy.
What be the joys for which t'enjoy they went to the pains?	Pains.
Then, to an earnest love, what doth best victory lend?	End.
End? But I can never end; love will not give me the leave.	Leave.
How be the minds disposed that cannot taste the physic?	Sick.
Yet say again th'advice for th'ills that I told thee.	I told thee.
Doth th'infected wretch of his ill th'extremity know?	No.
But if he know not his harms, what guides hath he whilst he be blind?	Blind.
What blind guides can he have that leads to a fancy?	A fancy.
Can fancies want eyes, or he fall that steppeth aloft?	Oft.
What causes first made these torments on me to light?	Light.
Can then a cause be so light that forceth a man to go die?	Aye.
Yet tell what light thing I had in me to draw me to die.	Eye.
Eyesight made me to yield; but what first pierced to my eyes?	Eyes.
Eyes' hurters eyes hurt. But what from them to me falls?	Falls.

---

[1] 'Tis: T'is 90

But when I first did fall, what brought most fall to my heart?   Art.
Art? What can be that art which thou doost mean by thy speech?   Speech.
What be the fruits of speaking art? What grows by the words?   Words.
Oh, much more than words! Those words served more me to bless.   Less.
5 Oh, when shall I be known where most to be known I do long?   Long.
Long be thy woes for such bad news! How recks she my thoughts?   Aughts.
Then, then what do I gain, since unt'her will I do wind?   Wind.
Wind, tempests, and storms[1] ! Yet, in end, what gives she desire?   Ire.
Silly reward – yet above women hath she a title.   A tittle.
10 What great name may I give to so heav'nly a woman?   A woe-man.
Woe – but seems to me joy, that agrees to my thought so.   I thought so.
Think so, for of my desired bliss it is only the course.   Course.
Cursed be thyself for cursing that which leads me to joys.   Toys.
What be the sweet creatures where lowly demands be not hard?   Hard.
15 Hard to be got, but got, constant; to be held, very steels.   Eels.
How be they held unkind? speak, for th'hast narrowly pried.   Pride.
How can pride come there, since springs of beauty be thence?   Thence.
Horrible is this blasphemy unto the most holy!   O lie!
Thou li'st, false echo; their minds, as virtue, be just.   Just.
20 Mockst thou those diamonds which only be matched[2] by the gods?   Odds.
Odds? What an odds is there! since them to the heav'ns I prefer.   Err.
Tell yet again, how name ye the goodly made evil?   A devil.
Devil? In hell where[3] such devil is, to that hell I do go.   Go.

After this well-placed echo, the other shepherds were offering themselves to have continued the sports, but the night had so quietly spent most part of herself that the king for that time licensed them; and so, bringing Zelmane to her lodging (who would much rather have done the same for Philoclea) of all sides they went to counterfeit a sleep in their beds, for a true one their agonies could not afford them. Yet there lay they (for so might they be most solitary) for the food of their thoughts, till it was near noon the next day, after which Basilius was to continue his Apollo devotions, and the other to meditate upon their private desires.

The end of the second Book.

---

[1] storms] scorns 90 (*uncorr.*)   [2] be matched: bematcht 90   [3] In hell where] where hell if 90 (*uncorr.*)

APPENDIX II

This dedication is printed in all editions, but belongs to the *Old Arcadia*; see Robertson, 3 and 418.

TO MY DEAR LADY AND SISTER, THE COUNTESS OF PEMBROKE

Here now have you (most dear, and most worthy to be most dear, lady) this idle work of mine, which I fear (like the spider's web) will be thought fitter to be swept away than worn to any other purpose. For my part, in very truth (as the cruel fathers among the Greeks were wont to do to the babes they would not foster) I could well find in my heart to cast out in some desert of forgetfulness this child which I am loath to father. But you desired me to do it, and your desire to my heart is an absolute commandment. Now it is done only for you, only to you; if you keep it to yourself, or to such friends who will weigh errors in the balance of goodwill, I hope, for the father's sake, it will be pardoned, perchance made much of, though in itself it have deformities. For indeed, for severer eyes it is not, being but a trifle, and that triflingly handled; your dear self can best witness the manner, being done in loose sheets of paper, most of it in your presence, the rest by sheets sent unto you as fast as they were done. In sum, a young head not so well stayed as I would it were (and shall be when God will) having many many fancies begotten in it, if it had not been in some way delivered, would have grown a monster, and more sorry might I be that they came in than that they gat out. But his chief safety shall be the not walking abroad; and his chief protection the bearing the livery of your name which (if much much goodwill do not deceive me) is worthy to be a sanctuary for a greater offender. This say I because I know the virtue so; and this say I because it may be ever so; or, to say better, because it will be ever so. Read it then at your idle times, and the follies your good judgement will find in it, blame not, but laugh at. And so, looking for no better stuff than, as in an haberdasher's shop, glasses or feathers, you will continue to love the writer who doth exceedingly love you, and most most heartily prays you may long live to be a principal ornament to the family of the Sidneys.

Your loving brother,
Philip Sidney

APPENDIX III

RINGLER, 367, argued from the persistence of apparent errors common to the manuscripts of the *Old Arcadia* that the manuscripts could not have been copied directly from the author's holograph. He suggested rather that their common source was a scribal transcript of the foul copy, and that the transcriber introduced the errors. To this hypothetical manuscript he assigned the siglum *T*. While supporting this hypothesis with examples from the prose, Robertson provided plausible explanations for some of the readings that Ringler had held to be in error. Four of these occur within the text of this volume.[1] In the following table I list the remaining evidence for *T*, and state the case for the validity of the manuscript tradition. My conclusion is that there are no errors common to the manuscripts of the *Old Arcadia* which clearly demonstrate that the manuscripts were copied from a single scribal intermediary between them and Sidney's foul copy. There is therefore no reason to suppose that such a scribal intermediary existed.

Page in   *Lemma*
Robertson

8, 24-7 But coming to that, his rude simplicity is either easily changed or easily deceived; and so grows that to be the last excuse of his fault *which seemed to have* been the first foundation of his faith.

which seemed to have *Cm, 90, 93*: which seemed might have *St, Cl, Da, Hm*; which ⟨ ⟩ might have *Bo*; which should have *Ph*

which seemed might have in the majority of the manuscripts is an ellipsis of the nominative, and may be expanded to 'which seemed it might have.' The reading *which seemed to have Cm, 90, 93* may be a revision to the less conditional made during the composition of the *New Arcadia* (see above, p. 17, 36).

76, 12-13 two dogs, whereof the elder was called Melampus, and the younger *Lælaps*

Lælaps 93: Lelanx *OA (ex. Da)*; Lenax *Da*

76, 25 What if *Lælaps* a better morsel finds

Lælaps 93: Lelanx *OA (ex. Da)*; Lenanx *Da*

76, 28 And thou, *Lælaps*, let not pride make thee brim

Lælaps 93: Lelanx *OA (ex. Da)*; Lenanx *Da*

76, 31 Here, *Lælaps*, here; indeed, against the foen

Lælaps 93: Lelanx *OA (ex. Da, Je)*; Lenanx *Da*; *Lilanx Je*

The name of Geron's younger dog, *Lælaps*, as in Ovid, *Met.* iii. 206, 211, and in *Met.* vii. 771, has been consistently mistranscribed as *Lelanx* through misreading the final *ps*. Sidney's 'p' with a faint downstroke and open-bottomed loop resembles the letter 'n,' and the final 's' with a loop at the top could be read as 'x'. Cf. Ringler, the plate facing p. lxiii, line 25, in the word 'palpable.'

---

[1] See above, pp. 14, 14; 198, 13; below, pp. 406, 28; 426, 16 and notes

77, 33   At blow point, hot cockles, or *else at* keels

else at 93: *om*. OA

else at was added in 93 to create a regular pentameter. But as Robertson, 432, notes, '*keels* is a variant spelling of *kayles*', often a disyllabic. In a line in which the silent 'e' in *blowe* may be pronounced and in which *point* may also have two syllables, the emendation in 93 is unnecessary (the old spelling is in Ringler, OA 10. 47, 'At blowe point, hotcocles, or els at keeles,' from 93). Cf. Robertson, 137, 27 where the manuscript spelling *muett* is retained to provide the necessary disyllable, followed in this text at p. 423, 7.

80, 7   Where thou, poor Nature, *left'st* all dry due glory to Fortune

left'st 93: left OA (*ex. Da*); lefts Da

left'st is an emendation in 93 to regularize the agreement between pronoun and verb; but *left* is supported by Abbott, 298, where by confusion of proximity the verb in the third person might be introduced following a noun, as in *Nature, left*.

82, 28   How to the woods love runs as well as *rides* to the palace

rides Da, Je, 93: ride St, Bo, Cl, Le, As, Ph, Hm

ride, the reading of the majority of the manuscripts, is supported by Abbott, 260, as the subjunctive meaning *it may ride*.

85, 14   Then by my high cedar, *rich* ruby, and only shining sun

rich ruby Cl, 93: right ruby St, Bo, Le, As, Ph, Je, Hm; ruby right Da

right in 'right ruby' means 'genuine' as in OED 17c, citing Sir Thomas More, 'whether a stone be right or counterfeit.'

94, 32–3   when thou (to me unfortunate guest) *camest* to draw me from myself

camest 90: came OA, Cm

See above, p. 105, 18 and note.

101, 18–20   O let not an excellent spirit do itself *such wrong as to think where* it is placed, embraced, and loved, there can be any unworthiness

as to think where Cl, 90, 93: as where St, Bo, Le, As, Ph, Je, Cm; as once to imagine where Da; as when Qu

See above, p. 113, 1 and note.

107, 6   *On* barren sweets they feed, and feeding starve

On Bo, 90, 93: In OA (*ex. Bo, Da*), Fl, Ma; O Da

See above, p. 119, 3 and note.

125, 28   *Leave leaving not* my mourning to maintain

Leave leaving not OA (*ex. Ph*); Leave off my sheep Ringler

Ringler, 397, regards *Leave leaving not* as an error in transcription which appears in all the manuscripts of the *Old Arcadia*, and therefore evidence for *T*. Robertson, 441, finds the reading viable, paraphrasing as 'Cease not ceasing to maintain my mourning.'

137, 19   Who others' virtue *doubt*, themselves are vicious

doubt 90: doubts OA

In the *Old Arcadia* the reading *doubts* appears to be the use of the third person plural ending in 's' described by Abbott, 235. In 90 the poem is in the Second Eclogues; see above, p. 422, 38.

140, 26–7   Which who doth miss his eyes are but delusions,
Barred from *their* chiefest object of delightfulness

their] his *As, Da, Je, Hm* (his *corr. to* their *Cl*) her *Ph*

Ringler, 367, rejects *his* as a scribal error, and uses it for evidence of *T*. But the relationship of *his* with *who … his* in the preceding line is regular, where 'his eyes' cannot see 'his chiefest object of delightfulness.' In a poem which shows signs of revision on several occasions, it is plausible that Sidney eventually changed the relationship in order to create a personification of *eyes*. See above, p. 425, 21.

162, 15–16   How can they be unkind? Speak for th'hast *narrowly* pried.

narrowly 90, 93: nearly *St, Bo, Cl, Le, As, Da, Je, Hm*; newly *Ph*

The reading in the *Old Arcadia* is reasonable and cannot be rejected. It occurs in the second section of a line of which the first part was evidently revised in two versions in A^5, that in 90, 'How be they held unkind?', somewhat more akin to its original than that in 93, 'What makes them be unkind?' The alteration to *narrowly* seems to have been made *in A^5* as well. See above, p. 434. 16.

163, 27   If *that to sing thou* art bent

that to sing 93: unto sing *St, Bo, Le, As, Je*; unto song *Cl, Da, Ph, Hm*

The reading *unto sing* means simply 'to sing' (cf. *OED unto* 29, meaning *to* with the infinitive), and has the support of the majority of manuscripts; *that to sing* in 93 resembles the other examples of editorial simplification in that edition listed above, pp. li-lii.

168, 27–9   who would ever have thought so good a schoolmaster as you were to me could for lack of *living have been* driven to shepherdry?

living have been *Robertson*: living been OA

Robertson, 448, defends the addition of *have* to the text:

'The insertion of *have* seems to be required by the other *haves* in this speech, and in the next; its omission by the copyist of T would have been an easy error to make.'

But Abbott, 297–8, cites examples of confusion of two constructions by combining them, similar to the one here in which *have* in 'have thought' is carried forward and understood before the next past participle, *been driven*.

APPENDIX III

177, 6–7   Apollo, since he (if he *know* anything) knows that my heart

know *Bo, Hm*, 93: knew *St, Cl, As, Da, Ph, Je*

Robertson, 450, sees *knew* as an error in *T*; but it is only an apparent irregularity in the sequences of tenses, for *knew* here means 'ever knew' (cf. Abbott, 269).

199, 19   Rising from *low*, are to the highest bent

low] love *Cl, As, Da, Ph, Hm (Je is missing)*

In *Rising from love* in the early manuscripts, 'rising' means 'arising.' The literal meaning in *Rising from low* in *St, Le, Bo, Le* 93 radically changes the interpretation and seems to be a revision.

207, 21–2   Because that thou, the author of our sight,
Disdainst we see thee stained with other's light.

Disdainst 93: Disdains *OA*

The manuscript reading *Disdains* is the third person agreement with *author*, resulting from the change of thought from *thou ... Disdainst* to *author ... Disdains*, according to Abbott, 301.

228, 24–5   those saucy *pangs* of love, doubts, griefs, languishing hopes, and threatening despairs

pangs *As, Hm*: pages *St, Bo, Cl, Da, Ph, Je*, 93

Robertson, p. lxvii, n. 2, and 458, rejects *pages* as a misreading of *pages*, though the meaning of *pages* as 'servants' is supported by Robertson, 20, 3–4 (see above, p. 60, 29–30), where similar characteristics of love are called 'his adjoined companions.'

234, 12–14   if ever in that profession they [i.e., my thoughts] received either spot or *falsehood*, then let their most horrible plagues fall upon me

falsehood 93: fellowship *OA*; friendship *Hm*

fellowship in the majority of manuscripts means 'kindred thoughts of love towards any other,' and as such is an acceptable parallel to *spot* without the emendation in 93 to the obvious *falsehood*.

238, 21   The matchless *pair*, e'en praise doth stain

pair 90, 93: praise *OA, Dd*

See above, p. 164, 16 and note.

260, 1–2   this is the right conceit of *young men who think* then they speak wiseliest

young men who think 90, 93: a young man, think *OA*; a young man, who think *Da*

The reading of the majority of the manuscripts, *conceit of a young man, think then they speak*, is an irregular construction reflecting change of thought. This moves from the singular and particular, 'young man' (Philisides), to the plural and general, 'they.' The abruptness caused by ellipsis of the relative *who* reflects Geron's disgruntled mood; see above, p. 414, 16–17.

261, 4-6   Either dull silence, or eternal chat;
Still contrary to what her husband says:
If he do praise the dog, she likes the cat.

om. Da, Ph, Je, Hm

Both Ringler, 415, and Robertson, 466, suggest that these lines were 'omitted by the transcriber of *T*', but later restored. It is equally plausible that the original lines were deleted by Sidney in his papers, and these lines not added until after the four early copies were made. Whatever the explanation, the omission did not necessarily arise from scribal error.

266, 1-3   could not *so suddenly* lose the colour that had so thoroughly dyed his thick brain but that he turned and tossed the poor bowels of the innocent earth

so suddenly *93*: suddenly *OA*

The simple construction in *not suddenly* in the manuscripts is followed by the conjunction *but* with its neutral affix *that* (cf. Abbott, 196), and the additional descriptive clause. The editor of *93* introduced a contrast in the structure *not so ... but that*, as in *OED* under but conj. 13.

278, 12-16   the furthest and only *limit* of his affection. He thanked the destinies that had wrought her honour out of his shame; and that had made his own *striving to* go amiss to be the best mean ever after to hold him in the right path.

limit *93*: limits *OA* striving *93*: finding *OA*

Robertson, 469, reads *limit* and *striving*. There is no evidence of error in *limits*. Whereas *striving* refers not to Basilius' shame but to the action which brings about his embarrassment, *finding* expresses his shame in finding himself to have gone amiss. The author's hand may be in both pairs of readings.

287, 22-3   he rose up, *so looking* upon the poor guiltless princess, transported with an unjust justice, that his eyes

so looking *93*: looking *OA*

Robertson, 470, notes that '*93*'s *so* is to be taken with *that* (line 23), and could easily have been overlooked by T' s copyist.' But *looking* alone is perfectly adequate when followed by *that*, which here accords with Abbott, 193, '*So* before *that* is very frequently omitted.'

371, 27-8   Since, *then*, eternity is not to be had in this conjunction

then *Cl, Je, 93*: the *St, Bo, Da, Ph, Hm*; their *As*

Robertson, 479, blames the confusion on the scribe of *T*, who must have written the word as *the*. But the majority of the manuscripts in reading *the eternity* follow the sense given in *OED* 2a, citing Golding's translation of de Mornay, 'The eternity hath not anything either afore or after it.'

APPENDIX IV

NEW ARCADIA – RHETORICAL FIGURES

NOTE: This is a non-comprehensive list of rhetorical figures employed by Sidney in the *New Arcadia*. Its aim is not so much to define the figures themselves (though brief definitions are given at the beginning of each entry) as to illustrate their importance for Sidney's style and to demonstrate the range of uses to which he puts them in his writing. Since the terminology of rhetorical figures is notoriously diverse, multiple names are listed where necessary. Closely related figures whose distinctions are only slight, such as oxymoron and synœciosis, have been grouped together. – EC

References

Ascham, Roger   *The Scholemaster*. 1570.
Burton, Gideon O.   *Silva Rhetoricae*. Brigham Young University, http://rhetoric.byu.edu/.
Fraunce, Abraham   *Arcadian Rhetorike*. 1588.
Gill, Alexander   *Logonomia Anglica*. 1619.
Lanham, Richard A.   *A Handlist of Rhetorical Terms*. 2nd ed., University of California Press, 1991.
Mulcaster, Richard   *The First Part of the Elementarie*. 1582.
Puttenham, George   *The Arte of English Poesie*. 1589.

ABUSIO: *see* CATACHRESIS

ACCUMULATIO or FREQUENTATIO: 'Heaping up praise or accusation to emphasize or summarize points or inferences already made' (Lanham 1).

1. 'as his adjoined companions be unquietness, longings, fond comforts, faint discomforts, hopes, jealousies, ungrounded rages, causeless yieldings' (60; Hoskyns 31, 'tending to the same end')
2. 'in that visage there was neither majesty, grace, favour, nor fairness; yet she wanted not a servant that would have made her fairer than the fair Artesia' (81)
3. 'This fight, being the more cruel since both love and hatred conspired to sharpen their humours, that hard it was to say whether love with one trumpet, or hatred with another, gave the louder alarum to their courages. Spite, rage, disdain, shame, revenge came waiting upon hatred.' (352; Hoskyns 31)

ADDUBITATION: *see* APORIA

ADNEXIO: *see* ZEUGMA

ADNOMINATIO / AGNOMINATIO: *see* PARONOMASIA

ALLEGORIA / INVERSIO or PERMUTATIO / ALLEGORY: 'Extending a metaphor through an entire speech or passage' (Lanham 4).

1. 'And herewith, the deep wound of his love being rubbed afresh with this new unkindness began as it were to bleed again, in such sort that he was not able to bear it any longer' (65; Fraunce B4^v)
2. 'when with pity once my heart was made tender, according to the aptness of the humour, it received quickly a cruel impression of that wonderful passion which to be defined is impossible' (66–7; Fraunce B4^v)
3. 'True it is that my reason, now grown a servant to passion, did yet often tell his master that he should more moderately use his delight, but he, that of a rebel was become a prince, disdained almost to allow him the place of councillor' (74)
4. 'but when that wish had once displayed his ensign in her mind, then followed whole squadrons of longings that so it might be, with a main battle of mislikings and repinings against their creation that so it was not.' (124–5; Hoskyns 9)
5. 'the sky of your virtue should be overclouded with sorrow' (279; Hoskyns 9)

ANABASIS: *see* **CLIMAX**

ANADIPLOSIS / (RE)DUPLICATIO: 'Repetition of the last word of one line or clause to begin the next' (Lanham 10).

1. 'For since you will not that he live – alas! alas! what followeth? What followeth of the most ruined Dorus but his end?' (133)
2. 'Plangus doth live, and shall Erona die?
    Erona die?' (173; Hoskyns 12)
3. 'Over these brooks, trusting to ease mine eyes
    (Mine eyes ev'n great in labour with their tears),
    I laid my face (my face wherein there lies
    Clusters of clouds which no sun ever clears).' (198; Fraunce C7^r)
4. 'reason to my passion yielded,
    Passion unto my rage, rage to a hasty revenge' (270; Gill 106)
5. 'Why lived I, alas? Alas, why loved I? To die wretched! and to be the example of the heavens' hate! And hate, and spare not! for your worst blow is stricken.' (375; Hoskyns 12)

ANAPHORA / REPETITIO: 'Repetition of the same word at the beginning of successive clauses or verses' (Lanham 11).

1. 'For nothing else did my husband take this strange resolution to live so solitarily, for nothing else have the winds delivered this strange guest to my country, for nothing else have the destinies reserved my life to this time, but that only I, most wretched I, should become a plague to myself, and a shame to womankind.' (103; Fraunce E6^r – cited as example of an exclamation of despair)
2. 'Old age is wise and full of constant truth;
    Old age well stayed from ranging humour lives;
    Old age hath known whatever was in youth;
    Old age orecome, the greater honour gives.' (106; Fraunce D^r)

3. 'though no man had less goodness in his soul than he, no man could better find the places whence arguments might grow of goodness to another; though no man felt less pity, no man could tell better how to stir pity; no man more impudent to deny, where proofs were not manifest; no man more ready to confess, with a repenting manner of aggravating his own evil, where denial would but make the fault fouler.' (159)
4. 'But be not, be not, most excellent lady, you that nature hath made to be a lodestar of comfort, be not the rock of shipwrack; you whom virtue hath made the princess of felicity, be not the minister of ruin; you whom my choice hath made the goddess of my safety' (200; Hoskyns 13)
5. 'It was not a pity; it was not an amazement; it was not a sorrow which then laid hold on Pyrocles, but a wild fury of desperate agony' (373)

ANTIMETABOLE or CHIASMUS / COMMUTATIO: '[I]nverting the order of repeated words (ABBA) to sharpen their sense or to contrast the ideas they convey, or both' (Lanham 14).

1. 'the sweetest fairness and fairest sweetness' (2; Hoskyns 15)
2. 'if extremity of love had not made your judgement partial, nor you could have loved me so entirely if you had not been apt to make so great (though undeserved) judgements of me.' (42; Hoskyns 15)
3. 'Zelmane, as much as Gynecia's jealousy would suffer, desired to be near Philoclea; Philoclea, as much as Gynecia's jealousy would suffer, desired to be near Zelmane.' (124; Hoskyns 15)
4. 'And Dorus the more blushed at her smiling; and she the more smiled at his blushing' (148; Hoskyns 15)
5. 'not as a purse for treasure, but as a treasure itself, worthy to be pursed up' (308; Hoskyns 15)
6. 'just to exercise his might, and mighty to perform his justice' (314; Hoskyns 15)
7. 'if before he languished because he could not obtain his desiring, he now lamented because he durst not desire the obtaining' (358; Hoskyns 14)

ANTISTROPHE: *see* **EPISTROPHE**

ANTITHESIS / CONTENTIO or OPPOSITIO: 'Conjoining contrasting ideas' (Lanham 16).

1. 'the universal lamenting his absented presence assured him of his present absence' (57; see also SYNŒCIOSIS)
2. 'neither that did hurt her, nor any contrary mean help her' (197; Hoskyns 37)
3. 'neither she could look on, nor would look off' (198; Hoskyns 37)
4. 'There was strength against nimbleness, rage against resolution, fury against virtue, confidence against courage, pride against nobleness' (402; Hoskyns 37)
5. 'but he was scarce down before he was up on his feet again, with brave gesture showing rising of courage in the falling of fortune' (353)

Aporia / Dubitatio / Addubitation: 'True or feigned doubt or deliberation about an issue' (Lanham 19).

1. 'Yet if my desire, how unjust so ever it be, might take effect, though a thousand deaths followed it, and every death were followed with a thousand shames, yet should not my sepulchre receive me without some contentment. But alas, though sure I am that Zelmane is such as can answer my love, yet as sure I am that this disguising must needs come for some foretaken conceit. And then, wretched Gynecia, where canst thou and any small groundplot for hope to dwell upon? No, no, it is Philoclea his heart is set upon; it is my daughter I have borne to supplant me. But if it be so, the life I have given thee, ungrateful Philoclea, I will sooner with these hands bereave thee of than my birth shall glory she hath bereaved me of my desires. In shame there is no comfort but to be beyond all bounds of shame.' (103; Fraunce G7^v-G8^r)

2. 'For yet if I found she contemned me, I would desperately labour both in fortune and virtue to overcome it; if she only misdoubted me, I were in heaven, for quickly I would bring sufficient assurance; lastly, if she hated me, yet I should know what passion to deal with, and either with infiniteness of desert I would take away the fuel from that fire, or if nothing would serve, then I would give her my heart-blood to quench it.'
(120; Hoskyns 50 – cited as an example of prevention by occupatio.)

3. 'Did I go to church? It seemed the very gods waited for me, their devotions not being solemnized till I was ready. Did I walk abroad to see any delight? Nay, my walking was the delight itself.'
(275; Hoskyns 50 – cited as an example of prevention by subjectio)

4. 'Shall death head his dart with the gold of Cupid's arrow? Shall death take his aim from the rest of beauty? O beloved-though-hating Philoclea, how, if thou beest merciful, hath cruelty stolen into thee? Or how, if thou beest cruel, doth cruelty look more merciful than ever mercy did? Or, alas, is it my destiny that makes mercy cruel, like an evil vessel which turns sweet liquor to sourness; so when thy grace falls upon me, my wretched constitution makes it become fierceness?' (284)

Apostrophe / Exclamatio / Exclamation: 'Breaking off a discourse to address some person or personified thing either present or absent' (Lanham 20); 'Exclamation expressing emotion' (Lanham 61).

1. ' "O only pearl!" said I, sobbing, "that so vile an oyster should keep thee!" ' (69)

2. 'Alas, poor lute, how much art thou deceived to think that in my miseries thou couldst ease my woes, as in my careless times thou wert wont to please my fancies!' (104; Fraunce G^v)

3. 'Alas, excellent Mopsa, consider that a virtuous prince requires the life of his meanest subject, and the heavenly sun disdains not to give light to the smallest worm.' (111; Fraunce F2^r – cited as exclamation of pity (though the pity is feigned))

4. ' "O Diana," said she, "I would either the cloud that now hides the light of my virtue would as easily pass away as you will quickly overcome this let; or else that you were for ever thus darkened, to serve for an excuse of my outrageous folly." '
(127; Fraunce E7^r – cited as exclamation of wishing)

5. 'O tyrant heaven! Traitor earth! Blind providence! No justice? How is this done?

How is this suffered? Hath this world a government?'
(373; Hoskyns 33)

6. 'O muse, historify
Her praise, whose praise to learn your skill hath framed me.'
(405; Fraunce G^r)

ASYNDETON / DISSOLUTIO: 'Omission of conjunctions between words, phrases, or clauses' (Lanham 25).

1. 'her face with beauty, her head with wisdom, her eyes with majesty, her countenance with gracefulness, her lips with loveliness, her tongue with victory' (119; Hoskyns 38)
2. 'a fair woman shall not only command without authority, but persuade without speaking.' (308; Hoskyns 38)

CATACHRESIS / ABUSIO / ABUSE: 'Implied metaphor, using words from common usage'; '[A]n extravagant, unexpected, farfetched metaphor' (Lanham 31).

1. 'I am afraid I have given your ears too great a surfeit with the gross discourses of that heavy piece of flesh' (15)
2. 'making a perpetual mansion of this poor baiting-place of man's life' (18)
3. 'but else neither in behaviour nor action accusing in himself any great trouble in mind whether he sped or no' (79; Hoskyns 11)
4. 'poor Zelmane yielded her ears to those tedious strokes, not warding them so much as with any one answer' (121)
5. 'Do you love your sorrow so well as to grudge me part of it?' (129; Hoskyns 11)
6. 'I gave order to some servants of mine, whom I thought as apt for such charities as myself, to lead him out into a forest, and there to kill him' (156; Hoskyns 11)

CHIASMUS: *see* **ANTIMETABOLE**

CLIMAX or ANABASIS / GRADATIO: 'Mounting by degrees through linked words or phrases, usually of increasing weight and in parallel construction' (Lanham 36).

1. 'let us think with consideration, and consider with acknowledging, and acknowledge with admiration, and admire with love, and love with joy in the midst of all woes' (2)
2. 'at length he grew content to mark their speeches, then to marvel at such wit in shepherds, after, to like their company, and lastly, to vouchsafe conference.' (7; Gill 106)
3. 'to have deceived me, and through the deceit abused me, and after the abuse forsaken me' (208; Hoskyns 13)
4. 'what doth better become wisdom than to discern what is worthy the loving? What more agreeable to goodness than to love it, so discerned; and what to greatness of heart than to be constant in it, once loved?'
(220; Hoskyns 13)

5. 'Do you think them fools that saw you should not enjoy your vines, your cattle, no, not your wives and children, without government? And that there could be no government without a magistrate, and no magistrate without obedience, and no obedience where every one upon his own private passion may interpret the doings of the rulers?' (247; Hoskyns 12)

6. 'finding himself not only unhappy, but unhappy after being fallen from happiness, and to be fallen from all happiness not by any misconceiving but by his own fault, and his fault to be done to no other but to Pamela' (267)

7. 'a young man of great beauty, beautified with great honour, honoured by great valure' (390; Hoskyns 12)

COMMUTATIO: *see* **ANTIMETABOLE**

COMPLEXIO: *see* **SYMPLOCE**

COMPAR: *see* **PARISON**

CONTENTIO: *see* **ANTITHESIS**

CONVERSIO: *see* **EPISTROPHE**

CORRECTIO: *see* **METANOIA**

DENOMINATIO or TRANSMUTATIO / METONYMY: 'Reference to something or someone by naming one of its attributes' (*Silva Rhetoricae*).

1. 'They loved – although for awhile the fire thereof (hope's wings being cut off) were blown by the bellows of despair' (22–3)

2. 'More white than Neptune's foamy face
When struggling rocks he would embrace.' (166; Fraunce A3^v)

3. 'Nay, ev'n cold death inflamed with hot desire Her to enjoy (where joy itself is thrall) Will spoil the earth of his most rich attire.'
(174; Fraunce A5^r)

4. 'Therefore, alas, you use vile Vulcan's spite,
Which nothing spares, to melt that virgin-wax
Which while it is, it is all Asia's light.' (174; Fraunce A3^v)

5. 'Bacchus, the learned say, was begot with thunder; I think that made him ever since so full of stir and debate. Bacchus indeed it was which sounded the first trumpet to this rude alarum' (251; Fraunce A3^v)

6. 'Hymen had not there his saffron-coloured coat' (260)

DIMINUTIO: *see* **LITOTES**

DISSOLUTIO: *see* **ASYNDETON**

DISTRIBUTION / DIVISIO: 'Dividing the whole into its parts' (Lanham 59).

1. 'Heretofore I have accused the sea, condemned the pirates, and hated my evil fortune that deprived me of thee; but now thyself is the sea which drowns my comfort; thyself is the pirate that robs thyself of me; thy own will becomes my evil fortune.'
(46; Hoskyns 46, cited as an example of prosapodosis, 'that overthroweth no part of the division, but returneth some reason to each member')

APPENDIX IV

2. 'to say "I cannot" is childish; and "I will not", womanish'
(60; Hoskyns 46, cited as an example of dilemma, 'which proposeth two sides and overthrows both')

3. 'time in one instant seeming both short and long unto them – short in the pleasingness of such presence, long in the stay of their desires.'
(76; Hoskyns 46, cited as an example of prosapodosis)

DIVISIO: *see* **DISTRIBUTION**

DUBITATIO: *see* **APORIA**

DUPLICATIO: *see* **ANADIPLOSIS**

EPANADIPLOSIS: *see* **EPANALEPSIS**

EPANALEPSIS or EPANADIPLOSIS / REPETITIO: 'Repetition at the end of a clause or sentence of the word or phrase with which it began' (Lanham 67).

1. 'she the overthrow of my desires and yet the recompense of my overthrow' (110; Hoskyns 14)
2. 'End then, evil-destinied Dorus, end! And end, thou woeful letter, end!' (133)
3. 'Each senseless thing had sense of pity – only they, that had sense, were senseless' (364)
4. 'He saw her alive; he was glad to see her alive. He saw her weep; he was sorry to see her weep.' (379)
5. 'their strength failed them sooner than their skill, and yet their breath failed them sooner than their strength' (402; Hoskyns 14)

EPISTROPHE or ANTISTROPHE / CONVERSIO: 'Repetition of a closing word or words at the end of several (usually successive) clauses, sentences, or verses'; 'The repetition of a word or phrase in a second context in the same position it held in an earlier and similar context' (Lanham 16).

1. '"Why," said she, "this is the picture of Amphialus! What need I say more to you? What ear is so barbarous but hath heard of Amphialus? Who follows deeds of arms, but everywhere finds monuments of Amphialus? Who is courteous, noble, liberal, but he that hath the example before his eyes of Amphialus? Where are all heroical parts, but in Amphialus?"'
(51; Hoskyns 13)
2. 'Nay, we are to resolve that if reason direct it, we must do it; and if we must do it, we will do it' (60; Fraunce D2^r)
3. 'Only reverence him and reward him, and with that bridle and saddle you shall well ride him.' (94)
4. 'a prince that indeed especially measured his greatness by his goodness – and if for anything he loved greatness it was because therein he might exercise his goodness' (136)
5. 'already half earth, and yet then most greedy of earth' (211–12)
6. 'where the richness did invite the eyes, the fashion did entertain the eyes, and the device did teach the eyes' (289; Hoskyns 13)

Epizeuxis / Geminatio: 'Emphatic repetition of a word with no other words between' (Lanham 71).

1. 'hither we are now come to pay the rent for which we are so called unto by overbusy remembrance – remembrance, restless remembrance, which claims not only this duty of us but, for it, will have us forget ourselves.' (1)
2. 'O you, the only, the only honour to women' (133)
3. 'o let not, let not, from you be poured upon me destruction.' (200; Hoskyns 12)
4. 'I am not the stay of your freedom, but love – love, which ties you in your own knots.' (279)
5. 'you fear lest you should offend. Offend! And how know you that you should offend? Because she doth deny. Deny! Now, by my truth! If your sadness would let me laugh, I could laugh heartily'
(348; Hoskyns 12; Hoskyns classifies this as anadiplosis, but the repetition of 'offend' and 'deny' serves the purpose of emphasizing the words rather than continuing the thought, and the 1590 punctuation (which attaches the exclamations to the preceding sentences through semicolons) suggests they are not intended to be read as clauses in their own right.)
6. 'Tormented! Tormented! Torment of my soul! Philoclea tormented!' (382; Hoskyns 12)

Erotema or Erotesis / Interrogatio / Interrogation: 'A "rhetorical question", one which implies an answer but does not give or lead us to expect one …' (Lanham 71).

1. 'the first word he spake to me was "Am not I Dametas? Why, am not I Dametas?"' (68)
2. 'did the sun ever bring you a fruitful harvest but that it was more hot than pleasant? Have any of you children that be not sometimes cumbersome? Have any of you fathers that be not sometime wearish? What, shall we curse the sun, hate our children, or disobey our fathers?'
(248; Hoskyns 33)
3. 'If you command your soldier to march foremost, and he for courtesy put others before him, would you praise his modesty?'
(348; Hoskyns 50, cited as an example of prevention)
4. 'how shall I believe mine eyes anymore? Or do you yet but appear thus unto me to stay me from some desperate end; for, alas! I saw the excellent Pamela beheaded, I saw your head – the head indeed, and chief part of all nature's works – standing in a dish of gold, too mean a shrine, God wot, for such a relic. How can this be, my only dear, and you live? Or if this be not so, how can I believe mine own senses? And if I cannot believe them, why should I now believe these blessed tidings they bring me?'
(377; Hoskyns 33)

Exclamatio: *see* **Apostrophe**

Frequentatio: *see* **Accumulatio**

Geminatio: *see* Epizeuxis

Gradatio: *see* Climax

Hyperbaton / Transgressio: 'A generic figure of various forms of departure from ordinary word order'; 'Separation of words usually belonging together' (Lanham 86).

1. 'By him am I sent unto you, as from a prince to his well-approved subjects' (245)
2. 'The fire, to see my woes, for anger burneth;
   The air, in rain, for my affliction weepeth;
   The sea, to ebb, for grief his flowing turneth;
   The earth, with pity dull, his centre keepeth'
   (340; Gill 118–19 cites the entire poem)

Hyperbole / Superlatio: 'Exaggerated or extravagant terms used for emphasis and not intended to be understood literally; self-conscious exaggeration' (Lanham 86).

1. 'the world sooner wanted occasions than he valour to go through them' (24; Hoskyns 29)
2. 'making their eyes, their ears, and their tongue serve almost for nothing but that inquiry' (48; Hoskyns 29)
3. 'though a thousand deaths followed it, and every death were followed with a thousand shames' (103; Hoskyns 29)
4. 'seeing such streams of blood as threatened a drowning of life, we galloped toward them to part them' (227)
5. 'beyond the bounds of conceit – much more, of uttering' (278; Hoskyns 29)
6. 'words and blows came so quick together as the one seemed a lightning of the other's thunder.' (351; Hoskyns 29)
7. 'of all ages came running up to see the beloved body, everybody thinking their safety bled in his wounds, and their honour died in his destruction.' (383)

Hysteron Proteron: 'Form of Hyperbaton; syntax or sense out of normal logical or temporal order' (Lanham 89).

1. 'the messenger came in with letters in his hand and haste in his countenance' (322)

Intellectio: *see* Synecdoche

Interpositio: *see* Parenthesis

Interrogatio: *see* Erotema

Inversio: *see* Allegoria

Isocolon: *see* Parison

Junctio: *see* Zeugma

Litotes or Meiosis / Diminutio: 'Denial of the contrary; understatement that intensifies' (Lanham 95); 'To belittle, often through a trope of one word; use a degrading epithet' (Lanham 98).

1. 'these fantastical mind-infected people that children and musicians call lovers' (44; Hoskyns 35)
2. 'not to show mislike' (79; Hoskyns 35)
3. 'no unfit branch to the noble stock whereof she came' (138; Hoskyns 35)
4. 'I was glad I had done so good a deed for a gentlewoman not unhandsome' (210)
5. 'this colour of mine which she (in the deceivable style of affection) would entitle beautiful' (216; Hoskyns 35)
6. 'not altogether unmodest' (231; Hoskyns 35)

MEIOSIS: see LITOTES

MESODIPLOSIS: 'Repetition of the same word or words in the middle of successive sentences' (*Silva Rhetoricae*).

1. 'The time full of danger, the person full of worthiness, the manner full of horror did greatly astonish all the beholders, so as by and by all the town was full of it' (383)

METANOIA / CORRECTIO: 'Qualification of a statement by recalling it and expressing it in a better way, often by using a negative' (Lanham 100).

1. 'Among the rest, or rather before the rest, was the Lord Philoxenus' (51)
2. 'her hair (alas, too poor a word; why should I not rather call them her beams?) drawn up into a net' (71)
3. 'oh that it had never been so! nay, oh that it might ever be so!' (91)
4. 'who will ever do any of you sacrifice, O you stars, if you do not succour me? No, no, you will not help me. No, no, you cannot help me!' (127; Hoskyns 30)
5. 'Methought – nay, sure, I was – I was in fairest wood
   Of Samothea land, a land which whilom stood
   An honour to the world, while honour was their end'
   (300–1; cited as anadiplosis in Fraunce B7ʳ and polyptoton in Gill 108)
6. 'persuade you to lose the hold of occasion while it may not only be taken, but offers, nay, sues to be taken' (310; Hoskyns 29)
7. ' "O Parthenia – no more Parthenia!" said she. "What are thou?" ' (327; Hoskyns 30)

METAPHORA / TRANSLATIO / METAPHOR: 'Changing a word from its literal meaning to one not properly applicable but analogous to it; assertion of identity rather than with Simile, likeness' (Lanham 100).

1. 'Argalus standing between them was it that most eclipsed her affection from shining upon Demagoras' (23)
2. 'for besides his eyes sometimes even great with tears' (43; Fraunce B2ʳ)
3. 'she longed to meet her friend Dorus, that upon the shoulders of friendship she might lay the burthen of sorrow' (108; Hoskyns 9)
4. 'pain fetching his ordinary companion, a fever, with him, drave her to entertain them both in her bed.' (122)

5. 'But now, perceiving the flood of their fury began to ebb, he thought it policy to take the first of the tide' (249)
6. 'keep love from looking through her eyes and going forth in her words, whom before as a close prisoner she had to her heart only committed.' (266; Hoskyns 8)
7. 'to divorce the fair marriage of the head and body' (369; Hoskyns 8)

METAPLASM: 'alterations of the words form and fauor' (Mulcaster 143).

1. 'You be the cause that I loved – what reason blameth a shadow
That with a body't goes, since by a body it is?' (270; Gill 131)
2. 'First let Cimmerian darkness be my onl' habitation' (270; Gill 131)
3. 'Unto Cupid – that boy! – shall a pedante be found?' (270; Gill 131)

METONYMY: *see* **DENOMINATIO**

OCCULTATIO: *see* **PARALIPSIS**

OPPOSITIO: *see* **ANTITHESIS**

OXYMORON: *see* **SYNŒCIOSIS**

PARALIPSIS / OCCULTATIO or OCCUPATIO: 'Emphasizing something by pointedly seeming to pass over it' (Lanham 104).

1. 'As for her parts unknown, which hidden sure are best,
Happy be they which well believe and never seek the rest' (14)
2. 'as his [love's] adjoined companions be unquietness, longings, fond comforts, faint discomforts, hopes, jealousies, ungrounded rages, causeless yieldings' (60; Hoskyns 31)
3. 'To tell you what pitiful mishaps fell to the young prince of Macedon, his cousin, I should too much fill your ears with strange horrors; neither will I stay upon those laboursome adventures, nor loathsome misadventures, to which and through which his fortune and courage conducted him – my speech hasteneth itself to come to the full point of Musidorus' infortunes.' (116; Fraunce B^r – cited as example of negatio)
4. 'I will not say unto you, how justly soever I may do it, that I am neither author nor accessory unto this your withholding, for since I do not redress it, I am as faulty as if I had begun it.' (279)

PARAPHRASIS: 'to turne rude and barbarus, into proper and eloquent' (Ascham 36^r).

1. 'making such a noise withal, as nobody could lay the stealing of a nap to her charge' (160; Hoskyns 44)
2. 'he is no such one over whom contempt may make any just challenge' (288; Hoskyns 44)
3. 'plentifully perjuring' (291; Hoskyns 47)
4. 'make his sword cursed by any widow'
(329; Hoskyns 47, 'by consequence')

5. 'make a muster of himself in the island' (330; Hoskyns 47)

6. 'made his spurs claim haste of his horse' (343; Hoskyns 44)

PARENTHESIS / INTERPOSITIO: 'Form of Hyperbaton: a word, phrase, or sentence inserted as an aside in a sentence complete in itself' (Lanham 108).

1. 'They therefore continued on their charitable office until, his spirits being well returned, he, without so much as thanking them for their pains, gate up' (3)

2. 'that what his wit could conceive (and his wit can conceive as far as the limits of reason stretch) was all directed to the setting forward the suit of his friend' (52; Hoskyns 44)

3. 'the moon then full, not thinking scorn to be a torch-bearer to such beauty, guided her steps' (122–3)

4. 'he (swelling in their humbleness like a bubble swollen up with a small breath, broken with a great), forgetting, or never knowing humanity, caused their heads to be stricken off' (151; Hoskyns 44)

5. 'till the next morning (known to be a morning better by the hour-glass than by the dayclearness), having run fortune' (143; Hoskyns 44)

6. 'assure thyself, most wicked woman, that hast so plaguily a corrupted mind as thou canst not keep thy sickness to thyself, but must most wickedly infect others, assure thyself, I say' (314; Hoskyns 44)

PARISON / COMPAR or ISOCOLON: 'the figure of euen' (Puttenham 178); 'the words match each other in rank ... verb to verb, adverb to adverb, substantive to substantive' (Hoskyns)

1. '"But those thoughts", replied Basilius, "cannot in this your loneliness neither warrant you from suspicion in others, nor defend you from melancholy in yourself."' (69; Hoskyns 38)

2. 'despair made fear valiant, and revenge gave shame countenance' (207)

3. 'rather seek to obtain that constantly by courtesy which you can never, assuredly, enjoy by violence' (306; Hoskyns 38)

4. 'If ever I could wish my faith untried and my counsel untrusted' (361; Hoskyns 37)

5. 'I have not lived so many years but that one death may be able to conclude them, neither have my faults, I hope, been so many but that one death may satisfy them.' (364; Hoskyns 38)

6. 'in the end Pamela yielded to her because she spake reason, and Philoclea yielded to her reason because she spake it' (395)

PARONOMASIA / ADNOMINATIO or AGNOMINATIO: 'Punning; playing on the sounds and meanings of words' (Lanham 110).

1. 'this place where we last (alas, that the word *last* should so long last!) did grace our eyes upon her ever-flourishing beauty' (1)

2. 'she would first be bedded in her grave than wedded to Demagoras' (23)

3. 'If I were princess of the whole world, and had withal all the blessings that ever the world brought forth, I should not make delay to lay myself and them under your feet' (26)
4. 'But her champion went away as much discomforted as discomfited.' (84)
5. 'But alas, what can saying make them believe, whom seeing cannot persuade?' (116; Hoskyns 16; Fraunce D5^v)
6. 'Waist it is called, for it doth waste
   Men's lives until it be embraced' (165)
7. 'she went away, repining but not repenting' (315; Hoskyns 16)

Periphrasis: 'Circumlocution' (Lanham 114).

1. 'when they had awhile hearkened to the persuasion of sleep' (48; Hoskyns 47)
2. 'Plangus' actions began to be translated into the language of suspicion' (190; Hoskyns 47)
3. 'having striven with the sun's earliness' (225; Hoskyns 47)
4. 'disgraced weeping with her countenance' (273; Hoskyns 47)
5. 'they lost the fortresses that nature had placed them in.' (298; Hoskyns 47)
6. 'none of Ceres' servants' (298; Hoskyns 47)
7. 'his blood, not daring to be in so dangerous a place, went out of his face and hid itself more inwardly' (329)

Permutatio: *see* **Allegoria**

Personification: *see* **Prosopopœia**

Polyptoton / Traductio: 'Repetition of words from the same root but with different endings' (Lanham 117).

1. 'that which made her fairness much the fairer was that it was but a fair embassador of a most fair mind' (22)
2. 'for likeness of manners is likely, in reason, to draw liking with affection' (22)
3. 'Much might be said in my defence, much more for love, and most of all for that divine creature which hath joined me and love together.' (63; Hoskyns 17)
4. 'by his faulty using of our faults' (206; Hoskyns 17)
5. 'exceedingly sorry for Pamela, but exceedingly exceeding that exceedingness in fear for Philoclea.' (370; Hoskyns 17)
6. 'reason cannot show itself more reasonable than to leave reasoning in things above reason' (396)
7. 'Thou art of blood; joy not to see things bleed.
   Thou fearest death; think they are loath to die.' (413; Fraunce D6^v)

PROSOPOPŒIA / PERSONIFICATION: 'An animal or an inanimate object is represented as having human attributes and addressed or made to speak as if it were human' (Lanham 123); 'The rhetorical exercise known as the speech in character or impersonation' (Lanham 124).

1. 'how the winds whistled and the seas danced for joy, how the sails did swell with pride' (2)
2. 'methought the lilies grew pale for envy; the roses, methought, blushed to see sweeter roses in her cheeks; and the apples, methought, fell down from the trees to do homage to the apples of her breast' (72)
3. 'But the night commanded truce for those sports' (86)
4. 'for now indeed love pulled off his mask, and showed his face unto her, and told her plainly that she was his prisoner' (125)
5. 'the ship ran upon it; and seeming willinger to perish than to have her course stayed, redoubled her blows till she had broken herself in pieces, and as it were tearing out her own bowels to feed the sea's greediness' (143)
6. 'Oh, what would your forefathers say if they lived at this time and saw their offspring defacing such an excellent principality, which they with much labour and blood so wisely have established?' (247; Hoskyns 48)
7. 'as if the needle itself would have been loath to have gone fromward such a mistress, but that it hoped to return thenceward very quickly again, the cloth looking with many eyes upon her, and lovingly embracing the wounds she gave it. The shears also were at hand to behead the silk that was grown too short' (307; Hoskyns 48)

REDUPLICATIO: *see* ANADIPLOSIS

REPETITIO: *see* ANAPHORA, EPANALEPSIS

SENTENTIA: 'Proverb' (Lanham 138).

1. 'to a heart fully resolute counsel is tedious, but reprehension is loathsome; and that there is nothing more terrible to a guilty heart than the eye of a respected friend.' (67; Hoskyns 40)
2. 'a good pleader makes a bad cause to prevail' (80)
3. 'for unlawful desires are punished after the effect of enjoying, but unpossible desires are punished in the desire itself.' (127; Hoskyns 40)
4. 'making his life the example of his laws, as it were his actions arising out of his deeds' (138; Hoskyns 40)
5. 'who stands only upon defence stands upon no defence' (169; Hoskyns 39)
6. 'men's experience is woman's best eyesight' (288; Hoskyns 39)
7. 'fearfulness, contrary to all other vices, making him think the better of another, the worse he found himself' (332; Hoskyns 40)

SIMILE / SIMILITUDO / SIMILITUDE: 'One thing is likened to another, dissimular thing by the use of like, as, etc.; distinguished from Metaphor in that the comparison is made explicit' (Lanham 140).

1. 'the mast whose proud height now lay along, like a widow having lost her make' (5)
2. 'you deal with me like a physician that, seeing his patient in a pestilent fever, should chide him instead of ministering help, and bid him be sick no more; or rather, like such a friend that, visiting his friend condemned to perpetual prison and loaden with grievous fetters, should will him to shake off his fetters, or he would leave him.' (64–5)
3. 'her breasts, which sweetly rase up like two fair mountainets in the pleasant vale of Tempe' (71)
4. 'she was like a horse desirous to run and miserably spurred, but so short-reined as he cannot stir forward' (76)
5. 'an exceeding red hair with small eyes did, like ill companions, disgrace the other assembly of most commendable beauties' (81)
6. 'Dorus drew Pamela behind a tree, where she stood quaking like the partridge on which the hawk is even ready to seize.' (96)
7. 'The wind was like a servant, waiting behind them so just that they might fill the sails as they listed' (141)
8. 'These words being spoken, like a furious storm presently carried away their well-inclined brains.' (252)
9. 'Basilius kissed her with more than fatherly thanks, and straight, like a hard-kept ward new come to his lands, would fain have used the benefit of that grant in laying his sickness before his only physician.' (257)
10 'Amphialus ... was utterly ignorant of all his mother's wicked devices – to which he would never have consented, being, like a rose out of a briar, an excellent son of an evil mother' (274)

SORITES: 'A chain of Categorical Syllogisms ... which can have any number of premises' (Lanham 143).

1. 'and seeing, to like; and liking, to love; and loving, straight to feel the most incident effects of love: to serve and preserve.'
   (260; Hoskyns 13)

SUPERLATIO: *see* **HYPERBOLE**

SYMPLOCE / COMPLEXIO: 'Repetition of one word or phrase at the beginning, and of another at the end, of successive clauses, sentences, or passages; a combination of Anaphora and Antistrophe' (Lanham 146).

1. 'Such was as then the state of the king as it was no time by direct means to seek her; and such was the state of his captived will as he could delay no time of seeking her.' (116; Fraunce D2^r)
2. 'The most covetous man longs not to get riches out of a ground which can never bear anything. Why? Because it is impossible. The most ambitious wight vexeth not his wits to climb into heaven. Why? Because it is impossible.' (128; Hoskyns 13)

SYNECDOCHE / INTELLECTIO: 'Substitution of part for whole, genus for species, or vice versa' (Lanham 148).

1. 'lances were put to silence, the swords were so busy.' (87)
2. 'For if my man must praises have,
   What then must I that keep the knave?'
   (98; Fraunce B7^v, 'of the general')
3. 'as if the stars would breathe themselves for a greater mischief'
   (115; Fraunce B7^r, 'of the integral')
4. '[Basilius] having combed and tricked himself more curiously than any time forty winters before' (195; Fraunce B5^v)

SYNŒCIOSIS: 'An expanded Oxymoron; a Paradox' (Lanham 148).

1. 'of an accompanable solitariness, and of a civil wildness' (8)
2. 'Warm snow' (167)
3. 'unkind carefulness' (241; Hoskyns 36)
4. 'that poisonous sugar of flattery' (258)
5. 'a wanton modesty, and an enticing soberness' (272; Hoskyns 36)
6. 'O foolish woman – and most miserably foolish, since wit makes you foolish' (311; Hoskyns 36)
7. 'captivity might seem to have authority over tyranny'
   (314; Hoskyns 36)
8. 'there was so perfect agreement in so mortal disagreement, like a music made of cunning discords' (319; Hoskyns 36)
9. 'seeking honour by dishonouring, and to build safety upon ruin'
   (357; Hoskyns 36)
10. 'And with that, she prettily smiled; which, mingled with her tears, one could not tell whether it were a mourning pleasure or a delightful sorrow'
    (379; Hoskyns 36)

TRADUCTIO: *see* **POLYPTOTON**

TRANSLATIO: *see* **METAPHORA**

TRANSMUTATIO: *see* **DENOMINATIO**

ZEUGMA / ADNEXIO or JUNCTIO: 'A kind of Ellipsis in which one word, usually a verb, governs several congruent words or clauses' (Lanham 159).

1. 'brought not only to this place but to my life' (19)
2. 'neither her fair picture nor his fair running could warrant him from overthrow, and her from becoming as then the last of Artesia's victories' (84)

COMMENTARY

NOTE: *new entries and additions to the 1987 commentary are indicated through square brackets. The only exception to this rule are references to* OED *entries changed since the first edition. Those references (approximately two thirds of the total) have been updated so they correspond to the most recent edition of the* OED. *– EC*

THE FIRST BOOK

PAGE 1, 1. *It was in the*. The opening is formulaic; see p. xxii.
1–2. *earth ... lover*. Earth's lover is the sun, Phoebus or Apollo. W. MacKeller, ed., *The Latin Poems of John Milton* (New Haven, 1930), 222, cites this among the analogues to Milton's 'elegia v', 55–6, along with Lucretius, i. 250–1; ii. 992–3; v. 318; and Virgil, *Georgics*, ii. 325–7.
2–3. *sun ... day*. This second periphrasis for spring sets the date at the vernal equinox when love infects the world, Virgil, *Georgics*, iii. 242–4.
4–7. *Strephon ... Claius*. The description of these characters in the *Old Arcadia* was adapted by the editors of *90* for the First Eclogues, p. 486, 9–10 and note. On the spelling *Claius*, see p. liii.
5. *Cythera*. This was the birthplace of Venus-Urania and home to a cult of Venus; see p. xxiv.
9–**PAGE 2**, 23. *pay ... memory*. The imagery of this passage is indebted to Montemayor's *Diana*; see p. xvii.
20. *grace*. See p. liii.
ever-flourishing beauty. Cf. p. 309, 25–9.
23. [*for respect of*. 'for the sake of'.]
26. *Urania*. On the allegorical associations of Urania, see K. Duncan-Jones, 'Sidney's Urania', *RES*, NS xvii (1966), 123–32.
30–**PAGE 2**, 23. *pay ... memory. place ... memory*. F. A. Yates, *The Art of Memory* (London, 1966), discusses the classical origins of this conceit used also in *A Defence of Poetry* (*Misc. Prose*, 101, 11 and 192) and in the *Old Arcadia* (Robertson, 372–3 and notes); cf. Boccaccio, *Filostrato*, v. 54 ff.; Chaucer, *Troilus and Criseyde*, v. 561–81, 603–16, echoes of Alcyone's memory of Ceyx in Ovid, *Met.* xi. 710–15, which Sidney appears to have known in Arthur Golding's translation, ed. W. H. D. Rouse, *Shakespeare's Ovid* (London, 1961), xi. 819–23:

> The morning came, and out she went right pensive to the shore,
> To that same place in which she took her leave of him before.
> While there she musing stood, and said: 'He kissed me even here,
> Here weighed he his anchors up, here loosed he from the pier';
> And while she called to mind the things there marked with her eyes,
> In looking on the open sea ...

PAGE 2, 11–12. *winds ... pride*. A similar prosopopoeia is used at p. 72, 3–6 and in *AS* 103.
14. *sweetest ... sweetness*. See p. xxxi; Hoskyns, 14, cites this as an example of antimetabole or *commutatio*.
16. *score*. See above, p. xvii.

17. *light ... place.* 'enlightenment derived from this place'. The obvious sight-place-memory relationships of the *ars memoriae* lie behind the conjectural emendation in 98 to *sight*.
22–3. *place ... places.* Hoskyns, 15, cites this as an example of antimetabole.
25–6. *consideration ... and love.* For other examples of gradatio or climax, see AS 1. 2–3, and below, pp. 163, 31–3; 247, 27–30; 266, 26–7; 267, 16–19; 326, 10–11; 390, 19–20.
29. *such that.* 'such a one that'.
36. *honey-flowing.* Cf. *A Defence of Poetry* (*Misc. Prose*, 117, 13–14): 'that honey-flowing matron Eloquence'.
38. *clover's grass.* Of the grasses, clover was among the highly esteemed; cf. p. 423, 13 and *OED* under *sweet-grass*.
40–PAGE **3**, 4. *better ... employed.* So Plato investigated his crux by analogy, *Laws*, x. 897, but the image was associated with the works of God as in Spenser, *An Hymn of Heavenly Beauty*, 114–47, and so contributes to the beatification of Urania.

PAGE **3**, 3. *sun-staining.* 'By being brighter, depriving the sun of lustre'.
6. *silly.* 'pitiable', as in OP 4. 6.
8–10. *when others ... when other.* Cf. the similar construction at p. 283, 24–5.
9. *viewing ... heavens.* It was traditional that 'the first shepherds of Egypt and other places were the bringers to light of astrology, physic, music, and many other liberal sciences ..., observing at leisure the courses of the stars' (C. Steevens [i.e., Estienne] and J. Liebault, *Maison Rustique*, trans. R. Surfleet (1600), L5^v); and see the Book of Jubilees, in R. H. Charles, ed., *The Apocrypha and Pseudepigraphia of the Old Testament* (Oxford, 1913), iv. 17, where Enoch, son of Seth, first 'wrote down the signs of heaven according to the order of their months in a book'. Sidney's Astrophil experiences quite opposite effects of love in AS 40. 3–4.
9–10. *running at base.* This is a game of chase in which two teams, each with a home or base, capture prisoners.
12. *eyes unto Cupid.* Cupid is one of the blind gods; see p. 14, 15 and note.
15–18. *thing ... man.* This continues the borrowing from Ovid begun on p. 1, 30; cf. *Met.* xi. 715–18, in Golding's trans., xi. 824–8, the implications of which are discussed on p. xxv:

> In looking on the open sea, a great way off she spies
> A certain thing, much like a corse, come hovering on the wave.
> At first she doubted what it was. As tide it nearer drave,
> Although it were a good way off, yet did it plainly show
> To be a corse.

19. *pity sake.* For this use of the uninflected genitive, see Abbott, 32; examples are listed on p. xxxii.
20. *memory.* 'record of his past, as a memorial'.
22. *board.* This is a synecdoche for the coffer; cf. p. 133, 39.
30–7. [*At length ... Pyrocles?* See p. lxxvii.]
37–8. *Pyrocles ... himself.* The cryptic phrasing of the figures zeugma in *cast* and syllepsis in *destruction* and *himself* expands to 'decided on his destruction and threw himself to his destruction', continuing the parody of the Alcyone and Ceyx story. Cf. George Pettie, *A Petite Palace of Pettie's Pleasure*, ed. H Hartman (London, 1938), 34: 'Did Alcyone seeing the dead carcass of her husband Ceyx cast on shore willingly cast herself into the sea to accompany his death'. See the syllepsis at p. 5, 4–5, the zeugma at p. 19, 7–8, 'brought ... life', and in AS 41. 1–2, 'Having this day my horse, my hand, my lance / Guided so well', and see p. lv above.

COMMENTARY 459

37. [*wilfully*. See note to p. 23, 28.]
39–PAGE 4, 1. *being ... should*. There is ellipsis both in *[he] being* and *[he] coming* where the subject is supplied from the following repeated possessive in 'his life', and in *[they] had* and *[they] should* where the meaning is evident; cf. p. xxxii above.

PAGE 4, 13. [*his own proof*. 'the fact that he was alive and well himself'. Cf. *proof* 5b in OED: 'the fact, condition, or quality of proving good, turning out well, or producing good results; thriving'.]
15. *attend*. 'expect'.
18. *a food*. 'to be a food', an ellipsis; cf. p. xxxii above.
19. *of value*. 'a sum'. This is the partitive genitive.
24. *by times*. 'at times'.

PAGE 5, 1. *wrinkles ... visage*. Cf. p. 339, 31–2 and *AS* 103. 1–3.
4. *storm or ill-footing*. 'storm and its attendant ill-footing', a syllepsis; cf. Shakespeare, *Richard III*, I. iv. 17, 'giddy footing of the hatches'.
9. *horseback*. Cf. Homer, *Odyssey*, trans. R. Lattimore (New York, 1967), v. 370–1: 'Odysseus / sat astride one beam, like a man riding on horseback'.
10. *blue ... gold*. The Sidney arms were *or, apheon azure*; see p. 48, 14–15 and note.
12–13. *hair ... long*. In addition to the classical appreciation of long hair in Homer, *Odyssey*, ii. 408; Heliodorus, II. xx. 5; Aristotle, *Rhetoric*, I. ix; Plutarch, *Moralia*, 189e and 'Life of Lycurgus', xxii, Thomas Nashe in *The Unfortunate Traveller*, in *Works*, ed. R. B. McKerrow, 2nd edn., ed. F. P. Wilson (Oxford, 1966), ii. 281, notes that contrary to the Roman style, youths 'of the English cut' wore their hair long and dressed in light colours. G. Puttenham, *Art of English Poesy*, ed. G. D. Willcock and A. Walker (Cambridge, 1936), 286–7, in discussing beards and hair, observed that 'at this time, the young gentlemen of the court have taken up the long hair trailing on their shoulders'; cf. Robertson, 26, 21 ff.
20–1. *simplicity ... superstition*. Cf. p. 149, 2 and the echo by George Sandys, on his translation of Ovid, *Met*. i (1632), D4^v–E1,

> Draconet Boniface ... saw a sea monster with the face and body like a man, but below the belly like a fish .... It had an old countenance, the hair and beard rough and shaggy, blue of colour, and high of stature, with fins between the arms and the body. These were held for gods of the sea and propitious to sailors: ignorance producing admiration, and admiration superstition.

Cf. Milton, *Comus*, 29, 'blue-haired deities'.
21–2. *begotten ... Venus*. Chivalry and love were Pyrocles' strong points; cf. p. xxiv. Neptune first broke horses and taught the art of riding (C. Stephanus [Estienne], *Dictionarium Historicum, Geographicum, Poeticum*, ed. N. Lloyd (London, 1686), Kk1^v).
32. *upon the stays*. 'abackstays'; the important sails are hauled round to the plane of the wind's direction, in order to stop.

PAGE 6, 6. *And alas*. *And* is emphatic.
21. *advise*. This is the historical present for 'advised'.
33. [*who ... haunted*. 'who so frequently entertains visitors'.]

PAGE 7, 5. *but in that respect*. 'if only for that reason'.
12. *by course*. 'in turns'.
28–30. *nightingales ... sorrow*. In Ovid, *Met*. vi. 424 ff., Tereus raped Philomela, who became the nightingale lamenting unjustly caused grief; see pp. 370, 12; 388, 10;

Robertson, 229, 10; *CS* 4; and *OP* 4. 474.

34. *humble valleys*. The earliest citation in *OED* for *humble* adj. 2b is in *humble dales* from Spenser, 'July', 13; cf. p. 419, 5.

35. *silver*. Spenser's use of *silver* to describe water is traced in his *Works*, vi. 246, with parallels in Shakespeare.

37. *were witnessed so to*. 'were attested to being so'.

deposition, disposition 93 (only) disagrees with the imagery of witnessing similarly used at pp. 128, 14; 200, 26.

40. *here ... there*. See p. xxvii.

shepherds boy ... old. The diminution from sheep to lambs is carried forward into this son of a shepherd, old enough to pipe but not to work. The recurrence of lambing and childbirth create the illusion of agelessness – quite a different concept to Polixenes' memory of his youthful *naïveté* in thinking he might 'be boy eternal' in Shakespeare's *Winter's Tale*, I. i. 64.

PAGE 8, 1–2. *shepherdess ... music*. Singing is common among woolworkers, with literary antecedents in Virgil, *Georgics*, i. 293–4, though knitting was not known in England until the sixteenth century.

4. [*th'other*. The contracted form in this line (the first of only five 'th'other's in the prose text of *Arcadia* – the second of which appears only a few lines later, in p. 8, 9) may have been the compositor's choice rather than Sidney's. In *90*, both appear towards the end of a paragraph whose final word would have been in danger of spilling over into an additional line. The use of contracted forms, along with macrons and '&' for 'and', were easy strategies for avoiding this without having to make adjustments to the spellings of words.]

5–6. *accompanable ... wildness*. These are examples of oxymoron.

14. *helots*. In the Greek states they stood between free men and slaves; a fuller description is in *The Oxford Classical Dictionary*, ed. N. G. L. Hammond and H. H. Scullard, 2nd edn. (Oxford, 1970).

14–15. *disfigured ... nature*. On this recurrent image, see M. Turner, 'The Disfigured Face of Nature: Image and Metaphor in the Revised *Arcadia*', *ELR* ii (1972), 116–35.

20. *peace ... husbandry*. Cf. Tilley, P139, 'By peace plenty'. [See also p. lxxxiv.]

23. *wanting ... much*. Cf. Tilley, L347a, 'He that desires but little has no need of much.'

28. *knowledge is darkness*. 'knowledge of it is obscure'.

39. *the house*. M. Girouard, *Robert Smythson* (London, 1966), 47, cites this description as evidence of a 'late 16th-century reaction against the decorated architecture which had been produced ... for the last fifteen years'; cf. J. C. A. Rathmell, 'Jonson, Lord Lisle, and Penshurst', *ELR* i (1971), 250–60, and G. R. Hibbard, 'The Country House Poem of the Seventeenth Century', *JWCI* xix (1956), 159–74.

PAGE 9, 3. *thrift ... magnificence*. Cf. *ODEP*, 'Frugality is the mother of liberality', for 1596.

13–14. *care to ... serve*. The editor of *13* made the charitable emendation, 'care of them that did serve, as to be served'. [The purpose of the convoluted original sentence is to avoid having Kalander take care of his servants first, which would be inappropriate, since the central idea here is that he is a good master, but nevertheless a master.]

17–18. [*tokens ... greatness*. 'signs of nobility'. Since Strephon and Claius are not motivated by financial gain, this is as likely to refer to Musidorus' noble appearance and bearing as to his chest of jewels. Kalander, who is 'no herald to inquire of men's pedigrees' but, like Strephon and Claius, knows how to read the signs, immediately

COMMENTARY 461

interprets Musidorus' face as a clue to his nobility – although he subsequently also observes the jewels that Musidorus offers to the two shepherds, which confirm his initial impression that his guest is 'of no mean calling' (p. 10, 1).]

PAGE 10, 9. *of Laconia pirates*. Abbott, 31, notes that 'any noun could be prefixed to another with the force of an adjective ... sometimes used where we should prefer the genitive', and on p. 318 compares Shakespeare's usage, 'Our Rome gates', in *Coriolanus*, III. iii. 104 and IV. v. 214.

PAGE 11, 1. *mosaical*. 'resembling mosaic'; this is the earliest citation in *OED* and how Yong translated Montemayor's *Mosayca* (Montemayor, 173; Yong, 139).
7–9. *Venus ... Aeneas*. See p. xxx.
9. *veins*. See p. xxvii.
Aeneas. He was the son of Anchises and Venus.
11. *breast running*. Cf. the fountains in Francesco Colonna, *Hypnerotomachia*, trans. R. D., ed. L. Gent (New York, 1973), 75, 'her round breasts did sprout out small streamings of pure and clear fresh water'; and in Montemayor, *Diana* (Montemayor, 178; Yong, 143), 'at her fair breasts through nipples of rubies spouted out water'; and in the Cambridge University device.
14. *pictures*. See p. xxv for the uses to which Sidney put them.
14–15. *Diana ... Actaeon*. When the hunter Actaeon came upon Diana bathing, she transformed him into a stag which was devoured by his dogs; cf. Ovid, *Met*. iii. 230 ff.
18. *Atalanta*. Atalanta, who determined to kill all suitors that could not outrun her, was secured as his wife by Hippomenes when he threw at her feet the golden apples given him by Venus. Cf. p. 161, 5–6 and note.
19. *eyes ... judges*. This is a common expression in Sidney's writings, perhaps from the concept of *judging eyes* in Venus' curse, p. 304, 21 (Robertson, 340, 14).
21. *Helena*. This is Helen of Troy.
Omphale, Iole. In his 1548 version of Sir Thomas Elyot's *Bibliotheca Eliotae* (New York, 1975), Thomas Cooper, like Sidney here, makes the post-classical distinction between Omphale and Iole in their relationship with Hercules: Omphale was 'a maiden ... whom Hercules did serve, and she caused him to spin on a rock' or distaff, while by contrast Iole was the princess 'whom Hercules loved so much that he served her in a women's apparel and span on a distaff'. A further confusion, stemming from lack of clarity in Ovid, *Heroides*, ix, is in Gavin Douglas, 'Prologue of the fourth Book' of his trans. of Virgil, *Aeneid* (1710), Aa1^v, where love taught 'Hercules go lerne to spin, / Reik Dejanire his mais and lioun skyn'. For the background and application, see above, p. xxv and V. Skretkowicz, 'Hercules in Sidney and Spenser', *N & Q* xxvii (1980), 306–10, with further examples in P. G. Schmidt, 'Hercules indutus vestibus Ioles', in D. H. Green, ed., *From Wolfram and Petrarch to Goethe and Grass* (Baden-Baden, 1982), 103–7.
34. *made by*. 'designed by'.

PAGE 12, 12. *Arcadia*. The *Old Arcadia* begins here.
20–1. *ravening ... muses*. Pastoral verse often celebrates the patience of common men living amid the contentions of the powerful; cf. *A Defence of Poetry* (*Misc. Prose*, 95).
27. *sufficient skill*. The ease of maintaining a hereditary princedom by an unexceptional prince, and the love of his subjects for such a leader, are treated in Machiavelli, *The Prince*, ii.

34–5. *magnificence ... liberality.* According to Aristotle, *Nicomachean Ethics*, trans. H. Rackham (London, 1926), IV. ii. 1, magnificence 'consists in suitable expenditure on a great scale', whereas, IV. i. 1, liberality is 'the observance of the mean in relation to wealth'.

36. *stricken in years.* 'advanced in years'.

PAGE 13, 3. *nature ... stepmother.* Cf. *AS* song vii. 1, 'stepdame nature'.

34. *bauble.* Cf. Tilley, F511, 'What is a fool without a bauble?'

PAGE 14, 8. *without book.* 'from memory'; cf. *AS* 56. 2 and Tilley, B532.

9–22. Ringler, *OA* 3, and 384; Robertson, 30, 23 ff. The tradition of the mock encomium is traced in Ringler, 384, and in H. K. Miller, 'The Paradoxical Encomium with Special Reference to its Vogue in England, 1600–1800', *MP* liii (1956), 145–78. C. W. Lemmi, 'Italian Borrowings in Sidney', *MLN* xlii (1927), 77–9, suggests a parallel with Berni's sonnet ii; see also T. N. Marsh, 'Elizabethan Wit in Metaphor and Conceit, Sidney, Shakespeare, Donne', *English Miscellany*, xiii (1962), 25–9. Texts with substantive variants are *OA* (*Je* has only ll. 1–4); *Dd*, f. 37^v; *Ha*, f. 145^v; *Hy*, f. 75; *Cm*, 90, 93 (Ringler, 554–7). Other texts are Bodleian Library MS Rawl. poet. 142, f. 26^v (Ringler, 558); National Library of Scotland MS 2059 (Ringler, 366, 560); *England's Parnassus* (1600), no. 2058 (Ringler, 565). Ringler, 351, notes the imitation beginning 'Philoclea and Pamela sweet' printed with *the Arcadia* from 1655 onwards, though probably by Sir John Mennes or James Smith as it was in Sir J. M. and Ja. S., *Musarum Deliciae* (1655), 13–15, of which copies are in Phillipps MS 8270, ff. 125–6^v (Rosenbach Cat. (1941), 194); British Library MS Add. 25303, ff. 137–8; British Library MS Harl. 6057, ff. 10^v–11^v; and Emmanuel College, Cambridge, MS 1. 3. 16, ff. 4–5^v (W. A. Ringler, 'Poems Attributed to Sir Philip Sidney', *SP* xlvii (1950), 126–51). Another adaptation for a poem on Besse Griffin is in Bodleian Library MS Eng. Poet. f. 27, pp. 99–101 (Robertson, 424).

9. *verse.* Parodying popular taste, Sidney uses the metre so desperately described by George Gascoigne, *Certain Notes of Instruction*, in *Works*, ed. J. W. Cunliffe (Cambridge, 1910), i. 472: 'the commonest sort of verse which we use nowadays (*viz.* the long verse of twelve and fourteen syllables) I know not certainly how to name it, unless I should say that it doth consist of poulter's measure, which giveth xii for one dozen and xiiii for another'.

[*Mopsa's. Englands Parnassus* reads 'Mopsus' and omits the phrase 'can serue'. Ringler claims the poetry in *Englands Parnassus* was based on 98, but the a/o confusion here indicates the poem may have been set from a manuscript source by an inattentive compositor (in print, a and o are not easily confused, and it is clear both from the poem itself and from the section in which it appears – 'Descriptions of Beautie & personage' – that Mopsa is female). A manuscript copy text, perhaps badly copied from 98, might also account for several textual differences in *Englands Parnassus*' versions of this poem and 'What tongue ...', the most significant of which are described below. See also the notes to pp. 14, 14; 14, 15; 165, 4–5.]

13. *Saturn ... Venus.* Saturn is portrayed as bowed with age; Venus is patroness of courtesans; see p. xxiv.

14. *Pan ... fast.* Pan was hairy; Juno severe and demanding; Iris, the rainbow, inconstant. Ringler's emendation of *Iris* to *Isis* was rejected by Robertson, 424, because '*Iris* is the reading of all the texts, and *fast* as well as "swift" also means "steadfast"'. [*Englands Parnassus* has the rhyme word as 'gracst', perhaps caused by an eyeskip to 'Momus' grace' two lines below.]

15. *Cupid ... pace.* See 'Blind Cupid' in E. Panofsky, *Studies in Iconology* (New York,

1939), 95–108; Vulcan is lame. [*Englands Parnassus* reads 'Gods (*sic*) Vulcans'.]

16. *Momus' grace.* Momus was banished from heaven for excessively criticizing perversion of the godly lineage by the offspring of mortals. This may be a comment on Mopsa's mongrelism.

17. *jacinth ... opal.* The jacinth was reddish-orange; the iridescent opal frequently changed colour (this is the earliest citation in *OED* for *opal* adj. 3).

18. *twinkling ... pearl.* The old verb *twinkle*, 'blink', in this participial form was first noted in *OED* 3 to have been used in 1740; *pearl* was an opaque, white cataract on the eye.

19. *crapal stone,* 'crapaud-stone' or 'toad-stone'. This was either white, or brown to black with a green eye in the centre, and could be set as a jewel, as the 'one which was black and spotted with red spots which I did set in a ring of gold', in British Library MS Sloane 2539, f. 34, cited in Joan Evans, *Magical Jewels* (Oxford, 1922), 150. [Mostly, however, toad-stones, supposedly found in the heads of toads, were not used as ornaments but for medicinal purposes. A stone's power as an antidote was sometimes believed to be proportional to the poisonousness of the toad from whose head it had been retrieved, so the analogy may be yet another slight against Mopsa. Cf. Lyly, *Euphues his England* (1580) fol. 53^v: 'for experience teacheth me, that straight trees haue crooked rootes, smooth baytes sharpe hooks, that the fayrer the stone is in the Toads head, ye more pestilent the poyson is in hir bowells.']

mouth ... wide. Cf. Berni's *bocca ampia celeste*; O describes the shape of her mouth; *heav'nly*, 'to the extent of heaven'. This is the earliest citation in *OED* 2.

[*heav'nly*. In Sidney's poetry, the word 'heavenly' is consistently disyllabic, with the exception of the quantitative poem 'Unto a caitiff wretch', where it is twice used trisyllabically, in pp. 269, 15 and 270, 21. For disyllabic uses of the word in the *New Arcadia* see pp. 105, 34; 126, 18; 164, 13; 165, 12; 300, 1, 18, 32; 301, 7; 406, 13; 411, 40; 417, 39; 422, 18; 423, 12; 434, 10. Correspondingly, 'heaven' or 'heavens' is usually monosyllabic, except in cases where the metre requires an additional syllable, as in p. 425, 19 and p. 432, 8.]

20. *silver ore.* This is black with silver flecks, and rough.

21–2. *As ... rest.* Cf. Ovid, *Met.* i. 502, 'Si qua latent, meliora putat', which Golding, i. 605–6, translates,

> And sure he thought such other parts as garments then did hide
> Excelled greatly all the rest the which he had espied.

27. [*often soothed ... success.* 98 and later editions read 'smoothed.']

29–PAGE 15, 4. *credit ... mended.* Such a situation is described by Castiglione, *The Cour-tier*, trans. Hoby (London, 1956), 123, 'if a prince be inclined to one that is most ignorant'.

PAGE 15, 6. [*principal herdman.* Kalander later implies that this is not the greatest of advancements, by calling Dametas '*but* chief herdman' (see p. 20, 13–14, emphasis added). In his challenge to Clinias in Book III, however, Dametas proudly refers to himself as 'Chief Governor of All the Royal Cattle (and also of Pamela ...)'. Cf. the note to p. 329, 22–3.]

7. [*strange determination.* See note to p. 23, 28.]

8–9. *great ... boat.* Cf. Tilley, S24, 'Make not your sail too big for the boat'.

11–12. *office ... men are.* Cf. Aristotle, *Politics*, trans. H. Rackham (London, 1932), I. iii. 21, 'statesmanship does not create human beings but having received them from nature makes use of them', and Plato, *Republic*, IV. iii.

13. *ass to manage.* [See *OED*, manage v., 2b: 'Of a horse: to perform an exercise of the manège.' The absurd image of an ass being trained in a riding school is the first of many references to horsemanship in the book. This example is not currently included in the OED entry, perhaps because it is technically not being used 'of a horse'.] On the futility of trying to teach an ass to obey the rein, see Horace, *Satires*, I. i. 90–1, from which Sidney adapted line 63 for *A Defence of Poetry* (*Misc. Prose*, 105, 32).

13–15. [*given your ears ... flesh.* See p. lxxxiii.]

21–2. *Clitophon ... marriage.* See p. xlviii.

preparing ... celebrated. This is omitted in 13; see p. xxxvii.

23. [*of his bedchamber.* 'one of his personal attendants'. This detail explains how Clitophon was able to gain access to the king's private correspondence.]

PAGE 16, 7–**PAGE 18**, 3. *Most ... imagined.* This letter is compared with Sidney's to Queen Elizabeth (*Misc. Prose*, 46–57) in W. R. Davis and R. A. Lanham, *Sidney's Arcadia* (New Haven, 1965), 241–4.

11–12. *wisdom and virtue.* Though these be the epitome of man's powers (see p. 128, 12–13), Philanax's notion of dependence upon human rather than divine wisdom is condemned implicitly by the dying Argalus at p. 327, 35–7 and by the second oracle at p. 396, 35–7.

19. *these ... soothsayers.* In this common construction, *kind of* was regarded as a single adjective when the following noun was plural, preceded by a plural pronoun, and followed by a plural verb; cf. *OED* under *kind* n. 8b.

they. 'the heavenly powers'.

21–2. *respected ... prevented.* Cf. Tiresias' reply to Ulysses in Horace, *Satires*, II. v. 59: 'quidquid dicam, aut erit, aut non'.

25–6. [*your determination.* See note to p. 23, 28.]

29–30. [*so hurtlessly strong ... of your enmity.* In early modern usage, 'hurtless', like its synonym 'harmless', does not imply incapability of inflicting harm. Consequently, the idea conveyed here is that Basilius is only 'hurtlessly' strong because his enemies are aware of his strength and prefer not to test it.]

38. *fear of death.* Cf. p. 143, 31–2.

PAGE 17, 9. *kill ... posterity.* Cf. p. 416, 23.

12. *Once.* 'In short'.

21–2. *cage ... bird.* Cf. Tilley, B361, 'Better to be a bird of the wood than of the cage'.

22. *dog ... tying.* Cf. Tilley, M742, 'A mastiff grows the fiercer for being tied up'.

32–3. *ignorance ... faithfulness.* This is cited both in Tilley, I17 and in *ODEP*.

33. *cannot ... is good.* Cf. Tilley, K181; cited in *ODEP*.

39. *valley ... hills.* Cf. Tilley, V7, 'The vale best discovers the hill'.

PAGE 18, 6. *baiting-place.* The conceit of earthly life as a short stay in a humble inn was commonplace; parallels are in B. Stevenson, *Stevenson's Book of Proverbs, Maxims and Familiar Phrases* (London, 1949), 1399. Cf. Sidney's translation of Psalm 39. 39–40, 'For I with Thee on earth a stranger am / But baiting'; the first line of William Crashaw's poem, AT 15 (Ringler, 350), 'It is not I that die, I do but leave an inn'; and p. 175, 23.

7–8. *certain ... uncertainty.* Cf. Montaigne, *Essays*, II. xiv, trans. Florio (London, 1910), ii. 333, citing Pliny, *Natural History*, II. 5. 25 (formerly II. 7). 'This only is sure, that there is nothing sure'; Robertson, 419, compares de Guevara, *Dispraise of the Life of a Courtier* (1548), C1, 'there is nothing in this world so certain as that all things is

uncertain'. This passage is cited in C. G. Smith, *Spenser's Proverb Lore* (Cambridge, Mass., 1970), 91.
9. *Philanax*. This is the uninflected genitive; see p. lxii.
12. *left the stern*. Cf. Tilley, S347, 'Like a ship without a stern'.
14. *for current*. 'as genuine'.
18. *hidden his head*. Cf. *ODEP*, 'Ostrich policy', and Tilley, O83. The image recurs on pp. 259, 7–8; 274, 31–2.
21. *priest*. This character remains unseen.
27–8. *old age ... talkative*. Cf. Aristotle, *Rhetoric*, trans. J. H. Freese (London, 1926), II. xiii, 'Older men ... are incessantly talking of the past, because they take pleasure in recollection'; Chaucer, 'Reeve's Prologue', 3896–8, in *Works*, ed. F. N. Robinson, 2nd edn. (Cambridge, Mass., 1961), 'The sely tonge ... with olde folk, save dotage, is namoore!'; and Shakespeare, sonnet 17. 10, 'old men of less truth than tongue'.
31–3. *eternize ... children*. Cf. p. 155, 36–8 and p. 287, 17–8.

PAGE 19, 4–5. *last ... least*. Cf. Tilley, L82, 'Last but not least'.
9. *shepherds ... governors*. 'Shepherd of the people' was a Homeric epithet applied to Grecian kings such as Agamemnon and Menelaus.
19. [*the meanest sort*. See the note to p. 39, 16.]
20. *dialogues in metre*. Cf. Virgil, *Eclogues*, iii. 59, 'alternis dicetis; amant alterna Camenae'.
23. [*no sort of people*. See the note to p. 39, 16.]
25. *ease ... poetry*. Cf. Tilley, P450, 'A poet in adversity can hardly make verses'.

PAGE 20, 13–14. [*being but chief herdman*. See notes to pp. 15, 6 and 329, 22–3.]
17–19. *supper ... Homer*. Heliodorus, II. xxii. 5, refers to Homer, *Odyssey*, xvii. 286–7 (and cf. *Iliad*, xxiv. 601 ff.):

> Maintenant, il convient de satisfaire notre ventre: ce ventre, qu'Homère a merveilleusement appelé un damné Tyran, parce qu'il veut toujours être le premier servi.

19–21. *Homer ... stopped*. Cf. *Odyssey*, i. 123–4; iii. 79; iv. 60–4, etc.
23. *parlour ... sup*. M. Girouard, *Life in the English Country House* (New Haven, 1978), 103, cites this passage in discussing parlours, 'informal sitting and eating rooms'.
24–5. *trencher-men of Media*. Cyrus was disgusted by the excessive eating habits of the Medes, Xenophon, *Cyropaedia*, 1. iii. 4–6. This is the only citation in *OED* under trencher-man n. 1, 'cook or caterer'. [The lack of other citations suggests the definition was based exclusively on this example, however. All other examples use 'trencher-man' to refer to a glutton or parasite at a patron's table, so as with other words in which the *OED* records no other example of a word used in the sense in which it appears in *Arcadia*, Sidney may either have mistaken the precise meaning of the word or deliberately misused it.]
27. *and attend*. See p. lvi.
33. *his sudden*. 'Kalander's sudden'.
35–6. *before ... marriage*. 13 substitutes 'not long since'; see p. xlviii.

PAGE 21, 33–4. [*with better success than expectation*. i.e. nobody expected the elderly Basilius to father an heir at this point. For Cecropia's version of the story, see p. 275, 20–31.]
27. *sees not*. 'does not have experience of'; cf. Chaucer, *The Book of the Duchess*, in *Works*, ed. F. N. Robinson, 2nd edn. (Cambridge, Mass., 1961), 799–804, 'in my firste youthe .../ Al were to me yliche good / That I knew thoo'; and Tilley, T162, 'All things are good unseyed'. See p. 123, 6–7.

40. *plant.* 'young person'. [The steward's word choice here highlights the passage of time, as Argalus (who is of a similar age as his cousin Gynecia) is no longer a young man at the time of telling.]

PAGE 22, 2–3. *factiousness.* 'disposition towards factions'.
5. [*two princes ... Macedon.* i.e. Musidorus and Pyrocles, who have as yet only been introduced by their names.]
10. *sad.* 'serious'.
11. *word ... deed.* Cf. p. 78, 2 and note.
11–12. *liberal than magnificent.* See p. 12, 34–5 and note.
14–15. [*was, ... is.* The lapse of tense and the subsequent correction indicate the steward's fear that Argalus may already be dead.]
27. *he brought him.* 'Clitophon brought Argalus'.
38–9. [*likeness ... affection.* See p. lxxx.]
39–40. *cross with.* 'go counter to'; this is the earliest citation in *OED* 15a.
40. [*it did so indeed.* i.e. Argalus' and Parthenia's likeness of manners did draw liking with affection and they fell in love.]

PAGE 23, 14–15. *well-judging eyes.* Cf. p. 11, 19 and note.
19–20. *she ... miss Parthenia.* Hoskyns, 15, cites this as an example of antimetabole.
25. *bedded ... wedded.* This is the earliest citation in Tilley, G426; see Robertson, 220, 19–20.
28. [*determinately – lest I say ... wilfully.* While the word 'determinately' merely stresses the single-mindedness of Parthenia's mother, the word 'wilfully' has connotations of obstinacy and perverseness, so the steward checks his impulse to apply it to 'a great lady', who is also his master's sister. Kalander uses the same euphemism as his steward when referring to Basilius' 'strange determination' to leave his court (p. 15, 7), as does Philanax in his letter (p. 16, 6). Parthenia's refusal of Demagoras is also described as 'determinate' (p. 24, 15). Elsewhere in *Arcadia*, the words 'wilfulness', 'wilful' and 'wilfully' are usually connoted with behaviour that is (or is perceived as) impulsive, irrational and self-sabotaging. Hence those words are applied to Musidorus' self-destructive impulse to drown himself directly after having been rescued from drowning (p. 3, 37), Erona's obstinate refusal of Tiridates for Antiphilus' sake, which will prompt Tiridates' slaughter of her subjects (p. 177, 31), and Amphialus' breaking of his 'good sword' after having unwittingly killed Parthenia – at least viewed in retrospect, when his inferior sword breaks (p. 356, 25). Similarly, Cecropia attributes wilfulness both to her son's reluctance to take advantage of the fact that Pamela and Philoclea are in his power (p. 276, 33) and to Philoclea's refusal to be persuaded by her (pp. 286, 2–3 and 367, 28), although being a wicked character, she misinterprets virtuous determination as wilfulness.]
37–8. *Juno ... Hercules.* Juno, jealous that her husband Jupiter begot Hercules by Alcmene, vowed that Hercules might gain immortality only by executing twelve great labours in the service of Eurystheus. See p. xxv.

PAGE 24, 4. *conquered ... conquests.* See. p. xxviii.
8–9. *world ... them.* Hoskyns, 29, cites this as an example of hyperbole.
11–12. [*so passed over all.* 'pass over' in the sense of surpass is a rare variant form of 'overpass'. The *OED* only cites one other example, from Gower's *Confessio Amantis*.]
15–16. [*her own determinate answer.* See note to p. 23, 28.]
17. *narrow eyes.* This is Sidney's adaptation of Horace, *Epistles*, I. xiv. 37–8, 'obliquo oculo ... Limat', glossed by Lambinus, ed. (Paris, 1567), Yy3, as 'aspecto maligno,

& invido', with a spiteful and envious look. Following the explanation by H. R. Fairclough, trans., *Satires, Epistles, and Ars Poetica* (London, 1970), 'The verb *limat* (lit. "files away"), as used with *obliquo oculo*, involves a play upon *limis oculis*', this would easily convert to 'narrow eyes'.

PAGE 25, 2. *he did not.* K. Myrick, *Sir Philip Sidney as a Literary Craftsman*, 2nd edn. (Lincoln, 1965), 235, compares Sir Henry Sidney's reaction in seeing his wife 'as foul a lady as the small-pox could make her', letter to Walsingham, 1 March 1582/3, *CSP Domestic 1581–90*, 98.
22. *affects and effects.* For examples of this common formula, see *OED* under *affect* n. I 1b.
33–4. *marshal ... harbinger.* 'officer of ceremonies to arrange that Argalus provide accomodation for her'. This love was now housed so successfully that no benefit could be gained by retaining a harbinger or purveyor of lodgings. The earliest citation in *OED* under *marshal* n. 4 *fig.* is from Chaucer.
36. *skin.* Cf. Tilley, B170, 'Beauty is but skin-deep'.
38. *loveliness.* 'lovingness'.

PAGE 26, 31. *king's nephew.* See p. 39, 6–11.

PAGE 27, 13. *close ... prison.* Cf. John Aubrey, '*Brief Lives*', ed. A. Clark (Oxford, 1898), i. 422, where John Hoskyns's stay in the Tower as a 'close prisoner' is described: 'his windows were boarded up. Through a small chink he saw once a crow, and another time a kite, the sight whereof, he said, was a great pleasure to him.'
31. *and that.* 'with the result that'.

PAGE 28, 1. [*more determinate ... do.* i.e. despite their large number and their fierce loyalty towards Kalander, they are an inefficient and unpractised force. Musidorus favours quality over quantity, so his plan casts most of those three or four thousand men as mere extras, who will be left outside the walls of Cardamyla while he attempts to free Clitophon and Argalus with 'two hundred of the best-chosen gentlemen for courage and strength' (p. 29, 2–3).]
4–5. *weapons ... encamping.* 'The action of war consisteth in three principal points, that is, in lodging or encamping, in marching, and in fighting' (T. Blundeville, *The True Order and Method of Writing and Reading Histories* (1574), ed. H. G. Dick, *HLQ* iii (1939–40), 163, drawing on F. Patrizi, *Della Historia Diece Dialoghi* (1560) and dedicated to Leicester). The earliest citation in *OED* under *encamping* n. 1 is from 1590, but see Blunderville's *True Order*, 167. See p. xxxix.
29–30. *against ... for whom.* This was a commonplace of strategy; cf. Xenophon, *Cyropaedia*, II. i. 4, and Sidney's letter to Robert Sidney, 'you cannot tell what the queen of England is able to do defensively or offensively but by through comparing what they are able to do with whom she is to be matched' (*Works*, iii. 125).
34–5. *experience.* As part of his education, Languet advised Sidney on 18 June 1574 to serve under Schwendi for his first military experience, and Robert Sidney wrote to his father that 'My brother ... wrote that if there were any good wars I should go to them'; see C. S. Levy. 'The Correspondence of Sir Philip Sidney and Hubert Languet, 1573–1576' (unpublished Ph.D. thesis, Cornell University, 1962), p. 197; and A. Collins, *Letters and Memorials of State* (1746), i. 286.
35–6. *reading ... stratagems.* In his letter of 22 May 1580, in J. Buxton, 'An Elizabethan Reading-List', *TLS* (24 March 1972), 343–4, Sidney advised Edward Denny, 'for the histories ... read the Greek and Roman writers, for they were the wisest and fullest

of excellent examples both of discipline and stratagems'; and on 18 October 1580 wrote to Robert Sidney advising him to note in his reading of histories, among other things, 'the enterings and endings of wars, and therein the stratagems against the enemy and the discipline upon the soldier' (*Works*, iii. 131).

37. [*poorest sort of people*. The helots are characterized by their lower-class origins (see p. 28, 8–19), so Musidorus' plan relies on the assumption that they are likely to be sympathetic towards lower-class Arcadians who have followed their example and risen against the nobility. See also the note to p. 39, 16.]

PAGE 29, 1. [*make ... ill-favouredly*. 'make them appear so shabby and unappealing'. The construction look + adverb was common in the sixteenth century. This is the earliest citation for *rustily* in *OED*.]

11. [*weeded out ... rhetoric*. See p. lxxiv.]

24. *such men ... peace*. Eminent hostages guaranteed immunity from attack.

PAGE 30, 36. *eyes ... judged*. Cf. p. 11, 19 and note.

PAGE 31, 38. *parter ... night*. Cf. Shakespeare, *Troilus and Cressida*, V. viii. 17–18, 'The dragon wing of night ... the armies separates.'

PAGE 32, 25. *Laconia*. This is interchangeable with *Lacedaemon* or with *Sparta*, its capital. Throughout this passage the scribe of *Cm* has *Lacedaemon*; see p. liii.

35. [*well on of their way*. Although the wording is both odd and ungrammatical (there are no comparable examples in the EEBO / TCP corpus, suggesting this may be an error in *90*), the sentence is reproduced exactly like this in all subsequent editions. Although compositors and proofreaders did occasionally correct passages they regarded as mistakes (see pp. lvi–lvii), they were perhaps wary of interfering with the complex grammar of Sidney's sentences any more than necessary and thus preferred to err on the side of caution.]

PAGE 33, 8. *only his benefit*, 'only to be due to his noble action'.

PAGE 34, 8. *kings*. The Lacedaemonians had two kings from two families; cf. Aristotle, *Politics*, v. ix. 1; and Pausanias, *Description of Greece*, III. i. 5 ff.

13. *pay*. Many cities of Laconia paid tribute to Sparta; cf. Pausanias, *Description of Greece*, III. xxi. 6.

18. *Spartan discipline*. Lycurgus' system of public education is described in Plutarch, *Life of Lycurgus*, xvi–xxv.

20. *decreed of*. 'determined'; the earliest citation in *OED* 5 is from Edmund Spenser's *Ruines of Rome* (1591).

PAGE 35, 4. *demigod*. Through God's grace, the courtier 'shall attain unto that heroical and noble virtue that shall make him pass the bounds of the nature of man, and shall rather be called a demigod than a man mortal' (Castiglione, *The Courtier*, trans. Hoby (London, 1956), 276); cf. p. 397, 23.

18. *no hair ... face*. Cf. p. 293, 17–18.

26. *moist*. With reference to the humour, 'easily changing'.

PAGE 36, 14–15. *she ... gone*. The tale begins on p. 48, 21.

PAGE 37, 13–14. *love ... finish*. Cf. Tilley, L539, 'A perfect love does last eternally'; cited in C. G. Smith, *Spenser's Proverb Lore*, 312.

25. *lonely*. As this is a 'solitary place', the emendation in *93* has been accepted; see p. 123, 23 and note. The earliest citation in *OED* 3 is from 1645.

27. *physician.* Ariston's wife 'was the ugliest maiden in Sparta, but became the most beautiful of her women, because Helen changed her' (Pausanias, *Description of Greece*, trans. W. H. S. Jones (London, 1918–35), III. vii. 7); Herodotus, vi. 61–7, tells of such a transformation at the chapel of Helen at Therapne.

PAGE 38, 14. *Messena.* This was the capital of Messenia, south-west of Arcadia and west of Laconia.

17–18. [*upon occasion … present.* The phrase 'upon occasion' highlights the element of chance. Since it is important for the narrative (Pyrocles needs to see Philoclea's picture in order to fall in love with her and have a motivation to leave Kalander's house), the presence of the pictures is also stressed at the beginning of this scene (p. 38, 1–2).]

32. *that place.* Cf. Tilley, W171, 'The way to heaven is as ready by water as by land'.

33. [*among … shrouds.* Shrouds in the naval sense are ropes that form part of a ship's rigging (cf. *shroud* n² in *OED*), but the literal meaning of 'shroud' is clearly implied given the context: Pyrocles, surrounded by floating bodies and the 'carcass' of the ship (cf. p. 4, 33–5), has just been considering the possibility of his own death.]

37. *underboard.* 'under deck'; the earliest citation in *OED* 1b is from 1588.

PAGE 39, 10. *admiral.* 'flagship'.

16. [*the popular sort.* 'the common people' – as opposed to 'the better sort', people of rank and nobility. In early modern English, the word 'sort' is often used to describe class distinctions, especially when combined with adjectives denoting quality. Cf. pp. 19, 19, 23; 28, 37; 149, 1–2; 242, 8–9; 244, 33; 246, 10–11.]

32. *Amiclas.* Cf. Pausanias, *Description of Greece*, trans. W. H. S. Jones (London, 1918–35), III. i. 2–3, 'Lacedaemon was wedded to Sparta …. On the death of [his son] Amyclas the empire came to Argalus'.

PAGE 40, 14. *blushing.* Cf. Tilley, B480, 'Blushing is virtue's colour'; see pp. 148, 27–9; 223, 36–7; 322, 22–4.

18. [*'O Jupiter!'* Sidney, like most of his contemporaries, favours the god's Latin name even in a Greek context, where he should technically be 'Zeus'. Cf. Mor-nay, *A Woorke Concerning the Trewnesse of the Christian Religion* (1587), p. 379: 'Heere lyeth the great Zeus whom men call Iupiter.' See also Dametas' mixed references to the 'pantable of Pallas' and 'combcase of Diana', p. 68, 27 and p. 69, 14.]

24–5. *company … alone.* Cf. AS 27. 1–2, 'I …/ Seem most alone in greatest company'.

25–6. [*Even the colour … alteration.* i.e. he started to look pale and gaunt, a physical manifestation of melancholy. Cf. Robert Burton's definition of the symptoms of 'Love-melancholy' in *The Anatomy of Melancholy*, p. 597.]

32–3. *strength … laws.* Sidney instructed his brother Robert 'in the right informing your mind with those things which are most notable in those places you come to' in his letter in *Works*, iii. 124–7.

PAGE 41, 16. [*slacking … main career.* This is *main* adj.2 2c ('exerted to the full') and *career* n. 2a in the *OED*, so Musidorus is comparing Pyrocles' sudden loss of spirits to an abandoned attempt at a full gallop during a tournament, with the implication that in succumbing to melancholy, Pyrocles has let himself down.]

27. *virtue … clouds.* Cf. p. 279, 25.

28. *solitariness.* J. Zeitlin, Introduction to his translation of Petrarch, *The Life of Solitude* (Urbana, 1924), sketches the debate on solitariness from the ancients to Petrarch. Sidney in *A Defence of Poetry* (*Misc. Prose*, 93, 3) noted the popularity

among philosophers of 'wrangling' about 'whether the contemplative or the active life do excel', and see Robertson, 420, and P. A. Duhamel, 'Sidney's *Arcadia* and Elizabethan Rhetoric', *SP* xlv (1948), 134–50.

31–3. [*no more ... a passenger.* The preoccupied Pyrocles is alternately compared to a child neglecting his duties in order to play and a 'diligent pilot' who ignores a passenger's 'unskilful' words in order to perform his duty. The combination of these two incompatible images leaves it unclear whether his other devotion is more or less important than Musidorus' words, reflecting Pyrocles' own ambivalence.]

PAGE 42, 5–8. *if extremity ... of me.* Hoskyns, 15, cites this as an example of concealed antimetabole, 'where he returns for *extremity of love, loving entirely*, and for *partial judgement, great undeserved judgement.*'

15–17. *mind ... broken.* B. Stevenson, *Stevenson's Book of Proverbs*, 226, amasses analogues for this commonplace, but with particular reference to the need for man's relaxation, see Herodotus, ii. 173.

24. *Eagles ... alone.* This is cited in Tilley, E7.

25. *sheep ... together.* This is cited in Tilley, S314.

36–**PAGE 43**, 10. *Do ... perfection.* Robertson, 421, compares the description from Gil Polo's *Enamoured Diana*, in Yong, 292.

21–**PAGE 44**, 27. *oft changing ... 'guilty'.* Cf. Thomas Wilson, *Arte of Rhetorique*, ed. G. H. Mair (Oxford, 1909), 94, where he observes of a person betraying guilt, 'often his colour changeth, his body shaketh, and his tongue faltereth within his mouth'.

31. *action.* Cf. *A Defence of Poetry* (*Misc. Prose*, 83), 'the ending end of all earthly learning being virtuous action', 'with the end of well-doing and not of well-knowing only'.

34–6. *arms ... employ them.* Cf. Tilley, L195, 'Use legs and have legs'.

PAGE 44, 9. *keep company.* Petrarch, *De Vita Solitaria*, I. v. 4, cites Cicero, *De Amicitia*, xxiii and *De Officiis*, I. xlvi, to support his argument that the joy of solitude ought to be shared with friends.

11. *not unpleasant.* Hoskyns, 35, cites this as an example of diminution 'by denying the contrary'.

13–14. [*Tempe ... brought up together.* See note to p. 71, 22.]

17. *mountains as molehills.* Cf. Tilley, M1035, 'Of a molehill he makes a mountain'. [John Weever alludes to Sidney's creative inversion of the image to describe the elevation of a lowly subject through lofty style, in his *Epigrammes* (1599), F5^v: 'A Goodwit (right Worshipful) wil shew his vigour in any subiect, and trauell as easily ouer a mountaine as a molehill. But mine (vnworthy the title of wit) tyred within three steppes of the mountaines foote, lay plodding there this long, and now at the last, hath brought forth a mouse'. Cf. also p. 418, 15.]

19–20. *these fantastical ... lovers.* Hoskyns, 35, cites this as an example of diminution 'by denying the right use of the word but by error of some'.

22. *tarantula.* 'bite of the tarantula' or 'tarantism'; this is the earliest citation in *OED* 2 [(though note that the entry calls this usage 'erroneous')]. Sufferers responded only to lively music; see the examples under *OED* 1 and 2; O'Connor, 199, compares *Amadis de Gaule*, XI. lvi. 90.

36. *hunting.* Spenser, *Astrophel*, 79–84, remarked on Sidney's skill in hunting, but Sir John Harington, *Metamorphosis of Ajax*, ed. E. S. Donno (London, 1962), 108, recalled that 'Sir Philip Sidney was wont to say that next hunting he liked hawking worst'.

PAGE 45, 2. [*against their return.* 'to be read at their return'. Cf. *OED* 10: 'n anticipation of, in preparation for'.]

11–2. *oft . . . thinking.* This is cited in Tilley, D571. [Sir John Hayward's third devotion in *A Sanctuarie for a Troubled Soule* (1601), pp. 133–4 paraphrases this to: 'as it often happeneth, that whilest one thinketh too much of dooing, he leaueth to doe the effect of his thinking; soe whilest it lamenteth the losse of all the time that is past, it looseth that little which then remaineth'.]

15. *old-growing . . . worse.* Cf. Tilley, B27, 'To go from bad to worse'.

17–18. *pleasant . . . length.* Cf. Tilley, C566, 'Good company makes short miles'.

21. *green liveries.* Cf. Chaucer, *Knight's Tale*, in *Works*, ed. F. N. Robinson, 2nd edn. (Cambridge, Mass., 1961), 1684–7, where Theseus, Ypolita, 'And Emelye, clothed all in grene, / On huntyng be they riden roially'; and George Gascoigne, *The Noble Art of Venery* (1575), G3, 'Phoebus saith that they ought to be clad in green when they hunt the hart or buck'. On Gascoigne's authorship, see J. Robertson, 'George Gascoigne and "The Noble Art of Venerie and Hunting"', *MLR* xxxvii (1942), 484–5; J. Robertson, review of C. Prouty, *George Gascoigne*, *MLR* xxxviii (1943), 139–40; and C. and R. Prouty, 'George Gascoigne, *The Noble Art of Venerie*, and Queen Elizabeth at Kenilworth', in J. G. McManaway, ed., *Joseph Quincy Adams Memorial Studies* (Washington, 1948), 639–64.

PAGE 45, 23. *were at a fault.* 'had lost the scent'; the earliest citation in *OED* is from 1593. [*The Noble Art of Venery* (1575) contains multiple examples of the related form 'at default', however.]

30. *view.* 'power of vision'.

31–3. *cry . . . music.* M. Poirier, 'Sidney's Influence upon *A Midsummer Night's Dream*', *SP* xliv (1947), 484–5, compares Shakespeare, *MND*, IV. i. 114–31. See also Gervase Markham's instructions for compounding a 'kennel for sweetness of cry' in *Country Contentments* (1631), cited in E. S. Donno, ed., Sir John Harington, *Metamorphosis of Ajax* (London, 1962), 110 n.

37–PAGE 46, 1. *Echo . . . Narcissus.* Cf. Ovid, *Met.* iii. 407 ff.

PAGE 46 2–3. *courage of despair.* Cf. Tilley, D216, 'Despair makes cowards courageous'; cited in C. G. Smith, *Spenser's Proverb Lore*, 176.

7–8. [*not suffer . . . poor beast.* Kalander's intervention is not motivated by compassion for the hart, he is preventing an act of foolishness. Gascoigne notes in *The Noble Art of Venery* that harts at bay are particularly dangerous and may inflict mortal wounds, citing the example of 'an Emperor named Basill which had ouercome his enimies in many battels, and had done great deeds of Chiualrie in his Countrie and was neuerthelesse slayne with an Harte in breaking of a Bay' (pp. 124–5). Killing it from a safe distance is consequently the prudent thing to do.]

8. *tears.* This common image was based on the belief that during the chase the deer's eyes secreted a liquid. This dried, dropped away, and was collected for its prophylactic properties; cf. 'The woeful words of the hart to the hunter', in Gascoigne's *Noble Art of Venery* (1575), 15:

> My tears congealed to gum by pieces from me fall,
> And thee preserve from pestilence in pomander or ball.
> Such wholesome tears shed I, when thou pursuest me so,
> Thou (not content) dost seek my death, and then thou get'st no more.

Tears flowed down Actaeon's nose when he became a stag, Ovid, *Met.* iii. 222–3, 'lacrimaeque per ora / Non sua fluxerunt'; analogous passages are in Shakespeare,

As You Like It, II. i. 38–40; Montaigne, *Essays*, II. xi, trans. Florio (London, 1910), ii. 122; Drayton, *Polyolbion*, xiii. 161; Gorges, in *Poems*, ed. H. E. Sandison (Oxford, 1953), no. 45; Marvell, 'The Nymph Complaining for the Death of her Faun', 95–6. [A late-sixteenth-century portrait of an unknown lady, speculatively identified as the Countess of Pembroke in an article by Alison Sorbie, depicts a crying stag – also mentioned in the poem that features in the portrait – standing next to the lady ('The Persian Lady Portrait', *British Art Journal* 16 (2015), 30–41). The creator of the portrait, Marcus Gheeraerts the Younger, is best known as the artist of the Ditchley Portrait of Elizabeth.]

30. *love my memory.* 'love the memory of me'; cf. p. 372, 36.
33–6. *Heretofore ... fortune.* Hoskyns, 46, cites this as an example of the second sort of division, prosapodosis, 'that overthroweth no part of the division, but returneth some reason to each member'.

PAGE 47, 15–16. *badge ... mind.* Cf. p. 350, 10–11.
17. [*a few choice jewels.* Cf. p. 119, 36–7.]
37–8. [*more cumber than courtesy.* Cf. Austin Saker, *Narbonus* (1580), p. 106: 'Now is Fidelia on Horseback, and about to ride as she long desired, more curious than coy: more courteous than cumbersome, more trifling than troublesome.']

PAGE 48, 2. *withal.* 'with'.
with unkindness. 'because of the unkind treatment' he had received; cf. *OED* under *with* 39a.
3–6. *Mantinea ... Stygian.* These places are named together in Strabo, *Geography*, VIII. viii. 2.
6–7. *making ... inquiry.* Hoskyns, 29, cites this as an example of hyperbole.
eyes ... tongue. Each uses his eyes, ears, and tongue.
9. *succeed to.* 'follow'; the earliest citation in *OED* is from 1687; see also Robertson, 356, 20.
18. *they ... them down.* Examples of this reflexive form are in *OED* under *lay down* 3.
21–2. *when ... sleep.* Hoskyns, 47, cites this as an example of periphrasis.
28. *which was.* See p. xliii.

PAGE 49, 2–27. *coach ... eye.* O'Connor, 193–5, compares *Amadis*, I.xxii, and XI. xxvii and xlix, for the episode of a knight coming upon an ornate coach, being refused permission to approach, defeating the guard, and finding beautiful women inside; though in I. xxii there is only one girl, mourning beside a marble tomb. In VIII xxiv Niquée stares enchanted at an image of Amadis de Grèce until her view is disturbed.
5. *black and white.* The purity of white was balanced by the steadfastness or strength of black, which could not be altered (cf. Abraham Fraunce, *Insignium, Armorum* (1588), L3–M1). R. C. Strong, *Portraits of Queen Elizabeth I* (Oxford, 1963), 21, notes that Elizabeth's personal colours were black and white, comparing *CSP Spanish, 1558–67*, 368, and the 'Sieve' and 'Ermine' portraits.
9. *titles.* 'substantiations of their claims'.
33. [*accomplish ... the other.* This refers back to 'cruelty' and 'evil fortune' in the preceding sentence, so Helen is imploring Amphialus to put her out of her misery by bringing his cruelty to completion, i.e. by killing her. Cf. *accomplish* 2a in the *OED*: 'To bring to an end; to complete, finish.']

PAGE 50, 27. *Helen.* Hoskyns, 41, cites Helen as an illustration of 'true constant love unrespected'.

COMMENTARY 473

34. [*but once I know.* This is an unconventional usage of 'once', which here appears to mean 'at any rate' (cf. meaning 3b in *OED*, though note that the only two examples given are from the same eighteenth-century text), or perhaps 'one thing'. Helen's meaning is clear, however: while some of her suitors were no doubt motivated by the desire to marry a queen, and some others might have been genuinely in love with her, this distinction hardly mattered in practice, because regardless of their true motivations, all of them professed to love her for her beauty.]

PAGE 51, 12–13. *thinking ... scorn.* 'violently disdaining'.
24–8. *Why ... in Amphialus.* Hoskyns, 13, cites this as an example of epistrophe, 'when many clauses end with the same words'.
39. [*put ... young cousin.* Since Amphialus is obviously older than Basilius' daughters, 'young' has to refer to his not yet being of age when Pamela was born and he ceased to be his uncle's heir and is thus one of several indications of Helen's bias in her account. 'Put by' here means 'bar'. This is the earliest example for *put by* 1c in *OED*.]

PAGE 52, 2. *Argos.* The Argians and Arcadians are 'ancient enemies', p. 246, 37.
11. *Well ... years.* 'They prospered as they grew older'.
24. *with him.* 'as regards him'; cf. Abbott, 129.
24–6. *that what ... friend.* Hoskyns, 44, cites this as an example of parenthesis.
29–30. *For why.* 'wherefore'; cf. Abbott, 54.
33. *framed the way.* 'shaped the course'.
33–5. *mind ... keys.* See p. 123, 29.
38. [*daintiest.* 'most tender'.]

PAGE 53, 1. *waited of.* 'executed the commands of'; this is the earliest citation in *OED*.
16–17. *forgetfulness ... absence.* Cf. Tilley, F596, 'Long absent soon forgotten'.
33–5. [*in these ... determinations.* Rather than blaming herself, because she did not attempt to deter Philoxenus from challenging Amphialus, Helen conveniently chooses to regard his death as fate and herself as a mere 'accessary' – like the distressed lady who delayed Amphialus, or Amphialus himself, who killed his friend by accident. Amphialus (also rather conveniently) holds Helen solely responsible, calling her 'the cause of all this mischief' (p. 55, 14).]

PAGE 54, 21–2. *nature ... defend.* Cf. Tilley, S219, 'Self-preservation is nature's first law', and p. 238, 5.
34. *representation.* 'performance', as in a play; the earliest citation in *OED* 3a is from 1589.
37–8. *mountains ... upon him.* This is the punishment of the Giants in Ovid, *Met.* v. 347 ff.; cf. p. 418, 28.

PAGE 65, 10. *vainly.* 'conceitedly'; the earliest citation in *OED* 3 is from 1602. [Alternatively, this may be meaning 2 ('foolishly' or 'thoughtlessly' cf. 139, 16), whose earliest citation is from 1588. Either way, what Helen means is that at the sight of Amphialus' armour she briefly hoped, despite better knowledge, that he might be about to return to her.]
35. *framing ... constructions.* 'putting a friendly interpretation on the actions'.

PAGE 56, 31–2. *spaniel ... fawned.* Cf. Tilley, S704, 'As fawning as a spaniel'.
33. [*for old knowledge.* 'because he recognized him'. 'old' stresses the fact that although the dog still knows him as Philoxenus' friend (and greets him accordingly), Amphialus has become 'his master's murtherer' (34), which makes the dog's reaction inappropriate.]

Page 57, 1. *his dog ... places.* See p. xix. [Through Ismenus' choice of pronoun the dog's ownership quietly passes to Amphialus.]

17. *absented presence.* Hoskyns, 36, cites this as an example of synoeciosis, 'a composition of contraries'. [See pp. lxxv–lxxvi.]

18. *Olympian.* 'Olympic'; the earliest citation in *OED* is from Skelton.

21. *loneliness.* This is the earliest citation in *OED*. [Note, however, that Gaspar de Loarte's *Exercise of a Christian Life* (1579) contains an example that is earlier still.]

28. *resembling ... loved.* Repetition of this phrasing at pp. 66, 31–2; 83, 30–1 and 232, 16 ties together the main and secondary plots. Such formulations were sanctioned by referring to precedents in the ancients by Ascham, *The Schoolmaster*, in *English Works*, ed. W. A. Wright (Cambridge, 1904), 247: 'The old and best authors that ever wrote were content, if occasion required to speak twice of one matter, not to change the words, but ... word for word to express it again'; see pp. xxvii–xxviii.

31. *discreet ... journeys.* This is cited in Tilley, W301.

Page 58, 1. *forgetting.* The earliest citation in *OED* is from 1847.

8. *careless.* 'untended'; the earliest citation in *OED* 4a is from Marlowe's *Hero and Leander*.

careless ... art. Cf. pp. 83, 7–8 and 285, 3.

art ... art. This is cited in Tilley, A335; cf. *A Defence of Poetry* (*Misc. Prose*, 119).

9–10. *lay ... excellent.* 'arrange them as a perfect example of the conflict between nature and art'.

14–15. *sky-colour ... gold.* Pyrocles continues to wear the same colours as on p. 5, 10; cf. Urania's clothing in du Bartas, *L'Uranie*, in *The Works*, ed. U. T. Holmes, Jr. (Chapel Hill, 1935–40), 45^a–47^a:

> Son cors est affublé d'une mante azurée,
> Semée haut et bas d'un milion de feus
> Qui d'un bel art sans art, distinctement confus ...

See also C. T. Wright, 'The Amazons in Elizabethan Literature', *SP* xxxvii (1940), 433–56; and R. Tuve, 'Spenser and Some Pictorial Conventions with Particular Reference to Illuminated manuscripts', *SP* xxxvii (1940), 149–76, on the depiction of Amazons.

25–6. *Hercules ... Omphale's.* See the note to p. 11, 21, and p. xxv.

25–7. *set with ... word.* See p. lv.

32. *arbour.* See R. Strong, *The Renaissance Garden in England* (London, 1979), 122–3.

35–6. *a voice ... ears.* Hoskyns, 11, cites this as an example of catachresis, 'the abuse of a word drawn from things far different'.

35 *beautiful.* This is the earliest citation in *OED* 2 [(referring to senses other than sight, specifically to hearing)].

Page 59, 1–14. Ringler, *OA* 2, and 384; Robertson, 28, 30 ff. Texts with substantive variants are *OA*; *Dd*, f. 38 (Ringler, 554); *Cm*, 90, 93. Non-substantive copies are in British Library MS Add. 34064, f. 28 (Ringler, 555) and in manuscript in Bodleian Library printed book 27980. e. 86, p. viii (M. Crum, *First-line Index of English Poetry* (Oxford, 1969), T3305).

3. [*powers.* See the notes to pp. 59, 12 and 126, 6.]

7. [*conspired.* Disyllabic. In 90, this is indicated through the spelling 'conspird' ('conspir'd' in subsequent editions).]

12. [*power.* Consistently pronounced as one syllable in the poetry of *Arcadia* – though note that the plural 'powers' may be either monosyllabic or disyllabic, depending on metrical requirements.]

19–20. *Apollo ... Daphne.* Cf. Ovid, *Met.* i. 553–65; there is a lengthy iconographical tradition in manuscripts and printed books. [Here the analogy slyly subverts that tradition: while Apollo is amazed that Daphne has become unavailable to him through her transformation, Musidorus is amazed to discover that the 'lady' he has been pursuing is his friend and cousin (and thus unavailable for other reasons), so the transformation takes place in his mind.]

23. *insinuation.* This is the kind of exordium to a speech used to win over the audience; cf. 'A Letter to Queen Elizabeth' (*Misc. Prose*, 46, 12–13), and *A Defence of Poetry* (*Misc. Prose*, 93, 21).

division. This is the statement of the topics to be treated in an oration.

24. *narration.* This is that part of an oration in which the facts are stated.

38–9. *father ... country.* See p. 200, 1 and p. xxiii.

PAGE 60, 2–3. *drown ... haven.* Cf. Tilley, H219, 'To shipwreck in a haven'. [See p. lxxxii.]

3. *like an.* 'even as an'.

act. The earliest citation in *OED* II 9a is from c1520. Examples abound in Bandello, *Certain Tragical Discourses* (1567), trans. GV. Fenton, and Underdowne added it to Heliodorus' already theatrical images; see p. xxiii.

3. [*ill player ... tragedy.* 'ill' may mean wicked or morally depraved (cf. *OED* 1a and 1b), so while the primary image is that of a bad actor failing to move his audience, there is an undertone of moral censorship here that chimes with Musidorus' vehement disapproval of Pyrocles' 'unnatural' (i.e. perverted) behaviour. Pyrocles later echoes his friend's theatre imagery in the phrase 'my first act' (p. 74, 15) – although of course he secretly prefers to think of himself as an actor in a comedy rather than a tragedy. Cf. p. 75, 21–3: 'And thus, my Musidorus, you have my tragedy played unto you by myself, which, I pray the gods, may not indeed prove a tragedy'. Later Musidorus refers to his feigned wooing of Mopsa as a 'tragedy', p. 119, 3–5).]

4–5. *men ... commandment.* See p. xxviii. On this commonplace, see Burton, *Anatomy of Melancholy*, 1. 1. 2. 8; Ringler, 461, compares AS 5. 1–4.

10–11. *to say ... womanish.* Hoskyns, 46, cites this as the third kind of division, dilemma, 'which proposeth two sides and overthrows both'.

14–15. [*behaviour ... unto it.* i.e. an outward disguise is not enough; in order to truly pass for a woman, Pyrocles needs to think and behave like a woman. This suggests that the first line of Pyrocles' song has alarmed Musidorus.]

18–19. *there is ... evil.* This is cited in *ODEP* under 'No man ever became thoroughly bad all at once'; Tilley, M316.

19. *grows either.* Cf. Shakespeare, *Othello*, I. iii. 319, 'Virtue? a fig! 'tis in ourselves that we are thus or thus'.

22–3. *fear ... wit.* Cf. Tilley, F135, 'Fear is one part of prudence'.

26. *right.* See p. lvi.

28. *idleness.* Cf. Ovid, *Remedio Amoris*, 142, 'Venus otia amat', and an abundance of parallels collected by Burton, *Anatomy of Melancholy*, 3. 2. 2. 1. For the puritan view of idleness, see L. B. Wright, *Middle-Class Culture in Elizabethan England* (Chapel Hill, 1935), 231 ff., 256. Cf. pp. 283, 36; 433, 20.

30–1. *companions ... yieldings.* Similar lists of these emotions which accompany sensual love are common; cf. Burton, *Anatomy of Melancholy*, 3. 2. 1. 2. Hoskyns, 31, cites this as an example of accumulation of matter 'tending to the same end'.

32–3. *pleasure ... after.* This old theme (cf. Ovid, *Heroides*, xix. 64, 'Quae fecisse juvat, facta referre pudet') is taken up by Shakespeare in sonnet 129. 5, 'Enjoy'd no sooner but despised straight'.

Page 61, 7. *kind of loves*. Abbott, 299, notes that 'two nouns together connected by "of" seem regarded as a compound noun with plural termination'.

10. *womanize*. The earliest citation in *OED* 1 is from 93.

11–12. *distaff-spinner*. See the note to p. 11, 21, and compare the similar ruse by young Achilles, disguised as a maiden and working with wool, in order to sleep with Deidamia in Bion, Idyl ii.

31–2. *born ... woman*. Cf. Tilley, W637, 'To be born of woman'.

33–4. [*unmanlike cruelty of mankind*. See the note to p. 204, 27–8.]

Page 62, 1–16. *framed ... lodging*. Robertson, 422, notes the imitation in *England's Parnassus*, no., 1754, 'Women be Framed with the same parts of the mind as we', 'And in her fairest lodging virtue rests'.

8–9. *kite ... hawk*. Cf. Tilley, K114, 'A carrion kite will never be a good hawk'. [For the inferiority of kites to other birds of prey see also the notes on pp. 77, 6–7 and 242, 26.]

14. *yourselves*. 'who oppose me'.

15–16. *it likes ... lodging*. In his letter to Robert Sidney of 18 October 1580 (*Works*, iii. 133), Sidney urged him to 'have care of your diet, and consequently of your complexion; remember, *gratior est veniens in pulchro corpore virtus*'; cf. C. G. Smith, *Spenser's Proverb Lore*, 819, citing Leonard Culman, *Sententiae Pueriles* (1685 edn.), *Gratior est pulchro veniens e corpore virtus*.

25–7. [*transported ... womankind*. The words 'transported' and 'it seemed him' hint that Musidorus' fears that his friend has indeed been 'transformed in mind' may not be entirely unfounded.]

Page 63, 4–5. *virtue ... book*. Cf. p. 102, 26–8 and note, and p. 369, 33.

18–19. *Much ... most*. Hoskyns, 17, cites this as an example of polyptoton, or traductio, with 'the same adjective in several comparisons'.

20–1. *disputations ... schools*. Cf. p. 423, 38.

37–**Page 64**, 2. *Enjoying ... nothing*. 'Enjoying' is synonymous with 'happiness', which in Aristotle, *Politics*, trans. H. Rackham (London, 1932), VII. xii. 3, 'is the complete activity and employment of virtue' (cf. *Ethics*, I. x. 15); Musidorus sees only the Epicurean interpretation, as in Dido's account of Pamphilus, p. 239, 4. Pyrocles uses this same argument against Basilius, p. 196, 8–9; cf. Burton, *Anatomy of Melancholy*, 3. 1. 1. 2 for a variety of opinions. See p. xxiii.

Page 64, 12–13. [*very white ... visage*. Musidorus' word choice implies that unlike Argalus' love, Pyrocles' is so superficial as to go no further than the skin: 'white and red' evokes Philoclea's complexion, 'visage' connotes her facial features, and 'painterly gloss' both compares the thin coat of paint to her skin and hints that the painting may reflect the skill of the painter rather than Philoclea's actual beauty. This is of course in contrast to the initial description of the painting, 'it seemed ... that the beauty of her bestowed new skill of the painter' (p. 11, 28–30).]

13. *painterly gloss*. 'the picture of Philoclea'.

16. *fading*. Cf. Tilley, B165, 'Beauty does fade like a flower'.

25. [*purge*. Cf. Pyrocles' comparing Musidorus to a physician in p. 64, 38.]

self. Cf. Abbott, 30, 'The use of "self" as a noun is common in Shakespeare'. [In practice, however, the absence of standardized spelling in early modern English meant that 'your self' was routinely conflated with the reflexive pronoun – as is illustrated by the fact that 90 uses the spelling 'your self' throughout this passage.]

34. *Alas*. Pyrocles' despair is similar to that experienced by Astrophil; Robertson, 423, compares *AS* 14 and 21.

37-8. *crow ... feathers*. Cf. Tilley, C851, 'The crow thinks her own bird whitest'. [Thomas Blague's *A Schole of Wise Conceytes* (1569) features a tale 'Of the Swan and the Crowe', in which the opposite happens: the jealous crow attempts to turn the swan's white feathers black, but the swan simply washes off the dirt.]

PAGE 65, 2. *friend*. Cf. AS 106. 12–14, 'he / That bad his friend, but then new maim'd, to be / Merry with him, and not think of his woe'.

11–12. *crossing his arms*. This posture is assumed by melancholy lovers; see pp. 124, 20; 283, 25; 348, 23.

12–13. *as if ... burthen*. See p. lvi.

21–2. [*manlike tears*. See the note to p. 204, 27–8.]

24. *strook*. 'struck'. [90 reads 'strooke' both here and on p. 87, 34.]

29. *shake ... friend*. Cf. Shakespeare, *Timon of Athens*, I. i. 100–1, 'I am not of that feather to shake off / My friend'. [See also the description of Amphialus' spaniel, p. 162, 22.]

33–4. [*unperfect ... perfect men*. Musidorus, finally able to see the humorous side of the situation, tries to defuse the tension by jokingly suggesting that as an 'unperfect' woman, Pyrocles should submit to Musidorus' male authority. This joke has the intended effect of making Pyrocles' grieved heart 'yiel[d] to some mirth' (p. 66, 4), which in turn prompts their reconciliation. Cf. Spenser, *Faerie Queene*, II. ix. 22 for a similar contrasting of masculine perfection and feminine imperfection.]

36. *evil*. 'malady'. [This is an example of the semantic overlap between 'ill' and 'evil' in early modern usage. Cf. also the notes to p. 64, 25 and p. 239, 32.]

PAGE 66, 20. *like as*. 'as'.

30–**PAGE 68**, 15. *pictures ... Amazon*. See p. xvii.

31. *much resembling*. See p. 57, 27 and note.

PAGE 67, 9–10. *architecture ... learning*. Pyrocles misses the symbolism entirely, as he does at p. 225, 30; see pp. 73, 14–19 and note.

21. *gnaw ... chain*. Cf. Chaucer, *Troilus and Criseyde*, in *Works*, ed. F. N. Robinson, 2nd edn. (Cambridge, Mass., 1961), i. 507–9:

> O fool, now artow in the snare,
> That whilom japedest at loves peyne.
> Now artow hent, now gnaw thin owen cheyne!

32–9. *to a heart ... friend*. Hoskyns, 40, cites this as an example of a double sententia with parison.

PAGE 68, 6. [*scape*. This is the only time Sidney uses the variant 'scape' in a prose passage of the *New Arcadia*. Typically, he favours 'escape' in verse as well, unless the metre requires one fewer syllable, as on p. 427, 27. Cf. also AS 12, 2 and AS 36, 14. Its use here is consequently surprising but could be explained as a compositor's choice caused by space constraints. Adding the 'e' to the line in 90 would either have left the compositor with only minimal spaces between words or forced him to move the word 'you' to a new line. Space constraints might also explain the use of 'scape' in one of the added chapter summaries (see p. 94, 8–9 (var.)).]

7. *Ithonia*. See p. liii.

27. *swearing ... Pallas*. Cf. Nashe, *The Unfortunate Traveller*, 'The Induction to the dapper Mounsier Pages of the Court', in *Works*, ed. R. B. McKerrow, 2nd edn., ed. F. P. Wilson (Oxford, 1966), ii. 207, 'whereas you were wont to swear men on a pantofle to be true to your puissant order'; iv. 256, the note comparing Massinger's

Unnatural Combat, III. ii. 107–8; and the examples in *OED* under *pantofle*. The irony is continued through Dametas' improbable association with Pallas or Minerva, goddess of wisdom, war, and all the liberal arts.

31–2. *Hercules ... head.* Robertson, 425, notes that Shakespeare similarly commented upon the disparity between the character of Hercules and the nature of the actor playing him, in *A Midsummer Night's Dream*, I. ii. 25 and in *Love's Labours Lost*, V. ii. 584.

34. [*Kalander's description.* Kalander intensely dislikes Dametas and earlier described him to Musidorus as a clown and a vain fool (see p. 13, 33–4 and p. 15, 6–10).]

PAGE 69, 1. *standing ... tiptoes.* This is the standard posture of pretension or haughtiness; cf. *OED* under *tiptoe* n. 1b. [Cf. also the ape 'uprearing' himself on his tiptoes to succeed at court in Edmund Spenser's *Mother Hubberds Tale* 663–4.]

7. *taking ... manner.* 'catching himself in a guilty act'; cf. Tilley, M633, 'To take one with the manner'.

14. [*combcase of Diana.* Dametas' oath is comical because of the incongruity of a goddess carrying a combcase, but also because he associates it with a hunting goddess, who is unlikely to spend a lot of time styling her hair.]

combcase. This is the earliest citation in *OED*; cf. Robertson, 32, 23, [but note that it also appears in Thomas North's translation of *The Morall Philosophie of Doni* (1570).]

21. *sword ... backward.* Cf. p. 333, 7–8.

22–3. *grace ... prayers.* By analogy Pyrocles' passion for Philoclea is compared with Latona's unquenched thirst when, by their excessive defiance, the rustics muddied the pond; but whereas Latona prayed that they forever inhabit that water, Dametas cannot so easily be got rid of. See Ovid, *Met.* vi. 313 ff.

34–5. *They ... thoughts.* This is cited in Tilley, A228.

36–8. *loneliness ... yourself.* Hoskyns, 38, cites this as an example of parison where 'the words match each other in rank ... verb to verb, adverb to adverb, substantive to substantive'.

PAGE 70, 15–16. *nest ... birds.* Cf. Tilley, B381, 'Such bird such nest'.

32. *Senicia.* Robertson, 425, compares the similar coinage in *Gynecia*.

32–3. *Penthesilea ... Pyrrhus.* The queen of the Amazons was killed before Troy by Achilles or by his son Neoptolemus or Pyrrhus. He was called *Pyrrhus* in Benoît de Sainte-Maure, *Roman de Troie*, battle xxiii; Guido delle Colonne, *Historia Trojana*, and in his successors; cf. Upton's note in Spenser, *Works*, ii. 218–19.

PAGE 71, 15. *as Dametas.* 'as Dametas is', an ellipsis. See p. xxxii.

16. *russet cloth.* This was a coarse, homespun woollen cloth of reddish-brown, grey, or neutral colour, worn by countryfolk.

21. *mountainets.* 'hillocks'. This is the earliest citation in *OED* (see Robertson, 37, 14), but *montagnette* was well established in French erotica – examples are in E. Huguet, *Dictionnaire de la langue française du seizième siècle* (Paris, 1925–67). [The compositors of the 1674 folio, who were perhaps unfamiliar with the word, changed this to 'Mountains', inadvertently making Pamela much chestier.]

22. [*the pleasant vale of Tempe.* The place in Thessalia where Musidorus and Pyrocles grew up (cf. p. 44, 13). Musidorus is prince of Thessalia, so the comparison indirectly signals that Pamela is intended for him.]

22–3. *diamond ... black horn.* The symbolism of this pendant implies steadfastness (see the note to p. 49, 5) and represents the diamond-like Pamela's setting among shepherds whose sheep provide horn for utensils.

23. *Yet still myself. Semper* or some variant upon this was a commonplace motto for imprese; see Henkel and Schöne, 1918.
30–1. *hair ... net.* Ringler, 465, compares *AS* 12. 2 where the image of larks attracted by mirrors into a day-net parallels Cupid's use of Stella's eyes and locks. Here Philoclea's beauty draws Pyrocles into an irresistable trap.
31–2. *Jupiter ... eagle.* Jupiter transformed himself into an eagle in order to snatch Ganymede (Ovid, *Met.* x. 155–61), seen by mythographers such as G. Sandys, *Met.*(1632), Tt4, as the elevation of 'a wise and understanding soul, uncontaminated with the vices of the flesh, and drawing nearest unto the nature of God'; cf. E. Panofsky, *Studies in Iconology* (New York, 1962), 213–17, and *AS* 13. 3–4. Pyrocles implies that Philoclea is more physically and spiritually elevated than Ganymede.
35–**PAGE 72**, 5 [*black eyes ... apples of her breast.* The physical attributes Pyrocles here singles out in his description of Philoclea – black eyes, perfect red and white complexion and apple-like breasts – are later echoed in his song (pp. 164, 1–168, 11).]
35. *black eyes.* See p. 164, 15 and note.
36–**PAGE 72**, 2. *nature ... beauty.* The same imagery is used in *AS* 7. 5–11.
PAGE 72, 3–4. *lilies ... cheeks.* Analogues to this commonplace are collected in Spenser, *Works*, v. 189.
5. *apples ... breast.* Some examples of earlier usage of this image are in Sannazaro, *Arcadia*, Prosa 4; Ariosto, *Orlando Furioso*, VII. xiv; and see E. Huguet, *Dictionnaire*, under *pommeler*, *pommelette*, *pommelu*, and *pommette*. [Cf. also p. 165, 23: 'Like pommels round of marble clear'.]
13. *prince.* 'royal personage'.
PAGE 73, 14–16. *lodge ... lodge.* M. Girouard, *Life in the English Country House* (New Haven, 1978), 108, cites this passage in his discussion of the emblematic architecture of lodges. [See also p. lxxiii.]
14–18. *star ... comet.* Although Henry Wotton in his 'Elements of Architecture' in *Reliquae Wottonianae* (1651), 304, condemns this design as an 'incommodious figure', between 1555 and 1557 the archduke Ferdinand of Tirol built a star-shaped lodge near Prague which Sidney could have seen in either 1575 or 1577; see V. Skretkowicz, 'Symbolic Architecture in Sidney's *New Arcadia*', *RES*, NS xxxiii (1982), 175–80, and above, p. xxi. Comets herald the death of princes; see p. xxv and cf. Shakespeare, *Julius Caesar*, II. ii. 30–1 and *1 Henry VI*, I. i. 1–5.
18–19. [*comet ... greatness.* Cf. John Blagrave, *The Mathematical Iewel* (1585), p. 62: 'it hath always been obserued of learned men, as namely, Apian and others, that the tayle of euery Comet extendeth it selfe directly from the Sunne'. In Pyrocles' version, the comet's tail points to a star of less greatness, partly because Dametas' lodge is of course smaller than the king's, but also to stress that the beauty of Philoclea, who is housed in the bigger, star-shaped lodge, exceeds that of the sun.]
25–34. *waterwork ... mill.* See R. Strong, *The Renaissance Garden in England* (London, 1979), 75 ff. and 132 ff., for descriptions of hydraulic effects including rainbows and singing birds; cf. Thomas Nashe, *The Unfortunate Traveller*, in *Works*, ed. R. B. McKerrow, 2nd edn., ed. F. P. Wilson (Oxford, 1966), ii. 282–4 and notes, including the Supplement.
PAGE 74, 15. [*having ... well played my first act.* Cf. p. 78, 22–3 and the notes to pp. 60, 3 and 119, 34.]
23–34. *first ... Gynecia also.* See p. xvii above.
30–1. [*a salad of wormwood.* The food analogy is consistent with the setting of this

scene during a banquet. While the main idea is of course that Basilius' attentions are unwelcome to Pyrocles, wormwood was believed to comfort the stomach and procure an appetite, so the implication is that Basilius is unwittingly heightening Pyrocles' passion for Philoclea. Cf. Tobias Venner, *Via Recta ad Vitam Longam* (1620), pp. 165-6:

> Wherefore in regard of the great commoditie that Wormewood bringeth to the stomacke and liuer that are weake and oppressed through the redundancie of choler or melancholy, I aduise all those in whom those humors exceede their limits, to eat oftentimes the young and tender tops, or leaues of Wormwood in sallads with other hearbes; but specially to drinke mornings fasting, and sometimes also before meales a draught of Wormewood wine, or Beere.]

PAGE 75, 8. *busy ... bee.* This is cited in Tilley, B202.
10. [*carried ... violent love.* An example of catachresis. Sidney here combines the expression 'to be carried with', meaning to be rapt with violent – generally negative – emotions, such as hatred or rage, with an image of Gynecia being more literally carried away as on a bier or litter (probably with an intentional pun on 'beer' and intoxication). In 90, the two references to biers are spelt 'beere' (p. 3, 22) and 'beer' (p. 255, 35) respectively. From 1655 onwards, *Arcadia* editions change the spelling of Musidorus' 'beere' – the most unambiguous of the three – to 'Bier', but leave the other two as 'beer', possibly an indication that the compositors preferred to err on the side of caution and so left the spellings unmodernized. For examples of the word 'bier' in a non-funereal context, see *OED* 1.]
11. *runs thorough.* The earliest citation in *OED* under *run* v. 31c *fig* ('stab or pierce'). is from Shakespeare, *Romeo and Juliet*, II. iv. 14.
12. *unevitable.* 'whom one could not avoid'; cf. *unresistable* at pp. 127, 32; 232, 20; 279, 28. [See also 309, 4.]
22-3. [*my tragedy ... indeed prove a tragedy.* Cf. the notes to pp. 60, 3; 74, 15 and 119, 34.]
24. *full point ... sigh.* Cf. *AS* 54. 4, 'Nor give each speech a full point of a groan'.
33. *as that.* 'except that'.

PAGE 76, 11-12. [*no ... my name.* This marks the near-complete transformation of Pyrocles into Zelmane. Although it features prominently in Musidorus' account of their lives, the name 'Pyrocles' otherwise all but disappears from the text after this point. It is next mentioned in p. 92, 4, when Musidorus recalls his thoughts, and in p. 107, 26 and 30, when Zelmane begins to soliloquize. Later, finding that Amphialus does not take her seriously as an adversary, Zelmane tells him her 'near kinsman' Pyrocles will fight with him on her behalf (p. 170, 10-12), which is the last mention of Pyrocles' name outside narrative accounts of his past accomplishments until he dramatically reveals his true identity to Philoclea in p. 199, 36-7.]
14. *coast was clear.* Cf. Tilley, C469, 'The coast is clear', and see p. 254, 30-1.
18. *spurred ... short-reined.* Analogues to this comparison of man to a horse ruled by emotions are in Ringler, notes to *AS* 49 and 98. [Cf. p. 41, 16 and p. 193, 16-17. *A Sanctuarie for a Troubled Soule*, p. 137 borrows this image:

> O, if [the soul] had but a smal time more of amendment, how seriously would it conuerte? what a sharpe and seuere course would it set into? but it is like vnto a horse, desirous to runne, & miserably spurred, but soe short reined that hee cannot stirre.]

19–22. *Zelmane ... four parts*. For the pursuit of one ill-suited lover after another, see Moschus, Idyl vi; Virgil, *Eclogues*, ii. 63–5; Horace, *Odes*, I. xxxiii; and Montemayor, 52 (Yong, 42):

> If Ismenia went by chance to the field, Alanius went after her; if Montanus went to his flocks, Ismenia after him; if I went to the hills with my sheep, Montanus after me; if I knew that Alanius was in the wood, ... thither I hied me after him. And it was the strangest thing in the world to hear how Alanius sighing said, 'Ah my Ismenia', and how Ismenia said, 'Ah my Montanus', and how Montanus said, 'Ah my Selvagia', and how Selvagia said, 'Ah my Alanius'.

27–9. *time ... desires*. Hoskyns, 46, cites this as an example of prosapodosis, the second part of division that 'overthroweth no part ... but returneth some reason to each member'.

PAGE 77, 3. *seeled*. 'whose eyes had been stitched up'. This is the earliest citation for the participial form in *seel* v. 2 in *OED*; see p. 287, 39 and *CS* 15.

5–7. *who ... made*. See p. lv.

6–7. [*thinking ... dangerous*. The 'recreation' consists of the irony that the injured kite is killed by her fellow kites' attempts to take her supposed prey from her. Kites were believed to frequently feed on carrion, particularly animal guts, and were often negatively connoted (applied to a person, 'kite' means 'parasite').]

8. *recreations*. Falconry and angling in Elizabethan times are examined in *Shakespeare's England*, ed. C. T. Onions (Oxford, 1916), ii. 351–75.

14–**PAGE 89**, 7. *Phalantus ... concluded*. G. Kipling, *The Triumph of Honour* (Leiden, 1977), 116–36, discusses this episode in its historical context, describing similar tournaments in fifteenth-century Burgundy where they were accompanied by narratives, and in early sixteenth-century England. O'Connor, 195, compares *Amadis de Gaule*, VII. lvi, the defence of the beauty of Onorie by Birmartes.

17. *proof ... affirm*. These are parts of an oration.

31–2. *his own good*. See p. lvi.

32. *Man-of-Arms*. 'man-at-arms', especially a heavily armed, mounted soldier; cf. *AS* 41. 9–11, 'Others ... Think nature me a man-of-arms did make'.

38. *unpersuadable*. 'not removable by persuasion'. This is the only citation in *OED* 1. [The definition was consequently tailored to Sidney's usage.]

PAGE 78, 2. *durst and knew*. In *A Defence of Poetry* (*Misc. Prose*, 83, 2), Sidney stated the purpose of knowledge to be 'well-doing and not of well-knowing only'. How this was to be achieved was described in his comment upon this passage by Robert Dallington, *The View of France* (1604), S3, where he says that Sidney's *durst and knew* 'well symbolizeth ... all requisite virtues in a gentleman: for if he have not valour to dare, and wisdom to know how and when, he wanteth one of the principal supporters of his honour'; see F. P. Wilson, *Elizabethan and Jacobean* (Oxford, 1945), 51–2, 137, cited in W. Milgate, ed., John Donne, *The Satires, Epigrams, and Verse Letters*, 270, comparing 'To the Countess of Bedford', 33, 'And *virtue's* whole *sum* is but *know* and *dare*', and compare the examples of the formula *sapientia et fortitudo* in E. R. Curtius, *European Literature and the Latin Middle Ages*, trans. W. R. Trask (London, 1979), 174–9, citing Shakespeare, *Macbeth*, III. i. 50–3, ' 'tis much he dares; ... He hath a wisdom that doth guide his valour / To act in safety'.

13. *companions*. 'fellows'; a term of contempt.

16. *lean*. 'incline in affection'.

18–19. *pay … money*. Cf. Tilley, C507, 'To pay one in his own coin'; cited in C. G. Smith, *Spenser's Proverb Lore*, 601.
21. *little … by*. 'having little esteem for'.
25. *who having*. 'Cecropia having', *who* being the redundant supplementary pronoun inserted to bridge the syntactical gap caused by completion of the preceding parallel construction in 'had bent her … had confirmed her'; cf. Abbott, 170.
[*having … charge*. While Amphialus spent his formative years with Timotheus and Philoxenus, which positively affected his education and his character (cf. p. 52, 1–9), Artesia was principally raised by Cecropia, who was a bad influence on her.]

PAGE 79, 11. *tongue-delight*. Cf. p. 89, 12, 'mouth-love'.
12. *not … mislike*. Hoskyns, 35, cites this as an example of diminution 'by denying the contrary'.
16–17. *Mercury … Venus*. See p. xxvi.
18–19. *accusing … or no*. Hoskyns, 11, cites this as an example of catachresis.
19. *sped*. 'succeeded'.
20–1. *foolish … thinks*. Hoskyns, 40, cites this as an example of sententia with synoeciosis.

PAGE 80, 3. *wives*. 'wife's'. This is the obsolete genitive singular form; cf. pp. 107, 3; 192, 23; 351, 29.
20. [*a blunt lance*. Here used to signify old age. Cf. Thomas North's 1568 translation of Antonio de Guevara's *The Diall of Princes*, 86:

> What is this (my lord) now that the wall is decayed ready to fall, the flower is withered, the grape dooth rotte, the teeth are loose, the gown is worn, the launce is blunt the knife is dull, and doost thou desire to return into the world, as if thou hadst neuer knowen the world?

The double entendre in Basilius' claim that Zelmane's eyes can 'sharpen a blunt lance' is probably meant to be read as unintentional (if comically Freudian) rather than as openly suggestive. Cf. his mortification when Zelmane challenges him about his use of 'enjoy' on p. 196, 3–9.]
21–2. *grey … care*. Cf. Tilley, C82, 'Care brings gray hair'. [Here used by Basilius to play down his age – cf. his use of 'only'.]
28–**PAGE 84**, 10. *tree … shield*. This was the traditional ritual of the Tree of Chivalry, of which the history is summarized by G. Kipling, *The Triumph of Honour* (Leiden, 1977), 117 ff. Kipling, 130, notes that the sequence of action here follows the precedent established by the Marquis of Dorset in 1501: after the shield is hung on the tree, Artesia enters, followed by Phalantus 'behind the chariot in the champion's position, just as Dorset had. After delivering the lady to a tent, … Phalantus takes his place in the lists, waiting'.
30–1. *impresa … stars*. See p. xxvi, and the resemblances with Sidney's starred imprese noted in K. Duncan-Jones, 'Sidney's Personal *Imprese*', *JWCI* xxxiii (1970), 322.
33. *next after*. 'immediately following'.
carnation. This is the colour of desire; see p. xxii and p. 318, 19 and note. [The association may be etymological: 'carnation' is 'the colour of flesh'. See *OED, carnation* n.², 1: '(a) The colour of human "flesh" or skin; flesh-colour. *Obsolete*. (b) A light rosy pink, but sometimes used for a deeper crimson colour as in the carnation flower'.]
34–5. *four … horses*. George Sandys describes them in Ovid, *Met.* (1632), E2ᵛ (i.e., F2ᵛ), embellishing ii. 454–5 as 'hot Pyröus, / Light / Æthon, fiery Phlegon, bright Eöus'; see the note to p. 324, 25–6.

36. *borrowed... Phoebus.* Artesia is portrayed as Phaeton, the example of the presumptuous seeker of advancement who brings destruction on himself; cf. E. Panofsky, *Studies in Iconology* (New York, 1962), 219 and notes, and see above, p. xxvi.

PAGE 81, 8–9. [*time had not yet... store thereof.* The referent of 'thereof' is grammatically unclear – most likely, the word is being used in the sense of 'for that reason'. The phrase appears to mean that Andromana's inferior looks cannot be blamed on her age, because her defects consist either of attributes independent of age (her small eyes) or of attributes that have not yet been affected by age (her exceeding red hair).]
14. *liketh.* 'pleases'. [Cf. p. 62, 15.]
31. *symmetrians.* 'advocates of symmetry'. This is the earliest citation in OED.

PAGE 82, 9. *more pity.* 'more one would be sorry'. [Cf. the phrase 'the more's the pity'.]
14. *conquered... conquered.* See p. xxviii.
19. *fast and loose.* This is an old cheating game involving the false intertwining of two objects; see the examples in OED a.
36. [*she might have sit.* 'sit' used as the past participle is a (rare) sixteenth-century variant.]

PAGE 83, 2. *great-mindedness... humbleness.* Cf. Tilley, N195, 'The more noble the more humble'.
8. *carelessness... artificial.* See p. 58, 8.
19. *their coupled.* See p. lv.
24. *bottle.* 'leather flask'.
But with. 'But in the midst of'.
30–1. *Zelmane... resembling.* See p. 57, 28 and note.
31. [*with more marking.* 'on closer inspection'.]

PAGE 84, 15–16. *waving... fishes.* See p. xxvi.
21. *juniper... sweet.* Seeds of juniper were burned to sweeten the air, and the coals reputed to glow for a year; see the examples in OED 1, and cf. OA 13. 120, 'Sweet juniper saith this, "Though I burn, yet I burn in a sweet fire"'.
33. [*discomforted... discomfited.* See p. lxxxii.]

PAGE 85, 3–4. [*brown... sun's familiarity.* Cf. p. 272, 5–6.]
5–6. *doth not... account.* 'does not, in the manner of men (who deal carelessly with things of little value)'. ['slubber up' means 'make a mess of'. Cf. p. 9, 9.]
10. *heart... well.* Cf. Tilley, N299, 'Nothing is impossible to a willing heart'.

PAGE 86, 6–7. *sepia... escape.* As the sepia could be recognized by its inky disguise, so Phebilus' love was known 'because he denied it'. On the emblem, see Henkel and Schöne, 702–4, and cf. Camerarius, *Symbolorum et Emblematum*, IV. xlvii. [Cf. also the contrast to Phalantus' caparison whose fish remain trapped (p. 84, 15–18).]
25. *night... sleep.* This periphrasis for 'the length of the night seemed shortened by sleeping through it' was based on the term for an unfair measure of length. The English ell was 45 inches; the *short ell* something less. This is the earliest citation in OED ell n¹ 2a; ODEP cites this under 'Measure with the long (short) ell'.
33–5. *gilt... rivers.* Cf. Queen Helen's hair, p. 82, 16–19.
35–6. *picture... ermion.* Iconographical analogues are the 'Ermine' portrait of Elizabeth I, which R. Strong, *The Cult of Elizabeth* (London, 1977), 149, suggests may have been influenced by Sidney's description as early as 1585; and Leonardo da Vinci's 'Lady with an Ermine'. This use of the ermine as an emblem of chastity depends

upon Petrarch's *Trionfo della Morte*, 19–21, where on the green banner was a white ermine with a collar of refined gold and topaz. In the same manner, then, that Elizabeth was associated through this emblem with Laura, as argued by F. A. Yates, *Astraea* (London, 1975), 114, 215–16, so is Queen Helen, and as such she becomes the unidentified Mira of Amphialus' dream in Book III. See p. xxiii.

36. *Rather ... spotted.* The emblem from which Sidney drew Clitophon's motto is an ermine surrounded by dung with the motto 'Malo mori quam foedari', from P. Giovio, *Dialogo dell'Imprese*. It was included in the manuscript given to Sidney by Abraham Fraunce, 'Emblemata Varia', Bodleian Library MS Rawl. D. 345, f. 56; in Camerarius, *Symbolorum et Emblematum*, II. lxxxi; and in Samuel Daniel's translation of Giovio, *The Worthy Tract* (1585), C4ᵛ–C5, where the explanation is given: 'being the proper nature of the *Armelui* rather to perish by hunger and thirst than, by escaping through the mire, to defile herself, and spot the polished white of her precious skin'. See Henkel and Schöne, 465. The image recurs on pp. 167, 15; 412, 14 and in AS 86. 5.

38. *terms of affection.* Clitophon was soon to be married; see p. xlviii.

PAGE 87, 6. *upon the head.* In 1466, John Tiptoft, Earl of Worcester, formulated the rules for assessing a knight's score in the tilt, either by the number of lances shattered upon an opponent (one staff broken on the head being equal to two broken on the body) or by attaints (lances not shattered, but which hit a legitimate target); see S. Anglo, 'Archives of the English Tournament: Score Cheques and Lists', *Journal of the Society of Archivists*, ii (1956), 155–6. See p. 221, 16–17.

15. *rusty.* Rapidly rusting armour was a perpetual problem; see Viscount Dillon, 'Armour Notes', *The Archaeological Journal*, lx (2nd ser. x) (1903), 118.

24. [*Ill-appointed Knight.* This is *appointed* 3 in the OED: 'provided with requisites, fitted out, equipped'. Although he is introduced as 'ill-appointed', the knight is most frequently referred to as 'ill-apparelled' (the chapter summary also has the additional variants 'ill-arrayed' and 'ill-furnished'). While all adjectives may mean 'badly equipped', their emphasis is subtly different. Collectively, they express the idea that the knight is both shabby-looking and inadequately furnished. See also p. xxviii]

32. *matachin dance.* This was a sword dance, often performed by three in a feigned battle. See p. 132, 27.

33. *had adversaries.* See p. lvi.

PAGE 88, 14. *Aesculapius.* He was god of medicine.

24–6. *sun... clouded.* Cf. p. 162, 35.

36. *broken girths.* This was not uncommon; see the triumph of 'Gereint son of Erbin', in *The Mabinogion*, trans. G. Jones and T. Jones (London, 1977), 273.

38–9. *disgrace ... known.* See p. xxvi.

PAGE 89, 30. *all ... thinking.* This is the noun absolute with the participle (Abbott, 275), compounded with *besides love*, where the infinitive *love* is used without *to* as the equivalent of the participle *loving* (Abbott, 248–50): 'all, besides loving, thinking'.

PAGE 90, 13–22. Ringler, *OA* 4, and 385; Robertson, 40, 3 ff. Substantive texts are *OA* (*ex. Je*), *Cm*, 90, 93; published in *England's Helicon* from a copy of 98 (Ringler, 564); and the second stanza set to music for five voices by Francis Pilkington, *The Second Set of Madrigals and Pastorals* (1624), no. 14, taken from a printed edition; cf. the edn. by E. H. Fellowes, in *The English Madrigal School*, xxvi (1923), and in id., *English Madrigal Verse*, 3rd edn., rev. by F. W. Sternfeld and D. Greer (1967), 197.

18. *Menalcas'*. The clothes were accustomed to the voice of their owner, Menalcas; see p. 93, 11.
31–2. *all ... experience*. This is cited in Tilley, A135, and in C. G. Smith, *Spenser's Proverb Lore*, 226. [This is the earliest example of 'lip-wisdom' in *OED*, though there are earlier examples, such as Thomas Rogers' 1580 translation of Thomas à Kempis' *Of the Imitation of Christ*, where it is used twice in the preface (B1ᵛ)]
34–5. *Beasts ... beauty*. Cf. p. 308, 24–6 and *A Defence of Poetry* (*Misc. Prose*, 104), 'only man, and no beast, hath that gift to discern beauty'.

PAGE 91, 13. *take ... earnest*. Cf. Tilley, J46, 'Leave jesting while it pleases lest it turn to earnest'; cited in C. G. Smith, *Spenser's Proverb Lore*, 201. [Cf. also Spenser, *Faerie Queene*, II. i. 31, where the image is reversed.]
23. *in right*. 'as her prerogative'.

PAGE 92, 4. [*O sweet Pyrocles*. See the note to p. 76, 11–12.]
18. *exaltation*. This was the position of the planet in the zodiac in which it was supposed to exert its greatest influence.
23–4. *love ... tyrant*. Hoskyns, 40, cites this as an example of sententia with parison and contentio.
24–5. *shaked ... into it*. Cf. Montaigne, *Essays*, I. xxxviii, trans. Florio (London, 1910), i. 253: 'you settle an evil in removing the same; as stakes or poles, the more they are stirred and shaken, the faster they stick, and sink deeper into the ground'; and *AS* song xi. 33–5, 'the more fools it [love] do shake, ... / Deeper still they drive the stake'.

PAGE 94, 11. *forest-bill*. This is much heavier weaponry than the mere hedging-bill he used to carry; cf. p. 68, 26–7.
32. *golden eloquence*. Cf. Tilley, G285a, 'Gold speaks'. [Sidney may have recalled the phrase from John Foxe's *Actes and Monuments* (1583), where it is used as a euphemism for bribery on p. 285.]

PAGE 95, 17. *pibble-stones*. 'pebbles'.
35. *hand ... book*. This is one of the methods listed in G. K. Hunter, 'The Marking of *Sententiae* in Elizabethan Printed Plays, Poems, and Romances', *The Library*, 5th Ser. vi (1951), 171–88. In 90 inverted commas were printed in the margin. [For a discussion of the inverted commas, see pp. lxv–lxvi. Typically, manicules were used by readers to draw attention to the words of others. Pyrocles here self-importantly inverts the idea by using someone else's hand to mark his own words.]

PAGE 96, 1. [*she-bear ... little less fierceness*. i.e. the lion is the fiercer of the two, though not by much. See the note to p. 98, 19.]
7. *but that*. 'than'. This is among the earliest citations in *OED* 10f (the earliest is from 1449).
22. *Arethusa ... Alpheus*. A. B. Taylor, 'A Note on Ovid in *Arcadia*', *N & Q*, NS xvi (1969), 455, noted the discrepancy between Arethusa and Alpheus in Ovid, *Met*. v. 603–5 and this description which is borrowed from Daphne's flight from Apollo in *Met*. i. 527–30. See p. xxxiii.
34. *she ... run*. 'she had no desire but to run'.

PAGE 97, 5. *unnatural ... blood*. See the analogues in A. R. Humphreys, ed., Shakespeare, *1 Henry IV* (London, 1978), II. iv. 267–8, 'the lion will not touch the true prince', citing E. Kölbing, 'Zu Shakespeare's King Henry IV', *Englische Studien*, xvi (1892), 454–9, for the tradition from Pliny, and adding *Mirror For Magistrates*, 'Lord

Hastings', 282–3; *Palmerin d'Oliva*, trans. Munday, II. v; Topsell, *History of Four-Footed Beasts* (1658 edn.), 370. Examples as in Spenser, *Works*, i. 396–8, do not distinguish between the lion's gratitude to a benefactor, his recognition of and obedience to a virgin, and his care for those of royal blood.

6. *her*. See p. lv.
21. [*surgery*. The outward treatment of wounds (as opposed to physic, which involved healing through treatments that typically had to be taken internally).]
32. *courage*. 'haughtiness', 'pride'; cf. Spenser, *Faerie Queene*, III. x. 30, Braggadochio's 'great courage', and p. lv.

PAGE 98, 1–12. Ringler, *OA* 5, and 385; Robertson, 51, 9 ff. Texts with substantive variants are *OA (ex. Le)*, *Cm*, 90, 93. See p. xxvi.
1–6. Ringler, 567, notes that Thomas Ravenscroft set these lines as a round for six voices in *Pammelia. Music's Miscellany* (1609), no. 95. This was transcribed by David Melvill in 1612 in *The Melvill Book of Roundels*, ed. G. Bantock and H. O. Anderton (London, 1916). See J. P. Cutts, 'Dametas' Song in Sidney's *Arcadia*', *Renaissance News*, xi (1958), 183–8, and E. H. Fellowes, *English Madrigal Verse*, 3rd edn., rev. by F. W. Sternfeld and D. Greer (Oxford, 1967), 218.
4. *bloody*. See p. li.
19. [*fearing belike ... present*. The text emphasizes that the lion is the stronger of the two beasts – which is why Pyrocles fights the lion and Musidorus the she-bear. See the note to p. 96, 1.]
21. *not guilty of*. Hoskyns, II, adapts this in an example of catachresis.
35. [*fell ... on my face*. Versions of this widely held belief (derived from one of Aesop's fables) can be found in a number of early modern texts, including Thomas Blague's *A Schole of Wise Conceytes* (1569), 232–4: 'Of a Currier and a Hunter' (in which an injured hunter escapes by playing dead, 'knowing the nature of the beast to bee, to take pitie of a carcase'); Lodowick Lloyd's *Pilgrimage of Princes* (1573) fol. 130: 'Examples of friendshippe' (in which a man abandoned by a disloyal friend during a bear-attack survives by playing dead, 'for it is sayde that the Lion or the Beare will spare their yeelded praies, and specially the Beare, if a man hold hys breth as though he were deade'); and Austin Saker's *Narbonus* (1580), 71: 'The Lion will deuoure no dead thing, nor the foule Beare touch a man lying on the Earth.' Cf. also the emblem 'In Amicos falsos' in Henry Peacham's *Minerua Britanna*, 148.]
24. *But this ... knife*. See p. lv–lvi.
30. [*ill-weaponed*. 'inadequately armed'. Cf. 'Ill-appointed Knight' (p. 87, 24).]
32–3. *manner ... feet*. An engraving by Cornelius Galle in Johannes Stradanus, *Venationes Ferarium, Avium, Piscium* (Antwerp, 1556), no. 26, shows these three steps in killing a bear; see G. Gascoigne, *The Noble Art of Venery*, published as *Turberville's Book of Hunting, 1576* (Oxford, 1908), 218.

PAGE 99, 5. *discern*. See p. lv.
14–15. *Dametas ... bush*. Robertson, 427, compares this posture with that of cowards in Ariosto, *Orlando Furioso*, II. iii. 34, and Spenser, *Faerie Queene*, II. iii. 21; see also Shakespeare, *A Midsummer Night's Dream*, III. ii. 405–6, 'coward, art thou fled? Speak! In some bush? Where dost thou hide thy head?'
16–17. *kind ... himself*. Cf. Tilley, P372, 'He that pities another remembers himself'.
34–5. *Pallas ... Gorgon*. In comparing Zelmane with Pallas Athena, who carried the head of Medusa which turned to stone whoever looked at it (Homer, *Iliad*, v. 733–43), Basilius reveals his total submission to her.

35-6. *Hercules ... lion*. This was the first labour of Hercules; see p. 23, 37-8 and note. [Just as Basilius' choice of analogy reveals his infatuation, Gynecia's reveals her growing suspicion that Zelmane is a young man in disguise. Cf. p. 103, 12-13.]

PAGE 100, 22. *to fall ... own*. 'to come into than he already had'.
33. *seeming*. Clinias' deception is indicated.

PAGE 101, 13. *good man*. 'simple, trusting man'.

THE SECOND BOOK

PAGE 102, 11. *eyes ... judgement*. See p. 11, 19 and note.
13-14. [*long-exercised virtue ... deformity*. Kalander's assessment of Gynecia's character (p. 12, 38-41) had hinted at misapplied virtues.]
15. *was a mortal*. See p. li.
19-**PAGE 103**, 1. *O sun ... proportion*. Hoskyns, 33, cites this as an example of exclamation.
20-1. [*unspotted light*. Recalling 'most unspotted chastity' (p. 12, 39).]
26-8. *virtue ... thing*. Cf. Horace, *Epistles*, I. xvii. 41, 'virtus nomen inane est', translated by Thomas Drant, *Horace's Art of Poetry, Pistles, and Satires Englished* (1567), 'But if that virtue be a thing and not an idle name'; cf. *A Defence of Poetry* (*Misc. Prose*, 93, 7), 'men who think virtue a school name'; Robertson, 322, 10, 'virtue, he counted it but a school name'; and *AS* 4. Cf. pp. 63, 5; 369, 33.

PAGE 103, 5-9. [*For nothing else ... womankind*. See pp. lxxviii-lxxix.]
10-11. *though ... shames*. Hoskyns, 29, cites this as an example of hyperbole.
18. *bereave thee of* See Robertson's note on this crux, 437.
birth. 'offspring'.
19. [*In shame ... shame*. Glossed as a sententia in 90. Fraunce G7ᵛ-G8 cites the *OA* equivalent of lines 9-19 as an example of addubitation.]
23-4. [*lamentable ... woeful mind*. Glossed as a sententia through inverted commas in 90 and cited on Cc8 of Nicholas Ling's *Politeuphuia*, in the section headed 'Of Dauncing'.]
24. *near away*. 'a short distance away'.
24-5. *companion ... misery*. Cf. Tilley, C571, 'It is good to have company in misery'.
32-**PAGE 104**, 10. Ringler, *OA* 14; Robertson, 93, 3 ff. Substantive texts are *OA*, *Cm*, 90, 93. Texts with non-substantive variants are in British Library MS Add. 34064, f. 29, and in Bodleian Library printed book 27980. e. 86, p. viii, a manuscript copy noted in M. Crum, *First-line Index* (Oxford, 1969), I1619; see Ringler, 555.

PAGE 104, 1 & 3. [*burned / turned*. In 90 and 93, the spellings 'burnd' and 'turnd' indicate monosyllabic pronunciation. From 98, the more common spellings 'burn'd' and 'turn'd' are used.]
22. *of; and alas*. See p. lv.
30. *indicted*. 'accused'.

PAGE 105, 18. *came*. This is an example of confusion by proximity (Abbot, 299) where the verb agrees with its preceding noun *guest* rather than with its subject in the second person.

33–Page 106, 10. Ringler, *OA* 15, and 395; Robertson, 95, 15 ff. Texts with substantive variants are *OA*, *Ha*, *Cm*, *90*, *93*. Non-substantive variants are in British Library MS Add. 34064, f. 28 (Ringler, 555), and Bodleian Library MS Rawl. Poet. 172, f. 6 (Ringler, 558). Two imitations are in the former Rosenbach MS 197, p. 81 (Ringler, 560) and in Ford's *Love's Sacrifice*, II. i (Robertson, 437).

34. [*heav'nly*. See the note to p. 14, 19.]

35–6. [*Old wood... virtue spend*. In an example of poetic commonplacing, *Quaternio* (1633) by Thomas Nash – not identical to the author of *Pierce Penilesse* – splices these lines with lines from Thomas Churchyard's 'A Discourse of an Old Souldiour and a Young' to create a composite poem attributed to Epicharmus (p. 137).]

35. *Old wood... fire*. Cf. Tilley, W740, 'Old wood best to burn...'; cited in *ODEP* and in C. G. Smith, *Spenser's Proverb Lore*, 875.

Page 106, 4. *homage*. See p. lv.

5. *Old... wise*. Cf. Tilley, O37, 'Older and wiser'; cited in C. G. Smith, *Spenser's Proverb Lore*, 9.

8. *orecome*. 'overcome'. [The spelling 'ore' for monosyllabic 'over' is common in early printed books, perhaps because compositors found it quicker to set than 'o'er'.]

12. [*sometimes fetching a little skip*. Cf *fetch* v. 9a in *OED*: 'to make or perform (a movement); to take (a walk, run, leap, etc.)'.]

24. [*brought to an exigent*. 'in an extremely difficult position'.]

36–7. *wait... passion*. 'attend upon passion's victory procession'.

Page 107, 3. *wives*. 'wife's'; see p. 80, 3 and note.

4. *knees*. See p. 195, 24 and p. xxii.

26. [*poor Pyrocles!*. See the note to p. 76, 11–12.]

Page 108, 3. *alone... company*. Cf. Tilley, C571, 'It is good to have company in trouble'.

4–5. *changing... objects*. Cf. Tilley, P374, 'One may change place but not change the grief', and Robertson, 41, 13–14, 'hoping... that the change of places might ease his grief' and the parallel in the *Defence of the Earl of Leicester* (*Misc. Prose*, 133, 12–13).

7. *eyes... judges*. See p. 11, 19 and note.

8–9. *shoulders of friendship*. Hoskyns, 9, cites this as an example of a metaphor which is 'too base'.

11–12. *laurel... cypress*. This mixture of triumph and mourning may symbolize Musidorus' predicament, or may indicate his resolve to 'win or die', as does the more traditional combination of palm and cypress in Camerarius, *Symbolorum et Emblematum*, I. xxiii. Cf. Fraunce's emblem in Bodleian Library MS Rawl. D. 345, f. 46; Daniel's translation of Giovio, *The Worthy Tract*, D6; Henkel and Schöne, 201. See pp. 162, 11; 342, 34 and notes.

24. *unfeatly... clerks*. Cf. Tilley, C409, 'The greatest clerks are not the wisest men'. In *unfeatly* Dametas uses the adverb meaning 'unfitly', 'unaptly' as an adjective. The passage is cited in *OED* under the proper adjectival usage *unfeaty* introduced in *93*. [In a letter to Walsingham dated 14 December 1585, Sidney jokingly (and perhaps unfairly) referred to Leicester's assistant Bartholomew Clerke as one of 'those great clerkes that are not alwaies the wisest' (MS Harleian 285, 164; a full transcription of the letter can be found in Roger Kuin (ed.), *The Correspondence of Sir Philip Sidney*, vol. II (Oxford, 2012), pp. 1143–6).]

Page 109, 1. *palm... loving*. See note to p. 324, 24.

25–7. [*scholar... ignorant*. *A Sanctuarie for a Troubled Soule*, p. 161 borrows this image: 'Gracious God, I haue noe goodnesse in my selfe, but onely to finde that I haue no

COMMENTARY

goodnesse like a scholler, who is come to that degree of knowledge, to knowe him selfe vtterly ignorante'.]

34–5. [*unlikely ... beauty*. While the main meaning of 'unlikely' here is 'disagreeable', there is also an undertone of 'inappropriate', reminding readers that it is not proper of Mopsa to envy Pamela, who is her superior in rank as well as beauty.]

PAGE 110, 1. *palm*. See note to p. 324, 24.

3–4. *testify his love*. Cf. p. 132, 27.

17–18. *nothing ... attempted*. Cf. Tilley, N320, 'Nothing venture nothing win'; cited in C. G. Smith, *Spenser's Proverb Lore*, 797.

27. *place of my memory*. 'the subject of my thoughts'. [Musidorus describes his mental substitution of Mopsa for Pamela by borrowing vocabulary typically used to describe the art of memorizing through 'places' (which need to remain the same to be more readily accessible) and 'images' (which may be substituted).]

35–6. *overthrow ... overthrow*. Hoskyns, 14, cites this as an example of epanalepsis, where a sentence has the same beginning and ending.

PAGE 111, 9. *cuckoo ... nightingale*. There is a contrast of their virtues implied, as in Spenser, *Works*, iii. 185, Raleigh's commendatory verse to the *Faerie Queene*, 'The praise of meaner wits this work like profit brings, / As doth the cuckoo's song delight when Philomela sings'.

11. *cloudy fancies*. 'sullen appearances'.

12–21. Ringler, *OA* 16, and 395; Robertson, 99, 21 ff. Texts with substantive variants are *OA, Cm,* 90, 93. Non-substantive texts are in British Library MS Add. 34064, f. 28 (Ringler, 555) and in Bodleian Library MS Eng. Poet. e. 14, f. 9, recorded in M. Crum, *First-line Index* (Oxford, 1969), S602.

PAGE 112, 9. [*wagging her lips*. Typically the expression implies (incoherent) speech, but here it appears to mean that Mopsa is opening and closing her mouth like a fish to express her surprise in a characteristically unrefined manner.]

15–16. *you blame ... fortune*. Cf. Tilley, A231, 'What cannot be altered must be borne not blamed'; cited in C. G. Smith, *Spenser's Proverb Lore*, 4. [Cf. p. 26, 15.]

24. *patronage. patrociny Bo, As, Je, Qu* is a synonym for 'patronage'; *patrony St, Cl* and *pattern Le* confuse spellings used for both 'patron' and 'pattern'; *patrimony Da* is an error; cf. p. 58, 9.

PAGE 113, 1. *as where*. 'as if where'. By reading *such ... as* as a comparative, the scribes of *Cl, Da* and the editor or compositor of 90 felt it necessary to supply an infinitive. Cf. p. 327, 2–5 and note; Robertson, p. xlvii and note; and *OED* under *as* B 1b.

14. *by my hallidame*. This is a dialectal form of the common oath, 'by my halidom' (holiness).

14–15. *throwing ... upon*. 'looking amorously at'. [The expression (chosen by Musidorus as a particularly apt description of an amorous shepherdess) was proverbial and the topic of epigram 99 of John Heywood's *Two Hundred Epigrammes* (1555).]

27–8. *I ... love*. Robertson, 437, compares *AS* 61. 14, 'That I love not, without I leave to love'.

30. *best part ... life*. 'the soul within my living being'.

31. *making ... passage*. 'dying'.

PAGE 114, 12. *rage*. See p. lxix. Robertson, 438, compares the use of this image in Languet's letters to Sidney of 14 June 1577 and 2 May 1578. C. S. Levy, unpublished

Ph.D. thesis, Cornell University, 1962, p. 248, compares Languet's letter of 12 June 1575, and refers to the analogue in Cicero, *In Catilinam*, I. xiii. 31.

24–5. *her blindness*. Recall Kalander's description of her cataracts, p. 14, 18 and note.

31. [*woes ... long* Glossed as a sententia in 90 through inverted commas, which were dropped in 98. Two printed commonplace books, Ralph Venning's *Things Worth Thinking On* (1664), p. 11 and George Liddell's *Divine Meditations* (1700), p. 18, contain versions but do not cite *Arcadia* as their source.]

PAGE 115, 1. (var.) [*octave*. Ottava rima, or more generally a stanza of eight lines of verse. The earliest example cited in *OED* for octave n.² 2a. is from 93.]

11. [*silly successor*. A reference to Musidorus' tender age. Musidorus' father died before the birth of Pyrocles, who is three or four years his junior (see p. 140, 33–4).]

25. *widowhead*. 'widowed'. [See glossary.]

PAGE 116, 27. *what power ... hath*. This is cited in C. G. Smith, *Spenser's Proverb Lore*, 48.

31–2. *But alas ... persuade*. Hoskyns, 16, cites this as an example of agnomination of syllables, a kind of pun.

PAGE 117, 29. *not deny*. Hoskyns, 35, cites this as an example of diminution 'by denying the contrary'.

36. *certainty ... knowledge*. 'written account of my mind', a metaphor designed to pass over Mopsa's head.

PAGE 118, 5–6. *songs ... Lamon*. Evidently Sidney intended Lamon to sing one of the Strephon and Claius songs from the *Old Arcadia* in the never completed First Eclogues. Barring a lost poem, the choice rested on *OA* 71 and 74, the editors of 90 opting for *OA* 71. The editor of 93 printed OP 4, a poem about Strephon and Claius though not one of theirs, but did not change this reference. See p. 417, 31 ff.

7. *his marriage*. 13 omits this; see p. xlviii.

17. [*any's*. 'anyone's'. Cf. also Spenser, *Mother Hubberds Tale*, 719–20: 'Doth loath such base condition, to backbite / Anies good name for enuie or despite'. All editions between 90 and the 1638 folio used the spelling 'anies'. The compositors of the 1655 edition, in an apparent attempt to clarify the form (which had by then become largely replaced by 'any mans'), added an apostrophe before the genitive s ('anie's'). In the 1674 edition, this was further amended to 'any's'.]

24. *Lastly*. The indirect speech is continued.

33–4. [*not accusing ... inward motion*. 'revealing no emotion'. Cf. *accuse* 4 in *OED*: 'to betray, disclose (a fault, crime, or offence); (hence) to reveal, show, or make known'.]

PAGE 119, 1–8. Ringler, *OA* 17 and 395; Robertson, 107, 4 ff. Substantive texts are *OA*, *Fl*, *Ma*, *Cm*, 90, 93.

3. *On*. The reading in Bo, 90 *On barren sweets* indicates what Musidorus' thoughts feed on, and is treated as a revision of *In barren sweets OA* (*ex. Bo*), describing how his thoughts feed 'in empty pleasures'.

14–16. *her face ... loveliness*. Hoskyns, 38, cites this as an example of asyndeton, but reads 'skull' for *face* and 'lovingness' for *loveliness*.

22. *Take heed*. In this transformation from the indirect speech of the *Old Arcadia* to direct speech, this agreement with *Ph* is mere chance; cf. Robertson, 107, 31.

26. [*in my conscience*. 'as far as I could tell'.]

far spent. 'to a great degree'; cf. *OED* under *far* adv. 3b. ['spent' here means 'smitten'.]

27. *quaint*. 'clever'.

34. [*actor in this tragedy*. Like Pyrocles in p. 74, 15 and p. 75, 22-3, Musidorus compares his story to a tragedy, while secretly hoping it may yet turn out a comedy.]

37-9. *crabfish ... choice*. The crab was commonly used in emblems to denote this antithesis, as in Camerarius, *Symbolorum et Emblematum*, IV. lv, 'Simul Ante Retroque'. Musidorus' motto is an inversion of those which usually demonstrate freedom, as in Camerarius, III. xxix, 'Sponte Mea, Non Vi', 'by free will, not force'. See W. Deonna, 'The Crab and the Butterfly: A Study in Animal Symbolism', *JWCI* xvii (1954), 47-86, and *ODEP* under 'Crab'.

PAGE 120, 2-6. [*that toy ... betwixt us*. Musidorus is pretending to have found the 'choice jewels' that he took with him after leaving Kalander's house in p. 47, 17.]

9. *slide*. 'take its own course'; cited in *OED* under *slide* v. 5b.

justly ... do. 'as we do with justice'.

12-18. *For ... quench it*. Hoskyns, 50, cites this as an example of prevention by occupatio.

18-19. *neither ... favour*. 'neither moving away from disliking, nor moving towards partiality'.

21-2. *neither ... horses*. See p. lv.

29. [*king in a tragedy*. See the note to p. 119, 34.]

32. *beat ... foam*. The metaphor is of waves pounding rocks, as in Shakespeare, *Rape of Lucrece*, 589-95.

34-5. [*counting ... a year*. i.e. a calculation that almost certainly exceeds Dametas' arithmetical skill (as well as the number of available fingers).]

35. [*desired ... that*. 'informed Zelmane that the king desired'. The construction is unusual.]

PAGE 121, 7. *wild method*. 'disorderly arrangement of topics'.

9-10. [*yielded ... answer*. See p. lxxxiii.]

19-20. *Zelmane's ... her body*. Philoclea is the magnet and Zelmane's soul the needle.

26. *proceeding*. 'advancing to a higher university degree', [with an added pun on the title 'Master of Arts' and (probably) 'Doctor of the Church', a term for a church father distinguished through his learning.]

28-PAGE 122, 25. *coach ... coach*. The earliest reference to a coach such as this in L. Tarr, *History of the Carriage*, trans. E. Hoch (New York, 1969), 210-11, is from Johann Coler, *Oeconomica Ruralis et Domestica* (c.1591-1601); an Austrian engraving of 1593 is reproduced. The novelty of such a coach from which one could see in all directions, and apprehension about the safety of its retractable top, seem to be current topics. J. Nichols, *The Progresses and Public Processions of Queen Elizabeth* (London, 1823), ii. 309, notes that coaches were first introduced into England in 1585.

29. *close*. 'shut'.

31. *discovered and open-sighted*. 'uncovered and with an unobstructed view'.

37. *mounty*. 'the action of rising in pursuit of a quarry'. Although this is the earliest citation in *OED*, there are several examples in G. Turberville, *Book of Falconry* (1575).

hern. 'heron'.

38. *with pain*. 'with difficulty'.

PAGE 122, 2. *after her*. See p. lv.

6. *towering*. 'soaring'. The earliest citation in *OED* n. b is from 1646.

10. *turn tail*. 'turn her back'. The earliest citation in *OED* under *turn* v. 59a is from Turberville's *Book of Falconry* (1575).

33. *sickness*. Further references to Gynecia's sickness are on pp. 161, 34; 271, 15–16.

PAGE 123, 14–15. *which tender youth*. See p. lv.
19. *wind ... hunters*. 'wind carrying the scent of the hunters'.
23. *lonely*. Cf. *lonely* in Robertson, 109, 11 and the variants, and see above, p. 37, 25 and note.
29. *keys ... mind*. This image was used on p. 52, 33–5.

PAGE 124, 3. *pattern ... proceeding*. 'model of excellent conduct'.
4–7. *enacted ... statute*. The metaphor is of the three estates, the commons (passions), the lords (noble thoughts), and the king (reason), passing an act.
5–6. *by reason ... had granted*. 'by reason itself, it had granted to it his royal assent'. The elliptical construction takes 'it' from 'it was enacted' (above) as the subject of the passive verb 'had granted'.
8. *grew on*. 'it occurred by degrees'.
9–10. *gestures ... eye her*. See p. xxxi.
13–15. *Zelmane ... near Zelmane*. Hoskyns, 15, cites this as an example of antimetabole.
16–17. *softly strained ... sweet fastness*. 'softly squeezed ... sweet gripping'.
20. *crossed ... eyes*. These are traditional postures of the melancholy lover; see p. 65, 11–12 and note.
24. *in continuance*. 'in the course of time'.
30–PAGE 125, 2. *First ... was not*. Hoskyns, 49, cites this as an example of deliberation.
33. *part*. 'share'.
39–PAGE 125, 2. *but when ... creation*. Hoskyns, 9, cites this as an example of allegory.

PAGE 125, 1. *main battle*. 'pitched battle'.
5–7. *diseases ... cured*. Cf. Machiavelli, *The Prince*, trans. N. H. Thomson, 3rd edn., (Oxford, 1913), 13, 'physicians tell us of hectic fever, that in its beginning it is easy to cure, but hard to recognize; whereas, after a time ... it becomes easy to recognize but impossible to cure'.
7–8. *prevent ... preventing*. Hoskyns, 15, cites this as an example of antimetabole.

PAGE 126, 4. *suspicion*. She seems to indicate that she thought her parents felt she was not to be trusted with men.
6–23. Ringler, *OA* 18, and 396; Robertson, 109, 30 ff. Substantive texts are *OA*, 90, 93.
6. [*pow'rs*. The word 'powers' is monosyllabic here, as in p. 173, 23 and p. 303, 3, but cf. pp. 59, 3; 300, 17; 410, 32, where it is disyllabic. See also the note to p. 59, 12.]
18. [*heav'nly*. See the note to p. 14, 19.]
19. *makst*. The second person agreement is with *chastity*.

PAGE 127, 1–12. Ringler, *OA* 19, and 396; Robertson, 110, 29 ff. Substantive texts are *OA*, 90, 93.
29–30. *idle lusts*. See note to p. 60, 28.
32. *unresistable*. 'irresistible'. The earliest citation in *OED* is from Udall's translation of Erasmus (1548).
33–4. *you stars ... help me*. Hoskyns, 30, cites this as an example of correctio.
36–8. *unlawful ... itself*. Hoskyns, 40, cites this as an example of sententia with *distinctio* and *contentio*.

PAGE 128, 2–5. *The most ... impossible*. Hoskyns, 13, cites this as an example of symploce or complexio, 'when several sentences have the same beginning and the same ending'.

COMMENTARY 493

5–6. *sampler ... take out*. 'pattern ... to copy'; the imagery is from embroidery.
13. *wisdom and virtue*. See p. 16, 11–12 and note.
22. *round about*. 'in all directions'.
26. *chicken ... kite's foot*. Kites commonly seized chickens; cf. the lengthy metaphor in Gavin Douglas's trans. of M. Vegio's 'Thretteene Booke of *Eneados*' (1710), Yyyyy2, and Shakespeare, 2 *Henry VI*, III. i. 249.
33. *serve herself*. 'minister to her own comforts'.
36. *doth*. The verb has shifted to the singular through its proximity to *night*; cf. Abbott, 298. The image is repeated at p. 134, 19–20, and in *AS* 38. 1–2 and PS 16. 21–2; cf. p. 31, 38 and note.

PAGE 129, 3. *circles*. Eyes are commonly described thus; cf. Shakespeare, *Rape of Lucrece*, 1229, 'circled eyne; Marlowe, *1 Tamburlaine*, II. i. 15, 'fiery circles'.
3–4. *red ... hottest*. 'red streaks in the evening sky during the hottest part of the summer', when the days are longest. Cf. *OED* under *fleck* v.¹ and *ODEP*, 741, 'Sky red'. As a sign of fair weather, this reflects Pamela's changing attitude towards Musidorus.
4. *element*. 'sky'; also used at Robertson, 374, 33.
12–13. *Do you ... of it*. Hoskyns, 11, adapts this in an example of catachresis.
21. [*love ... play him there*. This is *play* v. 11b in *OED* ('to engage in amorous play'), used with the archaic reflexive. The construction is uncommon.]
24. *curtain*. This is the curtain around the tester bed.
29. *since that*. 'since'.
30. *love ... eyes*. Cf. Tilley, L506, 'Love is blind'; cited in C. G. Smith, *Spenser's Proverb Lore*, 484, and see above, p. 14, 15 and note.
32–3. *but belike*. 'except that perhaps'.
33. *stained*. 'eclipsed'.
40. *shade*. 'place in the shade'. This is the earliest citation in *OED* v.¹ 2b.

PAGE 130, 9. *should*. 'should have had this knowledge'.
11. *of proof*. 'tested for impenetrability'; see Viscount Dillon, 'Armour Notes', *The Archaeological Journal*, lx (2nd Ser. x) (1903), 116–17.
13–14. *clip ... flown*. Cf. Tilley, W498, 'To clip one's wings' and B364, 'The bird is flown'.
19. *mind*. 'intentions'.
32. *matched ... together*. 'joined in combat within yourself those rarely regarded as equal'.
34. *ungratefulness*. Cf. *AS* song v. 42, 'Ungrateful who is called, the worst of evils is spok'n'.
37. *abase himself*. This was a token of greatness; cf. Spenser, *Faerie Queene*, VI. ix. xxxvii. 9, Sir Calidore as a shepherd because 'love so much could'; and Shakespeare, *The Winter's Tale*, IV. iv. 25–7, spoken by Prince Florizel to Perdita, 'The gods themselves / Humbling their deities to love, have taken / The shapes of beasts upon them'.
38. *Musidorus?* This is the punctuation in *Cm*.
38–9. *handmaid ... belief*. Cf. Ovid, *Heroides*, xvii. 130, 'Tarda solet magnis rebus inesse fides'; this is cited in C. G. Smith, *Spenser's Proverb Lore*, 382.

PAGE 131, 11. *run ... ring*. See the note to p. 132, 7–11.
11–12. *like ... lambskins*. 'take pleasure in rich cloth, especially considering that it was trimmed with lambskins'. [The lambskin acts as a cheap substitute for fur, exemplifying Dametas' characteristic clownish vanity.]
12. *did*. 'fared'.
14. *wait upon*. 'accompany'.

18–39. *come ... me-wards.* Cf. Blundeville, *The Four Chiefest Offices Belonging to Horsemanship* (c.1570), K2^v–K3:

> Ride first fair and softly toward the prince to do your reverence; that done, depart with a good round trot toward the farthest end of the career path, bearing your rod with the point upward ... and so observing always one time and measure, manage him to and fro ... but let the last stop be at the end where the prince standeth.

18. *dancer.* This indicates the gallop galliard in imitation of the dance in triple time (Blundeville, 18^v).

21. *one piece ... horse.* Cf. Shakespeare, *Hamlet*, IV. vii. 86–7, 'As had he been incorps'd and demi-natur'd / With the brave beast', noted in H. Jenkins, ed. (London, 1982).

33–4. *turn ... mouse.* This is the chambetta in which the horse 'shall carry both his forefeet clean above the ground' in a low turn on bent hocks (Blundeville, H7).

35. *rising before.* This turn is the volte in which the forefeet are raised high while the horse performs an about-face on its hind quarters.

raven. This is the curvet which, by an assimilation of meanings as in John Florio, *Queen Anna's New World of Words* (1611), 'Corbétta, a little panier. Also a young-raven. Also a corvet of a horse', gave Sidney the image. In the curvet the horse raises itself upon its hind legs to the vertical, and leaps along in the manner of a raven.

ridge. This is the agricultural term for the division formed in the field by several furrows, separated from another ridge by a water-furrow. Cf. Spenser, *Faerie Queene*, V. vi. 36: 'Streight was the passage like a ploughed ridge, / That if two met, the one mote needes fall ouer the lidge.'

36. *kids ... hillocks.* This is the capriole in which the horse leaps horizontally into the air, jerking his hind legs straight behind, the hooves bottom up. Blundeville, K1, calls it the goat's leap: 'behold our little lambs whilst they run and play together, and you shall see them lively to do the same'; cf. the Countess of Pembroke's trans. of Psalm 114. 15–16, which is the earliest citation in *OED* under *capriole* v.: 'Hillocks why caprioled ye, as wanton by their dams / We capriole see the lusty lambs?'

37–8. *roughness ... idleness.* 'severity ... lack of attention', on the part of the rider.

38. *still.* 'ever'.

Page 132, 8–10. *ring ... ring.* Running at the ring developed skill with the lance (see the exaggerated account in Rabelais, *Gargantua*, i. 23), but it became a sport under James; so, whereas Elizabethan treatises on horsemanship did not mention it, Gervase Markham, *Cavelarice, or the English Horseman* (1607), Ss3^v–Tt3^v, described and provided a diagram of the four steps and angles of execution as here. A manuscript depiction from 1493 is in G. Wickham, *Early English Stages 1300–1600* (1963–81), i. 292 and plate v. See E. M. Parkinson, 'Sidney's Portrayal of Mounted Combat with Lances', *Spenser Studies*, v (1985), 241–3 and plates 28–30; and above, pp. xv and 293, 26–7. [Cf. also l. 742 of *Mother Hubberds Tale*.]

10. *rest.* See Glossary.

14. *clearness.* 'purity'. This is cited in *OED* under the variant in 93, *cleanness*.

16–17. [*my delight ... window.* Pamela did not allow her delight to show in her eyes, the 'windows' of her soul, i.e. she was secretly delighted but looked indifferent.]

19–20. [*some physicians ... not inwardly.* Antiperistasis, as described by Hippocrates. Thomas Elyot's *Dictionary* (1538) defines it as 'that thinge, whereby where heate commeth colde is expelled, where colde is, heate is expelled.' This was also believed to be the underlying principle of ague fits (cf. the note to p. 218, 33).]

27. *testify his love.* Cf. p. 110, 3–4.

matachin... armour. On the matachin, see p. 87, 32 and note. Dancing in armour was an exhibition of fitness; cf. p. 209, 32–8 and note.

30. *dialogue*. This would be Musidorus' word, in order to persuade Dametas to participate, for Priam's role in the life of Paris was only to send him as an infant to be slain, and much later to recognize him as his son; cf. T. C. W. Stinton, *Euripides and the Judgement of Paris* (London, 1965). Presumably, then, Dametas stood dumbly by.

35. *Oenone*. Brought up as a shepherd, Paris wooed and married Oenone, a nymph of Mount Ida. He was subsequently recognized by Priam and set out on his voyage to Greece. The wooing is recounted by Oenone in Ovid, *Heroides*, v. The version in George Peele's *Arraignment of Paris* (1584), I. ii, is insufficiently eloquent to have been alluded to here.

38. *parents*. See p. 395, 5–6.

PAGE 133, 7. *iron stomach*. 'unyielding obstinacy'.
28. *poorly*. 'humbly'.
33–5. [*alas!... end!* See p. lxxviii.]
39–**PAGE 134**, 1. *coffin... sepulchre*. Cf. p. 3, 22–3.

PAGE 134, 9. [*rent*. A variant form of 'rend', i.e. tear apart.]
18–19. *being... fortune*. Hoskyns, 11, cites this as an example of catachresis.
31. *time a day*. See p. lv.

PAGE 135, 25. [*famous of victories*. The construction 'famous of' (for 'famous for') was already uncommon in the late sixteenth century, except in the phrase 'famous of renown'. This may explain why 93 changed the phrase to 'famous for victories', which persisted in all subsequent editions.]
26. *more lovely*. 'more worthy of love'.
35–7 *Who... bush*. Tilley, M1115, cites this.

PAGE 136, 15–18. [*would never... placed him*. i.e. rather than fighting wars over his historical claim to rule Greece, Euarchus was content to be king of Macedonia only. For similar imagery, cf. for example M. G. Haddon's letter to Sir Thomas Smith in *A Panoplie of Epistles* (1576), pp. 422–3:

> Wherefore, euen as Gouernours of shippes, keepe that course in sayling which they can, not that which they would: and cut the waues as they are furthered with a merrie winde: euen so let vs frame our studie and labour, to that wherevnto we are constrained by necessitie: and shewe our selues not discontent, with that wherevnto we are appointed by Gods gratious prouidence, bycause we must be ruled thereby.]

20. [*enow bleeding witnesses*. 'enow', a variant of 'enough' that survives in modern Scots, is an uncommon spelling in late sixteenth-century texts. The EEBO / TCP corpus lists only 79 examples of 'enow' in texts printed between 1570 and 1600, compared to 1,273 of 'enough' (for the variant spellings 'ynow' and 'inow' there are 53 and 40 examples respectively, compared to 573 for 'ynough' and 1,000 for 'inough'). In 90, the form may have been a compositor's choice, since it appears only five times: spelt 'enow' here and in p. 146, 11, 'inow' in p. 296, 13 and 'ennow' (an extremely uncommon spelling variant, probably chosen by the compositor to balance out the lines) in p. 323, 5. The remaining 70 instances of 'enough' are evenly divided between the spellings 'enough' and 'inough'. The 1628/9 folio standardized 'inow' and 'ennow' to 'enow', which was preserved by all subsequent editions – although the 1662 edition changed the 'enow's in p. 136, 20 and p. 146, 11 to 'enough'.]

PAGE 137, 5. *farms*. 'contracts to collect taxes'.
38–9. *love ... fear*. The concept hinges upon Horace, *Epistles*, I. xvi. 52–3, 'virtutis amore' and 'formidinae poenae', cited in *A Defence of Poetry* (*Misc. Prose*, 84, 33–4); cf. p. 309, 1 and Shakespeare, *Rape of Lucrece*, 610–11, 'This deed will make thee only lov'd for fear; / But happy monarchs still are fear'd for love'.

PAGE 138, 2–3. *making ... deeds*. Hoskyns, 40, cites this as an example of sententia.
life ... laws. Cf, p. 390, 6 and Tilley, E213, 'Examples teach more than precepts'.
3. *actions*. See p. lv. The earliest citation in *OED* under *action* n. I 2, 'conduct', is from Gower's *Confessio Amantis*.
6. [*even in reason*. 'quite rightly'.]
15–16. [*politic body ... own limbs*. Typically, the analogy between the human body and the body politic is invoked to remind the 'limbs' of their duty to the 'head'. Here, however, it is used to show Euarchus is a good ruler who cares about his subjects.]
18. *employed to*. In altering to 'employed but to' the proof corrector of *90* annihilated the contrast with p. 137, 8–10; see p. lii.
27. *no unfit*. Hoskyns, 35, cites this as an example of diminution 'by denying the contrary'.

PAGE 139, 22–3. *they begat ... peace*. This is cited in Tilley, W42, and in *ODEP*.
35. *truth*. 'reality'.

PAGE 140, 18. *dispense*. 'do without', 'forgo'; cited in *OED* under *dispense* v. 7.
18–20. *delight ... nobly*. Cf. *A Defence of Poetry* (*Misc. Prose*, 98, 14–15), 'the lofty image of such worthies most inflameth the mind with desire to be worthy, and informs with counsel how to be worthy'.
20. *beauty of virtue*. Cf. p. 147, 10. and *A Defence of Poetry* (*Misc. Prose*, 98, 6–7), 'who could see virtue would be wonderfully ravished with the love of her beauty', and *AS* 25.
24. *servile fear*. 'fear of punishment'. [Typically used in a theological context in the sixteenth century to signify the 'wrong' fear of God instilled by Catholicism.]
29–32. [*memorable ... aspire to*. See the note to pp. 103, 25–204, 1. 'nearness of their blood' stresses that the friends are also linked through close kinship: Pyrocles and Musidorus share both sets of grandparents, which makes them genetic siblings.]

PAGE 141, 9. *At which time*. 'At this time'.
10. [*all Pannonia and almost Thrace*. 'all of Pannonia and nearly all of Thrace'.]
20. *bid*. This is the past participle of *bide* v. 9, 'endure'.
21–2. *now ... able*. See p. lvi.
25. [*their dear parent Euarchus*. Musidorus' phrase uses 'parent' in the extended sense, highlighting that Euarchus – who is Pyrocles' father and Musidorus' uncle – is guardian to both. Thus it reinforces the idea that their parents' 'cross-marriage' and the fact that they had only one set of parents between them throughout their childhood effectively make the two princes more like brothers than cousins.]
30. *best sailers*. 'those most skilled in sailing'.
32. [*beautiful ... pipe*. This comparison of a fleet to a flock of sheep is Musidorus' only concession to his disguise as the shepherd 'Dorus' in this scene, so it sits oddly with the rest of his speech, which is full of obvious hints about his true identity.]
38. *run away*. 'run along'.
39–PAGE 142, 1. *trinkets ... attired*. 'tackle ... outfitted', but the imagery of 'ornaments ... adorned' is implicit.

PAGE 142, 10–11. *as pleasing... to.* Hoskyns, 29, cites this as an example of hyperbole.
12. *by that.* 'by the time that'.
13–15. *veil... heaven.* Cf. Ovid, *Met.* xi. 548–9, 'et inducta piceis e nubibus umbra / Omne latet coelum, duplicataque noctis imago est', and p. 142, 33–5.
21–3. *mountains... darkness.* Cf. Ovid, *Met.* xi. 505–9:

> Et modo sublimis, veluti de vertice montis,
> Despicere in valles, imumque Acheronta videtur:
> Nunc, ibi demissam curvum circumstetit aequor,
> Suspicere inferno summum de gurgite coelum...

24–5. *darkness... right.* See p. 142, 13–15 and note.
36–7. *masters... direct.* Cf. Ovid, *Met.* xi. 494–6:

> Ipse pavet, nec se, qui sit status, ipse fatetur
> Scire ratis rector, nec quid jubeatve, vetetve
> Tanta mali moles, totaque potentior arte est...

37–8. *when... hear.* Cf. Ovid, *Met.* xi. 486–7: 'Hic jubet: impediunt adversae jussa pro-cellae; / Nec sinit audiri vocem fragor aequoris ullam'.
42. [*the shrouds of the ship.* See the note to p. 38, 33.]

PAGE 143, 6. *dissolution.* 'desolation'. The last entry under 'dissolute' in *OED* notes that it is often used for 'desolate'.
11. *stricken.* 'lowered'. This is the only citation in *OED* 5, noting the variant in *90*; cf. Robertson, 125, 7. [There are of course numerous citations for the nautical sense of 'strike' (17a), from which the form 'stricken' is derived, going back as far as the medieval romance *King Horn*.]
19–20. *till... fortune.* Hoskyns, 44, cites this as an example of parenthesis.
20. *run fortune.* 'been exposed to chance'. This is the earliest citation in *OED run* v.
20–1 *blindly... painted.* Fortuna is often depicted as a blind goddess; cf. pp. 185, 4; 259, 18; 276, 11; 285, 23, and the note to p. 14, 15.
31–2. [*more able... drowning.* Cf. *A Sanctuarie for a Troubled Soule*, pp. 145–6:

> Somtimes the sinner, more able to abide death then the feare of death, wisheth to bee discharged, from beeinge guided by soe euell a soule; not in full hope that his tormentes shall thereby either end or abate; but according to the nature of greife, the present being most painfull, hee desireth to chang, and to put in aduenture the ensuing.]

34. *vows.* 'praying and cursing'.

PAGE 144, 28. *they... had left.* See p. liii.

PAGE 145, 35–6. *toad-like... of odiousness.* The toad was regarded as poisonous (see quotations in *OED*); its poison was hateful to others, who hated it in return.
35. *retiredness.* 'reservedness'. This is the earliest citation in *OED* 1a.

PAGE 146, 5–6. [*unsuccessings... prosper.* 'unsuccessing' is an obscure variant form of 'unsuccess', itself a relatively uncommon synonym for 'failure'. The only known instance of 'unsuccessing' is in *90*; *93* corrects this to 'unsuccess' (which is in turn the earliest example listed in the *OED*). 'Unsuccessings' may have been Sidney's coinage, to make the word a closer counterpart to 'unwillingness'.]
6–7. [*countermine against.* 'means of preventing'. A countermine is a military defence strategy, usually a passage dug by the besieged to intercept a mine dug by besiegers.

Here the image is used to illustrate the king of Phrygia's paranoia; he believes himself to be surrounded by potential enemies. See also the note to p. 174, 20.]

10–11. *honour ... serviceable.* 'high position to which those made shameless by poverty cannot make themselves useful'.

11. [*enow.* See the note to p. 136, 20.]

11–12. *of those desperate ambition.* 'of such desperate ambition'. Cf. *OED* under *those* II, demonstrative adj. 5; see p. liii.

12. *build ... ruins.* Cf. p. 189, 12–13.

19. *tyrant.* It was in a tyranny that the personality of the ruler had its greatest effect upon government; see W. D. Briggs, 'Political Ideas in Sidney's *Arcadia*', *SP* xxviii (1931), 137–61; I. Ribner, 'Machiavelli and Sidney: The *Arcadia* of 1590', *SP* xlvii (1950), 152–72; and id., 'Sir Philip Sidney on Civil Insurrection', *Journal of the History of Ideas*, xiii (1952), 257–65.

PAGE 147, 27–8. *conquest ... conquered.* Cf. C. G. Smith, *Spenser's Proverb Lore*, 114, 'Often the conquered conquer the victor', and p. xxviii.

29–30. *king ... and.* See p. lvi.

30–1. [*cheerfully ... fromward) his death.* The incongruous contrast and alliteration add a humorous element to the scene (which is not inappropriate, because both Pamela and the reader already know that Pyrocles and Musidorus escaped). For a similar usage cf. Robert Greene's *Planetomachia* (1585), C2ᵛ:

> He was pained with strange and vncertaine thoughts, thinking if he should with rigor reproue his daughters folly, it were but to make her ouer feruent in affection, knowing that women flie frowardly from those things whereunto they are perswaded, and wilfully attempt those actions, from which with sensible reasons they are forewarned.]

33. *one ... other.* 'Musidorus ... Pyrocles'; see p. 139, 12–24.

36. *suspected.* That is, suspected to be traitors.

PAGE 148, 10. [*some few crowns.* The first reference to this anachronistic currency (cf. p. xvii). Here used to refer to only a moderate sum of money for a nobleman – and thus perhaps intended to evoke English crowns, which were worth five shillings, i.e. a quarter of a pound – the same fictional currency is later employed to the opposite effect when Artaxia offers a bounty of 'an hundreth thousand crowns' to anyone who will deliver Pyrocles to her in p. 212, 13.]

16. *bad.* He accepted Pyrocles' bribe.

24. *Die nobly.* Cf. 395, 20–1.

27–9. *blushed ... blushing.* See p. 40, 14 and note. Hoskyns, 15, cites this as an example of antimetabole.

33. *turning backs.* This was the conventional defensive posture; cf. p. 357, 21.

40. *though ... been.* 'even if he had been'.

PAGE 149, 1–2. [*popular sort ... beholders.* See the note to p. 39, 16.]

2–3. *superstitiously ... mortal.* See p. 5, 20–1.

3. *from out.* 'from'. The earliest citation in *OED* for *from* with the pleonastic preposition, 15c, is from Marlowe's *Massacre at Paris.* [Cf. also pp. 86, 13; 162, 34; 317, 15; 416, 7.]

7. *conquered ... conquering.* See p. xxviii.

12. *pick a thank.* 'curry favour', as in B. J. Whiting and H. W. Whiting, *Proverbs, Sentences, and Proverbial Phrases From English Writings Mainly Before 1500* (Cambridge,

Mass., 1968), T62. [This is 'pick' in the sense of 'steal', hence the phrase implies dishonesty. Cf. *Nashes Lenten Stuffe* (1599), p. 68:

> I am not against it, ... that it behooues all loyall true subiects to bee vigilant and iealous for their princes safetie, and certaine too iealous and vigilant of it they cannot bee, ... but vppon the least wagging of a straw to put them in feare where no feare is, and make a hurliburlie in the realme vpon had I wist, not so much for any zeale or loue to their princes, or tender care of theyr preseruation, as to picke thankes, and curry a little fauour, that thereby they may lay the foundation to build a sute on, or crosse some great enemie they haue, I will maintaine it is most lewd and detestable.]

12–13. *strake ... face*. This seems to have been the appropriate treatment of a coward; cf. p. 250, 11.

30. *many-headed*. Cf. Tilley, M1308, 'A multitude of people is a beast of many heads'; and see p. 249, 3 and *A Letter to Queen Elizabeth* (*Misc. Prose*, 54, 23). *OED* compares Horace, *Epistles*, I. i. 76, 'Bellua multorum es capitum'; cf. Shakespeare, *Coriolanus*, II. iii. 16.

PAGE 150, 26. *tenant*. He held his title from them.

27. *liege man*. 'vassal', sworn to serve his lord, who in return protects him.

35. *unrevengefulness*. 'because he was not unrevengeful'. This is the earliest citation in *OED*, which also gives *revengefulness* from 93 as the earliest citation of that word.

36–PAGE 151, 1. [*wanton ... playfellow*. Sidney's use of 'playfellow' and 'wanton cruelty' creates an analogy between the tyrant of Pontus and an unruly child.]

PAGE 151, 10–11. [*a man ... ever infected the air with his breath ... plagued with others' well-being*. The man's envy is being compared to the plague (widely believed to spread through 'vapours' and infected air). Cf. p. 240, 6–7. and p. 430, 33.]

33. *in his liking*. 'according to his wish'.

36–8. *he ... off*. Hoskyns, 44, cites this as an example of parenthesis.

36–PAGE 152, 1. [*swelling ... masters*. See p. lxxvii.]

PAGE 152, 10. *royal expenses*. 'magnificent expenditure'. [Compensating for the 'unroyal reproaches' with which the servants' heads were sent to the princes (p. 152, 1).]

36. *discarded*. 'dismissed from service'. The earliest citation in *OED* 1a ('to reject as being no longer wanted or needed') is from 1578.

PAGE 153, 4. *glass of reason*. 'reason's mirror'. [Sidney uses the same image in the *Defence of Poetry*, when he suggests that those who enjoy writing poetry should 'look themselves in an unflattering glass of reason' to see if they are really cut out to be poets.]

5. *country*. 'the people of that country'.

12–13. *blind judge*. Cf. p. 11, 19 and note.

17. *suffered them*. 'consented'. This is the archaic reflexive form in *OED* 15a.

34. *passed ... cumber*. 'gone beyond all the burden'. [Alternatively, 'passed' may be used as a variant of 'past' here (as in pp. 168, 34; 248, 1; 253, 13; 257, 17; 335, 32; 344, 17, all of which read 'passed' in 90). Either way, the phrase implies that the wars were over, so the princes needed to look elsewhere for heroic opportunities.]

36. *Ulysses and Aeneas*. See p. xxix. [Technically those two were enemies, so the main purpose of the analogy is perhaps to stress that each was a hero in his own right.]

38. *to leave them*. 'to allow them to [go]'.

Page 154, 6. *Galatia*. This is a province of Paphlagonia. Sidney uses both names synonymously.
17. *blind ... leading*. See p. xviii.
32. *fits*. 'befits'.

Page 155, 36. *in the world*. 'among the people'.
38–9. [*carried by ... mother*. Although the king of Paphlagonia claims to blame only himself for his miserable condition, his wording here nevertheless implies he thinks of Plexirtus as the chief culprit – cf. 'carried with' (see the note to p. 75, 10). He also implicitly blames his bastard son's deficiencies of character on his 'base' mother, while hinting she might even have lied about his fatherhood.]

Page 156, 9. *charities*. Hoskyns, 11, cites this as an example of catachresis, 'where *charity* is used for *cruelty*'.
11. *thieves*. 'scoundrels'.
better ... myself. 'better natured than me to my son'.
15. *unlawful and unnatural*. 'illegitimate and wicked'. [Cf. 'unnatural dealings' on p. 155, 12.]
17. *passed ... distributed*. 'were passed ... were distributed'. [This is the early modern trope of the wicked counsellor seizing control (cf. the king's admission in the preceding line that he allowed himself to be 'governed by' Plexirtus).]
23–4. [*full ... guiltiness*. *A Sanctuarie for a Troubled Soule*, p. 120 paraphrases this to: 'Oh my soule, full of wretchednesse, ful of shame, but fullest of guiltines'.]
25. *stranger*. 'foreign'.
citadels. 'fortresses'. This is the earliest citation in *OED* for the figurative sense (3a).

Page 157, 2. *so well-deserving*. 'so highly meritorious'; see p. liii.
15. [*never ... ending me*. 'killing me would be an act of compassion comparable to (or greater than) saving someone else's life'.]
19. *gestures*. See p. xxxi.

Page 159, 13–18. [*no man ... fouler*. See p. lxxix.]
13. *turningness of sleights*. 'the twisting ways of deception'. This is the only citation in *OED*. [Cf. the note to p. 249, 12.]
22. *rope ... neck*. This was a token of submission; cf. Shakespeare, *2 Henry VI*, IV. ix. 11–12.

Page 160, 6. [*but private chivalries*. 'valorous deeds that benefited only individuals' (as opposed to whole kingdoms).]
7. [*puissant*. 'powerful', 'mighty'. An adjective with archaic connotations, favoured by Spenser (who also frequently uses the noun 'puissance'), but rare in Sidney.]
king of Armenia. 'Tiridates'.
13–14. *though ... him*. 'though their titles were derived from the king of Armenia'. [This is 'holding' in the sense of 'beholding', i.e. 'indebted'. Cf. Holinshed's *Chronicles* (1587), where an English baron is defined as 'such a free lord as hath a lordship or baronie, whereof he beareth his name, & hath diuerse knights or freeholders holding of him, who with him did serue the king in his wars' (p. 157).]
30. *story*. See p. 171, 19 ff.
of. 'from'.
33. *happily*. 'by chance'.
35–6. *making ... charge*. Hoskyns, 44, cites this as an example of paraphrasis. [Mopsa has evidently inherited the 'plainness and honesty' Basilius values so much in her father (p. 99, 27), so rather than stealing a nap she snores openly.]

PAGE 161, 1. *hardy*. 'bold'.
1–2. *printed … graces*. 'plainly seen among his attractive qualities'.
5–6. *dragon … fruit*. To steal the golden apples given by Juno to Jupiter on their wedding day, and guarded by the Hesperides and their dragon, was Hercules' twelfth labour. From this same tree came the golden apples used by Hippomenes to deceive Atalanta; see p. xxv and p. 11, 18 and note, and cf. pp. 356, 39–357, 3 and note.

PAGE 162, 11. *There … but*. On the lacunae in all texts, see p. li. There is a traditional tree-list in Robertson, 86, 20 ff., with others collected in Spenser, *Works*, i. 179, and in D. Bush, *Mythology and the Renaissance Tradition in English Poetry*, rev. edn. (New York, 1963), 162 n.
11. *cypress*. See notes to pp. 108, 11–12; 342, 34, and Robertson, 86, 23, 'Cypress promiseth help, but a help where comes no recomfort', with the gloss, 'Death'. It is a symbol of foreboding.
17–18. [*water spaniel … duck*. The spaniel mentioned in p. 56, 31 ff. Water-spaniels are dogs bred for hunting water-fowl. Abraham Fleming's translation of John Caius' *Of Englishe Dogges* (1576), pp. 16–18 praises their skill at retrieving injured birds and stray arrows and bolts (which may be why the dog first fetches the glove used to house 'the bloody shafts of Cupid's war').]
18. *with … grace*. 'with a gracefulness characterized by loud sniffing'. This is the earliest citation in *OED* under *snuffling* pres. p. adj.
27. *the eclipsing*. 'the concealment'.
30. *forswat melters*. 'sweaty metal melters'.
30–1. [*getting … garments*. Comparing Miso and Mopsa to hard-working smelters heightens the contrast to the undressed Philoclea, who shines effortlessly like a diamond or the sun (p. 162, 24–5). 'pure' is an unlikely adjective considering the earlier description of Mopsa's skin (p. 14, 20), but cf. Philoclea's 'silver skin' on p. 167, 14.]
40. *unwonted*. 'unaccustomed'. This is the earliest citation in *OED* 2a.

PAGE 163, 2. *fairest*. The brightest is Sirius.
3. *fixed stars*. Cf. Macrobius, *Commentary on the Dream of Scipio*, trans. W. H. Stahl (New York, 1966), I. xvii. 16, 'with the exception of the two brilliant luminaries and of the five errant planets, the stars move only with the celestial sphere, being fixed in it'. Between the stationary, heavy earth and this outermost sphere, and running contrary to it, were the wanderers whose motion could easily be discerned, and the sun and moon, in this order: earth, moon, Mercury, Venus, sun, Mars, Jupiter, Saturn.
16. *niggards … weirs*. They would be hoarding water for their own use. E. Kerridge, *The Farmers of Old England* (London, 1973), 110–15, discusses the rise of the floated watermeadow from 1560 onwards, with recent aerial photographs on plates 20 and 22 of the remains of those at Wilton.
23. *twenty*. This was a hyperbole for a larger number; cf. *OED* adj. 1d.
24. *in large*. 'on a large scale'. The earliest citation for the phrase in *OED* under *large* n. is from 1601.
27. *at one stay*. 'constant'.
31–3. *her wit … music*. Hoskyns, 13, refers to this as an example of climax 'where the last word or some one word in the last sentence begets the next clause'.
31. *divine fury*. Cf. *A Defence of Poetry* (*Misc. Prose*, 109), Plato 'attributeth unto poesy more than myself do, namely, to be a very inspiring of a divine force, far above man's

wit', and the notes, comparing *AS* 3 and 74, and Spenser, 'October', Argument and Gloss.

37–9. [*speedily write ... utterance.* See p. lxxxi.]

PAGE 164, 1–PAGE 168, 11. Ringler, *OA* 62, and 409–11; Robertson, 238, 6 ff. Texts with substantive variants are *OA* (additions in *Ph* are from *93* or a later edition – Ringler, 526), *Dd* (f. 26, ll. 1–2, and ff. 36ᵛ–37), *Eg* (f. 46ᵛ, last four lines), *Cm* (f. 100, ll. 1–8), *90*, *93* (Ringler, 554–5). Non-substantive copies are in British Library MS Add. 27406, f. 117 (ll. 1–4, from *93* or later); British Library MS Add. 34064, ff. 30–1 from *93* (Ringler, 555); British Library MS Sloane 1925, ff. 13–14, lines from a printed edition (Ringler, 557) in the following order in this text: pp. 191, 30–1; 193, 26–7; 194, 23–4; 194, 21–2; 193, 4–7; 192, 29–30; 192, 1–2; 191, 16–17; Corpus Christi College, Oxford, MS 328, ff. 85–86ᵛ, from *93* or later (Ringler, 559); Folger Shakespeare Library MS V.a.162 [452.4], ff. 93–96ᵛ (Ringler, 560; Robertson, 459). It is printed in *England's Parnassus*, no. 2012. This was referred to under 'Icon, or Resemblance by Imagery', by George Puttenham, *The Art of English Poesy*, ed. G. D. Willcock and A. Walker (Cambridge, 1936), 244 (cited in Robertson, 459). See A. Saunders, 'Sixteenth-century Collected Editions of *Blasons Anatomiques*', *The Library*, 5th Ser. xxxi (1976), 351–68. Robertson's arrangement of the verse paragraphs is followed here. [Additionally, paraphrases of 41 lines from the poem (interspersed with lines from other poems, taken from *Englands Parnassus*) appear in the section on 'Encomions on the Beauty of his Mistresse' on p. 129 and pp. 131–7 of *The Academy of Complements* (1640) by 'Philomusus' (probably William Elder, author of a near-identical collection published in 1656 as *Pearls of Eloquence*, which contains the same extracts in the same order). While the lines describing Philoclea's eyelids, cheeks, ears, lips, teeth, shoulders, hands and waist are only lightly modified to contextualize the couplets better, Philomusus' paraphrases of the lines describing her navel, belly and thighs noticeably change the tone of the poem, making its eroticism more explicit, so his paraphrase of p. 166, 8–11 reads:

> Most beauteous seale of Virgin wax,
> Pittie tis still the impression lackes;
> This place my sence with joy doth fill,
> Since tis intitled Cupids hill: (136)

In case this is still too subtle, Philomusus then adds a slighly modified couplet from Thomas Lodge's 'Forbonius and Prisceria' (published with *An Alarum Against Vsurers* (1584)): 'From hence a seemely passage there doth flow, / To stranger pleasures that are plac'd below.']

7. *more ... snow.* This is cited in C. G. Smith, *Spenser's Proverb Lore*, 843.

9. *even.* 'smooth'; cf. Spenser, *Faerie Queene*, II. xxv, Belphoebe's 'euen browes'. These are the unwrinkled brows on which the 'equal lines' of the eyebrows sit. Robertson, 459, notes the corresponding convention which uses *ebon* to describe black eyebrows. [Unlike the emphatic adverb 'even' (which is typically used monosyllabically in early modern verse), the adjective is usually disyllabic – cf. the manuscript variants 'eben' or 'pretty', which are disyllabic words that cannot easily be contracted.]

13. [*heav'nly.* See the note to p. 14, 19.]

15. *black stars.* Ringler, 410, compares with this line (along with pp. 165, 28 and 167, 30) the couplet in *AS* song v. 10–11, 'I said thine eyes were stars, thy breasts the milk'n way, / Thy fingers Cupid's shafts, thy voice the angel's lay' (see above, p. xv). Burton, *Anatomy of Melancholy*, 3. 2. 2. 2, lists commendations of black eyes, and notes the

comparison with stars in Balthasar Castilio, 'aemula lumina stellis', but not that in Ovid, *Met.* i. 499, 'Sideribus similes, oculos'.

16. *matchless ... stain.* 'unequalled pair which even praise belittles'. Robertson, 82, 7, 'the due praise of her praise', Robertson, 84, 33–85, 1, 'Ere that I leave with song of praise her praise to solemnize, / Her praise, whence to the world all praise had his only beginning', and p. 178, 24–6 below support the genuineness of *matchless praise* OA, Dd, however subsequently revised. See Ringler, 410; Robertson, 459–60.

21–2. *only ... see.* Cf. H. Goldwell, *Brief Declaration*, the speech of the herald representing the Four Foster Children of Desire at The Fortress of Perfect Beauty, 'that this death or overthrow may be seen by those eyes, who are only unhappy in that they can neither find fellows nor see themselves', in J. Nichols, *Progresses of Queen Elizabeth* (1823), ii. 328. Robertson, 460, compares OP 4. 451, 'Those eyes which nothing like themselves can see'.

25. *queen-apple's side.* Cf. Jonson, *Volpone*, IV. ii. 72–3, 'Your nose inclines – / That side that's next the sun – to the queen apple'; and Robertson, 460, comparing Spenser, 'June', 43.

29. *So that.* 'in such a way that'.

31. [*incirclets.* Probably coined by Sidney as a trisyllabic variant of 'circlets' (small circles) with a possible pun on 'encircle' (cf. also the similar formation 'incaved' in p. 166, 30). No other examples are cited in *OED*, although it appears in Joshua Poole's *The English Parnassus* (1657), which quotes this line in the section on ways to describe the ear (p. 265), lists 'incirclet' as a synonym for 'crown' (p. 242) and includes the phrase 'Verdant incirclets' in the cryptically titled section 'Garden v. flowers: Pleasant place. Garland v. Crown' (p. 319). *Englands Parnassus* has 'incircles'. Cf. also Spenser's 'circulet' (*Mother Hubberds Tale* 624).]

PAGE 165, 4–5 [*tip ... tip. Englands Parnassus* reads 'lippe' for both, perhaps caused by an eyeskip to 'ruddy lips' two lines below. The strangeness of the image suggests an absent-minded or hasty compositor (as well as perhaps a sloppily written copy text). See also the note to p. 14, 9.]

5–10. *ruddy ... row.* Robertson, 460, compares AS song v. 38, 'nor pearl's ruby-hidden row'. Pearl teeth and ruby lips are in Spenser, *Faerie Queene*, II. iii. 24; in *Amoretti*, 81; and in analogues provided in Spenser, *Works*, ii. 215 from Tasso and from Phineas Fletcher's *Purple Island*, and ibid. viii. 451–2 where Tasso's *Rime*, II. xxv. 17 is printed. G. Sandys, translating Ovid, *Met.* i. 499 (1632), B2, 'videt oscula, quae non / Est vidisse satis', may have imitated Sidney in 'her lips which kiss / Their happy selves'.

7. [*Rubies ... new.* The line noticeably deviates from the otherwise regular iambic metre of the poem. This cannot easily be resolved through spondees, because it would lead to too many syllables. To become iambic, the line would consequently have required a syllable before the word 'rubies' and the omission of 'and' – e.g. '*Such* rubies, cherries, roses new' – although none of the manuscript variants appear to have 'corrected' it in this fashion. George Wither alludes to the line in *Faire-virtue* (1622), F3: 'For, from thence he onely sips, / The pure *Nectar*, of her lips. / And at once with these he closes, / Melting Rubies, Cherries, Roses'.]

10–12. *pearl ... guard.* Cf. Tilley, T424, 'Good that the teeth guard the tongue'; cited in *ODEP*.

12. [*heav'nly-dewed.* See the note to p. 14, 19.]

23. *pommels.* Robertson, 460, compares Sannazaro, *Arcadia*, Prosa 4, 'duo ritondi pomi', *pomi* being equally translatable as apples or as pommels, ornamental knobs. See p. 74, 4–5 and note. Earlier uses of *pommel* for a woman's breast are cited in *OED* 3b and E. Huguet, *Dictionnaire*, under *pommelle*.

23-4. *marble ... veins.* See p. xxvii.
33-4. [*Waist ... embraced.* See p. lxxxi.]

PAGE 166, 13-14. *alablaster.* 'alabaster'. See p. lxi.
18-19. *world ... forgotten.* Robertson, 460, notes the similarity with Phineas Fletcher, *Venus and Anchises*, xxix, 'the shameless world of best things is ashamed'; cf. Tilley, N317, 'The best things may be abused'. [Glossed as a *sententia* in 90 through inverted commas, which are preserved in 93, 98 and the 1605 folio.]
21. *Her.* The compositor of 90 appears to have seen a mark deleting *Those* OA but failed to make the substitution printed in 93.
21-2. *Ovid's ... flanks.* Robertson, 460, compares Ovid, *Amores*, I. v. 22, 'Quantum et quale latus, quam juvenile femur!', translated by Marlowe, *Ovid's Elegies*, 'How large a leg, and what a lusty thigh', though Sidney more literally translates *latus* as *flank*.
22. *flanked.* The earliest citation in *OED* is from 1651. [There are earlier examples, however, for example in *The benefit of the aunciente bathes of Buckstones* (1572).]
24. *Albion clives.* The reference is to the chalk cliffs near Dover. [While *Englands Parnassus* regularizes to 'cliffes', Amour 24 of Michael Drayton's *Ideas Mirrour* (1594) preserves the less common form, perhaps as a more overt nod to Sidney: 'And *Auons* fame, to *Albyons* Cliues is raysed' (D4ᵛ).]
30. *bought incaved.* 'inward bend of the knee'. This is the only citation in *OED* for *incave* in this sense.
31. *shadowing.* 'shading'. The earliest citation in *OED* 9 is from 1603. Further references to chiaroscuro are on pp. 260, 35-7; 277, 38-278, 2; 342, 32-3; 380, 7-8.

PAGE 167, 1-2. *skies ... small.* As Atlas supported the heavens, so that most slender small of her leg supports the round skies of her calves; cf. *OED* under *small* n. B. 2. 7a; and p. 58, 18.
9. *Where ... mews.* 'Where Zeus, no longer needing his disguise, moults and leaves behind his feathers'. This is a periphrastic expression for the whiteness of her back.
11. *Like ... set.* 'Like round marzipan-covered sweetmeats'.
13. *within ... rooves.* The impression meant to be conveyed is of a dovecot with a high pitched roof having dormers on each side for entrances. [*Englands Parnassus* has 'in' for 'within', perhaps caused by an eyeskip to 'in marchpane' two lines above. See also the notes to p. 14, 9 and p. 165, 4-5.]
14. *leaded.* 'covered', as with sheets of lead roofing.
15. *hate-spot ermelin.* See p. 86, 36 and note.
17. *phoenix.* This is the uninflected genitive; see p. xxxii.
25. *Warm snow.* Ringler, 411, notes Petrarch's use of this oxymoron in 30. 10, 57. 5, and 157. 9, and compares *AS* song v. 37, 'warm, fine-odoured snow'. Robertson, 461, cites A. Davenport's comparison in *N & Q.* cxciv (1949), 555, with Shakespeare, *A Midsummer Night's Dream*, V. i. 59, 'hot ice and wondrous strange snow'. [Sir William Alexander, author of the *Supplement*, borrowed the phrase in Sonnet 78 of *Aurora* (1604).]
28. *Sweet islands.* See p. xxvii.
30. *shafts ... Cupid's.* See the note to p. 164, 15.
30. *amatists.* 'amethysts'; purple or violet gems.

PAGE 168, 4. [*How. Englands Parnassus* reads 'Now', indicating a misreading of the manuscript copy text. See also the notes to p. 14, 9 and p. 165, 4-5.]
8. *the ... lend.* 'Immortal fame lends the ink'. On the enduring property of verse perpetuated by its fame, see Ovid, *Met.* xv. 872-80; Virgil, *Aeneid*, ix. 446-7; and see *A Defence of Poetry* (*Misc. Prose*, 121, 18 ff.).

10–11. *No tongue ... all tongues.* Duplication of the opening lines seems to have been rejected from this contrasting repetition, which is similar to the construction used in the early version of p. 164, 16 (see note), *praise ... praise.* [*Englands Parnassus* does duplicate the opening lines. See the notes to p. 14, 9 and p. 165, 4–5.]
28. [*a right manlike man.* See the note to p. 204, 27–8.]

PAGE 169, 3–4. [*madded ... messenger.* Zelmane is angry both because her 'unlooked-for rival' Amphialus does not consider her a rival and because he has asked her to convey his declaration of love to Philoclea.]
6–7. [*Amazon-like.* 'in the manner of Amazons' – but also a reminder that 'Zelmane' is not really an Amazon.]
15. [*this courtesy ... Zelmane.* Amphialus' 'courtesy' here largely manifests itself in his insistence on treating even a belligerent Amazon as a 'fair lady' and thus only serves to make Pyrocles – who is not used to being patronized – angrier.]
20. *witty fury.* 'rational anger', an example of synoeciosis.
22–3. [*courtesy ... heart.* The text keeps stressing this as Amphialus' defining quality. See also lines 15 above and 29 below]
24–7. *sometimes ... sometimes.* Cf. *OED* under *sometime* 1b for examples of 'sometime' and 'sometimes' used together to introduce antithetical clauses.
26. *well-met.* This is the only citation in *OED* A2 [('*apparently*: designating a skilfully executed defensive stroke or movement, which parries blows effectively'), although it might also be A1 ('evenly matched in an encounter; well-matched').]
29. [*more spited ... courtesy.* See the notes to lines 15 and 22–3 above.]
33–4. [*seeming ... violence.* 'seeming' hints that the emblematic impression of innocence vs. violence is misleading – Amphialus is not as innocent and 'courteous' as he appears, and Pyrocles not as impulsive and violent. See also pp. lxxxiii–lxxxiv.]
35. *who ... no defence.* Hoskyns, 39, cites this as an example of sententia, with synoeciosis and epanodos.

PAGE 170, 2. *retiring.* 'drawing back'. The earliest citation in *OED* 5b is from Shakespeare, *Rape of Lucrece*, 303.
3. *conquered ... before-conquered.* See p. xxviii.
23–4. [*near ... Macedon.* See the note to p. 76, 11–12. Cf. p. 393, 29–30, where Zelmane tries to persuade Anaxius to fight her by claiming to be Pyrocles' half-sister.]
29–30. *solitary ... spaniel.* See p. xxiii.
32–3. *dream ... dreamed.* See p. xxiii.

PAGE 171, 8. *he ... them.* 'placing himself in their charge'.
12. [*naked simplicity.* i.e. improper clothing, dishabillé. Cf. p. 170, 22–3, which implies the princesses dressed after emerging from the river, but only minimally so.]
16–17. [*having ... fingers.* In sixteenth-century English, 'his' is also used as the genitive form of 'it' (the earliest example of 'its' in *OED* is only from 1577). Here the contrasting pronouns may be deliberate to heighten the eroticism of the image, however.]
20. *Dorus had told.* See p. 117, 19 ff.
31. *forced.* 'cared'. Cf. *OED* under *force* v. 14a(c), with the infinitive as object.

PAGE 172, 1–PAGE 176, 36. Ringler *OA* 30, and 401–2; Robertson, 146, 26 ff. Texts with substantive variants are *OA (ex. O), Cm* (ll. 1–33),90, 93. In the *Old Arcadia (ex. Le)* it is preceded by four lines and followed by six lines by the narrator, Histor. F. J. Fabry, 'Sidney's Poetry and Italian Song-Form', *ELR* iii (1973), 244 f., demonstrates that this lament 'is the kind of matter most favoured by composers of *capitoli*', songs in terza rima.

5-6. *my voice ... cries.* Robertson, 445, compares J. Wilbye, *The First Set of English Madrigals* (1598), no. 26. 9, in E. H. Fellowes, *English Madrigal Verse*, 3rd edn., rev. by F. W. Sternfeld and D. Greer (Oxford, 1967), 309, 'My throat is sore, my voice is hoarse, with skriking'.

9. *vessel of the mind.* 'receptacle of the soul'. Cf. *OED* under *vessel* n.¹ 3b, citing G. Du Wes, 'The body ... is the vessel of the soul', from 1532.

11. *mansions blind.* 'out of the way mansions'.

14. *Balls ... stars.* Cf. below, p. 395, 5, and Robertson, 386, 1-2, mankind 'are but like tennis balls tossed by the racket of the higher powers'. The classical allusion is to football (see Lewis and Short, *Latin Dictionary*, under *pila*, and *OED*), but later references are to tennis; cf. Shakespeare, *Pericles*, II. i. 63-4. [Tennis imagery gained popularity during the 1570s and 1580s. Examples include Churchyard's poem 'A Tragicall Discourse of the Vnhappy Mans Life' (in *The First Part of Churchyardes Chippes* (1575)), and Arthur Golding's translations of John Calvin's sermons on Job (1574) and Deuteronomy (1583). English translations of Calvin's sermons during this period are noticeably idiomatic, so the presence of multiple tennis analogies in the translations of Golding and others perhaps says more about the popularity of tennis imagery in English than it does about Calvin's own partiality to the sport.]

17. *filthy stage.* Cf. *A Defence of Poetry* (*Misc. Prose*, 95, 30-1), 'naughty play-makers and stage-keepers have justly made odious' English comedy. Ringler, 401, notes the similarity with Stephen Gosson's criticism of the commercial stage in *The School of Abuse* (1579), dedicated to Sidney.

20-1. *man ... life.* This is cited in Tilley, W889, 'We weeping come into the world and weeping hence we go'; in *ODEP*, 876; and in C. G. Smith, *Spenser's Proverb Lore*, 870. [Cf. also Melpomene's lament in Spenser's *Teares of the Muses* 157-9.]

21. [*presage.* 'omen'. Cf. pp. 190, 17; 200, 3; 256, 6; 277, 25; 323, 15; 347, 3.]

23. *shop of shame.* 'a place where what is morally disgraceful is produced'. Robertson, 445, cites the comparison by M. Poirier, in *Études Anglaises*, xi (1958), 153, with 'shops of shame' in Spenser, 'September', 36.

25-8. *strife ... reposed.* Cf. Marlowe, *1 Tamburlaine*, II. vii. 18-20:

> Nature that fram'd us of four elements,
> Warring within our breasts for regiment,
> Doth teach us all to have aspiring minds,

and James Howell, Δενδρολογια. *Dodona's Grove* (1640), I3-I3ᵛ, 'The philosophers teach that in natural bodies all things decay by the inward conflict of their principles, and reluctancy of the predominant elements; for if a body were evenly balanced by the four elements whence the humours are derived, it would be unperishable'.

30. *top ... whipping.* Fulke Greville used this image in his *Letter to an Honourable Lady*, ch. 4, 'Our flesh being like a top which only goes upright with whipping'; in *Caelica*, 86. 10, 'Life is a top which whipping sorrow driveth'; and in *Caelica*, 96. 49, 'Flesh but the *Top*, which only *Whips* make go'.

31. *man ... tree.* This describes the tripartite soul in man, containing the sensible soul of animals and the vegetal soul of plants.

17-18. *stone ... brain.* 'Anything the least bit more intelligent than a stone will feel grief'; cf. Arthur Golding's Preface, in *Shakespeare's Ovid*, 113-14: 'And if we be so drowned in vice that feeling once be gone, / Then may it well of us be said, we are a block or stone.'

32-3. These lines were set as a song for four voices in John Ward, *The First Set of English Madrigals* (1613), no. 12, ed. E. H. Fellowes, *The English Madrigal School*, xix (1922), and the words reprinted in E. H. Fellowes, *English Madrigal Verse*, 3rd edn., rev. by F. W. Sternfeld and D. Greer (Oxford, 1967), 268.

PAGE 173, 18–19. *Erona ... die*. Hoskyns, 12, cites this as an example of anadiplosis, 'repetition in the end of the former sentence and beginning of the next'.

19. *if heav'n*. Cf. p. 311, 9–10.

23. [*pow'rs*. See the notes to pp. 59, 12 and 126, 6.]

24. *virtue ... neglect*. See p. 16, 11–12 and note.

35. *sweet scourge*. Ringler, 401, compares St Augustine, *De Patientia*, I. xiv, which draws on Proverbs 3: 11–12 and Wisdom 3: 4–6; cf. also Job 5: 17 and Hebrews 12: 5. Parallels are cited in *ODEP* 5, under 'Afflictions are sent to us by God for our good' (Tilley, A53).

PAGE 174, 6. *moan ... bemoan*. Cf. Tilley, W924, 'The worth of a thing is best known by the want', and *ODEP*, 922.

10–14. *death ... get*. Cf. Shakespeare, *Romeo and Juliet*, V. iii. 102–5:

> Shall I believe
> That unsubstantial death is amorous,
> And that the lean abhorred monster keeps
> Thee here in dark to be his paramour?

and see E. Wind, *Pagan Mysteries in the Renaissance*, rev. edn. (Harmondsworth, 1967), 160–1.

20. [*what mine ... tower?*. A passage dug under an enemy position to make it collapse (hence 'undermine'). Cf. Arthur Hall's *Ten Books of Homer's Iliades, Translated out of French* (1581), p. 73, in which Echepolus' death is described in the line 'He fell as doth a tower hie, whych men do mine about'.]

21. *hath ... disgraced?* 'has dishonoured such a saint?'

29–30. *which ... grave*. 'which might have the power to remind the sun, Apollo, of Phaeton's mother, Clymene'; cf. Ovid, *Met*. i. 756 ff. 17.

31 *Vulcan's spite*. 'fire', over which Vulcan presided.

32. [*melt that virgin-wax*. Cf. p. 166, 8.]

35. *wittold beast*. Vulcan; see Glossary, and p. xxxii.

36. *Thy Venus' child*. Erona was Venus' child in spirit. Mars was Venus' paramour, Ovid, *Met*. iv. 171 ff.; cf. *A Defence of Poetry* (*Misc. Prose*, 110, 35–6).

PAGE 175, 1. *get ... grace*. Cf. p. 351, 29–30.

2. [*Sweet ... reclaims*. Glossed as a sententia in 90 through inverted commas, which are preserved in 93, 98, and the 1605 folio.]

PAGE 176, 6. *unlacing her*. Such an intimate act was construed by Puttenham, *The Art of English Poesy*, ed. G. D. Willcock and A. Walker (Cambridge, 1936), 196, as a synecdoche for 'the taking of a woman's maidenhead away'.

7. *mourning plainfulness*. 'sorrowful grieving'. This is the only citation in *OED* under *plainfulness*.

8. *diamond ... graved*. Cf. p. 335, 36 and Queen Elizabeth I, 'written with a diamond on her window at Woodstock', in *Poems*, ed. L. Bradner (Providence, RI, 1964), and Donne, 'A Valediction of My Name in the Window'. This is the earliest citation in *OED* 5a under *window-glass*.

PAGE 177, 12. *great request*. To help him rescue Erona; see p. 265, 12–13.

17–26. *Lycia ... Lycians*. See p. liii.

20. [*he punished*. This refers to Cupid.]

31. [*wilfully persevered* ... *in it*. See note to p. 23, 28.]

PAGE 178, 29. *barbarous*. 'non-Hellenic' and 'savagely cruel'.

38–9. *languishing consumption*. 'lingering disease'. The earliest citation in *OED* under *languishing* adj. 2 is from 1567.

PAGE 179, 7. [*he saw it like enough*. Either 'he very likely saw' or 'he saw that it was very likely'. The syntax is ambiguous, but the punctuation in 90 (commas before and after the phrase, rather than brackets around 'like enough') points to the latter reading.]

14. *Musidorus ... Barzanes*. Cf. p. 229, 29–30.

Pyrocles Euardes. Cf. pp. 203, 1–2; 337, 34–5.

PAGE 180, 14. *married*. Cf. Pamela's attitude, p. 366, 15–18.

22–3. *As for ... were*. 'As for ... they were'. Cf. *OED* under *as for*, 'Formerly occasionally with omission of the anaphoric pronoun in the main clause', a practice unacceptable to the editor of 93.

25. *furder*. 'further'. See p. lxi.

PAGE 181, 14 (*var*.). [*of the old cut*. 'outmoded', 'old-fashioned'. This is *cut* n.², 17b ('fashion, style, make'). Cf. Thomas Nashe's *Strange Newes* (1593) A2, which calls Gabriel Harvey a man who 'hath made many proper rimes of the old Cutte in his daies'. In *An Almond for a Parrat* (1589) F^v, Nashe had used the opposite image in the phrase 'apeece of scholershippe of the new cut'. The imagery is of clothes made according to fashion (see also Spenser's *Mother Hubberds Tale* 211–12: 'His breeches were made after the new cut, / Al Portugese, loose like an emptie gut'). The 1987 edition glossed 'cut' as 'a term of abuse' (meaning 30 in *OED*), but it is less likely that the chapter summary would use a disparaging term for Mopsa's heroine than that it would use a disparaging term for her story.]

14. *poets ... shun*. Cf. Ovid, *Met*. x. 280, 'Dira canam: natae procul hinc, procul este parentes', trans. Golding, x. 327–8, 'Of wicked and most cursed things to speak I now commence, / Ye daughters and ye parents all, go get ye far from hence.'

27. *I beshrow me*. 'I curse myself'.

28–32. *I have ... husbands*. When away from Dametas, Miso insists upon speaking first, believing that in marriage opening and concluding debates is the privilege of husbands.

31. *this ... suffered*. 'this can be endured'.

34. *ferret-eyes*. Cf. Tilley, E255, 'Eyes as red as a ferret's', and *ODEP*, 236.

38. *quavering*. 'as if sung with a trill'.

PAGE 182, 2. *simple ... here*. This is an idiomatic invocation of honesty, though Miso has adapted it to her sitting posture: 'simple as I stand here' seems to be the convention. The earliest citation for the phrase in *OED* under *simple* adj. is from 1589.

thought ... silver. This is cited in Tilley, P194. [As with 'simple as I sit here', Miso seems to adapt the expression to suit her purposes; in earlier examples it implies foolish vanity (i.e. the belief that other people's money is worth less). Cf. John Lyly, *Euphues* (1579), fol. 7^v: 'Heere ye may beholde gentlemen, how lewdly wit standeth in his owne lyght, howe he deemeth no pennye good siluer but his owne'. Cf. also Austin Saker, *Narbonus* (1580), p. 92:

> she so flattered him to the will of his fancie, and so bragged alwayes of hir honestie, which he thought to be most true, and that he had found some singu-

ler peece: and to make him beleeue the better of hir honestie, and to thinke that she could not be but good, she would hit him in the teeth with some one man of his profession, or some woman so honest as hir selfe, that had bin plagued for their wickednes, and punished for their sinnes. My maister Merchant thought hir pennie good Siluer, and that there was no better hay in Denshire, determined therefore to abide the brunt of this bargaine, and to dispatch his mariage'.]

3. [*if ... hasty fool*. 'if he had not rashly married me off at the first opportunity'. By her own account, Miso was still unmarried and beleaguered with suitors as a 'young girl' of twenty-seven (twice Philoclea's age) when the wise old woman offered her advice. What Miso presents as her father's rush to see her married young, then, was really his rush to see her married at all, so he was being 'hasty' in a different sense.]

4. *another-gaines*. 'of another kind'. This is Miso's coinage. *OED* suggests 'a corruption of *anotherkins* or *another-gates*, or a mixture of the two'; see p. xxxi.

9. [*in*. i.e. 'written on the flyleaves of' (cf. p. 183, 11). Manuscript notes added to Bibles or prayer-books in this manner were typically used to record births, deaths, marriages and other notable events in the owner's family, so Miso's inclusion of the ballad in this place highlights the significance she attaches to it.]

prayer-book. The earliest citation in *OED* is from 1529. *Cm* reads the more common 'paper book', but all texts have 'prayer-book' at p. 183, 11.

11. *No ... good*. 'haste is not good'. This is Tilley, H199.

13–14. *pretty little eyes*. See p. 330, 29 and note. [The narrator's disparaging comment about Andromana's 'small eyes' (p. 81, 9–11) suggests that Miso is proud of a physical feature generally considered to detract from beauty.]

16. *wink ... eye*. 'close one eye, as in aiming at a target'. On this idiomatic use, see *OED* under *wink* v. 4.

daisies. This is a debased usage of the emblem of true love. Cf. Chaucer, Prologue to *The Legend of Good Women*, 40 ff.; and H. Jenkins, ed., Shakespeare, *Hamlet* (London, 1982), 540, on IV. v. 181.

17. *peacock's tail*. This is an emblem of vanity; cf. Tilley, P157, 'As proud as a peacock'; cited in C. G. Smith, *Spenser's Proverb Lore*, 603. See p. 78, 38, and Robertson, 78, 27; 248, 1.

19. *wold*. 'old'. This is Miso's dialectal form.

22. *sop*. 'drink', of the wine used for dipping or steeping bread.

23. *Candia*. 'Crete'. Its wines enjoyed a high reputation.

23–4. [*which ... good cheap*. Miso's comments about the cheapness of wine from Crete in her youth may be a humorous reference to the fact that by the late sixteenth century, wines from Spain (which were significantly cheaper) had become widely available in England, making the wine from Crete seem more expensive by comparison. Additionally, Greek wines were no longer 'good cheap' in the sense of 'easily obtained' (cf. the note on p. 298, 8) during this period, due to the presence of pirates in the Mediterranean.]

28–9. *horns ... eyes*. These attributes befit the offspring of the heifer Io and her hundred-eyed guardian, Argus; see p. 212, 31. G. Kipling, *The Triumph of Honour* (Leiden, 1977), 110, notes a Burgundian pageant from the late fifteenth century in which the god of love was 'decked out in peacock's wings and feathers'; cf. Ronsard, 'L'Amour oyseau', followed by Spenser, 'March', 80, Cupid 'With spotted wings like peacock's train'.

30-1. *pair of gallows.* OED suggests that 'pair' might refer 'to the two posts of which the apparatus mainly consisted'.

31-2. *laurel... money.* See p. 184, 13–14; cf. Jacopo Zucchi, *Discorso sopra li dei de'gentili e loro imprese* (Rome, 1602), 51, ' "Just as the eye-spangled peacock's tail and the rainbow" – attributes of Juno – "dissolve into nothing, so do ambition and wealth" '; cited in J. Seznec, *The Survival of the Pagan Gods*, trans. B. F. Sessions (New York, 1961), 272.

32. *lace, of.* 'noose, on'.

PAGE 183, 2. *between... me.* 'in private' and 'by our joint action'.

3–4. [*this book.* Miso's prayer-book is unlikely to originate from the ballad-maker (and the wording on p. 182, 9 implies she considers the poem and the book separate entities), so she probably means the broadsheet containing the poem. The entry for *book* 1b in OED notes that '[I]n general, a short literary composition... receives some other name', but given Miso's lack of education it is not inconceivable that she might consider any printed text a 'book'.]

4. *ballets.* 'ballads'. See p. lv.

4–5. *for... pleasure.* 'in return for a little sensual gratification'. [A bawdy pun on the common expression 'to do (or show) someone a pleasure', in which 'pleasure' simply meant 'favour' (see P3 in OED). The verb 'pleasure' could be used similarly.]

6. *cow... Argus.* This may represent the debasing of learning through ignorance, as Argus was anything but false; cf. Ovid, *Met.* i. 568 ff. Robertson, 429–30, cites Florio's *Second Fruits* (1591), Y4, where Sidney's originality in this version of Cupid's pedigree is alluded to.

11. [*latter end.* 'flyleaf'. See the note to p. 182, 9.]

prayer-book. See p. 182, 9 and note.

13–**PAGE 184**, 24. Ringler, *OA* 8, and 387–8; Robertson, 65, 9 ff. Texts with substantive variants are *OA* (ex. As, O), *Cm* (incipit only), 90, 93. See p. lix.

16. *glozes of.* 'false appearances for'.

21. *blind.* See p. 14, 15 and note.

22. *young.* Cupid or Eros is portrayed as young, and, beginning with Hesiod, the oldest of the gods along with Earth and Tartarus; cf. *The Oxford Classical Dictionary*, ed. N. G. L. Hammond and H. H. Scullard, 2nd edn. (Oxford, 1973), under *Eros*.

22–4. *Phoebus'... head.* Angry Cupid caused Phoebus' love for Daphne, Ovid, *Met.* i. 452 ff. Cupid's two arrows are described in *Met.* i. 470–1: one is sharp, bright, gold, and causes love (see p. 283, 13); the other is dull, tipped with lead, and causes hatred. In the third, signifying cuckoldry (Ringler, 387), Sidney adapted military reality, for 'many countries both of old time and now use heads of horn', Ascham, *Toxophilus*, in *English Works*, ed. W. A. Wright (Cambridge, 1904), 93.

27–8. *Juno... Argus.* See Ovid, *Met.* i. 568 ff., and note to p. 183, 6.

35. *To... accuse.* This line falls into two parts: verbs of self-defence through deceit, and verbs of aggression through stealth, spying, and accusation.

36. *each other.* 'every other'.

PAGE 184, 2 & 5. [*horned.* Monosyllabic in l. 2 and disyllabic in l. 5, for metrical reasons.]

3. *winking wily shifts.* 'closing in crafty substitutions'. Argus' eyes slept in unnoticed succession, one pair always open.

13–14. *narrow... fire.* See p. 182, 31–2 and note.

17. *for that.* 'because'.

COMMENTARY

18. *name*. Latin *cupido* means 'desire'.
19. [*drivel*. A foolish or loathsome person. The metre suggests that the word should be monosyllabic, perhaps in imitation of 'devil', for which it may be a euphemism (cf. the note to p. 504, 30 and Spenser's *Faerie Queene* IV. ii. 3, where Duessa and Ate are called 'that false witch and that foule aged dreuill / The one a feend, the other an incarnate deuill'). See also Zelmane's claim that these are 'blasphemies'.]
20. *more ... wicked*. 'the more he was driven into exile, the more wicked he became'.

PAGE 185, 4. *blind*. See p. 143, 20–1 and note.
5. *And so*. Although this series of connectives parodies rustic style, even in heroic passages the narrator is not immune from such repetitions; cf. pp. 169, 28–32.
9. *keep ... house*. 'entertain in a grand manner'. [Cf. Kalander's 'great house' on p. 9, 1.]
13. *one ... silver*. The knight was blond, the horse was a grey.
15. *going ... head*. 'going past'. Cf. *OED* under *head* n. P1 k.(c).
17. *May ... rejoice*. On this commonplace, cf. Gavin Douglas's extensive description in the Prologue to the twelfth book of his translation of Virgil's *Aeneid*.
18. [*without ... breakfast*. Mopsa's many references to food suggest a preoccupation. Cf. also Dametas' culinary insults of Clinias in Book III (p. 329, 21–2).]
22. *upon his blessing*. 'on condition of receiving his favour'.
[*what*. 'who'. Formulaic phrases along the lines of 'what he was, whence he was and whither he would' (who he was, where he was from, and where he was going) were common and feature for example in Lyly's *Euphues and his England* (1580), Foxe's *Actes and Monuments* and Thomas Nashe's *The Vnfortunate Traueller* (1594). In this context 'what he was ...' builds up to the punchline and highlights that Mopsa's 'old wives tale' is cobbled together from tropes.]
23. *nor ... would*. That is, vanish away.
24. *dark as pitch*. This is Tilley, P357.
25. [*the question*. i.e. unable to see in the dark, she had to ask him where he had gone.]
26–27. [*that ... them*. An odd substitute for the more conventional heart of flint, iron or adamant; apparently Mopsa's coinage.]
37. *marriage-day*. The earliest citation in *OED* is from 1447.

PAGE 186, 2. *purposing with herself*. 'resolving'.
20. *eyes ... judge*. See p. 11, 19 and note.
28. [*such ... caught*. i.e. she only feigned resistance to Plangus' advances.]
33–6. [*sleeping ... accident*. Lethargy or the 'drowsy evil' was believed to originate in the brain and was associated with memory loss. *A Sanctuarie for a Troubled Soule*, pp. 107–8, paraphrases to: 'But as one that is sicke of a sleepie disease cannot bee awaked but by pinching; soe out of this lethargie of sinne, my sleepy soule (neither vnworthie nor vnwilling to haue perished) could not be called to it selfe, but by some sharpe and sensible accident'.]

PAGE 187, 2. *princes' ears*. Cf. Tilley, K87, 'Kings have long ears'. [Cf. also Robert Norton's translation of Rudolf Gwalther's *Certaine Godlie Homelies* (1573), pp. 245–6: 'For it is the maner of kings to haue many eares, many eies, and many hands, namely officers, by whome they know, & administer all things.']
13. *prodigal protestations*. The prodigal Plangus proclaims her chastity. Cf. *OED* under *prodigal* adj. 2, 'In Shakespeare ... by a kind of hypallage attributed to another noun in the sentence'.
29. *hoping of him*. 'supposing by him'.

29-32. [*left ... swallowed*. *A Sanctuarie for a Troubled Soule*, pp. 129-30, paraphrases to: 'how cunningly doth the deuell seeke to delay mee? what arte hath he vsed to keepe the line from breaking wherat the fish was caught? not drawing him violently, but letting him play vpon the hooke which hee soe greedely had swallowed.']
33. *mourning*. See p. lvi.
35-6. *affection ... pity*. Cf. *AS* 1. 4, 'Knowledge might pity win, and pity grace obtain'.

PAGE 188, 5. *weep ... would*. Cf. Tilley, W713, 'Women laugh when they can and weep when they will'.
7. [*teach ... blushing*. Blushing at will was regarded as a mark of particular duplicity.]
9-10. [*spur ... have it*. Andromana's manipulation of Plangus' father is being compared to the training of a horse. Cf. p. 94, 1-2. See also *ride* 19b in *OED*.]
31-2 *shunning ... sycophants*. 'instead of openly accusing him, as would paid slanderers'; cf. p. 145, 30-4.

PAGE 189, 4-5. *favours ... favours*. 'goodwill ... aid'.
11. *like might*. 'similar greatness'.
12-13. *loved ... ruin*. Cf. p. 146, 12.
17-18. *power ... hurt*. This is the earliest citation in Tilley, H170.

PAGE 190, 3-4. *Plangus' ... suspicion*. Hoskyns, 47, cites this as an example of periphrasis.
9-10. *as many ... Proteus*. Cf. Tilley, S285, 'As many shapes as Proteus'; cited in C. G. Smith, *Spenser's Proverb Lore*, 683.
10. *tedious*. See p. lvi.

PAGE 191, 15-16. [*that ... credulity*. Although 'credulity' is used in a negative sense here, 'credulity' in the positive sense was regarded as the foundation of faith. The 1598 edition of Nicholas Ling's *Politeuphuia*, whose section on credulity is based on the positive definition of credulity as 'a certaine ground and vnfained trust which wee repose in the obiect propounded to our imagination' consequently misquotes this passage as 'Credulity is the onely *aduantage* of honest harts. S. P. S.' (fol. 143, emphasis added). Unfortunately, this adjustment results in a commonplace that implies honest hearts are otherwise undesirable.]
34. [*his ... naked*. i.e. despite the minister's claim to have seen 'a man with sword *drawn*' (32, emphasis added), Plangus' sword was still sheathed.]

PAGE 192, 21. [*autentically*. The earliest examples of 'authentically' date to the 1560s, but it is relatively rare before 1600. Of the pre-1600 examples in the EEBO / TCP corpus, one third are spelt 'autentically'. Later, 'authentically' became the standard spelling, so the 1621-3 folio inserted an h that was kept by all subsequent editions.]
23. *wives*. 'wife's'. See p. 80, 3 and note.
24. [*so as*. 'so that'.]
32. *brought ... Artaxia*. See p. 181, 3-4.
36. *stolen ... daughters*. See p. xxiii.
39-**PAGE 193**, 1. *whose ... tendered*. This is legal terminology for 'whose suit she forcefully advanced'.

PAGE 193, 2. *her rotten voice*. This may mean 'her obscene turn of phrase'. In Robertson, 33, 10, Miso's reply to Dametas' demand 'that in a whore's name she should come out to him' was in a 'hollow rotten voice that bid him let her alone, like a knave as he was', which may be euphemistic. The earliest citation in *OED* under *rotten* adj. 6b ('morally offensive, obscene', referring to language) is from 1589.

5. [*that youthful error.* Amphialus is several years older than his two cousins (and consequently older than Musidorus and Pyrocles), so this may be a veiled insult.]
6. [*so as.* 'provided that'.]
16-17. [*whom ... bridle.* See the note to p. 76, 17-18.]
28-9. *physician ... taste.* Cf. Tilley, A282, 'Apothecaries would not give pills in sugar unless they were bitter'. [Sidney uses the image of foul-tasting medicine again in the *Defence of Poetry*:

> even as the child is often brought to take most wholesome things by hiding them in such other as have a pleasant taste: which if one should begin to tell them the nature of the Aloes or Rhabarbarum they should receive, wold sooner take their physic at their ears than at their mouth

The difference is that in the *Defence* scenario the wholesome taste of the educational 'physic' really is disguised by the pleasantness of poetry; in Zelmane's case, however, the blow is not softened by the father's protestations of love, and the physician's well-meant lie does not improve the taste of the medicine (i.e. the fact that Basilius and Gynecia are motivated by love does not make her situation any better).]

PAGE 194, 13. *chastest.* OED under *chasted* pp. adj. cites the variant in the 1605 and 1674 editions as the earliest usage meaning 'kept chaste', 'pure'.
15-16. [*Happy ... no feeling.* Cf. *Phisicke Against Fortune* (1579) – Thomas Twyne's translation of Petrarch's *De remediis utriusque fortunae* – in which Reason argues that the dead cannot be fortunate in their burial, because they can no longer feel:

> For what happinesse can this be in hym that hath no feelyng, or as a man woulde say, in one stone not couered with another? For yf it were otherwyse, that a graue or Tumbe made a man fortunate, who were more happie then Mausolus? (340ᵛ)]

16. *respect ... that thou.* This is the punctuation indicated by 90.
30-1. *river ... stopped.* Cf. Tilley, S929, 'The stream stopped swells the higher'; cited in C. G. Smith, *Spenser's Proverb Lore*, 731, who compares p. 363, 37-8.
34. *There ... ground.* Cf. Tilley, D651, 'To kiss the ground'; cited in C. G. Smith, *Spenser's Proverb Lore*, 438.
bliss. 'bless'.

PAGE 195, 3-4. [*tricked himself ... before.* 'dressed up', with an undertone of artifice and (self-)deception. 'forty winters before' hints that even forty years ago, Basilius was no longer a young man and thus had to resort to trickery to impress young women.]
8-21. Ringler, OA 20, and 396; Robertson, 114, 6 ff. Texts with substantive variants are *OA, Cm, 90, 93*. A non-substantive copy is in British Library MS Sloane 1925, f. 13 (Ringler, 557). The 'grammatical texture' of this poem is discussed by R. Jakobson, in M. Brahmer, ed., *Studies in Language and Literature in Honour of M. Schlauch* (Warsaw, 1966), 165-73.
15. *I wail ... store.* Cf. Tilley, M1287, 'Much would have more', and M1144, 'The more a man has the more he desires'; cited in C. G. Smith, *Spenser's Proverb Lore*, 559.
16-17. *blind ... old.* See p. 183, 22 and note.
24. *knees.* See p. 107, 3-4 and p. xxii.
25-6. *old ... shower.* It was in the form of a shower of gold that Jupiter begot Perseus upon Danae, Ovid, *Met.* iv. 611. In paintings by Titian and Tintoretto Danae's ugly old nurse tries to catch the shower in her apron or on a plate – but as Jupiter's

attention is fixed upon the beautiful nude Danae, as has been Pyrocles' mind upon the nude Philoclea, the nurse, like Basilius, is spurned. See p. xxiv.

PAGE 196, 2. *and a swaging.* 'and an assuagement'. As 'assuagement' rather than 'assuaging' was the more common form, the reading of *90*, *93* which was a regular usage has been preferred.

8. *Enjoying.* See p. xxiii and p. 63, 37–64, 2 and note. [Here the situation is more overtly comical, however, because Zelmane deliberately pretends to misunderstand Basilius' phrase 'enjoying those your excellencies' as meaning he came there hoping to consummate his love (cf. 'such base fancies'). She then feigns shock that Basilius would try to take advantage of his position of power (cf. 'disdain of my estate') or think of her as unchaste (cf. 'the opinion of my lightness'). Basilius' 'appalled' reaction suggests that he was not aware of his ambiguous word choice.]

30–1. *save... despair.* Hoskyns, 38, cites this as an example of parison.

PAGE 197, 13–14. [*performing... virtue.* Perhaps a sly reference to the fact that Pyrocles is the character most persistently associated with virtue. Shortly after this scene, Philoclea does end up embracing Pyrocles, after telling him 'thy virtue wan me; thy virtue preserve me' (p. 201, 20–1).]

20. *Alecto ... Proserpina.* One of the Furies, Alecto was the daughter of Proserpina by Pluto. Here, in Alecto's role as causer of grief, Miso is prevented from following Philoclea, the beautiful figure of Proserpina who presided over life and death – in this case Basilius'. See p. xxxiii.

29–30. *neither ... help her.* Hoskyns, 37, cites this as an example of contentio. [See also p. lxxv.]

33. *meltingly ... metamorphosed.* Having failed to discourage Pluto from taking Proserpina, Cyane melted into tears and became metamorphosed into the pool in which she stood; cf. Ovid, *Met.* v. 430 ff. [This is the earliest citation in *OED* for *meltingly*.]

PAGE 198, 8. *willow.* Sidney's marginal note to *OA* 13. 118, 'my request is crowned with a willow', equates the willow with refusal (Robertson, 86, 22); cf. Spenser, *Faerie Queene*, I. i. ix. 3, 'The willow worne of forlorne Paramours', and the note in Spenser, *Works*, i. 181; and Shakespeare, *Othello*, IV. iii. 40 ff.

9–26. Ringler, *OA* 21, and 396; Robertson, 118, 15 ff. Texts with substantive variants are *OA*, *Ra*, *Cm*, *90*, *93*. Non-substantive texts (Ringler, 555–8) are British Library MS Add. 34064, f. 28; British Library MS Harl. 3511, ff. 74^v–75; Bodleian Library MS Rawl. Poet. 148, ff. 99–100; and, noted in M. Crum, *First-Line Index* (Oxford, 1969), O1368, Bodleian Library MS *e. Mus. 37, f. 67. A setting in three parts is in Robert Jones, *The Second Book of Songs and Airs* (1601), no. 11, ed. E. H. Fellowes, *The English School of Lutenist Song Writers*, v (1926). The words are in E. H. Fellowes, *English Madrigal Verse*, 3rd edn., rev. by F. W. Sternfeld and D. Greer (Oxford, 1967), 566–7.

13. *watered eyes.* Robertson, 118, 19 and note, rejected Ringler's argument that this was an error in a scribal copy of Sidney's text, correctly emended by the scribes of *Bo*, *Cl* and in *90*, *93* to *watery eyes*, and analogous to *OA* 36. 8 (Robertson, 170, 26) where the texts read *watered St, As, Da, Je; wat'ry Bo, Cl, Le, Ph, Hm*.

25–6. *stream ... fire.* Ringler, p. lvii, notes the imagery of the four elements.

27–8. [*swarm ... mind. A Sanctuarie for a Troubled Soule*, p. 135, borrows this image.]

28. *new-born.* The earliest citation in *OED* 1b, the figurative senses is from *AS*.

31. *lightening.* 'illumination'.

31–2. *neither ... off.* Hoskyns, 37, cites this as an example of contentio.

PAGE 199, 10–12. [*making ... nature.* 'they sat down'. Terms typically used to describe the location of a building in relation to nature ('situation' is the location of the building itself, 'prospect' is the view from the building) are here applied to the 'most beautiful buildings of nature', i.e. their bodies.]

28. [*strange tragedies.* See the note to p. 60, 3.]

36–7. [*Behold ... Macedon.* See the note to p. 76, 11–12.]

PAGE 200, 1. *country ... father.* See p. 59, 37–8 and p. xxiii.

6–10. *But ... destruction.* Hoskyns, 13, cites this as an example of anaphora, 'when many clauses have the like beginning'.

9–10. *oh ... destruction.* Hoskyns, 12, cites this as an example of epizeuxis, 'repetition of the same word or sound immediately or without interposition of any other'.

18–22. *was ... creepingly.* This passage has been considerably rewritten from its form in the *Old Arcadia* (Robertson, 120, 25–8), 'wax little and little both softer ... stealingly', and the literalness of the image from Ovid, *Met.* x. 285, 'Cera remollescit' replaced by the synonymous 'creepingly'. Cf. the parallel change on p. 196, 11 above, 'looked as though he would gladly hide himself' which in Robertson, 115, 15 had been 'waxed staring dead'.

35. [*with ... tremor.* 'trembling'. Cf. p. 163, 1–3.]

PAGE 201, 11. *labour ... ruinous.* See p. l. Robertson, p. xxx n., discusses the revisions to this metaphor; cf. *A Letter to Queen Elizabeth* (*Misc. Prose*, 46, 10), 'to hope with laying on better colours to make it more acceptable'.

16. *eye ... me.* To emphasize the irony of this reference to p. 200, 4–6, *me* has been italicized.

23–4. *self-accusing ... finding that.* 'Philoclea accused herself and brought in the verdict that'.

25. [*minded to have done.* 'had intended to do'.]

26–8. [*presented ... quality.* In the *New Arcadia*, the princes' real identities are closely associated with their jewels. They continue to carry them even while in disguise, so when 'Dorus' presents Mopsa with the crab jewel, he needs an excuse as to why a shepherd would own something so valuable (p. 119, 36–120, 6), while the centrepiece of Pyrocles' Amazon disguise is a jewel that hints at his true identity because it features a carving of Hercules with a distaff and the motto 'Never more valiant' (p. 58, 24–7). Other references to the jewels are made on pp. 9, 35–6; 35, 8–9; 40, 4–5; 47, 16–17; 68, 4. Cf. also Pyrocles' and Musidorus' 'selling all the jewels they had of great price' in order to free Leucippus and Nelsus on p. 144, 17, and Pyrocles' angry reaction when he sees the jewel he received from his aunt and foster mother (and later gave to Philoclea as a love token) holding up Lycurgus' garter on p. 401, 1–3.]

31–5. *so ... passed.* In this elliptical construction the subject 'they', to be understood from repetition of 'their', has been transposed from the initial position, 'so that they', in order to give it the additional role of subject of the final adverbial clause. See p. xxxii.

33–5. *sealed ... marriage.* They would both have to affix their seals to render binding the agreement to unite made between their souls, hearts, and mouths (cf. *AS* 81. 5, 'O kiss, which souls, even souls, together ties'); Pyrocles was willing but Philoclea unwilling, so they agreed on marriage instead.

PAGE 202, 10. *you of you.* 'about you from your own lips'.

19–20. *kiss his rod.* 'kiss the cane he would be punished by', cited in Tilley, R156.

36. [*wickedness ... pit.* Typically, such hell analogies locate wickedness in the pit itself rather than comparing the two, but cf. Thomas Stocker's translation of *Two and Twentie Sermons of Maister Iohn Caluin* (1580), fol. 40: 'No doubt, there is not that man, which hath not in him selfe some one roote of all kinde of wickednesse, and this is a bottomlesse pitte wherein we are all confounded'.]

PAGE 203, 1. *Euardes ... kill.* Cf. pp. 179, 14; 337, 34–5.

15–16. *so ... service.* 'by so much would he have had Tiridates give him credit or superiority over Plangus'.

20. *Lycia.* This is where Euardes was killed, p. 179, 14.

24–6. *Amphialus ... master him.* Cf. p. 338, 10–11.

29–30. [*needs ... he was.* Pyrocles believed that Anaxius intended to meet him alone (i.e. not aided by his brothers, as in Book III), so Pyrocles not only wanted to prove himself, he also felt it would be unfair to have Musidorus join him.]

35–PAGE 204, 1. [*taught ... requite.* As Musidorus has done before him (see p. 140, 28–32), Pyrocles stresses that the basis of their friendship is their innate virtue, not their shared childhood. Cf. Tydeus and Telenor, who remain blindly loyal to their foster-brother Plexirtus despite secretly disapproving of his evil deeds, because they never learnt to 'make friendship a child, not the father, of virtue'. See p. 158, 14–15.]

PAGE 204, 12. [*as it were forefeeling.* Sidney's wording suggests he did not consider 'forefeel' an existing word. *OED* cites this as the earliest example, although Sidney was technically not the first to coin this analogous formation to 'foresee'. Cf. John Polemon, *All the Famous Battels* (1578), p. 8: 'Neither bycause that I do promise that in the successe all things will be easie for you, nor do despaire of the victorie, would I seeme to foresee in mind more than the rest, and more arrogantly to forefeele the whole euent of thys instante matter'.]

18. [*laund.* See glossary. The word is etymologically related to 'lawn' and relatively rare in this form, so the folio editions of 1655, 1662 and 1674 change this word to 'land'.]

21. *by pauses.* 'intermittently'.

25–6. *gentleman, bound.* O'Connor, 193, compares *Amadis*, XI. xxii, where Daraïde discovers a naked knight tied to a tree, being beaten by two women with whom he has made love and whom he has promised to marry.

27–8. [*eagles upon an ox.* 'ox' – as opposed to bull – hints at Pamphilus' 'unmanlike' nature. He is associated with the adjective three times (pp. 204, 24; 206, 26; 209, 21); cf. also Pyrocles' passionate defence of womankind after Musidorus has discovered him in his Amazon outfit (p. 61, 33). By contrast, Amphialus and Pyrocles are referred to as 'manlike', the latter even while disguised as Zelmane (pp. 65, 21; 168, 28; 359, 29). At the same time, 'eagles' highlights the fierceness of the gentlewomen (who use their bodkins like talons), but also their nobility.]

29. *bodkins.* These were knives such as those carried by Philoclea; see pp. 274, 8; 329, 24–5 and notes.

PAGE 205, 10. *impatient patient.* Hoskyns, 36, cites this as an example of synoeciosis. [Pamphilus is a 'patient' in the literal sense of suffering pain but 'impatient' because his unmanlike nature renders him unable to endure this pain with composure.]

26–35. *This ... companion.* This sentence is constructed from four complimentary descriptions, each followed by a critical qualification contrasting an idyllic appearance with a harsh reality.

26. *Pamphilus.* This was the common name for a lover mistreated by women in ballads of the sixteenth century; cf. T. J. Garbáty, 'The *Pamphilus* Tradition in Ruiz and Chaucer', *Ph. Q* xlvi (1967), 457–70.

31. *whose head ... mischievously.* 'whose mind one would not deem so constant in anything as in plotting harm'. See Abbott, 356, on the infinitive used as a gerund. See p. xxxii.
35. [*at arm's end.* An early version of 'at arm's length' (which did not become current until the mid-seventeenth century). This is the earliest example cited in *OED*.]

PAGE 206, 2–3. [*one bird ... more.* Mary Wroth uses a similar image in *The Countesse of Montgomeries Urania* (1621):

> nor doubted we; but like the silly birds, who hearing the sweet singing of other birds set for stales, thinking by that mirth they had no imprisonment, fall by innocent beliefe into the nets: so did we, seeing smiles, and hearing nothing but welcome and ioy speake. (p. 234)]

17. *tempest ... judgement.* Hoskyns, 9, adapts this into an example of a metaphor which is too base: 'the tempest of judgement had broken the main-mast of his will'.
33. [*bitter sauce.* Cf. George Gascoigne, 'The Fable of Philomela' (published with *The Steele Glas*, 1576):

> Thus men (my Lord) be Metamorphosed,
> From seemely shape, to byrds, and ougly beastes:
> Yea brauest dames, (if they amisse once tredde)
> Finde bitter sauce, for al their pleasant feasts. (Qiiij^v)]

24–5. *faulty ... faults.* Hoskyns, 17, cites this as an example of polyptoton or traductio, where the words differ only in termination.
26. [*unmanlike bravery.* See the note to p. 204, 27–8.]
31. *enjoy.* See p. 63, 37–64, 2 and note.

PAGE 207, 6–7. *despair ... valiant.* Cf. Tilley, D216, 'Despair makes cowards courageous'; cited in C. G. Smith, *Spenser's Proverb Lore*, 176.
12–13. [*as if ... delighted.* i.e. he thought he was God's gift to women.]
19–20. *change ... constancy.* See p. xxiii. The theme is expanded in Thomas Stanley, 'Changed, yet Constant', in *The Poems and Translations of Thomas Stanley*, ed. G. M. Crump (Oxford, 1962), 7–9.
34–5. *sixt ... eight.* 'sixth ... eighth'.
37. *Dido ... Aeneas.* See p. xxv. In Virgil, *Aeneid*, iv. 305 ff., before his intended marriage to Dido, Aeneas was instructed by the gods to pursue his search for Italy. Dido regarded herself as abandoned by a false Aeneas, cf. Ovid, *Heroides*, vii and Chaucer, *The Legend of Good Women*, 924 ff., and became the symbol of virtue destroyed by vicious love in Gavin Douglas, Prologue to his translation *of Aeneid*, iv.

PAGE 208, 1. *played ... prince.* 'played the heedless tyrant'; cf. Tilley, R96, 'To play rex'.
2. [*manfully overcame.* As opposed to 'unmanlike' Pamphilus. See the note to p. 204, 27–8.]
7–8. *deceived ... forsaken me.* Hoskyns, 13, cites this as an example of climax.
10–11. *judgement ... eyes.* See p. 11, 19 and note.

PAGE 209, 14–15. *threatened ... my horse.* To kill a knight's horse was regarded as unknightly; cf. p. 294, 22–3 and note.
16. *fortune ... victory.* See p. xxviii.
14. [*most unmanlike cruelty.* See the note to p. p. 204, 27–8.]
33–8. *use ... leapt on.* Vaulting fully armed onto a moving horse was standard training; cf. Rabelais, *Gargantua*, i. 23, and Elyot, *The Governor*, ed. H. H. S. Croft (London,

1883), i. 186, comparing Xenophon, *Hipparchicus*, i. 5. See Viscount Dillon, 'Armour Notes', *The Archaeological Journal*, IX (2nd ser. x) (1903), 122.
39. *fear ... wings*. This is cited in Tilley, F133, and in C. G. Smith, *Spenser's Proverb Lore*, 247.

PAGE 210, 16. *false-hearted*. 'lacking conviction'.
36. *not unhandsome*. This is the earliest citation in *OED* 1b. [While Pyrocles is more courteous in his choice of words than Pamphilus, his muted praise suggests that he privately agrees with Pamphilus' verdict that there are 'many fairer' than Dido.]

PAGE 211, 5. *thieves ... among them*. Hoskyns, 46, cites this as an example of periphrasis.
10. *Chremes*. Terence in *Andria*, *Heautontimorumenos*, and *Phormio* used the Greek for 'wallet' for his miserly old man. Through Roman authors the name became common for this type.
12. *evil-received opinion*. 'wrongly believed judgement'.
24. *to her-wards*. 'on her part'.
25-6. *abound ... thereof*. Her many reasons for welcoming him would be matched by her father's lack of hospitality.
40–PAGE 212, 1. [*half ... earth*. 'covetous of gold, though already old and decrepit'.]

PAGE 212, 5-6. *displeasure ... company*. 'annoyance caused him by her guest'.
8-9. [*company ... dust*. Compare the servants of Kalander (the epitome of a good host), who are described as 'cleanly in apparel and serviceable in behaviour' (p. 9, 12).]
13. *young borrower*. 'a young profligate already run through his fortune'. Cf. Tilley, C737, 'A young courtier an old beggar'.
14. *bid*. 'endured', 'suffered'.
33. [*the sum of an hundreth thousand crowns*. See the note to p. 148, 10.]

PAGE 213, 8. *churl's courtesy ... falsehood*. Cf. Tilley, C732, 'Full of courtesy full of craft'.
8-9. [*rathely comes but*. See glossary. The word order and the fact that 'rathely' is qualified by 'but' makes it unlikely that it is being used correctly here, which explains the emendation to 'rarely' in 93. The word was uncommon in the late sixteenth century, so it is possible that Sidney mistook it for a variant form of 'rarely'.]
25-6. *valuing ... oppressed*. Hoskyns, 39, cites this as an example of sententia, 'where there is meiosis, *not always with ease* for *ever* and *hardly*'. [Glossed as a sententia through inverted commas in 90.]

PAGE 214, 7. *if ever ... man*. 'if at any time (and at all times, if any man at all did)'.
20-1. [*niece ... hated*. i.e. Artaxia. 'wrongfully' here does not imply that Artaxia is undeserving of hatred, only that the King of Iberia is wrong to hate her for supporting Plangus' alleged plot against him.]

PAGE 215, 7. *rareness of affection*. 'exceptional nature of his affection'.
7-8. *use of directing*. 'being accustomed to being directed'.
16-17. *hope ... harm*. Cf. Tilley, B328, 'We must hope for the best and fear the worst'; cited in C. G. Smith, *Spenser's Proverb Lore*, 399.
18-19. *striving ... strive*. Hoskyns, 14, cites this as an example of antimetabole.
19. *contented ... contented*. 'did not desire any more ... satisfied with his present condition'. For the latter, the earliest citation in *OED* 3 is from Shakespeare's *Richard III* I. iii. 84.

22. [*brought known unto*. The expression is a hapax legomenon, which may have been used here as a synonym for 'to bring acquainted' (a variant of 'to make acquainted'), because the sentence already contains two other instances of 'acquainted'.]
25. *haunted us*. 'was in our company'. [Cf. p. 6, 33.]
26–8. [*evil mind ... thought of*. Glossed as a sententia through inverted commas in 90.]
29. *affected us both*. Arsace openly declares her love for both Thyamis and Theagenes in Heliodorus, VII. iv. 2.
32. *to ... shame*. 'in order to shame her husband'.
33. *reproach*. 'censure of her activities'. She deliberately created the scandalous reputation by which she shamed her husband.
hoodwinked. 'blindfolded'. The earliest citation in OED pp. adj. is from 1640. [Note, however, that the word also appears in Thomas Newton's translation of Levinus Lemnius' *Touchstone of Complexions* (1576).]
35–7. [*in nature ... by art*. i.e. she was not naturally unattractive, but she excessively tried to enhance her beauty by artificial means, which made her less attractive.]

PAGE 216, 3. *suburbs*. A. D[avenport]., 'Possible Echoes from Sidney's *Arcadia* in Shakespeare, Milton and Others', *N & Q* cxciv (1949), 554–5, compares Shakespeare, *Julius Caesar*, II. i. 285–6. The earliest citation in OED 2b is from 1568.
7. *which yet while*. 'which still to that time'. Cf. Abbott, 93.
15–16. *this colour ... beautiful*. Hoskyns, 35, cites this as an example of diminution 'by denying the right use of the word but by error of some'.
15. *style*. 'manner of speech'.
20. *a request*. 'on request'. See p. lv.
tennis. The image is of one player serving, then the other.

PAGE 217, 2–3. *which ... answering*. This is a flirtatious aside to persuade Philoclea that she cannot help returning his affection.
17. *good*. 'trustfully simple'.
17–18. *not knowing ... that*. 'only knowing'.
18 *pleasures to*. 'desires to be towards'. See p. liv.
19. *to ... us*. 'to treating us like slaves'.
33. *unworthy*. 'not deserving'.
35. *set ... wind*. This is the earliest citation in Tilley, S25.

PAGE 218, 6. *motherside*. This is the uninflected genitive of *mother*; cf. OED C5a.
18. *for the pity*. 'out of pity'.
33. [*ague*. Illnesses classified as agues were characterized by recurring fever or shivering fits. Early modern medical texts often distinguished between 'tertian' or 'quartain' ague, according to the intervals (or 'intermission') between fits, and advised different treatments for them. The image implies that Andromana's whims follow a predictable pattern. Note also the pun in 'a fit time to deliver us'.]
35–**PAGE 219**, 3. *every year ... justs*. Comparisons have been drawn with the annual Accession Day tilts commemorating Elizabeth's coming to the throne on 17 November 1558 by F. A. Yates, *Astraea* (London, 1975), 88–111, and by R. Strong, *The Cult of Elizabeth* (London, 1977), 147–50. [Here the festivities do not celebrate the king's own accession to the throne. Instead, they are in honour of his wife, which is why the Iberians regard them as an expression of his excessive fondness for her.]

PAGE 219, 4. [*a seven-night*. A period of seven days. The word was often contracted to 'sennight'. Cf. the analogously formed (and still current) 'fortnight'.]

5. *neighbour*. See p. xxxii.
8–10. *fame ... trumpet*. The goddess Fama was depicted blowing a trumpet.
21. *threatens*. The verb *threaten* is used as a noun here in the plural form; see above, p. xxxii, and cf. Abbott, 327. [The 1628/9 edition's dubious correction to 'threatned' (rather than the more logical 'threatenings') was reprinted in subsequent editions.]
24. *martial exercises*. See p. xx.
29–30. *marriage ... Venus*. See p. xxiii. The union of chastity and love in Diana and Venus is related to Queen Elizabeth in E. Wind, *Pagan Mysteries in the Renaissance*, rev. edn. (Harmondsworth, 1967), 77–8, and R. Strong, *The Cult of Elizabeth*, 47–52.
31–2. [*for yet ... seen her*. This is technically true, although Pyrocles did of course see Helen's portrait on display during Phalantus' challenge in Book I.]

PAGE 220, 2–4. *what doth ... loved*. Hoskyns, 13, cites this as an example of climax.
12. *honour sake*. See p. 3, 19 and note.
15–16. [*not ... him*. Andromana is fond of her son (cf. p. 218, 29–30) but surprisingly unconcerned about letting him fight in a tournament without fighting experience.]
25. *chained*. This represents his binding promise not to strike Philisides, p. 221, 22–3.
was .... See p. xliii.
28. *rich in stuff*. 'of costly fabric'.
29. [*lancely*. 'as from a (proper) lance'. This is the only known example of 'lancely', which stresses that although Philisides' lances are decoratively fashioned, they are as strong and functional as regular lances, so he is a serious opponent.]
33. *sheep ... pitch*. This was a common method of signalling ownership; cf. *OED* under *pitch-brand*.
34. *Spotted ... known*. The brand was probably in the form of a star, representing the owner. The device is similar to one recorded by Abraham Fraunce as being Sidney's, in which a sheep has been marked by a star, by which it is known to be Saturn's: 'Ovis Saturni sidere notata', with the motto, 'Macular modo noscar'; see D. Coulman, '"Spotted to be Known"', *JWCI* xx (1957), 179–80.
36–7. *windows ... 'star'*. See p. xv. Emphasis on 'star' is indicated by upright script in *Cm* and by italics in *90*, *93*.
36. *among there*. This ellipsis avoids repetition of 'the ladies', indicated by 'among'. See p. xxxii.
38. *Philisides*. See pp. xiv–xv, and V. Skretkowicz, '"A more lively monument": Philisides in *Arcadia*', in M. J. B. Allen, Dominic Baker Smith, Arthur F. Kinney and Margaret Sullivan eds. *Sir Philip Sidney's Achievements* (New York, 1990), 194–200.

PAGE 221, 6–11. Ringler, OP 1 and 493. Texts are *Cm*, *90*, *93*. Cf. Ringler, PP 4 and 5 and p. 518 for Sidney's poems in Goldwell's *Brief Declaration* of the assault upon The Fortress of Perfect Beauty. P. Beal, 'Poems by Sir Philip Sidney: The Ottley Manuscript', *The Library*, 5th Ser. xxxiii (1978), 287–9, adds to the Sidney canon the poem 'Waynd [weaned] from the hope', sent by a 'desert knight' 'in a letter sealed with a green leaf and superscribed ... To her that is Mistress of men'. In the manner of these shepherds, a ploughman whose impresa 'should have been a harrow' was to sing AT 21 while Sidney rode through the tilt as the shepherd Philisides, and then AT 19 'was to be said' after he left.
8. *brake across*. This is an inferior blow, the lance being broken across the body of the opponent rather than shattering from striking with the point. Cf. p. 332, 28.
13. *Lelius*. See p. xiv.

16. *head*. See p. 87, 6 and note.
18–20. [*swimming ... Mars*. 'swim' is an unusual choice of verb in this context and stresses the smoothness of the motion (as do 'gallant' and 'kiss').]
23. *whose disgraces to him*. 'Lelius' affronts to Philisides'.
24–5. *whose injuries ... honours*. 'Lelius' insults to which any repayment would be re-ceived as an honour'.
31. *wild man*. See p. xix.
33. *mill-horse*. Cf. Tilley, H697, 'To go round like a blind horse in a mill'.
34. *Data ... sequutus*. 'conforming to an ordained destiny'.
36. *without any device*. This was not uncommon. R. Strong, *The Cult of Elizabeth*, 141, records the appearance of an Unknown Knight in tilts of 1593 and 1600. Goldwell, *Brief Declaration* (1581), in J. Nichols, *Progresses of Queen Elizabeth* (1823), ii. 319, notes that 'in the midst of the running came in Sir Henry Lee, as unknown'; see also Nichols, iii. 196.
37. *white ... knight*. Unornamented steel or silver armour was described as 'white'. R. Strong, *The Cult of Elizabeth*, 156, notes that Robert Radcliffe, later 5th Earl of Sussex, wore white when he first tilted at court in 1593.
39. *bird ... fly*. G. Wickham, *Early English Stages* (London, 1963–81), i. 97, cites an example of a mechanical falcon descending from the roof of a pageant to a tree in Ann Boleyn's coronation reception, 1533.

PAGE 222, 2–3. *fire ... consumed*. The fabric of the phoenix would have been artfully burned away from the horseman which it covered.
4. *Frozen Knight*. There was such a knight in at least two tilts in which Sidney took part, on 22 January 1581, where it was Sir John Parrot's disguise, and on 15–16 May 1581 at The Fortress of Perfect Beauty. See R. Strong, 'Elizabethan Jousting Cheques in the Possession of the College of Arms', *The Coat of Arms*, v (1958–9), 8, and Nichols, *Progresses of Queen Elizabeth* (1823), ii. 319.
11. *in troops*. 'en masse', mounted and with the sword in the tourney.
13. *in the trial*. 'when put to the test'.
28. *stumble*. Cf. Tilley, H198, 'The more haste the less speed'.

PAGE 223, 5–10. [*taking ... other world*. 'with a traitorous blow' stresses that although it was not intentional, the slaying of Palladius was particularly unjust because it was done by one of his own subjects. Musidorus' and Pyrocles' avenging of Palladius' death is consequently framed in terms of restoring the hierarchy.]
14–15. [*no more ... hurt*. Because they were already outside Iberian territory and most of her troops were dead.]
16–17. *reasonable ... sensible*. Palladius is almost two-thirds dead; cf. Burton, *Anatomy of Melancholy*, 1. 1. 2. 5: 'The common division of the soul is into three principal faculties – vegetal, sensitive, and rational, which make three distinct kinds of living creatures – vegetal plants, sensible beasts, rational men .... The inferior may be alone, but the superior includes vegetal, rational both .... Necessary concomitants or affections of this vegetal faculty are life and his privation, death'.
28–9. *and only fear*. 'but it is only a slight fear'. This is another flirtatious aside, as on pp. 217, 2–3; 219, 11–12.
37. *blushed ... blushing*. See p. 40, 14 and note.

PAGE 224, 1. *go on*. 'take up'. Cf. *OED* under *go on* 1.
6. *gesture*. See p. xxxi.

16–19. *swear... false*. Such exaggerated vows are common, cf. Ovid, *Heroides*, v. 29–32, but the combination of sun and rocks is in Aeneas Silvius, *De Duobus Amantibus* in Burton, *Anatomy of Melancholy*, 3. 2. 4, 'bid the mountains come down into the plains, bid the rivers run back to their fountains; I can as soon leave to love as the sun leave his course', and in Chaucer, *Troilus and Criseyde*, iii. 1495–8.

22. *water... wind*. Cf. CS 13, where the words of a fickle woman to her lover 'In wind or water stream do require to be writ', and p. 367, 5.

26. *Well yet*. 'Yet'; *Well* is merely a preliminary word, as in OED under *well* adv. V.20.

PAGE 225, 4–5. [*not stick... folly*. In this, Baccha is a true match for Pamphilus, who previously used a similar strategy. Cf. p. 206, 2–3.]

11. *left his faith*. 'abandoned inconstancy', by marriage to Baccha.

13. *his cruel Dido*. See p. liv and p. 205, 8–9, 'her cruelty'.

17. *Vestal nuns*. These were virgin priestesses who had charge of the sacred fire in the temple of Vesta, goddess of the hearth, at Rome. The earliest citation in OED under *Vestal* adj. 2 is from 1599 (though an example of the phrase 'vestal nun' is listed in the figurative sense (3) and dated 1595).

20. *having... earliness*. Hoskyns, 47, cites this as an example of periphrasis.

30. *broken knots*. 'untied knots or bows', signifying unfulfilled love. Cf. Argalus' armour, p. 324, 14–15, and see p. 67, 9–11 and note.

31. *daring... do*. See p. 78, 1–2 and note.

PAGE 226, 5. [*liking... to be*. Pyrocles is anxious to stress to Philoclea that although he pitied Zelmane and was fond of 'Daiphantus', he did not love her and never saw through her disguise.]

8. *unapt to service*. 'unable to perform knightly duties'.

24. *dividing... side*. 'one going to each party'.

24–5. *trial... ourselves*. 'inquiry we had made, each by himself'.

28. [*our father and mother*. i.e Pyrocles' father and Musidorus' mother, who raised the two princes together and are thus effectively the parents of both. See the notes to p. 141, 25 and p. 235, 2.]

34. *stretching... length*. 'extending narrowly in length'.

37. *the martial story*. 'martial history'.

PAGE 227, 3. [*knights... villains*. Although it is more frequently used in the sense of 'scoundrel' or 'criminal', the primary meaning of 'villain' is 'low-born rustic' or 'feudal serf'. The latter is usually distinguished through the spelling 'villein' in modern texts, although both forms were used interchangeably by Sidney's contemporaries; while 90 mostly uses the spelling 'villaine' or 'villayne', the edition of Spenser's *Faerie Queene* that was published in the same year favours the spelling 'villein', while the 1596 *Faerie Queene* is more or less evenly divided between 'villein' and 'villain / villaine' (with the former dominating in the first and the latter in the second half of the book). The phrase here consequently stresses that their dishonourable behaviour revealed those knights to be unworthy of their knightly status, indirectly linking them to Chremes' inadequate servants, who were previously described as 'rustical villains full of sweat and dust', p. 212, 8–9.]

8–9. *astonishment* 'dismay'. This is the earliest citation in OED 3.

19. *is... thee*. 'is discovered to be done by you'.

26. *Trebizond*. The ancient name was Trapezus, a city of Pontus on the Euxine Sea.

PAGE 229, 1–2. [*wishing... virtue*. See the note to p. 203, 35–204, 1.]

COMMENTARY

2-3. *since ... heart.* Hoskyns, 39, cites this as an example of sententia, within which are asyndeton, zeugma, and metaphors.

28. *While ... understood.* In lieu of the normal 'While returning ... we understood', the pronoun *we* has been transposed from the following principal clause to the stress position at the beginning of the adverbial clause, permitting it to be directly influenced by *While* and by the participial *returning*, cf. Abbott, 161, 288.

29. *Otanes.* There is a character of this name in the *Old Arcadia*.
Barzanes ... Musidorus. Cf. p. 179, 40.

PAGE 230, 6. [*Daiphantus ... her constitution.* Unlike Pyrocles himself, who is referred to by feminine pronouns while disguised as 'Zelmane', the disguised Zelmane always remains 'she' even when she is specifically referred to as 'Daiphantus'.]

PAGE 231, 5-6. [*had ... oppress her.* 'felt she was about to die'. Cf. also the description of Parthenia's death in p. 344, 35-6.]
6. *said she.* The position of *said* in the midst rather than before the quotation requires the insertion of the otherwise redundant pronoun; see above, p. xxxii, and cf. Abbott, 162, 303.
8. *had it been reason.* 'had it been agreeable to reason'. Cf. *OED* under *reason* n. 6a.
11-12. *not ... unmodest.* Hoskyns, 35, though reading 'not ... modest', cites this as an example of diminution 'by denying the contrary'.
20. *placed affection.* This is opposed to his present unplaced affection.
22. *of my life.* 'upon my life'. This asseverative usage is indicated by the punctuation in Cm.

PAGE 232, 16. *resemble you.* See p. 57, 28 and note.

PAGE 233, 21-2. *no more ... hopes.* 'as unable to use his judgement in forming expectations, as in assessing them once conceived of'.
22. *blind to judge.* See p. 11, 19 and note.
39-40. *me ... adventure.* 'begged of me that perilous enterprise'. Cf. *OED* under *bid* v. 7a, with accusative of person and genitive of thing.

PAGE 234, 1-2. *journey ... ways.* Cf. Tilley, D35, 'The more danger the more honour'. [Glossed as a sententia in 90 through inverted commas that were preserved in 93 but dropped in 98.]
4-5. (*to ... matter*). The parentheses in this passage are in all texts.
12. *faith given.* 'assurance given'.
35-6. *unkindness and importunity.* 'the charge of ingratitude, and forcing others too greatly to solicit us to accept'.

PAGE 235, 2. [*our parents.* See the notes to p. 141, 25 and p. 226, 28.]
7. *Renowmed.* 'renowned'.
7-9. *no ... thereof.* Hoskyns, 47, cites this as an example of periphrasis.
35-PAGE 236, 1. *our safeties ... desires.* 'our safety to be what they chiefly desired'.

PAGE 236, 10. *he.* 'Plexirtus'.
10-11. *which ... knowledge.* 'who hated all other intimacy'.
13. *told us.* See p. xviii.
27-8. [*if it come to the push.* 'if worst comes to worst'. 'to come to the push', meaning 'to reach a critical point', gained popularity during the 1570s and featured in a number of texts, including the translations of Calvin's sermons by Golding and others. Cf. also the still current expression 'at a push'.]

PAGE 237, 20. *highest ... lowest*. This is cited in C. G. Smith, *Spenser's Proverb Lore*, 387.
26. [*death ... hire*. i.e. 'they rewarded them for their common sense by killing them'.]
26-7. *hope ... alive*. 'how to direct his life, but rather just of keeping it'. [Alternatively, the phrase may be read to mean that since anyone who called for a truce was killed, those who wished to live had no choice but to keep fighting and hope to survive until the end (this reading likely prompted 93's change to 'being last alive').]
33. *children of Cadmus*. When an army sprang out of the ground from the dragon's teeth sown by Cadmus, he set them to fight with one another, Ovid, *Met*. iii. 1 ff.

PAGE 238, 1. *little all*. 'all of us, however few'.
5. *nature ... life*. Cf. p. 54, 21 and note.
27-8. *ride ... mare*. 'see-saw'. Two motions are expressed, up and down as he bounces along the mast, and forwards as if moving up to make room for a rider behind him. This is the earliest citation in *OED* under *mare* n.¹ 4c. A variety of usages is mixed in Tilley, M655, 'To ride the wild mare', and *ODEP*, 725.

PAGE 239, 12. *Nay*. This is a mere introductory word with no sense of negation. Cf. *OED* A. 1c.
13. *And if*. 'If'.
32. [*evil at ease*. A rare sixteenth-century variant of 'ill at ease'. In early modern usage, there is a degree of semantic overlap between 'ill' and 'evil'.]

PAGE 240, 6. *like ... husband*. See p. xxv.
13. *valiant shrew*. This is a case of the malignant shrew taking on, as it was known to do, a large benign beast. See the examples in *OED*.
19. *side-look*. Cf. Spenser, *Faerie Queene*, IV. xxiv. 3, 'whally eyes (the sign of gelosy)', and Ovid, *Met*. ii. 767, 'Invidiam: visaque oculos avertit'. Cf. Tilley, L498, 'Love, being jealous, makes a good eye look asquint', and see pp. 151, 11-12; 315, 8-9; 334, 17.
12. [*metal*. The main meaning of 'mettle' is 'stuff' or 'character', but it is strongly connoted with traditionally 'masculine' virtues, i.e. courage, spirit or valour. As Zelmane has those qualities, Basilius' joke hinges on the more literal meaning of 'virility' (cf. *OED* 2b), but the joke is on him – and Gynecia nearly tells him so.]

PAGE 241, 2-3. *well-wishing ... carefulness*. Hoskyns, 36, cites this as two examples of synoeciosis.
6. [*thy breeder's power*. i.e. that of love, the father of jealousy.]
14-27. Ringler, *OA* 22, and 396; Robertson, 123, 3 ff. Texts with substantive variants are *OA*, *Ra*, *Cm*, 90, 93. The stanzas are in rhyme royal.
34. *Pallas ... Arachne*. Insisting on a competition with her teacher of weaving, Arachne depicted the crimes of the gods, while Pallas Athena wove examples of mortals being punished for presumption. Athena destroyed Arachne's work and, when she tried to kill herself, turned her into a spider, Ovid, *Met*. vi. 1 ff. Like Athena, Gynecia is jealous, vengeful, and possesses absolute authority.

PAGE 242, 8-9. [*unruly sort ... other rebels*. See the note to p. 39, 16.]
10-11. [*within perfect discerning*. 'within earshot of'.]
12. [*right villains*. See the note to p. 227, 3. These are 'villains' both because they are low-born rustics (cf. 'clowns') and because it is villainous to attack the ladies, who ought to be spared due to their sex and 'estates' – i.e. their social status as gentlewomen.]
13-14. *so many as ... minds*. Cf. Tilley, M583, 'So many men so many minds'; cited in C. G. Smith, *Spenser's Proverb Lore*, 371.

20. *lightening.* 'flashing'. One of the earliest citation in *OED* under *lighten* v. 7 is from the Countess of Pembroke's Psalm lxix [(the earliest example listed is from the romance *Greenes Menaphon* (1589), also known as *Greenes Arcadia*).]
22. [*long untried*. Basilius has reigned peacefully for thirty years. Cf. p. 16, 27–30.]
26. [*the odds... kite*. This image of Zelmane putting the rabble in their place contains a contrast of strength as well as rank: an eagle is larger and stronger than a kite and consequently more likely to prevail; at the same time it is a bird associated with royalty and one of the 'noblest' birds of prey, ranking far above kites.]
26–7. *nimble... nimbleness*. 'agile but steady conduct, and such a confident dexterity'.
36. [*would... father*. Dametas is not merely being a coward (as when he met the bear); he is bent exclusively on self-preservation, which implies he would not have opened the entry to his daughter and foster-daughter either, so Pamela and Mopsa were fortunate to be inside the cave when Dametas closed the entrance.]

PAGE 243, 4–5. [*helped... losing it*. 'killed him before he could regret having lost it'.]
6. *arms and legs*. They were symbolic of triumph in battle. Cf. p. 330, 19, and Thomas Churchyard, *A Discourse of the Queen's Majesty's Entertainment in Suffolk and Norfolk* [1587], cited in J. Nichols, *Progresses of Queen Elizabeth* (1823), ii. 200, where Fortune's six defenders triumphed in mock battle over six representing Manhood, Favour, and Desert, 'in which time was legs and arms of men (well and lively wrought) to be let fall in numbers on the ground, as bloody as might be'.
9. *conquered... conquering*. See p. xxviii.
10. *mastiff*. Mastiffs were renowned for their tenacity and used in bear- and bull-baiting. See J. Nichols, *Progresses of Queen Elizabeth* (1823), i. 67, ii. 459–60, *Progresses of King James* (1828), i. 320, ii. 259, and p. 354, 4–5 below.
13. *backward... forward*. So Turnus retreated like a lion, facing the Trojans, Virgil, *Aeneid*, ix. 792–4.
18–20. [*began... crown*. The description stresses the tailor's foolishness and lack of skill at using his chosen weapon. 'very fencer-*like*' (emphasis added) suggests he is simply imitating a pose he may have seen in a stage fight, while 'very nicely' implies that he handles his sword gingerly. Twirling his sword about his head is equally ineffective for attacking (he has no chance of hitting an opponent) as it is for defending (it exposes most of his body – including, but not limited to, his nose).]
25. [*butcherly*. The butcher is portrayed as rough and coarse, i.e. the opposite of the 'nice' tailor, although both are equally clumsy fighters.]
27. *lever*. This is the weapon, *vecte*, used by the Lapidi Macareus to kill the Centaur Erygdupus, Ovid, *Met*. xii. 452.
31–2. *See... good-fellow*. 'Now, watch me!'
36. *one ear... other*. Cf. Ovid, *Met*. xii. 336, 'Et missum a dextra laevam penetravit in aurem'.
38–PAGE 244, 1. *vomit... blood*. Cf. Ovid, *Met*. xii. 238–9, 'Sanguinis ille globos pariter cerebrumque, merumque, / Vulnere et ore vomens'; and Virgil, *Aeneid*, ix. 349–50.

PAGE 244, 6. *Centaurs and Lapiths*. Their grotesque battle at the wedding feast of Pirithous and Hippodamia is described in Ovid, *Met*. xii. 210 ff.
11–12. [*well-skilled... skill*. A pun on 'hand' in the sense of ability or skill. Cf. *Batman vppon Bartholome* (1582), Stephen Batman's revision of John Trevisa's translation of Bartholomaeus' *De proprietatibus rerum*: 'as it is sometime sayde of a Painter or a writer: He hath a good hand, that is to vnderstand, a good skill of writing, eyther of painting' (fol. 50). While the painter's punishment may appear cruel, it is worth

remembering that he was callous enough to attend a battle and be pleased to witness serious injuries in order to reproduce them in a painting.]
13–14. [*gave ... outside.* i.e. they closed the gate to the lodge, locking out the rebels.]
33. [*the country sort.* See the note to p. 39, 16.]

PAGE 245, 2–3. *by ... ones.* 'not by any minor gods'.
5. *hear ... little.* Cf. Tilley, M1277, 'Hear much but speak little'.
22. [*By him am I sent.* The word order is inverted in order to stress the word 'him', as a reminder of Basilius' authority as their ruler.]
well-approved subjects. 'subjects of well-proven loyalty'.

PAGE 246, 10–11. [*finer sort of burgesses.* See the note to p. 39, 16.]
17. [*made tokens.* 'signalled'.]
26. *country people.* 'people of that country'.
37. *Argians ... enemies.* Cecropia is daughter to the king of Argos.

PAGE 247, 18. *hateful.* 'hateful to him', as in the *Old Arcadia*, Robertson, 130, 21.
25–8. *what ... established.* Hoskyns, 48, adapts this as an example of prosopopoeia, 'as to make dead men speak'.
28–32. *you should ... rulers.* Hoskyns, 12, adapts this in an example of climax.

PAGE 248, 2–3. *did ... pleasant.* Cf. Tilley, H183, 'He that has a good harvest may be content with some thistles'.
2–5. *did ... fathers.* Hoskyns, 33, cites this as an example of interrogation.
4. *wearish.* 'peevish', 'crabbed'. The word describing a person's appearance under *OED* 4 seems to have been transferred to connote his personality [(although the definition is based on this passage alone).]
9–10. *action ... action.* Hoskyns, 15, cites this as an example of antimetabole.
12. *uncertainty ... arms.* See p. xxiii.
19–21. *gestures ... falling.* This corresponds with the description given by Thomas Wilson, *The Arte of Rhetorique*, ed. G. H. Mair (Oxford, 1909), 219–20.
31–2. *but how ... knots.* Cf. Tilley, K167, 'He has tied a knot with his tongue that he can't untie with all his teeth'; cited in C. G. Smith, *Spenser's Proverb Lore*, 50.

PAGE 249, 3 *many-headed.* This is cited in Tilley, M1308. See p. 149, 30–1 and note.
9 (var.). *Sinon.* He betrayed Troy. Cf. Virgil, *Aeneid*, ii. 57 ff. and Shakespeare, *Rape of Lucrece*, 1500 ff.
10. *words than manners.* He learned the words without understanding their bearing upon conduct.
12. [*slidingness of language.* 'smoothness of tongue'. Like 'turningness' in p. 159, 13 and 'whisperingness' in p. 292, 6–7, this is the only known instance of the word and the only example in its *OED* entry, so all three forms are likely Sidney's invention.]
15–16. *more ... rarely.* 'rather in an unusual manner than seldom'.
30–1. [*as if ... audience.* 'nice' highlights that Clinias' 'gravity' is not genuine but a calculated performance, while the reference to a stage prologue and word 'audience' evoke his past as an actor and his untrustworthiness as an orator. Cf. also p. 250, 10.]
34. *Giants.* See note to p. 54, 37.
37. *Pelops of wisdom.* Pelops, whose name was synonymous with wisdom, gave his name to Peloponnesus, of which Arcadia was a small part.
Minos ... government. Minos was celebrated for the fair laws he brought to Crete.

PAGE 250, 11. *strake ... face.* See p. 149, 12–13 and note.

15. *Aeolus.* He was the god of the winds.
20. *ungracious motion.* 'wicked motive'.
22-4. [*None ... leaders.* i.e. the ringleaders who had spurred on the others were the first to be killed, because they had taught them disobedience towards leaders.]
31. *coldly.* See p. li.
35. *policy sake.* See p. 3, 19 and note.
39. *share-marks.* 'shear-marks', marks left on an animal's hide from shearing or clipping. This is the earliest citation in *OED* under *shear* n.¹.

PAGE 251, 4. [*dipping... wound.* A theatrical gesture consistent with Clinias' exaggerated performance.]
17. *thunder.* That is, Jupiter; cf. Ovid, *Met.* iii. 260 ff.

PAGE 252, 11. *plain-headed.* 'ignorant', 'simple'; the claim is ironic.
31. *so general.* The text follows the syntax of *Cm*, supported by *OA*. *90*, *93* begin a new sentence here.

PAGE 253, 4-6. *spits ... mischief.* Cf. Ovid, *Met.* xii. 244, 'Res epulis quondam, tum bello et caedibus aptae'.
24. [*wring ... tears.* Stressing the theatricality and insincerity of Clinias' gestures.]
35-6. *fire ... bell.* For this system of firing beacons and ringing bells in the event of invasion, see L. Boynton, *The Elizabethan Militia* (Newton Abbot, 1971), 132 ff. and plates 10, 11.

PAGE 254, 12-13. [*sing maugre the muses.* i.e. Dametas' 'poetry' does not deserve the name. Cf. Spenser's description of the ape's poetic attempts in *Mother Hubberds Tale*, 814-16:

> Ne let such verses Poetrie be named:
> Yet he the name on him would rashly take,
> Maugre the sacred Muses ....]

15-21. Ringler, *OA* 25, and 397; Robertson, 132, 24 ff. Substantive texts are *OA* (*ex. Le*), *Cm*, *90*, *93*. See p. xxii.
15. *hateful ... hate.* Cf. Tilley, S950, 'He that is hated of his subjects cannot be counted a king'.
16. *bloody ... save.* Cf. Tilley, V52, 'It is a great victory that comes without blood'.
17. *foolish ... deal.* Cf. Tilley, F486, more concisely expressed in *ODEP*, 275, 'Thou art ane fule gif thow with fulis dalis'.
18. *bobbed.* 'hit with blows'. See pp. li.
20 & 26. [*It is even I.* Since the metre here emphasizes the last two words of the line – corresponding to Dametas' wish to highlight his own wisdom – 'even' needs to be disyllabic. 'It is' may be contracted to ' 'tis' to avoid an additional syllable in the line (as in some manuscript variants), although this is not strictly necessary.]
22. *brave lame.* 'splendid but defective', with a pun on 'lame'.
25. *But.* 'But with'.
28. [*passed ... enemies.* 'vanquished all his foes'. For a similar image, cf. the Life of Otho in Thomas North's translation of Plutarch's *Lives* (1579): 'and it seemeth, that if they had comen in time, they had not left one of their enemies aliue, but had marched vpon the bellies of all Cecinnaes armie' (p. 1125).]
30-1. *coast ... clear.* See p. 76, 14 and note.
31-2. *after ... drops.* Cf. Tilley, T275, 'After thunder comes rain'.
35. *be assured.* See p. l.

Page 255, 3. *fawning ... hope*. See p. 395, 14–15 and note.
4. *now his own*. 'now that he was once again his own master'.
30–9. Ringler, *OA* 1, and 383; Robertson, 5, 15 ff. Substantive texts are *OA*, 90, 93.

Page 256, 13–14. *pulley ... run on*. 'mechanism to make the bell of his praises continue sounding'. See Glossary under *pulley* and *run*.
37–**Page 257**, 14. Ringler, *OA* 26, and 397; Robertson, 134, 7 ff. Substantive texts are *OA* (ex. Le), *Cm* (ll. 1–4), 90, 93.
37–**Page 257**, 2. *Apollo ... fade*. As the sun lights the universe, so God lights man's spirit; as the sun shines even during the night when it has passed behind the earth, though in the geocentric universe hidden from view to those within the shadow cast by the earth, so God's perpetual light is hidden from man by his own spiritual night.

Page 257, 1. *earthly shade*. Cf. Macrobius, *Commentary on the Dream of Scipio*, trans. W. H. Stahl (New York, 1966), I. xx. 18: 'the earth's shadow, which the sun after setting and passing into the lower hemisphere sends upwards, creating on earth the darkness called night'; Lucan, *The Civil War*, ix. 690 ff.; Sandys, on his translation of Ovid, *Met*. i (1632), C3^v, 'the whole sky being all the night long in the beams of the sun (that little spire, the shadow of the earth, excepted)'. J. Norton-Smith, 'Marlowe's "Faustus" (I. iii. 1–4)', *N & Q*, NS xxv (1978), 436, discusses the variant in 1604, 'shadow of the earth', and 1616, 'shadow of the night'. Caxton, *Mirrour of the World*, ed. O. H. Prior, EETS, ES cx (1913), 130, called it 'shadow of the night', and printed illustrations on p. 135; cf. Milton, *Paradise Lost*, iv. 777–8, 'Now had night measur'd with her shaddowy Cone / Half way up Hill this vast Sublunar Vault'. See p. 350, 17–20.
3. *God*. For the image of God as the sun, see pp. 2, 40–3, 4 and note.
Python's skin. Apollo killed Python, Ovid, *Met*. i. 434 ff. Ringler, 398, notes that in the *Ovide Moralisé en Prose*, ed. C. de Boer (Amsterdam, 1954), 64, Python is the devil and Apollo is Christ. Cf. Sandys, on his translation of Ovid, *Met*. i (1632), F2^v, 'So serpentine error by the light of truth is confounded'. See p. xviii n.
4. [*humble ... sin*. Glossed as a sententia through inverted commas in 90 (which reads 'snakish kinne'). 'snakish' is an uncommon word that Sidney may have recalled from Golding's translation of Ovid, which uses it five times.]
5. *Latona's ... long*. Latona was in labour nine days and nights, and Eileithyia, the goddess of birth, was forbidden to attend her by the jealous Juno. The example is of goodness being achieved through effort and sacrifice. See Ovid, *Met*. vi. 332 ff.
7. *travail*. This may be 'travel' as proverbs support both concepts. [The line is glossed as a sententia through inverted commas in 90.]
8. *brickle hour-glass*. The sand of life may run out, or the glass holding it be shattered. See the examples in *OED* under *hour-glass* n. b. [Cf. also Abraham Fleming's *A Panoplie of Epistles* (1576): 'calling to remembrance the estate of mans life, how fraile it is, how brickle, how vncertaine & variable' (p. 447).]
race. Sidney alludes to the race of life in PS 11. 23, 26. 2, and 30. 19.
14. [*nothing wins ... forsake*. Glossed as a sententia through inverted commas in 90.]
26–7. [*like ... lands*. 'eagerly'. The image is of a young heir who has been controlled by a close-fisted guardian finally coming of age and being able to manage his own possessions. See also pp. lxxxii–lxxxiii.]
34. *for so far as*. 'as much as'.

Page 258, 8–9. [*could not ... subject*. i.e. Basilius was so moved by Plangus' story that

he felt compelled to write his 'Complaint of Plangus' (see p. 172, 1–176, 36).]
32. [*nothing... flattery.* For the opposite of this image, see the description of Kalander, to whom 'no music is so sweet to his ear as deserved thanks' (7, 2–3).]
33–4. *dogs fawning.* See p. 56, 31–2 and note.

PAGE 259, 7. *bird... head.* See p. 18, 18 and note.
11–12. [*within... barrenness.* Antiphilus' claim to the throne is only through his wife, so his attempt to justify a second marriage through the need to produce an heir is absurd (hence he needs to go to the lengths of passing an 'unlawful law' sanctioning bigamy to remain married to Erona). Cf. the account of the scandalous annulment of Louis XII's marriage in Thomas Beard's translation of Jean Chassanion's *Theatre of Gods Iudgements* (1597), which perhaps deliberately echoes Sidney's wording:

> pope *Alexander* the sixt... for the aduancement of his hautie desires, to gratifie and flatter *Lewis* the twelft king of France, sent him by his son a dispensation to put away his wife (daughter to king *Lewis* the eleuenth) because shee was barren and counterfait; and to recontract *Anne* of Bretaigne, the widdow of *Charles* the eight lately deceased. But herein though barrennesse of the former was pretended, yet the dutchie of the latter was aimed at, which before this time, he could neuer attaine vnto. (p. 355)]

18. *fortune... eyes.* See p. 143, 20 and note.

PAGE 260, 8. *Hymen... coat.* Cf. Ovid, *Met.* x. 1 ff. That the god of marriage should lack one of his main attributes was a sign of foreboding.
36. *shadows.* This is the art of chiaroscuro. See p. 166, 31 and note.
38. *seeing... loving.* Hoskyns, 13, cites this as an example of 'sorites, or climbing argument'.

PAGE 262, 37. *pyramis.* 'pyramid'. ['pyramis' (plural: 'pyramides') is the Greek form of the word.]
38. *than... fear.* 'than her sex gave her fear'.

PAGE 263, 4–5. *of her brother's.* This is the double possessive.
5. [*whom she dearly affected.* 'whom she was very fond of'.]
22. *like the other two.* 'in addition to the two knights Artaxia appointed to fight them'.
29. *his.* 'Antiphilus'.

PAGE 264, 18–32. [*It was... forth.* Perhaps in order to convey a sense of the nobleman's urgency, his message is reported in a single sprawling sentence that in 90 takes up more than half a page.]

PAGE 265, 4–5 & 24. [*his children's.* See the notes to p. 141, 25 and p. 226, 28.]
16. *dialogue-wise.* See p. 171, 38–9.

THE THIRD BOOK

PAGE 266, 3–5. *keep... prisoner.* Hoskyns, 8, cites 'to keep love close prisoner', an erroneous conflation of two of Sidney's images, as a metaphor for 'concealing love'. [The image of love 'looking through' Pamela's eyes once again implies the idea of her eyes as windows to her soul – an idea which 93's addition 'out' seeks to enhance. Cf. p. 132, 16–17 and note.]

4–5. *close prisoner.* See p. 27, 11 and note.

14–15. [*nothing ... virtue.* Glossed as a sententia through inverted commas in 90.]

21–2. [*never acquainted with mediocrity.* In late sixteenth-century usage, 'mediocrity' is less negatively connoted and closer to meaning simply 'intermediateness'. The narrator's word choice frames Musidorus' moral shortcomings comparatively positively, describing his inability to control his passions as the absence of 'mediocrity' rather than evidence of intemperateness, boldness or lack of moderation.]

PAGE 267, 5. [*only fall of my judgement.* 'fall' here appears to mean 'lapse', although the phrase 'fall of judgement' is uncommon. However, *A Sanctuarie for a Troubled Soule* borrows the phrase and recontextualizes it by merging it with phrases from Book V ('tread vpon my desolate ruins', 232^v in 93) and Book III ('nowe thou hast the full sack of my conquered spirits ... set not stil new fire to thy owne spoiles'. 174^v in 93): 'O sinne, the onlye fall of my iudgment and staine of my conscience, now thou hast sacked my soule, now thou hast beaten it downe vnder thy tiranny, rest thy selfe, forbeare a while, treade not vpon my ruins, set not fire to thine owne spoiles' (p. 125).]

9–10. *It was ... Dorus.* See p. xxviii.

16–17. [*finding himself ... all happiness.* *A Sanctuarie for a Troubled Soule* paraphrases this passage to 'but nowe I am not onely vnhappie, but vnhappy after the falle from some degree of happinesse' (p. 123).]

24–5. *image ... Dorus.* Cf. p. 432, 12–19 and *OA* 45. 5–6, 'His heart in me ... / My heart in him', Robertson, 190, 29–30, but the image is common. See, for example, Shakespeare, sonnets 22, 24, 31, 46–8, 133; Donne, 'The Blossom', 'The Legacy'.

35–6. [*counterfeit ... saw it.* Pamela might recognize his handwriting from his earlier letter, in which he pretended to address Mopsa (cf. p. 133, 5–6).]

38. *elegiac.* In *A Defence of Poetry* (*Misc. Prose*, 95, 12) Sidney called it 'the lamenting Elegiac'. See p. lii. [This is the earliest example of the noun 'elegiac' in the sense of elegiac metre in *OED* (B1). The example from *A Defence of Poetry* is cited in the same *OED* entry, although it is classified as an example of 'elegiac' used in the sense of elegiac poet (B2, for which it is likewise the earliest example). The same entry also cites a different passage from *A Defence of Poetry* as the earliest example of the adjective 'elegiac' (A1).]

never ... quakingly. On directions on how to compose love letters, see Ovid, *Ars Amatoria*, i. 467 ff.; Chaucer, *Troilus and Criseyde*, ii. 1002–43. On the difficulty of composition, see Ovid, *Met.* ix. 522–9.

39–**PAGE 268**, 1. *ink and tears.* Cf. Ovid, *Heroides*, iii. 3; xi. 1; and xv. 97; and Chaucer, *Troilus and Criseyde*, v. 1335–7 and 1599.

PAGE 268, 20. [*and therefore ... to again.* i.e. realizing it contained a letter from Musidorus, she abruptly closed the standish again.]

32–**PAGE 271**, 10. Ringler, *OA* 74, and 419; Robertson, 341, 11 ff. Texts with substantive variants are *OA* (*Je om.* ll. 1–28), *Hn*, *Cm* (ll. 1–16), 90, 93. Elegiac metre is illustrated in William Webbe, *A Discourse of English Poetry* (1586), in G. G. Smith, *Elizabethan Critical Essays* (Oxford, 1904), i. 285; and in A. Fraunce, *The Arcadian Rhetoric* (1588), C3–C3^v, citing p. 270, 26–7 as an example of 'hexameters joined with pentameters'. [Since the poem is written in quantitative verse but largely follows ordinary early modern syntax, it contains more contracted forms and uncommon forms (such as 'ne ... ne', 'hugy', or 'unendly') than the rest of the verse in *Arcadia*. Some of the manuscript variants – such as 'moment' for 'monument' – may be explained by the fact that owing to the use of spondees, lines are not all metrically identical, which led some scribes to attempt to 'correct' what they perceived as metrical errors.]

32. *caitiff*. 'captive'. The metaphor of 'prisoner to ... sorrow', p. 268, 16, is continued here. [Additionally, the adjective 'caitiff' has strong connotations of 'miserable' or 'wretched' (see meaning 2 in the *OED* entry), so there is a tautological element to the phrase 'caitiff wretch'.]

PAGE 269, 5. *deadly*. 'made by a person in danger of death'.
15. [*heavenly*. See the note to p. 14, 19.]
23. *where ... he lived*. That is, within her breast; cf. p. 267, 24–5 and note.

PAGE 270, 3. *to be loved*. 'someone to love'. The passive infinitive is the direct object.
9. *but ... miracle*. 'except it be to demonstrate a greater miracle'.
18. *Cimmerian darkness*. The Cimmerians lived in darkness and foggy gloom beyond the reach of the sun; cf. Homer, *Odyssey*, xi. 14 ff. and Ovid, *Met*. xi. 594. The earliest citation in *OED* is from 1598; Robertson, 476, gives other early examples. See B. Stevenson, *Stevenson's Book of Proverbs* (London, 1949), 486.
11. [*heavenly*. See the note to p. 14, 19.]
23. *rage's events*. 'actions prompted by sexual desire'.
25. *pedante*. 'tutor'. This is the earliest citation in *OED*. Robertson, 476, gives earlier examples of the synonymous *pedant*. [Alexander Gill in *Logonomia Anglica* (1619), p. 131 cites this line as an example of metaplasm.]
27. *rage ... revenge*. His sexual desire drove him to embrace her. As *revenge* was previously defined, p. 269, 32–3, he returned her signs of affection with increased strength, hoping for similar revenge from her.

PAGE 271, 14–15. *two ... turned*. The stars, as fixed points, appear to revolve around the celestial poles. The 'sky of beauty' was replete with stars; cf. p. 80, 30–1 and note, and p. 357, 7.
31. *tucked ... knees*. See p. 301, 28–9 and note.

PAGE 272, 4. *in excellency fair*. 'beautiful to a degree of perfection'.
5–6. [*beautiful ... kiss them*. i.e. while Artesia is fair (cf. Basilius' comments in p. 80, 10–11), the Arcadian maids are too sunburnt to be truly described as beautiful. The image hints at a lack of virtue on the maids' part, while also echoing Musidorus' attempt to 'establish a trophy of his victory' with Pamela a few pages earlier. Cf. also p. 85, 3–4.]
8. *wanton modesty*. Hoskyns, 36, cites this as an example of synoeciosis; cf. Shakespeare, *Rape of Lucrece*, 401, 'O modest wantons, wanton modesty!' [Greville also used the phrase in his *Letter to an Honourable Lady*, ch. 2: 'For in this crafty forge are framed wanton modesty, entising shamefac'dnesse, faint reproofes, with what other charmes soeuer are fit to stirre vp the blindnesse of our Selfe-loue, or Pitty' (*Certaine Learned and Elegant Workes* (1633), p. 263).]
22. *not disdained*. Hoskyns, 35, cites this as an example of diminution 'by denying the contrary'.

PAGE 273, 3–4. *wound ... heart*. Cf. OA 45. 10, 'My heart was wounded, with his wounded heart', in Robertson, 191, 2.
6. *disgraced ... countenance*. Hoskyns, 47, cites this as an example of periphrasis.

19. [*collation*. The word is here being used in the sense of *collation* 9 in *OED*: 'A light meal or repast: one consisting of light viands or delicacies (e.g. fruit, sweets, and wine)'.]
34. *of torches*. 'with torches'.
37–8. *making ... mischief.* Hoskyns, 47, cites this as an example of paraphrasis 'by similitude or metaphor'.

PAGE 274, 3. *high ... injury*. 'lofty spirit scorning meekness when confronted by ill-treatment'.
8. *knives*. On Philoclea's knives, see pp. 277, 19–20; 280, 12; 350, 20–1; 382, 27–8.
17. *rose ... briar*. Cf. Tilley, R179, 'Every rose grows from prickles'. [For a different version of this commonplace, see Francis Meres' *Palladis Tamia* (1598), fol. 211ᵛ: As of one roote springeth both the Rose and the brier: so of one mother may descend both a bad sonne and a good; for a man may bee borne of a noble byrth, and yet himselfe become vile and dishonorable'. William Winstanley's *The New Help to Discourse* (1680), p. 154 adapts and recontextualizes the image: '*Edward* the third, that true pattern of vertue and valor, was like a rose out of a Bryar, an excellent Son of an evil Father'.]
29. *younger than*. See p. liv.
31. *puts ... head*. See p. 18, 18 and note.
36. [*base name of subjection*. Cecropia repeatedly uses the word 'subjection' in the sense of 'being a subject' (as opposed to a ruler, which she believes to be her due). The earliest example cited in *OED* 5b is Shakespeare's *Henry V* IV. i. 145.]

PAGE 275, 6–7. *Did ... itself*. Hoskyns, 50, cites this as an example of prevention by *subjectio*, a figure in which the speaker answers his own question.
7. [*to it ... concourse*. i.e. people would come to see Cecropia take her walk.]
13. *that pass*. That is, Amphialus being a prince.
23. *turn her shoulder*. Sitting on the same side of the table, when both faced the head Gynecia's back was to Cecropia.
25–6. *strangers ... allies*. Cf. p. 395, 5–9. [Glossed as a sententia through inverted commas in 90.]
32. *look*. 'set their sights'.

PAGE 276, 4–5. [*weeping ... folks*. Glossed as a sententia through inverted commas in 90. Cecropia is the character most prone to speaking in commonplaces, but like Clinias, she deliberately misuses them (cf. p. 281, 6).]
5–6. [*the mire of subjection*. See the note to p. 274, 36.]
11. *blind fortune*. See p. 143, 20 and note.
15. [*I thought ... quit*. 'I decided to take a chance'. The phrase appears in a number of texts from the 1570s and 1580s, including Golding's translation of Calvin's sermons on the Book of Job. Cecropia is using it to make an elaborate pun on 'double' (she has seized both of Basilius' daughters at once) and requital ('to quit' may mean to repay a debt); getting quit of them would allow her son to succeed to the throne.]
18. *their ... Pluto*. They would have been dead when contesting Amphialus' claim to the throne.
21–2. [*hate ... subjection*. Glossed as a sententia through inverted commas in 90. See also the note to p. 274, 36.]
29. *highly entitled*. 'possessed of a high-ranking title'. [Amphialus is responding to his mother's caution that love may lead to 'subjection' by arguing that to serve Philoclea would be the opposite of subjection. Cf. also Cecropia's reply (p. 276, 32) in which she refers to his love as a 'base' weakness.]

32-3. [*since ... so wilful a knot*. See note to p. 23, 28.]
33. *I have brought*. See p. lvi.

PAGE 277, 16-17. [*Company confirms ... of one's thoughts*. 90 glossed this as a sententia through inverted commas. Anthony Walker in *The Great Evil of Procrastination* (1682), p. 66 uses a variant form of this commonplace: 'Good Company confirms Good Resolutions'.]
24. *his injury ... wrong*. 'his wrongful act, and her unjust treatment'.
28. *tuffs*. 'tufts'.
28-9. *black ... stars*. His virtue is clouded over; cf. p. 365, 21-2.
34. *fear and desire*. Cf. p. 348, 6-7.

PAGE 278, 1. *shadow*. See p. 166, 31 and note.
1-2. *Venus ... Adonis*. The intensity of Philoclea's preoccupation with thoughts of Pyrocles is suggested by the passionate mourning of the goddess of love for the courageous Adonis; cf. Ovid, *Met*. x. 708 ff. See p. xxxiii.
23-4. *beyond ... uttering*. Hoskyns, 29, cites this as an example of hyperbole.

PAGE 279, 2. *But*. 'Only'.
26. *sky ... sorrow*. Hoskyns, 9, adapts this as an example of an allegory; cf. p. 41, 27.

PAGE 280, 12-13. [*the house ... into it*. For a variation of this image cf. Sir Walter Raleigh, *The First Part of the History of the World* (1617), p. 31: 'but by what crooked path soeuer we walke, the same leadeth on directly to the house of death: whose dores lye open at all houres, and to all persons'.]
28. *with ... duty*. 'with intimate feelings, away from their usual duties'.
34-6. [*wrapping ... necessity*. i.e. he framed his requests for assistance so cunningly that the recipients of his letters would think he was doing them a favour rather than asking a favour of them. 'give over' is being used in the sense of 'yield' here.]
35. *they*. 'fulfilment of their aspirations'.
37-8. *from ... succour*. 'from that quarter Amphialus could expect little help'.

PAGE 281, 4. [*sowed abroad*. 'distributed, scattered'. The phrase was frequently used to refer to the transmission of the gospel, but also to the spreading of false rumours. Cf. Thomas Lupton's preface to *The Christian Against the Iesuite* (1582):
> For the children of God doe sowe the good corne of Gods word: and the seruants of Satan haue and will, scatter abroad Darnel, the Diuels doctrine. But as the godly sowers shall dwell for euer with God, whose good seede they did sow: So the throwers abroad of the Darnell, shall dwell with the Diuel, except they cease from their sowing. (¶2)]

33-4. [*new necessities require new remedies*. Glossed as a sententia through inverted commas in 90. William Cornwallis cites this commonplace in his 'Prayse of King Richard the Third' in *Essayes of Certaine Paradoxes* (1616), C4ᵛ, without mentioning *Arcadia* as its source. Cf. also Richard Hooker, who invokes it in the context of spiritual jurisdiction:
> so it were absurd to imagine the Church it self, the most glorious amongst them, abridged of this liberty, or to think that no Law, Constitution or Canon, can be further made, either for Limitation or Amplification, in the practice of our Saviours Ordinances whatsoever occasion be offered through variety of times, and things, during the state of this inconstant world, which bringeth forth daily such new evills, as must of necessity by new remedies be redrest (*The Works of Mr. Richard Hooker* (1666), p. 327).]

PAGE 282, 12. *false-minded ... issue.* 'posture of neutrality while awaiting the issue'.

PAGE 283, 5–6. *particularly and throughly.* 'as individuals and as a whole group'.
32–3. *Gorgon's ... stone.* Through this image Amphialus' paralysis contrasts with Pyrocles' active attitude towards love; cf. p. 99, 34–5 and note.
36. *idleness.* See p. 60, 27–8 and note.
39. *piping in a shadow.* The conventional posture of lazy shepherds was of lying beneath a tree piping tunes.
39–40. *do ... enwrap me.* 'am I in a feather bed?'

PAGE 284, 13–14. *gold ... arrow.* See the note to p. 183, 22–4.
14. *rest.* See Glossary.
26. *disdained ... 'desire'.* She hated even the idea that Amphialus should desire rather than command.
29. *counterpease.* 'counterpoise'.
29–32. [*youthful thoughts ... thirstily.* As a young girl, Cecropia was persuaded to marry Basilius' brother, because she was led to believe she would then be the next queen of Arcadia (see p. 274, 32–8), so she hopes that this experience will enable her to persuade Philoclea to marry Amphialus, with the prospect of later becoming queen herself. Although Cecropia anticipates that her niece will require more persuasion ('sweet liquor') than her own youthful self, she has failed to consider that although Philoclea is a younger daughter, she is not motivated by the same ambitions, so Cecropia's efforts are doomed to fail.]
34. *given-over.* 'resigned'. [This is the earliest example cited in *OED*. Cf. also the note to p. 280, 34–6.]

PAGE 285, 3–4. *careful ... chance.* Cf. p. 58, 8.
23. *fortune ... see.* See p. 143, 20–1 and note.
25. [*misconster.* A sixteenth-century variant that became less common during the seventeenth century. The compositors of the 1628/9 folio consequently changed this to 'misconstrue', which is also the form that appears in all subsequent editions.]
36. [*upon ... king's daughter.* Cecropia's choice of phrase is both an attempt to appeal to her niece – who is also a king's daugher – and an indication that her royal blood (which she repeatedly refers to) is her chief point of pride.]

PAGE 286, 2–3. [*let not ... wilfulness.* See note to p. 23, 28.]
17. [*such niceness.* An example of paranomasia playing on the sound of 'niece' / 'nice': during her speech, Cecropia keeps pointedly addressing Philoclea as 'niece'. Each of her successive appeals begins with 'niece', 'sweet niece', or 'dear niece', culminating in this chiding for 'niceness' (i.e. coyness; see *OED* 3), before Cecropia strikes a more conciliatory note again.]
19. *bow ... yew.* Resilient yew was the best wood for bows; see the examples in *OED* under *yew* 1b.
30–1. [*no small king's daughter.* Again, Cecropia stresses her royal birth. See the note to p. 285, 36.]
37–8. [*but who will cry out, 'The sun shines!'?* 'But why state the obvious?']

PAGE 287, 12–13. *child ... child.* Hoskyns, 14, cites this as an example of antimetabole.
19–20. *your own ... them.* Cf. Shakespeare, sonnets 9 and 13, and Thomas Wilson, *Arte of Rhetorique*, ed. G. H. Mair (Oxford, 1909), 56, 'what a joy shall this be unto you ... where you shall have a pretty little boy running up and down your house, such

a one as shall express your look, and your wife's look, such a one as shall call you "dad" with his sweet lisping words'.
33. *cloddy cumbers*. 'clod-like hindrances'. This continues the metaphor of a team of oxen. [Cloddy earth is hardened, so the oxen pulling the plough need to labour harder in order to break the soil.]
35–8. *my bed ... home*. Cf. Ovid, *Heroides*, x. 53–4, Ariadne to Theseus: 'et tua, quae possum pro te, vestigia tango / strataque quae membris intepuere tuis', followed by Ariadne's lament that, because she has betrayed Crete, 'accessus terra paterna negat' (64).
39. *seeled dove*. See p. 77, 3 and note.

PAGE 288, 1–2. *man's ... eyesight*. Hoskyns, 39, cites this as an example of sententia. [It is cited in John Webster's *The Devil's Law-Case* (1623), I. i. (B^v). After having been gallantly told that her judgement 'is perfect in all things', the litigious widow Leonora replies 'Indeed Sir, I am a Widdow, / And want the addition to make it so: / For mans Experience has still been held / Womans best eyesight'. See also p. lxxxiv.]
12. [*can one ... consort*. Cecropia is punning on 'consort' in the sense of 'concert', i.e. several instruments playing in harmony, and 'consort' in the sense of partner or spouse.]
16–17. *he ... challenge*. Hoskyns, 44, cites this as an example of paraphrasis.
35. *neither her*. 'neither Cecropia's'.

PAGE 289, 2–3. [*sucking ... denial*. The image is of a spider sucking poison, to illustrate the idea that a truly malicious person will see malice everywhere and use anything as an excuse for further spite. Cf. 'The Printer to the Gentle Reader' in George Gascoigne's *A Hundreth Sundrie Flowres* (1573):

> the well minded man may reape some commoditie out of the most friuolous works that are written. And as the venemous spider wil sucke poison out of the most holesome herbe, and the industrious Bee can gather hony out of the most stinking weede: Euen so the discrete reader may take a happie example by the most lasciuious histories, although the captious and harebraind heads can neither be encoraged by the good, nor forewarned by the bad

Sidney's unconventional variant of the image (sucking spite rather than poison) was echoed in the fourth riddle of N. B.'s 'Excellent Dreame of Ladies and their Riddles' in *The Phoenix Nest* (1593), 26: 'In sorrowes seede is secret paine, / Which spite the Spider onely sucks, / Which poison gone, then wittie braine / The wilie Bee, hir honie plucks'.]
13. *invention*. 'design'.
15–16. *where ... eyes*. Hoskyns, 13, cites this as an example of epistrophe.
17. *awfully serviceable*. 'filled with both awe and servility'.
26–7. *only ... servitude*. These are feudal terms: 'only judging her subordination to be his own, believing what he did to be a true, and truly painful, service'.

PAGE 291, 15. *fortune ... would*. See p. liv.
20. *plentifully perjuring*. Hoskyns, 47, cites this as an example of paraphrasis.

PAGE 292, 6–7. [*whisperingness*. The only known instance of the word. Grammatically, 'whispering' would suffice, but the unusual form turns Clinias' habitual whispering into his defining quality, so Sidney's coinage may be intended to express this idea. See also the notes on p. 159, 13 and p. 249, 12.]

536   COMMENTARY

16. *unassailed*. 'untroubled'. This is the earliest citation in OED [though the word also appears in Thomas Becon's *The Sycke Mans Salue* (1561).]

29-30. *fear ... fear*. Hoskyns, 17, cites this as an example of polyptoton or traductio, where the words differ in case.

PAGE 293, 17-18. *face ... hair*. Cf. p. 35, 18.

17–PAGE 294, 7. *face ... together*. Cf. Virgil, *Aeneid*, ix, describing Euryalus, the most beautiful boy to serve Aeneas, who had no hair on his face, 'quo pulchrior alter / Non fuit Aeneadum ... Ora puer prima signans intonsa juventa' (180-1), whose friendship and love for Nisus, 'His amor unus erat' (182), ended in their death together, 'Fortunati ambo!' (444-6).

18-19. *mind ... fear*. Cf. p. 21, 38 and note, and Tilley, F135, 'Fear is one part of prudence'.

26-7. [*but a ring ... lookers-on ladies*. The image emphasizes Agenor's lack of fighting experience and the contrast between the aestheticism of his looks and movements – more suitable for showing off before an audience of admiring ladies, like Dorus showing off his horsemanship before Pamela – and the bloody reality of the battle he is joining.]

26. *ring*. See p. 132, 7-10 and note.

28. *descending line*. This is the line of descent traced by the tip of a lance as it is lowered and aimed.

31-2. [*spared ... vamplate*. Instead of aiming for Agenor's unprotected (and beardless) face, Amphialus takes pity on his youth and deliberately aims for his vamplate, which is attached to his lance. In doing so, however, he ends up marring the youthful beauty he was trying to spare, because his own lance – which, unlike Amphialus himself, is 'pitiless' – splinters in Agenor's face.]

35. *splinters ... face*. The most notable occurrence of this type of accident was the death of King Henry II of France during the tournament celebrating the betrothal of his daughter Elizabeth to King Philip II of Spain; cf. C. D. O'Malley, *Andreas Vesalius of Brussels 1514-1564* (Berkeley, 1964), 248-8.

fitter ... Venus. Cf. Ovid, *Heroides*, xvii. 253, 'Apta magis Veneri, quam sint tua corpora Marti'.

PAGE 294, 13. [*prince ... sword*. Following the publication of *Arcadia*, this became a popular commonplace and was invoked in a wide range of contexts. It appears in Sir John Hayward's account of the life of William the Conqueror in *The Liues of the III Normans* (1613), as well as the life of St Elphegus in Jerome Porter's *Flowers of the Liues of the Most Renowned Saincts of the Three Kingdoms* (1632), John Fletcher's play *The False One* (first published in the 1647 folio edition of Beaumont and Fletcher's works), George Lawson's *Exposition of the Epistle to the Hebrewes* (1662), and Sir James Turner's collection of military essays, *Pallas Armata* (1683). See also p. lxxxiv.]

16. *justling*. 'jostling'.

23. *unknightly wounds*. It was esteemed cowardly to kill the horse rather than the man. At p. 299, 9-10 Amphialus feels dishonoured that his old governor kills Musidorus' horse, and at p. 353, 14-15 is apologetic for accidentally killing another. At p. 209, 14-15 Anaxius threatens to kill Pyrocles' horse after his own has died on a spear. See p. xxviii, and cf. Spenser, *Faerie Queene*, II. v. 4 5, and Spenser, *Works*, ii. 234, comparing Malory, *Morte Darthur*, x. 42.

24-5. *borne ... borne*. Hoskyns, 17, cites this as an example of polyptoton or traductio, with the same verb used in several voices.

26. *burthens*. Cf. p. 319, 36.

30-1. *heads ... seigniories.* Hoskyns, 8, cites this as an example of how a metaphor 'enricheth our knowledge with two things at once, with truth and with similitude'.
30-5. *heads ... legs.* Cf. p. 243, 6 and note, and Kyd, *Spanish Tragedy*, I. ii. 59-60, 'Here falls a body sund'red from his head, / There legs and arms lie bleeding on the grass'.
34. *trailing guts.* See p. 356, 9-10 and note.
arms ... feel. Cf. Virgil, *Aeneid*, x. 395-6, 'Te decisa suum, Laride, dextera quaerit: / Semianimesque; micant digiti, ferrumque; retractant'.

PAGE 295, 4. *wisdom ... courage.* See p. 78, 2 and note.
11. [*he thought himself abused.* i.e. he felt cheated, because he had taken the prophecy at face value and assumed that dying in the arms of his son meant he would die at home, not in battle.]
24. *unriddle.* This is the earliest citation in OED. On prophesies, see the note to p. 16, 21-2 and p. xxv.
30. *grew a proverb.* See p. 329, 6-7 and note.

PAGE 296, 12. [*lionets.* 'young lions', 'cubs'. This is the earliest example in *OED*.]
13-14. *chases ... line.* In royal tennis, when an opponent returns the service and his ball is either missed or left, the ball makes a chase at the point of its second bounce on the service side. At the end of a game, or when two chases have been made during a game, the players change ends.
13. [*enow.* Spelt 'inow' in 90. See the note to p. 136, 20.]
28-9. *asking ... courage.* Cf. Shakespeare, *Pericles*, I. i. 62-3, 'Nor ask advice of any other thought / But faithfulness and courage'.
31. *succour.* 'assist in capturing Amphialus'.

PAGE 297, 10. *well-set.* 'well-delivered'.
33. *valiantest ... vilest.* Hoskyns, 16, cites this as an example of agnomination of syllables, a kind of pun.

PAGE 298, 5. *lost ... them in.* Hoskyns, 47, cites this as an example of periphrasis.
8. [*cruelty ... glory.* The phrase is glossed as a *sententia* through inverted commas in 90.]
good cheap. 'easily obtained'.
36. *none ... servants.* Hoskyns, 47, cites this as an example of periphrasis.
37. *his flail.* For similar threshing images, see Ariosto, *Orlando Furioso*, trans. Harington, xxix. 6, and Shakespeare, *3 Henry VI*, II. i. 131-2. [Cf. Also Spenser, *Faerie Queene*, V. xi. 47, in which Talus' iron flail scatters his enemies so they run 'diffused .../ Like scattred chaffe'.]

PAGE 299, 9-10. *slew ... dishonoured.* See the note to p. 294, 23.
11. *private soldier.* This complaint is reiterated at p. 317, 21.
35. *his dream.* See p. xxiii.

PAGE 300, 1-PAGE 304, 35. Ringler, *OA* 73, and 417-19; Robertson, 335, 13 ff. Texts with substantive variants are *OA* (*ex.* O), 90, 93. Ringler compares with this variant on the judgement of Paris the preference for Ariadne over Venus in *Greek Anthology*, v. 222. In England the queen triumphed over Venus in the Hampton Court painting of 1569, see F. A. Yates, *Astraea* (London, 1975), 63; in Peele's *Arraignment of Paris* (1584); and in Bernard Garter, *The Joyful Receiving of the Queen's ... Majesty into ... Norwich* [1578], cited in J. Nichols, *Progresses of Queen Elizabeth* (1823), ii. 149-50, where in a dream vision in verse Jove judged that Juno, Venus, Diana, Ceres, Pallas, and Minerva [sic] end their strife because he had included their qualities equally within the heart of Elizabeth.

The first and last lines are adaptations of the version of Petrarch's sonnet 3 printed in the second edition of Tottel's *Songs and Sonnets*, 31 July 1557 (H. E. Rollins, ed., rev. edn. (Cambridge, Mass., 1965), i. 277):

> It was the day on which the sun deprived of his light,
> To rue Christ's death amid his course gave place unto the night
> ....
> Now vaunt thee, love, which fleest a maid defenced with virtues rare,
> And wounded hast a wight unwise, unweaponed, and unware.

See p. xxiii. 1. [*heav'nly*. See the note to p. 14, 19.]
17. [*powers*. See the notes to pp. 59, 12 and 126, 6.]
18. [*heav'nly*. See the note to p. 14, 19.]
26–32. *blind ... blind*. Deliberate repetition for contrast may not be ruled out despite the predominance of manuscripts of *OA* reading *bind* at l. 27.
32. [*heav'nly*. See the note to p. 14, 19.]
36. *Samothea*. According to Annius of Viterbo (late fifteenth century), Samothes, first son of Japhet, was the earliest king of Britain, shortly after the flood, when it was known as Samothea. See K. Duncan-Jones, 'Sidney in Samothea: A Forgotten National Myth', *RES*, NS xxv (1974), 174–7; supplemented by W. L. Godshalk, in *RES*, NS xxix (1978), 325–6 and xxxi (1980), 192, and cf. AT 20. 10, 'those that honour Samos Isle'.

PAGE 301, 7–8. *lamps ... ground*. See p. 163, 2–3 and note.
7. [*heav'nly*. See the note to p. 14, 19.]
28–9. *tucked ... knees*. This was Diana's fashion, Ovid, *Met*. x. 536, 'Nuda genu, vestem ritu succincta Dianae'.
31. *meagre cheer*. 'thin face'.
38. *mountains ... mouse*. Cf. Tilley, M1215, 'The mountain was in labour and brought forth a mouse'.

PAGE 302, 3. *hard*. 'heard'.
8. *mother ... seed*. 'mother of pearl ... seed pearl'.
hight. 'is called'.
17. *Mira*. See p. xxiii.

PAGE 303, 3. [*pow'rs*. See the notes to pp. 59, 12 and 126, 6.]
23. [*precedence*. Stressed on the second syllable.]
26–7. *better ... Becometh us*. 'judgement is more appropriate to us than chance'.
28. *amber*. Amber was worn as an amulet to attract lovers; cf. *OED* under *amber* n.¹ 4.
34. [*smirkly*. 'smirkingly'. There are no known instances of this variant outside *Arcadia*, so this may be a form of metaplasm, the deliberate omission of a syllable in order to make a word conform to the metre.]

PAGE 304, 9. *near ... fear*. Cf. Tilley, F47, 'Too much familiarity breeds contempt'; cited in B. Stevenson, *Stevenson's Book of Proverbs* (London, 1949), 756.
10. *by Styx*. To the Greek and Roman gods such an oath was inviolable; cf. Herodotus, vi. 74, and see *CS* 17. 6 and *AS* 74. 7. The reference is commonplace.
21. *judging*. One of the earliest citations in *OED* under *judging* pres. p. adj. is from *A Defence of Poetry* (*Misc. Prose*, 86, 7); see p. 11, 19 and note.

25. *seek ... case*. 'ask her to take pity on your miserable condition'.
36–**PAGE 305**, 1. *feet .... But*. Cm leaves a blank space from p. 299, 36 'with her' to p. 305, 1, 'But'. The printed texts have three asterisks, thus: 'feet * * * But'. See p. xxxiii.

PAGE 305, 24. [*his pretended speech*. 'the speech he had intended to give'. 'pretend', which is usually associated with duplicity and injustice – and has consequently been used to describe the actions of characters like Antiphilus, Plexirtus and Clinias – acts as a reminder that Amphialus was about to have the King's regent executed out of personal revenge (after persuading himself this would not be an act of rebellion).]

PAGE 306, 2–5. *rather ... violence*. Hoskyns, 38, cites this as an example of parison.
27. *not unvisited*. The princesses' condition of being held 'unvisited' was not lifted for Philanax; see p. liv.
31–2. *her ... tune*. See p. lii, and cf. p. 380, 17–18.

PAGE 307, 5. *ragged race*. 'uneven course'; that is, 'less direct'.
14–18. *as if ... silk*. Hoskyns, 48, cites this as an example of prosopopoeia.
26–7. [*though ... principal work*. While even the background of Pamela's purse is skilfully embroidered, it is nevertheless only there to highlight the flowers. In his *Life of Sidney* (published posthumously in 1651), Greville was probably drawing on this famous image when noting that *Arcadia* was marginal among Sidney's 'works': 'my Noble Friend had that dexterity, even with the dashes of his pen to make the Arcadian Antiques beautifie the Margents of his works' (p. 244).]
34. [*not rejected ... glass*. Cf. p. 285, 18–19.]
36–**PAGE 308**, 1. *who ... guest*. 'who rather tolerated that sorrow make itself miserable (that is, make itself at home) in her beauty than, like Pamela, make comfortable such an unwelcome guest' by grooming. See pp. lii.

PAGE 308, 3. *squaring out*. 'form'. The earliest citation in *OED* under *squaring* vbl. n. 1b is from 1611.
3–4. *beauty ... harborough*. Cf. Tilley, B163, 'Beauty and chastity seldom meet'; 'harborough' is the form in all texts for 'harbour'.
9–10. *purse ... pursed up*. Hoskyns, 15, cites this as an example of antimetabole.
13. [*but even as a very purse*. 'simply as a purse'. Pamela's use of 'very' stresses that this is really all it is, contradicting Cecropia's fanciful interpretation of the embroidered purse as a treasure in itself.]
20–5. *beasts ... persons*. This represents the spectrum of the created world, from man to stone; cf. p. 172, 31–3 and notes.
26–7. *judgement ... beauty*. See p. 90, 34–5 and note.
34–5. *fair ... speaking*. Hoskyns, 38, cites this as an example of asyndeton; cited in C. G. Smith, *Spenser's Proverb Lore*, 48.
36. *chain their ears*. The Gallic Hercules is depicted with the ears of his audience chained to his persuasive tongue. Here woman's beauty is given greater power than eloquence. Cf. AS 58. 1–8; Henkel and Schöne, 1651–2; and especially M. R. Jung, *Hercule dans la littérature française du xvie siècle* (Geneva, 1966), 73–93.
36–7. *venture ... venturing*. Hoskyns, 15, cites this as an example of antimetabole.
36–**PAGE 357**, 14. *conquer ... conquering*. See p. xxviii.

PAGE 309, 1. *govern ... love*. See p. 137, 38–9 and note.
14–15. *cranes ... Pygmies*. The annual attack by the cranes on the Pygmies was an ancient commonplace; *battles* are 'armies'.
16. *and that*. 'and as'.

16–17. *babes ... babies.* 'babies (unable to walk or speak) ... young children'.
27–8. *beauty ... ever flourishing.* Cf. p. 1, 20. [See also p. lxxxiv.]
34. *parent's.* 'father's'.
36. *How ... devotion.* 'How youth turns to religion before its natural time!' – which would be in old age, when preparing for death.
38. *heaven ... sure.* The innocence of youth was certain, and near to heaven because unsullied.

PAGE 310, 5. *April ... age.* This is cited in Tilley, A310. A long list of analogues is in H. E. Rollins, ed., *A New Variorum Edition of Shakespeare, The Sonnets* (Philadelphia, 1944), i. 13–14, on sonnet 3. 10. The earliest citation in *OED* under *April* 2a is from 1583.
5–9. *Let not ... overtaken.* Cf. Tilley, N54, 'He that will not when he may, when he would he shall have nay'; cited in C. G. Smith, *Spenser's Proverb Lore*, 369.
7–8. *persuade ... be taken.* Hoskyns, 29, cites this as an example of correctio.
11. *hidden.* See p. liii.
26–7. *children ... know.* But cf. Montaigne, *Essays*, I. xxv, trans. Florio (London, 1910), i. 175, 'How wide are they which go about to allure a child's mind to go to his book, being yet but tender and fearful, with a stern-frowning countenance and with handsful of rods! Oh, wicked and pernicious manner of teaching!'
32. *virtue.* See p. 63, 4–5 and p. 102, 26 and note.
35–PAGE 314, 19. *Fear ... destruction.* On this debate, see D. P. Walker, *The Ancient Theology* (London, 1972), 132–63, and the summary of scholarly comment in M. Rose, *Heroic Love* (Cambridge, Mass., 1968), 56–62.
35–6. *Fear ... inventor.* Cf. Chaucer, *Troilus and Criseyde*, iv. 1408, in *Works*, ed. F. N. Robinson, 2nd edn. (Cambridge, Mass., 1961), 'Eke drede first fond goddes', and the lengthy note.

PAGE 311, 8. *wisdom ... god.* See p. 16, 11–12 and note.
9–10. *if ... such.* Cf. p. 173, 19.
14–17. *enlarged ... interrupted.* See p. xxxi.
20. *your affection.* Cf. p. 310, 22.
22–3. *O ... you foolish.* Hoskyns, 36, cites this as an example of indirect synoeciosis.
23. *constancy.* See p. xxiii.
26. *not seen.* Cf. p. 310, 33.
29–30. *fruit ... heart.* The image is of an old fruit tree.
31–2. [*my ears ... blasphemy.* 'I will not listen to my creator being blasphemed'. The grammatical construction Pamela uses highlights her point that passively suffering blasphemous statements to be uttered in her presence without countering them would be equivalent to actively committing blasphemy (which would make her ears 'guilty' just for listening to Cecropia).]

PAGE 312, 2–3. *eternal ... not being.* See p. lvi.
20–1. *round ... centre.* Cf. Macrobius, *Commentary on the Dream of Scipio*, trans. W. H. Stahl (New York, 1966), I. xxii. 5–8:

> Of all the matter that went into the creation of the universe, that which was purest and clearest took the highest position ..., the dregs and off-scourings ... settled to the bottom ...; perhaps the spherical nature of the sky itself keeps the earth from moving in one direction or another .... To this point which is the bottom and middle, so to speak, and is stationary because it is the centre,

all weights must be drawn since the earth itself, like a weight, has fallen to this place.

And see the note to p. 163, 2–3.

22–4. *chance ... inconstancy*. See p. lvi.

PAGE 313, 25–7. *Each ... mankind.* 'As the only purpose of things below the order of man is self-preservation, so man alone possesses reason or judgement, with its attributes, speech and laughter'.

31–2. *this ... absurdities.* See p. liv.

32. *our bodies.* 'one's body'. The singular 'body' has become plural through association with 'our'; cf. Abbott, 298.

PAGE 314, 24–5. *just ... justice.* Hoskyns, 15, cites this as an example of antimetabole.

25–7. *assure ... assure thyself.* Hoskyns, 44, cites this as an example of a long parenthesis which requires 'a retreat to the matter' through antanaclasis.

25. [*plaguily.* 'extremely', with a pun on the literal meaning, 'in a plague-like manner', since Pamela is comparing Cecropia's blasphemous thoughts to a sickness that she seeks to pass on to others. This is the earliest citation in *OED*.]

29. *manifesting.* 'revealing'. The earliest citation in *OED* is from 1536.

30. *ugly shamefastness.* 'morally offensive propriety', a synoeciosis similar to that at p. 272, 8, 'wanton modesty', and p. 350, 21, 'forward favour'. See pp. 162, 39–40; 188, 7–8, and liv; cf. Nashe, *The Anatomy of Absurdity*, in *Works*, ed. R. B. McKerrow, 2nd edn., ed. F. P. Wilson (Oxford, 1966), i. 18, 'impudent shamefastness', but the figure is misunderstood and cited in *OED* 2 as the unique example of a misuse for 'shamelessness'.

33. *captivity ... tyranny.* Hoskyns, 36, though writing 'captivity ... captivity', cites this as an example of indirect synoeciosis.

17. *eyes ... judges.* See p. 11, 19 and note.

PAGE 315, 5. *to envy.* 'to envying'. See p. 205, 31–2 and note, and p. xxxii.

8. *eyes cast.* See p. 240, 19 and note.

9. *with colour ... yellowness.* 'reddening in anger, colouring her natural yellowness'. Yellowness was a sign of jealousy.

14. *repining ... repenting.* Hoskyns, 16, cites this as an example of agnomination of syllables, a kind of pun.

as she thought. 'what she thought to be'.

19–20. *both ... sorrow.* 'Sorrow' is personified as a hanging judge.

27. *carried before him.* 'continued forwards'.

32. *more ... choler.* 'more sullenness than irascibility'.

PAGE 316, 3–4. *marching ... fighting.* See p. 28, 5 and note, and p. xxix.

29. *love ... love.* Hoskyns, 14, cites this as an example of antimetabole.

30. *win.* 'would win'. This is the subjunctive in a subordinate sentence; cf. Abbott, 267.

33. *island.* The arena for fighting in the Spartan games was similarly surrounded by a moat; cf. Pausanias, *Description of Greece*, III. xiv. 8.

PAGE 317, 19. *private fighter.* Cf. p. 299, 11. [While Cecropia and Clinias have personal interests in discouraging Amphialus from accepting the challenge, the governor is accusing Amphialus of inadequate leadership, because he is putting his personal vanity above his responsibility for the 'Amphialians' who depend on him as their general. The governor's concerns turn out to be justified, because in offering to fight anyone willing to challenge him, Amphialus' behaviour mirrors that of Phalantus.]

34–6. *colour… before.* T. Blundeville, *The Four Chiefest Offices Belonging to Horsemanship* [c.1570], E4^v–E5^v, in adapting Grisone's treatise lists among perfect horses the brown bay and the pure black. Well coloured horses are improved by 'some black mark, at the least in their nethermost parts'. A brown bay or 'any other colour betokening colour a dust' needs a white mark 'to mitigate his fierceness'. This first of the good white-footed horses 'hath a white forefoot on the far [right] side', while the first of the bad ones has 'a white forefoot on the near [left] side.… It is an excellent good mark also for a horse to have a white star in his forehead.' See pp. xx–xxi, xxvi.

38. *tawny and gold.* Tawny symbolizes despair and languishing (see C. Marot, *Œuvres Diverses*, ed. C. A. Mayer (1966), 109, and the anonymous *Blason des couleurs*, 102 n.), with particular reference to love as in G. Whitney, *A Choice of Emblems* (1586), R3^v, 'The man refus'd, in tawny doth delight'. Gold is symbolic of virtue. At the assault upon The Fortress of Perfect Beauty in 1581, Fulke Greville's pages, trumpeters, gentlemen, and yeomen wore tawny and gold; see J. Nichols, *Progresses of Queen Elizabeth* (1823), ii. 316–17.

PAGE 318, 1. *leaves were falling.* Bradamante's 'desperation and will to die' was symbolized by 'the colour of her bases …/ Like to the falling whitish leaves and dry' in Ariosto, *Orlando Furioso*, trans. Harington (1591), xxxii. 46 (noted by K. Duncan-Jones, 'Sidney's Pictorial Imagination' (unpublished B.Litt. thesis, Oxford University, 1964), p. 126). See also P. Beal, 'Poems by Sir Philip Sidney: The Ottley Manuscript', *The Library*, 5th Ser. xxxiii (1978), 288, citing Sidney's poem describing a 'desert knight' in 'armour, bark and moss of faded tree', who had been 'Weaned from the hope which made affection glad', and the note to p. 221, 6–11.

3. *cloth of gold.* This was used for the withered leaves on the Tree of Honour at the Field of Cloth of Gold, 1520; see S. Anglo, *Spectacle Pageantry, and Early Tudor Policy* (Oxford, 1969), 151.

6. *torpedo fish.* On the cramp-fish or electric ray which numbed and stupefied when touched, and which transmitted its effects through an object to the hand, see p. 431, 38 and Robertson, 332, 33; E. M. Denkinger, 'The *Arcadia* and "The Fish Torpedo Faire"', *SP* xxviii (1931), 162–83; Camerarius, *Symbolorum et Emblematum*, IV. xl; and Henkel and Schöne, 693–4.

13–15. *could … party.* See p. xxiv.

16–18. *horse … stains.* On the humours of horses, Blundeville, *The Four Chiefest Offices* (c.1570), E4^v–5^v, says, 'if he hath more of the water, then is he phlegmatic, slow, dull, and apt to lose flesh, and of colour most commonly milk-white.… The horse that is flea-bitten [red, as if from flea-bites] only on the shoulders or on the flanks can neither be strong nor able to endure any hardness.'

17. *fretened.* 'adorned'. The editor of 93 altered the verb to *freck*. 'dapple', for which the earliest citation in *OED* is from 1621.

19. *carnation.* 'deep red', 'crimson'. Carnation symbolizes desire. At The Fortress of Perfect Beauty, virtuous Desire's chariot was drawn by horses 'apparelled in white and carnation silk'; see J. Nichols, *Progresses of Queen Elizabeth* (1823), ii. 327. Thomas Nashe recalls in *Have With You to Saffron-Walden* (1596) 'some 18 years since, when these Italianate carnation painted horse tails were in fashion', in *Works*, ed. R. B. McKerrow, 2nd edn., ed. F. P. Wilson (Oxford, 1966), iii. 54; cf. Fynes Moryson, *Itinerary* (1903), 83, 'Commonly painting the mane and tail … of their horses with light colours, as carnation and the like'. See p. xxvi and the note to p. 80, 33.

19–21. *vine ... grapes.* See p. xxvi.
27–8. *proportionately delivered.* 'evenly distributed'.
30. *glory ... prey.* Cf. Camerarius, *Symbolorum et Emblematum*, II. lxiii; Henkel and Schöne, 583, with the motto 'Gloria finis', but where the hare is killed. See p. xxvi.
32–3. *anything to him.* See p. lv.
37–8. *corvetting.* 'curvetting'. See the note to p. 131, 34–5. The earliest citation in *OED* 1a is from 1584.
39. *sun shines.* See p. lvi.
40. *upon the ground.* This is in contrast to the leaps of Phalantus' mount.
further foot before. See p. xxvi.

PAGE 319, 1. *master's ... angry.* Cf. p. 294, 20–21.
5–6. *there ... discords.* Hoskyns, 37, cites this as an example of indirect synoeciosis.
10. *mark ... meet.* The targets were approaching the lances.
24. *feeling sense.* See p. 223, 16–17 and note.
32–6. *corvet ... art.* 'curvet'. The spelling in the text reflects the association made with ravens on p. 131, 34–5 and note; cf. Christopher Clifford, *The School of Horsemanship* (1585), 'To the Reader',

> it is naught to teach a horse to curvet ... for that when you would encounter your enemy at hand strokes with your sword, these mistaught jades will fall a-dancing, which is a thing very dangerous in fighting with one horse against another, for that he never standeth surely, and therefore is in peril to be thrown down or else to give the rider's back to the enemy ...

See p. xx. 36. *burdening his burden.* Cf. p. 294, 23–4.

PAGE 320, 4–5. *never ... fortune.* See p. xxvi. [The operative word here is 'man': by making this distinction, Phalantus' claim is technically not an outright lie, because the opponent who unhorsed him (saddle and all) in p. 88, 36–9 was Zelmane.]
14. *great ... remnants.* Cf. Tilley, T260, 'Their thrift waxes thin that spend more than they win'.
19. *disdained.* 'disdainful'; see p. lxxvii. The earliest citation in *OED* is from Shakespeare, *1 Henry IV*, I. iii. 183.
20. *use his fortune.* This is cited in C. G. Smith, *Spenser's Proverb Lore*, 292.
33. [*went ... otherwhere.* This is in character for Phalantus, who fights primarily for personal glory but will move on 'as soon as the spur of honour cease[s]' (cf. p. 78, 3). Consequently, he has no interest in remaining at the siege after his defeat by Amphialus.]

PAGE 321, 1–2. *Philoclea ... combat.* See p. xxiv.
5. [*a simple service.* 'small service', 'not much of a service'.]
10–11. *if her ... with her.* See p. xxiv.
30. *weathercocks.* Their shifting in the wind symbolizes inconstancy.

PAGE 322, 5. *parlour.* See the note to p. 20, 23.
5–6. *stories of Hercules.* See p. xxv.
9–14. *happy ... ruling.* Cf. Chaucer, *The Book of the Duchess*, 1288–95, in *Works*, ed. F. N. Robinson, 2nd edn. (Cambridge, Mass., 1961),

> Our joye was every ylyche newe;
> Oure hertes wern so evene a payre,
> That never nas that oon contrayre

> To that other, for no woo.
> For some, ylyche they suffred thoo
> Oo blysse, and eke oo sorwe bothe;
> Ylyche they were bothe glad and wrothe;
> Al was us oon, withoute were.

See also Chaucer's source in G. de Machaut, *Le Jugement Dou Roy de Behaingne*, 166–76; and cf. below, pp. 346, 14–22.
12. *never ... never*. The double negative is used for emphasis; cf. Abbott, 295.
23–4. *blushed ... blushed*. See p. 40, 14 and note.
26. *like ... affection*. See p. xxv.
on sleep. This is an early form of 'asleep'.

PAGE 323, 3–4. [*which ... adventured*. 'which I will never allow to be risked like that'.]
5. [*Enow, enow there are*. 90 uses the spelling 'ennow', which only appears in two other texts in the EEBO / TCP corpus. See the note to p. 136, 20.]
15. *presage*. See p. xxvii.

PAGE 324, 2. *sword of justice*. The figure of Justice holds a sword; cf. p. xlvi.
3. *quickly received*. This elliptical form was expanded in the printed editions. See p. liv.
8–9. [*him ... conquered*. i.e. love.]
14. *gilded ... hair*. See p. xxvii and cf. the broken knots on Zelmane's apparel, p. 225, 30 and note. Gold symbolizes divine perfection, as in Abraham Fraunce, *Insignium, Armorum* (1588), L4.
woman's hair. Hair was cut off as a token of mourning; cf. Homer, *Iliad*, xxiii. 135.
16. *eagle*. The eagle symbolizes victory, perfection, and truth.
21. *sleeve*. This was a separate article of dress, often worn by knights as a love-token.
23. *full of*. 'covered with'.
bleeding hearts. See p. xxvii.
24. *palm trees*. Palm trees are the emblem of harmonious, faithful love; cf. pp. 109, 2; 110, 1. See Henkel and Schöne, 199, for the motto *Vivite Concordes* in J. Cats, *Emblemata* (1627), 1. Many examples are given in R. Burton, *Anatomy of Melancholy*, 3. 2. 1. 1. See p. xxvii.
25–6. *horse ... back*. T. Blundeville, *The Four Chiefest Offices* (c.1570), E4^v, in relating colour to the temperaments or complexions of horses, says, 'if of the fire, then is he choleric and therefore light, hot, fiery ... seldom of any great strength, and is wont to be of colour a bright sorrel'. Among the most commendable of horses is the 'bright sorrel ... having his outermost parts black, as the tips of his ears, his mane, his tail, or all four feet. And if he hath a list [a stripe of colour] from his mane to his tail, he is so much the better.'

PAGE 325, 8–9. *cruellest ... seen*. Hoskyns, 29, cites this as an example of hyperbole.
17. [*accused*. 'betrayed'.]

PAGE 326, 1–2. [*small ... quarrel*. i.e. he had no reason to hate Argalus personally.]
4. *filling ... blood*. See p. xxix.
5–6. *candle ... blaze*. Cf. Tilley, L277, 'A lightening before death'.
6–8. [*casting ... his shield*. In the description of the heated battle between Amphialus and Argalus, the referent of 'his' becomes deliberately mingled, so that in the same sentence, the phrase 'his shield' refers first to Argalus' and then to Amphialus' shield.]
15. *dreamed*. See p. xxv.

17–18. *fear ... nature.* 'fear for the safety of a loved one overcame the natural concern for her own preservation'; cf. p. 54, 20 and note.
25. *his affection.* 'love's power'.
38–PAGE 327, 2. *conqueror ... dishonour.* See p. xxviii.

PAGE 327, 2–5. *so that ... forward.* 'so that Argalus not so much disputing with Amphialus (for he would have done the same if he had had Amphialus in the same position, as though it were Amphialus struggling against *his* own might, which Amphialus above all held in contempt) set out against him'. As at p. 113, 1 the editor or compositor of 90 interpreted the construction in 'so much ... as' to be a comparative and punctuated accordingly with two parentheses, the first including *(for if ... with him)* and the second *(which ... despised).* On the other hand *Cm* has no punctuation from *in like sort* to *forward.* See p. xxxiii, and *OED* under *as* B 1b.
9. *dance of death.* The skeletal figure of death leads his dancing partners towards the grave in this popular artistic motif; cf. J. M. Clark, *The Dance of Death* (Glasgow, 1950).
14. *herself.* 'itself'. The emphatic pronoun has apparently become feminine through association with the possessive.
18. *O ... art thou.* Hoskyns, 30, cites this as an example of *correctio.*
31. *my better half.* This is cited in Tilley, H49; cf. Ovid, *Heroides,* x. 58, 'Perfide, pars nostri, lectule, major ubi est'. [This is the earliest known example of the phrase 'better half' used for a spouse, although there are earlier instances of it being used in the sense of 'larger part'.]
35. *wisdom and goodness.* Cf. p. 16, 11–12 and note.

PAGE 328, 6–7. *last breath ... mouth.* 'Just before death the soul was supposed to hover in the throat or the nose of the dying man ... so that it might be caught in the mouth of kinsmen or successors of the dying', comments A. S. Pease, ed., *Publi Vergili Maronis Aeneidos Liber Quartus* (Cambridge, Mass., 1935), note to iv. 684–5, with many examples. See below, p. 375, 14; Marlowe, *2 Tamburlaine,* II. iv. 69–70; Shakespeare, *Antony and Cleopatra,* IV. xv. 20–1 and 39. See also S. Gaselee, 'The Soul in the Kiss', *The Criterion,* ii (1924), 349 ff., and the Cabbalistic tradition in E. Wind, *Pagan Mysteries in the Renaissance,* rev. edn. (Harmondsworth, 1967), 152–70.
37. [*whether ... Miso.* Dametas' challenge to Clinias and the subsequent 'combat of cowards' is a comical reworking of Argalus' combat with Amphialus, which directly precedes it. Dametas' readiness to leave Miso behind (and even to consider absence from his wife an incentive to joining Basilius' campaign) contrasts with the cruel separation of the happy couple Argalus and Parthenia.]

PAGE 329, 1. *make ... widow.* Hoskyns, 47, cites this as an example of paraphrasis 'by consequence'.
6. *cowardice.* O'Connor, 190–1, compares the feud between the cowardly Darinel and Mardoquée in *Amadis de Gaule,* IX. xxxii and xxxiv.
proverb. 'phrase of contempt'. Cf. p. 295, 30–1.
9–10. [*favourable conceit of Basilius.* Sidney's choice of 'conceit' is apt here. Basilius' faith in Dametas' wisdom has repeatedly proved ill-conceived, so the primary meaning is 'opinion', but with undertones of 'conceitedness' and 'fanciful thinking'.]
15. *hare sitting.* 'an easy target'.
21–2. *fritter ... pot.* These are culinary metaphors.

21. *fritter ... iniquity*. Hoskyns, 9, cites this as an example of a metaphor which is 'too base', noting that 'they that speak of a scornful thing speak grossly'.

22-3. [*Chief Governor ... Pamela*. Seeking to intimidate Clinias, Dametas inflates his role as Basilius' principal herdsman (cf. the notes to pp. 15, 6 and 20, 13–14) into an official title. Since Dametas thinks of himself primarily as a shepherd, he mentions his guardianship of the king's eldest daughter only as an afterthought. The fact that she was abducted while in his care does not prevent him from boasting about his position of trust.]

24-5. *bodkin ... pike*. These weapons are of the least sophistication, being those of the herdsman and of the lowest rank of foot-soldier.

PAGE 330, 14–17. [*coming from ... furnitures*. This is a comical contrast to the armour and devices of the other knights, which are designed to express a specific idea (even the armour of the 'Ill-apparelled Knight' in Book I had a consistent theme), whereas for the self-important Dametas, more is more. He takes a similar approach to the design of his device, in insisting on 'a great many' arms and legs and 'a great army' of pens, inkhorns and books, and is pleased to be lifted onto his horse by several young gentlemen, which he takes as a sign of his importance but which is in fact a sign of his comical lack of horsemanship (cf. p. 132, 2–7 and the note to p. 209, 33–8).]

19. *arms and legs*. Cf. p. 243, 6–7 and note.

25. *Here ... hare*. Cf. Sir Thomas More's epigram 'In Malum Pictorem', in *Opera* (1566), E4, where in order to supplement his deficiency in skill he wrote on the painting, 'est hic canus, iste lepus'. See p. xviii.

29. Ringler, OP 2, and 493. Substantive texts are *Cm*, 90, 93. Dametas' wit is shown to be even further astonishing in his ability to compose this hexameter line. [Cf. p. 19, 19–23.]

mine own pigsney. Reference to any small eye was a term of endearment. Here 'pig's eye' contains ironic overtones, being a reference to Miso's recollection of being praised for her 'pretty little eyes', p. 182, 13–14, which she evidently had. Cf. p. 181, 35, 'her ferret-eyes', and note.

31-2. *make ... island*. Hoskyns, 47, cites this as an example of paraphrasis.

34-5. [*divers ... horseback*. Dametas is such a terrible rider (cf. p. 132, 2–7) he cannot even mount by himself, so he has to be 'lifted up' by several pages – which he takes pride ('no small glory') in, because it makes him feel important.]

35. [*comes me a page*. 'there came a page'. The word 'me' here functions as an 'ethic dative' used as a narrative expletive (see *me* 2d in *OED*), a form that was frequently combined with a switch to the historical present. Cf. Golding's translation of Ovid's *Metamorphoses* (1567), fol. 91 ('Now while I musing on the same supposde it to haue been / Some fancie of the foolish dreame which lately I had seen, / Behold, in comes me *Telamon* in hast...') and Puttenham's *The Arte of English Poesie* (1589), pp. 111–12: 'Comes me to the Court one *Polemon* an honest plaine man of the country ....']

PAGE 331, 34–5. [*contrary to his complexion*. 'unlike his nature'. 'complexion' here refers to the humours of the body, which were believed to define a person's temperament.]

PAGE 332, 4–6. *fearfulness ..., himself* Hoskyns, 40, cites this as an example of sententia. [Thomas Blount's *Academie of Eloquence* (1654) cites it as an example of compar and contentio (p. 35).]

28. *flat bastinado*. Cf. p. 221, 8 and note.

28-9. [*went ... his helmet*. Dametas is being dragged along by his horse, his head almost touching the ground. The image is a humorous reference to his earlier boast that he had 'left off the plough to do such bloody deeds with his sword as many inkhorns and books should be employed about historifying them' (p. 330, 21–3).]

35–9. [*horse fell ... behind*. A comical echo of the earlier combat between Amphialus and Phalantus. Amphialus, seeing Phalantus trapped underneath his fallen horse, had got off his own horse intending to help him. Dametas has no such knightly impulses, however, so only his extreme cowardice (he does not dare to attack Clinias except from behind) prevents him from achieving an unsporting victory by killing his helpless adversary while he is still on the ground.]

39. *pawing*. The earliest citation in *OED* for this verbal noun is from 1726; at p. 318, 39–40 *panting*, 98, 13 read *pawing*.

40. *that Dametas*. 'so that Dametas'. On the omission of 'so' before 'that', see Abbott, 193.

PAGE 333, 7. *went back*. Cf. p. 69, 20–1.

12. *ungratefully*. 'without striking back'; see Glossary.

16–17. *winking*. 'closing his eyes'.

18. *flail*. See the note to p. 298, 37.

PAGE 334, 17. *eye ... side*. See p. 240, 18–19 and note.

29. *among ... Amphialus*. 'among all of Amphialus' people'.

31–3. [*dig ... lure*. The images reflect Clinias' consideration of the different approaches he will need to take to recruit different groups of people as his allies: those with unsatisfied ambitions, who feel the tediousness of the siege, he tries to persuade to 'dig in the same mine' (a military strategy that would normally be employed by the besiegers, so the image also captures the switching of sides), while his winning over of the 'wealthy, weary folks' and 'unconstant youths' is expressed in an image from falconry.]

PAGE 335, 20. [*hardly brooking ... misery*. 'hardly able to bear the presence of Artesia, who had been instrumental in getting them imprisoned'.]

36. *graved ... windows*. See p. 176, 8 and note.

PAGE 336, 5. *the rather*. 'the more readily'.

8. *well-intended*. This is the earliest citation in *OED* 2 (of an action, utterance, etc).

36. *admonished*. 'exhorted' or 'urged'. See p. liv.

PAGE 337, 16. *thy ... net*. See p. xxvi. Cf. Tilley, F626, 'The fowler is caught in his own net'; cited in C. G. Smith, *Spenser's Proverb Lore*, 88.

26–7. *who do ... inferiors*. See the examples in B. Stevenson, *Stevenson's Book of Proverbs* (London, 1949), 1965, especially Seneca, *Thyestes*, 311, 'Saepe in magistrum scelera redierunt sua'.

34. *occasionable*. 'likely to have been caused'. This is the earliest citation in *OED*. See p. liv.

35. *Euardes*. Cf. pp. 179, 14; 203, 1.

PAGE 338, 6. *Thraso-like*. The adjective is based upon the name of the braggart soldier in Terence, *Eunuchus*; cf. *A Defence of Poetry* (*Misc. Prose*, 96, 9; 116, 15–16), 'a vainglorious Thraso', 'a heartless threatening Thraso'.

10. *four ... Amphialus*. See p. xxx, and p. 203, 25–8.

28. *courage ... wisdom*. See the note to p. 78, 1–2. [Glossed as a sententia through inverted commas in 90.]

37–8. [*make Anaxius ... grateful*. i.e. despite the circumstances, Amphialus tried to be a good host and to welcome Anaxius as a friend.]

PAGE 339, 15. *ladies ... me.* Cf. Shakespeare, *Twelfth Night*, II. iii. 151-2, 'it is his grounds of faith that all that look on him love him'.
23-4. *gave the watchword.* 'gave him the password'.
31-2. *smooth ... lake.* This is in contrast to p. 5, 1.

PAGE 340, 1-24. Ringler, CS 3, and 426. Texts with substantive variants are *St, Bo, Cl, Dd, Hn, Hy, Ra, Cm* (*incipit only*), 90, 93, 98; N. Breton, *The Arbour of Amorous Devices* (1597), B3ᵛ-B4 (Ringler, 564); A. Fraunce, *The Arcadian Rhetoric* (1588), E1-E1ᵛ (Ringler, 562). This poem formed part of Sidney's collection of *Certain Sonnets* before being used here. In his note to OA 43, Ringler, 406, describes the fashion for correlative verse. On the musical models, see F. J. Fabry, 'Sidney's Verse Adaptations of Two Sixteenth-Century Italian Art Songs', *Renaissance Quarterly*, xxiii (1970), 237-55; and 'Sidney's Poetry and Italian Song-Form', *ELR* iii (1973), 232-48.
1-4. *fire ... earth.* On this use of the elements, Ringler, 426, compares OA 13. 29-32, Robertson, 83, 23-7; and Shakespeare, sonnets 44 and 45.
1. [*fire.* The word is monosyllabic throughout this poem. This is especially apparent in p. 340, 20, which consists entirely of monosyllables.]
woes. This has been accepted into the text as an authorial adaptation, made to bring the poem into line with Amphialus' feelings; see p. li.
4. *earth ... keepeth.* See the notes to pp. 163, 2-3; 312, 20-1, and cf. p. 301, 8.
9. *alonely.* 'solely'.
12. *her eyes ... fuel.* This is cited in C. G. Smith, *Spenser's Proverb Lore*, 315.
24. *she ... me.* See p. li.

PAGE 341, 7. *from within.* 'from inside Amphialus' castle'.
37. *walls-ward.* 'towards the walls'. [Cf. 'to me-wards' (p. 131, 39).]

PAGE 342, 1-2. *blaspheming ... him.* See p.xxiii.
5. *requiting ... life.* Cf. p. 338, 12-13; and see p. xxx.
8. *his.* 'Amphialus'.
11-12. [*courage ... manhood.* Glossed as a sententia through inverted commas in 90.]
12. *hungry ... blood.* Hoskyns, 8, cites this as an example of metaphor.
25. [*unwelcome ... injury.* Glossed as a sententia through inverted commas in 90.]
33. *shadow.* See the note to p. 166, 31.
34-5. *cypress ... graves.* In the commentary 'Upon the Tenth Book' in his trans. of Ovid, *Met.* (1632), Tt 3, George Sandys noted that 'Because the Cypress tree, being cut down or lopped (as man by the scythe of death) reflourisheth no more, it was therefore used at funerals'. See the notes to pp. 108, 11-12; 162, 11.
36. *black worms.* In the grave, 'Wormes blake wol vs enbrase', cited from *Minor Poems of the Vernon MS.*, Part II, ed. F. J. Furnivall, EETS, os cxvii (1901), 661. 114.

PAGE 343, 1-3. *two ... death.* An analogous emblem is in Camerarius, *Symbolorum et Emblematum*, IV. lxxxix, the two-headed serpent, the amphisbaena, with one head lopped off and the motto, 'Nec mors, nec vita relicta', used in mourning the death of a spouse; cf. Henkel and Schöne, 651. Such emblems became fashionable in France in the fifteenth century; see D. S. Russell, *The Emblem and Device in France* (Lexington, 1985), 27, citing Brantôme, *Œuvres complètes*, ed. L. Lalanne (Paris 1864-82), vii. 349 ff.
1. *whereon.* 'on the impresa'.
6-7. *as glad.* 'as Basilius was glad that'.
13-14. [*if ... between them.* Amphialus responds to the challenge with a wry joke: if

the 'Knight of the Tomb' is indeed looking for a tomb, there is no cause for enmity between them, because they are both pursuing the same goal.]
22. *made ... horse.* Hoskyns, 44, cites this as an example of paraphrasis.
24. [*he perceived ... rest.* The purpose of the rest was to stabilize the lance during the encounter. Cf. William Segar's summary of jousting rules in *Honor Military and Ciuill* (1602), p. 188: 'He that conueyeth his Lance into the Rest in due time, is worthy commendation: but he that carieth it shaking in his hand, or vnstayedly in the Rest, meriteth blame'. Earlier in the book, missing his rest is the mistake Clinias is so anxious to avoid that he prefers to charge at Dametas with his unsupported lance dangling from his rest. That the first action of the 'Knight of the Tomb' is to miss his rest is a sign of his inexperience (and a first hint that this knight might not be a real knight), so 'courteous' Amphialus responds by deliberately missing his opponent, so as not to benefit from a foolish mistake, which he considers dishonourable.]
27. *blessed ... window.* Cf. *AS* 53. 8–9.
31–2. [*esteeming ... purchased.* To win through an opponent's mistake is dishonourable. Glossed as a sententia through inverted commas in 90.]

PAGE 344, 6. *in whom ... rage.* Hoskyns, 40, cites this as an example of sententia. [Cf. p. 342, 25–6 for a sententia expressing the opposite idea.]
8. *thy tongue ... no.* 'your words have acted as traitors to your life'.
12. *give ... lie.* 'accuse himself of lying'.
22. *alablaster.* 'alabaster'. See p. lxi.
22–9. [*the wound ... fairness.* Through the use of superlatives typically reserved for praise ('most dainty', 'purest', 'perfittest'), this description of the fatally wounded Parthenia implies that her beauty not only transcends injury but that her natural beauty is enhanced by her wounds. See also p. xxvii.]
24. *river ... island.* See p. xxvii, and cf. Shakespeare, *The Rape of Lucrece*, 1737–40:

> And bubbling from her breast, it doth divide
> In two slow rivers, that the crimson blood
> Circles her body in on every side,
> Who like a late-sack'd island vastly stood ...

32–3. *by-himself-accursed hands.* See p. 382, 16.
35. [*inward messengers.* Cf. Pyrocles' description of Zelmane's death in p. 231, 5.]
PAGE 345, 10. *I come.* This either was, or became, a formula; cf. Marlowe, *1 Tamburlaine*, V. i. 316, Zabina's 'I come, I come, I come, I come!'; Shakespeare, *Antony and Cleopatra*, V. ii. 290, 'husband, I come'; and Lady Mary Wroth, *The Countess of Montgomery's Urania* (1621), 3Q2, 'O my dear Amphilanthus, I come, I come'. [One of the earliest examples appears to have been Thomas Marsh's 1581 translation of the *Thebaid* (in *Seneca his Tenne Tragedies*):

> Oh stay me not I thee desire, behold, behold, I heare
> My Fathers ghost to bidde me come apace, and not to feare.
> O Father myne I come, I come, now father ceasse thy rage ... (41^v)

13. *Atropos cut.* Atropos is one of the three Parcae. She cuts the thread of life.
casting ... hands. This was the common description of a dying person's final affirmation of faith; cf. Gifford (?), *The Manner of Sidney's Death* (*Misc. Prose*, 170, 8 and 22), 'he lift up his eyes and hands ... he did ever and anon lift up his hands and eyes', and the description of the death of the Earl of Essex from Holinshed, *Chronicles* (1587), 143, cited in *Misc. Prose*, 163, 'when his tongue gave over to speak any more, he lifted up his hands and eyes to the Lord'.

PAGE 346, 14–22. Ringler, OP 3, and 493. The sole substantive text is 93, from which it was reprinted in succeeding editions. Non-substantive texts are in manuscript additions to 90 in both copies in the Huntington Library (69441 and 69442) and in the Houghton copy; in Bodleian Library printed book Douce D 238 (3), A6 (Ringler, 493). The first two lines are in Bodleian Library MSS Don. e. 6, f. 28 and Rawl. D. 954, f. 26; and ll. 1–6 were printed in Henry Hawkins, *Parthenia Sacra* (1633), L6^v, 'on the emblem of the palm' (M. Crum, *First-Line Index* (Oxford, 1969), H620 and H1216). It was printed from an unlocated manuscript in A. Clifford, *Tixall Poetry* (Edinburgh, 1813), 276 (P. Beal, *Index of English Literary Manuscripts* (London, 1980), SiP 69). The authenticity of the poem is substantiated by its role within the form of the *New Arcadia*; see p. li.

14–15. *His ... none.* Cf. *The Lady of May* (*Misc. Prose*, 29, 10), 'a man coupled to his wife, two bodies but one soul'.

23 (var.). *ghosty counsel.* This is an ironic adaptation of the idiom 'ghostly counsel', given by a priest to a penitent near death in order to relieve his conscience.

PAGE 347, 27–8. [*when ... former promises.* Cecropia's failure to help her son to win Philoclea is described using medical imagery. Cf. William Lambard, *A Perambulation of Kent* (1576), p. 271:

> But (as the Poet saith) *Male sarta gratia, nequicquam coit, & rescinditur, Fauour,* that is, euill peeced, will not ioyne close, but falleth a sunder againe. And therefore this their opinion fayled them, & that their cure was but patched: for soone after the sore brake out of newe, and the Canterbury Monkes reuiued their displeasure with suche a heate, that Hubert of Borrow (the chief Iustice of the Realme) was driuen to come into the Chapter house to coole it.]

PAGE 348, 4–5. [*Lust ... servant.* Glossed as a sententia through inverted commas in 90.]

6–7. *freezed ... desire.* Cf. Amphialus' symbolic collar, p. 277, 29–34.

12–14. *you fear lest ... laugh.* Hoskyns, 12, cites this as an example of anadiplosis.

15. *"no" ... mouth.* Cf. Tilley, W660, 'A woman says nay and means aye'. [A variation of Sidney's wording – 'In women's mouths, no is no negative' – appeared in John Weever's *Faunus and Melliflora* (1600), as well as in *Englands Parnassus*, which falsely attributed the sententia to Weever ('I. W.'). See also p. lxxxiv.]

16–17. [*lover's modesty ... liked.* Glossed as a sententia through inverted commas in 90 and 93.]

17. *for marring.* 'as a precaution against marring'.

19–21. *If ... modesty.* Hoskyns, 50, cites this as an example of prevention, in this instance by Cecropia presupposing the objection and bringing an argument 'to the contrary'. [See also p. lxxxiv.]

22–5. *Theseus ... child.* After Theseus captured Antiope (Hippolyte), Queen of the Amazons, they fell in love and had a son, Hyppolytus.

16–17. *crossing his arms.* See p. 65, 11–12 and note.

23–36. *ravished ... by force enjoys.* Cecropia lies in order to influence Amphialus towards rape, for there is no account of rape in either of these instances of abduction. See p. xxiv.

26–30. *Iole ... club.* After killing King Eurytus, Hercules carried away his daughter Iole. As part of their amorous exercises, they exchanged roles, she wearing his lion's skin and playing with his weapons. See p. 11, 21 and note.

32-6. *Helen ... enjoys her*. Helen was the daughter of Leda by Jupiter when he was disguised as a swan. She chose King Menelaus as her husband over many rivals. Paris, partly for her beauty, partly in retribution for the Greeks keeping his aunt, wooed and won Helen, abducted her to Troy, and caused the Trojan war. In the ninth year of the war Paris was killed, and Menelaus through his love for Helen forgave her all.

PAGE 349, 35-6. *nameless ... estate*. As the law of chivalry ensured that honour be maintained by requiring adversaries to be of equal rank, there was no onus to accept a challenge from one who would not declare his; cf. Shakespeare, *King Lear*, V. iii. 145-6, Edmund's reply to the unidentified Edgar, 'What safe and nicely I might well delay / By rule of knighthood, I disdain and spurn'.

PAGE 350, 10. *not ... furniture*. See p. xxvi.
12. *dainty*. 'excellently'. For the use of the adjective as adverb, see Abbott, 17. See p. xxxii.
13. *brave raggedness*. Hoskyns, 36, cites this as an example of synoeciosis.
15. *rusty*. See p. xxiv.
17-20. *night ... banished*. The shadow existed only because of the sun's light; cf. the description in the note to p. 257, 1.
20. *From whose*. 'From her whose'.
21. *forward favour*. 'immodest friendliness'. This is an ironic usage, suggesting the significance with which the knives became endowed when given Amphialus by Cecropia; cf. pp. 274, 8; 382, 27-8. [Alternatively, 'forward' in 90 text may be a typographical error for 'froward', which is perhaps a more fitting description of how Amphialus might view Philoclea's behaviour towards him. Rather than being a token *from* Philoclea (given voluntarily as a sign of affection, like the jewel that Pyrocles presents to her), the knives, which were taken from her by force and passed on to him, are merely a token of her refusal. The editors or the compositors of 93 tried to address the apparent incongruity of 'forward favour' by changing 'forward' to 'forced'.]
23. *attired ... livery*. 'in dress of the same symbolic import'.
25-6. *ravens ... snakes*. These symbolize foreboding.
26. *snakes*. Croesus' horses ate 'great store of snakes and serpents', which, 'as Herodotus saith, was an ill-boding prodigy into his affairs'; see Montaigne, *Essays*, I. xlviii, trans. Florio (London, 1910), i. 334.
30-2. *catoblepta ... light*. According to Pliny, *Natural History*, VIII. xxi, trans. Philemon Holland (1601), Tt1^v, the catoblepas was a small, slow creature with heavy limbs and an almost insupportably heavy head, which, because of its weight, was carried looking towards the earth; 'for if he did not so, he were able to kill all mankind, for there is not one that looketh upon his eyes but he dieth presently. The like property hath the serpent called a basilisk.' These two creatures were often not distinguished from one another or from the cockatrice, itself associated with the nocturnal ichneumon (see *OED* under *cockatrice*), sure to be aroused to its most dangerous state by seeing night approaching in the form of Amphialus' impresa. That it derived life from moonlight is not conventional.
33-4. *whip ... repentance*. Sidney's New Year's gift to the queen for 1580-1 was 'a jewel of gold, being a whip, garnished with small diamonds in four rows and cords of small seed pearl'; see J. Nichols, *Progresses of Queen Elizabeth* (1823), ii. 301.

34–5. *coal-black ... blackness*. The colour was chosen to match the costumes, but see the note to p. 317, 34–6.

PAGE 351, 4–5. *men ... reason*. See p. xxviii.
20. *rival*. See p. xxiv.
23–4. *words ... thunder*. Hoskyns, 29, cites this as an example of hyperbole.
29–30. *courteous ... armour*. See pp. xxix–xxx and cf. Virgil, *Aeneid*, viii. 381–4, where Venus' request is made.
29. *wives*. 'wife's'; see p. 80, 3, and note.
34. *that was*. See p. liv.

PAGE 352, 6. *Spite ... hatred*. Hoskyns, 31, cites this as an example of accumulation of matter 'tending to the same end'.

PAGE 353, 15. *killed his horse*. See p. 294, 23 and note.
21. *fortune ... victory*. See p. xxviii.
24. *sufficient ... nature*. The bond which his good nature placed upon him was rendered void. See Glossary, under *defeasance*.
26–7. *eye ... imagine*. Hoskyns, 29, cites this as an example of hyperbole.
29. *being themselves*. That is, without horses.
30–1. *to fetch feeding*. 'to go and receive food'. [The EEBO / TCP corpus suggests that the expression is unique to 90, which may explain 93's decision to change 'fetch' to 'fresh', although 'fresh feeding' was not a common phrase either.]

PAGE 354, 4. *mastiff*. See p. 243, 10 and note.
9. *conquered ... conquering*. See p. xxviii.
15–16. *leave ... fury*. 'abandon the continuous, directed assault controlled by cunning for the sporadic violence of fury'.
15. *storm*. See p. liv.
25. *rival*. See p. xxx.
32. *Barzanes*. See p. 179, 14.

PAGE 355, 4–5. *lion ... angry*. See p. xxx and Homer, *Iliad*, trans. R. Lattimore (Chicago, 1951), xx. 164–71, the battle where Achilles 'rose like a lion against' Aeneas: 'he lashes his own ribs with his tail and the flanks on both sides / as he rouses himself to fury for the fight'.
12–13. *filling ... blood*. See p. xxix.

PAGE 356, 10. *guts came out*. This is a well-documented injury; cf. p. 294, 34, and see Homer, *Iliad*, xxi. 180; Lucan, *The Civil War*, vii. 619–20.
25–6. *breaking ... sword*. See p. xxiv [and cf. also the note to p. 23, 28.]
39–PAGE 357, 3. *garden ... envy*. Unlike the Hesperides (see note to p. 161, 5–6), this garden of oranges, emblems of love, is guarded only by a sheep whose blissful state reflects that of the Arcadian shepherds (p. 12, 14–18). In this device the knight expresses confidence in his beloved.

PAGE 357, 2. *sheep*. Cf. Camerarius, *Symbolorum et Emblematum*, II. lxxi, a sheep lying in a field with the motto 'Undique Inermis', 'everywhere unarmed', an emblem of piety and innocence.
5. *cut in stars*. Cf. *AS* 104, the stars on Astrophil's armour to 'prove that I / Do Stella love'.
6. *aspects*. See Glossary.
pole. Cf. pp. 142, 2; 271, 14 and note.

7. *void ... reserved*. The space was for Polaris, the pole-star; see p. xxvi.
12–13. *seeking ... ruin*. Hoskyns, 36, cites this as an example of indirect synoeciosis.
17. *soldiers sent*. See p. xxiv.
21. *turning ... back*. Cf. p. 148, 33–4 and note.

PAGE 358, 2–3. *used ... inheritance*. Hoskyns, 29, cites this as an example of hyperbole.
28–9. *obtain ... obtaining*. Hoskyns, 14, cites this as an example of antimetabole.

PAGE 359, 18. *he should*. See pp. lvi.
29. [*setting ... valour*. See the note to p. 204, 27–8.]
34. *innate*. See p. lii.

PAGE 360, 1–2. *spite ... remedy*. 'insult that sees no means of redress'.
2. [*blood ... nose*. A sign of Pyrocles' barely suppressed anger. Spontaneous nosebleeds were thought to be caused by an excess of heat in the blood.]
6–7. *misliked ... misliked*. Hoskyns, 14, cites this as an example of antimetabole.
18. *heard him*. 'himself heard'. Cf. *OED* under *hear* v. IIa, and Abbott, 147, the verb used reflexively as an intensifier. See p. xxxii.
29–30. [*nothing ... done*. Glossed as a sententia through inverted commas in *90*.]
34. *winning ... life*. Cf. Tilley, T293, 'He that has time has life'. [Glossed as a sententia through inverted commas in *90*. Cf. also Matthew Mainwaring's romance *Vienna* (1628), which adapts it to: 'In extremities, the winning of time, is the purchase both of life and love' (p. 32 [i.e. 40]).]

PAGE 361, 3. *If ... untrusted*. Hoskyns, 37, cites this as an example of parison.
14–15. *hath ... incongruity*. Hoskyns, 47, cites this as an example of periphrasis.
20–1. [*promise ... threatening*. Glossed as a sententia through inverted commas in *90*. Cf. also Ralph Venning, *Things Worth Thinking On* (1664), 99: 'Of the two, Promises bind Faith more than threatnings do; and we should ever be (as God is) more ready to promise than threaten, and to perform them, rather than execute these, *Psal.* 103.8, 9'.]
21–3. [*prince ... reason will do*. *90* glosses these lines as a separate sententia through inverted commas.]
33–5. [*no man ... desperate folks*. Glossed as a sententia in *90* through inverted commas preserved in *93*, although in some copies (such as W. Blount's copy), the inverted commas were misplaced and so inadvertently glossed the not particularly aphoristic phrase 'Only let it suffice to take away their despair, which may be by granting pardon for what is past, so as the ladies may be freely delivered'. *98* was evidently based on such a copy, because it preserves the mistake, which was subsequently reproduced in *13* (though not in the 1605 folio).]

PAGE 362, 7. *words ... fear-babes*. This is cited in C. G. Smith, *Spenser's Proverb Lore*, 880. [*OED* cites this as the earliest example, but cf. L. Tomson's translation of Pierre de la Place's *Treatise of the Excellencie of a Christian Man* (1576), which includes the phrase 'all creatures are but fansies and vaine fearebabes, which haue no power, but as pleaseth God to giue them' (Gi).]
11–13. [*a prince ... profitable*. Glossed as a sententia through inverted commas in *90*. *93* preserved the inverted commas, but accidentally placed the first set one line higher than it should be. The mistake was reproduced in *98* and *13*.]
14–15. [*amazed for ... Zelmane*. Philoclea's name is missing, perhaps because Gynecia is still jealous of her younger daughter.]

PAGE 363, 3–4. *fair ... fair*. 'promising ... clear'.

8–9. *Philoclea ... undermined.* Hoskyns, 9–10, cites this as an example of allegory. [Cf. also the lines directly above, which also use military imagery and compare Pamela's determination to a lofty fortress.]

22. *by a contempt.* 'by treating them as of little account'.

23–4. *disgraced.* 'discredited'.

25. *diseasefulness.* 'discomfort'. This is the only citation in *OED*.

35. *fail.* See p. lii.

36. *rugged.* 'harsh'. The earliest citation in *OED* 2b is from 1533.
new and new. 'ever anew'.

37–8. *swelling ... stopped.* Cf. p. 194, 30–1 and note.

PAGE 364, 5. *Fury.* The Furies would have delighted in destroying an idol of chaste love. See p. xxxiii and p. 197, 20 and note.

10. [*senseless thing ... senseless.* See pp. lxxxi–lxxxii.]

16. *pity.* 'her pitiable state'.

20–23. [*common course ... prince's daughter.* Philoclea is listing the various reasons why Cecropia's treatment of her is shameful, culminating in a reminder of her status as a princess – an appeal to her aunt, who is so conscious of her own status as a king's daughter, but also a source of irritation to Cecropia, since it reminds her that Amphialus will never succeed Basilius. Cecropia retorts by calling Philoclea a 'wench', a word that has lower-class associations and is consequently an inappropriate way of addressing a woman she ought to consider at least her social equal, if not her superior.]

25–7. *I have ... satisfy them.* Hoskyns, 38, cites this as an example of parison.

32. *hellish monsters.* The Furies carried a burning torch in one hand and a whip of scorpions in the other with which they acted as punishers for the gods. See the note to p. 198, 15–16.

36. *armour ... smith.* See p. xxx.

PAGE 365, 37. [*as many sorts of pains as might rather vex them than spoil them.* i.e. forms of torture that would leave no long-term marks, such as scars, that might mar their beauty.]

PAGE 366, 9–10. [*prayed ... together.* 'virtuous' is the operative word here, acting as a reminder of what happened during the last encounter between Musidorus and Pamela. The distinction is important to highlight Pamela's own virtuousness, because it indicates that despite her miserable state, she does not regret rebuking him. Cf. Philoclea's being 'content to receive a kiss – and but a kiss – from Pyrocles' on their release (p. 380, 9).]

15. *no ... woman.* Cf. Erona's dilemma, p. 180, 14–15.

21. *set ... her.* See p. l. The earliest citation in *OED* under *set* v. 63a *fig.* is from Shakespeare, *The Merchant of Venice*, II. vii. 55.

35. *farder.* 'farther'. See p. lxi.

PAGE 367, 5. *water ... grasped.* Cf. p. 224, 22 and note.

28. [*rather ... wilful.* See note to p. 23, 28.]

29–30. [*despising ... despised.* Glossed as a sententia through inverted commas in 90. Cf. also Robert Sanderson's sermon on *Rom.* 14. 3 in *Two Sermons* (1622), 13: 'Thus you see *Despising* is hurtfull to the *despiser*, as a sinne: it is hurtfull also, as a *scandall*, to the *despised*.']

PAGE 368, 3. *crossing her arms.* This is a posture of defiance rather than the conventional one of melancholy; cf. p. 65, 11–12 and note.

17–18. *since … getting*. See p. xxiv.
28–9. *out to another*. See p. liv.

PAGE 369, 14. *divorce … body*. Hoskyns, 8, cites this as an example of metaphor. [Cf. p. 375, 22–3.]
26 (*var.*). *beautified*. Once introduced, the reading persisted through subsequent editions.
33. *book of virtue*. Cf. pp. 63, 4–5; 102, 26–7.

PAGE 370, 12. *Philomela*. This refers to the sweetness of Philoclea's grief-stricken complaints. See p. 7, 28–30 and note.
23. *hit the needle*. 'found the needle'. Cf. Tilley, N97, 'To seek a needle in a bottle [bundle] of hay'. [However, the context in which the expression is used here suggests there is also an element of 'hitting the nail on the head', because the sentence contains both the idea that the woman intuitively finds the best strategy for shocking Zelmane and the idea that her prediction of Zelmane's reaction was exactly right.]
24–5. *exceedingly … exceedingness*. Hoskyns, 17, cites this as an example of polyptoton or traductio, where the words differ only in termination.

PAGE 371, 5–6. *while … limits*. 'as she drew her mind up to the level of her courageous feelings, she pulled herself back from her wit's end to contemplate courageous action'.
5–26. [*she … affection's tower*. At this point in the book, 'Zelmane', who until now has been consistently referred to as 'she', grammatically turns into Pyrocles again, as he tries to think of ways to save Philoclea. The sentence beginning 'At last …' alone contains six instances of 'he' / 'his'. This is initially continued in the next sentence ('Then how to prevent …'), but towards the end of the sentence, following the phrase 'procure liberty for Zelmane', the pronouns revert to 'she' / 'her'.]
34. *the beauty … unoverthrown*. That is, her 'spiritual beauty'.
40–**PAGE 372**, 6. *At last … words*. See p. xxxi.

PAGE 372, 17. *touch*. 'taint' or 'stain'.
17. *pretend … affection*. See p. xvi.
20. [*my Pyrocles*. Philoclea's constant repetition of Pyrocles' name in order to appeal to him – over the course of the scene she uses it ten times, including nine times in this speech – also has the effect of consolidating the transformation of 'Zelmane' into Pyrocles, which had begun in the previous scene. When the guardians re-enter the room, he changes back into 'Zelmane'.]
36. *love the remembrance*. Cf. p. 46, 30.
40. *sorrow*. Sorrow is one of the passions with little to redeem it, as on p. 60, 23–4, but here the higher faculties of wisdom and virtue (see p. 16, 11–12 and note) allow an exception.

PAGE 373, 2. *mind … merit*. Hoskyns, 16, cites this as an example of agnomination of syllables, a kind of pun. [William Ponsonby, expressing a certain sense of ownership over the books he published, invoked this phrase in the dedication to Sir Robert Needham that he prefixed to Spenser's *Amoretti* (1595):

> This gentle Muse for her former perfection long wished for in Englande, nowe at the length crossing the Seas in your happy companye, (though to your selfe vnknowne) seemeth to make choyse of you, as meetest to giue her deserued countenaunce, after her retourne: entertaine her, then, (Right worshipfull) in

sorte best beseeming your gentle minde, and her merite, and take in worth my good will herein ... (¶ᵛ–¶2)]

2–3. *forsaken ... forsaking*. Hoskyns, 17, cites this as an example of polyptoton or traductio, with the same verb used in several voices.

15. [*so as*. 'so that'.]

35–6. *It was ... agony*. See p. xxviii.

37–8. *O ... government*. Hoskyns, 33, cites this as an example of exclamation.

PAGE 375, 4–6. *Why lived ... stricken*. Hoskyns, 12, cites this as an example of anadiplosis.

6–7. *with thee ... in me*. See p. 267, 24–5 and note.

14. *kiss ... mouth*. See p. 328, 6–7 and note.

15–16. *hope ... for*. Hoskyns, 48, cites this as an example of apostrophe.

22–3. [*divorce ... nature*. Pamela's phrase directly mirrors the metaphor the narrator had used when describing the execution from Philoclea's perspective (p. 369, 14). There are multiple echoes between the two scenes, to highlight the close affinity between the two sisters – which Cecropia had counted on when devising her cruel scheme.]

23–5. [*Philoclea is dead ... O deadly word*. Cf. 'Pamela is dead!' (p. 369, 39). Colin's and Lycon's 'Pastorall Aeglogue' for Sidney included in Spenser's *Astrophel* (1595), H3–H4, echoes the form of Pamela's lament for her sister in its refrain, which keeps pairing the words 'Phillisides is dead' with an exclamation beginning with 'O' ('O harmfull death', 'O dolefull ryme', 'O lucklesse age' and 'O happie sprite').]

28 (*var.*). [*Chap. 17*. The puzzling lapse in the chapter numbering suggests a compositor's error, or perhaps a blot in the manuscript copy text. Although the numbers 17 and 23 are not easily confused in Arabic or Roman numerals, 'xvii' and 'xxii' may look similar in certain secretary hands. As there are nine pages between them, this chapter is contained in a different gathering than the preceding one (Ww rather than Vu), and may have been set by a different compositor who did not recall the number of the previous chapter.]

33–4. *all ... 'Philoclea!'* Hoskyns, 13, cites this as an example of epistrophe.

PAGE 376, 40. *of darkness*. 'from darkness'.

PAGE 377, 10. *seen to*. 'seen by'. Cf. *OED* under *to* prep. 33b.

30–6. *how ... bring me*. Hoskyns, 33, cites this as an example of interrogation.

PAGE 378, 28. *given over*. 'pronounced incurable'. See p. 386, 1.

PAGE 379, 27. *mourning ... sorrow*. Hoskyns, 36, cites this as an example of synoeciosis.

28. *Zephyrus*. 'west wind'.

fine-coloured. 'finely-coloured'.

34–6. *He saw ... gladsome*. Hoskyns, 50, cites this as an example of prevention by occupatio.

PAGE 380, 7. *paint ... shadows*. See the note to p. 166, 31.

10. *herself*. 'she'. This is the emphatic form, with the nominative pronoun understood; cf. *OED* 4.

32. *goodly*. This ironic usage is commonplace. All texts have the early spelling *godly*.

PAGE 381, 6–7. *untaught sighs*. Hoskyns, 8, cites this as an example of 'a metaphor, or translation'. [Cf. also p. 188, 5.]

17-18. [*carried ... strength*. A reminder that Amphialus is still recovering from the injuries Musidorus gave him.]
20-1. *empoison ... mitigated*. See p. xxiv.
29. *death's kiss*. Cecropia's spirit is condemned to live on only in the ground rather than in a living body. Cf. p. 328, 6-7 and note. [Additionally, the wording implies she dies at the moment of impact. Cf. *Clidamas, or The Sicilian Tale* (1637), which transfers Sidney's image to a military context: 'the ladders were set up to the walls, and the souldiers mounted up to the top of them, from whence they were thrust downe headlong by the defendants, to receive their deaths kisse at the ground' (p. 73).]

PAGE 382, 1-11. *Thou hast ... lived*. See pp. xxviii, xxxi.
13-14. *Tormented ... tormented*. Hoskyns, 12, cites this as an example of epizeuxis.
16. *filthy hand*. See pp. xxxi; 344, 32-3.
24. *Charon's boat*. The souls of the buried dead were ferried by Charon across the river Styx to their resting places; cf. Virgil, *Aeneid*, vi. 298 ff. [Cf. also 'Charon's ferry' on pp. 98, 27 and 296, 21.]
27. *Philoclea's knives*. Cf. pp. 274, 8; 350, 20-1 and note.
29. [*only relic ... saint*. While the comparison of Philoclea to a saint does not necessarily make Amphialus' love idolatrous, the word 'relic' in this context invites associations with Catholic saint worship. Cf. also p. 350, 21.]

PAGE 383, 2. *overflow*. 'surpass in flowing'. Cf. *OED* under *over-* 2a.
13-14. *conquest ... overthrow*. See p. xxviii.
18. *of all ages*. This is an ellipsis for 'people of all ages'.
27. *engrained*. 'scarlet'. See Glossary under *grain*.
28. *eyes levelling*. 'directing his looks'. The earliest citation in *OED* under *level* v. 1 7c is from 1594.
from ... toe. Cf. Tilley, T436, 'From top to toe'; cited in C. G. Smith, *Spenser's Proverb Lore*, 782.

PAGE 384, 3. *kill ... sisters*. See p. xxviii.
12-24. *humbly ... brother*. See p. xxxii.
18-19. [*excellentest surgeon ... country*. Surgeons and physicians were members of separate professions (cf. the note to p. 97, 21), so this 'excellentest' surgeon is not identical with the 'most excellent' physician who restored Parthenia's disfigured face, after others had declared this to be impossible (p. 37, 27-9). Corinth consequently appears to be a centre of excellence in several medical disciplines.]
19. [*so old ... travel*. This may be a white lie on Helen's part, as her intention is to take Amphialus with her.]

PAGE 385, 3. *woe worth*. 'a curse upon'.
36-7. *woman-lover*. 'womanly lover' or 'weak lover', as opposed to maintaining her queenly dignity. This is the earliest citation in *OED* under *woman* n. C1.b (b) ('depreciative use').
38. *straight*. 'immediately'.

PAGE 386, 1. *given him over*. Cf. p. 378, 26.
22-PAGE 390, 15. *Among ... glorious*. In 93 this passage is transferred to the Fourth Eclogues; see p. lix.
25-PAGE 390, 15. Ringler, *OA* 75, and 419-21; Robertson, 344, 24 ff. Texts with substantive variants are *OA* (ex. O), 90, 93. Ringler, 419, demonstrates parallels in form

(terza rima with a refrain) and imagery in Sannazaro, *Arcadia*, Eclogue 11. In the invocations to mourn, in nature's sympathy, and in the lament that nature is perpetual whereas man's life ends (and Amphialus' life in particular), Sidney adapts the classical and continental elegy, though he denies his characters the traditional consolation in the ending (cf. Spenser, 'November', 163 ff.; Milton, *Lycidas*, 165–81). Such consolation would have belied the dramatic tension of this scene, where the general grief is not solely for the dead Amphialus, but includes grief for the resulting vulnerability of those under him. This is even more poignant in the midst of this rebellion than in the poem's original context in the *Old Arcadia*, after the supposed death of Basilius.

37. *weeping myrrh*. Cf. Ovid, *Met.* x. 310, and the commentary by G. Sandys in his translation (1632), Vv2^v: 'Myrra ... changed into a tree ... sheds bitter tears (meant by the odorous gum which distilleth from thence) ... which preserves the bodies of the dead from corruption', and Camerarius, *Symbolorum et Emblematum*, I. xi.

PAGE 387, 12. *Lily ... black*. Ringler, 420, compares Sannazaro, *Arcadia*, Eclogue II, 17–18, 'Et tu, terra, depingi nel tuo manto / I gigli oscuri', similarly used by Marot, 'Eglogue sur le Trepas de ma Dame Loyse de Savoye', 123, 'le blanc Lys en print noire taincture'.

14. *hyacinth ... 'ai'*. The Greek cry of lament αἴ, in Latin *ai*, was placed in the flower when Hyacinth became metamorphosed, Ovid, *Met.* x. 215. Robertson, 477, compares Moschus, *Elegy on Bion*, 5 ff.

23. *inconstant constant*. See the note to p. 163, 2–3.

28. *in*. 'among'.

36. [*To well-felt ... pleasure*. Glossed as a sententia through inverted commas in 90.]

PAGE 388, 5. *all-beholding*. Cf. 'all-seeing', p. 290, 11, and PS 11. 15, 'all-seeing sight'.

10. *Philomela*. See p. 7, 28–9 and note.

31. *snake ... mend*. The image is common. Camerarius, *Symbolorum et Emblematum*, IV. lxxxii, lists numerous classical examples.

PAGE 389, 13. *virtue's fort*. Cf. p. 174, 15.

17–19. *elements ... dissension*. Cf. p. 172, 25–8 and note.

22. *Atropos*. Cf. p. 345, 12–13 and note.

24. *rooted moisture*. 'rooted' seems to be Sidney's adaptation of the philosophical term 'radical'. *Radical moisture* is the humour or moisture inherent in all living creatures, and a necessary condition of vitality.

27. *Aesculapius*. See p. 88, 14 and note.

30. *Bountifulness ... conclusion*. 'Liberality has been brought to its absolute end'.

38. *turn of hand*. 'sleight of hand'.

PAGE 390, 3–5. [*While he ... home-strife*. These lines are a less than perfect fit for Amphialus, who has just been involved in a rebellion, although they would of course have fitted Basilius, the original subject of the song, who has had a famously long and peaceful reign. See also the note to p. 242, 22. 'home-strife' (written as one word in 90) appears to have been Sidney's coinage and was echoed by Samuel Daniel in his *Ciuile Wars*.]

6. *His ... law*. Cf. p. 138, 2–3 and note.

16. *all ... men's*. See p. liv.

17. *times*. 'rhythms'.

19–20. *a young ... valure*. Hoskyns, 12, cites this as an example of climax, 'a kind of anadiplosis leading by degrees and making the last word a step to the further meaning'.
28. *unvisited*. See p. liv.
30–1. *with his ... father*. See pp. xxviii, xxxii.
34–5. [*no expectation ... hopes*. Glossed as a sententia through inverted commas in *90*.]

PAGE 391, 15–16. [*my schoolmistress ... truly*. i.e. 'that my sister might survive me to see me die well'.]
20. *sight*. 'sighed'.

PAGE 392, 6–7. *to kill ... father*. See pp. xxviii, xxxii.
22–37. [*thou doest weakly ... combat*. 'Zelmane's' speech is the verbal equivalent of a formal challenge (but Anaxius initially fails to recognize it as such).]
28. *and in*. 'if in'.

PAGE 393, 15. *slew ... Euardes*. See p. 179, 14.
18. *ran from me*. Cf. p. 209, 31.
26–7. *much less*. According to *OED* under *less* adv. P4, *much less* is 'used to characterize a statement or suggestion as still more unacceptable than one that has been already denied'. The earliest citation is from 1526.
38. [*terror of the world*. Anaxius is modestly referring to himself.]

PAGE 394, 9. [*to be my hangman*. Pamela is echoing 'Zelmane's' challenge to Anaxius: 'and therefore, as a hangman, I say thou art unworthy to be counted a knight'. Cf. also p. 23, 25–6.]
11. *pull his plumes*. 'pluck his feathers'. This was the way to humiliate a vain man; cf. Marlowe, *1 Tamburlaine*, I. i. 33; Shakespeare, *1 Henry VI*, III. iii. 7; and *Troilus and Cressida*, I. iii. 386, 'Ajax employ'd plucks down Achilles' plumes'. [Alternatively, this may be read as an image of frustrated love (i.e. Cupid pulling his own plumes). Cf. Erato's lament in Spenser's *Teares of the Muses*, 401–2: 'And [Venus'] gay Sonne, that winged God of Loue, / May now goe prune his plumes like ruffed Doue'.]
14–15. [*Zoilus ... love Zelmane*. i.e. after his two elder brothers had taken their pick, Zoilus would have to make do with Zelmane, whether he liked her or not.]
17. *braggard*. This was an early spelling of 'braggart' or 'boastful'. The earliest citation in *OED* under *braggart* B. adj. is from 1604. This is the earliest citation in *OED* under *bragged* pp. adj. taking the variant reading from the edition of 1605.
22. *play of virtue*. 'play on the subject of virtue'. See p. 63, 4–5 and the note to p. 102, 25–6.
witty ignorance. Hoskyns, 36, cites this as an example of synoeciosis.
30. *set ... revenge*. 'made a mental note that this was a debt owed to revenge'.
33 (*var.*). *his Mercury*. 'his messenger'. Mercury was the messenger of the gods.

PAGE 395, 5. *balls ... fortune*. See p. 172, 14 and note.
5–6. *Since ... kin*. The clause omitted from *90* restates Pamela's position at p. 132, 38–9 and adds the cruelty of one's relations as her circumstances have changed. Cf. p. 275, 25–6 and p. lv.
9. *our friends' means*. 'through the activities of our parents *and* kin'.
14–15. *Hope ... mind*. Cf. p. 255, 3 and Tilley, H608, 'Too much hope deceives'. [Glossed as a sententia through inverted commas in *90* and *93*.]
19. *time*. 'rhythm'. Cf. p. 390, 17.

20-1. [*then ... live nobly*. Glossed as a sententia through inverted commas in 90. 93 attempted to preserve this but accidentally misplaced one set of inverted commas, so it was placed next to the line 'yet the time, which ought always to be one, is not tuned for it'. Cf. also pp. 17, 5-6 and 148, 24.]

PAGE 396, 30. *plainly to be understood*. Cf. John Lyly, *Midas*, V. iii. 78, in *Works*, ed. R. W. Bond (Oxford, 1902), Apollo's second reply, 'I will not speak in riddles, all shall be plain'.

36-7. [*give tribute, ... wisdom*. Glossed as a sententia through inverted commas in 90. 93 attempted to preserve this but misplaced the inverted commas, so they glossed the phrase 'Philanax and Basilius fully agreed in the understanding of the former prophecy' instead.]

human wisdom. Cf. p. 16, 11-12 and note.

38-9. [*reason ... above reason*. Glossed as a sententia through inverted commas in 90 and 93. It subsequently became a popular commonplace that was frequently quoted and adapted in seventeenth-century texts, for example in Edward Maihew's *A Treatise of the Groundes of the Old and Newe Religion* (1608), p. 144; Nicholas Morgan's *The Perfection of Horse-manship* (1609), p. 44; Zacharie Boyd's *The Last Battell of the Soule in Death* (1629), pp. 839-40; William Lithgow's *The Gushing Teares of Godly Sorrow* (1640), B3^v (which adapts it into verse as 'Can reason show, more reasonable way, / Than leave to pry, where reason can not swey'); and Peter Talbot's *A Treatise of the Nature of Catholick Faith and Heresie* (1657), *3^v. It also featured in collections of commonplaces, including Ralph Venning's *Things Worth Thinking On*, p. 3; Robert Codrington's *The Second Part of Youths Behavior* (1664), pp. 209-10; and George Liddell's *Divine Meditations* (1700), pp. 17-18. See also p. lxxx.]

PAGE 397, 6-7. [*bemoan ... Zelmane*. Basilius makes a similar distinction to the one made by Gynecia at the beginning of the siege, when she was 'amazed for her daughter Pamela – but mad for Zelmane' (p. 362, 14-15).]

23. *demigods*. See the note to p. 35, 4.

26. [*another wisdom ... above*. The operative term is 'another': impressed by the oracle's supposed insight, atheist Anaxius is now willing to believe in the existence of divine wisdom that is equal to (though not greater than) his own.]

PAGE 398, 14-15. *either ... lives*. Hoskyns, 13, cites this as an example of epistrophe.

18. *mustachos*. 'mustachios'. Apart from *mustuchoes* 90 (*uncorr.*) this is the form in all texts.

29. *But that*. 'But Zoilus' coming towards her'.

29-30. *occasion ... forehead*. Cf. Tilley, T311, 'Take occasion by the forelock, for she is bald behind'.

PAGE 399, 25. *Proserpina ... ravishers*. The queen of the underworld had been raped by Pluto.

39. [*knew ... defence*. Glossed as a sententia through inverted commas in 90 and 93.]

PAGE 400, 6. *as to spoil*. 'as if to despoil one he had already killed'.

7-8. *made ... arguments*. 'gave proof, beyond whatever flattering arguments might be used to persuade one of its strength'.

24-5. [*meaning ... good fortune*. 'intending to use her advantage over Lycurgus rather than handing him his sword in order to ensure a fairer fight'. Compare pp. 209, 15-16 and 353, 20-1.]

COMMENTARY 561

30–PAGE **401**, 11. *But seeing ... heart.* This passage closely imitates the conclusion of Virgil's *Aeneid*, from xii. 930 ff. Cf. *A Defence of Poetry* (Misc. Prose, 92, 36–7), citing *Aeneid*, xii. 645–6; and see above, p. xxx.

PAGE **401**, 9. *It is Philoclea.* Cf. Virgil, *Aeneid*, xii. 948–9, 'Pallas te hoc vulnere, Pallas / Immolat'.
11–12. *prepared to excuse.* 'ready to obtain exemption'.
21–2. *blasphemed heaven ... him.* See p. xxiii.
38. *once before.* See p. 208, 32–3.

PAGE **402**, 3–4. *combat ... beholders.* See p. xxix.
6–8. *There ... nobleness.* Hoskyns, 37, cites this as an example of contentio.
16. *Pallas.* This is Pallas Athena, goddess of war.
19–20. [*models, and but models.* i.e. the combat between Pyrocles and Anaxius defied any such analogies.]
21. *cask.* 'casque' or 'helmet'. This is the earliest citation in *OED* 4a.
21–2. *bravely covered.* 'excellently ornamented'.
22–3. *shield ... Troy.* See p. xxx, and Homer, *Iliad*, trans. R. Lattimore (Chicago, 1951), xx. 259–72; Aeneas could not penetrate the centre layer of gold, 'the god's gift'.
32–3. *their strength ... strength.* Hoskyns, 14, cites this as an example of epanalepsis. [See also p. lxxv.]

PAGE **403**, 13. *fiery and aery.* 'pertaining to the elements of fire and air'.
35–6. [*having never ... life.* i.e. having never so much as thought about leaping aside to evade a blow. From the context, it is clear that the rest of the sentence must have concerned Anaxius' reaction to his brief cowardly impulse. Sir William Alexander's *Supplement* did not attempt to end the sentence itself, but continued: 'Thus the fire of rage then burning contempt out of his brest, did burst forth in flames through his eyes, & in smoake from his mouth ...', whereas James Johnstoun's second *Supplement* added to the 1638 edition not only continued the sentence ('He meant to have redoubled his blowes with more force and violence, when he might know by the sounding alarme, and hideous clamours of the besieged citizens, that his presence was more needfull in some other place ...') but reprinted the sentence fragment from 90 above it, as a reminder to readers of what it was supplementing. 'redoubled his blowes' was a shrewd choice, because Sidney was evidently fond of the phrase and had used it several times in the context of angry combatants. Cf. pp. 169, 2; 344, 9; 352, 33–4.]

THE ECLOGUES – APPENDIX II

PAGE **404**, 2–7. *because ... do.* Cf. Robertson, 56, 30–57, 5. The reference to 'the cowardice of the fugitive shepherds' is not applicable to the version in the *New Arcadia* which omits the episode of the shepherds running away at the sight of the lion and bear (Robertson, 46, 31–2).
7–PAGE **409**, 30. *Dametas ... commendations.* Cf. Robertson, 57, 22–64, 6.
15. *brawl.* This is a French dance; cf. the analogues in Spenser, *Works*, iii. 284.

PAGE **405**, 22. [*Be none ... fashion.* This line is a particularly clear example of the ending '-ion' pronounced disyllabically, because the 'challenge' between Lalus and

Dorus consists of having to frame responses in different stanza forms written in regular metre.]

Page 406, 3. *How ... touch!* 'How careful to censure!'
13. [*heav'nly*. See the note to p. 14, 19.]
28. *keep*. Ringler's conjectural emendation to *sheep* was rejected by Robertson, 429. This is the infinitive of *OED* 16b, 'to tend [sheep]'.

Page 408, 22. [*noblest kind ... woes*. The first *sententia* glossed with inverted commas in *90* (where it appears at the end of Book I).]

Page 409, 30. *when ... shepherd*. This is an addition to the text.
30-2. *who ... melancholy*. Cf. Robertson, 71, 31-4.
32-5. *as though ... guise*. Cf. Robertson, 159, 21-4.
35. *or else*. This is an addition to the text.
35-**Page 410**, 1. *declare ..., he*. Cf. Robertson, 159, 28-32.

Page 410, 1-**Page 414**, 17. *sang ... themselves*. Cf. Robertson, 254, 19-260, 2.
8. *scothe*. 'darken' or 'overcast'; cf. *OED* under *skew* v.¹, 'to become overcast'. [Alternatively, 'scothe' in *90* may be a typographical error for 'soothe' (caused by a confusion of lowercase c and o) that subsequent proofreaders and compositors mistook for an obscure rural term and reproduced as they saw it. 'soothe' (the reading of *Cl*) would both fit the rhyme scheme and suit the context.]
20. *fond*. 'found'.
27. *clerkly rede*. 'learned counsel'.
32. [*powers*. See the notes to pp. 59, 12 and 126, 6.]

Page 411, 18. [*leopard*. Pronounced as three syllables.]
40. [*heav'nly*. See the note to p. 14, 19.]

Page 412, 11. [*patience*. Pronounced as three syllables here, but note that the same word is disyllabic on p. 413, 39.]
25. *ought*. This is an archaic form of 'oft'.

Page 413, 31. *hungry teeth*. 'greedy tithe'.

Page 414, 3. *fortune's ... stours*. 'painful struggles brought about by fortune'.
14. *sport-meeting*. 'pleasant pastime'. This is the only citation for this compound in *OED* under *sport* n.¹.
17-20. *But ... pensiveness*. Cf. Robertson, 162, 29-163, 2.
21-**Page 417**, 22. *invited ... annoy*. Cf. Robertson, 260, 2-263, 21.
33. [*Which whoso wants, half of himself doth miss*. Cf. p. 327, 31.]

Page 415, 14. *Puiling*. 'puling', 'whining'.
23. *fremb'd*. This is cited in *OED* under *fremd* adj. 2a, 'strange, unknown, unfamiliar'.

Page 416, 21-6. *Thy commonwealth ... conserved*. Cf. Shakespeare, *Venus and Adonis*, 757-64.

Page 417, 2-3. *last ... testify*. In the *Old Arcadia* the story of Erona is told by Histor in the First Eclogues (Robertson, 67, 13 ff.) and then referred to in this poem in the Third Eclogues. The reference does not fit the *New Arcadia*.
23. *All ... fellow*. Cf. Robertson, 79, 14-15.
23-4. *easily ... person*. Cf. Robertson, 263, 26-7.

COMMENTARY 563

25-7. *But ... gone to.* This is an editorial adaptation of p. 9, 27-39 of this text.
27-9. *continue ... other.* Cf. Robertson, 328, 11-12.
27-8. *like ... runners.* This is the image used in *The Rhetorica Ad Herennium*, trans. H. Caplan (London, 1954), IV. xlvii. 60:
> A comparison will be used also for greater clarity - the presentation being ... as follows: 'In maintaining a friendship, as in a footrace, you must train yourself not only so that you succeed in running as far as is required, but so that, extending yourself by will and sinew, you easily run beyond that point.' Indeed ... a runner ought to have enough speed to carry him beyond the goal, and a friend so much goodwill that in the devotion of friendship he may reach even beyond what his friend is capable of perceiving.

29-30. *he called ... performed.* This is an editorial addition.
30-PAGE 419, 27. *in this ... evening.* Cf. Robertson, 328, 21-330, 33.
30. [*double sestine.* Since the *OED* variously dates examples from the *New Arcadia* to 1590 and 'a1586', this is the earliest citation for *sestine*, although in terms of publication date, Abraham Fraunce's *Arcadian Rhetorike* (1588), which also uses it to refer to poems by Petrarch, technically predates it.]
39. [*heav'nly.* See the note to p. 14, 19.]

PAGE 418, 28. *under mountains.* Cf. p. 54, 37-8 and note.

PAGE 419, 28-30. *Zelmane ... ears.* Cf. Robertson, 163, 2-5.
30-PAGE 420, 20. *laying ... yet.* Cf. Robertson, 81, 14-82, 14.

PAGE 420, 21-4. *What ... unto it.* Cf. Robertson, 88, 16-21.
25-7. *fell ... body.* Cf. Robertson, 164, 32-4.
27-32. *But ... death.* Cf. Robertson, 88, 21-6.
30. [*Zelmane's late hurt.* i.e. the 'little scratch' she received from the lion's paw. Cf. p. 96, 17-18.]

PAGE 421, 1-PAGE 430, 12. *The rude ... persons.* Cf. Robertson, 135, 2-146, 24.
6. [*forlorn hope.* Here used in the military sense of 'troop detached from the rest', in accordance with the idea that the dance resembles a 'skirmish'.]

PAGE 422, 18. [*heav'nly.* See the note to p. 14, 19.]
38. *doubt.* See below, p. 438.

PAGE 423, 7. *muet.* 'mute'; see p. 437.
12. [*heav'nly.* See the note to p. 14, 19.]

PAGE 425, 8. *sickman's.* As in 90, the *OED* spells this without a hyphen.
13. [*quiet mind ... thee.* Glossed as a *sententia* through inverted commas in 90.]
15-16. [*Well do I prove ... true heart.* Glossed as a *sententia* through inverted commas in 90.]
19. [*heaven.* Disyllabic. See the note to p. 14, 19.]
24. *The lovely, blown.* 'The amorous one, driven on'. He contrasts his position with that of Dicus, and counters with his own wish.
25. *sightfulness.* 'power of seeing', but with the nuance of how his eyes react to excessive beauty. This is the earliest citation in *OED*.
29. *surfeit-woes.* 'a surfeit of woes'.

PAGE 426, 2. *start.* This subjunctive introduces the dialectal tone of the following passage; cf. Abbott, 269.

3. *jolly younker*. 'lively young fellow'.
10. *thrive*. 'prosper'.
14. *but grey*. 'only of grey material'.
16. *rayed*. Robertson, 444, rejected Ringler's conjectural emendation to *raged*. This is the aphetic form of *array* v. 10b, 'afflicted', often used in association with love.
17. *greeny wroughten*. This is the earliest citation in *OED* under *greeny*; *ywroughten*, Robertson, 142, 2, is unrecorded.
19. *treen*. 'wooden'.
20. *crouch*. 'crutch'.
21. *crouch*. 'cross'.

PAGE 427, 10. *iwis*. 'indeed'.
24. [*Arcad*. i.e. Arcadian (shortened in order to conform to the metre).]
27. *Syrinx*. This is the uninflected genitive; see p. xxxii.

PAGE 428, 10. *rathe*. 'early'.
31. *yester-morning*. This is the earliest citation in *OED*.
37. [*stark nak'd*. An example of metaplasm. In early modern usage, the word 'naked' could be variously pronounced as one or two syllables. Sidney normally favours the disyllabic version, as can be seen not only in the other songs in which it appears (see pp. 183, 18 and 20; 412, 3 and 34; 428, 33) but also in prose passages, as for example in the balanced metricality of the phrase 'though he were naked, nakedness was to him an apparel' (p. 3, 25), which would be lost if the word were pronounced as one syllable.]
a little tine. 'a very short time'.

PAGE 430, 7–8. *Lamon ... Klaius*. This is altered from Robertson, 146, 16–20.
12–**PAGE 432**, 39. *began ... bend*. Cf. Robertson, 331, 2–334, 6.

PAGE 431, 4. *haste*. 'hast'. This archaic form rhymes with 'waste'.

PAGE 432, 28. [*heavens*. Disyllabic. See the note to p. 14, 19.]

PAGE 433, 1–4. *So ... troubles*. Cf. Robertson, 152, 19–22.
4–7. *And ... them*. This is an addition to the text, followed by an adaptation of Robertson, 334, 7–9.
7–**PAGE 504**, 24 *which he ... echo*. Cf. Robertson, 159, 31–162, 29.
20. *Ease*. Cf. p. 60, 28 and note.

PAGE 434, 10. [*heav'nly*. See the note to p. 14, 19.]
12. *Course*. This is a variant spelling of 'curse'.
14. *hard*. This is the obsolete past tense of 'hear'.
22. [*made evil? A devil*. Both 'evil' and 'devil' are typically monosyllabic in early modern verse (cf. the Scots word 'deil', whose pronunciation resembles that of 'deal').]
31–2. *the other ... desires*. Cf. Robertson, 167, 17–26.

GLOSSARY

The Glossary includes archaic words, words currently in use but with unfamiliar meanings, and words which antedate the earliest citation in *OED*. Following the page-and-line reference, 'etc.' indicates that the word is used again later in the text; '(*var.*)' that the word is found only among the variants in the textual apparatus; and 'n.' that a note is in the Commentary. Words explained in the Commentary are not in the Glossary.

NOTE: *there have been two editions of the* OED *since 1987 (the second print edition of 1989 and the ongoing third edition). Consequently, entries in the glossary of the 1987* New Arcadia *edition that referenced now obsolete* OED *entries have been updated accordingly, and a number of words for which* Arcadia *is cited as the earliest known example in their respective* OED *entries have been added to the glossary.* – EC

ableness *n.* ability **219**, 5.
abode *n.* temporary stay **48**, 4.
[**absented** *pp. adj.* withdrawn, absent (this is the earliest citation in *OED*) **47**, 17, etc.]
abuse *v.* to be deceived **192**, 1.
acceptation *n.* reception **131**, 9, etc; acceptance **217**, 31.
accident *n.* event **38**, 15.
accompanable *adj.* companionable **8**, 5.
accompany *v.* **accompany with**, join to **187**, 32.
accord *v.* arrange **232**, 30.
action *n.* oratorical management of the body and features in harmony with the subject **248**, 18.
adherent *n.* attached quality **252**, 17.
adub *v.* array **330**, 12.
adubment *n.* adornment **328**, 36 (*var.*).
advantageous *adj.* favourable **141**, 35.
advertise *v.* inform **118**, 30.
advertisements *n. pl.* information **21**, 11; notifications **45**, 29.
advise *v.* consult **280**, 24.
affect *n.* inward disposition **25**, 22 n.; feeling **141**, 14.
affect *v.* aim at **9**, 4; seek **12**, 15.
affected *pp. adj.* disposed, inclined **39**, 26; full of affectation **44**, 1.
affection *n.* good disposition towards **22**, **39**, etc.; emotion **34**, 38, etc.; passion, lust **215**, 26.
affectionate *adj.* expressing love **53**, 24, 25.

affectionated *pp. adj.* affectionate (this is the earliest citation in *OED* 2b) **25**, 29.
afford *v.* carry out, accomplish **346**, 19.
aggravate *v.* make the most of **159**, 18.
alarum *n.* call to arms **45**, 24, etc.; surprise attack **315**, 37.
allay *n.* admixture of something that detracts from the value **372**, 27.
ally *n.* relative **275**, 26.
along *adv.* lengthwise **5**, 6.
amain *adv.* with full speed **130**, 16.
amaze *v.* terrify **190**, 17, etc.
amazement *n.* overwhelming fear (the earliest citation in *OED* 3 is from Spenser's 1590 *Faerie Queene*) **305**, 37.
ambrosia *n.* the fabled food of the immortals (the earliest citation in *OED* for the figurative sense (1b) is from 1610) **74**, 31.
amplifying *adj.* exaggerating **259**, 2.
ancient-bearer *n.* standard-bearer **83**, 2.
angle *n.* rod, line, and hook **76**, 37; meeting-point of two lines **216**, 21.
animate *v.* fill with boldness **381**, 24.
anointment *v.* ointment **384**, 20.
answer *v.* correspond with **73**, 15, etc.
answerable *adj.* corresponding (this is the earliest citation in *OED* 2b) **83**, 33.
apparence *n.* likelihood, probability **18**, 14, etc.; appearance **240**, 4.
appoint *v.* bring oneself to the point of resolution **123**, 17.
apprenticeage *n.* apprenticeship

(the earliest citation in *OED* is from Francis Bacon's *Resuscitatio* (posthumously published in 1657) **94**, 9 (var.).

arrant *n.* errand **135**, 4.

arrant *adj.* unmitigated **209**, 37.

aside-hand *adv.* to one side **293**, 8.

askances *conj.* as though **195**, 33.

aspect *n.* expression **85**, 39; the relative positions of the heavenly bodies as they appear to an observer on the earth's surface at a given time, but popularly, their joint look upon the earth **284**, 10, etc.

assurance *n.* marriage engagement **23**, 12, etc.

astonied *pp. adj.* stunned **31**, 20.

astonished *pp. adj.* stunned, benumbed **7**, 9, etc.

astonishment *n.* dismay, dread, loss of presence of mind **5**, 25, etc.; amazement (the earliest citation in *OED* 4 is from 1594) **56**, 23.

attaint *v.* subject to attainder or forfeiture of estates **387**, 1.

attempt *n.* personal assault upon a woman's honour (the earliest citation in *OED* 3b is from Shakespeare, *Rape of Lucrece*, 491) **187**, 14.

attempter *n.* assailant (this is the earliest citation in *OED* 2) **227**, 6.

attend *v.* expect **4**, 15; await **36**, 37, etc.; listen to **54**, 20, etc.

autentically *adv.* authentically, in proper legal form **192**, 21.

authorize *v.* claim authority for oneself (this is the only citation in *OED* 2d) **216**, 4; afford just ground for (the earliest citation in *OED* 3b is from 1589) **235**, 6.

await *n.* ambush **228**, 27.

[**bachelorly** *adj.* bachelor-like, inclined to remain unmarried (this is the earliest citation in *OED*) **274**, 34.]

backside *n.* back premises **10**, 32.

backwardly *adv.* reluctantly (this is the earliest citation in *OED*) **261**, 16.

badly *adv.* wickedly **215**, 38.

bait *v.* harass **194**, 28.

baiting-place *n.* stopping place for refreshment and changing horses on a journey **18**, 6 n.

balance *n.* one scale of a balance **18**, 39.

band *n.* company of persons in movement (the earliest citation in *OED* 3 is from the King James Bible) **95**, 13; bond **124**, 23.

bands *n. pl.* agreements **52**, 4.

barefaced *adj.* beardless (the earliest citation in *OED* 1 is from Shakespeare, *A Midsummer Night's Dream*, I. ii. 100) **209**, 19.

bases *n. pl.* plaited skirt appended to the doublet, and reaching from the waist to the knee **84**, 15, etc.

bastinado *n.* a blow with a stick, a whack **169**, 15, etc.

battle *n.* body of troops in battle array **309**, 15.

bauble *n.* baton of the Court Fool **13**, 34 n.

beaver *n.* visor and face-guard of a helmet **55**, 36, etc.

beck *n.* mute signal **131**, 38.

become *v.* befit, suit **19**, 23, etc.; accord with **87**, 26; grace **161**, 12.

beer *n.* force, impetus **75**, 10.

beetle *adj.* (qualifying 'brows') louring, scowling **48**, 13.

beguile *v.* deprive by fraud **125**, 35.

behindhand *quasi-n.* state of being behind (this is the earliest citation in *OED* 5) **139**, 20.

beholding *pres. p. adj.* attractive (this is the only citation in *OED* 2) **68**, 29.

beholdingness *n.* indebtedness (the earliest citation in *OED* is from p. 337, 16) **214**, 34, etc.

behoofeful *adj.* behoveful, advantageous, expedient **259**, 34, etc.

beldam *n.* loathsome old woman, hag (this is the earliest citation in *OED* 3) **13**, 40.

beleaguered *pp. adj.* besieged (the earliest citation in *OED* is from 1644) **358**, 14 (var.).

belike *adv.* in all likelihood **98**, 19, etc.

GLOSSARY

bemire *v.* befoul with mire **1**, 22.
bend *n.* curvature **10**, 38.
benefit *n.* kindness **4**, 6, etc.
bent *n.* concentrated energy, impetus **199**, 20.
beside *adv.* besides **7**, 23.
bettering *vbl. n.* improvement **42**, 12, etc.
bewail *v.* utter lamentations **1**, 31.
bewonder *v.* fill with wonder (this and Robertson, 211, 6 are the earliest citations in *OED* 1) **226**, 38.
bewray *v.* reveal, make known, expose **48**, 37, etc.
bickering *vbl. n.* skirmishing with weapons **88**, 12.
biding *n.* residence **137**, 12.
birth *n.* offspring **103**, 18.
blame *v.* reprove, scold **15**, 28, etc.; censure **30**, 9.
blancher *n.* one who heads back deer **89**, 36.
blaze *v.* proclaim **223**, 30; decry, hold up to infamy **225**, 2.
bleeding *pres. p. adj.* full of anguish (the earliest citation in *OED* 2a is from Spenser's 1590 *Faerie Queene*) **253**, 16.
block *n.* blockhead **129**, 35.
blockish *adj.* excessively dull **172**, 33.
blood *v.* draw blood **236**, 37.
blubbered *pp. adj.* flooded with tears **197**, 34, etc.
board *n.* table **21**, 29.
bob *n.* a blow **254**, 18.
bob *v.* strike with the fist **254**, 18.
bond *n.* obligation **258**, 29.
boss *n.* one of the metal knobs on each side of the bit of a bridle **318**, 21.
[**bought** *n.* bend, curve (esp. of a body) **166**, 30.]
bound *pp. adj.* under obligations **39**, 34.
bravery *n.* bravado, swaggering **207**, 30, etc.
brawl *n.* a dance consisting of a variety of steps and figures **404**, 15.
break *v.* reveal (one's mind) **40**, 37, etc.; utter **67**, 31.
brickle *adj.* fragile **257**, 8 n.
brickwall *n.* bricole, a tennis stroke angled so that the ball rebounds off the side wall of the court, popularly associated with the brick wall of the court **339**, 28.
bruit *n.* rumour **18**, 13.
bugbear *n.* imaginary terror **310**, 28, etc.
burthen *n.* bass, or undersong **43**, 25.
burgess *n.* free denizen (this is the earliest citation in *OED* 3) **204**, 21.
business *n.* mischievous activity **376**, 23.
bustle *v.* rouse **80**, 23.

caitiff *n.* captive, prisoner **109**, 11, etc.; [wretch, villain **331**, 16; **358**, 37;] *adj.* captive **268**, 32.
call *v.* challenge **392**, 20.
calling *vbl. n.* station in life **10**, 1.
caparison *n.* cloth or covering spread over the saddle or harness of a horse (the earliest citation in *OED* 1a is from 1602, though note that it also appears in John Bossewell's *Workes of Armorie* (1572)) **84**, 15.
captious *adj.* designed to entrap **145**, 17.
care *n.* charge (the earliest citation in *OED* 5b (referring to a person) is from 1697; cf. Robertson, 5, 15) **255**, 30.
career *n.* course **188**, 10; short gallop at full speed **208**, 36; the space enclosed by the barriers at a tournament (this is the earliest citation in *OED* 1a) **343**, 21.
careful *adj.* full of care, anxious **38**, 17, etc.
careless *adj.* unconcerned **153**, 15.
carelessness *n.* having no care **39**, 19.
carlish *adj.* rude, mean **208**, 28 (*var.*).
cast *n.* hue (the earliest citation in *OED* 35a is from Shakespeare, *Hamlet*, III. i. 85; cf. Robertson, 37, 29) **71**, 35; (in hawking) a couple **121**, 34.
cast *v.* **cast about**, turn about (the earliest citation in *OED* is from 1591) **5**, 29; **cast off**, let fly (the earliest citation in *OED cast off* 5 is from 1602) **122**, 2.
caution *n.* guarantee **150**, 20.
[**cawing** *adj.* uttering caws (this is the earliest citation in *OED*) **426**, 25.]
chafe *n.* rage **83**, 15.
chafe *v.* warm **3**, 29; inflame (the

feelings), fret **68**, 27, etc.
challenge v. accuse **206**, 32; demand as a right **322**, 2.
changeling n. turncoat **194**, 14.
character n. distinctive mark **99**, 4.
chase n. object of pursuit **186**, 28; hunted animal **294**, 14.
cheek n. the ring at each end of the bit of a bridle **350**, 27.
cheer n. face **266**, 26, etc.
cheerful adj. cheering **33**, 30.
cherish v. gladden, inspirit, encourage **129**, 20, etc.; foster **388**, 34.
chine n. back **96**, 15.
choice n. **of choice**, by preference **247**, 34.
chop v. snap (the earliest citation in OED 3 is from 1599) **318**, 22.
chuff n. rude, coarse, churlish fellow **243**, 25.
circus n. large building for the exhibition of public spectacles **226**, 32.
clause n. conclusion **269**, 5.
cleanly adj. artful **91**, 33.
clock n. bell **256**, 14 n.
close adj. enclosed **27**, 11 n., etc.; shut **40**, 12; secret **68**, 15; adv. secretly **92**, 3, etc.
cloudy adj. darkened by grief **111**, 11.
clown n. ignorant, uncouth man **11**, 39, etc.
coast n. region **272**, 20.
coast v. travel across **46**, 5.
comfort n. relief in distress **274**, 11.
comfort v. invigorate **182**, 22.
comfortable adj. cheering **117**, 18; reassuring **362**, 32.
commonalty n. the Commons as an estate of the realm **124**, 4 n.
companableness n. companionableness **205**, 30.
complaint n. expression of grief, lamentation **37**, 24, etc.
complement n. courtesy (the earliest citation in OED 8b is from Shakespeare, *Romeo and Juliet*, II. i. 131) **208**, 24; observance of ceremony in social relations **356**, 28.
conceit n. faculty of apprehension, mind **3**, 3, etc.; idea **12**, 23, etc.; device **40**, 21; whim **48**, 31.
concent n. harmony of sounds **43**, 7; accord **300**, 7.
conclude v. make an agreement, resolve **32**, 37.
concourse n. assembly **57**, 19.
condescend v. agree **44**, 38; yield **255**, 17.
condignly adv. suitably **330**, 30.
condition n. state of being **11**, 36.
conference n. conversation **3**, 7.
confines n. pl. boundaries, borders **6**, 31, etc.
confusion n. destruction **161**, 11.
congruity n. grammatical correctness **175**, 29.
conjuration n. entreaty **50**, 22.
conscience n. conscientiousness **188**, 21; internal convictions **213**, 14.
consequent n. effect, result **312**, 12.
consist v. exist **314**, 4.
consort v. combine in musical harmony (the earliest citation in OED 7 is from 1590) **272**, 9.
contentation n. satisfaction **34**, 20, etc.
conversation n. behaviour **20**, 1, etc.
convey v. lead **354**, 2.
cony-berry n. rabbit-burrow **330**, 10.
cony-hole n. rabbit hole or burrow **393**, 21.
copse n. coppice, a small wood of small trees grown for periodical cutting **204**, 19.
corsie n. grievance **359**, 5.
[**couplet** n. pair of rhyming lines (this is the earliest citation in OED) **404**, 17.]
counsel n. secret **37**, 32.
countenance n. expression **81**, 38; patronage, moral support **192**, 15.
counterbalance n. the opposite scale of a balance (this is the earliest citation in OED 1) **138**, 12.
counterbuff n. rebuff **392**, 13.
counterfeit n. portrait **81**, 12.
counterfeit v. imitate **11**, 2, etc.; depict **11**, 27, etc.; disguise **267**, 35.
countervail v. counterbalance **187**, 27, etc.; be equivalent in value **317**, 10.
course n. charge of combatants in battle

or tournament **77**, 20; **by course**, in turns **7**, 12; in due course **211**, 35.
cousin-german *n.* first cousin **35**, 35, etc.
crupper *n.* rump of a horse **87**, 8.
crushing *vbl. n.* crashing, smashing **294**, 16.
cumber *n.* burden **47**, 37; distress **68**, 2, etc.; embarrassment **204**, 13.
crystalline *adj.* of the clarity and purity of crystal **288**, 6.
curiosity *n.* undue subtlety **9**, 8.
current *adj.* genuine **18**, 14.
cut *n.* lot **181**, 30.
cypress *n.* cypress lawn, a light transparent material which, when black, was used on mourning clothes **277**, 28.

dainty *adj.* fastidious **71**, 12.
danger *n.* risk **80**, 18.
dapple *n.* one of many small blotches by which a surface is diversified (this is the earliest citation in *OED* 1) **182**, 29.
daring *vbl. n.* boldness, hardihood **216**, 28.
dark *adj.* obscure in meaning **396**, 29.
dastard *n.* coward **348**, 22.
deal *v.* act **98**, 19.
death-blow *n.* blow that causes death (this is the earliest citation in *OED*) **96**, 18.
decent *adj.* becoming **225**, 25.
decking *n.* ornamental attire **350**, 11.
defeasance *n.* a condition, upon the performance of which a bond is made void **353**, 24 n.
defendant *n.* party who denies the charge and accepts the challenge of the appellant in wager of battle **77**, 18, etc.
defy *n.* challenge to a fight **323**, 30.
degenerating *pres. p. adj.* showing a degeneration from an anterior type (the earliest citation in *OED* is from 1611) **122**, 17.
delicate *adj.* ingenious **276**, 14.
delightfulness *n.* state of feeling delight **175**, 22.
deliver *adj.* agile **357**, 16, etc.

deliver *v.* declare **29**, 12; utter notes in singing **73**, 30; put forth freely (this is the earliest citation in *OED* 16) **141**, 5.
deliverance *n.* release, rescue **33**, 7.
delivery *n.* use of the limbs, action (this is the earliest citation in *OED* 9) **141**, 6; setting free, rescue **222**, 17.
denounce *v.* proclaim **45**, 31, etc.
derive *v.* impart, pass on **309**, 9.
descry *v.* catch sight of **5**, 33.
[**despairful** *adj.* hopeless, desperate (this is the earliest citation in *OED*) **404**, 25.]
determine *v.* come to a judicial decision **87**, 38.
determinate *adj.* resolute, determined **24**, 15, etc.
determinately *adv.* resolutely **23**, 28.
determination *n.* decision **15**, 7.
device *n.* something fancifully devised **14**, 24, etc.; emblematic figure or design usually accompanied by a motto, an impresa **58**, 24, etc.
devise *v.* discern **13**, 35.
devotion *n.* that to which a thing is devoted (the earliest citation in *OED* 7 is from Shakespeare, *Richard III*, IV. i. 9) **236**, 1 n.
disastered *pp. adj.* stricken with disaster (this is the earliest citation in *OED*) **194**, 14.
disburdened *pp. adj.* freed from burden (the earliest citation in *OED* is from 1598) **1**, 32.
discomfort *v.* distress **273**, 39.
discountenance *v.* disconcert (the earliest citation in *OED* 3 is from 1584) **95**, 32.
discourse *n.* faculty of reasoning **75**, 25, etc.; account **274**, 19; course **305**, 30.
discover *v.* reveal **12**, 6, etc.; uncover **273**, 33.
disdain *v.* be moved with indignation **289**, 30.
disease *n.* cause of distress **384**, 39.
[**disenchant** *v.* remove a spell from (this is the earliest citation in *OED*) **64**, 5.]
digest *v.* digest **137**, 34.
disgrace *n.* dishonour, affront **221**, 23 n.,

etc.; disfigurement **344**, 27.
disgrace *v.* cast discredit upon **239**, 8.
disguise *v.* disfigure **36**, 15 (*var.*), etc.
disguisement *n.* disguise (this is the earliest citation in *OED* 2) **74**, 16.
[**disjointed** *pp. adj.* (of speech) incoherent (this is the earliest citation for *OED* 3) **130**, 7.]
disobeying *pres. p. adj.* which refuses submission to (the earliest citation in *OED* is from 1649) **239**, 7.
disparagement *n.* marriage to one of inferior rank **112**, 18.
dispatch *v.* free **33**, 17; get rid of **76**, 9; be quick **169**, 4.
dissuade *v.* exhort against **392**, 8.
distil *v.* extract (the earliest citation in *OED* 5b is from Shakespeare, *Henry V*, IV. i. 5) **131**, 31.
distrain *v.* hold captive **389**, 22.
distress *v.* make miserable (the earliest citation in *OED* 4 is from 1586) **307**, 37 n.
disuse *v.* disaccustom **90**, 18.
diversifying *vbl. n.* variation (the earliest citation in *OED* is from 1611) **289**, 10.
divorce *v.* dissolve (a marriage) (this is the earliest citation in *OED* 3) **369**, 14.
do *v.* deliver **77**, 11.
dogtrick *n.* treacherous act **224**, 3 (*var.*).
doleful *adj.* expressing mourning **187**, 32, 34.
dote *n.* natural endowment **329**, 13.
double *v.* repeat, reiterate **297**, 10.
doubt *n.* fear **48**, 27.
doubt *v.* suspect **148**, 23; dread **324**, 6.
downcast *pp. adj.* directed downwards **217**, 13.
draught *n.* drink **22**, 13.
draw *v.* bring together **22**, 39; induce **93**, 34.
dreadlessness *n.* fearlessness (this is the earliest citation in *OED*) **96**, 12.
drivel *n.* imbecile **119**, 33; dirty or foul person, 'pig' **184**, 19.

earthy *adj.* having the properties of the element 'earth' **324**, 29.
easier *adj.* more gentle **131**, 37 n.
effect *n.* contemplated result, purpose **236**, 23.
effectually *adv.* in reality **62**, 22.
[**effectuate** *v.* accomplish (this is the earliest citation in *OED*) **147**, 8.]
election *n.* deliberate choice **225**, 16.
embassage *n.* deputation to a sovereign **192**, 22; message conveyed by an ambassador **221**, 39, etc.
embraced *pp. adj.* enclosed (the earliest citation in *OED* is from Francis Thynne's, *Animaduersions*, (1599)) **121**, 18.
embroder *v.* embroider **277**, 27, etc.
embush *v.* conceal among trees **293**, 6.
enable *v.* strengthen **60**, 23, etc.
enamel *v.* beautify with varied colours (the earliest citation in *OED* 1c is from 1650; cf. Dunbar, 'Tua mariit Wemen', 31, 'annamalit with flouris') **7**, 35.
endamask *v.* tinge with paler colour (this is the only citation in *OED* a) **359**, 33.
endear *v.* enhance the value of, render precious (this is the earliest citation in *OED* 2) **145**, 24, etc.; deepen (affection) (this is the earliest citation in *OED* 6a) **289**, 5.
endue *v.* invest, endow **19**, 15, etc.
enforce *v.* strive **338**, 36.
engraff *v.* implant **138**, 4.
engrave *v.* sculpt **57**, 16.
engrieve *v.* aggravate **89**, 2.
enlargement *n.* release from confinement **379**, 7.
enow *adj.* enough **136**, 20; persons enough **323**, 5.
ensample *n.* example **16**, 33, etc.
enter *v.* enter to, be brought to a state or condition **209**, 17.
entertain *v.* engage agreeably the attention of, amuse **20**, 20, etc.; receive as a guest, show hospitality to **10**, 2, etc.; occupy one's attention or time **45**, 3; keep (a person) in a certain state **202**, 19.
entertaining *vbl. n.* receiving as a guest, showing hospitality **73**, 6.

GLOSSARY

entertainment *n.* hospitable provision for the wants of a guest **8**, 31, etc.; treatment (of persons) **134**, 32.
entreat *v.* treat, handle **49**, 39, etc.
[**entrusted** *pp. adj.* subject to the care of (this is the earliest citation in *OED*) **107**, 2.]
equity *n.* what is fair and right **213**, 26.
estate *n.* chair, throne (cf. *OED* 4d) **216**, 30; body politic, state, kingdom (the earliest citation in *OED* 10 is from 1605) **8**, 13, etc.
estrayed *pp. adj.* strayed **399**, 25.
event *n.* consequence **270**, 23.
everyway *adv.* in every respect **228**, 9.
evident *adj.* conclusive **77**, 17.
evil *adj.* inferior in quality **274**, 17.
excellency *n.* excellence **161**, 13.
excuse *n.* pardon (the earliest citation in *OED* 1b is from 1655) **159**, 22.
exercise *n.* practice of duties **109**, 18; customary practice **221**, 38.
expectation *n.* **of expectation**, affording ground for favourable anticipations **59**, 37; forecasting of something to happen **148**, 13.
expected *pp. adj.* looked for **266**, 16.
experience *v.* learn by experience (this is the earliest citation in *OED* 2b) **254**, 33.
exprobrate *v.* manifest to a person's shame **289**, 24.
exquisite *adj.* over-laboured **265**, 15.
extremity *n.* condition of extreme urgency or need **5**, 18, etc.; extreme severity or rigour **24**, 5; extreme intensity **25**, 11, etc.

fact *n.* deed **24**, 27, etc.; course of conduct **183**, 30.
faction *n.* class of persons **39**, 18; self-interested intrigue **192**, 28.
fain *adj.* obliged **74**, 26; *adv.* gladly **201**, 33.
faint *adj.* producing faintness **60**, 30.
faintly *adv.* timidly **59**, 6.
fairly *adv.* gently, peaceably **351**, 1.
fall *v.* **fall out with**, quarrel with **201**, 30.
falling *n.* hollow **293**, 6.

falsely *adv.* deceitfully **275**, 22.
falsify *v.* break one's faith **224**, 17.
familiarize *v.* adopt a familiar demeanour [(this is the earliest citation in *OED*)] **336**, 4.
fancy *n.* imagination **12**, 23, etc.
fantastical *adj.* imaginary **44**, 19.
far-fet *adj.* far-fetched, strained **338**, 3.
fashion *n.* outward ceremony, pretence **220**, 28.
faulty *adj.* censurable **206**, 24.
favour *n.* appearance **3**, 24; comeliness **82**, 20; face **110**, 33.
fear-babe *n.* a thing fit only to frighten a baby (this is the earliest citation in *OED*) **362**, 7.
feeling *n.* knowledge of an object through having felt its effects **3**, 5, etc.
fellow *n.* person of no esteem or worth **191**, 8, etc.
felon *adj.* cruel, wicked **392**, 4.
fertilely *adv.* fruitfully (this is the earliest citation in *OED*) **186**, 20.
fetch *n.* stratagem **288**, 35 (*var.*).
figure *v.* **figure out**, represent (the earliest citation in *OED* 15b is from 1657) **67**, 16.
fine *adj.* artful **192**, 1.
[**fine** *n.* **in fine**, in short **196**, 33; **247**, 6-7.]
finely *adv.* cunningly **159**, 27.
firebrand *n.* a thing which inflames the passions **280**, 2.
first *n.* the first part, the beginning **249**, 27.
fit *v.* befit (this is the earliest citation in *OED* 3) **154**, 32.
flake *n.* streak (of cloud) (the earliest citation in *OED* 1b is from 1653) **129**, 4 n.
flannen *n.* flannel **108**, 11.
flatlong *adv.* with the flat side (this is the earliest citation in *OED* 2) **369**, 12.
flatter *v.* charm away (this is the earliest citation in *OED* 6) **73**, 8; try to win the favour of **194**, 7.
fleshed *pp.* **fleshed in**, hardened **153**, 15.
[**fling** *v.* rush **321**, 11.]
fly *v.* flee **5**, 37, etc.

foin *v.* make a thrust at with a pointed weapon **403**, 32.
fond *adj.* foolish **60**, 30.
footing *n.* foothold **32**, 16.
force *v.* strive **386**, 18.
forefeel *v.* feel beforehand, have a pre-sentiment of (this is the earliest citation in *OED*) **204**, 12.
[**fore-preparation** *n.* advance preparation **260**, 13.]
foresightful *adj.* full of or possessed of foresight (these are the earliest citations in *OED*, [though the word also appears in Hendrik Niclaes' *Prouerbia HN* (1575))] **115**, 10; **257**, 9.
forsworn *pp. adj.* falsely sworn (this is the only citation in *OED* 2) **227**, 32.
forthright *adv.* directly forward **131**, 28, etc.
fortifier *n.* upholder **148**, 2.
fortune *n.* condition or standing in life **55**, 10, etc.
fountain *n.* head-spring, source **134**, 8.
frame *v.* shape **11**, 8; compose **20**, 30, etc.; adapt **129**, 34.
frequentable *adj.* accessible (this is the earliest citation in *OED*) **145**, 38.
froward *adj.* unreasonable, perverse **14**, 2.
furnish *v.* equip **213**, 11.
furniture *n.* apparel **220**, 31; trappings of a horse **318**, 24.
further *adj.* of a horse, the off (right) side **318**, 40.

gainsay *v.* hinder **163**, 25.
gainsaying *pres. p. adj.* given to contradiction **190**, 19.
gainstand *v.* resist **202**, 17.
game *n.* joke, jest **210**, 7.
gay *adj.* showily dressed **85**, 16.
gesture *n.* employment of bodily movements, attitudes, expression of countenance, as a means of giving effect to oratory (cf. p. xxvii) **189**, 39, etc.
ghastful *adj.* terrible, frightful **59**, 26, etc.
gilden *adj.* golden **142**, 12.

[**gin** *n.* snare **408**, 14.]
gittern *n.* cithern, a guitar-like instrument **254**, 11.
give *v.* suggest (to one) that **85**, 20.
[**glaringly** *adv.* brightly, garishly (this is the earliest citation in *OED*) **307**, 25.]
glass *v.* see, as in a mirror (this and Robertson, 191, 33 are the earliest citations in *OED* 4a) **175**, 16.
gloire *n.* glory **413**, 35.
gloze *v.* deceive with smooth talk **183**, 35 n.
go *v.* **go upon**, of a judicial authority, to consider the case of **381**, 11.
good-fellow *n.* reveller **35**, 30, etc.
goodly *adj.* comely **25**, 13.
goll *n.* hand (this is the earliest citation in *OED*) **185**, 3.
goodman *n.* husband **194**, 22.
goodness *n.* benefit **159**, 15.
gorget *n.* armour for the throat **319**, 13.
governess *n.* a woman who has charge of a young person **184**, 31, etc.
government *n.* conduct **201**, 8; discretion **201**, 9.
governor *n.* military commander **299**, 7.
grace *n.* seemliness **196**, 20.
grace *v.* delight **1**, 20 n.; lend grace to **53**, 13.
graced *pp. adj.* **well-graced**, well endowed with grace (this is the earliest citation in *OED* **114**, 14.
[**gracefulness** *n.* (virtuous) beauty, charm (**119**, 16 is the earliest citation in *OED*) **254**, 7, etc.]
grain *n.* scarlet dye, from the insect 'kermes' or 'scarlet grain' **311**, 15.
grateful *adj.* agreeable **23**, 18; pleasing **219**, 2; welcome **338**, 38.
gratefulness *n.* the quality of being pleasing (the earliest citation in *OED* is from *A Defence of Poetry* (*Misc. Prose*, 98, 21, [though the word also appears in *Delectable Demaundes, and Pleasaunt Questions* (1566)]) **161**, 12.
grave *v.* engrave **1/4**, 30.
graver *n.* sculptor **11**, 7.
grief *n.* (*pl.* griefs, grieves) grievance **245**, 28; hardship, suffering **287**, 24.

GLOSSARY

gripe *v.* clutch tenaciously **3**, 20.
guard *v.* accompany as a guard (the earliest citation in *OED* 1d is from Shakespeare, *2 Henry IV* IV. ii. 122) **35**, 11.
guilty *adj.* conscious, cognizant of (the earliest citation in *OED* 7 is from 1599) **102**, 13.
guise *n.* custom **244**, 28.

hale *v.* draw forcibly **285**, 6.
hallow *v.* pursue with shouts **209**, 36.
halt *v.* limp **87**, 38.
halting *vbl. n.* limp **88**, 12.
handle *v.* treat artistically **86**, 34.
handmaid *n.* a female personal attendant **130**, 38.
handsome *adv.* suitable **129**, 40.
hap *n.* fortune **34**, 32; good fortune, prosperity **240**, 29.
harbinger *n.* purveyor of lodgings **25**, 34 n.; forerunner **86**, 10, etc.
harbour *v.* lodge, take shelter **44**, 36, etc.
hard *adv.* close **3**, 18, etc.
hardly *adv.* bravely **229**, 13 (*var.*).
harnish *v.* harness in armour **406**, 29.
hazardous *adj.* addicted to risks **400**, 4.
head *n.* **make a head**, raise a body of troops **30**, 5–6.
heart-side *n.* the left side **356**, 5.
heavy *adj.* severe **28**, 12.
her-ward *n.* her direction **96**, 11.
high-flying *n.* aiming high (this is the earliest citation in *OED* 2; the earliest citation of the adjective is from *A Defence of Poetry* (*Misc. Prose*, 77, 7)) **189**, 2.
hire *n.* payment **4**, 18; wages **411**, 39.
[**historify** *v.* relate the history of (this is the earliest citation in *OED* 1) **405**, 31.]
historiology *n.* knowledge and telling of history (this is the earliest citation in *OED*) **134**, 19 (*var.*), **197**, 26 (*var.*).
hold *n.* stronghold, fort **30**, 21.
hollow *adj.* insincere **212**, 4.
hoodwink *v.* blindfold mentally (the earliest citation in *OED* 3 is from 1610) **160**, 25, etc.
hopeless *adj.* despairing (the earliest citations in *OED* 1 are from Shakespeare, *Comedy of Errors*, I. i. 158 and *Cymbeline* IV. iv. 27) **1**, 4.
house *v.* drive into a house (the earliest citation in *OED* 1c is from *Albions England* (1592)) **30**, 15.
hugy *adj.* huge **269**, 21.
hull *v.* be driven by the wind or current **4**, 35.
humour *n.* temperament **34**, 31; state of mind **43**, 29; one of the four chief fluids (blood, phlegm, choler, and melancholy or black choler) which determined the temperament **256**, 4.
hundreth *adj.* hundred **158**, 2.
hurdle *n.* a portable, rectangular frame of woven boughs, used to construct temporary sheep-pens **242**, 30.
hurtlessly *adv.* without causing hurt (this is the earliest citation in *OED*) **16**, 29.

Iberian *n.* an inhabitant of ancient Iberia in Asia (the earliest citation in *OED* 2 is from 1601, though Thomas Lanquet's *Epitome of Chronicles* (1559) also mentions Asian Iberians) **255**, 5; *adj.* pertaining to ancient Iberia in Asia (the earliest citation in *OED* A2 is from 1671) **214**, 31 (*var.*), **218**, 34 (*var.*).
if *conj.* though **272**, 5.
ill-favoured *adj.* having an unpleasing appearance **13**, 37, etc.
ill-favouredly *adv.* in an unpleasing style **29**, 1.
image *n.* statue **72**, 8.
imagination *n.* thought **194**, 37.
imbrue *v.* stain **305**, 9.
impair *v.* grow worse **75**, 38.
[**impairer** *n.* hindrance (this is the earliest citation in *OED*) **425**, 26.]
impairing *n.* deterioration **42**, 11.
imparadised *pp. adj.* paradise-like (this is the earliest citation in *OED*) **121**, 19.
impatient *adj.* intolerable (the earliest citation in *OED* 3 is from 1590) **122**, 31; restless in desire (the earliest citation in *OED* 2 is from Shakespeare, *Romeo and Juliet*, III. ii. 30) **124**, 25.

imperiousness *n.* absolute rule **206**, 14; overbearing manner **225**, 4.
import *v.* concern **47**, 12.
importune *adj.* troublesome **47**, 25.
importunity *n.* troublesome pertinacity in solicitation **47**, 40.
impost *n.* tax **245**, 34.
impresa *n.* emblem, device, usually accompanied by a motto (the earliest citation in *OED* is from 1589, [although the word appears over a hundred times in Samuel Daniel's translation of *The Worthy Tract of Paulus Iouius* (1585)]; cf. Robertson, 37, 18 (*var.*) and note) **80**, 30, etc.
impudent *adj.* shameless **146**, 10, etc.
inconstantly *adv.* with fickleness **78**, 16.
inconvenience *n.* harm **48**, 27.
indifferently *adv.* without bias, impartially **263**, 28.
indite *v.* compose **163**, 38; suggest **208**, 35, etc.
inditer *n.* author **316**, 18.
infection *n.* corruption of loyalty **282**, 35.
infortune *n.* misfortune **116**, 21.
injury *v.* wrong **81**, 28, etc.
intelligencer *n.* spy (this is the earliest citation in *OED* 3 (*fig.*), 'a means or source of information') **132**, 25.
interknowledge *n.* mutual knowledge (the *OED* distinguishes between the forms '*inter*knowledge' and '*enter*knowledge'; this is the earliest citation for the latter) **27**, 17 (*var.*).
intermit *v.* suspend **89**, 10; discontinue **136**, 15.
invention *n.* power of mental creation **11**, 33; faculty of devising **234**, 34.
inward *adj.* intimate **77**, 33.
inwardly *adv.* fervently **62**, 13.
inweed *v.* hide in weeds (this is the only citation in *OED*) **162**, 23.
issue *v.* sally **27**, 6.

Jacinth *n.* a reddish-orange gem **14**, 17, etc.
jealous *adj.* ardently amorous **194**, 23.
join *v.* engage in conflict **31**, 1.
jollity *n.* insolent presumption **88**, 9.
jolly *adj.* arrogant **207**, 30.
jump *adj.* exactly agreeing **410**, 33.
just *adv.* exactly **98**, 35.
just *v.* joust **77**, 32 (*var.*), etc.
justice *v.* punish judicially **261**, 33.
justs *n. pl.* (as *sing.*) tournament **324**, 22.

kind *n.* family, stock **45**, 21; nature **97**, 6; *adj.* benevolent **99**, 16 n.
kindly *adj.* natural, not artificial **164**, 23.
kindly *adv.* lovingly **25**, 24; naturally, according to nature **60**, 14, etc.; fittingly, properly **248**, 21, etc.
kindness *n.* tenderness **124**, 13, etc.; affection **202**, 15, etc.; natural affection arising from kinship **203**, 17.
kinred *n.* kindred, kinship **278**, 38, etc.
knowledge *n.* acquaintance, intimacy, friendship **236**, 11.

lame *n.* one of the overlapping thin plates in armour (this is the earliest citation in *OED*) **319**, 13.
lame *v.* paralyse **432**, 2.
lamentable *adj.* mournful **90**, 11; full of grief **370**, 12.
land-service *n.* military, as opposed to naval, service (this is the earliest citation in *OED*) **142**, 9.
languishing *pres. p. adj.* expressive of emotion **90**, 8.
large *adj.* lavish **187**, 26.
largely *adv.* liberally **12**, 22; fully **147**, 7.
largeness *n.* abundance **12**, 34.
laund *n.* open space among woods **204**, 18.
launder *n.* laundress **61**, 11.
lay *v.* expound, set forth (this is the only citation in *OED* 26d) **18**, 35; put, commit (cf. *OED* 15d) **39**, 15.
leads *n. pl.* a lead roof **381**, 15.
leaguer *n.* military camp engaged in a siege **358**, 14 (*var.*).
leave *v.* allow **153**, 38.
lesson *n.* punishment **128**, 28.
let *n.* obstruction **53**, 27, etc.
liberal *adj.* free from restraint **44**, 17; licentious **207**, 36.

GLOSSARY

liberally *adv.* without reserve **234**, 36.
license *v.* give leave of departure (to), dismiss **122**, 39, etc.
light *n.* window **9**, 5.
lighten *v.* burn brightly **27**, 31.
lightening *vbl. n.* comforting, cheering **266**, 18.
light of love *n.* one inconstant in love (this is the earliest citation in *OED*) **203**, 1 (*var.*).
lightsomeness *n.* liveliness **2**, 3.
like *adv.* likely **262**, 16.
limit *v.* allot, apportion **290**, 14.
list *v.* wish **216**, 2.
lists *n. pl.* an enclosed space for tournaments **298**, 33.
lively *adj.* life-like **88**, 22; *adv.* in a lifelike manner, vividly **11**, 19, etc.
loathly *adv.* reluctantly **163**, 11.
lodestar *n.* guiding star **110**, 34, etc.
lout *n.* country fellow **88**, 18.
loutish *adj.* awkward and ill-mannered **13**, 37.
loveliness *n.* lovableness **123**, 27.
lovely *adj.* worthy of, or suited to attract, love **3**, 24, etc.; loving **272**, 20.
lusty *adj.* vigorous **131**, 37; active **249**, 28.

mad *adj.* foolish **81**, 38, etc.
magnes-stone *n.* magnet **293**, 10.
main *adj.* mighty **400**, 17.
mainly *adv.* vehemently **44**, 32; considerably **146**, 13.
maintain *v.* defend **83**, 11.
make *n.* mate **5**, 7.
makebate *n.* breeder of strife **179**, 29, etc.
malediction *n.* curse **175**, 35.
mankind *n.* the male sex **308**, 30.
mannerly *adj.* well-mannered **69**, 25.
marry *int.* why, to be sure **93**, 31, etc.
[**masterfulness** *n.* mastery (this is the earliest citation in *OED*) **349**, 7.]
master-spring *n.* mainspring **282**, 31.
matachin *n.* a dance performed by matachins, sword-dancers in fantastic costume **87**, 33.
mated *pp. adj.* confounded **292**, 10.
matter *v.* discharge fluids or pus **405**, 17.

maugre *prep.* in spite of **254**, 12 n.
maze *n.* state of bewilderment **305**, 38, etc.
meagre *adj.* deficient in quality **259**, 10.
[**meagrely** *adv.* sparingly, niggardly (this is the earliest citation in *OED*) **389**, 21.]
mean *adj.* average **171**, 28.
meanness *n.* lowness of rank **247**, 22.
medicine *v.* heal, cure **1**, 14, etc.
mediocrity *n.* moderation, temperance **266**, 21 n.
meet *v.* **to meet half-way**, compromise with (this is the earliest citation in *OED* 2c) **260**, 3.
merchandise *n.* the business of buying and selling **137**, 22.
merely *adv.* entirely **7**, 8.
message *n.* mission **186**, 15.
metal *n.* mettle, the 'stuff' of which a man is made **240**, 23 n.
[**methodized** *pp. adj.* coherently organized (**372**, 1 is the earliest citation in *OED* for both *methodized* and *methodize* v. 1a) **336**, 1; **372**, 1.]
milch-kine *n. pl.* cows giving milk **243**, 35.
militar *adj.* military martial **314**, 32 (*var.*).
[**miniature** *n.* small-scale likeness (this is the earliest citation in *OED* 1a) **163**, 25.]
minion *n.* darling **182**, 25.
misconster *v.* misconstrue **285**, 25.
miser *n.* miserable or wretched person **133**, 11, etc.; *adj.* miserable, wretched **183**, 34, etc.
miserableness *n.* miserliness **208**, 28 (*var.*).
mislike *n.* want of affection **41**, 35; dissension (this is the earliest citation in *OED* 4) **246**, 16.
mislike *v.* displease **81**, 38.
[**misunderstood** *pp. adj.* misinterpreted (this is the earliest citation in *OED* 1) **17**, 106.]
mo *quasi-n.* others **11**, 21, etc.
moaning *vbl. n.* lamenting **51**, 23.
molest *v.* vex, annoy **240**, 1.

monomachy *n.* single combat **208**, 28 (*var.*).

[**moony** *adj.* of the moon (this is the earliest citation in *OED* 1) **302**, 27.]

morne *n.* rebated head of a tilting-lance **220**, 30.

motion *n.* emotion **61**, 25; agitation (of the mind or feelings) **171**, 33.

mowing *pres. p.* making grimaces **412**, 22.

muffle *v.* prevent from seeing by covering the head **273**, 23.

[**mutinously** *adv.* defiantly (this is the earliest citation in *OED*) **219**, 15.]

nailed *pp. adj.* studded, as with nails **58**, 15.

nakedness *n.* openness to attack (this is the earliest citation in *OED* 4) **320**, 16.

namely *adv.* above all **321**, 28.

narrow *adj.* parsimonious **184**, 13 n.

naturalize *v.* make familiar (the earliest citation in *OED* 6b is from 1606) **140**, 26, etc.

nearly *adv.* in close intimacy **79**, 14.

nice *adj.* able to discriminate in a high degree (this is the earliest citation in *OED* 10b) **22**, 15.

niceness *n.* reserve **50**, 25.

niggardly *adj.* close-fisted, stingy **12**, 5.

niggardness *n.* niggardliness, stinginess **212**, 11.

nis *v.* is not **411**, 16.

noisome *adj.* annoying **122**, 32.

not *v.* know not **411**, 8.

[**not-being** *n.* non-existence (this is the earliest citation in *OED*) **313**, 21.]

nuzzle *v.* train, nurture **137**, 19.

obsequies *n. pl.* funeral rites **139**, 31.

of *prep.* on **11**, 30, etc.; by **50**, 29, etc.

omniregency *n.* all-ruling condition (this is the earliest citation in *OED* **214**, 32 (*var.*).

once *adv.* to sum up, in short **17**, 12, etc.

only *adv.* pre-eminently **194**, 15.

opinion *n.* esteem **77**, 7; expectation **159**, 32.

oracle *n.* message given by a priest of a god **16**, 5, etc.

ordinary *adj.* conformable to order **93**, 34.

[**orphancy** *n.* orphanhood (this is the earliest citation in *OED*) **275**, 18.]

outright *adv.* straight ahead **58**, 31.

overbalance *v.* outweigh (this is the earliest citation in *OED* 1a) **210**, 9.

overcloud *v.* cover with something that conceals like a cloud (this is the earliest citation in *OED* 2) **121**, 20, etc.

overcome *v.* exceed **82**, 3.

overlook *v.* slight **48**, 13.

[**overmastered** *pp. adj.* overcome, overpowered (**360**, 1 is the earliest citation in *OED*) **247**, 16, etc.]

overmastering *pres. p. adj.* overpowering (the earliest citation in *OED* is from 1613) **205**, 1.

over-modestly *adv.* too modestly (this the earliest citation in *OED* **339**, 7.

[**over-partial** *adj.* favourably biased (this is the earliest citation in *OED*) **392**, 19.]

overpress *v.* oppress **49**, 11.

[**over-pressing** *adj.* oppressively heavy (this is the earliest citation in *OED*) **65**, 13.]

overrule *v.* prevail over, overcome **204**, 5.

overrun *v.* run faster than, surpass **141**, 3, etc.

[**over-spended** *pp. adj.* overspent, exhausted (this is the only citation in *OED*) **280**, 31.]

over-superstitiously *adv.* over-scrupulously (**139**, 13 is the only citation in *OED*) **349**, 4–5.

oversway *v.* overpower (this is the earliest citation in *OED* 1a) **15**, 9.

[**over-trodden** *pp. adj.* downtrodden (this is the earliest citation in *OED*) **418**, 22.]

overwatched *pp. adj.* wearied with too much watching **170**, 32, etc.

over-wayward *adj.* too self-willed **207**, 31.

owe *v.* own **50**, 6, etc.

painterly *adj.* artistic (this is the earliest

citation in *OED*) **64**, 13 n.
palfrey *n.* small saddle-horse for ladies **209**, 21, etc.
pantable *n.* slipper **68**, 27 n.
paragon *v.* compare to (this is the earliest citation in *OED* 1) **88**, 2.
pardie *int.* verily, assuredly **207**, 39.
part *v.* set out, depart **37**, 22.
partaker *n.* supporter **139**, 31.
particle *n.* minor part of speech **66**, 21.
partlet *n.* apparel worn about the neck and upper part of the chest **327**, 13.
parts *n. pl.* abilities, talents **217**, 32.
parture *n.* departure **395**, 14.
party *n.* one of the two bodies of combatants in a tournament **222**, 11.
party-love *n.* divided love **214**, 32 (*var.*).
passage *n.* proceeding **207**, 17.
passenger *n.* traveller **17**, 39, etc.
passing *adv.* very **8**, 12.
past *prep.* **past himself**, beside himself, out of his senses **38**, 6.
pastorals *n. pl.* pastoral games or pastimes **94**, 16, etc.
patent *adj.* **joined [joint] patent**, sharing by letters patent in some privilege or office **259**, 30.
pathologies *n. pl.* sorrows, sufferings (this is the only citation in *OED* 1) **20**, 25 (*var.*).
patron *n.* supporter **350**, 7.
pattern *v.* parallel, compare (this is the earliest citation in *OED* 2) **115**, 29.
paven *n.* pavan, a grave and stately dance **398**, 19.
pay *v.* **pay home** punish **158**, 17.
peacock *v.* display, plume (this is the earliest citation in *OED* 1) **78**, 38.
peevish *adj.* foolish, senseless **175**, 27; headstrong, obstinate **310**, 11, etc.
peise *v.* weigh **406**, 3.
peitrel *n.* armour protecting the breast of a horse **324**, 19, etc.
pencel *n.* small pennon or streamer **298**, 15.
perfit *adj.* perfect **165**, 8, etc.
perfitly *adv.* perfectly **127**, 25.
perplexedness *n.* state of being troubled (this is the earliest citation in *OED*) **91**, 25.
pester *v.* overcrowd **282**, 34.
pioneer *n.* one of a body of foot-soldiers equipped for digging trenches and other labours in preparing the way for the main body **306**, 11, etc.
pitch *n.* the height to which a falcon soars before swooping down on its prey **122**, 11; highest point, summit **339**, 8.
pitiful *adj.* despicable **24**, 36; exciting pity **81**, 34.
pity *v.* be sorry **82**, 9 n.
place *n.* subject, topic **159**, 14.
place *v.* repose (the earliest citation in *OED* 5 is from 1621) **231**, 20 n.
plague-sore *n.* sore caused by the plague **122**, 31-2.
plain *adj.* free from obstructions or interruptions **234**, 2 n.
plain *v.* lament **133**, 30, etc.
play *v.* allow a fish to exhaust itself by pulling against the line (this is the earliest citation in *OED* 6e) **187**, 31.
plea *n.* claim **67**, 29.
pleasingness *n.* pleasantness (this is the earliest citation in *OED* 1) **76**, 28.
plot *v.* plan (this is the earliest citation in *OED* plot v^1 1a) **371**, 28.
plunge *n.* dilemma **191**, 23.
point *v.* appoint, nominate **398**, 1 (*var.*).
policy *n.* stratagem **52**, 18, etc.; prudent procedure **249**, 27.
polled *pp. adj.* cut off **231**, 15.
polygamy *n.* plurality of spouses **262**, 29.
poppet *n.* puppet, marionette **193**, 21.
possessioner *n.* owner **28**, 10.
post-horse *n.* a horse for hire from an inn **171**, 29.
postilion *n.* forerunner (this is the earliest citation in *OED* 1b (fig.) **353**, 37.
poverty *n.* inferiority **85**, 30.
powder *v.* season, spice **321**, 13.
practice *n.* treachery **252**, 21, etc.
praise *n.* praiseworthiness, merit **225**, 34.
prenticeage *n.* apprenticeship **320**, 9.
presagious *adj.* portentous **256**, 2.

present *n.* affair in hand **247**, 33; *adj.* immediate **233**, 17.
prest *adv.* ready for action **301**, 29.
pretence *n.* claim **229**, 31.
pretended *pp. adj.* intended **305**, 24.
prettily *adv.* cleverly **220**, 30.
pretty *adj.* considerable **73**, 9, etc.; comely **85**, 8; pleasing **85**, 25; artful **189**, 20.
price *n.* place of honour, first or highest place **19**, 33, etc.
proceeding *n.* conduct, behaviour **13**, 14, etc.; course of action **36**, 33.
procure *v.* induce, persuade **108**, 34.
profitable *adj.* serviceable **212**, 10.
proportionately *adv.* in due proportion **318** , 27 n.
prospect *n.* appearance presented by anything, aspect **119**, 31.
prove *v.* show the existence of **172**, 32 n.; experience **175**, 14.
providence *n.* thrift **12**, 17; foresight **236**, 32.
pry *v.* spy **183**, 35 n.; look for **332**, 38.
puddled, *pp. adj.* dirty, miry **110**, 29.
puing *pres. p.* 'pewing', crying in a plaintive manner, as a bird (this is the earliest citation in OED for *pewing* n²)**411**, 31.
pulley *n.* wheel or drum on a shaft, turned by a belt for the application or transmission of power (this is the earliest citation in OED 2) **256**, 13 n.
purl *n.* thread made of twisted gold or silver wire, used for bordering or embroidering **80**, 34.
purling *pres. p. adj.* murmuring (the earliest citation in OED is from AS 15.1) **95** 17.
purpose *v.* be resolved or determined **216**, 9.

quality *n.* rank in society **201**, 28.
quite *v.* quit, absolve **358**, 33.

race *n.* course in a tournament **80**, 38.
racking *pres. p. adj.* extortionate **2**, 18.
rage *n.* sexual desire **270**, 27, etc.
rageful *adj.* full of rage **169**, 16; frenzied (this is the earliest citation in OED 2) **328**, 9.
rampire *n.* dam (this is the earliest citation in OED 2) **125**, 9; rampart **341**, 9.
rase *v.* demolish, raze **133**, 29.
rathely *adv.* quickly **213**, 8.
ravening *vbl. n.* plundering **12**, 20.
[**ravingly** *adv.* frenziedly (this is the earliest citation in OED 1) **128**, 21.]
raze *v.* wound slightly (this is the earliest citation in OED 4cβ) **382**, 23.
reasonable *adj.* rational **13**, 2, etc.
rebate *v.* blunt (this is the earliest citation in OED 3a, *fig.*) **293**, 31.
[**rebuff** *v.* ungraciously reject (this is the earliest citation in OED *rebuff* v¹ 1) **393**, 7.]
receive *v.* confer **50**, 32.
reck *v.* take heed of, heed **84**, 32, etc.
recken *v.* reckon, regard **361**, 36.
recommend *v.* give in charge, commit **141**, 26.
re-embattle *v.* draw up again in battle array (this is the earliest citation in OED) **296**, 6 (*var.*).
refection *n.* recreation, refreshment **424**, 4.
regiment *n.* office of ruler **137**, 30.
regreet *n.* return of a salutation or greeting (this is the earliest citation in OED) **224**, 3 (*var.*).
relic *n.* the remains **4**, 27; surviving trace of some practice **306**, 2.
remember *v.* remind **131**, 26.
remembrance *n.* the surviving memory of a person **236**, 19.
remove *v.* abandon a siege **361**, 25, etc.
repair *v.* make one's way **33**, 17, etc.
repairing *pres. p. adj.* dwelling (cf. OED under **repair** *v.* 3b, 'dwell' or 'reside') **12**, 22.
repine *v.* fret, murmur at **89**, 15; manifest discontent **188**, 19.
repining *vbl. n.* grumbling **125**, 2.
require *v.* request **396**, 24.
resolution *n.* fixed determination (the earliest citation in OED 11b is from Book IV of 93) **41**, 10.

[**respectfully** *adv.* with respect or deference (this is the earliest citation in *OED*) **10**, 2.]
rest *n.* a hook-shaped contrivance fixed to the right side of the cuirass (breast and back plates) of armour, in which the butt of the lance is rested while aim is taken in the charge **132**, 10, etc.
retire *v.* give ground (*fencing*) (the earliest citation in *OED* 1c is from 1594) **56**, 1.
retiring-place *n.* a place devoted to retiring or privacy **11**, 12, **66**, 25; a stronghold to which to retreat for security (cf. *OED* under **place** *n.* 5c, though the combination is not noted) **29**, 17, **315**, 37; a place to which to withdraw for shelter (cf. *OED* under **retire** *v.* 3a, though the combination is not noted) **210**, 37.
retrait *n.* signal for retreating **31**, 32, etc.; retreat **296**, 6 (*var.*).
revenge *n.* punishment, chastisement **269**, 29.
reverberation *n.* returning a sound **339**, 33.
reverse *n.* back-handed stroke or cut **325**, 15.
richesse *n.* wealth, opulence **122**, 16.
riding *n.* green track or lane for riding cut through a wood **73**, 16.
rightfulness *n.* righteousness **175**, 24.
road *n.* raid **26**, 32.
[**rosiness** *n.* rosy colour (this is the earliest citation in *OED*) **344**, 21.]
round *v.* whisper, talk privately **20**, 26, etc.
roundy *adj.* rounded (this is the earliest citation in *OED* 1) **344**, 19.
rude *adj.* violent, severe **49**, 9; inexperienced **87**, 26.
rule *n.* government, management **121**, 28.
rumour *n.* clamour **242**, 4.
run *v.* tilt, just or joust **85**, 2, etc.; **run on**, continue going on **256**, 14 n.
runagate *n.* fugitive **183**, 33.
running *vbl. n.* running at tilt, justing or jousting (cf. *OED* 2a, restricted to the action of riding on horseback) **80**, 38, **220**, 35.
rustle *v.* move with a rustling sound **87**, 22.

salute *v.* strike (the eye or ear) (this is the earliest citation in *OED* 5b) **125**, 31.
say *n.* assay, foretaste **165**, 19.
scape *v.* escape **68**, 6.
scold *v.* quarrel noisily **393**, 38.
scope *n.* aim, purpose **68**, 24.
score *n.* account **2**, 16, etc.
scour *v.* rid **39**, 7.
[**scrip** *n.* shepherd's pouch **426**, 15.]
scutcheon *n.* heraldic shield **215**, 38.
see *v.* meet a bet **328**, 36 (*var.*).
seech *v.* seek **411**, 33.
[**self-accusing** *pres. p. adj.* blaming herself (this is the earliest citation in *OED*) **201**, 23 n., **314**, 36.]
[**self-killing** *vbl. n.* suicide (this is the earliest citation in *OED*) **380**, 6 (*var.*).
[**self-pride** *n.* vanity (this is the earliest citation in *OED*) **347**, 34.]
sepia *n.* cuttle **86**, 6 n.
serve *v.* wrap a bandage round an object (this is the earliest citation in *OED* 53a) **327**, 13.
serviceable *adj.* expressing readiness to serve **193**, 22, etc.
settled *pp. adj.* of the countenance, indicating a settled purpose (this is the earliest citation in *OED* 1c) **118**, 33.
shade *v.* place in the shade (this is the earliest citation in *OED* shade v^1 2b) **129**, 40.
shadow *n.* reflected image **11**, 6, etc.
shamefastness *n.* modesty **162**, 39, etc.
shewel *n.* scarecrow **310**, 29.
short *adv.* **to make short**, to be brief **234**, 4.
shorten *v.* supply insufficiently (the earliest citation in *OED* 4 is from 1599) **188**, 13.
show *n.* **in show**, in appearance **9**, 27; **bear show of**, appear to be **5**, 8, etc.
shrewd *adj.* harsh, stern **30**, 9, etc.
shrewdly *adv.* grievously **14**, 11.
shrewdness *n.* ill nature **271**, 16.

shritch-owl *n.* shriek-owl, screech-owl **185**, 28.
shue *v.* sue **197**, 26 (*var.*).
side-blow *n.* a blow directed sideways **243**, 20–1.
side-look *n.* oblique look (this is the earliest citation in *OED*) **240**, 19 n.
sightfulness *n.* power of seeing **175**, 26, etc.
silly *adj.* pitiable **3**, 6 n., etc.; feeble **365**, 32.
simper *v.* smirk **81**, 39.
singularity *n.* personal action to attract attention to oneself **72**, 20.
skill *n.* expertise **46**, 5, etc.
skill *v.* know how to do something (this is the earliest citation in *OED* 4c) **412**, 39, etc.
skilled *pp. adj.* experienced **122**, 39.
skrike *v.* utter a shrill harsh cry **182**, 35.
slidingness *n.* easy flow (this is the only citation in *OED*) **249**, 12.
slops *n. pl.* wide baggy breeches **85**, 7.
slubber *v.* **slubber up**, soil **9**, 9; deal carelessly with **85**, 6 n.
sluttish *adj.* despicable **212**, 11.
smackering *vbl. n.* inclination (this is the earliest citation in *OED* 2) **112**, 7.
sober *adj.* peaceful **7**, 38; showing no trace of haste **87**, 20.
soldiery *n.* the military **189**, 40.
soothe *v.* corroborate **14**, 27.
sorrel *n.* reddish brown **324**, 26 n.
sorry *adj.* causing distress or sorrow **366**, 26.
sort *v.* agree, be in harmony or conformity **45**, 32; allot, assign **316**, 21.
sound *n.* swoon, fainting fit **320**, 17, etc.
sounding *vbl. n.* swooning, fainting fit **230**, 19.
spoil *n.* pillaging **237**, 1.
spoil *v.* destroy **237**, 19.
[**sportfully** *adv.* playfully (this is the earliest citation in *OED*) **348**, 29.]
sprent *pp.* besprinkled **175**, 7.
spy *v.* discover **94**, 17.
squeamish *adj.* unwilling **94**, 35.
stain *n.* one who eclipses or casts into the shade (this is the earliest citation in *OED* 3c) **76**, 1.
stain *v.* deprive a feebler luminary of its lustre **3**, 3; impair the beauty of **164**, 16.
stale *n.* decoy-bird **206**, 2.
stand *v.* **stand upon**, trust to **31**, 26; insist upon (the earliest citation in *OED stand upon* 14 is from 1634) **34**, 29; consist of **59**, 24.
standish *n.* a stand to hold writing materials **268**, 14.
stark *adv.* absolutely **70**, 9.
stay *n.* large rope used to support a mast **5**, 32 n.; state, condition **303**, 2.
stay *v.* await (the earliest citation in *OED* 19a is from p. 351, 21) **45**, 19, etc.
stayed *pp. adj.* checked, restrained **162**, 37.
[**stead** *v.* serve, be of use to **6**, 29; **105**, 24.]
steal *v.* direct furtively (of a look) (this is the earliest citation in *OED* 5c) **74**, 2.
step *n.* footprint **1**, 26.
stern *n.* rudder **299**, 1.
stickle *v.* quell **4**, 2.
stickler *n.* umpire at a tournament **84**, 11.
still *adj.* averse from moving about, sedentary (this is the earliest citation in *OED* 1c) **283**, 2.
stoop *v.* (of a hawk) descend **334**, 33.
stopped *pp. adj.* caused to cease, brought to a standstill (this is the earliest citation in *OED* 6a) **362**, 17.
store *n.* supply, abundance **8**, 9, etc.
stout *adj.* arrogant **23**, 6.
straight *adv.* immediately **14**, 37, etc.
strait *adj.* close, intimate **52**, 4, etc.
straiten *v.* restrict the freedom of (this is the earliest citation in *OED* 5a) **17**, 19.
strength *n.* fortification **342**, 21.
strike *v.* stab **215**, 33; lash out with the hooves **315**, 9, etc.
strive *v.* contend in words **47**, 38; make one's way with effort (this is the earliest citation in *OED* 10a) **77**, 4.
subtile *adj.* crafty **289**, 39.
subtilty *n.* guile **228**, 23, etc.
suffer *v.* submit to death **228**, 37.

sufficiency *n.* adequacy **91**, 33; ability **189**, 27, etc.
suggest *v.* seduce away (this is the earliest citation in *OED* 2a) **329**, 23.
suit *n.* company of followers **158**, 7.
suitable *adj.* agreeing in nature, accordant **110**, 33, etc.; matching **317**, 36; *adv.* in agreement, conformity **41**, 9.
suitableness *n.* conformity **261**, 7.
[**sundry** *adj.* separate, different **338**, 10.]
support *v.* (heraldic) flanked by supporters **215**, 38.
surety *n.* safety **29**, 23; guarantee **58**, 6.
surmount *v.* surpass **275**, 25.
surquidry *n.* arrogance **203**, 1 (*var.*).
swink *n.* labour, toil **411**, 39.
sycophant *n.* informer **145**, 30; slanderer **188**, 32.

table *n.* painting **11**, 18, etc.
tablet *n.* flat jewel **88**, 1.
target *n.* light round shield **400**, 20, etc.
tedious *adj.* disagreeable **190**, 10.
tender *v.* hold dear, esteem, value **267**, 19, etc.; be concerned about **281**, 40.
tender-hearted *adj.* easily moved by fear, timid **182**, 35.
thilk *dem. adj.* these **410**, 32.
thorough-inquiry *n.* thorough-going inquiry **253**, 33.
thought *n.* trifle **81**, 31; anxiety, distress of mind **226**, 9.
through-handling *vbl. n.* management of details **216**, 33.
throughly *adv.* fully, completely, perfectly **34**, 37, etc.
thunderbolt *v.* astonish, amaze (this is the only citation in *OED*) **369**, 16.
tie *v.* restrain **90**, 19.
title *n.* claim **136**, 15.
[**tittle-tattling** *vbl. n.* gossip, idle chatting (this is the earliest citation in *OED*) **182**, 6.]
[**tomb** *v.* serve as a tomb for (this is the earliest citation in *OED* 2) **346**, 21.]
town-house *n.* municipal building containing the public offices, court-house, and town hall **312**, 28.

trace *n.* path, course **213**, 31.
traffic *v.* carry on negotiations **362**, 25.
train *v.* entice **306**, 5.
traitorly *adj.* traitorous (this is the earliest citation in *OED*) **393**, 18.
trapper *n.* covering put over a horse for defence or ornament **318**, 26, etc.
treasure *n.* treasury **245**, 38.
triumph *n.* spectacle, pageant **147**, 38.
triumphant *adj.* befitting a triumph or victory procession **80**, 33.
trophy *n.* memorial consisting of the spoils of war **266**, 31; monument **354**, 31.
trow *v.* believe **134**, 31, etc.; suppose (but merely expletive) **182**, 28; be assured **310**, 23.
trumpet *n.* trumpeter **318**, 7.
truncheon *n.* fragment of a lance **319**, 16.
try *v.* test **23**, 38; undergo **90**, 14.
tumble *v.* proceed hastily, without order or premeditation (the earliest citation in *OED* 7 is from 1590) **185**, 6.

unassayed *pp. adj.* untested **17**, 34; unattempted **53**, 13.
unbar *v.* unfasten, undo (the earliest citation in *OED* b (*fig.*) is from 1601) **195**, 1.
unbashed *pp. adj.* unabashed **246**, 24.
uncivil *adj.* impolite (the earliest citation in *OED* 3b is from 1611) **62**, 18.
unconscionable *adj.* unreasonably excessive **79**, 29.
unconsulting *pres. p. adj.* inconsiderate, rash (this is the only citation in *OED* 1) **225**, 23.
uncorrupted *pp. adj.* not debased **306**, 26.
undeserved *pp. adj.* undeserving **83**, 15.
undiscovered *pp. adj.* unobserved, undetected (the earliest citation in *OED* 4 is from Shakespeare, *2 Henry VI*, III. i. 369) **213**, 18.
undiscreet *adj.* without discernment or sound judgement **215**, 15, etc.
unendly *adj.* unending (this is the only citation in *OED*) **269**, 29.

unevitable *adj.* unavoidable **75**, 12 n., **309**, 4.
ungratefully *adv.* without due return or gratitude **217**, 34, etc.
unhap *n.* misfortune **194**, 33.
unhospital *adj.* inhospitable **8**, 15.
[**unknow** *v.* forget (this is the earliest citation in *OED* for *unknow* v²) **285**, 32.]
[**unleisured** *pp. adj.* busy (this is the earliest citation in *OED*) **241**, 28.]
[**unlevel** *v.* make no longer level (this is the earliest citation in *OED*) **318**, 10.]
unlikely *adj.* distasteful **109**, 34.
[**unloveliness** *n.* ugliness, unpleasantness (this is the earliest citation in *OED* 1) **187**, 27.]
unlucky *adj.* causing harm (this is the earliest citation in *OED* 4a) **54**, 22.
[**unmasking** *vbl. n.* exposing (this is the earliest citation in *OED*) **375**, 28 (*var.*).]
unmodest *adj.* immodest **231**, 12.
[**unrefusing** *pres. p. adj.* welcoming (this is the earliest citation in *OED*) **308**, 4.]
[**unrelievable** *adj.* impossible to relieve (this is the earliest citation in *OED*) **50**, 24.]
unremovable *adj.* constant **219**, 36.
unresistable *adj.* irresistable **232**, 20.
[**unrespected** *pp. adj.* disregarded (this is the earliest citation in *OED* 1) **401**, 18.]
[**unrewarding** *vbl. n.* lack of reward (this is the only citation in *OED*) **336**, 14.]
[**unroyal** *adj.* unworthy of a king (this is the earliest citation in *OED* 1a) **152**, 1.]
unsensible *adj.* destitute of intelligence **14**, 32; incapable of being understood **39**, 21; imperceptible **73**, 8; unmoved, indifferent (the earliest citation in *OED* 4a(a) is from 1611) **120**, 25.
unstaidness *n.* physical unsteadiness (this is the earliest citation in *OED* 2) **43**, 22.
unsuccessing *n.* failure **146**, 5.
untried *pp. adj.* unrefined **14**, 20.
unused *pp. adj.* unusual, etc. **154**, 4.
upbraid *v.* allege, as a ground for reproach **347**, 21.
upward *adv.* upright **209**, 13.
utter *v.* reveal **45**, 28.

valorously *adv.* bravely (the earliest citation in *OED* is from 1614) **28**, 25.
valour *n.* worth due to personal qualities **247**, 20.
value *n.* a sum of exchange **4**, 19; valour **32**, 13, etc.; worthiness **51**, 15.
valure *n.* courage **153**, 30, etc.; value, worth **390**, 20.
vamplate *n.* a plate fixed on a lance as a guard for the hand **293**, 32, etc.
vaward *n.* vanguard **40**, 16.
venter *v.* venture, go so far as **8**, 24.
vice *n.* mechanical contrivance by which a piece of apparatus is worked **73**, 32.
vie *n.* challenge or bid (the metaphor is of card-playing) **328**, 36 (*var.*).
vine-press *n.* wine-press **122**, 19.
virgin-wax *n.* white wax used in candles and torches **166**, 8, etc.
visor *n.* face **13**, 38.
vizard *n.* outward appearance **289**, 4.
vouchsafe *v.* deign to accept **1**, 35; confer, bestow **6**, 32; condescend to engage in **7**, 26; give, grant in a gracious manner **20**, 1; permit, as an act of condescension **26**, 8; show willingness **52**, 35.

wage *v.* hire **238**, 1.
wallowish *adj.* nauseous **193**, 28.
wand *n* stick for urging on a horse **131**, 23; stick for chastisement **209**, 22.
wanhope *n.* hopelessness, despair **119**, 5.
wanton *adj.* arbitrary, gratuitous (this is the earliest citation in *OED* 2b) **150**, 36.
ward *n.* guard **30**, 4; defensive posture, mode of parrying **169**, 26, etc.
warely *adv.* cautiously **58**, 34.
warrant *n.* defence **70**, 2.
warrant *v.* protect **69**, 37.
warrantable *adj.* acceptable **239**, 9.
waterwork *n.* ornamental fountain (this is the earliest citation in *OED* 5a) **73**, 25 n.
watery *adj.* **73**, 29.

way-beater *n.* one who frequents the highway for felonious purposes (this is the earliest citation in OED) **228**, 31.

way-leader *n.* one who conducts a traveller **337**, 18.

wayment *v.* lament **408**, 26.

wayward *adj.* untoward, awkward **403**, 5.

weak-breach *n.* a fortified place not possessed of sound defence **332**, 13.

weal-public *n.* the state **281**, 13.

weeping-ripe *adj.* ready to weep **85**, 28.

[**well-applied** *pp. adj.* skilfully administered (this is the earliest citation in OED) **357**, 38.]

well-being *vbl. n.* prosperous condition **151**, 13.

[**well-followed** *pp. adj.* followed through (this is the earliest citation in OED) **296**, 6.]

[**well mixed** *pp. adj.* skilfully mixed (this is the earliest citation in OED) **165**, 24.]

[**well-paying** *pres. p. adj.* paying a good price (this is the earliest citation in OED) **71**, 3.]

well-placed *pp. adj.* fittingly placed **231**, 20 (*var.*).

[**well shading** *pres. p. adj.* providing ample shade (this is the earliest citation in OED well-shading adj.) **48**, 18.]

well-succeeding *pres. p. adj.* having a happy issue **219**, 22.

[**well-waiting** *pres. p. adj.* patiently waiting (the only other citation in OED is from *A Defence of Poetry*) **407**, 1.]

[**well-weaving** *vbl. n.* skilful weaving (this is the only citation in OED well weaving) **241**, 35.]

wherewithal *adv.* by means of which, whereby **402**, 23.

whether *adj.* whichever of the two **341**, 34.

whittle *n.* a large knife **333**, 31.

[**widowed** *pp. adj.* (*fig.*) desolate (this is the earliest citation in OED) **375**, 1; deprived of a partner **115**, 25 n. (spelt 'widowhead').]

willing *pres. p. adj.* deliberate **221**, 26.

winning *adj.* alluring, attractive (the earliest citation in OED 3 is from 1596) **78**, 5.

winy *adj.* accompanied by the drinking of wine (this is the only citation in OED 2a) **251**, 25.

withal *adv.* in addition, moreover, as well **11**, 17, etc.; therewith **258**, 31; *prep.* with **4**, 31, etc.

withers *n. pl.* in a horse, the highest part of the back, lying between the shoulder blades **318**, 17.

within *adv.* inside the defence of **238**, 30.

without *prep.* outside, beyond **41**, 6, etc.; *conj.* unless, except **141**, 32.

wittold *n.* a contented cuckold **174**, 35.

won'd *pp. adj.* inhabited **411**, 10.

work *n.* business **22**, 17.

working *n.* actions **153**, 37; effect **229**, 23; *pres. p. adj.* active **12**, 39; operative **291**, 5.

wormwood *n.* bitter tasting plant *Artemisia absinthium*, used as an emblem of what is bitter and grievous to the soul **74**, 31.

wrack *n.* wrecked ship **6**, 5.

wrinkle *v.* manifest (something) in or by facial wrinkles (this is the earliest citation in OED 4) **212**, 24.

wronglessly *adv.* without doing wrong **77**, 36.

wrought *pp. adj.* embroidered **71**, 33.

wry *v.* divert **94**, 4; twist, contort **112**, 10.

wrying *vbl. n.* twisting, writhing **182**, 15.

ycleped *pp.* called **410**, 13.

yet *adv.* moreover **52**, 13.

yield *v.* exert **60**, 6.

young *adj.* immature **187**, 9.

young-master *v.* to address or treat as a young master (this is the only citation in OED) **259**, 22.

younker *n.* young man **426**, 3.

INDEX OF CHARACTERS

Æschylus, dies in his son's arms 295
Agenor, younger brother of Philanax, 291 (*var.*), killed by Amphialus 293, avenged by Philanax 297
Amiclas, king of Lacedaemon (Laconia), 26, 29, 32, 34, 39, 78–9
Amiclas, wife of, 79
Amphialus, Arcadian prince, son of Cecropia, nephew of Basilius, 18, 22, 45 (*var.*), 48–51, befriends Philoxenus; woos Helen for him **52–3**, kills Philoxenus **54**, withdraws in remorse **55–7**, 77–9, 101, 160 (*var.*), meets his cousins **168–71**, 181, 193, 203, 219–20, 235, 249, 271 (*var.*), 274–6, visits Philoclea in her chamber **277–9**, assembles an army **280–3**, 284, 289, 291, prepares for battle **291–2**, 293–306, 309, 314 (*var.*), 315, fights Phalantus **316–20**, 321, fights and kills Argalus **323–8**, 329–32, 334–41, fights and kills Parthenia **342–5**, 346–8, fights Musidorus; is injured **348–59**, 360, 368, 370–1, 378–80, confronts Cecropia **381**, stabs himself **382–3**, 384–6, mourned by the Amphialians **386–90**, 397
Amphialus, governor of, 299, 317
Anaxius, prince, nephew of Euardes, brother of Zoilus and Lycurgus, 203–4, 208–10, 212–14, 235, 258, joins Amphialus in the siege **337–42**, 349 (*var.*), 350, 356, 358, 362, vows to avenge Amphialus 'death' **383–4**, 385–6, threatens to kill the princesses **390–1**, 392–3, seeks to marry Pamela **394–6**, 397–9, fights Pyrocles **401–3**
Andromana, a widow, later queen of Iberia, daughter of the king of Galatia and his concubine, sister of Plexirtus, stepmother of Plangus, mother of Palladius and one daughter, 81, affair with Plangus **186–7**, marriage to Plangus' father **187–92**, 214 (*var.*), 215–18, 219–20, 222–3, 225–6, 230, 264

Andromana, first husband of, 186–7
Antiphilus, king of Lycia by marriage to Erona, 177–81, 192, 202, 234–5, seeks bigamous marriage to Artaxia **258–9**, 260–1, executed by Artaxia **262**, mourned by Erona **163–4**
Argalus, cousin of Gynecia, married to Parthenia, 20 (*var.*), 21–7, 33, reunited with Parthenia **35–7**, 39, 80, 83, 235, 320 (*var.*), reluctantly joins Basilius in the siege **321–4**, fights Amphialus **325–8**, 344–6, 355
Argos, king of, father of Cecropia, 52, 274–5, 286
Argos, king of, brother of Cecropia, 280
Armenia, queen of, sister of the king of Iberia, mother of Tiridates and Artaxia, 192
Artaxia, sister of Tiridates, later queen of Armenia, cousin of Plangus, second wife of Plexirtus, 81, 177 (*var.*), 178, 181, 192, 212–13, 233, 236, 258 (*var.*), 259–64
Artesia, sister of Ismenus, related to the queen of Lacedaemon, 76 (*var.*), 77, fostered by Cecropia **78**, 79–84, 86, 88–9, helps to abduct the princesses **272–3**, 276, 316, conspires with Clinias **334–7**, 378

Baccha, married to Pamphilus, 81, 224–5
Barzanes, king of Hyrcania, brother of Otanes, 160, 177 (*var.*), 178–9, 229, 354
Basilius, king of Arcadia, married to Gynecia, father of Pamela and Philoclea, brother-in-law of Cecropia, 10 (*var.*), introduced by Kalander **12–20**, 21, 52, 66 (*var.*), meets and falls in love with Zelmane **68–80**, 83–9, 94–7, 99–101, 102 (*var.*), 105–8, 116, 121–3, 161, 'Complaint of Plangus' **171–6**, 193–4, declares his love for Zelmane and is rebuked **195–7**, 239–40, fights the rebels **242–5**, 247, 249–50, 253–4, recites the oracle **255**, 256–7, 265, 271–2, Cecropia's account of his marriage 274–5, 276, 280–2, 292, 296 (*var.*), 299,

INDEX OF CHARACTERS

besieges Amphialus' castle **315–16**, 321, 323, 328–9, 331, 333–4, 338, 341–3, 346, 357–62, 383–4, 386, 391, 394 (*var.*), 395, consults the oracle again **396–7**, 398, 404, 409, 417, 420, 422, 430, 433–4

Basilius' brother, married to Cecropia, father of Amphialus, 52, 78, 101, 274, 287

Basilius' sister, wife of Kalander, mother of Clitophon, 86

Bithynia, new king of, succeeds Euardes, 234

Black Knight, *see* **Musidorus**

Calodoulus, servant of Musidorus, 93

Cecropia, daughter of the king of Argos, sister-in-law of Basilius, mother of Amphialus, 52, 78, 86, 89, 100–1, 249, 251, 253, 271, imprisons her nieces and Zelmane **273–7**, 280, tries to persuade Philoclea to marry Amphialus **284–9**, targets Pamela instead **289–91**, 299 (*var.*), reprimanded for atheism by Pamela **306–15**, 317, 320–1, 328, 335, imprisons Artesia **337**, 339, encourages Amphialus towards rape **347–9**, 350, 357, 358 (*var.*), 359, 362–3, tortures her nieces and threatens execution **364–8**, 370–1, 373, 375 (*var.*), 377–80, dies **381**, 382,

Chremes, father of Dido, 208 (*var.*), 210–4

Claius, a shepherd in love with Urania, 1–9, 19, 118, 417–19, 430–2

Clinias, 100, ringleader of the mutiny **249–53**, 276, 280, 283, 291 (*var.*), 292, 317, 328 (*var.*), fights Dametas **329–34**, plots with Artesia **336–7**

Clitophon, son of Kalander and Basilius' sister, 15, 20 (*var.*), 21–3, imprisoned by the helots **27–30**, freed by Musidorus **32–5**, 38–9, 45 (*var.*), accompanies Musidorus **47–9**, 50 (*var.*), 55–7, 84 (*var.*), fights in Phalantus' challenge **86–7**, 118, 360

Codrus, killed by Philanax 296

Coriden (Coredens in *OA*), 411

Cosma, a shepherdess, 426–9

Crete, king of, 139

Ctesiphon, killed by Philanax 296

Cyprus, king of, father of Gynecia, 12

Daiphantus, assumed name of Zelmane, daughter of Plexirtus (q.v.)

Daiphantus, assumed name of Pyrocles (q.v.)

Dametas, husband of Miso, father of Mopsa, 10 (*var.*), introduced by Kalander **13–15**, 17, 19–20, 66 (*var.*), meets Zelmane **68–9**, 71, meets and hires Dorus **93–5**, encounters the bear **97–100**, 108–10, 112, 119–21, overturns the coach **122**, 128–32, 135, 182, 242, 253 (*var.*), 254, fights Clinias **328–34**, 404

Demagoras, a Laconian, 20 (*var.*), 23, disfigures Parthenia **24**, 25–6, 28, killed by Argalus **39**

Dicus, an old shepherd, 422–7, 430

Dido, daughter of Chremes, 203 (*var.*), tortures Pamphilus **204–5**, 206–8, rescued by Pyrocles **209–10**, 211–14, 225

Dorcas, a shepherdess, 426

Dorilaus, king of Thessalia, father of Musidorus, 115, 134 (*var.*), 138–9

Dorus, assumed name of Musidorus (q.v.)

Drialus, killed by Amphialus 295

Elis, princess of, 81

Elpine, an Arcadian lady, 84

Erona, queen of Lycia, married to Antiphilus, 81, 154 (*var.*), 160, 171 (*var.*), 173–7, besieged by Tiridates **178–80**, 181, 186, 192, 202–4, 227, 235, 239, 257, 258 (*var.*), overthrown by Antiphilus **259**, imprisoned by Artaxia **260–5**

Euarchus, king of Macedon, father of Pyrocles, uncle of Musidorus, 59, 64, 115, 134 (*var.*), early reign and marriage **135–42**, 147, 152–3, 200–1, 226, 235, 265, 393

Euardes, king of Bithynia, uncle of Anaxius, Zoilus, and Lycurgus, 160, 177 (*var.*), 178–9, 203, 337, 393

Eurileon, nephew of Amiclas, 26, 34, 39

Eurileon, an Arcadian, 84

Forsaken Knight, *see* **Musidorus**

Frozen Knight, 222

INDEX OF CHARACTERS

Galatia (Paphlagonia), king of, father of Leonatus and Plexirtus, 154–9, 227
Geron, a shepherd, 414–17
Green Knight, *see* **Knight of the Sheep**
Gynecia, queen of Arcadia, daughter of the king of Cyprus, married to Basilius, mother of Pamela and Philoclea, 10 (*var.*), 12–13, 21, 51, 71–3, in love with Zelmane **74–7**, 84, 86, 89, 95–7, 99–101, woos Zelmane **102–7**, 120 (*var.*), injured in a coach accident **121–2**, 124–5, 128, 134, 161, 193–4, 196–7, her dream **239–40**, 241–2, 256, 271, 275, 286, 305, 346, 362, 422

Halting Knight, has his picture of Pamela stolen by Musidorus, 87–8
Helen (Helena), queen of Corinth, 22, 35–7, 45 (*var.*), 49, tells Musidorus her story **50–5**, 56–7, 77–8, 82, 86, 218 (*var.*), 219–20, 383 (*var.*), seeks to cure Amphialus' wounds **384–6**, 390–1
Hippolitus, killed by Musidorus 298
Histor, a shepherd, rejected by Kala for Lalus, 414–17

Iberia, king of, father of Plangus, later married to Andromana and father of Palladius and a daughter, 179, 186–7, manipulated by Andromana **188–92**, 208 (*var.*), 213–18, 223, 230, 262, 264
Iberia, queen of, mother of Plangus, 186
Ill-apparelled Knight, *see* **Pyrocles**
Ill-appointed Knight, *see* **Pyrocles**
Ill-arrayed Knight, *see* **Pyrocles**
Ismenus, brother of Artesia, squire of Amphialus, fights Musidorus while wearing his armour **55–6**, 57, 79 killed by Philanax **296–7**, 305, 318, 334–5, 337, 382

Kala, a shepherdess, marries Lalus, 405–8, 414
Kalander, brother-in-law of Basilius, father of Clitophon, 6–10, his garden-house **10–11**, 12–16, 18–22, 24, 27–8, 30–3, 35–6, 37–9, 40 (*var.*), the stag hunt **44–7**, 61–2, 66, 68–9, 86, 91, 118, 358 (*var.*), 360–1
Kalander's steward, tells the story of Argalus and Parthenia 21–7

Klaius, *see* **Claius**
Knight of the Sheep (Green Knight), 337 (*var.*), 341–2, 349 (*var.*), 356–8
Knight of the Tomb, *see* **Parthenia**

Lacedaemon (Laconia), king of, *see* **Amiclas**
Lacedaemon (Laconia), queen of, related to Artesia, 79, 82
Lacemon, a rich knight, in love with Urania, 83
Lalus, a young shepherd, 85
Lalus, a singer in the Eclogues, in love with Kala (*see* **OA**), 405–9, 414–5, 417, 426
Lamon, a shepherd, stands in for the absent Strephon and Klaius at the Eclogues, 118, 417, 430, 433
Languet, Hubert, 410
Lelius, a knight, 220–1
Leon, a knight, 84
Leonatus, prince, later king, of Galatia (Paphlagonia), half-brother of Plexirtus, leads his blind father **154–7**, 158–60, 224 (*var.*), sends Plexirtus to Trebizond **227–8**, 233–5
Leontius, friend of Agenor, 291 (*var.*), 293–4, 297
Leuca, a shepherdess, 428–9
Leucippe, a noble lady, forsaken by Pamphilus, 81–2, 224–5
Leucippus, loyal servant to the princes, brother of Nelsus, 140 (*var.*), 144, 150–2
Lycia, king of, father of Erona, 177–8
Lycia, new king of, successor to Erona, 261
Lycia, queen of, *see* **Erona**
Lycurgus, brother of Anaxius and Zoilus, 341, 358, 362, 384, 394, fights Pyrocles **398–401**
Lydia, king of, 139

Macedon, queen of, sister of Dorilaus, wife of Euarchus, mother of Pyrocles, 139–40
Megalus, killed by Musidorus 298
Memnon, killed by Amphialus 295
Menalcas, Dorus' 'brother' **90–5**, 100, 118–20, 426

INDEX OF CHARACTERS

Milo, killed by Philanax 296
Mira, appears to Amphialus in his dream, 302, 304
Miso, wife of Dametas, mother of Mopsa, 10 (*var.*), 13–14, 109, 122, 128, 134, 161–2, 168, the old wives' tale **181–4**, 193, 196–7, 235 (*var.*), 239–41, 271–3, 306, 328, 330
Mopsa, daughter of Dametas and Miso, 13–14, 108 (*var.*), 109–14, 115 (*var.*), 118–20, 128, 130–1, 133–5, 160–2, 168, 170–1, 181 her tale **185**, 196, 242, 266–8, 273, 329
Musidorus, prince of Thessalia, son of Dorilaus and Euarchus' sister, 1 (*var.*), 3–12, 18–21, expedition against the helots **27–33**, 35, **38–48**, finds Amphialus' armour and meets Helen **49–51**, 55–7, meets Zelmane **58–66**, 68, 73 (*var.*), 75–6, 84 (*var.*), 86, fights in Phalantus' challenge **87–9**, disguised as Dorus **90–2**, 93–5, kills the bear **96–100**, 108–9, pretends to woo Mopsa **110–114**, 115–20, 128 (*var.*), 129–36, tells his story **139–61**, 171, 177 (*var.*), 178–80, 193, 202–4, 208 (*var.*), 213–8, 220, 222–6, 228–32, 234–8, 239 (*var.*), fights the rebels **242–4**, 250, 254, 258–60, 263–4, tries to kiss Pamela **266-7**, his letter **268–71**, 273, 290, 296 (*var.*), disguised as Black Knight **297–9**, 337, (*var.*), 341–2, fights Amphialus **349–58**, 366, 373, 382, 384, 391–2, 398, eclogue with Lalus **404–409**, 422–5

Nelsus, loyal servant to the princes, brother of Leucippus, 140 (*var.*), 144, 150–2
Nestor, an Arcadian knight, in love with Urania 84
Nico, a jolly younker, 426–9
Nisus, killed by Amphialus 295

Otanes, brother of Barzanes, 229, 232, 234
Otaves, *see* **Otanes**

Palemon, killed by Musidorus 298
Palladius, prince of Iberia, son of Plangus' father and Andromana, 186 (*var.*), 192, 214 (*var.*), 217–20, 222–3, 230, 264
Palladius, assumed name of Musidorus (q.v.)
Pamela, elder daughter of Basilius and Gynecia, 10 (*var.*), 11, 13, 17, 71–3, 76, 87–9, 92, 94 (*var.*), 95–100, 108 (*var.*), 109–20, 122, in love with Musidorus **128–34**, 135, 138, 148, 160–1, 170–1, 181, 184–6, 196, 215, 242, 254–5, 266–8, 272, 274, 288 (*var.*), 289, her prayer **290**, 291, her purse **307-8**, rebukes Cecropia's atheism **309–15**, 321, 329–30, 334 (*var.*), 335, reveals the plot **336–7**, 354, 358–9, 362–3, 365–6, 368, the mock-execution **369–70**, 372, 374, 377–8, confronts Amphialus **380–1**, 390 (*var.*), 391–6, 398, 406–9, 422–5
Pamphilus, 203 (*var.*), 204–10, 224–5
Pannonia, king of, 139
Paphlagonia, king of, *see* **Galatia**, king of
Parthenia, daughter of Kalander's sister, married to Argalus, also the Knight of the Tomb, 20 (*var.*), refuses Demagoras **22–3**, is disfigured and leaves Argalus **24–6**, reunited with Argalus **35–7**, 40, 47–8, 67, 80, 82–3, 320 (*var.*), 322–4, 326–8, as Knight of the Tomb **342–7**, 355, 382
Pas, a friend of Nico's, 426–9
Phalantus, bastard brother of Helen, queen of Corinth, 76 (*var.*), his challenge **77–80**, 84–7, loses to Zelmane **88–9**, 169, 314 (*var.*), leaves the siege after losing to Amphialus **316–21**
Phebilus, loses Philoclea's picture at Phalantus' challenge 85–6, 88, spared by Amphialus 295–6
Philanax, regent of Arcadia, his letter **15–18**, 21, 40, 68, 100, 253, 255–7, 271, 276, 281–2, 293, fights in the siege **296–9**, pardoned and released by Amphialus **305–7**, 329, 335, 338, 341–2, 346, 357–8, 360–2, 391, 396
Philisides, a knight, formerly a shepherd, 220–1
Philisides, a melancholy young shepherd (*see OA*), 409–11, 413–14, 433–4

INDEX OF CHARACTERS

Philoclea, younger daughter of Basilius and Gynecia, 10 (*var.*), 11, 13, 57, 66-7, 71-6, 83, 85-6, 88-9, 91, 94 (*var.*), 95-7, 103, 107-8, 120 (*var.*), 121-2, in love with Zelmane **123-8**, 129-30, 132-4, goes bathing **161-3**, 164-8, 170-1, 177-8, 181-2, 185-6, 193-4, 196-7, learns that Zelmane's is Pyrocles **197-202**, 216, 223-4, 231-2, 238-41, 244, 249, 257, 271-4, 276-80, 284-5, 287-9, 291, 294-6, 298-9, 305-7, 317, 320-1, 325, 328-9, 335-7, 339, 343, 347-50, 354, 358-9, 362-3, whipped by Cecropia **364**, 365, 366 (*var.*), 367-8, mourns Pamela **369-70**, reunited with Pyrocles **371-3**, 374-83, 385, 391, 394-5, 401-2, 419, 422, 434

Philoxenus, son of Timotheus, 50 (*var.*), 51-6, 220, 347, 382

Phrygia, evil king of, 139, 144-51

Phrygia, nobleman, later king of, 150, 152, 234

Plangus, prince of Iberia, cousin of Tiridates and Artaxia, stepson of Andromana, 117-8, 130, 135, 160, 'Complaint of Plangus' **171-7**, 178-9, 181, affair with Andromana **186-7**, 188-92, 202-3, 214, 217, 239, 257, 258 (*var.*), attempts to save Antiphilus **260-4**

Plexirtus, bastard of the king of Galatia by his concubine (Andromana's mother), half-brother of Leonatus, father of Zelmane, later king of Armenia by his marriage to Artaxia, 83, 154 (*var.*), 155-60, 218, 224 (*var.*), 225, 227-8, 229 (*var.*), 230-6, 259, 263-4

Plexirtus' captain, 234 (*var.*), 273-6

Plexirtus' counsellor, 234 (*var.*), 273-4

Plistonax, killed by Musidorus 298

Policrates, killed by Amphialus 295

Polixena, an Arcadian lady 84

Polycetes, an Arcadian knight, honourably in love with Gynecia, 84

Pontus, evil king of, 150-3

Pontus, new queen of, sister of evil king, 152

Pontus, nobleman of, friend of Euarchus, later new king of, 147, 152, 154 (*var.*), 157-8, 160, 228, 230, 232, 234-5

Pontus, envious counsellor *of*, 150 (*var.*), 151-2

Pontus, giants of, 150 (*var.*), 152-3

Pyrocles, prince of Macedon, son of Euarchus and Dorilaus' sister, 1 (*var.*), 3-8, 10, 20 (*var.*), 21, 27 (*var.*), captain of the helots **31-33**, 34-5, 37 (*var.*), 38-48, 57, meets Musidorus again as Zelmane **58-66**, seeks out Philoclea **66-73**, pursued by Basilius and Gynecia **74-7**, 80, 83-4, fights at Phalantus' challenge **86-9**, meets Dorus **90-4**, 95, kills the lion **96-101**, 102 (*var.*), love-complaints of Gynecia and Basilius **103-7**, 108, 116-8, 120-6, 128, 130, 134 (*var.*), 135-6, 139-41, 144-8, 150, 152-3, 157-60, observes the bathers **161-8**, meets and attacks Amphialus **168-71**, 177-81, 184-5, 192-4, surprised by Basilius **195-7**, surprised by Philoclea; reveals his identity **197-202**, tells her of his adventures **203-38**, 239-40, fights the rebels **242-50**, 253 (*var.*), 254-60, 263-5, 271, captured with the princesses **273-4**, 277, 279, 288-9, 305-6, 334 (*var.*), humours Artesia to free Philoclea **335-7**, 338, 346, 354, 359-60, 362, 364-5, 366 (*var.*), sees the mock-execution **368-70**, 371-2, believes Philoclea is dead **373-6**, 377-80, 390-5, 397, fights Anaxius and his brothers **398-403**, 404, 419-20, 422, 425, 430, 434

Sarpedon, killed by Musidorus 298
Sicyonian knight, 83
Strephon, a shepherd, 1-3, 6-9, 19, 118, 417-19, 430-2
Strophilus, killed by Musidorus 298

Telamon, an Arcadian knight, 84
Telenor, brother of Tydeus, 154 (*var*), 158-60, 224 (*var.*), 227-30, 233
Thessalia, queen of, sister of Euarchus, wife of Dorilaus, mother of Musidorus, 115, 138-41, 226, 401
Thrace, king of, 139

Timotheus, Corinthian noble, father of Philoxenus, foster-father of Amphialus, 51–2, 54–5, 382

Tiridates, king of Armenia, brother of Artaxia, cousin of Plangus, 160, besieges Erona **177–8**, holds Antiphilus hostage **179–80**, 192, 202–3, 212, 214, 233, 260–3

Tiridates, son of, 263

Tressennius, injured by Anaxius, killed by Lycurgus 341

Tydeus, brother of Telenor, 154 (*var.*), 158–60, 224 (*var.*), 227–30, 233

Urania, beloved of Claius and Strephon, 1–3, 9, 83, 85, 417–19, 430–2

White Knight, 337 (*var.*), 341, 349 (*var.*), 357

Zelmane, daughter of Plexirtus, 57, 66, 68, 83, 214 (*var.*), 218, 222, 224 (*var.*), 225–6, 229–33, 235, 264

Zelmane, assumed name of Pyrocles (q.v.)

Zoana, an Arcadian lady, 84

Zoilus, brother of Anaxius and Lycurgus, 341, 358, 362, 393–4, fights, and is killed by, Pyrocles **398–9**

INDEX OF OTHER NAMES

(Mainly Classical; bolded page numbers refer to the main text)

Achilles, xxx, **402**, 476, 478, 552, 559
Actaeon, xxv, **11**, 461, 471–2
Adonis, xxxiii, **278**, 533
Aeneas, xxiv, xxix–xxx, xxxiii, **11**, **153**, **207**, **351**, 461, 517, 536, 552, 561
Aeolus, **250**, 527
Aesculapius, **88**, **389**, 484
Alcyone, xviii, xxv, 457–8
Alecto, **197**, 514
Alpheus, **96**, 485
Amazon, 58–9, 61–2, 66, 68, 70, 72, 89, 95, 97, 106, 169, **348**, 393, 399, 474, 478, 550
Antiope (Hippolyte), xxxiii, **348**, 550
Apollo, xxvi, xxxiv, **59**, **80**, 95, 125, **164**, **183**, 253 (*var.*), 265–6, 272, **303**, **388**, **396**, **427**, **429**, **434**, 457, 475, 485, 507, 510, 528, 560
Arachne, **241**, 524
Arethusa, xxxiii, **96**, 485
Argus, **183**–4, 509–10
Ariadne, 535, 537
Atalanta, xxv, **11**, 461, 501
Atlas, **167**, 504
Atropos, **345**, **389**, 549
Aurora, **164**

Bacchus, xxvi, **251**, **273**,

Cadmus, **237**, 524
Centaurs, xxxi, **244**, 525
Ceres, **298**, 537–8
Ceyx, xviii, xxv, 457–8
Charon, **98**, **296**, **382**, 557
Cimmerii (Cimmerians), **270**, 531
Croesus, 551
Cupid, xxiv, xxxiii, **3**, **14**, **35**, 74–5, 81, 92, 165–7, 177, 179, 181 (*var.*), **182**–4, 270, 280, 284, 304, 352, 364, 394, 406, 417, 458, 462, 479, 502, 509–10, 559
Cyane, 514

Danae, xxiv, xxxiii, **195**, 513–14

Daphne, xxxiii, **59**, 475, 485, 510
Diana (Diane), xxiii–xxv, xxxiii, **11**, **69**, **124**, **127**, **219**, 302–4, **364**, 461, 478, 520, 537–8
Dido, 517

Echo, **45**, 418, 429, 433–4
Eros, *see* Cupid
Eurytus, father of Iole, **348**, 550

Fama, 520
Fortuna (Fortune), 497, 525
Furies, **364**, 514, 554

Ganymede, 479
Giants, **249**, 473
Gorgon (Medusa), **99**, **283**, 486
Graces, **167**

Helen of Troy (Helena), xxv, xxx, xxxiii, **11**, **348**, 461, 469, 551
Hercules, xxv, **23**, **58**, **68**, **99**, **322**, **348**, 461, 466, 478, 487, 501, 539, 550
Hesperides, 501, 552
Homer, **19–20**; *see also* General Index
Hyacinth, 558
Hymen, **260**

Io, **183**, 509
Iole, xxv, xxxiii, **11**, **348**, 461, 550
Iris, **14**, **73**, 462

Jove, *see* Jupiter
Juno, **14**, **23**, **183**–4, 462, 466, 501, 510, 528, 537–8
Jupiter, xxiv, xxxiii, **40**, **71**, **167**, **183**–4, **195**, **303**, **348**, **411**, 466, 469, 479, 501, 513–14, 527, 537–8, 551

Lapiths, xxxi, **244**, 525
Latona, **69**, **257**, 478, 528
Leda, **167**, 551

Mars, **35**, **174**, **221**, **263**, 291 (*var.*), **338**, 352, 397, 400, 507, 536

INDEX OF OTHER NAMES

Medusa, *see* Gorgon
Menelaus, **348**, 465, 551
Mercury, xxiv, xxvi, **79**, **183**, **394** (*var.*), **417**, 559
Minerva, *see* Pallas Athena
Minos, **249**, 526
Momus, **14**, 463

Narcissus, **46**
Nemean lion, **99**
Neptune, xxiv, xxx, **5**, **141**, **166**, 459
Nereus, xxx
Nestor, **269**
Nisus, 536

Oenone, **132**, 495
Omphale, xxv, xxxiii, **11**, **58**, 461
Ovid, **166**; *see also* General Index

Pallas Athena, **68**, **99**, **241**, **402**, 478, 486, 524, 537–8, 561
Pan, **14**, **98**, **404**, **405**, **407**, **427**, **429**, 462
Paris, **132**, **303**, **348**, 495, 537, 551
Pelops, **249**, 526
Penthesilea, **70**
Perseus, 513
Phaeton, xxvi, **174**, 483, 507
Philomela, **370**, **388**, 459, 489
Phoebus, *see* Apollo
Pluto, **276**, 514, 560

Poseidon, *see* Neptune
Priamus (Priam), **132**, 495
Proserpina, xxxiii, **197**, **399**, 514, 560
Proteus, **190**, 512
Pygmalion, **200**
Pygmies, **309**, 539
Pyrrhus, **70**, 478
Python, **257**, 528

Saturn, **14**, **303**, 462, 520
Senicia, fictitious Amazon queen, **70**
Sinon, **249** (*var.*), 526
Syrinx, **427**

Theseus, **348**, 535, 550
Thetis, xxx
Thraso, **338**, 547
Turnus, xxx, 525

Ulysses, **153**, 464

Venus, xxiii–xxvii, xxx, xxxiii, **5**, **11**, **14**, **79**, **88**, **92**, **129**, **165**, **174**, **183**, **219**, **278**, **293**, **302–4**, **351**, **364**, **424**, 457, 461–2, 475, 507, 520, 533, 536–7, 552, 559
Vesta, **225**, 522
Vulcan, **14**, **174**, **351**, 463, 507

Zephyrus, **379**
Zeus, *see* Jupiter

INDEX OF PLACES

Achaia, 57
Albion, 166
Alps, 419
Arcadia, 6, 8, 10 (*var.*), 12, 18, 20–2, 28–35, 38, 40, 45, 48, 51, 57, 74, 77, 84, 91, 93, 98, 100, 108, 116, 118, 121, 136, 161, 170, 219, 235, 246–8, 252–3, 272, 274, 276, 285, 316, 415, 427
Argos, 52, 80, 131, 246, 275
Armenia, 81, 160, 177, 181, 233, 236, 259, 264
Asia, 130, 174, 225, 229 (*var.*), 234–5, 259, 354, 393
Athens, 94, 120

Bithynia, 179, 222, 226, 229, 234
Byzantium, 116, 141–2

Candia, 182
Cardamyla, 29
Corinth, 22, 35–7, 50, 57, 77, 80, 86, 219, 221, 222, 316
Crete, 139
Cyprus, 12
Cythera, 1

Delphos, 13, 16, 256, 396–7

Egypt, 354
Elis, 57, 80–1
Enispe, 48, 251, 421
Enispus, *see* Enispe

Galatia, 154, 216, 226–7, 233–4
Greece, 5, 11–12, 29, 36, 79, 136, 162, 178, 181, 229, 231, 235–6, 254, 258, 264, 328

Hyrcania, 179

Iberia, 81, 179, 186, 213–15, 218 (*var.*), 220–3, 225, 231
India, 165
Ister, River, 410
Ithonia, 68

Lacedaemon, *see* Laconia

Laconia, 6–8, 10, 21, 23, 24, 26–9, 32, 34, 39, 47, 57, 77–83, 117–18, 238, 246, 264
Ladon, River, 161–3, 197, 369
Lycia, 81, 154 (*var.*), 160, 177–8, 203, 234, 261
Lydia, 139, 177 (*var.*

Macedon, 22, 44, 59, 115, 116, 136, 178, 199
Maenalus, Mt., 57
Mantinea, 40, 48, 118
Media, 20
Megalopolis, 171
Messena, 38
Messenia, 10, 38 (*var.*), 68

Nemea, 99

Olympia, 57

Pannonia, 139, 141
Paphlagonia, *see* Galatia
Peloponnesus, 7, 235
Pheneus, 48
Phrygia, 139, 144–5, 147, 150–2, 158, 216, 234
Pontus, 147, 152, 154, 157–8, 160, 216, 228–30, 232, 234–5

Rhipa, 48

Samothea, 300
Sicyonia, 57, 83
Sparta, *see* Laconia
Stymphalus, 48
Styx, River, 48, 304

Taenaria, 39
Tegea, 48
Tempe, 44, 71
Thessalia, 22, 44, 46, 92–3, 115, 118, 131, 138–9, 141–2, 144, 146, 178, 202, 401
Thrace, 116, 139, 141, 226
Trebizond, 227, 233–4
Troy, 402

INDEX OF FIRST LINES OF POEMS

	Page	OA No.
A hateful cure with hate to heal	254	25
Alas, how long this pilgrimage doth last!	172	30
And are you there, old Pas? In troth, I ever thought	426	29
Apollo great, whose beams the greater world do light	256	26
As I my little flock on Ister bank	410	66
Come, Dorus, come, let songs thy sorrows signify	405	7
Come, shepherd's weeds, become your master's mind	90	4
Dorus, tell me, where is thy wonted motion	422	28
Fair rocks, goodly rivers, sweet woods, when shall I see peace? Peace	433	31
His being was in her alone	346	[OP 3]
I joy in grief, and do detest all joys	430	72
If mine eyes can speak to do hearty errand	419	12
In faith, good Histor, long is your delay	414	67
In vain, mine eyes, you labour to amend	103	14
Let not old age disgrace my high desire	105	15
Loved I am, and yet complain of love	195	20
Methought some staves he missed – if so, not much amiss	221	[OP 1]
Miso, mine own pigsney, thou shalt hear news of Dametas	330	[OP 2]
My sheep are thoughts, which I both guide and serve	119	17
My words, in hope to blaze my steadfast mind	127	19
Now thanked be the great god Pan	98	5
Now was our heav'nly vault deprived of the light	300	73
Over these brooks, trusting to ease mine eyes	198	21
Poor painters oft with silly poets join	183	8
Since so mine eyes are subject to your sight	111	16
Since that to death is gone the shepherd high	386	75
The fire, to see my woes, for anger burneth	340	[CS 3]
Thou rebel vile, come, to thy master yield	421	27
Thy elder care shall from thy careful face	255	1
Transformed in show, but more transformed in mind	59	2
Unto a caitiff wretch whom long affliction holdeth	268	74
We love, and have our loves rewarded	404	6
What length of verse can serve brave Mopsa's good to show	14	3
What tongue can her perfections tell	164	62
With two strange fires of equal heat possessed	241	22
You goat-herd gods, that love the grassy mountains	417	71
You living pow'rs enclosed in stately shrine	126	18

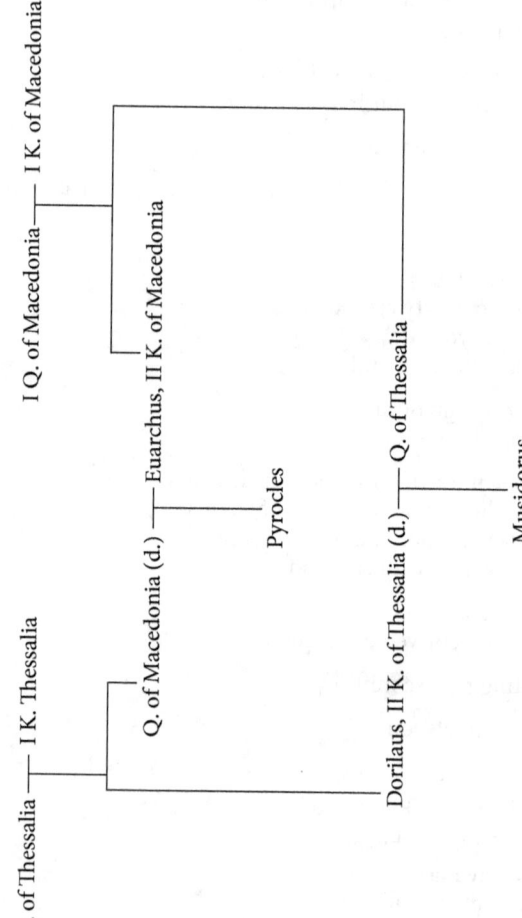

The royal families of Thessalia and Macedonia

GENEALOGICAL TABLES 595

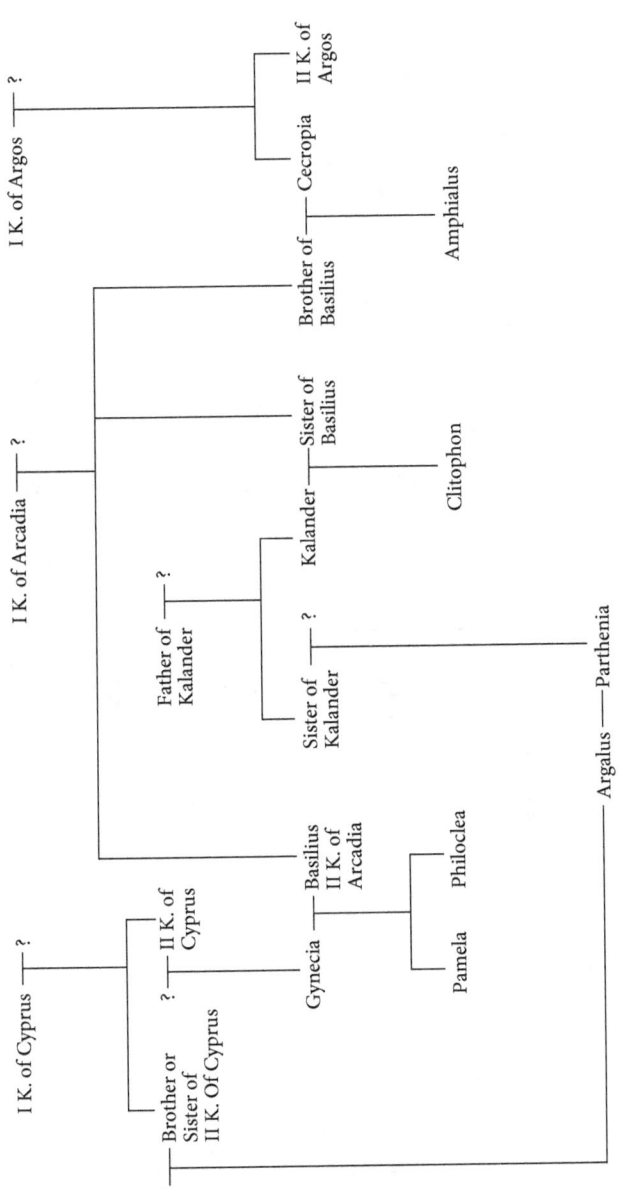

The royal families of Thessalia and Macedonia

596 GENEALOGICAL TABLES

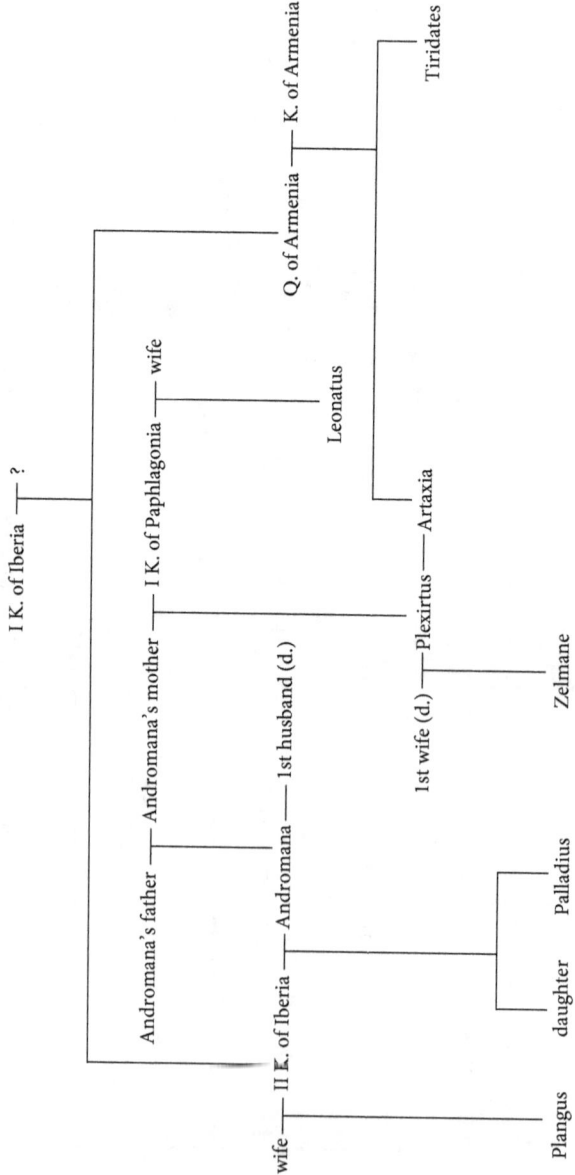

The royal families of Iberia, Armenia and Paphlagonia

GENERAL INDEX TO INTRODUCTION AND COMMENTARY

Aesop, 486
Alessandri, Livio, trans. Sidney, *Arcadia*, xxxiv
Alexander, Robert, xx
Alexander, Sir William, Supplement to Sidney's *Arcadia*, xxxvi–xxxvii, xlviii, lxvii n., lxviii–lxx, 521; *Aurora*, 504; *Tragedy of Croesus*, xxxviii
Allen, William, xliv
Amadis de Gaule, xvii–xviii, xxxiv, 470, 472, 481, 516, 545
Amyclas (king of Sparta), 469
Amyot, Jacques, trans. Heliodorus, *Aethiopian History*, xxi, xxxiii
Anderson, M. P., xxxiv
Angus, Earl of, *see* Douglas, Archibald
Anton, Robert, *Moriomachia*, xxxviii
Arcadia (country), xxvii, xxxix, 469, 473, 527, 552
'Arcadian Lovers or Metamorphosis of Princes', xxxvii
Argalus (king of Sparta), 469
Ariosto, Ludovico, *Orlando Furioso*, xxii, xxxiv, xxxvi, 479, 486, 537, 542
Ariston, 469
Aristotle, *Ethics*, 476; *Nicomachean Ethics*, 421–2; *Politics*, 463, 468, 476; *Rhetoric*, 459, 465
Arkadische Schäfer-Lust, xxxiv
Arundel, Earl of, xiv
Ascham, Roger, *The Schoolmaster*, 474; *Toxophilus*, 510
Aubrey, John, 'Brief Lives', 467; *The Natural History ... of Surrey*, xlvii
Augustine, St, *De Patientia*, 507

Bacon, Francis *Resuscitatio*, 566
Bandello, Matteo, xvii, xxii–xxiii; *Certain Tragical Discourses*, 475
Baron, Robert, *Apology for Paris*, xxxviii; *The Cyprian Academy*, xxxviii; *Mirza*, xxxviii; *Pocula Castalia*, xxxviii
Batman, Stephen, *Batman vppon Bartholome*, 525
Baudoin, Jean, trans. Sidney, *Arcadia*, xxxiv
Beard, Thomas, trans. Jean Chassanion, *The Theatre of Gods Iudgements*, 529
Beaumont, Francis, *Cupid's Revenge*, xxxvii; *Philaster*, xxxvii
Becon, Thomas, *The Sycke Mans Salue*, 536
Bedingfield, Thomas, trans. C. Corte, *The Art of Riding ... Reduced*, xx
Belling, Sir Richard, *A Sixth Book to ... Arcadia*, xxxvi, l
Belleforest, François de, xxii
Berni, Francesco, 462–3
Bible, Apocrypha – Book of Jubilees, 458; Book of Wisdom, 507; Hebrews, 507; *King James Bible*, 566; Proverbs, 507; Psalms, *see* Sidney, Mary, Countess of Pembroke; Sidney, Sir Philip
Bion, 476
Blagrave, John, *The Mathematical Iewel*, 479
Blague, Thomas, *A Schoole of Wise Conceytes*, 477, 486
Blason des couleurs, 542
Blount, Thomas, *Academy of Eloquence*, xxxv, 546,
Blount, W[illiam], xviii, lxvi, 553
Blundeville, Thomas, *The True Order and Method of Writing and Reading Histories*, 467; trans. F. Grisone, *The Art of Riding*, xx; trans. F. Grisone, *The Four Chiefest Offices ... Horsemanship*, xx, xxvi, 494, 542, 544
Boccaccio, Giovanni, *Filostrato*, 457
Boleyn, Ann, 521
Boniface, Draconet, 459
Bossewell, John, *Workes of Armorie*, 567
Boyd, Zacharie, *The Last Battell of the Soule in Death*, 560

Boyle, Roger, Earl of Orrery, *Parthenissa*, xxxix
Brantôme, Pierre de Bourdeilles de, 548
Brathwaite, Richard, *The Two Lancashire Lovers*, xxxix
Bressand, Friedrich Christian, *Der königliche Schäfer*, xxxv
Breton, Nicholas, *The Arbour of Amorous Devices*, xlii, lxiii, 548
Browne, William, of Tavistock, *Britannia's Pastorals*, xxxviii
Burleigh, Lord, *see* Cecil, Robert
Burton, Robert, *The Anatomy of Melancholy*, 469, 475–6, 502–3, 521–2, 544

Caballa, 545
Caius, John, *Of Englishe Dogges*, 501
Caldwell, James, *The Countess of Mar's Arcadia*, xxxiv
Calvin, John, *Sermons*, 506, 523, 532
Cambridge University, 461
Camden, William, *Annales*, lxx; *The Remains*, xix
Camerarius, Joachim, the younger, *Symbolorum et Emblematum*, xix, xxvi n., xlvii n., 483–4, 488, 491, 542–3, 548, 555, 558
Cantacuzenus, John (John VI), *Historiarum Libri IV*, xviii
Carracciolo, Pasqual, xx
Castiglione, Baldassare, 503; *The Courtier*, 463, 468
Castilio, Balthasar, *see* Castiglione, B.
Cats, Jacob, *Emblemata*, 544
Caxton, William, *Mirror of the World*, 528
Cecil, Robert, Lord Burleigh, xix
Chappelain, Geneviève, trans. Sidney, *Arcadia*, xxxiv, xl
Charles I, xxxix
Chassanion, Jean, *The Theatre of Gods Iudgements*, 529
Chaucer, Geoffrey, *The Book of the Duchess*, 465, 543–4; *Canterbury Tales*, 465, 467, 471; *The Legend of Good Women*, 509, 517; *Troilus and Criseyde*, 457, 477, 522, 530, 540
Churchyard, Thomas, *A Discourse of the Queen's Majesty's Entertainment in Suffolk and Norfolk*, 525; 'A Discourse of an Old Souldiour and a Young', 488; *The First Part of Churchyardes Chippes*, 506; 'A Tragicall Discourse of the Vnhappy Mans Life', 506
Cicero, *DeAmicitia*, xiv, 470; *De Officiis*, 470; *In Catilinam*, 490
Clerke, Bartholomew, 488–9
Clidamas, or The Sicilian Tale, 557
Clifford, Christopher, *School of Horsemanship*, xx, 543
Codrington, Robert, *The Second Part of Youths Behavior*, 560
Coldock, Francis, xliv
Coler, Johann, *Oeconomica Ruralis et Domestica*, 491
Colonna, Francesco, *Hypnerotomachia*, 461
Constable, Henry, xxxix
Cooper, Thomas, ed., Sir Thomas Elyot, *Bibliotheca Eliotae*, 461
Cornwallis, William, *Essayes of Certaine Paradoxes*, 533
Corte, Claudio, xx; *Il Cavallerizzo*, xx
Cotton, Charles, xxxix
Craig, Alexander, *Amorous Songs, Sonnets, and Elegies*, xxxvii; *The Poetical Recreations*, xxxvii
Crashaw, William, 464
Critz, Emanuel de, xl
Crowne, John, *Pandion andAmphigenia*, xxxix
Culman, Leonard, *Sententiae Pueriles*, 476
Curll, Edmund, lxx
Cyrus, 465

D., G., *A Brief Discovery of Doctor Allen's Seditious Drifts*, xliv
D., R., trans. F. Colonna, *Hypnerotomachia*, 461
Dallington, Robert, *The View of France*, 481
Daniel, Samuel, trans. P. Giovio, *The Worthy Tract of Paulus Jovius*, 484, 488, 574; *The Ciuile Wars*, 558
Day, John, *Isle of Gulls*, xxxvii
De Caede et Interitu... Henrici Tertii, xlv

Delectable Demaundes, and Pleasaunt Questions, 572
Delle Colonne, Guido, *Historia Trojana*, 478
Denny, Edward, xx
Devereux, Penelope, *see* Rich, Lady Penelope
Devereux, Walter, first Earl of Essex, 549
Donne, John, 481, 507, 530
Dorset, Marquis of, 482
Douglas, Archibald, eighth Earl of Angus, xiv
Douglas, Gavin, trans. Virgil, *Aeneid*, 461, 511, 517; trans. M. Vegio, 'The Threttene Booke of *Eneados*', 493
Drant, Thomas, trans. *Horace's Art of Poetry*, 487
'A Draught of ... Arcadia', xxxvii
Drayton, Michael, *Ideas Mirrour*, 506; *Polyolbion*, 472
Drummond, William, of Hawthornden, xxxi n., xxxix
Du Bartas, Guillaume de Saluste, sieur, *see* Saluste du Bartas, Guillaume de
Dudley, Robert, Earl of Leicester, xix n., xx, 467, 488
Dunbar, William, 570
Duplessis-Mornay, Philippe de Mornay, seigneur du Plessis, *see* Mornay, Philippe de
Du Wes, Giles, *An Introductory ... To Speak French Truly*, 506
Dyer, Edward, xiv, xlii

Edward III, 532
Eld, George, lxviii n.
Elder, William, *The Academy of Complements* 502; *Pearls of Eloquence*, 502
Elizabeth I, xx, xl, xlii, 467, 472, 483, 507, 519–21, 537–3, 551
Elyot, Sir Thomas, *Bibliotheca Eliotae*, 461; *The Dictionary of Syr Thomas Eliot, Knyght*, 494; *The Governor*, 517–8
England's Helicon, 484
England's Parnassus, 463, 476, 502–5, 550
Epicurus, 476
Essex, Earl of, *see* Devereux, Walter

Estienne, Charles, *Dictionarium*, 459; and Jean Liebault, *Praedium Rusticum*, trans. by C. Estienne, *L'Agriculture et Maison Rustique*, 458
Exequiae, xlv

The Famous History ... Being an Abstract of Pembroke's Arcadia, lxx
Fenton, Geoffrey, trans. M. Bandello, *Certain Tragical Discourses*, 475
Ferdinand of Tirol, xxi, 479,
Field of the Cloth of Gold, 542
Field, Richard, xlviii
Fleming, Abraham, *A Panoplie of Epistles*, 495, 528; trans. John Caius, *Of Englishe Dogges*, 501
Fletcher, John, *Cupid's Revenge*, xxxvii; *The False One*, 536; *Philaster*, xxxvii
Fletcher, Phineas, *Britain's Ida (Venus and Anchises)*, xxxviii, 504; *Piscatory Eclogues*, xxxviii; *Purple Island*, xxxviii, 503; *Siceledes*, xxxviii
Florio, John, xlvi; *Queen Anna's New World of Words*, 494; *Second Fruits*, 510; *World of Words*, xlvi; trans. Montaigne, *Essays*, xlv–xlvi, 464–5, 472, 485, 540, 551
Florio, Rose, xlvi
Ford, Emmanuel, *Parismus*, xxxviii
Ford, John, *Love's Sacrifice*, xxxviii, 488
The Fortress of Perfect Beauty, xvi, 503, 520–1, 542–3
Four Foster Children of Desire, 503
Foxe, John, *Actes and Monuments*, 485, 511
Fraunce, Abraham, xix; *Arcadian Rhetoric*, xxxv, xlii, lxiii, lxxiv, 487, 530, 548, 563; *The Countess of Pembroke's Ivychurch*, xiv; 'Emblemata Varia', xix, 484, 488; *Insignium, Armorum*, 472, 544; 'Symbolicae Philosophiae liber quartus et ultimis de Symbolis absolutis', 520; *The Third part of The Countess of Pembroke's Ivychurch*, xviii

Galle, Cornelius, 486
Garter, Bernard, *The Joyful Receiving of the Queen's ... Majesty ... into Norwich*, 537–8

Gascoigne, George, xxv n.; *Certain Notes of Instruction*, 462; 'The Fable of Philomela', 517; *A Hundreth Sundrie Flowres*, 535; *The Noble Art of Venery*, 471, 486; *The Steele Glas*, 517
Gaston III, Count de Foix and Béarn, 471
Gauden, John, *Eikon Basilike*, xxxix
Gentile, Alberico, *De Legationibus Libri Tres*, xiv
Gentile, Scipione, *Nereus ... Philippi Sidnaei Filiae*, xliv
Gheeraerts, Marcus, 472
Gifford, George, *The Manner of Sidney's Death*, 549–50
Gilbert, Sir Humphrey, xix
Gill, Alexander, *Logonomia Anglica*, xxxv, 531
Gil Polo, Gaspar, *Enamoured Diana*, xvii, 470
Giovio, Paulo, *Dialogo dell'Imprese*, xix, 484, 488
Glapthorne, Henry, *Argalus and Parthenia*, xxxvii
Gl'Ingannati, xvii
Golding, Arthur, trans. Calvin, *Sermons of Master Iohn Caluin, vpon the Booke of Iob*, 506, 523, 532; *Sermons of M. Iohn Caluin, vpon the Fifth Booke of Moses Called Deuteronomie*, 506, 523 trans. Ovid, *Metamorphoses*, 457–8, 463, 506–8, 528, 546
Goldwell, Henry, *Brief Declaration*, xvi, 503, 520
Gorges, Sir Arthur, 472
Gosson, Stephen, *The School of Abuse*, 506
Greaves, Paul, *Grammatica Anglicana*, xxxv
Greek Anthology, 537
Greene, Robert, *Menaphon (Greenes Arcadia)*, 525 *Planetomachia*, 498
Greville, Fulke, xvi, xix, xxxix, xlv–xlvi, l, 542; Letter to Walsingham, xiv, xvi, xxxiv, xlv, xlix; *Caelica*, 506; Dedication to Sir Philip Sidney, xlv; *Letter to an Honourable Lady*, 506, 531 *The Life of the Renowned Sr Philip Sidney*, 539
Grey, Henry, xiv

Griffin, Besse, 462
Grimmelshausen, H. J. C. von, *Simplicissimus*, xxxv
Grisone, Federico, xvi; *The Art of Riding*, xx; *The Four Chiefest Offices ... Horsemanship*, xx, xxvi, 494, 542, 544
Guarini, Giovanni Battista, xxxi
Guevara, Antonio de, *The Diall of Princes*, 482; *A Dispraise of the Life of a Courtier*, 464
Guilpin, Everard, *Skialetheia*, xxxv
Gwalther, Rudolf, *Certaine Godlie Homelies*, 511
Gwinne, Matthew, xlv–xlvi

Hall, Arthur, *Ten Books of Homer's Iliades, Translated out of French*, 507
Harington, Sir John, xli; *Metamorphosis of Ajax*, 470; trans. Ariosto, *Orlando Furioso*, xxii, 537, 542
Harvey, Gabriel, 508; *Four Letters*, xxxiv; *Pierces Supererogation*, xxxii, xxxiv
Hatton, Sir Christopher, xviii n.
Hawkins, Henry, *Parthenia Sacra*, 550
Hayward, Sir John, *The Liues of the III Normans*, 536; *A Sanctuarie for a Troubled Soule*, 471, 480, 488–9, 497, 500, 511–12, 514, 530,
Heliodorus, *Aethiopian History* xvi–xvii, xxi–xxiii, xxxiii, xl n., 459, 465, 475, 519
Henry II of France, 536
Henry III of France, xlv
Henry VIII, xx
Herodotus, *History*, 469–70, 538, 551
The Heroical Adventures of the Knight of the Sea, xxxix
Hesiod, *Theogony*, 510
Heylyn, Peter, *Cosmographie*, lxx
Heywood, John, *Two Hundred Epigrammes*, 489
Hippocrates, 494
Hoby, Sir Thomas, trans. B. Castiglione, *The Courtier*, 463, 468
Holdsworth, Richard, xliii
Holinshed, Raphael, *Chronicles*, xix n., 500, 549
Holland, Philemon, trans. Pliny, *Natural History*, 551

Homer, 465; *Iliad*, xxx, 465, 486, 507, 544, 550, 561; *Odyssey*, xxi, 459, 465, 531

Hooker, Richard, *Laws of Ecclesiastical Polity*, lxi; *The Works of Mr. Richard Hooker*, 533

Horace, *Art of Poetry*, 487; *Epistles*, 466–7, 487, 496, 503; *Odes*, 481; *Satires*, 464

Hoskyns, John, 531; *Directions for Speech and Style*, vii, xvi, xxi, xxxi, xxxiii, xxxv, lxxiv–lxxv, lxxxiii–lxxxiv, 457–8, 466–7, 470, 472–8, 481–2, 485–93, 495–501, 505, 507, 512, 514–20, 522–4, 526, 529, 531–33, 535–7, 539–41, 543–6, 548–57, 559–61; *see also* Appendix IV

Howell, James, Δενδρολογια. *Dodona's Grove*, 506

Hume, David, of Godscroft, *The History of the Houses of Douglas and Angus*, xiv

Ingelo, Nathaniel, *Bentivolio and Urania*, xxxix

James I, xxxiv, lxx, 494

Johnstoun, James, 'Supplement to the Third Book of *Arcadia*', xxxvi, lxx, 561

Jones, John, *The Benefit of the Auncient Bathes of Buckstones*, 504

Jones, Robert, *The Second Book of Songs and Airs*, 514

Jonghe, Felix van Sambix de, trans. *Arcadia*, xxxiv

Jonson, Ben, xxxi; 'Conversations', xxxi; *Every Man Out of His Humour*, xxxv; *Volpone*, 503

Kempis, Thomas à, *Of the Imitation of Christ*, 485

King, John, Bishop of London, xxxiv

King Horn, 497

Kyd, Thomas, *Spanish Tragedy*, 537

Lambard, William, *A Perambulation of Kent*, 550

Lambinus, Dionysius (Denis Lambin), 467

Lancelot Du Lak, lix

Langham, Robert, *A Letter*, xix n.

Languet, Hubert, xix, 467, 489–90

Lanquet, Thomas, *An Epitome of Chronicles*, 573

Laura (of Petrarch), xxiii, xxxiii, 484

Lawson, George, *An Exposition of the Epistle to the Hebrewes*, 536

Lee, Sir Henry, xiv–xv, 521

Leicester, Earl of, *see* Dudley, Robert

Leicester's Commonwealth, i.e., *The Copy of a Letter, Written by a Master of Art of Cambridge ... Concerning ... the Earl of Leicester and His Friends*, xv

Leland, John, *A Learned and True Assertion of... Prince Arthur*, xliv

Lemnius, Levinus, *The Touchstone of Complexions*, 519

Liddell, George, *Divine Meditations*, 490, 560

Liebault, Jean, and C. Estienne, *Praedium Rusticum*, 458

Ling, Nicholas, *Politeuphuia*, xxxv, 487, 512

Lithgow, William, *The Gushing Teares of Godly Sorrow*, 560

Lodge, Thomas, *An Alarum Against Vsurers*, 502

Lloyd, Lodowick, *The Pilgrimage of Princes*, 486

Lloyd, Nicholas, ed. C. Estienne, *Dictionarium*, 459

Loarte, Gaspar de, *The Exercise of a Christian Life*, 474

Louis XII, 529

Love's Changelings' Change, xxxvii

Lownes, Humphrey, xlviii, lxviii

Lownes, Matthew, xlviii, lxviii–lxx

Lucan, xxxi; *The Civil War*, 528, 552

Lucian, *Alexander*, xviii

Lucretius, *De Rerum Natura*, 457

Lupton, Thomas, *The Christian Against the Iesuite*, 533

Lycurgus, 459, 468

Lydgate, John, *Temple of Glas*, xxv

Lyly, John, *Euphues*, xxxii, lxxii n., lxvii–lxviii, 508; *Euphues his England*, 463, 511; *Midas*, 560; *Pappe With an Hatchet*, xxxii

The Mabinogion, 484

Machaut, Guillaume de, xxi, 544

Machiavelli, Niccolò, *The Prince*, 561, 492
Mackenzie, Sir George, *Aretina*, xxxix
Macrobius, Ambrosius Theodosius, *Commentary on the Dream of Scipio*, 501, 528, 540; *Saturnalia*, xviii
Maihew, Edward, *A Treatise of the Groundes of the Old and Newe Religion*, 560
Mainwaring, Matthew, *Vienna*, 553
Malory, Sir Thomas, *Morte Darthur*, 536
Mareschal, André, *La Cour Bergère*, xxxiv
Markham, Gervase, *Cavelarice*, 494; *Country Contentments*, 471; *The English Arcadia*, xvii, xxxvi
Marlowe, Christopher, xxxi; *Dr. Faustus*, 528; *Hero and Leander*, 474; *The Massacre at Paris*, 498; *1 Tamburlaine*, 493, 506, 549, 559; *2 Tamburlaine*, 545; trans. *Ovid's Elegies*, 504
Marmion, Edmund, xl
Marot, Clément, 542, 558
Marsh, Thomas, trans. *Seneca his Tenne Tragedies*, 549
Marston, John, *The Malcontent*, xxxix
Marvell, Andrew, xxxix, 472
Massinger, Philip, *The Unnatural Combat*, 477–8
Melvill, David, *The Melvill Book of Roundels*, 486
Mennes, Sir John, and James Smith, *Musarum Deliciae*, 462
Mercator, Gerard, xv
Meres, Francis, *Palladis Tamia*, 532
Milton, John, *Commonplace Book*, xviii n.; *Comus*, 459; *Eikonoklastes*, xxxix; 'elegia v', 457; *Lycidas*, xxxix, 558; *Paradise Lost*, xxxix, 528; *Samson Agonistes*, xxxix
Mirror for Magistrates, 485–6
Molyneux, Edmund, xix
Montaigne, Michel de, *Essays*, xlv, 464, 472, 485, 540, 551
Montemayor, Jorge de, *Diana*, xvi–xviii, xxi–xxii, xxxvi, xlv, 457, 461, 481
Moore, Richard, lxx
More, Sir Thomas, xviii, xxxiii, 546
Morgan, McNamara, *Philoclea*, xxxvii
Morgan, Nicholas, *The Perfection of Horse-manship*, 560
Mornay, Philippe de, *Traité de la vérité de la religion chrestienne*, xlv; *A Woorke Concerning the Trewnesse of Christian Religion*, 469
Moryson, Fynes, *Itinerary*, 542–3
Moschus, 481, 558
The Most Pleasant and Delightful History of Argalus and Parthenia, xxxvii
Mucedorus, xxxix
Munday, Anthony, trans. *Palmerin d'Oliva*, 486
Mynshew, xiv

Nash, Thomas (b. 1588), *Quaternio*, 488
Nashe, Thomas, *An Almond for a Parrat*, 508; *The Anatomy of Absurdity*, 541; *Have With You To Saffron-Walden*, 542; *Nashes Lenten Stuffe*, 499; *Pierce Penilesse*, 488; *Strange Newes*, 508; *The Unfortunate Traveller*, xl, 459, 477–8, 480, 511
Needham, Sir Robert, 555
Neoptolemus, *see* Pyrrhus
Neville, Alexander, *Academiae Cantabrigiensis Lachrymae*, xxxiii n.
The New Metamorphosis, xxxix
Newton, Thomas, trans. Levinus Lemnius, *The Touchstone of Complexions*, 519
Niclaes, Hendrik, *Prouerbia HN*, 572
North, Thomas, trans. A. de Guevara, *The Diall of Princes*, 482; trans. A. F. Doni, *The Morall Philosophie of Doni*, 478; trans. Plutarch, *Lives*, 527
Norton, Robert, trans. Rudolf Gwalther, *Certaine Godlie Homelies*, 511

Opitz, Martin, xxxiv
Ortelius, Abraham, xv
Ottley, Adam, xlii
Overbury, John, *Characters*, xxxviii
Ovid, *Amores*, 504; *Ars Amatoria*, 530; *Heroides*, 461, 476, 493, 495, 517, 522, 530, 535–6, 545; *Metamorphoses*, xviii, xxxiii, 457–9, 461, 463, 471–3, 475, 478–9, 482, 485, 497, 503–4, 507–8, 510, 513–15, 524–5, 527–31, 533, 538, 546, 548, 558; *Remedio Amoris*, 475

GENERAL INDEX

Ovide Moralisé en Prose, 528
Oxinden, Henry, xxxviii

Palmerin d'Oliva, 486
A Panoplie of Epistles, 495, 528
Parisetti, Flamineo, Il Re Pastore, xxxiv–xxxv
Parrot, Sir John, 521
Patrizi, Francesco, Della Historia Diece Dialoghi, 467
Pausanias, Description of Greece, 468–9, 541
Peacham, Henry, The Complete Gentleman, xix; Minerva Britanna, xix, 486
Peele, George, Arraignment of Paris, 495, 537
Pembroke, Countess of, see Sidney, Mary
Petrarch (Petrarca), Francesco, 563; De Vita Solitaria (The Life of Solitude), 470; Phisicke Against Fortune, 513; Rime, xxiii, xxxiii, 504, 538; Trionfo della Morte, 484
Pettie, George, A Petite Palace of Pettie's Pleasure, 458
Philip II of Spain, 536
Philomusus, see Elder, William
Phoebus, see Gaston III, Count de Foix and Béarn
The Phoenix Nest, 535
Pilkington, Francis, The Second Set of Madrigals and Pastorals, 484
Place, Pierre de la, Treatise of the Excellencie of a Christian Man, 553
Plato, 501–2; Laws, 458; Republic, 463
Pliny, Natural History, 464, 485, 551
Plutarch, Lives, 459, 468, 527; Moralia, 459
Polaris, 553
Polemon, John, All the Famous Battels, 516
Ponsonby, William, xliv, xlvi, xlviii, lxv n., lxvii–lxviii, 555–6
Poole, Joshua, The English Parnassus, 503
Porter, Jane, Aphorisms of Sir Philip Sidney, xxxv
Porter, Jerome, Flowers of the Liues of the Most Renowned Saincts of the Three Kingdoms, 536
Powell, Thomas, Tom of All Trades, xxxiv
Pugliano, John Pietro, xx
Puttenham, George, Art of English Poesy, 459, 502, 507, 546; see also Appendix IV

Quarles, Francis, Argalus and Parthenia, xxxvii, xl
Quarles, John, The History of ... Dimagoras, xxxvii

Rabelais, François, Gargantua, 494, 517
Radcliffe, Robert, fifth Earl of Sussex, 521
Raleigh, Sir Walter, 489; The First Part of the History of the World, 533
Ramus, Petrus (Pierre de La Ramée), xxxv
Ratis Raving, xliii
Ravenscroft, Thomas, Pammelia. Musics Miscellany, 486
Reusner, Nicolas, Emblemata, xlvii n.
Rhetorica Ad Herennium, 563
Rich, Lady Penelope (Devereux), xiv–xv, xxxix, xlv
Richard III, 533
Richardson, Samuel, Pamela, xxxix
Robinson, Richard, trans. John Leland, A Learned and True Assertion of ... Prince Arthur, xl
Rogers, Thomas, trans. Thomas à Kempis, Of the Imitation of Christ, 485
Ronsard, Pierre de, 509
Ruscelli, Girolamo, Le Imprese Illustri, xix

S., J., Andromana, xxxvii
St. John the Baptist, xv
Sainte-Maure, Benoît de, Roman de Troie, xviii, 478
Saker, Austin, Narbonus, 472, 486, 508–9
Saltonstall, Wye, Picturae Loquentes, xxxiv
Saluste du Bartas, Guillaume de, La semaine, xiv, xlv; L'Uranie, 474
Sanderson, Robert, Two Sermons, 554
Sandys, George, trans., Ovid, Metamorphoses, 459, 479, 482, 503, 528, 548, 558
Sanford, Hugh, xlvi–xlviii, li–lix

Sannazaro, Jacopo, *Arcadia*, xvi–xvii, xxi–xxii, xxxiii, 479, 503, 558
Scaliger, Julius Caesar, *Poetices Libri Septem*, xxii
Schalvius, Heinrich, xxxiv
Schottelius, Justus Georg, *Teutsche Sprachkunst*, xxxv
Schwendi, Lazarus von, 467
Scoloker, Anthony, *Daiphantus*, xxxix
Scot, Reginald, *Discovery of Witchcraft*, xv
Segar, William, *Honor Military and Ciuill*, 549
Seneca, *Phoenissae*, xviii; *Seneca his Tenne Tragedies*, 549; *Thyestes*, 547
Shakespeare, William, xxxi, xxxviii, 460, 476, 511; *Antony and Cleopatra*, 545, 549; *As You Like It*, 472; *Comedy of Errors*, 573; *Coriolanus*, 461, 499; *Cymbeline*, 573; *Hamlet*, 494, 509, 567; *1 Henry IV*, 485, 543; *2 Henry IV*, 573; *Henry V*, 532, 570; *1 Henry VI*, 479, 559; *2 Henry VI*, 493, 500, 581; *3 Henry VI*, 537; *Henry VIII*, 520; *Julius Caesar*, 479, 519; *King Lear*, xxxviii, xl, 551; *Love's Labours Lost*, 478; *Macbeth*, 482; *The Merchant of Venice*, 554; *A Midsummer Night's Dream*, 471, 478, 486, 504, 566; *Othello*, 475, 514; *Pericles*, xxxix n., xl, 506, 537; *The Rape of Lucrece*, 491, 493, 496, 505, 526, 531, 549, 566; *Richard III*, 459, 518, 569; *Romeo and Juliet*, xxxix n., 480, 507, 568, 573; *Sonnets*, xxxviii, 465, 476, 530, 534, 540, 548; *Timon of Athens*, 477; *Troilus and Cressida*, 468, 559; *Twelfth Night*, 548; *Venus and Adonis*, 562; *The Winter's Tale*, 460, 493
Shirley, James, *A Pastoral Called The Arcadia*, xxxvii
Sidney, Elizabeth, Countess of Rutland, xliv–xlv
Sidney, Sir Henry, 467
Sidney, Lady Mary, 467
Sidney, Mary, Countess of Pembroke, xiii, xlvi–xlvii, xlix, 472, 494, 525
Sidney, Sir Philip, *Astrophil and Stella*, xv n.; *AS* 1, 458, 512; *AS* 3, 502; *AS* 4, 487; *AS* 5, 475; *AS* 7, 479; *AS* 12, 477, 479; *AS* 13, 479; *AS* 14, 476; *AS* 15, 515, 578; *AS* 21, 476; *AS* 25, 496; *AS* 27, 469; *AS* 36, 477; *AS* 38, 493; *AS* 40, 458; *AS* 41, xv, 458, 481; *AS* 49, 480; *AS* 53, xv, 549; *AS* 54, 480; *AS* 56, 462; *AS* 58, 539; *AS* 61, 489; *AS* 73, xv; *AS* 74, 502, 538; *AS* 81, 515; *AS* 86, 484; *AS* song v, xv, 493, 502–4; *AS* song vii, 462; *AS* song viii, xv; *AS* 98, 480; *AS* 103, 457, 459; *AS* 104, 552; *AS* song xi, 485; *AS* 106, 477; *Certain Sonnets*, *CS* 1, xlii; *CS* 2, xlii; *CS* 3, xvi, xlii–xliii, xlix, li, 548; *CS* 4, 459; *CS* 13, xlii, 522; *CS* 14, xlii; *CS* 15, xlii, 481; *CS* 16, xlii; *CS* 17, xlii, 538; *CS* 18, xlii; *CS* 19, xlii; *CS* 20, xlii; *CS* 21, xlii; *CS* 22, xlii; *CS* 23, xlii; *CS* 24, xlii; *CS* 25, xlii; *CS* 28, xvii; *CS* 29, xvii; *CS* 31, xlii; *CS* 32, xlii; *A Defence of Poetry*, xvi, xx, xxxiii, lxvii, lxix n., 457–8, 461, 464, 470, 474–5, 481, 485, 487, 496, 499, 501–2, 504–7, 513, 530, 538, 547, 561, 572–3, 583; *Defence of the Earl of Leicester*, xv, 488; *The Lady of May*, 550; 'A Letter to Queen Elizabeth', 464, 475, 499, 515; Letter to Languet of 19. xii. 73, xix; Letter to Robert Sidney of ? ii. 79, 467–8; Letter to Robert Sidney of 18. x. 80, xix, 468, 476; Letter to Edward Denny of 22. v. 80, xx, 467–8; Letter to Sir Francis Walsingham of 14. xii. 85, 488–9; *Old Arcadia*, xiii–xvii, xxi, xxiii, xxv n., xxxii, xxxiv–xxxvi, xli–xlii, xlv–xlvi, xlix–liii, lv–lx, lxii–lxiii, lxxiv n.; 435, 457, 459, 461, 464, 466, 470, 472, 476–8, 486–8, 490–3, 497, 501–4, 506, 509–10, 512–15, 526, 530–1, 542, 561–4, 567, 572, 574; *OA* 1, xliii, 528; *OA* 2, xlii–xliii, 474; *OA* 3, xxxiii, xlii–xliii, 462; *OA* 4, xliii, 484; *OA* 5, xliii, li, lix, 486; *OA* 7, lxxxi, lxxxiv, lix, lxi; *OA* 8, xliii, lv, 510; *OA* 11, xlii; *OA* 12, xlii; *OA* 13, xlii, lix, 483, 514, 548; *OA* 14, xlii–xliii, 487; *OA* 15, xlii–xliii, lii, lix, 488; *OA* 16, xlii–xliii, 489; *OA* 17, xlii–xliii, 490; *OA* 18, xlii–xliii, 492; *OA* 19, xlii–xliii, 492; *OA* 20, xlii–xliii, 513; *OA* 21, xlii–xliii, 514; *OA* 22, xlii–xliii, 524; *OA* 25, lx, lxx, 527; *OA* 26, lx, 528; *OA* 27, xlii; *OA* 28, xlii;

OA 30, xliii, lix, 505; *OA* 31, xlii, lxxxi–lxxxii, lix; *OA* 33, xlii; *OA* 34, xlii; *OA* 35, xlii; *OA* 36, 515; *OA* 38, xlii; *OA* 43, 548; *OA* 45, 530–1; *OA* 60, xlii; *OA* 62, xv, xlii–xliii, l, 502–3; *OA* 63, lxxxi, lx; *OA* 66, xxxix; *OA* 71, 490; *OA* 72, 542; *OA* 73, xvi, xliii–xliv, 537; *OA* 74, xvi, xlii–xliii, 490, 530; *OA* 75, xvi–xvii, xliii, lix, 557; *OA* 77, xliii; 'Other Poems', OP 1, xliii, 520; OP 2, xliii, 546; OP 3, xliii, xlix, li, 550; OP 4, lix, lxi, 458–9, 490, 503; OP 5, lix, lxi; 'Poems Possibly by Sidney' (and here accepted as his), PP 4, 520; PP 5, 520; metrical versions of the Psalms, PS 11, 528, 558; PS 16, 493; PS 26, 528; PS 30, 520; PS 39, 464; 'Wrongly Attributed Poems (but here accepted as his), AT 19, xlii, 520; AT 20, 538; AT 21, xlii, 520

Sidney, Robert, xix, 467–8, 476
Silvius, Aeneas, *De Duobus Amantibus*, 522
Smith, James, and Sir John Mennes, *Musarum Deliciae*, 462
Smith, John, *Mystery of Rhetoric Unveil'd*, xxxv
Spenser, Edmund, 460, 478–9, 486, 489, 500–1, 503, 514, 536; *Amoretti*, 503, 555; *Astrophel*, 470, 556; *The Faerie Queene*, xxxiv, xliv, lxv n., 477, 485–7, 493–4, 502, 503, 511, 514, 522, 524, 536–7, 565, 567; *An Hymne of Heavenly Beauty*, 458; *Mother Hubberds Tale*, 478, 490, 494, 503, 508, 527; *The Ruines of Rome*, 468; *The Shepheardes Calender*, xlvi–xlvii, 460, 502–3, 506, 509, 558; *The Teares of the Muses*, 506, 559
Stafford, Anthony, *The Guide of Honour*, xxxiv
Stanley, Mrs., *Sir Philip Sidney's Arcadia Moderniz'd*, lxx–lxxi
Stanley, Thomas, 517
Steevens, C., *see* Estienne, Charles
Stephanus, C., *see* Estienne, Charles
Stephens, John, *Satirical Essays*, xxxv
Stocker, Thomas, trans. *Two and Twentie Sermons of Maister Iohn Caluin*, 516
Stow, John, continuation of Holinshed, *Chronicles*, xix n.

Strabo, *Geography*, 472
Stradanus, Johannes, *Venationes Ferarium, Avium, Piscium*, 486
Surfleet, Richard, trans. C. Steevens [Estienne] and J. Liebault, *Maison Rustique*, 458
Sylvester, Joshua, trans. Saluste du Bartas, *Divine Weeks*, xiv
Symeoni, Gabriel, *Imprese*, xix

Talbot, Peter, *A Treatise of the Nature of Catholick Faith and Heresie*, 560
Tasso, Torquato, *Aminta*, xxxvi; *Rime*, 503
Temple, William, xxxiii
Terence, *Andria*, 518; *Eunuchus*, 547; *Heautontimorumenos*, 518; *Phormio*, 518
Theophrastus, xxxiii
Thynne, Francis, *Animaduersions*, 570
Tintoretto, 513
Tiptoft, John, Earl of Worcester, 484
Titian, 513
Tomson, L., trans. Pierre de la Place, *Treatise of the Excellencie of a Christian Man*, 553
Topsell, Edward, *The History of Four-Footed Beasts*, 486
Torriano, Giovanni, *The Second Alphabet*, xlvi
Tottel, Richard, *Songs and Sonnets*, xxiii, xlvi n., xlviii n., 538
Tourval, Jean Loiseau de, trans. Sidney, *Arcadia*, xxxiv
Tree of Chivalry, xix, 482
Tree of Honour, 542
The Trial of Chivalry, xxxviii
Turberville, George, *Book of Falconry*, 491
Turner, Sir James, *Pallas Armata*, 536
Two Most Unnatural and Bloody Murthers, xxxviii–xxxix
Twyne, Thomas, trans. Petrarch, *Phisicke Against Fortune* (*De remediis utriusque fortunae*), 513
Tyrol, Ferdinand of, *see* Ferdinand of Tirol

Underdowne, Thomas, trans. Heliodorus, *An Aethiopian History*, 475

The Unfortunate Lovers ... Argalus and Parthenia, xxxvii

Valois, Elizabeth of, 536
Vegio, Maffeo (Maphaeus Vegius), 'The Threttene Booke of *Eneados*', xxx, 493
Venner, Tobias, *Via Recta ad Vitam Longam*, 480
Venning, Ralph, *Things Worth Thinking On*, 490, 553, 560
Vernon MS., 548
Vinci, Leonardo da, 483
Virgil, *Aeneid*, xviii, xxi, xxiv, xxix–xxx, xxxiii, liv, 461, 504, 511, 517, 525–6, 536, 537, 552, 557, 561; *Eclogues*, 465, 481; *Georgics*, 457, 460
Viterbo, Annius of, 538
von Hirschberg, Valentinus Theocritus, xxxiv
Vossius, Isaac, xviii

Waldegrave, Robert, lxix
Walker, Anthony, *The Great Evil of Procrastination*, 533
Walsingham, Sir Francis, xiv, xlv, xlix, 467, 488
Ward, John (vicar), lxxvi n., lxxxii
Ward, John, *The First Set of English Madrigals*, 506
Waterson, Simon, xlviii, lxviii–lxx
Weamys, Anne, *A Continuation of ... Arcadia*, xxxvii
Webbe, William, *A Discourse of English Poetry*, 530
Webster, John, *Characters* (additions to Overbury), xxxviii; *The Devil's Law-Case*, xxxviii, 535; *The Duchess of Malfi*, xxxviii; *A Monumental Column*, xxxviii; *The White Devil*, xxxviii
Weever, John, *Epigrammes*, 470; *Faunus and Melliflora*, xxxviii, 550
Whitney, Geoffrey, *A Choice of Emblems*, 542
Wilbye, John, *The First Set of English Madrigals*, 506
Wilkins, George, *The History of Justine*, xxxviii *The Painful Adventures of Pericles*, xxxviii
Wilson, Sir Thomas, *Arte of Rhetorique*, lxxiv, 470, 526, 534–5; trans. Montemayor, *Diana*, xvi, xlv
Windet, John, xliv, xlvi, xlviii n.
Windsor, Lord, xiv
Winstanley, William, *The New Help to Discourse*, 532
Wither, George, *Faire-virtue*, 503
Wolfe, John, xliv
Wotton, Henry, *Reliquiae Wottonianae*, 479
Wroth, Lady Mary, *The Countess of Montgomery's Urania*, xxxix, 517, 549

Xenophon, *Cyropaedia*, xxi, 465, 467; *Hipparchicus*, 518

Yong, Bartholomew, trans. Montemayor, *Diana*, and Gil Polo, *Enamoured Diana*, 461

Zelmane, or the Corinthian Queen, xxxix
Zucchi, Jacopo, *Discorso sopra li dei de'gentili e loro imprese*, 510

EU authorised representative for GPSR:
Easy Access System Europe, Mustamäe tee 50,
10621 Tallinn, Estonia
gpsr.requests@easproject.com

www.ingramcontent.com/pod-product-compliance
Lightning Source LLC
Chambersburg PA
CBHW052052300426
44117CB00013B/2092